The O

The Oxford Paperback German Dictionary

Third Edition

Second edition edited by
Gunhild Prowe
Jill Schneider

Third edition edited by
Roswitha Morris
Robin Sawers

OXFORD
UNIVERSITY PRESS

OXFORD
UNIVERSITY PRESS

Great Clarendon Street, Oxford OX2 6DP

Oxford University Press is a department of the University of Oxford.
It furthers the University's objective of excellence in research, scholarship,
and education by publishing worldwide in

Oxford New York

Athens Auckland Bangkok Bogotá Buenos Aires
Cape Town Chennai Dar es Salaam Delhi Florence Hong Kong Istanbul
Karachi Kolkata Kuala Lumpur Madrid Melbourne Mexico City Mumbai
Nairobi Paris São Paulo Shanghai Singapore Taipei Tokyo Toronto Warsaw

with associated companies in Berlin Ibadan

Oxford is a registered trade mark of Oxford University Press
in the UK and in certain other countries

© Oxford University Press 1993, 1997, 2002
First published 1993
Second edition published 1997
Third edition published 2002

British Library Cataloguing in Publication Data
Data available

Library of Congress Cataloging in Publication Data
Data available
ISBN 0-19-860515-3

10 9 8 7 6 5 4 3 2

Typeset by Morton Word Processing Ltd
Printed in Great Britain by
Clays Ltd, Bungay, Suffolk

Contents

Proprietary terms

This dictionary includes some words which are, or are asserted to be, proprietary names or trademarks. Their inclusion does not imply that they have acquired for legal purposes a non-proprietary or general significance, nor is any other judgement implied concerning their legal status. In cases where the editor has some evidence that a word is used as a proprietary name or trademark this is indicated by the letter (P), but no judgement concerning the legal status of such words is made or implied thereby.

Introduction

This dictionary reflects changes to the spelling of German ratified in July 1996. The symbol * has been introduced to refer from the old spelling to the new, preferred one:

> **As*** *nt* -ses, -se *s.* **Ass**
> **dasein*** *vi sep (sein)* **da sein,** *s.* **da**
> **Schiffahrt*** *f s.* **Schifffahrt**

Where both the old and new forms are valid, an equals sign = is used to refer to the preferred form:

> **aufwändig** *a* = **aufwendig**
> **Tunfisch** *m* = **Thunfisch**

When such forms follow each other alphabetically, they are given with commas, with the preferred form in first place:

> **Panther, Panter** *m* -s, - panther

In phrases, *od* (oder) is used:

> …**deine(r,s)** *poss pron* yours;
> **die D∼en** *od* **d∼en** *pl* your family *sg*

On the English–German side, only the preferred German form is given.

- A swung dash ∼ represents the headword or that part of the headword preceding a vertical bar |. The initial letter of a German headword is given to show whether or not it is a capital.

- The vertical bar | follows the part of the headword which is not repeated in compounds or derivatives.

- Square brackets [ ] are used for optional material.

- Angled brackets < > are used after a verb translation to indicate the object; before a verb translation to indicate the subject; before an adjective to indicate a typical noun which it qualifies.

- Round brackets ( ) are used for field or style labels
  (see list on pages xiii–xv), and for explanatory matter.
- A box □ indicates a new part of speech within an entry.
- *od* (oder) and *or* denote that words or portions of a phrase are
  synonymous. An oblique stroke / is used where there is a
  difference in usage or meaning.
- ≈ is used where no exact equivalent exists in the other language.
- A dagger † indicates that a German verb is irregular and that the
  parts can be found in the verb table on pages 499–502. Compound
  verbs are not listed there as they follow the pattern of the basic
  verb.
- The stressed vowel is marked in a German headword by _ (long) or .
  (short). A phonetic transcription is only given for words which do
  not follow the normal rules of pronunciation. These rules can be
  found on pages x–xi.
- German headword nouns are followed by the gender and, with the
  exception of compound nouns, by the genitive and plural. These
  are only given at compound nouns if they present some difficulty.
  Otherwise the user should refer to the final element.
- Nouns that decline like adjectives are entered as follows: **-e(r)** *m/f*,
  -e(s) *nt*.
- Adjectives which have no undeclined form are entered
  in the feminine form with the masculine and neuter in brackets
  -e(r,s).
- The reflexive pronoun **sich** is accusative unless marked (*dat*).

Phonetic symbols used for German words

a	Hand	hant	ŋ	lang	laŋ
a:	Bahn	ba:n	o	Moral	mo'ra:l
ɐ	Ober	'o:bɐ	o:	Boot	bo:t
ɐ̯	Uhr	u:ɐ̯	o̯	loyal	lo̯a'ja:l
ã	Conférencier	kõferã'si̯e:	õ	Konkurs	kõ'kʊrs
ã:	Abonnement	abɔnə'mã:	õ:	Ballon	ba'lõ:
ai̯	weit	vai̯t	ɔ	Post	pɔst
au̯	Haut	hau̯t	ø	Ökonom	øko'no:m
b	Ball	bal	ø:	Öl	ø:l
ç	ich	ɪç	œ	göttlich	'gœtliç
d	dann	dan	ɔy̯	heute	'hɔy̯tə
dʒ	Gin	dʒɪn	p	Pakt	pakt
e	Metall	me'tal	r	Rast	rast
e:	Beet	be:t	s	Hast	hast
ɛ	mästen	'mɛstən	ʃ	Schal	ʃa:l
ɛ:	wählen	'vɛ:lən	t	Tal	ta:l
ɛ̃	Cousin	ku'zɛ̃:	ts	Zahl	tsa:l
ə	Nase	'na:zə	tʃ	Couch	kau̯tʃ
f	Faß	fas	u	Kupon	ku'põ:
g	Gast	gast	u:	Hut	hu:t
h	haben	'ha:bən	u̯	aktuell	ak'tu̯ɛl
i	Rivale	ri'va:lə	ʊ	Pult	pʊlt
i:	viel	fi:l	v	was	vas
i̯	Aktion	ak'tsi̯o:n	x	Bach	bax
ɪ	Birke	'bɪrkə	y	Physik	fy'zi:k
j	ja	ja:	y:	Rübe	'ry:bə
k	kalt	kalt	ỹ	Nuance	'nỹã:sə
l	Last	last	Y	Fülle	'fYlə
m	Mast	mast	z	Nase	'na:zə
n	Naht	na:t	ʒ	Regime	re'ʒi:m

ˀ Glottal stop, e.g. Koordination / koˀɔrdinaˈtsi̯on /.

: Length sign after a vowel, e.g. Chrom / kro:m /.

ˈ Stress mark before stressed syllable, e.g. Balkon / balˈkõ:/.

Guide to German pronunciation

Consonants

Pronounced as in English with the following exceptions:

b	as	p	
d	as	t	*at the end of a word or syllable*
g	as	k	

ch	as in Scottish lo<u>ch</u>	*after a, o, u, au*
	like an exaggerated h as in <u>h</u>uge	*after i, e, ä, ö, ü, eu, ei*

-chs	as	x	(as in bo<u>x</u>)
-ig	as	-ich / ıç /	*when a suffix*
j	as	y	(as in <u>y</u>es)
ps			
pn			the p is pronounced
qu	as	k + v	
s	as	z	(as in <u>z</u>ero) *at the beginning of a word*
	as	s	(as in bu<u>s</u>) *at the end of a word or syllable, before a consonant, or when doubled*
sch	as	sh	
sp	as	shp	*at the beginning of a word*
st	as	sht	*at the beginning of a word*
v	as	f	(as in <u>f</u>or)
	as	v	(as in <u>v</u>ery) *within a word*
w	as	v	(as in <u>v</u>ery)
z	as	ts	

Vowels

Approximately as follows:

a	short	as	u	(as in b<u>u</u>t)
	long	as	a	(as in c<u>a</u>r)
e	short	as	e	(as in p<u>e</u>n)
	long	as	a	(as in p<u>a</u>per)
i	short	as	i	(as in b<u>i</u>t)
	long	as	ee	(as in qu<u>ee</u>n)
o	short	as	o	(as in h<u>o</u>t)
	long	as	o	(as in p<u>o</u>pe)
u	short	as	oo	(as in f<u>oo</u>t)
	long	as	oo	(as in b<u>oo</u>t)

Vowels are always short before a double consonant, and long when followed by an h or when double

ie	is pronounced	ee		(as in k<u>ee</u>p)

Diphthongs

au		as	ow	(as in h<u>ow</u>)
ei ai		as	y	(as in m<u>y</u>)
eu äu		as	oy	(as in b<u>oy</u>)

Pronunciation of the alphabet

English/Englisch		German/Deutsch
eɪ	a	aː
biː	b	beː
siː	c	tse̱ː
diː	d	deː
iː	e	eː
ef	f	ɛf
dʒiː	g	geː
eɪtʃ	h	haː
aɪ	i	iː
dʒeɪ	j	jɔt
keɪ	k	kaː
el	l	ɛl
em	m	ɛm
en	n	ɛn
əʊ	o	oː
piː	p	peː
kjuː	q	kuː
aː(r)	r	ɛr
es	s	ɛs
tiː	t	teː
juː	u	uː
viː	v	faṵ
'dʌbljuː	w	veː
eks	x	ɪks
waɪ	y	'ʏpsilɔn
zed	z	tsɛt
eɪ umlaut	ä	ɛː
əʊ umlaut	ö	øː
juː umlaut	ü	yː
es'zed	ß	ɛs'tsɛt

Abbreviations

adjective	*a*	Adjektiv
abbreviation	*abbr*	Abkürzung
accusative	*acc*	Akkusativ
Administration	*Admin*	Administration
adverb	*adv*	Adverb
American	*Amer*	amerikanisch
Anatomy	*Anat*	Anatomie
Archaeology	*Archaeol*	Archäologie
Architecture	*Archit*	Architektur
Astronomy	*Astr*	Astronomie
attributive	*attrib*	attributiv
Austrian	*Aust*	österreichisch
Motor vehicles	*Auto*	Automobil
Aviation	*Aviat*	Luftfahrt
Biology	*Biol*	Biologie
Botany	*Bot*	Botanik
Chemistry	*Chem*	Chemie
collective	*coll*	Kollektivum
Commerce	*Comm*	Handel
conjunction	*conj*	Konjunktion
Cookery	*Culin*	Kochkunst
dative	*dat*	Dativ
definite article	*def art*	bestimmter Artikel
demonstrative	*dem*	Demonstrativ-
dialect	*dial*	Dialekt
Electricity	*Electr*	Elektrizität
something	*etw*	etwas
feminine	*f*	Femininum
figurative	*fig*	figurativ
genitive	*gen*	Genitiv
Geography	*Geog*	Geographie
Geology	*Geol*	Geologie
Geometry	*Geom*	Geometrie
Grammar	*Gram*	Grammatik
Horticulture	*Hort*	Gartenbau
impersonal	*impers*	unpersönlich
indefinite article	*indef art*	unbestimmter Artikel
indefinite pronoun	*indef pron*	unbestimmtes Pronomen
infinitive	*inf*	Infinitiv
inseparable	*insep*	untrennbar
interjection	*int*	Interjektion
invariable	*inv*	unveränderlich
irregular	*irreg*	unregelmäßig
someone	*jd*	jemand
someone	*jdm*	jemandem
someone	*jdn*	jemanden
someone's	*jds*	jemandes
Journalism	*Journ*	Journalismus

Law	*Jur*	Jura
Language	*Lang*	Sprache
literary	*liter*	dichterisch
masculine	*m*	Maskulinum
Mathematics	*Math*	Mathematik
Medicine	*Med*	Medizin
Meteorology	*Meteorol*	Meteorologie
Military	*Mil*	Militär
Mineralogy	*Miner*	Mineralogie
Music	*Mus*	Musik
noun	*n*	Substantiv
Nautical	*Naut*	nautisch
North German	*N Ger*	Norddeutsch
nominative	*nom*	Nominativ
neuter	*nt*	Neutrum
or	*od*	oder
Proprietary term	*P*	Warenzeichen
pejorative	*pej*	abwertend
Photography	*Phot*	Fotografie
Physics	*Phys*	Physik
plural	*pl*	Plural
Politics	*Pol*	Politik
possessive	*poss*	Possessiv-
past participle	*pp*	zweites Partizip
predicative	*pred*	prädikativ
prefix	*pref*	Präfix
preposition	*prep*	Präposition
present	*pres*	Präsens
present participle	*pres p*	erstes Partizip
pronoun	*pron*	Pronomen
Psychology	*Psych*	Psychologie
past tense	*pt*	Präteritum
Railway	*Rail*	Eisenbahn
reflexive	*refl*	reflexiv
regular	*reg*	regelmäßig
relative	*rel*	Relativ-
Religion	*Relig*	Religion
see	*s.*	siehe
School	*Sch*	Schule
separable	*sep*	trennbar
singular	*sg*	Singular
South German	*S Ger*	Süddeutsch
someone	*s.o.*	jemand
something	*sth*	etwas
Technical	*Techn*	Technik
Telephone	*Teleph*	Telefon
Textiles	*Tex*	Textilien
Theatre	*Theat*	Theater
Television	*TV*	Fernsehen
Typography	*Typ*	Typographie
University	*Univ*	Universität
auxiliary verb	*v aux*	Hilfsverb
intransitive verb	*vi*	intransitives Verb
reflexive verb	*vr*	reflexives Verb
transitive verb	*vt*	transitives Verb

vulgar	*vulg*	vulgär
Zoology	*Zool*	Zoologie
familiar	🄸	familiär
slang	⊠	Slang

German–English Dictionary

Aa

Aal *m* -[e]s, -e eel

Aas *nt* -es carrion; ⊠ swine

ab *prep* (+ *dat*) from ● *adv* off; (*weg*) away; (*auf Fahrplan*) departs; **ab und zu** now and then; **auf und ab** up and down

abändern *vt sep* alter; (*abwandeln*) modify

Abbau *m* dismantling; (*Kohlen-*) mining. **a~en** *vt sep* dismantle; mine <*Kohle*>

abbeißen† *vt sep* bite off

abbeizen *vt sep* strip

abberufen† *vt sep* recall

abbestellen *vt sep* cancel; **jdn a~** put s.o. off

abbiegen† *vi sep* (*sein*) turn off; **[nach] links a~** turn left

Abbildung *f* -, -en illustration

abblättern *vi sep* (*sein*) flake off

abblend|en *vt/i sep* (*haben*) [die Scheinwerfer] **a~en** dip one's headlights. **A~licht** *nt* dipped headlights *pl*

abbrechen† *v sep* ● *vt* break off; (*abreißen*) demolish ● *vi* (*sein/haben*) break off

abbrennen† *v sep* ● *vt* burn off; (*niederbrennen*) burn down ● *vi* (*sein*) burn down

abbringen† *vt sep* dissuade (*von* from)

Abbruch *m* demolition; (*Beenden*) breaking off

abbuchen *vt sep* debit

abbürsten *vt sep* brush down; (*entfernen*) brush off

abdanken *vi sep* (*haben*) resign; <*Herrscher:*> abdicate

abdecken *vt sep* uncover; (*abnehmen*) take off; (*zudecken*) cover; **den Tisch a~** clear the table

abdichten *vt sep* seal

abdrehen *vt sep* turn off

Abdruck *m* (*pl* ⁻e) impression. **a~en** *vt sep* print

abdrücken *vt/i sep* (*haben*) fire; **sich a~** leave an impression

Abend *m* -s, -e evening; **am A~** in the evening; **heute A~** this evening, tonight; **gestern A~** yesterday evening, last night. **A~brot** *nt* supper. **A~essen** *nt* dinner; (*einfacher*) supper. **A~mahl** *nt* (*Relig*) [Holy] Communion. **a~s** *adv* in the evening

Abenteuer *nt* -s,- adventure; (*Liebes-*) affair. **a~lich** *a* fantastic

aber *conj* but; **oder a~** or else ● *adv* (*wirklich*) really

Aber|glaube *m* superstition. **a~gläubisch** *a* superstitious

abfahr|en† *v sep* ● *vi* (*sein*) leave; <*Auto:*> drive off ● *vt* take away; (*entlangfahren*) drive along; use <*Fahrkarte*>; **abgefahrene Reifen** worn tyres. **A~t** *f* departure; (*Talfahrt*) descent; (*Piste*) run; (*Ausfahrt*) exit

Abfall *m* refuse, rubbish; (*auf der Straße*) litter; (*Industrie-*) waste

abfallen† *vi sep* (*sein*) drop, fall; (*übrig bleiben*) be left (*für* for); (*sich neigen*) slope away. **a~d** *a* sloping

Abfallhaufen *m* rubbish-dump

abfällig *a* disparaging

abfangen† *vt sep* intercept

abfärben *vi sep* (*haben*) <*Farbe:*> run; <*Stoff:*> not be colour-fast

abfassen *vt sep* draft

abfertigen *vt sep* attend to; (*zollamtlich*) clear; **jdn kurz a~** 🗓 give s.o. short shrift

abfeuern *vt sep* fire

abfind|en† *vt sep* pay off; (*entschädigen*) compensate; **sich a~en mit** come to terms with. **A~ung** *f* -, -en compensation

abfliegen† *vi sep* (*sein*) fly off; (*Aviat*) take off

abfließen† *vi sep* (*sein*) drain *or* run away

Abflug *m* (*Aviat*) departure

Abfluss *m* drainage; (*Öffnung*) drain. **A~rohr** *nt* drain-pipe

abfragen *vt sep* jdn *od* jdm Vokabeln a~ test s.o. on vocabulary

Abfuhr *f* - removal; (*fig*) rebuff

abführ|en *vt sep* take *or* lead away. **A~mittel** *nt* laxative

abfüllen *vt sep* auf *od* in Flaschen a~ bottle

Abgase *ntpl* exhaust fumes

abgeben† *vt sep* hand in; (*abliefern*) deliver; (*verkaufen*) sell; (*zur Aufbewahrung*) leave; (*Fußball*) pass; (*ausströmen*) give off; (*abfeuern*) fire; (*verlauten lassen*) give; cast <*Stimme*>; jdm etw a~ give s.o. a share of sth

abgehen† *v sep* ● *vi* (*sein*) leave; (*Theat*) exit; (*sich lösen*) come off; (*abgezogen werden*) be deducted ● *vt* walk along

abgehetzt *a* harassed. **abgelegen** *a* remote. **abgeneigt** *a* etw (*dat*) nicht abgeneigt sein not be averse to sth. **abgenutzt** *a* worn.

Abgeordnete(r) *m/f* deputy; (*Pol*) Member of Parliament. **abgepackt** *a* pre-packed

abgeschieden *a* secluded

abgeschlossen *a* (*fig*) complete; <*Wohnung*> self-contained.

abgesehen *prep* apart (from von). **abgespannt** *a* exhausted. **abgestanden** *a* stale. **abgestorben** *a* dead; <*Glied*> numb. **abgetragen** *a* worn. **abgewetzt** *a* threadbare

abgewinnen† *vt sep* win (jdm from s.o.); etw (*dat*) Geschmack a~ get a taste for sth

abgewöhnen *vt sep* jdm/sich das Rauchen a~ cure s.o. of/ give up smoking

abgießen† *vt sep* pour off; drain <*Gemüse*>

Abgott *m* idol

abgöttisch *adv* a~ lieben idolize

abgrenz|en *vt sep* divide off; (*fig*) define. **A~ung** *f* - demarcation

Abgrund *m* abyss; (*fig*) depths *pl*

abgucken *vt sep* ① copy

Abguss *m* cast

abhacken *vt sep* chop off

abhaken *vt sep* tick off

abhalten† *vt sep* keep off; (*hindern*) keep, prevent (von from); (*veranstalten*) hold

abhanden *adv* a~ kommen get lost

Abhandlung *f* treatise

Abhang *m* slope

abhängen¹ *vt sep* (*reg*) take down; (*abkuppeln*) uncouple

abhäng|en²† *vi sep* (*haben*) depend (von on). **a~ig** *a* dependent (von on). **A~igkeit** *f* - dependence

abhärten *vt sep* toughen up

abheben† *v sep* ● *vt* take off; (*vom Konto*) withdraw; **sich a~** stand out (gegen against) ● *vi* (*haben*) (*Cards*) cut [the cards]; (*Aviat*) take off; <*Rakete:*> lift off

abheften *vt sep* file

Abhilfe *f* remedy

abholen *vt sep* collect

abhör|en *vt sep* listen to; (*überwachen*) tap; jdn *od* jdm Vokabeln a~en test s.o. on vocabulary. **A~gerät** *nt* bugging device

Abitur *nt* -s ≈ A levels *pl*

abkaufen *vt sep* buy (*dat* from)

abklingen† *vi sep* (*sein*) die away; (*nachlassen*) subside

abkochen *vt sep* boil

abkommen† *vi sep* (*sein*) a~ von stray from; (*aufgeben*) give up. **A~** *nt* -s,- agreement

Abkömmling *m* -s, -e descendant

abkratzen *vt sep* scrape off

abkühlen *vt/i sep* (*sein*) cool; **sich a~** cool [down]

Abkunft *f* - origin

abkuppeln *vt sep* uncouple

abkürz|en *vt sep* shorten; abbreviate <*Wort*>. **A~ung** *f* short cut; (*Wort*) abbreviation

abladen† *vt sep* unload

Ablage *f* shelf; (*für Akten*) tray

ablager|n *vt sep* deposit. **A∼ung** *f* -, -en deposit

ablassen† *vt sep* drain [off]; let off *<Dampf>*

Ablauf *m* drain; (*Verlauf*) course; (*Ende*) end; (*einer Frist*) expiry. **a∼en**† *v sep* ● *vi* (*sein*) run *or* drain off; (*verlaufen*) go off; (*enden*) expire; *<Zeit:>* run out; *<Uhrwerk:>* run down ● *vt* walk along; (*absuchen*) scour (**nach** for)

ableg|en *v sep* ● *vt* put down; discard *<Karte>*; (*abheften*) file; (*ausziehen*) take off; sit, take *<Prüfung>*; **abgelegte Kleidung** cast-offs *pl* ● *vi* (*haben*) take off one's coat; (*Naut*) cast off. **A∼er** *m* -s,- (*Bot*) cutting; (*Schössling*) shoot

ablehn|en *vt sep* refuse; (*missbilligen*) reject. **A∼ung** *f* -, -en refusal; rejection

ableit|en *vt sep* divert; **sich a∼en** be derived (**von/aus** from). **A∼ung** *f* derivation; (*Wort*) derivative

ablenk|en *vt sep* deflect; divert *<Aufmerksamkeit>*. **A∼ung** *f* -, -en distraction

ablesen† *vt sep* read

ablicht|en *vt sep* photocopy. **A∼ung** *f* photocopy

abliefern *vt sep* deliver

ablös|en *vt sep* detach; (*abwechseln*) relieve; **sich a∼en** come off; (*sich abwechseln*) take turns. **A∼ung** *f* relief

abmach|en *vt sep* remove; (*ausmachen*) arrange; (*vereinbaren*) agree. **A∼ung** *f* -, -en agreement

abmager|n *vi sep* (*sein*) lose weight. **A∼ungskur** *f* slimming diet

abmelden *vt sep* cancel; (*im Hotel*) check out

abmessen† *vt sep* measure

abmühen (sich) *vr sep* struggle

Abnäher *m* -s,- dart

abnehm|en† *v sep* ● *vt* take off, remove; pick up *<Hörer>*; **jdm etw a∼en** take/(*kaufen*) buy sth from s.o. ● *vi* (*haben*) decrease; (*nachlassen*) decline; *<Person:>* lose weight; *<Mond:>* wane. **A∼er** *m* -s,- buyer

Abneigung *f* dislike (**gegen** of)

abnorm *a* abnormal

abnutz|en *vt sep* wear out. **A∼ung** *f* - wear [and tear]

Abon|nement /abonə'mã:/ *nt* -s, -s subscription. **A∼nent** *m* -en, -en subscriber. **a∼nieren** *vt* take out a subscription to

Abordnung *f* -, -en deputation

abpassen *vt sep* wait for; **gut a∼** time well

abraten† *vi sep* (*haben*) **jdm von etw a∼** advise s.o. against sth

abräumen *vt/i* (*haben*) clear away

abrechn|en *v sep* ● *vt* deduct ● *vi* (*haben*) settle up. **A∼ung** *f* settlement; (*Rechnung*) account

Abreise *f* departure. **a∼n** *vi sep* (*sein*) leave

abreißen† *v sep* ● *vt* tear off; (*demolieren*) pull down ● *vi* (*sein*) come off

abrichten *vt sep* train

Abriss *m* demolition; (*Übersicht*) summary

abrufen† *vt sep* call away; (*Computer*) retrieve

abrunden *vt sep* round off

abrüst|en *vi sep* (*haben*) disarm. **A∼ung** *f* disarmament

abrutschen *vi sep* (*sein*) slip

Absage *f* -, -n cancellation; (*Ablehnung*) refusal. **a∼n** *v sep* ● *vt* cancel ● *vi* (*haben*) **[jdm] a∼n** cancel an appointment [with s.o.]; (*auf Einladung*) refuse [s.o.'s invitation]

Absatz *m* heel; (*Abschnitt*) paragraph; (*Verkauf*) sale

abschaffen *vt sep* abolish; get rid of *<Auto, Hund>*

abschalten *vt/i sep* (*haben*) switch off

Abscheu *m* - revulsion

abscheulich *a* revolting

abschicken *vt sep* send off

Abschied *m* -[e]s, -e farewell; (*Trennung*) parting; **A∼ nehmen** say goodbye (**von** to)

abschießen† *vt sep* shoot down; (*abfeuern*) fire; launch *<Rakete>*

a

abschirmen *vt sep* shield

abschlagen† *vt sep* knock off; (*verweigern*) refuse

Abschlepp|dienst *m* breakdown service. **a~en** *vt sep* tow away. **A~seil** *nt* tow-rope

abschließen† *v sep* ● *vt* lock; (*beenden, abmachen*) conclude; make <*Wette*>; balance <*Bücher*> ● *vi* (*haben*) lock up; (*enden*) end. **a~d** *adv* in conclusion

Abschluss *m* conclusion. **A~zeugnis** *nt* diploma

abschmecken *vt sep* season

abschmieren *vt sep* lubricate

abschneiden† *v sep* ● *vt* cut off ● *vi* (*haben*) **gut/schlecht a~** do well/badly

Abschnitt *m* section; (*Stadium*) stage; (*Absatz*) paragraph

abschöpfen *vt sep* skim off

abschrauben *vt sep* unscrew

abschreck|en *vt sep* deter; (*Culin*) put in cold water <*Ei*>. **a~end** *a* repulsive. **A~ungsmittel** *nt* deterrent

abschreib|en† *v sep* ● *vt* copy; (*Comm & fig*) write off ● *vi* (*haben*) copy. **A~ung** *f* (*Comm*) depreciation

Abschrift *f* copy

Abschuss *m* shooting down; (*Abfeuern*) firing; (*Raketen-*) launch

abschüssig *a* sloping; (*steil*) steep

abschwellen† *vi sep* (*sein*) go down

abseh|bar *a* **in a~barer Zeit** in the foreseeable future. **a~en**† *vt/i sep* (*haben*) copy; (*voraussehen*) foresee; **a~en von** disregard; (*aufgeben*) refrain from

abseits *adv* apart; (*Sport*) offside ● *prep* (+ *gen*) away from. **A~** *nt* - (*Sport*) offside

absend|en† *vt sep* send off. **A~er** *m* sender

absetzen *v sep* ● *vt* put *or* set down; (*ablagern*) deposit; (*abnehmen*) take off; (*abbrechen*) stop; (*entlassen*) dismiss; (*verkaufen*) sell; (*abziehen*) deduct ● *vi* (*haben*) pause

Absicht *f* -, -en intention; **mit A~** intentionally, on purpose

absichtlich *a* intentional

absitzen† *v sep* ● *vi* (*sein*) dismount ● *vt* Ⓣ serve <*Strafe*>

absolut *a* absolute

absolvieren *vt* complete; (*bestehen*) pass

absonder|n *vt sep* separate; (*ausscheiden*) secrete. **A~ung** *f* -, -en secretion

absorbieren *vt* absorb

abspeisen *vt sep* fob off (**mit** with)

absperr|en *vt sep* cordon off; (*abstellen*) turn off; (*SGer*) lock. **A~ung** *f* -, -en barrier

abspielen *vt sep* play; (*Fußball*) pass; **sich a~** take place

Absprache *f* agreement

absprechen† *vt sep* arrange; **sich a~** agree

abspringen† *vi sep* (*sein*) jump off; (*mit Fallschirm*) parachute; (*abgehen*) come off

Absprung *m* jump

abspülen *vt sep* rinse

abstamm|en *vi sep* (*haben*) be descended (**von** from). **A~ung** *f* - descent

Abstand *m* distance; (*zeitlich*) interval; **A~ halten** keep one's distance

abstatten *vt sep* **jdm einen Besuch a~** pay s.o. a visit

Abstecher *m* -s,- detour

abstehen† *vi sep* (*haben*) stick out

absteigen† *vi sep* (*sein*) dismount; (*niedersteigen*) descend; (*Fußball*) be relegated

abstell|en *vt sep* put down; (*lagern*) store; (*parken*) park; (*abschalten*) turn off. **A~gleis** *nt* siding. **A~raum** *m* box-room

absterben† *vi sep* (*sein*) die; (*gefühllos werden*) go numb

Abstieg *m* -[e]s, -e descent; (*Fußball*) relegation

---

*old spelling

abstimm|en *v sep* ● *vi* (*haben*) vote (**über** + *acc* on) ● *vt* coordinate (**auf** + *acc* with). **A~ung** *f* vote

Abstinenzler *m* -s, - teetotaller

abstoßen† *vt sep* knock off; (*verkaufen*) sell; (*fig: ekeln*) repel. **a~d** *a* repulsive

abstreiten† *vt sep* deny

Abstrich *m* (*Med*) smear

abstufen *vt sep* grade

Absturz *m* fall; (*Aviat*) crash

abstürzen *vi sep* (*sein*) fall; (*Aviat*) crash

absuchen *vt sep* search

absurd *a* absurd

Abszess *m* -es, -e abscess

Abt *m* -[e]s,¨-e abbot

abtasten *vt sep* feel; (*Techn*) scan

abtauen *vt/i sep* (*sein*) thaw; (*entfrosten*) defrost

Abtei *f* -, -en abbey

Abteil *nt* compartment

Abteilung *f* -, -en section; (*Admin, Comm*) department

abtragen† *vt sep* clear; (*einebnen*) level; (*abnutzen*) wear out

abträglich *a* detrimental (*dat* to)

abtreib|en† *vt sep* (*Naut*) drive off course; **ein Kind a~en lassen** have an abortion. **A~ung** *f* -, -en abortion

abtrennen *vt sep* detach; (*abteilen*) divide off

Abtreter *m* -s,- doormat

abtrocknen *vt/i sep* (*haben*) dry; **sich a~** dry oneself

abtropfen *vi sep* (*sein*) drain

abtun† *vt sep* (*fig*) dismiss

abwägen† *vt sep* (*fig*) weigh

abwandeln *vt sep* modify

abwarten *v sep* ● *vt* wait for ● *vi* (*haben*) wait [and see]

abwärts *adv* down[wards]

Abwasch *m* -[e]s washing-up; (*Geschirr*) dirty dishes *pl*. **a~en†** *v sep* ● *vt* wash; wash up <*Geschirr*>; (*entfernen*) wash off ● *vi* (*haben*) wash up. **A~lappen** *m* dishcloth

Abwasser *nt* -s,¨- sewage. **A~kanal** *m* sewer

abwechseln *vi/r sep* (*haben*) [**sich**] a~ alternate; <*Personen:*> take turns. **a~d** *a* alternate

Abwechslung *f* -, -en change; **zur A~** for a change

abwegig *a* absurd

Abwehr *f* - defence; (*Widerstand*) resistance; (*Pol*) counter-espionage. **a~en** *vt sep* ward off. **A~system** *nt* immune system

abweich|en† *vi sep* (*sein*) deviate/ (*von Regel*) depart (**von** from); (*sich unterscheiden*) differ (**von** from). **a~end** *a* divergent; (*verschieden*) different. **A~ung** *f* -, -en deviation

abweis|en† *vt sep* turn down; turn away <*Person*>. **a~end** *a* unfriendly. **A~ung** *f* rejection

abwenden† *vt sep* turn away; (*verhindern*) avert

abwerfen† *vt sep* throw off; throw <*Reiter*>; (*Aviat*) drop; (*Kartenspiel*) discard; shed <*Haut, Blätter*>; yield <*Gewinn*>

abwert|en *vt sep* devalue. **A~ung** *f* -, -en devaluation

Abwesenheit *f* - absence; absent-mindedness

abwickeln *vt sep* unwind; (*erledigen*) settle

abwischen *vt sep* wipe

abzahlen *vt sep* pay off

abzählen *vt sep* count

Abzahlung *f* instalment

Abzeichen *nt* badge

abzeichnen *vt sep* copy

Abzieh|bild *nt* transfer. **a~en†** *v sep* ● *vt* pull off; take off <*Laken*>; strip <*Bett*>; (*häuten*) skin; (*Phot*) print; run off <*Kopien*>; (*zurückziehen*) withdraw; (*abrechnen*) deduct ● *vi* (*sein*) go away, <*Rauch:*> escape

Abzug *m* withdrawal; (*Abrechnung*) deduction; (*Phot*) print (*Korrektur-*) proof; (*am Gewehr*) trigger; (*A~söffnung*) vent; **A~e** *pl* deductions

abzüglich *prep* (+ *gen*) less

Abzugshaube *f* [cooker] hood

a

abzweig|en *v sep* ● *vi* (*sein*) branch off ● *vt* divert. **A~ung** *f* -, -en junction; (*Gabelung*) fork

ach *int* oh; **a~ je!** oh dear! **a~ so I** see

Achse *f* -, -n axis; (*Rad-*) axle

Achsel *f* -, -n shoulder. **A~höhle** *f* armpit. **A~zucken** *nt* -s shrug

acht *inv a*, **A~** *f* -, -en eight

Acht *f* **A~ geben** be careful; **A~ geben auf** (+ *acc*) look after; **außer A~ lassen** disregard; **sich in A~ nehmen** be careful

acht|e(r,s) *a* eighth. **a~eckig** *a* octagonal. **A~el** *nt* -s,- eighth

achten *vt* respect ● *vi* (*haben*) **a~ auf** (+ *acc*) pay attention to; (*aufpassen*) look after

Achterbahn *f* roller-coaster

achtlos *a* careless

achtsam *a* careful

Achtung *f* - respect (**vor** + *dat* for); **A~!** look out!

acht|zehn *inv a* eighteen. **a~zehnte(r,s)** *a* eighteenth. **a~zig** *a inv* eighty. **a~zigste(r,s)** *a* eightieth

Acker *m* -s,⸗ field. **A~bau** *m* agriculture. **A~land** *nt* arable land

addieren *vt/i* (*haben*) add

Addition /-'tsjo:n/ *f* -, -en addition

ade *int* goodbye

Adel *m* -s nobility

Ader *f* -, -n vein

Adjektiv *nt* -s, -e adjective

Adler *m* -s,- eagle

adlig *a* noble. **A~e(r)** *m* nobleman

Administration /-'tsjo:n/ *f* - administration

Admiral *m* -s,⸗e admiral

adop|tieren *vt* adopt. **A~tion** /-'tsjo:n/ *f* -, -en adoption. **A~tiveltern** *pl* adoptive parents. **A~tivkind** *nt* adopted child

Adrenalin *nt* -s adrenalin

Adres|se *f* -, -n address. **a~sieren** *vt* address

Adria *f* - Adriatic

Adverb *nt* -s, -ien /-jən/ adverb

Affäre *f* -, -n affair

Affe *m* -n, -n monkey; (*Menschen-*) ape

affektiert *a* affected

affig *a* affected; (*eitel*) vain

Afrika *nt* -s Africa

Afrikan|er(in) *m* -s,- (*f* -, -nen) African. **a~isch** *a* African

After *m* -s,- anus

Agen|t(in) *m* -en, -en (*f* -, -nen) agent. **A~tur** *f* -, -en agency

Aggres|sion *f* -, -en aggression. **a~siv** *a* aggressive

Agnostiker *m* -s,- agnostic

Ägypt|en /ɛ'gʏptən/ *nt* -s Egypt. **Ä~er(in)** *m* -s,- (*f* -, -nen) Egyptian. **ä~isch** *a* Egyptian

ähneln *vi* (*haben*) (+ *dat*) resemble; **sich ä~** be alike

ahnen *vt* have a presentiment of; (*vermuten*) suspect

Ahnen *mpl* ancestors. **A~forschung** *f* genealogy

ähnlich *a* similar; **jdm ä~ sehen** resemble s.o. **Ä~keit** *f* -, -en similarity; resemblance

Ahnung *f* -, -en premonition; (*Vermutung*) idea, hunch

Ahorn *m* -s, -e maple

Ähre *f* -, -n ear [of corn]

Aids /e:ts/ *nt* - Aids

Akademie *f* -, -n academy

Akadem|iker(in) *m* -s,- (*f* -, -nen) university graduate. **a~isch** *a* academic

akklimatisieren (sich) *vr* become acclimatized

Akkord *m* -[e]s, -e (*Mus*) chord. **A~arbeit** *f* piece-work

Akkordeon *nt* -s, -s accordion

Akkumulator *m* -s, -en /-'to:rən/ (*Electr*) accumulator

Akkusativ *m* -s, -e accusative. **A~objekt** *nt* direct object

Akrobat|(in) *m* -en, -en (*f* -, -nen) acrobat. **a~isch** *a* acrobatic

Akt *m* -[e]s, -e act; (*Kunst*) nude

Akte *f* -, -n file; **A~n** documents. **A~ntasche** *f* briefcase

Aktie /'aktsiə/ *f* -, -n (*Comm*) share. **A∼ngesellschaft** *f* joint-stock company

Aktion /ak'tsio:n/ *f* -, -en action. **A∼är** *m* -s, -e shareholder

aktiv *a* active

aktuell *a* topical; (*gegenwärtig*) current

Akupunktur *f* - acupuncture

Akustik *f* - acoustics *pl*

akut *a* acute

Akzent *m* -[e]s, -e accent

akzept|abel *a* acceptable. **a∼ieren** *vt* accept

Alarm *m* -s alarm; (*Mil*) alert. **a∼ieren** *vt* alert; (*beunruhigen*) alarm

Albdruck *m* nightmare

albern *a* silly ● *vi* (*haben*) play the fool

Albtraum *m* nightmare

Album *nt* -s, -ben album

Algebra *f* - algebra

Algen *fpl* algae

Algerien /-iən/ *nt* -s Algeria

Alibi *nt* -s, -s alibi

Alimente *pl* maintenance *sg*

Alkohol *m* -s alcohol. **a∼frei** *a* non-alcoholic

Alkohol|iker(in) *m* -s,- (*f* -, -nen) alcoholic. **a∼isch** *a* alcoholic

all *inv pron* all das/mein Geld all the/my money; **all dies** all this

All *nt* -s universe

alle *pred a* finished

all|e(r,s) *pron* all; (*jeder*) every; **a∼es** everything, all; (*alle Leute*) everyone; **a∼e** *pl* all; **a∼es Geld** all the money; **a∼e beide** both [of them/us]; **a∼e Tage** every day; **a∼e drei Jahre** every three years; **ohne a∼en Grund** without any reason; **vor a∼em** above all; **a∼es in a∼em** all in all; **a∼es aussteigen!** all change!

Allee *f* -, -n avenue

allein *adv* alone; (*nur*) only; **a∼stehend** single; **a∼ der Gedanke** the mere thought; **von a∼[e]** of its/ <*Person*> one's own accord; (*automatisch*) automatically ● *conj* but. **A∼erziehende(r)** *m/f* single parent. **a∼ig** *a* sole. **A∼stehende** *pl* single people

allemal *adv* every time; (*gewiss*) certainly

allenfalls *adv* at most; (*eventuell*) possibly

aller|beste(r,s) *a* very best; **am a∼besten** best of all. **a∼dings** *adv* indeed; (*zwar*) admittedly. **a∼erste(r,s)** *a* very first

Allergie *f* -, -n allergy

allergisch *a* allergic (**gegen** to)

Aller|heiligen *nt* -s All Saints Day. **a∼höchstens** *adv* at the very most. **a∼lei** *inv a* all sorts of ● *pron* all sorts of things. **a∼letzte(r,s)** *a* very last. **a∼liebste(r,s)** *a* favourite ● *adv* **am a∼liebsten** for preference; **am a∼liebsten haben** like best of all. **a∼meiste(r,s)** *a* most ● *adv* **am a∼meisten** most of all. **A∼seelen** *nt* -s All Souls Day. **a∼wenigste(r,s)** *a* very least ● *adv* **am a∼wenigsten** least of all

allgemein *a* general, *adv* -ly; **im A∼en** (**a∼en**) in general. **A∼heit** *f* - community; (*Öffentlichkeit*) general public

Allianz *f* -, -en alliance

Alligator *m* -s, -en /-'to:rən/ alligator

alliiert *a* allied; **die A∼en** *pl* the Allies

all|jährlich *a* annual. **a∼mählich** *a* gradual

Alltag *m* working day; **der A∼** (*fig*) everyday life

alltäglich *a* daily; (*gewöhnlich*) everyday; <*Mensch*> ordinary

alltags *adv* on weekdays

allzu *adv* [far] too; **a∼ oft** all too often; **a∼ vorsichtig** over-cautious

Alm *f* -, -en alpine pasture

Almosen *ntpl* alms

Alpdruck *m* = Albdruck

Alpen *pl* Alps

Alphabet *nt* -[e]s, -e alphabet. **a∼isch** *a* alphabetical, *adv* -ly

Alptraum *m* = Albtraum

als *conj* as; (*zeitlich*) when; (*mit Komparativ*) than; **nichts als** nothing but; **als ob** as if *or* though

also *adv & conj* so; **a~ gut** all right then; **na a~!** there you are!

alt *a* old; (*gebraucht*) second-hand; (*ehemalig*) former; **alt werden** grow old

Alt *m* -s (*Mus*) contralto

Altar *m* -s,-̈e altar

Alt|e(r) *m/f* old man/woman; **die A~en** old people. **A~eisen** *nt* scrap iron. **A~enheim** *nt* old people's home

Alter *nt* -s,- age; (*Bejahrtheit*) old age; **im A~ von** at the age of

älter *a* older; **mein ä~er Bruder** my elder brother

altern *vi* (*sein*) age

Alternative *f* -, -n alternative

Alters|grenze *f* age limit. **A~heim** *nt* old people's home. **A~rente** *f* old-age pension. **a~schwach** *a* old and infirm

Alter|tum *nt* -s,-̈er antiquity. **a~tümlich** *a* old; (*altmodisch*) old-fashioned

altklug *a* precocious

alt|modisch *a* old-fashioned. **A~papier** *nt* waste paper. **A~warenhändler** *m* second-hand dealer

Alufolie *f* [aluminium] foil

Aluminium *nt* -s aluminium, (*Amer*) aluminum

am *prep* = **an dem**; **am Montag** on Monday; **am Morgen** in the morning; **am besten** [the] best

Amateur /-'tøːɐ̯/ *m* -s, -e amateur

Ambition /-'tsi̯oːn/ *f* -, -en ambition

Amboss *m* -es, -e anvil

ambulan|t *a* out-patient ... ● *adv* **a~t behandeln** treat as an out-patient. **A~z** *f* -, -en out-patients' department

Ameise *f* -, -n ant

amen *int*, **A~** *nt* -s amen

Amerika *nt* -s America

Amerikan|er(in) *m* -s,- (*f* -, -nen) American. **a~isch** *a* American

Ammoniak *nt* -s ammonia

Amnestie *f* -, -n amnesty

amoralisch *a* amoral

Ampel *f* -, -n traffic lights *pl*

Amphitheater *nt* amphitheatre

Amput|ation /-'tsi̯oːn/ *f* -, -en amputation. **a~ieren** *vt* amputate

Amsel *f* -, -n blackbird

Amt *nt* -[e]s,-̈er office; (*Aufgabe*) task; (*Teleph*) exchange. **a~lich** *a* official. **A~szeichen** *nt* dialling tone

Amulett *nt* -[e]s, -e [lucky] charm

amüs|ant *a* amusing. **a~ieren** *vt* amuse; **sich a~ieren** be amused (**über** + *acc* at); (*sich vergnügen*) enjoy oneself

---

an
● *preposition* (+ *dative*)

!   Note that **an** plus **dem** can become **am**

····▸ (*räumlich*) on; (*Gebäude, Ort*) at. **an der Wand** on the wall. **Frankfurt an der Oder** Frankfurt on [the] Oder. **an der Ecke** at the corner. **am Bahnhof** at the station. **an ... vorbei** past

····▸ (*zeitlich*) on. **am Montag** on Monday. **an jedem Sonntag** every Sunday. **am 24. Mai** on May 24th

····▸ (*sonstige Verwendungen*) **arm/reich an Vitaminen** low/rich in vitamins. **jdn an etw erkennen** recognize s.o. by sth. **an etw leiden** suffer from sth. **an einer Krankheit sterben** die of a disease. **an [und für] sich** actually

● *preposition* (+ *accusative*)

!   Note that **an** plus **das** can become **ans**

····▸ to. **schicke es an deinen Bruder** send it to your brother. **er ging ans Fenster** he went to the window

····▸ (*auf, gegen*) on. **etw an die Wand hängen** to hang sth on the wall. **lehne es an den Baum** lean it on *or* against the tree

····▸ (*sonstige Verwendungen*) **an etw/ jdn glauben** believe in sth/s.o. **an etw denken** think of sth. **sich an etw erinnern** remember sth

● *adverb*

····➤ *(auf Fahrplan)* **Köln an: 9.15** arriving Cologne 09.15

····➤ *(angeschaltet)* on. **die Waschmaschine/der Fernseher/das Licht/das Gas ist an** the washing machine/television/light/gas is on

····➤ *(ungefähr)* around; about. **an [die] 20 000 DM** around *or* about 20,000 DM

····➤ *(in die Zukunft)* **von heute an** from today (onwards)

analog *a* analogous; *(Computer)* analog. **A∼ie** *f* -, -n analogy

Analphabet *m* -en, -en illiterate person. **A∼entum** *nt* -s illiteracy

Analy|se *f* -, -n analysis. **a∼sieren** *vt* analyse. **A∼tiker** *m* -s,- analyst. **a∼tisch** *a* analytical

Anämie *f* - anaemia

Ananas *f* -, -[se] pineapple

Anatomie *f* - anatomy

Anbau *m* cultivation; *(Gebäude)* extension. **a∼en** *vt sep* build on; *(anpflanzen)* cultivate, grow

anbei *adv* enclosed

anbeißen† *v sep* ● *vt* take a bite of ● *vi (haben)* <Fisch:> bite

anbeten *vt sep* worship

Anbetracht *m* **in A∼** (+ *gen*) in view of

anbieten† *vt sep* offer; **sich a∼** offer (**zu** to)

anbinden† *vt sep* tie up

Anblick *m* sight. **a∼en** *vt sep* look at

anbrechen† *v sep* ● *vt* start on; break into <Vorräte> ● *vi (sein)* begin; <Tag:> break; <Nacht:> fall

anbrennen† *v sep* ● *vt* light ● *vi (sein)* burn

anbringen† *vt sep* bring [along]; *(befestigen)* fix

Anbruch *m (fig)* dawn; **bei A∼ des Tages/der Nacht** at daybreak/ nightfall

Andacht *f* -, -en reverence; *(Gottesdienst)* prayers *pl*

andächtig *a* reverent; *(fig)* rapt

andauern *vi sep (haben)* last; *(anhalten)* continue. **a∼d** *a* persistent; *(ständig)* constant

Andenken *nt* -s,- memory; *(Souvenir)* souvenir

ander|e(r,s) *a* other; *(verschieden)* different; *(nächste)* next; **ein a∼er, eine a∼e** another ● *pron* **der a∼e/ die a∼en** the other/others; **ein a∼er** another [one]; *(Person)* someone else; **kein a∼er** no one else; **einer nach dem a∼en** one after the other; **alles a∼e/nichts a∼es** everything/nothing else; **unter a∼em** among other things. **a∼enfalls** *adv* otherwise. **a∼erseits** *adv* on the other hand. **a∼mal** *adv* **ein a∼mal** another time

ändern *vt* alter; *(wechseln)* change; **sich ä∼** change

andernfalls *adv* otherwise

anders *pred a* different; **a∼ werden** change ● *adv* differently; <riechen, schmecken> different; *(sonst)* else; **jemand a∼** someone else

anderseits *adv* on the other hand

andersherum *adv* the other way round

anderthalb *inv a* one and a half; **a∼ Stunden** an hour and a half

Änderung *f* -, -en alteration; *(Wechsel)* change

andeut|en *vt sep* indicate; *(anspielen)* hint at. **A∼ung** *f* -, -en indication; hint

Andrang *m* rush (**nach** for); *(Gedränge)* crush

androhen *vt sep* **jdm etw a∼** threaten s.o. with sth

aneignen *vt sep* **sich** *(dat)* **a∼** appropriate; *(lernen)* learn

aneinander *adv & pref* together; <denken> of one another; **a∼ vorbei** past one another; **a∼ geraten** quarrel

Anekdote *f* -, -n anecdote

anerkannt *a* acknowledged

anerkenn|en† *vt sep* acknowledge, recognize; *(würdigen)* appreciate. **a∼end** *a* approving. **A∼ung** *f* - acknowledgement, recognition; appreciation

anfahren† _v sep_ ● _vt_ deliver;
(_streifen_) hit ● _vi_ (_sein_) start

Anfall _m_ fit, attack. **a~en**† _v sep_
● _vt_ attack ● _vi_ (_sein_) arise;
<_Zinsen:_> accrue

anfällig _a_ susceptible (**für** to); (_zart_)
delicate

Anfang _m_ -s,-̈e beginning, start; **zu**
_od_ **am A~** at the beginning;
(_anfangs_) at first. **a~en**† _vt/i sep_
(_haben_) begin, start; (_tun_) do

Anfänger(in) _m_ -s,- (_f_ -, -nen)
beginner

anfangs _adv_ at first.
A~buchstabe _m_ initial letter.
A~gehalt _nt_ starting salary

anfassen _vt sep_ touch; (_behandeln_)
treat; tackle <_Arbeit_>; **sich a~** hold
hands

anfechten† _vt sep_ contest

anfertigen _vt sep_ make

anfeuchten _vt sep_ moisten

anflehen _vt sep_ implore, beg

Anflug _m_ (_Avia_) approach

anforder|n _vt sep_ demand; (_Comm_)
order. **A~ung** _f_ demand

Anfrage _f_ enquiry. **a~n** _vi sep_
(_haben_) enquire, ask

anfreunden (sich) _vr sep_ make
friends (**mit** with)

anfügen _vt sep_ add

anfühlen _vt sep_ feel; **sich weich a~**
feel soft

anführ|en _vt sep_ lead; (_zitieren_)
quote; (_angeben_) give. **A~er** _m_
leader. **A~ungszeichen** _ntpl_
quotation marks

Angabe _f_ statement; (_Anweisung_)
instruction; (_Tennis_) service; **nähere
A~n** particulars

angeb|en† _v sep_ ● _vt_ state; give
<_Namen, Grund_>; (_anzeigen_)
indicate; set <_Tempo_> ● _vi_ (_haben_)
(_Tennis_) serve; (🔲 _protzen_) show off.
A~er(in) _m_ -s,- (_f_ -, -nen) 🔲 show-
off. **A~erei** _f_ - 🔲 showing-off

angeblich _a_ alleged

angeboren _a_ innate; (_Med_)
congenital

Angebot _nt_ offer; (_Auswahl_) range;
A~ und Nachfrage supply and
demand

angebracht _a_ appropriate

angeheiratet _a_ <_Onkel, Tante_> by
marriage

angeheitert _a_ 🔲 tipsy

angehen† _v sep_ ● _vi_ (_sein_) begin,
start; <_Licht, Radio:_> come on;
(_anwachsen_) take root; **a~ gegen**
fight ● _vt_ attack; tackle <_Arbeit_>;
(_bitten_) ask (**um** for); (_betreffen_)
concern

angehör|en _vi sep_ (_haben_) (+ _dat_)
belong to. **A~ige(r)** _m/f_ relative

Angeklagte(r) _m/f_ accused

Angel _f_ -, -n fishing-rod; (_Tür-_) hinge

Angelegenheit _f_ matter

Angel|haken _m_ fish-hook. **a~n** _vi_
(_haben_) fish (**nach** for); **a~n gehen**
go fishing ● _vt_ (_fangen_) catch.
A~rute _f_ fishing-rod

angelsächsisch _a_ Anglo-Saxon

angemessen _a_ commensurate
(_dat_ with); (_passend_) appropriate

angenehm _a_ pleasant; (_bei
Vorstellung_) **a~!** delighted to meet
you!

angeregt _a_ animated

angesehen _a_ respected; <_Firma_>
reputable

angesichts _prep_ (+ _gen_) in view of

angespannt _a_ intent; <_Lage_>
tense

Angestellte(r) _m/f_ employee

angewandt _a_ applied

angewiesen _a_ dependent (**auf** +
acc on); **auf sich selbst a~** on one's
own

angewöhnen _vt sep_ **jdm etw a~**
get s.o. used to sth; **sich** (_dat_) **etw a~**
get into the habit of doing sth

Angewohnheit _f_ habit

Angina _f_ - tonsillitis

angleichen† _vt sep_ adjust (_dat_ to)

anglikanisch _a_ Anglican

Anglistik _f_ - English [language and
literature]

Angorakatze _f_ Persian cat

angreif|en† *vt sep* attack; tackle
<*Arbeit*>; (*schädigen*) damage. **A~er**
m **-s,-** attacker; (*Pol*) aggressor

angrenzen *vi sep* (*haben*) adjoin
(**an** *etw acc* sth). **a~d** *a* adjoining

Angriff *m* attack; **in A~ nehmen**
tackle. **a~slustig** *a* aggressive

Angst *f* -,̈e fear; (*Psych*) anxiety;
(*Sorge*) worry (**um** about); **A~ haben**
be afraid (**vor** + *dat* of); (*sich sorgen*)
be worried (**um** about); **jdm A~
machen** frighten s.o.

ängstigen *vt* frighten; (*Sorge
machen*) worry; **sich ä~** be
frightened; be worried (**um** about)

ängstlich *a* nervous; (*scheu*) timid;
(*verängstigt*) frightened, scared;
(*besorgt*) anxious

angucken *vt sep* 🔲 look at

angurten (sich) *vr sep* fasten one's
seat-belt

anhaben† *vt sep* have on; **er/es
kann mir nichts a~** (*fig*) he/it cannot
hurt me

anhalt|en† *v sep* ● *vt* stop; hold
<*Atem*>; **jdn zur Arbeit a~en** urge
s.o. to work ● *vi* (*haben*) stop;
(*andauern*) continue. **a~end** *a*
persistent. **A~er(in)** *m* **-s,-** (*f* -,
-nen) hitchhiker; **per A~er fahren**
hitchhike. **A~spunkt** *m* clue

anhand *prep* (+ *gen*) with the aid of

Anhang *m* appendix

anhängen¹ *vt sep* (*reg*) hang up;
(*befestigen*) attach

anhäng|en²† *vi* (*haben*) be a
follower of. **A~er** *m* **-s,-** follower;
(*Auto*) trailer; (*Schild*) [tie-on] label;
(*Schmuck*) pendant. **A~erin** *f* -, **-nen**
follower. **a~lich** *a* affectionate

anhäufen *vt sep* pile up

Anhieb *m* **auf A~** straight away

Anhöhe *f* hill

anhören *vt sep* listen to; **sich gut
a~** sound good

animieren *vt* encourage (**zu** to)

Anis *m* **-es** aniseed

Anker *m* **-s,-** anchor; **vor A~ gehen**
drop anchor. **a~n** *vi* (*haben*)
anchor; (*liegen*) be anchored

anketten *vt sep* chain up

Anklage *f* accusation; (*Jur*) charge;
(*Ankläger*) prosecution. **A~bank** *f*
dock. **a~n** *vt sep* accuse (*gen* of);
(*Jur*) charge (*gen* with)

Ankläger *m* accuser; (*Jur*)
prosecutor

anklammern *vt sep* clip on; **sich
a~** cling (**an** + *acc* to)

ankleben *v sep* ● *vt* stick on ● *vi*
(*sein*) stick (**an** + *dat* to)

anklopfen *vi sep* (*haben*) knock

anknipsen *vt sep* 🔲 switch on

ankommen† *vi sep* (*sein*) arrive;
(*sich nähern*) approach; **gut a~**
arrive safely; (*fig*) go down well (**bei**
with); **nicht a~ gegen** (*fig*) be no
match for; **a~ auf** (+ *acc*) depend on;
das kommt darauf an it [all] depends

ankreuzen *vt sep* mark with a
cross

ankündig|en *vt sep* announce.
A~ung *f* announcement

Ankunft *f* - arrival

ankurbeln *vt sep* (*fig*) boost

anlächeln *vt sep* smile at

anlachen *vt sep* smile at

Anlage *f* -, **-n** installation;
(*Industrie-*) plant; (*Komplex*)
complex; (*Geld-*) investment; (*Plan*)
layout; (*Beilage*) enclosure;
(*Veranlagung*) aptitude; (*Neigung*)
predisposition; **öffentliche A~n**
[public] gardens; **als A~** enclosed

Anlass *m* **-es,**̈**e** reason; (*Gelegenheit*)
occasion; **A~ geben zu** give cause
for

anlass|en† *vt sep* (*Auto*) start; 🔲
leave on <*Licht*>; keep on <*Mantel*>.
A~er *m* **-s,-** starter

anlässlich *prep* (+ *gen*) on the
occasion of

Anlauf *m* (*Sport*) run-up; (*fig*)
attempt. **a~en†** *v sep* ● *vi* (*sein*)
start; (*beschlagen*) mist up; <*Metall:*>
tarnish; **rot a~en** blush ● *vt* (*Naut*)
call at

anlegen *v sep* ● *vt* put (**an** + *acc*
against); put on <*Kleidung,
Verband*>; lay back <*Ohren*>; aim
<*Gewehr*>; (*investieren*) invest;
(*ausgeben*) spend (**für** on); draw up

<Liste>; **es darauf a~** *(fig)* aim **(zu** to) ● *vi (haben) <Schiff:>* moor; **a~ auf** *(+ acc)* aim at

anlehnen *vt sep* lean **(an** + *acc* against); **sich a~** lean **(an** + *acc* on)

Anleihe *f -, -n* loan

anleit|en *vt sep* instruct. **A~ung** *f* instructions *pl*

anlernen *vt sep* train

Anliegen *nt -s,-* request; *(Wunsch)* desire

anlieg|en† *vi sep (haben)* [eng] **a~en** fit closely; [eng] **a~end** close-fitting. **A~er** *mpl* residents; **'A~er frei'** 'access for residents only'

anlügen† *vt sep* lie to

anmachen *vt sep* Ⅰ fix; *(anschalten)* turn on; dress *<Salat>*

anmalen *vt sep* paint

Anmarsch *m (Mil)* approach

anmeld|en *vt sep* announce; *(Admin)* register; **sich a~en** say that one is coming; *(Admin)* register; *(Sch)* enrol; *(im Hotel)* check in; *(beim Arzt)* make an appointment. **A~ung** *f* announcement; *(Admin)* registration; *(Sch)* enrolment; *(Termin)* appointment

anmerk|en *vt sep* mark; **sich** *(dat)* **etw a~en lassen** show sth. **A~ung** *f -, -en* note

Anmut *f -* grace; *(Charme)* charm

anmutig *a* graceful

annähen *vt sep* sew on

annäher|nd *a* approximate. **A~ungsversuche** *mpl* advances

Annahme *f -, -n* acceptance; *(Adoption)* adoption; *(Vermutung)* assumption

annehm|bar *a* acceptable. **a~en†** *vt sep* accept; *(adoptieren)* adopt; acquire *<Gewohnheit>*; *(sich zulegen, vermuten)* assume; **angenommen, dass** assuming that. **A~lichkeiten** *fpl* comforts

Anno *adv* **A~ 1920** in the year 1920

Annon|ce /a'nõːsə/ *f -, -n* advertisement. **a~cieren** /-'siː-/ *vt/i (haben)* advertise

annullieren *vt* annul; cancel

Anomalie *f -, -n* anomaly

anonym *a* anonymous

Anorak *m -s, -s* anorak

anordn|en *vt sep* arrange; *(befehlen)* order. **A~ung** *f* arrangement; order

anorganisch *a* inorganic

anormal *a* abnormal

anpass|en *vt sep* try on; *(angleichen)* adapt *(dat* to); **sich a~** adapt *(dat* to). **A~ung** *f -* adaptation. **a~ungsfähig** *a* adaptable. **A~ungsfähigkeit** *f* adaptability

Anpfiff *m (Sport)* kick-off

Anprall *m -[e]s* impact. **a~en** *vi sep (sein)* strike **(an etw** *acc* sth)

anpreisen† *vt sep* commend

Anprob|e *f* fitting. **a~ieren** *vt sep* try on

anrechnen *vt sep* count **(als** as); *(berechnen)* charge for; *(verrechnen)* allow *<Summe>*

Anrecht *nt* right **(auf** + *acc* to)

Anrede *f* [form of] address. **a~n** *vt sep* address; speak to

anreg|en *vt sep* stimulate; *(ermuntern)* encourage **(zu** to); *(vorschlagen)* suggest. **a~end** *a* stimulating. **A~ung** *f* stimulation; *(Vorschlag)* suggestion

Anreise *f* journey; *(Ankunft)* arrival. **a~n** *vi sep (sein)* arrive

Anreiz *m* incentive

Anrichte *f -, -n* sideboard. **a~n** *vt sep (Culin)* prepare; *(garnieren)* garnish **(mit** with); *(verursachen)* cause

anrüchig *a* disreputable

Anruf *m* call. **A~beantworter** *m -s,-* answering machine. **a~en†** *v sep* ● *vt* call to; *(bitten)* call on **(um** for); *(Teleph)* ring ● *vi (haben)* ring **(bei jdm** s.o.)

anrühren *vt sep* touch; *(verrühren)* mix

ans *prep* = **an das**

Ansage *f* announcement. **a~n** *vt sep* announce

ansamm|eln *vt sep* collect; *(anhäufen)* accumulate; **sich a~eln**

---

collect; *(sich häufen)* accumulate; *‹Leute:›* gather. **A~lung** *f* collection; *(Menschen-)* crowd

ansässig *a* resident

Ansatz *m* beginning; *(Versuch)* attempt

anschaffen *vt sep* [sich *dat*] etw a~ acquire/*(kaufen)* buy sth

anschalten *vt sep* switch on

anschau|en *vt sep* look at. **a~lich** *a* vivid, *adv* -ly. **A~ung** *f* -, -en *(fig)* view

Anschein *m* appearance. **a~end** *adv* apparently

anschirren *vt sep* harness

Anschlag *m* notice; *(Vor-)* estimate; *(Überfall)* attack (auf + *acc* on); *(Mus)* touch; *(Techn)* stop. **a~en†** *v sep* ● *vt* put up ‹Aushang›; strike ‹Note, Taste›; cast on ‹Masche›; *(beschädigen)* chip ● *vi (haben)* strike/*(stoßen)* knock (an + *acc* against); *(wirken)* be effective ● *vi (sein)* knock (an + *acc* against)

anschließen† *v sep* ● *vt* connect (an + *acc* to); *(zufügen)* add; sich a~ an (+ *acc*) *(anstoßen)* adjoin; *(folgen)* follow; *(sich anfreunden)* become friendly with; sich jdm a~ join s.o. ● *vi (haben)* a~ an (+ *acc*) adjoin; *(folgen)* follow. **a~d** *a* adjoining; *(zeitlich)* following ● *adv* afterwards

Anschluss *m* connection; *(Kontakt)* contact; A~ finden make friends; im A~ an (+ *acc*) after

anschmiegsam *a* affectionate

anschmieren *vt sep* smear

anschnallen *vt sep* strap on; sich a~ fasten one's seat-belt

anschneiden† *vt sep* cut into; broach ‹Thema›

anschreiben† *vt sep* write (an + *acc* on); *(Comm)* put on s.o.'s account; *(sich wenden)* write to

Anschrift *f* address

anschuldig|en *vt sep* accuse. **A~ung** *f* -, -en accusation

anschwellen† *vi sep (sein)* swell

ansehen† *vt sep* look at; *(einschätzen)* regard (als as); [sich *dat*] etw a~ look at sth; *(TV)* watch

sth. **A~** *nt* -s respect; *(Ruf)* reputation

ansehnlich *a* considerable

ansetzen *v sep* ● *vt* join (an + *acc* to); *(veranschlagen)* estimate ● *vi (haben) (anbrennen)* burn; zum Sprung a~ get ready to jump

Ansicht *f* view; meiner A~ nach in my view; zur A~ *(Comm)* on approval. **A~s[post]karte** *f* picture postcard. **A~ssache** *f* matter of opinion

ansiedeln (sich) *vr sep* settle

ansonsten *adv* apart from that

anspannen *vt sep* hitch up; *(anstrengen)* strain; tense ‹Muskel›

Anspielung *f* -, -en allusion; hint

Anspitzer *m* -s,- pencil-sharpener

Ansprache *f* address

ansprechen† *v sep* ● *vt* speak to; *(fig)* appeal to ● *vi (haben)* respond (auf + *acc* to)

anspringen† *v sep* ● *vt* jump at ● *vi (sein) (Auto)* start

Anspruch *m* claim/*(Recht)* right (auf + *acc* to); A~ haben be entitled (auf + *acc* to); in A~ nehmen make use of; *(erfordern)* demand; take up ‹Zeit›; occupy ‹Person›; hohe A~e stellen be very demanding. **a~slos** *a* undemanding. **a~svoll** *a* demanding; *(kritisch)* discriminating; *(vornehm)* upmarket

anstacheln *vt sep (fig)* spur on

Anstalt *f* -, -en institution

Anstand *m* decency; *(Benehmen)* [good] manners *pl*

anständig *a* decent; *(ehrbar)* respectable; *(richtig)* proper

anstandslos *adv* without any trouble

anstarren *vt sep* stare at

anstatt *conj & prep* (+ *gen*) instead of

ansteck|en *v sep* ● *vt* pin (an + *acc* to/on); put on ‹Ring›; *(anzünden)* light; *(in Brand stecken)* set fire to; *(Med)* infect; sich a~en catch an infection (bei from) ● *vi (haben)* be infectious. **a~end** *a* infectious. **A~ung** *f* -, -en infection

anstehen† *vi sep* (*haben*) queue

anstelle *prep* (+ *gen*) instead of

anstell|en *vt sep* put, stand (**an** + *acc* against); (*einstellen*) employ; (*anschalten*) turn on; (*tun*) do; **sich a~en** queue [up]. **A~ung** *f* employment; (*Stelle*) job

Anstieg *m* -[e]s, -e climb; (*fig*) rise

anstiften *vt sep* cause; (*anzetteln*) instigate

Anstoß *m* (*Anregung*) impetus; (*Stoß*) knock; (*Fußball*) kick-off; **A~ erregen** give offence (**an** + *dat* at). **a~en**† *v sep* ● *vt* knock; (*mit dem Ellbogen*) nudge ● *vi* (*sein*) knock (**an** + *acc* against) ● *vi* (*haben*) adjoin (**an** etw *acc* sth); **a~en auf** (+ *acc*) drink to; **mit der Zunge a~en** lisp

anstößig *a* offensive

anstrahlen *vt sep* floodlight

anstreichen† *vt sep* paint; (*anmerken*) mark

anstreng|en *vt sep* strain; (*ermüden*) tire; **sich a~en** exert oneself; (*sich bemühen*) make an effort (**zu** to). **a~end** *a* strenuous; (*ermüdend*) tiring. **A~ung** *f* -, -en strain; (*Mühe*) effort

Anstrich *m* coat [of paint]

Ansturm *m* rush; (*Mil*) assault

Ansuchen *nt* -s, - request

Antarktis *f* - Antarctic

Anteil *m* share; **A~ nehmen** take an interest (**an** + *dat* in). **A~nahme** *f* - interest (**an** + *dat* in); (*Mitgefühl*) sympathy

Antenne *f* -, -n aerial

Anthologie *f* -, -n anthology

Anthropologie *f* - anthropology

Anti|alkoholiker *m* teetotaller. **A~biotikum** *nt* -s, -ka antibiotic

antik *a* antique. **A~e** *f* - [classical] antiquity

Antikörper *m* antibody

Antilope *f* -, -n antelope

Antipathie *f* - antipathy

Antiquariat *nt* -[e]s, -e antiquarian bookshop

Antiquitäten *fpl* antiques. **A~händler** *m* antique dealer

Antrag *m* -[e]s,¨-e proposal; (*Pol*) motion; (*Gesuch*) application. **A~steller** *m* -s, - applicant

antreffen† *vt sep* find

antreten† *v sep* ● *vt* start; take up <*Amt*> ● *vi* (*sein*) line up

Antrieb *m* urge; (*Techn*) drive; **aus eigenem A~** of one's own accord

Antritt *m* start; **bei A~ eines Amtes** when taking office

antun† *vt sep* jdm etw **a~** do sth to s.o.; **sich** (*dat*) etwas **a~** take one's own life

Antwort *f* -, -en answer, reply (**auf** + *acc* to). **a~en** *vt/i* (*haben*) answer (jdm s.o.)

anvertrauen *vt sep* entrust/ (*mitteilen*) confide (jdm to s.o.)

Anwalt *m* -[e]s,¨-e, **Anwältin** *f* -, -nen lawyer; (*vor Gericht*) counsel

Anwandlung *f* -, -en fit (**von** of)

Anwärter(in) *m(f)* candidate

anweis|en† *vt sep* assign (*dat* to); (*beauftragen*) instruct. **A~ung** *f* instruction; (*Geld-*) money order

anwend|en *vt sep* apply (**auf** + *acc* to); (*gebrauchen*) use. **A~ung** *f* application; use

anwerben† *vt sep* recruit

Anwesen *nt* -s, - property

anwesen|d *a* present (**bei** at); **die A~den** those present. **A~heit** *f* - presence

anwidern *vt sep* disgust

Anwohner *mpl* residents

Anzahl *f* number

anzahl|en *vt sep* pay a deposit on. **A~ung** *f* deposit

anzapfen *vt sep* tap

Anzeichen *nt* sign

Anzeige *f* -, -n announcement; (*Inserat*) advertisement; **A~ erstatten gegen jdn** report s.o. to the police. **a~n** *vt sep* announce; (*inserieren*) advertise; (*melden*) report [to the police]; (*angeben*) indicate

anzieh|en† *vt sep* ● *vt* attract; (*festziehen*) tighten; put on <*Kleider*,

Bremse>; (*ankleiden*) dress; **sich a~en** get dressed. **a~end** *a* attractive. **A~ungskraft** *f* attraction; (*Phys*) gravity

Anzug *m* suit

anzüglich *a* suggestive

anzünden *vt sep* light; (*in Brand stecken*) set fire to

anzweifeln *vt sep* question

apart *a* striking

Apathie *f* - apathy

apathisch *a* apathetic

Aperitif *m* -s, -s aperitif

Apfel *m* -s,- apple

Apfelsine *f* -, -n orange

Apostel *m* -s,- apostle

Apostroph *m* -s, -e apostrophe

Apotheke *f* -, -n pharmacy. **A~er(in)** *m* -s,- (*f* -, -nen) pharmacist, [dispensing] chemist

Apparat *m* -[e]s, -e device; (*Phot*) camera; (*Radio, TV*) set; (*Teleph*) telephone; **am A~!** speaking!

Appell *m* -s, -e appeal; (*Mil*) roll-call. **a~ieren** *vi* (*haben*) appeal (**an** + *acc* to)

Appetit *m* -s appetite; **guten A~!** enjoy your meal! **a~lich** *a* appetizing

Applaus *m* -es applause

Aprikose *f* -, -n apricot

April *m* -[s] April

Aquarell *nt* -s, -e water-colour

Aquarium *nt* -s, -ien aquarium

Äquator *m* -s equator

Ära *f* - era

Araber(in) *m* -s,- (*f* -, -nen) Arab

arabisch *a* Arab; (*Geog*) Arabian; <*Ziffer*> Arabic

Arbeit *f* -, -en work; (*Anstellung*) employment, job; (*Aufgabe*) task; (*Sch*) [written] test; (*Abhandlung*) treatise; (*Qualität*) workmanship; **sich an die A~ machen** set to work; **sich** (*dat*) **viel A~ machen** go to a lot of trouble. **a~en** *v sep* ● *vi* (*haben*) work (**an** + *dat* on) ● *vt* make. **A~er(in)** *m* -s,- (*f* -, -nen) worker; (*Land-, Hilfs-*) labourer. **A~erklasse** *f* working class

Arbeitgeber *m* -s,- employer. **A~nehmer** *m* -s,- employee

Arbeitsamt *nt* employment exchange. **A~erlaubnis, A~genehmigung** *f* work permit. **A~kraft** *f* worker. **a~los** *a* unemployed; **~los sein** be out of work. **A~lose(r)** *m/f* unemployed person; **die A~losen** the unemployed *pl*. **A~losenunterstützung** *f* unemployment benefit. **A~losigkeit** *f* - unemployment

arbeitsparend *a* labour-saving

Arbeitsplatz *m* job

Archäologe *m* -n, -n archaeologist. **A~logie** *f* - archaeology

Arche *f* - **die A~** Noah Noah's Ark

Architekt(in) *m* -en, -en (*f* -, -nen) architect. **a~tonisch** *a* architectural. **A~tur** *f* - architecture

Archiv *nt* -s, -e archives *pl*

Arena *f* -, -nen arena

arg *a* bad; (*groß*) terrible

Argentinien /-iən/ *nt* -s Argentina. **a~isch** *a* Argentinian

Ärger *m* -s annoyance; (*Unannehmlichkeit*) trouble. **ä~lich** *a* annoyed; (*leidig*) annoying; **ä~lich sein** be annoyed. **ä~n** *vt* annoy; (*necken*) tease; **sich ä~n** get annoyed (**über jdn/etw** with s.o./ about sth). **Ä~nis** *nt* -ses, -se annoyance; **öffentliches Ä~nis** public nuisance

Arglist *f* - malice

arglos *a* unsuspecting

Argument *nt* -[e]s, -e argument. **a~ieren** *vi* (*haben*) argue (**dass** that)

Arie /'a:riə/ *f* -, -n aria

Aristokrat *m* -en, -en aristocrat. **A~kratie** *f* - aristocracy. **a~kratisch** *a* aristocratic

Arktis *f* - Arctic. **a~isch** *a* Arctic

arm *a* poor

Arm *m* -[e]s, -e arm; **jdn auf den Arm nehmen** Ⅱ pull s.o.'s leg

Armaturenbrett *nt* instrument panel; (*Auto*) dashboard

Armband nt (pl -bänder) bracelet; (Uhr-) watch-strap. **A~uhr** f wristwatch

Arm|e(r) m/f poor man/woman; die **A~en** the poor pl

Armee f -, -n army

Ärmel m -s,- sleeve. **Ä~kanal** m [English] Channel. **ä~los** a sleeveless

Arm|lehne f arm. **A~leuchter** m candelabra

ärmlich a poor; (elend) miserable

armselig a miserable

Armut f - poverty

Arran|gement /arãʒə'mã:/ nt -s, -s arrangement. **a~gieren** /-'ʒi:rən/ vt arrange

arrogant a arrogant

Arsch m -[e]s,̈-e (vulg) arse

Arsen nt -s arsenic

Art f -, -en manner; (Weise) way; (Natur) nature; (Sorte) kind; (Biol) species; **auf diese Art** in this way

Arterie /-i̯ə/ f -, -n artery

Arthritis f - arthritis

artig a well-behaved

Artikel m -s,- article

Artillerie f - artillery

Artischocke f -, -n artichoke

Arznei f -, -en medicine

Arzt m -[e]s,̈-e doctor

Ärzt|in f -, -nen [woman] doctor. **ä~lich** a medical

As* nt -ses, -se s. Ass

Asbest m -[e]s asbestos

Asche f - ash. **A~nbecher** m ashtray. **A~rmittwoch** m Ash Wednesday

Asiat|(in) m -en, -en (f -, -nen) Asian. **a~isch** a Asian

Asien /'a:zi̯ən/ nt -s Asia

asozial a antisocial

Aspekt m -[e]s, -e aspect

Asphalt m -[e]s asphalt. **a~ieren** vt asphalt

Ass nt -es, -e ace

Assistent(in) m -en, -en (f -, -nen) assistant

Ast m -[e]s,̈-e branch

asthetisch a aesthetic

Asthma nt -s asthma. **a~matisch** a asthmatic

Astro|loge m -n, -n astrologer. **A~logie** f - astrology. **A~naut** m -en, -en astronaut. **A~nomie** f - astronomy

Asyl nt -s, -e home; (Pol) asylum. **A~ant** m -en, -en asylum-seeker

Atelier /-'li̯e:/ nt -s, -s studio

Atem m -s breath. **a~los** a breathless. **A~zug** m breath

Atheist m -en, -en atheist

Äther m -s ether

Athiopien /-i̯ən/ nt -s Ethiopia

Athlet|(in) m -en, -en (f -, -nen) athlete. **a~isch** a athletic

Atlant|ik m -s Atlantic. **a~isch** a Atlantic; der **A~ische Ozean** the Atlantic Ocean

Atlas m -lasses, -lanten atlas

atmen vt/i (haben) breathe

Atmosphäre f -, -n atmosphere

Atmung f - breathing

Atom nt -s, -e atom. **A~bombe** f atom bomb. **A~krieg** m nuclear war

Atten|tat nt -[e]s, -e assassination attempt. **A~täter** m assassin

Attest nt -[e]s, -e certificate

Attrak|tion /-'tsi̯o:n/ f -, -en attraction. **a~tiv** a attractive

Attribut nt -[e]s, -e attribute

ätzen vt corrode; (Med) cauterize; (Kunst) etch. **ä~d** a corrosive; <Spott> caustic

au int ouch; au fein! oh good!

Aubergine /obɛr'ʒi:nə/ f -, -n aubergine

auch adv & conj also, too; (außerdem) what's more; (selbst) even; a~ wenn even if; sie weiß es a~ nicht she doesn't know either; wer/wie/was a~ immer whoever/however/whatever

Audienz f -, -en audience

audiovisuell a audio-visual

Auditorium nt -s, -ien (Univ) lecture hall

auf

● *preposition* (+ *dative*)

····▸ (*nicht unter*) on. **auf dem Tisch** on the table. **auf Deck** on deck. **auf der Erde** on earth. **auf der Welt** in the world. **auf der Straße** in the street

····▸ (*bei Institution, Veranstaltung usw.*) at; (*bei Gebäude, Zimmer*) in. **auf der Schule/Uni** at school/university. **auf einer Party/Hochzeit** at a party/wedding. **Geld auf der Bank haben** have money in the bank. **sie ist auf ihrem Zimmer** she's in her room. **auf Urlaub** on holiday

● *preposition* (+ *accusative*)

····▸ (*nicht unter*) on[to]. **er legte das Buch auf den Tisch** he laid the book on the table. **auf eine Mauer steigen** climb onto a wall. **auf die Straße gehen** go [out] into the street

····▸ (*bei Institution, Veranstaltung usw.*) to. **auf eine Party/die Toilette gehen** go to a party/the toilet. **auf die Schule/Uni gehen** go to school/university. **auf Urlaub schicken** send on holiday

····▸ (*bei Entfernung*) **auf 10 km [Entfernung] zu sehen/hören** visible/audible for [a distance of] 10 km

····▸ (*zeitlich*) (*wie lange*) for; (*bis*) until; (*wann*) on. **auf Jahre [hinaus]** for years [to come]. **auf ein paar Tage** for a few days. **etw auf nächsten Mittwoch verschieben** postpone sth until next Wednesday. **das fällt auf einen Montag** it falls on a Monday

····▸ (*Art und Weise*) in. **auf diese [Art und] Weise** in this way. **auf Deutsch/Englisch** in German/English

····▸ (*aufgrund*) **auf Wunsch** on request. **auf meine Bitte** on *or* at my request. **auf Befehl** on command

····▸ (*Proportion*) to. **ein Teelöffel auf einen Liter Wasser** one teaspoon to one litre of water. **auf die Sekunde/den Millimeter [genau]** [precise] to the nearest second/millimetre

····▸ (*Toast*) to. **auf deine Gesundheit!** your health!

● *adverb*

····▸ (*aufgerichtet, aufgestanden*) up. **auf!** (*steh auf!*) up you get! **auf und ab** (*hin und her*) up and down

····▸ (*aufgesetzt*) **Helm/Hut/Brille auf!** helmet/hat/glasses on!

····▸ (*geöffnet, offen*) open. **Fenster/Mund auf!** open the window/your mouth!

aufatmen *vi sep* (*haben*) heave a sigh of relief

aufbahren *vt sep* lay out

Aufbau *m* construction; (*Struktur*) structure. **a∼en** *v sep* ● *vt* construct, build; (*errichten*) erect; (*schaffen*) build up; (*arrangieren*) arrange; **sich a∼en** (*fig*) be based (**auf** + *dat* on) ● *vi* (*haben*) be based (**auf** + *dat* on)

aufbauschen *vt sep* puff out; (*fig*) exaggerate

aufbekommen† *vt sep* get open; (*Sch*) be given [as homework]

aufbessern *vt sep* improve; (*erhöhen*) increase

aufbewahr|en *vt sep* keep; (*lagern*) store. **A∼ung** *f* - safe keeping; storage; (*Gepäck-*) left-luggage office

aufblas|bar *a* inflatable. **a∼en†** *vt sep* inflate

aufbleiben† *vi sep* (*sein*) stay open; <*Person:*> stay up

aufblenden *vt/i sep* (*haben*) (*Auto*) switch to full beam

aufblühen *vi sep* (*sein*) flower

aufbocken *vt sep* jack up

aufbrauchen *vt sep* use up

aufbrechen† *v sep* ● *vt* break open ● *vi* (*sein*) <*Knospe:*> open; (*sich aufmachen*) set out, start

aufbringen† *vt sep* raise <*Geld*>; find <*Kraft*>

Aufbruch *m* start, departure

aufbrühen *vt sep* make <*Tee*>

aufbürden *vt sep* **jdm etw a∼** (*fig*) burden s.o. with sth

aufdecken *vt sep* (*auflegen*) put on; (*abdecken*) uncover; (*fig*) expose

aufdrehen *vt sep* turn on

aufdringlich *a* persistent

a

aufeinander *adv* one on top of the other; *<schießen>* at each other; *<warten>* for each other; **a~ folgend** successive; *<Tage>* consecutive.

Aufenthalt *m* stay; **10 Minuten A~ haben** *<Zug:>* stop for 10 minutes. **A~serlaubnis, A~sgenehmigung** *f* residence permit. **A~sraum** *m* recreation room; *(im Hotel)* lounge

Auferstehung *f* - resurrection

aufessen† *vt sep* eat up

auffahr|en† *vi sep (sein)* drive up; *(aufprallen)* crash, run (**auf** + *acc* into). **A~t** *f* drive; *(Autobahn-)* access road, slip road; *(Bergfahrt)* ascent

auffallen† *vi sep (sein)* be conspicuous; **unangenehm a~** make a bad impression

auffällig *a* conspicuous

auffangen† *vt sep* catch; pick up

auffass|en *vt sep* understand; *(deuten)* take. **A~ung** *f* understanding; *(Ansicht)* view

aufforder|n *vt sep* ask; *(einladen)* invite. **A~ung** *f* request; invitation

auffrischen *v sep* ● *vt* freshen up; revive *<Erinnerung>*; **seine Englischkenntnisse a~** brush up one's English

aufführ|en *vt sep* perform; *(angeben)* list; **sich a~en** behave. **A~ung** *f* performance

auffüllen *vt sep* fill up

Aufgabe *f* task; *(Rechen-)* problem; *(Verzicht)* giving up; **A~n** *(Sch)* homework *sg*

Aufgang *m* way up; *(Treppe)* stairs *pl*; *(Astr)* rise

aufgeben† *v sep* ● *vt* give up; post *<Brief>*; send *<Telegramm>*; place *<Bestellung>*; register *<Gepäck>*; put in the paper *<Annonce>*; **jdm eine Aufgabe a~** set s.o. a task; **jdm Suppe a~** serve s.o. with soup ● *vi* *(haben)* give up

Aufgebot *nt* contingent (**an** + *dat* of); *(Relig)* banns *pl*

---

*alte Schreibung

aufgedunsen *a* bloated

aufgehen† *vi sep (sein)* open; *(sich lösen)* come undone; *<Teig, Sonne:>* rise; *<Saat:>* come up; *(Math)* come out exactly; **in Flammen a~** go up in flames

aufgelegt *a* **gut/schlecht a~ sein** be in a good/bad mood

aufgeregt *a* excited; *(erregt)* agitated

aufgeschlossen *a* *(fig)* openminded

aufgeweckt *a* *(fig)* bright

aufgießen† *vt sep* pour on; *(aufbrühen)* make *<Tee>*

aufgreifen† *vt sep* pick up; take up *<Vorschlag, Thema>*

aufgrund *prep* (+ *gen*) on the strength of

Aufguss *m* infusion

aufhaben† *v sep* ● *vt* have on; **den Mund a~** have one's mouth open; **viel a~** *(Sch)* have a lot of homework ● *vi* *(haben)* be open

aufhalten† *vt sep* hold up; *(anhalten)* stop; *(abhalten)* keep; *(offenhalten)* hold out *<Hand>*; **sich a~** stay; *(sich befassen)* spend one's time (**mit** on)

aufhäng|en *vt/i sep (haben)* hang up; *(henken)* hang; **sich a~en** hang oneself. **A~er** *m* **-s,-** loop

aufheben† *vt sep* pick up; *(hochheben)* raise; *(aufbewahren)* keep; *(beenden)* end; *(rückgängig machen)* lift; *(abschaffen)* abolish; *(Jur)* quash *<Urteil>*; repeal *<Gesetz>*; *(ausgleichen)* cancel out; **gut aufgehoben sein** be well looked after

aufheitern *vt sep* cheer up; **sich a~** *<Wetter:>* brighten up

aufhellen *vt sep* lighten; **sich a~** *<Himmel:>* brighten

aufhetzen *vt sep* incite

aufholen *v sep* ● *vt* make up ● *vi* *(haben)* catch up; *(zeitlich)* make up time

aufhören *vi sep (haben)* stop

aufklappen *vt/i sep (sein)* open

aufklär|en *vt sep* solve; **jdn a~en** enlighten s.o.; **sich a~en** be solved; <*Wetter:*> clear up. **A~ung** *f* solution; enlightenment; (*Mil*) reconnaissance; **sexuelle A~ung** sex education

aufkleb|en *vt sep* stick on. **A~er** *m* -s,- sticker

aufknöpfen *vt sep* unbutton

aufkochen *v sep* ● *vt* bring to the boil ● *vi* (*sein*) come to the boil

aufkommen† *vi sep* (*sein*) start; <*Wind:*> spring up; <*Mode:*> come in

aufkrempeln *vt sep* roll up

aufladen† *vt sep* load; (*Electr*) charge

Auflage *f* impression; (*Ausgabe*) edition; (*Zeitungs-*) circulation

auflassen† *vt sep* leave open; leave on <*Hut*>

Auflauf *m* crowd; (*Culin*) ≈ soufflé

auflegen *v sep* ● *vt* apply (**auf** + *acc* to); put down <*Hörer:*>; **neu a~** reprint ● *vi* (*haben*) ring off

auflehn|en (sich) *vr sep* (*fig*) rebel. **A~ung** *f* - rebellion

auflesen† *vt sep* pick up

aufleuchten *vi sep* (*haben*) light up

auflös|en *vt sep* dissolve; close <*Konto*>; **sich a~en** dissolve; <*Nebel:*> clear. **A~ung** *f* dissolution; (*Lösung*) solution

aufmach|en *v sep* ● *vt* open; (*lösen*) undo; **sich a~en** set out (**nach** for) ● *vi* (*haben*) open; **jdm a~en** open the door to s.o. **A~ung** *f* -, -en get-up

aufmerksam *a* attentive; **a~ werden auf** (+ *acc*) notice; **jdn a~ machen auf** (+ *acc*) draw s.o.'s attention to. **A~keit** *f* -, -en attention; (*Höflichkeit*) courtesy

aufmuntern *vt sep* cheer up

Aufnahme *f* -, -n acceptance; (*Empfang*) reception; (*in Klub, Krankenhaus*) admission; (*Einbeziehung*) inclusion; (*Beginn*) start; (*Foto*) photograph; (*Film-*) shot; (*Mus*) recording; (*Band-*) tape recording. **a~fähig** *a* receptive. **A~prüfung** *f* entrance examination

aufnehmen† *vt sep* pick up; (*absorbieren*) absorb; take <*Nahrung, Foto*>; (*fassen*) hold; (*annehmen*) accept; (*leihen*) borrow; (*empfangen*) receive; (*in Klub, Krankenhaus*) admit; (*beherbergen, geistig erfassen*) take in; (*einbeziehen*) include; (*beginnen*) take up; (*niederschreiben*) take down; (*filmen*) film, shoot; (*Mus*) record; **auf Band a~** tape[-record]

aufopfer|n *vt sep* sacrifice; **sich a~n** sacrifice oneself. **A~ung** *f* self-sacrifice

aufpassen *vi sep* (*haben*) pay attention; (*sich vorsehen*) take care; **a~ auf** (+ *acc*) look after

Aufprall *m* -[e]s impact. **a~en** *vi sep* (*sein*) **a~en auf** (+ *acc*) hit

aufpumpen *vt sep* pump up, inflate

aufputsch|en *vt sep* incite. **A~mittel** *nt* stimulant

aufquellen† *vi sep* (*sein*) swell

aufraffen *vt sep* pick up; **sich a~** pick oneself up; (*fig*) pull oneself together

aufragen *vi sep* (*sein*) rise [up]

aufräumen *vt/i sep* (*haben*) tidy up; (*wegräumen*) put away

aufrecht *a & adv* upright. **a~erhalten**† *vt sep* (*fig*) maintain

aufreg|en *vt* excite; (*beunruhigen*) upset; (*ärgern*) annoy; **sich a~en** get excited; (*sich erregen*) get worked up. **a~end** *a* exciting. **A~ung** *f* excitement

aufreiben† *vt sep* chafe; (*fig*) wear down. **a~d** *a* trying

aufreißen† *v sep* ● *vt* tear open; dig up <*Straße*>; open wide <*Augen, Mund*> ● *vi* (*sein*) split open

aufrichtig *a* sincere. **A~keit** *f* - sincerity

aufrollen *vt sep* roll up; (*entrollen*) unroll

aufrücken *vi sep* (*sein*) move up; (*fig*) be promoted

Aufruf *m* appeal (**an** + *dat* to). **a~en**† *vt sep* call out <*Namen*>; **jdn a~en** call s.o.'s name

a

Aufruhr *m* -s, -e turmoil; (*Empörung*) revolt

aufrühr|en *vt sep* stir up. **A~er** *m* -s,- rebel. **a~erisch** *a* inflammatory; (*rebellisch*) rebellious

aufrunden *vt sep* round up

aufrüsten *vi sep* (*haben*) arm

aufsagen *vt sep* recite

aufsässig *a* rebellious

Aufsatz *m* top; (*Sch*) essay

aufsaugen† *vt sep* soak up

aufschauen *vi sep* (*haben*) look up (zu at/(*fig*) to)

aufschichten *vt sep* stack up

aufschieben† *vt sep* slide open; (*verschieben*) put off, postpone

Aufschlag *m* impact; (*Tennis*) service; (*Hosen-*) turn-up; (*Ärmel-*) upturned cuff; (*Revers*) lapel; (*Comm*) surcharge. **a~en**† *v sep* ● *vt* open; crack <*Ei*>; (*hochschlagen*) turn up; (*errichten*) put up; (*erhöhen*) increase; cast on <*Masche*>; sich (*dat*) das Knie a~en cut [open] one's knee ● *vi* (*haben*) hit (**auf etw** *acc/dat* sth); (*Tennis*) serve; (*teurer werden*) go up

aufschließen† *v sep* ● *vt* unlock ● *vi* (*haben*) unlock the door

aufschlussreich *a* revealing; (*lehrreich*) informative

aufschneiden† *v sep* ● *vt* cut open; (*in Scheiben*) slice ● *vi* (*haben*) ⚠ exaggerate

Aufschnitt *m* sliced sausage, cold meat [and cheese]

aufschrauben *vt sep* screw on; (*abschrauben*) unscrew

Aufschrei *m* [sudden] cry

aufschreiben† *vt sep* write down; jdn a~ <*Polizist:*> book s.o.

Aufschrift *f* inscription; (*Etikett*) label

Aufschub *m* delay; (*Frist*) grace

aufschürfen *vt sep* sich (*dat*) das Knie a~ graze one's knee

aufschwingen† (*sich*) *vr sep* find the energy (**zu** for)

Aufschwung *m* (*fig*) upturn

aufsehen† *vi sep* (*haben*) look up (zu at/(*fig*) to). **A~** *nt* -s **A~ erregen** cause a sensation; **A~ erregend** sensational

Aufseher(in) *m* -s,- (*f* -, -nen) supervisor; (*Gefängnis-*) warder

aufsetzen *vt sep* put on; (*verfassen*) draw up; (*entwerfen*) draft; sich a~ sit up

Aufsicht *f* supervision; (*Person*) supervisor. **A~srat** *m* board of directors

aufsperren *vt sep* open wide

aufspielen *v sep* ● *vi* (*haben*) play ● *vr* sich a~ show off

aufspießen *vt sep* spear

aufspringen† *vi sep* (*sein*) jump up; (*aufprallen*) bounce; (*sich öffnen*) burst open

aufspüren *vt sep* track down

aufstacheln *vt sep* incite

Aufstand *m* uprising, rebellion

aufständisch *a* rebellious

aufstehen† *vi sep* (*sein*) get up; (*offen sein*) be open; (*fig*) rise up

aufsteigen† *vi sep* (*sein*) get on; <*Reiter:*> mount; <*Bergsteiger:*> climb up; (*hochsteigen*) rise [up]; (*fig: befördert werden*) rise (**zu** to); (*Sport*) be promoted

aufstell|en *vt sep* put up; (*Culin*) put on; (*postieren*) post; (*in einer Reihe*) line up; (*nominieren*) nominate; (*Sport*) select <*Mannschaft*>; make out <*Liste*>; lay down <*Regel*>; make <*Behauptung*>; set up <*Rekord*>. **A~ung** *f* nomination; (*Liste*) list

Aufstieg *m* -[e]s, -e ascent; (*fig*) rise; (*Sport*) promotion

Aufstoßen *nt* -s burping

aufstrebend *a* (*fig*) ambitious

Aufstrich *m* [sandwich] spread

aufstützen *vt sep* rest (**auf** + *acc* on); sich a~ lean (**auf** + *acc* on)

Auftakt *m* (*fig*) start

auftauchen *vi sep* (*sein*) emerge; (*fig*) turn up; <*Frage:*> crop up

auftauen *vt/i sep* (*sein*) thaw

aufteil|en *vt sep* divide [up]. **A~ung** *f* division

auftischen *vt sep* serve [up]

Auftrag *m* -[e]s,-̈e task; (*Kunst*) commission; (*Comm*) order; **im A~** (+ *gen*) on behalf of. **a~en†** *vt sep* apply; (*servieren*) serve; (*abtragen*) wear out; **jdm a~en** instruct s.o. (**zu** to). **A~ geber** *m* -s,- client

auftrennen *vt sep* unpick, undo

auftreten† *vi sep* (*sein*) tread; (*sich benehmen*) behave, act; (*Theat*) appear; (*die Bühne betreten*) enter; (*vorkommen*) occur

Auftrieb *m* buoyancy; (*fig*) boost

Auftritt *m* (*Theat*) appearance; (*auf die Bühne*) entrance; (*Szene*) scene

aufwachen *vi sep* (*sein*) wake up

aufwachsen† *vi sep* (*sein*) grow up

Aufwand *m* -[e]s expenditure; (*Luxus*) extravagance; (*Mühe*) trouble; **A~ treiben** be extravagant

aufwändig *a* = aufwendig

aufwärmen *vt sep* heat up; (*fig*) rake up; **sich a~** warm oneself; (*Sport*) warm up

Aufwartefrau *f* cleaner

aufwärts *adv* upwards; (*bergauf*) uphill; **es geht a~ mit jdm/etw** s.o./ sth is improving

Aufwartung *f* - cleaner

aufwecken *vt sep* wake up

aufweichen *v sep* ● *vt* soften ● *vi* (*sein*) become soft

aufweisen† *vt sep* have, show

aufwend|en† *vt sep* spend; **Mühe a~en** take pains. **a~ig** *a* lavish; (*teuer*) expensive

aufwert|en *vt sep* revalue. **A~ung** *f* revaluation

aufwickeln *vt sep* roll up; (*auswickeln*) unwrap

Aufwiegler *m* -s,- agitator

aufwisch|en *vt sep* wipe up; wash <*Fußboden*>. **A~lappen** *m* floorcloth

aufwühlen *vt sep* churn up

aufzähl|en *vt sep* enumerate, list. **A~ung** *f* list

aufzeichn|en *vt sep* record; (*zeichnen*) draw. **A~ung** *f* recording; **A~ungen** notes

aufziehen† *v sep* ● *vt* pull up; hoist <*Segel*>; (*öffnen*) open; draw <*Vorhang*>; (*großziehen*) bring up; rear <*Tier*>; mount <*Bild*>; thread <*Perlen*>; wind up <*Uhr*>; (**!**) *necken*) tease ● *vi* (*sein*) approach

Aufzug *m* hoist; (*Fahrstuhl*) lift, (*Amer*) elevator; (*Prozession*) procession; (*Theat*) act

Augapfel *m* eyeball

Auge *nt* -s, -n eye; (*Punkt*) spot; **vier A~n werfen** throw a four; **gute A~n** good eyesight; **unter vier A~n** in private; **im A~ behalten** keep in sight; (*fig*) bear in mind

Augenblick *m* moment; **A~!** just a moment! **a~lich** *a* immediate; (*derzeitig*) present ● *adv* immediately; (*derzeit*) at present

Augen|braue *f* eyebrow. **A~höhle** *f* eye socket. **A~licht** *nt* sight. **A~lid** *nt* eyelid

August *m* -[s] August

Auktion /-'tsi̯o:n/ *f* -, -en auction

Aula *f* -, -len (*Sch*) [assembly] hall

Au-pair-Mädchen /o'pɛːr-/ *nt* aupair

aus *prep* (+ *dat*) out of; (*von*) from; (*bestehend*) [made] of; **aus Angst** from *or* out of fear; **aus Spaß** for fun ● *adv* out; <*Licht, Radio*> off; **aus sein auf** (+ *acc*) be after; **aus und ein** in and out; **von sich aus** of one's own accord; **von mir aus** as far as I'm concerned

ausarbeiten *vt sep* work out

ausarten *vi sep* (*sein*) degenerate (**in** + *acc* into)

ausatmen *vt/i sep* (*haben*) breathe out

ausbauen *vt sep* remove; (*vergrößern*) extend; (*fig*) expand

ausbedingen† *vt sep* **sich** (*dat*) **a~** insist on; (*zur Bedingung machen*) stipulate

ausbesser|n *vt sep* mend, repair. **A~ung** *f* repair

ausbeulen *vt sep* remove the dents from; (*dehnen*) make baggy

ausbild|en *vt sep* train; (*formen*) form; (*entwickeln*) develop; **sich**

a~en train (**als/zu** as); (*entstehen*) develop. **A~ung** f training; (*Sch*) education

ausbitten† vt sep **sich** (dat) **a~** ask for; (*verlangen*) insist on

ausblasen† vt sep blow out

ausbleiben† vi sep (sein) fail to appear/ <*Erfolg:*> materialize; (*nicht heimkommen*) stay out

Ausblick m view

ausbrech|en† vi sep (sein) break out; <*Vulkan:*> erupt; (*fliehen*) escape; **in Tränen a~en** burst into tears. **A~er** m runaway

ausbreit|en vt sep spread [out]. **A~ung** f spread

Ausbruch m outbreak; (*Vulkan-*) eruption; (*Wut-*) outburst; (*Flucht*) escape, break-out

ausbrüten vt sep hatch

Ausdauer f perseverance; (*körperlich*) stamina. **a~nd** a persevering; (*unermüdlich*) untiring

ausdehnen vt sep stretch; (*fig*) extend; **sich a~** stretch; (*Phys & fig*) expand; (*dauern*) last

ausdenken† vt sep **sich** (dat) **a~** think up; (*sich vorstellen*) imagine

Ausdruck m expression; (*Fach-*) term; (*Computer*) printout. **a~en** vt sep print

ausdrücken vt sep squeeze out; squeeze <*Zitrone*>; stub out <*Zigarette*>; (*äußern*) express

ausdrucks|los a expressionless. **a~voll** a expressive

auseinander adv apart; (*entzwei*) in pieces; **a~ falten** unfold; **a~ gehen** part; <*Linien, Meinungen:*> diverge; <*Ehe:*> break up; **a~ halten** tell apart; **a~ nehmen** take apart or to pieces; **a~ setzen** explain (**jdm** to s.o.); **sich a~ setzen** sit apart; (*sich aussprechen*) have it out (**mit jdm** with s.o.); come to grips (**mit einem Problem** with a problem). **A~setzung** f -, -en discussion; (*Streit*) argument

auserlesen a select, choice

Ausfahrt f drive; (*Autobahn-, Garagen-*) exit

Ausfall m failure; (*Absage*) cancellation; (*Comm*) loss. **a~en**† vi sep (sein) fall out; (*versagen*) fail; (*abgesagt werden*) be cancelled; **gut/ schlecht a~en** turn out to be good/ poor

ausfallend, ausfällig a abusive

ausfertig|en vt sep make out. **A~ung** f -, -en **in doppelter A~ung** in duplicate

ausfindig a **a~ machen** find

Ausflug m excursion, outing

Ausflügler m -s,- [day-]tripper

Ausfluss m outlet; (*Abfluss*) drain; (*Med*) discharge

ausfragen vt sep question

Ausfuhr f -, -en (*Comm*) export

ausführ|en vt sep take out; (*Comm*) export; (*erklären*) explain. **a~lich** a detailed ● adv in detail. **A~ung** f execution; (*Comm*) version; (*äußere*) finish; (*Qualität*) workmanship; (*Erklärung*) explanation

Ausgabe f issue; (*Buch-*) edition; (*Comm*) version

Ausgang m way out, exit; (*Flugsteig*) gate; (*Ende*) end; (*Ergebnis*) outcome. **A~spunkt** m starting-point. **A~ssperre** f curfew

ausgeben† vt sep hand out; issue <*Fahrkarten*>; spend <*Geld*>; **sich a~ als** pretend to be

ausgebildet a trained

ausgebucht a fully booked; <*Vorstellung*> sold out

ausgefallen a unusual

ausgefranst a frayed

ausgeglichen a [well-]balanced

ausgeh|en† vi sep (sein) go out; <*Haare:*> fall out; <*Vorräte, Geld:*> run out; (*verblassen*) fade; **gut/ schlecht a~en** end well/badly; **davon a~en, dass** assume that. **A~verbot** nt curfew

ausgelassen a high-spirited

ausgemacht a agreed

ausgenommen conj except; **a~ wenn** unless

ausgeprägt a marked

ausgeschlossen *pred a* out of the question

ausgeschnitten *a* low-cut

ausgesprochen *a* marked ● *adv* decidedly

ausgestorben *a* extinct; [wie] a~ <*Straße:*> deserted

Ausgestoßene(r) *m/f* outcast

ausgezeichnet *a* excellent

ausgiebig *a* extensive; (*ausgedehnt*) long; a~ **Gebrauch machen von** make full use of

ausgießen† *vt sep* pour out

Ausgleich *m* -[e]s balance; (*Entschädigung*) compensation. **a~en**† *v sep* ● *vt* balance; even out <*Höhe*>; (*wettmachen*) compensate for; **sich a~en** balance out ● *vi* (*haben*) (*Sport*) equalize. **A~streffer** *m* equalizer

ausgrab|en† *vt sep* dig up; (*Archaeol*) excavate. **A~ung** *f* -, -en excavation

Ausguss *m* [kitchen] sink

aushaben† *vt sep* have finished <*Buch*>

aushalten† *vt sep* bear, stand; hold <*Note*>; (*Unterhalt zahlen für*) keep; **nicht auszuhalten, nicht zum A~** unbearable

aushändigen *vt sep* hand over

aushängen¹ *vt sep* (*reg*) display; take off its hinges <*Tür*>

aushäng|en² *vi sep* (*haben*) be displayed. **A~eschild** *nt* sign

ausheben† *vt sep* excavate

aushecken *vt sep* (*fig*) hatch

aushelfen† *vi sep* (*haben*) help out (jdm s.o.)

Aushilf|e *f* [temporary] assistant; **zur A~e** to help out. **A~skraft** *f* temporary worker. **a~sweise** *adv* temporarily

aushöhlen *vt sep* hollow out

auskennen† (**sich**) *vr sep* know one's way around; **sich mit/in etw** (*dat*) a~ know all about sth

auskommen† *vi sep* (*sein*) manage (mit/ohne with/without); (*sich vertragen*) get on (**gut** well)

auskugeln *vt sep* **sich** (*dat*) **den Arm a~** dislocate one's shoulder

auskühlen *vt/i sep* (*sein*) cool

auskundschaften *vt sep* spy out

Auskunft *f* -, -̈e information; (*A~sstelle*) information desk/ (*Büro*) bureau; (*Teleph*) enquiries *pl*; **eine A~** a piece of information

auslachen *vt sep* laugh at

Auslage *f* [window] display; **A~n** expenses

Ausland *nt* im/ins A~ abroad

Ausländ|er(in) *m* -s,- (*f* -, -nen) foreigner. **a~isch** *a* foreign

Auslandsgespräch *nt* international call

auslass|en† *vt sep* let out; let down <*Saum*>; (*weglassen*) leave out; (*versäumen*) miss; (*Culin*) melt; (*fig*) vent <*Ärger*> (**an** + *dat* on). **A~ungszeichen** *nt* apostrophe

Auslauf *m* run. **a~en**† *vi sep* (*sein*) run out; <*Farbe:*> run; (*Naut*) put to sea; <*Modell:*> be discontinued

ausleeren *vt sep* empty [out]

ausleg|en *vt sep* lay out; display <*Waren*>; (*auskleiden*) line (**mit** with); (*bezahlen*) pay; (*deuten*) interpret. **A~ung** *f* -, -en interpretation

ausleihen† *vt sep* lend; **sich** (*dat*) a~ borrow

Auslese *f* - selection; (*fig*) pick; (*Elite*) elite

ausliefer|n *vt sep* hand over; (*Jur*) extradite. **A~ung** *f* handing over; (*Jur*) extradition; (*Comm*) distribution

ausloggen *vi sep* log off *or* out

auslosen *vt sep* draw lots for

auslös|en *vt sep* set off, trigger; (*fig*) cause; arouse <*Begeisterung*>; (*einlösen*) redeem; pay a ransom for <*Gefangene*>. **A~er** *m* -s,- trigger; (*Phot*) shutter release

Auslosung *f* draw

auslüften *vt/i sep* (*haben*) air

ausmachen *vt sep* put out; (*abschalten*) turn off; (*abmachen*) arrange; (*erkennen*) make out;

a

(*betragen*) amount to; (*wichtig sein*) matter

Ausmaß *nt* extent; **A~e** dimensions

Ausnahme| *f* -, -n exception. **A~ezustand** *m* state of emergency. **a~slos** *adv* without exception. **a~sweise** *adv* as an exception

ausnehmen† *vt sep* take out; gut <*Fisch*>; **sich gut a~** look good. **a~d** *adv* exceptionally

ausnutz|en, ausnütz|en *vt sep* exploit. **A~ung** *f* exploitation

auspacken *vt sep* unpack; (*auswickeln*) unwrap

ausplaudern *vt sep* let out, blab

ausprobieren *vt sep* try out

Auspuff *m* -s exhaust [system]. **A~gase** *ntpl* exhaust fumes. **A~rohr** *nt* exhaust pipe

auspusten *vt sep* blow out

ausradieren *vt sep* rub out

ausrauben *vt sep* rob

ausräuchern *vt sep* smoke out; fumigate <*Zimmer*>

ausräumen *vt sep* clear out

ausrechnen *vt sep* work out

Ausrede *f* excuse. **a~n** *v sep* ● *vi* (*haben*) finish speaking ● *vt* jdm etw a~n talk s.o. out of sth

ausreichen *vi sep* (*haben*) be enough. **a~d** *a* adequate

Ausreise *f* departure. **a~n** *vi sep* (*sein*) leave the country. **A~visum** *nt* exit visa

ausreißen† *v sep* ● *vt* pull *or* tear out ● *vi* (*sein*) 🄵 run away

ausrenken *vt sep* dislocate

ausrichten *vt sep* align; (*bestellen*) deliver; (*erreichen*) achieve; jdm a~ tell s.o. (**dass** that); **ich soll Ihnen Grüße von X a~** X sends [you] his regards

ausrotten *vt sep* exterminate; (*fig*) eradicate

Ausruf *m* exclamation. **a~en†** *vt sep* exclaim; call out <*Namen*>; (*verkünden*) proclaim; jdn a~en lassen have s.o. paged. **A~ezeichen** *nt* exclamation mark

ausruhen *vt/i sep* (*haben*) rest; **sich a~** have a rest

ausrüst|en *vt sep* equip. **A~ung** *f* equipment; (*Mil*) kit

ausrutschen *vi sep* (*sein*) slip

Aussage *f* -, -n statement; (*Jur*) testimony, evidence; (*Gram*) predicate. **a~n** *vt/i sep* (*haben*) state; (*Jur*) give evidence, testify

ausschalten *vt sep* switch off

Ausschank *m* sale of alcoholic drinks; (*Bar*) bar

Ausschau *f* - **A~ halten nach** look out for

ausscheiden† *vi sep* (*sein*) leave; (*Sport*) drop out; (*nicht in Frage kommen*) be excluded

ausschenken *vt sep* pour out

ausscheren *vi sep* (*sein*) (*Auto*) pull out

ausschildern *vt sep* signpost

ausschimpfen *vt sep* tell off

ausschlafen† *vi/r sep* (*haben*) [sich] a~ get enough sleep; (*morgens*) sleep late

Ausschlag *m* (*Med*) rash; den A~ geben (*fig*) tip the balance. **a~gebend** *a* decisive

ausschließ|en† *vt sep* lock out; (*fig*) exclude; (*entfernen*) expel. **a~lich** *a* exclusive

ausschlüpfen *vi sep* (*sein*) hatch

Ausschluss *m* exclusion; expulsion; **unter A~ der Öffentlichkeit** in camera

ausschneiden† *vt sep* cut out

Ausschnitt *m* excerpt, extract; (*Zeitungs-*) cutting; (*Hals-*) neckline

ausschöpfen *vt sep* ladle out; (*Naut*) bail out; exhaust <*Möglichkeiten*>

ausschreiben† *vt sep* write out; (*ausstellen*) make out; (*bekanntgeben*) announce; put out to tender <*Auftrag*>

Ausschreitungen *fpl* riots; (*Exzesse*) excesses

Ausschuss *m* committee; (*Comm*) rejects *pl*

ausschütten *vt sep* tip out; (*verschütten*) spill; (*leeren*) empty

---

*old spelling

aussehen† *vi sep* (*haben*) look; **wie sieht er/es aus?** what does he/it look like? **A∼** *nt* **-s** appearance

außen *adv* [on the] outside; **nach a∼** outwards. **A∼bordmotor** *m* outboard motor. **A∼handel** *m* foreign trade. **A∼minister** *m* Foreign Minister. **A∼politik** *f* foreign policy. **A∼seite** *f* outside. **A∼seiter** *m* **-s,-** outsider; (*fig*) misfit. **A∼stände** *mpl* outstanding debts

außer *prep* (+ *dat*) except [for], apart from; (*außerhalb*) out of; **a∼ sich** (*fig*) beside oneself ● *conj* except; **a∼ wenn** unless. **a∼dem** *adv* in addition, as well ● *conj* moreover

äußer|e(r,s) *a* external; <*Teil, Schicht*> outer. **Ä∼e(s)** *nt* exterior; (*Aussehen*) appearance

außer|ehelich *a* extramarital. **a∼gewöhnlich** *a* exceptional. **a∼halb** *prep* (+ *gen*) outside ● *adv* **a∼halb wohnen** live outside town

äußer|lich *a* external; (*fig*) outward. **ä∼n** *vt* express; **sich ä∼n** comment; (*sich zeigen*) manifest itself

außerordentlich *a* extraordinary

äußerst *adv* extremely

äußerste|(r,s) *a* outermost; (*weiteste*) furthest; (*höchste*) utmost, extreme; (*letzte*) last; (*schlimmste*) worst. **Ä∼(s)** *nt* **das Ä∼** the limit; (*Schlimmste*) the worst; **sein Ä∼s tun** do one's utmost; **aufs Ä∼** extremely

Äußerung *f* **-, -en** comment; (*Bemerkung*) remark

aussetzen *v sep* ● *vt* expose (*dat* to); abandon <*Kind*>; launch <*Boot*>; offer <*Belohnung*>; **etwas auszusetzen haben an** (+ *dat*) find fault with ● *vi* (*haben*) stop; <*Motor:*> cut out

Aussicht *f* **-, -en** view/(*fig*) prospect (**auf** + *acc* of); **weitere A∼en** (*Meteorol*) further outlook *sg*. **a∼slos** *a* hopeless

ausspannen *v sep* ● *vt* spread out; unhitch <*Pferd*> ● *vi* (*haben*) rest

aussperren *vt sep* lock out

ausspielen *v sep* ● *vt* play <*Karte*>; (*fig*) play off (**gegen** against) ● *vi* (*haben*) (*Kartenspiel*) lead

Aussprache *f* pronunciation; (*Gespräch*) talk

aussprechen† *vt sep* pronounce; (*äußern*) express; **sich a∼** talk; come out (**für/gegen** in favour of/against)

Ausspruch *m* saying

ausspucken *v sep* ● *vt* spit out ● *vi* (*haben*) spit

ausspülen *vt sep* rinse out

ausstatt|en *vt sep* equip. **A∼ung** *f* **-, -en** equipment; (*Innen-*) furnishings *pl*; (*Theat*) scenery and costumes *pl*

ausstehen† *v sep* ● *vt* suffer; **Angst a∼** be frightened; **ich kann sie nicht a∼** I can't stand her ● *vi* (*haben*) be outstanding

aussteigen† *vi sep* (*sein*) get out; (*aus Bus, Zug*) get off; **alles a∼!** all change!

ausstell|en *vt sep* exhibit; (*Comm*) display; (*ausfertigen*) make out; issue <*Pass*>. **A∼ung** *f* exhibition; (*Comm*) display

aussterben† *vi sep* (*sein*) die out; (*Biol*) become extinct

Aussteuer *f* trousseau

Ausstieg *m* **-[e]s, -e** exit

ausstopfen *vt sep* stuff

ausstoßen† *vt sep* emit; utter <*Fluch*>; heave <*Seufzer*>; (*ausschließen*) expel

ausstrahl|en *vt/i sep* (*sein*) radiate, emit; (*Radio, TV*) broadcast. **A∼ung** *f* radiation

ausstrecken *vt sep* stretch out; put out <*Hand*>

ausstreichen† *vt sep* cross out

ausströmen *v sep* ● *vi* (*sein*) pour out; (*entweichen*) escape ● *vt* emit; (*ausstrahlen*) radiate

aussuchen *vt sep* pick, choose

Austausch *m* exchange. **a∼bar** *a* interchangeable. **a∼en** *vt sep* exchange; (*auswechseln*) replace

austeilen *vt sep* distribute

Auster *f* **-, -n** oyster

austragen† *vt sep* deliver; hold <*Wettkampf*>; play <*Spiel*>

Austral|ien /-i̯ən/ *nt* -s Australia. **A∼ier(in)** *m* -s,- (*f* -, -nen) Australian. **a∼isch** *a* Australian

austreiben† *vt sep* drive out; (*Relig*) exorcize

austreten† *v sep* ● *vt* stamp out; (*abnutzen*) wear down ● *vi* (*sein*) come out; (*ausscheiden*) leave (**aus** etw sth); [**mal**] **a∼** 🚻 go to the loo

austrinken† *vt/i sep* (*haben*) drink up; (*leeren*) drain

Austritt *m* resignation

austrocknen *vt/i sep* (*sein*) dry out

ausüben *vt sep* practise; carry on <*Handwerk*>; exercise <*Recht*>; exert <*Druck, Einfluss*>

Ausverkauf *m* [clearance] sale. **a∼t** *a* sold out

Auswahl *f* choice, selection; (*Comm*) range; (*Sport*) team

auswählen *vt sep* choose, select

Auswander|er *m* emigrant. **a∼n** *vi sep* (*sein*) emigrate. **A∼ung** *f* emigration

auswärt|ig *a* non-local; (*ausländisch*) foreign. **a∼s** *adv* outwards; (*Sport*) away. **A∼sspiel** *nt* away game

auswaschen† *vt sep* wash out

auswechseln *vt sep* change; (*ersetzen*) replace; (*Sport*) substitute

Ausweg *m* (*fig*) way out

ausweichen† *vi sep* (*sein*) get out of the way; **jdm/etw a∼en** avoid/ (*sich entziehen*) evade s.o./sth

Ausweis *m* -es, -e pass; (*Mitglieds-, Studenten-*) card. **a∼en**† *vt sep* deport; **sich a∼en** prove one's identity. **A∼papiere** *ntpl* identification papers. **A∼ung** *f* deportation

auswendig *adv* by heart

auswerten *vt sep* evaluate

auswickeln *vt sep* unwrap

auswirk|en (sich) *vr sep* have an effect (**auf** + *acc* on). **A∼ung** *f* effect; (*Folge*) consequence

auswringen *vt sep* wring out

auszahlen *vt sep* pay out; (*entlohnen*) pay off; (*abfinden*) buy out; **sich a∼** (*fig*) pay off

auszählen *vt sep* count; (*Boxen*) count out

Auszahlung *f* payment

auszeichn|en *vt sep* (*Comm*) price; (*ehren*) honour; (*mit einem Preis*) award a prize to; (*Mil*) decorate; **sich a∼en** distinguish oneself. **A∼ung** *f* honour; (*Preis*) award; (*Mil*) decoration; (*Sch*) distinction

ausziehen† *v sep* ● *vt* pull out; (*auskleiden*) undress; take off <*Mantel, Schuhe*> ● *vi* (*sein*) move out; (*sich aufmachen*) set out

Auszug *m* departure; (*Umzug*) move; (*Ausschnitt*) extract; (*Bank-*) statement

Auto *nt* -s, -s car; **A∼ fahren** drive; (*mitfahren*) go in the car. **A∼bahn** *f* motorway

Autobiographie *f* autobiography

Auto|bus *m* bus. **A∼fahrer(in)** *m(f)* driver, motorist. **A∼fahrt** *f* drive

Autogramm *nt* -s, -e autograph

Automat *m* -en, -en automatic device; (*Münz-*) slot-machine; (*Verkaufs-*) vending-machine; (*Fahrkarten-*) machine; (*Techn*) robot. **A∼ik** *f* - automatic mechanism; (*Auto*) automatic transmission

automatisch *a* automatic

Autonummer *f* registration number

Autopsie *f* -, -n autopsy

Autor *m* -s, -en /-'to:rən/ author

Auto|reisezug *m* Motorail. **A∼rennen** *nt* motor race

Autorin *f* -, -nen author[ess]

Autori|sation /-'tsi̯o:n/ *f* - authorization. **A∼tät** *f* -, -en authority

Auto|schlosser *m* motor mechanic. **A∼skooter** /-sku:tɐ/ *m* -s,- dodgem. **A∼stopp** *m* -s per **A∼stopp fahren** hitch-hike. **A∼verleih** *m* car hire [firm]. **A∼waschanlage** *f* car wash

autsch *int* ouch

Axt *f* -,-̈e axe

Bb

B, b /be:/ *nt* - (*Mus*) B flat

Baby /'be:bi/ *nt* -s, -s baby. **B~ausstattung** *f* layette. **B~sitter** /-sɪtɐ/ *m* -s,- babysitter

Bach *m* -[e]s,-̈e stream

Backbord *nt* -[e]s port [side]

Backe *f* -, -n cheek

backen *vt/i*† (*haben*) bake; (*braten*) fry

Backenzahn *m* molar

Bäcker *m* -s,- baker. **B~ei** *f* -, -en, **B~laden** *m* baker's shop

Back|obst *nt* dried fruit. **B~ofen** *m* oven. **B~pfeife** *f* ⚀ slap in the face. **B~pflaume** *f* prune. **B~pulver** *nt* baking-powder. **B~stein** *m* brick

Bad *nt* -[e]s,-̈er bath; (*Zimmer*) bathroom; (*Schwimm-*) pool; (*Ort*) spa

Bade|anstalt *f* swimming baths *pl*. **B~anzug** *m* swim-suit. **B~hose** *f* swimming trunks *pl*. **B~kappe** *f* bathing-cap. **B~mantel** *m* bathrobe. **b~n** *vi* (*haben*) have a bath; (*im Meer*) bathe ● *vt* bath; (*waschen*) bathe. **B~ort** *m* seaside resort. **B~wanne** *f* bath. **B~zimmer** *nt* bathroom

Bagger *m* -s,- excavator; (*Nass-*) dredger. **B~see** *m* flooded gravel-pit

Bahn *f* -, -en path; (*Astr*) orbit; (*Sport*) track; (*einzelne*) lane; (*Rodel-*) run; (*Stoff-*) width; (*Eisen-*) railway; (*Zug*) train; (*Straßen-*) tram. **b~brechend** *a* (*fig*) pioneering. **B~hof** *m* [railway] station. **B~steig** *m* -[e]s, -e platform. **B~übergang** *m* level crossing

Bahre *f* -, -n stretcher

Baiser /bɛ'ze:/ *nt* -s, -s meringue

Bake *f* -, -n (*Naut, Aviat*) beacon

Bakterien /-iən/ *fpl* bacteria

Balanc|e /ba'lã:sə/ *f* - balance. **b~ieren** *vt/i* (*haben/sein*) balance

bald *adv* soon; (*fast*) almost

Baldachin /-xi:n/ *m* -s, -e canopy

bald|ig *a* early; <*Besserung*> speedy. **b~möglichst** *adv* as soon as possible

Balg *nt & m* -[e]s,-̈er ⚀ brat

Balkan *m* -s Balkans *pl*

Balken *m* -s,- beam

Balkon /bal'kõ:/ *m* -s, -s balcony; (*Theat*) circle

Ball¹ *m* -[e]s,-̈e ball

Ball² *m* -[e]s,-̈e (*Tanz*) ball

Ballade *f* -, -n ballad

Ballast *m* -[e]s ballast. **B~stoffe** *mpl* roughage *sg*

Ballen *m* -s,- bale; (*Anat*) ball of the hand/(*Fuß-*) foot; (*Med*) bunion

Ballerina *f* -, -nen ballerina

Ballett *nt* -s, -e ballet

Ballon /ba'lõ:/ *m* -s, -s balloon

Balsam *m* -s balm

Balt|ikum *nt* -s Baltic States *pl*. **b~isch** *a* Baltic

Bambus *m* -ses, -se bamboo

banal *a* banal

Banane *f* -, -n banana

Banause *m* -n, -n philistine

Band¹ *nt* -[e]s,-̈er ribbon; (*Naht-, Ton-, Ziel-*) tape; **am laufenden B~** ⚀ non-stop

Band² *m* -[e]s,-̈e volume

Band³ *nt* -[e]s, -e (*fig*) bond

Band⁴ /bɛnt/ *f* -, -s [jazz] band

Bandag|e /ban'da:ʒə/ *f* -, -n bandage. **b~ieren** *vt* bandage

Bande *f* -, -n gang

bändigen *vt* control, restrain; (*zähmen*) tame

Bandit *m* -en, -en bandit

Band|maß *nt* tape-measure. **B~scheibe** *f* (*Anat*) disc. **B~wurm** *m* tapeworm

Bang|e f B~e haben be afraid; jdm B~e machen frighten s.o. **b~en** vi (haben) fear (um for)

Banjo nt -s, -s banjo

Bank¹ f -, ¨e bench

Bank² f -, -en (Comm) bank. **B~einzug** m direct debit

Bankett nt -s, -e banquet

Bankier /baŋ'kie:/ m -s, -s banker

Bankkonto nt bank account

Bankrott m -s, -s bankruptcy. **b~** a bankrupt

Bankwesen nt banking

Bann m -[e]s, -e (fig) spell. **b~en** vt exorcize; (abwenden) avert; [wie] gebannt spellbound

Banner nt -s, - banner

bar a (rein) sheer; <Gold> pure; b~es Geld cash; [in] bar bezahlen pay cash

Bar f -, -s bar

Bär m -en, -en bear

Baracke f -, -n (Mil) hut

Barb|ar m -en, -en barbarian. **b~arisch** a barbaric

bar|fuß adv barefoot. **B~geld** nt cash

barmherzig a merciful

barock a baroque. **B~** nt & m -[s] baroque

Barometer nt -s, - barometer

Baron m -s, -e baron. **B~in** f -, -nen baroness

Barren m -s, - (Gold-) bar, ingot; (Sport) parallel bars pl. **B~gold** nt gold bullion

Barriere f -, -n barrier

Barrikade f -, -n barricade

barsch a gruff

Barsch m -[e]s, -e (Zool) perch

Bart m -[e]s, ¨e beard; (der Katze) whiskers pl

bärtig a bearded

Barzahlung f cash payment

Basar m -s, -e bazaar

Base¹ f -, -n [female] cousin

Base² f -, -n (Chem) alkali, base

Basel nt -s Basle

basieren vi (haben) be based (auf + dat on)

Basilikum nt -s basil

Basis f -, Basen base; (fig) basis

basisch a (Chem) alkaline

Bask|enmütze f beret. **b~isch** a Basque

Bass m -es, ¨e bass

Bassin /ba'sɛ̃:/ nt -s, -s pond; (Brunnen-) basin; (Schwimm-) pool

Bassist m -en, -en bass player; (Sänger) bass

Bast m -[e]s raffia

basteln vt make ● vi (haben) do handicrafts

Batterie f -, -n battery

Bau¹ m -[e]s, -e burrow; (Fuchs-) earth

Bau² m -[e]s, -ten construction; (Gebäude) building; (Auf-) structure; (Körper-) build; (B~stelle) building site. **B~arbeiten** fpl building work sg; (Straßen-) road-works

Bauch m -[e]s, Bäuche abdomen, belly; (Magen) stomach; (Bauchung) bulge. **b~ig** a bulbous. **B~nabel** m navel. **B~redner** m ventriloquist. **B~schmerzen** mpl stomach-ache sg. **B~speicheldrüse** f pancreas

bauen vt build; (konstruieren) construct ● vi (haben) build (an etw dat sth); b~ auf (+ acc) (fig) rely on

Bauer¹ m -s, -n farmer; (Schach) pawn

Bauer² nt -s, - [bird]cage

bäuerlich a rustic

Bauern|haus nt farmhouse. **B~hof** m farm

bau|fällig a dilapidated. **B~genehmigung** f planning permission. **B~gerüst** nt scaffolding. **B~jahr** nt year of construction. **B~kunst** f architecture. **b~lich** a structural

Baum m -[e]s, Bäume tree

baumeln vi (haben) dangle

bäumen (sich) vr rear [up]

Baum|schule f [tree] nursery. **B~wolle** f cotton

---

*old spelling

Bausch *m* -[e]s, Bäusche wad; in
B∼ und Bogen (*fig*) wholesale.
b∼en *vt* puff out

Bau|sparkasse *f* building society.
B∼stein *m* building brick.
B∼stelle *f* building site; (*Straßen-*)
roadworks *pl.* **B∼unternehmer** *m*
building contractor

Bayer|(in) *m* -s, -n (*f* -, -nen)
Bavarian. **B∼n** *nt* -s Bavaria

bay[e]risch *a* Bavarian

Bazillus *m* -, -len bacillus

beabsichtig|en *vt* intend. **b∼t** *a*
intended; intentional

beacht|en *vt* take notice of;
(*einhalten*) observe; (*folgen*) follow;
nicht b∼en ignore. **b∼lich** *a*
considerable. **B∼ung** *f* -
observance; etw (*dat*) keine B∼ung
schenken take no notice of sth

Beamte(r) *m*, **Beamtin** *f* -, -nen
official; (*Staats-*) civil servant;
(*Schalter-*) clerk

beanspruchen *vt* claim;
(*erfordern*) demand

beanstand|en *vt* find fault with;
(*Comm*) make a complaint about.
B∼ung *f* -, -en complaint

beantragen *vt* apply for

beantworten *vt* answer

bearbeiten *vt* work; (*weiter-*)
process; (*behandeln*) treat (mit with);
(*Admin*) deal with; (*redigieren*) edit;
(*Theat*) adapt; (*Mus*) arrange

Beatmungsgerät *nt* ventilator

beaufsichtig|en *vt* supervise.
B∼ung *f* - supervision

beauftragen *vt* instruct;
commission <*Künstler*>

bebauen *vt* build on; (*bestellen*)
cultivate

beben *vi* (*haben*) tremble

Becher *m* -s,- beaker; (*Henkel-*) mug;
(*Joghurt-, Sahne-*) carton

Becken *nt* -s,- basin; pool; (*Mus*)
cymbals *pl*; (*Anat*) pelvis

bedacht *a* careful; darauf b∼
anxious (zu to)

bedächtig *a* careful; slow

bedanken (sich) *vr* thank (bei jdm
s.o.)

Bedarf *m* -s need/(*Comm*) demand
(an + *dat* for); bei B∼ if required.
B∼shaltestelle *f* request stop

bedauer|lich *a* regrettable.
b∼licherweise *adv* unfortunately.
b∼n *vt* regret; (*bemitleiden*) feel
sorry for; bedaure! sorry!
b∼nswert *a* pitiful; (*bedauerlich*)
regrettable

bedeckt *a* covered; <*Himmel*>
overcast

bedenken† *vt* consider; (*überlegen*)
think over. **B∼** *pl* misgivings; ohne
B∼ without hesitation

bedenklich *a* doubtful; (*verdächtig*)
dubious; (*ernst*) serious

bedeut|en *vi* (*haben*) mean.
b∼end *a* important; (*beträchtlich*)
considerable. **B∼ung** *f* -, -en
meaning; (*Wichtigkeit*) importance.
b∼ungslos *a* meaningless;
(*unwichtig*) unimportant.
b∼ungsvoll *a* significant;
(*vielsagend*) meaningful

bedien|en *vt* serve; (*betätigen*)
operate; sich [selbst] b∼en help
oneself. **B∼ung** *f* -, -en service;
(*Betätigung*) operation; (*Kellner*)
waiter; (*Kellnerin*) *f* waitress.
B∼ungsgeld *nt* service charge

Bedingung *f* -, -en condition; B∼en
conditions; (*Comm*) terms. **b∼slos**
a unconditional

bedrohen *vt* threaten. **b∼lich** *a*
threatening. **B∼ung** *f* threat

bedrücken *vt* depress

bedruckt *a* printed

bedürf|en† *vi* (*haben*) (+ *gen*) need.
B∼nis *nt* -ses, -se need

Beefsteak /'bi:fste:k/ *nt* -s, -s
steak; deutsches B∼ hamburger

beeilen (sich) *vr* hurry; hasten (zu
to)

beeindrucken *vt* impress

beeinflussen *vt* influence

beeinträchtigen *vt* mar;
(*schädigen*) impair

beengen *vt* restrict

beerdig|en *vt* bury. **B∼ung** *f* -, -en
funeral

Beere *f* -, -n berry

Beet *nt* -[e]s, -e (*Hort*) bed

Beete *f* -, -n rote B~ beetroot

befähig|en *vt* enable; (*qualifizieren*) qualify. **B~ung** *f* - qualification; (*Fähigkeit*) ability

befahrbar *a* passable

befallen† *vt* attack; <*Angst:*> seize

befangen *a* shy; (*gehemmt*) self-conscious; (*Jur*) biased. **B~heit** *f* - shyness; self-consciousness; bias

befassen (sich) *vr* concern oneself/(*behandeln*) deal (**mit** with)

Befehl *m* -[e]s, -e order; (*Leitung*) command (**über** + *acc* of). **b~en†** *vt* jdm etw b~en order s.o. to do sth ● *vi* (*haben*) give the orders. **B~sform** *f* (*Gram*) imperative. **B~shaber** *m* -s,- commander

befestigen *vt* fasten (**an** + *dat* to); (*Mil*) fortify

befeuchten *vt* moisten

befinden† (sich) *vr* be. **B~** *nt* -s [state of] health

beflecken *vt* stain

befolgen *vt* follow

beförder|n *vt* transport; (*im Rang*) promote. **B~ung** *f* -, -en transport; promotion

befragen *vt* question

befrei|en *vt* free; (*räumen*) clear (**von** of); (*freistellen*) exempt (**von** from); **sich b~en** free oneself. **B~er** *m* -s,- liberator. **B~ung** *f* - liberation; exemption

befreunden (sich) *vr* make friends; **befreundet sein** be friends

befriedig|en *vt* satisfy. **b~end** *a* satisfying; (*zufrieden stellend*) satisfactory. **B~ung** *f* - satisfaction

befrucht|en *vt* fertilize. **B~ung** *f* - fertilization; **künstliche B~ung** artificial insemination

Befugnis *f* -, -se authority

Befund *m* result

befürcht|en *vt* fear. **B~ung** *f* -, -en fear

befürworten *vt* support

begab|t *a* gifted. **B~ung** *f* -, -en gift, talent

begeben† (sich) *vr* go; **sich in Gefahr b~** expose oneself to danger

begegn|en *vi* (*sein*) jdm/etw b~en meet s.o./sth. **B~ung** *f* -, -en meeting

begehr|en *vt* desire. **b~t** *a* sought-after

begeister|n *vt* jdn b~n arouse s.o.'s enthusiasm. **b~t** *a* enthusiastic; (*eifrig*) keen. **B~ung** *f* - enthusiasm

Begierde *f* -, -n desire

Beginn *m* -s beginning. **b~en†** *vt/i* (*haben*) start, begin

beglaubigen *vt* authenticate

begleichen† *vt* settle

begleit|en *vt* accompany. **B~er** *m* -s, - companion; (*Mus*) accompanist. **B~ung** *f* -, -en company; (*Mus*) accompaniment

beglück|en *vt* make happy. **b~wünschen** *vt* congratulate (**zu** on)

begnadig|en *vt* (*Jur*) pardon. **B~ung** *f* -, -en (*Jur*) pardon

begraben† *vt* bury

Begräbnis *n* -ses, -se burial; (*Feier*) funeral

begreif|en† *vt* understand; **nicht zu b~en** incomprehensible. **b~lich** *a* understandable

begrenz|en *vt* form the boundary of; (*beschränken*) restrict. **b~t** *a* limited. **B~ung** *f* -, -en restriction; (*Grenze*) boundary

Begriff *m* -[e]s, -e concept; (*Ausdruck*) term; (*Vorstellung*) idea

begründ|en *vt* give one's reason for. **b~et** *a* justified. **B~ung** *f* -, -en reason

begrüß|en *vt* greet; (*billigen*) welcome. **b~enswert** *a* welcome. **B~ung** *f* - greeting; welcome

begünstigen *vt* favour

begütert *a* wealthy

behaart *a* hairy

behäbig *a* portly

behag|en *vi* (*haben*) please (jdm s.o.). **B~en** *nt* -s contentment; (*Genuss*) enjoyment. **b~lich** *a* comfortable. **B~lichkeit** *f* - comfort

behalten† vt keep; (*sich merken*) remember

Behälter m -s,- container

behandeln vt treat; (*sich befassen*) deal with. **B~lung** f treatment

beharren vi (*haben*) persist (**auf** + *dat* in). **b~lich** a persistent

behaupten vt maintain; (*vorgeben*) claim; (*sagen*) say; (*bewahren*) retain; **sich b~en** hold one's own. **B~ung** f -, -en assertion; claim; (*Äußerung*) statement

beheben† vt remedy

behelfen† (**sich**) vr make do (**mit** with). **b~smäßig** a makeshift ● adv provisionally

beherbergen vt put up

beherrschen vt rule over; (*dominieren*) dominate; (*meistern, zügeln*) control; (*können*) know. **b~t** a self-controlled. **B~ung** f - control

beherzigen vt heed

behilflich a **jdm b~ sein** help s.o.

behindern vt hinder; (*blockieren*) obstruct. **b~t** a handicapped; (*schwer*) disabled. **B~te(r)** m/f handicapped/disabled person. **B~ung** f -, -en obstruction; (*Med*) handicap; disability

Behörde f -, -n [public] authority

behüten vt protect. **b~t** a sheltered

behutsam a careful; (*zart*) gentle

bei
● *preposition* (+ *dative*)

! Note that **bei** plus **dem** can become **beim**

····▸ (*nahe*) near; (*dicht an, neben*) by; (*als Begleitung*) with. **wer steht da bei ihm?** who is standing there next to *or* with him? **etw bei sich haben** have sth with *or* on one. **bleiben Sie beim Gepäck/bei den Kindern** stay with the luggage/the children. **war heute ein Brief für mich bei der Post?** was there a letter for me in the post today?

····▸ (*an*) by. **jdn bei der Hand nehmen** take s.o. by the hand

····▸ (*in der Wohnung von*) at ...'s home *or* house/flat. **bei mir [zu Hause]** at my home *or* 🅸 place. **bei seinen Eltern leben** live with one's parents. **wir sind bei Ulrike eingeladen** we have been invited to Ulrike's. **bei Schmidt** at the Schmidts'; (*Geschäft*) at Schmidts'; (*auf Briefen*) c/o Schmidt. **bei jdm/einer Firma arbeiten** work for s.o./a firm. **bei uns tut man das nicht** we don't do that where I come from.

····▸ (*gegenwärtig*) at; (*verwickelt*) in. **bei einer Hochzeit/einem Empfang** at a wedding/reception. **bei einem Unfall** in an accident

····▸ (*im Falle von*) in the case of, with; (*bei Wetter*) in. **wie bei den Römern** as with the Romans. **bei Nebel** in fog, if there is fog. **bei dieser Hitze** in this heat

····▸ (*angesichts*) with; (*trotz*) in spite of. **bei deinen guten Augen** with your good eyesight. **bei all seinen Bemühungen** in spite of *or* despite all his efforts

····▸ (*Zeitpunkt*) at, on. **bei diesen Worten errötete er** he blushed at this *or* on hearing this. **bei seiner Ankunft** on his arrival. **bei Tag/Nacht** by day/night.

····▸ (*Gleichzeitigkeit, mit Verbalsubstantiv*) **beim ...en** while *or* when ...ing. **beim Spazierengehen im Walde** while walking in the woods. **beim Überqueren der Straße** when crossing the road. **sie war beim Lesen** she was reading. **wir waren beim Frühstück** we were having breakfast

beibehalten† vt sep keep

beibringen† vt sep **jdm etw b~** teach s.o. sth; (*mitteilen*) break sth to s.o.; (*zufügen*) inflict sth on s.o.

Beichte f -, -n confession. **b~en** vt/i (*haben*) confess. **B~stuhl** m confessional

beide a & pron both; **b~s** both; **dreißig b~** (*Tennis*) thirty all. **b~rseitig** a mutual. **b~rseits** adv & prep (+ gen) on both sides (of)

beieinander adv together

b

Beifahrer(in) *m(f)* [front-seat] passenger; (*Motorrad*) pillion passenger

Beifall *m* -[e]s applause; (*Billigung*) approval; **B~ klatschen** applaud

beifügen *vt sep* add; (*beilegen*) enclose

beige /bɛːʒ/ *inv a* beige

beigeben† *vt sep* add

Beihilfe *f* financial aid; (*Studien-*) grant; (*Jur*) aiding and abetting

Beil *nt* -[e]s, -e hatchet, axe

Beilage *f* supplement; (*Gemüse*) vegetable

beiläufig *a* casual

beilegen *vt sep* enclose; (*schlichten*) settle

Beileid *nt* condolences *pl.* **B~sbrief** *m* letter of condolence

beiliegend *a* enclosed

beim *prep* = **bei dem; b~ Militär** in the army; **b~ Frühstück** at breakfast

beimessen† *vt sep* (*fig*) attach (*dat* to)

Bein *nt* -[e]s, -e leg; **jdm ein B~ stellen** trip s.o. up

beinah[e] *adv* nearly, almost

Beiname *m* epithet

beipflichten *vi sep* (*haben*) agree (*dat* with)

Beirat *m* advisory committee

beisammen *adv* together; **b~ sein** be together

Beisein *nt* presence

beiseite *adv* aside; (*abseits*) apart; **b~ legen** put aside; (*sparen*) put by

beisetz|en *vt sep* bury. **B~ung** *f* -, -en funeral

Beispiel *nt* example; **zum B~** for example. **b~sweise** *adv* for example

beißen† *vt/i* (*haben*) bite; (*brennen*) sting; **sich b~** <*Farben:*> clash

Bei|stand *m* -[e]s help. **b~stehen†** *vi sep* (*haben*) **jdm b~stehen** help s.o.

beistimmen *vi sep* (*haben*) agree

Beistrich *m* comma

Beitrag *m* -[e]s,-̈e contribution; (*Mitglieds-*) subscription; (*Versicherungs-*) premium; (*Zeitungs-*) article. **b~en†** *vt/i sep* (*haben*) contribute

bei|treten† *vi sep* (*sein*) (+ *dat*) join. **B~tritt** *m* joining

Beize *f* -, -n (*Holz-*) stain

beizeiten *adv* in good time

beizen *vt* stain <*Holz*>

bejahen *vt* answer in the affirmative; (*billigen*) approve of

bejahrt *a* aged, old

bekämpf|en *vt* fight. **B~ung** *f* fight (*gen* against)

bekannt *a* well-known; (*vertraut*) familiar; **jdn b~ machen** introduce s.o.; **etw b~ machen** *od* **geben** announce sth; **b~ werden** become known. **B~e(r)** *m/f* acquaintance; (*Freund*) friend. **B~gabe** *f* announcement. **b~lich** *adv* as is well known. **B~machung** *f* -, -en announcement; (*Anschlag*) notice. **B~schaft** *f* - acquaintance; (*Leute*) acquaintances *pl*; (*Freunde*) friends *pl*

bekehr|en *vt* convert. **B~ung** *f* -, -en conversion

bekenn|en† *vt* confess, profess <*Glauben*>; **sich [für] schuldig b~en** admit one's guilt. **B~tnis** *nt* -ses, -se confession; (*Konfession*) denomination

beklag|en *vt* lament; (*bedauern*) deplore; **sich b~en** complain. **b~enswert** *a* unfortunate. **B~te(r)** *m/f* (*Jur*) defendant

bekleid|en *vt* hold <*Amt*>. **B~ung** *f* clothing

Beklemmung *f* -, -en feeling of oppression

bekommen† *vt* get; have <*Baby*>; catch <*Erkältung*> ● *vi* (*sein*) **jdm gut b~** do s.o. good; <*Essen:*> agree with s.o.

beköstig|en *vt* feed. **B~ung** *f* - board; (*Essen*) food

bekräftigen *vt* reaffirm

bekreuzigen (sich) *vr* cross oneself

---

*old spelling

bekümmert a troubled; (*besorgt*) worried

bekunden vt show

Belag m -[e]s,¨e coating; (*Fußboden-*) covering; (*Brot-*) topping; (*Zahn-*) tartar; (*Brems-*) lining

belager|n vt besiege. **B~ung** f -, -en siege

Belang m von B~ of importance; **B~e** pl interests. **B~los** a irrelevant; (*unwichtig*) trivial

belassen† vt leave; es dabei b~ leave it at that

belasten vt load; (*fig*) burden; (*beanspruchen*) put a strain on; (*Comm*) debit; (*Jur*) incriminate

belästigen vt bother; (*bedrängen*) pester; (*unsittlich*) molest

Belastung f -, -en load; (*fig*) strain; (*Comm*) debit. **B~smaterial** nt incriminating evidence. **B~szeuge** m prosecution witness

belaufen† (sich) vr amount (auf + acc to)

belauschen vt eavesdrop on

beleb|en vt (*fig*) revive; (*lebhaft machen*) enliven. **b~t** a lively; <*Straße*> busy

Beleg m -[e]s, -e evidence; (*Beispiel*) instance (für of); (*Quittung*) receipt. **b~en** vt cover/(*garnieren*) garnish (mit with); (*besetzen*) reserve; (*Univ*) enrol for; (*nachweisen*) provide evidence for; den ersten Platz b~en (*Sport*) take first place. **B~schaft** f -, -en work-force. **b~t** a occupied; <*Zunge*> coated; <*Stimme*> husky; b~te Brote open sandwiches

belehren vt instruct

beleidig|en vt offend; (*absichtlich*) insult. **B~ung** f -, -en insult

belesen a well-read

beleucht|en vt light; (*anleuchten*) illuminate. **B~ung** f -, -en illumination

Belg|ien /-jən/ nt -s Belgium. **B~ier(in)** m -s,- (f -, -nen) Belgian. **b~isch** a Belgian

belicht|en vt (*Phot*) expose. **B~ung** f - exposure

Belieb|en nt -s nach B~en [just] as one likes. **b~ig** a eine b~ige Zahl any number you like ● adv b~ig oft as often as one likes. **b~t** a popular

bellen vi (*haben*) bark

belohn|en vt reward. **B~ung** f -, -en reward

belustig|en vt amuse. **B~ung** f -, -en amusement

bemalen vt paint

bemängeln vt criticize

bemannt a manned

bemerk|bar a sich b~bar machen attract attention. **b~en** vt notice; (*äußern*) remark. **b~enswert** a remarkable. **B~ung** f -, -en remark

bemitleiden vt pity

bemüh|en vt trouble; sich b~en try (zu to; um etw to get sth); (*sich kümmern*) attend (um to); b~t sein endeavour (zu to). **B~ung** f -, -en effort

benachbart a neighbouring

benachrichtig|en vt inform; (*amtlich*) notify. **B~ung** f -, -en notification

benachteiligen vt discriminate against; (*ungerecht sein*) treat unfairly

benehmen† (sich) vr behave. **B~** nt -s behaviour

beneiden vt envy (um etw sth)

Bengel m -s,- boy; (*Rüpel*) lout

benötigen vt need

benutz|en, (SGer) benütz|en vt use; take <*Bahn*> **B~ung** f use

Benzin nt -s petrol

beobacht|en vt observe. **B~er** m -s,- observer. **B~ung** f -, -en observation

bequem a comfortable; (*mühelos*) easy; (*faul*) lazy. **b~en (sich)** vr deign (zu to). **B~lichkeit** f -, -en comfort; (*Faulheit*) laziness

berat|en† vt advise; (*überlegen*) discuss; sich b~en confer ● vi (*haben*) discuss (über etw acc sth); (*beratschlagen*) confer. **B~er(in)** m -s,- (f -, -nen) adviser. **B~ung** f -, -en guidance; (*Rat*) advice;

(*Besprechung*) discussion; (*Med, Jur*) consultation

berechn|en *vt* calculate; (*anrechnen*) charge for; (*abfordern*) charge. **B~ung** *f* calculation

berechtig|en *vt* entitle; (*befugen*) authorize; (*fig*) justify. **b~t** *a* justified, justifiable. **B~ung** *f* -, -en authorization; (*Recht*) right; (*Rechtmäßigkeit*) justification

bered|en *vt* talk about; **sich b~en** talk. **B~samkeit** *f* - eloquence

beredt *a* eloquent

Bereich *m* -[e]s, -e area; (*fig*) realm; (*Fach-*) field

bereichern *vi* enrich

bereit *a* ready. **b~en** *vt* prepare; (*verursachen*) cause; give <*Überraschung*>. **b~halten†** *vt sep* have/(*ständig*) keep ready. **b~legen** *vt sep* put out [ready]. **b~machen** *vt sep* get ready. **b~s** *adv* already

Bereitschaft *f* -, -en readiness; (*Einheit*) squad. **B~sdienst** *m* **B~sdienst haben** (*Mil*) be on stand-by; <*Arzt*> be on call. **B~spolizei** *f* riot police

bereit|stehen† *vi sep* (*haben*) be ready. **b~stellen** *vt sep* put out ready; (*verfügbar machen*) make available. **B~ung** *f* - preparation. **b~willig** *a* willing

bereuen *vt* regret

Berg *m* -[e]s, -e mountain; (*Anhöhe*) hill; **in den B~en** in the mountains. **b~ab** *adv* downhill. **B~arbeiter** *m* miner. **b~auf** *adv* uphill. **B~bau** *m* -[e]s mining

bergen† *vt* recover; (*Naut*) salvage; (*retten*) rescue

Berg|führer *m* mountain guide. **b~ig** *a* mountainous. **B~kette** *f* mountain range. **B~mann** *m* (*pl* -leute) miner. **B~steiger(in)** *m* -s,- (*f* -, -nen) mountaineer, climber

Bergung *f* - recovery; (*Naut*) salvage; (*Rettung*) rescue

Berg|wacht *f* mountain rescue service. **B~werk** *nt* mine

Bericht *m* -[e]s, -e report; (*Reise-*) account. **b~en** *vt/i* (*haben*) report; (*erzählen*) tell (von of). **B~erstatter(in)** *m* -s,- (*f* -, -nen) reporter

berichtigen *vt* correct

beriesel|n *vt* irrigate. **B~ungsanlage** *f* sprinkler system

Berlin *nt* -s Berlin. **B~er** *m* -s,- Berliner

Bernhardiner *m* -s,- St Bernard

Bernstein *m* amber

berüchtigt *a* notorious

berücksichtig|en *vt* take into consideration. **B~ung** *f* - consideration

Beruf *m* profession; (*Tätigkeit*) occupation; (*Handwerk*) trade. **b~en†** *vt* appoint; **sich b~en** refer (auf + acc to); (*vorgeben*) plead (auf etw acc sth); ● *a* competent; **b~en sein** be destined (zu to). **b~lich** *a* professional; <*Ausbildung*> vocational ● *adv* professionally; **b~lich tätig sein** work, have a job. **B~sberatung** *f* vocational guidance. **b~smäßig** *adv* professionally. **B~sschule** *f* vocational school. **B~ssoldat** *m* regular soldier. **b~stätig** *a* working; **b~stätig sein** work, have a job. **B~stätige(r)** *m/f* working man/woman. **B~ung** *f* -, -en appointment; (*Bestimmung*) vocation; (*Jur*) appeal; **B~ung einlegen** appeal. **B~ungsgericht** *nt* appeal court

beruhen *vi* (*haben*) be based (auf + dat on)

beruhig|en *vt* calm [down]; (*zuversichtlich machen*) reassure. **b~end** *a* calming; (*tröstend*) reassuring; (*Med*) sedative. **B~ung** *f* - calming; reassurance; (*Med*) sedation. **B~ungsmittel** *nt* sedative; (*bei Psychosen*) tranquillizer

berühmt *a* famous. **B~heit** *f* -, -en fame; (*Person*) celebrity

berühr|en *vt* touch; (*erwähnen*) touch on. **B~ung** *f* -, -en touch; (*Kontakt*) contact

besänftigen vt soothe

Besatz m -es,ⸯe trimming

Besatzung f -, -en crew; (Mil) occupying force

beschädig|en vt damage. **B~ung** f -, -en damage

beschaffen vt obtain, get ● a so b~ sein, dass be such that. **B~heit** f - consistency

beschäftig|en vt occupy; <Arbeitgeber:> employ; sich b~en occupy oneself. **b~t** a busy; (angestellt) employed (bei at). **B~ung** f -, -en occupation; (Anstellung) employment

beschämt a ashamed; (verlegen) embarrassed

beschatten vt shade; (überwachen) shadow

Bescheid m -[e]s information; jdm B~ sagen od geben let s.o. know; B~ wissen know

bescheiden a modest. **B~heit** f - modesty

bescheinen† vt shine on; von der Sonne beschienen sunlit

bescheinig|en vt certify. **B~ung** f -, -en [written] confirmation; (Schein) certificate

beschenken vt give a present/ presents to

Bescherung f -, -en distribution of Christmas presents

beschildern vt signpost

beschimpf|en vt abuse, swear at. **B~ung** f -, -en abuse

beschirmen vt protect

Beschlag m in B~ nehmen monopolize. **b~en†** vt shoe ● vi (sein) steam or mist up ● a steamed or misted up. **B~nahme** f -, -n confiscation; (Jur) seizure. **b~nahmen** vt confiscate; (Jur) seize

beschleunig|en vt hasten; (schneller machen) speed up <Schritt> ● vi (haben) accelerate. **B~ung** f - acceleration

beschließen† vt decide; (beenden) end ● vi (haben) decide (über + acc about)

Beschluss m decision

beschmutzen vt make dirty

beschneid|en† vt trim; (Hort) prune; (Relig) circumcise. **B~ung** f - circumcision

beschnüffeln vt sniff at

beschönigen vt (fig) gloss over

beschränken vt limit, restrict; sich b~ auf (+ acc) confine oneself to

beschrankt a <Bahnübergang> with barrier[s]

beschränk|t a limited; (geistig) dull-witted. **B~ung** f -, -en limitation, restriction

beschreib|en† vt describe. **B~ung** f -, -en description

beschuldig|en vt accuse. **B~ung** f -, -en accusation

beschummeln vt 🗓 cheat

Beschuss m (Mil) fire; (Artillerie-) shelling

beschütz|en vt protect. **B~er** m -s,- protector

Beschwer|de f -, -n complaint; B~den (Med) trouble sg. **b~en** vt weight down; sich b~en complain. **b~lich** a difficult

beschwindeln vt cheat (um out of); (belügen) lie to

beschwipst a 🗓 tipsy

beseitig|en vt remove. **B~ung** f - removal

Besen m -s,- broom

besessen a obsessed (von by)

besetz|en vt occupy; fill <Posten>; (Theat) cast <Rolle>; (verzieren) trim (mit with). **b~t** a occupied; <Toilette, Leitung> engaged; <Zug, Bus> full up; der Platz ist b~t this seat is taken. **B~tzeichen** nt engaged tone. **B~ung** f -, -en occupation; (Theat) cast

besichtig|en vt look round <Stadt>; (prüfen) inspect; (besuchen) visit. **B~ung** f -, -en visit; (Prüfung) inspection; (Stadt-) sightseeing

besiedelt a dünn/dicht b~ sparsely/densely populated

besiegen vt defeat

besinn|en† (sich) vr think, reflect; (sich erinnern) remember (**auf jdn**/

etw s.o./sth). **B~ung** f - reflection; (*Bewusstsein*) consciousness; **bei/ ohne B~ung** conscious/unconscious. **b~ungslos** a unconscious

Besitz m possession; (*Eigentum, Land-*) property; (*Gut*) estate. **b~en**† vt own, possess; (*haben*) have. **B~er(in)** m -s,- (f -, -nen) owner; (*Comm*) proprietor

besoffen a ⊠ drunken; **b~ sein** be drunk

besonder|e(r,s) a special; (*bestimmt*) particular; (*gesondert*) separate. **b~s** adv [e]specially, particularly; (*gesondert*) separately

besonnen a calm

besorg|en vt get; (*kaufen*) buy; (*erledigen*) attend to; (*versorgen*) look after. **b~t** a worried/(*bedacht*) concerned (**um** about). **B~ung** f -, -en errand; **B~ungen machen** do shopping

bespitzeln vt spy on

besprech|en† vt discuss; (*rezensieren*) review. **B~ung** f -, -en discussion; review; (*Konferenz*) meeting

besser a & adv better. **b~n** vt improve; **sich b~n** get better. **B~ung** f - improvement; **gute B~ung!** get well soon!

Bestand m -[e]s,"e existence; (*Vorrat*) stock (**an** + dat of)

beständig a constant; <*Wetter*> settled; **b~ gegen** resistant to

Bestand|saufnahme f stocktaking. **B~teil** m part

bestätig|en vt confirm; acknowledge <*Empfang*>; **sich b~en** prove to be true. **B~ung** f -, -en confirmation

bestatt|en vt bury. **B~ung** f -, -en funeral

Bestäubung f - pollination

bestaunen vt gaze at in amazement; (*bewundern*) admire

best|e(r,s) a best; **b~en Dank!** many thanks! **B~e(r,s)** m/f/nt best; **sein B~es tun** do one's best

bestech|en† vt bribe; (*bezaubern*) captivate. **b~end** a captivating. **b~lich** a corruptible. **B~ung** f - bribery. **B~ungsgeld** nt bribe

Besteck nt -[e]s, -e [set of] knife, fork and spoon; (*coll*) cutlery

bestehen† vi (*haben*) exist; (*fortdauern*) last; (*bei Prüfung*) pass; **~ aus** consist/(*gemacht sein*) be made of; **~ auf** (+ dat) insist on ● vt pass <*Prüfung*>

besteig|en† vt climb; (*aufsteigen*) mount; ascend <*Thron*>. **B~ung** f ascent

bestell|en vt order; (*vor-*) book; (*ernennen*) appoint; (*bebauen*) cultivate; (*ausrichten*) tell; **zu sich b~en** send for; **b~t sein** have an appointment; **kann ich etwas b~en?** can I take a message? **B~schein** m order form. **B~ung** f order; (*Botschaft*) message; (*Bebauung*) cultivation

besteuer|n vt tax. **B~ung** f - taxation

Bestie /'bɛstiə/ f -, -n beast

bestimm|en vt fix; (*entscheiden*) decide; (*vorsehen*) intend; (*ernennen*) appoint; (*ermitteln*) determine; (*definieren*) define; (*Gram*) qualify ● vi (*haben*) be in charge (**über** + acc of). **b~t** a definite; (*gewiss*) certain; (*fest*) firm,. **B~ung** f fixing; (*Vorschrift*) regulation; (*Ermittlung*) determination; (*Definition*) definition; (*Zweck*) purpose; (*Schicksal*) destiny. **B~ungsort** m destination

Bestleistung f (*Sport*) record

bestraf|en vt punish. **B~ung** f -, -en punishment

Bestrahlung f radiotherapy

Bestreb|en nt -s endeavour; (*Absicht*) aim. **B~ung** f -, -en effort

bestreiten† vt dispute; (*leugnen*) deny; (*bezahlen*) pay for

bestürz|t a dismayed; (*erschüttert*) stunned. **B~ung** f - dismay, consternation

Bestzeit f (*Sport*) record [time]

Besuch m -[e]s, -e visit; (*kurz*) call; (*Schul-*) attendance; (*Gast*) visitor;

(*Gäste*) visitors *pl*; **B~ haben** have a visitor/visitors; **bei jdm zu** *od* **auf B~ sein** be staying with s.o. **b~en** *vt* visit; (*kurz*) call on; (*teilnehmen*) attend; go to <*Schule, Ausstellung*>. **B~er(in)** *m* -s,- (*f* -, -nen) visitor; caller. **B~szeit** *f* visiting hours *pl*

betagt *a* aged, old

betätig|en *vt* operate; **sich b~en** work (**als** as). **B~ung** *f* -, **-en** operation; (*Tätigkeit*) activity

betäub|en *vt* stun; <*Lärm:*> deafen; (*Med*) anaesthetize; (*lindern*) ease, deaden <*Schmerz*>; **wie b~t** dazed. **B~ung** *f* - daze; (*Med*) anaesthesia. **B~ungsmittel** *nt* anaesthetic

Bete *f* -, **-n** Rote **B~** beetroot

beteilig|en *vt* give a share to; **sich b~en** take part (**an** + *dat* in); (*beitragen*) contribute (**an** + *dat* to). **b~t** *a* **b~t sein** take part/(*an Unfall*) be involved/(*Comm*) have a share (**an** + *dat* in); **alle B~ten** all those involved. **B~ung** *f* -, **-en** participation; involvement; (*Anteil*) share

beten *vi* (*haben*) pray

Beton /be'tɔŋ/ *m* **-s** concrete

betonen *vt* stressed, emphasize

beton|t *a* stressed; (*fig*) pointed. **B~ung** *f* -, **-en** stress

Betracht *m* **in B~ ziehen** consider; **außer B~ lassen** disregard; **nicht in B~ kommen** be out of the question. **b~en** *vt* look at; (*fig*) regard (**als** as)

beträchtlich *a* considerable

Betrachtung *f* -, **-en** contemplation; (*Überlegung*) reflection

Betrag *m* **-[e]s,-̈e** amount. **b~en†** *vt* amount to; **sich b~en** behave. **B~en** *nt* **-s** behaviour; (*Sch*) conduct

betreff|en† *vt* affect; (*angehen*) concern. **b~end** *a* relevant. **b~s** *prep* (+ *gen*) concerning

betreiben† *vt* (*leiten*) run; (*ausüben*) carry on

betreten† *vt* step on; (*eintreten*) enter; '**B~ verboten**' 'no entry'; (*bei Rasen*) 'keep off [the grass]'

betreu|en *vt* look after. **B~er(in)** *m* -s,- (*f* -, -nen) helper; (*Kranken-*) nurse. **B~ung** *f* - care

Betrieb *m* business; (*Firma*) firm; (*Treiben*) activity; (*Verkehr*) traffic; **außer B~** not in use; (*defekt*) out of order

Betriebs|anleitung, B~anweisung *f* operating instructions *pl*. **B~ferien** *pl* firm's holiday. **B~leitung** *f* management. **B~rat** *m* works committee. **B~störung** *f* breakdown

betrinken† (sich) *vr* get drunk

betroffen *a* disconcerted; **b~ sein** be affected (**von** by)

betrüb|en *vt* sadden. **b~t** *a* sad

Betrug *m* **-[e]s** deception; (*Jur*) fraud

betrüg|en† *vt* cheat, swindle; (*Jur*) defraud; (*in der Ehe*) be unfaithful to. **B~er(in)** *m* -s,- (*f* -, -nen) swindler. **B~erei** *f* -, **-en** fraud

betrunken *a* drunken; **b~ sein** be drunk. **B~e(r)** *m* drunk

Bett *nt* **-[e]s, -en** bed. **B~couch** *f* sofa-bed. **B~decke** *f* blanket; (*Tages-*) bedspread

Bettel|ei *f* - begging. **b~n** *vi* (*haben*) beg

Bettler(in) *m* -s,- (*f* -, -nen) beggar

Bettpfanne *f* bedpan

Betttuch (**Bettuch**) *nt* sheet

Bett|wäsche *f* bed linen. **B~zeug** *nt* bedding

betupfen *vt* dab (**mit** with)

beug|en *vt* bend; (*Gram*) decline; conjugate <*Verb*>; **sich b~en** bend; (*lehnen*) lean; (*sich fügen*) submit (*dat* to). **B~ung** *f* -, **-en** (*Gram*) declension; conjugation

Beule *f* -, **-n** bump; (*Delle*) dent

beunruhig|en *vt* worry; **sich b~en** worry. **B~ung** *f* - worry

beurlauben *vt* give leave to

beurteil|en *vt* judge. **B~ung** *f* -, **-en** judgement; (*Ansicht*) opinion

Beute *f* - booty, haul; (*Jagd-*) bag; (*eines Raubtiers*) prey

Beutel *m* -s,- bag; (*Tabak- & Zool*) pouch. **B~tier** *nt* marsupial

Bevölkerung f -, -en population

bevollmächtigen vt authorize

bevor conj before; b~ nicht until

bevormunden vt treat like a child

bevorstehen† vi sep (haben) approach; (unmittelbar) be imminent. **b~d** a approaching, forthcoming; unmittelbar b~d imminent

bevorzug|en vt prefer; (begünstigen) favour. **b~t** a privileged; <Behandlung> preferential

bewachen vt guard

Bewachung f - guard; unter B~ under guard

bewaffn|en vt arm. **b~et** a armed. **B~ung** f - armament; (Waffen) arms pl

bewahren vt protect (vor + dat from); (behalten) keep; die Ruhe b~ keep calm

bewähren (sich) vr prove one's/ <Ding:> its worth; (erfolgreich sein) prove a success

bewähr|t a reliable; (erprobt) proven. **B~ung** f - (Jur) probation. **B~ungsfrist** f [period of] probation. **B~ungsprobe** f (fig) test

bewältigen vt cope with; (überwinden) overcome

bewässer|n vt irrigate. **B~ung** f - irrigation

bewegen[1] vt (reg) move; sich b~ move; (körperlich) take exercise

bewegen[2]† vt jdn dazu b~, etw zu tun induce s.o. to do sth

Beweg|grund m motive. **b~lich** a movable, mobile; (wendig) agile. **B~lichkeit** f - mobility; agility. **B~ung** f -, -en movement; (Phys) motion; (Rührung) emotion; (Gruppe) movement; körperliche B~ung physical exercise. **b~ungslos** a motionless

Beweis m -es, -e proof; (Zeichen) token; B~e evidence sg. **b~en**† vt prove; (zeigen) show; sich b~en

prove oneself/<Ding:> itself. **B~material** nt evidence

bewerb|en† (sich) vr apply (um for; bei to). **B~er(in)** m -s,- (f -, -nen) applicant. **B~ung** f -, -en application

bewerten vt value; (einschätzen) rate; (Sch) mark, grade

bewilligen vt grant

bewirken vt cause; (herbeiführen) bring about

bewirt|en vt entertain. **B~ung** f - hospitality

bewohn|bar a habitable. **b~en** vt inhabit, live in. **B~er(in)** m -s,- (f -, -nen) resident, occupant; (Einwohner) inhabitant

bewölk|en (sich) vr cloud over; b~t cloudy. **B~ung** f - clouds pl

bewunder|n vt admire. **b~nswert** a admirable. **B~ung** f - admiration

bewusst a conscious (gen of); (absichtlich) deliberate. **b~los** a unconscious. **B~losigkeit** f - unconsciousness; **B~sein** nt -s consciousness; (Gewissheit) awareness; bei B~sein conscious

bezahl|en vt/i (haben) pay; pay for <Ware, Essen>. **B~ung** f - payment; (Lohn) pay. **B~fernsehen** nt pay television; pay TV

bezaubern vt enchant

bezeichn|en vt mark; (bedeuten) denote; (beschreiben, nennen) describe (als as). **b~end** a typical. **B~ung** f marking; (Beschreibung) description (als as); (Ausdruck) term; (Name) name

bezeugen vt testify to

bezichtigen vt accuse (gen of)

bezieh|en† vt cover; (einziehen) move into; (beschaffen) obtain; (erhalten) get; (in Verbindung bringen) relate (auf + acc to); sich b~en cloud over; sich b~en auf (+ acc) refer to; das Bett frisch b~en put clean sheets on the bed. **B~ung** f -, -en relation; (Verhältnis) relationship; (Bezug) respect; B~ungen haben have

---

*alte Schreibung

connections. **b~ungsweise** *adv* respectively; (*vielmehr*) or rather

Bezirk *m* -[e]s, -e district

Bezug *m* cover; (*Kissen-*) case; (*Beschaffung*) obtaining; (*Kauf*) purchase; (*Zusammenhang*) reference; **B~̈e** *pl* earnings; **B~ nehmen** refer (**auf** + *acc* to); **in B~ auf** (+ *acc*) regarding

bezüglich *prep* (+ *gen*) regarding ● *a* relating (**auf** + *acc* to)

bezwecken *vt* (*fig*) aim at

bezweifeln *vt* doubt

BH /beː'haː/ *m* -[s], -[s] bra

Bibel *f* -, -n Bible

Biber *m* -s,- beaver

Biblio|thek *f* -, -en library. **B~thekar(in)** *m* -s,- (*f* -, -nen) librarian

biblisch *a* biblical

bieg|en† *vt* bend; **sich b~en** bend ● *vi* (*sein*) curve (**nach** to); **um die Ecke b~en** turn the corner. **b~sam** *a* flexible, supple. **B~ung** *f* -, -en bend

Biene *f* -, -n bee. **B~nstock** *m* beehive. **B~nwabe** *f* honeycomb

Bier *nt* -s, -e beer. **B~deckel** *m* beer-mat. **B~krug** *m* beer-mug

bieten† *vt* offer; (*bei Auktion*) bid

Bifokalbrille *f* bifocals *pl*

Bigamie *f* - bigamy

bigott *a* over-pious

Bikini *m* -s, -s bikini

Bilanz *f* -, -en balance sheet; (*fig*) result; **die B~ ziehen** (*fig*) draw conclusions (**aus** from)

Bild *nt* -[e]s, -er picture; (*Theat*) scene

bilden *vt* form; (*sein*) be; (*erziehen*) educate

Bild|erbuch *nt* picture-book. **B~fläche** *f* screen. **B~hauer** *m* -s,- sculptor. **b~lich** *a* pictorial; (*figurativ*) figurative. **B~nis** *nt* -ses, -se portrait. **B~schirm** *m* (*TV*) screen. **B~schirmgerät** *nt* visual display unit, VDU. **b~schön** *a* very beautiful

Bildung *f* - formation; (*Erziehung*) education; (*Kultur*) culture

Billard /'brljart/ *nt* -s billiards *sg*. **B~tisch** *m* billiard table

Billett /brl'jɛt/ *nt* -[e]s, -e & -s ticket

Billiarde *f* -, -n thousand million million

billig *a* cheap; (*dürftig*) poor; **recht und b~** right and proper. **b~en** *vt* approve. **B~ung** *f* - approval

Billion /brlio:n/ *f* -, -en million million, billion

Bimsstein *m* pumice stone

Binde *f* -, -n band; (*Verband*) bandage; (*Damen-*) sanitary towel. **B~hautentzündung** *f* conjunctivitis. **b~n**† *vt* tie (**an** + *acc* to); make <*Strauß*>; bind <*Buch*>; (*fesseln*) tie up; (*Culin*) thicken; **sich b~n** commit oneself. **B~strich** *m* hyphen. **B~wort** *nt* (*pl* -wörter) (*Gram*) conjunction

Bind|faden *m* string. **B~ung** *f* -, -en (*fig*) tie; (*Beziehung*) relationship; (*Verpflichtung*) commitment; (*Ski-*) binding; (*Tex*) weave

binnen *prep* (+ *dat*) within. **B~handel** *m* home trade

Bio- *pref* organic

Bio|chemie *f* biochemistry. **b~dynamisch** *m* organic. **B~graphie**, **B~grafie** *f* -, -n biography

Bio|hof *m* organic farm. **B~laden** *m* health-food store

Biolog|e *m* -n, -n biologist. **B~ie** *f* - biology. **b~isch** *a* biological; **b~ischer Anbau** organic farming; **b~isch angebaut** organically grown

Birke *f* -, -n birch [tree]

Birm|a *nt* -s Burma. **b~anisch** *a* Burmese

Birn|baum *m* pear-tree. **B~e** *f* -, -n pear; (*Electr*) bulb

bis *prep* (+ *acc*) as far as, [up] to; (*zeitlich*) until, till; (*spätestens*) by; **bis zu** up to; **bis auf** (+ *acc*) (*einschließlich*) [down] to; (*ausgenommen*) except [for]; **drei bis vier Mark** three to four marks; **bis morgen!** see you tomorrow! ● *conj* until

Bischof *m* -s, -̈e bishop

b

bish<u>e</u>r *adv* so far, up to now

Biskuit|rolle /bɪsˈkviːt-/ *f* Swiss roll. **B~teig** *m* sponge mixture

B<u>i</u>ss *m* -es, -e bite

b<u>i</u>sschen *inv pron* **ein b~** a bit, a little; **kein b~** not a bit

B<u>i</u>ss|en *m* -s,- bite, mouthful. **b~ig** *a* vicious; (*fig*) caustic

bisw<u>ei</u>len *adv* from time to time

b<u>i</u>tt|e *adv* please; (*nach Klopfen*) come in; (*als Antwort auf 'danke'*) don't mention it, you're welcome; **wie b~e?** pardon? **B~e** *f* -, -n request/(*dringend*) plea (**um** for). **b~en†** *vt/i* (*haben*) ask/(*dringend*) beg (**um** for); (*einladen*) invite, ask. **b~end** *a* pleading

b<u>i</u>tter *a* bitter. **B~keit** *f* - bitterness. **b~lich** *adv* bitterly

B<u>i</u>ttschrift *f* petition

biz<u>a</u>rr *a* bizarre

bl<u>ä</u>h|en *vt* swell; <*Vorhang, Segel*:> billow ● *vi* (*haben*) cause flatulence. **B~ungen** *fpl* flatulence *sg*, ⚙ wind *sg*

Blam<u>a</u>ge /blaˈmaːʒə/ *f* -, -n humiliation; (*Schande*) disgrace

blam<u>ie</u>ren *vt* disgrace; **sich b~** disgrace oneself; (*sich lächerlich machen*) make a fool of oneself

blanch<u>ie</u>ren /blãˈʃiːrən/ *vt* (*Culin*) blanch

bl<u>a</u>nk *a* shiny. **B~oscheck** *m* blank cheque

Bl<u>a</u>se *f* -, -n bubble; (*Med*) blister; (*Anat*) bladder. **b~n†** *vt/i* (*haben*) blow; play <*Flöte*>. **B~nentzündung** *f* cystitis

Bl<u>a</u>s|instrument *nt* wind instrument. **B~kapelle** *f* brass band

bl<u>a</u>ss *a* pale; (*schwach*) faint

Bl<u>ä</u>sse *f* - pallor

Bl<u>a</u>tt *nt* -[e]s,¨-er (*Bot*) leaf; (*Papier*) sheet; (*Zeitung*) paper

Bl<u>a</u>ttlaus *f* greenfly

bl<u>au</u> *a*, **B~** *nt* -s,- blue; **b~er Fleck** bruise; **b~es Auge** black eye; **b~ sein** ⚙ be tight; **Fahrt ins B~e**

mystery tour. **B~beere** *f* bilberry. **B~licht** *nt* blue flashing light

Bl<u>e</u>ch *nt* -[e]s, -e sheet metal; (*Weiß-*) tin; (*Platte*) metal sheet; (*Back-*) baking sheet; (*Mus*) brass; (⚙ *Unsinn*) rubbish. **B~schaden** *m* (*Auto*) damage to the bodywork

Bl<u>ei</u> *nt* -[e]s lead

Bl<u>ei</u>be *f* - place to stay. **b~n†** *vi* (*sein*) remain, stay; (*übrig-*) be left; **ruhig b~n** keep calm; **bei etw b~n** (*fig*) stick to sth; **b~n Sie am Apparat** hold the line; **etw b~n lassen** not to do sth. **b~nd** *a* permanent; (*anhaltend*) lasting

bl<u>ei</u>ch *a* pale. **b~en†** *vi* (*sein*) bleach; (*ver-*) fade ● *vt* (*reg*) bleach. **B~mittel** *nt* bleach

bl<u>ei</u>|ern *a* leaden. **b~frei** *a* unleaded. **B~stift** *m* pencil. **B~stiftabsatz** *m* stiletto heel. **B~stiftspitzer** *m* -s,- pencil sharpener

Bl<u>e</u>nde *f* -, -n shade, shield; (*Sonnen-*) [sun] visor; (*Phot*) diaphragm; (*Öffnung*) aperture; (*an Kleid*) facing. **b~n** *vt* dazzle, blind

Bl<u>i</u>ck *m* -[e]s, -e look; (*kurz*) glance; (*Aussicht*) view; **auf den ersten B~** at first sight. **b~en** *vi* (*haben*) look/(*kurz*) glance (**auf** + *acc* at). **B~punkt** *m* (*fig*) point of view

bl<u>i</u>nd *a* blind; (*trübe*) dull; **b~er Alarm** false alarm; **b~er Passagier** stowaway. **B~darm** *m* appendix. **B~darmentzündung** *f* appendicitis. **B~e(r)** *m/f* blind man/woman; **die B~en** the blind *pl*. **B~enhund** *m* guidedog. **B~enschrift** *f* braille. **B~gänger** *m* -s,- (*Mil*) dud. **B~heit** *f* - blindness

bl<u>i</u>nk|en *vi* (*haben*) flash; (*funkeln*) gleam; (*Auto*) indicate. **B~er** *m* -s,- (*Auto*) indicator. **B~licht** *nt* flashing light

bl<u>i</u>nzeln *vi* (*haben*) blink

Bl<u>i</u>tz *m* -es, -e [flash of] lightning; (*Phot*) flash. **B~ableiter** *m* lightning-conductor. **b~artig** *a* lightning ... ● *adv* like lightning. **b~en** *vi* (*haben*) flash; (*funkeln*)

---

*old spelling

sparkle; **es hat geblitzt** there was a flash of lightning. **B~licht** nt (Phot) flash. **b~sauber** a spick and span. **b~schnell** a lightning ... ● adv like lightning

Block m -[e]s, ̈e block ● -[e]s, -s & ̈e pad; (Häuser-) block

Blockade f -, -n blockade

Blockflöte f recorder

blockieren vt block; (Mil) blockade

Blockschrift f block letters pl

blöd[e] a feeble-minded; (dumm) stupid

Blödsinn m -[e]s idiocy; (Unsinn) nonsense

blöken vi (haben) bleat

blond a fair-haired; <Haar> fair

bloß a bare; (alleinig) mere ● adv only, just

bloß|legen vt sep uncover. **b~stellen** vt sep compromise

Bluff m -s, -s bluff. **b~en** vt/i (haben) bluff

blühen vi (haben) flower; (fig) flourish. **b~d** a flowering; (fig) flourishing, thriving

Blume f -, -n flower; (vom Wein) bouquet. **B~nbeet** nt flower-bed. **B~ngeschäft** nt flower-shop, florist's. **B~nkohl** m cauliflower. **B~nmuster** nt floral design. **B~nstrauß** m bunch of flowers. **B~ntopf** m flowerpot; (Pflanze) pot plant. **B~nzwiebel** f bulb

blumig a (fig) flowery

Bluse f -, -n blouse

Blut nt -[e]s blood. **b~arm** a anaemic. **B~bahn** f blood-stream. **B~bild** nt blood count. **B~druck** m blood pressure. **b~dürstig** a bloodthirsty

Blüte f -, -n flower, bloom; (vom Baum) blossom; (B~zeit) flowering period; (Baum-) blossom time; (Höhepunkt) peak, prime

Blut|egel m -s,- leech. **b~en** vi (haben) bleed

Blüten|blatt nt petal. **B~staub** m pollen

Blut|er m -s,- haemophiliac. **B~erguss** m bruise. **B~gefäß** nt

blood-vessel. **B~gruppe** f blood group. **b~ig** a bloody. **B~körperchen** nt -s,- corpuscle. **B~probe** f blood test. **b~rünstig** a (fig) bloody, gory. **B~schande** f incest. **B~spender** m blood donor. **B~sturz** m haemorrhage. **B~transfusion, B~übertragung** f blood transfusion. **B~ung** f -, -en bleeding; (Med) haemorrhage; (Regel-) period. **b~unterlaufen** a bruised; <Auge> bloodshot. **B~vergiftung** f blood-poisoning. **B~wurst** f black pudding

Bö f -, -en gust; (Regen-) squall

Bob m -s, -s bob[-sleigh]

Bock m -[e]s, ̈e buck; (Ziege) billy goat; (Schaf) ram; (Gestell) support. **b~ig** a 🔲 stubborn. **B~springen** nt leap-frog

Boden m -s, ̈ ground; (Erde) soil; (Fuß-) floor; (Grundfläche) bottom; (Dach-) loft, attic. **B~satz** m sediment. **B~schätze** mpl mineral deposits. **B~see** (der) Lake Constance

Bogen m -s, & ̈ curve; (Geom) arc; (beim Skilauf) turn; (Archit) arch; (Waffe, Geigen-) bow; (Papier) sheet; **einen großen B~ um jdn/etw machen** 🔲 give s.o./sth a wide berth. **B~schießen** nt archery

Bohle f -, -n [thick] plank

Böhm|en nt -s Bohemia. **b~isch** a Bohemian

Bohne f -, -n bean; **grüne B~n** French beans

bohner|n vt polish. **B~wachs** nt floor-polish

bohr|en vt/i (haben) drill (nach for); drive <Tunnel>; sink <Brunnen>; <Insekt:> bore. **B~er** m -s,- drill. **B~insel** f [offshore] drilling rig. **B~turm** m derrick

Boje f -, -n buoy

Böllerschuss m gun salute

Bolzen m -s,- bolt; (Stift) pin

bombardieren vt bomb; (fig) bombard (mit with)

Bombe *f* -, -n bomb. **B∼nangriff** *m* bombing raid. **B∼nerfolg** *m* huge success

Bon /bɔŋ/ *m* -s, -s voucher; (*Kassen-*) receipt

Bonbon /bɔŋ'bɔŋ/ *m & nt* -s, -s sweet

Bonus *m* -[sses], -[sse] bonus

Boot *nt* -[e]s, -e boat. **B∼ssteg** *m* landing-stage

Bord[1] *nt* -[e]s, -e shelf

Bord[2] *m* (*Naut*) **an B∼** aboard, on board; **über B∼** overboard. **B∼buch** *nt* log[-book]

Bordell *nt* -s, -e brothel

Bordkarte *f* boarding-pass

borgen *vt* borrow; **jdm etw b∼** lend s.o. sth

Borke *f* -, -n bark

Börse *f* -, -n purse; (*Comm*) stock exchange. **B∼nmakler** *m* stockbroker

Borst|e *f* -, -n bristle. **b∼ig** *a* bristly

Borte *f* -, -n braid

Böschung *f* -, -en embankment

böse *a* wicked, evil; (*unartig*) naughty; (*schlimm*) bad; (*zornig*) cross; **jdm** *od* **auf jdn b∼ sein** be cross with s.o.

bos|haft *a* malicious, spiteful. **B∼heit** *f* -, -en malice; spite; (*Handlung*) spiteful act/(*Bemerkung*) remark

böswillig *a* malicious

Botani|k *f* - botany. **B∼ker(in)** *m* -s,- (*f* -, -nen) botanist

Bot|e *m* -n, -n messenger. **B∼engang** *m* errand. **B∼schaft** *f* -, -en message; (*Pol*) embassy. **B∼schafter** *m* -s,- ambassador

Bouillon /bʊl'jɔŋ/ *f* -, -s clear soup. **B∼würfel** *m* stock cube

Bowle /'boːlə/ *f* -, -n punch

box|en *vi* (*haben*) box ● *vt* punch. **B∼en** *nt* -s boxing. **B∼er** *m* -s,- boxer

brachliegen† *vi sep* (*haben*) lie fallow

Branche /'brãːʃə/ *f* -, -n [line of] business. **B∼nverzeichnis** *nt* (*Teleph*) classified directory

Brand *m* -[e]s,¨e fire; (*Med*) gangrene; (*Bot*) blight; **in B∼ geraten** catch fire; **in B∼ setzen** *od* **stecken** set on fire. **B∼bombe** *f* incendiary bomb

Brand|stifter *m* arsonist. **B∼stiftung** *f* arson

Brandung *f* - surf

Brand|wunde *f* burn. **B∼zeichen** *nt* brand

Branntwein *m* spirit; (*coll*) spirits *pl*. **B∼brennerei** *f* distillery

bras|ilianisch *a* Brazilian. **B∼ilien** /-iən/ *nt* -s Brazil

Brat|apfel *m* baked apple. **b∼en†** *vt/i* (*haben*) roast; (*in der Pfanne*) fry. **B∼en** *m* -s,- roast; (*B∼stück*) joint. **b∼fertig** *a* oven-ready. **B∼hähnchen** *nt* roasting chicken. **B∼kartoffeln** *fpl* fried potatoes. **B∼pfanne** *f* frying-pan

Bratsche *f* -, -n (*Mus*) viola

Bratspieß *m* spit

Brauch *m* -[e]s, Bräuche custom. **b∼bar** *a* usable; (*nützlich*) useful. **b∼en** *vt* need; (*ge-, verbrauchen*) use; take <*Zeit*>; **er b∼t es nur zu sagen** he only has to say

Braue *f* -, -n eyebrow

brau|en *vt* brew. **B∼er** *m* -s,- brewer. **B∼erei** *f* -, -en brewery

braun *a*, **B∼** *nt* -s,- brown; **b∼ werden** <*Person.*> get a tan; **b∼ [gebrannt] sein** be [sun-]tanned

Bräune *f* - [sun-]tan. **b∼n** *vt/i* (*haben*) brown; (*in der Sonne*) tan

Braunschweig *nt* -s Brunswick

Brause *f* -, -n (*Dusche*) shower; (*an Gießkanne*) rose; (*B∼limonade*) fizzy drink

Braut *f* -,¨e bride; (*Verlobte*) fiancée

Bräutigam *m* -s, -e bridegroom; (*Verlobter*) fiancé

Brautkleid *nt* wedding dress

Brautpaar *nt* bridal couple; (*Verlobte*) engaged couple

brav *a* good; (*redlich*) honest ● *adv* dutifully; (*redlich*) honestly

---

*alte Schreibung

bravo int bravo!

BRD abbr (Bundesrepublik Deutschland) FRG

Brech|eisen nt jemmy; (B~stange) crowbar. **b~en**† vt break; (Phys) refract <Licht>; (erbrechen) vomit; sich b~en <Wellen:> break; <Licht:> be refracted; sich (dat) den Arm b~en break one's arm ● vi (sein) break ● vi (haben) vomit, be sick. **B~reiz** m nausea. **B~stange** f crowbar

Brei m -[e]s, -e paste; (Culin) purée; (Hafer-) porridge

breit a wide; <Schultern, Grinsen> broad. **B~e** f -, -n width; breadth; (Geog) latitude. **b~en** vt spread (über + acc over). **B~engrad** m [degree of] latitude. **B~enkreis** m parallel

Bremse¹ f -, -n horsefly

Bremse² f -, -n brake. **b~n** vt slow down; (fig) restrain ● vi (haben) brake

Bremslicht nt brake-light

brenn|bar a combustible; leicht b~bar highly [in]flammable. **b~en**† vi (haben) burn; <Licht:> be on; <Zigarette:> be alight; (weh tun) smart, sting ● vt burn; (rösten) roast; (im Brennofen) fire; (destillieren) distil. **b~end** a burning; (angezündet) lighted; (fig) fervent **B~erei** f -, -en distillery

Brennessel* f s. Brennnessel

Brenn|holz nt firewood. **B~ofen** m kiln. **B~nessel** f stinging nettle. **B~punkt** m (Phys) focus. **B~spiritus** m methylated spirits. **B~stoff** m fuel

Bretagne /breˈtanjə/ (die) - Brittany

Brett nt -[e]s, -er board; (im Regal) shelf; schwarzes B~ notice board. **B~spiel** nt board game

Brezel f -, -n pretzel

Bridge /brɪtʃ/ nt - (Spiel) bridge

Brief m -[e]s, -e letter. **B~beschwerer** m -s,- paperweight. **B~freund(in)** m(f) penfriend. **B~kasten** m letter-box. **B~kopf** m letter-head. **b~lich** a &

adv by letter. **B~marke** f [postage] stamp. **B~öffner** m paper-knife. **B~papier** nt notepaper. **B~tasche** f wallet. **B~träger** m postman. **B~umschlag** m envelope. **B~wahl** f postal vote. **B~wechsel** m correspondence

Brikett nt -s, -s briquette

Brillant m -en, -en [cut] diamond

Brille f -, -n glasses pl, spectacles pl; (Schutz-) goggles pl; (Klosett-) toilet seat

bringen† vt bring; (fort-) take; (ein-) yield; (veröffentlichen) publish; (im Radio) broadcast; show <Film>; ins Bett b~ put to bed; jdn nach Hause b~ take/(begleiten) see s.o. home; um etw b~ deprive of sth; jdn dazu b~, etw zu tun get s.o. to do sth; es weit b~ (fig) go far

Brise f -, -n breeze

Brit|e m -n, -n, **B~in** f -, -nen Briton. **b~isch** a British

Bröck|chen nt -s,- (Culin) crouton. **b~elig** a crumbly; <Gestein> friable. **b~eln** vt/i (haben/sein) crumble

Brocken m -s,- chunk; (Erde, Kohle) lump

Brokat m -[e]s, -e brocade

Brokkoli pl broccoli sg

Brombeere f blackberry

Bronchitis f - bronchitis

Bronze /ˈbrõːsə/ f -, -n bronze

Brosch|e f -, -n brooch. **b~iert** a paperback. **B~üre** f -, -n brochure; (Heft) booklet

Brösel mpl (Culin) breadcrumbs

Brot n -[e]s, -e bread; ein B~ a loaf [of bread]; (Scheibe) a slice of bread

Brötchen n -s,- [bread] roll

Brotkrümel m breadcrumb

Bruch m -[e]s,ⁿe break; (Brechen) breaking; (Rohr-) burst; (Med) fracture; (Eingeweide-) rupture, hernia; (Math) fraction; (fig) breach; (in Beziehung) break-up

brüchig a brittle

Bruch|landung f crash-landing. **B~rechnung** f fractions pl.

B∼stück nt fragment. **B∼teil** m fraction

Brücke f -, -n bridge; (*Teppich*) rug

Bruder m -s,- brother

brüderlich a brotherly, fraternal

Brügge nt -s Bruges

Brüh|e f -, -n broth, stock. **B∼würfel** m stock cube

brüllen vt/i (*haben*) roar

brumm|eln vt/i (*haben*) mumble. **b∼en** vi (*haben*) <*Insekt:*> buzz; <*Bär:*> growl; <*Motor:*> hum; (*murren*) grumble **B∼er** m -s,- 🔲 bluebottle. **b∼ig** a 🔲 grumpy

brünett a dark-haired

Brunnen m -s,- well; (*Spring-*) fountain; (*Heil-*) spa water

brüsk a brusque

Brüssel nt -s Brussels

Brust f -,⸚e chest; (*weibliche, Culin: B∼stück*) breast. **B∼bein** nt breastbone

brüsten (sich) vr boast

Brust|fellentzündung f pleurisy. **B∼schwimmen** nt breaststroke

Brüstung f -, -en parapet

Brustwarze f nipple

Brut f -, -en incubation

brutal a brutal

brüten vi (*haben*) sit (*on eggs*); (*fig*) ponder (**über** + *dat* over)

Brutkasten m (*Med*) incubator

brutto adv, **B∼-** pref gross

Bub m -en, -en (*SGer*) boy. **B∼e** m -n, -n (*Karte*) jack, knave

Buch nt -[e]s,⸚er book; **B∼ führen** keep a record (**über** + *acc* of); **die B∼er führen** keep the accounts

Buche f -, -n beech

buchen vt book; (*Comm*) enter

Bücher|ei f -, -en library. **B∼regal** nt bookcase, bookshelves pl. **B∼schrank** m bookcase

Buchfink m chaffinch

Buch|führung f bookkeeping. **B∼halter(in)** m -s,- (f -, -nen) bookkeeper, accountant. **B∼haltung** f bookkeeping,

accountancy; (*Abteilung*) accounts department. **B∼handlung** f bookshop

Büchse f -, -n box; (*Konserven-*) tin, can

Buch|stabe m -n, -n letter. **b∼stabieren** vt spell [out]. **b∼stäblich** adv literally

Bucht f -, -en (*Geog*) bay

Buchung f -, -en booking, reservation; (*Comm*) entry

Buckel m -s,- hump; (*Beule*) bump; (*Hügel*) hillock

bücken (sich) vr bend down

bucklig a hunchbacked

Bückling m -s, -e smoked herring

Buddhis|mus m - Buddhism. **B∼t(in)** m -en, -en (f -, -nen) Buddhist. **b∼tisch** a Buddhist

Bude f -, -n hut; (*Kiosk*) kiosk; (*Markt-*) stall; (🔲 *Zimmer*) room

Budget /bY'dʒe:/ nt -s, -s budget

Büfett nt -[e]s, -e sideboard; (*Theke*) bar; **kaltes B∼** cold buffet

Büffel m -s,- buffalo

Bügel m -s,- frame; (*Kleider-*) coathanger; (*Steig-*) stirrup; (*Brillen-*) sidepiece. **B∼brett** nt ironing-board. **B∼eisen** nt iron. **B∼falte** f crease. **b∼frei** a non-iron. **b∼n** vt/i (*haben*) iron

Bühne f -, -n stage. **B∼nbild** nt set. **B∼neingang** m stage door

Buhrufe mpl boos

Bukett nt -[e]s, -e bouquet

Bulgarien /-iən/ nt -s Bulgaria

Bull|auge nt (*Naut*) porthole. **B∼dogge** f bulldog. **B∼dozer** /-do:zɐ/ m -s,- bulldozer. **B∼e** m -n, -n bull; (🔲 *Polizist*) cop

Bummel m -s,- 🔲 stroll. **B∼lei** f - 🔲 dawdling

bummel|ig a 🔲 slow; (*nachlässig*) careless. **b∼n** vi (*sein*) 🔲 stroll ● vi (*haben*) 🔲 dawdle. **B∼streik** m go-slow. **B∼zug** m 🔲 slow train

Bums m -es, -e 🔲 bump, thump

Bund¹ nt -[e]s, -e bunch

Bund² m -[e]s,⸚e association; (*Bündnis*) alliance; (*Pol*) federation;

(*Rock-, Hosen-*) waistband; **der B∼** the Federal Government

Bündel *nt* **-s,-** bundle. **b∼n** *vt* bundle [up]

Bundes|- *pref* Federal. **B∼genosse** *m* ally. **B∼kanzler** *m* Federal Chancellor. **B∼land** *nt* [federal] state; (*Aust*) province. **B∼liga** *f* German national league. **B∼rat** *m* Upper House of Parliament. **B∼regierung** *f* Federal Government. **B∼republik** *f* **die B∼republik Deutschland** the Federal Republic of Germany. **B∼tag** *m* Lower House of Parliament. **B∼wehr** *f* [Federal German] Army

bünd|ig *a & adv* **kurz und b∼ig** short and to the point. **B∼nis** *nt* **-sses, -sse** alliance

Bunker *m* **-s,-** bunker; (*Luftschutz-*) shelter

bunt *a* coloured; (*farbenfroh*) colourful; (*grell*) gaudy; (*gemischt*) varied; (*wirr*) confused; **b∼e Platte** assorted cold meats. **B∼stift** *m* crayon

Bürde *f* **-, -n** (*fig*) burden

Burg *f* **-, -en** castle

Bürge *m* **-n, -n** guarantor. **b∼n** *vi* (*haben*) **b∼n für** vouch for; (*fig*) guarantee

Bürger|(in) *m* **-s,-** (*f* **-, -nen**) citizen. **B∼krieg** *m* civil war. **b∼lich** *a* civil; <*Pflicht*> civic; (*mittelständisch*) middle-class. **B∼liche(r)** *m/f* commoner. **B∼meister** *m* mayor. **B∼rechte** *npl* civil rights. **B∼steig** *m* **-[e]s, -e** pavement

Bürgschaft *f* **-, -en** surety

Burgunder *m* **-s,-** (*Wein*) Burgundy

Büro *nt* **-s, -s** office. **B∼angestellte(r)** *m/f* office-worker. **B∼klammer** *f* paper-clip. **B∼kratie** *f* **-, -n** bureaucracy. **b∼kratisch** *a* bureaucratic

Bursche *m* **-n, -n** lad, youth

Bürste *f* **-, -n** brush. **b∼n** *vt* brush. **B∼nschnitt** *m* crew cut

Bus *m* **-ses, -se** bus; (*Reise-*) coach

Busch *m* **-[e]s, ̈-e** bush

Büschel *nt* **-s,-** tuft

buschig *a* bushy

Busen *m* **-s,-** bosom

Bussard *m* **-s, -e** buzzard

Buße *f* **-, -n** penance; (*Jur*) fine

Bußgeld *nt* (*Jur*) fine

Büste *f* **-, -n** bust; (*Schneider-*) dummy. **B∼nhalter** *m* **-s,-** bra

Butter *f* **-** butter. **B∼blume** *f* buttercup. **B∼brot** *nt* slice of bread and butter. **B∼milch** *f* buttermilk. **b∼n** *vt* butter

b.w. *abbr* (**bitte wenden**) P.T.O.

Cc

ca. *abbr* (**circa**) about

Café /ka'fe:/ *nt* **-s, -s** café

camp|en /'kɛmpən/ *vi* (*haben*) go camping. **C∼ing** *nt* **-s** camping. **C∼ingplatz** *m* campsite

Caravan /'ka[:]ravan/ *m* **-s, -s** (*Auto*) caravan; (*Kombi*) estate car

CD /tse:'de:/ *f* **-, -s** compact disc, CD. **CD-ROM** /tse:de:'rɔm/ *f* **-,-(s)** CD-ROM

Cell|ist(in) /tʃɛ'lɪst(ɪn)/ *m* **-en, -en** (*f* **-, -nen**) cellist. **C∼o** /'tʃɛlo/ *nt* **-, -los & -li** cello

Celsius /'tsɛlziʊs/ *inv* Celsius, centigrade

Champagner /ʃam'panjɐ/ *m* **-s** champagne

Champignon /'ʃampɪnjɔŋ/ *m* **-s, -s** [field] mushroom

Chance /'ʃã:s(ə)/ *f* **-, -n** chance

Chaos /'ka:ɔs/ *nt* **-** chaos

Charakter /ka'raktɐ/ *m* **-s, -e** /-'te:rə/ character. **c∼isieren** *vt* characterize. **c∼istisch** *a* characteristic (**für** of)

charm|ant /ʃar'mant/ *a* charming. **C∼e** /ʃarm/ *m* **-s** charm

Charter|flug /ˈtʃ-, ˈʃartɐ-/ m charter flight. **c∼n** vt charter

Chassis /ʃaˈsiː/ nt -,- /-ˈsiː[s], -ˈsiːs/ chassis

Chauffeur /ʃɔˈføːɐ/ m -s, -e chauffeur; (Taxi-) driver

Chauvinist /ʃoviˈnɪst/ m -en, -en chauvinist

Chef /ʃɛf/ m -s, -s head; 𝕋 boss

Chemie /çeˈmiː/ f - chemistry

Chem|iker(in) /ˈçe-/ m -s,- (f -, -nen) chemist. **c∼isch** a chemical; c∼ische Reinigung dry-cleaning; (Geschäft) dry-cleaner's

Chicorée /ˈʃikoreː/ m -s chicory

Chiffre /ˈʃɪfɐ, ˈʃɪfrə/ f -, -n cipher

Chile /ˈçiːle/ nt -s Chile

Chin|a /ˈçiːna/ nt -s China. **C∼ese** m -n, -n, **C∼esin** f -, -nen Chinese. c∼esisch a Chinese. **C∼esisch** nt -[s] (Lang) Chinese

Chip /tʃɪp/ m -s, -s [micro]chip. **C∼s** pl crisps

Chirurg /çiˈrʊrk/ m -en, -en surgeon. **C∼ie** /-ˈgiː/ f - surgery

Chlor /kloːɐ/ nt -s chlorine

Choke /tʃoːk/ m -s, -s (Auto) choke

Cholera /ˈkoːlera/ f - cholera

cholerisch /koˈleːrɪʃ/ a irascible

Cholesterin /ço-, kolɛsteˈriːn/ nt -s cholesterol

Chor /koːɐ/ m -[e]s,ːe choir

Choreographie, Choreografie /koreograˈfiː/ f -, -n choreography

Christ /krɪst/ m -en, -en Christian. **C∼baum** m Christmas tree. **C∼entum** nt -s Christianity c∼lich a Christian

Christus /ˈkrɪstʊs/ m -ti Christ

Chrom /kroːm/ nt -s chromium

Chromosom /kromoˈzoːm/ nt -s, -en chromosome

Chronik /ˈkroːnɪk/ f -, -en chronicle

chronisch /ˈkroːnɪʃ/ a chronic

Chrysantheme /kryzanˈteːmə/ f -, -n chrysanthemum

circa /ˈtsɪrka/ adv about

Clique /ˈklɪkə/ f -, -n clique

Clou /kluː/ m -s, -s highlight, 𝕋 high spot

Clown /klaʊn/ m -s, -s clown

Club /klʊp/ m -s, -s club

Cocktail /ˈkɔkteːl/ m -s, -s cocktail

Code /ˈkoːt/ m -s, -s code

Comic-Heft /ˈkɔmɪk-/ nt comic

Computer /kɔmˈpjuːtɐ/ m -s,- computer. **c∼isieren** vt computerize. **C∼spiel** nt computer game

Conférencier /kõferãˈsi̯eː/ m -s,- compère

Cord /kɔrt/ m -s, **C∼samt** m corduroy

Couch /kaʊtʃ/ f -, -es settee

Cousin /kuˈzɛ̃ː/ m -s, -s [male] cousin. **C∼e** /-ˈziːnə/ f -, -n [female] cousin

Creme /kreːm/ f -, -s cream; (Speise) cream dessert

Curry /ˈkari, ˈkœri/ nt & m -s curry powder ● nt -s, -s (Gericht) curry

Dd

da adv there; (hier) here; (zeitlich) then; (in dem Fall) in that case; **von da an** from then on; **da sein** be there/(hier) here; (existieren) exist; **wieder da sein** be back ● conj as, since

dabei (emphatic: **dabei**) adv nearby; (daran) with it; (eingeschlossen) included; (hinsichtlich) about it; (währenddem) during this; (gleichzeitig) at the same time; (doch) and yet; **dicht d∼** close by; **d∼ sein** be present; (mitmachen) be involved; **d∼ sein, etw zu tun** be just doing sth

Dach nt -[e]s,ːer roof. **D∼boden** m loft. **D∼luke** f skylight. **D∼rinne** f gutter

Dachs m -es, -e badger

Dachsparren m -s,- rafter

Dackel *m* -s,- dachshund

dadurch (*emphatic:* dadurch) *adv* through it/them; (*Ursache*) by it; (*deshalb*) because of that; d∼, dass because

dafür (*emphatic:* dafür) *adv* for it/ them; (*anstatt*) instead; (*als Ausgleich*) but [on the other hand]; d∼, dass considering that; ich kann nichts dafür it's not my fault

dagegen (*emphatic:* dagegen) *adv* against it/them; (*Mittel, Tausch*) for it; (*verglichen damit*) by comparison; (*jedoch*) however; hast du was d∼? do you mind?

daheim *adv* at home

daher (*emphatic:* daher) *adv* from there; (*deshalb*) for that reason; das kommt d∼, weil that's because ● *conj* that is why

dahin (*emphatic:* dahin) *adv* there; bis d∼ up to there; (*bis dann*) until/ (*Zukunft*) by then; jdn d∼bringen, dass er etw tut get s.o. to do sth

dahinten *adv* back there

dahinter (*emphatic:* dahinter) *adv* behind it/them; d∼ kommen (*fig*) get to the bottom of it

Dahlie /-ɪə/ *f* -, -n dahlia

dalassen† *vt sep* leave there

daliegen† *vi sep* (*haben*) lie there

damalig *a* at that time; der d∼e Minister the then minister

damals *adv* at that time

Damast *m* -es, -e damask

Dame *f* -, -n lady; (*Karte, Schach*) queen; (*D∼spiel*) draughts *sg.* d∼nhaft *a* ladylike

damit (*emphatic:* damit) *adv* with it/ them; (*dadurch*) by it; hör auf d∼! stop it! ● *conj* so that

Damm *m* -[e]s,¨e dam

dämmerig *a* dim. D∼licht *nt* twilight. d∼n *vi* <*haben*> <*Morgen:*> dawn; es d∼t it is getting light/(*abends*) dark. D∼ung *f* dawn; (*Abend-*) dusk

Dämon *m* -s, -en /-'moːnən/ demon

Dampf *m* -es,¨e steam; (*Chem*) vapour. d∼en *vi* (*haben*) steam

dämpfen *vt* (*Culin*) steam; (*fig*) muffle <*Ton*>; lower <*Stimme*>

Dampf|er *m* -s,- steamer. D∼kochtopf *m* pressure-cooker. D∼maschine *f* steam engine. D∼walze *f* steamroller

danach (*emphatic:* danach) *adv* after it/them; <*suchen*> for it/them; <*riechen*> of it; (*später*) afterwards; (*entsprechend*) accordingly; es sieht d∼ aus it looks like it

Däne *m* -n, -n Dane

daneben (*emphatic:* daneben) *adv* beside it/them; (*außerdem*) in addition; (*verglichen damit*) by comparison

Dän|emark *nt* -s Denmark. D∼in *f* -, -nen Dane. d∼isch *a* Danish

Dank *m* -es thanks *pl*; vielen D∼! thank you very much! d∼ *prep* (+ *dat or gen*) thanks to. d∼bar *a* grateful; (*erleichtert*) thankful; (*lohnend*) rewarding. D∼barkeit *f* - gratitude. d∼e *adv* d∼e [schön *od* sehr]! thank you [very much]! d∼en *vi* (*haben*) thank (jdm s.o.); (*ablehnen*) decline; nichts zu d∼en! don't mention it!

dann *adv* then; selbst d∼, wenn even if

daran (*emphatic:* daran) *adv* on it/ them; at it/them; <*denken*> of it; nahe d∼ on the point of (etw zu tun of doing sth). d∼setzen *vt sep* alles d∼setzen do one's utmost (zu to)

darauf (*emphatic:* darauf) *adv* on it/ them; <*warten*> for it; <*antworten*> to it; (*danach*) after that; (d∼hin) as a result. d∼hin *adv* as a result

daraus (*emphatic:* daraus) *adv* out of or from it/them; er macht sich nichts d∼ he doesn't care for it

darlegen *vt sep* expound; (*erklären*) explain

Darlehen *nt* -s,- loan

Darm *m* -[e]s,¨e intestine

darstell|en *vt sep* represent; (*bildlich*) portray; (*Theat*) interpret; (*spielen*) play; (*schildern*) describe. D∼er *m* -s,- actor. D∼erin *f* -, -nen actress. D∼ung *f* representation; interpretation; description

darüber (*emphatic:* **da**rüber) *adv* over it/them; (*höher*) above it/them; <*sprechen, lachen, sich freuen*> about it; (*mehr*) more; **d∼ hinaus** beyond [it]; (*dazu*) on top of that

darum (*emphatic:* **da**rum) *adv* round it/them; <*bitten, kämpfen*> for it; (*deshalb*) that is why; **d∼, weil** because

darunter (*emphatic:* **da**runter) *adv* under it/them; (*tiefer*) below it/them; (*weniger*) less; (*dazwischen*) among them

das *def art & pron s.* **der**

dasein* *vi sep* (*sein*) **da sein,** *s.* **da. D∼** *nt* **-s** existence

dass *conj* that

dasselbe *pron s.* **derselbe**

Daten|sichtgerät *nt* visual display unit, VDU. **D∼verarbeitung** *f* data processing

datieren *vt/i* (*haben*) date

Dativ *m* **-s, -e** dative. **D∼objekt** *nt* indirect object

Dattel *f* **-, -n** date

Datum *nt* **s, -ten** date; **Daten** dates; (*Angaben*) data

Dauer *f* **-** duration, length; (*Jur*) term; **auf die D∼** in the long run. **D∼auftrag** *m* standing order. **d∼haft** *a* lasting, enduring; (*fest*) durable. **D∼karte** *f* season ticket. **d∼n** *vi* (*haben*) last; **lange d∼n** take a long time. **d∼nd** *a* lasting; (*ständig*) constant. **D∼welle** *f* perm

Daumen *m* **-s,-** thumb; **jdm den D∼ drücken** *od* **halten** keep one's fingers crossed for s.o.

Daunen *fpl* down *sg.* **D∼decke** *f* [down-filled] duvet

davon (*emphatic:* **da**von) *adv* from it/them; (*dadurch*) by it; (*damit*) with it/them; (*darüber*) about it; (*Menge*) of it/them; **das kommt d∼!** it serves you right! **d∼kommen†** *vi sep* (*sein*) escape (**mit dem Leben** with one's life). **d∼laufen†** *vi sep* (*sein*) run away. **d∼machen** (**sich**) *vr sep* Ⓘ make off. **d∼tragen†** *vt sep*

carry off; (*erleiden*) suffer; (*gewinnen*) win

davor (*emphatic:* **da**vor) *adv* in front of it/them; <*sich fürchten*> of it; (*zeitlich*) before it/them

dazu (*emphatic:* **da**zu) *adv* to it/them; (*damit*) with it/them; (*dafür*) for it; **noch d∼** in addition to that; **jdn d∼ bringen, etw zu tun** get s.o. to do sth; **ich kam nicht d∼** I didn't get round to [doing] it. **d∼kommen†** *vi sep* (*sein*) arrive [on the scene]; (*hinzukommen*) be added. **d∼rechnen** *vt sep* add to it/them

dazwischen (*emphatic:* **da**zwischen) *adv* between them; in between; (*darunter*) among them. **d∼kommen†** *vi sep* (*sein*) (*fig*) crop up; **wenn nichts d∼kommt** if all goes well

Debat|te *f* **-, -n** debate; **zur D∼te stehen** be at issue. **d∼tieren** *vt/i* (*haben*) debate

Debüt /de'by:/ *nt* **-s, -s** début

Deck *nt* **-[e]s, -s** (*Naut*) deck; **an D∼** on deck. **D∼bett** *nt* duvet

Decke *f* **-, -n** cover; (*Tisch-*) table-cloth; (*Bett-*) blanket; (*Reise-*) rug; (*Zimmer-*) ceiling; **unter einer D∼stecken** Ⓘ be in league

Deckel *m* **-s,-** lid; (*Flaschen-*) top; (*Buch-*) cover

decken *vt* cover; tile <*Dach*>; lay <*Tisch*>; (*schützen*) shield; (*Sport*) mark; meet <*Bedarf*>; **jdn d∼** (*fig*) cover up for s.o.; **sich d∼** (*fig*) cover oneself (**gegen** against); (*übereinstimmen*) coincide

Deckname *m* pseudonym

Deckung *f* **-** (*Mil*) cover; (*Sport*) defence; (*Mann-*) marking; (*Boxen*) guard; (*Sicherheit*) security; **in D∼ gehen** take cover

defin|ieren *vt* define. **D∼ition** /-'tsio:n/ *f* **-, -en** definition

Defizit *nt* **-s, -e** deficit

deformiert *a* deformed

deftig *a* Ⓘ <*Mahlzeit*> hearty; <*Witz*> coarse

Degen *m* **-s,-** sword; (*Fecht-*) épée

degeneriert *a* (*fig*) degenerate

degradieren vt (Mil) demote; (fig) degrade

dehn|bar a elastic. **d~en** vt stretch; lengthen <Vokal>; sich **d~en** stretch

Deich m -[e]s, -e dike

dein poss pron your. **d~e(r,s)** poss pron yours; **die D~en** od **d~en** pl your family sg. **d~erseits** adv for your part. **d~etwegen** adv for your sake; (wegen dir) because of you, on your account. **d~etwillen** adv um **d~etwillen** for your sake. **d~ige** poss pron der/die/das d~ige yours. **d~s** poss pron yours

Dekan m -s, -e dean

Deklin|ation /-'tsio:n/ f -, -en declension. **d~ieren** vt decline

Dekolleté, Dekolletee /dekɔl'te:/ nt -s, -s low neckline

Dekor m & nt -s decoration. **D~ateur** /-'tø:ɐ/ m -s, -e interior decorator; (Schaufenster-) window-dresser. **D~ation** /-'tsio:n/ f -, -en decoration; (Schaufenster-) window-dressing; (Auslage) display. **d~ativ** a decorative. **d~ieren** vt decorate; dress <Schaufenster>

Deleg|ation /-'tsio:n/ f -, -en delegation. **D~ierte(r)** m/f delegate

delikat a delicate; (lecker) delicious; (taktvoll) tactful. **D~essengeschäft** nt delicatessen

Delikt nt -[e]s, -e offence

Delinquent m -en, -en offender

Delle f -, -n dent

Delphin m -s, -e dolphin

Delta nt -s, -s delta

dem def art & pron s. der

dementieren vt deny

dem|entsprechend a corresponding; (passend) appropriate ● adv accordingly; (passend) appropriately. **d~nächst** adv soon; (in Kürze) shortly

Demokrat m -en, -en democrat. **D~ie** f -, -n democracy. **d~isch** a democratic

demolieren vt wreck

Demonstr|ant m -en, -en demonstrator. **D~ation** /-'tsio:n/ f -, -en demonstration. **d~ieren** vt/i (haben) demonstrate

demontieren vt dismantle

Demoskopie f - opinion research

Demut f - humility

den def art & pron s. der. **d~en** pron s. der

denk|bar a conceivable. **d~en†** vt/i (haben) think (an + acc of); (sich erinnern) remember (an etw acc sth); das kann ich mir **d~en** I can imagine [that]; ich **d~e** nicht daran I have no intention of doing it. **D~mal** nt memorial; (Monument) monument. **d~würdig** a memorable

denn conj for; besser/mehr **d~** je better/more than ever ● adv wie/wo **d~**? but how/where? warum **d~** nicht? why ever not? es sei **d~** [, dass] unless

dennoch adv nevertheless

Denunz|iant m -en, -en informer. **d~ieren** vt denounce

Deodorant nt -s, -s deodorant

deplaciert, deplatziert /-'tsi:ɐt/ a (fig) out of place

Deponie f -, -n dump. **d~ren** vt deposit

deportieren vt deport

Depot /de'po:/ nt -s, -s depot; (Lager) warehouse; (Bank-) safe deposit

Depression f -, -en depression

deprimieren vt depress

der, die, das, pl **die**
● definite article

(acc den, die, das, pl die; gen des, der, des, pl der; dat dem, der, dem, pl den)

····▸ the. der Mensch the person; (als abstrakter Begriff) man. die Natur nature. das Leben life. das Lesen/ Tanzen reading/dancing. sich (dat) das Gesicht/die Hände waschen wash one's face/hands. 5 Mark das Pfund 5 marks a pound

● pronoun

(acc den, die, das, pl die; gen dessen, deren, dessen, pl deren; dat dem, der, dem, pl denen)

d

d

● *demonstrative pronoun*
····▸ that; (*pl*) those
····▸ (*attributiv*) **der Mann war es** it was 'that man
····▸ (*substantivisch*) he, she, it; (*pl*) they. **der war es** it was 'him. **die da** (*person*) that woman/girl; (*thing*) that one

● *relative pronoun*
····▸ (*Person*) who. **der Mann, der/dessen Sohn hier arbeitet** the man who/whose son works here. **die Frau, mit der ich Tennis spiele** the woman with whom I play tennis, the woman I play tennis with. **das Mädchen, das ich gestern sah** the girl I saw yesterday
····▸ (*Ding*) which, that. **ich sah ein Buch, das mich interessierte** I saw a book that interested me. **die CD, die ich mir anhöre** the CD I am listening to. **das Auto, mit dem wir nach Deutschland fahren** the car we are going to Germany in *or* in which we are going to Germany

derb *a* tough; (*kräftig*) strong; (*grob*) coarse; (*unsanft*) rough

deren *pron s.* der

dergleichen *inv a* such ● *pron* such a thing/such things

der-/die-/dasselbe, *pl* **dieselben** *pron* the same; **ein- und dasselbe** one and the same thing

derzeit *adv* at present

des *def art s.* der

Desert|eur /-'tø:ʀ/ *m* -s, -e deserter. **d~ieren** *vi* (*sein/haben*) desert

desgleichen *adv* likewise ● *pron* the like

deshalb *adv* for this reason; (*also*) therefore

Designer(in) /di'zaɪnɐ, -nərɪn/ *m* -s,- (*f*, -, -nen) designer

Desin|fektion /dɛs?ɪnfɛk'tsi̯oːn/ *f* disinfecting. **D~fektionsmittel** *nt* disinfectant. **d~fizieren** *vt* disinfect

dessen *pron s.* der

Destill|ation /-'tsi̯oːn/ *f* - distillation. **d~ieren** *vt* distil

desto *adv* **je mehr d~ besser** the more the better

deswegen *adv* = deshalb

Detektiv *m* -s, -e detective

Deton|ation /-'tsi̯oːn/ *f* -, -en explosion. **d~ieren** *vi* (*sein*) explode

deut|en *vt* interpret; predict <Zukunft> ● *vi* (*haben*) point (**auf** + *acc* at/(*fig*) to). **d~lich** *a* clear; (*eindeutig*) plain

deutsch *a* German. **D~** *nt* -[s] (*Lang*) German; **auf D~** in German. **D~e(r)** *m/f* German. **D~land** *nt* -s Germany

Deutung *f* -, -en interpretation

Devise *f* -, -n motto. **D~n** *pl* foreign currency *or* exchange *sg*

Dezember *m* -s,- December

dezent *a* unobtrusive; (*diskret*) discreet

Dezernat *nt* -[e]s, -e department

Dezimalzahl *f* decimal

d.h. *abbr* (*das heißt*) i.e.

Dia *nt* -s, -s (*Phot*) slide

Diabet|es *m* - diabetes. **D~iker** *m* -s,- diabetic

Diadem *nt* -s, -e tiara

Diagnose *f* -, -n diagnosis

diagonal *a* diagonal. **D~e** *f* -, -n diagonal

Diagramm *nt* -s, -e diagram; (*Kurven-*) graph

Diakon *m* -s, -e deacon

Dialekt *m* -[e]s, -e dialect

Dialog *m* -[e]s, -e dialogue

Diamant *m* -en, -en diamond

Diapositiv *nt* -s, -e (*Phot*) slide

Diaprojektor *m* slide projector

Diät *f* -, -en (*Med*) diet; **D~ leben** be on a diet

dich *pron* (*acc of* du) you; (*refl*) yourself

dicht *a* dense; (*dick*) thick; (*undurchlässig*) airtight; (*wasser-*) watertight ● *adv* densely; (*nahe*) close (**bei** to). **D~e** density. **d~en¹** *vt* make watertight

dicht|en² *vi* (*haben*) write poetry. ● *vt* write. **D~er(in)** *m* -s,- (*f* -, -en) poet. **d∼erisch** a poetic. **D∼ung¹** f -, -en poetry; (*Gedicht*) poem

Dichtung² f -, -en seal; (*Ring*) washer; (*Auto*) gasket

dick a thick; (*beleibt*) fat; (*geschwollen*) swollen; (*fam; eng*) close; **d∼ machen** be fattening. **d∼flüssig** a thick; (*Phys*) viscous. **D∼kopf** m 🎨 stubborn person; **einen D∼kopf haben** be stubborn

die *def art & pron* s. der

Dieb|(in) m -[e]s, -e (f -, -nen) thief. **d∼isch** a thieving; <*Freude*> malicious. **D∼stahl** m -[e]s,ˉe theft

Diele f -, -n floorboard; (*Flur*) hall

dien|en vi (haben) serve. **D∼er** m -s,- servant; (*Verbeugung*) bow. **D∼erin** f -, -nen maid, servant

Dienst m -[e]s, -e service; (*Arbeit*) work; (*Amtsausübung*) duty; **außer D∼** off duty; (*pensioniert*) retired; **D∼ haben** work; <*Soldat, Arzt:*> be on duty

Dienstag m Tuesday. **d∼s** adv on Tuesdays

Dienst|bote m servant. **d∼frei** a **d∼freier Tag** day off; **d∼frei haben** have time off; <*Soldat, Arzt:*> be off duty. **D∼grad** m rank. **D∼leistung** f service. **d∼lich** a official ● adv **d∼lich verreist** away on business. **D∼mädchen** nt maid. **D∼reise** f business trip. **D∼stelle** f office. **D∼stunden** fpl office hours

dies inv pron this. **d∼bezüglich** a relevant ● adv regarding this matter. **d∼e(r,s)** pron this; (pl) these; (*substantivisch*) this [one]; (pl) these; **d∼e Nacht** tonight; (*letzte*) last night

dieselbe pron s. derselbe

Dieselkraftstoff m diesel [oil]

diesmal adv this time

Dietrich m -s, -e skeleton key

Diffamation /-'tsio:n/ f - defamation

Differential* /-'tsia:l/ nt -s, -e s. Differenzial

Differenz f -, -en difference. **D∼ial** nt -s, -e differential. **d∼ieren** vt/i

(haben) differentiate (**zwischen** + dat between)

Digital- pref digital. **D∼uhr** f digital clock/watch

Dikt|at nt -[e]s, -e dictation. **D∼ator** m -s, -en /-'to:rən/ dictator. **D∼atur** f -, -en dictatorship. **d∼ieren** vt/i (haben) dictate

Dill m -s dill

Dimension f -, -en dimension

Ding nt -[e]s, -e & 🎨 -er thing; **guter D∼e sein** be cheerful; **vor allen D∼en** above all

Dinosaurier /-ie/ m -s,- dinosaur

Diözese f -, -n diocese

Diphtherie f - diphtheria

Diplom nt -s, -e diploma; (*Univ*) degree

Diplomat m -en, -en diplomat

dir pron (dat of du) [to] you; (refl) yourself; **ein Freund von dir** a friend of yours

direkt a direct ● adv directly; (*wirklich*) really. **D∼ion** /-'tsio:n/ f - management; (*Vorstand*) board of directors. **D∼or** m -s, -en /-'to:rən/, **D∼orin** f -, -nen director; (*Bank-, Theater-*) manager; (*Sch*) head; (*Gefängnis*) governor. **D∼übertragung** f live transmission

Dirig|ent m -en, -en (*Mus*) conductor. **d∼ieren** vt direct; (*Mus*) conduct

Dirndl nt -s,- dirndl [dress]

Diskette f -, -n floppy disc

Disko f -, -s 🎨 disco. **D∼thek** f -, -en discothèque

diskret a discreet

Diskus m -, -se & Disken discus

Disku|ssion f -, -en discussion. **d∼tieren** vt/i (haben) discuss

disponieren vi (haben) make arrangements; **d∼ [können] über** (+ acc) have at one's disposal

Disqualifi|kation /-'tsio:n/ f disqualification. **d∼zieren** vt disqualify

Dissertation /-'tsio:n/ f -, -en dissertation

Dissident m -en, -en dissident

Distanz f -, -en distance. **d~ieren (sich)** vr dissociate oneself (von from). **d~iert** a aloof

Distel f -, -n thistle

Disziplin f -, -en discipline. **d~arisch** a disciplinary. **d~iert** a disciplined

dito adv ditto

diverse attrib a pl various

Divid|ende f -, -en dividend. **d~ieren** vt divide (durch by)

Division f -, -en division

DJH abbr (Deutsche Jugendherberge) [German] youth hostel

DM abbr (Deutsche Mark) DM

doch conj & adv but; (dennoch) yet; (trotzdem) after all; **wenn d~** ...! if only ...! **nicht d~**! don't!

Docht m -[e]s, -e wick

Dock nt -s, -s dock. **d~en** vt/i (haben) dock

Dogge f -, -n Great Dane

Dogm|a nt -s, -men dogma. **d~atisch** a dogmatic

Dohle f -, -n jackdaw

Doktor m -s, -en /-'to:rən/ doctor. **D~arbeit** f [doctoral] thesis

Dokument nt -[e]s, -e document. **D~arbericht** m documentary. **D~arfilm** m documentary film

Dolch m -[e]s, -e dagger

Dollar m -s, -dollar

dolmetsch|en vt/i (haben) interpret. **D~er(in)** m -s,- (f -, -nen) interpreter

Dom m -[e]s, -e cathedral

Domino nt -s, -s dominoes sg. **D~stein** m domino

Dompfaff m -en, -en bullfinch

Donau f - Danube

Donner m -s thunder. **d~n** vi (haben) thunder

Donnerstag m Thursday. **d~s** adv on Thursdays

doof a 🗓 stupid

Doppel nt -s,- duplicate; (Tennis) doubles pl. **D~bett** nt double bed. **D~decker** m -s,- doubledecker

[bus]. **d~deutig** a ambiguous. **D~gänger** m -s,- double. **D~kinn** nt double chin. **D~name** m double-barrelled name. **D~punkt** m (Gram) colon. **D~stecker** m two-way adaptor. **d~t** a double; <Boden> false; **in d~ter Ausfertigung** in duplicate; **die d~te Menge** twice the amount ● adv doubly; (zweimal) twice; **d~t so viel** twice as much. **D~zimmer** nt double room

Dorf nt -[e]s,⸚er village. **D~bewohner** m villager

dörflich a rural

Dorn m -[e]s, -en thorn. **d~ig** a thorny

Dorsch m -[e]s, -e cod

dort adv there. **d~ig** a local

Dose f -, -n tin, can

dösen vi (haben) doze

Dosen|milch f evaporated milk. **D~öffner** m tin or can opener

dosieren vt measure out

Dosis f -, Dosen dose

Dot-com-Firma f dot-com (company)

Dotter m & nt -s,- [egg] yolk

Dozent(in) m -en, -en (f -, -nen) (Univ) lecturer

Dr. abbr (Doktor) Dr

Drache m -n, -n dragon. **D~n** m -s,- kite. **D~nfliegen** nt hang-gliding

Draht m -[e]s,⸚e wire; **auf D~** 🗓 on the ball. **D~seilbahn** f cable railway

Dram|a nt -s, -men drama. **D~atik** f - drama. **D~atiker** m -s,- dramatist. **d~atisch** a dramatic

dran adv 🗓 = daran; **gut/schlecht d~ sein** be well off/in a bad way; **ich bin d~** it's my turn

Drang m -[e]s urge; (Druck) pressure

dräng|eln vt/i (haben) push; (bedrängen) pester. **d~en** vt push; (bedrängen) urge; **sich d~en** crowd (um round) ● vi (haben) push; (eilen) be urgent; **d~en auf** (+ acc) press for

dran|halten† (sich) vr sep hurry. **d~kommen†** vi sep (sein) have one's turn

drauf adv 🔲 = darauf; d∼ und dran sein be on the point (etw zu tun of doing sth). **D∼gänger** m -s,- daredevil

draußen adv outside; (im Freien) out of doors

drechseln vt (Techn) turn

Dreck m -s dirt; (Morast) mud

Dreh m -s 🔲 knack; den D∼ heraushaben have got the hang of it. **D∼bank** f lathe. **D∼bleistift** m propelling pencil. **D∼buch** nt screenplay, script. **d∼en** vt turn; (im Kreis) rotate; (verschlingen) twist; roll <Zigarette>; shoot <Film>; lauter/leiser d∼en turn up/down; sich d∼en turn; (im Kreis) rotate; (schnell) spin; <Wind:> change; sich d∼en um revolve around; (sich handeln) be about ● vi (haben) turn; <Wind:> change; an etw (dat) d∼en turn sth. **D∼stuhl** m swivel chair. **D∼tür** f revolving door. **D∼ung** f -, -en turn; (im Kreis) rotation. **D∼zahl** f number of revolutions

drei inv a, **D∼** f -, -en three; (Sch) ≈ pass. **D∼eck** nt -[e]s, -e triangle. **d∼eckig** a triangular. **d∼erlei** inv a three kinds of ● pron three things. **d∼fach** a triple. **d∼mal** adv three times. **D∼rad** nt tricycle.

dreißig inv a thirty. **d∼ste(r,s)** a thirtieth

dreiviertel* inv a drei viertel, s. viertel. **D∼stunde** f three-quarters of an hour

dreizehn inv a thirteen **d∼te(r,s)** a thirteenth

dreschen† vt thresh

dress|ieren vt train. **D∼ur** f - training

dribbeln vi (haben) dribble

Drill m -[e]s (Mil) drill. **d∼en** vt drill

Drillinge mpl triplets

dringlich a urgent

Drink m -[s], -s [alcoholic] drink

drinnen adv inside

dritt adv zu d∼ in threes; wir waren zu d∼ there were three of us. **d∼e(r,s)** a third; ein D∼er a third person. **d∼el** inv a third. **D∼el** nt -s,- third. **d∼ens** adv thirdly. **d∼rangig** a third-rate

Drog|e f -, -n drug. **D∼enabhängige(r)** m/f drug addict. **D∼erie** f -, -n chemist's shop. **D∼ist** m -en, -en chemist

drohen vi (haben) threaten (jdm s.o.)

dröhnen vi (haben) resound; (tönen) boom

Drohung f -, -en threat

drollig a funny; (seltsam) odd

Drops m -,- [fruit] drop

Drossel f -, -n thrush

drosseln vt (Techn) throttle; (fig) cut back

drüben adv over there

Druck¹ m -[e]s,¨e pressure; unter D∼ setzen (fig) pressurize

Druck² m -[e]s, -e printing; (Schrift, Reproduktion) print. **D∼buchstabe** m block letter

drucken vt print

drücken vt/i (haben) press; (aus-) squeeze; <Schuh:> pinch; (umarmen) hug; Preise d∼ force down prices; (an Tür) d∼ push; sich d∼ 🔲 make oneself scarce; sich d∼ vor (+ dat) 🔲 shirk. **d∼d** a heavy; (schwül) oppressive

Drucker m -s,- printer

Druckerei f -, -en printing works

Druck|fehler m misprint. **D∼knopf** m press-stud. **D∼luft** f compressed air. **D∼sache** f printed matter. **D∼schrift** f type; (Veröffentlichung) publication; in D∼schrift in block letters pl

Druckstelle f bruise

Drüse f -, -n (Anat) gland

Dschungel m -s,- jungle

du pron (familiar address) you; auf Du und Du on familiar terms

Dübel m -s,- plug

Dudelsack m bagpipes pl

Duell nt -s, -e duel

Duett nt -s, -e [vocal] duet

Duft m -[e]s,¨e fragrance, scent; (Aroma) aroma. **d∼en** vi (haben) smell (nach of)

dulden vt tolerate; (*erleiden*) suffer ● vi (*haben*) suffer

dumm a stupid; (*unklug*) foolish; (🆃 *lästig*) awkward; **wie d~!**. **d~erweise** adv stupidly; (*leider*) unfortunately. **D~heit** f -, -en stupidity; (*Torheit*) foolishness; (*Handlung*) folly. **D~kopf** m 🆃 fool.

dumpf a dull

Düne f -, -n dune

Dung m -s manure

Düng|emittel nt fertilizer. **d~en** vt fertilize. **D~er** m -s,- fertilizer

dunk|el a dark; (*vage*) vague; (*fragwürdig*) shady; **d~les Bier** brown ale; **im D~eln** in the dark

Dunkel|heit f - darkness. **D~kammer** f dark-room. **d~n** vi (*haben*) get dark

dünn a thin; *<Buch>* slim; (*spärlich*) sparse; (*schwach*) weak

Dunst m -es,¨e mist, haze; (*Dampf*) vapour

dünsten vt steam

dunstig a misty, hazy

Duo nt -s, -s [instrumental] duet

Duplikat nt -[e]s, -e duplicate

Dur nt - (*Mus*) major [key]

durch prep (+ acc) through; (*mittels*) by; **[geteilt] d~** (*Math*) divided by ● adv **die Nacht d~** throughout the night; **d~ und d~ nass** wet through

durchaus adv absolutely; **d~ nicht** by no means

durchblättern vt sep leaf through

durchblicken vi sep (*haben*) look through; **d~ lassen** (*fig*) hint at

Durchblutung f circulation

durchbohren vt insep pierce

durchbrechen[1]† vt/i sep (*haben*) break [in two]

durchbrechen[2] vt insep break through; break *<Schallmauer>*

durchbrennen† vi sep (*sein*) burn through; *<Sicherung:>* blow

Durchbruch m breakthrough

durchdrehen v sep ● vt mince ● vi (*haben/sein*) 🆃 go crazy

durchdringen† vi sep (*sein*) penetrate; (*sich durchsetzen*) get one's way. **d~d** a penetrating; *<Schrei>* piercing

durcheinander adv in a muddle; *<Person>* confused; **d~ bringen** muddle [up]; confuse *<Person>*; **d~ geraten** get mixed up; **d~ reden** all talk at once. **D~** nt -s muddle

durchfahren vi sep (*sein*) drive through; *<Zug:>* go through

Durchfahrt f journey/drive through; **auf der D~** passing through; **'D~ verboten'** 'no thoroughfare'

Durchfall m diarrhoea. **d~en**† vi sep (*sein*) fall through; (🆃 *versagen*) flop; (*bei Prüfung*) fail

Durchfuhr f - (*Comm*) transit

durchführ|bar a feasible. **d~en** vt sep carry out

Durchgang m passage; (*Sport*) round; **'D~ verboten'** 'no entry' . **D~sverkehr** m through traffic

durchgeben† vt sep pass through; (*übermitteln*) transmit; (*Radio, TV*) broadcast

durchgebraten a gut **d~** well done

durchgehen† vi sep (*sein*) go through; (*davonlaufen*) run away; *<Pferd:>* bolt; **jdm etw d~ lassen** let s.o. get away with sth. **d~d** a continuous; **d~d geöffnet** open all day; **d~der Zug** through train

durchgreifen† vi sep (*haben*) reach through; (*vorgehen*) take drastic action. **d~d** a drastic

durchhalte|n† v sep (*fig*) ● vi (*haben*) hold out ● vt keep up. **D~vermögen** nt stamina

durchkommen† vi sep (*sein*) come through; (*gelangen, am Telefon*) get through

durchlassen† vt sep let through

durchlässig a permeable; (*undicht*) leaky

Durchlauferhitzer m -s,- geyser

durchlesen† vt sep read through

durchleuchten vt insep X-ray

durchlöchert a riddled with holes

durchmachen vt sep go through; (erleiden) undergo

Durchmesser m -s,- diameter

durchnässt a wet through

durchnehmen† vt sep (Sch) do

durchnummeriert a numbered consecutively

durchpausen vt sep trace

durchqueren vt insep cross

Durchreiche f -, -n hatch

Durchreise f journey through; auf der D∼ passing through. **d∼n** vi sep (sein) pass through

durchreißen† vt/i sep (sein) tear

Durchsage f -, -n announcement. **d∼n** vt sep announce

Durchschlag m carbon copy; (Culin) colander. **d∼en†** v sep ● vt (Culin) rub through a sieve; sich **d∼en** (fig) struggle through ● vi (sein) <Sicherung:> blow

durchschlagend a (fig) effective; <Erfolg> resounding

durchschneiden† vt sep cut

Durchschnitt m average; im D∼ on average. **d∼lich** a average ● adv on average. **D∼s-** pref average

Durchschrift f carbon copy

durchsehen† v sep ● vi (haben) see through ● vt look through

durchseihen vt sep strain

durchsetzen vt sep force through; sich **d∼** assert oneself; <Mode:> catch on

Durchsicht f check

durchsichtig a transparent

durchsickern vi sep (sein) seep through; <Neuigkeit:> leak out

durchstehen† vt sep (fig) come through

durchstreichen† vt sep cross out

durchsuch|en vt insep search. **D∼ung** f -, -en search

durchwachsen a <Speck> streaky; (🅸 gemischt) mixed

durchwählen vi sep (haben) (Teleph) dial direct

durchweg adv without exception

durchwühlen vt insep rummage through; ransack <Haus>

Durchzug m through draught

dürfen†

● transitive & auxiliary verb

····▸ (Erlaubnis haben zu) be allowed; may, can. etw [tun] dürfen be allowed to do sth. darf ich das tun? may or can I do that? nein, das darfst du nicht no you may not or cannot [do that]. er sagte mir, ich dürfte sofort gehen he told me I could go at once. hier darf man nicht rauchen smoking is prohibited here. sie darf/durfte es nicht sehen she must not/was not allowed to see it.

····▸ (in Höflichkeitsformeln) may. darf ich rauchen? may I smoke? darf/dürfte ich um diesen Tanz bitten? may/might I have the pleasure of this dance?

····▸ dürfte (sollte) should, ought. jetzt dürften sie dort angekommen sein they should or ought to be there by now. das dürfte nicht allzu schwer sein that should not be too difficult. ich hätte es nicht tun/sagen dürfen I ought not to have done/said it

● intransitive verb

····▸ (irgendwohin gehen dürfen) be allowed to go; may go; can go. darf ich nach Hause? may or can I go home? sie durfte nicht ins Theater she was not allowed to go the theatre

dürftig a poor; <Mahlzeit> scanty

dürr a dry; <Boden> arid; (mager) skinny. **D∼e** f -, -n drought

Durst m -[e]s thirst; D∼ haben be thirsty. **D∼ig** a thirsty

Dusche f -, -n shower. **d∼n** vi/r (haben) [sich] **d∼n** have a shower

Düse f -, -n nozzle. **D∼nflugzeug** nt jet

Dutzend nt -s, -e dozen. **d∼weise** adv by the dozen

duzen vt jdn **d∼** call s.o. 'du'

Dynam|ik f - dynamics sg; (fig) dynamism. **d∼isch** a dynamic; <Rente> index-linked

Dynamit nt -es dynamite

Dynamo m -s, -s dynamo

Dynastie f -, -n dynasty

D-Zug /'de:-/ m express [train]

Ee

Ebbe f -, -n low tide

eben a level; (*glatt*) smooth; **zu e~er Erde** on the ground floor ● adv just; (*genau*) exactly; **e~ noch** only just; (*gerade vorhin*) just now; **das ist es e~!** that's just it! **E~bild** nt image

Ebene f -, -n (*Geog*) plain; (*Geom*) plane; (*fig: Niveau*) level

eben|falls adv also; **danke, e~falls** thank you, [the] same to you. **E~holz** nt ebony. **e~so** adv just the same; (*ebenso sehr*) just as much; **e~so gut** just as good; adv just as well; **e~so sehr** just as much; **e~so viel** just as much/many; **e~so wenig** just as little/few; (*noch*) no more

Eber m -s,- boar

ebnen vt level; (*fig*) smooth

Echo nt -s, -s echo

echt a genuine, real; authentic ● adv 🄸 really; typically. **E~heit** f - authenticity

Eck|ball m (*Sport*) corner. **E~e** f -, -n corner; **um die E~e bringen** 🄸 bump off. **e~ig** a angular; <*Klammern*> square; (*unbeholfen*) awkward. **E~zahn** m canine tooth

Ecu, ECU /e'ky:/ m -[s], -[s] ecu

edel a noble; (*wertvoll*) precious; (*fein*) fine. **e~mütig** a magnanimous. **E~stahl** m stainless steel. **E~stein** m precious stone

Efeu m -s ivy

Effekt m -[e]s, -e effect. **E~en** pl securities. **e~iv** a actual, adv -ly; (*wirksam*) effective

EG f - abbr (**Europäische Gemeinschaft**) EC

egal a **das ist mir e~** 🄸 it's all the same to me ● adv **e~ wie/wo** no matter how/where

Egge f -, -n harrow

Ego|ismus m - selfishness. **E~ist(in)** m -en, -en (f -, -nen) egoist. **e~istisch** a selfish

eh adv (*Aust, fam*) anyway

ehe conj before; **ehe nicht** until

Ehe f -, -n marriage. **E~bett** nt double bed. **E~bruch** m adultery. **E~frau** f wife. **e~lich** a marital; <*Recht*> conjugal; <*Kind*> legitimate

ehemalig a former. **e~s** adv formerly

Ehe|mann m (pl -männer) husband. **E~paar** nt married couple

eher adv earlier, sooner; (*lieber, vielmehr*) rather; (*mehr*) more

Ehering m wedding ring

Ehr|e f -, -n honour. **e~en** vt honour. **e~enamtlich** a honorary ● adv in an honorary capacity. **E~engast** m guest of honour. **e~enhaft** a honourable. **E~ensache** f point of honour. **E~enwort** nt word of honour. **e~erbietig** a deferential. **E~furcht** f reverence; (*Scheu*) awe. **e~fürchtig** a reverent. **E~gefühl** nt sense of honour. **E~geiz** m ambition. **e~geizig** a ambitious. **e~lich** a honest; **e~lich gesagt** to be honest. **E~lichkeit** f - honesty. **e~los** a dishonourable. **e-würdig** a venerable; (*als Anrede*) Reverend

Ei nt -[e]s, -er egg

Eibe f -, -n yew

Eiche f -, -n oak. **E~l** f -, -n acorn

eichen vt standardize

Eichhörnchen nt -s,- squirrel

Eid m -[e]s, -e oath

Eidechse f -, -n lizard

eidlich a sworn ● adv on oath

Eidotter m & nt egg yolk

Eier|becher m egg-cup. **E~kuchen** m pancake; (*Omelett*) omelette. **E~schale** f eggshell. **E~schnee** m beaten egg-white. **E~stock** m ovary

Eifer *m* -s eagerness. **E∼sucht** *f* jealousy. **e∼süchtig** *a* jealous

eifrig *a* eager

Eigelb *nt* -[e]s, -e [egg] yolk

eigen *a* own; (*typisch*) characteristic (*dat* of); (*seltsam*) odd; (*genau*) particular. **E∼art** *f* peculiarity. **e∼artig** *a* peculiar. **e∼händig** *a* personal; <*Unterschrift*> own. **E∼heit** *f* -, -en peculiarity. **E∼name** *m* proper name. **e∼nützig** *a* selfish. **e∼s** *adv* specially. **E∼schaft** *f* -, -en quality; (*Phys*) property; (*Merkmal*) characteristic; (*Funktion*) capacity. **E∼schaftswort** *nt* (*pl* -wörter) adjective. **E∼sinn** *m* obstinacy. **e∼sinnig** *a* obstinate

eigentlich *a* actual, real; (*wahr*) true ● *adv* actually, really; (*streng genommen*) strictly speaking

Eigen|tor *nt* own goal. **E∼tum** *nt* -s property. **E∼tümer(in)** *m* -s, -(*f* -, -nen) owner. **E∼tumswohnung** *f* freehold flat. **e∼willig** *a* self-willed; <*Stil*> highly individual

eignen (sich) *vr* be suitable

Eil|brief *m* express letter. **E∼e** *f* - hurry; **E∼e haben** be in a hurry; <*Sache:*> be urgent. **e∼en** *vi* (*sein*) hurry ● (*haben*) (*drängen*) be urgent. **e∼ig** *a* hurried; (*dringend*) urgent; **es e∼ig haben** be in a hurry. **E∼zug** *m* semi-fast train

Eimer *m* -s,- bucket; (*Abfall-*) bin

. . . .

ein

● *indefinite article*

····➤ a, (*vor Vokal*) an. **ein Kleid/Apfel/ Hotel/Mensch** a dress/an apple/a[n] hotel/a human being. **so ein** such a. **was für ein …** (*Frage*) what kind of a …? (*Ausruf*) what a …!

● *adjective*

····➤ (*Ziffer*) one. **eine Mark** one mark. **wir haben nur eine Stunde** we only have an/(*betont*) one hour. **eines Tages/Abends** one day/evening

····➤ (*derselbe*) the same. **einer Meinung sein** be of the same opinion. **mit jdm in einem Zimmer schlafen** sleep in the same room as s.o.

einander *pron* one another

Einäscherung *f* -, -en cremation

einatmen *vt/i sep* (*haben*) inhale, breathe in

Einbahnstraße *f* one-way street

einbalsamieren *vt sep* embalm

Einband *m* binding

Einbau *m* installation; (*Montage*) fitting. **e∼en** *vt sep* install; (*montieren*) fit. **E∼küche** *f* fitted kitchen

einbegriffen *pred* a included

Einberufung *f* call-up

Einbettzimmer *nt* single room

einbeulen *vt sep* dent

einbeziehen† *vt sep* [*mit*] e∼ include; (*berücksichtigen*) take into account

einbiegen† *vi sep* (*sein*) turn

einbild|en *vt sep* **sich** (*dat*) **etw e∼en** imagine sth; **sich** (*dat*) **viel e∼en** be conceited. **E∼ung** *f* imagination; (*Dünkel*) conceit. **E∼ungskraft** *f* imagination

einblenden *vt sep* fade in

Einblick *m* insight

einbrech|en† *vi sep* (*haben/sein*) break in; **bei uns ist eingebrochen worden** we have been burgled. **E∼er** *m* burglar

einbringen† *vt sep* get in; bring in <*Geld*>

Einbruch *m* burglary; **bei E∼ der Nacht** at nightfall

einbürger|n *vt sep* naturalize. **E∼ung** *f* - naturalization

einchecken /-tʃɛkən/ *vt/i sep* (*haben*) check in

eindecken (sich) *vr sep* stock up

eindeutig *a* unambiguous; (*deutlich*) clear

eindicken *vt sep* (*Culin*) thicken

eindringen† *vi sep* (*sein*) **e∼en in** (+ *acc*) penetrate into; (*mit Gewalt*) force one's/<*Wasser:*> its way into; (*Mil*) invade

Eindruck *m* impression

eindrücken *vt sep* crush

eindrucksvoll *a* impressive

ein|e(r,s) *pron* one; *(jemand)* someone; *(man)* one, you

einebnen *vt sep* level

eineiig *a <Zwillinge>* identical

eineinhalb *inv a* one and a half; **e~ Stunden** an hour and a half

Einelternfamilie *f* one-parent family

einengen *vt sep* restrict

Einer *m* -s,- *(Math)* unit. **e~** *pron s.* **eine(r,s). e~lei** *inv a* ● *attrib a* one kind of; *(eintönig, einheitlich)* the same ● *pred a* Ⓣ immaterial; **es ist mir e~lei** it's all the same to me. **e~seits** *adv* on the one hand

einfach *a* simple; *<Essen>* plain; *<Faden, Fahrt>* single; **e~er Soldat** private. **E~heit** *f* - simplicity

einfädeln *vt sep* thread; *(fig; arrangieren)* arrange

einfahr|en† *v sep* ● *vi (sein)* arrive; *<Zug:>* pull in ● *vt (Auto)* run in. **E~t** *f* arrival; *(Eingang)* entrance, way in; *(Auffahrt)* drive; *(Autobahn-)* access road; **keine E~t** no entry

Einfall *m* idea; *(Mil)* invasion. **e~en**† *vi sep (sein)* collapse; *(eindringen)* invade; **jdm e~en** occur to s.o.; **was fällt ihm ein!** what does he think he is doing!

Einfalt *f* - naïvety

einfarbig *a* of one colour; *<Stoff, Kleid>* plain

einfass|en *vt sep* edge; set *<Edelstein>*. **E~ung** *f* border, edging

einfetten *vt sep* grease

Einfluss *m* influence. **e~reich** *a* influential

einförmig *a* monotonous. **E~keit** *f* - monotony

einfrieren† *vt/i sep (sein)* freeze

einfügen *vt sep* insert; *(einschieben)* interpolate; **sich e~** fit in

einfühlsam *a* sensitive

Einfuhr *f* -, -en import

einführ|en *vt sep* introduce; *(einstecken)* insert; *(einweisen)* initiate; *(Comm)* import. **e~end** *a*

introductory. **E~ung** *f* introduction; *(Einweisung)* initiation

Eingabe *f* petition; *(Computer)* input

Eingang *m* entrance, way in; *(Ankunft)* arrival

eingebaut *a* built-in; *<Schrank>* fitted

eingeben† *vt sep* hand in; *(Computer)* feed in

eingebildet *a* imaginary; *(überheblich)* conceited

Eingeborene(r) *m/f* native

eingehen† *v sep* ● *vi (sein)* come in; *(ankommen)* arrive; *(einlaufen)* shrink; *(sterben)* die; *<Zeitung, Firma:>* fold; **auf etw** *(acc)* **e~** go into sth; *(annehmen)* agree to sth ● *vt* enter into; contract *<Ehe>*; make *<Wette>*; take *<Risiko>*

eingemacht *a (Culin)* bottled

eingenommen *pred a (fig)* taken **(von** with); prejudiced **(gegen** against)

eingeschneit *a* snowbound

eingeschrieben *a* registered

Einge|ständnis *nt* admission. **e~stehen**† *vt sep* admit

eingetragen *a* registered

Eingeweide *pl* bowels, entrails

eingewöhnen (sich) *vr sep* settle in

eingießen† *vt sep* pour in; *(einschenken)* pour

eingleisig *a* single-track

einglieder|n *vt sep* integrate. **E~ung** *f* integration

eingravieren *vt sep* engrave

eingreifen† *vi sep (haben)* intervene. **E~** *nt* -s intervention

Eingriff *m* intervention; *(Med)* operation

einhaken *vt/r sep* **jdn e~** *od* **sich bei jdm e~** take s.o.'s arm

einhalten† *v sep* ● *vt* keep; *(befolgen)* observe ● *vi (haben)* stop

einhändigen *vt sep* hand in

einhängen *vt sep* hang; put down *<Hörer>*

einheimisch a local; (*eines Landes*) native; (*Comm*) home-produced. **E~e(r)** m/f local native

Einheit f -, -en unity; (*Maß-, Mil*) unit. **e~lich** a uniform. **E~spreis** m standard price; (*Fahrpreis*) flat fare

einholen vt sep catch up with; (*aufholen*) make up for; (*erbitten*) seek; (*einkaufen*) buy

einhüllen vt sep wrap

einhundert inv a one hundred

einig a united; [sich (*dat*)] e~ sein be in agreement

einig|e(r,s) pron some; (*ziemlich viel*) quite a lot of; (*substantivisch*) **e~e** pl some; (*mehrere*) several; (*ziemlich viele*) quite a lot; **e~es** sg some things; **vor e~er Zeit** some time ago

einigen vt unite; unify <*Land*>; **sich e~** come to an agreement

einigermaßen adv to some extent; (*ziemlich*) fairly; (*ziemlich gut*) fairly well

Einigkeit f - unity; (*Übereinstimmung*) agreement

einjährig a one-year-old; **e~e Pflanze** annual

einkalkulieren vt sep take into account

einkassieren vt sep collect

Einkauf m purchase; (*Einkaufen*) shopping; **Einkäufe machen** do some shopping. **e~en** vt sep buy; **e~en gehen** go shopping. **E~swagen** m shopping trolley

einklammern vt sep bracket

Einklang m harmony; **in E~ stehen** be in accord (**mit** with)

einkleben vt sep stick in

einkleiden vt sep fit out

einklemmen vt sep clamp

einkochen v sep ● vi (*sein*) boil down ● vt preserve, bottle

Einkommen nt -s income. **E~[s]steuer** f income tax

Einkünfte pl income sg; (*Einnahmen*) revenue sg

einlad|en† vt sep load; (*auffordern*) invite; (*bezahlen für*) treat. **E~ung** f invitation

Einlage f enclosure; (*Schuh-*) arch support; (*Programm-*) interlude; (*Comm*) investment; (*Bank-*) deposit; **Suppe mit E~** soup with noodles/ dumplings

Ein|lass m -es admittance. **e~lassen†** vt sep let in; run <*Bad, Wasser*>; **sich auf etw** (*acc*) **e~lassen** get involved in sth

einleben (sich) vr sep settle in

Einlege|arbeit f inlaid work. **e~n** vt sep put in; lay in <*Vorrat*>; lodge <*Protest*>; (*einfügen*) insert; (*Auto*) engage <*Gang*>; (*Culin*) pickle; (*marinieren*) marinade; **eine Pause e~n** have a break. **E~sohle** f insole

einleit|en vt sep initiate; (*eröffnen*) begin. **E~ung** f introduction

einleuchten vi sep (*haben*) be clear (*dat* to). **e~d** a convincing

einliefer|n vt sep take (**ins Krankenhaus** to hospital). **E~ung** f admission

einlösen vt sep cash <*Scheck*>; redeem <*Pfand*>; (*fig*) keep

einmachen vt sep preserve

einmal adv once; (*eines Tages*) or some day; **noch/schon e~** again/ before; **noch e~ so teuer** twice as expensive; **auf e~** at the same time; (*plötzlich*) suddenly; **nicht e~** not even. **E~eins** nt - [multiplication] tables pl. **e~ig** a (*einzigartig*) unique; (**I** *großartig*) fantastic

einmarschieren vi sep (*sein*) march in

einmisch|en (sich) vr sep interfere. **E~ung** f interference

Einnahme f -, -n taking; (*Mil*) capture; **E~n** pl income sg; (*Einkünfte*) revenue sg; (*Comm*) receipts; (*eines Ladens*) takings

einnehmen† vt sep take; have <*Mahlzeit*>; (*Mil*) capture; take up <*Platz*>

einordnen vt sep put in its proper place; (*klassifizieren*) classify; **sich e~** fit in; (*Auto*) get in lane

einpacken *vt sep* pack
einparken *vt sep* park
einpflanzen *vt sep* plant; implant <*Organ*>
einplanen *vt sep* allow for
einprägen *vt sep* impress (**jdm** [up]on s.o.); **sich** (*dat*) **etw e~en** memorize sth.
einrahmen *vt sep* frame
einrasten *vi sep* (*sein*) engage
einräumen *vt sep* put away; (*zugeben*) admit; (*zugestehen*) grant
einrechnen *vt sep* include
einreden *v sep* ● *vt* **jdm/sich** (*dat*) **etw e~** persuade s.o./oneself of sth.
einreiben† *vt sep* rub (**mit** with)
einreichen *vt sep* submit; **die Scheidung e~** file for divorce
Einreih|er *m* **-s,-** single-breasted suit. **e~ig** *a* single-breasted
Einreise *f* entry. **e~n** *vi sep* (*sein*) enter (**nach Irland** Ireland)
einrenken *vt sep* (*Med*) set
einricht|en *vt sep* fit out; (*möblieren*) furnish; (*anordnen*) arrange; (*Med*) set <*Bruch*>; (*eröffnen*) set up; **sich e~en** furnish one's home; (*sich einschränken*) economize; (*sich vorbereiten*) prepare (**auf** + *acc* for). **E~ung** *f* furnishing; (*Möbel*) furnishings *pl*; (*Techn*) equipment; (*Vorrichtung*) device; (*Eröffnung*) setting up; (*Institution*) institution; (*Gewohnheit*) practice
einrosten *vi sep* (*sein*) rust; (*fig*) get rusty
eins *inv a & pron* one; **noch e~** one other thing; **mir ist alles e~** 🆃 it's all the same to me. **E~** *f* **-, -en** one; (*Sch*) ≈ A
einsam *a* lonely; (*allein*) solitary; (*abgelegen*) isolated. **E~keit** *f* **-** loneliness; solitude; isolation
einsammeln *vt sep* collect
Einsatz *m* use; (*Mil*) mission; (*Wett-*) stake; (*E~teil*) insert; **im E~** in action
einschalt|en *vt sep* switch on; (*einschieben*) interpolate; (*fig:*

beteiligen) call in; **sich e~en** (*fig*) intervene. **E~quote** *f* (*TV*) viewing figures *pl*; ≈ ratings *pl*
einschätzen *vt sep* assess; (*bewerten*) rate
einschenken *vt sep* pour
einscheren *vi sep* (*sein*) pull in
einschicken *vt sep* send in
einschieben† *vt sep* push in; (*einfügen*) insert
einschiff|en (sich) *vr sep* embark. **E~ung** *f* **-** embarkation
einschlafen† *vi sep* (*sein*) go to sleep; (*aufhören*) peter out
einschläfern *vt sep* lull to sleep; (*betäuben*) put out; (*töten*) put to sleep. **e~d** *a* soporific
Einschlag *m* impact. **e~en**† *v sep* ● *vt* knock in; (*zerschlagen*) smash; (*drehen*) turn; take <*Weg*>; take up <*Laufbahn*> ● *vi* (*haben*) hit/ <*Blitz:*> strike (**in etw** *acc* sth); (*Erfolg haben*) be a hit
einschleusen *vt sep* infiltrate
einschließ|en† *vt sep* lock in; (*umgeben*) enclose; (*einkreisen*) surround; (*einbeziehen*) include; **sich e~en** lock oneself in; **Bedienung eingeschlossen** service included. **e~lich** *adv* inclusive ● *prep* (+ *gen*) including
einschneiden† *vt/i sep* (*haben*) **[in] etw** *acc* **e~** cut into sth. **e~d** *a* (*fig*) drastic
Einschnitt *m* cut; (*Med*) incision; (*Lücke*) gap; (*fig*) decisive event
einschränk|en *vt sep* restrict; (*reduzieren*) cut back; **sich e~en** economize. **E~ung** *f* **-, -en** restriction; (*Reduzierung*) reduction; (*Vorbehalt*) reservation
Einschreib|[e]brief *m* registered letter. **e~en**† *vt sep* enter; register <*Brief*>; **sich e~en** put one's name down; (*sich anmelden*) enrol. **E~en** *nt* registered letter/packet; **als** *od* **per E~en** by registered post
einschüchtern *vt sep* intimidate
Einsegnung *f* **-, -en** confirmation
einsehen† *vt sep* inspect; (*lesen*) consult; (*begreifen*) see

---
*old spelling

einseitig *a* one-sided; (*Pol*) unilateral ● *adv* on one side; (*fig*) one-sidedly; (*Pol*) unilaterally

einsenden† *vt sep* send in

einsetzen *v sep* ● *vt* put in; (*einfügen*) insert; (*verwenden*) use; put on <*Zug*>; call out <*Truppen*>; (*Mil*) deploy; (*ernennen*) appoint; (*wetten*) stake; (*riskieren*) risk ● *vi* (*haben*) start; <*Winter, Regen:*> set in

Einsicht *f* insight; (*Verständnis*) understanding; (*Vernunft*) reason. **e~ig** *a* understanding

Einsiedler *m* hermit

einsinken† *vi sep* (*sein*) sink in

einspannen *vt sep* harness; **jdn e~** 🔟 rope s.o. in

einsparen *vt sep* save

einsperren *vt sep* shut/(*im Gefängnis*) lock up

einsprachig *a* monolingual

einspritzen *vt sep* inject

Einspruch *m* objection; **E~ erheben** object; (*Jur*) appeal

einspurig *a* single-track; (*Auto*) single-lane

einst *adv* once; (*Zukunft*) one day

Einstand *m* (*Tennis*) deuce

einstecken *vt sep* put in; post <*Brief*>; (*Electr*) plug in; (🔟 *behalten*) pocket; (🔟 *hinnehmen*) take; suffer <*Niederlage*>; **etw e~** put sth in one's pocket

einsteigen† *vi sep* (*sein*) get in; (*in Bus/Zug*) get on

einstell|en *vt sep* put in; (*anstellen*) employ; (*aufhören*) stop; (*regulieren*) adjust, set; (*Optik*) focus; tune <*Motor, Zündung*>; tune to <*Sender*>; **sich e~en** turn up; <*Schwierigkeiten:*> arise; **sich e~en auf** (+ *acc*) adjust to; (*sich vorbereiten*) prepare for. **E~ung** *f* employment; (*Regulierung*) adjustment; (*TV, Auto*) tuning; (*Haltung*) attitude

einstig *a* former

einstimmig *a* unanimous. **E~keit** *f* - unanimity

einstöckig *a* single-storey

einstudieren *vt sep* rehearse

einstufen *vt sep* classify

Ein|sturz *m* collapse. **e~stürzen** *vi sep* (*sein*) collapse

einstweilen *adv* for the time being; (*inzwischen*) meanwhile

eintasten *vt sep* key in

eintauchen *vt/i sep* (*sein*) dip in

eintauschen *vt sep* exchange

eintausend *inv a* one thousand

einteil|en *vt sep* divide (**in** + *acc* into); (*Biol*) classify; **sich** (*dat*) **seine Zeit gut e~en** organize one's time well. **e~ig** *a* one piece. **E~ung** *f* division

eintönig *a* monotonous. **E~keit** *f* - monotony

Eintopf *m*, **E~gericht** *nt* stew

Eintracht *f* - harmony

Eintrag *m* -[e]s,⸚e entry. **e~en**† *vt sep* enter; (*Admin*) register; **sich e~en** put one's name down

einträglich *a* profitable

Eintragung *f* -, -en registration

eintreffen† *vi sep* (*sein*) arrive; (*fig*) come true

eintreiben† *vt sep* drive in; (*einziehen*) collect

eintreten† *v sep* ● *vi* (*sein*) enter; (*geschehen*) occur; **in einen Klub e~** join a club; **e~ für** (*fig*) stand up for ● *vt* kick in

Eintritt *m* entrance; (*zu Veranstaltung*) admission; (*Beitritt*) joining; (*Beginn*) beginning. **E~skarte** *f* [admission] ticket

einüben *vt sep* practise

einundachtzig *inv a* eighty-one

Einvernehmen *nt* -s understanding; (*Übereinstimmung*) agreement

einverstanden *a* **e~ sein** agree

Einverständnis *nt* agreement; (*Zustimmung*) consent

Einwand *m* -[e]s,⸚e objection

Einwander|er *m* immigrant. **e~n** *vi sep* (*sein*) immigrate. **E~ung** *f* immigration

einwandfrei *a* perfect

einwärts *adv* inwards

einwechseln *vt sep* change

einwecken *vt sep* preserve, bottle

Einweg- *pref* non-returnable

einweichen *vt sep* soak

einweih|en *vt sep* inaugurate; (*Relig*) consecrate; (*einführen*) initiate; **in ein Geheimnis e~en** let into a secret. **E~ung** *f* -, **-en** inauguration; consecration; initiation

einweisen† *vt sep* direct; (*einführen*) initiate; **ins Krankenhaus e~** send to hospital

einwerfen† *vt sep* insert; post <*Brief*>; (*Sport*) throw in

einwickeln *vt sep* wrap [up]

einwillig|en *vi sep* (*haben*) consent, agree (**in** + *acc* to). **E~ung** *f* - consent

Einwohner|(in) *m* -s,- (*f* -, -nen) inhabitant. **E~zahl** *f* population

Einwurf *m* interjection; (*Einwand*) objection; (*Sport*) throw-in; (*Münz-*) slot

Einzahl *f* (*Gram*) singular

einzahl|en *vt sep* pay in. **E~ung** *f* payment; (*Einlage*) deposit

einzäunen *vt sep* fence in

Einzel *nt* -s,- (*Tennis*) singles *pl*. **E~bett** *nt* single bed. **E~gänger** *m* -s,- loner. **E~haft** *f* solitary confinement. **E~handel** *m* retail trade. **E~händler** *m* retailer. **E~haus** *nt* detached house. **E~heit** *f* -, -en detail. **E~karte** *f* single ticket. **E~kind** *nt* only child

einzeln *a* single; (*individuell*) individual; (*gesondert*) separate; odd <*Handschuh, Socken*>; **e~e Fälle** some cases. **E~e(r,s)** *pron* der/die **E~e** the individual; **E~e** *pl* some; **im E~en** in detail

Einzel|teil *nt* [component] part. **E~zimmer** *nt* single room

einziehen† *v sep* ● *vt* pull in; draw in <*Atem, Krallen*>; (*Zool, Techn*) retract; indent <*Zeile*>; (*aus dem Verkehr ziehen*) withdraw; (*beschlagnahmen*) confiscate; (*eintreiben*) collect; make <*Erkundigungen*>; (*Mil*) call up ● *vi* (*sein*) enter; (*umziehen*) move in; (*eindringen*) penetrate

einzig *a* only; (*einmalig*) unique; **eine e~e Frage** a a single question ● *adv* only; **e~ und allein** solely. **E~e(r,s)** *pron* der/die/das **E~e** the only one; **ein/kein E~er** a/not a single one; **das E~e, was mich stört** the only thing that bothers me

Eis *nt* -es ice; (*Speise-*) ice-cream; **Eis am Stiel** ice lolly; **Eis laufen** skate. **E~bahn** *f* ice rink. **E~bär** *m* polar bear. **E~becher** *m* ice-cream sundae. **E~berg** *m* iceberg. **E~diele** *f* ice-cream parlour

Eisen *nt* -s,- iron. **E~bahn** *f* railway

eisern *a* iron; (*fest*) resolute; **e~er Vorhang** (*Theat*) safety curtain; (*Pol*) Iron Curtain

Eis|fach *nt* freezer compartment. **e~gekühlt** *a* chilled. **e~ig** *a* icy. **E~kaffee** *m* iced coffee. **E~lauf** *m* skating. **E~läufer(in)** *m(f)* skater. **E~pickel** *m* ice-axe. **E~scholle** *f* ice-floe. **E~vogel** *m* kingfisher. **E~würfel** *m* ice-cube. **E~zapfen** *m* icicle. **E~zeit** *f* ice age

eitel *a* vain; (*rein*) pure. **E~keit** *f* - vanity

Eiter *m* -s pus. **e~n** *vi* (*haben*) discharge pus

Eiweiß *nt* -es, -e egg-white

Ekel *m* -s disgust; (*Widerwille*) revulsion. **e~haft** *a* nauseating; (*widerlich*) repulsive. **e~n** *vt/i* (*haben*) **mich** *od* **mir e~t [es] davor** it makes me feel sick ● *vr* **sich e~n vor** (+ *dat*) find repulsive

eklig *a* disgusting, repulsive

Ekzem *nt* -s, -e eczema

elastisch *a* elastic; (*federnd*) springy; (*fig*) flexible

Elch *m* -[e]s, -e elk

Elefant *m* -en, -en elephant

elegan|t *a* elegant. **E~z** *f* - elegance

Elektri|ker *m* -s,- electrician. **e~sch** *a* electric

Elektrizität f - electricity.
E~swerk nt power station
Elektr|oartikel mpl electrical
appliances. E~ode f -, -n electrode.
E~onik f - electronics sg.
e~onisch a electronic
Elend nt -s misery; (Armut) poverty.
e~ a miserable; (krank) poorly;
(gemein) contemptible. E~sviertel
nt slum
elf inv a, E~ f -, -en eleven
Elfe f -, -n fairy
Elfenbein nt ivory
Elfmeter m (Fußball) penalty
elfte(r,s) a eleventh
Ell[en]bogen m elbow
Ellip|se f -, -n ellipse. e~tisch a
elliptical
Elsass nt - Alsace
elsässisch a Alsatian
Elster f -, -n magpie
elter|lich a parental. E~n pl
parents. e~nlos a orphaned.
E~nteil m parent
Email /e'ma|/ nt -s, -s, E~le
/e'maljə/ f -, -n enamel
E-Mail /'i:me:l/ f -, -s e-mail; e-mail
message
Emanzi|pation /-'tsio:n/ f -
emancipation. e~piert a
emancipated
Embargo nt -s, -s embargo
Embryo m -s, -s embryo
Emigr|ant(in) m -en, -en (f -, -nen)
emigrant. E~ation /-'tsio:n/ f -
emigration. e~ieren vi (sein)
emigrate
Empfang m -[e]s,ˮe reception;
(Erhalt) receipt; in E~ nehmen
receive; (annehmen) accept. e~en†
vt receive; (Biol) conceive
Empfäng|er m -s,- recipient; (Post-)
addressee; (Zahlungs-) payee; (Radio,
TV) receiver. E~nis f - (Biol)
conception
Empfängnisverhütung f
contraception. E~smittel nt
contraceptive
Empfangs|bestätigung f
receipt. E~dame f receptionist.
E~halle f [hotel] foyer

empfehl|en† vt recommend.
E~ung f -, -en recommendation;
(Gruß) regards pl
empfind|en† vt feel. e~lich a
sensitive (gegen to); (zart) delicate.
E~lichkeit f - sensitivity; delicacy;
tenderness; touchiness. E~ung f -,
-en sensation; (Regung) feeling
empor adv (liter) up[wards]
empören vt incense; sich e~ be
indignant; (sich auflehnen) rebel
Emporkömmling m -s, -e upstart
empör|t a indignant. E~ung f -
indignation; (Auflehnung) rebellion
Ende nt -s, -n end; (eines Films,
Romans) ending; (ᵾ Stück) bit; zu
E~ sein be finished; etw zu E~
schreiben finish writing sth; am E~
at the end; (schließlich) in the end;
(ᵾ vielleicht) perhaps; (ᵾ erschöpft)
at the end of one's tether
end|en vi (haben) end. e~gültig a
final; (bestimmt) definite
Endivie /-i̯ə/ f -, -n endive
end|lich adv at last, finally;
(schließlich) in the end. e~los a
endless. E~station f terminus.
E~ung f -, -en (Gram) ending
Energie f - energy
energisch a resolute;
(nachdrücklich) vigorous
eng a narrow; (beengt) cramped;
(anliegend) tight; (nah) close; e~
anliegend tight-fitting
Engagement /ãgaʒə'mã:/ nt -s, -s
(Theat) engagement; (fig)
commitment
Engel m -s,- angel
England nt -s England
Engländer m -s,- Englishman;
(Techn) monkey-wrench; die E~ the
English pl. E~in f -, -nen
Englishwoman
englisch a English. E~ nt -[s]
(Lang) English; auf E~ in English
Engpass m (fig) bottle-neck
en gros /ã'gro:/ adv wholesale
Enkel m -s,- grandson; E~ pl
grandchildren. E~in f -, -nen
granddaughter. E~kind nt

grandchild. **E~sohn** *m* grandson.
E~tochter *f* granddaughter

Ensemble /ã'sã:bəl/ *nt* -s, -s
ensemble; (*Theat*) company

entart|en *vi* (*sein*) degenerate.
e~et *a* degenerate

entbehren *vt* do without;
(*vermissen*) miss

entbind|en† *vt* release (**von** from);
(*Med*) deliver (**von** of) ● *vi* (*haben*)
give birth. **E~ung** *f* delivery.
E~ungsstation *f* maternity ward

entdeck|en *vt* discover. **E~er** *m*
-s,- discoverer; (*Forscher*) explorer.
E~ung *f* -, -en discovery

Ente *f* -, -n duck

entehren *vt* dishonour

enteignen *vt* dispossess;
expropriate <*Eigentum*>

enterben *vt* disinherit

Enterich *m* -s, -e drake

entfallen† *vi* (*sein*) not apply; **auf**
jdn e~ be s.o.'s share

entfern|en *vt* remove; **sich e~en**
leave. **e~t** *a* distant; (*schwach*)
vague; **2 Kilometer e~t** 2 kilometres
away; **e~t verwandt** distantly
related. **E~ung** *f* -, -en removal;
(*Abstand*) distance; (*Reichweite*)
range

entfliehen† *vi* (*sein*) escape

entfremden *vt* alienate

entfrosten *vt* defrost

entführ|en *vt* abduct, kidnap;
hijack <*Flugzeug*>. **E~er** *m*
abductor, kidnapper; hijacker.
E~ung *f* abduction, kidnapping;
hijacking

entgegen *adv* towards ● *prep* (+
dat) contrary to. **e~gehen**† *vi sep*
(*sein*) (+ *dat*) go to meet; (*fig*) be
heading for. **e~gesetzt** *a* opposite;
(*gegensätzlich*) opposing.
e~kommen† *vi sep* (*sein*) (+ *dat*)
come to meet; (*zukommen auf*) come
towards; (*fig*) oblige. **E~kommen**
nt -s helpfulness; (*Zugeständnis*)
concession. **e~kommend** *a*
approaching; <*Verkehr*> oncoming;

(*fig*) obliging. **e~nehmen**† *vt sep*
accept. **e~wirken** *vi sep* (*haben*) (+
dat) counteract; (*fig*) oppose

entgegn|en *vt* reply (**auf** + *acc* to).
E~ung *f* -, -en reply

entgehen† *vi sep* (*sein*) (+ *dat*)
escape; **jdm e~** (*unbemerkt bleiben*)
escape s.o.'s notice; **sich** (*dat*) **etw**
e~ lassen miss sth

Entgelt *nt* -[e]s payment; **gegen E~**
for money

entgleis|en *vi* (*sein*) be derailed;
(*fig*) make a gaffe. **E~ung** *f* -, -en
derailment; (*fig*) gaffe

entgräten *vt* fillet, bone

Enthaarungsmittel *nt* depilatory

enthalt|en† *vt* contain; **in etw** (*dat*)
e~en sein be contained/
(*eingeschlossen*) included in sth; **sich**
der Stimme e~en (*Pol*) abstain.
e~sam *a* abstemious. **E~ung** *f*
(*Pol*) abstention

enthaupten *vt* behead

entheben† *vt* **jdn seines Amtes e~**
relieve s.o. of his post

Enthüllung *f* -, -en revelation

Enthusias|mus *m* - enthusiast.
E~t *m* -en, -en enthusiast

entkernen *vt* stone; core <*Apfel*>

entkleiden *vt* undress; **sich e~en**
undress

entkommen† *vi* (*sein*) escape

entkorken *vt* uncork

entladen† *vt* unload; (*Electr*)
discharge; **sich e~** discharge;
<*Gewitter:*> break; <*Zorn:*> explode

entlang *adv & prep* (+ *preceding acc*
or following dat) along; **die Straße**
e~ along the road; **an etw** (*dat*) **e~**
along sth. **e~fahren**† *vi sep* (*sein*)
drive along. **e~gehen**† *vi sep* (*sein*)
walk along

entlarven *vt* unmask

entlass|en† *vt* dismiss; (*aus*
Krankenhaus) discharge; (*aus der*
Haft) release. **E~ung** *f* -, -en
dismissal; discharge; release

entlast|en *vt* relieve the strain on;
ease <*Gewissen, Verkehr*>; relieve
(**von** of); (*Jur*) exonerate. **E~ung** *f* -
relief; exoneration

entlaufen† *vi* (sein) run away

entleeren *vt* empty

entlegen *a* remote

entlohnen *vt* pay

entlüft|en *vt* ventilate. **E~er** *m* -s,- extractor fan. **E~ung** *f* ventilation

entmündigen *vt* declare incapable of managing one's own affairs

entmutigen *vt* discourage

entnehmen† *vt* take (*dat* from); (*schließen*) gather (*dat* from)

entpuppen (sich) *vr* (*fig*) turn out (**als etw** to be sth)

entrahmt *a* skimmed

entrichten *vt* pay

entrinnen† *vi* (sein) escape

entrüst|en *vt* fill with indignation; **sich e~en** be indignant (**über** + *acc* at). **e~et** *a* indignant. **E~ung** *f* - indignation

entsaft|en *vt* extract the juice from. **E~er** *m* -s,- juice extractor

entsagen *vi* (haben) (+ *dat*) renounce

entschädig|en *vt* compensate. **E~ung** *f* -,-en compensation

entschärfen *vt* defuse

entscheid|en† *vt/i* (haben) decide; **sich e~en** decide; <*Sache:*> be decided. **e~end** *a* decisive; (*kritisch*) crucial. **E~ung** *f* decision

entschließen† (**sich**) *vr* decide, make up one's mind; **sich anders e~** change one's mind

entschlossen *a* determined; (*energisch*) resolute; **kurz e~** without hesitation. **E~heit** *f* - determination

Entschluss *m* decision

entschlüsseln *vt* decode

entschuld|bar *a* excusable. **e~igen** *vt* excuse; **sich e~igen** apologize (**bei** to); **e~igen Sie [bitte]!** sorry! (*bei Frage*) excuse me. **E~igung** *f* -,-en apology; (*Ausrede*) excuse; **um E~igung bitten** apologize

entsetz|en *vt* horrify. **E~en** *nt* -s horror. **e~lich** *a* horrible; (*schrecklich*) terrible

Entsorgung *f* - waste disposal

entspann|en *vt* relax; **sich e~en** relax; <*Lage:*> ease. **E~ung** *f* - relaxation; easing; (*Pol*) détente

entsprech|en† *vi* (haben) (+ *dat*) correspond to; (*übereinstimmen*) agree with. **e~end** *a* corresponding; (*angemessen*) appropriate; (*zuständig*) relevant ● *adv* correspondingly; appropriately; (*demgemäß*) accordingly ● *prep* (+ *dat*) in accordance with

entspringen† *vi* (sein) <*Fluss:*> rise; (*fig*) arise, spring (*dat* from)

entstammen *vi* (sein) come/ (*abstammen*) be descended (*dat* from)

entsteh|en† *vi* (sein) come into being; (*sich bilden*) form; (*sich entwickeln*) develop; <*Brand:*> start; (*stammen*) originate. **E~ung** *f* - origin; formation; development

entstell|en *vt* disfigure; (*verzerren*) distort. **E~ung** *f* disfigurement; distortion

entstört *a* (*Electr*) suppressed

enttäusch|en *vt* disappoint. **E~ung** *f* disappointment

entwaffnen *vt* disarm

entwässer|n *vt* drain. **E~ung** *f* - drainage

entweder *conj* & *adv* either

entwerfen† *vt* design; (*aufsetzen*) draft; (*skizzieren*) sketch

entwert|en *vt* devalue; (*ungültig machen*) cancel. **E~er** *m* -s,- ticket-cancelling machine. **E~ung** *f* devaluation; cancelling

entwick|eln *vt* develop; **sich e~eln** develop. **E~lung** *f* -,-en development; (*Biol*) evolution. **E~lungsland** *nt* developing country

entwöhnen *vt* wean (*gen* from); cure <*Süchtige*>

entwürdigend *a* degrading

Entwurf *m* design; (*Konzept*) draft; (*Skizze*) sketch

entwurzeln *vt* uproot

entzie|hen† *vt* take away (*dat* from); **jdm den Führerschein e~hen** disqualify s.o. from driving; **sich**

e~hen (+ *dat*) withdraw from.
E~hungskur *f* treatment for drug/alcohol addiction

entziffern *vt* decipher

Entzug *m* withdrawal; (*Vorenthaltung*) deprivation

entzünd|en *vt* ignite; (*anstecken*) light; (*fig: erregen*) inflame; **sich e~en** ignite; (*Med*) become inflamed. **e~et** *a* (*Med*) inflamed. **e~lich** *a* inflammable. **E~ung** *f* (*Med*) inflammation

entzwei *a* broken

Enzian *m* -s, -e gentian

Enzyklo|pädie *f* -, -en encyclopaedia. **e~pädisch** *a* encyclopaedic

Enzym *nt* -s, -e enzyme

Epidemie *f* -, -n epidemic

Epi|lepsie *f* - epilepsy. **E~leptiker(in)** *m* -s,- (*f* -, -nen) epileptic. **e~leptisch** *a* epileptic

Epilog *m* -s, -e epilogue

Episode *f* -, -n episode

Epoche *f* -, -n epoch

Epos *nt* -/Epen epic

er *pron* he; (*Ding, Tier*) it

erachten *vt* consider (**für nötig** necessary). **E~** *nt* -s **meines E~s** in my opinion

erbarmen (sich) *vr* have pity/ <*Gott:*> mercy (*gen* on). **E~** *nt* -s pity; mercy

erbärmlich *a* wretched

erbauen *vt* build; (*fig*) edify; **nicht erbaut von** Ⓘ not pleased about

Erbe¹ *m* -n, -n heir

Erbe² *nt* -s inheritance; (*fig*) heritage. **e~n** *vt* inherit

erbeuten *vt* get; (*Mil*) capture

Erbfolge *f* (*Jur*) succession

erbieten† (sich) *vr* offer (**zu** to)

Erbin *f* -, -nen heiress

erbitten† *vt* ask for

erbittert *a* bitter; (*heftig*) fierce

erblassen *vi* (*sein*) turn pale

erblich *a* hereditary

erblicken *vt* catch sight of

erblinden *vi* (*sein*) go blind

erbrechen† *vt* vomit ● *vi/r* [sich] e~ vomit. **E~** *nt* -s vomiting

Erbschaft *f* -, -en inheritance

Erbse *f* -, -n pea

Erb|stück *nt* heirloom. **E~teil** *nt* inheritance

Erd|apfel *m* (*Aust*) potato. **E~beben** *nt* -s,- earthquake. **E~beere** *f* strawberry

Erde *f* -, -n earth; (*Erdboden*) ground; (*Fußboden*) floor. **e~n** *vt* (*Electr*) earth

erdenklich *a* imaginable

Erd|gas *nt* natural gas. **E~geschoss** *nt* ground floor. **E~kugel** *f* globe. **E~kunde** *f* geography. **E~nuss** *f* peanut. **E~öl** *nt* [mineral] oil

erdrosseln *vt* strangle

erdrücken *vt* crush to death

Erd|rutsch *m* landslide. **E~teil** *m* continent

erdulden *vt* endure

ereignen (sich) *vr* happen

Ereignis *nt* -ses, -se event. **e~los** *a* uneventful. **e~reich** *a* eventful

Eremit *m* -en, -en hermit

erfahr|en† *vt* learn, hear; (*erleben*) experience ● *a* experienced. **E~ung** *f* -, -en experience; **in E~ung bringen** find out

erfassen *vt* seize; (*begreifen*) grasp; (*einbeziehen*) include; (*aufzeichnen*) record

erfind|en† *vt* invent. **E~er** *m* -s,- inventor. **e~erisch** *a* inventive. **E~ung** *f* -, -en invention

Erfolg *m* -[e]s, -e success; (*Folge*) result; **E~ haben** be successful. **e~en** *vi* (*sein*) take place; (*geschehen*) happen. **e~los** *a* unsuccessful. **e~reich** *a* successful

erforder|lich *a* required, necessary. **e~n** *vt* require, demand

erforsch|en *vt* explore; (*untersuchen*) investigate. **E~ung** *f* exploration; investigation

erfreu|en *vt* please. **e~lich** *a* pleasing. **e~licherweise** *adv* happily. **e~t** *a* pleased

erfrier|en† vi (sein) freeze to death; <Glied:> become frostbitten; <Pflanze:> be killed by the frost. **E~ung** f -, -en frostbite

erfrisch|en vt refresh. **E~ung** f -, -en refreshment

erfüll|en vt fill; (nachkommen) fulfil; serve <Zweck>; discharge <Pflicht:> **sich e~en** come true. **E~ung** f fulfilment

erfunden a invented

ergänz|en vt complement; (hinzufügen) add. **E~ung** f complement; supplement; (Zusatz) addition

ergeben† vt produce; (zeigen) show, establish; **sich e~en** result; <Schwierigkeit:> arise; (kapitulieren) surrender; (sich fügen) submit ● a devoted; (resigniert) resigned

Ergebnis nt -ses, -se result. **e~los** a fruitless

ergiebig a productive; (fig) rich

ergreifen† vt seize; take <Maßnahme, Gelegenheit>; take up <Beruf>; (rühren) move; **die Flucht e~** flee. **e~d** a moving

ergriffen a deeply moved. **E~heit** f - emotion

ergründen vt (fig) get to the bottom of

erhaben a raised; (fig) sublime

Erhalt m -[e]s receipt. **e~en**† vt receive, get; (gewinnen) obtain; (bewahren) preserve, keep; (instand halten) maintain; (unterhalten) support; **am Leben e~en** keep alive ● a gut/schlecht **e~en** in good/bad condition; **e~en bleiben** survive

erhältlich a obtainable

Erhaltung f - preservation; maintenance

erhängen (sich) vr hang oneself

erheb|en† vt raise; levy <Steuer>; charge <Gebühr>; **Anspruch e~en** lay claim (auf + acc to); **Protest e~en** protest; **sich e~en** rise; <Frage:> arise. **e~lich** a considerable. **E~ung** f -, -en elevation; (Anhöhe) rise; (Aufstand) uprising; (Ermittlung) survey

erheiter|n vt amuse. **E~ung** f - amusement

erhitzen vt heat

erhöh|en vt raise; (fig) increase; **sich e~en** rise, increase. **E~ung** f -, -en increase

erhol|en (sich) vr recover (von from); (nach Krankheit) convalesce; (sich ausruhen) have a rest. **e~sam** a restful. **E~ung** f - recovery; (Ruhe) rest

erinner|n vt remind (an + acc of); **sich e~n** remember (an jdn/etw s.o./ sth). **E~ung** f -, -en memory; (Andenken) souvenir

erkält|en (sich) vr catch a cold; **e~et sein** have a cold. **E~ung** f -, -en cold

erkenn|bar a recognizable; (sichtbar) visible. **e~en**† vt recognize; (wahrnehmen) distinguish. **E~tnis** f -, -se recognition; realization; (Wissen) knowledge; **die neuesten E~tnisse** the latest findings

Erker m -s,- bay

erklär|en vt declare; (erläutern) explain; **sich bereit e~en** agree (zu to). **e~end** a explanatory. **e~lich** a explicable; (verständlich) understandable. **e~licherweise** adv understandably. **E~ung** f -, -en declaration; explanation; **öffentliche E~ung** public statement

erkrank|en vi (sein) fall ill; be taken ill (an + dat with). **E~ung** f -, -en illness

erkundig|en (sich) vr enquire (nach jdm/etw after s.o./about sth). **E~ung** f -, -en enquiry

erlangen vt attain, get

Erlass m -es,-̈e (Admin) decree; (Befreiung) exemption; (Straf-) remission

erlassen† vt (Admin) issue; **jdm etw e~** exempt s.o. from sth; let s.o. off <Strafe>

erlauben vt allow, permit; **ich kann es mir nicht e~** I can't afford it

Erlaubnis f - permission. **E~schein** m permit

erläutern vt explain

Erle *f* -, -n alder

erleb|en *vt* experience; (*mit-*) see; have <*Überraschung*>. **E~nis** *nt* -ses, -se experience

erledigen *vt* do; (*sich befassen mit*) deal with; (*beenden*) finish; (*entscheiden*) settle; (*töten*) kill

erleichter|n *vt* lighten; (*vereinfachen*) make easier; (*befreien*) relieve; (*lindern*) ease. **e~t** *a* relieved. **E~ung** *f* - relief

erleiden† *vt* suffer

erleuchten *vt* illuminate; **hell erleuchtet** brightly lit

erlogen *a* untrue, false

Erlös *m* -es proceeds *pl*

erlöschen† *vi* (*sein*) go out; (*vergehen*) die; (*aussterben*) die out; (*ungültig werden*) expire; **erloschener Vulkan** extinct volcano

erlös|en *vt* save; (*befreien*) release (**von** from); (*Relig*) redeem. **e~t** *a* relieved. **E~ung** *f* release; (*Erleichterung*) relief; (*Relig*) redemption

ermächtig|en *vt* authorize. **E~ung** *f* -, -en authorization

Ermahnung *f* exhortation; admonition

ermäßig|en *vt* reduce. **E~ung** *f* -, -en reduction

ermessen† *vt* judge; (*begreifen*) appreciate. **E~** *nt* -s discretion; (*Urteil*) judgement; **nach eigenem E~** at one's own discretion

ermitt|eln *vt* establish; (*herausfinden*) find out ● *vi* (*haben*) investigate (**gegen jdn** s.o.). **E~lungen** *fpl* investigations. **E~lungsverfahren** *nt* (*Jur*) preliminary inquiry

ermöglichen *vt* make possible

ermord|en *vt* murder. **E~ung** *f* -, -en murder

ermüd|en *vt* tire ● *vi* (*sein*) get tired. **E~ung** *f* - tiredness

ermutigen *vt* encourage. **e~d** *a* encouraging

---

ernähr|en *vt* feed; (*unterhalten*) support, keep; **sich e~en von** live/ <*Tier:*> feed on. **E~er** *m* -s,- breadwinner. **E~ung** *f* - nourishment; nutrition; (*Kost*) diet

ernenn|en† *vt* appoint. **E~ung** *f* -, -en appointment

erneu|ern *vt* renew; (*auswechseln*) replace; change <*Verband*>; (*renovieren*) renovate. **E~erung** *f* renewal; replacement; renovation. **e~t** *a* renewed; (*neu*) new ● *adv* again

ernst *a* serious; **e~ nehmen** take seriously. **E~** *m* -es seriousness; **im E~** seriously; **mit einer Drohung E~ machen** carry out a threat; **ist das dein E~?** are you serious? **e~haft** *a* serious. **e~lich** *a* serious

Ernte *f* -, -n harvest; (*Ertrag*) crop. **E~dankfest** *nt* harvest festival. **e~n** *vt* harvest; (*fig*) reap, win

ernüchter|n *vt* sober up; (*fig*) bring down to earth. **e~nd** *a* (*fig*) sobering

Erober|er *m* -s,- conqueror. **e~n** *vt* conquer. **E~ung** *f* -, -en conquest

eröffn|en *vt* open; **jdm etw e~en** announce sth to s.o. **E~ung** *f* opening; (*Mitteilung*) announcement

erörter|n *vt* discuss. **E~ung** *f* -, -en discussion

Erot|ik *f* - eroticism. **e~isch** *a* erotic

Erpel *m* -s,- drake

erpicht *a* **e~ auf** (+ *acc*) keen on

erpress|en *vt* extort; blackmail <*Person*>. **E~er** *m* -s,- blackmailer. **E~ung** *f* - extortion; blackmail

erprob|en *vt* test. **e~t** *a* proven

erraten† *vt* guess

erreg|bar *a* excitable. **e~en** *vt* excite; (*hervorrufen*) arouse; **sich e~en** get worked up. **e~end** *a* exciting. **E~er** *m* -s,- (*Med*) germ. **e~t** *a* agitated; (*hitzig*) heated. **E~ung** *f* - excitement

erreich|bar *a* within reach; <*Ziel*> attainable; <*Person*> available. **e~en** *vt* reach; catch <*Zug*>; live to <*Alter*>; (*durchsetzen*) achieve

errichten vt erect

erringen† vt gain, win

erröten vi (sein) blush

Errungenschaft f -, -en achievement; (☐ Anschaffung) acquisition

Ersatz m -es replacement, substitute; (Entschädigung) compensation. **E~reifen** m spare tyre. **E~teil** nt spare part

erschaffen† vt create

erschein|en† vi (sein) appear; <Buch:> be published. **E~ung** f -, -en appearance; (Person) figure; (Phänomen) phenomenon; (Symptom) symptom; (Geist) apparition

erschieß|en† vt shoot [dead]. **E~ungskommando** nt firing squad

erschlaffen vi (sein) go limp

erschlagen† vt beat to death; (tödlich treffen) strike dead; **vom Blitz e~ werden** be killed by lightning

erschließen† vt develop

erschöpf|en vt exhaust. **e~t** a exhausted. **E~ung** f - exhaustion

erschrecken† vi (sein) get a fright ● vt (reg) startle; (beunruhigen) alarm; **du hast mich erschreckt** you gave me a fright

erschrocken a frightened; (erschreckt) startled

erschütter|n vt shake; (ergreifen) upset deeply. **E~ung** f -, -en shock

erschwinglich a affordable

ersehen† vt (fig) see (**aus** from)

ersetzen vt replace; make good <Schaden>; refund <Kosten>; **jdm etw e~** compensate s.o. for sth

ersichtlich a obvious, apparent

erspar|en vt save. **E~nis** f -, -se saving; **E~nisse** savings

erst adv (zuerst) first; (noch nicht mehr als) only; (nicht vor) not until; **e~ dann** only then; **eben e~** [only] just

erstarren vi (sein) solidify; (gefrieren) freeze; (steif werden) go stiff; (vor Schreck) be paralysed

erstatten vt (zurück-) refund; **Bericht e~** report (**jdm** to s.o.)

Erstaufführung f first performance, première

erstaun|en vt amaze, astonish. **E~en** nt amazement, astonishment. **e~lich** a amazing

Erst|ausgabe f first edition. **e~e(r,s)** a first; (beste) best; **e~e Hilfe** first aid. **E~e(r)** m/f first; (Beste) best; **fürs E~e** for the time being; **als E~es** first of all; **er kam als E~er** he arrived first

erstechen† vt stab to death

ersteigern vt buy at an auction

erstens adv firstly, in the first place. **e~ere(r,s)** a the former; **der/die/das E~ere** the former

erstick|en vt suffocate; smother <Flammen> ● vi (sein) suffocate. **E~nt** -s suffocation; **zum E~** stifling

erstklassig a first-class

ersuchen vt ask, request. **E~** nt -s request

ertappen vt ☐ catch

erteilen vt give (**jdm** s.o.)

ertönen vi (sein) sound; (erschallen) ring out

Ertrag m -[e]s, ̈e yield. **e~en**† vt bear

erträglich a bearable; (leidlich) tolerable

ertränken vt drown

ertrinken† vi (sein) drown

erübrigen (sich) vr be unnecessary

erwachsen a grown-up. **E~e(r)** m/f adult, grown-up

erwäg|en† vt consider. **E~ung** f -, -en consideration; **in E~ung ziehen** consider

erwähn|en vt mention. **E~ung** f -, -en mention

erwärmen vt warm; **sich e~** warm up; (fig) warm (**für** to)

erwart|en vt expect; (warten auf) wait for. **E~ung** f -, -en expectation

erweisen† vt prove; (bezeigen) do <Gefallen, Dienst, Ehre>; **sich e~ als** prove to be

erweitern *vt* widen; dilate
<*Pupille*>; (*fig*) extend, expand

Erwerb *m* -[e]s acquisition; (*Kauf*)
purchase; (*Brot-*) livelihood;
(*Verdienst*) earnings *pl.* **e~en†** *vt*
acquire; (*kaufen*) purchase. **e~slos**
a unemployed. **e~stätig** *a*
employed

erwider|n *vt* reply; return <*Besuch,
Gruß*>. **E~ung** *f* -, -en reply

erwirken *vt* obtain

erwürgen *vt* strangle

Erz *nt* -es, -e ore

erzähl|en *vt* tell (jdm s.o.) ● *vi*
(*haben*) talk (**von** about). **E~er** *m*
-s,- narrator. **E~ung** *f* -, -en story,
tale

Erzbischof *m* archbishop

erzeug|en *vt* produce; (*Electr*)
generate. **E~er** *m* -s,- producer.
E~nis *nt* -ses, -se product;
landwirtschaftliche E~nisse farm
produce *sg.*

erzieh|en† *vt* bring up; (*Sch*)
educate. **E~er** *m* -s,- [private] tutor.
E~erin *f* -, -nen governess. **E~ung**
f - upbringing; education

erzielen *vt* achieve; score <*Tor*>

erzogen *a* **gut/schlecht e~** well/
badly brought up

es
● *pronoun*
····▸ (*Sache*) it; (*weibliche Person*) she/
her; (*männliche Person*) he/him. **ich
bin es** it's me. **wir sind traurig, ihr
seid es auch** we are sad, and so are
you. **er ist es, der …** he is the one
who …. **es sind Studenten** they are
students
····▸ (*impers*) it. **es hat geklopft** there
was a knock. **es klingelt** someone is
ringing. **es wird schöner** the weather
is improving. **es geht ihm gut/
schlecht** he is well/unwell. **es lässt
sich aushalten** it is bearable. **es gibt**
there is *or* (*pl*) are
····▸ (*als formales Objekt*) **er hat es gut**
he has it made; he's well off. **er**

---

meinte es gut he meant well. **ich
hoffe/glaube es** I hope/think so

Esche *f* -, -n ash

Esel *m* -s,- donkey; (fig *Person*) ass

Eskimo *m* -[s], -[s] Eskimo

Eskort|e *f* -, -n (*Mil*) escort.
e~ieren *vt* escort

essbar *a* edible

essen† *vt/i* (*haben*) eat; **zu Mittag/
Abend e~** have lunch/supper; **e~
gehen** eat out. **E~** *nt* -s,- food;
(*Mahl*) meal; (*festlich*) dinner

Esser(in) *m* -s,- (*f* -, -nen) eater

Essig *m* -s vinegar. **E~gurke** *f*
[pickled] gherkin

Esslöffel *m* ≈ dessertspoon.
Essstäbchen *ntpl* chopsticks.
Esstisch *m* dining-table.
Esswaren *fpl* food *sg*; (*Vorräte*)
provisions. **Esszimmer** *nt* dining-
room

Estland *nt* -s Estonia

Estragon *m* -s tarragon

etablieren (sich) *vr* establish
oneself/<*Geschäft:*> itself

Etage /e'ta:ʒə/ *f* -, -n storey.
E~nbett *nt* bunk-beds *pl.*
E~nwohnung *f* flat

Etappe *f* -, -n stage

Etat /e'ta:/ *m* -s, -s budget

Eth|ik *f* - ethic; (*Sittenlehre*) ethics
sg. **e~isch** *a* ethical

ethnisch *a* ethnic; **e~e Säuberung**
ethnic cleansing

Etikett *nt* -[e]s, -e[n] label; (*Preis-*)
tag. **e~ieren** *vt* label

Etui /e'tvi:/ *nt* -s, -s case

etwa *adv* (*ungefähr*) about; (*zum
Beispiel*) for instance; (*womöglich*)
perhaps; **nicht e~, dass …** not that
…; **denkt nicht e~ …** don't imagine
…

etwas *pron* something; (*fragend/
verneint*) anything; (*ein bisschen*)
some, a little; **sonst noch e~?**
anything else? **so e~ Ärgerliches!**
what a nuisance! ● *adv* a bit

Etymologie *f* - etymology

euch *pron (acc of* ihr *pl)* you; *(dat)* [to] you; *(refl)* yourselves; *(einander)* each other

euer *poss pron pl* your. e∼e, e∼t- s. eure, euret-

Eule *f* -, -n owl

Euphorie *f* - euphoria

eur|e *poss pron pl* your. e∼e(r,s) *poss pron* yours. e∼etwegen *adv* for your sake; *(wegen euch)* because of you, on your account. e∼etwillen *adv* um e∼etwillen for your sake. e∼ige *poss pron* der/die/das e∼ige yours

Euro *m* -[s], -[s] Euro. E∼- *pref* Euro-

Europa *nt* -s Europe. E∼- *pref* European

Europä|er(in) *m* -s,- *(f* -, -nen) European. e∼isch *a* European

Euter *nt* -s,- udder

evakuier|en *vt* evacuate. E∼ung *f* - evacuation

evan|gelisch *a* Protestant. E∼gelium *nt* -s, -ien gospel

eventuell *a* possible ● *adv* possibly; *(vielleicht)* perhaps

Evolution /-'tsio:n/ *f* - evolution

ewig *a* eternal; *(endlos)* never-ending; e∼ dauern 🈂 take ages. E∼keit *f* - eternity

Examen *nt* -s,- & -mina *(Sch)* examination

Exemplar *nt* -s, -e specimen; *(Buch)* copy. e∼isch *a* exemplary

exerzieren *vt/i (haben) (Mil)* drill; *(üben)* practise

exhumieren *vt* exhume

Exil *nt* -s exile

Existenz *f* -, -en existence; *(Lebensgrundlage)* livelihood

existieren *vi (haben)* exist

exklusiv *a* exclusive. e∼e *prep (+ gen)* excluding

exkommunizieren *vt* excommunicate

Exkremente *npl* excrement *sg*

Expedition /-'tsio:n/ *f* -, -en expedition

Experiment *nt* -[e]s, -e experiment. e∼ieren *vi (haben)* experiment

Experte *m* -n, -n expert

explo|dieren *vi (sein)* explode. E∼sion *f* -, -en explosion

Expor|t *m* -[e]s, -e export. E∼teur /-'tø:ɐ/ *m* -s, -e exporter. e∼tieren *vt* export

extra *adv* separately; *(zusätzlich)* extra; *(eigens)* specially; (🈂 *absichtlich)* on purpose

extravagan|t *a* flamboyant; *(übertrieben)* extravagant

extravertiert *a* extrovert

extrem *a* extreme. E∼ist *m* -en, -en extremist

Exzellenz *f* - *(title)* Excellency

Exzentr|iker *m* -s,- eccentric. e∼isch *a* eccentric

Ff

Fabel *f* -, -n fable. f∼haft *a* 🈂 fantastic

Fabrik *f* -, -en factory. F∼ant *m* -en, -en manufacturer. F∼at *nt* -[e]s, -e product; *(Marke)* make. F∼ation /-'tsio:n/ *f* - manufacture

Fach *nt* -[e]s,-̈er compartment; *(Schub-)* drawer; *(Gebiet)* field; *(Sch)* subject. F∼arbeiter *m* skilled worker. F∼arzt *m*, F∼ärztin *f* specialist. F∼ausdruck *m* technical term

Fächer *m* -s,- fan

Fach|gebiet *nt* field. f∼kundig *a* expert. f∼lich *a* technical; *(beruflich)* professional. F∼mann *m* *(pl* -leute) expert. f∼männisch *a* expert. F∼schule *f* technical college. F∼werkhaus *nt* half-timbered house. F∼wort *nt (pl* -wörter) technical term

Fackel *f* -, -n torch

fade *a* insipid; *(langweilig)* dull

Faden *m* -s,- thread; (*Bohnen-*) string; (*Naut*) fathom

Fagott *nt* -[e]s, -e bassoon

fähig *a* capable (**zu**/*gen* of); (*tüchtig*) able, competent. **F~keit** *f* -, -en ability; competence

fahl *a* pale

fahnd|en *vi* (*haben*) search (**nach** for). **F~ung** *f* -, -en search

Fahne *f* -, -n flag; (*Druck-*) galley [proof]; **eine F~ haben** 🔲 reek of alcohol. **F~nflucht** *f* desertion

Fahr|ausweis *m* ticket. **F~bahn** *f* carriageway; (*Straße*) road. **f~bar** *a* mobile

Fähre *f* -, -n ferry

fahr|en† *vi* (*sein*) go, travel; <*Fahrer:*> drive; <*Radfahrer:*> ride; (*verkehren*) run, (*ab-*) leave; <*Schiff:*> sail; **mit dem Auto/Zug f~en** go by car/train; **was ist in ihn gefahren?** 🔲 what has got into him? ● *vt* drive; ride <*Fahrrad*>; take <*Kurve*>. **f~end** *a* moving; (*f~bar*) mobile; (*nicht sesshaft*) travelling. **F~er** *m* -s,- driver. **F~erflucht** *f* failure to stop after an accident. **F~erhaus** *nt* driver's cab. **F~erin** *f* -, -nen woman driver. **F~gast** *m* passenger. **F~geld** *nt* fare. **F~gestell** *nt* chassis; (*Aviat*) undercarriage. **F~karte** *f* ticket. **F~kartenschalter** *m* ticket office. **f~lässig** *a* negligent. **F~lässigkeit** *f* - negligence. **F~lehrer** *m* driving instructor. **F~plan** *m* timetable. **f~planmäßig** *a* scheduled ● *adv* according to/(*pünktlich*) on schedule. **F~preis** *m* fare. **F~prüfung** *f* driving test. **F~rad** *nt* bicycle. **F~schein** *m* ticket. **F~schule** *f* driving school. **F~schüler(in)** *m(f)* learner driver. **F~stuhl** *m* lift

Fahrt *f* -, -en journey; (*Auto*) drive; (*Ausflug*) trip; (*Tempo*) speed

Fährte *f* -, -n track; (*Witterung*) scent

Fahr|tkosten *pl* travelling expenses. **F~werk** *nt*

---

undercarriage. **F~zeug** *nt* -[e]s, -e vehicle; (*Wasser-*) craft, vessel

fair /fɛːɐ/ *a* fair

Fakultät *f* -, -en faculty

Falke *m* -n, -n falcon

Fall *m* -[e]s,-̈e fall; (*Jur, Med, Gram*) case; **im F~[e]** in case (*gen* of); **auf jeden F~** in any case; (*bestimmt*) definitely; **für alle F~e** just in case; **auf keinen F~** on no account

Falle *f* -, -n trap

fallen† *vi* (*sein*) fall; (*sinken*) go down; [**im Krieg**] **f~** be killed in the war; **f~ lassen** drop <*etw, fig: Plan, jdn*>; make <*Bemerkung*>

fällen *vt* fell; (*fig*) pass <*Urteil*>

fällig *a* due; <*Wechsel*> mature; **längst f~** long overdue. **F~keit** *f* - (*Comm*) maturity

falls *conj* in case; (*wenn*) if

Fallschirm *m* parachute. **F~jäger** *m* paratrooper. **F~springer** *m* parachutist

Falltür *f* trapdoor

falsch *a* wrong; (*nicht echt, unaufrichtig*) false; (*gefälscht*) forged; <*Geld*> counterfeit; <*Schmuck*> fake ● *adv* wrongly; falsely; <*singen*> out of tune; **f~ gehen** <*Uhr:*> be wrong

fälschen *vt* forge, fake

Falschgeld *nt* counterfeit money

fälschlich *a* wrong; (*irrtümlich*) mistaken

Falsch|meldung *f* false report; (*absichtlich*) hoax report. **F~münzer** *m* -s,- counterfeiter

Fälschung *f* -, -en forgery, fake

Falte *f* -, -n fold; (*Rock-*) pleat; (*Knitter-*) crease; (*im Gesicht*) line; wrinkle

falten *vt* fold

Falter *m* -s,- butterfly; moth

faltig *a* creased; <*Gesicht*> lined; wrinkled

familiär *a* family ...; (*vertraut, zudringlich*) familiar; (*zwanglos*) informal

Familie /-iə/ *f* -, -n family. **F~nforschung** *f* genealogy. **F~nname** *m* surname.

---

*old spelling

F~nplanung f family planning.
F~nstand m marital status
Fan /fɛn/ m -s, -s fan
Fana|tiker m -s,- fanatic. **f~tisch**
a fanatical
Fanfare f -, -n trumpet; (*Signal*)
fanfare
Fang m -[e]s,ːe capture; (*Beute*)
catch; F~e (*Krallen*) talons; (*Zähne*)
fangs. **F~arm** m tentacle. **f~en†** vt
catch; (*ein-*) capture; **gefangen
nehmen** take prisoner. **F~en** nt -s
F~en **spielen** play tag. **F~frage** f
catch question
Fantasie f -, -n = Phantasie
Farb|aufnahme f colour
photograph. **F~band** nt (pl -bänder)
typewriter ribbon. **F~e** f -, -n
colour; (*Maler-*) paint; (*zum Färben*)
dye; (*Karten*) suit. **f~echt** a colour-
fast
färben vt colour; dye <*Textilien,
Haare*> ● vi (*haben*) not be colour-
fast
farb|enblind a colour-blind.
f~enfroh a colourful. **F~film** m
colour film. **f~ig** a coloured ● adv
in colour. **F~ige(r)** m/f coloured
man/woman. **F~kasten** m box of
paints. **f~los** a colourless. **F~stift**
m crayon. **F~stoff** m dye;
(*Lebensmittel-*) colouring. **F~ton** m
shade
Färbung f -, -en colouring
Farn m -[e]s, -e fern
Färse f -, -n heifer
Fasan m -[e]s, -e[n] pheasant
Faschierte(s) nt (*Aust*) mince
Fasching m -s (*SGer*) carnival
Faschis|mus m - fascism. **F~t** m
-en, -en fascist. **f~tisch** a fascist
Faser f -, -n fibre
Fass nt -es,ːer barrel, cask; **Bier vom
F~** draught beer
Fassade f -, -n façade
fassbar a comprehensible;
(*greifbar*) tangible
fassen vt take [hold of], grasp;
(*ergreifen*) seize; (*fangen*) catch; (*ein-*)
set; (*enthalten*) hold; (*fig: begreifen*)
take in, grasp; conceive <*Plan*>;

make <*Entschluss*>; **sich f~** compose
oneself; **sich kurz f~** be brief; **nicht
zu f~** (*fig*) unbelievable ● vi (*haben*)
f~ an (+ acc) touch
Fassung f -, -en mount; (*Edelstein-*)
setting; (*Electr*) socket; (*Version*)
version; (*Beherrschung*) composure;
aus der F~ bringen disconcert.
f~slos a shaken; (*erstaunt*)
flabbergasted. **F~svermögen** nt
capacity
fast adv almost, nearly; **f~ nie**
hardly ever
fast|en vi (*haben*) fast. **F~enzeit** f
Lent. **F~nacht** f Shrovetide;
(*Karneval*) carnival.
F~nachtsdienstag m Shrove
Tuesday
fatal a fatal; (*peinlich*) embarrassing
Fata Morgana f - -/- -nen mirage
fauchen vi (*haben*) spit, hiss ● vt
snarl
faul a lazy; (*verdorben*) rotten, bad;
<*Ausrede*> lame
faul|en vi (*sein*) rot; <*Zahn:*> decay;
(*verwesen*) putrefy. **f~enzen** vi
(*haben*) be lazy. **F~enzer** m -s,-
lazy-bones sg. **F~heit** f - laziness
Fäulnis f - decay
Fauna f - fauna
Faust f -,Fäuste fist; **auf eigene F~**
(*fig*) off one's own bat.
F~handschuh m mitten.
F~schlag m punch
Fauxpas /foˈpa/ m -,- /-[s], -s/ gaffe
Favorit(in) /favoˈriːt(m)/ m -en, -en
(f -, -nen) (*Sport*) favourite
Fax nt -, -[e] fax. **f~en** vt fax
Faxen fpl 🔲 antics; **f~ machen** fool
about
Faxgerät nt fax machine
Februar m -s, -e February
fecht|en† vi (*haben*) fence. **F~er** m
-s,- fencer
Feder f -, -n feather; (*Schreib-*) pen;
(*Spitze*) nib; (*Techn*) spring. **F~ball**
m shuttlecock; (*Spiel*) badminton.
F~busch m plume. **f~leicht** a as
light as a feather. **f~n** vi (*haben*) be
springy; (*nachgeben*) give; (*hoch-*)
bounce. **f~nd** a springy; (*elastisch*)

elastic. **F∼ung** f - (Techn) springs
pl; (Auto) suspension

Fee f -, -n fairy

Fegefeuer nt purgatory

fegen vt sweep

Fehde f -, -n feud

fehl a **f∼ am Platze** out of place.
F∼betrag m deficit. **f∼en** vi
(haben) be missing/(Sch) absent;
(mangeln) be lacking; **mir f∼t die
Zeit** I haven't got the time; **was f∼t
ihm?** what's the matter with him?
das hat uns noch gefehlt! that's all
we need! **f∼end** a missing; (Sch)
absent

Fehler m -s,- mistake, error; (Sport
& fig) fault; (Makel) flaw. **f∼frei** a
faultless. **f∼haft** a faulty. **f∼los** a
flawless

Fehl|geburt f miscarriage.
F∼griff m mistake.
F∼kalkulation f miscalculation.
F∼schlag m failure.
f∼schlagen† vi sep (sein) fail.
F∼start m (Sport) false start.
F∼zündung f (Auto) misfire

Feier f -, -n celebration; (Zeremonie)
ceremony; (Party) party. **F∼abend**
m end of the working day; **F∼abend
machen** stop work. **f∼lich** a
solemn; (förmlich) formal. **f∼n** vt
celebrate; hold <Fest> ● vi (haben)
celebrate. **F∼tag** m [public]
holiday; (kirchlicher) feast-day;
erster/zweiter F∼tag Christmas Day
/ Boxing Day. **f∼tags** adv on public
holidays

feige a cowardly; **f∼ sein** be a
coward ● adv in a cowardly way

Feige f -, -n fig

Feig|heit f - cowardice. **F∼ling** m
-s, -e coward

Feile f -, -n file. **f∼n** vt/i (haben) file

feilschen vi (haben) haggle

fein a fine; (zart) delicate;
<Strümpfe> sheer; <Unterschied>
subtle; (scharf) keen; (vornehm)
refined; (prima) great; **sich f∼
machen** dress up. **F∼arbeit** f
precision work

Feind(in) m -es, -e (f -, -nen) enemy.
f∼lich a enemy; (f∼selig) hostile.
F∼schaft f -, -en enmity

fein|fühlig a sensitive. **F∼gefühl**
nt sensitivity; (Takt) delicacy.
F∼heit f -, -en fineness; delicacy;
subtlety; refinement; **F∼heiten**
subtleties. **F∼kostgeschäft** nt
delicatessen [shop]

feist a fat

Feld nt -[e]s, -er field; (Fläche)
ground; (Sport) pitch; (Schach-)
square; (auf Formular) box. **F∼bett**
nt camp-bed. **F∼forschung** f
fieldwork. **F∼herr** m commander.
F∼stecher m -s,- field-glasses pl.
F∼webel m -s,-(Mil) sergeant.
F∼zug m campaign

Felge f -, -n [wheel] rim

Fell nt -[e]s, -e (Zool) coat; (Pelz) fur;
(abgezogen) skin, pelt

Fels m -en, -en rock. **F∼block** m
boulder. **F∼en** m -s,- rock

Femininum nt -s, -na (Gram)
feminine

Feminist|(in) m -en, -en (f -, -nen)
feminist. **f∼isch** a feminist

Fenchel m -s fennel

Fenster nt -s,- window. **F∼brett** nt
window-sill. **F∼scheibe** f
[window-]pane

Ferien /'fe:riən/ pl holidays; (Univ)
vacation sg; **F∼ haben** be on
holiday. **F∼ort** m holiday resort

Ferkel nt -s,- piglet

fern a distant; **der F∼e Osten** the Far
East; **sich f∼ halten** keep away
● adv far away; **von f∼** from a
distance ● prep (+ dat) far [away]
from. **F∼bedienung** f remote
control. **F∼e** f - distance; **in weiter
F∼e** far away; (zeitlich) in the
distant future. **f∼er** a further ● adv
(außerdem) furthermore; (in
Zukunft) in future. **f∼gelenkt** a
remote-controlled; <Rakete> guided.
F∼gespräch nt long-distance call.
F∼glas nt binoculars pl.
F∼kurs[us] m correspondence
course. **F∼licht** nt (Auto) full beam.
F∼meldewesen nt

telecommunications *pl*. **F∼rohr** *nt* telescope. **F∼schreiben** *nt* telex

Fernseh|apparat *m* television set. **f∼en†** *vi sep* (*haben*) watch television. **F∼en** *nt* -s television. **F∼er** *m* -s,- [television] viewer; (*Gerät*) television set

Fernsprech|amt *nt* telephone exchange. **F∼er** *m* telephone

Fernsteuerung *f* remote control

Ferse *f* -, -n heel

fertig *a* finished; (*bereit*) ready; (*Comm*) ready-made; <*Gericht*> ready-to-serve; **f∼ werden mit** finish; (*bewältigen*) cope with; **f∼ sein** have finished; (*fig*) be through (**mit jdm** with s.o.); (🔳 *erschöpft*) be all in/ (*seelisch*) shattered; **etw f∼ bringen** manage to do sth; (*beenden*) finish sth; **etw/jdn f∼ machen** finish sth; (*bereitmachen*) get sth/s.o. ready; (🔳 *erschöpfen*) wear s.o. out; (*seelisch*) shatter s.o.; **sich f∼ machen** get ready; **etw f∼ stellen** complete sth ● *adv* **f∼ essen/lesen** finish eating/ reading. **F∼bau** *m* (*pl* -bauten) prefabricated building. **f∼en** *vt* make. **F∼gericht** *nt* ready-to-serve meal. **F∼haus** *nt* prefabricated house. **F∼keit** *f* -, -en skill. **F∼stellung** *f* completion. **F∼ung** *f* - manufacture

fesch *a* 🔳 attractive

Fessel *f* -, -n ankle

fesseln *vt* tie up; tie (**an** + *acc* to); (*fig*) fascinate

fest *a* firm; (*nicht flüssig*) solid; (*erstarrt*) set; (*haltbar*) strong; (*nicht locker*) tight; (*feststehend*) fixed; (*ständig*) steady; <*Anstellung*> permanent; <*Schlaf*> sound; <*Blick, Stimme*> steady; **f∼ werden** harden; <*Gelee:*> set; **f∼e Nahrung** solids *pl* ● *adv* firmly; tightly; steadily; soundly; (*kräftig, tüchtig*) hard; **f∼ schlafen** be fast asleep; **f∼ angestellt** permanent

Fest *nt* -[e]s, -e celebration; (*Party*) party; (*Relig*) festival; **frohes F∼!** happy Christmas!

fest|binden† *vt sep* tie (**an** + *dat* to). **f∼bleiben†** *vi sep* (*sein*) (*fig*)

remain firm. **f∼halten†** *v sep* ● *vt* hold on to; (*aufzeichnen*) record; **sich f∼halten** hold on ● *vi* (*haben*) **f∼halten an** (+ *dat*) (*fig*) stick to; cling to <*Tradition*>. **f∼igen** *vt* strengthen. **F∼iger** *m* -s,- styling lotion/(*Schaum-*) mousse. **F∼igkeit** *f* - firmness; solidity; strength; steadiness. **F∼land** *nt* mainland; (*Kontinent*) continent. **f∼legen** *vt sep* (*fig*) fix, settle; lay down <*Regeln*>; tie up <*Geld*>; **sich f∼legen** commit oneself

festlich *a* festive **F∼keiten** *fpl* festivities

fest|liegen† *vi sep* (*haben*) be fixed, settled. **f∼machen** *v sep* ● *vt* fasten/(*binden*) tie (**an** + *dat* to); (*f∼legen*) fix, settle ● *vi* (*haben*) (*Naut*) moor. **F∼mahl** *nt* feast. **F∼nahme** *f* -, -n arrest. **f∼nehmen†** *vt sep* arrest. **f∼setzen** *vt sep* fix, settle; (*inhaftieren*) gaol; **sich f∼setzen** collect. **f∼sitzen†** *vi sep* (*haben*) be firm/<*Schraube:*> tight; (*haften*) stick; (*nicht weiterkommen*) be stuck. **F∼spiele** *npl* festival *sg*. **f∼stehen†** *vi sep* (*haben*) be certain. **f∼stellen** *vt sep* fix; (*ermitteln*) establish; (*bemerken*) notice; (*sagen*) state. **F∼tag** *m* special day

Festung *f* -, -en fortress

Festzug *m* [grand] procession

Fete /'fe:tə, 'fɛ:tə/ *f* -, -n party

fett *a* fat; fatty; (*fettig*) greasy; (*üppig*) rich; <*Druck*> bold. **F∼** *nt* -[e]s, -e fat; (*flüssig*) grease. **f∼arm** *a* low-fat. **f∼en** *vt* grease ● *vi* (*haben*) be greasy. **F∼fleck** *m* grease mark. **f∼ig** *a* greasy

Fetzen *m* -s,- scrap; (*Stoff*) rag

feucht *a* damp, moist; <*Luft*> humid. **F∼igkeit** *f* - dampness; (*Nässe*) moisture; (*Luft-*) humidity. **F∼igkeitscreme** *f* moisturizer

Feuer *nt* -s,- fire; (*für Zigarette*) light; (*Begeisterung*) passion; **F∼ machen** light a fire. **F∼alarm** *m* fire alarm. **f∼gefährlich** *a* [in]flammable. **F∼leiter** *f* fire-escape. **F~löscher** m -s,- fire extinguisher. **F~melder** m -s,- fire alarm. **f~n** vi (haben) fire (auf + acc on). **F~probe** f (fig) test. **f~rot** a crimson. **F~stein** m flint. **F~stelle** f hearth. **F~treppe** f fire-escape. **F~wache** f fire station. **F~waffe** f firearm. **F~wehr** f -, -en fire brigade. **F~wehrauto** nt fire-engine. **F~wehrmann** m (pl -männer & -leute) fireman. **F~werk** nt firework display, fireworks pl. **F~zeug** nt lighter

feurig a fiery; (fig) passionate

Fiaker m -s,- (Aust) horse-drawn cab

Fichte f -, -n spruce

Fieber nt -s [raised] temperature; **F~ haben** have a temperature. **f~n** vi (haben) be feverish. **F~thermometer** nt thermometer

fiebrig a feverish

Figur f -, -en figure; (Roman-, Film-) character; (Schach-) piece

Filet /fi'le:/ nt -s, -s fillet

Filiale f -, -n (Comm) branch

Filigran nt -s filigree

Film m -[e]s, -e film; (Kino-) film; (Schicht) coating. **f~en** vt/i (haben) film. **F~kamera** f cine-/(für Kinofilm) film camera

Filt|er m & (Techn) nt -s,- filter; (Zigaretten-) filter-tip. **f~ern** vt filter. **F~erzigarette** f filter-tipped cigarette. **f~rieren** vt filter

Filz m -es felt. **F~stift** m felt-tipped pen

Fimmel m -s,- 🔲 obsession

Finale nt -s,- (Mus) finale; (Sport) final

Finanz f -, -en finance. **F~amt** nt tax office. **f~iell** a financial. **f~ieren** vt finance. **F~minister** m minister of finance

find|en† vt find; (meinen) think; **den Tod f~en** meet one's death; **wie f~est du das?** what do you think of that? **es wird sich f~en** it'll turn up; (fig) it'll be all right ● vi (haben) find one's way. **F~er** m -s,- finder.

F~erlohn m reward. **f~ig** a resourceful

Finesse f -, -n (Kniff) trick; **F~n** (Techn) refinements

Finger m -s,- finger; **die F~ lassen von** 🔲 leave alone. **F~abdruck** m finger-mark; (Admin) fingerprint. **F~hut** m thimble. **F~nagel** m finger-nail. **F~spitze** f fingertip. **F~zeig** m -[e]s, -e hint

Fink m -en, -en finch

Finn|e m -n, -n, **F~in** f -, -nen Finn. **f~isch** a Finnish. **F~land** nt -s Finland

finster a dark; (düster) gloomy; (unheildrohend) sinister. **F~nis** f - darkness; (Astr) eclipse

Firma f -, -men firm, company

Firmen|wagen m company car. **F~zeichen** nt trade mark, logo

Firmung f -, -en (Relig) confirmation

Firnis m -ses, -se varnish. **f~sen** vt varnish

First m -[e]s, -e [roof] ridge

Fisch m -[e]s, -e fish; **F~e** (Astr) Pisces. **F~dampfer** m trawler. **f~en** vt/i (haben) fish. **F~er** m -s,- fisherman. **F~erei** f - fishing. **F~händler** m fishmonger. **F~reiher** m heron

Fiskus m - der F~ the Treasury

fit a fit. **Fitness** f - fitness

fix a 🔲 quick; (geistig) bright; **f~e Idee** obsession; **fix und fertig** all finished; (bereit) all ready; (🔲 erschöpft) shattered. **F~er** m -s,- 🗙 junkie

fixieren vt stare at; (Phot) fix

Fjord m -[e]s, -e fiord

flach a flat; (eben) level; (niedrig) low; (nicht tief) shallow

Fläche f -, -n area; (Ober-) surface; (Seite) face. **F~nmaß** nt square measure

Flachs m -es flax. **f~blond** a flaxen-haired; <Haar> flaxen

flackern vi (haben) flicker

Flagge f -, -n flag

Flair /flɛːɐ̯/ nt -s air, aura

Flak f -, -[s] anti-aircraft artillery/ (Geschütz) gun

flämisch *a* Flemish

Flamme *f* -, -n flame; (*Koch-*) burner

Flanell *m* -s (*Tex*) flannel

Flank|e *f* -, -n flank. **f~ieren** *vt* flank

Flasche *f* -, -n bottle. **F~nbier** *nt* bottled beer. **F~nöffner** *m* bottle-opener

flatter|haft *a* fickle. **f~n** *vi* (*sein/haben*) flutter; <*Segel:*> flap

flau *a* (*schwach*) faint; (*Comm*) slack

Flaum *m* -[e]s down. **f~ig** *a* downy; f~ig rühren (*Aust Culin*) cream

flauschig *a* fleecy; <*Spielzeug*> fluffy

Flausen *fpl* 🔲 silly ideas

Flaute *f* -, -n (*Naut*) calm; (*Comm*) slack period; (*Schwäche*) low

fläzen (sich) *vr* 🔲 sprawl

Flechte *f* -, -n (*Med*) eczema; (*Bot*) lichen; (*Zopf*) plait. **f~n**† *vt* plait; weave <*Korb*>

Fleck *m* -[e]s, -e[n] spot; (*größer*) patch; (*Schmutz-*) stain, mark; **blauer F~** bruise. **f~en** *vi* (*haben*) stain. **f~enlos** *a* spotless. **F~entferner** *m* -s,- stain remover. **f~ig** *a* stained

Fledermaus *f* bat

Flegel *m* -s,- lout. **f~haft** *a* loutish

flehen *vi* (*haben*) beg (um for)

Fleisch *nt* -[e]s flesh; (*Culin*) meat; (*Frucht-*) pulp; **F~ fressend** carnivorous. **F~er** *m* -s,- butcher. **F~fresser** *m* -s,- carnivore. **f~ig** *a* fleshy. **f~lich** *a* carnal. **F~wolf** *m* mincer

Fleiß *m* -es diligence; **mit F~** diligently; (*absichtlich*) on purpose. **f~ig** *a* diligent; (*arbeitsam*) industrious

fletschen *vt* die Zähne f~ <*Tier:*> bare its teeth

flex|ibel *a* flexible; <*Einband*> limp. **F~ibilität** *f* - flexibility

flicken *vt* mend; (*mit Flicken*) patch. **F~** *m* -s,- patch

Flieder *m* -s lilac

Fliege *f* -, -n fly; (*Schleife*) bow-tie. **f~n**† *vi* (*sein*) fly; (*geworfen werden*) be thrown; (🔲 *fallen*) fall; (🔲 *entlassen werden*) be fired/(von der

Schule) expelled; **in die Luft f~n** blow up ● *vt* fly. **f~nd** *a* flying. **F~r** *m* -s,- airman; (*Pilot*); pilot; (🔲 *Flugzeug*) plane. **F~rangriff** *m* air raid

flieh|en† *vi* (*sein*) flee (**vor** + *dat* from); (*entweichen*) escape ● *vt* shun. **f~end** *a* fleeing; <*Kinn, Stirn*> receding

Fliese *f* -, -n tile

Fließ|band *nt* assembly line. **f~en**† *vi* (*sein*) flow; (*aus Wasserhahn*) run. **f~end** *a* flowing; <*Wasser*> running; <*Verkehr*> moving; (*geläufig*) fluent

flimmern *vi* (*haben*) shimmer; (*TV*) flicker

flink *a* nimble; (*schnell*) quick

Flinte *f* -, -n shotgun

Flirt /flœɐ̯t/ *m* -s, -s flirtation. **f~en** *vi* (*haben*) flirt

Flitter *m* -s sequins *pl*. **F~wochen** *fpl* honeymoon *sg*

flitzen *vi* (*sein*) 🔲 dash

Flock|e *f* -, -n flake; (*Wolle*) tuft. **f~ig** *a* fluffy

Floh *m* -[e]s,̈-e flea. **F~spiel** *nt* tiddly-winks *sg*

Flora *f* - flora

Florett *nt* -[e]s, -e foil

florieren *vi* (*haben*) flourish

Floskel *f* -, -n [empty] phrase

Floß *nt* -es,̈-e raft

Flosse *f* -, -n fin; (*Seehund-, Gummi-*) flipper; (⊠ *Hand*) paw

Flöt|e *f* -, -n flute; (*Block-*) recorder. **f~en** *vi* (*haben*) play the flute/recorder; (🔲 *pfeifen*) whistle ● *vt* play on the flute/recorder. **F~ist(in)** *m* -en, -en (*f* -, -nen) flautist

flott *a* quick; (*lebhaft*) lively; (*schick*) smart

Flotte *f* -, -n fleet

flottmachen *vt sep* **wieder f~** (*Naut*) refloat; get going again <*Auto*>; put back on its feet <*Unternehmen*>

Flöz *nt* -es, -e [coal] seam

Fluch *m* -[e]s,̈-e curse. **f~en** *vi* (*haben*) curse, swear

Flucht f - flight; (*Entweichen*) escape; die F~ ergreifen take flight. **f~artig** a hasty

flücht|en vi (*sein*) flee (**vor** + *dat* from); (*entweichen*) escape ● vr **sich f~en** take refuge. **f~ig** a fugitive; (*kurz*) brief; <*Blick*> fleeting; <*Bekanntschaft*> passing; (*oberflächlich*) cursory; (*nicht sorgfältig*) careless. **f~ig kennen** know slightly. **F~igkeitsfehler** m slip. **F~ling** m -s, -e fugitive; (*Pol*) refugee

Fluchwort nt (*pl* -wörter) swear-word

Flug m -[e]s,-̈e flight. **F~abwehr** f anti-aircraft defence

Flügel m -s,- wing; (*Fenster*-) casement; (*Mus*) grand piano

Fluggast m [air] passenger

flügge a fully-fledged

Flug|gesellschaft f airline. **F~hafen** m airport. **F~lotse** m air-traffic controller. **F~platz** m airport; (*klein*) airfield. **F~preis** m air fare. **F~schein** m air ticket. **F~schneise** f flight path. **F~schreiber** m -s,- flight recorder. **F~schrift** f pamphlet. **F~steig** m -[e]s, -e gate. **F~zeug** nt -[e]s, -e aircraft, plane

Flunder f -, -n flounder

flunkern vi (*haben*) 🔲 tell fibs

Flur m -[e]s, -e [entrance] hall; (*Gang*) corridor

Fluss m -es,-̈e river; (*Fließen*) flow; **im F~** (*fig*) in a state of flux. **f~abwärts** adv downstream. **f~aufwärts** adv upstream

flüssig a liquid; <*Lava*> molten; (*fließend*) fluent; <*Verkehr*> freely moving. **F~keit** f -, -en liquid; (*Anat*) fluid

Flusspferd nt hippopotamus

flüstern vt/i (*haben*) whisper

Flut f -, -en high tide; (*fig*) flood

Föderation /-'tsio:n/ f -, -en federation

Fohlen nt -s,- foal

*alte Schreibung

Föhn m -s föhn [wind]; (*Haartrockner*) hair-drier. **f~en** vt [blow-]dry

Folg|e f -, -n consequence; (*Reihe*) succession; (*Fortsetzung*) instalment; (*Teil*) part. **f~en** vi (*sein*) follow (**jdm/etw** s.o./sth); (*zuhören*) listen (*dat* to); **wie f~t** as follows ● (*haben*) (*gehorchen*) obey (**jdm** s.o.). **f~end** a following; **F~endes** the following

folger|n vt conclude (**aus** from). **F~ung** f -, -en conclusion

folg|lich adv consequently. **f~sam** a obedient

Folie /'fo:liə/ f -, -n foil; (*Plastik*-) film

Folklore f - folklore

Folter f -, -n torture. **f~n** vt torture

Fön (P) m -s, -e hair-drier

Fonds /fõ:/ m -,- /-[s], -s/ fund

fönen* vt s. föhnen

Förder|band nt (*pl* -bänder) conveyor belt. **f~lich** a beneficial

fordern vt demand; (*beanspruchen*) claim; (*zum Kampf*) challenge

fördern vt promote; (*unterstützen*) encourage; (*finanziell*) sponsor; (*gewinnen*) extract

Forderung f -, -en demand; (*Anspruch*) claim

Förderung f - promotion; encouragement; (*Techn*) production

Forelle f -, -n trout

Form f -, -en form; (*Gestalt*) shape; (*Culin, Techn*) mould; (*Back*-) tin; [**gut**] **in F~** in good form

Formalität f -, -en formality

Format nt -[e]s, -e format; (*Größe*) size; (*fig: Bedeutung*) stature

formatieren vt format

Formel f -, -n formula

formen vt shape, mould; (*bilden*) form; **sich f~** take shape

förmlich a formal

form|los a shapeless; (*zwanglos*) informal. **F~sache** f formality

Formular nt -s, -e [printed] form

formulier|en vt formulate, word. **F~ung** f -, -en wording

forsch|en *vi (haben)* search (nach
  for). **f~end** *a* searching. **F~er** *m*
  -s,- research scientist; *(Reisender)*
  explorer. **F~ung** *f* -, -en research

Forst *m* -[e]s, -e forest

Förster *m* -s,- forester

Forstwirtschaft *f* forestry

Fort *nt* -s, -s *(Mil)* fort

fort *adv* away; **f~ sein** be away;
  (gegangen/verschwunden) have gone;
  und so f~ and so on; **in einem f~**
  continuously. **F~bewegung** *f*
  locomotion. **F~bildung** *f* further
  education/training. **f~bleiben†** *vi*
  sep (sein) stay away. **f~bringen†** *vt*
  sep take away. **f~fahren†** *vi sep*
  (sein) go away ● *(haben/sein)*
  continue (zu to). **f~fallen†** *vi sep*
  (sein) be dropped/*(ausgelassen)*
  omitted; *(entfallen)* no longer apply;
  (aufhören) cease. **f~führen** *vt sep*
  continue. **f~gehen†** *vi sep (sein)*
  leave, go away; *(ausgehen)* go out;
  (andauern) go on. **f~geschritten** *a*
  advanced; *(spät)* late.
  F~geschrittene(r) *m/f* advanced
  student. **f~lassen†** *vt sep* let go;
  (auslassen) omit. **f~laufen†** *vi sep*
  (sein) run away; *(sich f~setzen)*
  continue. **f~laufend** *a* consecutive.
  f~pflanzen (sich) *vr sep*
  reproduce; *<Ton, Licht:>* travel.
  F~pflanzung *f* - reproduction.
  F~pflanzungsorgan *nt*
  reproductive organ. **f~schicken** *vt*
  sep send away; *(abschicken)* send off.
  f~schreiten† *vi sep (sein)*
  continue; *(Fortschritte machen)*
  progress, advance. **f~schreitend** *a*
  progressive; *<Alter>* advancing.
  F~schritt *m* progress; **F~schritte**
  machen make progress.
  f~schrittlich *a* progressive.
  f~setzen *vt sep* continue; **sich**
  f~setzen continue. **F~setzung** *f* -,
  -en continuation; *(Folge)* instalment;
  F~setzung folgt to be continued.
  F~setzungsroman *m* serialized
  novel, serial. **f~während** *a*
  constant. **f~ziehen†** *v sep* ● *vt* pull
  away ● *vi (sein)* move away

Fossil *nt* -, -ien /-iən/ fossil

Foto *nt* -s, -s photo. **F~apparat** *m*
  camera. **f~gen** *a* photogenic

Fotograf|(in) *m* -en, -en *(f* -, -nen)
  photographer. **F~ie** *f* -, -n
  photography; *(Bild)* photograph.
  f~ieren *vt* take a photo[graph] of
  ● *vi (haben)* take photographs.
  f~isch *a* photographic

Fotokopie *f* photocopy. **f~ren** *vt*
  photocopy. **F~rgerät** *nt*
  photocopier

Fötus *m* -, -ten foetus

Foul /faul/ *nt* -s, -s *(Sport)* foul.
  f~en *vt* foul

Fracht *f* -, -en freight. **F~er** *m* -s,-
  freighter. **F~gut** *nt* freight.
  F~schiff *nt* cargo boat

Frack *m* -[e]s,¨e & -s tailcoat

Frage *f* -, -n question; **nicht in F~**
  kommen *s.* infrage. **F~bogen** *m*
  questionnaire. **f~n** *vt (haben)* ask;
  sich f~n wonder *(ob* whether).
  f~nd *a* questioning. **F~zeichen** *nt*
  question mark

frag|lich *a* doubtful; *<Person,*
  Sache> in question. **f~los** *adv*
  undoubtedly

Fragment *nt* -[e]s, -e fragment

fragwürdig *a* questionable;
  (verdächtig) dubious

Fraktion /-'tsio:n/ *f* -, -en
  parliamentary party

Franken¹ *m* -s,- *(Swiss)* franc

Franken² *nt* -s Franconia

frankieren *vt* stamp, frank

Frankreich *nt* -s France

Fransen *fpl* fringe *sg*

Franz|ose *m* -n, -n Frenchman; **die**
  F~osen the French *pl.* **F~ösin** *f* -,
  -nen Frenchwoman. **f~ösisch** *a*
  French. **F~ösisch** *nt* -[s] *(Lang)*
  French

Fraß *m* -es feed; *(pej: Essen)* muck

Fratze *f* -, -n grotesque face;
  (Grimasse) grimace

Frau *f* -, -en woman; *(Ehe-)* wife;
  F~Thomas Mrs Thomas; **Unsere**
  Liebe F~ *(Relig)* Our Lady

Frauen|arzt *m,* **F~ärztin** *f*
  gynaecologist. **F~rechtlerin** *f* -,
  -nen feminist

Fräulein *nt* -s,- single woman; (*jung*) young lady; (*Anrede*) Miss

frech *a* cheeky; (*unverschämt*) impudent. **F~heit** *f* -, -en cheekiness; impudence; (*Äußerung*) impertinence

frei *a* free; (*freischaffend*) freelance; <*Künstler*> independent; (*nicht besetzt*) (*offen*) open; (*bloß*) bare; **f~er Tag** day off; **sich** (*dat*) **f~ nehmen** take time off; **f~ machen** (*räumen*) clear; vacate <*Platz*>; (*befreien*) liberate; **f~ lassen** leave free; **ist dieser Platz f~?** is this seat taken? '**Zimmer f~**' 'vacancies' ● *adv* freely; (*ohne Notizen*) without notes; (*umsonst*) free

Frei|bad *nt* open-air swimming pool. **f~beruflich** *a & adv* freelance. **F~e** *nt* **im F~en** in the open air, out of doors. **F~gabe** *f* release. **f~geben†** *v sep* ● *vt* release; (*eröffnen*) open; **jdm einen Tag f~geben** give s.o. a day off ● *vi* (*haben*) **jdm f~geben** give s.o. time off. **f~gebig** *a* generous. **F~gebigkeit** *f* - generosity. **f~haben†** *v sep* ● *vt* **eine Stunde f~haben** have an hour off; (*Sch*) have a free period ● *vi* (*haben*) be off work/(*Sch*) school; (*beurlaubt sein*) have time off. **f~händig** *adv* without holding on

Freiheit *f* -, -en freedom, liberty. **F~sstrafe** *f* prison sentence

Frei|herr *m* baron. **F~körperkultur** *f* naturism. **F~lassung** *f* - release. **F~lauf** *m* free-wheel. **f~legen** *vt sep* expose. **f~lich** *adv* admittedly; (*natürlich*) of course. **F~lichttheater** *nt* open-air theatre. **f~machen** *vt sep* (*frankieren*) frank; (*entkleiden*) bare; **einen Tag f~machen** take a day off. **F~maurer** *m* Freemason. **f~schaffend** *a* freelance. **f~schwimmen†** (**sich**) *v sep* pass one's swimming test. **f~sprechen†** *vt sep* acquit. **F~spruch** *m* acquittal. **f~stehen†** *vi sep* (*haben*) stand empty; **es steht ihm f~** (*fig*) he

is free (**zu** to). **f~stellen** *vt sep* exempt (**von** from); **jdm etw f~stellen** leave sth up to s.o. **F~stil** *m* freestyle. **F~stoß** *m* free kick

Freitag *m* Friday. **f~s** *adv* on Fridays

Frei|tod *m* suicide. **F~umschlag** *m* stamped envelope. **f~weg** *adv* freely; (*offen*) openly. **f~willig** *a* voluntary. **F~willige(r)** *m/f* volunteer. **F~zeichen** *nt* ringing tone; (*Rufzeichen*) dialling tone. **F~zeit** *f* free *or* spare time; (*Muße*) leisure. **F~zeit-** *pref* leisure … **F~zeitbekleidung** *f* casual wear. **f~zügig** *a* unrestricted; (*großzügig*) liberal

fremd *a* foreign; (*unbekannt*) strange; (*nicht das eigene*) other people's; **ein f~er Mann** a stranger; **f~e Leute** strangers; **unter f~em Namen** under an assumed name; **ich bin hier f~** I'm a stranger here. **F~e** *f* - **in der F~e** away from home; (*im Ausland*) in a foreign country. **F~e(r)** *m/f* stranger; (*Ausländer*) foreigner; (*Tourist*) tourist. **F~enführer** *m* [tourist] guide. **F~enverkehr** *m* tourism. **F~enzimmer** *nt* room [to let]; (*Gäste-*) guest room. **f~gehen†** *vi sep* (*sein*) 🄸 be unfaithful. **F~sprache** *f* foreign language. **F~wort** *nt* (*pl* -wörter) foreign word

Freske *f* -, -n, **Fresko** *nt* -s, -ken fresco

Fresse *f* -, -n ⊠ (*Mund*) gob; (*Gesicht*) mug. **f~n†** *vt/i* (*haben*) eat. **F~n** *nt* -s feed; (⊠ *Essen*) grub

Fressnapf *m* feeding bowl

Freud|e *f* -, -n pleasure; (*innere*) joy; **mit F~en** with pleasure; **jdm eine F~e machen** please s.o. **f~ig** *a* joyful

freuen *vt* please; **sich f~** be pleased (**über** + *acc* about); **sich f~ auf** (+ *acc*) look forward to; **es freut mich** I'm glad (**dass** that)

Freund *m* -es, -e friend; (*Verehrer*) boyfriend. **F~in** *f* -, -nen friend; (*Liebste*) girlfriend. **f~lich** *a* kind; (*umgänglich*) friendly; (*angenehm*)

pleasant. **f~licherweise** *adv*
kindly. **F~lichkeit** *f* -, -en
kindness; friendliness; pleasantness

Freund|schaft *f* -, -en friendship;
F~schaft schließen become friends.
f~lich *a* friendly

Frieden *m* -s peace; **F~ schließen**
make peace; **im F~** in peace-time;
lass mich in F~! leave me alone!
F~svertrag *m* peace treaty

Fried|hof *m* cemetery. **f~lich** *a*
peaceful

frieren† *vi* (*haben*) <*Person:*> be
cold; *impers* **es friert/hat gefroren** it
is freezing/there has been a frost;
frierst du? are you cold? ● (*sein*)
(*gefrieren*) freeze

Fries *m* -es, -e frieze

frisch *a* fresh; (*sauber*) clean;
(*leuchtend*) bright; (*munter*) lively;
(*rüstig*) fit; **sich f~ machen** freshen
up ● *adv* freshly, newly; **ein Bett f~**
beziehen put clean sheets on a bed;
f~ gestrichen! wet paint! **F~e** *f* -
freshness; brightness; liveliness;
fitness. **F~haltepackung** *f*
vacuum pack

Fri|seur /fri'zø:ɐ̯/ *m* -s, -e
hairdresser; (*Herren-*) barber.
F~seursalon *m* hairdressing
salon. **F~seuse** /-'zø:zə/ *f* -, -n
hairdresser

frisier|en *vt* **jdn/sich f~en** do s.o.'s/
one's hair; **die Bilanz/einen Motor**
f~en Ⓘ fiddle the accounts/soup up
an engine

Frisör *m* -s, -e = Friseur

Frist *f* -, -en period; (*Termin*)
deadline; (*Aufschub*) time; **drei Tage**
F~ three days' grace. **f~los** *a*
instant

Frisur *f* -, -en hairstyle

frittieren *vt* deep-fry

frivol /fri'vo:l/ *a* frivolous

froh *a* happy; (*freudig*) joyful;
(*erleichtert*) glad

fröhlich *a* cheerful; (*vergnügt*)
merry. **F~keit** *f* - cheerfulness;
merriment

fromm *a* devout; (*gutartig*) docile

Frömmigkeit *f* - devoutness

Fronleichnam *m* Corpus Christi

Front *f* -, -en front. **f~al** *a* frontal;
<*Zusammenstoß*> head-on ● *adv*
from the front; <*zusammenstoßen*>
head-on. **F~alzusammenstoß** *m*
head-on collision

Frosch *m* -[e]s, -̈e frog. **F~laich** *m*
frog-spawn. **F~mann** *m* (*pl*
-männer) frogman

Frost *m* -[e]s, -̈e frost. **F~beule** *f*
chilblain

frösteln *vi* (*haben*) shiver

frostig *a* frosty. **F~schutzmittel**
nt antifreeze

Frottee *nt* & *m* -s towelling

frottier|en *vt* rub down.
F~[hand]tuch *nt* terry towel

Frucht *f* -, -̈e fruit; **F~ tragen** bear
fruit. **f~bar** *a* fertile; (*fig*) fruitful.
F~barkeit *f* - fertility

früh *a* early ● *adv* early; (*morgens*) in
the morning; **heute f~** this morning;
von f~ an *od* **auf** from an early age.
F~aufsteher *m* -s,- early riser.
F~e *f* - **in aller F~e** bright and
early; **in der F~e** (*SGer*) in the
morning. **f~er** *adv* earlier; (*eher*)
sooner; (*ehemals*) formerly; (*vor*
langer Zeit) in the old days; **f~er**
oder später sooner or later; **ich**
wohnte f~er in X I used to live in X.
f~ere(r,s) *a* earlier; (*ehemalig*)
former; (*vorige*) previous; **in f~eren**
Zeiten in former times. **f~estens**
adv at the earliest. **F~geburt** *f*
premature birth/(*Kind*) baby.
F~jahr *nt* spring. **F~ling** *m* -s, -e
spring. **f~morgens** *adv* early in
the morning. **f~reif** *a* precocious

Frühstück *nt* breakfast. **f~en** *vi*
(*haben*) have breakfast

frühzeitig *a* & *adv* early; (*vorzeitig*)
premature

Frustr|ation /-'tsio:n/ *f* -, -en
frustration. **f~ieren** *vt* frustrate

Fuchs *m* -es, -̈e fox; (*Pferd*) chestnut.
f~en *vt* Ⓘ annoy

Füchsin *f* -, -nen vixen

Fuge¹ *f* -, -n joint

Fuge² *f* -, -n (*Mus*) fugue

füg|en vt fit (in + acc into); (an-) join (an + acc on to); (dazu-) add (zu to); **sich f~en** fit (in + acc into); adjoin/ (folgen) follow (an etw acc sth); (fig: gehorchen) submit (dat to). **f~sam** a obedient. **F~ung** f -, -en eine F~ung des Schicksals a stroke of fate

fühl|bar a noticeable. **f~en** vt/i (haben) feel; **sich f~en** feel (krank/einsam ill/lonely); (🔲 stolz sein) fancy oneself. **F~er** m -s,- feeler. **F~ung** f - contact

Fuhre f -, -n load

führ|en vt lead; guide <Tourist>; (geleiten) take; (leiten) run; (befehligen) command; (verkaufen) stock; bear <Namen>; keep <Liste, Bücher>; **bei od mit sich f~en** carry ● vi (haben) lead; (verlaufen) go, run; **zu etw f~en** lead to sth. **f~end** a leading. **F~er** m -s,- leader; (Fremden-) guide; (Buch) guide[book]. **F~erhaus** nt driver's cab. **F~erschein** m driving licence; **den F~erschein machen** take one's driving test. **F~erscheinentzug** m disqualification from driving. **F~ung** f -, -en leadership; (Leitung) management; (Mil) command; (Betragen) conduct; (Besichtigung) guided tour; (Vorsprung) lead; **in F~ung gehen** go into the lead

Fuhr|unternehmer m haulage contractor. **F~werk** nt cart

Fülle f -, -n abundance, wealth (an + dat of); (Körper-) plumpness. **f~n** vt fill; (Culin) stuff

Füllen nt -s,- foal

Füll|er m -s,-, 🔲, **F~federhalter** m fountain pen. **F~ung** f -, -en filling; (Braten-) stuffing

fummeln vi (haben) fumble (an + dat with)

Fund m -[e]s, -e find

Fundament nt -[e]s, -e foundations pl. **f~al** a fundamental

Fundbüro nt lost-property office

fünf inv a, **F~** f -, -en five; (Sch) ≈ fail mark. **F~linge** mpl quintuplets. **f~te(r,s)** a fifth. **f~zehn** inv a fifteen. **f~zehnte(r,s)** a fifteenth. **f~zig** inv a fifty. **f~zigste(r,s)** a fiftieth

fungieren vi (haben) act (als as)

Funk m -s radio. **F~e** m -n, -n spark. **f~eln** vi (haben) sparkle; <Stern:> twinkle. **F~en** m -s,- spark. **f~en** vt radio. **F~sprechgerät** nt walkie-talkie. **F~spruch** m radio message. **F~streife** f [police] radio patrol

Funktion /-'tsio:n/ f -, -en function; (Stellung) position; (Funktionieren) working; **außer F~** out of action. **F~är** m -s, -e official. **f~ieren** vi (haben) work

für prep (+ acc) for; **Schritt für Schritt** step by step; **was für [ein]** what [a]! (fragend) what sort of [a]? **Für** nt **das Für und Wider** the pros and cons pl

Furche f -, -n furrow

Furcht f - fear (vor + dat of); **F~erregend** terrifying. **f~bar** a terrible

fürcht|en vt/i (haben) fear; **sich f~en** be afraid (vor + dat of). **f~erlich** a dreadful

füreinander adv for each other

Furnier nt -s, -e veneer. **f~t** a veneered

Fürsorg|e f care; (Admin) welfare; (🔲 Geld) ≈ social security. **F~er(in)** m -s,- (f -, -nen) social worker. **f~lich** a solicitous

Fürst m -en, -en prince. **F~entum** nt -s,̈-er principality. **F~in** f -, -nen princess

Furt f -, -en ford

Furunkel m -s,- (Med) boil

Fürwort nt (pl -wörter) pronoun

Furz m -es, -e (vulg) fart

Fusion f -, -en fusion; (Comm) merger

Fuß m -es,̈-e foot; (Aust: Bein) leg; (Lampen-) base; (von Weinglas) stem; **zu Fuß** on foot; **zu Fuß gehen** walk; **auf freiem Fuß** free. **F~abdruck** m

---

*alte Schreibung

footprint. **F~abtreter** *m* -s,-
doormat. **F~ball** *m* football.
F~ballspieler *m* footballer.
F~balltoto *nt* football pools *pl.*
F~bank *f* footstool. **F~boden** *m*
floor

Fussel *f* -, -n & *m* -s, -[n] piece of
fluff; **F~n** fluff *sg.* **f~n** *vi* (*haben*)
shed fluff

fußen *vi* (*haben*) be based (**auf** + *dat*
on)

Fußgänger|(in) *m* -s,- (*f* -, -nen)
pedestrian. **F~brücke** *f* footbridge.
F~zone *f* pedestrian precinct

Fuß|geher *m* -s,- (*Aust*) =
F~gänger. F~gelenk *nt* ankle.
F~hebel *m* pedal. **F~nagel** *m*
toenail. **F~note** *f* footnote.
F~pflege *f* chiropody. **F~rücken**
m instep. **F~sohle** *f* sole of the
foot. **F~tritt** *m* kick. **F~weg** *m*
footpath; **eine Stunde F~weg** an
hour's walk

futsch *pred a* 🔲 gone

Futter¹ *nt* -s feed; (*Trocken-*) fodder

Futter² *nt* -s,- (*Kleider-*) lining

Futteral *nt* -s, -e case

füttern¹ *vt* feed

füttern² *vt* line

Futur *nt* -s (*Gram*) future

Gg

Gabe *f* -, -n gift; (*Dosis*) dose

Gabel *f* -, -n fork. **g~n (sich)** *vr*
fork. **G~stapler** *m* -s,- fork-lift
truck. **G~ung** *f* -, -en fork

gackern *vi* (*haben*) cackle

gaffen *vi* (*haben*) gape, stare

Gage /'ga:ʒə/ *f* -, -n (*Theat*) fee

gähnen *vi* (*haben*) yawn

Gala *f* - ceremonial dress

Galavorstellung *f* gala
performance

Galerie *f* -, -n gallery

Galgen *m* -s,- gallows *sg.* **G~frist** *f*
🔲 reprieve

Galionsfigur *f* figurehead

Galle *f* - bile; (*G~nblase*) gall-
bladder. **G~nblase** *f* gall-bladder.
G~nstein *m* gallstone

Galopp *m* -s gallop; **im G~** at a
gallop. **g~ieren** *vi* (*sein*) gallop

gamm|eln *vi* (*haben*) 🔲 loaf
around. **G~ler(in)** *m* -s,- (*f* -, -nen)
drop-out

Gams *f* -, -en (*Aust*) chamois

Gämse *f* -, -n chamois

Gang *m* -[e]s,ˉe walk; (*G~art*) gait;
(*Boten-*) errand; (*Funktionieren*)
running; (*Verlauf, Culin*) course;
(*Durch-*) passage; (*Korridor*)
corridor; (*zwischen Sitzreihen*) aisle,
gangway; (*Anat*) duct; (*Auto*) gear; **in
G~ bringen** get going; **im G~e sein**
be in progress; **Essen mit vier G~ˉen**
four-course meal

gängig *a* common; (*Comm*) popular

Gangschaltung *f* gear change

Gangster /'gɛnstɐ/ *m* -s,- gangster

Ganove *m* -n, -n 🔲 crook

Gans *f* -,ˉe goose

Gänse|blümchen *nt* -s,- daisy.
G~füßchen *ntpl* inverted commas.
G~haut *f* goose-pimples *pl.*
G~rich *m* -s, -e gander

ganz *a* whole, entire; (*vollständig*)
complete; (🔲 *heil*) undamaged,
intact; **die g~e Zeit** all the time, the
whole time; **eine g~e Weile/Menge**
quite a while/lot; *inv* **g~
Deutschland** the whole of Germany;
wieder g~ machen 🔲 mend; **im
Großen und G~en** on the whole
● *adv* quite; (*völlig*) completely,
entirely; (*sehr*) very; **nicht g~** not
quite; **g~ allein** all on one's own; **g~
und gar** completely, totally; **g~ und
gar nicht** not at all. **G~e(s)** *nt*
whole. **g~jährig** *adv* all the year
round. **g~tägig** *a & adv* full-time;
<*geöffnet*> all day. **g~tags** *adv* all
day; <*arbeiten*> full-time

gar¹ *a* done, cooked

gar² *adv* gar nicht/nichts/niemand not/nothing/no one at all

Garage /ga'ra:ʒə/ *f* -, -n garage

Garantie *f* -, -n guarantee. **g~ren** *vt/i (haben)* [für] etw g~ren guarantee sth. **G~schein** *m* guarantee

Garderobe *f* -, -n *(Kleider)* wardrobe; *(Ablage)* cloakroom; *(Künstler-)* dressing-room. **G~nfrau** *f* cloakroom attendant

Gardine *f* -, -n curtain

garen *vt/i (haben)* cook

gären† *vi (haben)* ferment; *(fig)* seethe

Garn *nt* -[e]s, -e yarn; *(Näh-)* cotton

Garnele *f* -, -n shrimp; prawn

garnieren *vt* decorate; *(Culin)* garnish

Garnison *f* -, -en garrison

Garnitur *f* -, -en set; *(Möbel-)* suite

Garten *m* -s,-¨ garden. **G~arbeit** *f* gardening. **G~bau** *m* horticulture. **G~haus** *nt,* **G~laube** *f* summerhouse. **G~schere** *f* secateurs *pl*

Gärtner|(in) *m* -s,- *(f* -, -nen*)* gardener. **G~ei** *f* -, -en nursery

Gärung *f* - fermentation

Gas *nt* -es, -e gas; Gas geben Ⓘ accelerate. **G~maske** *f* gas mask. **G~pedal** *nt (Auto)* accelerator

Gasse *f* -, -n alley; *(Aust)* street

Gast *m* -[e]s,-¨e guest; *(Hotel-)* visitor; *(im Lokal)* patron; zum Mittag G~e haben have people to lunch; bei jdm zu G~ sein be staying with s.o. **G~arbeiter** *m* foreign worker. **G~bett** *nt* spare bed

Gäste|bett *nt* spare bed. **G~buch** *nt* visitors' book. **G~zimmer** *nt* [hotel] room; *(privat)* spare room

gast|freundlich *a* hospitable. **G~freundschaft** *f* hospitality. **G~geber** *m* -s,- host. **G~geberin** *f* -, -nen hostess. **G~haus** *nt,* **G~hof** *m* inn, hotel

gastlich *a* hospitable

Gastronomie *f* - gastronomy

Gast|spiel *nt* guest performance. **G~spielreise** *f (Theat)* tour. **G~stätte** *f* restaurant. **G~wirt** *m* landlord. **G~wirtin** *f* landlady. **G~wirtschaft** *f* restaurant

Gas|werk *nt* gasworks *sg.* **G~zähler** *m* gas-meter

Gatte *m* -n, -n husband

Gattin *f* -, -nen wife

Gattung *f* -, -en kind; *(Biol)* genus; *(Kunst)* genre

Gaudi *f* - *(Aust, fam)* fun

Gaumen *m* -s,- palate

Gauner *m* -s,- crook, swindler. **G~ei** *f* -, -en swindle

Gaze /'ga:zə/ *f* - gauze

Gazelle *f* -, -n gazelle

Gebäck *nt* -s [cakes and] pastries *pl; (Kekse)* biscuits *pl*

Gebälk *nt* -s timbers *pl*

geballt *a <Faust>* clenched

Gebärde *f* -, -n gesture

gebär|en† *vt* give birth to, bear; geboren werden be born. **G~mutter** *f* womb, uterus

Gebäude *nt* -s,- building

Gebeine *ntpl* [mortal] remains

Gebell *nt* -s barking

geben† *vt* give; *(tun, bringen)* put; *(Karten)* deal; *(aufführen)* perform; *(unterrichten)* teach; etw verloren g~ give sth up as lost; viel/wenig g~ auf *(+ acc)* set great/little store by; sich g~ *(nachlassen)* wear off; *(besser werden)* get better; *(sich verhalten)* behave ● *impers* es gibt there is/are; was gibt es Neues/zum Mittag/im Kino? what's the news/for lunch/on at the cinema? es wird Regen g~ it's going to rain ● *vi (haben) (Karten)* deal

Gebet *nt* -[e]s, -e prayer

Gebiet *nt* -[e]s, -e area; *(Hoheits-)* territory; *(Sach-)* field

gebieten† *vt* command; *(erfordern)* demand ● *vi (haben)* rule

Gebilde *nt* -s,- structure

gebildet *a* educated; *(kultiviert)* cultured

Gebirg|e *nt* -s,- mountains *pl.* **g~ig** *a* mountainous

Gebiss nt -es, -e teeth pl; (künstliches) false teeth pl; dentures pl, (des Zaumes) bit

geblümt a floral, flowered

gebogen a curved

geboren a born; g~er Deutscher German by birth; Frau X, g~e Y Mrs X, née Y

Gebot nt -[e]s, -e rule

gebraten a fried

Gebrauch m use; (Sprach-) usage; Gebräuche customs; in G~ in use; G~ machen von make use of. g~en vt use; zu nichts zu g~en useless

gebräuchlich a common; <Wort> in common use

Gebrauch|sanleitung, G~sanweisung f directions pl for use. g~t a used; (Comm) secondhand. G~twagen m used car

gebrechlich a frail, infirm

gebrochen a broken ● adv g~ Englisch sprechen speak broken English

Gebrüll nt -s roaring

Gebühr f -, -en charge, fee; über G~ excessively. g~end a due; (geziemend) proper. g~enfrei a free ● adv free of charge. g~enpflichtig a & adv subject to a charge; g~enpflichtige Straße toll road

Geburt f -, -en birth; von G~ by birth. G~enkontrolle, G~enregelung f birth-control. G~enziffer f birth-rate

gebürtig a native (aus of); g~er Deutscher German by birth

Geburts|datum nt date of birth. G~helfer m obstetrician. G~hilfe f obstetrics sg. G~ort m place of birth. G~tag m birthday. G~urkunde f birth certificate

Gebüsch nt -[e]s, -e bushes pl

Gedächtnis nt -ses memory; aus dem G~ from memory

Gedanke m -ns, -n thought (an + acc of); (Idee) idea; sich (dat) G~n machen worry (über + acc about).

g~nlos a thoughtless; (zerstreut) absent-minded. G~nstrich m dash

Gedärme ntpl intestines; (Tier-) entrails

Gedeck nt -[e]s, -e place setting; (auf Speisekarte) set meal

gedeihen† vi (sein) thrive, flourish

gedenken† vi (haben) propose (etw zu tun to do sth); jds g~ remember s.o. G~ nt -s memory

Gedenk|feier f commemoration. G~gottesdienst m memorial service

Gedicht nt -[e]s, -e poem

Gedräng|e nt -s crush, crowd. g~t a (knapp) concise ● adv g~t voll packed

Geduld f - patience; G~ haben be patient. g~en (sich) vr be patient. g~ig a patient. G~[s]spiel nt puzzle

gedunsen a bloated

geehrt a honoured; Sehr g~er Herr X Dear Mr X

geeignet a suitable; im g~en Moment at the right moment

Gefahr f -, -en danger; in G~ in danger; auf eigene G~ at one's own risk; G~ laufen run the risk (etw zu tun of doing sth)

gefähr|den vt endanger; (fig) jeopardize. g~lich a dangerous

gefahrlos a safe

Gefährt nt -[e]s, -e vehicle

Gefährte m -n, -n, Gefährtin f -, -nen companion

gefahrvoll a dangerous, perilous

Gefälle nt -s,- slope; (Straßen-) gradient

gefallen† vi (haben) jdm g~ please s.o.; er/es gefällt mir I like him/it; sich (dat) etw g~ lassen put up with sth

Gefallen¹ m -s,- favour

Gefallen² nt -s pleasure (an + dat in); dir zu G~ to please you

Gefallene(r) m soldier killed in the war

gefällig a pleasing; (hübsch) attractive; (hilfsbereit) obliging; noch etwas g~? will there be anything else? **G~keit** *f* -, -en favour; (*Freundlichkeit*) kindness

Gefangen|e(r) *m/f* prisoner. **G~nahme** *f* - capture. **g~nehmen*** *vt sep* g~ nehmen, *s.* fangen. **G~schaft** *f* - captivity

Gefängnis *nt* -ses, -se prison; (*Strafe*) imprisonment. **G~strafe** *f* imprisonment; (*Urteil*) prison sentence. **G~wärter** *m* [prison] warder

Gefäß *nt* -es, -e container; (*Blut-*) vessel

gefasst *a* composed; (*ruhig*) calm; **g~ sein auf** (+ *acc*) be prepared for

gefedert *a* sprung

gefeiert *a* celebrated

Gefieder *nt* -s plumage

gefleckt *a* spotted

Geflügel *nt* -s poultry. **G~klein** *nt* -s giblets *pl.* **g~t** *a* winged

Geflüster *nt* -s whispering

Gefolge *nt* -s retinue, entourage

gefragt *a* popular

Gefreite(r) *m* lance-corporal

gefrier|en† *vi* (*sein*) freeze. **G~fach** *nt* freezer compartment. **G~punkt** *m* freezing point. **G~schrank** *m* upright freezer. **G~truhe** *f* chest freezer

gefroren *a* frozen

gefügig *a* compliant; (*gehorsam*) obedient

Gefühl *nt* -[e]s, -e feeling; (*Empfindung*) sensation; (*G~sregung*) emotion; **im G~ haben** know instinctively. **g~los** *a* insensitive; (*herzlos*) unfeeling; (*taub*) numb. **g~smäßig** *a* emotional; (*instinktiv*) instinctive. **G~sregung** *f* emotion. **g~voll** *a* sensitive; (*sentimental*) sentimental

gefüllt *a* filled; (*voll*) full

gefürchtet *a* feared, dreaded

gefüttert *a* lined

gegeben *a* given; (*bestehend*) present; (*passend*) appropriate. **g~enfalls** *adv* if need be

gegen *prep* (+ *acc*) against; (*Sport*) versus; (*g~über*) to[wards]; (*Vergleich*) compared with; (*Richtung, Zeit*) towards; (*ungefähr*) around; **ein Mittel g~** a remedy for ● *adv* **g~ 100 Leute** about 100 people. **G~angriff** *m* counter-attack

Gegend *f* -, -en area, region; (*Umgebung*) neighbourhood

gegeneinander *adv* against/ (*gegenüber*) towards one another

Gegen|fahrbahn *f* opposite carriageway. **G~gift** *nt* antidote. **G~maßnahme** *f* countermeasure. **G~satz** *m* contrast; (*Widerspruch*) contradiction; (*G~teil*) opposite; **im G~satz zu** unlike. **g~seitig** *a* mutual; **sich g~seitig hassen** hate one another. **G~stand** *m* object; (*Gram, Gesprächs-*) subject. **G~stück** *nt* counterpart; (*G~teil*) opposite. **G~teil** *nt* opposite, contrary; **im G~teil** on the contrary. **g~teilig** *a* opposite

gegenüber *prep* (+ *dat*) opposite; (*Vergleich*) compared with; **jdm g~ höflich sein** be polite to s.o. ● *adv* opposite. **G~** *nt* -s person opposite. **g~liegend** *a* opposite. **g~stehen†** *vi sep* (*haben*) (+ *dat*) face; **feindlich g~stehen** (+ *dat*) be hostile to. **g~stellen** *vt sep* confront; (*vergleichen*) compare

Gegen|verkehr *m* oncoming traffic. **G~vorschlag** *m* counterproposal. **G~wart** *f* - present; (*Anwesenheit*) presence. **g~wärtig** *a* present ● *adv* at present. **G~wehr** *f* - resistance. **G~wert** *m* equivalent. **G~wind** *m* head wind. **g~zeichnen** *vt sep* countersign

geglückt *a* successful

Gegner|(in) *m* -s,- (*f* -, -nen) opponent. **g~isch** *a* opposing

Gehabe *nt* -s affected behaviour

Gehackte(s) *nt* mince

Gehalt *nt* -[e]s,¨er salary. **G~serhöhung** *f* rise

gehässig *a* spiteful

gehäuft *a* heaped

Gehäuse *nt* -s,- case; (*TV, Radio*) cabinet; (*Schnecken-*) shell

Geh̲e̲ge *nt* -s,- enclosure

geheim *a* secret; **g~ halten** keep secret; **im G~en** secretly. **G~dienst** *m* Secret Service. **G~nis** *nt* -ses, -se secret. **g~nisvoll** *a* mysterious

geh̲e̲mmt *a* (*fig*) inhibited

geh̲e̲n†
● *intransitive verb* (*sein*)
····▸ (*sich irgendwohin begeben*) go; (*zu Fuß*) walk. **tanzen/schwimmen/ einkaufen gehen** go dancing/ swimming/shopping. **schlafen gehen** go to bed. **zum Arzt gehen** go to the doctor's. **in die Schule gehen** go to school. **auf und ab gehen** walk up and down. **über die Straße gehen** cross the street
····▸ (*weggehen; fam: abfahren*) go; leave. **ich muss bald gehen** I must go soon. **Sie können gehen** you may go. **der Zug geht um zehn Uhr** 🔢 the train leaves *or* goes at ten o'clock
····▸ (*funktionieren*) work. **der Computer geht wieder/nicht mehr** the computer is working again/has stopped working. **meine Uhr geht falsch/richtig** my watch is wrong/ right
····▸ (*möglich sein*) be possible. **ja, das geht** yes, I *or* we can manage that. **das geht nicht** that can't be done; (🔢 *ist nicht akzeptabel*) it's not good enough, it's not on 🔢. **es geht einfach nicht, dass du so spät nach Hause kommst** it simply won't do for you to come home so late
····▸ (🔢 *gerade noch angehen*) **es geht [so]** it is all right. **Wie war die Party? — Es ging so** How was the party? — Not bad *or* So-so
····▸ (*sich entwickeln*) do; go. **der Laden geht gut** the shop is doing well. **es geht alles nach Wunsch** everything is going to plan
····▸ (*impers*) **wie geht es Ihnen?** how are you? **es geht ihm gut/schlecht** (*gesundheitlich*) he is well/not well; (*geschäftlich*) he is doing well/badly; **ein gut g~des Geschäft** a thriving business

····▸ (*impers; sich um etw handeln*) **es geht um** it concerns. **worum geht es hier?** what is this all about? **es geht ihr nur ums Geld** she is only interested in money

Geh̲e̲ul *nt* -s howling

Geh̲i̲lfe *m* -n, -n, **Geh̲i̲lfin** *f* -, -nen trainee; (*Helfer*) assistant

Geh̲i̲rn *nt* -s brain; (*Verstand*) brains *pl* **G~erschütterung** *f* concussion. **G~hautentzündung** *f* meningitis. **G~wäsche** *f* brainwashing

geh̲o̲ben *a* (*fig*) superior

Geh̲ö̲ft *nt* -[e]s, -e farm

Geh̲ö̲r *nt* -s hearing

geh̲o̲rchen *vi* (*haben*) (+ *dat*) obey

geh̲ö̲ren *vi* (*haben*) belong (*dat* to); **dazu gehört Mut** that takes courage; **es gehört sich nicht** it isn't done

geh̲ö̲rlos *a* deaf

Geh̲ö̲rn *nt* -s, -e horns *pl*; (*Geweih*) antlers *pl*

geh̲o̲rsam *a* obedient. **G~** *m* -s obedience

Geh̲|steig *m* -[e]s, -e pavement. **G~weg** *m* = **Gehsteig**; (*Fußweg*) footpath

Geier *m* -s,- vulture

Geig̲|e *f* -, -n violin. **g~en** *vi* (*haben*) play the violin ● *vt* play on the violin. **G~er(in)** *m* -s,- (*f* -, -nen) violinist

geil *a* lecherous; randy; (🔢 *toll*) great

Geisel *f* -, -n hostage

Geiß *f* -, -en (*SGer*) [nanny-]goat. **G~blatt** *nt* honeysuckle

Geist *m* -[e]s, -er mind; (*Witz*) wit; (*Gesinnung*) spirit; (*Gespenst*) ghost; **der Heilige G~** the Holy Ghost *or* Spirit

geistes|abwesend *a* absent-minded. **G~blitz** *m* brainwave. **g~gegenwärtig** *adv* with great presence of mind. **g~gestört** *a* [mentally] deranged. **g~krank** *a* mentally ill. **G~krankheit** *f* mental illness. **G~wissenschaften** *fpl* arts. **G~zustand** *m* mental state

geist̲|ig *a* mental; (*intellektuell*) intellectual. **g~lich** *a* spiritual; (*religiös*) religious; <*Musik*> sacred;

<Tracht> clerical. **G~liche(r)** *m* clergyman. **G~lichkeit** *f* - clergy. **g~reich** *a* clever; (*witzig*) witty

Geiz *m* -es meanness. **g~en** *vi* (*haben*) be mean (**mit** with). **G~hals** *m* ▣ miser. **g~ig** *a* mean, miserly. **G~kragen** *m* ▣ miser

Gekicher *nt* -s giggling

geknickt *a* ▣ dejected

gekonnt *a* accomplished ● *adv* expertly

gekränkt *a* offended, hurt

Gekritzel *nt* -s scribble

Gelächter *nt* -s laughter

geladen *a* loaded

gelähmt *a* paralysed

Geländer *nt* -s,- railings *pl*; (*Treppen-*) banisters

gelangen *vi* (*sein*) reach/(*fig*) attain (**zu etw/an etw** *acc* sth)

gelassen *a* composed; (*ruhig*) calm. **G~heit** *f* - equanimity; (*Fassung*) composure

Gelatine /ʒela-/ *f* - gelatine

geläufig *a* common, current; (*fließend*) fluent; **jdm g~ sein** be familiar to s.o.

gelaunt *a* **gut/schlecht g~ sein** in a good/bad mood

gelb *a* yellow; (*bei Ampel*) amber; **das G~e vom Ei** the yolk of the egg. **G~** *nt* -s,- yellow. **g~lich** *a* yellowish. **G~sucht** *f* jaundice

Geld *nt* -es, -er money; **öffentliche G~er** public funds. **G~beutel** *m*, **G~börse** *f* purse. **G~geber** *m* -s,- backer. **g~lich** *a* financial. **G~mittel** *ntpl* funds. **G~schein** *m* banknote. **G~schrank** *m* safe. **G~strafe** *f* fine. **G~stück** *nt* coin

Gelee /ʒe'le:/ *nt* -s, -s jelly

gelegen *a* situated; (*passend*) convenient

Gelegenheit *f* -, -en opportunity, chance; (*Anlass*) occasion; (*Comm*) bargain; **bei G~** some time. **G~sarbeit** *f* casual work. **G~skauf** *m* bargain

gelegentlich *a* occasional ● *adv* occasionally; (*bei Gelegenheit*) some time

Gelehrte(r) *m/f* scholar

Geleit *nt* -[e]s escort; **freies G~** safe conduct. **g~en** *vt* escort

Gelenk *nt* -[e]s, -e joint. **g~ig** *a* supple; (*Techn*) flexible

gelernt *a* skilled

Geliebte(r) *m/f* lover

gelingen† *vi* (*sein*) succeed, be successful. **G~** *nt* -s success

gellend *a* shrill

geloben *vt* promise [solemnly]; **das Gelobte Land** the Promised Land

Gelöbnis *nt* -ses, -se vow

gelöst *a* (*fig*) relaxed

gelten† *vi* (*haben*) be valid; <*Regel:*> apply; **g~ als** be regarded as; **etw nicht g~ lassen** not accept sth; **wenig/viel g~** be worth/(*fig*) count for little/a lot; **jdm g~** be meant for s.o.; **das gilt nicht** that doesn't count. **g~d** *a* valid; <*Preise*> current; <*Meinung*> prevailing; **g~d machen** assert <*Recht, Forderung*>; bring to bear <*Einfluss*>

Geltung *f* - validity; (*Ansehen*) prestige; **zur G~ bringen** set off

Gelübde *nt* -s,- vow

gelungen *a* successful

Gelüst *nt* -[e]s, -e desire

gemächlich *a* leisurely ● *adv* in a leisurely manner

Gemahl *m* -s, -e husband. **G~in** *f* -, -nen wife

Gemälde *nt* -s,- painting. **G~galerie** *f* picture gallery

gemäß *prep* (+ *dat*) in accordance with

gemäßigt *a* moderate; <*Klima*> temperate

gemein *a* common; (*unanständig*) vulgar; (*niederträchtig*) mean; **g~er Soldat** private

Gemeinde *f* -, -n [local] community; (*Admin*) borough; (*Pfarr-*) parish; (*bei Gottesdienst*) congregation. **G~rat** *m* local council/(*Person*) councillor. **G~wahlen** *fpl* local elections

gemein|gefährlich a dangerous.
G~heit f -, -en commonness;
vulgarity; meanness; (*Bemerkung,
Handlung*) mean thing [to say/do];
so eine G~heit! how mean!
G~kosten pl overheads.
g~nützig a charitable. **g~sam** a
common ● adv together

Gemeinschaft f -, -en community.
g~lich a joint; <*Besitz*> communal
● adv jointly; (*zusammen*) together.
G~sarbeit f team-work

Gemenge nt -s,- mixture

Gemisch nt -[e]s, -e mixture. **g~t**
a mixed

Gemme f -, -n engraved gem

Gemse* f -, -n s.Gämse

Gemurmel nt -s murmuring

Gemüse nt -s,- vegetable; (*coll*)
vegetables pl. **G~händler** m
greengrocer

gemustert a patterned

Gemüt nt -[e]s, -er nature,
disposition; (*Gefühl*) feelings pl

gemütlich a cosy; (*gemächlich*)
leisurely; (*zwanglos*) informal;
<*Person*> genial; **es sich** (*dat*) **g~
machen** make oneself comfortable.
G~keit f - cosiness

Gen nt -s, -e gene

genau a exact, precise; <*Waage,
Messung*> accurate; (*sorgfältig*)
meticulous; (*ausführlich*) detailed;
nichts G~es wissen not know any
details; **g~ genommen** strictly
speaking; **g~! exactly! G~igkeit** f -
exactitude; precision; accuracy;
meticulousness

genauso adv just the same;
(*g~sehr*) just as much; **g~ teuer** just
as expensive; **g~ gut** just as good;
adv just as well; **g~ sehr** just as
much; **g~ viel** just as much/many;
g~ wenig just as little/few; (*noch*) no
more

Gendarm /ʒãˈdarm/ m -en, -en
(*Aust*) policeman

Genealogie f - genealogy

genehmig|en vt grant; approve
<*Plan*>. **G~ung** f -, -en permission;
(*Schein*) permit

geneigt a sloping, inclined; (*fig*)
well-disposed (*dat* towards)

General m -s, ̈-e general.
G~direktor m managing director.
G~probe f dress rehearsal.
G~streik m general strike

Generation /-ˈtsi̯oːn/ f -, -en
generation

Generator m -s, -en /-ˈtoːrən/
generator

generell a general

genes|en† vi (*sein*) recover.
G~ung f - recovery; (*Erholung*)
convalescence

Genetik f - genetics sg

Genf nt -s Geneva. **G~er** a Geneva
...; **G~er See** Lake Geneva

genial a brilliant. **G~ität** f genius

Genick nt -s, -e [back of the] neck;
sich (*dat*) **das G~ brechen** break
one's neck

Genie /ʒeˈniː/ nt -s, -s genius

genieren /ʒeˈniːrən/ vt embarrass;
sich g~ feel or be embarrassed

genieß|bar a fit to eat/drink.
g~en† vt enjoy; (*verzehren*) eat/
drink

Genitiv m -s, -e genitive

Genosse m -n, -n (*Pol*) comrade.
G~nschaft f -, -en cooperative

genug inv a & adv enough

Genüge f **zur G~** sufficiently. **g~n**
vi (*haben*) be enough. **g~nd** inv a
sufficient, enough; (*Sch*) fair ● adv
sufficiently, enough

Genuss m -es, ̈-e enjoyment;
(*Vergnügen*) pleasure; (*Verzehr*)
consumption

geöffnet a open

Geo|graphie, G~grafie f -
geography. **g~graphisch,
g~grafisch** a geographical.
G~logie f - geology. **g~logisch** a
geological. **G~meter** m -s,-
surveyor. **G~metrie** f - geometry.
g~metrisch a geometric[al]

geordnet a well-ordered; (*stabil*)
stable; **alphabetisch g~** in
alphabetical order

Gepäck nt -s luggage, baggage.
G~ablage f luggage-rack.

G~aufbewahrung f left-luggage office. **G~schein** m left-luggage ticket; (*Aviat*) baggage check. **G~träger** m porter; (*Fahrrad-*) luggage carrier; (*Dach-*) roof-rack

Gepard m -s, -e cheetah

gepflegt a well-kept; (*Person*) well-groomed; (*Hotel*) first-class

gepunktet a spotted

gerade a straight; (*direkt*) direct; (*aufrecht*) upright; (*aufrichtig*) straightforward; (*Zahl*) even ● adv straight; directly; (*eben*) just; (*genau*) exactly; (*besonders*) especially; g~ sitzen/stehen sit/stand [up] straight; g~ erst only just. **G~f~, -n** straight line. **g~aus** adv straight ahead/on. **g~heraus** adv (*fig*) straight out. **g~so** adv just the same; g~so gut just as good; adv just as well. **g~stehen†** vi sep (*haben*) (*fig*) accept responsibility (für for). **g~zu** adv virtually; (*wirklich*) absolutely

Geranie /-iə/ f -, -n geranium

Gerät nt -[e]s, -e tool; (*Acker-*) implement; (*Küchen-*) utensil; (*Elektro-*) appliance; (*Radio-, Fernseh-*) set; (*Turn-*) piece of apparatus; (*coll*) equipment

geraten† vi (*sein*) get; in Brand g~ catch fire; in Wut g~ get angry; gut g~ turn out well

Geratewohl nt aufs G~ at random

geräuchert a smoked

geräumig a spacious, roomy

Geräusch nt -[e]s, -e noise. **g~los** a noiseless

gerben vt tan

gerecht a just; (*fair*) fair. **g~fertigt** a justified. **G~igkeit** f - justice; fairness

Gerede nt -s talk

geregelt a regular

gereizt a irritable

Geriatrie f - geriatrics sg

Gericht¹ nt -[e]s, -e (*Culin*) dish

Gericht² nt -[e]s, -e court [of law]; vor G~ in court; das Jüngste G~ the Last Judgement. **g~lich** a

judicial; (*Verfahren*) legal ● adv g~lich vorgehen take legal action. **G~shof** m court of justice. **G~smedizin** f forensic medicine. **G~ssaal** m court-room. **G~svollzieher** m -s,- bailiff

gerieben a grated; (⊡ *schlau*) crafty

gering a small; (*niedrig*) low; (g~fügig) slight. **g~fügig** a slight. **g~schätzig** a contemptuous; (*Bemerkung*) disparaging. **g~ste(r,s)** a least; nicht im G~sten not in the least

gerinnen† vi (*sein*) curdle; (*Blut:*) clot

Gerippe nt -s,- skeleton; (*fig*) framework

gerissen a ⊡ crafty

Germ m -[e]s & (*Aust*) f - yeast

German|e m -n, -n [ancient] German. **g~isch** a Germanic. **G~istik** f - German [language and literature]

gern[e] adv gladly; g~ haben like; (*lieben*) be fond of; ich tanze g~ I like dancing; willst du mit?—g~! do you want to come?—I'd love to!

Gerste f - barley. **G~nkorn** nt (*Med*) stye

Geruch m -[e]s,-̈e smell (von/nach of). **g~los** a odourless. **G~ssinn** m sense of smell

Gerücht nt -[e]s, -e rumour

gerührt a (*fig*) moved, touched

Gerümpel nt -s lumber, junk

Gerüst nt -[e]s, -e scaffolding; (*fig*) framework

gesammelt a collected; (*gefasst*) composed

gesamt a entire, whole. **G~ausgabe** f complete edition. **G~eindruck** m overall impression. **G~heit** f - whole. **G~schule** f comprehensive school. **G~summe** f total

Gesandte(r) m/f envoy

Gesang m -[e]s,-̈e singing; (*Lied*) song; (*Kirchen-*) hymn. **G~verein** m choral society

Gesäß nt -es buttocks pl

Geschäft nt -[e]s, -e business; (*Laden*) shop, store; (*Transaktion*) deal; **schmutzige G~e** shady dealings; **ein gutes G~machen** do very well (**mit** out of). **g~ig** a busy; <*Treiben*> bustling. **G~igkeit** f - activity. **g~lich** a business ... ● adv on business

Geschäfts|brief m business letter. **G~führer** m manager; (*Vereins-*) secretary. **G~mann** m (pl -leute) businessman. **G~stelle** f office; (*Zweigstelle*) branch. **g~tüchtig** a **g~tüchtig sein** be a good businessman/-woman. **G~zeiten** fpl hours of business

geschehen† vi (sein) happen (*dat* to); **das geschieht dir recht!** it serves you right! **gern g~!** you're welcome! **G~** nt -s events pl

gescheit a clever

Geschenk nt -[e]s, -e present, gift

Geschicht|e f -, -n history; (*Erzählung*) story; (Ⅱ *Sache*) business. **g~lich** a historical

Geschick nt -[e]s fate; (*Talent*) skill. **G~lichkeit** f - skilfulness, skill. **g~t** a skilful; (*klug*) clever

geschieden a divorced

Geschirr nt -s, -e (*coll*) crockery; (*Porzellan*) china; (*Service*) service; (*Pferde-*) harness; **schmutziges G~** dirty dishes pl. **G~spülmaschine** f dishwasher. **G~tuch** nt tea-towel

Geschlecht nt -[e]s, -er sex; (*Gram*) gender; (*Generation*) generation. **g~lich** a sexual. **G~skrankheit** f venereal disease. **G~steile** ntpl genitals. **G~sverkehr** m sexual intercourse. **G~swort** nt (pl -wörter) article

geschliffen a (*fig*) polished

Geschmack m -[e]s,-̈e taste; (*Aroma*) flavour; (*G~ssinn*) sense of taste; **einen guten G~ haben** (*fig*) have good taste. **g~los** a tasteless; **g~los sein** (*fig*) be in bad taste. **g~voll** a (*fig*) tasteful

Geschoss nt -es, -e missile; (*Stockwerk*) storey, floor

Geschrei nt -s screaming; (*fig*) fuss

Geschütz nt -es, -e gun, cannon

geschützt a protected; <*Stelle*> sheltered

Geschwader nt -s,- squadron

Geschwätz nt -es talk

geschweige conj **g~ denn** let alone

Geschwindigkeit f -, -en speed; (*Phys*) velocity. **G~sbegrenzung, G~sbeschränkung** f speed limit

Geschwister pl brother[s] and sister[s]; siblings

geschwollen a swollen; (*fig*) pompous

Geschworene|(r) m/f juror; **die G~n** the jury sg

Geschwulst f -,-̈e swelling; (*Tumor*) tumour

geschwungen a curved

Geschwür nt -s, -e ulcer

gesellig a sociable; (*Zool*) gregarious; (*unterhaltsam*) convivial; **g~er Abend** social evening

Gesellschaft f -, -en company; (*Veranstaltung*) party; **die G~** society; **jdm G~ leisten** keep s.o. company. **g~lich** a social. **G~sspiel** nt party game

Gesetz nt -es, -e law. **G~entwurf** m bill. **g~gebend** a legislative. **G~gebung** f - legislation. **g~lich** a legal. **g~mäßig** a lawful; (*gesetzlich*) legal. **g~widrig** a illegal

gesichert a secure

Gesicht nt -[e]s, -er face; (*Aussehen*) appearance. **G~sfarbe** f complexion. **G~spunkt** m point of view. **G~szüge** mpl features

Gesindel nt -s riff-raff

Gesinnung f -, -en mind; (*Einstellung*) attitude

gesondert a separate

Gespann nt -[e]s, -e team; (*Wagen*) horse and cart/carriage

gespannt a taut; (*fig*) tense; <*Beziehungen*> strained; (*neugierig*) eager; (*erwartungsvoll*) expectant; **g~ sein, ob** wonder whether; **auf etw g~ sein** look forward eagerly to sth

Gespenst nt -[e]s, -er ghost. **g~isch** a ghostly; (*unheimlich*) eerie

g

Gespött *nt* -[e]s mockery; **zum G~ werden** become a laughing-stock

Gespräch *nt* -[e]s-e conversation; (*Telefon-*) call; **ins G~ kommen** get talking; **im G~ sein** be under discussion. **g~ig** *a* talkative, **G~sthema** *nt* topic of conversation

Gestalt *f* -, -en figure; (*Form*) shape, form; **G~ annehmen** (*fig*) take shape. **g~en** *vt* shape; (*organisieren*) arrange; (*schaffen*) create; (*entwerfen*) design; **sich g~en** turn out

Geständnis *nt* -ses, -se confession

Gestank *m* -s stench, [bad] smell

gestatten *vt* allow, permit; **nicht gestattet** prohibited; **g~ Sie?** may I?

Geste /'gɛ-, 'ge:stə/ *f* -, -n gesture

Gesteck *nt* -[e]s, -e flower arrangement

gestehen† *vt/i* (*haben*) confess; confess to <*Verbrechen*>

Gestein *nt* -[e]s, -e rock

Gestell *nt* -[e]s, -e stand; (*Flaschen-*) rack; (*Rahmen*) frame

gesteppt *a* quilted

gestern *adv* yesterday; **g~ Nacht** last night

gestrandet *a* stranded

gestreift *a* striped

gestrichelt *a* <*Linie*> dotted

gestrichen *a* **g~er Teelöffel** level teaspoon[ful]

gestrig /'gɛstrɪç/ *a* yesterday's; **am g~en Tag** yesterday

Gestrüpp *nt* -s, -e undergrowth

Gestüt *nt* -[e]s, -e stud [farm]

Gesuch *nt* -[e]s, -e request; (*Admin*) application. **g~t** *a* sought-after

gesund *a* healthy; **g~ sein** be in good health; <*Sport, Getränk:*> be good for one; **wieder g~ werden** get well again

Gesundheit *f* - health; **G~!** (*bei Niesen*) bless you! **g~lich** *a* health ...; **g~licher Zustand** state of health ● *adv* **es geht ihm g~lich gut/**

schlecht he is in good/poor health. **g~sschädlich** *a* harmful

getäfelt *a* panelled

Getöse *nt* -s racket, din

Getränk *nt* -[e]s, -e drink. **G~ekarte** *f* wine-list

getrauen *vt* sich (*dat*) etw **g~** dare [to] do sth; **sich g~** dare

Getreide *nt* -s (*coll*) grain

getrennt *a* separate; **g~ leben** live apart; **g~ schreiben** write as two words

getreu *a* faithful ● *prep* (+ *dat*) true to. **g~lich** *adv* faithfully

Getriebe *nt* -s,- bustle; (*Techn*) gear; (*Auto*) transmission; (*Gehäuse*) gearbox

getrost *adv* with confidence

Getto *nt* -s, -s ghetto

Getue *nt* -s ⓘ fuss

Getümmel *nt* -s tumult

geübt *a* skilled

Gewächs *nt* -es, -e plant

gewachsen *a* **jdm g~ sein** be a match for s.o.

Gewächshaus *nt* greenhouse

gewagt *a* daring

gewählt *a* refined

gewahr *a* **g~ werden** become aware (*acc/gen*) of

Gewähr *f* - guarantee

gewähr|en *vt* grant; (*geben*) offer. **g~leisten** *vt* guarantee

Gewahrsam *m* -s safekeeping; (*Haft*) custody

Gewalt *f* -, -en power; (*Kraft*) force; (*Brutalität*) violence; **mit G~** by force. **G~herrschaft** *f* tyranny. **g~ig** *a* powerful; (ⓘ *groß*) enormous; (*stark*) tremendous. **g~sam** *a* forcible; <*Tod*> violent. **g~tätig** *a* violent. **G~tätigkeit** *f* -, -en violence; (*Handlung*) act of violence

Gewand *nt* -[e]s,-̈er robe

gewandt *a* skilful. **G~heit** *f* - skill

Gewebe *nt* -s,- fabric; (*Anat*) tissue

Gewehr *nt* -s, -e rifle, gun

Geweih *nt* -[e]s, -e antlers *pl*

Gewerb|e *nt* -s,- trade. **g~lich** *a* commercial. **g~smäßig** *a* professional

Gewerkschaft *f* -, -en trade union. **G~ler(in)** *m* -s,- (*f* -, -nen) trade unionist

Gewicht *nt* -[e]s, -e weight; (*Bedeutung*) importance. **G~heben** *nt* -s weight-lifting

Gewinde *nt* -s,- [screw] thread

Gewinn *m* -[e]s, -e profit; (*fig*) gain, benefit; (*beim Spiel*) winnings *pl*; (*Preis*) prize; (*Los*) winning ticket. **G~beteiligung** *f* profit-sharing. **g~en†** *vt* win; (*erlangen*) gain; (*fördern*) extract ● *vi* (*haben*) win; **g~en an** (+ *dat*) gain in. **g~end** *a* engaging. **G~er(in)** *m* -s,- (*f* -, -nen) winner

Gewirr *nt* -s, -e tangle; (*Straßen-*) maze

gewiss *a* certain

Gewissen *nt* -s,- conscience. **g~haft** *a* conscientious. **g~los** *a* unscrupulous. **G~sbisse** *mpl* pangs of conscience

gewissermaßen *adv* to a certain extent; (*sozusagen*) as it were

Gewissheit *f* - certainty

Gewitt|er *nt* -s,- thunderstorm. **g~rig** *a* thundery

gewogen *a* (*fig*) well-disposed (*dat* towards)

gewöhnen *vt* jdn/sich **g~ an** (+ *acc*) get s.o. used to/get used to; [an] jdn/etw gewöhnt sein be used to s.o./ sth

Gewohnheit *f* -, -en habit. **G~srecht** *nt* common law

gewöhnlich *a* ordinary; (*üblich*) usual; (*ordinär*) common

gewohnt *a* customary; (*vertraut*) familiar; (*üblich*) usual; etw (*acc*) **g~ sein** be used to sth

Gewölbe *nt* -s,- vault

Gewühl *nt* -[e]s crush

gewunden *a* winding

Gewürz *nt* -es, -e spice. **G~nelke** *f* clove

gezackt *a* serrated

gezähnt *a* serrated; (*Säge*) toothed

Gezeiten *fpl* tides

gezielt *a* specific; (*Frage*) pointed

geziert *a* affected

gezwungen *a* forced. **g~ermaßen** *adv* of necessity

Gicht *f* - gout

Giebel *m* -s,- gable

Gier *f* - greed (nach for). **g~ig** *a* greedy

gieß|en† *vt* pour; water <*Blumen, Garten*>; (*Techn*) cast ● *v impers* es **g~t** it is pouring [with rain]. **G~kanne** *f* watering-can

Gift *nt* -[e]s, -e poison; (*Schlangen-*) venom; (*Biol, Med*) toxin. **g~ig** *a* poisonous; <*Schlange*> venomous; (*Med, Chem*) toxic; (*fig*) spiteful. **G~müll** *m* toxic waste. **G~pilz** *m* toadstool

Gilde *f* -, -n guild

Gin /dʒɪn/ *m* -s gin

Ginster *m* -s (*Bot*) broom

Gipfel *m* -s,- summit, top; (*fig*) peak. **G~konferenz** *f* summit conference. **g~n** *vi* (*haben*) culminate (in + *dat* in)

Gips *m* -es plaster. **G~verband** *m* (*Med*) plaster cast

Giraffe *f* -, -n giraffe

Girlande *f* -, -n garland

Girokonto /ˈʒiːro-/ *nt* current account

Gischt *m* -[e]s & *f* - spray

Gitar|re *f* -, -n guitar. **G~rist(in)** *m* -en, -en (*f* -, -nen) guitarist

Gitter *nt* -s,- bars *pl*; (*Rost*) gratting, grid; (*Geländer, Zaun*) railings *pl*; (*Fenster-*) grille; (*Draht-*) wire screen

Glanz *m* -es shine; (*von Farbe, Papier*) gloss; (*Seiden-*) sheen; (*Politur*) polish; (*fig*) brilliance; (*Pracht*) splendour

glänzen *vi* (*haben*) shine. **g~d** *a* shining, bright; <*Papier*> glossy; (*fig*) brilliant

glanz|los *a* dull. **G~stück** *nt* masterpiece

Glas *nt* -es,ˮer glass; (*Brillen-*) lens; (*Fern-*) binoculars *pl*; (*Marmeladen-*) [glass] jar. **G~er** *m* -s,- glazier

glasieren *vt* glaze; ice <*Kuchen*>

glas|ig a glassy; (*durchsichtig*) transparent. **G~scheibe** f pane

Glasur f -, -en glaze; (*Culin*) icing

glatt a smooth; (*eben*) even; <*Haar*> straight; (*rutschig*) slippery; (*einfach*) straightforward; <*Absage*> flat; **g~ streichen** smooth out; **g~ rasiert** clean-shaven; **g~ gehen** go off smoothly; **das ist g~ gelogen** it's a downright lie

Glätte f - smoothness; (*Rutschigkeit*) slipperiness

Glatt|eis nt [black] ice. **g~weg** adv 🔲 outright

Glatz|e f -, -n bald patch; (*Voll-*) bald head; **eine G~e bekommen** go bald. **g~köpfig** a bald

Glaube m -ns belief (**an** + *acc* in); (*Relig*) faith; **G~n schenken** (+ *dat*) believe. **g~n** vt/i (*haben*) believe (**an** + *acc* in); (*vermuten*) think; **jdm g~n** believe s.o; **nicht zu g~n** unbelievable, incredible. **G~nsbekenntnis** nt creed

gläubig a religious; (*vertrauend*) trusting. **G~e(r)** m/f (*Relig*) believer; **die G~en** the faithful. **G~er** m -s,- (*Comm*) creditor

glaub|lich a **kaum g~lich** scarcely believable. **g~würdig** a credible; <*Person*> reliable

gleich a same; (*identisch*) identical; (*g~wertig*) equal; **g~ bleibend** constant; **2 mal 5 [ist] g~ 10** two times 5 equals 10; **das ist mir g~** it's all the same to me; **ganz g~, wo/wer** no matter where/who ● adv equally; (*übereinstimmend*) identically, the same; (*sofort*) immediately; (*in Kürze*) in a minute; (*fast*) nearly; (*direkt*) right. **g~altrig** a [of] the same age. **g~bedeutend** a synonymous. **g~berechtigt** a equal. **G~berechtigung** f equality

gleichen† vi (*haben*) **jdm/etw g~** be like or resemble s.o./sth

gleich|ermaßen adv equally. **g~falls** adv also, likewise; **danke g~falls** thank you, the same to you. **G~gewicht** nt balance; (*Phys &*

fig) equilibrium. **g~gültig** a indifferent; (*unwichtig*) unimportant. **G~gültigkeit** f indifference. **g~machen** vt sep make equal; **dem Erdboden g~machen** raze to the ground. **g~mäßig** a even, regular; (*beständig*) constant. **G~mäßigkeit** f - regularity

Gleichnis nt -ses, -se parable

Gleich|schritt m **im G~schritt** in step. **g~setzen** vt sep equate/ (*g~stellen*) place on a par (*dat*/mit with). **g~stellen** vt sep place on a par (*dat* with). **G~strom** m direct current

Gleichung f -, -en equation

gleichwertig adv of equal value. **g~zeitig** a simultaneous

Gleis nt -es, -e track; (*Bahnsteig*) platform; **G~ 5** platform 5

gleiten† vi (*sein*) glide; (*rutschen*) slide. **g~d** a sliding; **g~de Arbeitszeit** flexitime

Gleitzeit f flexitime

Gletscher m -s,- glacier

Glied nt -[e]s, -er limb; (*Teil*) part; (*Ketten-*) link; (*Mitglied*) member; (*Mil*) rank. **g~ern** vt arrange; (*einteilen*) divide. **G~maßen** fpl limbs

glitschig a slippery

glitzern vi (*haben*) glitter

globalisier|en vt globalize. **G~ung** f -, -en globalization

Globus m - & -busses, -ben & -busse globe

Glocke f -, -n bell. **G~nturm** m bell-tower, belfry

glorreich a glorious

Glossar nt -s, -e glossary

Glosse f -, -n comment

glotzen vi (*haben*) stare

Glück nt -[e]s [good] luck; (*Zufriedenheit*) happiness; **G~ bringend** lucky; **G~/kein G~ haben** be lucky/unlucky; **zum G~** luckily, fortunately; **auf gut G~** on the off chance; (*wahllos*) at random. **g~en** vi (*sein*) succeed

glücklich a lucky, fortunate; (*zufrieden*) happy; (*sicher*) safe ● adv happily; safely. **g~erweise** *adv* luckily, fortunately

Glücksspiel *nt* game of chance; (*Spielen*) gambling

Glückwunsch *m* good wishes *pl*; (*Gratulation*) congratulations *pl*; **herzlichen G~!** congratulations! (*zum Geburtstag*) happy birthday! **G~karte** *f* greetings card

Glüh|birne *f* light-bulb. **g~en** *vi* (*haben*) glow. **g~end** *a* glowing; (*rot-*) red-hot; <*Hitze*> scorching; (*leidenschaftlich*) fervent. **G~faden** *m* filament. **G~wein** *m* mulled wine. **G~würmchen** *nt* -s,- glow-worm

Glukose *f* - glucose

Glut *f* - embers *pl*; (*Röte*) glow; (*Hitze*) heat; (*fig*) ardour

Glyzinie /-iə/ *f* -, -n wisteria

GmbH *abbr* (**Gesellschaft mit beschränkter Haftung**) ≈ plc

Gnade *f* - mercy; (*Gunst*) favour; (*Relig*) grace. **G~nfrist** *f* reprieve

gnädig *a* gracious; (*mild*) lenient; **g~e Frau** Madam

Gnom *m* -en, -en gnome

Gobelin /gobə'lɛ̃:/ *m* -s, -s tapestry

Gold *nt* -[e]s gold. **g~en** *a* gold ...; (*g~farben*) golden. **G~fisch** *m* goldfish. **g~ig** *a* sweet, lovely. **G~lack** *m* wallflower. **G~regen** *m* laburnum. **G~schmied** *m* goldsmith

Golf[1] *m* -[e]s, -e (*Geog*) gulf

Golf[2] *nt* -s golf. **G~platz** *m* golf-course. **G~schläger** *m* golf-club. **G~spieler(in)** *m(f)* golfer

Gondel *f* -, -n gondola; (*Kabine*) cabin

gönnen *vt* jdm etw g~ not begrudge s.o. sth; **jdm etw nicht g~** begrudge s.o. sth

Gör *nt* -s, -en, **Göre** *f* -, -n 🄸 kid

Gorilla *m* -s, -s gorilla

Gosse *f* -, -n gutter

Got|ik *f* - Gothic. **g~isch** *a* Gothic

Gott *m* -[e]s,-̈er God; (*Myth*) god

Götterspeise *f* jelly

Gottes|dienst *m* service. **G~lästerung** *f* blasphemy

Gottheit *f* -, -en deity

Göttin *f* -, -nen goddess

göttlich *a* divine

gottlos *a* ungodly; (*atheistisch*) godless

Grab *nt* -[e]s,-̈er grave

graben† *vi* (*haben*) dig

Graben *m* -s,-̈ ditch; (*Mil*) trench

Grab|mal *nt* tomb. **G~stein** *m* gravestone, tombstone

Grad *m* -[e]s, -e degree

Graf *m* -en, -en count

Grafik *f* -, -en graphics *sg*; (*Kunst*) graphic arts *pl*; (*Druck*) print

Gräfin *f* -, -nen countess

grafisch *a* graphic; **g~e Darstellung** diagram

Grafschaft *f* -, -en county

Gram *m* -s grief

grämen (sich) *vr* grieve

Gramm *nt* -s, -e gram

Gram|matik *f* -, -en grammar. **g~matikalisch** *a* grammatical

Granat *m* -[e]s, -e (*Miner*) garnet. **G~e** *f* -, -n shell; (*Hand-*) grenade

Granit *m* -s, -e granite

Gras *nt* -es,-̈er grass. **g~en** *vi* (*haben*) graze. **G~hüpfer** *m* -s,- grasshopper

grässlich *a* dreadful

Grat *m* -[e]s, -e [mountain] ridge

Gräte *f* -, -n fishbone

Gratifikation /-'tsio:n/ *f* -, -en bonus

gratis *adv* free [of charge]. **G~probe** *f* free sample

Gratu|lant(in) *m* -en, -en (*f* -, -nen) well-wisher. **G~lation** /-'tsio:n/ *f* -, -en congratulations *pl*; (*Glückwünsche*) best wishes *pl*. **g~lieren** *vi* (*haben*) jdm g~lieren congratulate s.o. (**zu** on); (*zum Geburtstag*) wish s.o. happy birthday

grau *a*, **G~** *nt* -s,- grey

Gräuel *m* -s,- horror

grauen *v impers* mir graut [es] davor I dread it. **G~** *nt* -s dread. **g~haft** *a* gruesome; (*grässlich*) horrible

gräulich *a* horrible

grausam *a* cruel. **G~keit** *f* -, **-en** cruelty

graus|en *v impers* mir graust davor I dread it. **G~en** *nt* **-s** horror, dread. **g~ig** *a* gruesome

gravieren *vt* engrave. **g~d** *a* (*fig*) serious

graziös *a* graceful

greifen† *vt* take hold of; (*fangen*) catch ● *vi* (*haben*) reach (**nach** for); **um sich g~** (*fig*) spread

Greis *m* **-es, -e** old man. **G~in** *f* -, **-nen** old woman

grell *a* glaring; <*Farbe*> garish; (*schrill*) shrill

Gremium *nt* **-s, -ien** committee

Grenz|e *f* -, **-n** border; (*Staats-*) frontier; (*Grundstücks-*) boundary; (*fig*) limit. **g~en** *vi* (*haben*) border (**an** + *acc* on). **g~enlos** *a* boundless; (*maßlos*) infinite

Griech|e *m* **-n, -n** Greek. **G~enland** *nt* **-s** Greece. **G~in** *f* -, **-nen** Greek woman. **g~isch** *a* Greek. **G~isch** *nt* **-[s]** (*Lang*) Greek

Grieß *m* **-es** semolina

Griff *m* **-[e]s, -e** grasp, hold; (*Hand-*) movement of the hand; (*Tür-, Messer-*) handle; (*Schwert-*) hilt. **g~bereit** *a* handy

Grill *m* **-s, -s** grill; (*Garten-*) barbecue

Grille *f* -, **-n** (*Zool*) cricket

grill|en *vt* grill; (*im Freien*) barbecue ● *vi* (*haben*) have a barbecue. **G~fest** *nt* barbecue

Grimasse *f* -, **-n** grimace; **G~n schneiden** pull faces

grimmig *a* furious; <*Kälte*> bitter

grinsen *vi* (*haben*) grin

Grippe *f* -, **-n** influenza, 🔲 flu

grob *a* coarse; (*unsanft, ungefähr*) rough; (*unhöflich*) rude; (*schwer*) gross; <*Fehler*> bad; **g~ geschätzt** roughly. **G~ian** *m* **-s, -e** brute

Groll *m* **-[e]s** resentment. **g~en** *vi* (*haben*) be angry (*dat* with); <*Donner:*> rumble

Grönland *nt* **-s** Greenland

Gros *nt* **-ses,-** (*Maß*) gross

Groschen *m* **-s,-** (*Aust*) groschen; 🔲 ten-pfennig piece

groß *a* big; <*Anzahl, Summe*> large; (*bedeutend, stark*) great; (*g~artig*) grand; <*Buchstabe*> capital; **g~e Ferien** summer holidays; **der größte Teil** the majority *or* bulk; **g~ werden** <*Person:*> grow up; **g~ in etw** (*dat*) **sein** be good at sth; **G~ und Klein** young and old; **im G~en und Ganzen** on the whole ● *adv* <*feiern*> in style; (🔲 *viel*) much

groß|artig *a* magnificent. **G~aufnahme** *f* close-up. **G~britannien** *nt* **-s** Great Britain. **G~buchstabe** *m* capital letter. **G~e(r)** *m/f* **unser G~er** our eldest; **die G~en** the grown-ups; (*fig*) the great *pl*

Größe *f* -, **-n** size; (*Ausmaß*) extent; (*Körper-*) height; (*Bedeutsamkeit*) greatness; (*Math*) quantity; (*Person*) great figure

Großeltern *pl* grandparents

Groß|handel *m* wholesale trade. **G~händler** *m* wholesaler. **G~macht** *f* superpower. **g~mütig** *a* magnanimous. **G~mutter** *f* grandmother. **G~schreibung** *f* capitalization. **g~spurig** *a* pompous; (*überheblich*) arrogant. **G~stadt** *f* [large] city. **g~städtisch** *a* city ... **G~teil** *m* large proportion; (*Hauptteil*) bulk

größtenteils *adv* for the most part

groß|tun† (**sich**) *vr sep* brag. **G~vater** *m* grandfather. **g~ziehen**† *vt sep* bring up; rear <*Tier*>. **g~zügig** *a* generous. **G~zügigkeit** *f* - generosity

Grotte *f* -, **-n** grotto

Grübchen *nt* **-s,-** dimple

Grube *f* -, **-n** pit

grübeln *vi* (*haben*) brood

Gruft *f* -,**-̈e** [burial] vault

grün *a* green; **im G~en** out in the country; **die G~en** the Greens

Grund *m* **-[e]s,̈-e** ground; (*Boden*) bottom; (*Hinter-*) background; (*Ursache*) reason; **aus diesem G~e** for this reason; **im G~e [genommen]** basically; **auf G~ laufen** (*Naut*) run

g

aground; **zu G~e richten/gehen** *s.* **zugrunde. G~begriffe** *mpl* basics. **G~besitzer** *m* landowner

gründ|en *vt* found, set up; start <*Familie*>; (*fig*) base (**auf** + *acc* on); **sich g~en** be based (**auf** + *acc* on). **G~er(in)** *m* -s,- (*f* -, -nen) founder

Grund|farbe *f* primary colour. **G~form** *f* (*Gram*) infinitive. **G~gesetz** *nt* (*Pol*) constitution. **G~lage** *f* basis, foundation

gründlich *a* thorough. **G~keit** *f* - thoroughness

Gründonnerstag *m* Maundy Thursday

Grund|regel *f* basic rule. **G~riss** *m* ground-plan; (*fig*) outline. **G~satz** *m* principle. **g~sätzlich** *a* fundamental; (*im Allgemeinen*) in principle; (*prinzipiell*) on principle; **G~schule** *f* primary school. **G~stück** *nt* plot [of land]

Gründung *f* -, -en foundation

Grün|span *m* verdigris. **G~streifen** *m* grass verge; (*Mittel-*) central reservation

grunzen *vi* (*haben*) grunt

Gruppe *f* -, -n group; (*Reise-*) party

gruppieren *vt* group

Grusel|geschichte *f* horror story. **g~ig** *a* creepy

Gruß *m* -es,ⁱ̈e greeting; (*Mil*) salute; **einen schönen G~ an X** give my regards to X; **viele/herzliche G~e** regards; **Mit freundlichen G~en** Yours sincerely/faithfully

grüßen *vt/i* (*haben*) say hallo (**jdn** to s.o.); (*Mil*) salute; **g~Sie X von mir** give my regards to X; **grüß Gott!** (*SGer, Aust*) good morning/afternoon/evening!

gucken *vi* (*haben*) 🔲 look

Guerilla /ge'rɪlja/ *f* - guerrilla warfare. **G~kämpfer** *m* guerrilla

Gulasch *nt & m* -[e]s goulash

gültig *a* valid

Gummi *m & nt* -s, -[s] rubber; (*Harz*) gum. **G~band** *nt* (*pl* -bänder) elastic *or* rubber band

gummiert *a* gummed

Gummi|knüppel *m* truncheon. **G~stiefel** *m* gumboot, wellington. **G~zug** *m* elastic

Gunst *f* - favour

günstig *a* favourable; (*passend*) convenient

Gurgel *f* -, -n throat. **g~n** *vi* (*haben*) gargle

Gurke *f* -, -n cucumber; (*Essig-*) gherkin

Gurt *m* -[e]s, -e strap; (*Gürtel*) belt; (*Auto*) safety-belt. **G~band** *nt* (*pl* -bänder) waistband

Gürtel *m* -s,- belt. **G~linie** *f* waistline. **G~rose** *f* shingles *sg*

Guss *m* -es,ⁱ̈e (*Techn*) casting; (*Strom*) stream; (*Regen-*) downpour; (*Torten-*) icing. **G~eisen** *nt* cast iron

gut *a* good; <*Gewissen*> clear; (*gütig*) kind (**zu** to); **jdm gut sein** be fond of s.o.; **im G~en** amicably; **schon gut** that's all right ● *adv* well; <*schmecken, riechen*> good; (*leicht*) easily; **gut zu sehen** clearly visible; **gut drei Stunden** a good three hours

Gut *nt* -[e]s,ⁱ̈er possession, property; (*Land-*) estate; **Gut und Böse** good and evil; **Güter** (*Comm*) goods

Gutacht|en *nt* -s,- expert's report. **G~er** *m* -s,- expert

gutartig *a* good-natured; (*Med*) benign

Gute|(s) *nt* etwas/nichts **G~s** something/nothing good; **G~s tun** do good; **alles G~!** all the best!

Güte *f* -, -n goodness, kindness; (*Qualität*) quality

Güterzug *m* goods train

gut|gehen* *vi sep* (*sein*) gut gehen, *s.* gehen. **g~gehend*** *a* gut gehend, *s.* gehen. **g~gläubig** *a* trusting. **g~haben†** *vt sep* fünfzig Mark **g~haben** have fifty marks credit (**bei** with). **G~haben** *nt* -s,- [credit] balance; (*Kredit*) credit

gut|machen *vt sep* make up for; make good <*Schaden*>. **g~mütig** *a* good-natured. **G~mütigkeit** *f* - good nature. **G~schein** *m* credit note; (*Bon*) voucher; (*Geschenk-*) gift

token. **g~schreiben†** vt sep credit.
G~schrift f credit

Guts|haus nt manor house

gut|tun* vi sep (haben) gut tun, s.
tun. **g~willig** a willing

Gymnasium nt -s, -ien ≈ grammar
school

Gymnastik f - [keep-fit] exercises
pl; (Turnen) gymnastics sg

Gynäko|loge m -n, -n
gynaecologist. **G~logie** f -
gynaecology

Hh

H, h /ha:/ nt, -,- (Mus) B, b

Haar nt -[e]s, -e hair; sich (dat) die
Haare od das H~ waschen wash
one's hair; um ein H~ 🛈 very
nearly. **H~bürste** f hairbrush.
h~en vi (haben) shed hairs; <Tier:>
moult ● vr sich h~en moult. **h~ig**
a hairy; 🛈 tricky. **H~klemme** f
hair-grip. **H~nadelkurve** f hairpin
bend. **H~schnitt** m haircut.
H~spange f slide.
H~waschmittel nt shampoo

Habe f - possessions pl

haben†
● transitive verb
····▶ have; (im Präsens) have got 🛈. er
hat kein Geld he has no money or 🛈
he hasn't got any money. ich habe/
hatte die Grippe I've got flu/had flu.
was haben Sie da? what have you
got there? wenn ich die Zeit hätte if I
had the time
····▶ (empfinden) Angst/Hunger/Durst
haben be frightened/hungry/thirsty.
was hat er? what's wrong with him?
····▶ (+ Adj., es) es gut/schlecht haben
be well/badly off. es schwer haben
be having a difficult time

····▶ (+ zu) (müssen) du hast zu
gehorchen you must obey
● auxiliary verb
····▶ have. ich habe/hatte ihn eben
gesehen I have or I've/I had or I'd
just seen him. er hat es gewusst he
knew it. er hätte ihr geholfen he
would have helped her
● reflexive verb
····▶ (🛈 sich aufregen) make a fuss.
hab dich nicht so! don't make such a
fuss!

Habgier f greed. **h~ig** a greedy

Habicht m -[e]s, -e hawk

Hachse f -, -n (Culin) knuckle

Hackbraten m meat loaf

Hacke¹ f -, -n hoe; (Spitz-) pick

Hacke² f -, -n, **Hacken** m -s,- heel

hack|en vt hoe; (schlagen,
zerkleinern) chop; <Vogel:> peck.
H~fleisch nt mince

Hafen m -s, - harbour; (See-) port.
H~arbeiter m docker. **H~stadt** f
port

Hafer m -s oats pl. **H~flocken** fpl
[rolled] oats

Haft f - (Jur) custody; (H~strafe)
imprisonment. **h~bar** a (Jur)
liable. **H~befehl** m warrant

haften vi (haben) cling; (kleben)
stick; (bürgen) vouch/(Jur) be liable
(für for)

Häftling m -s, -e detainee

Haftpflicht f (Jur) liability.
H~versicherung f (Auto) third-
party insurance

Haftung f - (Jur) liability

Hagebutte f -, -n rose-hip

Hagel m -s hail. **h~n** vi (haben) hail

hager a gaunt

Hahn m -[e]s, -e cock; (Techn) tap

Hähnchen nt -s,- (Culin) chicken

Hai[fisch] m -[e]s, -e shark

Häkchen nt -s,- tick

häkel|n vt/i (haben) crochet.
H~nadel f crochet-hook

Haken m -s,- hook; (Häkchen) tick;
(🛈 Schwierigkeit) snag. **h~** vt hook
(an + acc to). **H~kreuz** nt swastika

halb *a* half; **auf h~em Weg** half-way ● *adv* half; **h~drei** half past two; **fünf [Minuten] vor/nach h~vier** twenty-five [minutes] past three/to four. **H~e(r,s)** *f/m/nt* half [a litre]

halber *prep* (+ *gen*) for the sake of; **Geschäfte h~** on business

Halbfinale *nt* semifinal

halbieren *vt* halve, divide in half; (*Geom*) bisect

Halb|insel *f* peninsula. **H~kreis** *m* semicircle. **H~kugel** *f* hemisphere. **h~laut** *a* low ● *adv* in an undertone. **h~mast** *adv* at half-mast. **H~mond** *m* half moon. **H~pension** *f* half-board. **h~rund** *a* semicircular. **H~schuh** *m* [flat] shoe. **h~tags** *adv* [for] half a day; **h~tags arbeiten** ≈ work part-time. **H~ton** *m* semitone. **h~wegs** *adv* half-way; (*ziemlich*) more or less. **h~wüchsig** *a* adolescent. **H~zeit** *f* (*Sport*) half-time; (*Spielzeit*) half

Halde *f* -, -n dump, tip

Hälfte *f* -, -n half; **zur H~** half

Halfter *f* -, -n & *nt* -s,- holster

Halle *f* -, -n hall; (*Hotel-*) lobby; (*Bahnhofs-*) station concourse

hallen *vi* (*haben*) resound; (*wider-*) echo

Hallen- *pref* indoor

hallo *int* hallo

Halluzination /-'tsio:n/ *f* -, -en hallucination

Halm *m* -[e]s, -e stalk; (*Gras-*) blade

Hals *m* -es,¨e neck; (*Kehle*) throat; **aus vollem H~e** at the top of one's voice; <*lachen*> out loud. **H~band** *nt* (*pl* -bänder) collar. **H~schmerzen** *mpl* sore throat *sg*

halt *int* stop! (*Mil*) halt! 🔲 wait a minute!

Halt *m* -[e]s, -e hold; (*Stütze*) support; (*innerer*) stability; (*Anhalten*) stop; **H~ machen** stop. **h~bar** *a* durable; (*Tex*) hard-wearing; (*fig*) tenable; **h~bar bis …** (*Comm*) use by …

halten† *vt* hold; make <*Rede*>; give <*Vortrag*>; (*einhalten, bewahren*) keep; [**sich** (*dat*)] **etw h~** keep <*Hund*>; take <*Zeitung*>; **h~ für** regard as; **viel h~ von** think highly of; **sich links h~** keep left; **sich h~ an** (+ *acc*) (*fig*) keep to ● *vi* (*haben*) hold; (*haltbar sein, bestehen bleiben*) keep; <*Freundschaft, Blumen:*> last; (*Halt machen*) stop; **auf sich** (*acc*) **h~** take pride in oneself; **zu jdm h~** be loyal to s.o.

Halte|stelle *f* stop. **H~verbot** *nt* waiting restriction; 'H~verbot' 'no waiting'

Haltung *f* -, -en (*Körper-*) posture; (*Verhalten*) manner; (*Einstellung*) attitude; (*Fassung*) composure; (*Halten*) keeping

Hammel *m* -s,- ram; (*Culin*) mutton. **H~fleisch** *nt* mutton

Hammer *m* -s,¨ hammer

hämmern *vt/i* (*haben*) hammer

Hamster *m* -s,- hamster. **h~n** *vt/i* 🔲 hoard

Hand *f* -,¨e hand; **jdm die H~ geben** shake hands with s.o.; **rechter/linker H~** on the right/left; **zweiter H~** second-hand; **unter der H~** unofficially; (*geheim*) secretly; **H~ und Fuß haben** (*fig*) be sound. **H~arbeit** *f* manual work; (*handwerklich*) handicraft; (*Nadelarbeit*) needlework; (*Gegenstand*) handmade article. **H~ball** *m* [German] handball. **H~bewegung** *f* gesture. **H~bremse** *f* handbrake. **H~buch** *nt* handbook, manual

Händedruck *m* handshake

Handel *m* -s trade, commerce; (*Unternehmen*) business; (*Geschäft*) deal; **H~ treiben** trade. **h~n** *vi* (*haben*) act; (*Handel treiben*) trade (*mit in*); **von etw** *od* **über etw** (*acc*) **h~n** deal with sth; **sich h~n um** be about, concern. **H~smarine** *f* merchant navy. **H~sschiff** *nt* merchant vessel. **H~sschule** *f* commercial college. **H~sware** *f* merchandise

Hand|feger *m* -s,- brush. **H~fläche** *f* palm. **H~gelenk** *nt* wrist. **H~gemenge** *nt* -s,- scuffle. **H~gepäck** *nt* hand-luggage. **h~geschrieben** *a* hand-written.

h~greiflich *a* tangible; **h~greiflich werden** become violent. **H~griff** *m* handle

handhaben *vt insep* (*reg*) handle

Handikap /'hɛndikɛp/ *nt* -s, -s handicap

Handkuss *m* kiss on the hand

Händler *m* -s,- dealer, trader

handlich *a* handy

Handlung *f* -, -en act; (*Handeln*) action; (*Roman-*) plot; (*Geschäft*) shop. **H~sweise** *f* conduct

Hand|schellen *fpl* handcuffs. **H~schlag** *m* handshake. **H~schrift** *f* handwriting; (*Text*) manuscript. **H~schuh** *m* glove. **H~stand** *m* handstand. **H~tasche** *f* handbag. **H~tuch** *nt* towel

Handwerk *nt* craft, trade. **H~er** *m* -s,- craftsman; (*Arbeiter*) workman

Handy /'hɛndi/ *nt* -s, -s mobile phone

Hanf *m* -[e]s hemp

Hang *m* -[e]s,ᵉe slope; (*fig*) inclination

Hänge|brücke *f* suspension bridge. **H~matte** *f* hammock

hängen¹ *vt* (*reg*) hang

hängen²† *vi* (*haben*) hang; **h~ an** (+ *dat*) (*fig*) be attached to; **h~ lassen** leave

Hannover *nt* -s Hanover

hänseln *vt* tease

hantieren *vi* (*haben*) busy oneself

Happen *m* -s,- mouthful; **einen H~ essen** have a bite to eat

Harfe *f* -, -n harp

Harke *f* -, -n rake. **h~n** *vt/i* (*haben*) rake

harmlos *a* harmless; (*arglos*) innocent

Harmonie *f* -, -n harmony

Harmonika *f* -, -s accordion; (*Mund-*) mouth-organ

harmonisch *a* harmonious

Harn *m* -[e]s urine. **H~blase** *f* bladder

Harpune *f* -, -n harpoon

hart *a* hard; (*heftig*) violent; (*streng*) harsh

Härte *f* -, -n hardness; (*Strenge*) harshness; (*Not*) hardship. **h~n** *vt* harden

Hart|faserplatte *f* hardboard. **h~näckig** *a* stubborn; (*ausdauernd*) persistent. **H~näckigkeit** *f* - stubbornness; persistence

Harz *nt* -es, -e resin

Haschee *nt* -s, -s (*Culin*) hash

Haschisch *nt* & *m* -[s] hashish

Hase *m* -n, -n hare

Hasel *f* -, -n hazel. **H~maus** *f* dormouse. **H~nuss** *f* hazel-nut

Hass *m* -es hatred

hassen *vt* hate

hässlich *a* ugly; (*unfreundlich*) nasty. **H~keit** *f* - ugliness; nastiness

Hast *f* - haste. **h~ig** *a* hasty, hurried

hast, hat, hatte, hätte *s.* haben

Haube *f* -, -n cap; (*Trocken-*) drier; (*Kühler-*) bonnet

Hauch *m* -[e]s breath; (*Luft-*) breeze; (*Duft*) whiff; (*Spur*) tinge. **h~dünn** *a* very thin

Haue *f* -, -n pick; (Ⓐ *Prügel*) beating. **h~n**† *vt* beat; (*hämmern*) knock; (*meißeln*) hew; **sich h~n** fight; **übers Ohr h~n** Ⓐ cheat ● *vi* (*haben*) bang (**auf** + *acc* on); **jdm ins Gesicht h~n** hit s.o. in the face

Haufen *m* -s,- heap, pile; (*Leute*) crowd

häufen *vt* heap *or* pile [up]; **sich h~** pile up; (*zunehmen*) increase

häufig *a* frequent

Haupt *nt* -[e]s, Häupter head. **H~bahnhof** *m* main station. **H~fach** *nt* main subject. **H~gericht** *nt* main course

Häuptling *m* -s, -e chief

Haupt|mahlzeit *f* main meal **H~mann** *m* (*pl* -leute) captain. **H~post** *f* main post office. **H~quartier** *nt* headquarters *pl.* **H~rolle** *f* lead; (*fig*) leading role. **H~sache** *f* main thing; **in der**

H~sache in the main. **h~sächlich** *a* main. **H~satz** *m* main clause. **H~stadt** *f* capital. **H~verkehrsstraße** *f* main road. **H~verkehrszeit** *f* rush-hour. **H~wort** *nt* (*pl* -wörter) noun

Haus *nt* -es, Häuser house; (*Gebäude*) building; (*Schnecken-*) shell; **zu H~e** at home; **nach H~e** home. **H~arbeit** *f* housework; (*Sch*) homework. **H~arzt** *m* family doctor. **H~aufgaben** *fpl* homework *sg.* **H~besetzer** *m* -s,- squatter **hausen** *vi* (*haben*) live; (*wüten*) wreak havoc

Haus|frau *f* housewife. **h~gemacht** *a* home-made. **H~halt** *m* -[e]s, -e household; (*Pol*) budget. **h~halten†** *vi sep* (*haben*) **h~halten mit** manage carefully; conserve <*Kraft*>. **H~hälterin** *f* -, -nen housekeeper. **H~haltsgeld** *nt* housekeeping [money]. **H~haltsplan** *m* budget. **H~herr** *m* head of the household; (*Gastgeber*) host

Hausierer *m* -s,- hawker

Haus|lehrer *m* [private] tutor. **H~in** *f* governess

häuslich *a* domestic, <*Person*> domesticated

Haus|meister *m* caretaker. **H~ordnung** *f* house rules *pl.* **H~putz** *m* cleaning. **H~rat** *m* -[e]s household effects *pl.* **H~schlüssel** *m* front-door key. **H~schuh** *m* slipper. **H~suchung** *f* [police] search. **H~suchungsbefehl** *m* search-warrant. **H~tier** *nt* domestic animal; (*Hund, Katze*) pet. **H~tür** *f* front door. **H~wirt** *m* landlord. **H~wirtin** *f* landlady

Haut *f* -,Häute skin; (*Tier-*) hide. **H~arzt** *m* dermatologist

häuten *vt* skin; **sich h~** moult

haut|eng *a* skin-tight. **H~farbe** *f* colour; (*Teint*) complexion

Hebamme *f* -, -n midwife

Hebel *m* -s,- lever

heben† *vt* lift; (*hoch-, steigern*) raise; **sich h~** rise; <*Nebel:*> lift; (*sich verbessern*) improve

hebräisch *a* Hebrew

hecheln *vi* (*haben*) pant

Hecht *m* -[e]s, -e pike

Heck *nt* -s, -s (*Naut*) stern; (*Aviat*) tail; (*Auto*) rear

Hecke *f* -, -n hedge

Heck|fenster *nt* rear window. **H~tür** *f* hatchback

Heer *nt* -[e]s, -e army

Hefe *f* - yeast

Heft *nt* -[e]s, -e booklet; (*Sch*) exercise book; (*Zeitschrift*) issue. **h~en** *vt* (*nähen*) tack; (*stecken*) pin/ (*klammern*) clip/(*mit Heftmaschine*) staple (**an** + *acc* to). **H~er** *m* -s,- file

heftig *a* fierce, violent; <*Regen*> heavy; <*Schmerz, Gefühl*> intense

Heft|klammer *f* staple; (*Büro-*) paper-clip. **H~maschine** *f* stapler. **H~zwecke** *f* -, -n drawing-pin

Heide¹ *m* -n, -n heathen

Heide² *f* -, -n heath; (*Bot*) heather. **H~kraut** *nt* heather

Heidelbeere *f* bilberry

Heidin *f* -, -nen heathen

heikel *a* difficult, tricky

heil *a* undamaged, intact; <*Person*> unhurt; **mit h~er Haut** 🄸 unscathed

Heil *nt* -s salvation

Heiland *m* -s (*Relig*) Saviour

Heil|anstalt *f* sanatorium; (*Nerven-*) mental hospital. **H~bad** *nt* spa. **h~bar** *a* curable

Heilbutt *m* -[e]s, -e halibut

heilen *vt* cure; heal <*Wunde*> ● *vi* (*sein*) heal

Heilgymnastik *f* physiotherapy

heilig *a* holy; (*geweiht*) sacred; **der H~e Abend** Christmas Eve; **die h~e Anna** Saint Anne; **h~ sprechen** canonize. **H~abend** *m* Christmas Eve. **H~e(r)** *m/f* saint. **H~enschein** *m* halo. **H~keit** *f* - sanctity, holiness. **H~tum** *nt* -s,-̈er shrine

heil|kräftig *a* medicinal. **H~kräuter** *ntpl* medicinal herbs. **H~mittel** *nt* remedy. **H~praktiker** *m* -s,- practitioner of alternative medicine. **H~sarmee** *f* Salvation Army. **H~ung** *f* - cure

Heim nt -[e]s, -e home; (Studenten-)
hostel. **h~** adv home

Heimat f -, -en home; (Land) native
land. **H~stadt** f home town

heim|begleiten vt sep see home.
H~computer m home computer.
h~fahren† v sep ● vi (sein) go/
drive home ● vt take/drive home.
H~fahrt f way home. **h~gehen**†
vi sep (sein) go home

heimisch a native, indigenous;
(Pol) domestic

Heim|kehr f - return [home].
h~kehren vi sep (sein) return
home. **h~kommen**† vi sep (sein)
come home

heimlich a secret; etw h~ tun do
sth secretly. **H~keit** f -, -en secrecy;
H~keiten secrets

Heim|reise f journey home.
H~spiel nt home game.
h~suchen vt sep afflict.
h~tückisch a treacherous;
<Krankheit> insidious. **h~wärts**
adv home. **H~weg** m way home.
H~weh nt -s homesickness;
H~weh haben be homesick.
H~werker m -s,- [home]
handyman. **h~zahlen** vt sep jdm
etw h~zahlen (fig) pay s.o. back for
sth

Heirat f -, -en marriage. **h~en** vt/i
(haben) marry. **H~santrag** m
proposal; jdm einen H~santrag
machen propose to s.o.

heiser a hoarse. **H~keit** f -
hoarseness

heiß a hot; (hitzig) heated;
(leidenschaftlich) fervent

heißen† vi (haben) be called;
(bedeuten) mean; ich heiße ... my
name is ...; wie h~Sie? what is your
name? wie heißt ... auf Englisch?
what's the English for ...? ● vt call;
jdn etw tun h~ tell s.o. to do sth

heiter a cheerful; <Wetter> bright;
(amüsant) amusing; aus h~em
Himmel (fig) out of the blue

Heiz|anlage f heating; (Auto)
heater. **H~decke** f electric blanket.

h~en vt heat; light <Ofen> ● vi
(haben) put the heating on; <Ofen:>
give out heat. **H~gerät** nt heater.
H~kessel m boiler. **H~körper** m
radiator. **H~lüfter** m -s,- fan
heater. **H~material** nt fuel.
H~ung f -, -en heating; (Heizkörper)
radiator

Hektar nt & m -s,- hectare

Held m -en, -en hero. **h~enhaft** a
heroic. **H~entum** nt -s heroism.
H~in f -, -nen heroine

helf|en† vi (haben) help (jdm s.o.);
(nützen) be effective; sich (dat) nicht
zu h~en wissen not know what to
do; es hilft nichts it's no use.
H~er(in) m -s,- (f -, -nen) helper,
assistant

hell a light; (Licht ausstrahlend, klug)
bright; <Stimme> clear; (🔲 völlig)
utter; h~es Bier ≈ lager ● adv
brightly

Hell|igkeit f - brightness.
H~seher(in) m -s,- (f -, -nen)
clairvoyant

Helm m -[e]s, -e helmet

Hemd nt -[e]s, -en vest; (Ober-) shirt

Hemisphäre f -, -n hemisphere

hemm|en vt check; (verzögern)
impede; (fig) inhibit. **H~ung** f -, -en
(fig) inhibition; (Skrupel) scruple;
H~ungen haben be inhibited.
h~ungslos a unrestrained

Hendl nt -s, -[n] (Aust) chicken

Hengst m -[e]s, -e stallion

Henkel m -s,- handle

Henne f -, -n hen

her adv here; (zeitlich) ago; her mit ...!
give me ...! von Norden/weit her
from the north/far away; vom Thema
her as far as the subject is
concerned; her sein come (von from);
es ist schon lange her it was a long
time ago

herab adv down [here]; von oben h~
from above; (fig) condescending

herablassen† vt sep let down; sich
h~ condescend (zu to)

herab|sehen† vi sep (haben) look
down (auf + acc on). **h~setzen** vt
sep reduce, cut; (fig) belittle

Heraldik f - heraldry

heran adv near; [bis] h~ an (+ acc) up to. **h~kommen**† vi sep (sein) approach; h~kommen an (+ acc) come up to; (erreichen) get at; (fig) measure up to. **h~machen (sich)** vr sep sich h~machen an (+ acc) approach; get down to <Arbeit>. **h~wachsen**† vi sep (sein) grow up. **h~ziehen** v sep ● vt pull up (an + acc to); (züchten) raise; (h~bilden) train; (hinzuziehen) call in ● vi (sein) approach

herauf adv up [here]; die Treppe h~ up the stairs. **h~setzen** vt sep raise, increase

heraus adv out (aus of); h~ damit od mit der Sprache! out with it! **h~bekommen**† vt sep get out; (ausfindig machen) find out; (lösen) solve; Geld h~bekommen get change. **h~finden**† v sep ● vt find out ● vi (haben) find one's way out. **h~fordern** vt sep provoke; challenge <Person>. **H~forderung** f provocation; challenge. **H~gabe** f handing over; (Admin) issue; (Veröffentlichung) publication. **h~geben**† vt sep hand over; (Admin) issue; (veröffentlichen) publish; edit <Zeitschrift>; jdm Geld h~geben give s.o. change ● vi (haben) give change (auf + acc for). **H~geber** m -s,- publisher; editor. **h~halten**† (sich) vr sep (fig) keep out (aus of). **h~kommen**† vi sep (sein) come out; (aus Schwierigkeit, Takt) get out; auf eins od dasselbe h~kommen 🛈 come to the same thing. **h~lassen**† vt sep let out. **h~nehmen**† vt sep take out; sich zu viel h~nehmen (fig) take liberties. **h~reden (sich)** vr sep make excuses. **h~rücken** v sep ● vt move out; (hergeben) hand over ● vi (sein) h~rücken mit hand over; (fig: sagen) come out with. **h~schlagen**† vt sep knock out; (fig) gain. **h~stellen** vt sep put out; sich h~stellen turn out (als to be; dass that). **h~ziehen**† vt sep pull out

herb a sharp; <Wein> dry; (fig) harsh

herbei adv here. **h~führen** vt sep (fig) bring about. **h~schaffen** vt sep get. **h~sehnen** vt sep long for

Herberg|e f -, -n [youth] hostel; (Unterkunft) lodging. **H~svater** m warden

herbestellen vt sep summon

herbitten† vt sep ask to come

herbringen† vt sep bring [here]

Herbst m -[e]s, -e autumn. **h~lich** a autumnal

Herd m -[e]s, -e stove, cooker

Herde f -, -n herd; (Schaf-) flock

herein adv in [here]; h~! come in! **h~bitten**† vt sep ask in. **h~fallen**† vi sep (sein) 🛈 be taken in (auf + acc by). **h~kommen**† vi sep (sein) come in. **h~lassen**† vt sep let in. **h~legen** vt sep 🛈 take for a ride

Herfahrt f journey/drive here

herfallen† vi sep (sein) ~ über (+ acc) attack; fall upon <Essen>

hergeben† vt sep hand over; (fig) give up

hergehen† vi sep (sein) h~ vor (+ dat) walk along in front of; es ging lustig her 🛈 there was a lot of merriment

herholen vt sep fetch; weit hergeholt (fig) far-fetched

Hering m -s, -e herring; (Zeltpflock) tent-peg

her|kommen† vi sep (sein) come here; wo kommt das her? where does it come from? **h~kömmlich** a traditional. **H~kunft** f - origin

herleiten vt sep derive

hermachen vt sep viel/wenig h~ be impressive/unimpressive; (wichtig nehmen) make a lot of/little fuss (von of); sich h~ über (+ acc) fall upon; tackle <Arbeit>

Hermelin[1] nt -s, -e (Zool) stoat

Hermelin[2] m -s, -e (Pelz) ermine

Hernie /'hɛrniə/ f -, -n hernia

Heroin nt -s heroin

heroisch a heroic

Herr m -n, -en gentleman; (Gebieter) master (über + acc of); [Gott,] der H~ the Lord [God]; H~ Meier Mr Meier;

Sehr geehrte H~en Dear Sirs.
H~enhaus nt manor [house].
h~enlos a ownerless; <*Tier*> stray

Herrgott m der H~ the Lord

herrichten vt sep prepare; **wieder h~** renovate

Herrin f -, -nen mistress

herrlich a marvellous; (*großartig*) magnificent

Herrschaft f -, -en rule; (*Macht*) power; (*Kontrolle*) control; **meine H~en!** ladies and gentlemen!

herrsch|en vi (*haben*) rule; (*verbreitet sein*) prevail; **es h~te Stille** there was silence. **H~er(in)** m -s,- (f -, -nen) ruler

herrühren vi sep (*haben*) stem (**von** from)

herstammen vi sep (*haben*) come (**aus/von** from)

herstell|en vt sep establish; (*Comm*) manufacture, make. **H~er** m -s,- manufacturer, maker. **H~ung** f - establishment; manufacture

herüber adv over [here]

herum adv **im Kreis h~** [round] in a circle; **falsch h~** the wrong way round; **um ... h~** round ...; (*ungefähr*) [round] about ...; **h~ sein** be over. **h~drehen** vt sep turn round/(*wenden*) over; turn <*Schlüssel*>. **h~gehen**† vi sep (*sein*) walk around; <*Zeit*:> pass; **h~gehen um** go round. **h~kommen**† vi sep (*sein*) get about; **h~kommen um** get round; come round <*Ecke*>; **um etw [nicht] h~kommen** (*fig*) [not] get out of sth. **h~sitzen**† vi sep (*haben*) sit around; **h~sitzen um** sit round. **h~sprechen**† (**sich**) vr sep <*Gerücht*:> get about. **h~treiben**† (**sich**) vr sep hang around. **h~ziehen**† vi sep (*sein*) move around; (*ziellos*) wander about

herunter adv down [here]; **die Treppe h~** down the stairs. **h~fallen**† vi fall off. **h~gekommen** a (*fig*) run-down; <*Gebäude*> dilapidated; <*Person*>

down-at-heel. **h~kommen**† vi sep (*sein*) come down; (*fig*) go to rack and ruin; <*Firma, Person*:> go downhill; (*gesundheitlich*) get run down. **h~lassen**† vt sep let down, lower. **h~machen** vt sep 🗉 reprimand; (*herabsetzen*) run down. **h~spielen** vt sep (*fig*) play down

hervor adv out (**aus** of). **h~bringen**† vt sep produce; utter <*Wort*>. **h~gehen**† vi sep (*sein*) come/(*sich ergeben*) emerge/(*folgen*) follow (**aus** from). **h~heben**† vt sep (*fig*) stress, emphasize. **h~ragen** vi sep (*haben*) jut out; (*fig*) stand out. **h~ragend** a (*fig*) outstanding. **h~rufen**† vt sep (*fig*) cause. **h~stehen**† vi sep (*haben*) protrude. **h~treten**† vi sep (*sein*) protrude, bulge; (*fig*) stand out. **h~tun**† (**sich**) vr sep (*fig*) distinguish oneself; (*angeben*) show off

Herweg m way here

Herz nt -ens, -en heart; (*Kartenspiel*) hearts pl; **sich** (*dat*) **ein H~ fassen** pluck up courage. **H~anfall** m heart attack

herzhaft a hearty; (*würzig*) savoury

herziehen† v sep ● vt **hinter sich** (*dat*) **h~** pull along [behind one] ● vi (*sein*) **hinter jdm h~** follow along behind s.o.; **über jdn h~** 🗉 run s.o. down

herz|ig a sweet, adorable. **H~infarkt** m heart attack. **H~klopfen** nt -s palpitations pl

herzlich a cordial; (*warm*) warm; (*aufrichtig*) sincere; **h~en Dank!** many thanks! **h~e Grüße** kind regards

herzlos a heartless

Herzog m -s,-̈e duke. **H~in** f -, -nen duchess. **H~tum** nt -s,-̈er duchy

Herzschlag m heartbeat; (*Med*) heart failure

Hessen nt -s Hesse

heterosexuell a heterosexual

Hetze f - rush; (*Kampagne*) virulent campaign (**gegen** against). **h~n** vt chase; **sich h~n** hurry

Heu nt -s hay

Heuchelei f - hypocrisy

heuch|eln vt feign ● vi (haben) pretend. **H∼ler(in)** m -s,- (f -, -nen) hypocrite. **h∼lerisch** a hypocritical

heuer adv (Aust) this year

heulen vi (haben) howl; (🛈 weinen) cry

Heu|schnupfen m hay fever. **H∼schober** m -s,- haystack. **H∼schrecke** f -, -n grasshopper

heut|e adv today; (heutzutage) nowadays; h∼e früh od Morgen this morning; von h∼e auf morgen from one day to the next. **h∼ig** a today's ...; (gegenwärtig) present; der h∼ige Tag today. **h∼zutage** adv nowadays

Hexe f -, -n witch. **h∼n** vi (haben) work magic. **H∼nschuss** m lumbago

Hieb m -[e]s, -e blow; (Peitschen-) lash; H∼e hiding sg

hier adv here; h∼ sein/bleiben/ lassen/behalten be/stay/leave/keep here; h∼ und da here and there; (zeitlich) now and again

hier|auf adv on this/these; (antworten) to this; (zeitlich) after this. **h∼aus** adv out of or from this/these. **h∼durch** adv through this/these; (Ursache) as a result of this. **h∼her** adv here. **h∼hin** adv here. **h∼in** adv in this/these. **h∼mit** adv with this/these; (Comm) herewith; (Admin) hereby. **h∼nach** adv after this/these; (demgemäß) according to this/these. **h∼über** adv over/(höher) above this/these; <sprechen, streiten> about this/these. **h∼von** adv from this/these; (h∼über) about this/these; (Menge) of this/these. **h∼zu** adv to this/ these; (h∼für) for this/these. **h∼zulande** adv here

hiesig a local. **H∼e(r)** m/f local

Hilf|e f -, -n help, aid; um H∼e rufen call for help. **h∼los** a helpless. **H∼losigkeit** f - helplessness. **h∼reich** a helpful

Hilfs|arbeiter m unskilled labourer. **h∼bedürftig** a needy; h∼bedürftig sein be in need of help. **h∼bereit** a helpful. **H∼kraft** f

helper. **H∼mittel** nt aid. **H∼verb** nt auxiliary verb

Himbeere f raspberry

Himmel m -s,- sky; (Relig & fig) heaven; (Bett-) canopy; unter freiem H∼ in the open air. **H∼bett** nt four-poster [bed]. **H∼fahrt** f Ascension

himmlisch a heavenly

hin adv there; hin und her to and fro; hin und zurück there and back; (Rail) return; hin und wieder now and again; an (+ dat) ... hin along; auf (+ acc) ... hin in reply to <Brief, Anzeige>; on <jds Rat>; zu od nach ... hin towards; hin sein 🛈 be gone; es ist noch lange hin it's a long time yet

hinauf adv up [there]. **h∼gehen†** vi sep (sein) go up. **h∼setzen** vt sep raise

hinaus adv out [there]; (nach draußen) outside; zur Tür h∼ out of the door; auf Jahre h∼ for years to come; über etw (acc) h∼ beyond sth; (Menge) [over and] above sth; über etw (acc) h∼ sein (fig) be past sth. **h∼gehen†** vi sep (sein) go out; <Zimmer:> face (nach Norden north); h∼gehen über (+ acc) go beyond, exceed. **h∼laufen†** vi sep (sein) run out; h∼laufen auf (+ acc) (fig) amount to. **h∼lehnen (sich)** vr sep lean out. **h∼schieben†** vt sep push out; (fig) put off. **h∼werfen†** vt sep throw out; (🛈 entlassen) fire. **h∼wollen†** vi sep (haben) want to go out; h∼wollen auf (+ acc) (fig) aim at. **h∼ziehen†** v sep ● vt pull out; (in die Länge ziehen) drag out; (verzögern) delay; sich h∼ziehen drag on; be delayed ● vi (sein) move out. **h∼zögern** vt delay; sich h∼zögern be delayed

Hinblick m im H∼ auf (+ acc) in view of; (hinsichtlich) regarding

hinder|lich a awkward; jdm h∼lich sein hamper s.o. **h∼n** vt hamper; (verhindern) prevent. **H∼nis** nt -ses, -se obstacle. **H∼nisrennen** nt steeplechase

Hindu *m* -s, -s Hindu. **H~ismus** *m*
- Hinduism

hindurch *adv* through it/them

hinein *adv* in [there]; (*nach drinnen*)
inside; **h~ in** (+ *acc*) into.
h~fallen† *vi sep* (*sein*) fall in.
h~gehen† *vi sep* (*sein*) go in;
h~gehen in (+ *acc*) go into.
h~reden *vi sep* (*haben*) **jdm
h~reden** interrupt s.o.; (*sich
einmischen*) interfere in s.o.'s affairs.
h~versetzen (sich) *vr sep* **sich in
jds Lage h~versetzen** put oneself in
s.o.'s position. **h~ziehen**† *vt sep*
pull in; **h~ziehen in** (+ *acc*) pull into;
in etw (*acc*) **h~gezogen werden** (*fig*)
become involved in sth

hin|fahren† *v sep* ● *vi* (*sein*) go/
drive there ● *vt* take/drive there.
H~fahrt *f* journey/drive there;
(*Rail*) outward journey. **h~fallen**†
vi sep (*sein*) fall. **h~fliegen**† *v sep*
● *vi* (*sein*) fly there; [Ⓣ] fall ● *vt* fly
there. **H~flug** *m* flight there;
(*Admin*) outward flight

Hingeb|ung *f* - devotion.
h~ungsvoll *a* devoted

hingehen† *vi sep* (*sein*) go/(*zu Fuß*)
walk there; (*vergehen*) pass; **h~ zu**
go up to; **wo gehst du hin?** where are
you going?

hingerissen *a* rapt; **h~ sein** be
carried away (**von** by)

hinhalten† *vt sep* hold out; (*warten
lassen*) keep waiting

hinken *vi* (*haben/sein*) limp

hin|knien (sich) *vr sep* kneel down.
h~kommen† *vi sep* (*sein*) get there;
(*h~gehören*) belong, go; ([Ⓣ]
auskommen) manage (**mit** with); ([Ⓣ]
stimmen) be right. **h~laufen**† *vi sep*
(*sein*) run/(*gehen*) walk there.
h~legen *vt sep* lay *or* put down;
sich h~legen lie down.
h~nehmen† *vt sep* (*fig*) accept

hinreichen *v sep* ● *vt* hand (*dat* to)
● *vi* (*haben*) extend (**bis** to);
(*ausreichen*) be adequate. **h~d** *a*
adequate

Hinreise *f* journey there; (*Rail*)
outward journey

hinreißen† *vt sep* (*fig*) carry away;
sich h~ lassen get carried away.
h~d *a* ravishing

hinricht|en *vt sep* execute. **H~ung**
f execution

hinschreiben† *vt sep* write there;
(*aufschreiben*) write down

hinsehen† *vi sep* (*haben*) look

hinsetzen *vt sep* put down; **sich h~**
sit down

Hinsicht *f* - **in dieser H~** in this
respect; **in finanzieller H~**
financially. **h~lich** *prep* (+ *gen*)
regarding

hinstellen *vt sep* put *or* set down;
park <*Auto*>

hinstrecken *vt sep* hold out; **sich
h~** extend

hinten *adv* at the back; **dort h~**
back there; **nach/von h~** to the
back/from behind. **h~herum** *adv*
round the back; [Ⓣ] by devious means

hinter *prep* (+ *dat*/*acc*) behind;
(*nach*) after; **h~ jdm/etw herlaufen**
run after s.o./sth; **h~ etw** (*dat*)
stecken (*fig*) be behind sth; **h~ etw**
(*acc*) **kommen** (*fig*) get to the bottom
of sth; **etw h~ sich** (*acc*) **bringen** get
sth over [and done] with

Hinterbliebene *pl* (*Admin*)
surviving dependants; **die H~n** the
bereaved family *sg*

hintere(r,s) *a* back, rear; **h~s
Ende** far end

hintereinander *adv* one behind/
(*zeitlich*) after the other; **dreimal h~**
three times in succession

Hintergedanke *m* ulterior motive

hintergehen† *vt* deceive

Hinter|grund *m* background.
H~halt *m* -[e]s, -e ambush.
h~hältig *a* underhand

hinterher *adv* behind, after;
(*zeitlich*) afterwards

Hinter|hof *m* back yard. **H~kopf**
m back of the head

hinterlassen† *vt* leave [behind];
(*Jur*) leave, bequeath (*dat* to).
H~schaft *f* -, -en (*Jur*) estate

hinterlegen *vt* deposit

Hinter|leib *m* (*Zool*) abdomen.
H~list *f* deceit. **h~listig** *a*
deceitful. **H~n** *m* -s,- ⚠ bottom,
backside. **H~rad** *nt* rear *or* back
wheel. **h~rücks** *adv* from behind.
h~ste(r,s) *a* last; **h~ste Reihe**
back row. **H~teil** *nt* ⚠ behind.
H~treppe *f* back stairs *pl*

hinterziehen† *vt* (*Admin*) evade

hinüber *adv* over *or* across [*there*];
h~ sein (⚠ *unbrauchbar, tot*) have
had it. **h~gehen†** *vi sep* (*sein*) go
over *or* across; **h~gehen über** (+ *acc*)
cross

hinunter *adv* down [*there*].
h~gehen† *vi sep* (*sein*) go down.
h~schlucken *vt sep* swallow

Hinweg *m* way there

hinweg *adv* away, off; **h~ über** (+
acc) over; **über eine Zeit h~** over a
period. **h~kommen†** *vt sep* (*sein*)
h~kommen über (+ *acc*) (*fig*) get
over. **h~sehen†** *vi sep* (*haben*)
h~sehen über (+ *acc*) see over; (*fig*)
overlook. **h~setzen** (sich) *vr sep*
sich **h~setzen über** (+ *acc*) ignore

Hinweis *m* -es, -e reference;
(*Andeutung*) hint; (*Anzeichen*)
indication; **unter H~ auf** (+ *acc*) with
reference to. **h~en†** *v sep* ● *vi*
(*haben*) point (**auf** + *acc* to) ● *vt* **jdn
auf etw** (*acc*) **h~en** point sth out to
s.o.

hinwieder *adv* on the other hand

hin|zeigen *vi sep* (*haben*) point (**auf**
+ *acc* to). **h~ziehen†** *vt sep* pull;
(*fig: in die Länge ziehen*) drag out;
(*verzögern*) delay; **sich h~ziehen**
drag on

hinzu *adv* in addition. **h~fügen** *vt
sep* add. **h~kommen†** *vt sep* (*sein*)
be added; (*ankommen*) arrive [on the
scene]; join (**zu jdm** s.o.).
h~ziehen† *vt sep* call in

Hiobsbotschaft *f* bad news *sg*

Hirn *nt* -s brain; (*Culin*) brains *pl*.
H~hautentzündung *f* meningitis

Hirsch *m* -[e]s, -e deer; (*männlich*)
stag; (*Culin*) venison

Hirse *f* - millet

Hirt *m* -en, -en, **Hirte** *m* -n, -n
shepherd

hissen *vt* hoist

Histor|iker *m* -s,- historian.
h~isch *a* historical; (*bedeutend*)
historic

Hitz|e *f* - heat. **h~ig** *a* (*fig*) heated;
<*Person*> hot-headed; (*jähzornig*)
hot-tempered. **H~schlag** *m* heat-
stroke

H-Milch /'ha:-/ *f* long-life milk

Hobby *nt* -s, -s hobby

Hobel *m* -s,- (*Techn*) plane; (*Culin*)
slicer. **h~n** *vt/i* (*haben*) plane.
H~späne *mpl* shavings

hoch *a* (*attrib* **hohe(r,s)**) high;
<*Baum, Mast*> tall; <*Offizier*> high-
ranking; <*Alter*> great; <*Summe*>
large; <*Strafe*> heavy; **hohe Schuhe**
ankle boots ● *adv* high; (*sehr*)
highly; **h~ gewachsen** tall; **h~
begabt** highly gifted; **h~ gestellte
Persönlichkeit** important person; **die
Treppe h~** up the stairs; **sechs Mann
h~** six of us/them. **H~** *nt* -s, -s
cheer; (*Meteorol*) high

Hoch|achtung *f* high esteem.
H~achtungsvoll *adv* Yours
faithfully. **H~betrieb** *m* great
activity; **in den Geschäften herrscht
H~betrieb** the shops are terribly
busy. **H~deutsch** *nt* High German.
H~druck *m* high pressure.
H~ebene *f* plateau. **h~fahren†** *vi
sep* (*sein*) go up; (*auffahren*) start up;
(*aufbrausen*) flare up. **h~gehen†** *vi
sep* (*sein*) go up; (*explodieren*) blow
up; (*aufbrausen*) flare up.
h~gestellt *attrib a* <*Zahl*>
superior; (*fig*) *****h~ gestellt, s. hoch.
H~glanz *m* high gloss. **h~gradig**
a extreme. **h~hackig** *a* high-
heeled. **h~halten†** *vt sep* hold up;
(*fig*) uphold. **H~haus** *nt* high-rise
building. **h~heben†** *vt sep* lift up;
raise <*Hand*>. **h~kant** *adv* on end.
h~kommen† *vi sep* (*sein*) come up;
(*aufstehen*) get up; (*fig*) get on [in the
world]. **H~konjunktur** *f* boom.
h~krempeln *vt sep* roll up.
h~leben *vi sep* (*haben*) **h~leben
lassen** give three cheers for;
H~mut *m* pride, arrogance.

h∼näsig *a* 🄸 snooty. **H∼ofen** *m* blast-furnace. **h∼ragen** *vi sep* rise [up]; <*Turm:*> soar. **H∼ruf** *m* cheer. **H∼saison** *f* high season. **h∼schlagen**† *vt sep* turn up <*Kragen*>. **H∼schule** *f* university; (*Musik-, Kunst-*) academy. **H∼sommer** *m* midsummer. **H∼spannung** *f* high/(*fig*) great tension. **h∼spielen** *vt sep* (*fig*) magnify. **H∼sprung** *m* high jump

höchst *adv* extremely, most

Hochstapler *m* -s,- confidence trickster

höchst|e(r,s) *a* highest; <*Baum, Turm*> tallest; (*oberste, größte*) top; es ist h∼e Zeit it is high time. **h∼ens** *adv* at most; (*es sei denn*) except perhaps. **H∼geschwindigkeit** *f* top or maximum speed. **H∼maß** *nt* maximum. **h∼persönlich** *adv* in person. **H∼preis** *m* top price. **H∼temperatur** *f* maximum temperature

Hoch|verrat *m* high treason. **H∼wasser** *nt* high tide; (*Überschwemmung*) floods *pl*. **H∼würden** *m* -s Reverend; (*Anrede*) Father

Hochzeit *f* -, -en wedding. **H∼skleid** *nt* wedding dress. **H∼sreise** *f* honeymoon [trip]. **H∼stag** *m* wedding day/(*Jahrestag*) anniversary

Hocke *f* - in der H∼sitzen squat. **h∼n** *vi* (*haben*) squat ● *vr* sich h∼n squat down

Hocker *m* -s,- stool

Höcker *m* -s,- bump; (*Kamel-*) hump

Hockey /'hɔki/ *nt* -s hockey

Hode *f* -, -n, **Hoden** *m* -s,- testicle

Hof *m* -[e]s,⸚e [court]yard; (*Bauern-*) farm; (*Königs-*) court; (*Schul-*) playground; (*Astr*) halo

hoffen *vt/i* (*haben*) hope (auf + *acc* for). **h∼tlich** *adv* I hope, let us hope

Hoffnung *f* -, -en hope. **h∼slos** *a* hopeless. **h∼svoll** *a* hopeful

höflich *a* polite. **H∼keit** *f* -, -en politeness, courtesy

hohe(r,s) *a s.* hoch

Höhe *f* -, -n height; (*Aviat, Geog*) altitude; (*Niveau*) level; (*einer Summe*) size; (*An-*) hill

Hoheit *f* -, -en (*Staats-*) sovereignty; (*Titel*) Highness. **H∼sgebiet** *nt* [sovereign] territory. **H∼szeichen** *nt* national emblem

Höhe|nlinie *f* contour line. **H∼nsonne** *f* sun-lamp. **H∼punkt** *m* (*fig*) climax, peak. **h∼r** *a & adv* higher; h∼re Schule secondary school

hohl *a* hollow; (*leer*) empty

Höhle *f* -, -n cave; (*Tier-*) den; (*Hohlraum*) cavity; (*Augen-*) socket

Hohl|maß *nt* measure of capacity. **H∼raum** *m* cavity

Hohn *m* -s scorn, derision

höhnen *vt* deride

holen *vt* fetch, get; (*kaufen*) buy; (*nehmen*) take (aus from)

Holland *nt* -s Holland

Holländ|er *m* -s,- Dutchman; die H∼er the Dutch *pl*. **H∼erin** *f* -, -nen Dutchwoman. **h∼isch** *a* Dutch

Höll|e *f* - hell. **h∼isch** *a* infernal; (*schrecklich*) terrible

Holunder *m* -s (*Bot*) elder

Holz *nt* -es,⸚er wood; (*Nutz-*) timber. **H∼blasinstrument** *nt* woodwind instrument

hölzern *a* wooden

Holz|hammer *m* mallet. **h∼ig** *a* woody. **H∼kohle** *f* charcoal. **H∼schnitt** *m* woodcut. **H∼wolle** *f* wood shavings *pl*

Homöopathie *f* - homoeopathy

homosexuell *a* homosexual. **H∼e(r)** *m/f* homosexual

Honig *m* -s honey. **H∼wabe** *f* honeycomb

Hono|rar *nt* -s, -e fee. **h∼rieren** *vt* remunerate; (*fig*) reward

Hopfen *m* -s hops *pl*; (*Bot*) hop

hopsen *vi* (*sein*) jump

horchen *vi* (*haben*) listen (auf + *acc* to); (*heimlich*) eavesdrop

hören vt hear; (an-) listen to ● vi (haben) hear; (horchen) listen; (gehorchen) obey; h~ auf (+ acc) listen to

Hör|er m -s,- listener; (Teleph) receiver. **H~funk** m radio. **H~gerät** nt hearing-aid

Horizon|t m -[e]s horizon. **h~tal** a horizontal

Hormon nt -s, -e hormone

Horn nt -s,"er horn. **H~haut** f hard skin; (Augen-) cornea

Hornisse f -, -n hornet

Horoskop nt -[e]s, -e horoscope

Horrorfilm m horror film

Hör|saal m (Univ) lecture hall. **H~spiel** nt radio play

Hort m -[e]s, -e (Schatz) hoard; (fig) refuge. **h~en** vt hoard

Hortensie /-iə/ f -, -n hydrangea

Hose f -, -n, **Hosen** pl trousers pl. **H~nrock** m culottes pl. **H~nschlitz** m fly, flies pl. **H~nträger** mpl braces

Hostess f -, -tessen hostess; (Aviat) air hostess

Hostie /'hɔstiə/ f -, -n (Relig) host

Hotel nt -s, -s hotel

hübsch a pretty; (nett) nice

Hubschrauber m -s,- helicopter

Huf m -[e]s, -e hoof. **H~eisen** nt horseshoe

Hüft|e f -, -n hip. **H~gürtel** m -s,- girdle

Hügel m -s,- hill. **h~ig** a hilly

Huhn nt -s,"er chicken; (Henne) hen

Hühn|chen nt -s,- chicken. **H~erauge** nt corn **H~erstall** m henhouse

Hülle f -, -n cover; (Verpackung) wrapping; (Platten-) sleeve. **h~n** vt wrap

Hülse f -, -n (Bot) pod; (Etui) case. **H~nfrüchte** fpl pulses

human a humane. **H~ität** f - humanity

Hummel f -, -n bumble-bee

Hummer m -s,- lobster

Hum|or m -s humour; **H~or haben** have a sense of humour. **h~orvoll** a humorous

humpeln vi (sein/haben) hobble

Humpen m -s,- tankard

Hund m -[e]s, -e dog; (Jagd-) hound. **H~ehütte** f kennel

hundert inv a one/a hundred. **H~** nt -s, -e hundred; **H~e** od **h~e von** hundreds of. **H~jahrfeier** f centenary. **h~prozentig** a & adv one hundred per cent. **h~ste(r,s)** a hundredth. **H~stel** nt -s,- hundredth

Hündin f -, -nen bitch

Hüne m -n, -n giant

Hunger m -s hunger; **H~ haben** be hungry. **h~n** vi (haben) starve. **H~snot** f famine

hungrig a hungry

Hupe f -, -n (Auto) horn. **h~n** vi (haben) sound one's horn

hüpfen vi (sein) skip; <Frosch:> hop; <Grashüpfer:> jump

Hürde f -, -n (Sport & fig) hurdle; (Schaf-) pen, fold

Hure f -, -n whore

hurra int hurray

husten vi (haben) cough. **H~** m -s cough. **H~saft** m cough mixture

Hut¹ m -[e]s,"e hat; (Pilz-) cap

Hut² f - auf der **H~sein** be on one's guard (vor + dat against)

hüten vt watch over; tend <Tiere>; (aufpassen) look after; **das Bett h~ müssen** be confined to bed; **sich h~** be on one's guard (vor + dat against); **sich h~, etw zu tun** take care not to do sth

Hütte f -, -n hut; (Hunde-) kennel; (Techn) iron and steel works. **H~nkäse** m cottage cheese. **H~nkunde** f metallurgy

Hyäne f -, -n hyena

hydraulisch a hydraulic

Hygien|e /hy'giːnə/ f - hygiene. **h~isch** a hygienic

Hypno|se f - hypnosis. **h~tisch** a hypnotic. **H~tiseur** /-'zøːr/ m -s, -e hypnotist. **h~tisieren** vt hypnotize

Hypochonder /hypo'xɔndɐ/ m -s,- hypochondriac

Hypothek f -, -en mortgage

Hypothese f -, -n hypothesis

Hys|terie f - hysteria. **h~terisch** a hysterical

....

I i

ich pron I; **ich bins** it's me. **Ich** nt -[s], -[s] self; (Psych) ego

IC-Zug /i'tse:-/ m inter-city train

ideal a ideal. **I~** nt -s, -e ideal. **I~ismus** m - idealism. **I~ist(in)** m -en, -en (f -, -nen) idealist. **i~istisch** a idealistic

Idee f -, -n idea; **fixe I~** obsession

identifizieren vt identify

identisch a identical

Ideo|logie f -, -n ideology. **i~logisch** a ideological

idiomatisch a idiomatic

Idiot m -en, -en idiot. **i~isch** a idiotic

idyllisch /i'dylɪʃ/ a idyllic

Igel m -s,- hedgehog

ihm pron (dat of er, es) [to] him; (Ding, Tier) [to] it

ihn pron (acc of er) him; (Ding, Tier) it. **i~en** pron (dat of sie pl) [to] them. **I~en** pron (dat of Sie) [to] you

ihr pron (2nd pers pl) you ● (dat of sie sg) [to] her; (Ding, Tier) [to] it ● poss pron her; (Ding, Tier) its; (pl) their. **Ihr** poss pron your. **i~e(r,s)** poss pron hers; (pl) theirs. **I~e(r,s)** poss pron yours. **i~erseits** adv for her/(pl) their part. **I~erseits** adv on your part. **i~etwegen** adv for her/(Ding, Tier) its/(pl) their sake; (wegen) because of her/it/them, on her/its/their account. **I~etwegen** adv for your sake; (wegen) because of you, on your account. **i~ige** poss pron der/die/das i~ige hers; (pl) theirs. **I~ige** poss pron der/die/das I~ige yours. **i~s** poss pron hers; (pl) theirs. **I~s** poss pron yours

Ikone f -, -n icon

illegal a illegal

Illus|ion f -, -en illusion. **i~orisch** a illusory

Illustr|ation /-'tsio:n/ f -, -en illustration. **i~ieren** vt illustrate. **I~ierte** f -n, -[n] [illustrated] magazine

Iltis m -ses, -se polecat

im prep = in dem

Imbiss m snack. **I~stube** f snack-bar

Imit|ation /-'tsio:n/ f -, -en imitation. **i~ieren** vt imitate

Imker m -s,- bee-keeper

Immatrikul|ation /-'tsio:n/ f - (Univ) enrolment. **i~ieren** vt (Univ) enrol; **sich i~ieren** enrol

immer adv always; **für i~** for ever; (endgültig) for good; **i~ noch** still; **i~ mehr** more and more; **was i~** whatever. **i~hin** adv (wenigstens) at least; (trotzdem) all the same; (schließlich) after all. **i~zu** adv all the time

Immobilien /-iən/ pl real estate sg. **I~makler** m estate agent

immun a immune (gegen to)

Imperialismus m - imperialism

impf|en vt vaccinate, inoculate. **I~stoff** m vaccine. **I~ung** f -, -en vaccination, inoculation

imponieren vi (haben) impress (jdm s.o.)

Impor|t m -[e]s, -e import. **I~teur** /-'tø:ɐ/ m -s, -e importer. **i~tieren** vt import

impoten|t a (Med) impotent. **I~z** f - (Med) impotence

imprägnieren vt waterproof

Impressionismus m - impressionism

improvisieren vt/i (haben) improvise

imstande *pred a* able (**zu** to);
capable (**etw zu tun** of doing sth)

in *prep* (+ *dat*) in; (+ *acc*) into, in; (*bei
Bus, Zug*) on; **in der Schule** at school;
in die Schule to school ● *a* **in sein**
be in

Inbegriff *m* embodiment

indem *conj* (*während*) while;
(*dadurch*) by (+ -ing)

Inder(in) *m* -s,- (*f* -, -nen) Indian

indessen *conj* while ● *adv*
(*unterdessen*) meanwhile

Indian|er(in) *m* -s,- (*f* -, -nen)
(American) Indian. **i~isch** *a* Indian

Indien /'ɪndiən/ *nt* -s India

indirekt *a* indirect

indisch *a* Indian

indiskret *a* indiscreet

indiskutabel *a* out of the question

Individu|alist *m* -en, -en
individualist. **I~alität** *f* -
individuality. **i~ell** *a* individual

Indizienbeweis /ɪn'diːtsiən-/ *m*
circumstantial evidence

industr|ialisiert *a* industrialized.
I~ie *f* -, -n industry. **i~iell** *a*
industrial

ineinander *adv* in/into one another

Infanterie *f* - infantry

Infektion /-'tsioːn/ *f* -, -en
infection. **I~skrankheit** *f*
infectious disease

infizieren *vt* infect; **sich i~** become/
<*Person.*> be infected

Inflation /-'tsioːn/ *f* - inflation.
i~är *a* inflationary

infolge *prep* (+ *gen*) as a result of.
i~dessen *adv* consequently

Inform|atik *f* - information science.
I~ation /-'tsioːn/ *f* -, -en
information; **I~ationen** information
sg. **i~ieren** *vt* inform; **sich i~ieren**
find out (**über** + *acc* about)

infrage *adv* **etw i~** stellen question
sth; (*ungewiss machen*) make sth
doubtful; **nicht i~** kommen be out of
the question

infrarot *a* infra-red

Ingenieur /ɪnʒe'nioːɐ̯/ *m* -s, -e
engineer

Ingwer *m* -s ginger

Inhaber(in) *m* -s,- (*f* -, -nen) holder;
(*Besitzer*) proprietor; (*Scheck-*) bearer

inhaftieren *vt* take into custody

inhalieren *vt/i* (*haben*) inhale

Inhalt *m* -[e]s, -e contents *pl*;
(*Bedeutung, Gehalt*) content;
(*Geschichte*) story. **I~sangabe** *f*
summary. **I~sverzeichnis** *nt* list/
(*in Buch*) table of contents

Initiative /initsia'tiːvə/ *f* -, -n
initiative

inklusive *prep* (+ *gen*) including
● *adv* inclusive

inkonsequent *a* inconsistent

inkorrekt *a* incorrect

Inkubationszeit /-'tsioːns-/ *f*
(*Med*) incubation period

Inland *nt* -[e]s home country;
(*Binnenland*) interior.
I~sgespräch *nt* inland call

inmitten *prep* (+ *gen*) in the middle
of; (*unter*) amongst

innen *adv* inside; **nach i~** inwards.
I~architekt(in) *m(f)* interior
designer. **I~minister** *m* Minister of
the Interior; (*in UK*) Home
Secretary. **I~politik** *f* domestic
policy. **I~stadt** *f* town centre

inner|e(r,s) *a* inner; (*Med, Pol*)
internal. **I~e(s)** *nt* interior; (*Mitte*)
centre; (*fig: Seele*) inner being.
I~eien *fpl* (*Culin*) offal *sg*. **i~halb**
prep (+ *gen*) inside; (*zeitlich & fig*)
within; (*während*) during ● *adv*
i~halb von within. **i~lich** *a*
internal

innig *a* sincere

innovativ *a* innovative

Innung *f* -, -en guild

ins *prep* = **in das**

Insasse *m* -n, -n inmate; (*im Auto*)
occupant; (*Passagier*) passenger

insbesondere *adv* especially

Inschrift *f* inscription

Insekt *nt* -[e]s, -en insect.
I~envertilgungsmittel *nt*
insecticide

Insel *f* -, -n island

Inser|at *nt* -[e]s, -e [newspaper] advertisement. **i~ieren** *vt/i* (*haben*) advertise

insge|heim *adv* secretly. **i~samt** *adv* [all] in all

insofern, insoweit *adv* /-'zo:-/ in this respect; **i~ als** in as much as

Insp|ektion /ɪnspɛk'tsio:n/ *f* -, -en inspection. **I~ektor** *m* -en, -en /-'to:rən/ inspector

Install|ateur /ɪnstala'tø:ɐ/ *m* -s, -e fitter; (*Klempner*) plumber. **i~ieren** *vt* install

instand *adv* **i~** halten maintain; (*pflegen*) look after. **I~haltung** *f* - maintenance, upkeep

Instandsetzung *f* - repair

Instanz /-st-/ *f* -, -en authority

Instinkt /-st-/ *m* -[e]s, -e instinct. **i~iv** *a* instinctive

Institut /-st-/ *nt* -[e]s, -e institute

Instrument /-st-/ *nt* -[e]s, -e instrument. **I~almusik** *f* instrumental music

Insulin *nt* -s insulin

inszenier|en *vt* (*Theat*) produce. **I~ung** *f* -, -en production

Integr|ation /-'tsio:n/ *f* - integration. **i~ieren** *vt* integrate; sich **i~ieren** integrate

Intellekt *m* -[e]s intellect. **i~uell** *a* intellectual

intelligen|t *a* intelligent. **I~z** *f* - intelligence

Intendant *m* -en, -en director

Intensivstation *f* intensive-care unit

interaktiv *a* interactive

inter|essant *a* interesting. **I~esse** *nt* -s, -n interest; **I~esse** haben be interested (**an** + *dat* in). **I~essengruppe** *f* pressure group. **I~essent** *m* -en, -en interested party; (*Käufer*) prospective buyer. **i~essieren** *vt* interest; sich **i~essieren** be interested (**für** in)

Inter|nat *nt* -[e]s, -e boarding school. **i~national** *a* international. **I~nist** *m* -en, -en specialist in

internal diseases. **I~pretation** /-'tsio:n/ *f* -, -en interpretation. **i~pretieren** *vt* interpret. **I~vall** *nt* -s, -e interval. **I~vention** /-'tsio:n/ *f* -, -en intervention

Internet *nt* -s, -s Internet; im **I~** on the Internet

Interview /'ɪntɛvju:/ *nt* -s, -s interview. **i~en** /-'vju:ən/ *vt* interview

intim *a* intimate

intoleran|t *a* intolerant. **I~z** *f* - intolerance

intravenös *a* intravenous

Intrige *f* -, -n intrigue

introvertiert *a* introverted

Invalidenrente *f* disability pension

Invasion *f* -, -en invasion

Inven|tar *nt* -s, -e furnishings and fittings *pl*; (*Techn*) equipment; (*Bestand*) stock; (*Liste*) inventory. **I~tur** *f* -, -en stock-taking

investieren *vt* invest

inwie|fern *adv* in what way. **i~weit** *adv* how far, to what extent

Inzest *m* -[e]s incest

inzwischen *adv* in the meantime

Irak (der) -[s] Iraq. **i~isch** *a* Iraqi

Iran (der) -[s] Iran. **i~isch** *a* Iranian

irdisch *a* earthly

Ire *m* -n, -n Irishman; die **I~n** the Irish *pl*

irgend *adv* wenn **i~** möglich if at all possible. **i~ein** *indef art* some/any; **i~ein** anderer someone/anyone else. **i~eine(r,s)** *pron* any one; (*jemand*) someone/anyone. **i~etwas** *pron* something; anything. **i~jemand** *pron* someone; anyone. **i~wann** *pron* at some time [or other]/at any time. **i~was** *pron* 🔟 something [or other]/anything. **i~welche(r,s)** *pron* any. **i~wer** *pron* someone/ anyone. **i~wie** *adv* somehow [or other]. **i~wo** *adv* somewhere/ anywhere

Irin *f* -, -nen Irishwoman

irisch *a* Irish

Irland *nt* -s Ireland

Ironie *f* - irony

ironisch *a* ironic

irre *a* mad, crazy; (🗵 *gewaltig*) incredible. **I~(r)** *m/f* lunatic. **i~führen** *vt sep* (*fig*) mislead

irre|machen *vt sep* confuse. **i~n** *vi/r* (*haben*) [sich] **i~n** be mistaken ● *vi* (*sein*) wander. **I~nanstalt** *f*, **I~nhaus** *nt* lunatic asylum. **i~werden**† *vi sep* (*sein*) get confused

Irrgarten *m* maze

irritieren *vt* irritate

Irr|sinn *m* madness, lunacy. **i~sinnig** *a* mad; (🗵 *gewaltig*) incredible. **I~tum** *m* -s,-̈er mistake

Ischias *m* & *nt* - sciatica

Islam (der) -[s] Islam. **islamisch** *a* Islamic

Island *nt* -s Iceland

Isolier|band *nt* insulating tape. **i~en** *vt* isolate; (*Phys, Electr*) insulate; (*gegen Schall*) soundproof. **I~ung** *f* - isolation; insulation; soundproofing

Israel /'ɪsraɛ:l/ *nt* -s Israel. **I~eli** *m* -[s], -s & *f* -, -[s] Israeli. **i~elisch** *a* Israeli

ist *s.* sein; **er ist** he is

Ital|ien /-iən/ *nt* -s Italy. **I~iener(in)** *m* -s,- (*f* -, -nen) Italian. **i~ienisch** *a* Italian. **I~ienisch** *nt* -[s] (*Lang*) Italian

Jj

ja *adv*, **Ja** *nt* -[s] yes; **ich glaube ja** I think so; **ja nicht!** not on any account! **da seid ihr ja!** there you are!

Jacht *f* -, -en yacht

Jacke *f* -, -n jacket; (*Strick-*) cardigan

Jackett /ʒa'kɛt/ *nt* -s, -s jacket

Jade *m* -[s] & *f* - jade

Jagd *f* -, -en hunt; (*Schießen*) shoot; (*Jagen*) hunting; shooting; (*fig*) pursuit (**nach** of); **auf die J~ gehen** go hunting/shooting. **J~gewehr** *nt* sporting gun. **J~hund** *m* gun-dog; (*Hetzhund*) hound

jagen *vt* hunt; (*schießen*) shoot; (*verfolgen, wegjagen*) chase; (*treiben*) drive; **sich j~** chase each other; **in die Luft j~** blow up ● *vi* (*haben*) hunt, go hunting/shooting; (*fig*) chase (**nach** after) ● *vi* (*sein*) race, dash

Jäger *m* -s,- hunter

Jahr *nt* -[e]s, -e year. **j~elang** *adv* for years. **J~eszahl** *f* year. **J~eszeit** *f* season. **J~gang** *m* year; (*Wein*) vintage. **J~hundert** *nt* century

jährlich *a* annual, yearly

Jahr|markt *m* fair. **J~tausend** *nt* millennium. **J~zehnt** *nt* -[e]s, -e decade

Jähzorn *m* violent temper. **j~ig** *a* hot-tempered

Jalousie /ʒalu'zi:/ *f* -, -n venetian blind

Jammer *m* -s misery

jämmerlich *a* miserable; (*Mitleid erregend*) pitiful

jammern *vi* (*haben*) lament ● *vt* **jdn j~n** arouse s.o.'s pity

Jänner *m* -s,- (*Aust*) January

Januar *m* -s, -e January

Jap|an *nt* -s Japan. **J~aner(in)** *m* -s,- (*f* -, -nen) Japanese. **j~anisch** *a* Japanese. **J~anisch** *nt* -[s] (*Lang*) Japanese

jäten *vt/i* (*haben*) **weed**

jaulen *vi* (*haben*) yelp

Jause *f* -, -n (*Aust*) snack

jawohl *adv* yes

Jazz /jats, dʒɛs/ *m* - jazz

je *adv* (*jemals*) ever; (*jeweils*) each; (*pro*) per; **je nach** according to; **seit eh und je** always ● *conj* **je mehr, desto besser** the more the better ● *prep* (+ *acc*) per

Jeans /dʒi:ns/ *pl* jeans

jede(r,s) *pron* every; (*j~er Einzelne*) each; (*j~er Beliebige*) any;

(*substantivisch*) everyone; each one; anyone; **ohne j~en Grund** without any reason. **j~enfalls** *adv* in any case; (*wenigstens*) at least. **j~ermann** *pron* everyone. **j~erzeit** *adv* at any time. **j~esmal** *adv* every time

jedoch *adv & conj* however

jemals *adv* ever

jemand *pron* someone, somebody; (*fragend, verneint*) anyone, anybody

jen|e(r,s) *pron* that; (*pl*) those; (*substantivisch*) that one; (*pl*) those. **j~seits** *prep* (+ *gen*) [on] the other side of

jetzt *adv* now

jiddisch *a*, **J~** *nt* -[s] Yiddish

Job /dʒɔp/ *m* -s, -s job. **j~ben** *vi* (*haben*) 🗉 work

Joch *nt* -[e]s, -e yoke

Jockei, Jockey /'dʒɔki/ *m* -s, -s jockey

Jod *nt* -[e]s iodine

jodeln *vi* (*haben*) yodel

Joga *m & nt* -[s] yoga

joggen /'dʒɔgən/ *vi* (*haben/sein*) jog

Joghurt, Jogurt *m & nt* -[s] yoghurt

Johannisbeere *f* redcurrant

Joker *m* -s,- (*Karte*) joker

Jolle *f* -, -n dinghy

Jongleur /ʒõ'gløːɐ̯/ *m* -s, -e juggler

Jordanien /-iən/ *nt* -s Jordan

Journalis|mus /ʒʊrna'lɪsmʊs/ *m* - journalism. **J~t(in)** *m* -en, -en (*f* -, -nen) journalist

Jubel *m* -s rejoicing, jubilation. **j~n** *vi* (*haben*) rejoice

Jubiläum *nt* -s,-äen jubilee; (*Jahrestag*) anniversary

jucken *vi* (*haben*) itch; **sich j~en** scratch; **es j~t mich** I have an itch

Jude *m* -n, -n Jew. **J~ntum** *nt* -s Judaism; (*Juden*) Jewry

Jüd|in *f* -, -nen Jewess. **j~isch** *a* Jewish

Judo *nt* -[s] judo

---
*alte Schreibung

Jugend *f* - youth; (*junge Leute*) young people *pl*. **J~herberge** *f* youth hostel. **J~kriminalität** *f* juvenile delinquency. **j~lich** *a* youthful. **J~liche(r)** *m/f* young man/woman. **J~liche** *pl* young people. **J~stil** *m* art nouveau

Jugoslaw|ien /-iən/ *nt* -s Yugoslavia. **j~isch** *a* Yugoslav

Juli *m* -[s], -s July

jung *a* young; <*Wein*> new ● *pron* **J~ und Alt** young and old. **J~e** *m* -n, -n boy. **J~e(s)** *nt* young animal/bird; (*Katzen-*) kitten; (*Bären-*) cub; (*Hunde-*) pup; **die J~en** the young *pl*

Jünger *m* -s,- disciple

Jung|frau *f* virgin; (*Astr*) Virgo. **J~geselle** *m* bachelor

Jüngling *m* -s, -e youth

jüngst|e(r,s) *a* youngest; (*neueste*) latest; **in j~er Zeit** recently

Juni *m* -[s], -s June

Jura *pl* law *sg*

Jurist|(in) *m* -en, -en (*f* -, -nen) lawyer. **j~isch** *a* legal

Jury /ʒy'riː/ *f* -, -s jury; (*Sport*) judges *pl*

Justiz *f* - **die J~** justice

Juwel *nt* -s, -en & (*fig*) -e jewel. **J~ier** *m* -es, -e jeweller

Jux *m* -es, -e 🗉 joke; **aus Jux** for fun

....

Kk

....

Kabarett *nt* -s, -s & -e cabaret

Kabel *nt* -s,- cable. **K~fernsehen** *nt* cable television

Kabeljau *m* -s, -e & -s cod

Kabine *f* -, -n cabin; (*Umkleide-*) cubicle; (*Telefon-*) booth; (*einer K~nbahn*) car. **K~nbahn** *f* cable-car

Kabinett *nt* -s, -e (*Pol*) Cabinet

Kabriolett nt -s, -s convertible

Kachel f -, -n tile. **k~n** vt tile

Kadenz f -, -en (Mus) cadence

Käfer m -s,- beetle

Kaffee /'kafe:, ka'fe:/ m -s, -s coffee. **K~kanne** f coffee-pot. **K~maschine** f coffee-maker. **K~mühle** f coffee-grinder

Käfig m -s, -e cage

kahl a bare; (haarlos) bald; **k~ geschoren** shaven

Kahn m -s, ̈-e boat; (Last-) barge

Kai m -s, -s quay

Kaiser m -s,- emperor. **K~in** f -, -nen empress. **k~lich** a imperial. **K~reich** nt empire. **K~schnitt** m Caesarean [section]

Kajüte f -, -n (Naut) cabin

Kakao /ka'kau/ m -s cocoa

Kakerlak m -s & -en, -en cockroach

Kaktus m -, -teen /-'te:ən/ cactus

Kalb nt -[e]s, ̈-er calf. **K~fleisch** nt veal

Kalender m -s,- calendar; (Termin-) diary

Kaliber nt -s,- calibre; (Gewehr-) bore

Kalium nt -s potassium

Kalk m -[e]s, -e lime; (Kalzium) calcium. **K~en** vt whitewash. **K~stein** m limestone

Kalkulation /-'tsio:n/ f -, -en calculation. **k~ieren** vt/i (haben) calculate

Kalorie f -, -n calorie

kalt a cold; mir ist **k~** I am cold

Kälte f - cold; (Gefühls-) coldness; **10** Grad **K~** 10 degrees below zero

Kalzium nt -s calcium

Kamel nt -s, -e camel

Kamera f -, -s camera

Kamerad(in) m -en, -en (f -, -nen) companion; (Freund) mate; (Mil, Pol) comrade

Kameramann m (pl -männer & -leute) cameraman

Kamille f - camomile

Kamin m -s, -e fireplace; (SGer: Schornstein) chimney

Kamm m -[e]s, ̈-e comb; (Berg-) ridge; (Zool, Wellen-) crest

kämmen vt comb; jdn/sich **k~** comb s.o.'s/one's hair

Kammer f -, -n small room; (Techn, Biol, Pol) chamber. **K~musik** f chamber music

Kammgarn nt (Tex) worsted

Kampagne /kam'panjə/ f -, -n (Pol, Comm) campaign

Kampf m -es, ̈-e fight; (Schlacht) battle; (Wett-) contest; (fig) struggle

kämpf|en vi (haben) fight; sich **k~en durch** fight one's way through. **K~er(in)** m -s,- (f -, -nen) fighter

Kampfrichter m (Sport) judge

Kanada nt -s Canada

Kanad|ier(in) /-iɐ, -iərɪn/ m -s,- (f -, -nen) Canadian. **k~isch** a Canadian

Kanal m -s, ̈-e canal; (Abfluss-) drain, sewer; (Radio, TV) channel; der **K~** the [English] Channel

Kanalisation /-'tsio:n/ f - sewerage system, drains pl

Kanarienvogel /-iən-/ m canary

Kanarisch a **K~e Inseln** Canaries

Kandidat(in) m -en, -en (f -, -nen) candidate

kandiert a candied

Känguru nt -s, -s kangaroo

Kaninchen nt -s,- rabbit

Kanister m -s,- canister; (Benzin-) can

Kännchen nt -s,- [small] jug; (Kaffee-) pot

Kanne f -, -n jug; (Tee-) pot; (Öl-) can; (große Milch-) churn

Kannibal|e m -n, -n cannibal. **K~ismus** m - cannibalism

Kanon m -s, -s canon; (Lied) round

Kanone f -, -n cannon, gun

kanonisieren vt canonize

Kantate f -, -n cantata

Kante f -, -n edge

Kanten m -s,- crust [of bread]

Kanter m -s,- canter

kantig a angular

Kantine f -, -n canteen

Kanton m -s, -e (Swiss) canton

Kanu nt -s, -s canoe

Kanzel f -, -n pulpit; (*Aviat*) cockpit

Kanzler m -s,- chancellor

Kap nt -s, -s (*Geog*) cape

Kapazität f -, -en capacity

Kapelle f -, -n chapel; (*Mus*) band

kapern vt (*Naut*) seize

kapieren vt ⚏ understand

Kapital nt -s capital. **K~ismus** m - capitalism. **K~ist** m -en, -en capitalist. **k~istisch** a capitalist

Kapitän m -s, -e captain

Kapitel nt -s,- chapter

Kaplan m -s, -e curate

Kappe f -, -n cap

Kapsel f -, -n capsule; (*Flaschen-*) top

kaputt a ⚏ broken; (*zerrissen*) torn; (*defekt*) out of order; (*ruiniert*) ruined; (*erschöpft*) worn out. **k~gehen†** vi sep (*sein*) ⚏ break; (*zerreißen*) tear; (*defekt werden*) pack up; <*Ehe, Freundschaft:*> break up. **k~lachen (sich)** vr sep ⚏ be in stitches. **k~machen** vt sep ⚏ break; (*zerreißen*) tear; (*defekt machen*) put out of order; (*erschöpfen*) wear out; **sich k~machen** wear oneself out

Kapuze f -, -n hood

Kapuzinerkresse f nasturtium

Karaffe f -, -n carafe; (*mit Stöpsel*) decanter

Karamell m -s caramel. **K~bonbon** m & nt ≈ toffee

Karat nt -[e]s, -e carat

Karawane f -, -n caravan

Kardinal m -s,-̈e cardinal. **K~zahl** f cardinal number

Karfreitag m Good Friday

karg a meagre; (*frugal*) frugal; (*spärlich*) sparse; (*unfruchtbar*) barren; (*gering*) scant

Karibik f - Caribbean

kariert a check[ed]; <*Papier*> squared; **schottisch k~** tartan

Karik|atur f -, -en caricature; (*Journ*) cartoon. **k~ieren** vt caricature

Karneval m -s, -e & -s carnival

Kärnten nt -s Carinthia

Karo nt -s, -s (*Raute*) diamond; (*Viereck*) square; (*Muster*) check (*Kartenspiel*) diamonds pl

Karosserie f -, -n bodywork

Karotte f -, -n carrot

Karpfen m -s,-, carp

Karren m -s,- cart; (*Hand-*) barrow. **k~** vt cart

Karriere /ka'rie:rə/ f -, -n career; **K~ machen** get to the top

Karte f -, -n card; (*Eintritts-, Fahr-*) ticket; (*Speise-*) menu; (*Land-*) map

Kartei f -, -en card index

Karten|spiel nt card-game; (*Spielkarten*) pack of cards. **K~vorverkauf** m advance booking

Kartoffel f -, -n potato. **K~brei** m nt mashed potatoes

Karton /kar'tɔŋ/ m -s, -s cardboard; (*Schachtel*) carton

Karussell nt -s, -s & -e roundabout

Käse m -s,- cheese

Kaserne f -, -n barracks pl

Kasino nt -s, -s casino

Kasperle nt & m -s,- Punch. **K~theater** nt Punch and Judy show

Kasse f -, -n till; (*Registrier-*) cash register; (*Zahlstelle*) cash desk; (*im Supermarkt*) check-out; (*Theater-*) box-office; (*Geld*) pool [of money], ⚏ kitty; (*Kranken-*) health insurance scheme; **knapp bei K~ sein** ⚏ be short of cash. **K~nwart** m -[e]s, -e treasurer. **K~nzettel** m receipt

Kasserolle f -, -n saucepan

Kassette f -, -n cassette; (*Film-, Farbband-*) cartridge. **K~nrekorder** /-rəkɔrdə/ m -s,- cassette recorder

kassier|en vi (*haben*) collect the money/(*im Bus*) the fares ● vt collect. **K~er(in)** m -s,- (f -, -nen) cashier

Kastanie /kas'ta:niə/ f -, -n [horse] chestnut, ⚏ conker

Kasten m -s,⁻ box; (*Brot-*) bin; (*Flaschen-*) crate; (*Brief-*) letter-box; (*Aust: Schrank*) cupboard

kastrieren vt castrate; neuter

Katalog m -[e]s, -e catalogue

Katalysator m -s, -en /-'to:rən/ catalyst; (*Auto*) catalytic converter

Katapult nt -[e]s, -e catapult

Katarrh, Katarr m -s, -e catarrh

Katastrophe f -, -n catastrophe

Katechismus m - catechism

Kategorie f -, -n category

Kater m -s,- tom-cat; (🔟 *Katzenjammer*) hangover

Kathedrale f -, -n cathedral

Kath|olik(in) m -en, -en (f -, -nen) Catholic. **K~olisch** a Catholic. **K~olizismus** m - Catholicism

Kätzchen nt -s,- kitten; (*Bot*) catkin

Katze f -, -n cat. **K~njammer** m 🔟 hangover. **K~nsprung** m ein K~nsprung 🔟 a stone's throw

Kauderwelsch nt -[s] gibberish

kauen vt/i (*haben*) chew; bite <*Nägel*>

Kauf m -[e]s, Käufe purchase; **guter K~** bargain; **in K~nehmen** (*fig*) put up with. **k~en** vt/i (*haben*) buy; k~en bei shop at

Käufer(in) m -s,- (f -, -nen) buyer; (*im Geschäft*) shopper

Kauf|haus nt department store. **K~laden** m shop

käuflich a saleable; (*bestechlich*) corruptible; k~ erwerben buy

Kauf|mann m (pl -leute) businessman; (*Händler*) dealer; (*dial*) grocer. **K~preis** m purchase price

Kaugummi m chewing-gum

Kaulquappe f -, -n tadpole

kaum adv hardly

Kaution /-'tsio:n/ f -, -en surety; (*Jur*) bail; (*Miet-*) deposit

Kautschuk m -s rubber

Kauz m -es, Käuze owl

Kavalier m -s, -e gentleman

Kavallerie f - cavalry

Kaviar m -s caviare

keck a bold; cheeky

Kegel m -s,- skittle; (*Geom*) cone. **K~bahn** f skittle-alley. **k~n** vi (*haben*) play skittles

Kehl|e f -, -n throat; **aus voller K~e** at the top of one's voice. **K~kopf** m larynx. **K~kopfentzündung** f laryngitis

Kehr|e f -, -n [hairpin] bend. **k~en** vi (*haben*) (*fegen*) sweep ● vt sweep; (*wenden*) turn; **sich nicht k~en an** (+ *acc*) not care about. **K~icht** m -[e]s sweepings pl. **K~reim** m refrain. **K~seite** f (*fig*) drawback. **k~tmachen** vi sep (*haben*) turn back; (*sich umdrehen*) turn round

Keil m -[e]s, -e wedge

Keilriemen m fan belt

Keim m -[e]s, -e (*Bot*) sprout; (*Med*) germ. **k~en** vi (*haben*) germinate; (*austreiben*) sprout. **k~frei** a sterile

kein pron no; not a; k~e fünf Minuten less than five minutes. **k~e(r,s)** pron no one, nobody; (*Ding*) none, not one. **k~esfalls** adv on no account. **k~eswegs** adv by no means. **k~mal** adv not once. **k~s** pron none, not one

Keks m -[es], -[e] biscuit

Kelch m -[e]s, -e goblet, cup; (*Relig*) chalice; (*Bot*) calyx

Kelle f -, -n ladle; (*Maurer*) trowel

Keller m -s,- cellar. **K~ei** f -, -en winery. **K~wohnung** f basement flat

Kellner m -s,- waiter. **K~in** f -, -nen waitress

keltern vt press

keltisch a Celtic

Kenia nt -s Kenya

kenn|en† vt know; k~en lernen get to know; (*treffen*) meet; **sich k~en lernen** meet; (*näher*) get to know one another. **K~er** m -s,-, **K~erin** f -, -nen connoisseur; (*Experte*) expert. **k~tlich** a recognizable; k~tlich machen mark. **K~tnis** f -, -se knowledge; **zur K~tnis nehmen** take note of; **in K~tnis setzen** inform (*von* of). **K~wort** nt (pl -wörter) reference; (*geheimes*) password. **K~zeichen** nt distinguishing mark or feature; (*Merkmal*) characteristic,

(*Markierung*) marking; (*Auto*) registration. **k~zeichnen** *vt* distinguish; (*markieren*) mark

kentern *vi* (*sein*) capsize

Keramik *f* -, -en pottery

Kerbe *f* -, -n notch

Kerker *m* -s,- dungeon; (*Gefängnis*) prison

Kerl *m* -s, -e & -s 🔠 fellow, bloke

Kern *m* -s, -e pip; (*Kirsch-*) stone; (*Nuss-*) kernel; (*Techn*) core; (*Atom-, Zell- & fig*) nucleus; (*Stadt-*) centre; (*einer Sache*) heart. **K~energie** *f* nuclear energy. **K~gehäuse** *nt* core. **k~los** *a* seedless. **K~physik** *f* nuclear physics *sg*

Kerze *f* -, -n candle. **K~nhalter** *m* -s,- candlestick

kess *a* pert

Kessel *m* -s,- kettle

Kette *f* -, -n chain; (*Hals-*) necklace. **k~n** *vt* chain (an + *acc* to). **K~nladen** *m* chain store

Ketze|r(in) *m* -s,- (*f* -, -nen) heretic. **K~rei** *f* - heresy

keuch|en *vi* (*haben*) pant. **K~husten** *m* whooping cough

Keule *f* -, -n club; (*Culin*) leg; (*Hühner-*) drumstick

keusch *a* chaste

Khaki *nt* - khaki

kichern *vi* (*haben*) giggle

Kiefer[1] *f* -, -n pine[-tree]

Kiefer[2] *m* -s,- jaw

Kiel *m* -s, -e (*Naut*) keel

Kiemen *fpl* gills

Kies *m* -es gravel. **K~el** *m* -s,-, **K~elstein** *m* pebble

Kilo *nt* -s, -[s] kilo. **K~gramm** *nt* kilogram. **K~hertz** *nt* kilohertz. **K~meter** *m* kilometre. **K~meterstand** *m* ≈ mileage. **K~watt** *nt* kilowatt

Kind *nt* -es, -er child; **von K~ auf** from childhood

Kinder|arzt *m*, **K~ärztin** *f* paediatrician. **K~bett** *nt* child's cot. **K~garten** *m* nursery school. **K~geld** *nt* child benefit.

K~lähmung *f* polio. **k~leicht** *a* very easy. **k~los** *a* childless. **K~mädchen** *nt* nanny. **K~reim** *m* nursery rhyme. **K~spiel** *nt* children's game. **K~tagesstätte** *f* day nursery. **K~teller** *m* children's menu. **K~wagen** *m* pram. **K~zimmer** *nt* child's/children's room; (*für Baby*) nursery

Kind|heit *f* - childhood. **k~isch** *a* childish. **k~lich** *a* childlike

kinetisch *a* kinetic

Kinn *nt* -[e]s, -e chin. **K~lade** *f* jaw

Kino *nt* -s, -s cinema

Kiosk *m* -[e]s, -e kiosk

Kippe *f* -, -n (*Müll-*) dump; (🔠 *Zigaretten-*) fag-end. **k~n** *vt* tilt; (*schütten*) tip (in + *acc* into) ● *vi* (*sein*) topple

Kirch|e *f* -, -n church. **K~enbank** *f* pew. **K~endiener** *m* verger. **K~enlied** *nt* hymn. **K~enschiff** *nt* nave. **K~hof** *m* churchyard. **k~lich** *a* church ... ● *adv* **k~lich getraut werden** be married in church. **K~turm** *m* church tower, steeple. **K~weih** *f* -, -en [village] fair

Kirmes *f* -, -sen = **Kirchweih**

Kirsche *f* -, -n cherry

Kissen *nt* -s,- cushion; (*Kopf-*) pillow

Kiste *f* -, -n crate; (*Zigarren-*) box

Kitsch *m* -es sentimental rubbish; (*Kunst*) kitsch

Kitt *m* -s [adhesive] cement; (*Fenster-*) putty

Kittel *m* -s,- overall, smock

Kitz *nt* -es, -e (*Zool*) kid

Kitz|el *m* -s,- tickle; (*Nerven-*) thrill. **k~eln** *vt/i* (*haben*) tickle. **k~lig** *a* ticklish

kläffen *vi* (*haben*) yap

Klage *f* -, -n lament; (*Beschwerde*) complaint; (*Jur*) action. **k~n** *vi* (*haben*) lament; (*sich beklagen*) complaint; (*Jur*) sue

Kläger(in) *m* -s,- (*f* -, -nen) (*Jur*) plaintiff

klamm *a* cold and damp; (*steif*) stiff. **K~** *f* -, -en (*Geog*) gorge

Klammer f -, -n (Wäsche-) peg; (Büro-) paper-clip; (Heft-) staple; (Haar-) grip; (für Zähne) brace; (Techn) clamp; (Typ) bracket. **k~n (sich)** vr cling (an + acc to)

Klang m -[e]s,⁓e sound; (K~farbe) tone

Klapp|e f -, -n flap; (▣ Mund) trap. **k~en** vt fold; (hoch-) tip up ● vi (haben) ▣ work out

Klapper f -, -n rattle. **k~n** vi (haben) rattle. **K~schlange** f rattlesnake

klapp|rig a rickety; (schwach) decrepit. **K~stuhl** m folding chair

Klaps m -es, -e pat, smack

klar a clear; sich (dat) k~ werden make up one's mind; (erkennen) realize (dass that); sich (dat) k~ od im K~en sein realize (dass that) ● adv clearly; (▣ natürlich) of course

klären vt clarify; sich k~ clear; (fig: sich lösen) resolve itself

Klarheit f -,- clarity

Klarinette f -, -n clarinet

klar|machen vt sep make clear (dat to); sich (dat) etw k~machen understand sth. **k~stellen** vt sep clarify

Klärung f - clarification

Klasse f -, -n class; (Sch) class, form; (Zimmer) classroom. **k~** inv a ▣ super. **K~narbeit** f [written] test. **K~nzimmer** nt classroom

Klassik f - classicism; (Epoche) classical period. **K~iker** m -s,- classical author/(Mus) composer. **k~isch** a classical; (typisch) classic

Klatsch m -[e]s gossip. **K~base** f ▣ gossip. **k~en** vt slap; Beifall k~en applaud ● vi (haben) make a slapping sound; (im Wasser) splash; (tratschen) gossip; (applaudieren) clap. **k~nass** a ▣ soaking wet

klauen vt/i (haben) ▣ steal

Klausel f -, -n clause

Klaustrophobie f - claustrophobia

Klausur f -, -en (Univ) paper

Klavier nt -s, -e piano. **K~spieler(in)** m(f) pianist

kleb|en vt stick/(mit Klebstoff) glue (an + acc to) ● vi (haben) stick (an + dat to). **k~rig** a sticky. **K~stoff** m adhesive, glue. **K~streifen** m adhesive tape

Klecks m -es, -e stain; (Tinten-) blot; (kleine Menge) dab. **k~en** vi (haben) make a mess

Klee m -s clover

Kleid nt -[e]s, -er dress; K~er dresses; (Kleidung) clothes. **k~en** vt dress; (gut stehen) suit. **K~erbügel** m coat-hanger. **K~erbürste** f clothes-brush. **K~erhaken** m coat-hook. **K~erschrank** m wardrobe. **k~sam** a becoming. **K~ung** f - clothes pl, clothing. **K~ungsstück** nt garment

Kleie f - bran

klein a small, little; (von kleinem Wuchs) short; k~ schneiden cut up small. von k~ auf from childhood. **K~arbeit** f painstaking work. **K~e(r,s)** m/f/nt little one. **K~geld** nt [small] change. **K~handel** m retail trade. **K~heit** f - smallness; (Wuchs) short stature. **K~holz** nt firewood. **K~igkeit** f -, -en trifle; (Mahl) snack. **K~kind** nt infant. **k~laut** a subdued. **k~lich** a petty

klein|schreiben† vt sep write with a small [initial] letter. **K~stadt** f small town. **k~städtisch** a provincial

Kleister m -s paste. **k~n** vt paste

Klemme f -, -n [hair-]grip. **k~n** vt jam; sich (dat) den Finger k~n get one's finger caught ● vi (haben) jam, stick

Klempner m -s,- plumber

Klerus (der) - the clergy

Klette f -, -n burr

kletter|n vi (sein) climb. **K~pflanze** f climber

Klettverschluss m Velcro (P) fastening

klicken vi (haben) click

Klient(in)/ kli'ɛnt(m)/ m -en, -en (f -, -nen) (Jur) client

Kliff nt -[e]s, -e cliff

Klima nt -s climate. **K~anlage** f air-conditioning

klimat|isch a climatic. **k~isiert** a air-conditioned

klimpern vi (haben) jingle; **k~ auf** (+ dat) tinkle on <Klavier>; strum <Gitarre>

Klinge f -, -n blade

Klingel f -, -n bell. **k~n** vi (haben) ring; **es k~t** there's a ring at the door

klingen† vi (haben) sound

Klinik f -, -en clinic

Klinke f -, -n [door] handle

Klippe f -, -n [submerged] rock

Klips m -es, -e clip; (Ohr-) clip-on ear-ring

klirren vi (haben) rattle <Glas:> chink

Klo nt -s, -s ▣ loo

klopfen vi (haben) knock; (leicht) tap; <Herz:> pound; **es k~te** there was a knock at the door

Klops m -es, -e meatball

Klosett nt -s, -s lavatory

Kloß m -es, ̈e dumpling

Kloster nt -s, ̈ monastery; (Nonnen-) convent

klösterlich a monastic

Klotz m -es, ̈e block

Klub m -s, -s club

Kluft f -, ̈e cleft; (fig: Gegensatz) gulf

klug a intelligent; (schlau) clever. **K~heit** f - cleverness

Klump|en m -s, - lump

knabbern vt/i (haben) nibble

Knabe m -n, -n boy. **k~nhaft** a boyish

Knäckebrot nt crispbread

knack|en vt/i (haben) crack. **K~s** m -es, -e crack

Knall m -[e]s, -e bang. **K~bonbon** m cracker. **k~en** vi (haben) go bang; <Peitsche:> crack ● vt (▣ werfen) chuck; **jdm eine k~en** ▣ clout s.o. **k~ig** a ▣ gaudy

knapp a (gering) scant; (kurz) short; (mangelnd) scarce; (gerade ausreichend) bare; (eng) tight. **K~heit** f - scarcity

knarren vi (haben) creak

Knast m -[e]s ▣ prison

knattern vi (haben) crackle; <Gewehr:> stutter

Knäuel m & nt -s, - ball

Knauf m -[e]s, Knäufe knob

knauserig a ▣ stingy

knautschen vt ▣ crumple ● vi (haben) crease

Knebel m -s, - gag. **k~n** vt gag

Knecht m -[e]s, -e farm-hand; (fig) slave

kneif|en† vt pinch ● vi (haben) pinch; (▣ sich drücken) chicken out. **K~zange** f pincers pl

Kneipe f -, -n ▣ pub

knet|en vt knead; (formen) mould. **K~masse** f Plasticine(P)

Knick m -[e]s, -e bend; (Kniff) crease. **k~en** vt bend; (kniffen) fold; **geknickt sein** ▣ be dejected

Knicks m -es, -e curtsy. **k~en** vi (haben) curtsy

Knie nt -s, - /'kni:ə/ knee

knien /'kni:ən/ vi (haben) kneel ● vr **sich k~** kneel [down]

Kniescheibe f kneecap

Kniff m -[e]s, -e pinch; (Falte) crease; (▣ Trick) trick. **k~en** vt fold

knipsen vt (lochen) punch; (Phot) photograph ● vi (haben) take a photograph/photographs

Knirps m -es, -e ▣ little chap; (P) (Schirm) telescopic umbrella

knirschen vi (haben) grate; <Schnee, Kies:> crunch

knistern vi (haben) crackle; <Papier:> rustle

Knitter|falte f crease. **k~frei** a crease-resistant. **k~n** vi (haben) crease

knobeln vi (haben) toss (um for)

Knoblauch m -s garlic

Knöchel m -s, - ankle; (Finger-) knuckle

Knochen m -s,- bone. **K~mark** nt bone marrow

knochig a bony

Knödel m -s,- (SGer) dumpling

Knoll|e f -, -n tuber

Knopf m -[e]s,⸚e button; (Griff) knob

knöpfen vt button

Knopfloch nt buttonhole

Knorpel m -s gristle; (Anat) cartilage

Knospe f bud

Knoten m -s,- knot; (Med) lump; (Haar-) bun, chignon. **k~** vt knot. **K~punkt** m junction

knüll|en vt crumple ● vi (haben) crease. **K~er** m -s,- 🛈 sensation

knüpfen vt knot; (verbinden) attach (an + acc to)

Knüppel m -s,- club; (Gummi-) truncheon

knurren vi (haben) growl; <Magen:> rumble

knusprig a crunchy, crisp

knutschen vi (haben) 🛈 smooch

k.o. /ka'ʔo:/ a k.o. **schlagen** knock out; **k.o. sein** 🛈 be worn out

Koalition /koali'tsi̯o:n/ f -, -en coalition

Kobold m -[e]s, -e goblin, imp

Koch m -[e]s,⸚e cook; (im Restaurant) chef. **K~buch** nt cookery book. **k~en** vt cook; (sieden) boil; make <Kaffee, Tee>; **hart gekochtes Ei** hard-boiled egg ● vi (haben) cook; (sieden) boil; 🛈 seethe (**vor** + dat with). **K~en** nt -s cooking; (Sieden) boiling. **k~end** a boiling. **K~herd** m cooker, stove

Köchin f -, -nen [woman] cook

Koch|löffel m wooden spoon. **K~nische** f kitchenette. **K~platte** f hotplate. **K~topf** m saucepan

Köder m -s,- bait

Koffein /kofe'i:n/ nt -s caffeine. **k~frei** a decaffeinated

Koffer m -s,- suitcase. **K~kuli** m luggage trolley. **K~raum** m (Auto) boot

Kognak /'kɔnjak/ m -s, -s brandy

Kohl m -[e]s cabbage

Kohle f -, -n coal. **K~[n]hydrat** nt -[e]s, -e carbohydrate. **K~nbergwerk** nt coal-mine, colliery. **K~ndioxid** nt carbon dioxide. **K~nsäure** f carbon dioxide. **K~nstoff** m carbon

Koje f -, -n (Naut) bunk

Kokain /koka'i:n/ nt -s cocaine

kokett a flirtatious. **k~ieren** vi (haben) flirt

Kokon /ko'kõ:/ m -s, -s cocoon

Kokosnuss (f) coconut

Koks m -es coke

Kolben m -s,- (Gewehr-) butt; (Mais-) cob; (Techn) piston; (Chem) flask

Kolibri m -s, -s humming-bird

Kolik f -, -en colic

Kollaborateur /-'tø:ɐ̯/ m -s, -e collaborator

Kolleg nt -s, -s & -ien /-i̯ən/ (Univ) course of lectures

Kolleg|e m -n, -n, **K~in** f -, -nen colleague. **K~ium** nt -s, -ien staff

Kollek|te f -, -n (Relig) collection. **K~tion** /-'tsi̯o:n/ f -, -en collection

Köln nt -s Cologne. **K~ischwasser, K~isch Wasser** nt eau-de-Cologne

Kolonie f -, -n colony

Kolonne f -, -n column; (Mil) convoy

Koloss m -es, -e giant

Koma nt -s, -s coma

Kombi m -s, -s = **K~wagen**. **K~nation** /-'tsi̯o:n/ f -, -en combination; (Folgerung) deduction; (Kleidung) co-ordinating outfit. **k~nieren** vt combine; (fig) reason; (folgern) deduce. **K~wagen** m estate car

Kombüse f -, -n (Naut) galley

Komet m -en, -en comet

Komfort /kɔm'fo:ɐ̯/ m -s comfort; (Luxus) luxury

Komik f - humour. **K~er** m -s,- comic, comedian

komisch a funny; <Oper> comic; (sonderbar) odd, funny. **k~erweise** adv funnily enough

k

Komitee *nt* -s, -s committee

Komma *nt* -s, -s & -ta comma; (*Dezimal-*) decimal point; **drei K~ fünf** three point five

Kommando *nt* -s, -s order; (*Befehlsgewalt*) command; (*Einheit*) detachment. **K~brücke** *f* bridge

kommen† *vi* (*sein*) come; (*eintreffen*) arrive; (*gelangen*) get (**nach** to); **k~ lassen** send for; **auf/ hinter etw** (*acc*) **k~** think of/find out about sth; **um/zu etw k~** lose/ acquire sth; **wieder zu sich k~** come round; **wie kommt das?** why is that? **k~d** *a* coming; **k~den Montag** next Monday

Kommen|tar *m* -s, -e commentary; (*Bemerkung*) comment. **k~tieren** *vt* comment on

kommerziell *a* commercial

Kommissar *m* -s, -e commissioner; (*Polizei-*) superintendent

Kommission *f* -, -en commission; (*Gremium*) committee

Kommode *f* -, -n chest of drawers

Kommunalwahlen *fpl* local elections

Kommunion *f* -, -en [Holy] Communion

Kommun|ismus *m* - Communism. **K~ist(in)** *m* -en, -en (*f* -, -nen) Communist. **k~istisch** *a* Communist

kommunizieren *vi* (*haben*) receive [Holy] Communion

Komödie /ko'møːdiə/ *f* -, -n comedy

Kompagnon /'kɔmpanjõː/ *m* -s, -s (*Comm*) partner

Kompanie *f* -, -n (*Mil*) company

Komparse *m* -n, -n (*Theat*) extra

Kompass *m* -es, -e compass

komplett *a* complete

Komplex *m* -es, -e complex

Komplikation /-'tsioːn/ *f* -, -en complication

Kompliment *nt* -[e]s, -e compliment

Komplize *m* -n, -n accomplice

komplizier|en *vt* complicate. **k~t** *a* complicated

Komplott *nt* -[e]s, -e plot

kompo|nieren *vt/i* (*haben*) compose. **K~nist** *m* -en, -en composer

Kompost *m* -[e]s compost

Kompott *nt* -[e]s, -e stewed fruit

Kompromiss *m* -es, -e compromise; **einen K~ schließen** compromise. **k~los** *a* uncompromising

Konden|sation /-'tsioːn/ *f* - condensation. **k~sieren** *vt* condense

Kondensmilch *f* evaporated/ (*gesüßt*) condensed milk

Kondition /-'tsioːn/ *f* - (*Sport*) fitness; **in K~** in form

Konditor *m* -s, -en /-'toːrən/ confectioner. **K~ei** *f* -, -en patisserie

Kondo|lenzbrief *m* letter of condolence. **k~lieren** *vi* (*haben*) express one's condolences

Kondom *nt* & *m* -s, -e condom

Konfekt *nt* -[e]s confectionery; (*Pralinen*) chocolates *pl*

Konfektion /-'tsioːn/ *f* - ready-to-wear clothes *pl*

Konferenz *f* -, -en conference; (*Besprechung*) meeting

Konfession *f* -, -en [religious] denomination. **k~ell** *a* denominational

Konfetti *nt* -s confetti

Konfirm|and(in) *m* -en, -en (*f* -, -nen) candidate for confirmation. **K~ation** /-'tsioːn/ *f* -, -en (*Relig*) confirmation. **k~ieren** *vt* (*Relig*) confirm

Konfitüre *f* -, -n jam

Konflikt *m* -[e]s, -e conflict

Konföderation /-'tsioːn/ *f* confederation

konfus *a* confused

Kongress *m* -es, -e congress

König *m* -s, -e king. **K~in** *f* -, -nen queen. **k~lich** *a* royal; (*hoheitsvoll*) regal; (*großzügig*) handsome. **K~reich** *nt* kingdom

k

Konjunktiv *m* -s, -e subjunctive

Konjunktur *f* - economic situation; (*Hoch-*) boom

konkret *a* concrete

Konkurrent(in) *m* -en, -en (*f* -, -nen) competitor, rival. **K~z** *f* - competition; **jdm K~z machen** compete with s.o. **K~zkampf** *m* competition, rivalry

konkurrieren *vi* (*haben*) compete

Konkurs *m* -es, -e bankruptcy

können†
● *auxiliary verb*
····▶ (*vermögen*) be able to; (*Präsens*) can; (*Vergangenheit, Konditional*) could. **ich kann nicht schlafen** I cannot *or* can't sleep. **kann ich Ihnen helfen?** can I help you? **kann/könnte das explodieren?** can/could it explode? **es kann sein, dass er kommt** he may come

! Distinguish **konnte** and **könnte** (both can be 'could'): **er konnte sie nicht retten** he couldn't *or* was unable to rescue them. **er konnte sie noch retten** he was able to rescue them. **er könnte sie noch retten, wenn ...** he could still rescue them if ...

····▶ (*dürfen*) can, may. **kann ich gehen?** can *or* may I go? **können wir mit[kommen]?** can *or* may we come too?
● *transitive verb*
····▶ (*beherrschen*) know <language>; be able to play <game>. **können Sie Deutsch?** do you know any German? **sie kann das [gut]** she can do that [well]. **ich kann nichts dafür** I can't help that, I'm not to blame
● *intransitive verb*
····▶ (*fähig sein*) **ich kann [heute] nicht** I can't [today]. **er kann nicht anders** there's nothing else he can do; (*es ist seine Art*) he can't help it. **er kann nicht mehr** 🗓 he can't go on; (*nicht mehr essen*) he can't eat any more
····▶ (*irgendwohin gehen können*) be able to go; can go. **ich kann nicht ins Kino** I can't go to the cinema. **er**

konnte endlich nach Florenz at last he was able to go to Florence

konsequen|t *a* consistent; (*logisch*) logical. **K~z** *f* -, -en consequence

konservativ *a* conservative

Konserv|en *fpl* tinned or canned food *sg.* **K~endose** *f* tin, can. **K~ierungsmittel** *nt* preservative

Konsonant *m* -en, -en consonant

Konstitution /-'tsio:n/ *f* -, -en constitution. **k~ell** *a* constitutional

konstruieren *vt* construct; (*entwerfen*) design

Konstruk|tion /-'tsio:n/ *f* -, -en construction; (*Entwurf*) design. **k~tiv** *a* constructive

Konsul *m* -s, -n consul. **K~at** *nt* -[e]s, -e consulate

Konsum *m* -s consumption. **K~güter** *npl* consumer goods

Kontakt *m* -[e]s, -e contact. **K~linsen** *fpl* contact lenses. **K~person** *f* contact

kontern *vt/i* (*haben*) counter

Kontinent /'kon-, konti'nɛnt/ *m* -[e]s, -e continent

Konto *nt* -s, -s account. **K~auszug** *m* [bank] statement. **K~nummer** *f* account number. **K~stand** *m* [bank] balance

Kontrabass *m* double-bass

Kontroll|abschnitt *m* counterfoil. **K~e** *f* -, -n control; (*Prüfung*) check. **K~eur** /-'lø:ɐ/ *m* -s, -e [ticket] inspector. **k~ieren** *vt* check; inspect <*Fahrkarten*>; (*beherrschen*) control

Kontroverse *f* -, -n controversy

Kontur *f* -, -en contour

konventionell *a* conventional

Konversationslexikon *nt* encyclopaedia

konvert|ieren *vi* (*haben*) (*Relig*) convert. **K~it** *m* -en, -en convert

Konzentration /-'tsio:n/ *f* -, -en concentration. **K~slager** *nt* concentration camp

konzentrieren *vt* concentrate; **sich k~** concentrate (**auf** + *acc* on)

Konzept *nt* -[e]s, -e [rough] draft; jdn aus dem K~bringen put s.o. off his stroke

Konzern *m* -s, -e (*Comm*) group [of companies]

Konzert *nt* -[e]s, -e concert; (*Klavier-*) concerto

Konzession *f* -, -en licence; (*Zugeständnis*) concession

Konzil *nt* -s, -e (*Relig*) council

Kooperation /koˀɔpera'tsi̯oːn/ *f* co-operation

Koordin|ation /koˀɔrdina'tsi̯oːn/ *f* - co-ordination. **k~ieren** *vt* co-ordinate

Kopf *m* -[e]s, ⸚e head; ein K~ Kohl/ Salat a cabbage/lettuce; aus dem K~ from memory; (*auswendig*) by heart; auf den K~ (*verkehrt*) upside down; K~ stehen stand on one's head; sich (*dat*) den K~ waschen wash one's hair; sich (*dat*) den K~ zerbrechen rack one's brains. **K~ball** *m* header

köpfen *vt* behead; (*Fußball*) head

Kopf|ende *nt* head. **K~haut** *f* scalp. **K~hörer** *m* headphones *pl*. **K~kissen** *nt* pillow. **k~los** *a* panic-stricken. **K~rechnen** *nt* mental arithmetic. **K~salat** *m* lettuce. **K~schmerzen** *mpl* headache *sg*. **K~sprung** *m* header, dive. **K~stand** *m* headstand. **K~steinpflaster** *nt* cobble-stones *pl*. **K~tuch** *nt* headscarf. **k~über** *adv* head first; (*fig*) headlong. **K~wäsche** *f* shampoo. **K~weh** *nt* headache

Kopie *f* -, -n copy. **k~ren** *vt* copy

Koppel[1] *f* -, -n enclosure; (*Pferde-*) paddock

Koppel[2] *nt* -s,- (*Mil*) belt. **k~n** *vt* couple

Koralle *f* -, -n coral

Korb *m* -[e]s, ⸚e basket; jdm einen K~ geben (*fig*) turn s.o. down. **K~ball** *m* [kind of] netball

Kord *m* -s (*Tex*) corduroy

Kordel *f* -, -n cord

Korinthe *f* -, -n currant

Kork *m* -s,- cork. **K~en** *m* -s,- cork. **K~enzieher** *m* -s,- corkscrew

Korn *nt* -[e]s, ⸚er grain, (*Samen-*) seed; (*am Visier*) front sight

Körn|chen *nt* -s,- granule. **k~ig** *a* granular

Körper *m* -s,- body; (*Geom*) solid. **K~bau** *m* build, physique. **k~behindert** *a* physically disabled. **k~lich** *a* physical; <*Strafe*> corporal. **K~pflege** *f* personal hygiene. **K~schaft** *f* -, -en corporation, body

korrekt *a* correct. **K~or** *m* -s, -en /-'toːrən/ proof-reader. **K~ur** *f* -, -en correction. **K~urabzug** *m* proof

Korrespon|dent(in) *m* -en, -en (*f* -, -nen) correspondent. **K~denz** *f* -, -en correspondence

Korridor *m* -s, -e corridor

korrigieren *vt* correct

Korrosion *f* - corrosion

korrup|t *a* corrupt. **K~tion** /-'tsi̯oːn/ *f* - corruption

Korsett *nt* -[e]s, -e corset

koscher *a* kosher

Kosename *m* pet name

Kosmet|ik *f* - beauty culture. **K~ika** *ntpl* cosmetics. **K~ikerin** *f* -, -nen beautician. **k~isch** *a* cosmetic; <*Chirurgie*> plastic

kosm|isch *a* cosmic. **K~onaut(in)** *m* -en, -en (*f* -, -nen) cosmonaut

Kosmos *m* - cosmos

Kost *f* - food; (*Ernährung*) diet; (*Verpflegung*) board

kostbar *a* precious. **K~keit** *f* -, -en treasure

kosten[1] *vt/i* (*haben*) [von] etw k~ taste sth

kosten[2] *vt* cost; (*brauchen*) take; wie viel kostet es? how much is it? **K~** *pl* expense *sg*, cost *sg*; (*Jur*) costs; auf meine K~ at my expense. **K~[vor]anschlag** *m* estimate. **k~los** *a* free ● *adv* free [of charge]

köstlich *a* delicious; (*entzückend*) delightful

Kostprobe *f* taste; (*fig*) sample

Kostüm nt -s, -e (Theat) costume; (Verkleidung) fancy dress; (Schneider-) suit. **k~iert** a k~iert sein be in fancy dress

Kot m -[e]s excrement

Kotelett /kɔt'lɛt/ nt -s, -s chop, cutlet. **K~en** pl sideburns

Köter m -s,- (pej) dog

Kotflügel m (Auto) wing

kotzen vi (haben) 🗵 throw up

Krabbe f -, -n crab, shrimp

krabbeln vi (sein) crawl

Krach m -[e]s,⸚e din, racket; (Knall) crash; (🗵 Streit) row; (🗵 Ruin) crash. **k~en** vi (haben) crash; es hat gekracht there was a bang/(🗵 Unfall) a crash ● (sein) break, crack; (auftreffen) crash (**gegen** into)

krächzen vi (haben) croak

Kraft f -,⸚e strength; (Gewalt) force; (Arbeits-) worker; **in/außer K~** in/no longer in force. **K~fahrer** m driver. **K~fahrzeug** nt motor vehicle. **K~fahrzeugbrief** m [vehicle] registration document

kräftig a strong; (gut entwickelt) sturdy; (nahrhaft) nutritious; (heftig) hard

kraft|los a weak. **K~probe** f trial of strength. **K~stoff** m (Auto) fuel. **K~wagen** m motor car. **K~werk** nt power station

Kragen m -s,- collar

Krähe f -, -n crow

krähen vi (haben) crow

Kralle f -, -n claw

Kram m -s 🗵 things pl, 🗵 stuff; (Angelegenheiten) business. **k~en** vi (haben) rummage about (**in** + dat in; **nach** for)

Krampf m -[e]s,⸚e cramp. **K~adern** fpl varicose veins. **k~haft** a convulsive; (verbissen) desperate

Kran m -[e]s,⸚e (Techn) crane

Kranich m -s, -e (Zool) crane

krank a sick; <Knie, Herz> bad; k~ sein/werden be/fall ill. **K~e(r)** m/f sick man/woman, invalid; **die K~en** the sick pl

kränken vt offend, hurt

Kranken|bett nt sick-bed. **K~geld** nt sickness benefit. **K~gymnast(in)** m -en, -en (f -, -nen) physiotherapist. **K~gymnastik** f physiotherapy. **K~haus** nt hospital. **K~kasse** f health insurance scheme/(Amer) office. **K~pflege** f nursing. **K~saal** m [hospital] ward. **K~schein** m certificate of entitlement to medical treatment. **K~schwester** f nurse. **K~versicherung** f health insurance. **K~wagen** m ambulance

Krankheit f -, -en illness, disease

kränklich a sickly

krank|melden vt sep jdn k~melden report s.o. sick; **sich** k~melden report sick

Kranz m -es,⸚e wreath

Krapfen m -s,- doughnut

Krater m -s,- crater

kratzen vt/i (haben) scratch. **K~er** m -s,- scratch

Kraul nt -s (Sport) crawl. **k~en¹** vi (haben/sein) (Sport) do the crawl

kraulen² vt tickle; **sich am Kopf k~** scratch one's head

kraus a wrinkled; <Haar> frizzy; (verworren) muddled. **K~e** f -, -n frill

kräuseln vt wrinkle; frizz <Haar->; gather <Stoff>; **sich k~** wrinkle; (sich kringeln) curl; <Haar:> go frizzy

Kraut nt -[e]s, Kräuter herb; (SGer) cabbage; (Sauer-) sauerkraut

Krawall m -s, -e riot; (Lärm) row

Krawatte f -, -n [neck]tie

krea|tiv /krea'ti:f/ a creative. **K~tur** f -, -en creature

Krebs m -es, -e crayfish; (Med) cancer; (Astr) Cancer

Kredit m -s, -e credit; (Darlehen) loan; **auf K~** on credit. **K~karte** f credit card

Kreide f - chalk. **k~ig** a chalky

kreieren /kre'i:rən/ vt create

Kreis m -es, -e circle; (Admin) district

k

kreischen vt/i (haben) screech; (schreien) shriek

Kreisel m -s,- [spinning] top

kreis|en vi (haben) circle; revolve (um around). **k~förmig** a circular. **K~lauf** m cycle; (Med) circulation. **K~säge** f circular saw. **K~verkehr** m [traffic] roundabout

Krem f -, -s & m -s, -e cream

Krematorium nt -s, -ien crematorium

Krempe f -, -n [hat] brim

krempeln vt turn (nach oben up)

Krepp m -s, -s & -e crêpe

Krepppapier nt crêpe paper

Kresse f -, -n cress; (Kapuziner-) nasturtium

Kreta nt -s Crete

Kreuz nt -es, -e cross; (Kreuzung) intersection; (Mus) sharp; (Kartenspiel) clubs pl; (Anat) small of the back; über K~ crosswise; das K~ schlagen cross oneself. **k~en** vt cross; sich k~en cross; <Straßen:> intersect; <Meinungen:> clash ● vi (haben/sein) cruise. **K~fahrt** f (Naut) cruise. **K~gang** m cloister

kreuzig|en vt crucify. **K~ung** f -, -en crucifixion

Kreuz|otter f adder, common viper. **K~ung** f -, -en intersection; (Straßen-) crossroads sg. **K~verhör** nt cross-examination. **k~weise** adv crosswise. **K~worträtsel** nt crossword [puzzle]. **K~zug** m crusade

kribbel|ig a 🔟 edgy. **k~n** vi (haben) tingle; (kitzeln) tickle

kriech|en† vi (sein) crawl; (fig) grovel (vor + dat to). **K~spur** f (Auto) crawler lane. **K~tier** nt reptile

Krieg m -[e]s, -e war

kriegen vt 🔟 get; ein Kind k~ have a baby

kriegs|beschädigt a war-disabled. **K~dienstverweigerer** m -s,- conscientious objector. **K~gefangene(r)** m prisoner of war. **K~gefangenschaft** f captivity. **K~gericht** nt court martial. **K~list** f stratagem. **K~rat** m council of war. **K~recht** nt martial law

Krimi m -s, -s 🔟 crime story/film. **K~nalität** f - crime; (Vorkommen) crime rate. **K~nalpolizei** f criminal investigation department. **K~nalroman** m crime novel. **k~nell** a criminal

Krippe f -, -n manger; (Weihnachts-) crib; (Kinder-) crèche. **K~nspiel** nt Nativity play

Krise f -, -n crisis

Kristall nt -s crystal; (geschliffen) cut glass

Kritik f -, -en criticism; (Rezension) review; unter aller K~ 🔟 abysmal

Kriti|ker m -s,- critic; (Rezensent) reviewer. **k~sch** a critical. **k~sieren** vt criticize; review

kritzeln vt/i (haben) scribble

Krokodil nt -s, -e crocodile

Krokus m -, -[se] crocus

Krone f -, -n crown; (Baum-) top

krönen vt crown

Kronleuchter m chandelier

Krönung f -, -en coronation; (fig: Höhepunkt) crowning event

Kropf m -[e]s,̈-e (Zool) crop; (Med) goitre

Kröte f -, -n toad

Krücke f -, -n crutch

Krug m -[e]s,̈-e jug; (Bier-) tankard

Krümel m -s,- crumb. **k~ig** a crumbly. **k~n** vt crumble ● vi (haben) be crumbly

krumm a crooked; (gebogen) curved; (verbogen) bent

krümmen vt bend; crook <Finger>; sich k~ bend; (sich winden) writhe; (vor Lachen) double up

Krümmung f -, -en bend, curve

Krüppel m -s,- cripple

Kruste f -, -n crust; (Schorf) scab

Kruzifix nt -es, -e crucifix

Kub|a nt -s Cuba. **k~anisch** a Cuban

Kübel *m* -s,- tub; (*Eimer*) bucket; (*Techn*) skip

Küche *f* -, -n kitchen; (*Kochkunst*) cooking; **kalte/warme K~** cold/hot food

Kuchen *m* -s,- cake

Küchen|herd *m* cooker, stove. **K~maschine** *f* food processor, mixer. **K~schabe** *f* -, -n cockroach

Kuckuck *m* -s, -e cuckoo

Kufe *f* -, -n [sledge] runner

Kugel *f* -, -n ball; (*Geom*) sphere; (*Gewehr-*) bullet; (*Sport*) shot. **k~förmig** *a* spherical. **K~lager** *nt* ball-bearing. **k~n** *vt/i* (*haben*) roll; **sich k~n** (*vor Lachen*) fall about. **K~schreiber** *m* -s,-, ballpoint [pen]. **k~sicher** *a* bullet-proof. **K~stoßen** *nt* -s shot-putting

Kuh *f* -,̈-e cow

kühl *a* cool; (*kalt*) chilly. **K~box** *f* -, -en cool-box. **K~e** *f* - coolness; chilliness. **k~en** *vt* cool; refrigerate <*Lebensmittel*>; chill <*Wein*>. **K~er** *m* -s,-; (*Auto*) radiator. **K~erhaube** *f* bonnet. **K~fach** *nt* frozen-food compartment. **K~raum** *m* cold store. **K~schrank** *m* refrigerator. **K~truhe** *f* freezer. **K~wasser** *nt* [radiator] water

kühn *a* bold

Kuhstall *m* cowshed

Küken *nt* -s,- chick; (*Enten-*) duckling

Kulissen *fpl* (*Theat*) scenery *sg*; (*seitlich*) wings; **hinter den K~** (*fig*) behind the scenes

Kult *m* -[e]s, -e cult

kultivier|en *vt* cultivate. **k~t** *a* cultured

Kultur *f* -, -en culture. **K~beutel** *m* toiletbag. **k~ell** *a* cultural. **K~film** *m* documentary film

Kultusminister *m* Minister of Education and Arts

Kümmel *m* -s caraway; (*Getränk*) kümmel

Kummer *m* -s sorrow, grief; (*Sorge*) worry; (*Ärger*) trouble

kümmer|lich *a* puny; (*dürftig*) meagre; (*armselig*) wretched. **k~n** *vt*

concern; **sich k~n um** look after; (*sich befassen*) concern oneself with; (*beachten*) take notice of

kummervoll *a* sorrowful

Kumpel *m* -s,- [I] mate

Kunde *m* -n, -n customer. **K~ndienst** *m* [after-sales] service

Kundgebung *f* -, -en (*Pol*) rally

kündig|en *vt* cancel <*Vertrag*>; give notice of withdrawal for <*Geld*>; give notice to quit <*Wohnung*>; **seine Stellung k~en** give [in one's] notice ● *vi* (*haben*) give [in one's] notice; **jdm k~en** give s.o. notice. **K~ung** *f* -, -en cancellation; notice [of withdrawal/dismissal/to quit]; (*Entlassung*) dismissal. **K~ungsfrist** *f* period of notice

Kund|in *f* -, -nen [woman] customer. **K~schaft** *f* - clientele, customers *pl*

künftig *a* future ● *adv* in future

Kunst *f* -,̈-e art; (*Können*) skill. **K~faser** *f* synthetic fibre. **K~galerie** *f* art gallery. **K~geschichte** *f* history of art. **K~gewerbe** *nt* arts and crafts *pl*. **K~griff** *m* trick

Künstler *m* -s,- artist; (*Könner*) master. **K~in** *f* -, -nen [woman] artist. **k~isch** *a* artistic

künstlich *a* artificial

Kunst|stoff *m* plastic. **K~stück** *nt* trick; (*große Leistung*) feat. **k~voll** *a* artistic; (*geschickt*) skilful

kunterbunt *a* multicoloured; (*gemischt*) mixed

Kupfer *nt* -s copper

Kupon /ku'põ:/ *m* -s, -s voucher; (*Zins-*) coupon; (*Stoff-*) length

Kuppe *f* -, -n [rounded] top

Kuppel *f* -, -n dome

kuppeln *vt* couple (**an** + *acc* to) ● *vi* (*haben*) (*Auto*) operate the clutch. **K~lung** *f* -, -en coupling; (*Auto*) clutch

Kur *f* -, -en course of treatment, cure

Kür *f* -, -en (*Sport*) free exercise; (*Eislauf*) free programme

Kurbel *f* -, -n crank. **K~welle** *f* crankshaft

Kürbis *m* -ses, -se pumpkin

Kurier *m* -s, -e courier

kurieren *vt* cure

kurios *a* curious, odd. **K~ität** *f* -, -en oddness; (*Objekt*) curiosity

Kurort *m* health resort; (*Badeort*) spa

Kurs *m* -es, -e course; (*Aktien-*) price. **K~buch** *nt* timetable

kursieren *vi* (*haben*) circulate

kursiv *a* italic ● *adv* in italics. **K~schrift** *f* italics *pl*

Kursus *m* -,Kurse course

Kurswagen *m* through carriage

Kurtaxe *f* visitors' tax

Kurve *f* -, -n curve; (*Straßen-*) bend

kurz *a* short; (*knapp*) brief; (*rasch*) quick; (*schroff*) curt; **k~e Hosen** shorts; **vor k~em** a short time ago; **seit k~em** lately; **den Kürzeren ziehen** get the worst of it; **k~ vor** shortly before; **sich k~ fassen** be brief; **k~ und gut** in short; **zu k~ kommen** get less than one's fair share. **k~ärmelig** *a* short-sleeved. **k~atmig** *a* **k~atmig sein** be short of breath

Kürze *f* - shortness; (*Knappheit*) brevity; **in K~** shortly. **k~n** *vt* shorten; (*verringern*) cut

kurzfristig *a* short-term ● *adv* at short notice

kürzlich *adv* recently

Kurz|meldung *f* newsflash. **K~schluss** *m* short circuit. **K~schrift** *f* shorthand. **k~sichtig** *a* short-sighted. **K~sichtigkeit** *f* - short-sightedness. **K~streckenrakete** *f* short-range missile

Kürzung *f* -, -en shortening; (*Verringerung*) cut (*gen* in)

Kurz|waren *fpl* haberdashery *sg*. **K~welle** *f* short wave

kuscheln (sich) *vr* snuggle (**an** + *acc* up to)

Kusine *f* -, -n [female] cousin

Kuss *m* -es,¨e kiss

küssen *vt/i* (*haben*) kiss; **sich k~** kiss

Küste *f* -, -n coast

Küster *m* -s,- verger

Kutsch|e *f* -, -n [horse-drawn] carriage/(*geschlossen*) coach. **K~er** *m* -s,- coachman, driver

Kutte *f* -, -n (*Relig*) habit

Kutter *m* -s,- (*Naut*) cutter

Kuvert /ku've:ɐ̯/ *nt* -s, -s envelope

LI

Labor *nt* -s, -s & -e laboratory. **L~ant(in)** *m* -en, -en (*f* -, -nen) laboratory assistant

Labyrinth *nt* -[e]s, -e maze, labyrinth

Lache *f* -, -n puddle; (*Blut-*) pool

lächeln *vi* (*haben*) smile. **L~** *nt* -s smile. **l~d** *a* smiling

lachen *vi* (*haben*) laugh. **L~** *nt* -s laugh; (*Gelächter*) laughter

lächerlich *a* ridiculous; **sich l~ machen** make a fool of oneself. **L~keit** *f* -, -en ridiculousness; (*Kleinigkeit*) triviality

Lachs *m* -es, -e salmon

Lack *m* -[e]s, -e varnish; (*Japan-*) lacquer; (*Auto*) paint. **l~en** *vt* varnish. **l~ieren** *vt* varnish; (*spritzen*) spray. **L~schuhe** *mpl* patent-leather shoes

laden† *vt* load; (*Electr*) charge; (*Jur: vor-*) summon

Laden *m* -s,¨ shop; (*Fenster-*) shutter. **L~dieb** *m* shop-lifter. **L~schluss** *m* [shop] closing-time. **L~tisch** *m* counter

Laderaum *m* (*Naut*) hold

lädieren *vt* damage

Ladung *f* -, -en load; (*Naut, Aviat*) cargo; (*elektrische*) charge

Lage *f* -, -n position, situation; (*Schicht*) layer; **nicht in der L∼ sein** not be in a position (**zu** to)

Lager *nt* -s,- camp; (*L∼haus*) warehouse; (*Vorrat*) stock; (*Techn*) bearing; (*Erz-, Ruhe-*) bed; (*eines Tieres*) lair; [**nicht**] **auf L∼** [not] in stock. **L∼haus** *nt* warehouse. **l∼n** *vt* store; (*legen*) lay; **sich l∼n** settle. **L∼raum** *m* store-room. **L∼ung** *f* - storage

Lagune *f* -, -n lagoon

lahm *a* lame. **l∼en** *vi* (*haben*) be lame

lähmen *vt* paralyse

Lähmung *f* -, -en paralysis

Laib *m* -[e]s, -e loaf

Laich *m* -[e]s (*Zool*) spawn

Laie *m* -n, -n layman; (*Theat*) amateur. **l∼nhaft** *a* amateurish

Laken *nt* -s,- sheet

Lakritze *f* - liquorice

lallen *vt/i* (*haben*) mumble; <*Baby:*> babble

Lametta *nt* -s tinsel

Lamm *nt* -[e]s,¨-er lamb

Lampe *f* -, -n lamp; (*Decken-, Wand-*) light; (*Glüh-*) bulb. **L∼nfieber** *nt* stage fright

Lampion /lamˈpiɔŋ/ *m* -s, -s Chinese lantern

Land *nt* -[e]s,¨-er country; (*Fest-*) land; (*Bundes-*) state, Land; (*Aust*) province; **auf dem L∼e** in the country; **an L∼ gehen** (*Naut*) go ashore. **L∼arbeiter** *m* agricultural worker. **L∼ebahn** *f* runway. **l∼en** *vt/i* (*sein*) land; (🄳 *gelangen*) end up

Ländereien *pl* estates

Länderspiel *nt* international

Landesverrat *m* treason

Landkarte *f* map

ländlich *a* rural

Land|schaft *f* -, -en scenery; (*Geog, Kunst*) landscape; (*Gegend*) country[side]. **l∼schaftlich** *a* scenic; (*regional*) regional. **L∼streicher** *m* -s,- tramp. **L∼tag** *m* state/(*Aust*) provincial parliament

Landung *f* -, -en landing

Land|vermesser *m* -s,- surveyor. **L∼weg** *m* country lane; **auf dem L∼weg** overland. **L∼wirt** *m* farmer. **L∼wirtschaft** *f* agriculture; (*Hof*) farm. **l∼wirtschaftlich** *a* agricultural

lang¹ *adv & prep* (+ *preceding acc or preceding an* + *dat*) along; **den** *od* **am Fluss l∼** along the river

lang² *a* long; (*groß*) tall; **seit l∼em** for a long time ● *adv* **eine Stunde l∼** for an hour; **mein Leben l∼** all my life. **l∼ärmelig** *a* long-sleeved. **l∼atmig** *a* long-winded. **l∼e** *adv* a long time; <*schlafen*> late; **schon l∼e** [for] a long time; (*zurückliegend*) a long time ago; **l∼e nicht** not for a long time; (*bei weitem nicht*) nowhere near

Länge *f* -, -n length; (*Geog*) longitude; **der L∼nach** lengthways

Läng|engrad *m* degree of longitude. **l∼er** *a & adv* longer; (*längere Zeit*) [for] some time

Langeweile *f* - boredom; **L∼ haben** be bored

lang|fristig *a* long-term; <*Vorhersage*> long-range. **l∼jährig** *a* long-standing; <*Erfahrung*> long

länglich *a* oblong; **l∼ rund** oval

längs *adv & prep* (+ *gen/dat*) along; (*der Länge nach*) lengthways

lang|sam *a* slow. **L∼samkeit** *f* - slowness

längst *adv* [**schon**] **l∼** for a long time; (*zurückliegend*) a long time ago; **l∼ nicht** nowhere near

Lang|strecken- *pref* long-distance; (*Mil, Aviat*) long-range. **l∼weilen** *vt* bore; **sich l∼weilen** be bored. **l∼weilig** *a* boring

Lanze *f* -, -n lance

Lappalie /la'pa:liə/ *f* -, -n trifle

Lappen *m* -s,- cloth; (*Anat*) lobe

Lärche *f* -, -n larch

Lärm *m* -s noise. **l∼end** *a* noisy

Larve /ˈlarfə/ *f* -, -n larva; (*Maske*) mask

lasch *a* listless; (*schlaff*) limp

Lasche *f* -, -n tab, flap

Laser /ˈleː-, ˈlaːzɐ/ *m* -s,- laser

lassen†

● *transitive verb*

····▶ (+ *inf; veranlassen*) etw tun lassen have *or* get sth done. **jdn etw tun lassen** make s.o. do sth.; get s.o. to do sth. **sich** *dat* **die Haare schneiden lassen** have *or* get one's hair cut. **jdn warten lassen** make *or* let s.o. wait; keep s.o. waiting. **jdn grüßen lassen** send one's regards to s.o. **jdn kommen/rufen lassen** send for s.o.

····▶ (+ *inf; erlauben*) let; allow; (*hineinlassen/herauslassen*) let *or* allow (**in** + *acc* into, **aus** + *dat* out of). **jdn etw tun lassen** let s.o. do sth; allow s.o. to do sth. **er ließ mich nicht ausreden** he didn't let me finish [what I was saying]

····▶ (*belassen, bleiben lassen*) leave. **jdn in Frieden lassen** leave s.o. in peace. **etw ungesagt lassen** leave sth unsaid

····▶ (*unterlassen*) stop. **das Rauchen lassen** stop smoking. **er kann es nicht lassen, sie zu quälen** he can't stop *or* he is forever tormenting her

····▶ (*überlassen*) **jdm etw lassen** let s.o. have sth

····▶ (*als Aufforderung*) **lass/lasst uns gehen/fahren!** let's go!

● *reflexive verb*

····▶ **das lässt sich machen** that can be done. **das lässt sich nicht beweisen** it can't be proved. **die Tür lässt sich leicht öffnen** the door opens easily

● *intransitive verb*

····▶ 🛈 **Lass mal. Ich mache das schon** Leave it. I'll do it

lässig *a* casual. **L~keit** *f* - casualness

Lasso *nt* -s, -s lasso

Last *f* -, -en load; (*Gewicht*) weight; (*fig*) burden; **L~en** charges; (*Steuern*) taxes. **L~auto** *nt* lorry. **l~en** *vi* (*haben*) weigh heavily/(*liegen*) rest (**auf** + *dat* on)

Laster¹ *m* -s,- 🛈 lorry

Laster² *nt* -s,- vice

*alte Schreibung

läster|n *vt* blaspheme ● *vi* (*haben*) make disparaging remarks (**über** + *acc* about). **L~ung** *f* -, -en blasphemy

lästig *a* troublesome; **l~ sein/werden** be/become a nuisance

Last|kahn *m* barge. **L~[kraft]wagen** *m* lorry

Latein *nt* -[s] Latin. **L~amerika** *nt* Latin America. **l~isch** *a* Latin

Laterne *f* -, -n lantern; (*Straßen-*) street lamp. **L~npfahl** *m* lamp-post

latschen *vi* (*sein*) 🛈 traipse

Latte *f* -, -n slat; (*Tor-, Hochsprung-*) bar

Latz *m* -es,¨e bib

Lätzchen *nt* -s,- [baby's] bib

Latzhose *f* dungarees *pl*

Laub *nt* -[e]s leaves *pl*; (*L~werk*) foliage. **L~baum** *m* deciduous tree

Laube *f* -, -n summer-house

Laub|säge *f* fretsaw. **L~wald** *m* deciduous forest

Lauch *m* -[e]s leeks *pl*

Lauer *f* **auf der L~ liegen** lie in wait. **l~n** *vi* (*haben*) lurk; **l~n auf** (+ *acc*) lie in wait for

Lauf *m* -[e]s, Läufe run; (*Laufen*) running; (*Verlauf*) course; (*Wett-*) race; (*Sport: Durchgang*) heat; (*Gewehr-*) barrel; **im L~[e]** (+ *gen*) in the course of. **L~bahn** *f* career. **l~en†** *vi* (*sein*) run; (*zu Fuß gehen*) walk; (*gelten*) be valid; **Ski/Schlittschuh l~en** ski/skate. **l~end** *a* running; (*gegenwärtig*) current; (*regelmäßig*) regular; **auf dem L~enden sein** be up to date ● *adv* continually

Läufer *m* -s,- (*Person, Teppich*) runner; (*Schach*) bishop

Lauf|gitter *nt* play-pen. **L~masche** *f* ladder. **L~zettel** *m* circular

Lauge *f* -, -n soapy water

Laun|e *f* -, -n mood; (*Einfall*) whim; **guter L~e sein, gute L~e haben** be in a good mood. **l~isch** *a* moody

Laus *f* -, Läuse louse; (*Blatt-*) greenfly

lauschen *vi* (*haben*) listen

laut *a* loud; *(geräuschvoll)* noisy; **l∼ lesen** read aloud; **l∼er stellen** turn up ● *prep* (+ *gen/dat*) according to. **L∼** *m* **-es, -e** sound

Laute *f* **-, -n** *(Mus)* lute

lauten *vi (haben)* *<Text:>* run, read

läuten *vt/i (haben)* ring

lauter *a* pure; *(ehrlich)* honest; *<Wahrheit>* plain ● *a inv* sheer; *(nichts als)* nothing but

laut|hals *adv* at the top of one's voice, *<lachen>* out loud. **l∼los** *a* silent, *<Stille>* hushed. **L∼schrift** *f* phonetics *pl*. **L∼sprecher** *m* loudspeaker. **L∼stärke** *f* volume

lauwarm *a* lukewarm

Lava *f* **-, -ven** lava

Lavendel *m* **-s** lavender

lavieren *vi (haben)* manœuvre

Lawine *f* **-, -n** avalanche

Lazarett *nt* **-[e]s, -e** military hospital

leasen /'li:sən/ *vt* rent

Lebehoch *nt* cheer

leben *vt/i (haben)* live (**von** on); **leb wohl!** farewell! **L∼** *nt* **-s,-** life, *(Treiben)* bustle; **am L∼** alive. **l∼d** *a* living

lebendig *a* live; *(lebhaft)* lively; *(anschaulich)* vivid; **l∼ sein** be alive. **L∼keit** *f* **-** liveliness; vividness

Lebens|abend *m* old age. **L∼alter** *nt* age. **l∼fähig** *a* viable. **L∼gefahr** *f* mortal danger; **in L∼gefahr** in mortal danger; *<Patient>* critically ill. **l∼gefährlich** *a* extremely dangerous; *<Verletzung>* critical. **L∼haltungskosten** *pl* cost of living *sg*. **l∼länglich** *a* life ... ● *adv* for life. **L∼lauf** *m* curriculum vitae. **L∼mittel** *ntpl* food *sg*. **L∼mittelgeschäft** *nt* food shop. **L∼mittelhändler** *m* grocer. **L∼retter** *m* rescuer; *(beim Schwimmen)* life-guard. **L∼unterhalt** *m* livelihood; **seinen L∼unterhalt verdienen** earn one's living. **L∼versicherung** *f* life assurance. **L∼wandel** *m* conduct. **l∼wichtig** *a* vital. **L∼zeit** *f* **auf L∼zeit** for life

Leber *f* **-, -n** liver. **L∼fleck** *m* mole

Lebe|wesen *nt* living being. **L∼wohl** *nt* **-s, -s &** **-e** farewell

leb|haft *a* lively; *<Farbe>* vivid. **L∼kuchen** *m* gingerbread. **l∼los** *a* lifeless. **L∼zeiten** *fpl* **zu jds L∼zeiten** in s.o.'s lifetime

leck *a* leaking. **L∼** *nt* **-s, -s** leak. **l∼en**[1] *vi (haben)* leak

lecken[2] *vi (haben)* lick

lecker *a* tasty. **L∼ bissen** *m* delicacy

Leder *nt* **-s,-** leather

ledig *a* single

leer *a* empty; *(unbesetzt)* vacant; **l∼ laufen** *(Auto)* idle. **l∼en** *vt* empty; **sich l∼en** empty. **L∼lauf** *m* *(Auto)* neutral. **L∼ung** *f* **-, -en** *(Post)* collection

legal *a* legal. **l∼isieren** *vt* legalize. **L∼ität** *f* **-** legality

Legas|thenie *f* **-** dyslexia. **L∼theniker** *m* **-s,-** dyslexic

legen *vt* put; *(hin-, ver-)* lay; set *<Haare>*; **sich l∼** lie down; *(nachlassen)* subside

Legende *f* **-, -n** legend

leger /le'ʒe:ɐ/ *a* casual

Legierung *f* **-, -en** alloy

Legion *f* **-, -en** legion

Legislative *f* **-** legislature

legitim *a* legitimate. **L∼ität** *f* **-** legitimacy

Lehm *m* **-s** clay

Lehn|e *f* **-, -n** *(Rücken-)* back; *(Arm-)* arm. **l∼en** *vt* lean (**an** + *acc against*); **sich l∼en** lean (**an** + *acc against*) ● *vi (haben)* be leaning (**an** + *acc against*)

Lehr|buch *nt* textbook. **L∼e** *f* **-, -n** apprenticeship; *(Anschauung)* doctrine; *(Theorie)* theory; *(Wissenschaft)* science; *(Erfahrung)* lesson. **l∼en** *vt/i (haben)* teach. **L∼er** *m* **-s,-** teacher; *(Fahr-)* instructor. **L∼erin** *f* **-, -nen** teacher. **L∼erzimmer** *nt* staff-room. **L∼fach** *nt* *(Sch)* subject. **L∼gang** *m* course. **L∼kraft** *f* teacher. **L∼ling** *m* **-s, -e** apprentice; *(Auszubildender)* trainee. **L∼plan** *m*

syllabus. **l~reich** a instructive.
L~stelle f apprenticeship.
L~stuhl m (*Univ*) chair. **L~zeit** f
apprenticeship

Leib m -es, -er body; (*Bauch*) belly.
L~eserziehung f (*Sch*) physical
education. **L~gericht** nt favourite
dish. **l~lich** a physical;
(*blutsverwandt*) real, natural.
L~wächter m bodyguard

Leiche f -, -n [dead] body; corpse.
L~nbestatter m -s,- undertaker.
L~nhalle f mortuary. **L~nwagen**
m hearse. **L~nzug** m funeral
procession, cortège

Leichnam m -s, -e [dead] body

leicht a light; <*Stoff*> lightweight;
(*gering*) slight; (*mühelos*) easy; **jdm**
l~ fallen be easy for s.o.; **etw l~**
machen make sth easy (**dat** for); **es**
sich (*dat*) **l~ machen** take the easy
way out; **etw l~ nehmen** (*fig*) take
sth lightly. **L~athletik** f [track and
field] athletics *sg*. **L~gewicht** nt
(*Boxen*) lightweight. **l~gläubig** a
gullible. **l~hin** adv casually.
L~igkeit f - lightness;
(*Mühelosigkeit*) ease; (*L~sein*)
easiness; **mit L~igkeit** with ease.
L~sinn m carelessness;
recklessness; (*Frivolität*) frivolity.
l~sinnig a careless; (*unvorsichtig*)
reckless

Leid nt -[e]s sorrow, grief; (*Böses*)
harm; **es tut mir L~** I am sorry; **er**
tut mir L~ I feel sorry for him. **l~** a
jdn/etw l~ sein/werden be/get tired
of s.o./sth

Leide|form f passive. **l~n†** vt/i
(*haben*) suffer (**an** + *dat* from); **jdn/**
etw nicht l~n können dislike s.o./sth.
L~n nt -s,- suffering; (*Med*)
complaint; (*Krankheit*) disease.
l~nd a suffering. **L~nschaft** f -,
-en passion. **l~nschaftlich** a
passionate

leider adv unfortunately; **l~er ja/**
nicht I'm afraid so/not

Leier|kasten m barrel-organ. **l~n**
vt/i (*haben*) wind; (*herunter-*) drone
out

Leih|e f -, -n loan. **l~en†** vt lend;
sich (*dat*) **etw l~en** borrow sth.
L~gabe f loan. **L~gebühr** f
rental; lending charge. **L~haus** nt
pawnshop. **L~wagen** m hire-car.
l~weise adv on loan

Leim m -s glue. **l~en** vt glue

Leine f -, -n rope; (*Wäsche-*) line;
(*Hunde-*) lead, leash

Leinen nt -s linen. **L~wand** f
linen; (*Kunst*) canvas; (*Film-*) screen

leise a quiet; <*Stimme, Berührung*>
soft; (*schwach*) faint; (*leicht*) light;
l~r stellen turn down

Leiste f -, -n strip; (*Holz-*) batten;
(*Anat*) groin

leist|en vt achieve, accomplish; **sich**
(*dat*) **etw l~en** treat oneself to sth;
(⊞ *anstellen*) get up to sth; **ich kann**
es mir nicht l~en I can't afford it.
L~ung f -, -en achievement; (*Sport,*
Techn) performance; (*Produktion*)
output; (*Zahlung*) payment

Leit|artikel m leader, editorial.
l~en vt run, manage; (*an-/*
hinführen) lead; (*Mus, Techn, Phys*)
conduct; (*lenken, schicken*) direct.
l~end a leading; <*Posten*>
executive

Leiter¹ f -, -n ladder

Leit|er² m -s,- director; (*Comm*)
manager; (*Führer*) leader; (*Mus,*
Phys) conductor. **L~erin** f -, -nen
director; manageress; leader.
L~planke f crash barrier.
L~spruch m motto. **L~ung** f -, -en
(*Führung*) direction; (*Comm*)
management; (*Aufsicht*) control;
(*Electr: Schnur*) lead, flex; (*Kabel*)
cable; (*Telefon-*) line; (*Rohr-*) pipe;
(*Haupt-*) main. **L~ungswasser** nt
tap water

Lektion /-'tsio:n/ f -, -en lesson

Lekt|or m -s, -en /-'to:ran/, **L~orin** f
-, -nen (*Univ*) assistant lecturer;
(*Verlags-*) editor. **L~üre** f -, -n
reading matter

Lende f -, -n loin

lenk|en vt guide; (*steuern*) steer;
(*regeln*) control; **jds Aufmerksamkeit**
auf sich (*acc*) **l~en** attract s.o.'s
attention. **L~rad** nt steering-wheel.

---

*old spelling

L~stange f handlebars pl. **L~ung** f - steering

Leopard m -en, -en leopard

Lepra f - leprosy

Lerche f -, -n lark

lernen vt/i (haben) learn; (für die Schule) study

Lesb|ierin /'lɛsbiərɪn/ f -, -nen lesbian. **l~isch** a lesbian

les|en† vt/i (haben) read; (Univ) lecture • vt pick, gather. **L~en** nt -s reading. **L~er(in)** m -s,- (f -, -nen) reader. **l~erlich** a legible. **L~ezeichen** nt bookmark

lethargisch a lethargic

Lettland nt -s Latvia

letzt|e(r,s) a last; (neueste) latest; in **l~er Zeit** recently; **l~en Endes** in the end. **l~ens** adv recently; (zuletzt) lastly. **l~ere(r,s)** a the latter; **der/die/das L~ere** the latter

Leucht|e f -, -n light. **l~en** vi (haben) shine. **l~end** a shining. **L~er** m -s,- candlestick. **L~feuer** nt beacon. **L~rakete** f flare. **L~reklame** f neon sign. **L~röhre** f fluorescent tube. **L~turm** m lighthouse

leugnen vt deny

Leukämie f - leukaemia

Leumund m -s reputation

Leute pl people; (Mil) men; (Arbeiter) workers

Leutnant m -s, -s second lieutenant

Lexikon nt -s, -ka encyclopaedia; (Wörterbuch) dictionary

Libanon (der) -s Lebanon

Libelle f -, -n dragonfly

liberal a (Pol) Liberal

Libyen nt -s Libya

Licht nt -[e]s, -er light; (Kerze) candle; **L~ machen** turn on the light. **l~** a bright; (Med) lucid; (spärlich) sparse. **L~bild** nt [passport] photograph; (Dia) slide. **L~blick** m (fig) ray of hope. **l~en** vt thin out; **den Anker l~en** (Naut) weigh anchor; **sich l~en** become less dense; thin. **L~hupe** f headlight flasher; **die L~hupe betätigen** flash one's headlights. **L~maschine** f dynamo. **L~ung** f -, -en clearing

Lid nt -[e]s, -er [eye]lid. **L~schatten** m eye-shadow

lieb a dear; (nett) nice; (artig) good; **jdn l~ haben** be fond of s.o.; (lieben) love s.o.; **es wäre mir l~er** I should prefer it (wenn if)

Liebe f -, -n love. **l~n** vt love; (mögen) like; **sich l~n** love each other; (körperlich) make love. **l~nd** a loving. **l~nswert** a lovable. **l~nswürdig** a kind. **l~nswürdigerweise** adv very kindly

lieber adv rather; (besser) better; **l~ mögen** like better; **ich trinke l~ Tee** I prefer tea

Liebes|brief m love letter. **L~dienst** m favour. **L~kummer** m heartache. **L~paar** nt [pair of] lovers pl

lieb|evoll a loving, affectionate. **L~haber** m -s,- lover; (Sammler) collector. **L~haberei** f -, -en hobby. **L~kosung** f -, -en caress. **l~lich** a lovely; (sanft) gentle; (süß) sweet. **L~ling** m -s, -e darling; (Bevorzugte) favourite. **L~lingspref** favourite. **l~los** a loveless; <Eltern> uncaring; (unfreundlich) unkind. **L~schaft** f -, -en [love] affair. **l~ste(r,s)** a dearest; (bevorzugt) favourite • adv am **l~sten** best [of all]; **jdn/etw am l~sten mögen** like s.o./sth best [of all]. **L~ste(r)** m/f beloved; (Schatz) sweetheart

Lied nt -[e]s, -er song

liederlich a slovenly; (unordentlich) untidy. **L~keit** f - slovenliness; untidiness

Lieferant m -en, -en supplier

liefer|bar a (Comm) available. **l~n** vt supply; (zustellen) deliver; (hervorbringen) yield. **L~ung** f -, -en delivery; (Sendung) consignment

Liege f -, -n couch. **l~n**† vi (haben) lie; (gelegen sein) be situated; **l~n bleiben** remain lying [there]; (im Bett) stay in bed; <Ding:> be left; <Schnee:> settle; <Arbeit:> remain undone; (*zurückgelassen werden*) be left behind; **l∼n lassen** leave; (*zurücklassen*) leave behind; (*nicht fortführen*) leave undone; **l∼n an** (+ *dat*) (*fig*) be due to; (*abhängen*) depend on; **jdm [nicht] l∼n** [not] suit s.o.; **mir liegt viel daran** it is very important to me. **L∼stuhl** *m* deckchair. **L∼stütz** *m* -es, -e press-up, (*Amer*) push-up. **L∼wagen** *m* couchette car

Lift *m* -[e]s, -e & -s lift

Liga *f* -, -gen league

Likör *m* -s, -e liqueur

lila *inv a* mauve; (*dunkel*) purple

Lilie /'li:liə/ *f* -, -n lily

Liliputaner(in) *m* -s,- (*f* -, -nen) dwarf

Limo *f* -, -[s] 🄸, **L∼nade** *f* -, -n fizzy drink; lemonade

Limousine /limu'zi:nə/ *f* -, -n saloon

lind *a* mild

Linde *f* -, -n lime tree

lindern *vt* relieve, ease. **L∼ung** *f* - relief

Lineal *nt* -s, -e ruler

Linie /-iə/ *f* -, -n line; (*Zweig*) branch; (*Bus-*) route; **L∼ 4** number 4 [bus/ tram]; **in erster L∼** primarily. **L∼nflug** *m* scheduled flight. **L∼nrichter** *m* linesman

lin[i]iert *a* lined, ruled

Linke *f* -n, -n left side; (*Hand*) left hand; (*Boxen*) left; **die L∼e** (*Pol*) the left. **l∼e(r,s)** *a* left; (*Pol*) leftwing; **l∼e Masche** purl

links *adv* on the left; (*bei Stoff*) on the wrong side; (*verkehrt*) inside out; **l∼ stricken** purl. **L∼händer(in)** *m* -s,- (*f* -, -nen) lefthander. **l∼händig** *a* & *adv* lefthanded

Linoleum /-leʊm/ *nt* -s lino, linoleum

Linse *f* -, -n lens; (*Bot*) lentil

Lippe *f* -, -n lip. **L∼nstift** *m* lipstick

Liquid|ation /-'tsio:n/ *f* -, -en liquidation. **l∼ieren** *vt* liquidate

lispeln *vt/i* (*haben*) lisp

List *f* -, -en trick, ruse

Liste *f* -, -n list

listig *a* cunning, crafty

Litanei *f* -, -en litany

Litauen *nt* -s Lithuania

Liter *m* & *nt* -s,- litre

Literatur *f* - literature

Liturgie *f* -, -n liturgy

Litze *f* -, -n braid

Lizenz *f* -, -en licence

Lob *nt* -[e]s praise

Lobby /'lɔbi/ *f* - (*Pol*) lobby

loben *vt* praise

löblich *a* praiseworthy

Lobrede *f* eulogy

Loch *nt* -[e]s, ¨er hole. **l∼en** *vt* punch a hole/holes in; punch <*Fahrkarte*>. **L∼er** *m* -s,- punch

löcherig *a* full of holes

Locke *f* -, -n curl. **l∼n¹** *vt* curl; **sich l∼n** curl

locken² *vt* lure, entice; (*reizen*) tempt. **l∼d** *a* tempting

Lockenwickler *m* -s,- curler; (*Rolle*) roller

locker *a* loose; <*Seil*> slack; <*Erde*> light; (*zwanglos*) casual; (*zu frei*) lax. **l∼n** *vt* loosen; slacken <*Seil*>; break up <*Boden*>; relax <*Griff*>; **sich l∼n** become loose; <*Seil:*> slacken; (*sich entspannen*) relax

lockig *a* curly

Lockmittel *nt* bait

Loden *m* -s (*Tex*) loden

Löffel *m* -s,- spoon; (*L∼ voll*) spoonful. **l∼n** *vt* spoon up

Logarithmus *m* -, -men logarithm

Logbuch *nt* (*Naut*) log-book

Loge /'lo:ʒə/ *f* -, -n lodge; (*Theat*) box

Log|ik *f* - logic. **l∼isch** *a* logical

Logo *nt* -s, -s logo

Lohn *m* -[e]s, ¨e wages *pl*, pay; (*fig*) reward. **L∼empfänger** *m* wageearner. **l∼en** *vi|r* (*haben*) [sich] **l∼en** be worth it *or* worth while ● *vt* be worth. **l∼end** *a* worthwhile; (*befriedigend*) rewarding. **L∼erhöhung** *f* [pay] rise. **L∼steuer** *f* income tax

Lok *f* -, -s 🄸 = **Lokomotive**

Lokal *nt* -s, -e restaurant; (*Trink-*) bar

Lokomotiv|e *f* -, -n engine, locomotive. **L~führer** *m* engine driver

London *nt* -s London. **L~er** *a* London ... ● *m* -s,- Londoner

Lorbeer *m* -s, -en laurel. **L~blatt** *nt* (*Culin*) bay-leaf

Lore *f* -, -n (*Rail*) truck

Los *nt* -es, -e lot; (*Lotterie-*) ticket; (*Schicksal*) fate

los *pred a* los sein be loose; jdn/etw los sein be rid of s.o./sth; was ist [mit ihm] los? what's the matter [with him]? ● *adv* los! go on! Achtung, fertig, los! ready, steady, go!

lösbar *a* soluble

losbinden† *vt sep* untie

Lösch|blatt *nt* sheet of blotting-paper. **l~en** *vt* put out, extinguish; quench <*Durst*>; blot <*Tinte*>; (*tilgen*) cancel; (*streichen*) delete

Löschfahrzeug *nt* fire-engine

lose *a* loose

Lösegeld *nt* ransom

losen *vt* (*haben*) draw lots (um for)

lösen *vt* undo; (*lockern*) loosen; (*entfernen*) detach; (*klären*) solve; (*auflösen*) dissolve; cancel <*Vertrag*>; break off <*Beziehung*>; (*kaufen*) buy; sich l~ come off; (*sich trennen*) detach oneself/itself; (*lose werden*) come undone; (*sich klären*) resolve itself; (*sich auflösen*) dissolve

los|fahren† *vi sep* (*sein*) start; <*Auto:*> drive off; **l~fahren auf** (+ *acc*) head for. **l~gehen**† *vi sep* (*sein*) set off; (🔲 *anfangen*) start; <*Bombe:*> go off; **l~gehen auf** (+ *acc*) head for; (*fig: angreifen*) go for. **l~kommen**† *vi sep* (*sein*) get away (von from). **l~lassen**† *vt sep* let go of; (*freilassen*) release

löslich *a* soluble

los|lösen *vt sep* detach; sich l~lösen become detached; (*fig*) break away (von from). **l~machen** *vt sep* detach; untie. **l~reißen**† *vt sep* tear off; sich l~reißen break free; (*fig*) tear oneself away. **l~schicken** *vt*

sep send off. **l~sprechen**† *vt sep* absolve (von from)

Losung *f* -, -en (*Pol*) slogan; (*Mil*) password

Lösung *f* -, -en solution. **L~smittel** *nt* solvent

loswerden† *vt sep* get rid of

Lot *nt* -[e]s, -e perpendicular; (*Blei-*) plumb[-bob]. **l~en** *vt* plumb

löt|en *vt* solder. **L~lampe** *f* blow-lamp

lotrecht *a* perpendicular

Lotse *m* -n, -n (*Naut*) pilot. **l~n** *vt* (*Naut*) pilot; (*fig*) guide

Lotterie *f* -, -n lottery

Lotto *nt* -s, -s lotto; (*Lotterie*) lottery

Löw|e *m* -n, -n lion; (*Astr*) Leo. **L~enzahn** *m* (*Bot*) dandelion. **L~in** *f* -, -nen lioness

loyal /loaˈjaːl/ *a* loyal. **L~ität** *f* - loyalty

Luchs *m* -es, -e lynx

Lücke *f* -, -n gap. **l~nhaft** *a* incomplete; <*Wissen*> patchy. **l~nlos** *a* complete; <*Folge*> unbroken

Luder *nt* -s,- ✕ (*Frau*) bitch

Luft *f* -,ˆe air; tief L~ holen take a deep breath; in die L~ gehen explode. **L~angriff** *m* air raid. **L~aufnahme** *f* aerial photograph. **L~ballon** *m* balloon. **L~blase** *f* air bubble. **L~druck** *m* atmospheric pressure

lüften *vt* air; raise <*Hut*>; reveal <*Geheimnis*>

Luft|fahrt *f* aviation. **L~fahrtgesellschaft** *f* airline. **L~gewehr** *nt* airgun. **l~ig** *a* airy; <*Kleid*> light. **L~kissenfahrzeug** *nt* hovercraft. **L~krieg** *m* aerial warfare. **l~leer** *a* leer Raum vacuum. **L~linie** *f* 100 km L~linie 100 km as the crow flies. **L~matratze** *f* air-bed, inflatable mattress. **L~pirat** *m* hijacker. **L~post** *f* airmail. **L~röhre** *f* windpipe. **L~schiff** *nt* airship. **L~schlange** *f* [paper] streamer. **L~schutzbunker** *m* air-raid shelter

Lüftung f - ventilation

Luft|veränderung f change of air.
L~waffe f air force. **L~zug** m
draught

Lüg|e f -, -n lie. **l~en†** vt/i (haben)
lie. **L~ner(in)** m -s,- (f -, -nen) liar.
l~nerisch a untrue; <Person>
untruthful

Luke f -, -n hatch; (Dach-) skylight

Lümmel m -s,- lout

Lump m -en, -en scoundrel. **L~en** m
-s,- rag; in **L~en** in rags.
L~enpack nt riff-raff.
L~ensammler m rag-and-bone
man. **l~ig** a mean, shabby

Lunge f -, -n lungs pl; (L~nflügel)
lung. **L~nentzündung** f
pneumonia

Lupe f -, -n magnifying glass

Lurch m -[e]s, -e amphibian

Lust f -,-̈e pleasure; (Verlangen)
desire; (sinnliche Begierde) lust; **L~**
haben feel like (**auf etw** acc sth); **ich**
habe keine L~ I don't feel like it;
(will nicht) I don't want to

lustig a jolly; (komisch) funny; **sich**
l~ machen über (+ acc) make fun of

Lüstling m -s, -e lecher

lust|los a listless. **L~mörder** m
sex killer. **L~spiel** nt comedy

lutsch|en vt/i (haben) suck. **L~er**
m -s,- lollipop

Lüttich nt -s Liège

Luv f & nt - nach Luv (Naut) to
windward

luxuriös a luxurious

Luxus m - luxury

Lymph|drüse /ˈlymf-/ f,
L~knoten m lymph gland

lynchen /ˈlynçən/ vt lynch

Lyr|ik f - lyric poetry. **L~iker** m -s,-
lyric poet. **l~isch** a lyrical

M m

Machart f style

machen
● transitive verb
····▸ (herstellen, zubereiten) make
<money, beds, music, exception, etc>.
aus Plastik/Holz gemacht made of
plastic/wood. **sich** (dat) **etw machen**
lassen have sth made. **etw aus jdm**
machen make s.o. into sth. **jdn zum**
Präsidenten machen make s.o.
president. **er machte sich** (dat) **viele**
Freunde/Feinde he made a lot of
friends/enemies. **jdm/sich** (dat)
[einen] Kaffee machen make [some]
coffee for s.o./oneself. **ein Foto**
machen take a photo
····▸ (verursachen) make, cause
<difficulties>; cause <pain, anxiety>.
jdm Arbeit machen make [extra]
work for s.o., cause s.o. extra work.
jdm Mut/Hoffnung machen give s.o.
courage/hope. **das macht Hunger/**
Durst this makes you hungry/
thirsty. **das macht das Wetter** that's
[because of] the weather
····▸ (ausführen, ordnen) do <job,
repair ①: room, washing, etc.>; take
<walk, trip, exam, course>. **sie**
machte mir die Haare ① she did my
hair for me. **einen Besuch [bei jdm]**
machen pay [s.o.] a visit
····▸ (tun) do <nothing, everything>.
was machst du [da]? what are you
doing? **so etwas macht man nicht**
that [just] isn't done
····▸ **was macht ...?** (wie ist es um ...
bestellt?) how is ...? **was macht die**
Gesundheit/Arbeit? how are you
keeping/how is the job [getting on]?
····▸ (Math: ergeben) be. **zwei mal zwei**
macht vier two times two is four. **das**
macht 6 Mark [zusammen] that's or
that comes to six marks [altogether]

·····➤ (*schaden*) was macht das schon? what does it matter? **[das] macht nichts!** ⓘ it doesn't matter

·····➤ **machs gut!** ⓘ look after yourself!; (*auf Wiedersehen*) so long!

● *reflexive verb*

·····➤ **sich machen** ⓘ do well

·····➤ **sich an etw** (*acc*) **machen** get down to sth. **sie machte sich an die Arbeit** she got down to work

● *intransitive verb*

·····➤ **das macht hungrig/durstig** it makes you hungry/thirsty. **das macht dick** it's fattening

Macht *f* -,-̈e power. **M~haber** *m* -s,- ruler

mächtig *a* powerful ● *adv* ⓘ terribly

machtlos *a* powerless

Mädchen *nt* -s,- girl; (*Dienst-*) maid. **m~haft** *a* girlish. **M~name** *m* girl's name; (*vor der Ehe*) maiden name

Made *f* -,-n maggot

madig *a* maggoty

Madonna *f* -,-nen madonna

Magazin *nt* -s,-e magazine; (*Lager*) warehouse; store-room

Magd *f* -,-̈e maid

Magen *m* -s,-̈ stomach. **M~verstimmung** *f* stomach upset

mager *a* thin; <*Fleisch*> lean; <*Boden*> poor; (*dürftig*) meagre. **M~keit** *f* - thinness; leanness. **M~sucht** *f* anorexia

Magie *f* - magic

Magier /'ma:giɐ/ *m* -s,- magician. **m~isch** *a* magic

Magistrat *m* -s,-e city council

Magnet *m* -en & -[e]s,-e magnet. **m~isch** *a* magnetic

Mahagoni *nt* -s mahogany

Mäh|drescher *m* -s,- combine harvester. **m~en** *vt/i* (*haben*) mow

Mahl *nt* -[e]s,-̈er & -e meal

mahlen† *vt* grind

Mahlzeit *f* meal; **M~!** enjoy your meal!

Mähne *f* -,-n mane

mahn|en *vt/i* (*haben*) remind (*wegen* about); (*ermahnen*) admonish; (*auffordern*) urge (**zu** to). **M~ung** *f* -,-en reminder; admonition

Mai *m* -[e]s,-e May; **der Erste Mai** May Day. **M~glöckchen** *nt* -s,- lily of the valley

Mailand *nt* -s Milan

Mais *m* -es maize; (*Culin*) sweet corn

Majestät *f* -,-en majesty. **m~isch** *a* majestic

Major *m* -s,-e major

Majoran *m* -s marjoram

makaber *a* macabre

Makel *m* -s,- blemish; (*Defekt*) flaw

Makkaroni *pl* macaroni *sg*

Makler *m* -s,- (*Comm*) broker

Makrele *f* -,-n mackerel

Makrone *f* -,-n macaroon

mal *adv* (*Math*) times; (*bei Maßen*) by; (ⓘ *einmal*) once; (*eines Tages*) one day; **nicht mal** not even

Mal *nt* -[e]s,-e time; **zum ersten/ letzten Mal** for the first/last time; **ein für alle Mal** once and for all; **jedes Mal** every time; **jedes Mal, wenn** whenever

Mal|buch *nt* colouring book. **m~en** *vt/i* (*haben*) paint. **M~er** *m* -s,- painter. **M~erei** *f* -,-en painting. **M~erin** *f* -,-nen painter. **m~erisch** *a* picturesque

Mallorca /ma'lɔrka, -'jɔrka/ *nt* -s Majorca

malnehmen† *vt sep* multiply (**mit** by)

Malz *nt* -es malt

Mama /'mama, ma'ma:/ *f* -s,-s mummy

Mammut *nt* -s,-e & -s mammoth

mampfen *vt* ⓘ munch

man *pron* one, you; (*die Leute*) people, they; **man sagt** they say, it is said

manch|e(r,s) *pron* many a; [**so**] **m~es Mal** many a time; **m~e Leute** some people ● (*substantivisch*) **m~er/m~e** many a man/woman; **m~e** *pl* some; (*Leute*) some people; (*viele*) many [people]; **m~es** some

things; (*vieles*) many things.
m~erlei *inv* a various ● *pron* various things

manchmal *adv* sometimes

Mandant(in) *m* -en, -en (*f* -, -nen) (*Jur*) client

Mandarine *f* -, -n mandarin

Mandat *nt* -[e]s, -e mandate; (*Jur*) brief; (*Pol*) seat

Mandel *f* -, -n almond; (*Anat*) tonsil. **M~entzündung** *f* tonsillitis

Manege /ma'ne:ʒə/ *f* -, -n ring; (*Reit-*) arena

Mangel¹ *m* -s,= lack; (*Knappheit*) shortage; (*Med*) deficiency; (*Fehler*) defect

Mangel² *f* -, -n mangle

mangel|haft *a* faulty, defective; (*Sch*) unsatisfactory. **m~n¹** *vi* (*haben*) **es m~t an** (+ *dat*) there is a lack/(*Knappheit*) shortage of

mangeln² *vt* put through the mangle

Manie *f* -, -n mania

Manier *f* -, -en manner; **M~en** manners. **m~lich** *a* well-mannered ● *adv* properly

Manifest *nt* -[e]s, -e manifesto

Maniküre *f* -, -n manicure; (*Person*) manicurist. **m~n** *vt* manicure

Manko *nt* -s, -s disadvantage; (*Fehlbetrag*) deficit

Mann *m* -[e]s,=er man; (*Ehe-*) husband

Männchen *nt* -s,- little man; (*Zool*) male

Mannequin /'manəkɛ̃/ *nt* -s, -s model

männlich *a* male; (*Gram & fig*) masculine; (*mannhaft*) manly; <*Frau*> mannish. **M~keit** *f* - masculinity; (*fig*) manhood

Mannschaft *f* -, -en team; (*Naut*) crew

Manöv|er *nt* -s,- manœuvre; (*Winkelzug*) trick. **m~rieren** *vt/i* (*haben*) manœuvre

Mansarde *f* -, -n attic room; (*Wohnung*) attic flat

Manschette *f* -, -n cuff. **M~nknopf** *m* cuff-link

Mantel *m* -s,= coat; overcoat

Manuskript *nt* -[e]s, -e manuscript

Mappe *f* -, -n folder; (*Akten-*) briefcase; (*Schul-*) bag

Märchen *nt* -s,- fairy-tales

Margarine *f* - margarine

Marienkäfer /ma'ri:ən-/ *m* lady-bird

Marihuana *nt* -s marijuana

Marine *f* marine; (*Kriegs-*) navy. **m~blau** *a* navy [blue]

marinieren *vt* marinade

Marionette *f* -, -n puppet, marionette

Mark¹ *f* -,- mark; **drei M~** three marks

Mark² *nt* -[e]s (*Knochen-*) marrow (*Bot*)pith; (*Frucht-*) pulp

markant *a* striking

Marke *f* -, -n token; (*rund*) disc; (*Erkennungs-*) tag; (*Brief-*) stamp; (*Lebensmittel-*) coupon; (*Spiel-*) counter; (*Markierung*) mark; (*Fabrikat*) make; (*Tabak-*) brand. **M~nartikel** *m* branded article

markieren *vt* mark; (🔲 *vortäuschen*) fake

Markise *f* -, -n awning

Markstück *nt* one-mark piece

Markt *m* -[e]s,=e market; (*M~platz*) market-place. **M~forschung** *f* market research

Marmelade *f* -, -n jam; (*Orangen-*) marmalade

Marmor *m* -s marble

Marokko *nt* -s Morocco

Marone *f* -, -n [sweet] chestnut

Marsch *m* -[e]s,=e march. **m~** *int* (*Mil*) march!

Marschall *m* -s,=e marshal

marschieren *vi* (*sein*) march

Marter *f* -, -n torture. **m~n** *vt* torture

Märtyrer(in) *m* -s,- (*f* -, -nen) martyr

Marxismus *m* - Marxism

März *m* -, -e March

Marzipan *nt* -s marzipan

Masche f -, -n stitch; (*im Netz*) mesh; (⚡ *Trick*) dodge. **M~ndraht** m wire netting

Maschin|e f -, -n machine; (*Flugzeug*) plane; (*Schreib-*) typewriter; **M~e schreiben** type. **m~egeschrieben** a typewritten, typed. **m~ell** a machine ... ● *adv* by machine. **M~enbau** m mechanical engineering. **M~engewehr** nt machine-gun. **M~ist** m -en, -en machinist; (*Naut*) engineer

Masern pl measles sg

Maserung f -, -en [wood] grain

Maske f -, -n mask; (*Theat*) make-up

maskieren vt mask; **sich m~** dress up (**als** as)

maskulin a masculine

Masochist m -en, -en masochist

Maß[1] nt -es, -e measure; (*Abmessung*) measurement; (*Grad*) degree; (*Mäßigung*) moderation; **in hohem Maße** to a high degree

Maß[2] f -,- (*SGer*) litre [of beer]

Massage /ma'saːʒə/ f -, -n massage

Massaker nt -s,- massacre

Maßband nt (*pl* -bänder) tape-measure

Masse f -, -n mass; (*Culin*) mixture; (*Menschen-*) crowd; **eine M~ Arbeit** ⚡ masses of work. **m~nhaft** adv in huge quantities. **M~nproduktion** f mass production. **m~nweise** adv in huge numbers

Masseu|r /ma'søːɐ̯/ m -s, -e masseur. **M~se** /-'søːzə/ f -, -n masseuse

maß|gebend a authoritative; (*einflussreich*) influential. **m~geblich** a decisive. **m~geschneidert** a made-to-measure

massieren vt massage

massig a massive

mäßig a moderate; (*mittelmäßig*) indifferent. **m~en** vt moderate; **sich m~en** moderate; (*sich beherrschen*) restrain oneself. **M~ung** f - moderation

massiv a solid; (*stark*) heavy

Maß|krug m beer mug. **m~los** a excessive; (*grenzenlos*) boundless; (*äußerst*) extreme. **M~nahme** f -, -n measure

Maßstab m scale; (*Norm & fig*) standard. **m~sgerecht, m~sgetreu** a scale ... ● *adv* to scale

Mast[1] m -[e]s, -en pole; (*Überland-*) pylon; (*Naut*) mast

Mast[2] f - fattening

mästen vt fatten

masturbieren vi (*haben*) masturbate

Material nt -s, -ien /-jən/ material; (*coll*) materials pl. **M~ismus** m - materialism. **m~istisch** a materialistic

Mathe f - ⚡ maths sg

Mathe|matik f - mathematics sg. **M~matiker** m -s,- mathematician. **m~matisch** a mathematical

Matinee f -, -n (*Theat*) morning performance

Matratze f -, -n mattress

Matrose m -n, -n sailor

Matsch m -[e]s mud; (*Schnee-*) slush

matt a weak; (*gedämpft*) dim; (*glanzlos*) dull; <*Politur, Farbe*> matt. **M~** nt -s (*Schach*) mate

Matte f -, -n mat

Mattglas nt frosted glass

Matura f - (*Aust*) ≈ A levels pl

Mauer f -, -n wall. **M~werk** nt masonry

Maul nt -[e]s, Mäuler (*Zool*) mouth; **halts M~!** ⚡ shut up! **M~korb** m muzzle. **M~tier** nt mule. **M~wurf** m mole

Maurer m -s,- bricklayer

Maus f -,Mäuse mouse

Maut f -, -en (*Aust*) toll. **M~straße** f toll road

maximal a maximum

Maximum nt -s, -ma maximum

Mayonnaise /majɔ'nɛːzə/ f -, -n mayonnaise

Mechan|ik /me'çaːnɪk/ f - mechanics sg; (*Mechanismus*) mechanism. **M~iker** m -s,-

m

mechanic. **m~isch** *a* mechanical.
m~isieren *vt* mechanize.
M~ismus *m* -, -men mechanism

meckern *vi* (*haben*) bleat; (🔢 *nörgeln*) grumble

Medaill|e /me'daljə/ *f* -, -n medal.
M~on /-'jõ:/ *nt* -s, -s medallion (*Schmuck*) locket

Medikament *nt* -[e]s, -e medicine

Medit|ation /-'tsio:n/ *f* -, -en meditation. **m~ieren** *vi* (*haben*) meditate

Medium *nt* -s, -ien medium; die Medien the media

Medizin *f* -, -en medicine. **M~er** *m* -s,- doctor; (*Student*) medical student. **m~isch** *a* medical; (*heilkräftig*) medicinal

Meer *nt* -[e]s, -e sea. **M~busen** *m* gulf. **M~enge** *f* strait.
M~esspiegel *m* sea-level.
M~jungfrau *f* mermaid.
M~rettich *m* horseradish.
M~schweinchen *nt* -s,- guinea-pig

Mehl *nt* -[e]s flour. **M~schwitze** *f* (*Culin*) roux

mehr *pron & adv* more; nicht m~ no more; (*zeitlich*) no longer; nichts m~ no more; (*nichtsweiter*) nothing else; nie m~ never again. **m~eres** *pron* several things *pl*. **m~fach** *a* multiple; (*mehrmalig*) repeated. ● *adv* several times.
M~fahrtenkarte *f* book of tickets.
M~heit *f* -, -en majority.
m~malig *a* repeated. **m~mals** *adv* several times. **m~sprachig** *a* multilingual. **M~wertsteuer** *f* value-added tax, VAT. **M~zahl** *f* majority; (*Gram*) plural.
M~zweck- *pref* multi-purpose

meiden† *vt* avoid, shun

Meile *f* -, -n mile. **m~nweit** *adv* [for] miles

mein *poss pron* my. **m~e(r,s)** *poss pron* mine; die M~en *od* m~en *pl* my family *sg*

Meineid *m* perjury

meinen *vt* mean; (*glauben*) think; (*sagen*) say

mein|erseits *adv* for my part.
m~etwegen *adv* for my sake; (*wegen mir*) because of me; (🔢 *von mir aus*) as far as I'm concerned

Meinung *f* -, -en opinion; jdm die M~ sagen give s.o. a piece of one's mind. **M~sumfrage** *f* opinion poll

Meise *f* -, -n (*Zool*) tit

Meißel *m* -s,- chisel. **m~n** *vt/i* (*haben*) chisel

meist *adv* mostly; (*gewöhnlich*) usually. **m~e** *a* der/die/das m~e most; die m~en Leute most people; am m~en [the] most ● *pron* das m~e most [of it]; die m~en most. **m~ens** *adv* mostly; (*gewöhnlich*) usually

Meister *m* -s,- master craftsman; (*Könner*) master; (*Sport*) champion. **m~n** *vt* master. **M~schaft** *f* -, -en mastery; (*Sport*) championship

meld|en *vt* report; (*anmelden*) register; (*ankündigen*) announce; sich m~en report (bei to); (*zum Militär*) enlist; (*freiwillig*) volunteer; (*Teleph*) answer; (*Sch*) put up one's hand; (*von sich hören lassen*) get in touch (bei with). **M~ung** *f* -, -en report; (*Anmeldung*) registration

melken† *vt* milk

Melodie *f* -, -n tune, melody

melodisch *a* melodic; melodious

Melone *f* -, -n melon

Memoiren /me'moa:rən/ *pl* memoirs

Menge *f* -, -n amount, quantity; (*Menschen*-) crowd; (*Math*) set; eine M~ Geld a lot of money. **m~n** *vt* mix

Mensa *f* -, -sen (*Univ*) refectory

Mensch *m* -en, -en human being; der M~ man; die M~en people; jeder/kein M~ everybody/nobody. **M~enaffe** *m* ape.
m~enfeindlich *a* antisocial.
M~enfresser *m* -s,- cannibal; (*Zool*) man-eater. **m~enfreundlich** *a* philanthropic. **M~enleben** *nt* human life; (*Lebenszeit*) lifetime. **m~enleer** *a* deserted.

M~enmenge f crowd. **M~enraub** m kidnapping. **M~enrechte** ntpl human rights. **m~enscheu** a unsociable. **m~enwürdig** a humane. **M~heit** f - die M~heit mankind, humanity. **m~lich** a human; (human) humane. **M~lichkeit** f - humanity

Menstru|ation /-'tsio:n/ f - menstruation. **m~ieren** vi (haben) menstruate

Mentalität f -, -en mentality

Menü nt -s, -s menu; (festes M~) set meal

Meridian m -s, -e meridian

merk|bar a noticeable. **M~blatt** nt [explanatory] leaflet. **m~en** vt notice; **sich** (dat) etw m~en remember sth. **M~mal** nt feature

merkwürdig a odd, strange

Messe¹ f -, -n (Relig) mass; (Comm) [trade] fair

Messe² f -, -n (Mil) mess

messen† vt/i (haben) measure; (ansehen) look at; [bei jdm] Fieber m~ take s.o.'s temperature; **sich mit** jdm m~ können be a match for s.o.

Messer nt -s,- knife

Messias m - Messiah

Messing nt -s brass

Messung f -, -en measurement

Metabolismus m - metabolism

Metall nt -s, -e metal. **m~isch** a metallic

Metamorphose f -, -n metamorphosis

metaphorisch a metaphorical

Meteor m -s, -e meteor. **M~ologie** f - meteorology

Meter m & nt -s,- metre. **M~maß** nt tape-measure

Method|e f -, -n method. **m~isch** a methodical

Metropole f -, -n metropolis

Metzger m -s,- butcher. **M~ei** f -, -en butcher's shop

Meuterei f -, -en mutiny

meutern vi (haben) mutiny; (🗓 schimpfen) grumble

Mexikan|er(in) m -s,- (f -, -nen) Mexican. **m~isch** a Mexican

Mexiko nt -s Mexico

miauen vi (haben) mew, miaow

mich pron (acc of ich) me; (refl) myself

Mieder nt -s,- bodice

Miene f -, -n expression

mies a 🗓 lousy

Miet|e f -, -n rent; (Mietgebühr) hire charge; **zur M~e wohnen** live in rented accommodation. **m~en** vt rent <Haus, Zimmer>; hire <Auto, Boot>. **M~er(in)** m -s,- (f -, -nen) tenant. **m~frei** a & adv rent-free. **M~shaus** nt block of rented flats. **M~vertrag** m lease. **M~wagen** m hire-car. **M~wohnung** f rented flat; (zu vermieten) flat to let

Migräne f -, -n migraine

Mikro|chip m microchip. **M~computer** m microcomputer. **M~film** m microfilm

Mikro|fon, M~phon nt -s, -e microphone. **M~skop** nt -s, -e microscope. **m~skopisch** a microscopic

Mikrowelle f microwave. **M~nherd** m microwave oven

Milbe f -, -n mite

Milch f - milk. **M~glas** nt opal glass. **m~ig** a milky. **M~mann** m (pl -männer) milkman. **M~straße** f Milky Way

mild a mild; (nachsichtig) lenient. **M~e** f - mildness; leniency. **m~ern** vt make milder; (mäßigen) moderate; (lindern) ease; **sich m~ern** become milder; (sich mäßigen) moderate; <Schmerz:> ease; **m~ernde Umstände** mitigating circumstances

Milieu /mi'liø:/ nt -s, -s [social] environment

Militär nt -s army; (Soldaten) troops pl; **beim M~** in the army. **m~isch** a military

Miliz f -, -en militia

Milliarde /mr'liardə/ f -, -n thousand million, billion

Milli|gramm *nt* milligram. **M~meter** *m & nt* millimetre. **M~meterpapier** *nt* graph paper

Million /mɪˈli̯oːn/ *f* **-, -en** million. **M~är** *m* **-s, -e** millionaire

Milz *f* **-** (*Anat*) spleen

mimen *vt* ([!] *vortäuschen*) act

Mimose *f* **-, -n** mimosa

Minderheit *f* **-, -en** minority

minderjährig *a* (*Jur*) under-age. **M~e(r)** *m/f* (*Jur*) minor

mindern *vt* diminish; decrease

minderwertig *a* inferior. **M~keit** *f* **-** inferiority. **M~keitskomplex** *m* inferiority complex

Mindest- *pref* minimum. **m~e** *a & pron* **der/die/das M~e** *od* **m~e** the least; **nicht im M~en** not in the least. **m~ens** *adv* at least. **M~lohn** *m* minimum wage. **M~maß** *nt* minimum

Mine *f* **-, -n** mine; (*Bleistift-*) lead; (*Kugelschreiber-*) refill. **M~nräumboot** *nt* minesweeper

Mineral *nt* **-s, -e & -ien** /-i̯ən/ mineral. **m~isch** *a* mineral. **M~wasser** *nt* mineral water

Miniatur *f* **-, -en** miniature

Minigolf *nt* miniature golf

minimal *a* minimal

Minimum *nt* **-s, -ma** minimum

Mini|ster *m*, **-s,-** minister. **m~steriell** *a* ministerial. **M~sterium** *nt* **-s, -ien** ministry

minus *conj, adv & prep* (+ *gen*) minus. **M~** *nt* **-** deficit; (*Nachteil*) disadvantage. **M~zeichen** *nt* minus [sign]

Minute *f* **-, -n** minute

mir *pron* (*dat of* **ich**) [to] me; (*refl*) myself

Misch|ehe *f* mixed marriage. **m~en** *vt* mix; blend <*Tee, Kaffee*>; toss <*Salat*>; shuffle <*Karten*>; **sich m~en** mix; <*Person,*> mingle (**unter** + *acc* with); **sich m~en in** (+ *acc*) join in <*Gespräch*>; meddle in <*Angelegenheit*> ● *vi* (*haben*) shuffle the cards. **M~ling** *m* **-s, -e** half-caste. **M~ung** *f* **-, -en** mixture; blend

miserabel *a* abominable

missachten *vt* disregard

Miss|achtung *f* disregard. **M~bildung** *f* deformity

missbilligen *vt* disapprove of

Miss|billigung *f* disapproval. **M~brauch** *m* abuse

missbrauchen *vt* abuse; (*vergewaltigen*) rape

Misserfolg *m* failure

Misse|tat *f* misdeed. **M~täter** *m* [!] culprit

missfallen† *vi* (*haben*) displease (**jdm** s.o.)

Miss|fallen *nt* **-s** displeasure; (*Missbilligung*) disapproval. **M~geburt** *f* freak; (*fig*) monstrosity. **M~geschick** *nt* mishap; (*Unglück*) misfortune

miss|glücken *vi* (*sein*) fail. **m~gönnen** *vt* begrudge

misshandeln *vt* ill-treat

Misshandlung *f* ill-treatment

Mission *f* **-, -en** mission

Missionar(in) *m* **-s, -e** (*f* **-, -nen**) missionary

Missklang *m* discord

misslingen† *vi* (*sein*) fail; **es misslang ihr** she failed. **M~** *nt* **-s** failure

Missmut *m* ill humour. **m~ig** *a* morose

missraten† *vi* (*sein*) turn out badly

Miss|stand *m* abuse; (*Zustand*) undesirable state of affairs. **M~stimmung** *f* discord; (*Laune*) bad mood

misstrauen *vi* (*haben*) **jdm/etw m~** mistrust s.o./sth; (*Argwohn hegen*) distrust s.o./sth

Misstrau|en *nt* **-s** mistrust; (*Argwohn*) distrust. **M~ensvotum** *nt* vote of no confidence. **m~isch** *a* distrustful; (*argwöhnisch*) suspicious

Miss|verständnis *nt* misunderstanding. **m~verstehen**† *vt* misunderstand. **M~wirtschaft** *f* mismanagement

Mist *m* **-[e]s** manure; [!] rubbish

*alte Schreibung

Mistel f -, -n mistletoe

Misthaufen m dungheap

mit prep (+ dat) with; <sprechen> to; (mittels) by; (inklusive) including; (bei) at; **mit Bleistift** in pencil; **mit lauter Stimme** in a loud voice; **mit drei Jahren** at the age of three ● adv (auch) as well; **mit anfassen** (fig) lend a hand

Mitarbeit f collaboration. **m~en** vi sep collaborate (**an** + dat on). **M~er(in)** m(f) collaborator; (Kollege) colleague; employee

Mitbestimmung f co-determination

mitbringen† vt sep bring [along]

miteinander adv with each other

Mitesser m (Med) blackhead

mitfahren† vi sep (sein) go/come along; **mit jdm m~** go with s.o.; (mitgenommen werden) be given a lift by s.o.

mitfühlen vi sep (haben) sympathize

mitgeben† vt sep **jdm etw m~** give s.o. sth to take with him

Mitgefühl nt sympathy

mitgehen† vi sep (sein) **mit jdm m~** go with s.o.

Mitgift f -, -en dowry

Mitglied nt member. **M~schaft** f - membership

mithilfe prep (+ gen) with the aid of

Mithilfe f assistance

mitkommen† vi sep (sein) come [along] too; (fig: folgen können) keep up; (verstehen) follow

Mitlaut m consonant

Mitleid nt pity, compassion; **M~ erregend** pitiful. **m~ig** a pitying; (mitfühlend) compassionate. **m~slos** a pitiless

mitmachen v sep ● vt take part in; (erleben) go through ● vi (haben) join in

Mitmensch m fellow man

mitnehmen† vt sep take along; (mitfahren lassen) give a lift to; (fig: schädigen) affect badly; (erschöpfen) exhaust; '**zum M~**' 'to take away'

mitreden vi sep (haben) join in [the conversation]; (mit entscheiden) have a say (**bei** in)

mitreißen† vt sep sweep along; (fig: begeistern) carry away; **m~d** rousing

mitsamt prep (+ dat) together with

mitschreiben† vt sep (haben) take down

Mitschuld f partial blame. **m~ig** a **m~ig sein** be partly to blame

Mitschüler(in) m(f) fellow pupil

mitspielen vi sep (haben) join in; (Theat) be in the cast; (beitragen) play a part

Mittag m midday, noon; (Mahlzeit) lunch; (Pause) lunch-break; **heute/ gestern M~** at lunch-time today/ yesterday; [**zu**] **M~ essen** have lunch. **M~essen** nt lunch. **m~s** adv at noon; (als Mahlzeit) for lunch; **um 12 Uhr m~s** at noon. **M~spause** f lunch-hour; (Pause) lunch-break. **M~sschlaf** m after-lunch nap

Mittäter|(in) m(f) accomplice. **M~schaft** f - complicity

Mitte f -, -n middle; (Zentrum) centre; **die goldene M~** the golden mean; **M~ Mai** in mid-May; **in unserer M~** in our midst

mitteil|en vt sep **jdm etw m~en** tell s.o. sth; (amtlich) inform s.o. of sth. **M~ung** f -, -en communication; (Nachricht) piece of news

Mittel nt -s,- means sg; (Heil) remedy; (Medikament) medicine; (M~wert) mean; (Durchschnitt) average; **M~ pl** (Geld-) funds, resources. **m~** pred a medium; (m~mäßig) middling. **M~alter** nt Middle Ages pl. **m~alterlich** a medieval. **M~ding** nt (fig) cross. **m~europäisch** a Central European. **M~finger** m middle finger. **m~los** a destitute. **m~mäßig** a middling; [nur] **m~mäßig** mediocre. **M~meer** nt Mediterranean. **M~punkt** m centre; (fig) centre of attention

mittels prep (+ gen) by means of

Mittel|schule f = Realschule. **M~smann** m (pl -männer)

intermediary, go-between.
M~stand m middle class.
m~ste(r,s) a middle. **M~streifen**
m (*Auto*) central reservation.
M~stürmer m centre-forward.
M~welle f medium wave.
M~wort nt (pl -wörter) participle

mitten adv m~ **in/auf** (*dat/acc*) in
the middle of. **m~durch** adv [right]
through the middle

Mitternacht f midnight

mittler|e(r,s) a middle; <*Größe,
Qualität*> medium; (*durchschnittlich*)
mean, average. **m~weile** adv
meanwhile; (*seitdem*) by now

Mittwoch m -s, -e Wednesday.
m~s adv on Wednesdays

mitunter adv now and again

mitwirk|en vi sep (*haben*) take part;
(*helfen*) contribute. **M~ung** f
participation

mix|en vt mix. **M~er** m -s,- (*Culin*)
liquidizer, blender

Möbel pl furniture sg. **M~stück** nt
piece of furniture. **M~wagen** m
removal van

Mobiliar nt -s furniture

mobilisier|en vt mobilize. **M~ung**
f - mobilization

Mobil|machung f - mobilization.
M~telefon nt mobile phone

möblier|en vt furnish; m~tes
Zimmer furnished room

mochte, möchte s. mögen

Mode f -, -n fashion; **M~ sein** be
fashionable

Modell nt -s, -e model. **m~ieren** vt
model

Modenschau f fashion show

Modera|tor m -s, -en /-'to:rən/,
M~torin f -, -nen (*TV*) presenter

modern a modern; (*modisch*)
fashionable. **m~isieren** vt
modernize

Mode|schmuck m costume
jewellery. **M~schöpfer** m fashion
designer

modisch a fashionable

Modistin f -, -nen milliner

modrig a musty

modulieren vt modulate

Mofa nt -s, -s moped

mogeln vi (*haben*) 🄸 cheat

mögen†
● *transitive verb*
····▸ like. **sie mag ihn sehr [gern]** she
likes him very much. **möchten Sie
ein Glas Wein?** would you like a
glass of wine? **lieber mögen** prefer.
ich möchte lieber Tee I would prefer
tea
● *auxiliary verb*
····▸ (*wollen*) want to. **sie mochte nicht
länger bleiben** she didn't want to
stay any longer. **ich möchte ihn
[gerne] sprechen** I'd like to speak to
him. **möchtest du nach Hause?** do
you want to go home? *or* would you
like to go home?
····▸ (*Vermutung, Möglichkeit*) may. **ich
mag mich irren** I may be wrong.
wer/was mag das sein? whoever/
whatever can it be? **[das] mag sein**
that may well be. **mag kommen, was
da will** come what may

möglich a possible; **alle m~en** all
sorts of; **über alles M~e sprechen**
talk about all sorts of things.
m~erweise adv possibly. **M~keit**
f -, -en possibility. **M~keitsform** f
subjunctive. **m~st** adv if possible;
m~st viel as much as possible

Mohammedan|er(in) m -s,- (f -,
-nen) Muslim. **m~isch** a Muslim

Mohn m -s poppy

Möhre, Mohrrübe f -, -n carrot

Mokka m -s mocha; (*Geschmack*)
coffee

Molch m -[e]s, -e newt

Mole f -, -n (*Naut*) mole

Molekül nt -s, -e molecule

Molkerei f -, -en dairy

Moll nt - (*Mus*) minor

mollig a cosy; (*warm*) warm;
(*rundlich*) plump

Moment m -s, -e moment; **M~[mal]!**
just a moment! **m~an** a
momentary; (*gegenwärtig*) at the
moment

Monarch *m* -en, -en monarch.
M~ie *f* -, -n monarchy
Monat *m* -s, -e month. **m~elang**
adv for months. **m~lich** *a* & *adv*
monthly
Mönch *m* -[e]s, -e monk
Mond *m* -[e]s, -e moon
mondän *a* fashionable
Mond|finsternis *f* lunar eclipse.
m~hell *a* moonlit. **M~sichel** *f*
crescent moon. **M~schein** *m*
moonlight
monieren *vt* criticize
Monitor *m* -s, -en /-'to:rən/ (*Techn*)
monitor
Monogramm *nt* -s, -e monogram
Mono|log *m* -s, -e monologue.
M~pol *nt* -s, -e monopoly. **m~ton**
a monotonous
Monster *nt* -s,- monster
Monstrum *nt* -s, -stren monster
Monsun *m* -s, -e monsoon
Montag *m* Monday
Montage /mɔn'ta:ʒə/ *f* -, -n fitting;
(*Zusammenbau*) assembly; (*Film-*)
editing; (*Kunst*) montage
montags *adv* on Mondays
Montanindustrie *f* coal and steel
industry
Monteur /mɔn'tøːɐ/ *m* -s, -e
fitter.**M~anzug** *m* overalls *pl*
montieren *vt* fit; (*zusammenbauen*)
assemble
Monument *nt* -[e]s, -e monument.
m~al *a* monumental
Moor *nt* -[e]s, -e bog; (*Heide-*) moor
Moos *nt* es, -e moss **m~ig** *a* mossy
Moped *nt* -s, -s moped
Mopp *m* -s, -s mop
Moral *f* -, morals *pl*, (*Selbstvertrauen*)
morale; (*Lehre*) moral. **m~isch** *a*
moral
Mord *m* -[e]s, -e murder, (*Pol*)
assassination. **M~anschlag** *m*
murder/assassination attempt.
m~en *vt/i* (*haben*) murder, kill
Mörder *m* -s,- murderer, (*Pol*)
assassin. **M~in** *f* -, -nen murderess.
m~isch *a* murderous; (🛈 *schlimm*)
dreadful

morgen *adv* tomorrow; **m~ Abend**
tomorrow evening
Morgen *m* -s,- morning; (*Maß*) ≈
acre; **am M~** in the morning; **heute/**
Montag M~ this/Monday morning.
M~dämmerung *f* dawn. **M~rock**
m dressing-gown. **M~rot** *nt* red sky
in the morning. **m~s** *a* in the
morning
morgig *a* tomorrow's; **der m~e Tag**
tomorrow
Morphium *nt* -s morphine
morsch *a* rotten
Morsealphabet *nt* Morse code
Mörtel *m* -s mortar
Mosaik /moza'i:k/ *nt* -s, -e[n] mosaic
Moschee *f* -, -n mosque
Mosel *f* - Moselle
Moskau *nt* -s Moscow
Moskito *m* -s, -s mosquito
Moslem *m* -s, -s Muslim
Motiv *nt* -s, -e motive; (*Kunst*) motif
Motor /'mo:tɔr, mo'to:ɐ/ *m* -s, -en
/-'to:rən/ engine; (*Elektro-*) motor.
M~boot *nt* motor boat
motorisieren *vt* motorize
Motor|rad *nt* motor cycle.
M~roller *m* motor scooter
Motte *f* -, -n moth. **M~nkugel** *f*
mothball
Motto *nt* -s, -s motto
Möwe *f* -, -n gull
Mücke *f* -, -n gnat; (*kleine*) midge;
(*Stech-*) mosquito
müd|e *a* tired; **es m~e sein** be tired
(*etw zu tun* of doing sth). **M~igkeit**
f - tiredness
muffig *a* musty; (🛈 *mürrisch*)
grumpy
Mühe *f* -, -n effort; (*Aufwand*)
trouble; **sich** (*dat*) **M~ geben** make
an effort; (*sich bemühen*) try; **nicht**
der M~ wert not worth while; **mit**
M~ und Not with great difficulty;
(*gerade noch*) only just. **m~los** *a*
effortless
muhen *vi* (*haben*) moo
Mühl|e *f* -, -n mill; (*Kaffee-*) grinder.
M~stein *m* millstone

m

Müh|sal f -, -e (liter) toil; (Mühe) trouble. **m~sam** a laborious; (beschwerlich) difficult

Mulde f -, -n hollow

Müll m -s refuse. **M~abfuhr** f refuse collection

Mullbinde f gauze bandage

Mülleimer m waste bin; (Mülltonne) dustbin

Müller m -s,- miller

Müll|halde f [rubbish] dump. **M~schlucker** m refuse chute. **M~tonne** f dustbin

multi|national a multinational. **M~plikation** /-'tsio:n/ f -, -en multiplication. **m~plizieren** vt multiply

Mumie /'mu:miə/ f -, -n mummy

Mumm m -s 🄸 energy

Mumps m - mumps

Mund m -[e]s,¨-er mouth; ein M~ voll Suppe a mouthful of soup; halt den M~! 🗵 shut up! **M~art** f dialect. **m~artlich** a dialect

Mündel nt & m -s,- (Jur) ward. **m~sicher** a gilt-edged

münden vi (sein) flow;/<Straße:> lead (in + acc into)

Mundharmonika f mouth-organ

mündig a m~ sein/werden (Jur) be/come of age. **M~keit** f - (Jur) majority

mündlich a verbal; m~e Prüfung oral

Mündung f -, -en (Fluss-) mouth; (Gewehr-) muzzle

Mundwinkel m corner of the mouth

Munition /-'tsio:n/ f - ammunition

munkeln vt/i (haben) talk (von of); es wird gemunkelt rumour has it (dass that)

Münster nt -s,- cathedral

munter a lively; (heiter) merry; m~ sein (wach) be wide awake ; gesund und m~ fit and well

Münz|e f -, -n coin; (M~stätte) mint. **M~fernsprecher** m payphone

mürbe a crumbly; <Obst> mellow; <Fleisch> tender. **M~teig** m short pastry

Murmel f -, -n marble

murmeln vt/i (haben) murmur; (undeutlich) mumble

Murmeltier nt marmot

murren vt/i (haben) grumble

mürrisch a surly

Mus nt -es purée

Muschel f -, -n mussel; [sea] shell

Museum /mu'ze:ʊm/ nt -s, -seen /-'ze:ən/ museum

Musik f - music. **m~alisch** a musical

Musiker(in) m -s,- (f -, -nen) musician

Musik|instrument nt musical instrument. **M~kapelle** f band. **M~pavillon** m bandstand

musisch a artistic

musizieren vi (haben) make music

Muskat m -[e]s nutmeg

Muskel m -s, -n muscle. **M~kater** m stiff and aching muscles pl

muskulös a muscular

muss s. müssen

Muße f - leisure

müssen†
● auxiliary verb
····▸ (gezwungen/verpflichtet/notwendig sein) have to; must. er muss es tun he must or has to do it; 🄸 he's got to do it. ich musste schnell fahren I had to drive fast. das muss 1968 gewesen sein it must have been in 1968. er muss gleich hier sein he must be here at any moment
····▸ (in negativen Sätzen; ungezwungen) sie muss es nicht tun she does not have to or 🄸 she hasn't got to do it. es musste nicht so sein it didn't have to be like that
····▸ es müsste (sollte) doch möglich sein it ought to or should be possible. du müsstest es mal versuchen you ought to or should try it
● intransitive verb

····▸ *(irgendwohin gehen müssen)* have to *or* must go. **ich muss nach Hause/ zum Arzt** I have to *or* must go home/ to the doctor. **ich musste mal [aufs Klo]** I had to go [to the loo]

müßig *a* idle

musste, müßte *s.* müssen

Muster *nt* -s,- pattern; *(Probe)* sample; *(Vorbild)* model. **M~beispiel** *nt* typical example; *(Vorbild)* perfect example. **m~gültig, m~haft** *a* exemplary. **m~n** *vt* eye; *(inspizieren)* inspect. **M~ung** *f* -, -en inspection; *(Mil)* medical; *(Muster)* pattern

Mut *m* -[e]s courage; **jdm Mut machen** encourage s.o.; **zu M~e sein** = **zumute sein**, *s.* zumute

mut|ig *a* courageous. **m~los** *a* despondent

mutmaßen *vt* presume; *(Vermutungen anstellen)* speculate

Mutprobe *f* test of courage

Mutter[1] *f* -,-̈ mother

Mutter[2] *f* -, -n *(Techn)* nut

Muttergottes *f* -,- madonna

Mutterland *nt* motherland

mütterlich *a* maternal; *(fürsorglich)* motherly. **m~erseits** *adv* on one's/the mother's side

Mutter|mal *nt* birthmark; *(dunkel)* mole. **M~schaft** *f* - motherhood. **m~seelenallein** *a & adv* all alone. **M~sprache** *f* mother tongue. **M~tag** *m* Mother's Day

Mütze *f* -, -n cap; **wollene M~** woolly hat

MwSt. *abbr* **(Mehrwertsteuer)** VAT

mysteriös *a* mysterious

Mystik /'mystɪk/ *f* - mysticism

myth|isch *a* mythical. **M~ologie** *f* - mythology

Nn

na *int* well; **na gut** all right then

Nabel *m* -s,- navel. **N~schnur** *f* umbilical cord

nach
● *preposition (+ dative)*
····▸ *(räumlich)* to. **nach London fahren** go to London. **der Zug nach München** the train to Munich; *(noch nicht abgefahren)* the train for Munich; the Munich train. **nach Hause gehen** go home. **nach Osten [zu]** eastwards; towards the east
····▸ *(zeitlich)* after; *(Uhrzeit)* past. **nach fünf Minuten/dem Frühstück** after five minutes/breakfast. **zehn [Minuten] nach zwei** ten [minutes] past two
····▸ *([räumliche und zeitliche] Reihenfolge)* after. **nach Ihnen/dir!** after you!
····▸ *(mit bestimmten Verben)* for. **greifen/streben/schicken nach** grasp/strive/send for
····▸ *(gemäß)* according to. **nach der neuesten Mode gekleidet** dressed in [accordance with] the latest fashion. **dem Gesetz nach** in accordance with the law; by law. **nach meiner Ansicht** *od* **Meinung, meiner Ansicht** *od* **Meinung nach** in my view *or* opinion. **nach etwas schmecken/ riechen** taste/smell of sth
● *adverb*
····▸ *(zeitlich)* **nach und nach** little by little; gradually. **nach wie vor** still

nachahm|en *vt sep* imitate. **N~ung** *f* -, -en imitation

Nachbar|(in) *m* -n, -n *(f* -, -nen*)* neighbour. **N~haus** *nt* house next door. **n~lich** *a* neighbourly; *(Nachbar-)* neighbouring. **N~schaft** *f* - neighbourhood

nachbestell|en *vt sep* reorder. **N~ung** *f* repeat order

nachbild|en vt sep copy, reproduce. **N~ung** f copy, reproduction

nachdatieren vt sep backdate

nachdem conj after; **je n~** it depends

nachdenk|en† vi sep (haben) think (über + acc about). **n~lich** a thoughtful

nachdrücklich a emphatic

nacheinander adv one after the other

Nachfahre m -n, -n descendant

Nachfolg|e f succession. **N~er(in)** m -s,- (f -, -nen) successor

nachforsch|en vi sep (haben) make enquiries. **N~ung** f enquiry

Nachfrage f (Comm) demand. **n~n** vi sep (haben) enquire

nachfüllen vt sep refill

nachgeben† v sep ● vi (haben) give way; (sich fügen) give in, yield ● vt jdm Suppe n~ give s.o. more soup

Nachgebühr f surcharge

nachgehen† vi sep (sein) <Uhr:> be slow; jdm/etw n~ follow s.o./sth; follow up <Spur, Angelegenheit>; pursue <Angelegenheit>

Nachgeschmack m after-taste

nachgiebig a indulgent; (gefällig) compliant. **N~keit** f - indulgence; compliance

nachgrübeln vi sep (haben) ponder (über + acc on)

nachhaltig a lasting

nachhelfen† vi sep (haben) help

nachher adv later; (danach) afterwards; **bis n~!** see you later!

Nachhilfeunterricht m coaching

Nachhinein adv im N~ afterwards

nachhinken vi sep (sein) (fig) lag behind

nachholen vt sep (später holen) fetch later; (mehr holen) get more; (später machen) do later; (aufholen) catch up on

Nachkomme m -n, -n descendant. **n~n**† vi sep (sein) follow [later],

come later; **etw** (dat) **n~n** (fig) comply with <Bitte>; carry out <Pflicht>. **N~nschaft** f - descendants pl, progeny

Nachkriegszeit f post-war period

Nachlass m -es,̈e discount; (Jur) [deceased's] estate

nachlassen† v sep ● vi (haben) decrease; <Regen, Hitze:> let up; <Schmerz:> ease; <Sturm:> abate; <Augen, Leistungen:> deteriorate ● vt etw vom Preis n~ take sth off the price

nachlässig a careless; (leger) casual; (unordentlich) sloppy. **N~keit** f - carelessness; sloppiness

nachlesen† vt sep look up

nachlöse|n vi sep (haben) pay one's fare on the train/on arrival. **N~schalter** m excess-fare office

nachmachen vt sep (später machen) do later; (imitieren) imitate, copy; (fälschen) forge

Nachmittag m afternoon; **heute/ gestern N~** this/yesterday afternoon. **n~s** adv in the afternoon

Nachnahme f etw per N~ schicken send sth cash on delivery or COD

Nachname m surname

Nachporto nt excess postage

nachprüfen vt sep check, verify

Nachricht f -, -en [piece of] news sg; **N~en** news sg; **eine N~ hinterlassen** leave a message; **jdm N~ geben** inform s.o. **N~endienst** m (Mil) intelligence service

nachrücken vi sep (sein) move up

Nachruf m obituary

nachsagen vt sep repeat (jdm after s.o.); **jdm Schlechtes/Gutes n~** speak ill/well of s.o.

Nachsaison f late season

nachschicken vt sep (später schicken) send later; (hinterher-) send after (jdm s.o.); send on <Post> (jdm to s.o.)

nachschlagen† v sep ● vt look up ● vi (haben) in einem Wörterbuch n~en consult a dictionary; jdm n~en take after s.o.

n

Nachschrift f transcript; (*Nachsatz*) postscript

Nachschub m (*Mil*) supplies pl

nachsehen† v sep ● vt (*prüfen*) check; (*nachschlagen*) look up; (*hinwegsehen über*) overlook ● vi (*haben*) have a look; (*prüfen*) check; **im Wörterbuch n~** consult a dictionary

nachsenden† vt sep forward <*Post*> (jdm to s.o.); '**bitte n~**' 'please forward'

nachsichtig a forbearing; lenient; indulgent

Nachsilbe f suffix

nachsitzen† vi sep (*haben*) **n~ müssen** be kept in [after school]; **jdn n~ lassen** give s.o. detention. **N~** nt **-s** (*Sch*) detention

Nachspeise f dessert, sweet

nachsprechen† vt sep repeat (jdm after s.o.)

nachspülen vt sep rinse

nächst /-çst/ prep (+ dat) next to. **n~beste(r,s)** a first [available]; (*zweitbeste*) next best. **n~e(r,s)** a next; (*nächstgelegene*) nearest; <*Verwandte*> closest; **in n~er Nähe** close by; **am n~en sein** be nearest or closest ● pron **der/die/das N~e** the next; **der N~e bitte** next please; **als N~es** next; **fürs N~e** for the time being. **N~e(r)** m fellow man

nachstehend a following ● adv below

Nächst|enliebe f charity. **n~ens** adv shortly. **n~gelegen** a nearest

nachsuchen vi sep (*haben*) search; **n~ um** request

Nacht f -ë night; **über/bei N~** overnight/at night; **morgen N~** tomorrow night; **heute N~** tonight; (*letzte Nacht*) last night; **gestern N~** last night; (*vorletzte Nacht*) the night before last. **N~dienst** m night duty

Nachteil m disadvantage; **zum N~** to the detriment (*gen* of)

Nacht|falter m moth. **N~hemd** nt night-dress; (*Männer-*) night-shirt

Nachtigall f -, -en nightingale

Nachtisch m dessert

Nachtklub m night-club

nächtlich a nocturnal, night ...

Nacht|lokal nt night-club. **N~mahl** nt (*Aust*) supper

Nachtrag m postscript; (*Ergänzung*) supplement. **n~en**† vt sep add; **jdm etw n~en** (*fig*) bear a grudge against s.o. for sth. **n~end** a vindictive; **n~end sein** bear grudges

nachträglich a subsequent, later; (*verspätet*) belated ● adv later; (*nachher*) afterwards; (*verspätet*) belatedly

Nacht|ruhe f night's rest; **angenehme N~ruhe!** sleep well! **n~s** adv at night; **2 Uhr n~s** 2 o'clock in the morning. **N~schicht** f night-shift. **N~tisch** m bedside table. **N~tischlampe** f bedside lamp. **N~topf** m chamber-pot. **N~wächter** m night-watchman. **N~zeit** f night-time

Nachuntersuchung f check-up

Nachwahl f by-election

Nachweis m -es, -e proof. **n~bar** a demonstrable. **n~en**† vt sep prove; (*aufzeigen*) show; (*vermitteln*) give details of; **jdm nichts n~en können** have no proof against s.o.

Nachwelt f posterity

Nachwirkung f after-effect

Nachwuchs m new generation; (⚏ *Kinder*) offspring. **N~spieler** m young player

nachzahlen vt/i sep (*haben*) pay extra; (*später zahlen*) pay later; **Steuern n~** pay tax arrears

nachzählen vt/i sep (*haben*) count again; (*prüfen*) check

Nachzahlung f extra/later payment; (*Gehalts-*) back-payment

nachzeichnen vt sep copy

Nachzügler m -s,- latecomer; (*Zurückgebliebener*) straggler

Nacken m -s,- nape or back of the neck

nackt a naked; (*bloß, kahl*) bare; <*Wahrheit*> plain. **N~heit** f - nakedness, nudity. **N~kultur** f nudism. **N~schnecke** f slug

Nadel *f* -, -n needle; (*Häkel-*) hook; (*Schmuck-, Hut-*) pin. **N~arbeit** *f* needlework. **N~baum** *m* conifer. **N~stich** *m* stitch; (*fig*) pinprick. **N~wald** *m* coniferous forest

Nagel *m* -s,̈ nail. **N~haut** *f* cuticle. **N~lack** *m* nail varnish. **n~n** *vt* nail. **n~neu** *a* brand-new

nagen *vt/i* (*haben*) gnaw (**an** + *dat* at); **n~d** (*fig*) nagging

Nagetier *nt* rodent

nah *a, adv & prep* = nahe

Näharbeit *f* sewing

Nahaufnahme *f* close-up

nahe *a* nearby; (*zeitlich*) imminent; (*eng*) close; **der N~ Osten** the Middle East; **in n~r Zukunft** in the near future; **von n~m** [from] close to; **n~ sein** be close (*dat* to) ● *adv* near, close; (*verwandt*) closely; **n~ an** (+ *acc/dat*) near [to], close to; **n~ daran sein, etw zu tun** nearly do sth; **n~ liegen** be close; (*fig*) be highly likely; **n~ legen** (*fig*) recommend (*dat* to); **jdm n~ legen, etw zu tun** urge s.o. to do sth; **jdm n~ gehen** (*fig*) affect s.o. deeply; **jdm zu n~ treten** (*fig*) offend s.o. ● *prep* (+ *dat*) near [to], close to

Nähe *f* - nearness, proximity; **aus der N~** [from] close to; **in der N~** near *or* close by

nahe|gehen* *vi sep* (*sein*) **n~ gehen**, *s.* nahe. **n~legen*** *vt sep* **n~ legen**, *s.* nahe. **n~liegen*** *vi sep* (*haben*) **n~ liegen**, *s.* nahe

nähen *vt/i* (*haben*) sew; (*anfertigen*) make; (*Med*) stitch [up]

näher *a* closer; (*Weg*) shorter; (*Einzelheiten*) further ● *adv* closer; (*genauer*) more closely; **n~ kommen** come closer; (*fig*) get closer (*dat* to); **sich n~ erkundigen** make further enquiries; **n~ an** (+ *acc/dat*) nearer [to], closer to ● *prep* (+ *dat*) nearer [to], closer to. **N~e[s]** *nt* [further] details *pl*. **n~n (sich)** *vr* approach

nahezu *adv* almost

Nähgarn *nt* [sewing] cotton

Nahkampf *m* close combat

Näh|maschine *f* sewing machine. **N~nadel** *f* sewing-needle

nähren *vt* feed; (*fig*) nurture

nahrhaft *a* nutritious

Nährstoff *m* nutrient

Nahrung *f* - food, nourishment. **N~smittel** *nt* food

Nährwert *m* nutritional value

Naht *f* -,̈e seam; (*Med*) suture. **n~los** *a* seamless

Nahverkehr *m* local service

Nähzeug *nt* sewing; (*Zubehör*) sewing kit

naiv /na'i:f/ *a* naïve. **N~ität** /-vi'tɛ:t/ *f* - naïvety

Name *m* -ns, -n name; **im N~n** (+ *gen*) in the name of; <*handeln*> on behalf of. **n~nlos** *a* nameless; (*unbekannt*) unknown, anonymous. **N~nstag** *m* name-day. **N~nsvetter** *m* namesake. **N~nszug** *m* signature. **n~ntlich** *adv* by name; (*besonders*) especially

namhaft *a* noted; (*ansehnlich*) considerable; **n~ machen** name

nämlich *adv* (*und zwar*) namely; (*denn*) because

nanu *int* hallo

Napf *m* -[e]s,̈e bowl

Narbe *f* -, -n scar

Narkose *f* -, -n general anaesthetic. **N~arzt** *m* anaesthetist. **N~mittel** *nt* anaesthetic

Narr *m* -en, -en fool; **zum N~en halten** make a fool of s.o. **n~en** *vt* fool

Närr|in *f* -, -nen fool. **n~isch** *a* foolish; (🅷 *verrückt*) crazy (**auf** + *acc* about)

Narzisse *f* -, -n narcissus

naschen *vt/i* (*haben*) nibble (**an** + *dat* at)

Nase *f* -, -n nose

näseln *vi* (*haben*) speak through one's nose; **n~d** nasal

Nasen|bluten *nt* -s nosebleed. **N~loch** *nt* nostril

Nashorn *nt* rhinoceros

nass *a* wet

Nässe *f* - wet; wetness. **n~n** *vt* wet

Nation /na'tsio:n/ f -, -en nation.
n~al a national. N~alhymne f
national anthem. N~alismus m -
nationalism. N~alität f -, -en
nationality. N~alspieler m
international

Natrium nt -s sodium

Natron nt -s doppeltkohlensaures
N~ bicarbonate of soda

Natter f -, -n snake; (Gift-) viper

Natur f -, -en nature; von N~ aus by
nature. n~alisieren vt naturalize.
N~alisierung f -, -en
naturalization

Naturell nt -s, -e disposition

Natur|erscheinung f natural
phenomenon. N~forscher m
naturalist. N~kunde f natural
history

natürlich a natural ● adv
naturally; (selbstverständlich) of
course. N~keit f - naturalness

natur|rein a pure. N~schutz m
nature conservation; unter N~schutz
stehen be protected.
N~schutzgebiet nt nature
reserve. N~wissenschaft f
[natural] science.
N~wissenschaftler m scientist

nautisch a nautical

Navigation /-'tsio:n/ f - navigation

Nazi m -s, -s Nazi

n.Chr. abbr (nach Christus) AD

Nebel m -s,- fog; (leicht) mist

neben prep (+ dat/acc) next to,
beside; (+ dat) (außer) apart from.
n~an adv next door

Neben|anschluss m (Teleph)
extension. N~ausgaben fpl
incidental expenses

nebenbei adv in addition;
(beiläufig) casually

Neben|bemerkung f passing
remark. N~beruf m second job

nebeneinander adv next to each
other, side by side

Neben|eingang m side entrance.
N~fach nt (Univ) subsidiary
subject. N~fluss m tributary

nebenher adv in addition

nebenhin adv casually

Neben|höhle f sinus. N~kosten
pl additional costs. N~produkt nt
by-product. N~rolle f supporting
role; (Kleine) minor role. N~sache
f unimportant matter. n~sächlich
a unimportant. N~satz m
subordinate clause. N~straße f
minor road; (Seiten-) side street.
N~wirkung f side-effect.
N~zimmer nt room next door

neblig a foggy; (leicht) misty

neck|en vt tease. N~erei f -
teasing. n~isch a teasing

Neffe m -n, -n nephew

negativ a negative. N~ nt -s, -e
(Phot) negative

Neger m -s,- Negro

nehmen† vt take (dat from); sich
(dat) etw n~ take sth; help oneself to
<Essen>

Neid m -[e]s envy, jealousy. n~isch
a envious, jealous (auf + acc of); auf
jdn n~isch sein envy s.o.

neig|en vt incline; (zur Seite) tilt;
(beugen) bend; sich n~en incline;
<Boden:> slope; <Person:> bend
(über + acc over) ● vi (haben) n~en
zu (fig) have a tendency towards; be
prone to <Krankheit>; incline
towards <Ansicht>; dazu n~en, etw
zu tun tend to do sth. N~ung f -, -en
inclination; (Gefälle) slope; (fig)
tendency

nein adv, N~ nt -s no

Nektar m -s nectar

Nelke f -, -n carnation; (Culin) clove

nenn|en† vt call; (taufen) name;
(angeben) give; (erwähnen) mention;
sich n~en call oneself. n~enswert
a significant

Neon nt -s neon. N~beleuchtung
f fluorescent lighting

Nerv m -s, -en /-fən/ nerve; die N~en
verlieren lose control of oneself.
n~en vt jdn n~en 🗵 get on s.o.'s
nerves. N~enarzt m neurologist.
n~enaufreibend a nerve-racking.
N~enkitzel m 🖪 thrill.
N~ensystem nt nervous system.
N~enzusammenbruch m
nervous breakdown

nervös a nervy, edgy; (*Med*) nervous; n~ **sein** be on edge

Nervosität f - nerviness, edginess

Nerz m -es, -e mink

Nessel f -, -n nettle

Nest nt -[e]s, -er nest; (🗊 *Ort*) small place

nett a nice; (*freundlich*) kind

netto adv net

Netz nt -es, -e net; (*Einkaufs-*) string bag; (*Spinnen-*) web; (*auf Landkarte*) grid; (*System*) network; (*Electr*) mains pl. **N~haut** f retina. **N~karte** f area season ticket. **N~werk** nt network

neu a new; (*modern*) modern; **wie neu** as good as new; **das ist mir neu** it's news to me; **von n~em** all over again ● adv newly; (*gerade erst*) only just; (*erneut*) again; **etw neu schreiben** rewrite sth; **neu vermähltes Paar** newly-weds pl. **N~auflage** f new edition; (*unverändert*) reprint. **N~bau** m (pl -ten) new house/building

Neu|e(r) m/f new person, newcomer; (*Schüler*) new boy/girl. **N~e(s)** nt das **N~e** the new; **etwas N~es** something new; (*Neuigkeit*) a piece of news; **was gibts N~es?** what's the news?

neuerdings adv [just] recently

neuest|e(r,s) a newest; (*letzte*) latest; **seit n~em** just recently. **N~e** nt das **N~e** the latest thing; (*Neuigkeit*) the latest news sg

neugeboren a newborn

Neugier, Neugierde f - curiosity; (*Wissbegierde*) inquisitiveness

neugierig a curious (**auf** + acc about); (*wissbegierig*) inquisitive

Neuheit f -, -en novelty; newness

Neuigkeit f -, -en piece of news; **N~en** news sg

Neujahr nt New Year's Day; **über N~** over the New Year

neulich adv the other day

Neumond m new moon

neun inv a, **N~** f -, -en nine. **n~te(r,s)** a ninth. **n~zehn** inv a nineteen. **n~zehnte(r,s)** a nineteenth. **n~zig** inv a ninety. **n~zigste(r,s)** a ninetieth

Neuralgie f -, -n neuralgia

neureich a nouveau riche

Neurologe m -n, -n neurologist

Neurose f -, -n neurosis

Neuschnee m fresh snow

Neuseeland nt -s New Zealand

neuste(r,s) a = neueste(r,s)

neutral a neutral. **N~ität** f - neutrality

Neutrum nt -s, -tra neuter noun

neu|vermählt* a n~ **vermählt**, s. neu. **N~zeit** f modern times pl

nicht adv not; **ich kann n~** I cannot or can't; **er ist n~ gekommen** he hasn't come; **bitte n~!** please don't! n~ **berühren!** do not touch! **du kennst ihn doch, n~?** you know him, don't you?

Nichte f -, -n niece

Nichtraucher m non-smoker

nichts pron & a nothing; n~ **mehr** no more; n~ **ahnend** unsuspecting; n~ **sagend** meaningless; (*uninteressant*) nondescript. **N~** nt - nothingness; (*fig: Leere*) void

Nichtschwimmer m non-swimmer

nichts|nutzig a good-for-nothing; (🗊 *unartig*) naughty. **n~sagend*** a n~ sagend, s. nichts. **N~tun** nt -s idleness

Nickel nt -s nickel

nicken vi (haben) nod

Nickerchen nt -s,-, 🗊 nap

nie adv never

nieder a low ● adv down. **n~brennen**† vt/i sep (sein) burn down. **N~deutsch** nt Low German. **N~gang** m (*fig*) decline. **n~gedrückt** a (*fig*) depressed. **n~geschlagen** a dejected, despondent. **N~kunft** f -,¨-e confinement. **N~lage** f defeat

Niederlande (die) pl the Netherlands

Niederländ|er *m* -s,- Dutchman; die N~er the Dutch *pl*. **N~erin** *f* -, -nen Dutchwoman. **n~isch** *a* Dutch

nieder|lassen† *vt sep* let down; sich n~lassen settle; (*sich setzen*) sit down. **N~lassung** *f* -, -en settlement; (*Zweigstelle*) branch. **n~legen** *vt sep* put *or* lay down; resign <*Amt*>; die Arbeit n~legen go on strike. **n~metzeln** *vt sep* massacre. **N~sachsen** *nt* Lower Saxony. **N~schlag** *m* precipitation; (*Regen*) rainfall; (*radioaktiver*) fallout. **n~schlagen†** *vt sep* knock down; lower <*Augen*>; (*unterdrücken*) crush. **n~schmettern** *vt sep* (*fig*) shatter. **n~setzen** *vt sep* put *or* set down; sich n~setzen sit down. **n~strecken** *vt sep* fell; (*durch Schuss*) gun down. **n~trächtig** *a* base, vile. **n~walzen** *vt sep* flatten

niedlich *a* pretty; sweet

niedrig *a* low; (*fig: gemein*) base ● *adv* low

niemals *adv* never

niemand *pron* nobody, no one

Niere *f* -, -n kidney; künstliche N~ kidney machine

niesel|n *vi* (*haben*) drizzle. **N~regen** *m* drizzle

niesen *vi* (*haben*) sneeze. **N~** *nt* -s sneezing; (*Nieser*) sneeze

Niete[1] *f* -, -n rivet; (*an Jeans*) stud

Niete[2] *f* -, -n blank; 🄵 failure

nieten *vt* rivet

Nikotin *nt* -s nicotine

Nil *m* -[s] Nile. **N~pferd** *nt* hippopotamus

nimmer *adv* (*SGer*) not any more; nie und n~ never

nirgend|s, n~wo *adv* nowhere

Nische *f* -, -n recess, niche

nisten *vi* (*haben*) nest

Nitrat *nt* -[e]s, -e nitrate

Niveau /ni'vo:/ *nt* -s, -s level; (*geistig, künstlerisch*) standard

nix *adv* 🄵 nothing

Nixe *f* -, -n mermaid

nobel *a* noble; (🄵 *luxuriös*) luxurious; (🄵 *großzügig*) generous

noch *adv* still; (*zusätzlich*) as well; (*mit Komparativ*) even; n~ nicht not yet; gerade n~ only just; n~ immer *od* immer n~ still; n~ letzte Woche only last week; wer n~? who else? n~ etwas something else; (*Frage*) anything else? n~ einmal again; n~ ein Bier another beer; n~ größer even bigger; n~ so sehr however much ● *conj* weder ... n~ neither ... nor

nochmals *adv* again

Nomad|e *m* -n, -n nomad. **n~isch** *a* nomadic

nominier|en *vt* nominate. **N~ung** *f* -, -en nomination

Nonne *f* -, -n nun. **N~nkloster** *nt* convent

Nonstopflug *m* direct flight

Nord *m* -[e]s north. **N~amerika** *nt* North America

Norden *m* -s north

nordisch *a* Nordic

nördlich *a* northern; <*Richtung*> northerly ● *adv & prep* (+ *gen*) n~ [von] der Stadt [to the] north of the town

Nordosten *m* north-east

Nord|pol *m* North Pole. **N~see** *f* - North Sea. **N~westen** *m* north-west

Nörgelei *f* -, -en grumbling

nörgeln *vi* (*haben*) grumble

Norm *f* -, -en norm; (*Techn*) standard; (*Soll*) quota

normal *a* normal. **n~erweise** *adv* normally

normen *vt* standardize

Norwe|gen *nt* -s Norway. **N~ger(in)** *m* -s,- (*f* -, -nen) Norwegian. **n~gisch** *a* Norwegian

Nost|algie *f* - nostalgia. **n~algisch** *a* nostalgic

Not *f* -,-̈e need; (*Notwendigkeit*) necessity; (*Entbehrung*) hardship; (*seelisch*) trouble; **Not leiden** be in need, suffer hardship; **Not leidende Menschen** needy people; **zur Not** if need be; (*äußerstenfalls*) at a pinch

Notar *m* -s, -e notary public

Not|arzt m emergency doctor.
  N~ausgang m emergency exit.
  N~behelf m -[e]s, -e makeshift.
  N~bremse f emergency brake.
  N~dienst m **N~dienst haben** be on
  call

Note f -, -n note; (*Zensur*) mark;
  ganze/halbe N~ (*Mus*) semi-breve/
  minim; **N~n lesen** read music;
  persönliche N~ personal touch.
  N~nblatt nt sheet of music.
  N~nschlüssel m clef

Notfall m emergency; **für den N~**
  just in case. **n~s** adv if need be

notieren vt note down; (*Comm*)
  quote; **sich** (*dat*) **etw n~** make a note
  of sth

nötig a necessary; **n~ haben** need;
  das N~ste the essentials pl ● adv
  urgently. **n~enfalls** adv if need be.
  N~ung f - coercion

Notiz f -, -en note; (*Zeitungs-*) item;
  [keine] N~ nehmen von take [no]
  notice of. **N~buch** nt notebook.
  N~kalender m diary

Not|lage f plight. **n~landen** vi
  (*sein*) make a forced landing.
  N~landung f forced landing.
  n~leidend* a Not leidend, s. Not.
  N~lösung f stopgap

Not|ruf m emergency call; (*Naut,
  Aviat*) distress call; (*Nummer*)
  emergency services number.
  N~signal nt distress signal.
  N~stand m state of emergency.
  N~unterkunft f emergency
  accommodation. **N~wehr** f - (*Jur*)
  self-defence

notwendig a necessary; essential
  ● adv urgently. **N~keit** f -, -en
  necessity

Notzucht f - (*Jur*) rape

Nougat /'nu:gat/ m & nt -s nougat

Novelle f -, -n novella; (*Pol*)
  amendment

November m -s,- November

Novize m -n, -n, **Novizin** f -, -nen
  (*Relig*) novice

Nu m **im Nu** 🔟 in a flash

nüchtern a sober; (*sachlich*)
  matter-of-fact; (*schmucklos*) bare;
  (*ohne Würze*) bland; **auf n~en Magen**
  on an empty stomach

Nudel f -, -n piece of pasta; **N~n**
  pasta sg; (*Band-*) noodles. **N~holz**
  nt rolling-pin

Nudist m -en, -en nudist

nuklear a nuclear

null inv a zero, nought; (*Teleph*) O;
  (*Sport*) nil; (*Tennis*) love; **n~ Fehler**
  no mistakes; **n~ und nichtig** (*Jur*)
  null and void. **N~** f -, -en nought,
  zero; (*fig: Person*) nonentity.
  N~punkt m zero

numerieren* vt s. nummerieren

Nummer f -, -n number; (*Ausgabe*)
  issue; (*Darbietung*) item; (*Zirkus-*)
  act; (*Größe*) size. **n~ieren** vt
  number. **N~nschild** nt number-
  plate

nun adv now; (*na*) well; (*halt*) just;
  nun gut! very well then!

nur adv only, just; **wo kann sie nur
  sein?** wherever can she be? **er soll
  es nur versuchen!** just let him try!

Nürnberg nt -s Nuremberg

nuscheln vt/i (*haben*) mumble

Nuss f -,-̈e nut. **N~knacker** m -s,-
  nutcrackers pl

Nüstern fpl nostrils

Nut f -, -en, **Nute** f -, -n groove

Nutte f -, -n 🔲 tart 🔲

nutz|bar a usable; **n~bar machen**
  utilize; cultivate <*Boden*>.
  n~bringend a profitable

nutzen vt use, utilize; (*aus-*) take
  advantage of ● vi (*haben*) = nützen.
  N~ m -s benefit; (*Comm*) profit; **N~
  ziehen aus** benefit from; **von N~ sein**
  be useful

nützen vi (*haben*) be useful or of use
  (*dat* to); <*Mittel*> be effective; **nichts
  n~** be useless or no use; **was nützt
  mir das?** what good is that to me?
  ● vt = nutzen

nützlich a useful. **N~keit** f -
  usefulness

nutz|los a useless; (*vergeblich*) vain.
  N~losigkeit f - uselessness.
  N~ung f - use, utilization

Nylon /'naɪlɔn/ *nt* -s nylon

Nymphe /'nymfə/ *f* -, **-n** nymph

O o

o *int* o ja/nein! oh yes/no!

Oase *f* -, **-n** oasis

ob *conj* whether; **ob reich, ob arm** rich or poor; **und ob!** 🄸 you bet!

Obacht *f* O~ **geben** pay attention; **O~!** look out!

Obdach *nt* -[e]s shelter. **o~los** *a* homeless. **O~lose(r)** *m/f* homeless person; **die O~losen** the homeless *pl*

Obduktion /-'tsi̯oːn/ *f* -, **-en** post-mortem

O-Beine *ntpl* 🄸 bow-legs, bandy legs

oben *adv* at the top; (*auf der Oberseite*) on top; (*eine Treppe hoch*) upstairs; (*im Text*) above; **da o~** up there; **o~ im Norden** up in the north; **siehe o~** see above; **o~ auf** (+ *acc/dat*) on top of; **nach o~** up[wards]; (*die Treppe hinauf*) upstairs; **von o~** from above/upstairs; **von o~ bis unten** from top to bottom/<*Person*> to toe; **jdn von o~ bis unten mustern** look s.o. up and down; **o~ erwähnt** *od* **genannt** above-mentioned. **o~drein** *adv* on top of that

Ober *m* -s,- waiter

Ober|arm *m* upper arm. **O~arzt** *m* ≈ senior registrar. **O~deck** *nt* upper deck. **o~e(r,s)** *a* upper; (*höhere*) higher. **O~fläche** *f* surface. **o~flächlich** *a* superficial. **O~geschoss** *nt* upper storey. **o~halb** *adv & prep* (+ *gen*) above. **O~haupt** *nt* (*fig*) head. **O~haus** *nt* (*Pol*) upper house; (*in UK*) House of Lords. **O~hemd** *nt* [man's] shirt. **o~irdisch** *a* surface ... ● *adv* above ground. **O~kiefer** *m* upper jaw. **O~körper** *m* upper part of the body. **O~leutnant** *m* lieutenant. **O~lippe** *f* upper lip

Obers *nt* - (*Aust*) cream

Ober|schenkel *m* thigh. **O~schule** *f* grammar school. **O~seite** *f* upper/(*rechte Seite*) right side

Oberst *m* -en & -s, -en colonel

oberste(r,s) *a* top; (*höchste*) highest; <*Befehlshaber, Gerichtshof*> supreme; (*wichtigste*) first

Ober|stimme *f* treble. **O~teil** *nt* top. **O~weite** *f* chest/(*der Frau*) bust size

obgleich *conj* although

Obhut *f* - care

obig *a* above

Objekt *nt* -[e]s, -e object; (*Haus, Grundstück*) property

Objektiv *nt* -s, -e lens. **o~** *a* objective. **O~ität** *f* - objectivity

Oblate *f* -, **-n** (*Relig*) wafer

Obmann *m* (*pl* -männer) [jury] foreman; (*Sport*) referee

Oboe /o'boːə/ *f* -, **-n** oboe

Obrigkeit *f* - authorities *pl*

obschon *conj* although

Observatorium *nt* -s, -ien observatory

obskur *a* obscure; dubious

Obst *nt* -es (*coll*) fruit. **O~baum** *m* fruit-tree. **O~garten** *m* orchard. **O~händler** *m* fruiterer

obszön *a* obscene

O-Bus *m* trolley bus

obwohl *conj* although

Ochse *m* -n, -n ox

öde *a* desolate; (*unfruchtbar*) barren; (*langweilig*) dull. **Öde** *f* - desolation; barrenness; dullness

oder *conj* or; **du kennst ihn doch, o~?** you know him, don't you?

Ofen *m* -s, ̈- stove; (*Heiz-*) heater; (*Back-*) oven; (*Techn*) furnace

offen *a* open; <*Flamme*> naked; (*o~herzig*) frank; (*o~ gezeigt*) overt; (*unentschieden*) unsettled; **o~e Stelle** vacancy; **Wein o~ verkaufen** sell wine by the glass; **o~ bleiben** remain open; **o~ halten**

hold open <*Tör*>; keep open <*Mund, Augen*>; o~ **lassen** leave open; leave vacant <*Stelle*>; o~ **stehen** be open; <*Rechnung:*> be outstanding; jdm o~ **stehen** (*fig*) be open to s.o.; *adv* o~ **gesagt** *od* **gestanden** to be honest. **o~bar** *a* obvious ● *adv* apparently. **o~baren** *vt* reveal. **O~barung** *f* -, -en revelation. **O~heit** *f* - frankness, openness. **o~sichtlich** *a* obvious

offenstehen* *vi sep* (*haben*) offen stehen, *s.* offen

öffentlich *a* public. **Ö~keit** *f* - public; **in aller Ö~keit** in public, publicly

Offerte *f* -, -n (*Comm*) offer

offiziell *a* official

Offizier *m* -s, -e (*Mil*) officer

öffn|en *vt/i* (*haben*) open; **sich ö~en** open. **Ö~er** *m* -s,- opener. **Ö~ung** *f* -, -en opening. **Ö~ungszeiten** *fpl* opening hours

oft *adv* often

öfter *adv* quite often. **ö~e(r,s)** *a* frequent; **des Ö~en** frequently. **ö~s** *adv* Ⓣ quite often

oh *int* oh!

o **ohne** *prep* (+ *acc*) without; **o~ mich!** count me out! **oben o~** topless ● *conj* **o~ zu überlegen** without thinking; **o~ dass ich es merkte** without my noticing it. **o~dies** *adv* anyway. **o~gleichen** *pred a* unparalleled. **o~hin** *adv* anyway

Ohn|macht *f* -, -en faint; (*fig*) powerlessness; **in O~macht fallen** faint. **o~mächtig** *a* unconscious; (*fig*) powerless; **o~mächtig werden** faint

Ohr *nt* -[e]s, -en ear

Öhr *nt* -[e]s, -e eye

Ohrenschmalz *nt* ear-wax. **O~schmerzen** *mpl* earache *sg*

Ohrfeige *f* slap in the face. **o~n** *vt* jdn **o~n** slap s.o.'s face

Ohr|läppchen *nt* -s,- ear-lobe. **O~ring** *m* ear-ring. **O~wurm** *m* earwig

oje *int* oh dear!

okay /o'ke:/ *a & adv* Ⓣ OK

Öko|logie *f* - ecology. **ö~logisch** *a* ecological. **Ö~nomie** *f* - economy; (*Wissenschaft*) economics *sg*. **ö~nomisch** *a* economic; (*sparsam*) economical

Oktave *f* -, -n octave

Oktober *m* -s,- October

ökumenisch *a* ecumenical

Öl *nt* -[e]s, -e oil; **in Öl malen** paint in oils. **Ölbaum** *m* olivetree. **ölen** *vt* oil. **Ölfarbe** *f* oil-paint. **Ölfeld** *nt* oilfield. **Ölgemälde** *nt* oil-painting. **ölig** *a* oily

Oliv|e *f* -, -n olive. **O~enöl** *nt* olive oil

Ölmessstab *m* dip-stick. **Ölsardinen** *fpl* sardines in oil. **Ölstand** *m* oil-level. **Öltanker** *m* oil-tanker. **Ölteppich** *m* oil-slick

Olympiade *f* -, -n Olympic Games *pl*, Olympics *pl*

Olymp|iasieger(in) /o'lympia-/ *m(f)* Olympic champion. **o~isch** *a* Olympic; **O~ische Spiele** Olympic Games

Ölzeug *nt* oilskins *pl*

Oma *f* -, -s Ⓣ granny

Omnibus *m* bus; (*Reise-*) coach

onanieren *vi* (*haben*) masturbate

Onkel *m* -s,- uncle

Opa *m* -s, -s Ⓣ grandad

Opal *m* -s, -e opal

Oper *f* -, -n opera

Operation /-'tsio:n/ *f* -, -en operation. **O~ssaal** *m* operating theatre

Operette *f* -, -n operetta

operieren *vt* operate on <*Patient, Herz*>; **sich o~ lassen** have an operation ● *vi* (*haben*) operate

Opernglas *nt* opera-glasses *pl*

Opfer *nt* -s,- sacrifice; (*eines Unglücks*) victim; **ein O~ bringen** make a sacrifice; **jdm/etw zum O~ fallen** fall victim to s.o./sth. **o~n** *vt* sacrifice

Opium *nt* -s opium

Opposition /-'tsio:n/ f - opposition. **O~spartei** f opposition party

Optik f - optics sg, (🔲 *Objektiv*) lens. **O~er** m -s,- optician

optimal a optimum

Optimis|mus m - optimism. **O~t** m -en, -en optimist. **o~tisch** a optimistic

optisch a optical; <*Eindruck*> visual

Orakel nt -s,- oracle

Orange /o'rã:ʒə/ f -, -n orange. **o~** inv a orange. **O~ade** /orã'ʒa:də/ f -, -n orangeade. **O~nmarmelade** f [orange] marmalade

Oratorium nt -s, -ien oratorio

Orchester /ɔr'kɛstɐ/ nt -s,- orchestra

Orchidee /ɔrçi'de:ə/ f -, -n orchid

Orden m -s,- (*Ritter-, Kloster-*) order; (*Auszeichnung*) medal, decoration

ordentlich a neat. tidy; (*anständig*) respectable; (*ordnungsgemäß* 🔲: *richtig*) proper; <*Mitglied, Versammlung*> ordinary; (🔲 *gut*) decent; (🔲 *gehörig*) good

Order f -, -s & -n order

ordinär a common

Ordination /-'tsio:n/ f -, -en (*Relig*) ordination; (*Aust*) surgery

ordn|en vt put in order; tidy; (*an-*) arrange. **O~er** m -s,- steward; (*Akten-*) file

Ordnung f - order; **O~ machen** tidy up; **in O~ bringen** put in order; (*aufräumen*) tidy; (*reparieren*) mend; (*fig*) put right; **in O~ sein** be in order; (*ordentlich sein*) be tidy; (*fig*) be all right; [geht] **in O~!** OK! **o~sgemäß** a proper. **O~sstrafe** f (*Jur*) fine. **o~swidrig** a improper

Ordonnanz, Ordonanz f -, -en (*Mil*) orderly

Organ nt -s, -e organ; voice

Organisation /-'tsio:n/ f -, -en organization

organisch a organic

organisieren vt organize; (🔲 *beschaffen*) get [hold of]

Organismus m -, -men organism; (*System*) system

Organspenderkarte f donor card

Orgasmus m -, -men orgasm

Orgel f -, -n (*Mus*) organ. **O~pfeife** f organ-pipe

Orgie /'ɔrgiə/ f -, -n orgy

Orien|t /'o:riɛnt/ m -s Orient. **o~talisch** a Oriental

orientier|en /oriɛn'ti:rən/ vt inform (über + *acc* about); **sich o~en** get one's bearings, orientate oneself; (*unterrichten*) inform oneself (über + *acc* about). **O~ung** f - orientation; **die O~ung verlieren** lose one's bearings

original a original. **O~** nt -s, -e original. **O~übertragung** f live transmission

originell a original; (*eigenartig*) unusual

Orkan m -s, -e hurricane

Ornament nt -[e]s, -e ornament

Ort m -[e]s, -e place; (*Ortschaft*) [small] town; **am Ort** locally; **am Ort des Verbrechens** at the scene of the crime

ortho|dox a orthodox. **O~graphie, O~grafie** f - spelling. **O~päde** m -n, -n orthopaedic specialist

örtlich a local

Ortschaft f -, -en [small] town; (*Dorf*) village; **geschlossene O~** (*Auto*) built-up area

Orts|gespräch nt (*Teleph*) local call. **O~verkehr** m local traffic. **O~zeit** f local time

Öse f -, -n eyelet; (*Schlinge*) loop; **Haken und Öse** hook and eye

Ost m -[e]s east

Osten m -s east; **nach O~** east

ostentativ a pointed

Osteopath m -en, -en osteopath

Oster|ei /'o:stɐʔai/ nt Easter egg. **O~fest** nt Easter. **O~glocke** f daffodil. **O~n** nt -,- Easter; **frohe O~n!** happy Easter!

Österreich nt -s Austria. **Ö~er** m, -s,-, **Ö~erin** f -, -nen Austrian. **ö~isch** a Austrian

östlich a eastern; <*Richtung*> easterly ● *adv & prep* (+ *gen*) **ö~**

[von] der Stadt [to the] east of the town

Ostsee *f* Baltic [Sea]

Otter¹ *m* -s,- otter

Otter² *f* -, -n adder

Ouverture /uvɛrˈtyːrə/ *f* -, -n overture

oval *a* oval. **O~** *nt* -s, -e oval

Oxid, Oxyd *nt* -[e]s, -e oxide

Ozean *m* -s, -e ocean

Ozon *nt* -s ozone. **O~loch** *nt* hole in the ozone layer. **O~schicht** *f* ozone layer

P p

paar *pron inv* ein p~ a few; ein p~ Mal a few times; alle p~ Tage every few days. **P~** *nt* -[e]s, -e pair; (*Ehe-, Liebes-*) couple. **p~en** *vt* mate; (*verbinden*) combine; sich p~en mate. **P~ung** *f* -, -en mating. **p~weise** *adv* in pairs, in twos

Pacht *f* -, -en lease; (*P~summe*) rent. **p~en** *vt* lease

Pächter *m* -s,- lessee; (*eines Hofes*) tenant

Pachtvertrag *m* lease

Päckchen *nt* -s,- package, small packet

pack|en *vt/i* (*haben*) pack; (*ergreifen*) seize; (*fig: fesseln*) grip. **P~en** *m* -s,- bundle. **p~end** *a* (*fig*) gripping. **P~papier** *nt* [strong] wrapping paper. **P~ung** *f* -, -en packet; (*Med*) pack

Pädagog|e *m* -n, -n educationalist; (*Lehrer*) teacher. **P~ik** *f* - educational science

Paddel *nt* -s,- paddle. **P~boot** *nt* canoe. **p~n** *vt/i* (*haben/sein*) paddle. **P~sport** *m* canoeing

Page /ˈpaːʒə/ *m* -n, -n page

Paillette /pajˈjɛtə/ *f* -, -n sequin

Paket *nt* -[e]s, -e packet; (*Post-*) parcel

Pakist|an *nt* -s Pakistan. **P~aner(in)** *m* -s,- (*f* -, -nen) Pakistani. **p~anisch** *a* Pakistani

Palast *m* -[e]s,-̈e palace

Paläst|ina *nt* -s Palestine. **P~inenser(in)** *m* -s,- (*f* -, -nen) Palestinian. **p~inensisch** *a* Palestinian

Palette *f* -, -n palette

Palme *f* -, -n palm[-tree]

Pampelmuse *f* -, -n grapefruit

Panier|mehl *nt* (*Culin*) breadcrumbs *pl*. **p~t** *a* (*Culin*) breaded

Panik *f* - panic

Panne *f* -, -n breakdown; (*Reifen-*) flat tyre; (*Missgeschick*) mishap

Panther, Panter *m* -s,- panther

Pantine *f* -, -n [wooden] clog

Pantoffel *m* -s, -n slipper; mule

Pantomime¹ *f* -, -n mime

Pantomime² *m* -n, -n mime artist

Panzer *m* -s,- armour; (*Mil*) tank; (*Zool*) shell. **p~n** *vt* armourplate. **P~schrank** *m* safe

Papa /ˈpapa, paˈpaː/ *m* -s, -s daddy

Papagei *m* -s & -en, -en parrot

Papier *nt* -[e]s, -e paper. **P~korb** *m* waste-paper basket. **P~schlange** *f* streamer. **P~waren** *fpl* stationery *sg*

Pappe *f* - cardboard

Pappel *f* -, -n poplar

pappig *a* ⓘ sticky

Papp|karton *m*, **P~schachtel** *f* cardboard box

Papst *m* -[e]s,-̈e pope

päpstlich *a* papal

Parade *f* -, -n parade

Paradies *nt* -es, -e paradise

Paraffin *nt* -s paraffin

Paragraph, Paragraf *m* -en, -en section

parallel *a & adv* parallel. **P~e** *f* -, -n parallel

Paranuss f Brazil nut

Parasit m -en, -en parasite

parat a ready

Parcours /par'kuːɐ̯/ m -,- /-[s], -s/ (*Sport*) course

Pardon /par'dõː/ int sorry!

Parfüm nt -s, -e & -s perfume, scent. **p∼iert** a perfumed, scented

parieren vi (*haben*) 🗓 obey

Park m -s, -s park. **p∼en** vt/i (*haben*) park. **P∼en** nt -s parking; 'P∼en verboten' 'no parking'

Parkett nt -[e]s, -e parquet floor; (*Theat*) stalls pl

Park|haus nt multi-storey car park. **P∼lücke** f parking space. **P∼platz** m car park; parking space. **P∼scheibe** f parking-disc. **P∼schein** m car-park ticket. **P∼uhr** f parking-meter. **P∼verbot** nt parking ban; 'P∼verbot' 'no parking'

Parlament nt -[e]s, -e parliament. **p∼arisch** a parliamentary

Parodie f -, -n parody

Parole f -, -n slogan; (*Mil*) password

Partei f -, -en (*Pol, Jur*) party; (*Miet-*) tenant; **für jdn P∼ ergreifen** take s.o.'s part. **p∼isch** a biased

Parterre /par'tɛr/ nt -s, -s ground floor; (*Theat*) rear stalls pl

Partie f -, -n part; (*Tennis, Schach*) game; (*Golf*) round; (*Comm*) batch; **eine gute P∼ machen** marry well

Partikel nt -s,- particle

Partitur f -, -en (*Mus*) full score

Partizip nt -s, -ien /-i̯ən/ participle

Partner|(in) m -s,- (f -, -nen) partner. **P∼schaft** f -, -en partnership. **P∼stadt** f twin town

Party /'paːɐ̯ti/ f -, -s party

Parzelle f -, -n plot [of ground]

Pass m -es,ˉe passport; (*Geog, Sport*) pass

Passage /pa'saːʒə/ f -, -n passage; (*Einkaufs-*) shopping arcade

Passagier /pasa'ʒiːɐ̯/ m -s, -e passenger

Passant(in) m -en, -en (f -, -nen) passer-by

Passe f -, -n yoke

passen vi (*haben*) fit; (*geeignet sein*) be right (**für** for); (*Sport*) pass the ball; (*aufgeben*) pass; **p∼ zu** go [well] with; (*übereinstimmen*) match; **jdm p∼** fit s.o.; (*gelegen sein*) suit s.o.; **[ich] passe** pass. **p∼d** a suitable; (*angemessen*) appropriate; (*günstig*) convenient; (*übereinstimmend*) matching

passier|en vt pass; cross <*Grenze*>; (*Culin*) rub through a sieve ● vi (*sein*) happen (**jdm** to s.o.); **es ist ein Unglück p∼t** there has been an accident. **P∼schein** m pass

Passiv nt -s, -e (*Gram*) passive

Passstraße f pass

Paste f -, -n paste

Pastell nt -[e]s, -e pastel

Pastete f -, -n pie; (*Gänseleber-*) pâté

pasteurisieren /pastøri'ziːrən/ vt pasteurize

Pastor m -s, -en /-'toːrən/ pastor

Pate m -n, -n godfather; (*fig*) sponsor; **P∼n** godparents. **P∼nkind** nt godchild

Patent nt -[e]s, -e patent; (*Offiziers-*) commission. **p∼** a 🗓 clever; <*Person*> resourceful. **p∼ieren** vt patent

Pater m -s,- (*Relig*) Father

Patholog|e m -n, -n pathologist. **p∼isch** a pathological

Patience /pa'si̯ãːs/ f -, -n patience

Patient(in) /pa'tsi̯ɛnt(ɪn)/ m -en, -en (f -, -nen) patient

Patin f -, -nen godmother

Patriot|(in) m -en, -en (f -, -nen) patriot. **p∼isch** a patriotic. **P∼ismus** m - patriotism

Patrone f -, -n cartridge

Patrouille /pa'trʊljə/ f -, -n patrol

Patsch|e f **in der P∼e sitzen** 🗓 be in a jam. **p∼nass** a 🗓 soaking wet

Patt nt -s stalemate

Patz|er m -s,- 🗓 slip. **p∼ig** a 🗓 insolent

Pauk|e f -, -n kettledrum; **auf die P∼e hauen** 🗓 have a good time;

p

(*prahlen*) boast. **p~en** *vt/i* (*haben*) 🔧 swot

pauschal *a* all-inclusive; (*einheitlich*) flat-rate; (*fig*) sweeping <*Urteil*>; **p~e Summe** lump sum. **P~e** *f* -, -n lump sum. **P~reise** *f* package tour. **P~summe** *f* lump sum

Pause¹ *f* -, -n break; (*beim Sprechen*) pause; (*Theat*) interval; (*im Kino*) intermission; (*Mus*) rest; **P~ machen** have a break

Pause² *f* -, -n tracing. **p~n** *vt* trace

pausenlos *a* incessant

pausieren *vi* (*haben*) have a break; (*ausruhen*) rest

Pauspapier *nt* tracing-paper

Pavian *m* -s, -e baboon

Pavillon /'paviljõ/ *m* -s, -s pavilion

Pazifi|k *m* -s Pacific [Ocean]. **p~sch** *a* Pacific

Pazifist *m* -en, -en pacifist

Pech *nt* -s pitch; (*Unglück*) bad luck; **P~ haben** be unlucky

Pedal *nt* -s, -e pedal

Pedant *m* -en, -en pedant

Pediküre *f* -, -n pedicure

Pegel *m* -s,- level; (*Gerät*) water-level indicator. **P~stand** *m* [water] level

peilen *vt* take a bearing on

peinigen *vt* torment

peinlich *a* embarrassing, awkward; (*genau*) scrupulous; **es war mir sehr p~** I was very embarrassed

Peitsche *f* -, -n whip. **p~n** *vt* whip; (*fig*) lash ● *vi* (*sein*) lash (**an** + *acc* against). **P~nhieb** *m* lash

Pelikan *m* -s, -e pelican

Pell|e *f* -, -n skin. **p~en** *vt* peel; shell <*Ei*>; **sich p~en** peel

Pelz *m* -es, -e fur

Pendel *nt* -s,- pendulum. **p~n** *vi* (*haben*) swing ● *vi* (*sein*) commute. **P~verkehr** *m* shuttle-service; (*für Pendler*) commuter traffic

Pendler *m* -s,- commuter

penetrant *a* penetrating; (*fig*) obtrusive

Penis *m* -, -se penis

Penne *f* -, -n 🔧 school

Pension /pã'zio:n/ *f* -, -en pension; (*Hotel*) guest-house; **bei voller/halber P~** with full/half board. **P~är(in)** *m* -s, -e (*f* -, -nen) pensioner. **P~at** *nt* -[e]s, -e boarding-school. **p~ieren** *vt* retire. **P~ierung** *f* - retirement

Pensum *nt* -s [allotted] work

Peperoni *f* -,- chilli

per *prep* (+ *acc*) by

Perfekt *nt* -s (*Gram*) perfect

Perfektion /-'tsio:n/ *f* - perfection

perforiert *a* perforated

Pergament *nt* -[e]s, -e parchment. **P~papier** *nt* grease-proof paper

Period|e *f* -, -n period. **p~isch** *a* periodic

Perl|e *f* -, -n pearl; (*Glas-, Holz-*) bead; (*Sekt-*) bubble. **P~mutt** *nt* -s mother-of-pearl

Persi|en /-iən/ *nt* -s Persia. **p~isch** *a* Persian

Person *f* -, -en person; (*Theat*) character; **für vier P~en** for four people

Personal *nt* -s personnel, staff. **P~ausweis** *m* identity card. **P~chef** *m* personnel manager. **P~ien** /-iən/ *pl* personal particulars. **P~mangel** *m* staff shortage

persönlich *a* personal ● *adv* personally, in person. **P~keit** *f* -, -en personality

Perücke *f* -, -n wig

pervers *a* [sexually] perverted. **P~ion** *f* -, -en perversion

Pessimis|mus *m* - pessimism. **P~t** *m* -en, -en pessimist. **p~tisch** *a* pessimistic

Pest *f* - plague

Petersilie /-iə/ *f* - parsley

Petroleum /-leum/ *nt* -s paraffin

Petze *f* -, -n 🔧 sneak. **p~n** *vi* (*haben*) 🔧 sneak

Pfad *m* -[e]s, -e path. **P∼finder** *m* -s,- [Boy] Scout. **P∼finderin** *f* -, -nen [Girl] Guide

Pfahl *m* -[e]s, ̈-e stake, post

Pfalz (die) - the Palatinate

Pfand *nt* -[e]s, ̈-er pledge; (*beim Spiel*) forfeit; (*Flaschen-*) deposit

pfänd|en *vt* (*Jur*) seize. **P∼erspiel** *nt* game of forfeits

Pfandleiher *m* -s,- pawnbroker

Pfändung *f* -, -en (*Jur*) seizure

Pfann|e *f* -, -n [frying-]pan. **P∼kuchen** *m* pancake

Pfarr|er *m* -s,- vicar, parson; (*katholischer*) priest. **P∼haus** *nt* vicarage

Pfau *m* -s, -en peacock

Pfeffer *m* -s pepper. **P∼kuchen** *m* gingerbread. **P∼minze** *f* - (*Bot*) peppermint. **p∼n** *vt* pepper; (🔲 *schmeißen*) chuck. **P∼streuer** *m* -s,- pepperpot

Pfeif|e *f* -, -n whistle; (*Tabak-, Orgel-*) pipe. **p∼en†** *vt/i* (*haben*) whistle; (*als Signal*) blow the whistle

Pfeil *m* -[e]s, -e arrow

Pfeiler *m* -s,- pillar; (*Brücken-*) pier

Pfennig *m* -s, -e pfennig

Pferch *m* -[e]s, -e [sheep] pen

Pferd *nt* -es, -e horse; zu P∼e on horseback. **P∼erennen** *nt* horse-race; (*als Sport*) [horse-]racing. **P∼eschwanz** *m* horse's tail; (*Frisur*) pony-tail. **P∼estall** *m* stable. **P∼estärke** *f* horsepower

Pfiff *m* -[e]s, -e whistle

Pfifferling *m* -s, -e chanterelle

pfiffig *a* smart

Pfingst|en *nt* -s Whitsun. **P∼rose** *f* peony

Pfirsich *m* -s, -e peach

Pflanz|e *f* -, -n plant. **p∼en** *vt* plant. **P∼enfett** *nt* vegetable fat. **p∼lich** *a* vegetable

Pflaster *nt* -s,- pavement; (*Heft-*) plaster. **p∼n** *vt* pave

Pflaume *f* -, -n plum

Pflege *f* - care; (*Kranken-*) nursing; in P∼ nehmen look after; (*Admin*) foster <*Kind*>. **p∼bedürftig** *a* in need of care. **P∼eltern** *pl* foster-parents. **P∼kind** *nt* foster-child. **p∼leicht** *a* easy-care. **p∼n** *vt* look after, care for; nurse <*Kranke*>; cultivate <*Künste, Freundschaft*>. **P∼r(in)** *m* -s,- (*f* -, -nen) nurse; (*Tier-*) keeper

Pflicht *f* -, -en duty; (*Sport*) compulsory exercise/routine. **p∼bewusst** *a* conscientious. **P∼gefühl** *nt* sense of duty

pflücken *vt* pick

Pflug *m* -[e]s, ̈-e plough

pflügen *vt/i* (*haben*) plough

Pforte *f* -, -n gate

Pförtner *m* -s,- porter

Pfosten *m* -s,- post

Pfote *f* -, -n paw

Pfropfen *m* -s,- stopper; (*Korken*) cork. **p∼** *vt* graft (auf + *acc* on [to]); (🔲 *pressen*) cram (in + *acc* into)

pfui *int* ugh

Pfund *nt* -[e]s, -e & - pound

Pfusch|arbeit *f* 🔲 shoddy work. **p∼en** *vi* (*haben*) 🔲 botch one's work. **P∼erei** *f* -, -en 🔲 botch-up

Pfütze *f* -, -n puddle

Phantasie *f* -, -n imagination; P∼n fantasies; (*Fieber-*) hallucinations. **p∼los** *a* unimaginative. **p∼ren** *vi* (*haben*) fantasize; (*im Fieber*) be delirious. **p∼voll** *a* imaginative

phantastisch *a* fantastic

pharma|zeutisch *a* pharmaceutical. **P∼zie** *f* - pharmacy

Phase *f* -, -n phase

Philologie *f* - [study of] language and literature

Philosoph *m* -en, -en philosopher. **P∼ie** *f* -, -n philosophy

philosophisch *a* philosophical

Phobie *f* -, -n phobia

Phonet|ik *f* - phonetics *sg.* **p∼isch** *a* phonetic

Phosphor *m* -s phosphorus

Photo *nt*, **Photo-** = Foto, Foto-

Phrase *f* -, -n empty phrase

Physik *f* - physics *sg.* **p∼alisch** *a* physical

p

Physiker(in) *m* -s,- (*f* -, -nen) physicist

Physiologie *f* - physiology

physisch *a* physical

Pianist(in) *m* -en, -en (*f* -, -nen) pianist

Pickel *m* -s,- pimple, spot; (*Spitzhacke*) pick. **p~ig** *a* spotty

Picknick *nt* -s, -s picnic

piep[s]|en *vi* (*haben*) <*Vogel:*> cheep; <*Maus:*> squeak; (*Techn*) bleep. **P~er** *m* -s,- bleeper

Pier *m* -s, -e [harbour] pier

Pietät /pie'tɛ:t/ *f* - reverence. **p~los** *a* irreverent

Pigment *nt* -[e]s, -e pigment. **P~ierung** *f* - pigmentation

Pik *nt* -s, -s (*Karten*) spades *pl*

pikant *a* piquant; (*gewagt*) racy

piken *vt* Ⓔ prick

pikiert *a* offended, hurt

Pilger|(in) *m* -s,- (*f* -, -nen) pilgrim. **P~fahrt** *f* pilgrimage. **p~n** *vi* (*sein*) make a pilgrimage

Pille *f* -, -n pill

Pilot *m* -en, -en pilot

Pilz *m* -es, -e fungus; (*essbarer*) mushroom

pingelig *a* Ⓔ fussy

Pinguin *m* -s, -e penguin

Pinie /-iə/ *f* -, -n stone-pine

pinkeln *vi* (*haben*) Ⓔ pee

Pinsel *m* -s,- [paint]brush

Pinzette *f* -, -n tweezers *pl*

Pionier *m* -s, -e (*Mil*) sapper; (*fig*) pioneer

Pirat *m* -en, -en pirate

Piste *f* -, -n (*Ski-*) run, piste; (*Renn-*) track; (*Aviat*) runway

Pistole *f* -, -n pistol

pitschnass *a* Ⓔ soaking wet

pittoresk *a* picturesque

Pizza *f* -, -s pizza

Pkw /'pe:kave:/ *m* -s, -s car

plädieren *vi* (*haben*) plead (**für** for); **auf Freispruch p~** (*Jur*) ask for an acquittal

Plädoyer /plɛdoa'je:/ *nt* -s, -s (*Jur*) closing speech; (*fig*) plea

Plage *f* -, -n [hard] labour; (*Mühe*) trouble; (*Belästigung*) nuisance. **p~n** *vt* torment, plague; (*bedrängen*) pester; **sich p~n** struggle

Plakat *nt* -[e]s, -e poster

Plakette *f* -, -n badge

Plan *m* -[e]s,¨-e plan

Plane *f* -, -n tarpaulin; (*Boden-*) groundsheet

planen *vt/i* (*haben*) plan

Planet *m* -en, -en planet

planier|en *vt* level. **P~raupe** *f* bulldozer

Planke *f* -, -n plank

plan|los *a* unsystematic. **p~mäßig** *a* systematic; <*Ankunft:*> scheduled

Plansch|becken *nt* paddling pool. **p~en** *vi* (*haben*) splash about

Plantage /plan'ta:ʒə/ *f* -, -n plantation

Planung *f* - planning

plappern *vi* (*haben*) chatter ● *vt* talk <*Unsinn*>

plärren *vi* (*haben*) bawl

Plasma *nt* -s plasma

Plastik¹ *f* -, -en sculpture

Plast|ik² *nt* -s plastic. **p~isch** *a* three-dimensional; (*formbar*) plastic; (*anschaulich*) graphic

Plateau /pla'to:/ *nt* -s, -s plateau

Platin *nt* -s platinum

platonisch *a* platonic

plätschern *vi* (*haben*) splash; <*Bach:*> babble ● *vi* (*sein*) <*Bach:*> babble along

platt *a* & *adv* flat. **P~** *nt* -[s] (*Lang*) Low German

Plättbrett *nt* ironing-board

Platte *f* -, -n slab; (*Druck-*) plate; (*Metall-, Glas-*) sheet; (*Fliese*) tile; (*Koch-*) hotplate; (*Tisch-*) top; (*Schall-*) record, disc; (*zum Servieren*) [flat] dish, platter; **kalte P~** assorted cold meats and cheeses *pl*

Plätt|eisen *nt* iron. **p~en** *vt/i* (*haben*) iron

Plattenspieler *m* record-player

Platt|form f -, -en platform.
P~füße mpl flat feet

Platz m -es,-̈e place; (von Häusern
umgeben) square; (Sitz-) seat; (Sport-)
ground; (Fußball-) pitch; (Tennis-)
court; (Golf-) course; (freier Raum)
room, space; P~ nehmen take a seat;
P~ machen make room; vom P~
stellen (Sport) send off.
P~anweiserin f -, -nen usherette

Plätzchen nt -s,- spot; (Culin)
biscuit

platzen vi (sein) burst; (auf-) split;
(🅘 scheitern) fall through;
<Verlobung:> be off

Platz|karte f seat reservation
ticket. P~mangel m lack of space.
P~patrone f blank. P~verweis
m (Sport) sending off. P~wunde f
laceration

Plauderei f -, -en chat

plaudern vi (haben) chat

plausibel a plausible

pleite a 🅘 p~ sein be broke:
<Firma:> be bankrupt. P~ f -, -n 🅘
bankruptcy; (Misserfolg) flop; P~
gehen od machen go bankrupt

plissiert a [finely] pleated

Plomb|e f -, -n seal; (Zahn-) filling.
p~ieren vt seal; fill <Zahn>

plötzlich a sudden

plump a plump; clumsy

plumpsen vi (sein) 🅘 fall

plündern vt/i (haben) loot

Plunderstück nt Danish pastry

Plural m -s, -e plural

plus adv, conj & prep (+ dat) plus.
P~ nt - surplus; (Gewinn) profit
(Vorteil) advantage, plus. P~punkt
m (Sport) point; (fig) plus

Po m -s, -s 🅘 bottom

Pöbel m -s mob, rabble. p~haft a
loutish

pochen vi (haben) knock, <Herz:>
pound; p~ auf (+ acc) (fig) insist on

pochieren /pɔˈʃiːrən/ vt poach

Pocken pl smallpox sg

Podest nt -[e]s, -e rostrum

Podium nt -s, -ien /-i̯ən/ platform;
(Podest) rostrum

Poesie /poeˈziː/ f - poetry

poetisch a poetic

Pointe /ˈpoɛ̃ːtə/ f -, -n point (of a
joke)

Pokal m -s, -e goblet; (Sport) cup

pökeln vt (Culin) salt

Poker nt -s poker

Pol m -s, -e pole. p~ar a polar

Polarstern m pole-star

Pole m, -n, -n Pole. P~n nt -s Poland

Police /poˈliːsə/ f -, -n policy

Polier m -s, -e foreman

polieren vt polish

Polin f -, -nen Pole

Politesse f -, -n [woman] traffic
warden

Politik f - politics sg; (Vorgehen,
Maßnahme) policy

Polit|iker(in) m -s,- (f, -, -nen)
politician. p~isch a political

Politur f -, -en polish

Polizei f - police pl. p~lich a police
... ● adv by the police; <sich
anmelden> with the police.
P~streife f police patrol.
P~stunde f closing time.
P~wache f police station

Polizist m -en, -en policeman. P~in
f -, -nen policewoman

Pollen m -s pollen

polnisch a Polish

Polster nt -s,- pad; (Kissen) cushion;
(Möbel-) upholstery. p~n vt pad;
upholster <Möbel>. P~ung f -
padding; upholstery

Polter|abend m wedding-eve
party. p~n vi (haben) thump bang

Polyäthylen nt -s polythene

Polyester m -s polyester

Polyp m -en, -en polyp. P~en
adenoids pl

Pommes frites /pɔmˈfriːt/ pl
chips; (dünner) French fries

Pomp m -s pomp

Pompon /põˈpõː/ m -s, -s pompon

pompös a ostentatious

Pony¹ nt -s, -s pony

Pony² m -s, -s fringe

Pop m -[s] pop

Popo *m* -s, -s 🔲 bottom

populär *a* popular

Pore *f* -, -n pore

Porno|graphie, Pornografie *f* - pornography. **p~graphisch, p~grafisch** *a* pornographic

Porree *m* -s leeks *pl*

Portal *nt* -s, -e portal

Portemonnaie /pɔrtmɔ'neː/ *nt*-s, -s purse

Portier /pɔr'tieː/ *m* -s, -s doorman, porter

Portion /-'tsioːn/ *f* -, -en helping, portion

Portmonee *nt* -s, -s = Portemonnaie

Porto *nt* -s postage. **p~frei** *adv* post free, post paid

Porträt /pɔr'trɛː/ *nt* -s, -s portrait. **p~tieren** *vt* paint a portrait of

Portugal *nt* -s Portugal

Portugies|e *m* -n, -n, **P~in** *f* -, -nen Portuguese. **p~isch** *a* Portuguese

Portwein *m* port

Porzellan *nt* -s china, porcelain

Posaune *f* -, -n trombone

Position /-'tsioːn/ *f* -, -en position

positiv *a* positive. **P~** *nt* -s, -e (*Phot*) positive

Post *f* - post office; (*Briefe*) mail, post; **mit der P~** by post

postalisch *a* postal

Post|amt *nt* post office. **P~anweisung** *f* postal money order. **P~bote** *m* postman

Posten *m* -s,- post; (*Wache*) sentry; (*Waren-*) batch; (*Rechnungs-*) item, entry

Poster *nt* & *m* -s,- poster

Postfach *nt* post-office *or* PO box

Post|karte *f* postcard. **p~lagernd** *adv* poste restante. **P~leitzahl** *f* postcode. **P~scheckkonto** *nt* ≈ National Girobank account. **P~stempel** *m* postmark

postum *a* posthumous

post|wendend *adv* by return of post. **P~wertzeichen** *nt* [postage] stamp

Potenz *f* -, -en potency; (*Math & fig*) power

Pracht *f* - magnificence, splendour

prächtig *a* magnificent; splendid

prachtvoll *a* magnificent

Prädikat *nt* -[e]s, -e rating; (*Comm*) grade; (*Gram*) predicate

prägen *vt* stamp (**auf** + *acc* on); emboss <*Leder*>; mint <*Münze*>; coin <*Wort*>; (*fig*) shape

prägnant *a* succinct

prähistorisch *a* prehistoric

prahl|en *vi* (*haben*) boast, brag (**mit** about)

Prakti|k *f* -, -en practice. **P~kant(in)** *m* -en, -en (*f* -, -nen) trainee

Prakti|kum *nt* -s, -ka practical training. **p~sch** *a* practical; (*nützlich*) handy; (*tatsächlich*) virtual; **p~scher Arzt** general practitioner ● *adv* practically; virtually; (*in der Praxis*) in practice. **p~zieren** *vt/i* (*haben*) practise; (*anwenden*) put into practice; (🔲 *bekommen*) get

Praline *f* -, -n chocolate

prall *a* bulging; (*dick*) plump; <*Sonne*> blazing ● *adv* **p~ gefüllt** full to bursting. **p~en** *vi* (*sein*) **p~ auf** (+ *acc*)/**gegen** collide with, hit; <*Sonne*:> blaze down on

Prämie /-iə/ *f* -, -n premium; (*Preis*) award

präm[i]ieren *vt* award a prize to

Pranger *m* -s,- pillory

Pranke *f* -, -n paw

Präparat *nt* -[e]s, -e preparation

Präsens *nt* - (*Gram*) present

präsentieren *vt* present

Präsenz *f* - presence

Präservativ *nt* -s, -e condom

Präsident|(in) *m* -en, -en (*f* -, -nen) president. **P~schaft** *f* - presidency

Präsidium *nt* -s presidency; (*Gremium*) executive committee; (*Polizei-*) headquarters *pl*

---

*old spelling

prasseln vi (haben) <Regen:> beat down; <Feuer:> crackle

Präteritum nt -s imperfect

Praxis f -, -xen practice; (Erfahrung) practical experience; (Arzt-) surgery; in der P~ in practice

Präzedenzfall m precedent

präzis[e] a precise

predig|en vt/i (haben) preach. **P~t** f -, -en sermon

Preis m -es, -e price; (Belohnung) prize. **P~ausschreiben** nt competition

Preiselbeere f (Bot) cowberry; (Culin) ≈ cranberry

preisen† vt praise

preisgeben† vt sep abandon (dat to); reveal <Geheimnis>

preis|gekrönt a award-winning. **p~günstig** a reasonably priced ● adv at a reasonable price. **P~lage** f price range. **p~lich** a price … ● adv in price. **P~richter** m judge. **P~schild** nt price-tag. **P~träger(in)** m(f) prize-winner. **p~wert** a reasonable

Prell|bock m buffers pl. **p~en** vt bounce; (verletzen) bruise; (🔟 betrügen) cheat. **P~ung** f -, -en bruise

Premiere /prə'mie:rə/ f -, -n première

Premierminister(in) /prə'mie:-/ m(f) Prime Minister

Presse f -, -n press. **p~n** vt press

Pressluftbohrer m pneumatic drill

Preuß|en nt -s Prussia. **p~isch** a Prussian

prickeln vi (haben) tingle

Priester m -s,- priest

prima inv a first-class, first-rate; (🔟 toll) fantastic

primär a primary

Primel f -, -n primula

primitiv a primitive

Prinz m -en, -en prince. **P~essin** f -, -nen princess

Prinzip nt -s, -ien /-iən/ principle. **p~iell** a <Frage> of principle ● adv on principle

Prise f -, -n P~ Salz pinch of salt

Prisma nt -s, -men prism

privat a private, personal. **P~adresse** f home address. **p~isieren** vt privatize

Privileg nt -[e]s, -ien /-iən/ privilege. **p~iert** a privileged

pro prep (+ dat) per. **Pro** nt - das Pro und Kontra the pros and cons pl

Probe f -, -n test, trial; (Menge, Muster) sample; (Theat) rehearsal; auf die P~ stellen put to the test; ein Auto P~ fahren test-drive a car. **p~n** vt/i (haben) (Theat) rehearse. **p~weise** adv on a trial basis. **P~zeit** f probationary period

probieren vt/i (haben) try; (kosten) taste; (proben) rehearse

Problem nt -s, -e problem. **p~atisch** a problematic

problemlos a problem-free ● adv without any problems

Produkt nt -[e]s, -e product

Produk|tion /-'tsio:n/ f -, -en production. **p~tiv** a productive

Produ|zent m -en, -en producer. **p~zieren** vt produce

Professor m -s, -en /-'so:rən/ professor

Profi m -s, -s (Sport) professional

Profil nt -s, -e profile; (Reifen-) tread; (fig) image

Profit m -[e]s, -e profit. **p~ieren** vi (haben) profit (von from)

Prognose f -, -n forecast; (Med) prognosis

Programm nt -s, -e programme; (Computer-) program; (TV) channel; (Comm: Sortiment) range. **p~ieren** vt/i (haben) (Computer) program. **P~ierer(in)** m -s,- (f -, -nen) [computer] programmer

Projekt nt -[e]s, -e project

Projektor m -s, -en /-'to:rən/ projector

Prolet m -en, -en boor. **P~ariat** nt -[e]s proletariat

Prolog m -s, -e prologue

Promenade f -, -n promenade

Promille *pl* 🔢 alcohol level *sg* in the blood; **zu viel P~ haben** 🔢 be over the limit

Prominenz *f* - prominent figures *pl*

Promiskuität *f* - promiscuity

promovieren *vi* (*haben*) obtain one's doctorate

prompt *a* prompt

Pronomen *nt* -s,- pronoun

Propaganda *f* - propaganda; (*Reklame*) publicity

Propeller *m* -s,- propeller

Prophet *m* -en, -en prophet

prophezei|en *vt* prophesy. **P~ung** *f* -, -en prophecy

Proportion /-'tsio:n/ *f* -, -en proportion

Prosa *f* - prose

prosit *int* cheers!

Prospekt *m* -[e]s, -e brochure; (*Comm*) prospectus

prost *int* cheers!

Prostitu|ierte *f* -n, -n prostitute. **P~tion** /-'tsio:n/ *f* - prostitution

Protest *m* -[e]s, -e protest

Protestant|(in) *m* -en, -en (*f* -, -nen) (*Relig*) Protestant. **p~isch** *a* (*Relig*) Protestant

protestieren *vi* (*haben*) protest

Prothese *f* -, -n artificial limb; (*Zahn-*) denture

Protokoll *nt* -s, -e record; (*Sitzungs-*) minutes *pl*; (*diplomatisches*) protocol

protz|en *vi* (*haben*) show off (**mit etw** sth). **p~ig** *a* ostentatious

Proviant *m* -s provisions *pl*

Provinz *f* -, -en province

Provision *f* -, -en (*Comm*) commission

provisorisch *a* provisional, temporary

Provokation /-'tsio:n/ *f* -, -en provocation

provozieren *vt* provoke

Prozedur *f* -, -en [lengthy] business

Prozent *nt* -[e]s, -e & - per cent; 5 **P~** 5 per cent. **P~satz** *m* percentage. **p~ual** *a* percentage ...

Prozess *m* -es, -e process; (*Jur*) lawsuit; (*Kriminal-*) trial

Prozession *f* -, -en procession

prüde *a* prudish

prüf|en *vt* test/(*über-*) check (**auf +** *acc* for); audit <*Bücher*>; (*Sch*) examine; **p~ender Blick** searching look. **P~er** *m* -s,- inspector; (*Buch-*) auditor; (*Sch*) examiner. **P~ling** *m* -s, -e examination candidate. **P~ung** *f* -, -en examination; (*Test*) test; (*Bücher-*) audit; (*fig*) trial

Prügel *m* -s,- cudgel; **P~** *pl* hiding *sg*, beating *sg*. **P~ei** *f* -, -en brawl, fight. **p~n** *vt* beat, thrash

Prunk *m* -[e]s magnificence, splendour

Psalm *m* -s, -en psalm

Pseudonym *nt* -s, -e pseudonym

pst *int* shush!

Psychi|ater *m* -s,- psychiatrist. **P~atrie** *f* - psychiatry. **p~atrisch** *a* psychiatric

psychisch *a* psychological

Psycho|analyse *f* psychoanalysis. **P~loge** *m* -n, -n psychologist. **P~logie** *f* - psychology. **p~logisch** *a* psychological

Pubertät *f* - puberty

Publi|kum *nt* -s public; (*Zuhörer*) audience; (*Zuschauer*) spectators *pl*. **p~zieren** *vt* publish

Pudding *m* -s, -s blancmange; (*im Wasserbad gekocht*) pudding

Pudel *m* -s,- poodle

Puder *m* & 🔢 *nt* -s,- powder. **P~dose** *f* [powder] compact. **p~n** *vt* powder. **P~zucker** *m* icing sugar

Puff *m* & *nt* -s, -s ⊠ brothel

Puffer *m* -s,- (*Rail*) buffer; (*Culin*) pancake. **P~zone** *f* buffer zone

Pull|i *m* -s, -s jumper. **P~over** *m* -s,- jumper; (*Herren-*) pullover

Puls *m* -es pulse. **P~ader** *f* artery

Pult *nt* -[e]s, -e desk

Pulver *nt* -s,- powder. **p~ig** *a* powdery

p

Pulverkaffee *m* instant coffee
pummelig *a* 🔲 chubby
Pumpe *f* -, -n pump. **p~n** *vt/i*
(*haben*) pump; (🔲 *leihen*) lend; [sich
(*dat*)] etw p~n (🔲 *borgen*) borrow
sth
Pumps /pœmps/ *pl* court shoes
Punkt *m* -[e]s, -e dot; (*Tex*) spot;
(*Geom, Sport & fig*) point; (*Gram*)
full stop, period; **P~ sechs Uhr** at six
o'clock sharp
pünktlich *a* punctual. **P~keit** *f* -
punctuality
Pupille *f* -, -n (*Anat*) pupil
Puppe *f* -, -n doll; (*Marionette*)
puppet; (*Schaufenster-, Schneider-*)
dummy; (*Zool*) chrysalis
pur *a* pure; (🔲 *bloß*) sheer
Püree *nt* -s, -s purée; (*Kartoffel-*)
mashed potatoes *pl*
purpurrot *a* crimson
Purzel|baum *m* 🔲 somersault.
p~n *vi* (*sein*) 🔲 tumble
Puste *f* - 🔲 breath. **p~n** *vt/i* (*haben*)
🔲 blow
Pute *f* -, -n turkey
Putsch *m* -[e]s, -e coup
Putz *m* -es plaster; (*Staat*) finery.
p~en *vt* clean; (*Aust*) dry-clean;
(*zieren*) adorn; **sich p~en** dress up;
sich (*dat*) **die Zähne/Nase p~en**
clean one's teeth/blow one's nose.
P~frau *f* cleaner, charwoman.
p~ig *a* 🔲 amusing, cute; (*seltsam*)
odd
Puzzlespiel /'pazl-/ *nt* jigsaw
Pyramide *f* -, -n pyramid

Qq

Quacksalber *m* -s,- quack
Quadrat *nt* -[e]s, -e square. **q~isch**
a square

quaken *vi* (*haben*) quack; <*Frosch:*>
croak
Quäker(in) *m* -s,- (*f* -, -nen) Quaker
Qual *f* -, -en torment; (*Schmerz*)
agony
quälen *vt* torment; (*foltern*) torture;
(*bedrängen*) pester; **sich q~** torment
oneself; (*leiden*) suffer; (*sich mühen*)
struggle
Quälerei *f* -, -en torture
Qualifi|kation /-'tsio:n/ *f* -, -en
qualification. **q~zieren** *vt* qualify.
q~ziert *a* qualified; (*fähig*)
competent; <*Arbeit*> skilled
Qualität *f* -, -en quality
Qualle *f* -, -n jellyfish
Qualm *m* -s [thick] smoke
qualvoll *a* agonizing
Quantum *nt* -s, -ten quantity;
(*Anteil*) share, quota
Quarantäne *f* - quarantine
Quark *m* -s quark, ≈ curd cheese
Quartal *nt* -s, -e quarter
Quartett *nt* -[e]s, -e quartet
Quartier *nt* -s, -e accommodation;
(*Mil*) quarters *pl*
Quarz *m* -es quartz
quasseln *vi* (*haben*) 🔲 jabber
Quaste *f* -, -n tassel
Quatsch *m* -[e]s 🔲 nonsense,
rubbish; **Q~ machen** (*Unfug*
machen) fool around; (*etw falsch*
machen) do a silly thing. **q~en** *vi*
(*haben*) talk; <*Wasser, Schlamm:*>
squelch ● *vt* talk
Quecksilber *nt* mercury
Quelle *f* -, -n spring; (*Fluss- & fig*)
source
quengeln *vi* 🔲 whine
quer *adv* across, crosswise; (*schräg*)
diagonally; **q~ gestreift** horizontally
striped
Quere *f* - **der Q~ nach** across,
crosswise; **jdm in die Q~ kommen**
get in s.o.'s way
Quer|latte *f* crossbar. **Q~schiff** *nt*
transept. **Q~schnitt** *m* cross-
section. **q~schnittsgelähmt** *a*
paraplegic. **Q~straße** *f* side-street.
Q~verweis *m* cross-reference

p

q

quetschen *vt* squash; (*drücken*) squeeze; (*zerdrücken*) crush; (*Culin*) mash; **sich q~ in** (+ *acc*) squeeze into

Queue /kø:/ *nt* **-s, -s** cue

quieken *vi* (*haben*) squeal; <*Maus:*> squeak

quietschen *vi* (*haben*) squeal; <*Tür, Dielen:*> creak

Quintett *nt* **-[e]s, -e** quintet

quirlen *vt* mix

Quitte *f* **-, -n** quince

quittieren *vt* receipt <*Rechnung*>; sign for <*Geldsumme, Sendung*>; **den Dienst q~** resign

Quittung *f* **-, -en** receipt

Quiz /kvɪs/ *nt* **-, -** quiz

Quote *f* **-, -n** proportion

Rr

Rabatt *m* **-[e]s, -e** discount

Rabatte *f* **-, -n** (*Hort*) border

Rabattmarke *f* trading stamp

Rabbiner *m* **-s, -** rabbi

Rabe *m* **-n, -n** raven

Rache *f* **-** revenge, vengeance

Rachen *m* **-s, -** pharynx

rächen *vt* avenge; **sich r~** take revenge (**an** + *dat* on); <*Fehler:*> cost s.o. dear

Rad *nt* **-[e]s, ̈er** wheel; (*Fahr-*) bicycle, 🅸 bike; **Rad fahren** cycle

Radar *m & nt* **-s** radar

Radau *m* **-s** 🅸 din, racket

radeln *vi* (*sein*) 🅸 cycle

Rädelsführer *m* ringleader

radfahr|en* *vi sep* (*sein*) Rad fahren, *s.* Rad. **R~er(in)** *m(f)* **-s, -** (*f* **-, -nen**) cyclist

---

*old spelling

radier|en *vt/i* (*haben*) rub out; (*Kunst*) etch. **R~gummi** *m* eraser, rubber. **R~ung** *f* **-, -en** etching

Radieschen /-'di:sçən/ *nt* **-s, -** radish

radikal *a* radical, drastic

Radio *nt* **-s, -s** radio

radioaktiv *a* radioactive. **R~ität** *f* **-** radioactivity

Radius *m* **-, -ien** /-iən/ radius

Rad|kappe *f* hub-cap. **R~ler** *m* **-s, -** cyclist; (*Getränk*) shandy

raffen *vt* grab; (*kräuseln*) gather; (*kürzen*) condense

Raffin|ade *f* **-** refined sugar. **R~erie** *f* **-, -n** refinery. **R~esse** *f* **-, -n** refinement; (*Schlauheit*) cunning. **r~iert** *a* ingenious; (*durchtrieben*) crafty

ragen *vi* (*haben*) rise [up]

Rahm *m* **-s** (*SGer*) cream

rahmen *vt* frame. **R~** *m* **-s, -** frame; (*fig*) framework; (*Grenze*) limits *pl*; (*einer Feier*) setting

Rakete *f* **-, -n** rocket; (*Mil*) missile

Rallye /'rali/ *nt* **-s, -s** rally

rammen *vt* ram

Rampe *f* **-, -n** ramp; (*Theat*) front of the stage

Ramsch *m* **-[e]s** junk

ran *adv* = heran

Rand *m* **-[e]s, ̈er** edge; (*Teller-, Gläser-, Brillen-*) rim; (*Zier-*) border, edging; (*Brief-*) margin; (*Stadt-*) outskirts *pl*; (*Ring*) ring

randalieren *vi* (*haben*) rampage

Randstreifen *m* (*Auto*) hard shoulder

Rang *m* **-[e]s, ̈e** rank; (*Theat*) tier; **erster/zweiter R~** (*Theat*) dress/upper circle; **ersten R~es** first-class

rangieren /raŋ'ʒi:rən/ *vt* shunt ● *vi* (*haben*) rank (**vor** + *dat* before)

Rangordnung *f* order of importance; (*Hierarchie*) hierarchy

Ranke *f* **-, -n** tendril; (*Trieb*) shoot

ranken (sich) *vr* (*Bot*) trail; (*in die Höhe*) climb

Ranzen *m* **-s, -** (*Sch*) satchel

ranzig *a* rancid

Rappe m -n, -n black horse

Raps m -es (Bot) rape

rar a rare; er macht sich rar 🖪 we don't see much of him. **R~ität** f -, -en rarity

rasant a fast; (schnittig, schick) stylish

rasch a quick

rascheln vi (haben) rustle

Rasen m -s,- lawn

rasen vi (sein) tear [along]; <Puls:> race; <Zeit:> fly; gegen eine Mauer r~ career into a wall ● vi (haben) rave; <Sturm:> rage. **r~d** a furious; (tobend) raving; <Sturm, Durst> raging; <Schmerz> excruciating; <Beifall> tumultuous

Rasenmäher m lawn-mower

Rasier|apparat m razor. **r~en** vt shave; sich r~en shave. **R~klinge** f razor blade. **R~wasser** nt aftershave [lotion]

Raspel f -, -n rasp; (Culin) grater. **r~n** vt grate

Rasse f -, -n race. **R~hund** m pedigree dog

Rassel f -, -n rattle. **r~n** vi (haben) rattle; <Schlüssel:> jangle; <Kette:> clank

Rassendiskriminierung f racial discrimination

Rassepferd nt thoroughbred. **rassisch** a racial

Rassis|mus m - racism. **r~tisch** a racist

Rast f -, -en rest. **R~platz** m picnic area. **R~stätte** f motorway restaurant [and services]

Rasur f -, -en shave

Rat m -[e]s (piece of) advice; sich (dat) keinen Rat wissen not know what to do; zu Rat[e] ziehen = zurate ziehen, s. zurate

Rate f -, -n instalment

raten† vt guess; (empfehlen) advise ● vi (haben) guess; jdm r~ advise s.o.

Ratenzahlung f payment by instalments

Rat|geber m -s,- adviser; (Buch) guide. **R~haus** nt town hall

ratifizier|en vt ratify. **R~ung** f -, -en ratification

Ration /ra'tsi̯o:n/ f -, -en ration. **r~ell** a efficient. **r~ieren** vt ration

rat|los a helpless; r~los sein not know what to do. **r~sam** pred a advisable; prudent. **R~schlag** m piece of advice; **R~schläge** advice sg

Rätsel nt -s,- riddle; (Kreuzwort-) puzzle; (Geheimnis) mystery. **r~haft** a puzzling, mysterious. **r~n** vi (haben) puzzle

Ratte f -, -n rat

rau a rough; (unfreundlich) gruff; <Klima> harsh, raw; (heiser) husky; <Hals> sore

Raub m -[e]s robbery; (Menschen-) abduction; (Beute) loot, booty. **r~en** vt steal; abduct <Menschen>

Räuber m -s,- robber

Raub|mord m robbery with murder. **R~tier** nt predator. **R~vogel** m bird of prey

Rauch m -[e]s smoke. **r~en** vt/i (haben) smoke. **R~en** nt -s smoking; 'R~en verboten' 'no smoking'. **R~er** m -s, -smoker

Räucher|lachs m smoked salmon. **r~n** vt (Culin) smoke

rauf adv = herauf, hinauf

rauf|en vt pull ● vr/i (haben) [sich] r~en fight. **R~erei** f -,-en fight

rauh* a s. rau

Raum m -[e]s, Räume room; (Gebiet) area; (Welt-) space

räumen vt clear; vacate <Wohnung>; evacuate <Gebäude, Gebiet, (Mil) Stellung>; (bringen) put (in/auf + acc into/on); (holen) get (aus out of)

Raum|fahrer m astronaut. **R~fahrt** f space travel. **R~inhalt** m volume

räumlich a spatial

Raum|pflegerin f cleaner. **R~schiff** nt spaceship

Räumung f - clearing; vacating; evacuation. **R~sverkauf** m clearance/closing-down sale

Raupe f -, -n caterpillar

raus adv = heraus, hinaus

r

Rausch m -[e]s, Räusche intoxication; (*fig*) exhilaration; **einen R~haben** be drunk

rauschen vi (*haben*) <*Wasser, Wind:*> rush; <*Bäume Blätter:*> rustle ● vi (*sein*) rush [along]

Rauschgift nt [narcotic] drug; (*coll*) drugs pl. **R~süchtige(r)** m/f drug addict

räuspern (sich) vr clear one's throat

rausschmeißen† vt sep ⊞ throw out; (*entlassen*) sack

Raute f -, -n diamond

Razzia f -, -ien /-i̯ən/ [police] raid

Reagenzglas nt test-tube

reagieren vi (*haben*) react (**auf** + acc to)

Reaktion /-'tsi̯o:n/ f -, -en reaction. **r~är** a reactionary

Reaktor m -s, -en /-'to:rən/ reactor

realisieren vt realize

Realis|mus m - realism. **R~t** m -en, -en realist. **r~tisch** a realistic

Realität f -, -en reality

Realschule f ≈ secondary modern school

Rebe f -, -n vine

Rebell m -en, -en rebel. **r~ieren** vi (*haben*) rebel. **R~ion** f -, -en rebellion

rebellisch a rebellious

Rebhuhn nt partridge

Rebstock m vine

Rechen m -s- rake

Rechen|aufgabe f arithmetical problem; (*Sch*) sum. **R~maschine** f calculator

recherchieren /reʃɛr'ʃi:rən/ vt/i (*haben*) investigate; (*Journ*) research

rechnen vi (*haben*) do arithmetic; (*schätzen*) reckon; (*zählen*) count (**zu** among; **auf** + acc on); **r~ mit** reckon with; (*erwarten*) expect ● vt calculate, work out; (*fig*) count (**zu** among). **R~** nt -s arithmetic

Rechner m -s,- calculator; (*Computer*) computer

Rechnung f -, -en bill; (*Comm*) invoice; (*Berechnung*) calculation; **R~ führen über** (+ acc) keep account of. **R~sjahr** nt financial year. **R~sprüfer** m auditor

Recht nt -[e]s, -e law; (*Berechtigung*) right (**auf** + acc to); **im R~ sein** be in the right; **R~ haben/behalten** be right; **R~ bekommen** be proved right; **jdm R~ geben** agree with s.o.; **mit** od **zu R~** rightly

recht a right; (*wirklich*) real; **ich habe keine r~e Lust** I don't really feel like it; **es jdm r~ machen** please s.o.; **jdm r~ sein** be all right with s.o. **r~ vielen Dank** many thanks

Recht|e f -n, -[n] right side; (*Hand*) right hand; (*Boxen*) right; **die R~e** (*Pol*) the right; **zu meiner R~en** on my right. **r~e(r,s)** a right; (*Pol*) right-wing; **r~e Masche** plain stitch. **R~e(r)** m/f der/die **R~e** the right man/woman; **R~e(s)** nt das **R~e** the right thing; **etwas R~es lernen** learn something useful; **nach dem R~en sehen** see that everything is all right

Rechteck nt -[e]s, -e rectangle. **r~ig** a rectangular

rechtfertigen vt justify; **sich r~en** justify oneself

recht|haberisch a opinionated. **r~lich** a legal. **r~mäßig** a legitimate

rechts adv on the right; (*bei Stoff*) on the right side; **von/nach r~** from/to the right; **zwei r~, zwei links stricken** knit two, purl two. **R~anwalt** m, **R~anwältin** f lawyer

Rechtschreibung f - spelling

Rechts|händer(in) m -s,- (f -, -nen) right-hander. **r~händig** a & adv right-handed. **r~kräftig** a legal. **R~streit** m law suit. **R~verkehr** m driving on the right. **r~widrig** a illegal. **R~wissenschaft** f jurisprudence

rechtzeitig a & adv in time

Reck nt -[e]s, -e horizontal bar

recken vt stretch

Redakteur /redak'tø:ɐ/ *m* -s, -e editor; (*Radio, TV*) producer

Redaktion /-'tsio:n/ *f* -, -en editing; (*Radio, TV*) production; (*Abteilung*) editorial/production department

Rede *f* -, -n speech; zur R~ stellen demand an explanation from; nicht der R~ wert not worth mentioning

reden *vi* (*haben*) talk (von about; mit to); (*eine Rede halten*) speak ● *vt* talk; speak <*Wahrheit*>. R~sart *f* saying

Redewendung *f* idiom

redigieren *vt* edit

Redner *m* -s,- speaker

reduzieren *vt* reduce

Reeder *m* -s,- shipowner. R~ei *f* -, -en shipping company

Refer|at *nt* -[e]s, -e report; (*Abhandlung*) paper; (*Abteilung*) section. R~ent(in) *m* -en, -en (*f* -, -nen) speaker; (*Sachbearbeiter*) expert. R~enz *f* -, -en reference

Reflex *m* -es, -e reflex; (*Widerschein*) reflection. R~ion *f* -, -en reflection. r~iv *a* reflexive

Reform *f* -, -en reform. R~ation /-'tsio:n/ *f* - (*Relig*) Reformation

Reform|haus *nt* health-food shop. r~ieren *vt* reform

Refrain /rə'frɛ̃:/ *m* -s, -s refrain

Regal *nt* -s, -e [set of] shelves *pl*

Regatta *f* -, -ten regatta

rege *a* active; (*lebhaft*) lively; (*geistig*) alert; (*Handel*) brisk

Regel *f* -, -n rule; (*Monats-*) period. r~mäßig *a* regular. r~n *vt* regulate; direct <*Verkehr*>; (*erledigen*) settle. r~recht *a* real, proper ● *adv* really. R~ung *f* -, -en regulation; settlement

regen *vt* move; sich r~ move; (*wach werden*) stir

Regen *m* -s,- rain. R~bogen *m* rainbow. R~bogenhaut *f* iris

Regener|ation /-'tsio:n/ *f* - regeneration. r~ieren *vt* regenerate

Regen|mantel *m* raincoat. R~schirm *m* umbrella. R~tag *m* rainy day. R~wetter *nt* wet weather. R~wurm *m* earthworm

Regie /re'ʒi:/ *f* - direction; R~ führen direct

regier|en *vt/i* (*haben*) govern, rule; <*Monarch:*> reign [over]; (*Gram*) take. R~ung *f* -, -en government; (*Herrschaft*) rule; (*eines Monarchen*) reign

Regiment *nt* -[e]s, -er regiment

Region *f* -, -en region. r~al *a* regional

Regisseur /reʒɪ'sø:ɐ/ *m* -s, -e director

Register *nt* -s,- register; (*Inhaltsverzeichnis*) index; (*Orgel-*) stop

Regler *m* -s,- regulator

reglos *a & adv* motionless

regn|en *vi* (*haben*) rain; es r~et it is raining. r~erisch *a* rainy

regul|är *a* normal; (*rechtmäßig*) legitimate. r~ieren *vt* regulate

Regung *f* -, -en movement; (*Gefühls-*) emotion. r~slos *a & adv* motionless

Reh *nt* -[e]s, -e roe-deer; (*Culin*) venison

Rehbock *m* roebuck

reib|en† *vt* rub; (*Culin*) grate ● *vi* (*haben*) rub. R~ung *f* - friction. r~ungslos *a* (*fig*) smooth

reich *a* rich (an + *dat* in)

Reich *nt* -[e]s, -e empire; (*König-*) kingdom; (*Bereich*) realm

Reiche(r) *m/f* rich man/woman; die R~en the rich *pl*

reichen *vt* hand; (*anbieten*) offer ● *vi* (*haben*) be enough; (*in der Länge*) be long enough; r~ bis zu reach [up to]; (*sich erstrecken*) extend to; mit dem Geld r~ have enough money

reich|haltig *a* extensive, large <*Mahlzeit*> substantial. r~lich *a* ample: <*Vorrat*> abundant. R~tum *m* -s, -tümer wealth (an + *dat* of); R~tümer riches. R~weite *f* reach; (*Techn, Mil*) range

Reif *m* -[e]s [hoar-]frost

reif *a* ripe; (*fig*) mature; r~ für ready for. r~en *vi* (*sein*) ripen; <*Wein, Käse & fig*> mature

r

Reifen *m* -s,- hoop; (*Arm-*) bangle; (*Auto-*) tyre. **R∼druck** *m* tyre pressure. **R∼panne** *f* puncture, flat tyre

reiflich *a* careful

Reihe *f* -, -n row; (*Anzahl & Math*) series; der R∼ nach in turn; wer ist an der R∼? whose turn is it? **r∼n (sich)** *vr* sich r∼n an (+ *acc*) follow. **R∼nfolge** *f* order. **R∼nhaus** *nt* terraced house

Reiher *m* -s,- heron

Reim *m* -[e]s, -e rhyme. **r∼en** *vt* rhyme; sich r∼en rhyme

rein[1] *a* pure; (*sauber*) clean; <*Unsinn, Dummheit*> sheer; ins R∼e schreiben make a fair copy of

rein[2] *adv* = herein, hinein

Reineclaude /rɛːnəˈkloːdə/ *f* -, -n greengage

Reinfall *m* 🔢 let-down; (*Misserfolg*) flop

Rein|gewinn *m* net profit. **R∼heit** *f* - purity

reinig|en *vt* clean; (*chemisch*) dryclean. **R∼ung** *f* -, -en cleaning; (*chemische*) dry-cleaning; (*Geschäft*) dry cleaner's

reinlegen *vt sep* put in; 🔢 dupe; (*betrügen*) take for a ride

reinlich *a* clean. **R∼keit** *f* - cleanliness

Reis *m* -es rice

Reise *f* -, -n journey; (*See-*) voyage; (*Urlaubs-, Geschäfts-*) trip. **R∼andenken** *nt* souvenir. **R∼büro** *nt* travel agency. **R∼bus** *m* coach. **R∼führer** *m* tourist guide; (*Buch*) guide. **R∼gesellschaft** *f* tourist group. **R∼leiter(in)** *m(f)* courier. **r∼n** *vi* (*sein*) travel. **R∼nde(r)** *m/f* traveller. **R∼pass** *m* passport. **R∼scheck** *m* traveller's cheque. **R∼veranstalter** *m* -s,- tour operator. **R∼ziel** *nt* destination

Reisig *nt* -s brushwood

Reißaus *m* R∼ nehmen 🔢 run away

Reißbrett *nt* drawing-board

reißen† *vt* tear; (*weg-*) snatch; (*töten*) kill; Witze r∼ crack jokes; an sich (*acc*) r∼snatch; seize <*Macht*>; sich r∼ um 🔢 fight for ● *vi* (*sein*) tear; <*Seil, Faden:*> break ● *vi* (*haben*) r∼ an (+ *dat*) pull at

Reißer *m* -s,- 🔢 thriller; (*Erfolg*) big hit

Reiß|nagel *m* = R∼zwecke. **R∼verschluss** *m* zip [fastener]. **R∼wolf** *m* shredder. **R∼zwecke** *f* -, -n drawing-pin

reit|en† *vt/i* (*sein*) ride. **R∼er(in)** *m* -s,- (*f* -, -nen) rider. **R∼hose** *f* riding breeches *pl*. **R∼pferd** *nt* saddle-horse. **R∼weg** *m* bridle-path

Reiz *m* -es, -e stimulus; (*Anziehungskraft*) attraction, appeal; (*Charme*) charm. **r∼bar** *a* irritable. **R∼barkeit** *f* - irritability. **r∼en** *vt* provoke; (*Med*) irritate; (*interessieren, locken*) appeal to, attract; arouse <*Neugier*>; (*beim Kartenspiel*) bid. **R∼ung** *f* -, -en (*Med*) irritation. **r∼voll** *a* attractive

rekeln (sich) *vr* stretch

Reklamation /-ˈtsi̯oːn/ *f* -, -en (*Comm*) complaint

Reklam|e *f* -, -n advertising, publicity; (*Anzeige*) advertisement; (*TV, Radio*) commercial; R∼e machen advertise (für etw sth). **r∼ieren** *vt* complain about; (*fordern*) claim ● *vi* (*haben*) complain

Rekord *m* -[e]s, -e record

Rekrut *m* -en, -en recruit

Rek|tor *m* -s, -en /-ˈtoːrən/ (*Sch*) head[master]; (*Univ*) vice-chancellor. **R∼torin** *f* -, -nen head, headmistress; vice-chancellor

Relais /rəˈlɛː/ *nt* -,- /-s, -s/ (*Electr*) relay

relativ *a* relative

Religi|on *f* -, -en religion; (*Sch*) religious education. **r∼ös** *a* religious

Reling *f* -, -s (*Naut*) rail

Reliquie /reˈliːkvi̯ə/ *f* -, -n relic

rempeln *vt* jostle; (*stoßen*) push

Reneklode *f* -, -n greengage

Renn|bahn *f* race-track; *(Pferde-)* racecourse. **R~boot** *nt* speedboat. **r~en†** *vt/i (sein)* run; **um die Wette r~en** have a race. **R~en** *nt* -s,- race. **R~pferd** *nt* racehorse. **R~sport** *m* racing. **R~wagen** *m* racing car

renommiert *a* renowned; *<Hotel, Firma>* of repute

renovier|en *vt* renovate; redecorate *<Zimmer>*. **R~ung** *f* - renovation; redecoration

rentabel *a* profitable

Rente *f* -, -n pension; **in R~ gehen** ☒ retire. **R~nversicherung** *f* pension scheme

Rentier *nt* reindeer

rentieren (sich) *vr* be profitable; *(sich lohnen)* be worth while

Rentner(in) *m* -s,- *(f* -, -nen) [old-age] pensioner

Reparatur *f* -, -en repair. **R~werkstatt** *f* repair workshop; *(Auto)* garage

reparieren *vt* repair, mend

Reportage /-'ta:ʒə/ *f* -, -n report

Reporter(in) *m* -s,- *(f* -, -nen) reporter

repräsentativ *a* representative (für of); *(eindrucksvoll)* imposing

Reprodu|ktion /-'tsio:n/ *f* -, -en reproduction. **r~zieren** *vt* reproduce

Reptil *nt* -s, -ien /-iən/ reptile

Republik *f* -, -en republic. **r~anisch** *a* republican

Requisiten *pl (Theat)* properties, ☒ props

Reservat *nt* -[e]s, -e reservation

Reserve *f* -, -n reserve; *(Mil, Sport)* reserves *pl*. **R~rad** *nt* spare wheel

reservier|en *vt* reserve; **r~en lassen** book. **r~t** *a* reserved. **R~ung** *f* -, -en reservation

Reservoir /rezɛr'voa:ɐ/ *nt* -s, -s reservoir

Residenz *f* -, -en residence

Resign|ation /-'tsio:n/ *f* - resignation. **r~ieren** *vi (haben)* give up. **r~iert** *a* resigned

resolut *a* resolute

Resonanz *f* -, -en resonance

Respekt /-sp-, -ʃp-/ *m* -[e]s respect (vor + *dat* for). **r~ieren** *vt* respect

respektlos *a* disrespectful

Ressort /rɛ'so:ɐ/ *nt* -s, -s department

Rest *m* -[e]s, -e remainder, rest; **R~e** remains; *(Essens-)* leftovers

Restaurant /rɛsto'rɑ̃:/ *nt* -s, -s restaurant

Restaur|ation /rɛstaura'tsio:n/ *f* - restoration. **r~ieren** *vt* restore

Rest|betrag *m* balance. **r~lich** *a* remaining

Resultat *nt* -[e]s, -e result

rett|en *vt* save (vor + *dat* from); *(aus Gefahr befreien)* rescue; **sich r~en** save oneself; *(flüchten)* escape. **R~er** *m* -s,- rescuer; *(fig)* saviour

Rettich *m* -s, -e white radish

Rettung *f* -, -en rescue; *(fig)* salvation; **jds letzte R~** s.o.'s last hope. **R~sboot** *nt* lifeboat. **R~sdienst** *m* rescue service. **R~sgürtel** *m* lifebelt. **r~slos** *adv* hopelessly. **R~sring** *m* lifebelt. **R~swagen** *m* ambulance

retuschieren *vt (Phot)* retouch

Reue *f* - remorse; *(Relig)* repentance

Revanch|e /re'vɑ̃:ʃə/ *f* -, -n revenge; **R~e fordern** *(Sport)* ask for a return match. **r~ieren (sich)** *vr* take revenge; *(sich erkenntlich zeigen)* reciprocate (mit with)

Revers /re've:ɐ/ *nt* -s, -,- /-[s], -s/ lapel

Revier *nt* -s, -e district; *(Zool & fig)* territory; *(Polizei-)* [police] station

Revision *f* -, -en revision; *(Prüfung)* check; *(Jur)* appeal

Revolution /-'tsio:n/ *f* -, -en revolution. **r~är** *a* revolutionary. **r~ieren** *vt* revolutionize

Revolver *m* -s,- revolver

rezen|sieren *vt* review. **R~sion** *f* -, -en review

Rezept *nt* -[e]s, -e prescription; *(Culin)* recipe

Rezession *f* -, -en recession

R-Gespräch *nt* reverse-charge call

Rhabarber *m* -s rhubarb

r

Rhein *m* -s Rhine. **R~land** *nt* -s
Rhineland. **R~wein** *m* hock

Rhetorik *f* - rhetoric

Rheum|a *nt* -s rheumatism.
r~atisch *a* rheumatic.
R~atismus *m* - rheumatism

Rhinozeros *nt* -[ses], -se
rhinoceros

rhyth|misch /'ryt-/ *a* rhythmic[al].
R~mus *m* -, -men rhythm

richten *vt* direct (auf + *acc* at);
address <*Frage*> (an + *acc* to); aim
<*Waffe*> (auf + *acc* at); (*einstellen*)
set; (*vorbereiten*) prepare;
(*reparieren*) mend; **in die Höhe r~**
raise [up]; **sich r~** be directed (auf +
acc at; **gegen** against); <*Blick:*> turn
(auf + *acc* on); **sich r~ nach** comply
with <*Vorschrift*>; fit in with <*jds*
Plänen>; (*abhängen*) depend on ● *vi*
(*haben*) **r~ über** (+ *acc*) judge

Richter *m* -s,- judge

richtig *a* right, correct; (*wirklich,*
echt) real; **das R~e** the right thing
● *adv* correctly; really; **r~ stellen**
put right <*Uhr*>; (*fig*) correct
<*Irrtum*>; **die Uhr geht r~** the clock
is right

Richtlinien *fpl* guidelines

Richtung *f* -, -en direction

riechen† *vt/i* (*haben*) smell (nach of;
an etw *dat* sth)

Riegel *m* -s,- bolt; (*Seife*) bar

Riemen *m* -s,- strap; (*Ruder*) oar

Riese *m* -n, -n giant

rieseln *vi* (*sein*) trickle; <*Schnee:*>
fall lightly

riesengroß *a* huge, enormous

riesig *a* huge; (*gewaltig*) enormous
● *adv* [1] terribly

Riff *nt* -[e]s, -e reef

Rille *f* -, -n groove

Rind *nt* -es, -er ox; (*Kuh*) cow; (*Stier*)
bull; (*R~fleisch*) beef; **R~er** cattle *pl*

Rinde *f* -, -n bark; (*Käse-*) rind;
(*Brot-*) crust

Rinderbraten *m* roast beef

Rindfleisch *nt* beef

Ring *m* -[e]s, -e ring

ringeln (sich) *vr* curl

ring|en† *vi* (*haben*) wrestle; (*fig*)
struggle (um/nach for) ● *vt* wring
<*Hände*>. **R~er** *m* -s,- wrestler.
R~kampf *m* wrestling match; (*als*
Sport) wrestling

rings|herum, r~um *adv* all
around

Rinn|e *f* -, -n channel; (*Dach-*) gutter.
r~en† *vi* (*sein*) run; <*Sand:*>
trickle. **R~stein** *m* gutter

Rippe *f* -, -n rib.
R~nfellentzündung *f* pleurisy

Risiko *nt* -s, -s & -ken risk

risk|ant *a* risky. **r~ieren** *vt* risk

Riss *m* -es, -e tear; (*Mauer-*) crack;
(*fig*) rift

rissig *a* cracked; <*Haut*> chapped

Rist *m* -[e]s, -e instep

Ritt *m* -[e]s, -e ride

Ritter *m* -s,- knight

Ritual *nt* -s, -e ritual

Ritz *m* -es, -e scratch. **R~e** *f* -, -n
crack; (*Fels-*) cleft; (*zwischen Betten,*
Vorhängen) gap. **r~en** *vt* scratch

Rival|e *m* -n, -n, **R~in** *f* -, -nen
rival. **R~ität** *f* -, -en rivalry

Robbe *f* -, -n seal

Robe *f* -, -n gown; (*Talar*) robe

Roboter *m* -s,- robot

robust *a* robust

röcheln *vi* (*haben*) breathe
stertorously

Rochen *m* -s,- (*Zool*) ray

Rock¹ *m* -[e]s,¨e skirt; (*Jacke*) jacket

Rock² *m* -[s] (*Mus*) rock

rodel|n *vi* (*sein/haben*) toboggan.
R~schlitten *m* toboggan

roden *vt* clear <*Land*>; grub up
<*Stumpf*>

Rogen *m* -s,- [hard] roe

Roggen *m* -s rye

roh *a* rough; (*ungekocht*) raw; <*Holz*>
bare; (*brutal*) brutal. **R~bau** *m*
-[e]s, -ten shell. **R~kost** *f* raw
[vegetarian] food. **R~ling** *m* -s, -e
brute. **R~öl** *nt* crude oil

Rohr *nt* -[e]s, -e pipe; (*Geschütz-*)
barrel; (*Bot*) reed; (*Zucker-, Bambus-*)
cane

Röhre f -, -n tube; (*Radio-*) valve; (*Back-*) oven

Rohstoff m raw material

Rokoko nt -s rococo

Rollbahn f taxiway; (*Start-/Landebahn*) runaway

Rolle f -, -n roll; (*Garn-*) reel; (*Draht-*) coil; (*Techn*) roller; (*Seil-*) pulley; (*Lauf-*) castor; (*Theat*) part, role; **das spielt keine R~** (*fig*) that doesn't matter. **r~n** vt roll; (*auf-*) roll up; **sich r~n** roll ● vi (*sein*) roll; <*Flugzeug:*> taxi. **R~r** m -s,- scooter

Roll|feld nt airfield. **R~kragen** m polo-neck. **R~mops** m rollmop[s] sg

Rollo nt -s, -s [roller] blind

Roll|schuh m roller-skate; **R~schuh laufen** roller-skate. **R~stuhl** m wheelchair. **R~treppe** f escalator

Rom nt -s Rome

Roman m -s, -e novel. **r~isch** a Romanesque; <*Sprache*> Romance

Romant|ik f - romanticism. **r~isch** a romantic

Röm|er(in) m -s,- (f -, -nen) Roman. **r~isch** a Roman

Rommé, Rommee /'rɔme:/ nt -s rummy

röntgen vt X-ray. **R~aufnahme** f, **R~bild** nt X-ray. **R~strahlen** mpl X-rays

rosa inv a, **R~** nt -[s],- pink

Rose f -, -n rose. **R~nkohl** m [Brussels] sprouts pl. **R~nkranz** m (*Relig*) rosary

Rosine f -, -n raisin

Rosmarin m -s rosemary

Ross nt -es,-̈er horse

Rost¹ m -[e]s, -e grating; (*Kamin-*) grate; (*Brat-*) grill

Rost² m -[e]s rust. **r~en** vi (*haben*) rust

rösten vt roast; toast <*Brot*>

rostfrei a stainless

rostig a rusty

rot a, **Rot** nt -s,- red; **rot werden** turn red; (*erröten*) go red, blush

Röte f - redness; (*Scham-*) blush

Röteln pl German measles sg

röten vt redden; **sich r~** turn red

rothaarig a red-haired

rotieren vi (*haben*) rotate

Rot|kehlchen nt -s,- robin. **R~kohl** m red cabbage

rötlich a reddish

Rotwein m red wine

Rou|lade /ru'la:də/ f -, -n beef olive. **R~leau** /-'lo:/ nt -s, -s [roller] blind

Routin|e /ru'ti:nə/ f -, -n routine; (*Erfahrung*) experience. **r~emäßig** a routine ... ● adv routinely. **r~iert** a experienced

Rowdy /'raudi/ m -s, -s hooligan

Rübe f -, -n beet; **rote R~** beetroot

Rubin m -s, -e ruby

Rubrik f -, -en column

Ruck m -[e]s, -e jerk

ruckartig a jerky

rück|bezüglich a (*Gram*) reflexive. **R~blende** f flashback. **R~blick** m (*fig*) review (**auf** + *acc* of). **r~blickend** adv in retrospect. **r~datieren** vt (*inf & pp only*) backdate

Rücken m -s,- back; (*Buch-*) spine; (*Berg-*) ridge. **R~lehne** f back. **R~mark** nt spinal cord. **R~schwimmen** nt backstroke. **R~wind** m following wind; (*Aviat*) tail wind

rückerstatten vt (*inf & pp only*) refund

Rückfahr|karte f return ticket. **R~t** f return journey

Rück|fall m relapse. **R~flug** m return flight. **R~frage** f [further] query. **r~fragen** vi (*haben*) (*inf & pp only*) check (**bei** with). **R~gabe** f return. **r~gängig** a **r~gängig machen** cancel; break off <*Verlobung*>. **R~grat** nt -[e]s, -e spine, backbone. **R~hand** f backhand. **R~kehr** return. **R~lagen** fpl reserves. **R~licht** nt rear-light. **R~reise** f return journey

Rucksack m rucksack

Rück|schau f review. **R~schlag** m (*Sport*) return; (*fig*) set-back. **r~schrittlich** a retrograde.

r

R~seite f back; (*einer Münze*) reverse

Rücksicht f -, -en consideration. **R~nahme** f - consideration. **r~slos** a inconsiderate; (*schonungslos*) ruthless. **r~svoll** a considerate

Rück|sitz m back seat; (*Sozius*) pillion. **R~spiegel** m rear-view mirror. **R~spiel** nt return match. **R~stand** m (*Chem*) residue; (*Arbeits-*) backlog; im R~stand sein be behind. **r~ständig** a (*fig*) backward. **R~stau** m (*Auto*) tailback. **R~strahler** m -s,- reflector. **R~tritt** m resignation; (*Fahrrad*) back pedalling

rückwärt|ig a back ..., rear ... **r~s** adv backwards. **R~sgang** m reverse [gear]

Rückweg m way back

rück|wirkend a retrospective. **R~wirkung** f retrospective force; mit R~wirkung vom backdated to. **R~zahlung** f repayment

Rüde m -n, -n [male] dog

Rudel nt -s,- herd; (*Wolfs-*) pack; (*Löwen-*) pride

Ruder nt -s,- oar; (*Steuer-*) rudder; am R~ (*Naut & fig*) at the helm. **R~boot** nt rowing boat. **r~n** vt/i (*haben/sein*) row

Ruf m -[e]s, -e call; (*laut*) shout; (*Telefon*) telephone number; (*Ansehen*) reputation. **r~en†** vt/i (*haben*) call (**nach** for); r~en lassen send for

Ruf|name m forename by which one is known. **R~nummer** f telephone number. **R~zeichen** nt dialling tone

Rüge f -, -n reprimand. **r~n** vt reprimand; (*kritisieren*) criticize

Ruhe f - rest; (*Stille*) quiet; (*Frieden*) peace; (*innere*) calm; (*Gelassenheit*) composure; R~ [da]! quiet! **r~los** a restless. **r~n** vi (*haben*) rest (**auf** + *dat* on); <*Arbeit, Verkehr:*> have stopped. **R~pause** f rest, break. **R~stand** m retirement; im

R~stand retired. **R~störung** f disturbance of the peace. **R~tag** m day of rest; 'Montag R~tag' 'closed on Mondays'

ruhig a quiet; (*erholsam*) restful; (*friedlich*) peaceful; (*unbewegt, gelassen*) calm; man kann r~ darüber sprechen there's no harm in talking about it

Ruhm m -[e]s fame; (*Ehre*) glory

rühmen vt praise

ruhmreich a glorious

Ruhr f - (*Med*) dysentery

Rühr|ei nt scrambled eggs pl. **r~en** vt move; (*Culin*) stir; **sich r~en** move ● vi (*haben*) stir; r~en an (+ acc) touch; (*fig*) touch on. **r~end** a touching

Rührung f - emotion

Ruin m -s ruin. **R~e** f -, -n ruin; ruins pl (*gen* of). **r~ieren** vt ruin

rülpsen vi (*haben*) 🔊 belch

Rum m -s rum

Rumän|ien /-jən/ nt -s Romania. **r~isch** a Romanian

Rummel m -s 🔊 hustle and bustle; (*Jahrmarkt*) funfair

Rumpelkammer f junk-room

Rumpf m -[e]s, ̈-e body, trunk; (*Schiffs-*) hull; (*Aviat*) fuselage

rund a round ● adv approximately; r~ um [a]round. **R~blick** m panoramic view. **R~brief** m circular [letter]

Runde f -, -n round; (*Kreis*) circle; (*eines Polizisten*) beat; (*beim Rennen*) lap; eine R~ Bier a round of beer

Rund|fahrt f tour. **R~frage** f poll

Rundfunk m radio; im R~ on the radio. **R~gerät** nt radio [set]

Rund|gang m round; (*Spaziergang*) walk (**durch** round). **r~heraus** adv straight out. **r~herum** adv all around. **r~lich** a rounded; (*mollig*) plump. **R~reise** f [circular] tour. **R~schreiben** nt circular. **r~um** adv all round. **R~ung** f -, -en curve

Runzel f -, -n wrinkle

runzlig a wrinkled

Rüpel m -s,- 🔊 lout

rupfen vt pull out; pluck <*Geflügel*>

Rüsche *f* -, -n frill

Ruß *m* -es soot

Russe *m* -n, -n Russian

Rüssel *m* -s,- (*Zool*) trunk

Russ|in *f* -, -nen Russian. **r~isch** *a* Russian. **R~isch** *nt* -[s] (*Lang*) Russian

Russland *nt* -s Russia

rüsten *vi* (*haben*) prepare (**zu/für** for) ● *vr* **sich r~** get ready

rüstig *a* sprightly

rustikal *a* rustic

Rüstung *f* -, -en armament; (*Harnisch*) armour. **R~skontrolle** *f* arms control

Rute *f* -, -n twig; (*Angel-, Wünschel-*) rod; (*zur Züchtigung*) birch; (*Schwanz*) tail

Rutsch *m* -[e]s, -e slide. **R~bahn** *f* slide. **R~e** *f* -, -n chute. **r~en** *vt* slide; (*rücken*) move ● *vi* (*sein*) slide; (*aus-, ab-*) slip; (*Auto*) skid. **r~ig** *a* slippery

rütteln *vt* shake ● *vi* (*haben*) **r~ an** (+ *dat*) rattle

Ss

Saal *m* -[e]s, Säle hall; (*Theat*) auditorium; (*Kranken-*) ward

Saat *f* -, -en seed; (*Säen*) sowing; (*Gesätes*) crop

sabbern *vi* (*haben*) 🄸 slobber; <*Baby:*> dribble; (*reden*) jabber

Säbel *m* -s,- sabre

Sabo|tage /zabo'ta:ʒə/ *f* - sabotage. **S~teur** /-'tø:ɐ̯/ *m* -s, -e saboteur. **s~tieren** *vt* sabotage

Sach|bearbeiter *m* expert. **S~buch** *nt* non-fiction book

Sache *f* -, -n matter, business; (*Ding*) thing; (*fig*) cause

Sach|gebiet *nt* (*fig*) area, field. **s~kundig** *a* expert. **s~lich** *a* factual; (*nüchtern*) matter-of-fact

sächlich *a* (*Gram*) neuter

Sachse *m* -n, -n Saxon. **S~n** *nt* -s Saxony

sächsisch *a* Saxon

Sach|verhalt *m* -[e]s facts *pl*. **S~verständige(r)** *m/f* expert

Sack *m* -[e]s, ̈e sack

Sack|gasse *f* cul-de-sac; (*fig*) impasse. **S~leinen** *nt* sacking

Sad|is|mus *m* - sadism. **S~t** *m* -en, -en sadist

säen *vt/i* (*haben*) sow

Safe /ze:f/ *m* -s, -s safe

Saft *m* -[e]s, ̈e juice; (*Bot*) sap. **s~ig** *a* juicy

Sage *f* -, -n legend

Säge *f* -, -n saw. **S~mehl** *nt* sawdust

sagen *vt* say; (*mitteilen*) tell; (*bedeuten*) mean

sägen *vt/i* (*haben*) saw

sagenhaft *a* legendary

Säge|späne *mpl* wood shavings. **S~werk** *nt* sawmill

Sahn|e *f* - cream. **S~ebonbon** *m* & *nt* ≈ toffee. **s~ig** *a* creamy

Saison /zɛ'zõ:/ *f* -, -s season

Saite *f* -, -n (*Mus, Sport*) string. **S~ninstrument** *nt* stringed instrument

Sakko *m* & *nt* -s, -s sports jacket

Sakrament *nt* -[e]s, -e sacrament

Sakristei *f* -, -en vestry

Salat *m* -[e]s, -e salad. **S~soße** *f* salad-dressing

Salbe *f* -, -n ointment

Salbei *m* -s & *f* - sage

salben *vt* anoint

Saldo *m* -s, -dos & -den balance

Salon /za'lõ:/ *m* -s, -s salon

salopp *a* casual; <*Benehmen*> informal

Salto *m* -s, -s somersault

Salut *m* -[e]s, -e salute. **s~ieren** *vi* (*haben*) salute

Salve *f* -, -n volley; (*Geschütz-*) salvo, (*von Gelächter*) burst

r

s

Salz *nt* -es, -e salt. **s∼en**† *vt* salt.
  S∼fass *nt* salt-cellar. **s∼ig** *a* salty.
  S∼kartoffeln *fpl* boiled potatoes.
  S∼säure *f* hydrochloric acid

Samen *m* -s,- seed; (*Anat*) semen,
sperm

Sammel|becken *nt* reservoir.
  s∼n *vt/i* (*haben*) collect; (*suchen*,
versammeln) gather; **sich s∼n**
collect; (*sich versammeln*) gather;
(*sich fassen*) collect oneself.
  S∼name *m* collective noun

Samm|ler(in) *m* -s,- (*f* -, -nen)
collector. **S∼lung** *f* -, -en collection;
(*innere*) composure

Samstag *m* -s, -e Saturday. **s∼s**
adv on Saturdays

samt *prep* (+ *dat*) together with

Samt *m* -[e]s velvet

sämtlich *indef pron inv* all.
  s∼e(r,s) *indef pron* all the; **s∼e**
Werke complete works

Sanatorium *nt* -s, -ien sanatorium

Sand *m* -[e]s sand

Sandale *f* -, -n sandal

Sand|bank *f* sandbank. **S∼kasten**
m sand-pit. **S∼papier** *nt* sandpaper

sanft *a* gentle

Sänger(in) *m* -s,-(*f* -, -nen) singer

sanieren *vt* clean up; redevelop
  <*Gebiet*>; (*modernisieren*) modernize;
make profitable <*Industrie, Firma*>;
sich s∼ become profitable

sanitär *a* sanitary

Sanität|er *m* -s,- first-aid man;
  (*Fahrer*) ambulance man; (*Mil*)
medical orderly. **S∼swagen** *m*
ambulance

Sanktion /zaŋk'tsˌio:n/ *f* -, -en
sanction. **s∼ieren** *vt* sanction

Saphir *m* -s, -e sapphire

Sardelle *f* -, -n anchovy

Sardine *f* -, -n sardine

Sarg *m* -[e]s,¨-e coffin

Sarkasmus *m* - sarcasm

Satan *m* -s Satan; (🔟 *Teufel*) devil

Satellit *m* -en, -en satellite.
  S∼enfernsehen *nt* satellite
television. **S∼enschüssel** *f*
satellite dish

Satin /za'tɛŋ/ *m* -s satin

Satire *f* -, -n satire

satt *a* full; <*Farbe*> rich; **s∼ sein**
have had enough [to eat]; **etw s∼**
haben 🔟 be fed up with sth

Sattel *m* -s,¨- saddle. **s∼n** *vt* saddle.
  S∼zug *m* articulated lorry

sättigen *vt* satisfy; (*Chem & fig*)
saturate ● *vi* (*haben*) be filling

Satz *m* -es,¨-e sentence; (*Teil-*) clause;
(*These*) proposition; (*Math*) theorem;
(*Mus*) movement; (*Tennis*,
Zusammengehöriges) set; (*Boden-*)
sediment; (*Kaffee-*) grounds *pl*;
(*Steuer-, Zins-*) rate; (*Druck-*) setting;
(*Schrift-*) type; (*Sprung-*) leap, bound.
  S∼aussage *f* predicate.
  S∼gegenstand *m* subject.
  S∼zeichen *nt* punctuation mark

Sau *f* -,Säue sow

sauber *a* clean; (*ordentlich*) neat;
(*anständig*) decent; **s∼ machen**
clean. **S∼keit** *f* - cleanliness;
neatness

säuberlich *a* neat

Sauce /'zo:sə/ *f* -, -n sauce; (*Braten-*)
gravy

Saudi-Arabien /-iən/ *nt* -s Saudi
Arabia

sauer *a* sour; (*Chem*) acid; (*eingelegt*)
pickled; (*schwer*) hard; **saurer Regen**
acid rain

Sauerkraut *nt* sauerkraut

säuerlich *a* slightly sour

Sauerstoff *m* oxygen

saufen† *vt/i* (*haben*) drink; ⊠ booze

Säufer *m* -s,- ⊠ boozer

saugen† *vt/i* (*haben*) suck; (*staub-*)
vacuum, hoover; **sich voll Wasser**
s∼ soak up water

säugen *vt* suckle

Säugetier *nt* mammal

saugfähig *a* absorbent

Säugling *m* -s, -e infant

Säule *f* -, -n column

Saum *m* -[e]s,Säume hem; (*Rand*)
edge

säumen *vt* hem; (*fig*) line

Sauna f -, -nas & -nen sauna

Säure f -, -n acidity; (*Chem*) acid

sausen vi (haben) rush; <*Ohren:*> buzz ● vi (sein) rush [along]

Saxophon, Saxofon nt -s, -e saxophone

S-Bahn f city and suburban railway

Scanner m -s,- scanner

sch int shush! (*fort*) shoo!

Schabe f -, -n cockroach

schaben vt/i (haben) scrape

schäbig a shabby

Schablone f -, -n stencil; (*Muster*) pattern; (*fig*) stereotype

Schach nt -s chess; **S~!** check! **S~brett** nt chessboard

Schachfigur f chess-man

schachmatt a s~ setzen checkmate; **s~!** checkmate!

Schachspiel nt game of chess

Schacht m -[e]s,-̈e shaft

Schachtel f -, -n box; (*Zigaretten-*) packet

Schachzug m move

schade a s~ sein be a pity or shame: zu s~ für too good for

Schädel m -s, skull. **S~bruch** m fractured skull

schaden vi (haben) (+ dat) damage; (*nachteilig sein*) hurt. **S~** m -s,-̈ damage; (*Defekt*) defect; (*Nachteil*) disadvantage. **S~ersatz** m damages pl. **S~freude** f malicious glee. **s~froh** a gloating

schädig|en vt damage, harm. **S~ung** f -, -en damage

schädlich a harmful

Schädling m -s, -e pest. **S~sbekämpfungsmittel** nt pesticide

Schaf nt -[e]s, -e sheep. **S~bock** m ram

Schäfer m -s,- shepherd. **S~hund** m sheepdog; Deutscher S~hund alsatian

schaffen[1]† vt create; (*herstellen*) establish; make <*Platz*>

schaffen[2] v (reg) ● vt manage [to do]; pass <*Prüfung*>; catch <*Zug*>; (*bringen*) take

Schaffner m -s,- conductor; (*Zug-*) ticket-inspector

Schaffung f - creation

Schaft m -[e]s,-̈e shaft; (*Gewehr-*) stock; (*Stiefel-*) leg

Schal m -s, -s scarf

Schale f -, -n skin; (*abgeschält*) peel; (*Eier-, Nuss-, Muschel-*) shell; (*Schüssel*) dish

schälen vt peel; sich s~ peel

Schall m -[e]s sound. **S~dämpfer** m silencer. **S~dicht** a soundproof. **s~en** vi (haben) ring out: (*nachhallen*) resound. **S~mauer** f sound barrier. **S~platte** f record, disc

schalt|en vt switch ● vi (haben) switch/<*Ampel:*> turn (auf + acc to); (*Auto*) change gear; (⌶ *begreifen*) catch on. **S~er** m -s,- switch; (*Post-, Bank-*) counter; (*Fahrkarten-*) ticket window. **S~hebel** m switch; (*Auto*) gear lever. **S~jahr** nt leap year. **S~ung** f -, -en circuit: (*Auto*) gear change

Scham f - shame; (*Anat*) private parts pl

schämen (sich) vr be ashamed

scham|haft a modest. **s~los** a shameless

Schampon nt -s shampoo. **s~ieren** vt shampoo

Schande f - disgrace, shame

schändlich a disgraceful

Schanktisch m bar

Schanze f, -, -n [ski-]jump

Schar f -, -en crowd; (*Vogel-*) flock

Scharade f -, -n charade

scharen vt um sich s~ gather round one; sich s~ um flock round. **s~weise** adv in droves

scharf a sharp; (*stark*) strong; (*stark gewürzt*) hot; <*Geruch*> pungent; <*Wind, Augen, Verstand*> keen; (*streng*) harsh; <*Galopp*> hard; <*Munition*> live; <*Hund*> fierce; s~ einstellen (*Phot*) focus; s~ sein (*Phot*) be in focus; s~ sein auf (+ acc) ⌶ be keen on

S

Schärfe f sharpness; strength; hotness; pungency; keenness; harshness. **s~n** vt sharpen

Scharf|richter m executioner. **S~schütze** m marksman. **S~sinn** m astutenes

Scharlach m -s scarlet fever

Scharlatan m -s, -e charlatan

Scharnier nt -s, -e hinge

Schärpe f -, -n sash

scharren vi (haben) scrape; <Huhn> scratch ● vt scrape

Schaschlik m & nt -s, -s kebab

Schatten m -s,- shadow; (schattige Stelle) shade. **S~riss** m silhouette. **S~seite** f shady side; (fig) disadvantage

schattier|en vt shade. **S~ung** f -, -en shading

schattig a shady

Schatz m -es, ̈e treasure; (Freund, Freundin) sweetheart

schätzen vt estimate; (taxieren) value; (achten) esteem; (würdigen) appreciate

Schätzung f -, -en estimate; (Taxierung) valuation

Schau f -, -en show. **S~ bild** nt diagram

Schauder m -s shiver; (vor Abscheu) shudder. **s~ haft** a dreadful. **s~n** vi (haben) shiver; (vor Abscheu) shudder

schauen vi (haben) (SGer, Aust) look; **s~, dass** make sure that

Schauer m -s,- shower; (Schauder) shiver. **S~geschichte** f horror story. **s~lich** a ghastly

Schaufel f -, -n shovel; (Kehr-) dustpan. **s~n** vt shovel; (graben) dig

Schaufenster nt shop-window. **S~puppe** f dummy

Schaukel f -, -n swing. **s~n** vt rock ● vi (haben) rock; (auf einer Schaukel) swing; (schwanken) sway. **S~pferd** nt rocking-horse. **S~stuhl** m rocking-chair

Schaum m -[e]s foam; (Seifen-) lather; (auf Bier) froth; (als Frisier-, Rasiermittel) mousse

schäumen vi (haben) foam, froth; <Seife:> lather

Schaum|gummi m foam rubber. **s~ig** a frothy; **s~ig rühren** (Culin) cream. **S~stoff** m [synthetic] foam. **S~wein** m sparkling wine

Schauplatz m scene

schaurig a dreadful; (unheimlich) eerie

Schauspiel nt play; (Anblick) spectacle. **S~er** m actor. **S~erin** f actress

Scheck m -s, -s cheque. **S~buch, S~heft** nt cheque-book. **S~karte** f cheque card

Scheibe f -, -n disc; (Schieß-) target; (Glas-) pane; (Brot-, Wurst-) slice. **S~nwischer** m -s,- windscreen-wiper

Scheich m -s, -e & -s sheikh

Scheide f -, -n sheath; (Anat) vagina

scheid|en† vt separate; (unterscheiden) distinguish; dissolve <Ehe>; **sich s~en lassen** get divorced ● vi (sein) leave; (voneinander) part. **S~ung** f -, -en divorce

Schein m -[e]s, -e light; (Anschein) appearance; (Bescheinigung) certificate; (Geld-) note. **s~bar** a apparent. **s~en†** vi (haben) shine; (den Anschein haben) seem, appear

scheinheilig a hypocritical

Scheinwerfer m -s,- floodlight; (Such-) searchlight; (Auto) headlight; (Theat) spotlight

Scheiße f - (vulg) shit. **s~n†** vi (haben) (vulg) shit

Scheit nt -[e]s, -e log

Scheitel m -s,- parting

scheitern vi (sein) fail

Schelle f -, -n bell. **s~n** vi (haben) ring

Schellfisch m haddock

Schelm m -s, -e rogue

Schelte f - scolding

Schema nt -s, -mata model, pattern; (Skizze) diagram

Schemel m -s,- stool

Schenke f -, -n tavern

Schenkel m -s,- thigh

schenken vt give [as a present]; jdm Vertrauen s~ trust s.o.

Scherbe f -, -n [broken] piece

Schere f -, -n scissors pl; (Techn) shears pl; (Hummer-) claw. s~n¹† vt shear; crop <Haar>

scheren² vt (reg) 🔲 bother; sich nicht s~ um not care about

Scherenschnitt m silhouette

Scherereien fpl 🔲 trouble sg

Scherz m -es, -e joke; im/zum S~ as a joke. s~en vi (haben) joke

scheu a shy; <Tier> timid; s~ werden <Pferd:> shy

scheuchen vt shoo

scheuen vt be afraid of; (meiden) shun; keine Mühe/Kosten s~ spare no effort/expense; sich s~ be afraid (vor + dat of); shrink (etw zu tun from doing sth)

scheuern vt scrub; (reiben) rub; [wund] s~n chafe ● vi (haben) rub, chafe

Scheuklappen fpl blinkers

Scheune f -, -n barn

Scheusal nt -s, -e monster

scheußlich a horrible

Schi m -s, -er ski; S~ fahren od laufen ski

Schicht f -, -en layer; (Geol) stratum; (Gesellschafts-) class; (Arbeits-) shift. S~arbeit f shift work. s~en vt stack [up]

schick a stylish; <Frau> chic. S~ m -[e]s style

schicken vt/i (haben) send; s~ nach send for

Schicksal nt -s, -e fate. S~sschlag m misfortune

Schieb|edach nt (Auto) sun-roof. s~en† vt push; (gleitend) slide; (🔲 handeln mit) traffic in; etw s~en auf (+ acc) (fig) put sth down to; shift <Schuld> on to ● vi (haben) push. S~etür f sliding door. S~ung f -, -en 🔲 illicit deal; (Betrug) rigging, fixing

Schieds|gericht nt panel of judges; (Jur) arbitration tribunal. S~richter m referee; (Tennis) umpire; (Jur) arbitrator

schief a crooked; (unsymmetrisch) lopsided; (geneigt) slanting, sloping; (nicht senkrecht) leaning; <Winkel> oblique; (fig) false; suspicious ● adv not straight; s~ gehen 🔲 go wrong

Schiefer m -s slate

schielen vi (haben) squint

Schienbein nt shin

Schiene f -, -n rail; (Gleit-) runner; (Med) splint. s~n vt (Med) put in a splint

Schieß|bude f shooting-gallery. s~en† vt shoot; fire <Kugel>; score <Tor> ● vi (haben) shoot, fire (auf + acc at). S~scheibe f target. S~stand m shooting-range

Schifahr|en nt skiing. S~er(in) m(f) skier

Schiff nt -[e]s, -e ship; (Kirchen-) nave; (Seiten-) aisle

Schiffahrt* f s. Schifffahrt

schiff|bar a navigable. S~bruch m shipwreck. s~brüchig a shipwrecked. S~fahrt f shipping

Schikan|e f -, -n harassment; mit allen S~en 🔲 with every refinement. s~ieren vt harass

Schi|laufen nt -s skiing. S~läufer(in) m(f) -s,- (f -, -nen) skier

Schild¹ m -[e]s, -e shield

Schild² nt -[e]s, -er sign; (Nummern-) plate; (Mützen-) badge; (Etikett) label

Schilddrüse f thyroid [gland]

schilder|n vt describe. S~ung f -, -en description

Schild|kröte f tortoise; (See-) turtle. S~patt nt -[e]s tortoiseshell

Schilf nt -[e]s reeds pl

schillern vi (haben) shimmer

Schimmel m -s,- mould; (Pferd) white horse. s~n vi (haben/sein) go mouldy

schimmern vi (haben) gleam

Schimpanse m -n, -n chimpanzee

schimpf|en vi (haben) grumble (mit at; über + acc about); scold (mit jdm s.o.) ● *vt* call. **S∼wort** *nt* (*pl* -wörter) swear-word

Schinken *m* -s,- ham. **S∼speck** *m* bacon

Schippe *f* -, -n shovel. **s∼n** *vt* shovel

Schirm *m* -[e]s, -e umbrella; (*Sonnen-*) sunshade; (*Lampen-*) shade; (*Augen-*) visor; (*Mützen-*) peak; (*Ofen-, Bild-*) screen; (*fig: Schutz*) shield. **S∼herrschaft** *f* patronage. **S∼mütze** *f* peaked cap

schizophren *a* schizophrenic. **S∼ie** *f* - schizophrenia

Schlacht *f* -, -en battle

schlachten *vt* slaughter, kill

Schlacht|feld *nt* battlefield. **S∼hof** *m* abattoir

Schlacke *f* -, -n slag

Schlaf *m* -[e]s sleep; im S∼ in one's sleep. **S∼fertig** *m* pyjamas *pl*

Schläfe *f* -, -n (*Anat*) temple

schlafen† *vi* (*haben*) sleep; s∼ gehen go to bed; er schläft noch he is still asleep

schlaff *a* limp; <*Seil*> slack; <*Muskel*> flabby

Schlaf|lied *nt* lullaby. **s∼los** *a* sleepless. **S∼losigkeit** *f* - insomnia. **S∼mittel** *nt* sleeping drug

schläfrig *a* sleepy

Schlaf|saal *m* dormitory. **S∼sack** *m* sleeping-bag. **S∼tablette** *f* sleeping-pill. **S∼wagen** *m* sleeping-car, sleeper. **s∼wandeln** *vi* (*haben/sein*) sleep-walk. **S∼zimmer** *nt* bedroom

Schlag *m* -[e]s,ⸯe blow; (*Faust-*) punch; (*Herz-, Puls-, Trommel-*) beat; (*einer Uhr*) chime; (*Glocken-, Gong- & Med*) stroke; (*elektrischer*) shock; (*Art*) type; S∼̈e bekommen get a beating; S∼ auf S∼ in rapid succession. **S∼ader** *f* artery. **S∼anfall** *m* stroke. **S∼baum** *m* barrier

schlagen† *vt* hit, strike; (*fällen*) fell; knock <*Loch, Nagel*> (in + *acc*

into); (*prügeln, besiegen*) beat; (*Culin*) whisk <*Eiweiß*>; whip <*Sahne*>; (*legen*) throw; (*wickeln*) wrap; sich s∼ fight ● *vi* (*haben*) beat; <*Tür:*> bang; <*Uhr:*> strike; (*melodisch*) chime; mit den Flügeln s∼ flap its wings ● *vi* (*sein*) in etw (*acc*) s∼ <*Blitz, Kugel:*> strike sth; nach jdm s∼ (*fig*) take after s.o.

Schlager *m* -s,- popular song; (*Erfolg*) hit

Schläger *m* -s,- racket; (*Tischtennis-*) bat; (*Golf-*) club; (*Hockey-*) stick. **S∼ei** *f* -, -en fight, brawl

schlag|fertig *a* quick-witted. **S∼loch** *nt* pot-hole. **S∼sahne** *f* whipped cream; (*ungeschlagen*) whipping cream. **S∼seite** *f* (*Naut*) list. **S∼stock** *m* truncheon. **S∼wort** *nt* (*pl* -worte) slogan. **S∼zeile** *f* headline. **S∼zeug** *nt* (*Mus*) percussion. **S∼zeuger** *m* -s,- percussionist; (*in Band*) drummer

Schlamm *m* -[e]s mud. **s∼ig** *a* muddy

Schlampe| *f* -, -n 🗓 slut. **s∼en** *vi* (*haben*) 🗓 be sloppy (bei in). **s∼ig** *a* slovenly; <*Arbeit*> sloppy

Schlange *f* -, -n snake; (*Menschen-, Auto-*) queue; S∼ stehen queue

schlängeln (sich) *vr* wind; <*Person:*> weave (durch through)

schlank *a* slim. **S∼heitskur** *f* slimming diet

schlapp *a* tired; (*schlaff*) limp

schlau *a* clever; (*gerissen*) crafty; ich werde nicht s∼ daraus I can't make head or tail of it

Schlauch *m* -[e]s,Schläuche tube; (*Wasser-*) hose|pipe]. **S∼boot** *nt* rubber dinghy

Schlaufe *f* -, -n loop

schlecht *a* bad; (*böse*) wicked; (*unzulänglich*) poor; s∼ werden go bad; <*Wetter:*> turn bad; mir ist s∼ I feel sick; s∼ machen 🗓 run down. **s∼gehen*** *vi sep* (*sein*) s∼ gehen, s. gehen

schlecken *vt/i* (*haben*) lick (an etw *dat* sth); (*auf-*) lap up

---

Schlegel *m* -s,- (*SGer: Keule*) leg; (*Hühner-*) drumstick

schleichen† *vi* (*sein*) creep; (*langsam gehen/fahren*) crawl ● *vr* sich s∼ creep. **s∼d** *a* creeping

Schleier *m* -s,- veil; (*fig*) haze

Schleife *f* -, -n bow; (*Fliege*) bowtie; (*Biegung*) loop

schleifen¹ *v* (*reg*) ● *vt* drag ● *vi* (*haben*) trail, drag

schleifen²† *vt* grind; (*schärfen*) sharpen; cut <*Edelstein, Glas*>

Schleim *m* -[e]s slime; (*Anat*) mucus; (*Med*) phlegm. **s∼ig** *a* slimy

schlendern *vi* (*sein*) stroll

schlenkern *vt/i* (*haben*) swing; s∼ mit swing; dangle <*Beine*>

Schlepp|dampfer *m* tug. **S∼e** *f* -, -n train. **s∼en** *vt* drag; (*tragen*) carry; (*ziehen*) tow; sich s∼en drag oneself; (*sich hinziehen*) drag on; sich s∼en mit carry. **S∼er** *m* -s,- tug; (*Traktor*) tractor. **S∼kahn** *m* barge. **S∼lift** *m* T-bar lift. **S∼tau** *nt* tow-rope; ins **S∼tau nehmen** take in tow

Schleuder *f* -, -n catapult; (*Wäsche-*) spin-drier. **s∼n** *vt* hurl; spin <*Wäsche*> ● *vi* (*sein*) skid; ins **S∼n geraten** skid. **S∼sitz** *m* ejector seat

Schleuse *f* -, -n lock; (*Sperre*) sluice[-gate]. **s∼n** *vt* steer

Schliche *pl* tricks

schlicht *a* plain; simple

Schlichtung *f* - settlement; (*Jur*) arbitration

Schließe *f* -, -n clasp; buckle

schließen† *vt* close (*ab-*) lock; fasten <*Kleid, Verschluss*>; (*stilllegen*) close down; (*beenden, folgern*) conclude; enter into <*Vertrag*>; sich s∼ close; etw s∼ an (+ *acc*) connect sth to; sich s∼ an (+ *acc*) follow ● *vi* (*haben*) close, (*den Betrieb einstellen*) close down, (*den Schlüssel drehen*) turn the key; (*enden, folgern*) conclude

Schließ|fach *nt* locker. **s∼lich** *adv* finally, in the end; (*immerhin*) after all. **S∼ung** *f* -, -en closure

Schliff *m* -[e]s cut; (*Schleifen*) cutting; (*fig*) polish

schlimm *a* bad

Schlinge *f* -, -n loop; (*Henkers-*) noose; (*Med*) sling; (*Falle*) snare

Schlingel *m* -s,- 🔟 rascal

schlingen† *vt* wind, wrap; tie <*Knoten*> ● *vi* (*haben*) bolt one's food

Schlips *m* -es, -e tie

Schlitten *m* -s,- sledge; (*Rodel-*) toboggan; (*Pferde-*) sleigh; **S∼ fahren** toboggan

schlittern *vi* (*haben/ sein*) slide

Schlittschuh *m* skate; **S∼ laufen** skate. **S∼läufer(in)** *m(f)* -s,- (*f* -, -nen) skater

Schlitz *m* -es, -e slit; (*für Münze*) slot; (*Jacken-*) vent; (*Hosen-*) flies *pl*. **s∼en** *vt* slit

Schloss *nt* -es,-̈er lock; (*Vorhänge-*) padlock; (*Verschluss*) clasp; (*Gebäude*) castle; palace

Schlosser *m* -s,- locksmith; (*Auto-*) mechanic

Schlucht *f* -, -en ravine, gorge

schluchzen *vi* (*haben*) sob

Schluck *m* -[e]s, -e mouthful; (*klein*) sip

Schluckauf *m* -s hiccups *pl*

schlucken *vt/i* (*haben*) swallow

Schlummer *m* -s slumber

Schlund *m* -[e]s [back of the] throat; (*fig*) mouth

schlüpf|en *vi* (*sein*) slip; [aus dem Ei] s∼en hatch. **S∼er** *m* -s,- knickers *pl*. **s∼rig** *a* slippery

schlürfen *vt/i* (*haben*) slurp

Schluss *m* -es,-̈e end; (*S∼folgerung*) conclusion; zum **S∼** finally; **S∼ machen** stop (mit etw sth); finish (mit jdm with s.o.)

Schlüssel *m* -s,- key; (*Schrauben-*) spanner; (*Geheim-*) code; (*Mus*) clef. **S∼bein** *nt* collar-bone. **S∼bund** *m* & **nt** bunch of keys. **S∼loch** *nt* keyhole

Schlussfolgerung *f* conclusion

schlüssig *a* conclusive

S

Schluss|licht *nt* rear-light.
  S~verkauf *m* sale

schmächtig *a* slight

schmackhaft *a* tasty

schmal *a* narrow; (*dünn*) thin;
  (*schlank*) slender; (*karg*) meagre

schmälern *vt* diminish;
  (*herabsetzen*) belittle

Schmalz¹ *nt* -es lard; (*Ohren-*) wax

Schmalz² *m* -es ▣ schmaltz

Schmarotzer *m* -s,- parasite;
  (*Person*) sponger

schmatzen *vi* (*haben*) eat noisily

schmausen *vi* (*haben*) feast

schmecken *vi* (*haben*) taste (**nach**
  of); [**gut**] **s~** taste good ● *vt* taste

Schmeichelei *f* -, -en flattery;
  (*Kompliment*) compliment

schmeichel|haft *a*
  complimentary, flattering. **s~n** *vi*
  (*haben*) (+ *dat*) flatter

schmeißen† *vt/i* (*haben*) **s~** [**mit**]
  ▣ chuck

Schmeißfliege *f* bluebottle

schmelz|en† *vt/i* (*sein*) melt; smelt
  <*Erze*>. **S~wasser** *nt* melted snow
  and ice

Schmerbauch *m* ▣ paunch

Schmerz *m* -es, -en pain; (*Kummer*)
  grief; **S~en haben** be in pain. **s~en**
  vt hurt; (*fig*) grieve ● *vi* (*haben*)
  hurt, be painful. **S~ensgeld** *nt*
  compensation for pain and suffering.
  s~haft *a* painful. **S~los** *a* painless
  s~stillend *a* pain-killing;
  s~stillendes Mittel analgesic, pain-
  killer. **S~tablette** *f* pain-killer

Schmetterball *m* (*Tennis*) smash

Schmetterling *m* -s, -e butterfly

schmettern *vt* hurl; (*Tennis*)
  smash; (*singen*) sing ● *vi* (*haben*)
  sound

Schmied *m* -[e]s, -e blacksmith

Schmiede *f* -, -n forge. **S~eisen**
  nt wrought iron. **s~n** *vt* forge

Schmier|e *f* -, -n grease; (*Schmutz*)
  mess. **s~en** *vt* lubricate; (*streichen*)
  spread; (*schlecht schreiben*) scrawl
  ● *vi* (*haben*) smudge; (*schreiben*)

scrawl. **S~geld** *nt* ▣ bribe. **s~ig** *a*
greasy; (*schmutzig*) grubby.
  S~mittel *nt* lubricant

Schminke *f* -, -n make-up. **s~n** *vt*
make up; **sich s~n** put on make-up;
sich (*dat*) **die Lippen s~n** put on
lipstick

schmirgel|n *vt* sand down.
  S~papier *nt* emery-paper

schmollen *vi* (*haben*) sulk

schmor|en *vt/i* (*haben*) braise.
  S~topf *m* casserole

Schmuck *m* -[e]s jewellery;
  (*Verzierung*) ornament, decoration

schmücken *vt* decorate, adorn

schmuck|los *a* plain. **S~stück**
  nt piece of jewellery

Schmuggel *m* -s smuggling. **s~n**
  vt smuggle. **S~ware** *f* contraband

Schmuggler *m* -s,- smuggler

schmunzeln *vi* (*haben*) smile

schmusen *vi* (*haben*) cuddle

Schmutz *m* -es dirt. **s~en** *vi*
  (*haben*) get dirty. **s~ig** *a* dirty

Schnabel *m* -s, ̈ beak, bill; (*eines
  Kruges*) lip; (*Tülle*) spout

Schnalle *f* -, -n buckle. **s~n** *vt*
  strap; (*zu-*) buckle

schnalzen *vi* (*haben*) **mit der Zunge
  s~** click one's tongue

schnapp|en *vi* (*haben*) **s~en nach**
  snap at; gasp for <*Luft*> ● *vt* snatch,
  grab; (▣ *festnehmen*) nab.
  S~schloss *nt* spring lock.
  S~schuss *m* snapshot

Schnaps *m* -es, ̈ e schnapps

schnarchen *vi* (*haben*) snore

schnaufen *vi* (*haben*) puff, pant

Schnauze *f* -, -n muzzle; (*eines
  Kruges*) lip; (*Tülle*) spout

schnäuzen (sich) *vr* blow one's
nose

Schnecke *f* -, -n snail; (*Nackt-*)
  slug; (*Spirale*) scroll. **S~nhaus** *nt*
snail-shell

Schnee *m* -s snow; (*Eier-*) beaten
egg-white. **S~besen** *m* whisk.
  S~brille *f* snow-goggles *pl*. **S~fall**
m snowfall. **S~flocke** *f* snowflake.
  S~glöckchen *nt* -s,- snowdrop.
  S~kette *f* snow chain. **S~mann**

m (*pl* -männer) snowman. **S~pflug** *m* snowplough. **S~schläger** *m* whisk. **S~sturm** *m* snowstorm, blizzard. **S~wehe** *f* -, -n snowdrift

Schneide *f* -, -n [cutting] edge; (*Klinge*) blade

schneiden† *vt* cut; (*in Scheiben*) slice; (*kreuzen*) cross; (*nicht beachten*) cut dead; Gesichter s~ pull faces; **sich** s~ cut oneself; (*über-*) intersect

Schneider *m* -s,- tailor. **S~in** *f* -, -nen dressmaker. **s~n** *vt* make <*Anzug, Kostüm*>

Schneidezahn *m* incisor

schneien *vi* (*haben*) snow; **es schneit** it is snowing

Schneise *f* -, -n path

schnell *a* quick; <*Auto, Tempo*> fast ● *adv* quickly; (*in s~em Tempo*) fast; (*bald*) soon; **mach** s~! hurry up! **S~igkeit** *f* - rapidity; (*Tempo*) speed. **S~kochtopf** *m* pressure-cooker. **s~stens** *adv* as quickly as possible. **S~zug** *m* express [train]

schnetzeln *vt* cut into thin strips

Schnipsel *m* & *nt* -s,- scrap

Schnitt *m* -[e]s, -e cut; (*Film-*) cutting; (*S~muster*) [paper] pattern; **im** S~ (*durchschnittlich*) on average

Schnitte *f* -, -n slice [of bread]

schnittig *a* stylish; (*stromlinienförmig*) streamlined

Schnitt|lauch *m* chives *pl*. **S~muster** *nt* [paper] pattern. **S~punkt** *m* [point of] intersection. **S~wunde** *f* cut

Schnitzel *nt* -s,- scrap; (*Culin*) escalope. **s~n** *vt* shred

schnitzen *vt/i* (*haben*) carve

schnodderig *a* 🔲 brash

Schnorchel *m* -s,- snorkel

Schnörkel *m* -s,- flourish; (*Kunst*) scroll. **s~ig** *a* ornate

schnüffeln *vi* (*haben*) sniff (**an etw** *dat* sth); (🔲 *spionieren*) snoop [around]

Schnuller *m* -s,- [baby's] dummy

Schnupf|en *m* -s,- [head] cold. **S~tabak** *m* snuff

schnuppern *vt/i* (*haben*) sniff (**an etw** *dat* sth)

Schnur *f* -,:-e string; (*Kordel*) cord; (*Electr*) flex

schnüren *vt* tie; lace [up] <*Schuhe*>

Schnurr|bart *m* moustache. **s~en** *vi* (*haben*) hum; <*Katze:*> purr

Schnürsenkel *m* [shoe-]lace

Schock *m* -[e]s, -s shock. **s~en** *vt* 🔲 shock. **s~ieren** *vt* shock

Schöffe *m* -n, -n lay judge

Schokolade *f* - chocolate

Scholle *f* -, -n clod [of earth]; (*Eis-*) [ice-]floe; (*Fisch*) plaice

schon *adv* already; (*allein*) just; (*sogar*) even; (*ohnehin*) anyway; s~ **einmal** before; (*jemals*) ever; s~ **immer/oft/wieder** always/often/again; s~ **deshalb** for that reason alone; **das ist** s~ **möglich** that's quite possible; **ja** s~, **aber** well yes, but

schön *a* beautiful; <*Wetter*> fine; (*angenehm, nett*) nice; (*gut*) good; (🔲 *beträchtlich*) pretty; **s~en Dank!** thank you very much!

schonen *vt* spare; (*gut behandeln*) look after. **s~d** *a* gentle

Schönheit *f* -, -en beauty. **S~sfehler** *m* blemish. **S~skonkurrenz** *f* beauty contest

Schonung *f* -, -en gentle care; (*nach Krankheit*) rest; (*Baum-*) plantation. **s~slos** *a* ruthless

Schonzeit *f* close season

schöpf|en *vt* scoop [up]; ladle <*Suppe*>; **Mut s~en** take heart. **s~erisch** *a* creative. **S~kelle** *f*. **S~löffel** *m* ladle. **S~ung** *f* -, -en creation

Schoppen *m* -s,- (*SGer*) ≈ pint

Schorf *m* -[e]s scab

Schornstein *m* chimney. **S~feger** *m* -s,- chimney-sweep

Schoß *m* -es,:-e lap; (*Frack-*) tail

Schössling *m* -s, -e (*Bot*) shoot

Schote *f* -, -n pod; (*Erbse*) pea

Schotte *m* -n, -n Scot, Scotsman

Schotter *m* -s gravel

schott|isch *a* Scottish, Scots. **S~land** *nt* -s Scotland

schraffieren *vt* hatch

schräg *a* diagonal; *(geneigt)* sloping; s~ halten tilt. **S~strich** *m* oblique stroke

Schramme *f* -, -n scratch

Schrank *m* -[e]s,-̈e cupboard; *(Kleider-)* wardrobe; *(Akten-, Glas-)* cabinet

Schranke *f* -, -n barrier

Schraube *f* -, -n screw; *(Schiffs-)* propeller. **s~n** *vt* screw; *(ab-)* unscrew; *(drehen)* turn. **S~nschlüssel** *m* spanner. **S~nzieher** *m* -s,- screwdriver

Schraubstock *m* vice

Schreck *m* -[e]s, -e fright. **S~en** *m* -s,- fright; *(Entsetzen)* horror

Schreck|gespenst *nt* spectre. **s~haft** *a* easily frightened; *(nervös)* jumpy. **s~lich** *a* terrible. **S~schuss** *m* warning shot

Schrei *m* -[e]s, -e cry, shout; *(gellend)* scream; der letzte S~ ⬛ the latest thing

schreib|en† *vt/i (haben)* write; *(auf der Maschine)* type; **richtig/falsch s~en** spell right/wrong; **sich s~en** <*Wort:*> be spelt; *(korrespondieren)* correspond. **S~en** *nt* -s,- writing; *(Brief)* letter. **S~fehler** *m* spelling mistake. **S~heft** *nt* exercise book. **S~kraft** *f* clerical assistant; *(für Maschineschreiben)* typist. **S~maschine** *f* typewriter. **S~tisch** *m* desk. **S~ung** *f* -, -en spelling. **S~waren** *fpl* stationery *sg.*

schreien† *vt/i (haben)* cry; *(gellend)* scream; *(rufen, laut sprechen)* shout

Schreiner *m* -s,- joiner

schreiten† *vi (sein)* walk

Schrift *f* -, -en writing; *(Druck-)* type; *(Abhandlung)* paper; die Heilige S~ the Scriptures *pl.* **S~führer** *m* secretary. **s~lich** *a* written ● *adv* in writing. **S~sprache** *f* written language. **S~steller(in)** *m* -s,- (*f* -, -nen) writer. **S~stück** *nt* document. **S~zeichen** *nt* character

schrill *a* shrill

Schritt *m* -[e]s, -e step; *(Entfernung)* pace; *(Gangart)* walk; *(der Hose)* crotch. **S~macher** *m* -s,- pacemaker. **s~weise** *adv* step by step

schroff *a* precipitous; *(abweisend)* brusque; *(unvermittelt)* abrupt; <*Gegensatz:*> stark

Schrot *m* & *nt* -[e]s coarse meal; *(Blei-)* small shot. **S~flinte** *f* shotgun

Schrott *m* -[e]s scrap[-metal]; zu S~ fahren ⬛ write off. **S~platz** *m* scrap-yard

schrubben *vt/i (haben)* scrub

Schrull|e *f* -, -n whim; alte S~e ⬛ old crone. **s~ig** *a* cranky

schrumpfen *vi (sein)* shrink

schrump[e]lig *a* wrinkled

Schub *m* -[e]s,-̈e *(Phys)* thrust; *(S~fach)* drawer; *(Menge)* batch. **S~fach** *nt* drawer. **S~karre** *f*, **S~karren** *m* wheelbarrow. **S~lade** *f* drawer

Schubs *m* -es, -e push, shove **s~en** *vt* push, shove

schüchtern *a* shy. **S~heit** *f* - shyness

Schuft *m* -[e]s, -e *(pej)* swine

Schuh *m* -[e]s, -e shoe. **S~anzieher** *m* -s,- shoehorn. **S~band** *nt* (*pl* -bänder) shoe-lace. **S~creme** *f* shoe-polish. **S~löffel** *m* shoehorn. **S~macher** *m* -s,- shoemaker

Schul|abgänger *m* -s,- schoolleaver. **S~arbeiten**, **S~aufgaben** *fpl* homework *sg.*

Schuld *f* -, -en guilt; *(Verantwortung)* blame; *(Geld-)* debt; **S~en machen** get into debt; **S~ haben** be to blame (an + *dat* for); **jdm S~ geben** blame s.o. ● **s~ sein** be to blame (an + *dat* for). **s~en** *vt* owe

schuldig *a* guilty *(gen of)*; *(gebührend)* due; **jdm etw s~ sein** owe s.o. sth. **S~keit** *f* - duty

schuld|los *a* innocent. **S~ner** *m* -s,- debtor. **S~spruch** *m* guilty verdict

Schule *f* -, -n school; in der/die S~ at/to school. **s~n** *vt* train

S

Schüler(in) *m* -s,- (*f* -, -nen) pupil

schul|frei *a* s~freier Tag day without school; **wir haben morgen s~frei** there's no school tomorrow. **S~hof** *m* [school] playground. **S~jahr** *nt* school year; (*Klasse*) form. **S~kind** *nt* schoolchild. **S~stunde** *f* lesson

Schulter *f* -, -n shoulder. **S~blatt** *nt* shoulder-blade

Schulung *f* - training

schummeln *vi* (*haben*) 🔲 cheat

Schund *m* -[e]s trash

Schuppe *f* -, -n scale; **S~n** *pl* dandruff *sg.* **s~n (sich)** *vr* flake [off]

Schuppen *m* -s,- shed

schürf|en *vt* mine; **sich** (*dat*) **das Knie s~en** graze one's knee ● *vi* (*haben*) **s~en nach** prospect for. **S~wunde** *f* abrasion, graze

Schürhaken *m* poker

Schurke *m* -n, -n villain

Schürze *f* -, -n apron

Schuss *m* -es,¨e shot; (*kleine Menge*) dash

Schüssel *f* -, -n bowl; (*TV*) dish

Schuss|fahrt *f* (*Ski*) schuss. **S~waffe** *f* firearm

Schuster *m* -s,- = Schuhmacher

Schutt *m* -[e]s rubble. **S~abladeplatz** *m* rubbish dump

Schüttel|frost *m* shivering fit. **s~n** *vt* shake; **sich s~n** shake oneself/itself; (*vor Ekel*) shudder; **jdm die Hand s~n** shake s.o.'s hand

schütten *vt* pour; (*kippen*) tip; (*ver-*) spill ● *vi* (*haben*) **es schüttet** it is pouring [with rain]

Schutz *m* -es protection; (*Zuflucht*) shelter; (*Techn*) guard; **S~ suchen** take refuge. **S~anzug** *m* protective suit. **S~blech** *nt* mudguard. **S~brille** *f* goggles *pl*

Schütze *m* -n, -n marksman; (*Tor-*) scorer; (*Astr*) Sagittarius

schützen *vt* protect/(*Zuflucht gewähren*) shelter (**vor** + *dat* from) ● *vi* (*haben*) give protection/shelter (**vor** + *dat* from)

Schutz|engel *m* guardian angel. **S~heilige(r)** *m/f* patron saint

Schützling *m* -s, -e charge

schutz|los *a* defenceless, helpless. **S~mann** *m* (*pl* -männer & -leute) policeman. **S~umschlag** *m* dust-jacket

Schwaben *nt* -s Swabia

schwäbisch *a* Swabian

schwach *a* weak; (*nicht gut; gering*) poor; (*leicht*) faint

Schwäche *f* -, -n weakness. **S~n** *vt* weaken

schwäch|lich *a* delicate. **S~ling** *m* -s, -e weakling

Schwachsinn *m* mental deficiency. **s~ig** *a* mentally deficient; 🔲 idiotic

Schwager *m* -s,¨ brother-in-law

Schwägerin *f* -, -nen sister-in-law

Schwalbe *f* -, -n swallow

Schwall *m* -[e]s torrent

Schwamm *m* -[e]s,¨e sponge; (*SGer: Pilz*) fungus; (*essbar*) mushroom. **s~ig** *a* spongy

Schwan *m* -[e]s,¨e swan

schwanger *a* pregnant

Schwangerschaft *f* -, -en pregnancy

Schwank *m* -[e]s,¨e (*Theat*) farce

schwank|en *vi* (*haben*) sway; <*Boot:*> rock; (*sich ändern*) fluctuate; (*unentschieden sein*) be undecided ● (*sein*) stagger. **S~ung** *f* -, -en fluctuation

Schwanz *m* -es,¨e tail

schwänzen *vt* 🔲 skip; **die Schule s~** play truant

Schwarm *m* -[e]s,¨e swarm; (*Fisch-*) shoal; (🔲 *Liebe*) idol

schwärmen *vi* (*haben*) swarm; **s~ für** 🔲 adore; (*verliebt sein*) have a crush on

Schwarte *f* -, -n (*Speck-*) rind

schwarz *a* black; (🔲 *illegal*) illegal; **s~er Markt** black market; **s~ gekleidet** dressed in black; **s~ auf weiß** in black and white; **s~ sehen** (*fig*) be pessimistic; **ins S~e treffen** score a bull's-eye. **S~** *nt* -[e]s,- black. **S~arbeit** *f* moonlighting.

S

s~arbeiten vi sep (haben) moonlight. **S~e(r)** m/f black

Schwärze f - blackness. **s~n** vt blacken

Schwarz|fahrer m fare-dodger. **S~handel** m black market (mit in). **S~händler** m black marketeer. **S~markt** m black market. **S~wald** m Black Forest. **s~weiß** a black and white

schwatzen, (SGer) **schwätzen** vi (haben) chat; (klatschen) gossip; (Sch) talk [in class] ● vt talk

Schwebe f - in der S~ (fig) undecided. **S~bahn** f cable railway. **s~n** vi (haben) float; (fig) be undecided; <Verfahren:> be pending; in Gefahr s~n be in danger ● (sein) float

Schwed|e m -n, -n Swede. **S~en** nt -s Sweden. **S~in** f -, -nen Swede. **s~isch** a Swedish

Schwefel m -s sulphur

schweigen† vi (haben) be silent; ganz zu s~ von let alone. **S~** nt -s silence; zum S~ bringen silence

schweigsam a silent; (wortkarg) taciturn

Schwein nt -[e]s, -e pig; (Culin) pork; (🗵 Schuft) swine; **S~ haben** (🄸) be lucky. **S~ebraten** m roast pork. **S~efleisch** nt pork. **S~erei** f -, -en (🗵) [dirty] mess; (Gemeinheit) dirty trick. **S~estall** m pigsty. **S~sleder** nt pigskin

Schweiß m -es sweat

schweißen vt weld

Schweiz (die) - Switzerland. **S~er** a & m -s,-, **S~erin** f -, -nen Swiss. **s~erisch** a Swiss

Schwelle f -, -n threshold; (Eisenbahn-) sleeper

schwellen† vi (sein) swell. **S~ung** f -, -en swelling

schwer a heavy; (schwierig) difficult; (mühsam) hard; (ernst) serious; (schlimm) bad; **3 Pfund s~ sein** weigh 3 pounds ● adv heavily; with difficulty; (mühsam) hard; (schlimm, sehr) badly, seriously; **s~**

krank/verletzt seriously ill/injured; **s~ hören** be hard of hearing; **etw s~ nehmen** take sth seriously; **jdm s~ fallen** be hard for s.o.; **es jdm s~ machen** make it or things difficult for s.o.; **sich s~ tun** have difficulty (mit with); **s~ zu sagen** difficult or hard to say

Schwere f - heaviness; (Gewicht) weight; (Schwierigkeit) difficulty; (Ernst) gravity. **S~losigkeit** f - weightlessness

schwer|fällig a ponderous, clumsy. **S~gewicht** nt heavyweight. **s~hörig** a s~hörig sein be hard of hearing. **S~kraft** f (Phys) gravity. **s~mütig** a melancholic. **S~punkt** m centre of gravity; (fig) emphasis

Schwert nt -[e]s, -er sword. **S~lilie** f iris

Schwer|verbrecher m serious offender. **s~wiegend** a weighty

Schwester f -, -n sister; (Kranken-) nurse. **s~lich** a sisterly

Schwieger|eltern pl parents-in-law. **S~mutter** f mother-in-law. **S~sohn** m son-in-law. **S~tochter** f daughter-in-law. **S~vater** m father-in-law

schwierig a difficult. **S~keit** f -, -en difficulty

Schwimm|bad nt swimming-baths pl. **S~becken** nt swimming-pool. **s~en†** vt/i (sein/haben) swim; (auf dem Wasser treiben) float. **S~weste** f life-jacket

Schwindel m -s dizziness, vertigo; (🄸 Betrug) fraud; (Lüge) lie. **S~anfall** m dizzy spell. **s~frei** a s~frei sein have a good head for heights. **s~n** vi (haben) lie

Schwindl|er m -s,- liar; (Betrüger) fraud, con-man. **s~ig** a dizzy; mir ist od wird s~ig I feel dizzy

schwing|en† vi (haben) swing; (Phys) oscillate; (vibrieren) vibrate ● vt swing; wave <Fahne>; (drohend) brandish. **S~ung** f -, -en oscillation; vibration

Schwips m -es, -e einen S~ haben (🄸) be tipsy

---

*old spelling

S

schwitzen vi (haben) sweat; **ich schwitze** I am hot

schwören† vt/i (haben) swear (**auf** + acc by)

schwul a (⊞ homosexuell) gay

schwül a close. **S~e** f - closeness

Schwung m -[e]s,ˬe swing; (Bogen) sweep; (Schnelligkeit) momentum; (Kraft) vigour. **s~los** a dull. **s~voll** a vigorous; <Bogen, Linie> sweeping; (mitreißend) spirited

Schwur m -[e]s,ˬe vow; (Eid) oath. **S~gericht** nt jury [court]

sechs inv a, **S~** f -, -en six; (Sch) ≈ fail mark. **s~eckig** a hexagonal. **s~te(r,s)** a sixth

sech|zehn inv a sixteen. **s~zehnte(r,s)** a sixteenth. **s~zig** inv a sixty. **s~zigste(r,s)** a sixtieth

See¹ m -s, -n /'ze:ən/ lake

See² f - sea; **an die/der See** to/at the seaside; **auf See** at sea. **S~fahrt** f [sea] voyage; (Schifffahrt) navigation. **S~gang** m schwerer **S~gang** rough sea. **S~hund** m seal. **s~krank** a seasick

Seele f -, -n soul

seelisch a psychological; (geistig) mental

See|macht f maritime power. **S~mann** m (pl -leute) seaman, sailor. **S~not** f in **S~not** in distress. **S~reise** f [sea] voyage. **S~rose** f water-lily. **S~sack** m kitbag. **S~stern** m starfish. **S~tang** m seaweed. **s~tüchtig** a seaworthy. **S~zunge** f sole

Segel nt -s,- sail. **S~boot** nt sailing-boat. **S~flugzeug** nt glider. **s~n** vt/i (sein/haben) sail. **S~schiff** nt sailing-ship. **S~sport** m sailing. **S~tuch** nt canvas

Segen m -s blessing

Segler m -s,- yachtsman

segnen vt bless

sehen† vt see; watch <Fernsehsendung>; **jdn/etw wieder s~** see s.o./sth again; **sich s~ lassen** show oneself ● vi (haben) see;

(blicken) look (**auf** + acc at); (ragen) show (**aus** above); **gut/schlecht s~** have good/bad eyesight; **vom S~ kennen** know by sight; **s~ nach** keep an eye on; (betreuen) look after; (suchen) look for. **s~swert, s~swürdig** a worth seeing. **S~swürdigkeit** f -, -en sight

Sehne f -, -n tendon; (eines Bogens) string

sehnen (sich) vr long (**nach** for)

Sehn|sucht f - longing (**nach** for). **s~süchtig** a longing; <Wunsch> dearest

sehr adv very; (mit Verb) very much; **so s~, dass** so much that

seicht a shallow

seid s. sein¹

Seide f -, -n silk

Seidel nt -s,- beer-mug

seiden a silk ... **S~papier** nt tissue paper. **S~raupe** f silk-worm

seidig a silky

Seife f -, -n soap. **S~npulver** nt soap powder. **S~nschaum** m lather

Seil nt -[e]s, -e rope; (Draht-) cable. **S~bahn** f cable railway. **s~springen**† vi (sein) (inf & pp only) skip. **S~tänzer(in)** m(f) tightrope walker

sein†¹
● intransitive verb (sein)
····▸ be. **ich bin glücklich** I am happy. **er ist Lehrer/Schwede** he is a teacher/Swedish. **bist du es?** is that you? **sei still!** be quiet! **sie waren in Paris** they were in Paris. **morgen bin ich zu Hause** I shall be at home tomorrow. **er ist aus Berlin** he is or comes from Berlin
····▸ (impers + dat) **mir ist kalt/besser** I am cold/better. **ihr ist schlecht** she feels sick
····▸ (existieren) be. **es ist/sind ...** there is/are .... **es ist keine Hoffnung mehr** there is no more hope. **es sind vier davon** there are four of them. **es war einmal ein Prinz** once upon a time there was a prince
● auxiliary verb

S

····▸ (*zur Perfektumschreibung*) have. **er ist gestorben** he has died. **sie sind angekommen** they have arrived. **sie war dort gewesen** she had been there. **ich wäre gefallen** I would have fallen

····▸ (*zur Bildung des Passivs*) be. **wir sind gerettet worden/wir waren gerettet** we were saved

····▸ (+ *zu* + *Infinitiv*) be to be. **es war niemand zu sehen** there was no one to be seen. **das war zu erwarten** that was to be expected. **er ist zu bemitleiden** he is to be pitied. **die Richtlinien sind strengstens zu beachten** the guidelines are to be strictly followed

sein² *poss pron* his; (*Ding, Tier*) its; (*nach man*) one's; **sein Glück versuchen** try one's luck. **s~e(r,s)** *poss pron* his; (*nach man*) one's own; **das S~e tun** do one's share. **s~erseits** *adv* for his part. **s~erzeit** *adv* in those days. **s~etwegen** *adv* for his sake; (*wegen ihm*) because of him, on his account. **s~ige** *poss pron der/die/das s~ige* his

seins *poss pron* his; (*nach man*) one's own

seit *conj & prep* (+ *dat*) since; **s~ einiger Zeit** for some time [past]; **ich wohne s~ zehn Jahren hier** I've lived here for ten years. **s~dem** *conj* since ● *adv* since then

Seite *f* -, -n side; (*Buch-*) page; **zur S~ treten** step aside; **auf der einen/ anderen S~** (*fig*) on the one/other hand

seitens *prep* (+ *gen*) on the part of

Seiten|schiff *nt* [side] aisle. **S~sprung** *m* infidelity. **S~stechen** *nt* -s (*Med*) stitch. **S~straße** *f* side-street. **S~streifen** *m* verge; (*Autobahn-*) hard shoulder

seither *adv* since then

seit|lich *a* side ... ● *adv* at/on the side; **s~lich von** to one side of ● *prep* (+ *gen*) to one side of.

─────────
*alte Schreibung

s~wärts *adv* on/to one side; (*zur Seite*) sideways

Sekret|är *m* -s, -e secretary; (*Schrank*) bureau. **S~ariat** *nt* -[e]s, -e secretary's office. **S~ärin** *f* -, -nen secretary

Sekt *m* -[e]s [German] sparkling wine

Sekte *f* -, -n sect

Sektor *m* -s, -en /-'to:rən/ sector

Sekunde *f* -, -n second

selber *pron* ⒤ = selbst

selbst *pron* oneself; **ich/du/er/sie s~** I myself /you yourself/ he himself/ she herself; **wir/ihr/sie s~** we ourselves/you yourselves/they themselves; **ich schneide mein Haar s~** I cut my own hair; **von s~** of one's own accord; (*automatisch*) automatically; **s~ gemacht** home-made ● *adv* even

selbständig *a* = selbstständig. **S~keit** *f* - = Selbstständigkeit

Selbst|bedienung *f* self-service. **S~befriedigung** *f* masturbation. **s~bewusst** *a* self-confident. **S~bewusstsein** *nt* self-confidence. **S~bildnis** *nt* self-portrait. **S~erhaltung** *f* self-preservation. **s~gemacht*** *a* s~ gemacht, *s.* selbst. **s~haftend** *a* self-adhesive. **S~hilfe** *f* self-help. **s~klebend** *a* self-adhesive. **S~kostenpreis** *m* cost price. **S~laut** *m* vowel. **s~los** *a* selfless. **S~mord** *m* suicide. **S~mörder(in)** *m(f)* suicide. **s~mörderisch** *a* suicidal. **S~porträt** *nt* self-portrait. **s~sicher** *a* self-assured. **s~ständig** *a* independent; self-employed <*Handwerker*>; **sich s~ständig machen** set up on one's own. **S~ständigkeit** *f* - independence. **s~süchtig** *a* selfish. **S~tanken** *nt* self-service (*for petrol*). **s~tätig** *a* automatic. **S~versorgung** *f* self-catering. **s~verständlich** *a* natural; **etw für s~ halten** take sth for granted; **das ist s~** that goes without saying; **s~!** of course! **S~verteidigung** *f* self-defence. **S~vertrauen** nt self-confidence. **S~verwaltung** f self-government

selig a blissfully happy; (Relig) blessed; (verstorben) late. **S~keit** f - bliss

Sellerie m -s, -s & f -,- celeriac; (Stangen-) celery

selten a rare ● adv rarely, seldom; (besonders) exceptionally. **S~heit** f -, -en rarity

seltsam a odd, strange. **s~erweise** adv oddly

Semester nt -s, - (Univ) semester

Semikolon nt -s, -s semicolon

Seminar nt -s, -e seminar; (Institut) department; (Priester-) seminary

Semmel f -, -n [bread] roll. **S~brösel** pl breadcrumbs

Senat m -[e]s, -e senate. **S~or** m -s, -en /-'to:rən/ senator

senden[1]† vt send

sende|n[2] vt (reg) broadcast; (über Funk) transmit. send. **S~r** m -s,- [broadcasting] station; (Anlage) transmitter. **S~reihe** f series

Sendung f -, -en consignment, shipment; (TV) programme

Senf m -s mustard

senil a senile. **S~ität** f - senility

Senior m -s, -en /-'o:rən/ senior; **S~en** senior citizens. **S~enheim** nt old people's home

senken vt lower; bring down <Fieber, Preise>; bow <Kopf>; sich **s~** come down, fall; (absinken) subside

senkrecht a vertical. **S~e** f -n, -n perpendicular

Sensation /-'tsio:n/ f -, -en sensation. **s~ell** a sensational

Sense f -, -n scythe

sensibel a sensitive

sentimental a sentimental

September m -s,- September

Serie /'ze:riə/ f -, -n series; (Briefmarken) set; (Comm) range. **S~nnummer** f serial number

seriös a respectable; (zuverlässig) reliable

Serpentine f -, -n winding road; (Kehre) hairpin bend

Serum nt -s,Sera serum

Service[1] /zɛr'vi:s/ nt -[s],- /-'vi:s[əs], -'vi:sə/ service, set

Service[2] /'zø:ɐvis/ m & nt -s /-vis[əs]/ (Comm, Tennis) service

servier|en vt/i (haben) serve. **S~erin** f -, -nen waitress

Serviette f -, -n napkin, serviette

Servus int (Aust) cheerio; (Begrüßung) hallo

Sessel m -s,- armchair. **S~bahn** f, **S~lift** m chair-lift

sesshaft a settled

Set /zɛt/ nt & m -[s], -s set; (Deckchen) place-mat

setz|en vt put; (abstellen) set down; (hin-) sit down <Kind>; move <Spielstein>; (pflanzen) plant; (schreiben, wetten) put; sich **s~en** sit down; (sinken) settle ● vi (sein) leap ● vi (haben) **s~en auf** (+ acc) back

Seuche f -, -n epidemic

seufz|en vi (haben) sigh. **S~er** m -s,- sigh

Sex /zɛks/ m -[es] sex

Sexu|alität f - sexuality. **s~ell** a sexual

sezieren vt dissect

Shampoo /ʃam'pu:/, **Shampoon** /ʃam'po:n/ nt -s shampoo

siamesisch a Siamese

sich refl pron oneself; (mit er/sie/es) himself/herself/itself; (mit sie pl) themselves; (mit Sie) yourself; (pl) yourselves; (einander) each other; **s~** kennen know oneself/(einander) each other; **s~** waschen have a wash; **s~** (dat) die Haare kämmen comb one's hair; **s~** wundern be surprised; **s~** gut verkaufen sell well; von **s~** aus of one's own accord

Sichel f -, -n sickle

sicher a safe; (gesichert) secure; (gewiss) certain; (zuverlässig) reliable; sure <Urteil>; steady <Hand>; (selbstbewusst) self-confident; bist du **s~**? are you sure? ● adv safely; securely; certainly;

S

reliably; self-confidently; (*wahrscheinlich*) most probably; **s~!** certainly! **s~gehen†** *vi sep* (*sein*) (*fig*) be sure

Sicherheit *f* - safety; (*Pol, Psych, Comm*) security; (*Gewissheit*) certainty; (*Zuverlässigkeit*) reliability; (*des Urteils*) surety; (*Selbstbewusstsein*) self-confidence. **S~sgurt** *m* safety-belt; (*Auto*) seat-belt. **S~snadel** *f* safety-pin

sicherlich *adv* certainly; (*wahrscheinlich*) most probably

sicher|n *vt* secure; (*garantieren*) safeguard; (*schützen*) protect; put the safety-catch on <*Pistole*>. **S~ung** *f* -, -en safeguard, protection; (*Gewehr-*) safety-catch; (*Electr*) fuse

Sicht *f* - view; (*S~weite*) visibility; **auf lange S~** in the long term. **s~bar** *a* visible. **S~vermerk** *m* visa. **S~weite** *f* visibility; **außer S~weite** out of sight

sie *pron* (*nom*) (*sg*) she; (*Ding, Tier*) it; (*pl*) they; (*acc*) (*sg*) her; (*Ding, Tier*) it; (*pl*) them

Sie *pron* you; **gehen/warten Sie!** go/wait!

Sieb *nt* -[e]s, -e sieve; (*Tee-*) strainer. **s~en¹** *vt* sieve, sift

sieben² *inv a*, **S~** *f* -, -en seven. **S~sachen** *fpl* Ⓘ belongings. **s~te(r,s)** *a* seventh

sieb|te(r,s) *a* seventh. **s~zehn** *inv a* seventeen. **s~zehnte(r,s)** *a* seventeenth. **s~zig** *inv a* seventy. **s~zigste(r,s)** *a* seventieth

siede|n† *vt/i* (*haben*) boil. **S~punkt** *m* boiling point

Siedlung *f* -, -en [housing] estate; (*Niederlassung*) settlement

Sieg *m* -[e]s, -e victory

Siegel *nt* -s,- seal. **S~ring** *m* signet-ring

sieg|en *vi* (*haben*) win. **S~er(in)** *m* -s,- (*f* -, -nen) winner. **s~reich** *a* victorious

siezen *vt* jdn s~ call s.o. 'Sie'

Signal *nt* -s, -e signal

Silbe *f* -, -n syllable

Silber *nt* -s silver. **s~n** *a* silver

Silhouette /zɪ'luɛtə/ *f* -, -n silhouette

Silizium *nt* -s silicon

Silo *m & nt* -s, -s silo

Silvester *nt* -s New Year's Eve

Sims *m & nt* -es, -e ledge

simultan *a* simultaneous

sind *s.* sein¹

Sinfonie *f* -, -n symphony

singen† *vt/i* (*haben*) sing

Singvogel *m* songbird

sinken† *vi* (*sein*) sink; (*nieder-*) drop; (*niedriger werden*) go down, fall; **den Mut s~ lassen** lose courage

Sinn *m* -[e]s, -e sense; (*Denken*) mind; (*Zweck*) point; **in gewissem S~e** in a sense; **es hat keinen S~** it is pointless. **S~bild** *nt* symbol

sinnlich *a* sensory; (*sexuell*) sensual; <*Genüsse*> sensuous. **S~keit** *f* - sensuality; sensuousness

sinn|los *a* senseless; (*zwecklos*) pointless. **s~voll** *a* meaningful; (*vernünftig*) sensible

Sintflut *f* flood

Siphon /'zi:fõ/ *m* -s, -s siphon

Sippe *f* -, -n clan

Sirene *f* -, -n siren

Sirup *m* -s, -e syrup; treacle

Sitte *f* -, -n custom; **S~n** manners

sittlich *a* moral. **S~keit** *f* - morality. **S~keitsverbrecher** *m* sex offender

sittsam *a* well-behaved; (*züchtig*) demure

Situ|ation /-'tsio:n/ *f* -, -en situation. **s~iert** *a* **gut/schlecht s~iert** well/badly off

Sitz *m* -es, -e seat; (*Passform*) fit

sitzen† *vi* (*haben*) sit; (*sich befinden*) be; (*passen*) fit; (Ⓘ *treffen*) hit home; **[im Gefängnis] s~** Ⓘ be in jail; **s~ bleiben** remain seated; Ⓘ (*Sch*) stay *or* be kept down; (*nicht heiraten*) be left on the shelf; **s~ bleiben auf** (+ *dat*) be left with

Sitz|gelegenheit *f* seat. **S~platz** *m* seat. **S~ung** *f* -, -en session

Sizilien /-iən/ nt -s Sicily

Skala f -, -len scale; (Reihe) range

Skalpell nt -s, -e scalpel

skalpieren vt scalp

Skandal m -s, -e scandal. **s~ös** a scandalous

Skandinav|ien /-iən/ nt -s Scandinavia. **s~isch** a Scandinavian

Skat m -s skat

Skelett nt -[e]s, -e skeleton

Skep|sis f - scepticism. **s~tisch** a sceptical

Ski /ʃiː/ m -s, -er ski; Ski fahren od laufen ski. **S~fahrer(in)**, **S~läufer(in)** m(f) -s,- (f -, -nen) skier. **S~sport** m skiing

Skizz|e f -, -n sketch. **s~ieren** vt sketch

Sklav|e m -n, -n slave. **S~erei** f - slavery. **S~in** f -, -nen slave

Skorpion m -s, -e scorpion; (Astr) Scorpio

Skrupel m -s,- scruple. **s~los** a unscrupulous

Skulptur f -, -en sculpture

Slalom m -s, -s slalom

Slaw|e m -n, -n, **S~in** f -, -nen Slav. **s~isch** a Slav; (Lang) Slavonic

Slip m -s, -s briefs pl

Smaragd m -[e]s, -e emerald

Smoking m -s, -s dinner jacket

Snob m -s, -s snob. **S~ismus** m - snobbery **s~istisch** a snobbish

so adv so; (so sehr) so much; (auf diese Weise) like this/that; (solch) such; (⚠ sowieso) anyway; (⚠ umsonst) free; (⚠ ungefähr) about; so viel so much; so gut/bald wie as good/soon as; so ein Zufall! what a coincidence! mir ist so, als ob I feel as if; so oder so in any case; so um zehn Mark ⚠ about ten marks; so? really? ● conj (also) so; (dann) then; so dass = sodass

sobald conj as soon as

Söckchen nt -s,- [ankle] sock

Socke f -, -n sock

Sockel m -s,- plinth, pedestal

Socken m -s,- sock

sodass conj so that

Sodawasser nt soda water

Sodbrennen nt -s heartburn

soeben adv just [now]

Sofa nt -s, -s settee, sofa

sofern adv provided [that]

sofort adv at once, immediately; (auf der Stelle) instantly

Software /ˈzɔftveːɐ̯/ f - software

sogar adv even

sogenannt a so-called

sogleich adv at once

Sohle f -, -n sole; (Tal-) bottom

Sohn m -[e]s,ːe son

Sojabohne f soya bean

solange conj as long as

solch inv pron such; **s~** ein(e) such a; **s~** einer/eine/eins one/(Person) someone like that. **s~e(r,s)** pron such ● (substantivisch) ein **s~er/eine s~e/ein s~es** one/(Person) someone like that; **s~e** pl those; (Leute) people like that

Soldat m -en, -en soldier

Söldner m -s,- mercenary

Solidarität f - solidarity

solide a solid; (haltbar) sturdy; (sicher) sound; (anständig) respectable

Solist(in) m -en, -en (f -, -nen) soloist

Soll nt -s (Comm) debit; (Produktions-) quota

sollen†
● auxiliary verb
····▸ (Verpflichtung) be [supposed or meant] to. er soll morgen zum Arzt gehen he is [supposed] to go to the doctor tomorrow. die beiden Flächen sollen fluchten the two surfaces are meant to be or should be in alignment. du solltest ihn anrufen you were meant to phone him or should have phoned him
····▸ (Befehl) du sollst sofort damit aufhören you're to stop that at once. er soll hereinkommen he is to come in; (sagen Sie es ihm) tell him to come in

····▸ **sollte** (*subjunctive*) should; ought to. **wir sollten früher aufstehen** we ought to *or* should get up earlier. **das hätte er nicht tun/sagen sollen** he shouldn't have done/said that

····▸ (*Zukunft, Geplantes*) be to. **ich soll die Abteilung übernehmen** I am to take over the department. **du sollst dein Geld zurückbekommen** you are to *or* shall get your money back. **es soll nicht wieder vorkommen** it won't happen again. **sie sollten ihr Reiseziel nie erreichen** they were never to reach their destination

····▸ (*Ratlosigkeit*) be to; shall. **was soll man nur machen?** what is one to do?; what shall I/we do? **ich weiß nicht, was ich machen soll** I don't know what I should do *or* what to do

····▸ (*nach Bericht*) be supposed to. **er soll sehr reich sein** he is supposed *or* is said to be very rich. **sie soll geheiratet haben** they say *or* I gather she has got married

····▸ (*Absicht*) be meant *or* supposed to. **was soll dieses Bild darstellen?** what is this picture supposed to represent? **das sollte ein Witz sein** that was meant *or* supposed to be a joke

····▸ (*in Bedingungssätzen*) should. **sollte er anrufen, falls** *od* **wenn er anrufen sollte** should he *or* if he should telephone

● *intransitive verb*

····▸ (*irgendwohin gehen sollen*) be [supposed] to go. **er soll morgen zum Arzt/nach Berlin** he is [supposed] to go to the doctor/to Berlin tomorrow. **ich sollte ins Theater** I was supposed to go to the theatre

····▸ (*sonstige Wendungen*) **soll er doch!** let him! **was soll das?** what's that in aid of? 🗓

Solo *nt* -s, -los & -li solo

somit *adv* therefore, so

Sommer *m* -s,- summer. **s∼lich** *a* summery; (*Sommer-*) summer ... ● *adv* **s∼lich warm** as warm as summer. **S∼sprossen** *fpl* freckles

Sonate *f* -, -n sonata

Sonde *f* -, -n probe

Sonder|angebot *nt* special offer. **s∼bar** *a* odd. **S∼fahrt** *f* special excursion. **S∼fall** *m* special case. **s∼gleichen** *adv* **eine Gemeinheit s∼gleichen** unparalleled meanness. **S∼ling** *m* -s, -e crank. **S∼marke** *f* special stamp

sondern *conj* but; **nicht nur ... s∼ auch** not only ... but also

Sonder|preis *m* special price. **S∼schule** *f* special school

Sonett *nt* -[e]s, -e sonnet

Sonnabend *m* -s, -e Saturday. **s∼s** *adv* on Saturdays

Sonne *f* -, -n sun. **s∼n (sich)** *vr* sun oneself

Sonnen|aufgang *m* sunrise. **s∼baden** *vi* (*haben*) sunbathe. **S∼bank** *f* sun-bed. **S∼blume** *f* sunflower. **S∼brand** *m* sunburn. **S∼brille** *f* sunglasses *pl*. **S∼energie** *f* solar energy. **S∼finsternis** *f* solar eclipse. **S∼milch** *f* sun-tan lotion. **S∼öl** *nt* sun-tan oil. **S∼schein** *m* sunshine. **S∼schirm** *m* sunshade. **S∼stich** *m* sunstroke. **S∼uhr** *f* sundial. **S∼untergang** *m* sunset. **S∼wende** *f* solstice

sonnig *a* sunny

Sonntag *m* -s, -e Sunday. **s∼s** *adv* on Sundays

sonst *adv* (*gewöhnlich*) usually; (*im Übrigen*) apart from that; (*andernfalls*) otherwise, or [else]; **wer/was/wie/wo s∼?** who/what/how/where else? **s∼ niemand** no one else; **s∼ noch etwas?** anything else? **s∼ noch Fragen?** any more questions? **s∼ jemand** *od* **wer** someone/(*fragend, verneint*) anyone else; (*irgendjemand*) [just] anyone; **s∼ wo** somewhere/(*fragend, verneint*) anywhere else; (*irgendwo*) [just] anywhere. **s∼ig** *a* other

sooft *conj* whenever

Sopran *m* -s, -e soprano

Sorge *f* -, -n worry (**um** about); (*Fürsorge*) care; **sich** (*dat*) **S∼n machen** worry. **s∼n** *vi* (*haben*) **s∼n für** look after, care for; (*vorsorgen*) provide for; (*sich kümmern*) see to; dafür s~n, dass see or make sure that ● *vr* sich s~n worry. **s~nfrei** *a* carefree. **s~nvoll** *a* worried. **S~recht** *nt* (*Jur*) custody

Sorg|falt *f* - care. **s~fältig** *a* careful

Sorte *f* -, -n kind, sort; (*Comm*) brand

sort|ieren *vt* sort [out]; (*Comm*) grade. **S~iment** *nt* -[e]s, -e range

sosehr *conj* however much

Soße *f* -, -n sauce; (*Braten-*) gravy; (*Salat-*) dressing

Souvenir /zuvə'niːɐ̯/ *nt* -s, -s souvenir

souverän /zuvə'rɛːn/ *a* sovereign

soviel *conj* however much; s~ ich weiß as far as I know ● *adv* *so viel, s. viel

soweit *conj* as far as; (*insoweit*) [in] so far as ● *adv* *so weit, s. weit

sowenig *conj* however little ● *adv* *so wenig, s. wenig

sowie *conj* as well as; (*sobald*) as soon as

sowieso *adv* anyway, in any case

sowjet|isch *a* Soviet. **S~union** *f* - Soviet Union

sowohl *adv* s~ ... als *od* wie auch ... ... as well as ...

sozial *a* social; (*Einstellung, Beruf*) caring. **S~arbeit** *f* social work. **S~demokrat** *m* social democrat. **S~hilfe** *f* social security

Sozialis|mus *m* - socialism. **S~t** *m* -en, -en socialist

Sozial|versicherung *f* National Insurance. **S~wohnung** *f* ≈ council flat

Soziologie *f* - sociology

Sozius *m* -, -se (*Comm*) partner; (*Beifahrersitz*) pillion

Spachtel *m* -s,- & *f* -, -n spatula

Spagat *m* -[e]s, -e (*Aust*) string; S~ machen do the splits *pl*

Spaghetti, Spagetti *pl* spaghetti *sg*

Spalier *nt* -s, -e trellis

Spalt|e *f* -, -n crack; (*Gletscher-*) crevasse; (*Druck-*) column;

(*Orangen-*) segment. **s~en†** *vt* split. **S~ung** *f* -, -en splitting; (*Kluft*) split; (*Phys*) fission

Span *m* -[e]s,̈e [wood] chip

Spange *f* -, -n clasp; (*Haar-*) slide; (*Zahn-*) brace

Span|ien /-iən/ *nt* -s Spain. **S~ier** *m* -s,-, **S~ierin** *f* -, -nen Spaniard. **s~isch** *a* Spanish. **S~isch** *nt* -[s] (*Lang*) Spanish

Spann *m* -[e]s instep

Spanne *f* -, -n span; (*Zeit-*) space; (*Comm*) margin

spann|en *vt* stretch; put up <*Leine*>; (*straffen*) tighten; (*an-*) harness (an + *acc* to); sich s~en tighten ● *vi* (*haben*) be too tight. **s~end** *a* exciting. **S~ung** *f* -, -en tension; (*Erwartung*) suspense; (*Electr*) voltage

Spar|buch *nt* savings book. **S~büchse** *f* money-box. **s~en** *vt/i* (*haben*) save; (*sparsam sein*) economize (mit/an + *dat* on). **S~er** *m* -s,- saver

Spargel *m* -s,- asparagus

Spar|kasse *f* savings bank. **S~konto** *nt* deposit account

sparsam *a* economical; <*Person*> thrifty. **S~keit** *f* - economy; thrift

Sparschwein *nt* piggy bank

Sparte *f* -, -n branch; (*Zeitungs-*) section; (*Rubrik*) column

Spaß *m* -es,̈e fun; (*Scherz*) joke; im/ aus/zum S~ for fun; S~ machen be fun; <*Person:*> be joking; viel S~! have a good time! **s~en** *vi* (*haben*) joke. **S~vogel** *m* joker

Spastiker *m* -s,- spastic

spät *a* & *adv* late; wie s~ ist es? what time is it? zu s~ kommen be late

Spaten *m* -s,- spade

später *a* later; (*zukünftig*) future ● *adv* later

spätestens *adv* at the latest

Spatz *m* -en, -en sparrow

Spätzle *pl* (*Culin*) noodles

spazieren *vi* (*sein*) stroll; s~ gehen go for a walk

S

Spazier|gang m walk; einen S~gang machen go for a walk. **S~gänger(in)** m -s,- (f -, -nen) walker. **S~stock** m walking-stick

Specht m -[e]s, -e woodpecker

Speck m -s bacon. **s~ig** a greasy

Spedi|teur /ʃpedi'tøːɐ̯/ m -s, -e haulage/(für Umzüge) removals contractor. **S~tion** /-'tsioːn/ f -, -en carriage, haulage; (Firma) haulage/(für Umzüge) removals firm

Speer m -[e]s, -e spear; (Sport) javelin

Speiche f -, -n spoke

Speichel m -s saliva

Speicher m -s,- warehouse; (dial: Dachboden) attic; (Computer) memory. **s~n** vt store

Speise f -, -n food; (Gericht) dish; (Pudding) blancmange. **S~eis** nt ice-cream. **S~kammer** f larder. **S~karte** f menu. **s~n** vi (haben) eat ● vt feed. **S~röhre** f oesophagus. **S~saal** m dining-room. **S~wagen** m dining-car

Spektrum nt -s, -tra spectrum

Spekul|ant m -en, -en speculator. **s~ieren** vi (haben) speculate; **s~ieren auf** (+ acc) hope to get

Spelze f -, -n husk

spendabel a generous

Spende f -, -n donation. **s~n** vt donate; give <Blut, Schatten>; Beifall s~n applaud. **S~r** m -s,- donor; (Behälter) dispenser

spendieren vt pay for

Sperling m -s, -e sparrow

Sperre f -, -n barrier; (Verbot) ban; (Comm) embargo. **s~n** vt close; (ver-) block; (verbieten) ban; cut off <Strom, Telefon>; stop <Scheck, Kredit>; **s~n in** (+ acc) put in <Gefängnis, Käfig>

Sperr|holz nt plywood. **S~müll** m bulky refuse. **S~stunde** f closing time

Spesen pl expenses

spezial|isieren (sich) vr specialize (auf + acc in). **S~ist** m -en, -en specialist. **S~ität** f -, -en speciality

spicken vt (Culin) lard; **gespickt mit** (fig) full of ● vi (haben) ⏣ crib (bei from)

Spiegel m -s,- mirror; (Wasser-, Alkohol-) level. **S~bild** nt reflection. **S~ei** nt fried egg. **s~n** vt reflect; **sich s~n** be reflected ● vi (haben) reflect [the light]; (glänzen) gleam. **S~ung** f -, -en reflection

Spiel nt -[e]s, -e game; (Spielen) playing; (Glücks-) gambling; (Schau-) play; (Satz) set; auf dem S~ stehen be at stake; aufs S~ setzen risk. **S~automat** m fruit machine. **S~bank** f casino. **S~dose** f musical box. **s~en** vt/i (haben) play; (im Glücksspiel) gamble; (vortäuschen) act; <Roman:> be set (in + dat in); **s~en mit** (fig) toy with

Spieler(in) m -s,- (f -, -nen) player; (Glücks-) gambler

Spiel|feld nt field, pitch. **S~marke** f chip. **S~plan** m programme. **S~platz** m playground. **S~raum** m (fig) scope; (Techn) clearance. **S~regeln** fpl rules [of the game]. **S~sachen** fpl toys. **S~verderber** m -s,- spoilsport. **S~waren** fpl toys. **S~warengeschäft** nt toyshop. **S~zeug** nt toy; (S~sachen) toys pl

Spieß m -es, -e spear; (Brat-) spit; skewer; (Fleisch-) kebab. **S~er** m -s,- [petit] bourgeois. **s~ig** a bourgeois

Spike[s]reifen /'ʃpaik[s]-/ m studded tyre

Spinat m -s spinach

Spindel f -, -n spindle

Spinne f -, -n spider

spinn|en† vt/i (haben) spin; er spinnt ⏣ he's crazy. **S~[en]gewebe** nt, **S~webe** f -, -n cobweb

Spion m -s, -e spy

Spionage /ʃpio'naːʒə/ f - espionage, spying. **S~abwehr** f counter-espionage

spionieren vi (haben) spy

Spionin f -, -nen [woman] spy

Spiral|e f -, -n spiral. **s~ig** a spiral

Spirituosen pl spirits

Spiritus m - alcohol; (Brenn-) methylated spirits pl. **S~kocher** m spirit stove

spitz a pointed; (scharf) sharp; (schrill) shrill; <Winkel> acute. **S~bube** m scoundrel

Spitze f -, -n point; (oberer Teil) top; (vorderer Teil) front; (Pfeil-, Finger-, Nasen-) tip; (Schuh-, Strumpf-) toe; (Zigarren-, Zigaretten-) holder; (Höchstleistung) maximum; (Tex) lace; (🔲 Anspielung) dig; **an der S~ liegen** be in the lead

Spitzel m -s, - informer

spitzen vt sharpen; purse <Lippen>; prick up <Ohren>. **S~geschwindigkeit** f top speed

Spitzname m nickname

Spleen /ʃpliːn/ m -s, -e obsession

Splitter m -s, - splinter. **s~n** vi (sein) shatter

sponsern vt sponsor

Spore f -, -n (Biol) spore

Sporn m -[e]s, Sporen spur

Sport m -[e]s sport; (Hobby) hobby. **S~art** f sport. **S~ler** m -s, - sportsman. **S~lerin** f -, -nen sportswoman. **s~lich** a sports ...; (fair) sporting; (schlank) sporty. **S~platz** m sports ground. **S~verein** m sports club. **S~wagen** m sports car; (Kinder-) push-chair, (Amer) stroller

Spott m -[e]s mockery

spotten vi (haben) mock; **s~ über** (+ acc) make fun of; (höhnend) ridicule

spöttisch a mocking

Sprach|e f -, -n language; (Sprechfähigkeit) speech; **zur S~e bringen** bring up. **S~fehler** m speech defect. **S~labor** nt language laboratory. **s~lich** a linguistic. **s~los** a speechless

Spray /ʃpreː/ nt & m -s, -s spray. **S~dose** f aerosol [can]

Sprechanlage f intercom

sprechen† vi (haben) speak/(sich unterhalten) talk (über + acc/von about/of); **Deutsch s~** speak German ● vt speak; (sagen) say; pronounce <Urteil>; **schuldig s~** find guilty; **Herr X ist nicht zu s~** Mr X is not available

Sprecher(in) m -s, - (f -, -nen) speaker; (Radio, TV) announcer; (Wortführer) spokesman, f spokeswoman

Sprechstunde f consulting hours pl; (Med) surgery. **S~nhilfe** f (Med) receptionist

Sprechzimmer nt consulting room

spreizen vt spread

spreng|en vt blow up; blast <Felsen>; (fig) burst; (begießen) water; (mit Sprenger) sprinkle; dampen <Wäsche>. **S~er** m -s, - sprinkler. **S~kopf** m warhead. **S~körper** m explosive device. **S~stoff** m explosive

Spreu f - chaff

Sprich|wort nt (pl -wörter) proverb. **s~wörtlich** a proverbial

Springbrunnen m fountain

spring|en† vi (sein) jump; (Schwimmsport) dive; <Ball:> bounce; (spritzen) spurt; (zer-) break; (rissig werden) crack; (SGer: laufen) run. **S~er** m -s, - jumper; (Kunst-) diver; (Schach) knight. **S~reiten** nt show-jumping

Sprint m -s, -s sprint

Spritz|e f -, -n syringe; (Injektion) injection; (Feuer-) hose. **s~en** vt spray; (be-, ver-) splash; (Culin) pipe; (Med) inject ● vi (haben) splash; <Fett:> spit ● vi (sein) splash; (hervor-) spurt. **S~er** m -s, - splash; (Schuss) dash

spröde a brittle; (trocken) dry

Sprosse f -, -n rung

Sprotte f -, -n sprat

Spruch m -[e]s, ̈e saying; (Denk-) motto; (Zitat) quotation. **S~band** nt (pl -bänder) banner

Sprudel m -s, - sparkling mineral water. **s~n** vi (haben/sein) bubble

S

Sprüh|dose f aerosol [can]. **s~en** vt spray ● vi (sein) <Funken:> fly; (fig) sparkle

Sprung m -[e]s,⸚e jump, leap; (Schwimmsport) dive; (🄸 Katzen-) stone's throw; (Riss) crack. **S~brett** nt springboard. **S~schanze** f ski-jump. **S~seil** nt skipping-rope

Spucke f - spit. **s~n** vt/i (haben) spit; (sich übergeben) be sick

Spuk m -[e]s, -e [ghostly] apparition. **s~en** vi (haben) <Geist:> walk; in diesem Haus s~t es this house is haunted

Spülbecken nt sink

Spule f -, -n spool

Spüle f -, -n sink

spulen vt spool

spül|en vt rinse; (schwemmen) wash; Geschirr s~en wash up ● vi (haben) flush [the toilet]. **S~kasten** m cistern. **S~mittel** nt washing-up liquid

Spur f -, -en track; (Fahr-) lane; (Fährte) trail; (Anzeichen) trace; (Hinweis) lead

spürbar a noticeable

spür|en vt feel; (seelisch) sense. **S~hund** m tracker dog

spurlos adv without trace

spurten vi (sein) put on a spurt

sputen (sich) vr hurry

Staat m -[e]s, -en state; (Land) country; (Putz) finery. **s~lich** a state … ● adv by the state

Staatsangehörig|e(r) m/f national. **S~keit** f - nationality

Staats|anwalt m state prosecutor. **S~beamte(r)** m civil servant. **S~besuch** m state visit. **S~bürger(in)** m(f) national. **S~mann** m (pl -männer) statesman. **S~streich** m coup

Stab m -[e]s,⸚e rod; (Gitter-) bar (Sport) baton; (Mil) staff

Stäbchen ntpl chopsticks

Stabhochsprung m pole-vault

---

stabil a stable; (gesund) robust; (solide) sturdy

Stachel m -s,- spine; (Gift-) sting; (Spitze) spike. **S~beere** f gooseberry. **S~draht** m barbed wire. **S~schwein** nt porcupine

Stadion nt -s, -ien stadium

Stadium nt -s, -ien stage

Stadt f -,⸚e town; (Groß-) city

städtisch a urban; (kommunal) municipal

Stadt|mitte f town centre. **S~plan** m street map. **S~teil** m district

Staffel f -, -n team; (S~lauf) relay; (Mil) squadron

Staffelei f -, -en easel

Staffel|lauf m relay race. **s~n** vt stagger; (abstufen) grade

Stahl m -s steel. **S~beton** m reinforced concrete

Stall m -[e]s,⸚e stable; (Kuh-) shed; (Schweine-) sty; (Hühner-) coop; (Kaninchen-) hutch

Stamm m -[e]s⸚e trunk; (Sippe) tribe; (Wort-) stem. **S~baum** m family tree; (eines Tieres) pedigree

stammeln vt/i (haben) stammer

stammen vi (haben) come/(zeitlich) date (von/aus from)

stämmig a sturdy

Stamm|kundschaft f regulars pl. **S~lokal** nt favourite pub

stampfen vi (haben) stamp; <Maschine:> pound ● vi (sein) tramp ● vt pound; mash <Kartoffeln>

Stand m -[e]s,⸚e standing position; (Zustand) state; (Spiel-) score; (Höhe) level; (gesellschaftlich) class; (Verkaufs-) stall; (Messe-) stand; (Taxi-) rank; auf den neuesten S~ bringen up-date

Standard m -s, -s standard

Standbild nt statue

Ständer m -s,- stand; (Geschirr-) rack; (Kerzen-) holder

Standes|amt nt registry office. **S~beamte(r)** m registrar

standhaft a steadfast

ständig a constant; (fest) permanent

Stand|licht nt sidelights pl. **S~ort** m position; (Firmen-) location; (Mil) garrison. **S~punkt** m point of view. **S~uhr** f grandfather clock

Stange f -, -n bar; (Holz-) pole; (Gardinen-) rail; (Hühner-) perch; (Zimt-) stick; **von der S~** ⊞ off the peg

Stängel m -s,- stalk, stem

Stangenbohne f runner bean

Stanniol nt -s tin foil. **S~papier** nt silver paper

stanzen vt stamp; punch <Loch>

Stapel m -s,- stack, pile. **S~lauf** m launch[ing]. **s~n** vt stack or pile up

Star¹ m -[e]s, -e starling

Star² m -[e]s (Med) [grauer] **S~** cataract; **grüner S~** glaucoma

Star³ m -s, -s (Theat, Sport) star

stark a strong; <Motor> powerful; <Verkehr, Regen> heavy; <Hitze, Kälte> severe; (groß) big; (schlimm) bad; (dick) thick; (korpulent) stout ● adv (sehr) very much

Stärk|e f -, -n strength; power; thickness; stoutness; (Größe) size; (Mais-, Wäsche-) starch. **S~emehl** nt cornflour. **s~en** vt strengthen; starch <Wäsche>; **sich s~en** fortify oneself. **S~ung** f -, -en strengthening; (Erfrischung) refreshment

starr a rigid; (steif) stiff

starren vi (haben) stare

Starr|sinn m obstinacy. **s~sinnig** a obstinate

Start m -s, -s start; (Aviat) take-off. **S~bahn** f runway. **s~en** vi (sein) start; (Aviat) take off ● vt start; (fig) launch

Station /-'tsio:n/ f -, -en station; (Haltestelle) stop; (Abschnitt) stage; (Med) ward; **S~ machen** break one's journey. **s~är** adv as an inpatient. **s~ieren** vt station

statisch a static

Statist(in) m -en, -en (f -, -nen) (Theat) extra

Statisti|k f -, -en statistics sg; (Aufstellung) statistics pl. **s~sch** a statistical

Stativ nt -s, -e (Phot) tripod

statt prep (+ gen) instead of; **an seiner s~** in his place; **an Kindes s~ annehmen** adopt ● conj **s~ etw zu tun** instead of doing sth. **s~dessen** adv instead

statt|finden† vi sep (haben) take place. **s~haft** a permitted

Statue /'ʃta:tuə/ f -, -n statue

Statur f - build, stature

Status m - status. **S~symbol** nt status symbol

Statut nt -[e]s, -en statute

Stau m -[e]s, -s congestion; (Auto) [traffic] jam; (Rück-) tailback

Staub m -[e]s dust; **S~ wischen** dust; **S~ saugen** vacuum, hoover

Staubecken nt reservoir

staub|ig a dusty. **s~saugen** vt/i (haben) vacuum, hoover. **S~sauger** m vacuum cleaner, Hoover (P)

Staudamm m dam

stauen vt dam up; **sich s~** accumulate; <Autos:> form a tailback

staunen vi (haben) be amazed or astonished

Stau|see m reservoir. **S~ung** f -, -en congestion; (Auto) [traffic] jam

Steak /ʃte:k, ste:k/ nt -s, -s steak

stechen† vt stick (in + acc in); (verletzen) prick; (mit Messer) stab; <Insekt:> sting; <Mücke:> bite ● vi (haben) prick; <Insekt:> sting; <Mücke:> bite; (mit Stechuhr) clock in/out; **in See s~** put to sea

Stech|ginster m gorse. **S~kahn** m punt. **S~palme** f holly. **S~uhr** f time clock

Steck|brief m 'wanted' poster. **S~dose** f socket. **s~en** vt put; (mit Nadel, Reißzwecke) pin; (pflanzen) plant ● vi (haben) be; (fest-) be stuck; **s~ bleiben** get stuck; **den Schlüssel s~ lassen** leave the key in the lock

Steckenpferd nt hobby-horse

Steck|er m -s,- (Electr) plug. **S~nadel** f pin

Steg m -[e]s, -e foot-bridge; (Boots-) landing-stage; (Brillen-) bridge

stehen† *vi* (*haben*) stand; (*sich befinden*) be; (*still-*) be stationary; <*Maschine, Uhr:*> have stopped; s~ **bleiben** remain standing; <*Gebäude:*> be left standing; (*anhalten*) stop; <*Motor:*> stall; <*Zeit:*> stand still; **vor dem Ruin** s~ face ruin; **zu jdm/etw** s~ (*fig*) stand by s.o./sth; **jdm [gut]** s~ suit s.o.; **sich gut** s~ be on good terms; **es steht 3 zu 1** the score is 3–1. **s~d** *a* standing; (*sich nicht bewegend*) stationary; <*Gewässer*> stagnant

Stehlampe *f* standard lamp

stehlen† *vt/i* (*haben*) steal; **sich** s~ steal, creep

Steh|platz *m* standing place. **S~vermögen** *nt* stamina, staying-power

steif *a* stiff

Steig|bügel *m* stirrup. **S~eisen** *nt* crampon

steigen† *vi* (*sein*) climb; (*hochgehen*) rise, go up; <*Schulden, Spannung:*> mount; s~ **auf** (+ *acc*) climb on [to] <*Stuhl*>; climb <*Berg, Leiter*>; get on <*Pferd, Fahrrad*>; s~ **in** (+ *acc*) climb into; get in <*Auto*>; get on <*Bus, Zug*>; s~ **aus** climb out of; get out of <*Bett, Auto*>; get off <*Bus, Zug*>; s~**de Preise** rising prices

steiger|n *vt* increase; **sich** s~**n** increase; (*sich verbessern*) improve. **S~ung** *f* -, -en increase; improvement; (*Gram*) comparison

steil *a* steep. **S~küste** *f* cliffs *pl*

Stein *m* -[e]s, -e stone; (*Ziegel-*) brick; (*Spiel-*) piece. **S~bock** *m* ibex; (*Astr*) Capricorn. **S~bruch** *m* quarry. **S~garten** *m* rockery. **S~gut** *nt* earthenware. **s~ig** *a* stony. **s~igen** *vt* stone. **S~kohle** *f* [hard] coal. **S~schlag** *m* rock fall

Stelle *f* -, -n place; (*Fleck*) spot; (*Abschnitt*) passage; (*Stellung*) job, post; (*Behörde*) authority; **auf der** S~ immediately

stellen *vt* put; (*aufrecht*) stand; set <*Wecker, Aufgabe*>; ask <*Frage*>; make <*Antrag, Forderung,*

Diagnose>; **zur Verfügung** s~ provide; **lauter/leiser** s~ turn up/down; **kalt/warm** s~ chill/keep hot; **sich** s~ [go and] stand; give oneself up (**der Polizei** to the police); **sich tot** s~ pretend to be dead; **gut gestellt sein** be well off

Stellen|anzeige *f* job advertisement. **S~vermittlung** *f* employment agency. **s~weise** *adv* in places

Stellung *f* -, -en position; (*Arbeit*) job; S~ **nehmen** make a statement (**zu** on). **S~suche** *f* job-hunting

Stellvertreter *m* deputy

Stelzen *fpl* stilts. s~ *vi* (*sein*) stalk

stemmen *vt* press; lift <*Gewicht*>

Stempel *m* -s,- stamp; (*Post-*) postmark; (*Präge-*) die; (*Feingehalts-*) hallmark. **s~n** *vt* stamp; hallmark <*Silber*>; cancel <*Marke*>

Stengel* *m* -s,- s. Stängel

Steno *f* - ⒤ shorthand

Steno|gramm *nt* -[e]s, -e shorthand text. **S~grafie** *f* - shorthand. **s~grafieren** *vt* take down in shorthand ● *vi* (*haben*) do shorthand

Steppdecke *f* quilt

Steppe *f* -, -n steppe

Stepptanz *m* tap-dance

sterben† *vi* (*sein*) die (**an** + *dat* of); **im** S~ **liegen** be dying

sterblich *a* mortal. **S~keit** *f* - mortality

stereo *adv* in stereo. **S~anlage** *f* stereo [system]

steril *a* sterile. **s~isieren** *vt* sterilize. **S~ität** *f* - sterility

Stern *m* -[e]s, -e star. **S~bild** *nt* constellation. **S~chen** *nt* -s,- asterisk. **S~kunde** *f* astronomy. **S~schnuppe** *f* -, -n shooting star. **S~warte** *f* -, -n observatory

stets *adv* always

Steuer[1] *nt* -s,- steering-wheel; (*Naut*) helm; **am** S~ at the wheel

Steuer[2] *f* -, -n tax

Steuer|bord *nt* -[e]s starboard [side]. **S~erklärung** *f* tax return. **s~frei** *a* & *adv* tax-free. **S~mann**

s

m (*pl* -**leute**) helmsman; (*beim
Rudern*) cox. **s~n** *vt* steer; (*Aviat*)
pilot; (*Techn*) control ● *vi* (*haben*) be
at the wheel/(*Naut*) helm.
s~pflichtig *a* taxable. **S~rad** *nt*
steering-wheel. **S~ruder** *nt* helm.
S~ung *f* - steering; (*Techn*) controls
pl. **S~zahler** *m* -s,- taxpayer

Stewardess /'stjuːɛdɛs/ *f* -, -en air
hostess, stewardess

Stich *m* -[e]s, -e prick; (*Messer-*) stab;
(*S~wunde*) stab wound; (*Bienen-*)
sting; (*Mücken-*) bite; (*Schmerz*)
stabbing pain; (*Näh-*) stitch; (*Kupfer-*)
engraving; (*Kartenspiel*) trick

stick|en *vt/i* (*haben*) embroider.
S~erei *f* - embroidery

Stickstoff *m* nitrogen

Stiefel *m* -s,- boot

Stief|kind *nt* stepchild. **S~mutter**
f stepmother. **S~mütterchen** *nt*
-s,- pansy. **S~sohn** *m* stepson.
S~tochter *f* stepdaughter.
S~vater *m* stepfather

Stiege *f* -, -n stairs *pl*

Stiel *m* -[e]s, -e handle; (*Blumen-,
Gläser-*) stem; (*Blatt-*) stalk

Stier *m* -[e]s, -e bull; (*Astr*) Taurus

Stierkampf *m* bullfight

Stift¹ *m* -[e]s, -e pin; (*Nagel*) tack;
(*Blei-*) pencil; (*Farb-*) crayon

Stift² *nt* -[e]s, -e [endowed]
foundation. **s~en** *vt* endow;
(*spenden*) donate; create <*Unheil,
Verwirrung*>; bring about
<*Frieden*>. **S~ung** *f* -, -en
foundation; (*Spende*) donation

Stil *m* -[e]s, -e style

still *a* quiet; (*reglos, ohne
Kohlensäure*) still; (*heimlich*) secret;
der **S~e** Ozean the Pacific; im **S~en**
secretly. **S~e** *f* - quiet; (*Schweigen*)
silence

Stilleben* *nt s.* **Stillleben**

stillen *vt* satisfy; quench <*Durst*>;
stop <*Schmerzen, Blutung*>; breast-
feed <*Kind*>

still|halten† *vi sep* (*haben*) keep
still. **S~leben** *nt* still life

Still|schweigen *nt* silence.
S~stand *m* standstill; **zum**

S~stand bringen/kommen stop.
s~stehen† *vi sep* (*haben*) stand
still; (*anhalten*) stop; <*Verkehr:*> be
at a standstill

Stimm|bänder *ntpl* vocal cords.
s~berechtigt *a* entitled to vote.
S~bruch *m* er ist im **S~bruch** his
voice is breaking

Stimme *f* -, -n voice; (*Wahl-*) vote

stimmen *vi* (*haben*) be right;
(*wählen*) vote ● *vt* tune

Stimmung *f* -, -en mood;
(*Atmosphäre*) atmosphere

Stimmzettel *m* ballot-paper

stink|en† *vi* (*haben*) smell/(*stark*)
stink (nach of). **S~tier** *nt* skunk

Stipendium *nt* -s, -ien scholarship;
(*Beihilfe*) grant

Stirn *f* -, -en forehead

stochern *vi* (*haben*) **s~ in** (+ *dat*)
poke <*Feuer*>; pick at <*Essen*>

Stock¹ *m* -[e]s, ̈e stick; (*Ski-*) pole;
(*Bienen-*) hive; (*Rosen-*) bush; (*Reb-*)
vine

Stock² *m* -[e]s,- storey, floor.
S~bett *nt* bunk-beds *pl*.

stock|en *vi* (*haben*) stop;
<*Verkehr:*> come to a standstill;
<*Person:*> falter. **S~ung** *f* -, -en
hold-up

Stockwerk *nt* storey, floor

Stoff *m* -[e]s, -e substance; (*Tex*)
fabric, material; (*Thema*) subject
[matter]; (*Gesprächs-*) topic.
S~wechsel *m* metabolism

stöhnen *vi* (*haben*) groan, moan

Stola *f* -, -len stole

Stollen *m* -s,- gallery; (*Kuchen*)
stollen

stolpern *vi* (*sein*) stumble; **s~ über**
(+ *acc*) trip over

stolz *a* proud (auf + *acc* of). **S~** *m*
-es pride

stopfen *vt* stuff; (*stecken*) put;
(*ausbessern*) darn ● *vi* (*haben*) be
constipating

Stopp *m* -s, -s stop. **s~** *int* stop!

stoppelig *a* stubbly

stopp|en *vt* stop; (*Sport*) time ● *vi*
(*haben*) stop. **S~uhr** *f* stop-watch

Stöpsel *m* -s,- plug; (*Flaschen-*) stopper

Storch *m* -[e]s,ⁱ e stork

Store /ʃtoːɐ̯/ *m* -s, -s net curtain

stören *vt* disturb; disrupt <*Rede*>; jam <*Sender*>; (*missfallen*) bother ● *vi* (*haben*) be a nuisance

stornieren *vt* cancel

störrisch *a* stubborn

Störung *f* -, -en disturbance; disruption; (*Med*) trouble; (*Radio*) interference; **technische S~** technical fault

Stoß *m* -es,ⁱ e push, knock; (*mit Ellbogen*) dig; (*Hörner-*) butt; (*mit Waffe*) thrust; (*Schwimm-*) stroke; (*Ruck*) jolt; (*Erd-*) shock; (*Stapel*) stack, pile. **S~dämpfer** *m* -s,- shock absorber

stoßen† *vt* push, knock; (*mit Füßen*) kick; (*mit Kopf*) butt; (*an-*) poke, nudge; (*treiben*) thrust; **sich s~** knock oneself; **sich** (*dat*) **den Kopf s~** hit one's head ● *vi* (*haben*) push; **s~ an** (+ *acc*) knock against; (*angrenzen*) adjoin ● *vi* (*sein*) **s~ gegen** knock against; bump into <*Tür*>; **s~ auf** (+ *acc*) bump into; (*entdecken*) come across; strike <*Öl*>

Stoß|stange *f* bumper. **S~verkehr** *m* rush-hour traffic. **S~zahn** *m* tusk. **S~zeit** *f* rush-hour

stottern *vt/i* (*haben*) stutter, stammer

Str. *abbr* (*Straße*) St

Strafanstalt *f* prison

Strafe *f* -, -n punishment; (*Jur & fig*) penalty; (*Geld-*) fine; (*Freiheits-*) sentence. **s~n** *vt* punish

straff *a* tight, taut. **s~en** *vt* tighten

Strafgesetz *nt* criminal law

sträf|lich *a* criminal. **S~ling** *m* -s, -e prisoner

Straf|mandat *nt* (*Auto*) [parking/ speeding] ticket. **S~porto** *nt* excess postage. **S~raum** *m* penalty area. **S~stoß** *m* penalty. **S~tat** *f* crime

Strahl *m* -[e]s, -en ray; (*einer Taschenlampe*) beam; (*Wasser-*) jet. **s~en** *vi* (*haben*) shine; (*funkeln*) sparkle; (*lächeln*) beam. **S~enbehandlung** *f* radiotherapy. **S~ung** *f* - radiation

Strähne *f* -, -n strand

stramm *a* tight

Strampel|höschen /-sç-/ *nt* -s,- rompers *pl*. **s~n** *vi* (*haben*) <*Baby:*> kick

Strand *m* -[e]s,ⁱ e beach. **s~en** *vi* (*sein*) run aground

Strang *m* -[e]s,ⁱ e rope

Strapaz|e *f* -, -n strain. **s~ieren** *vt* be hard on; tax <*Nerven*>

Strass *m* - & -es paste

Straße *f* -, -n road; (*in der Stadt auch*) street; (*Meeres-*) strait. **S~nbahn** *f* tram. **S~nkarte** *f* road-map. **S~nsperre** *f* road-block

Strat|egie *f* -, -n strategy. **s~egisch** *a* strategic

Strauch *m* -[e]s, Sträucher bush

Strauß¹ *m* -es, Sträuße bunch [of flowers]; (*Bukett*) bouquet

Strauß² *m* -es, -e ostrich

streben *vi* (*haben*) strive (**nach** for) ● *vi* (*sein*) head (**nach/zu** for)

Streber *m* -s,- pushy person

Strecke *f* -, -n stretch, section; (*Entfernung*) distance; (*Rail*) line; (*Route*) route

strecken *vt* stretch; (*aus-*) stretch out; (*gerade machen*) straighten; (*Culin*) thin down; **den Kopf aus dem Fenster s~** put one's head out of the window

Streich *m* -[e]s, -e prank, trick

streicheln *vt* stroke

streichen† *vt* spread; (*weg-*) smooth; (*an-*) paint; (*aus-*) delete; (*kürzen*) cut ● *vi* (*haben*) **s~ über** (+ *acc*) stroke

Streichholz *nt* match

Streich|instrument *nt* stringed instrument. **S~käse** *m* cheese spread. **S~orchester** *nt* string orchestra. **S~ung** *f* -, -en deletion; (*Kürzung*) cut

Streife *f* -, -n patrol

S

streifen *vt* brush against; (*berühren*) touch; (*verletzen*) graze; (*fig*) touch on <*Thema*>

Streifen *m* **-s,-** stripe; (*Licht-*) streak; (*auf der Fahrbahn*) line; (*schmales Stück*) strip

Streifenwagen *m* patrol car

Streik *m* **-s, -s** strike; **in den S~ treten** go on strike. **S~brecher** *m* strike-breaker, (*pej*) scab. **s~en** *vi* (*haben*) strike; [!] refuse; (*versagen*) pack up

Streit *m* **-[e]s, -e** quarrel; (*Auseinandersetzung*) dispute. **s~en**† *vr/i* (*haben*) **[sich] s~en** quarrel. **S~igkeiten** *fpl* quarrels. **S~kräfte** *fpl* armed forces

streng *a* strict; <*Blick, Ton*> stern; (*rau, nüchtern*) severe; <*Geschmack*> sharp; **s~ genommen** strictly speaking. **S~e** *f* **-** strictness; sternness; severity

Stress *m* **-es, -e** stress

streuen *vt* spread; (*ver-*) scatter; sprinkle <*Zucker, Salz*>; **die Straßen s~** grit the roads

streunen *vi* (*sein*) roam

Strich *m* **-[e]s, -e** line; (*Feder-, Pinsel-*) stroke; (*Morse-, Gedanken-*) dash. **S~kode** *m* bar code. **S~punkt** *m* semicolon

Strick *m* **-[e]s, -e** cord; (*Seil*) rope

strick|en *vt/i* (*haben*) knit. **S~jacke** *f* cardigan. **S~leiter** *f* rope-ladder. **S~nadel** *f* knitting-needle. **S~waren** *fpl* knitwear *sg*. **S~zeug** *nt* knitting

striegeln *vt* groom

strittig *a* contentious

Stroh *nt* **-[e]s** straw. **S~blumen** *fpl* everlasting flowers. **S~dach** *nt* thatched roof. **S~halm** *m* straw

Strolch *m* **-[e]s, -e** [!] rascal

Strom *m* **-[e]s,¨-e** river; (*Menschen-, Auto-, Blut-*) stream; (*Tränen-*) flood; (*Schwall*) torrent; (*Electr*) current, power; **gegen den S~** (*fig*) against the tide. **s~abwärts** *adv* downstream. **s~aufwärts** *adv* upstream

strömen *vi* (*sein*) flow; <*Menschen, Blut:*> stream, pour

Strom|kreis *m* circuit. **s~linienförmig** *a* streamlined. **S~sperre** *f* power cut

Strömung *f* **-, -en** current

Strophe *f* **-, -n** verse

Strudel *m* **-s,-** whirlpool; (*SGer Culin*) strudel

Strumpf *m* **-[e]s,¨-e** stocking; (*Knie-*) sock. **S~band** *nt* (*pl* **-bänder**) suspender. **S~hose** *f* tights *pl*

Strunk *m* **-[e]s,¨-e** stalk

struppig *a* shaggy

Stube *f* **-, -n** room. **s~nrein** *a* house-trained

Stuck *m* **-s** stucco

Stück *nt* **-[e]s, -e** piece; (*Zucker-*) lump; (*Seife*) tablet; (*Theater-*) play; (*Gegenstand*) item; (*Exemplar*) specimen; **ein S~** (*Entfernung*) some way. **S~chen** *nt* **-s,-** [little] bit. **s~weise** *adv* bit by bit; (*einzeln*) singly

Student|(in) *m* **-en, -en** (*f* **-, -nen**) student. **s~isch** *a* student ...

Studie /-i̯ə/ *f* **-, -n** study

studieren *vt/i* (*haben*) study

Studio *nt* **-s, -s** studio

Studium *nt* **-s, -ien** studies *pl*

Stufe *f* **-, -n** step; (*Treppen-*) stair; (*Raketen-*) stage; (*Niveau*) level. **s~n** *vt* terrace; (*staffeln*) grade

Stuhl *m* **-[e]s,¨-e** chair; (*Med*) stools *pl*. **S~gang** *m* bowel movement

stülpen *vt* put (**über** + *acc* over)

stumm *a* dumb; (*schweigsam*) silent

Stummel *m* **-s,-** stump; (*Zigaretten-*) butt; (*Bleistift-*) stub

Stümper *m* **-s,-** bungler

stumpf *a* blunt; <*Winkel*> obtuse; (*glanzlos*) dull; (*fig*) apathetic. **S~** *m* **-[e]s,¨-e** stump

Stumpfsinn *m* apathy; tedium

Stunde *f* **-, -n** hour; (*Sch*) lesson

stunden *vt* **jdm eine Schuld s~** give s.o. time to pay a debt

Stunden|kilometer *mpl* kilometres per hour. **s~lang** *adv* for hours. **S~lohn** *m* hourly rate.

S~plan *m* timetable. **s~weise** *adv* by the hour

stündlich *a & adv* hourly

stur *a* pigheaded

Sturm *m* -[e]s,ᵉe gale; storm; (*Mil*) assault

stürm|en *vi* (*haben*) <*Wind:*> blow hard ● *vi* (*sein*) rush ● *vt* storm; (*bedrängen*) besiege. **S~er** *m* -s,- forward. **s~isch** *a* stormy; <*Überfahrt*> rough

Sturz *m* -es,ᵉe [heavy] fall; (*Preis-*) sharp drop; (*Pol*) overthrow

stürzen *vi* (*sein*) fall [heavily]; (*in die Tiefe*) plunge; <*Preise:*> drop sharply; <*Regierung:*> fall; (*eilen*) rush ● *vt* throw; (*umkippen*) turn upside down; turn out <*Speise, Kuchen*>; (*Pol*) overthrow, topple; **sich s~** throw oneself (**aus/in** + *acc* out of/into)

Sturzhelm *m* crash-helmet

Stute *f* -, -n mare

Stütze *f* -, -n support

stützen *vt* support; (*auf-*) rest; **sich s~ auf** (+ *acc*) lean on

stutzig *a* puzzled; (*misstrauisch*) suspicious

Stützpunkt *m* (*Mil*) base

Substantiv *nt* -s, -e noun

Substanz *f* -, -en substance

Subvention /-'tsi̯oːn/ *f* -, -en subsidy. **s~ieren** *vt* subsidize

Such|e *f* - search; **auf der S~e nach** looking for. **s~en** *vt* look for; (*intensiv*) search for; seek <*Hilfe, Rat*>; 'Zimmer gesucht' 'room wanted' ● *vi* (*haben*) look, search (**nach** for). **S~er** *m* -s,- (*Phot*) viewfinder

Sucht *f* -,ᵉe addiction; (*fig*) mania

süchtig *a* addicted. **S~e(r)** *m/f* addict

Süd *m* -[e]s south. **S~afrika** *nt* South Africa. **S~amerika** *nt* South America. **s~deutsch** *a* South German

Süden *m* -s south; **nach S~** south

Süd|frucht *f* tropical fruit. **s~lich** *a* southern; <*Richtung*> southerly ● *adv & prep* (+ *gen*) **s~lich der Stadt** south of the town. **S~pol** *m* South Pole. **s~wärts** *adv* southwards

Sühne *f* -, -n atonement; (*Strafe*) penalty. **s~n** *vt* atone for

Sultanine *f* -, -n sultana

Sülze *f* -, -n [meat] jelly

Summe *f* -, -n sum

summen *vi* (*haben*) hum; <*Biene:*> buzz ● *vt* hum

summieren (sich) *vr* add up

Sumpf *m* -[e]s,ᵉe marsh, swamp

Sünd|e *f* -, -n sin. **S~enbock** *m* scapegoat. **S~er(in)** *m* -s,- (*f* -, -nen) sinner. **s~igen** *vi* (*haben*) sin

super *inv a* 🔢 great. **S~markt** *m* supermarket

Suppe *f* -, -n soup. **S~nlöffel** *m* soup-spoon. **S~nteller** *m* soup-plate. **S~nwürfel** *m* stock cube

Surf|brett /'sœːɐ̯f-/ *nt* surfboard. **S~en** *nt* -s surfing

surren *vi* (*haben*) whirr

süß *a* sweet. **S~e** *f* - sweetness. **s~en** *vt* sweeten. **S~igkeit** *f* -, -en sweet. **s~lich** *a* sweetish; (*fig*) sugary. **S~speise** *f* sweet. **S~stoff** *m* sweetener. **S~waren** *fpl* confectionery *sg*, sweets *pl*. **S~wasser-** *pref* freshwater …

Sylvester *nt* -s = Silvester

Symbol *nt* -s, -e symbol. **S~ik** *f* - symbolism. **s~isch** *a* symbolic

Sym|metrie *f* - symmetry. **s~metrisch** *a* symmetrical

Sympathie *f* -, -n sympathy

sympathisch *a* agreeable; <*Person*> likeable

Symptom *nt* -s, -e symptom. **s~atisch** *a* symptomatic

Synagoge *f* -, -n synagogue

synchronisieren /zʏnkroniˈziːrən/ *vt* synchronize; dub <*Film*>

Syndikat *nt* -[e]s, -e syndicate

Syndrom *nt* -s, -e syndrome

synonym *a* synonymous

Synthese f -, -n synthesis
Syrien /-iən/ nt -s Syria
System nt -s, -e system. **s~atisch** a systematic
Szene f -, -n scene

Tt

Tabak m -s, -e tobacco
Tabelle f -, -n table; (Sport) league table
Tablett nt -[e]s, -s tray
Tablette f -, -n tablet
tabu a taboo. **T~** nt -s, -s taboo
Tacho m -s, -s, **Tachometer** m & nt speedometer
Tadel m -s,- reprimand; (Kritik) censure; (Sch) black mark. **t~los** a impeccable. **t~n** vt reprimand; censure
Tafel f -, -n (Tisch, Tabelle) table; (Platte) slab; (Anschlag-, Hinweis-) board; (Gedenk-) plaque; (Schiefer-) slate; (Wand-) blackboard; (Bild-) plate; (Schokolade) bar
Täfelung f - panelling
Tag m -[e]s, -e day; unter T~e underground; es wird Tag it is getting light; guten Tag! good morning/afternoon!
Tage|buch nt diary. **t~lang** adv for days
Tages|anbruch m daybreak. **T~ausflug** m day trip. **T~decke** f bedspread. **T~karte** f day ticket; (Speise-) menu of the day. **T~licht** nt daylight. **T~mutter** f childminder. **T~ordnung** f agenda. **T~rückfahrkarte** f day return [ticket]. **T~zeit** f time of the day. **T~zeitung** f daily [news]paper
täglich a & adv daily; zweimal t~ twice a day
tags adv by day; t~ zuvor/darauf the day before/after

tagsüber adv during the day
tag|täglich a daily ● adv every single day. **T~ung** f -, -en meeting; conference
Taille /'taljə/ f -, -n waist. **t~iert** /ta'ji:ɐt/ a fitted
Takt m -[e]s, -e tact; (Mus) bar; (Tempo) time; (Rhythmus) rhythm; im T~ in time
Taktik f - tactics pl.
takt|los a tactless. **T~losigkeit** f - tactlessness. **T~stock** m baton. **t~voll** a tactful
Tal nt -[e]s, -e valley
Talar m -s, -e robe; (Univ) gown
Talent nt -[e]s, -e talent. **t~iert** a talented
Talg m -s tallow; (Culin) suet
Talsperre f dam
Tampon /tam'põ:/ m -s, -s tampon
Tank m -s, -s tank. **t~en** vt fill up with <Benzin> ● vi (haben) fill up with petrol; (Aviat) refuel. **T~er** m -s,- tanker. **T~stelle** f petrol station. **T~wart** m -[e]s, -e petrol-pump attendant
Tanne f -, -n fir [tree]. **T~nbaum** m fir tree; (Weihnachtsbaum) Christmas tree. **T~nzapfen** m fir cone
Tante f -, -n aunt
Tantiemen /tan'tie:mən/ pl royalties
Tanz m -es,-e dance. **t~en** vt/i (haben) dance
Tänzer(in) m -s,- (f -, -nen) dancer
Tapete f -, -n wallpaper
tapezieren vt paper
tapfer a brave. **T~keit** f - bravery
Tarif m -s, -e rate; (Verzeichnis) tariff
tarn|en vt disguise; (Mil) camouflage. **T~ung** f - disguise; camouflage
Tasche f -, -n bag; (Hosen-, Mantel-) pocket. **T~nbuch** nt paperback. **T~ndieb** m pickpocket. **T~ngeld** nt pocket-money. **T~nlampe** f torch. **T~nmesser** nt penknife. **T~ntuch** nt handkerchief
Tasse f -, -n cup

s

t

Tastatur f -, -en keyboard

Tast|e f -, -n key; (Druck-) push-button. **t~en** vi (haben) feel, grope (nach for) ● vt key in <Daten>; **sich t~en** feel one's way (zu to)

Tat f -, -en action; (Helden-) deed; (Straf-) crime; **auf frischer Tat ertappt** caught in the act

Täter(in) m -s,- (f -, -nen) culprit; (Jur) offender

tätig a active; **t~ sein** work. **T~keit** f -, -en activity; (Arbeit) work, job

Tatkraft f energy

Tatort m scene of the crime

tätowier|en vt tattoo. **T~ung** f -, -en tattooing; (Bild) tattoo

Tatsache f fact. **T~nbericht** m documentary

tatsächlich a actual

Tatze f -, -n paw

Tau¹ m -[e]s dew

Tau² nt -[e]s, -e rope

taub a deaf; (gefühllos) numb

Taube f -, -n pigeon; dove. **T~nschlag** m pigeon-loft

Taub|heit f - deafness. **t~stumm** a deaf and dumb

tauch|en vt dip, plunge; (unter-) duck ● vi (haben/sein) dive/(ein-) plunge (in + acc into); (auf-) appear (aus out of). **T~er** m -s,- diver. **T~eranzug** m diving-suit

tauen vi (sein) melt, thaw ● impers **es taut** it is thawing

Tauf|becken nt font. **T~e** f -, -n christening, baptism. **t~en** vt christen, baptize. **T~pate** m godfather

taugen vi (haben) **etwas/nichts t~n** be good/no good

tauglich a suitable; (Mil) fit

Tausch m -[e]s, -e exchange, 🔲 swap. **t~en** vt exchange/(handeln) barter (gegen for) ● vi (haben) swap (mit etw sth; mit jdm with s.o.)

täuschen vt deceive, fool; betray <Vertrauen>; **sich t~** delude oneself; (sich irren) be mistaken ● vi (haben)

be deceptive. **t~d** a deceptive; <Ähnlichkeit> striking

Täuschung f -, -en deception; (Irrtum) mistake; (Illusion) delusion

tausend inv a one/a thousand. **T~** nt -, -e thousand. **T~füßler** m -s,- centipede. **t~ste(r, s)** a thousandth. **T~stel** nt -s,- thousandth

Tau|tropfen m dewdrop. **T~wetter** nt thaw

Taxe f -, -n charge; (Kur-) tax; (Taxi) taxi

Taxi nt -s, -s taxi, cab

Taxi|fahrer m taxi driver. **T~stand** m taxi rank

Teakholz /'ti:k-/ nt teak

Team /ti:m/ nt -s, -s team

Techni|k f -, -en technology; (Methode) technique. **T~ker** m -s,- technician. **t~sch** a technical; (technologisch) technological; **T~sche Hochschule** Technical University

Techno|logie f -, -n technology. **t~logisch** a technological

Teddybär m teddy bear

Tee m -s, -s tea. **T~beutel** m tea-bag. **T~kanne** f teapot. **T~löffel** m teaspoon

Teer m -s tar. **t~en** vt tar

Tee|sieb nt tea-strainer. **T~wagen** m [tea] trolley

Teich m -[e]s, -e pond

Teig m -[e]s, -e pastry; (Knet-) dough; (Rühr-) mixture; (Pfannkuchen-) batter. **T~rolle** f rolling-pin. **T~waren** fpl pasta sg

Teil m -[e]s, -e part; (Bestand-) component; (Jur) party; **zum T~** partly; **zum großen/größten T~** for the most part ● m & nt -[e]s (Anteil) share; **ich für mein[en] T~** for my part ● nt -[e]s, -e part; (Ersatz-) spare part; (Anbau-) unit

teil|bar a divisible. **T~chen** nt -s,- particle. **t~en** vt divide; (auf-) share out; (gemeinsam haben) share; (Pol) partition <Land>; **sich (dat) etw t~en** share sth; **sich t~en** divide;

(*sich gabeln*) fork; <*Meinungen:*> differ ● *vi* (*haben*) share

Teilhaber *m* -s,- (*Comm*) partner

Teilnahme *f* - participation; (*innere*) interest; (*Mitgefühl*) sympathy

teilnehm|en† *vi sep* (*haben*) t~en an (+ *dat*) take part in; (*mitfühlen*) share [in]. **T~er(in)** *m* -s,- (*f* -, -nen) participant; (*an Wettbewerb*) competitor

teil|s *adv* partly. **T~ung** *f* -, -en division; (*Pol*) partition. **t~weise** *a* partial ● *adv* partially, partly. **T~zahlung** *f* part-payment; (*Rate*) instalment. **T~zeitbeschäftigung** *f* part-time job

Teint /tɛ̃:/ *m* -s, -s complexion

Telefax *nt* fax

Telefon *nt* -s, -e [tele]phone. **T~anruf** *m*, **T~at** *nt* -[e]s, -e [tele]phone call. **T~buch** *nt* [tele]phone book. **t~ieren** *vi* (*haben*) [tele]phone

telefon|isch *a* [tele]phone ... ● *adv* by [tele]phone. **T~ist(in)** *m* -en, -en (*f* -, -nen) telephonist. **T~karte** *f* phone card. **T~nummer** *f* [tele]phone number. **T~zelle** *f* [tele]phone box

Telegraf *m* -en, -en telegraph. **T~enmast** *m* telegraph pole. **t~ieren** *vi* (*haben*) send a telegram. **t~isch** *a* telegraphic ● *adv* by telegram

Telegramm *nt* -s, -e telegram

Teleobjektiv *nt* telephoto lens

Telepathie *f* - telepathy

Teleskop *nt* -s, -e telescope

Telex *nt* -, -[e] telex. **t~en** *vt* telex

Teller *m* -s,- plate

Tempel *m* -s,- temple

Temperament *nt* -s, -e temperament; (*Lebhaftigkeit*) vivacity

Temperatur *f* -, -en temperature

Tempo *nt* -s, -s speed; T~ [T~]! hurry up!

Tendenz *f* -, -en trend; (*Neigung*) tendency

Tennis *nt* - tennis. **T~platz** *m* tennis-court. **T~schläger** *m* tennis-racket

Teppich *m* -s, e carpet. **T~boden** *m* fitted carpet

Termin *m* -s, -e date; (*Arzt-*) appointment. **T~kalender** *m* [appointments] diary

Terpentin *nt* -s turpentine

Terrasse *f* -, -n terrace

Terrier /'tɛriɐ/ *m* -s,- terrier

Terrine *f* -, -n tureen

Territorium *nt* -s, -ien territory

Terror *m* -s terror. **t~isieren** *vt* terrorize. **T~ismus** *m* - terrorism. **T~ist** *m* -en, -en terrorist

Tesafilm (P) *m* ≈ Sellotape (P)

Test *m* -[e]s, -s & -e test

Testament *nt* -[e]s, -e will; Altes/ Neues T~ Old/New Testament. **T~svollstrecker** *m* -s,- executor

testen *vt* test

Tetanus *m* - tetanus

teuer *a* expensive; (*lieb*) dear; wie t~? how much?

Teufel *m* -s,- devil. **T~skreis** *m* vicious circle

teuflisch *a* fiendish

Text *m* -[e]s, -e text; (*Passage*) passage; (*Bild-*) caption; (*Lied-*) lyrics *pl*. **T~er** *m* -s,- copy-writer; (*Schlager-*) lyricist

Textilien /-iən/ *pl* textiles; (*Textilwaren*) textile goods

Textverarbeitungssystem *nt* word processor

Theater *nt* -s,- theatre; (🛈 *Getue*) fuss. **T~kasse** *f* box-office. **T~stück** *nt* play

Theke *f* -, -n bar; (*Ladentisch*) counter

Thema *nt* -s, -men subject

Themse *f* - Thames

Theolo|ge *m* -n, -n theologian. **T~gie** *f* - theology

theor|etisch *a* theoretical. **T~ie** *f* -, -n theory

Therapeut(in) *m* -en, -en (*f* -, -nen) therapist

Therapie *f* -, -n therapy

t

Thermalbad *nt* thermal bath

Thermometer *nt* -s,- thermometer

Thermosflasche (P) *f* Thermos flask (P)

Thermostat *m* -[e]s, -e thermostat

These *f* -, -n thesis

Thrombose *f* -, -n thrombosis

Thron *m* -[e]s, -e throne. **t∼en** *vi* (*haben*) sit [in state]. **T∼folge** *f* succession. **T∼folger** *m* -s,- heir to the throne

Thunfisch *m* tuna

Thymian *m* -s thyme

ticken *vi* (*haben*) tick

tief *a* deep; (*t∼ liegend, niedrig*) low; (*t∼gründig*) profound; **t∼er Teller** soup-plate ● *adv* deep; low; (*sehr*) deeply, profoundly; <*schlafen*> soundly. **T∼** *nt* -s, -s (*Meteorol*) depression. **T∼bau** *m* civil engineering. **T∼e** *f* -, -n depth. **T∼garage** *f* underground car park. **t∼gekühlt** *a* [deep-]frozen

Tiefkühl|fach *nt* freezer compartment. **T∼kost** *f* frozen food. **T∼truhe** *f* deep-freeze

Tiefsttemperatur *f* minimum temperature

Tier *nt* -[e]s, -e animal. **T∼arzt** *m*, **T∼ärztin** *f* vet, veterinary surgeon. **T∼garten** *m* zoo. **T∼kreis** *m* zodiac. **T∼kunde** *f* zoology. **T∼quälerei** *f* cruelty to animals

Tiger *m* -s,- tiger

tilgen *vt* pay off <*Schuld*>; (*streichen*) delete; (*fig: auslöschen*) wipe out

Tinte *f* -, -n ink. **T∼nfisch** *m* squid

Tipp *m* -s, -s 🔢 tip

tipp|en *vt* 🔢 type ● *vi* (*haben*) (*berühren*) touch (**auf/an etw** *acc* sth); (🔢 *Maschine schreiben*) type; **t∼en auf** (+ *acc*) (🔢 *wetten*) bet on. **T∼schein** *m* pools/lottery coupon

tipptopp *a* 🔢 immaculate

Tirol *nt* -s [the] Tyrol

Tisch *m* -[e]s, -e table; (*Schreib-*) desk; **nach T∼** after the meal. **T∼decke** *f* table-cloth. **T∼gebet**

nt grace. **T∼ler** *m* -s,- joiner; (*Möbel-*) cabinet-maker. **T∼rede** *f* after-dinner speech. **T∼tennis** *nt* table tennis

Titel *m* -s,- title

Toast /to:st/ *m* -[e]s, -e toast; (*Scheibe*) piece of toast. **T∼er** *m* -s,- toaster

toben *vi* (*haben*) rave; <*Sturm:*> rage; <*Kinder:*> play boisterously

Tochter *f* -,⸚ daughter. **T∼gesellschaft** *f* subsidiary

Tod *m* -es death

Todes|angst *f* mortal fear. **T∼anzeige** *f* death announcement; (*Zeitungs-*) obituary. **T∼fall** *m* death. **T∼opfer** *nt* fatality, casualty. **T∼strafe** *f* death penalty. **T∼urteil** *nt* death sentence

todkrank *a* dangerously ill

tödlich *a* fatal; <*Gefahr*> mortal

Toilette /toa'lεtə/ *f* -, -n toilet. **T∼npapier** *nt* toilet paper

toler|ant *a* tolerant. **T∼anz** *f* - tolerance. **t∼ieren** *vt* tolerate

toll *a* crazy, mad; (🔢 *prima*) fantastic; (*schlimm*) awful ● *adv* (*sehr*) very; (*schlimm*) badly. **t∼kühn** *a* foolhardy. **T∼wut** *f* rabies. **t∼wütig** *a* rabid

Tölpel *m* -s,- fool

Tomate *f* -, -n tomato. **T∼nmark** *nt* tomato purée

Tombola *f* -, -s raffle

Ton¹ *m* -[e]s clay

Ton² *m* -[e]s,⸚e tone; (*Klang*) sound; (*Note*) note; (*Betonung*) stress; (*Farb-*) shade; **der gute Ton** (*fig*) good form. **T∼abnehmer** *m* -s,- pick-up. **t∼angebend** *a* (*fig*) leading. **T∼art** *f* tone [of voice]; (*Mus*) key. **T∼band** *nt* (*pl* -bänder) tape. **T∼bandgerät** *nt* tape recorder

tönen *vi* (*haben*) sound ● *vt* tint

Tonleiter *f* scale

Tonne *f* -, -n barrel, cask; (*Müll-*) bin; (*Maß*) tonne, metric ton

Topf *m* -[e]s,⸚e pot; (*Koch-*) pan

Topfen *m* -s (*Aust*) ≈ curd cheese

Töpferei *f* -, -en pottery

Topf|lappen *m* oven-cloth.
T~pflanze *f* potted plant

Tor *nt* -[e]s, -e gate; (*Einfahrt*)
gateway; (*Sport*) goal

Torf *m* -s peat

torkeln *vi* (*sein/habe*) stagger

Tornister *m* -s,- knapsack; (*Sch*)
satchel

Torpedo *m* -s, -s torpedo

Torpfosten *m* goal-post

Torte *f* -, -n gateau; (*Obst-*) flan

Tortur *f* -, -en torture

Torwart *m* -s, -e goalkeeper

tot *a* dead; **tot geboren** stillborn; **sich
tot stellen** pretend to be dead

total *a* total. **T~schaden** *m* ≈
write-off

Tote|(r) *m/f* dead man/woman;
(*Todesopfer*) fatality; **die T~n** the
dead *pl*

töten *vt* kill

Toten|gräber *m* -s,- grave-digger.
T~kopf *m* skull. **T~schein** *m*
death certificate

totfahren† *vt sep* run over and kill

Toto *nt* & *m* -s football pools *pl*.
T~schein *m* pools coupon

tot|schießen† *vt sep* shoot dead.
T~schlag *m* (*Jur*) manslaughter.
t~schlagen† *vt sep* kill

Tötung *f* -, -en killing; **fahrlässige
T~** (*Jur*) manslaughter

Toup|et /tu'pe:/ *nt* -s, -s toupee.
t~ieren *vt* back-comb

Tour /tu:ɐ̯/ *f* -, -en tour; (*Ausflug*)
trip; (*Auto-*) drive; (*Rad-*) ride;
(*Strecke*) distance; (*Techn*)
revolution; (🅸 *Weise*) way

Touris|mus /tu'rɪsmʊs/ *m* -
tourism. **T~t** *m* -en, -en tourist

Tournee /tʊr'ne:/ *f* -, -n tour

Trab *m* -[e]s trot

Trabant *m* -en, -en satellite

traben *vi* (*haben/sein*) trot

Tracht *f* -, -en [national] costume

Tradition /-'tsio:n/ *f* -, -en tradition.
t~ell *a* traditional

Trag|bahre *f* stretcher. **t~bar** *a*
portable; <*Kleidung*> wearable

tragen† *vt* carry; (*an-/ aufhaben*)
wear; (*fig*) bear ● *vi* (*haben*) carry;
gut t~ <*Baum:*> produce a good
crop

Träger *m* -s,- porter; (*Inhaber*)
bearer; (*eines Ordens*) holder; (*Bau-*)
beam; (*Stahl-*) girder; (*Achsel-*)
[shoulder] strap. **T~kleid** *nt*
pinafore dress

Trag|etasche *f* carrier bag.
T~flächenboot, T~flügelboot
nt hydrofoil

Trägheit *f* - sluggishness; (*Faulheit*)
laziness; (*Phys*) inertia

Trag|ik *f* - tragedy. **t~isch** *a* tragic

Tragödie /-iə/ *f* -, -n tragedy

Train|er /'trɛːnɐ/ *m* -s,- trainer;
(*Tennis-*) coach. **t~ieren** *vt/i*
(*haben*) train

Training /'trɛːnɪŋ/ *nt* -s training.
T~sanzug *m* tracksuit. **T~s-
schuhe** *mpl* trainers

Traktor *m* -s, -en /-'to:rən/ tractor

trampeln *vi* (*haben*) stamp one's
feet ● *vi* (*sein*) trample (**auf** + *acc* on)
● *vt* trample

trampen /'trɛmpən/ *vi* (*sein*) 🅸
hitch-hike

Tranchiermesser /trãˈʃiːɐ̯-/ *nt*
carving-knife

Träne *f* -, -n tear. **t~n** *vi* (*haben*)
water. **T~ngas** *nt* tear-gas

Tränke *f* -, -n watering-place; (*Trog*)
drinking-trough. **t~n** *vt* water
<*Pferd*>; (*nässen*) soak (**mit** with)

Trans|formator *m* -s, -en /-'to:rən/
transformer. **T~fusion** *f* -, -en
[blood] transfusion

Transit /tran'zi:t/ *m* -s transit

Transparent *nt* -[e]s, -e banner;
(*Bild*) transparency

transpirieren *vi* (*haben*) perspire

Transport *m* -[e]s, -e transport;
(*Güter-*) consignment. **t~ieren** *vt*
transport

Trapez *nt* -es, -e trapeze

Tratte *f* -, -n (*Comm*) draft

Traube *f* -, -n bunch of grapes;
(*Beere*) grape; (*fig*) cluster.
T~nzucker *m* glucose

t

trauen vi (haben) (+ dat) trust ● vt marry; **sich t~** dare (**etw zu tun** [to] do sth); venture (**in** + acc/**aus** into/out of)

Trauer f - mourning; (Schmerz) grief (**um** for); **T~ tragen** be [dressed] in mourning. **T~fall** m bereavement. **T~feier** f funeral service. **t~n** vi (haben) grieve; **t~n um** mourn [for]. **T~spiel** nt tragedy. **T~weide** f weeping willow

Traum m -[e]s, Träume dream

Trauma nt -s, -men trauma

träumen vt/i (haben) dream

traumhaft a dreamlike; (schön) fabulous

traurig a sad; (erbärmlich) sorry. **T~keit** f - sadness

Trau|ring m wedding-ring. **T~schein** m marriage certificate. **T~ung** f -, -en wedding [ceremony]

Treff nt -s, -s (Karten) spades pl

treff|en† vt hit; <Blitz:> strike; (fig: verletzen) hurt; (zusammenkommen mit) meet; take <Maßnahme>; **t~en** meet (**mit jdm** s.o.); **sich gut t~en** be convenient; **es gut/schlecht t~en** be lucky/unlucky ● vi (haben) hit the target; **t~en auf** (+ acc) meet; (fig) meet with. **T~en** nt -s,- meeting. **T~er** m -s,- hit; (Los) winner. **T~punkt** m meeting-place

treiben† vt drive; (sich befassen mit) do; carry on <Gewerbe>; indulge in <Luxus>; get up to <Unfug>; **Handel t~** trade ● vi (sein) drift; (schwimmen) float ● vi (haben) (Bot) sprout. **T~** nt -s activity

Treib|haus nt hothouse. **T~hauseffekt** m greenhouse effect. **T~holz** nt driftwood. **T~riemen** m transmission belt. **T~sand** m quicksand. **T~stoff** m fuel

trenn|bar a separable. **t~en** vt separate/(abmachen) detach (**von** from); divide, split <Wort>; **sich t~en** separate; (auseinander gehen) part; **sich t~en von** leave; (fortgeben) part with. **T~ung** f -, -en

separation; (Silben-) division. **T~ungsstrich** m hyphen. **T~wand** f partition

trepp|ab adv downstairs. **t~auf** adv upstairs

Treppe f -, -n stairs pl; (Außen-) steps pl. **T~ngeländer** nt banisters pl

Tresor m -s, -e safe

Tresse f -, -n braid

Treteimer m pedal bin

treten† vi (sein/haben) step; (versehentlich) tread; (ausschlagen) kick (**nach** at); **in Verbindung t~** get in touch ● vt tread; (mit Füßen) kick

treu a faithful; (fest) loyal. **T~e** f - faithfulness; loyalty; (eheliche) fidelity. **T~händer** m -s,- trustee. **t~los** a disloyal; (untreu) unfaithful

Tribüne f -, -n platform; (Zuschauer-) stand

Trichter m -s,- funnel; (Bomben-) crater

Trick m -s, -s trick. **T~film** m cartoon. **t~reich** a clever

Trieb m -[e]s, -e drive, urge; (Instinkt) instinct; (Bot) shoot. **T~verbrecher** m sex offender. **T~werk** nt (Aviat) engine; (Uhr-) mechanism

triefen† vi (haben) drip; (nass sein) be dripping (**von/vor** + dat with)

Trigonometrie f - trigonometry

Trikot[1] /tri'ko:/ m -s (Tex) jersey

Trikot[2] nt -s, -s (Sport) jersey; (Fußball-) shirt

Trimester nt -s,- term

Trimm-dich nt -s keep-fit

trimmen vt trim; tune <Motor>; **sich t~** keep fit

trink|en† vt/i (haben) drink. **T~er(in)** m -s,- (f -, -nen) alcoholic. **T~geld** nt tip. **T~spruch** m toast

trist a dreary

Tritt m -[e]s, -e step; (Fuß-) kick. **T~brett** nt step

Triumph m -s, -e triumph. **t~ieren** vi (haben) rejoice

trocken a dry. **T~haube** f drier. **T~heit** f -, -en dryness; (Dürre) drought. **t~legen** vt sep change

<*Baby*>; drain <*Sumpf*>. **T∼milch** *f* powdered milk

trockn|en *vt/i* (*sein*) dry. **T∼er** *m* -s,- drier

Trödel *m* -s 🔲 junk. **t∼n** *vi* (*haben*) dawdle

Trödler *m* -s,- 🔲 slowcoach; (*Händler*) junk-dealer

Trog *m* -[e]s,ⁿe trough

Trommel *f* -, -n drum. **T∼fell** *nt* ear-drum. **t∼n** *vi* (*haben*) drum

Trommler *m* -s,- drummer

Trompete *f* -, -n trumpet. **T∼r** *m* -s,- trumpeter

Tropen *pl* tropics

Tropf *m* -[e]s, -e (*Med*) drip

tröpfeln *vt/i* (*sein*/*haben*) drip

tropfen *vt/i* (*sein*/*haben*) drip. **T∼** *m* -s,- drop; (*fallend*) drip. **t∼weise** *adv* drop by drop

Trophäe /tro'fɛ:ə/ *f* -, -n trophy

tropisch *a* tropical

Trost *m* -[e]s consolation, comfort

tröst|en *vt* console, comfort; **sich t∼en** console oneself. **t∼lich** *a* comforting

trost|los *a* desolate; (*elend*) wretched; (*reizlos*) dreary. **T∼preis** *m* consolation prize

Trott *m* -s amble; (*fig*) routine

Trottel *m* -s,- 🔲 idiot

Trottoir /trɔ'toa:ɐ/ *nt* -s, -s pavement

trotz *prep* (+ *gen*) despite, in spite of. **T∼** *m* -es defiance. **t∼dem** *adv* nevertheless. **t∼ig** *a* defiant; stubborn

trübe *a* dull; <*Licht*> dim; <*Flüssigkeit*> cloudy; (*fig*) gloomy

Trubel *m* -s bustle

trüben *vt* dull; make cloudy <*Flüssigkeit*>; (*fig*) spoil; strain <*Verhältnis*> **sich t∼** <*Flüssigkeit:*> become cloudy; <*Himmel:*> cloud over; <*Augen:*> dim

Trüb|sal *f* - misery. **T∼sinn** *m* melancholy. **t∼sinnig** *a* melancholy

trügen† *vt* deceive ● *vi* (*haben*) be deceptive

Trugschluss *m* fallacy

Truhe *f* -, -n chest

Trümmer *pl* rubble *sg*; (*T∼teile*) wreckage *sg*, (*fig*) ruins

Trumpf *m* -[e]s,ⁿe trump [card]. **t∼en** *vi* (*haben*) play trumps

Trunk *m* -[e]s drink. **T∼enheit** *f* - drunkenness; **T∼enheit am Steuer** drink-driving

Trupp *m* -s, -s group; (*Mil*) squad. **T∼e** *f* -, -n (*Mil*) unit; (*Theat*) troupe; **T∼en** troops

Truthahn *m* turkey

Tschech|e *m* -n, -n, **T∼in** *f* -, -nen Czech. **t∼isch** *a* Czech. **T∼oslowakei** (die) - Czechoslovakia

tschüs, tschüss *int* bye, cheerio

Tuba *f* -, -ben (*Mus*) tuba

Tube *f* -, -n tube

Tuberkulose *f* - tuberculosis

Tuch *nt* -[e]s,ⁿer cloth; (*Hals-*, *Kopf-*) scarf; (*Schulter-*) shawl

tüchtig *a* competent; (*reichlich, beträchtlich*) good; (*groß*) big ● *adv* competently; (*ausreichend*) well

Tück|e *f* -, -n malice. **t∼isch** *a* malicious; (*gefährlich*) treacherous

Tugend *f* -,en virtue. **t∼haft** *a* virtuous

Tülle *f* -, -n spout

Tulpe *f* -, -n tulip

Tümmler *m* -s,- porpoise

Tumor *m* -s, -en /-'mo:rən/ tumour

Tümpel *m* -[e]s,- pond

Tumult *m* -[e]s, -e commotion; (*Aufruhr*) riot

tun† *vt* do; take <*Schritt, Blick*>; work <*Wunder*>; (*bringen*) put (in + *acc* into); **sich tun** happen; **jdm etwas tun** hurt s.o.; **das tut nichts** it doesn't matter ● *vi* (*haben*) act (**als ob** as if); **er tut nur so** he's just pretending; **jdm/etw gut tun** do s.o./sth. good; **zu tun haben** have things/work to do; **[es] zu tun haben mit** have to deal with. **Tun** *nt* -s actions *pl*

Tünche *f* -, -n whitewash; (*fig*) veneer. **t∼n** *vt* whitewash

Tunesien /-iən/ *nt* -s Tunisia

Tunfisch *m* = Thunfisch

Tunnel *m* -s,- tunnel

tupf|en *vt* dab ● *vi* (haben) t~en an/auf (+ acc) touch. **T~en** *m* -s,- spot. **T~er** *m* -s,- spot; (Med) swab

Tür *f* -, -en door

Turban *m* -s, -e turban

Turbine *f* -, -n turbine

Türk|e *m* -n, -n Turk. **T~ei** (die) -Turkey. **T~in** *f* -, -nen Turk

türkis *inv a* turquoise

türkisch *a* Turkish

Turm *m* -[e]s,¨e tower; (Schach) rook, castle

Türm|chen *nt* -s,- turret. **t~en** *vt* pile [up]; sich t~en pile up

Turmspitze *f* spire

turn|en *vi* (haben) do gymnastics. **T~en** *nt* -s gymnastics sg; (Sch) physical education, ▣ gym. **T~er(in)** *m* -s,- (f -, -nen) gymnast. **T~halle** *f* gymnasium

Turnier *nt* -s, -e tournament; (Reit-) show

Turnschuhe *mpl* gym shoes; trainers

Türschwelle *f* doorstep, threshold

Tusche *f* -, -n [drawing] ink

tuscheln *vt/i* (haben) whisper

Tüte *f* -, -n bag; (Comm) packet; (Eis-) cornet; in die T~ blasen ▣ be breathalysed

TÜV *m* - ≈ MOT [test]

Typ *m* -s, -en type; (▣ Kerl) bloke. **T~e** *f* -, -n type

Typhus *m* - typhoid

typisch *a* typical (für of)

Typus *m* -, Typen type

Tyrann *m* -en, -en tyrant. **T~ei** *f* -tyranny. **t~isch** *a* tyrannical. **t~isieren** *vt* tyrannize

Uu

U-Bahn *f* underground

übel *a* bad; (hässlich) nasty; **mir ist ü~** I feel sick; jdm etw ü~ nehmen hold sth against s.o. **Ü~keit** *f* -nausea

üben *vt/i* (haben) practise

über *prep* (+ dat/acc) over; (höher als) above; (betreffend) about; <Buch, Vortrag> on; <Scheck, Rechnung> for; (quer ü~) across; ü~ Köln fahren go via Cologne; ü~ Ostern over Easter; die Woche ü~ during the week; Fehler ü~ Fehler mistake after mistake ● *adv* ü~ und ü~ all over; jdm ü~ sein be better/(stärker) stronger than s.o. ● *a* ▣ ü~ sein be left over; etw ü~ sein be fed up with sth

überall *adv* everywhere

überanstrengen *vt insep* overtax; strain <Augen>

überarbeiten *vt insep* revise; sich ü~en overwork

überbieten† *vt insep* outbid; (übertreffen) surpass

Überblick *m* overall view; (Abriss) summary

überblicken *vt insep* overlook; (abschätzen) assess

überbringen† *vt insep* deliver

überbrücken *vt insep* (fig) bridge

überdies *adv* moreover

überdimensional *a* oversized

Überdosis *f* overdose

überdrüssig *a* ü~ sein/werden be/grow tired (gen of)

übereignen *vt insep* transfer

übereilt *a* over-hasty

übereinander *adv* one on top of/above the other; <sprechen> about each other

überein|kommen† *vi sep* (sein) agree. **Ü~kunft** *f* - agreement.

ü~stimmen *vi sep* (*haben*) agree; *<Zahlen:>* tally; *<Ansichten:>* coincide; *<Farben:>* match.
Ü~stimmung *f* agreement

überfahren† *vt insep* run over

Überfahrt *f* crossing

Überfall *m* attack; (*Bank-*) raid

überfallen† *vt insep* attack; raid *<Bank>*; (*bestürmen*) bombard (**mit** with)

Überfluss *m* abundance; (*Wohlstand*) affluence

überflüssig *a* superfluous

überfordern *vt insep* overtax

überführ|en *vt insep* transfer; (*Jur*) convict (*gen* of). **Ü~ung** *f* transfer; (*Straße*) flyover; (*Fußgänger-*) footbridge

überfüllt *a* overcrowded

Übergabe *f* handing over; transfer

Übergang *m* crossing; (*Wechsel*) transition

übergeben† *vt insep* hand over; (*übereignen*) transfer; **sich ü~** be sick

übergehen† *vt insep* (*fig*) pass over; (*nicht beachten*) ignore; (*auslassen*) leave out

Übergewicht *nt* excess weight; (*fig*) predominance; **Ü~ haben** be overweight

über|greifen† *vi sep* (*haben*) spread (**auf** + *acc* to). **Ü~griff** *m* infringement

über|groß *a* outsize; (*übertrieben*) exaggerated. **Ü~größe** *f* outsize

überhand *adv* **ü~ nehmen** increase alarmingly

überhäufen *vt insep* inundate (**mit** with)

überhaupt *adv* (*im Allgemeinen*) altogether; (*eigentlich*) anyway; (*überdies*) besides; **ü~ nicht/nichts** not/nothing at all

überheblich *a* arrogant. **Ü~keit** *f* - arrogance

überhol|en *vt insep* overtake; (*reparieren*) overhaul. **ü~t** *a* outdated. **Ü~ung** *f* -, -en overhaul. **Ü~verbot** *nt* 'Ü~verbot' 'no overtaking'

überhören *vt insep* fail to hear; (*nicht beachten*) ignore

überirdisch *a* supernatural

überkochen *vi sep* (*sein*) boil over

überlassen† *vt insep* **jdm etw ü~** leave sth to s.o.; (*geben*) let s.o. have sth; **sich** (*dat*) **selbst ü~ sein** be left to one's own devices

Überlauf *m* overflow

überlaufen† *vi sep* (*sein*) overflow; (*Mil, Pol*) defect

Überläufer *m* defector

überleben *vt/i insep* (*haben*) survive. **Ü~de(r)** *m/f* survivor

überlegen¹ *vt sep* put over

überlegen² *v insep* ● *vt* [**sich** *dat*] **ü~** think over, consider; **es sich** (*dat*) **anders ü~** change one's mind ● *vi* (*haben*) think, reflect

überlegen³ *a* superior. **Ü~heit** *f* - superiority

Überlegung *f* -, -en reflection

überliefer|n *vt insep* hand down. **Ü~ung** *f* tradition

überlisten *vt insep* outwit

Übermacht *f* superiority

übermäßig *a* excessive

Übermensch *m* superman. **ü~lich** *a* superhuman

übermitteln *vt insep* convey; (*senden*) transmit

übermorgen *adv* the day after tomorrow

übermüdet *a* overtired

Über|mut *m* high spirits *pl.* **ü~mütig** *a* high-spirited

übernächst|e(r,s) *a* next ... but one; **ü~es Jahr** the year after next

übernacht|en *vi insep* (*haben*) stay overnight. **Ü~ung** *f* -, -en overnight stay; **Ü~ung und Frühstück** bed and breakfast

Übernahme *f* - taking over; (*Comm*) take-over

übernatürlich *a* supernatural

übernehmen† *vt insep* take over; (*annehmen*) take on; **sich ü~** overdo things; (*finanziell*) over-reach oneself

überqueren *vt insep* cross

u

überrasch|en *vt insep* surprise.
ü~end *a* surprising; (*unerwartet*)
unexpected. **Ü~ung** *f* -, -en surprise

überreden *vt insep* persuade

Überreste *mpl* remains

Überschall- *pref* supersonic

überschätzen *vt insep*
overestimate

Überschlag *m* rough estimate;
(*Sport*) somersault

überschlagen¹† *vt sep* cross
<*Beine*>

überschlagen²† *vt insep* estimate
roughly; (*auslassen*) skip; **sich ü~**
somersault; <*Ereignisse:*> happen
fast ● *a* tepid

überschneiden† (sich) *vr insep*
intersect, cross; (*zusammenfallen*)
overlap

überschreiten† *vt insep* cross;
(*fig*) exceed

Überschrift *f* heading; (*Zeitungs-*)
headline

Über|schuss *m* surplus.
ü~schüssig *a* surplus

überschwemm|en *vt insep* flood;
(*fig*) inundate. **Ü~ung** *f* -, -en flood

Übersee in/nach **Ü~** overseas;
aus/von **Ü~** from overseas.
Ü~dampfer *m* ocean liner.
ü~isch *a* overseas

übersehen† *vt insep* look out over;
(*abschätzen*) assess; (*nicht sehen*)
overlook, miss; (*ignorieren*) ignore

übersenden† *vt insep* send

übersetzen¹ *vi sep* (*haben/sein*)
cross [over]

übersetz|en² *vt insep* translate.
Ü~er(in) *m* -s,- (*f* -, -nen)
translator. **Ü~ung** *f* -, -en
translation

Übersicht *f* overall view; (*Abriss*)
summary; (*Tabelle*) table. **ü~lich** *a*
clear

Übersiedlung *f* move

überspielen *vt insep* (*fig*) cover up;
auf Band **ü~** tape

u

überstehen† *vt insep* come
through; get over <*Krankheit*>;
(*überleben*) survive

übersteigen† *vt insep* climb
[over]; (*fig*) exceed

überstimmen *vt insep* outvote

Überstunden *fpl* overtime *sg*; **Ü~**
machen work overtime

überstürz|en *vt insep* rush; **sich**
ü~en <*Ereignisse:*> happen fast.
ü~t *a* hasty

übertrag|bar *a* transferable; (*Med*)
infectious. **ü~en†** *vt insep* transfer;
(*übergeben*) assign (*dat* to); (*Techn,*
Med) transmit; (*Radio, TV*)
broadcast; (*übersetzen*) translate;
(*anwenden*) apply (auf + *acc* to) ● *a*
transferred, figurative. **Ü~ung** *f* -,
-en transfer; transmission;
broadcast; translation; application

übertreffen† *vt insep* surpass;
(*übersteigen*) exceed; **sich selbst ü~**
excel oneself

übertreib|en† *vt insep* exaggerate;
(*zu weit treiben*) overdo. **Ü~ung** *f* -,
-en exaggeration

übertreten¹† *vi sep* (*sein*) step over
the line; (*Pol*) go over/(*Relig*) convert
(zu to)

übertret|en²† *vt insep* infringe;
break <*Gesetz*>. **Ü~ung** *f* -, -en
infringement; breach

übertrieben *a* exaggerated

übervölkert *a* overpopulated

überwachen *vt insep* supervise;
(*kontrollieren*) monitor; (*bespitzeln*)
keep under surveillance

überwältigen *vt insep* overpower;
(*fig*) overwhelm

überweis|en† *vt insep* transfer;
refer <*Patienten*>. **Ü~ung** *f*
transfer; (*ärztliche*) referral

überwiegen† *v insep* ● *vi* (*haben*)
predominate, ● *vt* outweigh

überwind|en† *vt insep* overcome;
sich ü~en force oneself. **Ü~ung** *f*
effort

Über|zahl *f* majority. **ü~zählig** *a*
spare

überzeug|en *vt insep* convince;
sich [selbst] ü~en satisfy oneself.

ü~end *a* convincing. **Ü~ung** *f*,
-en conviction

überziehen¹† *vt sep* put on

überziehen²† *vt insep* cover;
overdraw *<Konto>*

Überzug *m* cover; *(Schicht)* coating

üblich *a* usual; *(gebräuchlich)*
customary

U-Boot *nt* submarine

übrig *a* remaining; *(andere)* other;
alles **Ü~e** [all] the rest; im **Ü~en**
besides; *(ansonsten)* apart from that;
ü~ **sein** *od* **bleiben** be left [over]; etw
ü~ **lassen** leave sth [over]; uns blieb
nichts anderes ü~ we had no choice

Übung *f* -, -en exercise; *(Üben)*
practice; außer *od* aus der **Ü~** out of
practice

Ufer *nt* -s,- shore; *(Fluss-)* bank

Uhr *f* -, -en clock; *(Armband-)* watch;
(Zähler) meter; um ein **U~** at one
o'clock; wie viel **U~** ist es? what's
the time? **U~macher** *m* -s,- watch
and clockmaker. **U~werk** *nt* clock/
watch mechanism. **U~zeiger** *m*
[clock-/watch-]hand. **U~zeit** *f* time

Uhu *m* -s, -s eagle owl

UKW *abbr (Ultrakurzwelle)* VHF

ulkig *a* funny; *(seltsam)* odd

Ulme *f* -, -n elm

Ultimatum *nt* -s, -ten ultimatum

Ultrakurzwelle *f* very high
frequency

Ultraschall *m* ultrasound

ultraviolett *a* ultraviolet

um *prep* (+ *acc*) [a]round; *(Uhrzeit)* at;
<bitten> for; *<streiten>* over; *<sich
sorgen>* about; *<betrügen>* out of;
(bei Angabe einer Differenz) by; um
[... herum] around, [round] about;
Tag um Tag day after day; um
seinetwillen for his sake ● *adv*
(ungefähr) around, about; um sein 🄸
be over; *<Zeit>* be up ● *conj* um zu
to; *(Absicht)* [in order] to; zu müde,
um zu ... too tired to ...

umarm|en *vt insep* embrace, hug.
U~ung *f* -, -en embrace, hug

Umbau *m* rebuilding; conversion
(zu into). **u~en** *vt sep* rebuild;
convert (zu into)

Umbildung *f* reorganization; *(Pol)*
reshuffle

umbinden† *vt sep* put on

umblättern *v sep* ● *vt* turn [over]
● *vi (haben)* turn the page

umbringen† *vt sep* kill; sich u~
kill oneself

umbuchen *v sep* ● *vt* change;
(Comm) transfer ● *vi (haben)* change
one's booking

umdrehen *v sep* ● *vt* turn round/
(wenden) over; turn *<Schlüssel>*;
(umkrempeln) turn inside out; sich
u~ turn round; *(im Liegen)* turn
over ● *vi (haben/sein)* turn back

Umdrehung *f* turn; *(Motor-)*
revolution

umeinander *adv* around each
other; sich u~ sorgen worry about
each other

umfahren¹† *vt sep* run over

umfahren²† *vt insep* go round;
bypass *<Ort>*

umfallen† *vi sep (sein)* fall over;
<Person:> fall down

Umfang *m* girth; *(Geom)*
circumference; *(Größe)* size

umfangreich *a* extensive; *(dick)*
big

umfassen *vt insep* consist of,
comprise; *(umgeben)* surround. **u~d**
a comprehensive

Umfrage *f* survey, poll

umfüllen *vt sep* transfer

umfunktionieren *vt sep* convert

Umgang *m* [social] contact;
(Umgehen) dealing (mit with)

Umgangssprache *f* colloquial
language

umgeb|en *vt/i insep (haben)*
surround ● *a* u~en von surrounded
by. **U~ung** *f* -, -en surroundings *pl*

umgehen† *vt insep* avoid; *(nicht
beachten)* evade; *<Straße:>* bypass

umgehend *a* immediate

Umgehungsstraße *f* bypass

umgekehrt *a* inverse;
<Reihenfolge> reverse; es war u~ it
was the other way round

umgraben† *vt sep* dig [over]

u

Umhang m cloak

umhauen† vt sep knock down; (fällen) chop down

umhören (sich) vr sep ask around

Umkehr f - turning back. **u~en** v sep ● vi (sein) turn back ● vt turn round; turn inside out <Tasche>; (fig) reverse

umkippen v sep ● vt tip over; (versehentlich) knock over ● vi (sein) fall over; <Boot:> capsize

Umkleide|kabine f changing-cubicle. **u~n (sich)** vr sep change. **U~raum** m changing-room

umknicken v sep ● vt bend; (falten) fold ● vi (sein) bend; (mit dem Fuß) go over on one's ankle

umkommen† vi sep (sein) perish

Umkreis m surroundings pl; im U~ von within a radius of

umkreisen vt insep circle; (Astr) revolve around; <Satellit:> orbit

umkrempeln vt sep turn up; (von innen nach außen) turn inside out; (ändern) change radically

Umlauf m circulation; (Astr) revolution. **U~bahn** f orbit

Umlaut m umlaut

umlegen vt sep lay or put down; flatten <Getreide>; turn down <Kragen>; put on <Schal>; throw <Hebel>; (verlegen) transfer; (🄸 töten) kill

umleit|en vt sep divert. **U~ung** f diversion

umliegend a surrounding

umpflanzen vt sep transplant

umranden vt insep edge

umräumen vt sep rearrange

umrechn|en vt sep convert. **U~ung** f conversion

umreißen† vt insep outline

Umriss m outline

umrühren vt/i sep (haben) stir

ums pron = um das

Umsatz m (Comm) turnover

umschalten vt/i sep (haben) switch over; **auf Rot u~** <Ampel:> change to red

Umschau f U~ halten nach look out for

Umschlag m cover; (Schutz-) jacket; (Brief-) envelope; (Med) compress; (Hosen-) turn-up. **u~en**† v sep ● vt turn up; turn over <Seite>; (fällen) chop down ● vi (sein) topple over; <Wetter:> change; <Wind:> veer

umschließen† vt insep enclose

umschreiben vt insep define; (anders ausdrücken) paraphrase

umschulen vt sep retrain; (Sch) transfer to another school

Umschwung m (fig) change; (Pol) U-turn

umsehen† (sich) vr sep look round; (zurück) look back; sich u~ nach look for

umsein* vi sep (sein) um sein, s. um

umseitig a & adv overleaf

umsetzen vt sep move; (umpflanzen) transplant; (Comm) sell

umsied|eln v sep ● vt resettle ● vi (sein) move. **U~lung** f resettlement

umso conj ~ besser/mehr all the better/more; je mehr, ~ besser the more the better

umsonst adv in vain; (grundlos) without reason; (gratis) free

Umstand m circumstance; (Tatsache) fact; (Aufwand) fuss; (Mühe) trouble; unter U~en possibly; jdm U~e machen put s.o. to trouble; in andern U~en pregnant

umständlich a laborious; (kompliziert) involved

Umstands|kleid nt maternity dress. **U~wort** nt (pl -wörter) adverb

Umstehende pl bystanders

umsteigen† vi sep (sein) change

umstellen¹ vt insep surround

umstell|en² vt sep rearrange; transpose <Wörter>; (anders einstellen) reset; (Techn) convert; (ändern) change; sich u~en adjust. **U~ung** f rearrangement;

---

*old spelling

transposition; resetting; conversion; change; adjustment

umstritten *a* controversial; (*ungeklärt*) disputed

umstülpen *vt sep* turn upside down; (*von innen nach außen*) turn inside out

Um|sturz *m* coup. **u~stürzen** *v sep* ● *vt* overturn; (*Pol*) overthrow ● *vi* (*sein*) fall over

umtaufen *vt sep* rename

Umtausch *m* exchange. **u~en** *vt sep* change; exchange (**gegen** for)

umwechseln *vt sep* change

Umweg *m* detour; **auf U~en** (*fig*) in a roundabout way

Umwelt *f* environment. **u~freundlich** *a* environmentally friendly. **U~schutz** *m* protection of the environment

umwerfen† *vt sep* knock over; (*fig*) upset <*Plan*>

umziehen† *v sep* ● *vi* (*sein*) move ● *vt* change; **sich u~** change

umzingeln *vt insep* surround

Umzug *m* move; (*Prozession*) procession

unabänderlich *a* irrevocable; <*Tatsache*> unalterable

unabhängig *a* independent; **u~ davon, ob** irrespective of whether. **U~keit** *f* - independence

unablässig *a* incessant

unabsehbar *a* incalculable

unabsichtlich *a* unintentional

unachtsam *a* careless

unangebracht *a* inappropriate

unangenehm *a* unpleasant; (*peinlich*) embarrassing

Unannehmlichkeiten *fpl* trouble *sg*

unansehnlich *a* shabby

unanständig *a* indecent

unappetitlich *a* unappetizing

Unart *f* -, -en bad habit. **u~ig** *a* naughty

unauffällig *a* inconspicuous; unobtrusive

unaufgefordert *adv* without being asked

unauf|haltsam *a* inexorable. **u~hörlich** *a* incessant

unaufmerksam *a* inattentive

unaufrichtig *a* insincere

unausbleiblich *a* inevitable

unausstehlich *a* insufferable

unbarmherzig *a* merciless

unbeabsichtigt *a* unintentional

unbedenklich *a* harmless ● *adv* without hesitation

unbedeutend *a* insignificant; (*geringfügig*) slight

unbedingt *a* absolute; **nicht u~** not necessarily

unbefriedig|end *a* unsatisfactory. **u~t** *a* dissatisfied

unbefugt *a* unauthorized ● *adv* without authorization

unbegreiflich *a* incomprehensible

unbegrenzt *a* unlimited ● *adv* indefinitely

unbegründet *a* unfounded

Unbehagen *nt* unease; (*körperlich*) discomfort

unbekannt *a* unknown; (*nicht vertraut*) unfamiliar. **U~e(r)** *m/f* stranger

unbekümmert *a* unconcerned; (*unbeschwert*) carefree

unbeliebt *a* unpopular. **U~heit** *f* unpopularity

unbemannt *a* unmanned

unbemerkt *a* & *adv* unnoticed

unbenutzt *a* unused

unbequem *a* uncomfortable; (*lästig*) awkward

unberechenbar *a* unpredictable

unberechtigt *a* unjustified; (*unbefugt*) unauthorized

unberührt *a* untouched; (*fig*) virgin; <*Landschaft*> unspoilt

unbescheiden *a* presumptuous

unbeschrankt *a* unguarded

unbeschränkt *a* unlimited ● *adv* without limit

unbeschwert *a* carefree

unbesiegt *a* undefeated

unbespielt *a* blank

unbeständig *a* inconsistent; <*Wetter*> unsettled

u

unbestechlich *a* incorruptible
unbestimmt *a* indefinite: <*Alter*> indeterminate; (*ungewiss*) uncertain; (*unklar*) vague
unbestritten *a* undisputed ● *adv* indisputably
unbeteiligt *a* indifferent; u~ an (+ *dat*) not involved in
unbetont *a* unstressed
unbewacht *a* unguarded
unbewaffnet *a* unarmed
unbeweglich *a* & *adv* motionless, still
unbewohnt *a* uninhabited
unbewusst *a* unconscious
unbezahlbar *a* priceless
unbrauchbar *a* useless
und *conj* and; **und so weiter** and so on; **nach und nach** bit by bit
Undank *m* ingratitude. **u~bar** *a* ungrateful; (*nicht lohnend*) thankless. **U~barkeit** *f* ingratitude
undeutlich *a* indistinct; vague
undicht *a* leaking; u~e Stelle leak
Unding *nt* absurdity
undiplomatisch *a* undiplomatic
unduldsam *a* intolerant
undurch|dringlich *a* impenetrable; <*Miene*> inscrutable. **u~führbar** *a* impracticable
undurch|lässig *a* impermeable. **u~sichtig** *a* opaque; (*fig*) doubtful
uneben *a* uneven. **U~heit** *f* -, -en unevenness; (*Buckel*) bump
unecht *a* false; u~er Schmuck imitation jewellery
unehelich *a* illegitimate
uneinig *a* (*fig*) divided; [sich (*dat*)] u~ sein disagree
uneins *a* u~ sein be at odds
unempfindlich *a* insensitive (gegen to); (*widerstandsfähig*) tough; (*Med*) immune
unendlich *a* infinite; (*endlos*) endless. **U~keit** *f* - infinity
unentbehrlich *a* indispensable
unentgeltlich *a* free, <*Arbeit*> unpaid ● *adv* free of charge

unentschieden *a* undecided; (*Sport*) drawn; u~ spielen draw. **U~ nt** -s,- draw
unentschlossen *a* indecisive; (*unentschieden*) undecided
unentwegt *a* persistent; (*unaufhörlich*) incessant
unerfahren *a* inexperienced. **U~heit** *f* - inexperience
unerfreulich *a* unpleasant
unerhört *a* enormous; (*empörend*) outrageous
unerklärlich *a* inexplicable
unerlässlich *a* essential
unerlaubt *a* unauthorized ● *adv* without permission
unerschwinglich *a* prohibitive
unersetzlich *a* irreplaceable; <*Verlust*> irreparable
unerträglich *a* unbearable
unerwartet *a* unexpected
unerwünscht *a* unwanted; <*Besuch*> unwelcome
unfähig *a* incompetent; u~, etw zu tun incapable of doing sth; (*nicht in der Lage*) unable to do sth. **U~keit** *f* incompetence; inability (zu to)
unfair *a* unfair
Unfall *m* accident. **U~flucht** *f* failure to stop after an accident. **U~station** *f* casualty department
unfassbar *a* incomprehensible
Unfehlbarkeit *f* - infallibility
unfolgsam *a* disobedient
unförmig *a* shapeless
unfreiwillig *a* involuntary; (*unbeabsichtigt*) unintentional
unfreundlich *a* unfriendly; (*unangenehm*) unpleasant. **U~keit** *f* unfriendliness; unpleasantness
Unfriede[n] *m* discord
unfruchtbar *a* infertile; (*fig*) unproductive. **U~keit** *f* infertility
Unfug *m* -s mischief; (*Unsinn*) nonsense
Ungar|(in) *m* -n, -n (*f* -, -nen) Hungarian. **u~isch** *a* Hungarian. **U~n** *nt* -s Hungary
ungeachtet *prep* (+ *gen*) in spite of; **dessen u~** notwithstanding [this].

u

---

ungebraucht *a* unused

ungedeckt *a* uncovered; (*Sport*) unmarked; *<Tisch>* unlaid

Ungeduld *f* impatience. **u~ig** *a* impatient

ungeeignet *a* unsuitable

ungefähr *a* approximate, rough

ungefährlich *a* harmless

ungeheuer *a* enormous. **U~** *nt* -s,- monster

ungehorsam *a* disobedient. **U~** *m* disobedience

ungeklärt *a* unsolved; *<Frage>* unsettled; *<Ursache>* unknown

ungelegen *a* inconvenient

ungelernt *a* unskilled

ungemütlich *a* uncomfortable; (*unangenehm*) unpleasant

ungenau *a* inaccurate; vague. **U~igkeit** *f* -, -en inaccuracy

ungeniert /'ʊnʒeni:ɐt/ *a* uninhibited ● *adv* openly

ungenießbar *a* inedible; *<Getränk>* undrinkable

ungenügend *a* inadequate; (*Sch*) unsatisfactory

ungepflegt *a* neglected; *<Person>* unkempt

ungerade *a* *<Zahl>* odd

ungerecht *a* unjust. **U~igkeit** *f* -, -en injustice

ungern *adv* reluctantly

ungesalzen *a* unsalted

Ungeschick|lichkeit *f* clumsiness. **u~t** *a* clumsy

ungeschminkt *a* without make-up; *<Wahrheit>* unvarnished

ungesetzlich *a* illegal

ungestört *a* undisturbed.

ungesund *a* unhealthy

ungesüßt *a* unsweetened

Ungetüm *nt* -s, -e monster

ungewiss *a* uncertain; **im Ungewissen sein/lassen** be/leave in the dark. **U~heit** *f* uncertainty

ungewöhnlich *a* unusual

ungewohnt *a* unaccustomed; (*nicht vertraut*) unfamiliar

Ungeziefer *nt* -s vermin

ungezogen *a* naughty

ungezwungen *a* informal; (*natürlich*) natural

ungläubig *a* incredulous

unglaublich *a* incredible, unbelievable

ungleich *a* unequal; (*verschieden*) different. **U~heit** *f* - inequality. **u~mäßig** *a* uneven

Unglück *nt* -s, -e misfortune; (*Pech*) bad luck; (*Missgeschick*) mishap; (*Unfall*) accident. **u~lich** *a* unhappy; (*ungünstig*) unfortunate. **u~licherweise** *adv* unfortunately

ungültig *a* invalid; (*Jur*) void

ungünstig *a* unfavourable; (*unpassend*) inconvenient

Unheil *nt* -s disaster; **U~ anrichten** cause havoc

unheilbar *a* incurable

unheimlich *a* eerie; (*gruselig*) creepy; (⊞ *groß*) terrific ● *adv* eerily; (⊞ *sehr*) terribly

unhöflich *a* rude. **U~keit** *f* rudeness

unhygienisch *a* unhygienic

Uni *f* -, -s ⊞ university

uni /y'ni:/ *inv a* plain

Uniform *f* -, -en uniform

uninteressant *a* uninteresting

Union *f* -, -en union

universell *a* universal

Universität *f* -, -en university

Universum *nt* -s universe

unkenntlich *a* unrecognizable

unklar *a* unclear; (*ungewiss*) uncertain; (*vage*) vague; **im U~en sein** be in the dark

unkompliziert *a* uncomplicated

Unkosten *pl* expenses

Unkraut *nt* weed; (*coll*) weeds *pl*; **U~ jäten** weed. **U~vertilgungsmittel** *nt* weed-killer

unlängst *adv* recently

unlauter *a* dishonest; (*unfair*) unfair

unleserlich *a* illegible

unleugbar *a* undeniable

unlogisch *a* illogical

u

Unmenge f enormous amount/ (*Anzahl*) number

Unmensch m 🔳 brute. **u~lich** a inhuman

unmerklich a imperceptible

unmittelbar a immediate; (*direkt*) direct

unmöbliert a unfurnished

unmodern a old-fashioned

unmöglich a impossible. **U~keit** f - impossibility

Unmoral f immorality. **u~isch** a immoral

unmündig a under-age

Unmut m displeasure

unnatürlich a unnatural

unnormal a abnormal

unnötig a unnecessary

unord|entlich a untidy; (*nachlässig*) sloppy. **U~nung** f disorder; (*Durcheinander*) muddle

unorthodox a unorthodox ● adv in an unorthodox manner

unparteiisch a impartial

unpassend a inappropriate; <*Moment*> inopportune

unpersönlich a impersonal

unpraktisch a impractical

unpünktlich a unpunctual ● adv late

unrealistisch a unrealistic

unrecht a wrong ● n jdm u~ tun do s.o. an injustice. **U~** nt wrong; **zu U~** wrongly; **U~ haben** be wrong; **jdm U~ geben** disagree with s.o. **u~mäßig** a unlawful

unregelmäßig a irregular

unreif a unripe; (*fig*) immature

unrein a impure; <*Luft*> polluted; <*Haut*> bad; **ins U~e schreiben** make a rough draft of

unrentabel a unprofitable

Unruh|e f -, -n restlessness; (*Erregung*) agitation; (*Besorgnis*) anxiety; **U~en** (*Pol*) unrest sg. **u~ig** a restless; (*laut*) noisy; (*besorgt*) anxious

uns pron (*acc/dat of* wir) us; (*refl*) ourselves; (*einander*) each other

unsauber a dirty; (*nachlässig*) sloppy

unschädlich a harmless

unscharf a blurred

unschätzbar a inestimable

unscheinbar a inconspicuous

unschlagbar a unbeatable

unschlüssig a undecided

Unschuld f - innocence; (*Jungfräulichkeit*) virginity. **u~ig** a innocent

unselbstständig, unselbständig a dependent ● adv **u~** denken not think for oneself

unser poss pron our. **u~e(r,s)** poss pron ours. **u~erseits** adv for our part. **u~twegen** adv for our sake; (*wegen uns*) because of us, on our account

unsicher a unsafe; (*ungewiss*) uncertain; (*nicht zuverlässig*) unreliable; <*Schritte, Hand*> unsteady; <*Person*> insecure ● adv unsteadily. **U~heit** f uncertainty; unreliability; insecurity

unsichtbar a invisible

Unsinn m nonsense. **u~ig** a nonsensical, absurd

Unsitt|e f bad habit. **u~lich** a indecent

unsportlich a not sporty; (*unfair*) unsporting

uns|re(r,s) poss pron = unsere(r,s). **u~rige** poss pron der/die/das **u~rige** ours

unsterblich a immortal. **U~keit** f immortality

Unsumme f vast sum

unsympathisch a unpleasant; **er ist mir u~** I don't like him

untätig a idle

untauglich a unsuitable; (*Mil*) unfit

unten adv at the bottom; (*auf der Unterseite*) underneath; (*eine Treppe tiefer*) downstairs; (*im Text*) below; **hier/da u~** down here/there; **nach u~** down[wards]; (*die Treppe hinunter*) downstairs; **siehe u~** see below

u

unter *prep* (+ *dat/acc*) under; (*niedriger als*) below; (*inmitten, zwischen*) among; **u~ anderem** among other things; **u~ der Woche** during the week; **u~ sich** by themselves

Unter|arm *m* forearm. **U~bewusstsein** *nt* subconscious

unterbieten† *vt insep* undercut; beat <*Rekord*>

unterbinden† *vt insep* stop

unterbrech|en† *vt insep* interrupt; break <*Reise*>. **U~ung** *f* -, -en interruption, break

unterbringen† *vt sep* put; (*beherbergen*) put up

unterdessen *adv* in the meantime

Unterdrückung *f* - suppression; oppression

untere(r,s) *a* lower

untereinander *adv* one below the other; (*miteinander*) among ourselves/yourselves/themselves

unterernähr|t *a* undernourished. **U~ung** *f* malnutrition

Unterführung *f* underpass; (*Fußgänger-*) subway

Untergang *m* (*Astr*) setting; (*Naut*) sinking; (*Zugrundegehen*) disappearance; (*der Welt*) end

Untergebene(r) *m/f* subordinate

untergehen† *vi sep* (sein) (*Astr*) set; (*versinken*) go under; <*Schiff:*> go down, sink; (*zugrunde gehen*) disappear; <*Welt:*> come to an end

Untergeschoss *nt* basement

Untergrund *m* foundation; (*Hintergrund*) background. **U~bahn** *f* underground [railway]

unterhaken *vt sep* **jdn u~** take s.o.'s arm; **untergehakt** arm in arm

unterhalb *adv & prep* (+ *gen*) below

Unterhalt *m* maintenance

unterhalt|en† *vt insep* maintain; (*ernähren*) support; (*betreiben*) run; (*erheitern*) entertain; **sich u~en** talk; (*sich vergnügen*) enjoy oneself. **U~ung** *f* -, -en maintenance; (*Gespräch*) conversation; (*Zeitvertreib*) entertainment

Unter|haus *nt* (*Pol*) lower house; (*in UK*) House of Commons. **U~hemd** *nt* vest. **U~hose** *f* underpants *pl*. **u~irdisch** *a & adv* underground

Unterkiefer *m* lower jaw

unterkommen† *vi sep* (sein) find accommodation; (*eine Stellung finden*) get a job

Unterkunft *f* -, -künfte accommodation

Unterlage *f* pad; **U~n** papers

Unterlass *m* **ohne U~** incessantly

Unterlassung *f* -, -en omission

unterlegen *a* inferior; (*Sport*) losing; **zahlenmäßig u~** outnumbered (*dat* by). **U~e(r)** *m/f* loser

Unterleib *m* abdomen

unterliegen† *vi insep* (sein) lose (*dat* to); (*unterworfen sein*) be subject (*dat* to)

Unterlippe *f* lower lip

Untermiete *f* **zur U~ wohnen** be a lodger. **U~r(in)** *m(f)* lodger

unternehm|en† *vt insep* undertake; take <*Schritte*>; **etw/ nichts u~en** do sth/nothing. **U~en** *nt* -s,- undertaking, enterprise (*Betrieb*) concern. **U~er** *m* -s,- employer; (*Bau-*) contractor; (*Industrieller*) industrialist. **u~ungslustig** *a* enterprising

Unteroffizier *m* non-commissioned officer

unterordnen *vt sep* subordinate

Unterredung *f* -, -en talk

Unterricht *m* -[e]s teaching; (*Privat-*) tuition; (*U~sstunden*) lessons *pl*

unterricht|en *vt/i insep* (*haben*) teach; (*informieren*) inform; **sich u~** inform oneself

Unterrock *m* slip

untersagen *vt insep* forbid

Untersatz *m* mat; (*mit Füßen*) stand; (*Gläser-*) coaster

unterscheid|en† *vt/i insep* (*haben*) distinguish; (*auseinander halten*) tell apart; **sich u~en** differ. **U~ung** *f* -, -en distinction

u

Unterschied *m* -[e]s, -e difference; (*Unterscheidung*) distinction; im U~ zu ihm unlike him. **u~lich** *a* different; (*wechselnd*) varying

unterschlag|en† *vt insep* embezzle; (*verheimlichen*) suppress. **U~ung** *f* -, -en embezzlement; suppression

Unterschlupf *m* -[e]s shelter; (*Versteck*) hiding-place

unterschreiben† *vt/i insep* (*haben*) sign

Unter|schrift *f* signature; (*Bild-*) caption. **U~seeboot** *nt* submarine

Unterstand *m* shelter

unterste(r,s) *a* lowest, bottom

unterstehen† *v insep* ● *vi* (*haben*) be answerable (*dat* to); (*unterliegen*) be subject (*dat* to)

unterstellen¹ *vt sep* put underneath; (*abstellen*) store; **sich u~** shelter

unterstellen² *vt insep* place under the control (*dat* of); (*annehmen*) assume; (*fälschlich zuschreiben*) impute (*dat* to)

unterstreichen† *vt insep* underline

unterstütz|en *vt insep* support; (*helfen*) aid. **U~ung** *f* -, -en support; (*finanziell*) aid; (*regelmäßiger Betrag*) allowance; (*Arbeitslosen-*) benefit

untersuch|en *vt insep* examine; (*Jur*) investigate; (*prüfen*) test; (*überprüfen*) check; (*durchsuchen*) search. **U~ung** *f* -, -en examination; investigation; test; check; search. **U~ungshaft** *f* detention on remand

Untertan *m* -s & -en, -en subject

Untertasse *f* saucer

Unterteil *nt* bottom (part)

Untertitel *m* subtitle

untervermieten *vt/i insep* (*haben*) sublet

Unterwäsche *f* underwear

unterwegs *adv* on the way; (*außer Haus*) out; (*verreist*) away

Unterwelt *f* underworld

unterzeichnen *vt insep* sign

unterziehen† *vt insep* etw einer Untersuchung/Überprüfung u~ examine/ check sth; **sich einer Operation/Prüfung u~** have an operation/take a test

Untier *nt* monster

untragbar *a* intolerable

untrennbar *a* inseparable

untreu *a* disloyal; (*in der Ehe*) unfaithful. **U~e** *f* disloyalty; infidelity

untröstlich *a* inconsolable

unübersehbar *a* obvious; (*groß*) immense

ununterbrochen *a* incessant

unveränderlich *a* invariable; (*gleichbleibend*) unchanging

unverändert *a* unchanged

unverantwortlich *a* irresponsible

unverbesserlich *a* incorrigible

unverbindlich *a* non-committal; (*Comm*) not binding ● *adv* without obligation

unverdaulich *a* indigestible

unver|gesslich *a* unforgettable. **u~gleichlich** *a* incomparable. **u~heiratet** *a* unmarried. **u~käuflich** *a* not for sale; <*Muster*> free

unverkennbar *a* unmistakable

unverletzt *a* unhurt

unvermeidlich *a* inevitable

unver|mindert *a* & *adv* undiminished. **u~mutet** *a* unexpected

Unver|nunft *f* folly. **u~nünftig** *a* foolish

unverschämt *a* insolent; (Ⅱ *ungeheuer*) outrageous. **U~heit** *f* -, -en insolence

unver|sehens *adv* suddenly. **u~sehrt** *a* unhurt; (*unbeschädigt*) intact

unverständlich *a* incomprehensible; (*undeutlich*) indistinct

unverträglich *a* incompatible; <*Person*> quarrelsome; (*unbekömmlich*) indigestible

unver|wundbar *a* invulnerable.
u~wüstlich *a* indestructible;
<Person, Humor> irrepressible;
<Gesundheit> robust. **u~zeihlich** *a*
unforgivable

unverzüglich *a* immediate

unvollendet *a* unfinished

unvollkommen *a* imperfect;
(unvollständig) incomplete

unvollständig *a* incomplete

unvor|bereitet *a* unprepared.
u~hergesehen *a* unforeseen

unvorsichtig *a* careless

unvorstellbar *a* unimaginable

unvorteilhaft *a* unfavourable;
(nicht hübsch) unattractive

unwahr *a* untrue. **U~heit** *f* -, -en
untruth. **u~scheinlich** *a* unlikely;
(unglaublich) improbable; (🔲 *groß*)
incredible

unweit *adv & prep* (+ *gen*) not far

unwesentlich *a* unimportant

Unwetter *nt* -s,- storm

unwichtig *a* unimportant

unwider|legbar *a* irrefutable.
u~stehlich *a* irresistible

Unwill|e *m* displeasure. **u~ig** *a*
angry; *(widerwillig)* reluctant

unwirklich *a* unreal

unwirksam *a* ineffective

unwirtschaftlich *a* uneconomic

unwissen|d *a* ignorant. **U~heit** *f* -
ignorance

unwohl *a* unwell; *(unbehaglich)*
uneasy

unwürdig *a* unworthy (*gen* of)

Unzahl *f* vast number. **unzählig** *a*
innumerable, countless

unzerbrechlich *a* unbreakable

unzerstörbar *a* indestructible

unzertrennlich *a* inseparable

Unzucht *f* sexual offence;
gewerbsmäßige U~ prostitution

unzüchtig *a* indecent; *<Schriften>*
obscene

unzufrieden *a* dissatisfied;
(innerlich) discontented. **U~heit** *f*
dissatisfaction

unzulässig *a* inadmissible

unzurechnungsfähig *a* insane.
U~keit *f* insanity

unzusammenhängend *a*
incoherent

unzutreffend *a* inapplicable;
(falsch) incorrect

unzuverlässig *a* unreliable

unzweifelhaft *a* undoubted

üppig *a* luxuriant; *(überreichlich)*
lavish

uralt *a* ancient

Uran *nt* -s uranium

Uraufführung *f* first performance

Urenkel *m* great-grandson; *(pl)*
great-grandchildren

Urgroß|mutter *f* great-
grandmother. **U~vater** *m* great-
grandfather

Urheber *m* -s,- originator;
(Verfasser) author. **U~recht** *nt*
copyright

Urin *m* -s, -e urine

Urkunde *f* -, -n certificate;
(Dokument) document

Urlaub *m* -s holiday; *(Mil, Admin)*
leave; **auf U~** on holiday/leave; **U~**
haben be on holiday/leave.
U~er(in) *m* -s,- (*f* -, -nen) holiday-
maker. **U~sort** *m* holiday resort

Urne *f* -, -n urn; *(Wahl-)* ballot-box

Ursache *f* cause; *(Grund)* reason;
keine U~! don't mention it!

Ursprung *m* origin

ursprünglich *a* original;
(anfänglich) initial; *(natürlich)*
natural

Urteil *nt* -s, -e judgement; *(Meinung)*
opinion; *(U~sspruch)* verdict;
(Strafe) sentence. **u~en** *vi* (*haben*)
judge

Urwald *m* primeval forest;
(tropischer) jungle

Urzeit *f* primeval times *pl*

USA *pl* USA *sg*

usw. *abbr* (**und so weiter**) etc.

utopisch *a* Utopian

Vv

Vakuum /'va:kuʊm/ *nt* **-s** vacuum.
  v~verpackt *a* vacuum-packed
Vanille /va'nɪljə/ *f* - vanilla
variieren *vt/i* (*haben*) vary
Vase /'va:zə/ *f* -, **-n** vase
Vater *m* **-s,**⁻ father. **V~land** *nt*
  fatherland
väterlich *a* paternal; (*fürsorglich*)
  fatherly. **v~erseits** *adv* on one's/
  the father's side
Vater|schaft *f* - fatherhood; (*Jur*)
  paternity. **V~unser** *nt* **-s,-** Lord's
  Prayer
v. Chr. *abbr* (**vor Christus**) BC
Vegetar|ier(in) /vege'ta:riɐ,
  -iərn/ *m(f)* **-s,-** (*f* -, **-nen**) vegetarian.
  v~isch *a* vegetarian
Veilchen *nt* **-s, -n** violet
Vene /'ve:nə/ *f* -, **-n** vein
Venedig /ve'ne:dɪç/ *nt* **-s** Venice
Ventil /vɛn'ti:l/ *nt* **-s, -e** valve.
  V~ator *m* **-s, -en** /-'to:rən/ fan
verabred|en *vt* arrange; **sich** [**mit
  jdm**] **v~en** arrange to meet [s.o.].
  V~ung *f* -, **-en** arrangement;
  (*Treffen*) appointment
verabschieden *vt* say goodbye to;
  (*aus dem Dienst*) retire; pass
  <*Gesetz*>; **sich v~** say goodbye
verachten *vt* despise
Verachtung *f* - contempt
verallgemeinern *vt/i* (*haben*)
  generalize
veränder|lich *a* changeable;
  (*Math*) variable. **v~n** *vt* change;
  sich v~n change; (*beruflich*) change
  one's job. **V~ung** *f* change
verängstigt *a* frightened, scared
verankern *vt* anchor
veranlag|t *a* künstlerisch/
  musikalisch **v~t sein** have an

artistic/a musical bent; **praktisch
  v~t** practically minded. **V~ung** *f* -,
  -en disposition; (*Neigung*) tendency;
  (*künstlerisch*) bent
veranlassen *vt* (*reg*) arrange for;
  (*einleiten*) institute; **jdn v~** prompt
  s.o. (**zu** to)
veranschlagen *vt* (*reg*) estimate
veranstalt|en *vt* organize; hold,
  give <*Party*>; make <*Lärm*>. **V~er**
  m **-s,-** organizer. **V~ung** *f* -, **-en**
  event
verantwort|lich *a* responsible;
  v~lich machen hold responsible.
  V~ung *f* - responsibility.
  v~ungsbewusst *a* responsible.
  v~ungslos *a* irresponsible.
  v~ungsvoll *a* responsible
verarbeiten *vt* use; (*Techn*)
  process; (*verdauen & fig*) digest
verärgern *vt* annoy
verausgaben (sich) *vr* spend all
  one's money
veräußern *vt* sell
Verb /vɛrp/ *nt* **-s, -en** verb
Verband *m* **-[e]s,⁻e** association;
  (*Mil*) unit; (*Med*) bandage; (*Wund-*)
  dressing. **V~szeug** *nt* first-aid kit
verbann|en *vt* exile; (*fig*) banish.
  V~ung *f* - exile
verbergen† *vt* hide; **sich v~** hide
verbesser|n *vt* improve;
  (*berichtigen*) correct. **V~ung** *f* -, **-en**
  improvement; correction
verbeug|en (sich) *vr* bow.
  V~ung *f* bow
verbeulen *vt* dent
verbiegen† *vt* bend
verbieten† *vt* forbid; (*Admin*)
  prohibit, ban
verbillig|en *vt* reduce [in price].
  v~t *a* reduced
verbinden† *vt* connect (**mit** to);
  (*zusammenfügen*) join; (*verknüpfen*)
  combine; (*in Verbindung bringen*)
  associate; (*Med*) bandage; dress
  <*Wunde*>; **jdn verbunden sein** (*fig*)
  be obliged to s.o.
verbindlich *a* friendly; (*bindend*)
  binding

Verbindung *f* connection; (*Verknüpfung*) combination; (*Kontakt*) contact; (*Vereinigung*) association; **chemiche V~** chemical compound; **in V~ stehen/sich in V~ setzen** be/get in touch

verbissen *a* grim

verbitter|n *vt* make bitter. **v~t** *a* bitter. **V~ung** *f* - bitterness

verblassen *vi* (*sein*) fade

Verbleib *m* -s whereabouts *pl*

verbleit *a* <*Benzin*> leaded

verblüff|en *vt* amaze, astound. **V~ung** *f* - amazement

verblühen *vi* (*sein*) wither, fade

verbluten *vi* (*sein*) bleed to death

verborgen *vt* lend

Verbot *nt* -[e]s, -e ban. **v~en** *a* forbidden; (*Admin*) prohibited

Verbrauch *m* -[e]s consumption. **v~en** *vt* use; consume <*Lebensmittel*>; (*erschöpfen*) use up. **V~er** *m* -s,- consumer

Verbrechen *nt* -s,- crime

Verbrecher *m* -s,- criminal

verbreit|en *vt* spread. **v~et** *a* widespread. **V~ung** *f* - spread; (*Verbreiten*) spreading

verbrenn|en† *vt/i* (*sein*) burn; cremate <*Leiche*>. **V~ung** *f* -, -en burning; cremation; (*Wunde*) burn

verbringen† *vt* spend

verbrühen *vt* scald

verbuchen *vt* enter

verbünd|en (sich) *vr* form an alliance. **V~ete(r)** *m/f* ally

verbürgen *vt* guarantee; **sich v~ für** vouch for

Verdacht *m* -[e]s suspicion; **in** *or* **im V~ haben** suspect

verdächtig *a* suspicious. **v~en** *vt* suspect (*gen* of). **V~te(r)** *m/f* suspect

verdamm|en *vt* condemn; (*Relig*) damn. **v~t** *a & adv* 🗷 damned; **v~t!** damn!

verdampfen *vt/i* (*sein*) evaporate

verdanken *vt* owe (*dat* to)

verdau|en *vt* digest. **v~lich** *a* digestible. **V~ung** *f* - digestion

Verdeck *nt* -[e]s, -e hood; (*Oberdeck*) top deck

verderb|en† *vi* (*sein*) spoil; <*Lebensmittel:*> go bad ● *vt* spoil; **ich habe mir den Magen verdorben** I have an upset stomach. **V~en** *nt* -s ruin. **v~lich** *a* perishable; (*schädlich*) pernicious

verdien|en *vt/i* (*haben*) earn; (*fig*) deserve. **V~er** *m* -s,- wage-earner

Verdienst[1] *m* -[e]s earnings *pl*

Verdienst[2] *nt* -[e]s, -e merit

verdient *a* well-deserved

verdoppeln *vt* double

verdorben *a* spoilt, ruined; <*Magen*> upset; (*moralisch*) corrupt; (*verkommen*) depraved

verdreh|en *vt* twist; roll <*Augen*>; (*fig*) distort. **v~t** *a* 🗉 crazy

verdreifachen *vt* treble, triple

verdrücken *vt* crumple; (🗉 *essen*) polish off; **sich v~** 🗉 slip away

Verdruss *m* -es annoyance

verdünnen *vt* dilute; **sich v~** taper off

verdunst|en *vi* (*sein*) evaporate. **V~ung** *f* - evaporation

verdursten *vi* (*sein*) die of thirst

veredeln *vt* refine; (*Hort*) graft

verehr|en *vt* revere; (*Relig*) worship; (*bewundern*) admire; (*schenken*) give. **V~er(in)** *m* -s,- (*f* -, -nen) admirer. **V~ung** *f* - veneration; worship; admiration

vereidigen *vt* swear in

Verein *m* -s, -e society; (*Sport-*) club

vereinbar *a* compatible. **v~en** *vt* arrange. **V~ung** *f* -, -en agreement

vereinfachen *vt* simplify

vereinheitlichen *vt* standardize

vereinig|en *vt* unite; merge <*Firmen*>; **wieder v~en** reunite; reunify <*Land*>; **sich v~en** unite; **V~te Staaten [von Amerika]** United States *sg* [of America]. **V~ung** *f* -, -en union; (*Organisation*) organization

vereinzelt *a* isolated ● *adv* occasionally

vereist *a* frozen; <*Straße*> icy

V

vereitert a septic

verenden vi (sein) die

verengen vt restrict; **sich v~** narrow; <Pupille:> contract

vererb|en vt leave (dat to); (Biol & fig) pass on (dat to). **V~ung** f - heredity

verfahren† vi (sein) proceed; **v~ mit** deal with ● vr **sich v~** lose one's way ● a muddled. **V~** nt -s,- procedure; (Techn) process; (Jur) proceedings pl

Verfall m decay; (eines Gebäudes) dilapidation; (körperlich & fig) decline; (Ablauf) expiry. **v~en**† vi (sein) decay; <Person, Sitten:> decline; (ablaufen) expire; **v~en in** (+ acc) lapse into; **v~en auf** (+ acc) hit on <Idee>

verfärben (sich) vr change colour; <Stoff:> discolour

verfass|en vt write; (Jur) draw up; (entwerfen) draft. **V~er** m -s,- author. **V~ung** f (Pol) constitution; (Zustand) state

verfaulen vi (sein) rot, decay

verfechten† vt advocate

verfehlen vt miss

verfeinde|n (sich) vr become enemies; **v~t sein** be enemies

verfeinern vt refine; (verbessern) improve

verfilmen vt film

verfluch|en vt curse. **v~t** a & adv ⚠ damned; **v~t!** damn!

verfolg|en vt pursue; (folgen) follow; (bedrängen) pester; (Pol) persecute; **strafrechtlich v~en** prosecute. **V~er** m -s,- pursuer. **V~ung** f - pursuit; persecution

verfrüht a premature

verfügbar a available

verfüg|en vt order; (Jur) decree ● vi (haben) **v~en über** (+ acc) have at one's disposal. **V~ung** f -, -en order; (Jur) decree; **jdm zur V~ung stehen** be at s.o.'s disposal

verführ|en vt seduce; tempt. **V~ung** f seduction; temptation

vergangen a past; (letzte) last. **V~heit** f - past; (Gram) past tense

vergänglich a transitory

vergas|en vt gas. **V~er** m -s,- carburettor

vergeb|en† vt award (an + dat to); (weggeben) give away; (verzeihen) forgive. **v~lich** a futile, vain ● adv in vain. **V~ung** f - forgiveness

vergehen† vi (sein) pass; **sich v~** violate (gegen etw sth). **V~** nt -s,- offence

vergelt|en† vt repay. **V~ung** f - retaliation; (Rache) revenge

vergessen† vt forget; (liegen lassen) leave behind

vergesslich a forgetful. **V~keit** f - forgetfulness

vergeuden vt waste, squander

vergewaltig|en vt rape. **V~ung** f -, -en rape

vergießen† vt spill; shed <Tränen, Blut>

vergift|en vt poison. **V~ung** f -, -en poisoning

Vergissmeinnicht nt -[e]s, -[e] forget-me-not

vergittert a barred

verglasen vt glaze

Vergleich m -[e]s, -e comparison; (Jur) settlement. **v~bar** a comparable. **v~en**† vt compare (mit with/to)

vergnüg|en (sich) vr enjoy oneself. **V~en** nt -s,- pleasure; (Spaß) fun; **viel V~en!** have a good time! **v~t** a cheerful; (zufrieden) happy. **V~ungen** fpl entertainments

vergolden vt gild; (plattieren) gold-plate

vergraben† vt bury

vergriffen a out of print

vergrößer|n vt enlarge; <Linse:> magnify; (vermehren) increase; (erweitern) extend; expand <Geschäft>; **sich v~n** grow bigger; <Firma:> expand; (zunehmen) increase. **V~ung** f -, -en magnification; increase; expansion;

V

(Phot) enlargement. **V∼ungsglas** *nt* magnifying glass

vergüt|en *vt* pay for; jdm etw v∼en reimburse s.o. for sth. **V∼ung** *f* -, -en remuneration; *(Erstattung)* reimbursement

verhaft|en *vt* arrest. **V∼ung** *f*-, -en arrest

verhalten† **(sich)** *vr* behave; *(handeln)* act; *(beschaffen sein)* be. **V∼** *nt* -s behaviour, conduct

Verhältnis *nt* -ses, -se relationship; *(Liebes-)* affair; *(Math)* ratio; **V∼se** circumstances; conditions. **v∼mäßig** *adv* comparatively, relatively

verhand|eln *vt* discuss; *(Jur)* try ● *vi (haben)* negotiate. **V∼lung** *f (Jur)* trial; **V∼lungen** negotiations

Verhängnis *nt* -ses fate, doom

verhärten *vt/i (sein)* harden

verhasst *a* hated

verhätscheln *vt* spoil

verhauen† *vt* 🄵 beat; make a mess of <*Prüfung*>

verheilen *vi (sein)* heal

verheimlichen *vt* keep secret

verheirat|en (sich) *vr* get married (mit to); sich wieder v∼en remarry. **v∼et** *a* married

verhelfen† *vi (haben)* jdm zu etw v∼ help s.o. get sth

verherrlichen *vt* glorify

verhexen *vt* bewitch

verhinder|n *vt* prevent; **v∼t sein** be unable to come

Verhör *nt* -s, -e interrogation; ins V∼ nehmen interrogate. **v∼en** *vt* interrogate; sich v∼en mishear

verhungern *vi (sein)* starve

verhüt|en *vt* prevent. **V∼ung** *f* - prevention. **V∼ungsmittel** *nt* contraceptive

verirren (sich) *vr* get lost

verjagen *vt* chase away

verjüngen *vt* rejuvenate

verkalkt *a* 🄵 senile

verkalkulieren (sich) *vr* miscalculate

Verkauf *m* sale; zum V∼ for sale. **v∼en** *vt* sell; zu v∼en for sale

Verkäufer(in) *m(f)* seller; *(im Geschäft)* shop assistant

Verkehr *m* -s traffic; *(Kontakt)* contact; *(Geschlechts-)* intercourse; aus dem V∼ ziehen take out of circulation. **v∼en** *vi (haben)* operate; <*Bus, Zug*:> run; *(Umgang haben)* associate, mix (mit with); *(Gast sein)* visit (bei jdm s.o.)

Verkehrs|ampel *f* traffic lights *pl*. **V∼unfall** *m* road accident. **V∼verein** *m* tourist office. **V∼zeichen** *nt* traffic sign

verkehrt *a* wrong; **v∼ herum** *adv* the wrong way round; *(links)* inside out

verklagen *vt* sue (auf + *acc* for)

verkleid|en *vt* disguise; *(Techn)* line; sich v∼en disguise oneself; *(für Kostümfest)* dress up. **V∼ung** *f* -, -en disguise; *(Kostüm)* fancy dress; *(Techn)* lining

verkleiner|n *vt* reduce [in size]. **V∼ung** *f* - reduction

verknittern *vt/i (sein)* crumple

verknüpfen *vt* knot together

verkommen† *vi (sein)* be neglected; *(sittlich)* go to the bad; *(verfallen)* decay; <*Haus*:> fall into disrepair; <*Gegend*:> become run-down; <*Lebensmittel*:> go bad ● *a* neglected; *(sittlich)* depraved; <*Haus*> dilapidated; <*Gegend*> run-down

verkörpern *vt* embody, personify

verkraften *vt* cope with

verkrampft *a (fig)* tense

verkriechen† **(sich)** *vr* hide

verkrümmt *a* crooked, bent

verkrüppelt *a* crippled; <*Glied*> deformed

verkühl|en (sich) *vr* catch a chill. **V∼ung** *f* -, -en chill

verkümmern *vi (sein)* waste/ <*Pflanze*:> wither away

verkünden *vt* announce; pronounce <*Urteil*>

V

verkürzen *vt* shorten; (*verringern*) reduce; (*abbrechen*) cut short; while away <*Zeit*>

Verlag *m* -[e]s, -e publishing firm

verlangen *vt* ask for; (*fordern*) demand; (*berechnen*) charge. **V∼** *nt* -s desire; (*Bitte*) request

verlänger|n *vt* extend; lengthen <*Kleid*>; (*zeitlich*) prolong; renew <*Pass, Vertrag*>; (*Culin*) thin down. **V∼ung** *f* -, -en extension; renewal. **V∼ungsschnur** *f* extension cable

verlassen† *vt* leave; (*im Stich lassen*) desert; **sich v∼ auf** (+ *acc*) rely *or* depend on ● *a* deserted. **V∼heit** *f* - desolation

verlässlich *a* reliable

Verlauf *m* course; **im V∼** (+ *gen*) in the course of. **v∼en†** *vi* (*sein*) run; (*ablaufen*) go; **gut v∼en** go [off] well ● *vr* **sich v∼en** lose one's way

verlegen *vt* move; (*verschieben*) postpone; (*vor-*) bring forward; (*verlieren*) mislay; (*versperren*) block; (*legen*) lay <*Teppich, Rohre*>; (*veröffentlichen*) publish; **sich v∼ auf** (+ *acc*) take up <*Beruf*>; resort to <*Bitten*> ● *a* embarrassed. **V∼heit** *f* - embarrassment

Verleger *m* -s,- publisher

verleihen† *vt* lend; (*gegen Gebühr*) hire out; (*überreichen*) award, confer; (*fig*) give

verlernen *vt* forget

verletz|en *vt* injure; (*kränken*) hurt; (*verstoßen gegen*) infringe; violate <*Grenze*>. **v∼end** *a* hurtful, wounding. **V∼te(r)** *m|f* injured person; (*bei Unfall*) casualty. **V∼ung** *f* -, -en (*Verstoß*) infringement; violation

verleugnen *vt* deny; disown <*Freund*>

verleumd|en *vt* slander; (*schriftlich*) libel. **v∼erisch** *a* slanderous; libellous. **V∼ung** *f* -, -en slander; (*schriftlich*) libel

verlieben (sich) *vr* fall in love (in + *acc* with); **verliebt sein** be in love (in + *acc* with)

verlier|en† *vt* lose; shed <*Laub*> ● *vi* (*haben*) lose (an etw *dat* sth). **V∼er** *m* -s,- loser

verlob|en (sich) *vr* get engaged (mit to); **v∼t sein** be engaged. **V∼te** *f* fiancée. **V∼te(r)** *m* fiancé. **V∼ung** *f* -, -en engagement

verlock|en *vt* tempt. **V∼ung** *f* -, -en temptation

verloren *a* lost; **v∼ gehen** get lost

verlos|en *vt* raffle. **V∼ung** *f* -, -en raffle; (*Ziehung*) draw

Verlust *m* -[e]s, -e loss

vermachen *vt* leave, bequeath

Vermächtnis *nt* -ses, -se legacy

vermähl|en (sich) *vr* marry. **V∼ung** *f* -, -en marriage

vermehren *vt* increase; propagate <*Pflanzen*>; **sich v∼** increase; (*sich fortpflanzen*) breed

vermeiden† *vt* avoid

Vermerk *m* -[e]s, -e note. **v∼en** note [down]

vermessen† *vt* measure; survey <*Gelände*> ● *a* presumptuous

vermiet|en *vt* let, rent [out]; hire out <*Boot, Auto*>; **zu v∼en** to let; <*Boot:*> for hire. **V∼er** *m* landlord. **V∼erin** *f* landlady

vermindern *vt* reduce

vermischen *vt* mix

vermissen *vt* miss

vermisst *a* missing

vermitteln *vi* (*haben*) mediate ● *vt* arrange; (*beschaffen*) find; place <*Arbeitskräfte*>

Vermittl|er *m* -s,- agent; (*Schlichter*) mediator. **V∼ung** *f* -, -en arrangement; (*Agentur*) agency; (*Teleph*) exchange; (*Schlichtung*) mediation

Vermögen *nt* -s,- fortune. **v∼d** *a* wealthy

vermut|en *vt* suspect; (*glauben*) presume. **v∼lich** *a* probable ● *adv* presumably. **V∼ung** *f* -, -en supposition; (*Verdacht*) suspicion

vernachlässigen *vt* neglect

vernehm|en† *vt* hear; (*verhören*) question; (*Jur*) examine. **V∼ung** *f* -, -en questioning

verneigen (sich) *vr* bow

vernein|en *vt* answer in the negative; (*ablehnen*) reject. **v~end** *a* negative. **V~ung** *f* -, -en negative answer

vernicht|en *vt* destroy; (*ausrotten*) exterminate. **V~ung** *f* - destruction; extermination

Vernunft *f* - reason

vernünftig *a* reasonable, sensible

veröffentlich|en *vt* publish. **V~ung** *f* -, -en publication

verordn|en *vt* prescribe (*dat* for). **V~ung** *f* -, -en prescription; (*Verfügung*) decree

verpachten *vt* lease [out]

verpack|en *vt* pack; (*einwickeln*) wrap. **V~ung** *f* packaging; wrapping

verpassen *vt* miss; (🄸 *geben*) give

verpfänden *vt* pawn

verpflanzen *vt* transplant

verpfleg|en *vt* feed: sich selbst v~en cater for oneself. **V~ung** *f* - board; (*Essen*) food; **Unterkunft und V~ung** board and lodging

verpflicht|en *vt* oblige; (*einstellen*) engage; (*Sport*) sign; sich v~en undertake/(*versprechen*) promise (**zu** to); (*vertraglich*) sign a contract. **V~ung** *f* -, -en obligation, commitment

verprügeln *vt* beat up, thrash

Verputz *m* -es plaster. **v~en** *vt* plaster

Verrat *m* -[e]s betrayal, treachery. **v~en†** *vt* betray; give away <*Geheimnis*>

Verräter *m* -s,- traitor

verrech|nen *vt* settle; clear <*Scheck*>; sich v~nen make a mistake; (*fig*) miscalculate. **V~nungsscheck** *m* crossed cheque

verreisen *vi* (*sein*) go away; **verreist sein** be away

verrenken *vt* dislocate

verrichten *vt* perform, do

verriegeln *vt* bolt

verringer|n *vt* reduce; sich v~n decrease. **V~ung** *f* - reduction; decrease

verrost|en *vi* (*sein*) rust. **v~et** *a* rusty

verrückt *a* crazy, mad. **V~e(r)** *m/f* lunatic, **V~heit** *f* -, -en madness; (*Torheit*) folly

verrühren *vt* mix

verrunzelt *a* wrinkled

verrutschen *vt* (*sein*) slip

Vers /fɛrs/ *m* -es, -e verse

versag|en *vi* (*haben*) fail ● *vt* sich etw v~en deny oneself sth. **V~en** *nt* -s,- failure. **V~er** *m* -s,- failure

versalzen† *vt* put too much salt in/on; (*fig*) spoil

versamm|eln *vt* assemble. **V~lung** *f* assembly, meeting

Versand *m* -[e]s dispatch. **V~haus** *nt* mail-order firm

versäumen *vt* miss; lose <*Zeit*>; (*unterlassen*) neglect; **[es] v~, etw zu tun** fail to do sth

verschärfen *vt* intensify; tighten <*Kontrolle*>; increase <*Tempo*>; aggravate <*Lage*>; sich v~ intensify; increase; <*Lage*> worsen

verschätzen (sich) *vr* sich v~ in (+ *dat*) misjudge

verschenken *vt* give away

verscheuchen *vt* shoo/(*jagen*) chase away

verschicken *vt* send; (*Comm*) dispatch

verschieb|en† *vt* move; (*aufschieben*) put off, postpone; sich v~en move, shift; (*verrutschen*) slip; (*zeitlich*) be postponed. **V~ung** *f* shift; postponement

verschieden *a* different; **v~e** *pl* different; (*mehrere*) various; **V~es** some things; (*dieses und jenes*) various things; **das ist v~** it varies ● *adv* differently; **v~ groß** of different sizes. **v~artig** *a* diverse

verschimmel|n *vi* (*sein*) go mouldy. **v~t** *a* mouldy

verschlafen† *vi* (*haben*) oversleep ● *vt* sleep through <*Tag*>; sich v~ oversleep ● *a* sleepy

verschlagen† *vt* lose <*Seite*>; **jdm die Sprache/den Atem v~** leave s.o. speechless/take s.o.'s breath away ● *a* sly

verschlechter|n *vt* make worse; **sich v~n** get worse, deteriorate. **V~ung** *f* -, -en deterioration

Verschleiß *m* -es wear and tear

verschleppen *vt* carry off; (*entführen*) abduct; spread <*Seuche*>; neglect <*Krankheit*>; (*hinausziehen*) delay

verschleudern *vt* sell at a loss

verschließen† *vt* close; (*abschließen*) lock; (*einschließen*) lock up

verschlimmer|n *vt* make worse; aggravate <*Lage*>; **sich v~n** get worse, deteriorate. **V~ung** *f* -, -en deterioration

verschlossen *a* reserved. **V~heit** *f* - reserve

verschlucken *vt* swallow; **sich v~** choke (**an** + *dat* on)

Verschluss *m* -es,-̈e fastener, clasp; (*Koffer-*) catch; (*Flaschen-*) top; (*luftdicht*) seal; (*Phot*) shutter

verschlüsselt *a* coded

verschmelzen† *vt/i* (sein) fuse

verschmerzen *vt* get over

verschmutz|en *vt* soil; pollute <*Luft*> ● *vi* (sein) get dirty. **V~ung** *f* - pollution

verschneit *a* snow-covered

verschnörkelt *a* ornate

verschnüren *vt* tie up

verschollen *a* missing

verschonen *vt* spare

verschossen *a* faded

verschränken *vt* cross

verschreiben† *vt* prescribe; **sich v~** make a slip of the pen

verschulden *vt* be to blame for. **V~** *nt* -s fault

verschuldet *a* **v~ sein** be in debt

verschütten *vt* spill; (*begraben*) bury

verschweigen† *vt* conceal, hide

verschwend|en *vt* waste. **V~ung** *f* - extravagance; (*Vergeudung*) waste

verschwiegen *a* discreet

verschwinden† *vi* (sein) disappear; [mal] **v~** 🛈 spend a penny

verschwommen *a* blurred

verschwör|en† (sich) *vr* conspire. **V~ung** *f* -, -en conspiracy

versehen† *vt* perform; hold <*Posten*>; keep <*Haushalt*>; **v~ mit** provide with; **sich v~** make a mistake. **V~** *nt* -s,- oversight; (*Fehler*) slip; **aus V~** by mistake. **v~tlich** *adv* by mistake

Versehrte(r) *m* disabled person

versengen *vt* singe; (*stärker*) scorch

versenken *vt* sink

versessen *a* keen (**auf** + *acc* on)

versetz|en *vt* move; transfer <*Person*>; (*Sch*) move up; (*verpfänden*) pawn; (*verkaufen*) sell; (*vermischen*) blend; **jdn v~en** (🛈 warten lassen) stand s.o. up; **jdm in Angst/Erstaunen v~en** frighten/ astonish s.o.; **sich in jds Lage v~en** put oneself in s.o.'s place. **V~ung** *f* -, -en move; transfer; (*Sch*) move to a higher class

verseuchen *vt* contaminate

versicher|n *vt* insure; (*bekräftigen*) affirm; **jdm v~n** assure s.o (**dass** that). **V~ung** *f* -, -en insurance; assurance

versiegeln *vt* seal

versiert /vɛrˈʒiːɐt/ *a* experienced

versilbert *a* silver-plated

Versmaß /ˈfɛrs-/ *nt* metre

versöhn|en *vt* reconcile; **sich v~en** become reconciled. **V~ung** *f* -, -en reconciliation

versorg|en *vt* provide, supply (**mit** with); provide for <*Familie*>; (*betreuen*) look after. **V~ung** *f* - provision, supply; (*Betreuung*) care

verspät|en (sich) *vr* be late. **v~et** *a* late; <*Zug*> delayed; <*Dank*> belated. **V~ung** *f* - lateness; **v~ung haben** be late

versperren *vt* block; bar <*Weg*>

verspiel|en vt gamble away. **v~t** a playful

verspotten vt mock, ridicule

versprech|en† vt promise; sich v~en make a slip of the tongue; sich (dat) viel v~en von have high hopes of; ein viel v~ender Anfang a promising start. **V~en** nt -s,- promise. **V~ungen** fpl promises

verstaatlich|en vt nationalize. **V~ung** f - nationalization

Verstand m -[e]s mind; (Vernunft) reason; den V~ verlieren go out of one's mind

verständig a sensible; (klug) intelligent. **v~en** vt notify, inform; sich v~en communicate; (sich verständlich machen) make oneself understood. **V~ung** f - notification; communication; (Einigung) agreement

verständlich a comprehensible; (deutlich) clear; (begreiflich) understandable; sich v~ machen make oneself understood. **v~erweise** adv understandably

Verständnis nt -ses understanding

verstärk|en vt strengthen, reinforce; (steigern) intensify, increase; amplify <Ton>. **V~er** m -s,- amplifier. **V~ung** f reinforcement; increase; amplification; (Truppen) reinforcements pl

verstaubt a dusty

verstauchen vt sprain

Versteck nt -[e]s, -e hiding-place. V~ spielen play hide-and-seek. **v~en** vt hide; sich v~en hide

verstehen† vt understand; (können) know; **falsch v~** misunderstand; sich v~en understand one another; (auskommen) get on

versteiger|n vt auction. **V~ung** f auction

versteinert a fossilized

verstell|en vt adjust; (versperren) block; (verändern) disguise; sich v~en pretend. **V~ung** f - pretence

versteuern vt pay tax on

verstimm|t a disgruntled; <Magen> upset; (Mus) out of tune. **V~ung** f - ill humour; (Magen-) upset

verstockt a stubborn

verstopf|en vt plug; (versperren) block; **v~t** blocked; <Person> constipated. **V~ung** f -, -en blockage; (Med) constipation

verstorben a late, deceased. **V~e(r)** m/f deceased

verstört a bewildered

Verstoß m infringement. **v~en**† vt disown ● vi (haben) v~en gegen contravene, infringe

verstreuen vt scatter

verstümmeln vt mutilate; garble <Text>

Versuch m -[e]s, -e attempt; (Experiment) experiment. **v~en** vt/i (haben) try; **v~t** sein be tempted (zu to). **V~ung** f -, -en temptation

vertagen vt adjourn; (aufschieben) postpone; sich v~ adjourn

vertauschen vt exchange; (verwechseln) mix up

verteidig|en vt defend. **V~er** m -s,- defender; (Jur) defence counsel. **V~ung** f -, -en defence

verteil|en vt distribute; (zuteilen) allocate; (ausgeben) hand out; (verstreichen) spread. **V~ung** f - distribution; allocation

vertief|en vt deepen; **v~t** sein in (+ acc) be engrossed in. **V~ung** f -, -en hollow, depression

vertikal /vɛrti'ka:l/ a vertical

vertilgen vt exterminate; kill [off] <Unkraut>

vertippen (sich) vr make a typing mistake

vertonen vt set to music

Vertrag m -[e]s, ̈-e contract; (Pol) treaty

vertragen† vt tolerate, stand; take <Kritik, Spaß>; sich v~ get on

vertraglich a contractual

verträglich a good-natured; (bekömmlich) digestible

vertrauen vi (haben) trust (jdm/etw s.o./sth; auf + acc in). **V~** nt -s trust, confidence (**zu** in); **im V**∼ in confidence. **v**∼**swürdig** *a* trustworthy

vertraulich *a* confidential; (*intim*) familiar

vertraut *a* intimate; (*bekannt*) familiar. **V**∼**heit** *f* - intimacy; familiarity

vertreib|en† *vt* drive away; drive out <*Feind*>; (*Comm*) sell; **sich** (*dat*) **die Zeit v**∼**en** pass the time. **V**∼**ung** *f* -, -en expulsion

vertret|en† *vt* represent; (*einspringen für*) stand in *or* deputize for; (*verfechten*) support; hold <*Meinung*>; **sich** (*dat*) **den Fuß v**∼**en** twist one's ankle. **V**∼**er** *m* -s,- representative; deputy; (*Arzt-*) locum; (*Verfechter*) supporter. **V**∼**ung** *f* -, -en representation; (*Person*) deputy; (*eines Arztes*) locum; (*Handels-*) agency

Vertrieb *m* -[e]s (*Comm*) sale

vertrocknen *vi* (*sein*) dry up

verüben *vt* commit

verunglücken *vi* (*sein*) be involved in an accident; (**ⓕ** *missglücken*) go wrong; **tödlich v**∼ be killed in an accident

verunreinigen *vt* pollute; (*verseuchen*) contaminate

verursachen *vt* cause

verurteil|en *vt* condemn; (*Jur*) convict (**wegen** of); sentence (**zum Tode** to death). **V**∼**ung** *f* - condemnation; (*Jur*) conviction

vervielfachen *vt* multiply

vervielfältigen *vt* duplicate

vervollständigen *vt* complete

verwählen (sich) *vr* misdial

verwahren *vt* keep; (*verstauen*) put away

verwahrlost *a* neglected; <*Haus*> dilapidated

Verwahrung *f* - keeping; **in V**∼ **nehmen** take into safe keeping

verwaist *a* orphaned

verwalt|en *vt* administer; (*leiten*) manage; govern <*Land*>. **V**∼**er** *m*

-s,- administrator; manager. **V**∼**ung** *f* -, -en administration; management; government

verwand|eln *vt* transform, change (**in** + *acc* into) **sich v**∼**eln** change, turn (**in** + *acc* into). **V**∼**lung** *f* transformation

verwandt *a* related (**mit** to). **V**∼**e(r)** *m/f* relative. **V**∼**schaft** *f* - relationship; (*Menschen*) relatives *pl*

verwarn|en *vt* warn, caution. **V**∼**ung** *f* warning, caution

verwechs|eln *vt* mix up, confuse; (*halten für*) mistake (**mit** for). **V**∼**lung** *f* -, -en mix-up

verweiger|n *vt/i* (*haben*) refuse (**jdm etw** s.o sth). **V**∼**ung** *f* refusal

Verweis *m* -es, -e reference (**auf** + *acc* to); (*Tadel*) reprimand; **v**∼**en†** *vt* refer (**auf/an** + *acc* to); (*tadeln*) reprimand; **von der Schule v**∼**en** expel

verwelken *vi* (*sein*) wilt

verwend|en† *vt* use; spend <*Zeit, Mühe*>. **V**∼**ung** *f* use

verwerten *vt* utilize, use

verwesen *vi* (*sein*) decompose

verwick|eln *vt* involve (**in** + *acc* in); **sich v**∼**eln** get tangled up. **v**∼**elt** *a* complicated

verwildert *a* wild; <*Garten*> overgrown; <*Aussehen*> unkempt

verwinden† *vt* (*fig*) get over

verwirklichen *vt* realize

verwirr|en *vt* tangle up; (*fig*) confuse; **sich v**∼**en** get tangled; (*fig*) become confused. **v**∼**t** *a* confused. **V**∼**ung** *f* - confusion

verwischen *vt* smudge

verwittert *a* weathered

verwitwet *a* widowed

verwöhn|en *vt* spoil. **v**∼**t** *a* spoilt

verworren *a* confused

verwund|bar *a* vulnerable. **v**∼**en** *vt* wound

verwunder|lich *a* surprising. **v**∼**n** *vt* surprise; **sich v**∼**n** be surprised. **V**∼**ung** *f* - surprise

Verwund|ete(r) *m* wounded soldier; **die V**∼**eten** the wounded *pl*. **V**∼**ung** *f* -, -en wound

verwüst|en *vt* devastate, ravage.
  V∼ung *f* -, -en devastation
verzählen (sich) *vr* miscount
verzaubern *vt* bewitch; (*fig*)
  enchant; **v∼ in** (+ *acc*) turn into
Verzehr *m* -s consumption. **v∼en**
  vt eat
verzeih|en† *vt* forgive; **v∼en Sie!**
  excuse me! **V∼ung** *f* - forgiveness;
  um V∼ung bitten apologize; **V∼ung!**
  sorry! (*bei Frage*) excuse me!
Verzicht *m* -[e]s renunciation (**auf** +
  acc of). **v∼en** *vi* (*haben*) do without;
  v∼en auf (+ *acc*) give up; renounce
  <*Recht, Erbe*>
verziehen† *vt* pull out of shape;
  (*verwöhnen*) spoil; **sich v∼** lose
  shape; <*Holz:*> warp; <*Gesicht:*>
  twist; (*verschwinden*) disappear;
  <*Nebel:*> disperse; <*Gewitter:*> pass
  ● *vi* (*sein*) move [away]
verzier|en *vt* decorate. **V∼ung** *f* -,
  -en decoration
verzinsen *vt* pay interest on
verzöger|n *vt* delay; (*verlangsamen*)
  slow down. **V∼ung** *f* -, -en delay
verzollen *vt* pay duty on; **haben Sie**
  etwas zu v∼? have you anything to
  declare?
verzweif|eln *vi* (*sein*) despair.
  v∼elt *a* desperate. **V∼lung** *f* -
  despair; (*Ratlosigkeit*) desperation
verzweigen (sich) *vr* branch [out]
Veto /'ve:to/ *nt* -s, -s veto
Vetter *m* -s, -n cousin
vgl. *abbr* (*vergleiche*) cf.
Viadukt /via'dʊkt/ *nt* -[e]s, -e
  viaduct
Video /'vi:deo/ *nt* -s, -s video.
  V∼kassette *f* video cassette.
  V∼recorder /-rəkɔrdɐ/ *m* -s,-
  video recorder
Vieh *nt* -[e]s livestock; (*Rinder*) cattle
  pl; (🄸 *Tier*) creature
viel *pron* a great deal/🄸 a lot of; (*pl*)
  many, 🄸 a lot of; (*substantivisch*)
  v∼[es] much, 🄸 a lot; **nicht/so/wie/**
  zu v∼ not/so/how/too much/ (*pl*)
  many; **v∼e** *pl* many; **das v∼e Geld**
  all that money ● *adv* much, 🄸 a lot;
  v∼ mehr/weniger much more/less;

v∼ zu groß/klein much *or* far too
  big/small; **so v∼ wie möglich** as
  much as possible; **so/zu v∼ arbeiten**
  work so/too much
viel|deutig *a* ambiguous. **v∼fach**
  a multiple ● *adv* many times; (🄸 *oft*)
  frequently. **V∼falt** *f* - diversity,
  [great] variety
vielleicht *adv* perhaps, maybe; (🄸
  wirklich) really
vielmals *adv* very much
vielmehr *adv* rather; (*im Gegenteil*)
  on the contrary
vielseitig *a* varied; <*Person*>
  versatile. **V∼keit** *f* - versatility
vielversprechend* *a* viel
  versprechend, s. versprechen
vier *inv a*, **V∼** *f* -, -en four; (*Sch*) ≈
  fair. **V∼eck** *nt* -[e]s, -e oblong,
  rectangle; (*Quadrat*) square.
  v∼eckig *a* oblong, rectangular;
  square. **V∼linge** *mpl* quadruplets
viertel /'fɪrtəl/ *inv a* quarter; **um v∼**
  neun at [a] quarter past eight; **um**
  drei v∼ neun at [a] quarter to nine.
  V∼ *nt* -s, - quarter; (*Wein*) quarter
  litre; **V∼ vor/nach sechs** [a] quarter
  to/past six. **V∼finale** *nt* quarter-
  final. **V∼jahr** *nt* three months *pl*;
  (*Comm*) quarter. **v∼jährlich** *a* &
  adv quarterly. **V∼stunde** *f* quarter
  of an hour
vier|zehn /'fɪr-/ *inv a* fourteen.
  v∼zehnte(r,s) *a* fourteenth.
  v∼zig *inv a* forty. **v∼zigste(r,s)** *a*
  fortieth
Villa /'vɪla/ *f* -, -len villa
violett /vio'lɛt/ *a* violet
Vio|line /vio'li:nə/ *f* -, -n violin.
  V∼linschlüssel *m* treble clef
Virus /'vi:rʊs/ *nt* -, -ren virus
Visier /vi'zi:ɐ/ *nt* -s, -e visor
Visite /vi'zi:tə/ *f* -, -n round; **V∼**
  machen do one's round
Visum /'vi:zʊm/ *nt* -s, -sa visa
Vitamin /vita'mi:n/ *nt* -s, -e vitamin
Vitrine /vi'tri:nə/ *f* -, -n display
  cabinet/(*im Museum*) case
Vizepräsident /'fi:tsə-/ *m* vice
  president

Vogel *m* -s,- bird; einen V∼ haben 🛈 have a screw loose. **V∼scheuche** *f* -, -n scarecrow

Vokabeln /vo'ka:bəln/ *fpl* vocabulary *sg*

Vokal /vo'ka:l/ *m* -s, -e vowel

Volant /vo'lã:/ *m* -s, -s flounce

Volk *nt* -[e]s,-̈er people *sg*; (*Bevölkerung*) people *pl*

Völker|kunde *f* ethnology. **V∼mord** *m* genocide. **V∼recht** *nt* international law

Volks|abstimmung *f* plebiscite. **V∼fest** *nt* public festival. **V∼hochschule** *f* adult education classes *pl*/(*Gebäude*) centre. **V∼lied** *nt* folk-song. **V∼tanz** *m* folk-dance. **v∼tümlich** *a* popular. **V∼wirt** *m* economist. **V∼wirtschaft** *f* economics *sg*. **V∼zählung** *f* [national] census

voll *a* full (von *od* mit of); <*Haar*> thick; <*Erfolg, Ernst*> complete; <*Wahrheit*> whole; **v∼ machen** fill up; **v∼ tanken** fill up with petrol ● *adv* (*ganz*) completely; <*arbeiten*> full-time; <*auszahlen*> in full; **v∼ und ganz** completely

Vollblut *nt* thoroughbred

vollende|n *vt insep* complete. **v∼t** *a* perfect

Vollendung *f* completion; (*Vollkommenheit*) perfection

voller *inv a* full of

Volleyball /'vɔli-/ *m* volleyball

vollführen *vt insep* perform

vollfüllen *vt sep* fill up

Vollgas *nt* V∼ **geben** put one's foot down; **mit V∼** flat out

völlig *a* complete

volljährig *a* **v∼ sein** (*Jur*) be of age. **V∼keit** *f* - (*Jur*) majority

Vollkaskoversicherung *f* fully comprehensive insurance

vollkommen *a* perfect; (*völlig*) complete

Voll|kornbrot *nt* wholemeal bread. **V∼macht** *f* -, -en authority; (*Jur*)

power of attorney. **V∼mond** *m* full moon. **V∼pension** *f* full board

vollständig *a* complete

vollstrecken *vt insep* execute; carry out <*Urteil*>

volltanken* *vi sep* (*haben*) **voll tanken**, *s.* **voll**

Volltreffer *m* direct hit

vollzählig *a* complete

vollziehen† *vt insep* carry out; perform <*Handlung*>; consummate <*Ehe*>; **sich v∼** take place

Volt /vɔlt/ *nt* -[s],- volt

Volumen /vo'lu:mən/ *nt* -s,- volume

vom *prep* = **von dem**

---

von
● *preposition* (+ *dative*)

❗ Note that **von dem** can become **vom**

····▶ (*räumlich*) from; (*nach Richtungen*) of. **von hier an** from here on[ward]. **von Wien aus** [starting] from Vienna. **nördlich/ südlich von Mannheim** [to the] north/south of Mannheim. **rechts/ links von mir** to the right/left of me; on my right/left

····▶ (*zeitlich*) from. **von jetzt an** from now on. **von heute/morgen an** [as] from today/tomorrow; starting today/tomorrow

····▶ (*zur Angabe des Urhebers, der Ursache; nach Passiv*) by. **der Roman ist von Fontane** the novel is by Fontane. **sie hat ein Kind von ihm.** she has a child by him. **er ist vom Blitz erschlagen worden** he was killed by lightning

····▶ (*anstelle eines Genitivs; Zugehörigkeit, Beschaffenheit, Menge etc.*) of. **ein Stück von dem Kuchen** a piece of the cake. **einer von euch** one of you. **eine Fahrt von drei Stunden** a drive of three hours; a three-hour drive. **das Brot von gestern** yesterday's bread. **ein Tal von erstaunlicher Schönheit** a valley of extraordinary beauty

····▶ (*betreffend*) about. **handeln/ wissen/erzählen** *od* **reden von …** be/ know/talk about …. **eine Geschichte**

*alte Schreibung

von zwei Elefanten a story about *or* of two elephants

voneinander *adv* from each other; <*abhängig*> on each other

vonseiten *prep* (+ *gen*) on the part of

vonstatten *adv* v~ **gehen** take place

vor *prep* (+ *dat/acc*) in front of; (*zeitlich, Reihenfolge*) before; (+ *dat*) (*bei Uhrzeit*) to; <*warnen, sich fürchten*> of; <*schützen, davonlaufen*> from; <*Respekt haben*> for; **vor Angst zittern** tremble with fear; **vor drei Tagen** three days ago; **vor allen Dingen** above all ● *adv* forward; **vor und zurück** backwards and forwards

Vorabend *m* eve

voran *adv* at the front; (*voraus*) ahead; (*vorwärts*) forward. **v~gehen**† *vi sep* (*sein*) lead the way; (*Fortschritte machen*) make progress. **v~kommen**† *vi sep* (*sein*) make progress; (*fig*) get on

Vor|anschlag *m* estimate. **V~anzeige** *f* advance notice. **V~arbeiter** *m* foreman

voraus *adv* ahead (*dat* of); (*vorn*) at the front; (*vorwärts*) forward ● **im Voraus** in advance. **v~bezahlen** *vt sep* pay in advance. **v~gehen**† *vi sep* (*sein*) go on ahead; **jdm/etw v~gehen** precede s.o./sth. **V~sage** *f* -, -n prediction. **v~sagen** *vt sep* predict

voraussetz|en *vt sep* take for granted; (*erfordern*) require; **vorausgesetzt, dass** provided that. **V~ung** *f* -, -en assumption; (*Erfordernis*) prerequisite

voraussichtlich *a* anticipated, expected ● *adv* probably

Vorbehalt *m* -[e]s, -e reservation

vorbei *adv* past (**an** jdm/etw s.o./sth); (*zu Ende*) over. **v~fahren**† *vi sep* (*sein*) drive/go past. **v~gehen**† *vi sep* (*sein*) go past; (*verfehlen*) miss; (*vergehen*) pass; (🛈 *besuchen*) drop in (**bei** on)

vorbereit|en *vt sep* prepare; prepare for <*Reise*>; **sich v~en** prepare [oneself] (**auf** + *acc* for). **V~ung** *f* -, -en preparation

vorbestellen *vt sep* order/(*im Theater, Hotel*) book in advance

vorbestraft *a* **v~ sein** have a [criminal] record

Vorbeugung *f* - prevention

Vorbild *nt* model. **v~lich** *a* exemplary, model ● *adv* in an exemplary manner

vorbringen† *vt sep* put forward; offer <*Entschuldigung*>

vordatieren *vt sep* post-date

Vorder|bein *nt* foreleg. **v~e(r,s)** *a* front. **V~grund** *m* foreground. **V~rad** *nt* front wheel. **V~seite** *f* front; (*einer Münze*) obverse. **v~ste(r,s)** *a* front, first. **V~teil** *nt* front

vor|drängeln (sich) *vr sep* 🛈 jump the queue. **v~drängen (sich)** *vr sep* push forward. **v~dringen**† *vi sep* (*sein*) advance

voreilig *a* rash

voreingenommen *a* biased, prejudiced. **V~heit** *f* - bias

vorenthalten† *vt sep* withhold

vorerst *adv* for the time being

Vorfahr *m* -en, -en ancestor

Vorfahrt *f* right of way; 'V~ beachten' 'give way'. **V~sstraße** *f* ≈ major road

Vorfall *m* incident. **v~en**† *vi sep* (*sein*) happen

vorfinden† *vt sep* find

Vorfreude *f* [happy] anticipation

vorführ|en *vt sep* present, show; (*demonstrieren*) demonstrate; (*aufführen*) perform. **V~ung** *f* presentation; demonstration; performance

Vor|gabe *f* (*Sport*) handicap. **V~gang** *m* occurrence; (*Techn*) process. **V~gänger(in)** *m* -s,- (*f* -, -nen) predecessor

vorgehen† *vi sep* (*sein*) go forward; (*voraus-*) go on ahead; <*Uhr*:> be fast; (*wichtig sein*) take precedence;

V

(*verfahren*) act, proceed; (*geschehen*) happen, go on. **V~** *nt* **-s** action

vor|geschichtlich *a* prehistoric. **V~geschmack** *m* foretaste. **V~gesetzte(r)** *m/f* superior. **v~gestern** *adv* the day before yesterday; **v~gestern Abend** the evening before last

vorhaben† *vt sep* propose, intend (**zu** to); **etw v~** have sth planned. **V~** *nt* **-s,-** plan

Vorhand *f* (*Sport*) forehand

vorhanden *a* existing; **v~ sein** exist; be available

Vorhang *m* curtain

Vorhängeschloss *nt* padlock

vorher *adv* before[hand]

vorhergehend *a* previous

vorherrschend *a* predominant

Vorher|sage *f* -, -n prediction; (*Wetter-*) forecast. **v~sagen** *vt sep* predict; forecast <*Wetter*>. **v~sehen**† *vt sep* foresee

vorhin *adv* just now

vorige(r,s) *a* last, previous

Vor|kehrungen *fpl* precautions. **V~kenntnisse** *fpl* previous knowledge *sg*

vorkommen† *vi sep* (*sein*) happen; (*vorhanden sein*) occur; (*nach vorn kommen*) come forward; (*hervorkommen*) come out; (*zu sehen sein*) show; **jdm bekannt v~** seem familiar to s.o.

Vorkriegszeit *f* pre-war period

vorlad|en† *vt sep* (*Jur*) summons. **V~ung** *f* summons

Vorlage *f* model; (*Muster*) pattern; (*Gesetzes-*) bill

vorlassen† *vt sep* admit; **jdn v~** Ⓘ let s.o. pass; (*den Vortritt lassen*) let s.o. go first

Vor|lauf *m* (*Sport*) heat. **V~läufer** *m* forerunner. **v~läufig** *a* provisional; (*zunächst*) for the time being. **v~laut** *a* forward. **V~leben** *nt* past

vorleg|en *vt sep* put on <*Kette*>; (*unterbreiten*) present; (*vorzeigen*) show. **V~er** *m* **-s,-** mat; (*Bett-*) rug

vorles|en† *vt sep* read [out]; **jdm v~en** read to s.o. **V~ung** *f* lecture

vorletzt|e(r,s) *a* last ... but one; **v~es Jahr** the year before last

Vorliebe *f* preference

vorliegen† *vt sep* (*haben*) be present/(*verfügbar*) available; (*bestehen*) exist, be

vorlügen† *vt sep* lie (*dat* to)

vormachen *vt sep* put up; put on <*Kette*>; push <*Riegel*>; (*zeigen*) demonstrate; **jdm etwas v~** (Ⓘ *täuschen*) kid s.o.

Vormacht *f* supremacy

vormals *adv* formerly

vormerken *vt sep* make a note of; (*reservieren*) reserve

Vormittag *m* morning; **gestern/ heute V~** yesterday/this morning. **v~s** *adv* in the morning

Vormund *m* **-[e]s, -munde** & **-münder** guardian

vorn *adv* at the front; **nach v~** to the front; **von v~** from the front/(*vom Anfang*) beginning; **von v~ anfangen** start afresh

Vorname *m* first name

vorne *adv* = **vorn**

vornehm *a* distinguished; smart

vornehmen† *vt sep* carry out; **sich** (*dat*) **v~, etw zu tun** plan to do sth

vornherein *adv* **von v~herein** from the start

Vor|ort *m* suburb. **V~rang** *m* priority, precedence (**vor** + *dat* over). **V~rat** *m* **-[e]s, -̈e** supply, stock (**an** + *dat* of). **v~rätig** *a* available; **v~rätig haben** have in stock. **V~ratskammer** *f* larder. **V~recht** *nt* privilege. **V~richtung** *f* device

Vorrunde *f* qualifying round

vorsagen *vt/i sep* (*haben*) recite; **jdm v~** tell s.o. the answer

Vor|satz *m* resolution. **v~sätzlich** *a* deliberate; (*Jur*) premeditated

Vorschau *f* preview; (*Film-*) trailer

Vorschein *m* zum V~kommen appear

Vorschlag *m* suggestion, proposal. **v~en†** *vt sep* suggest, propose

vorschnell *a* rash

vorschreiben† *vt sep* lay down; dictate (*dat* to); **vorgeschriebene Dosis** prescribed dose

Vorschrift *f* regulation; (*Anweisung*) instruction; **jdm V~en machen** tell s.o. what to do. **v~smäßig** *a* correct

Vorschule *f* nursery school

Vorschuss *m* advance

vorseh|en† *v sep* ● *vt* intend (**für/als** for/as); (*planen*) plan; **sich v~en** be careful (**vor** + *dat* of) ● *vi* (*haben*) peep out. **V~ung** *f* - providence

Vorsicht *f* - care; (*bei Gefahr*) caution; **V~!** careful! (*auf Schild*) 'caution'. **v~ig** *a* careful; cautious. **V~smaßnahme** *f* precaution

Vorsilbe *f* prefix

Vorsitz *m* chairmanship; **den V~ führen** be in the chair. **V~ende(r)** *m/f* chairman

Vorsorge *f* V~ **treffen** take precautions; make provisions (**für** for). **v~n** *vi sep* (*haben*) provide (**für** for)

Vorspeise *f* starter

Vorspiel *nt* prelude. **v~en** *v sep* ● *vt* perform/ (*Mus*) play (*dat* for) ● *vi* (*haben*) audition

vorsprechen† *v sep* ● *vt* recite; (*zum Nachsagen*) say (*dat* to) ● *vi* (*haben*) (*Theat*) audition; **bei jdm v~** call on s.o.

Vor|sprung *m* projection; (*Fels-*) ledge; (*Vorteil*) lead (**vor** + *dat* over). **V~stadt** *f* suburb. **V~stand** *m* board [of directors]; (*Vereins-*) committee; (*Partei-*) executive

vorsteh|en† *vi sep* (*haben*) project, protrude; **einer Abteilung v~en** be in charge of a department. **V~er** *m* -s,- head

vorstell|en *vt sep* put forward <*Bein, Uhr*>; (*darstellen*) represent; (*bekanntmachen*) introduce; **sich v~en** introduce oneself; (*als*

Bewerber) go for an interview; **sich** (*dat*) **etw v~en** imagine sth. **V~ung** *f* introduction; (*bei Bewerbung*) interview; (*Aufführung*) performance; (*Idee*) idea; (*Phantasie*) imagination. **V~ungsgespräch** *nt* interview

Vorstoß *m* advance

Vorstrafe *f* previous conviction

Vortag *m* day before

vortäuschen *vt sep* feign, fake

Vorteil *m* advantage. **v~haft** *a* advantageous; flattering

Vortrag *m* -[e]s,ⁿe talk; (*wissenschaftlich*) lecture. **v~en†** *vt sep* perform; (*aufsagen*) recite; (*singen*) sing; (*darlegen*) present (*dat* to)

vortrefflich *a* excellent

Vortritt *m* precedence; **jdm den V~ lassen** let s.o. go first

vorüber *adv* **v~ sein** be over; **an etw** (*dat*) **v~** past sth. **v~gehend** *a* temporary

Vor|urteil *nt* prejudice. **V~verkauf** *m* advance booking

vorverlegen *vt sep* bring forward

Vor|wahl[nummer] *f* dialling code. **V~wand** *m* -[e]s,ⁿe pretext; (*Ausrede*) excuse

vorwärts *adv* forward[s]; **v~ kommen** make progress; (*fig*) get on or ahead

vorwegnehmen† *vt sep* anticipate

vorweisen† *vt sep* show

vorwiegend *adv* predominantly

Vorwort *nt* (*pl* -worte) preface

Vorwurf *m* reproach; **jdm Vorwürfe machen** reproach s.o. **v~svoll** *a* reproachful

Vorzeichen *nt* sign; (*fig*) omen

vorzeigen *vt sep* show

vorzeitig *a* premature

vorziehen† *vt sep* pull forward; draw <*Vorhang*>; (*lieber mögen*) prefer; favour

Vor|zimmer *nt* ante-room; (*Büro*) outer office. **V~zug** *m* preference; (*gute Eigenschaft*) merit, virtue; (*Vorteil*) advantage

vorzüglich *a* excellent

vulgär /vʊlˈgɛːɐ̯/ *a* vulgar ● *adv* in a vulgar way

Vulkan /vʊlˈkaːn/ *m* **-s, -e** volcano

Ww

Waage *f* -, **-n** scales *pl*; (*Astr*) Libra. **w~recht** *a* horizontal

Wabe *f* -, **-n** honeycomb

wach *a* awake; (*aufgeweckt*) alert; **w~ werden** wake up

Wach|e *f* -, **-n** guard; (*Posten*) sentry; (*Dienst*) guard duty; (*Naut*) watch; (*Polizei-*) station; **W~e halten** keep watch. **W~hund** *m* guard-dog

Wacholder *m* **-s** juniper

Wachposten *m* sentry

Wachs *nt* **-es** wax

wachsam *a* vigilant. **W~keit** *f* - vigilance

wachsen†[1] *vi* (*sein*) grow

wachs|en[2] *vt* (*reg*) wax. **W~figur** *f* waxwork

Wachstum *nt* **-s** growth

Wächter *m* **-s,-** guard; (*Park-*) keeper; (*Parkplatz-*) attendant

Wacht|meister *m* [police] constable. **W~posten** *m* sentry

wackel|ig *a* wobbly; <*Stuhl*> rickety; <*Person*> shaky. **W~kontakt** *m* loose connection. **w~n** *vi* (*haben*) wobble; (*zittern*) shake

Wade *f* -, **-n** (*Anat*) calf

Waffe *f* -, **-n** weapon; **W~n** arms

Waffel *f* -, **-n** waffle; (*Eis-*) wafer

Waffen|ruhe *f* cease-fire. **W~schein** *m* firearms licence. **W~stillstand** *m* armistice

Wagemut *m* daring

wagen *vt* risk; **es w~,** etw zu tun dare [to] do sth; **sich w~** (*gehen*) venture

Wagen *m* **-s,-** cart; (*Eisenbahn-*) carriage, coach; (*Güter-*) wagon; (*Kinder-*) pram; (*Auto*) car. **W~heber** *m* **-s,-** jack

Waggon /vaˈgõː/ *m* **-s, -s** wagon

Wahl *f* -, **-en** choice; (*Pol, Admin*) election; (*geheime*) ballot; **zweite W~** (*Comm*) seconds *pl*

wähl|en *vt/i* (*haben*) choose; (*Pol, Admin*) elect; (*stimmen*) vote; (*Teleph*) dial. **W~er(in)** *m* **-s,-** (*f* -, **-nen**) voter. **w~erisch** *a* choosy, fussy

Wahl|fach *nt* optional subject. **w~frei** *a* optional. **W~kampf** *m* election campaign. **W~kreis** *m* constituency. **W~lokal** *nt* polling-station. **w~los** *a* indiscriminate

Wahl|spruch *m* motto. **W~urne** *f* ballot-box

Wahn *m* **-[e]s** delusion; (*Manie*) mania

Wahnsinn *m* madness. **w~ig** *a* mad, insane; (🄵 *unsinnig*) crazy; (🄵 *groß*) terrible; **w~ig werden** go mad ● *adv* 🄵 terribly. **W~ige(r)** *m/f* maniac

wahr *a* true; (*echt*) real; **du kommst doch, nicht w~?** you are coming, aren't you?

während *prep* (+ *gen*) during ● *conj* while; (*wohingegen*) whereas

Wahrheit *f* -, **-en** truth. **w~sgemäß** *a* truthful

wahrnehm|en† *vt sep* notice; (*nutzen*) take advantage of; exploit <*Vorteil*>; look after <*Interessen*>. **W~ung** *f* -, **-en** perception

Wahrsagerin *f* -, **-nen** fortune teller

wahrscheinlich *a* probable. **W~keit** *f* - probability

Währung *f* -, **-en** currency

Wahrzeichen *nt* symbol

Waise *f* -, **-n** orphan. **W~nhaus** *nt* orphanage. **W~nkind** *nt* orphan

Wal *m* **-[e]s, -e** whale

Wald m -[e]s,-̈er wood; (groß) forest.
w∼ig a wooded

Walis|er m -s,- Welshman. w∼isch
a Welsh

Wall m -[e]s,-̈e mound

Wallfahr|er(in) m(f) pilgrim. W∼t
f pilgrimage

Walnuss f walnut

Walze f -, -n roller. w∼n vt roll

Walzer m -s,- waltz

Wand f -,-̈e wall; (Trenn-) partition;
(Seite) side; (Fels-) face

Wandel m -s change

Wander|er m -s,-, W∼in f -, -nen
hiker, rambler. w∼n vi (sein) hike,
ramble; (ziehen) travel; (gemächlich
gehen) wander; (ziellos) roam.
W∼schaft f - travels pl. W∼ung f
-, -en hike, ramble. W∼weg m
footpath

Wandlung f -, -en change,
transformation

Wand|malerei f mural. W∼tafel
f blackboard. W∼teppich m
tapestry

Wange f -, -n cheek

wann adv when

Wanne f -, -n tub

Wanze f -, -n bug

Wappen nt -s,- coat of arms.
W∼kunde f heraldry

war, wäre s. sein[1]

Ware f -, -n article; (Comm)
commodity; (coll) merchandise; W∼n
goods. W∼nhaus nt department
store. W∼nprobe f sample.
W∼nzeichen nt trademark

warm a warm; <Mahlzeit> hot; w∼
machen heat ● adv warmly; w∼
essen have a hot meal

Wärm|e f - warmth; (Phys) heat; 10
Grad W∼e 10 degrees above zero.
w∼en vt warm; heat <Essen,
Wasser>. W∼flasche f hot-water
bottle

Warn|blinkanlage f hazard
[warning] lights pl. w∼en vt/i
(haben) warn (vor + dat of). W∼ung
f -, -en warning

Warteliste f waiting list

warten vi (haben) wait (auf + acc
for) ● vt service

Wärter(in) m -s,- (f -, -nen) keeper;
(Museums-) attendant; (Gefängnis-)
warder; (Kranken-) orderly

Warte|raum, W∼saal m
waiting-room. W∼zimmer nt (Med)
waiting-room

Wartung f - (Techn) service

warum adv why

Warze f -, -n wart

was pron what ● rel pron that; alles,
was ich brauche all [that] I need
● indef pron (🔲 etwas) something;
(fragend, verneint) anything; so was
Ärgerliches! what a nuisance! ● adv
🔲 (warum) why; (wie) how

wasch|bar a washable.
W∼becken nt wash-basin

Wäsche f -, washing; (Unter-)
underwear

waschecht a colour-fast

Wäscheklammer f clothes-peg

waschen† vt wash; sich w∼ have a
wash; W∼ und Legen shampoo and
set ● vi (haben) do the washing

Wäscherei f -, -en laundry

Wäsche|schleuder f spin-drier.
W∼trockner m tumble-drier

Wasch|küche f laundry-room.
W∼lappen m face-flannel.
W∼maschine f washing machine.
W∼mittel nt detergent. W∼pulver
nt washing-powder. W∼salon m
launderette. W∼zettel m blurb

Wasser nt -s water. W∼ball m
beach-ball; (Spiel) water polo.
w∼dicht a watertight; <Kleidung>
waterproof. W∼fall m waterfall.
W∼farbe f water-colour. W∼hahn
m tap. W∼kraft f water-power.
W∼kraftwerk nt hydroelectric
power-station. W∼leitung f water-
main; aus der W∼leitung from the
tap. W∼mann m (Astr) Aquarius

wässern vt soak; (begießen) water
● vi (haben) water

Wasser|ski nt -s water-skiing.
W∼stoff m hydrogen. W∼straße f
waterway. W∼waage f spirit-level

wässrig a watery

W

watscheln *vi* (*sein*) waddle

Watt *nt* -s,- (*Phys*) watt

Watt|e *f* - cotton wool. **w~iert** *a* padded; (*gesteppt*) quilted

WC /ve'tse:/ *nt* -s, -s WC

web|en *vt/i* (*haben*) weave. **W~er** *m* -s,- weaver. **W~stuhl** *m* loom

Website /web'sart/ *f* -s, -s web site

Wechsel *m* -s,- change; (*Tausch*) exchange; (*Comm*) bill of exchange. **W~geld** *nt* change. **w~haft** *a* changeable. **W~jahre** *npl* menopause *sg*. **W~kurs** *m* exchange rate. **w~n** *vt* change; (*tauschen*) exchange ● *vi* (*haben*) change; vary. **w~nd** *a* changing; varying. **W~strom** *m* alternating current. **W~stube** *f* bureau de change

weck|en *vt* wake [up]; (*fig*) awaken ● *vi* (*haben*) <*Wecker:*> go off. **W~er** *m* -s,- alarm [clock]

wedeln *vi* (*haben*) wave; mit dem Schwanz w~ wag its tail

weder *conj* w~ ... noch neither ... nor

Weg *m* -[e]s, -e way; (*Fuß-*) path; (*Fahr-*) track; (*Gang*) errand; sich auf den Weg machen set off

weg *adv* away, off; (*verschwunden*) gone; weg sein be away; (*gegangen/ verschwunden*) have gone; Hände weg! hands off!

wegen *prep* (+ *gen*) because of; (*um ... willen*) for the sake of; (*bezüglich*) about

weg|fahren† *vi sep* (*sein*) go away; (*abfahren*) leave. **w~fallen†** *vi sep* (*sein*) be dropped/(*ausgelassen*) omitted; (*entfallen*) no longer apply. **w~geben†** *vt sep* give away. **w~gehen†** *vi sep* (*sein*) leave, go away; (*ausgehen*) go out. **w~kommen†** *vi sep* (*sein*) get away; (*verloren gehen*) disappear; schlecht w~kommen 🔄 get a raw deal. **w~lassen†** *vt sep* let go; (*auslassen*) omit. **w~laufen†** *vi sep* (*sein*) run away. **w~räumen** *vt sep* put away; (*entfernen*) clear away.

w~schicken *vt sep* send away; (*abschicken*) send off. **w~tun†** *vt sep* put away; (*wegwerfen*) throw away

Wegweiser *m* -s,- signpost

weg|werfen† *vt sep* throw away. **w~ziehen†** *v sep* ● *vt* pull away ● *vi* (*sein*) move away

weh *a* sore; weh tun hurt; <*Kopf, Rücken:*> ache; jdm weh tun hurt s.o.

wehe *int* alas; w~ [dir/euch]! (*drohend*) don't you dare!

wehen *vi* (*haben*) blow; (*flattern*) flutter ● *vt* blow

Wehen *fpl* contractions

Wehr¹ *nt* -[e]s, -e weir

Wehr² *f* sich zur W~ setzen resist. **W~dienst** *m* military service. **W~dienstverweigerer** *m* -s,- conscientious objector

wehren (sich) *vr* resist; (*gegen Anschuldigung*) protest; (*sich sträuben*) refuse

wehr|los *a* defenceless. **W~macht** *f* armed forces *pl*. **W~pflicht** *f* conscription

Weib *nt* -[e]s, -er woman; (*Ehe-*) wife. **W~chen** *nt* -s,- (*Zool*) female. **w~lich** *a* feminine; (*Biol*) female

weich *a* soft; (*gar*) done

Weiche *f* -, -n (*Rail*) points *pl*

Weich|heit *f* - softness. **w~lich** *a* soft; <*Charakter:*> weak. **W~spüler** *m* -s,- (*Tex*) conditioner. **W~tier** *nt* mollusc

Weide¹ *f* -, -n (*Bot*) willow

Weide² *f* -, -n pasture. **w~n** *vt/i* (*haben*) graze

weiger|n (sich) *vr* refuse. **W~ung** *f* -, -en refusal

Weihe *f* -, -n consecration; (*Priester-*) ordination. **w~n** *vt* consecrate; (*zum Priester*) ordain

Weiher *m* -s,- pond

Weihnacht|en *nt* -s & *pl* Christmas. **w~lich** *a* Christmassy. **W~sbaum** *m* Christmas tree. **W~slied** *nt* Christmas carol. **W~smann** *m* (*pl* -männer) Father Christmas. **W~stag** *m* erster/ zweiter W~stag Christmas Day/ Boxing Day

---

*old spelling

Weih|rauch m incense.
  W~wasser nt holy water
weil conj because; (da) since
Weile f - while
Wein m -[e]s, -e wine; (Bot) vines pl;
  (Trauben) grapes pl. **W~bau** m
  wine-growing. **W~berg** m
  vineyard. **W~brand** m -[e]s brandy
weinen vt/i (haben) cry, weep
Wein|glas nt wineglass. **W~karte**
  f wine-list. **W~lese** f grape harvest.
  W~liste f wine-list. **W~probe** f
  wine-tasting. **W~rebe** f, **W~stock**
  m vine. **W~stube** f wine-bar.
  W~traube f bunch of grapes;
  (W~beere) grape
weise a wise
Weise f -, -n way; (Melodie) tune
Weisheit f -, -en wisdom.
  W~szahn m wisdom tooth
weiß a, **W~** nt -,- white
weissag|en vt/i insep (haben)
  prophesy. **W~ung** f -, -en prophecy
Weiß|brot nt white bread. **W~e(r)**
  m/f white man/woman. **w~en** vt
  whitewash. **W~wein** m white wine
Weisung f -, -en instruction;
  (Befehl) order
weit a wide; (ausgedehnt) extensive;
  (lang) long ● adv widely; <offen,
  öffnen> wide; (lang) far; von w~em
  from a distance; bei w~em by far;
  w~ und breit far and wide; ist es
  noch w~? is it much further? so
  w~ wie möglich as far as possible;
  ich bin so w~ I'm ready; w~
  verbreitet widespread; w~ reichende
  Folgen far-reaching consequences
Weite f -, -n expanse; (Entfernung)
  distance; (Größe) width. **w~n** vt
  widen; stretch <Schuhe>
weiter a further ● adv further;
  (außerdem) in addition;
  (anschließend) then; etw w~ tun go
  on doing sth; w~ nichts/niemand
  nothing/no one else; und so w~ and
  so on
weiter|e(r,s) a further; ohne w~es
  just like that; (leicht) easily
weiter|erzählen vt sep go on
  with; (w~sagen) repeat.

w~fahren† vi sep (sein) go on.
w~geben† vt sep pass on. **w~hin**
  adv (immer noch) still; (in Zukunft)
  in future; (außerdem) furthermore;
  etw w~hin tun go on doing sth.
w~machen vi sep (haben) carry
  on
weit|gehend a extensive ● adv to
  a large extent. **w~sichtig** a long-
  sighted; (fig) far-sighted.
  W~sprung m long jump.
  w~verbreitet* a w~ verbreitet, s.
  weit
Weizen m -s wheat
welch inv pron what; w~ ein(e)
  what a. **w~e(r,s)** pron which; um
  w~e Zeit? at what time? ● rel pron
  which; (Person) who ● indef pron
  some; (fragend) any; was für w~e?
  what sort of?
Wellblech nt corrugated iron
Well|e f -, -n wave; (Techn) shaft.
  W~enlänge f wavelength.
  W~enlinie f wavy line.
  W~enreiten nt surfing.
  W~ensittich m -s, -e budgerigar.
  w~ig a wavy
Welt f -, -en world; auf der W~ in the
  world; auf die od zur W~ kommen be
  born. **W~all** nt universe.
  w~berühmt a world-famous.
  w~fremd a unworldly. **W~kugel**
  f globe. **w~lich** a worldly; (nicht
  geistlich) secular
Weltmeister|(in) m(f) world
  champion. **W~schaft** f world
  championship
Weltraum m space. **W~fahrer** m
  astronaut
Weltrekord m world record
wem pron (dat of wer) to whom
wen pron (acc of wer) whom
Wende f -, -n change. **W~kreis** m
  (Geog) tropic
Wendeltreppe f spiral staircase
wenden¹ vt (reg) turn ● vi (haben)
  turn [round]
wenden²† (& reg) vt turn; sich w~
  turn; sich an jdn w~ turn/
  (schriftlich) write to s.o.
Wend|epunkt m (fig) turning-
  point. **W~ung** f -, -en turn;

(*Biegung*) bend; (*Veränderung*) change

wenig *pron* little; (*pl*) few; **so/zu w~** so/too little/(*pl*) few; **w~e** *pl* few ● *adv* little; (*kaum*) not much; **so w~ wie möglich** as little as possible. **w~er** *pron* less; (*pl*) fewer; **immer w~er** less and less ● *adv & conj* less. **w~ste(r,s)** least; **am w~sten** least [of all]. **w~stens** *adv* at least

wenn *conj* if; (*sobald*) when; **immer w~** whenever; **w~ nicht** *od* **außer w~** unless; **w~ auch** even though

wer *pron* who; (🎔 *jemand*) someone; (*fragend*) anyone

Werbe|agentur *f* advertising agency. **w~n†** *vt* recruit; attract <*Kunden, Besucher*> ● *vi* (*haben*) **w~n für** advertise; canvass for <*Partei*>. **W~spot** /-sp-/ *m* **-s, -s** commercial

Werbung *f* - advertising

werden†
● *intransitive verb* (*sein*)
····▸ (+ *adjective*) become; get; (*allmählich*) grow. **müde/alt/länger werden** become *or* get/grow tired/old/longer. **taub/blind/wahnsinnig werden** go deaf/blind/mad. **blass werden** become *or* turn pale. **krank werden** become *or* fall ill. **es wird warm/dunkel** it is getting warm/dark. **mir wurde schlecht/schwindlig** I began to feel sick/dizzy
····▸ (+ *noun*) become. **Arzt/Lehrer/Mutter werden** become a doctor/teacher/mother. **er will Lehrer werden** he wants to be a teacher. **was ist aus ihm geworden?** what has become of him?
····▸ **werden zu** become; turn into. **das Erlebnis wurde zu einem Albtraum** the experience became *or* turned into a nightmare. **zu Eis werden** turn into ice
● *auxiliary verb*
····▸ (*Zukunft*) will; shall. **er wird bald hier sein** he will *or* he'll soon be here. **wir werden sehen** we shall see.

es wird bald regnen it's going to rain soon
····▸ (*Konjunktiv*) **würde(n)** would. **ich würde es kaufen, wenn ...** I would buy it if .... **würden Sie so nett sein?** would you be so kind?
····▸ (*beim Passiv*; *pp* **worden**) be. **geliebt/geboren werden** be loved/born. **du wirst gerufen** you are being called. **er wurde gebeten** he was asked. **es wurde gemunkelt** it was rumoured. **mir wurde gesagt, dass ...** I was told that .... **das Haus ist soeben/1995 renoviert worden** the house has just been renovated/was renovated in 1995

werfen† *vt* throw; cast <*Blick, Schatten*>; **sich w~** <*Holz:*> warp

Werft *f* -, **-en** shipyard

Werk *nt* **-[e]s, -e** work; (*Fabrik*) works *sg*, factory; (*Trieb-*) mechanism. **W~en** *nt* **-s** (*Sch*) handicraft. **W~statt** *f* -,"-en workshop; (*Auto-*) garage. **W~tag** *m* weekday. **w~tags** *adv* on weekdays. **w~tätig** *a* working

Werkzeug *nt* tool; (*coll*) tools *pl*

Wermut *m* **-s** vermouth

wert *a* **viel w~** worth a lot; **nichts w~ sein** be worthless; **jds w~ sein** be worthy of s.o. **W~** *m* **-[e]s, -e** value; (*Nenn-*) denomination; **im W~ von** worth. **w~en** *vt* rate

Wert|gegenstand *m* object of value. **w~los** *a* worthless. **W~minderung** *f* depreciation. **W~papier** *nt* (*Comm*) security. **W~sachen** *fpl* valuables. **w~voll** *a* valuable

Wesen *nt* **-s,-** nature; (*Lebe-*) being; (*Mensch*) creature

wesentlich *a* essential; (*grundlegend*) fundamental ● *adv* considerably, much

weshalb *adv* why

Wespe *f* -, **-n** wasp

wessen *pron* (*gen of* **wer**) whose

westdeutsch *a* West German

Weste *f* -, **-n** waistcoat

Westen *m* **-s** west

Western *m* **-[s],-** western

w

Westfalen nt -s Westphalia

Westindien nt West Indies pl

westlich a western; <Richtung> westerly ● adv & prep (+ gen) w~lich [von] der Stadt [to the] west of the town. **w~wärts** adv westwards

weswegen adv why

Wettbewerb m -s, -e competition

Wette f -, -n bet; um die W~ laufen race (mit jdm s.o.)

wetten vt/i (haben) bet (auf + acc on); mit jdm w~ have a bet with s.o.

Wetter nt -s,- weather; (Un-) storm. **W~bericht** m weather report. **W~vorhersage** f weather forecast. **W~warte** f -, -n meteorological station

Wettkampf m contest. **W~kämpfer(in)** m(f) competitor. **W~lauf** m race. **W~rennen** nt race. **W~streit** m contest

Whisky m -s whisky

wichtig a important; w~ nehmen take seriously. **W~keit** f - importance

Wicke f -, -n sweet pea

Wickel m -s,- compress

wickeln vt wind; (ein-) wrap; (bandagieren) bandage; ein Kind frisch w~ change a baby

Widder m -s,- ram; (Astr) Aries

wider prep (+ acc) against; (entgegen) contrary to; w~ Willen against one's will

widerlegen vt insep refute

widerlich a repulsive. **W~rede** f contradiction; keine W~rede! don't argue!

widerrufen† vt/i insep (haben) retract; revoke <Befehl>

Widersacher m -s,- adversary

widersetzen (sich) vr insep resist (jdm/etw s.o./sth)

widerspiegeln vt sep reflect

widersprechen† vi insep (haben) contradict (jdm/etw s.o./sth)

Widerspruch m contradiction; (Protest) protest. **w~sprüchlich** a contradictory. **w~spruchslos** adv without protest

Widerstand m resistance; W~ leisten resist. **w~sfähig** a resistant; (Bot) hardy

widerstehen† vi insep (haben) resist (jdm/etw s.o./sth); (anwidern) be repugnant (jdm to s.o.)

Widerstreben nt -s reluctance

widerwärtig a disagreeable

Widerwille m aversion, repugnance. **w~ig** a reluctant

widmen vt dedicate (dat to); (verwenden) devote (dat to); sich w~en (+ dat) devote oneself to. **W~ung** f -, -en dedication

wie adv how; wie viel how much/(pl) many; um wie viel Uhr? at what time? wie viele? how many? wie ist Ihr Name? what is your name? wie ist das Wetter? what is the weather like? ● conj as; (gleich wie) like; (sowie) as well as; (als) when, as; so gut wie as good as; nichts wie nothing but

wieder adv again; jdn/etw w~ erkennen recognize s.o./sth; etw w~ verwenden/verwerten reuse/recycle sth; etw w~ gutmachen make up for <Schaden>; redress <Unrecht>; (bezahlen) pay for sth

Wiederaufbau m reconstruction

wieder|bekommen† vt sep get back. **W~belebung** f - resuscitation. **w~bringen†** vt sep bring back. **w~erkennen*** vt sep w~ erkennen, s. wieder. **w~geben†** vt sep give back; return; (darstellen) portray; (ausdrücken, übersetzen) render; (zitieren) quote. **W~geburt** f reincarnation

Wiedergutmachung f - reparation; (Entschädigung) compensation

wiederherstellen vt sep re-establish; restore <Gebäude>; restore to health <Kranke>

wiederholen vt insep repeat; (Sch) revise; sich w~en recur; <Person:> repeat oneself. **w~t** a repeated. **W~ung** f -, -en repetition; (Sch) revision

W

Wieder|hören nt auf W~hören! goodbye! **W~käuer** m -s,- ruminant. **W~kehr** f - return; (W~holung) recurrence. **w~kommen**† vi sep (sein) come back

wiedersehen* vt sep wieder sehen, s. sehen. **W~** nt -s,- reunion; auf W~! goodbye!

wiedervereinig|en* vt sep wieder vereinigen, s. vereinigen. **W~ung** f reunification

wieder|verwenden* vt sep w~ verwenden, s. wieder. **w~verwerten*** vt sep w~ verwerten, s. wieder

Wiege f -, -n cradle

wiegen¹† vt/i (haben) weigh

wiegen² vt (reg) rock. **W~lied** nt lullaby

wiehern vi (haben) neigh

Wien nt -s Vienna. **W~er** a Viennese ● m -s,- Viennese ● f -,- ≈ frankfurter. **w~erisch** a Viennese

Wiese f -, -n meadow

Wiesel nt -s,- weasel

wieso adv why

wieviel* pron wie viel, s. wie. **w~te(r,s)** a which; der W~te ist heute? what is the date today?

wieweit adv how far

wild a wild; <Stamm> savage; w~er Streik wildcat strike; w~ wachsen grow wild. **W~** nt -[e]s game; (Rot-) deer; (Culin) venison. **W~e(r)** m/f savage

Wilder|er m -s,- poacher. **w~n** vt/i (haben) poach

Wild|heger, W~hüter m -s,- gamekeeper. **W~leder** nt suede. **W~nis** f - wilderness. **W~schwein** nt wild boar. **W~westfilm** m western

Wille m -ns will

Willenskraft f will-power

willig a willing

willkommen a welcome; w~ heißen welcome. **W~** nt -s welcome

wimmeln vi (haben) swarm

wimmern vi (haben) whimper

Wimpel m -s,- pennant

Wimper f -, -n [eye]lash; **W~ntusche** f mascara

Wind m -[e]s, -e wind

Winde f -, -n (Techn) winch

Windel f -, -n nappy

winden† vt wind; make <Kranz>; in die Höhe w~ winch up; sich w~ wind (um round); (sich krümmen) writhe

Wind|hund m greyhound. **w~ig** a windy. **W~mühle** f windmill. **W~pocken** fpl chickenpox sg. **W~schutzscheibe** f windscreen. **W~stille** f calm. **W~stoß** m gust of wind. **W~surfen** nt windsurfing

Windung f -, -en bend; (Spirale) spiral

Winkel m -s,- angle; (Ecke) corner. **W~messer** m -s,- protractor

winken vi (haben) wave

Winter m -s,- winter. **w~lich** a wintry; (Winter-) winter ... **W~schlaf** m hibernation; **W~sport** m winter sports pl

Winzer m -s,- winegrower

winzig a tiny, minute

Wipfel m -s,- [tree-]top

Wippe f -, -n see-saw

wir pron we; wir sind es it's us

Wirbel m -s,- eddy; (Drehung) whirl; (Trommel-) roll; (Anat) vertebra; (Haar-) crown; (Aufsehen) fuss. **w~n** vt/i (sein/haben) whirl. **W~säule** f spine. **W~sturm** m cyclone. **W~tier** nt vertebrate. **W~wind** m whirlwind

wird s. werden

wirken vi (haben) have an effect (auf + acc on); (zur Geltung kommen) be effective; (tätig sein) work; (scheinen) seem ● vt (Tex) knit

wirklich a real. **W~keit** f -, -en reality

wirksam a effective

Wirkung f -, -en effect. **w~los** a ineffective. **w~svoll** a effective

wirr a tangled; <Haar> tousled; (verwirrt, verworren) confused

W

Wirt *m* -[e]s, -e landlord. **W~in** *f*-, -nen landlady

Wirtschaft *f* -, -en economy; (*Gast-*) restaurant; (*Kneipe*) pub. **w~en** *vi* (*haben*) manage one's finances. **w~lich** *a* economic; (*sparsam*) economical. **W~sgeld** *nt* housekeeping [money]. **W~sprüfer** *m* auditor

Wirtshaus *nt* inn; (*Kneipe*) pub

wischen *vt/i* (*haben*) wipe; wash <*Fußboden*>

wissen† *vt/i* (*haben*) know; **weißt du noch?** do you remember? **nichts w~ wollen von** not want anything to do with. **W~** *nt* -s knowledge; **meines W~s** to my knowledge

Wissenschaft *f* -, -en science. **W~ler** *m* -s,- academic; (*Natur-*) scientist. **w~lich** *a* academic; scientific

wissenswert *a* worth knowing

wittern *vt* scent; (*ahnen*) sense. **W~ung** *f* - scent; (*Wetter*) weather

Witwe *f* -, -n widow. **W~r** *m* -s,- widower

Witz *m* -es, -e joke; (*Geist*) wit. **W~bold** *m* -[e]s, -e joker. **w~ig** *a* funny; witty

wo *adv* where; (*als*) when; (*irgendwo*) somewhere; **wo immer** wherever ● *conj* seeing that; (*obwohl*) although; (*wenn*) if

woanders *adv* somewhere else

wobei *adv* how; (*relativ*) during the course of which

Woche *f* -, -n week. **W~nende** *nt* weekend. **W~nkarte** *f* weekly ticket. **w~nlang** *adv* for weeks. **W~ntag** *m* day of the week; (*Werktag*) weekday. **w~tags** *adv* on weekdays

wöchentlich *a* & *adv* weekly

Wodka *m* -s vodka

wofür *adv* what ... for; (*relativ*) for which

Woge *f* -, -n wave

woher *adv* where from; **woher weißt du das?** how do you know that?

wohin *adv* where [to]; **wohin gehst du?** where are you going?

wohl *adv* well; (*vermutlich*) probably; (*etwa*) about; (*zwar*) perhaps; **w~ kaum** hardly; **sich w~ fühlen** feel well/(*behaglich*) comfortable; **jdm w~ tun** do s.o. good. **W~** *nt* -[e]s welfare, well-being; **zum W~** (+ *gen*) for the good of; **zum W~!** cheers!

Wohl|befinden *nt* well-being. **W~behagen** *nt* feeling of well-being. **W~ergehen** *nt* -s welfare. **w~erzogen** *a* well brought-up

Wohlfahrt *f* - welfare. **W~sstaat** *m* Welfare State

wohl|habend *a* prosperous, well-to-do. **w~ig** *a* comfortable. **w~schmeckend** *a* tasty

Wohlstand *m* prosperity. **W~sgesellschaft** *f* affluent society

Wohltat *f* [act of] kindness; (*Annehmlichkeit*) treat; (*Genuss*) bliss

Wohltät|er *m* benefactor. **w~ig** *a* charitable

wohl|tuend *a* agreeable. **w~tun*** *vi sep* (*haben*) **w~ tun**, *s.* **wohl**

Wohlwollen *nt* -s goodwill; (*Gunst*) favour. **w~d** *a* benevolent

Wohn|block *m* block of flats. **w~en** *vi* (*haben*) live; (*vorübergehend*) stay. **W~gegend** *f* residential area. **w~haft** *a* resident. **W~haus** *nt* house. **W~heim** *nt* hostel; (*Alten-*) home. **w~lich** *a* comfortable. **W~mobil** *nt* -s, -e camper. **W~ort** *m* place of residence. **W~sitz** *m* place of residence

Wohnung *f* -, -en flat; (*Unterkunft*) accommodation. **W~snot** *f* housing shortage

Wohn|wagen *m* caravan. **W~zimmer** *nt* living-room

wölb|en *vt* curve; arch <*Rücken*>. **W~ung** *f* -, -en curve; (*Archit*) vault

Wolf *m* -[e]s, ̈e wolf; (*Fleisch-*) mincer; (*Reiß-*) shredder

Wolk|e *f* -, -n cloud. **W~enbruch** *m* cloudburst. **W~enkratzer** *m* skyscraper. **w~enlos** *a* cloudless. **w~ig** *a* cloudy

Woll|decke *f* blanket. **W~e** *f* -, -n wool

w

wollen†¹
- *auxiliary verb*
····▸ *(den Wunsch haben)* want to. **ich will nach Hause gehen** I want to go home. **ich wollte Sie fragen, ob ...** I wanted to ask you if ...
····▸ *(im Begriff sein)* be about to. **wir wollten gerade gehen** we were just about to go
····▸ *(sich in der gewünschten Weise verhalten)* will nicht refuses to. **der Motor will nicht anspringen** the engine won't *or* refuses to start
- *intransitive verb*
····▸ want to. **ob du willst oder nicht** whether you want to or not. **ganz wie du willst** just as you like
····▸ (🔢 *irgendwohin zu gehen wünschen)* **ich will nach Hause** I want to go home. **zu wem wollen Sie?** who[m] do you want to see?
····▸ (🔢 *funktionieren)* will nicht won't go. **meine Beine wollen nicht mehr** my legs are giving up 🔢
- *transitive verb*
····▸ want; *(beabsichtigen)* intend. **er will nicht, dass du ihm hilfst** he does not want you to help him. **das habe ich nicht gewollt** I never intended *or* meant that to happen

wollen² *a* woollen. **w~ig** *a* woolly. **W~sachen** *fpl* woollens.

womit *adv* what ... with; *(relativ)* with which. **wonach** *adv* what ... after/<*suchen*> for/<*riechen*> of; *(relativ)* after/for/of which

woran *adv* what ... on/<*denken, sterben*> of; *(relativ)* on/of which; **woran hast du ihn erkannt?** how did you recognize him? **worauf** *adv* what ... on/<*warten*> for; *(relativ)* on/for which; *(woraufhin)* whereupon. **woraus** *adv* what ... from; *(relativ)* from which

Wort *nt* -[e]s,⸚er & -e word; **jdm ins W~ fallen** interrupt s.o.

Wörterbuch *nt* dictionary

Wort|führer *m* spokesman. **w~getreu** *a* & *adv* word-for-word.

w~karg *a* taciturn. **W~laut** *m* wording

wörtlich *a* literal; *(wortgetreu)* word-for-word

wort|los *a* silent ● *adv* without a word. **W~schatz** *m* vocabulary. **W~spiel** *nt* pun, play on words

worüber *adv* what ... over/<*lachen, sprechen*> about; *(relativ)* over/about which. **worum** *adv* what ... round/<*bitten, kämpfen*> for; *(relativ)* round/for which; **worum geht es?** what is it about? **wovon** *adv* what ... from/<*sprechen*> about; *(relativ)* from/about which. **wovor** *adv* what ... in front of; <*sich fürchten*> what ... of; *(relativ)* in front of which; of which. **wozu** *adv* what ... to/<*brauchen, benutzen*> for; *(relativ)* to/for which; **wozu?** what for?

Wrack *nt* -s, -s wreck

wringen† *vt* wring

Wucher|preis *m* extortionate price. **W~ung** *f* -, -en growth

Wuchs *m* -es growth; *(Gestalt)* stature

Wucht *f* - force

wühlen *vi* *(haben)* rummage; *(in der Erde)* burrow ● *vt* dig

Wulst *m* -[e]s,⸚e bulge; *(Fett-)* roll

wund *a* sore; **w~ reiben** chafe; **sich w~ liegen** get bedsores. **W~brand** *m* gangrene

Wunde *f* -, -n wound

Wunder *nt* -s,- wonder, marvel; *(übernatürliches)* miracle; **kein W~!** no wonder! **w~bar** *a* miraculous; *(herrlich)* wonderful. **W~kind** *nt* infant prodigy. **w~n** *vt* surprise; **sich w~n** be surprised (über + *acc* at). **w~schön** *a* beautiful

Wundstarrkrampf *m* tetanus

Wunsch *m* -[e]s,⸚e wish; *(Verlangen)* desire; *(Bitte)* request

wünschen *vt* want; **sich** *(dat)* **etw w~** want sth; *(bitten um)* ask for sth; **jdm Glück/gute Nacht w~** wish s.o. luck/good night; **Sie w~?** can I help you? **w~swert** *a* desirable

Wunschkonzert *nt* musical request programme

---

wurde, würde s. werden

Würde f -, -n dignity; (*Ehrenrang*) honour. **w∼los** a undignified. **W∼nträger** m dignitary. **w∼voll** a dignified ● adv with dignity

würdig a dignified; (*wert*) worthy

Wurf m -[e]s,⸚e throw; (*Junge*) litter

Würfel m -s,- cube; (*Spiel-*) dice; (*Zucker-*) lump. **w∼n** vi (*haben*) throw the dice; w∼n um play dice for ● vt throw; (*in Würfel schneiden*) dice. **W∼zucker** m cube sugar

würgen vt choke ● vi (*haben*) retch; choke (an + *dat* on)

Wurm m -[e]s,⸚er worm; (*Made*) maggot. **w∼en** vi (*haben*) jdn w∼en 🛈 rankle [with s.o.]

Wurst f -,⸚e sausage; **das ist mir W∼** 🛈 I couldn't care less

Würze f -, -n spice; (*Aroma*) aroma

Wurzel f -, -n root; W∼n schlagen take root. **w∼n** vi (*haben*) root

würz|en vt season. **w∼ig** a tasty; (*aromatisch*) aromatic; (*pikant*) spicy

wüst a chaotic; (*wirr*) tangled; (*öde*) desolate; (*wild*) wild; (*schlimm*) terrible

Wüste f -, -n desert

Wut f - rage, fury. **W∼anfall** m fit of rage

wüten vi (*haben*) rage. **w∼d** a furious; w∼d machen infuriate

Xx

x /ɪks/ *inv* a (*Math*) x; 🛈 umpteen. **X-Beine** ntpl knock-knees. **x-beinig, X-beinig** a knock-kneed. **x-beliebig** a 🛈 any. **x-mal** adv 🛈 umpteen times

Yy

Yoga /ˈjoːga/ m & nt -[s] yoga

Zz

Zack|e f -, -n point; (*Berg-*) peak; (*Gabel-*) prong. **z∼ig** a jagged; (*gezackt*) serrated

zaghaft a timid; (*zögernd*) tentative

zäh a tough; (*hartnäckig*) tenacious. **z∼flüssig** a viscous; <*Verkehr*> slow-moving. **Z∼igkeit** f - toughness; tenacity

Zahl f -, -en number; (*Ziffer, Betrag*) figure

zahlen vt/i (*haben*) pay; (*bezahlen*) pay for; **bitte z∼!** the bill please!

zählen vi (*haben*) count; z∼ zu (*fig*) be one/(pl) some of ● vt count; z∼ zu add to; (*fig*) count among

zahlenmäßig a numerical

Zähler m -s,- meter

Zahl|grenze f fare-stage. **Z∼karte** f paying-in slip. **z∼los** a countless. **z∼reich** a numerous; <*Anzahl, Gruppe*> large ● adv in large numbers. **Z∼ung** f -, -en payment; in Z∼ung nehmen take in part-exchange

Zählung f -, -en count

Zahlwort nt (pl -wörter) numeral

zahm a tame

zähmen vt tame; (*fig*) restrain

Zahn m -[e]s,⸚e tooth; (*am Zahnrad*) cog. **Z∼arzt** m, **Z∼ärztin** f dentist. **Z∼belag** m plaque. **Z∼bürste** f toothbrush. **Z∼fleisch** nt gums pl. **z∼los** a toothless. **Z∼pasta** f -, -en

w
x
y
z

toothpaste. **Z~rad** nt cog-wheel.
Z~schmelz m enamel.
Z~schmerzen mpl toothache sg.
Z~spange f brace. **Z~stein** m
tartar. **Z~stocher** m -s,- toothpick

Zange f -, -n pliers pl; (Kneif-)
pincers pl; (Kohlen-, Zucker-) tongs
pl; (Geburts-) forceps pl

Zank m -[e]s squabble. **z~en** vr sich
z~en squabble

Zäpfchen nt -s,- (Anat) uvula;
(Med) suppository

zapfen vt tap, draw. **Z~streich** m
(Mil) tattoo

Zapf|hahn m tap. **Z~säule** f
petrol-pump

zappeln vi (haben) wriggle; <Kind:>
fidget

zart a delicate; (weich, zärtlich)
tender; (sanft) gentle. **Z~gefühl** nt
tact

zärtlich a tender; (liebevoll) loving.
Z~keit f -, -en tenderness;
(Liebkosung) caress

Zauber m -s magic; (Bann) spell.
Z~er m -s,- magician. **z~haft** a
enchanting. **Z~künstler** m
conjuror. **z~n** vi (haben) do magic;
(Zaubertricks ausführen) do
conjuring tricks ● vt produce as if
by magic. **Z~stab** m magic wand.
Z~trick m conjuring trick

Zaum m -[e]s, Zäume bridle

Zaun m -[e]s, Zäune fence

z.B. abbr (zum Beispiel) e.g.

Zebra nt -s, -s zebra. **Z~streifen** m
zebra crossing

Zeche f -, -n bill; (Bergwerk) pit

zechen vi (haben) 🛈 drink

Zeder f -, -n cedar

Zeh m -[e]s, -en toe. **Z~e** f -, -n toe;
(Knoblauch-) clove

zehn inv a, **Z~** f -, -en ten.
z~te(r,s) a tenth. **Z~tel** nt -s,-
tenth

Zeichen nt -s,- sign; (Signal) signal.
Z~setzung f - punctuation.
Z~trickfilm m cartoon

zeichn|en vt/i (haben) draw; (kenn-)
mark; (unter-) sign. **Z~ung** f -, -en
drawing

Zeige|finger m index finger. **z~n**
vt show; sich z~n appear; (sich
herausstellen) become clear ● vi
(haben) point (auf + acc to). **Z~r** m
-s,- pointer; (Uhr-) hand

Zeile f -, -n line; (Reihe) row

Zeit f -, -en time; sich (dat) Z~
lassen take one's time; es hat Z~
theres's no hurry; mit der Z~ in
time; in nächster Z~ in the near
future; zur Z~ (rechtzeitig) in time;
*(derzeit) s. zurzeit; eine Z~ lang for
a time or while

Zeit|alter nt age, era. **z~gemäß** a
modern, up-to-date. **Z~genosse** m,
Z~genossin f contemporary.
z~genössisch a contemporary.
z~ig a & adv early

zeitlich a <Dauer> in time; <Folge>
chronological. ● adv z~ begrenzt for
a limited time

zeit|los a timeless. **Z~lupe** f slow
motion. **Z~punkt** m time.
z~raubend a time-consuming.
Z~raum m period. **Z~schrift** f
magazine, periodical

Zeitung f -, -en newspaper.
Z~spapier nt newspaper

Zeit|verschwendung f waste of
time. **Z~vertreib** m pastime.
z~weise adv at times. **Z~wort** nt
(pl -wörter) verb. **Z~zünder** m time
fuse

Zelle f -, -n cell; (Telefon-) box

Zelt nt -[e]s, -e tent; (Fest-) marquee.
z~en vi (haben) camp. **Z~en** nt -s
camping. **Z~plane** f tarpaulin.
Z~platz m campsite

Zement m -[e]s cement

zen|sieren vt (Sch) mark; censor
<Presse, Film>. **Z~sur** f -, -en (Sch)
mark; (Presse-) censorship

Zentimeter m & nt centimetre.
Z~maß nt tape-measure

Zentner m -s,- [metric]
hundredweight (50 kg)

zentral a central. **Z~e** f -, -n
central office; (Partei-) headquarters

pl; (*Teleph*) exchange. **Z~heizung** *f* central heating

Zentrum *nt* -s, -tren centre

zerbrech|en† *vt/i* (*sein*) break. **z~lich** *a* fragile

zerdrücken *vt* crush

Zeremonie *f* -, -n ceremony

Zerfall *m* disintegration; (*Verfall*) decay. **z~en**† *vi* (*sein*) disintegrate; (*verfallen*) decay

zergehen† *vi* (*sein*) melt; (*sich auflösen*) dissolve

zerkleinern *vt* chop/(*schneiden*) cut up; (*mahlen*) grind

zerknüllen *vt* crumple [up]

zerkratzen *vt* scratch

zerlassen† *vt* melt

zerlegen *vt* take to pieces, dismantle; (*zerschneiden*) cut up; (*tranchieren*) carve

zerlumpt *a* ragged

zermalmen *vt* crush

zermürben *vt* (*fig*) wear down

zerplatzen *vi* (*sein*) burst

zerquetschen *vt* squash; crush

Zerrbild *nt* caricature

zerreißen† *vt* tear; (*in Stücke*) tear up; break <*Faden, Seil*> ● *vi* (*sein*) tear; break

zerren *vt* drag; pull <*Muskel*> ● *vi* (*haben*) pull (**an** + *dat* at)

zerrissen *a* torn

zerrütten *vt* ruin, wreck; shatter <*Nerven*>

zerschlagen† *vt* smash; smash up <*Möbel*>; **sich z~** (*fig*) fall through; <*Hoffnung:*> be dashed

zerschmettern *vt/i* (*sein*) smash

zerschneiden† *vt* cut; (*in Stücke*) cut up

zersplittern *vi* (*sein*) splinter; <*Glas:*> shatter ● *vt* shatter

zerspringen† *vi* (*sein*) shatter; (*bersten*) burst

Zerstäuber *m* -s,- atomizer

zerstör|en *vt* destroy; (*zunichte machen*) wreck. **Z~er** *m* -s,- destroyer. **Z~ung** *f* destruction

zerstreu|en *vt* scatter; disperse <*Menge*>; dispel <*Zweifel*>; **sich**

z~en disperse; (*sich unterhalten*) amuse oneself. **z~t** *a* absent-minded

Zertifikat *nt* -[e]s, -e certificate

zertrümmern *vt* smash [up]; wreck <*Gebäude, Stadt*>

Zettel *m* -s,- piece of paper; (*Notiz*) note; (*Bekanntmachung*) notice

Zeug *nt* -s 🔟 stuff; (*Sachen*) things *pl*; (*Ausrüstung*) gear; **dummes Z~** nonsense

Zeuge *m* -n, -n witness. **z~n** *vi* (*haben*) testify; **z~n von** (*fig*) show ● *vt* father. **Z~naussage** *f* testimony. **Z~nstand** *m* witness box

Zeugin *f* -, -nen witness

Zeugnis *nt* -ses, -se certificate; (*Sch*) report; (*Referenz*) reference; (*fig: Beweis*) evidence

Zickzack *m* -[e]s, -e zigzag

Ziege *f* -, -n goat

Ziegel *m* -s,- brick; (*Dach-*) tile. **Z~stein** *m* brick

ziehen† *vt* pull; (*sanfter; zücken; zeichnen*) draw; (*heraus-*) pull out; extract <*Zahn*>; raise <*Hut*>; put on <*Bremse*>; move <*Schachfigur*>; (*dehnen*) stretch; make <*Grimasse, Scheitel*>; (*züchten*) breed; grow <*Rosen*>; **nach sich z~** (*fig*) entail ● *vr* **sich z~** (*sich erstrecken*) run; (*sich verziehen*) warp ● *vi* (*haben*) pull (**an** + *dat* on/at); <*Tee, Ofen:*> draw; (*Culin*) simmer; **es zieht** there is a draught; **solche Filme z~ nicht mehr** films like that are no longer popular ● *vi* (*sein*) (*um-*) move (**nach** to); <*Menge:*> march; <*Vögel:*> migrate; <*Wolken, Nebel:*> drift

Ziehharmonika *f* accordion

Ziehung *f* -, -en draw

Ziel *nt* -[e]s, -e destination; (*Sport*) finish; (*Z~scheibe & Mil*) target; (*Zweck*) aim, goal. **z~bewusst** *a* purposeful. **z~en** *vi* (*haben*) aim (**auf** + *acc* at). **z~los** *a* aimless. **Z~scheibe** *f* target

ziemlich *a* 🔟 fair ● *adv* rather, fairly

Zier|de *f* -, -n ornament. **z~en** *vt* adorn

zierlich a dainty

Ziffer f -, -n figure, digit; (*Zahlzeichen*) numeral. **Z~blatt** nt dial

Zigarette f -, -n cigarette

Zigarre f -, -n cigar

Zigeuner(in) m -s,- (f -, -nen) gypsy

Zimmer nt -s,- room. **Z~mädchen** nt chambermaid. **Z~mann** m (pl -leute) carpenter. **Z~nachweis** m accommodation bureau. **Z~pflanze** f house plant

Zimt m -[e]s cinnamon

Zink nt -s zinc

Zinn m -s tin; (*Gefäße*) pewter

Zins|en mpl interest sg; **Z~en** tragen earn interest. **Z~eszins** m -es, -en compound interest. **Z~fuß,** **Z~satz** m interest rate

Zipfel m -s,- corner; (*Spitze*) point

zirka adv about

Zirkel m -s,- [pair of] compasses pl; (*Gruppe*) circle

Zirkul|ation /-'tsi̯o:n/ f - circulation. **z~ieren** vi (sein) circulate

Zirkus m -, -se circus

zirpen vi (haben) chirp

zischen vi (haben) hiss; <*Fett:*> sizzle ● vt hiss

Zit|at nt -[e]s, -e quotation. **z~ieren** vt/i (haben) quote

Zitr|onat nt -[e]s candied lemon-peel. **Z~one** f -, -n lemon

zittern vi (haben) tremble; (vor *Kälte*) shiver; (*beben*) shake

zittrig a shaky

Zitze f -, -n teat

zivil a civilian; <*Ehe, Recht*> civil. **Z~** nt -s civilian clothes pl. **Z~dienst** m community service

Zivili|sation /-'tsi̯o:n/ f -, -en civilization. **z~sieren** vt civilize. **z~siert** a civilized ● adv in a civilized manner

Zivilist m -en, -en civilian

zögern vi (haben) hesitate. **Z~** nt -s hesitation. **z~d** a hesitant

Zoll¹ m -[e]s,- inch

Zoll² m -[e]s,̈e [customs] duty; (*Behörde*) customs pl. **Z~abfertigung** f customs clearance. **Z~beamte(r)** m customs officer. **z~frei** a & adv duty-free. **Z~kontrolle** f customs check

Zone f -, -n zone

Zoo m -s, -s zoo

zoologisch a zoological

Zopf m -[e]s,̈e plait

Zorn m -[e]s anger. **z~ig** a angry

---

zu

● *preposition (+ dative)*

! Note that zu dem can become zum and zu der zur

····▸ (*Richtung*) to; (*bei Beruf*) into. wir gehen zur Schule we are going to school. ich muss zum Arzt I must go to the doctor's. zu ... hin towards. er geht zum Theater/Militär he is going into the theatre/army

····▸ (*zusammen mit*) with. zu dem Käse gab es Wein there was wine with the cheese. zu etw passen go with sth

····▸ (*räumlich; zeitlich*) at. zu Hause at home. zu ihren Füßen at her feet. zu Ostern at Easter. zur Zeit (+ gen) at the time of

····▸ (*preislich*) at; for. zum halben Preis at half price. das Stück zu zwei Mark at or for two marks each. eine Marke zu 60 Pfennig a 60-pfennig stamp

····▸ (*Zweck, Anlass*) for. zu diesem Zweck for this purpose. zum Spaß for fun. zum Lesen for reading. zum Geburtstag bekam ich ... for my birthday I got .... zum ersten Mal for the first time

····▸ (*Art und Weise*) zu meinem Erstaunen/Entsetzen to my surprise/horror. zu Fuß/Pferde on foot/horseback. zu Dutzenden by the dozen. wir waren zu dritt/viert there were three/four of us

····▸ (*Zahlenverhältnis*) to. es steht 5 zu 3 the score is 5–3

····▸ (*Ziel, Ergebnis*) into. zu etw werden turn into sth

····▸ (*gegenüber*) to; towards.
freundlich/hässlich zu jdm sein be
friendly/nasty to s.o.
····▸ (*über*) on; about. **sich zu etw
äußern** to comment on sth
● *adverb*
····▸ (*allzu*) too. **zu groß/viel/weit** too
big/much/far
····▸ (*Richtung*) towards. **nach dem
Fluss zu** towards the river
····▸ (*geschlossen*) closed; (*an Schalter,
Hahn*) off. **zu sein** be closed. **Augen
zu!** close your eyes! **Tür zu!** shut the
door!
● *conjunction*
····▸ to. **etwas zu essen** something to
eat. **nicht zu glauben** unbelievable.
zu erörternde Probleme problems to
be discussed

zualler|erst *adv* first of all.
z∼letzt *adv* last of all

Zubehör *nt* -s accessories *pl*

zubereit|en *vt sep* prepare.
Z∼ung *f* - preparation; (*in Rezept*)
method

zubinden† *vt sep* tie [up]

zubring|en† *vt sep* spend. **Z∼er** *m*
-s,- access road; (*Bus*) shuttle

Zucchini /tsuˈkiːni/ *pl* courgettes

Zucht *f* -, -en breeding; (*Pflanzen-*)
cultivation; (*Art, Rasse*) breed; (*von
Pflanzen*) strain; (*Z∼farm*) farm;
(*Pferde-*) stud

zücht|en *vt* breed; cultivate, grow
<*Rosen*>. **Z∼er** *m* -s,- breeder;
grower

Zuchthaus *nt* prison

Züchtung *f* -, -en breeding;
(*Pflanzen-*) cultivation; (*Art, Rasse*)
breed; (*von Pflanzen*) strain

zucken *vi* (*haben*) twitch; (*sich z∼d
bewegen*) jerk; <*Blitz:*> flash;
<*Flamme:*> flicker ● *vt* **die Achseln
z∼** shrug one's shoulders

Zucker *m* -s sugar. **Z∼dose** *f*
sugar basin. **Z∼guss** *m* icing.
z∼krank *a* diabetic. **Z∼krankheit**
f diabetes. **z∼n** *vt* sugar. **Z∼rohr** *nt*
sugar cane. **Z∼rübe** *f* sugar beet.
Z∼watte *f* candyfloss

zudecken *vt sep* cover up; (*im Bett*)
tuck up; cover <*Topf*>

zudem *adv* moreover

zudrehen *vt sep* turn off

zueinander *adv* to one another; **z∼
passen** go together; **z∼ halten** (*fig*)
stick together

zuerkennen† *vt sep* award (*dat* to)

zuerst *adv* first; (*anfangs*) at first

zufahr|en† *vi sep* (*sein*) **z∼en auf** (+
acc) drive towards. **Z∼t** *f* access;
(*Einfahrt*) drive

Zufall *m* chance; (*Zusammentreffen*)
coincidence; **durch Z∼** by chance/
coincidence. **z∼en**† *vi sep* (*sein*)
close, shut; **jdm z∼en** <*Aufgabe:*>
fall/<*Erbe:*> go to s.o.

zufällig *a* chance, accidental ● *adv*
by chance

Zuflucht *f* refuge; (*Schutz*) shelter

zufolge *prep* (+ *dat*) according to

zufrieden *a* contented; (*befriedigt*)
satisfied; **sich z∼ geben** be satisfied;
jdn z∼ lassen leave s.o. in peace; **jdn
z∼ stellen** satisfy s.o.; **z∼ stellend**
satisfactory. **Z∼heit** *f* -
contentment; satisfaction

zufrieren† *vi sep* (*sein*) freeze over

zufügen *vt sep* inflict (*dat* on); do
<*Unrecht*> (*dat* to)

Zufuhr *f* - supply

Zug *m* -[e]s,⸚e train; (*Kolonne*)
column; (*Um-*) procession; (*Mil*)
platoon; (*Vogelschar*) flock; (*Ziehen,
Zugkraft*) pull; (*Wandern, Ziehen*)
migration; (*Schluck, Luft-*) draught;
(*Atem-*) breath; (*beim Rauchen*) puff;
(*Schach-*) move; (*beim Schwimmen,
Rudern*) stroke; (*Gesichts-*) feature;
(*Wesens-*) trait

Zugabe *f* (*Geschenk*) [free] gift;
(*Mus*) encore

Zugang *m* access

zugänglich *a* accessible;
<*Mensch:*> approachable

Zugbrücke *f* drawbridge

zugeben† *vt sep* add; (*gestehen*)
admit; (*erlauben*) allow

zugehen† *vi sep* (*sein*) close; **jdm z∼**
be sent to s.o.; **z∼ auf** (+ *acc*) go
towards; **dem Ende z∼** draw to a

z

close; <*Vorräte:*> run low; **auf der Party ging es lebhaft zu** the party was pretty lively

Zugehörigkeit *f* - membership

Zügel *m* -s,- rein

zugelassen *a* registered

zügel|los *a* unrestrained. **z~n** *vt* rein in; (*fig*) curb

Zuge|ständnis *nt* concession. **z~stehen†** *vt sep* grant

zügig *a* quick

Zugkraft *f* pull; (*fig*) attraction

zugleich *adv* at the same time

Zugluft *f* draught

zugreifen† *vi sep* (*haben*) grab it/ them; (*bei Tisch*) help oneself; (*bei Angebot*) jump at it; (*helfen*) lend a hand

zugrunde *adv* **z~** **richten** destroy; **z~ gehen** be destroyed; (*sterben*) die; **z~ liegen** form the basis (*dat* of)

zugunsten *prep* (+ *gen*) in favour of; <*Sammlung*> in aid of

zugute *adv* **jdm/etw z~ kommen** benefit s.o./sth

Zugvogel *m* migratory bird

zuhalten† *v sep* ● *vt* keep closed; (*bedecken*) cover; **sich** (*dat*) **die Nase z~** hold one's nose

Zuhälter *m* -s,- pimp

zuhause *adv* = **zu Hause**, *s.* **Haus**. **Z~** *nt* -s,- home

zuhör|en *vi sep* (*haben*) listen (*dat* to). **Z~er(in)** *m(f)* listener

zujubeln *vi sep* (*haben*) **jdm z~** cheer s.o.

zukleben *vt sep* seal

zuknöpfen *vt sep* button up

zukommen† *vi sep* (*sein*) **z~ auf** (+ *acc*) come towards; (*sich nähern*) approach; **z~ lassen** send (**jdm** s.o.); devote <*Pflege*> (*dat* to); **jdm z~** be s.o.'s right

Zukunft *f* - future. **zukünftig** *a* future ● *adv* in future

zulächeln *vi sep* (*haben*) smile (*dat* at)

zulangen *vi sep* (*haben*) help oneself

zulassen† *vt sep* allow, permit; (*teilnehmen lassen*) admit; (*Admin*) license, register; (*geschlossen lassen*) leave closed; leave unopened <*Brief*>

zulässig *a* permissible

Zulassung *f* -, -en admission; registration; (*Lizenz*) licence

zuleide *adv* **jdm etwas z~ tun** hurt s.o.

zuletzt *adv* last; (*schließlich*) in the end

zuliebe *adv* **jdm/etw z~** for the sake of s.o./sth

zum *prep* = **zu dem**; **zum Spaß** for fun; **etw zum Lesen** sth to read

zumachen *v sep* ● *vt* close, shut; do up <*Jacke*>; seal <*Umschlag*>; turn off <*Hahn*>; (*stilllegen*) close down ● *vi* (*haben*) close, shut; (*stillgelegt werden*) close down

zumal *adv* especially ● *conj* especially since

zumindest *adv* at least

zumutbar *a* reasonable

zumute *adv* **mir ist nicht danach z~** I don't feel like it

zumut|en *vt sep* **jdm etw z~en** ask *or* expect sth of s.o.; **sich** (*dat*) **zu viel z~en** overdo things. **Z~ung** *f* - imposition

zunächst *adv* first [of all]; (*anfangs*) at first; (*vorläufig*) for the moment ● *prep* (+ *dat*) nearest to

Zunahme *f* -, -n increase

Zuname *m* surname

zünd|en *vt/i* (*haben*) ignite. **Z~er** *m* -s,- detonator, fuse. **Z~holz** *nt* match. **Z~kerze** *f* sparking-plug. **Z~schlüssel** *m* ignition key. **Z~schnur** *f* fuse. **Z~ung** *f* -, -en ignition

zunehmen† *vi sep* (*haben*) increase (**an** + *dat* in); <*Mond:*> wax; (*an Gewicht*) put on weight. **z~d** *a* increasing

Zuneigung *f* - affection

Zunft *f* -,⸚e guild

Zunge *f* -, -n tongue. **Z~nbrecher** *m* tongue-twister

zunutze *a* sich (*dat*) etw z~ machen make use of sth; (*ausnutzen*) take advantage of sth

zuoberst *adv* right at the top

zuordnen *vt sep* assign (*dat* to)

zupfen *vt/i* (*haben*) pluck (an + *dat* at); pull out <*Unkraut*>

zur *prep* = zu der; zur Schule to school; zur Zeit at present

zurate *adv* z~ ziehen consult

zurechnungsfähig *a* of sound mind

zurecht|finden† (sich) *vr sep* find one's way. z~kommen† *vi sep* (*sein*) cope (mit with); (*rechtzeitig kommen*) be in time. z~legen *vt sep* put out ready; sich (*dat*) eine Ausrede z~legen have an excuse all ready. z~machen *vt sep* get ready. Z~weisung *f* reprimand

zureden *vi sep* (*haben*) jdm z~ try to persuade s.o.

zurichten *vt sep* prepare; (*beschädigen*) damage; (*verletzen*) injure

zuriegeln *vt sep* bolt

zurück *adv* back; Berlin, hin und z~ return to Berlin. z~bekommen† *vt sep* get back. z~bleiben† *vi sep* (*sein*) stay behind; (*nicht mithalten*) lag behind. z~bringen† *vt sep* bring back; (*wieder hinbringen*) take back. z~erstatten *vt sep* refund. z~fahren† *v sep* ● *vt* drive back ● *vi* (*sein*) return, go back; (*im Auto*) drive back; (*zurückweichen*) recoil. z~finden† *vi sep* (*haben*) find one's way back. z~führen *v sep* ● *vt* take back; (*fig*) attribute (auf + *acc* to) ● *vi* (*haben*) lead back. z~geben† *vt sep* give back, return. z~geblieben *a* retarded. z~gehen† *vi sep* (*sein*) go back, return; (*abnehmen*) go down; z~gehen auf (+ *acc*) (*fig*) go back to

zurückgezogen *a* secluded. Z~heit *f* - seclusion

zurückhalt|en† *vt sep* hold back; (*abhalten*) stop; sich z~en restrain oneself. z~end *a* reserved. Z~ung *f* - reserve

zurück|kehren *vi sep* (*sein*) return. z~kommen† *vi sep* (*sein*) come back, return; (*ankommen*) get back. z~lassen† *vt sep* leave behind; (*z~kehren lassen*) allow back. z~legen *vt sep* put back; (*reservieren*) keep; (*sparen*) put by; cover <*Strecke*>. z~liegen† *vi sep* (*haben*) be in the past; (*Sport*) be behind; das liegt lange zurück that was long ago. z~melden (sich) *vr sep* report back. z~schicken *vt sep* send back. z~schlagen† *v sep* ● *vi* (*haben*) hit back. ● *vt* hit back; (*umschlagen*) turn back.

z~schrecken *vi sep* (*sein*) shrink back, recoil; (*fig*) shrink (vor + *dat* from). z~stellen *vt sep* put back; (*reservieren*) keep; (*fig*) put aside; (*aufschieben*) postpone. z~stoßen† *v sep* ● *vt* push back ● *vi* (*sein*) reverse, back. z~treten† *vi sep* (*sein*) step back; (*vom Amt*) resign; (*verzichten*) withdraw. z~weisen† *vt sep* turn away; (*fig*) reject. z~zahlen *vt sep* pay back. z~ziehen† *vt sep* draw back; (*fig*) withdraw; sich z~ziehen withdraw; (*vom Beruf*) retire

Zuruf *m* shout. z~en† *vt sep* shout (*dat* to)

zurzeit *adv* at present

Zusage *f* -, -n acceptance; (*Versprechen*) promise. z~n *v sep* ● *vt* promise ● *vi* (*haben*) accept

zusammen *adv* together; (*insgesamt*) altogether; z~ sein be together. Z~arbeit *f* co-operation. z~arbeiten *vi sep* (*haben*) co-operate. z~bauen *vt sep* assemble. z~bleiben† *vi sep* (*sein*) stay together. z~brechen† *vi sep* (*sein*) collapse. Z~bruch *m* collapse; (*Nerven- & fig*) breakdown. z~fallen† *vi sep* (*sein*) collapse; (*zeitlich*) coincide. z~fassen *vt sep* summarize, sum up. Z~fassung *f* summary. z~fügen *vt sep* fit together. z~gehören *vi sep* (*haben*) belong together; (*z~passen*) go together. z~gesetzt *a* (*Gram*) compound. z~halten *v sep* ● *vt* hold together; (*beisammenhalten*)

z

keep together ● *vi* (*haben*) (*fig*) stick together. **Z~hang** *m* connection; (*Kontext*) context. **z~hanglos** *a* incoherent. **z~klappen** *v sep* ● *vt* fold up ● *vi* (*sein*) collapse. **z~kommen**† *vi sep* (*sein*) meet; (*sich sammeln*) accumulate. **Z~kunft** *f* -,-ͤe meeting. **z~laufen**† *vi sep* (*sein*) gather; <*Flüssigkeit:*> collect; <*Linien:*> converge. **z~leben** *vi sep* (*haben*) live together. **z~legen** *v sep* ● *vt* put together; (*z~falten*) fold up; (*vereinigen*) amalgamate; pool <*Geld*> ● *vi* (*haben*) club together. **z~nehmen**† *vt sep* gather up; summon up <*Mut*>; collect <*Gedanken*>; sich z~nehmen pull oneself together. **z~passen** *vi sep* (*haben*) go together, match. **Z~prall** *m* collision. **z~rechnen** *vt sep* add up. **z~schlagen**† *vt sep* smash up; (*prügeln*) beat up. **z~schließen**† (sich) *vr sep* join together; <*Firmen:*> merge. **Z~schluss** *m* union; (*Comm*) merger

Zusammensein *nt* -s get-together

zusammensetz|en *vt sep* put together; (*Techn*) assemble; sich z~en sit [down] together; (*bestehen*) be made up (aus from). **Z~ung** *f* -, -en composition; (*Techn*) assembly; (*Wort*) compound

zusammen|stellen *vt sep* put together; (*gestalten*) compile. **Z~stoß** *m* collision; (*fig*) clash. **z~treffen**† *vi sep* (*sein*) meet; (*zeitlich*) coincide. **z~zählen** *vt sep* add up. **z~ziehen** *v sep* ● *vt* draw together; (*addieren*) add up; (*konzentrieren*) mass; sich z~ziehen contract; <*Gewitter:*> gather ● *vi* (*sein*) move in together; move in (mit with)

Zusatz *m* addition; (*Jur*) rider; (*Lebensmittel-*) additive. **zusätzlich** *a* additional ● *adv* in addition

zuschau|en *vi sep* (*haben*) watch. **Z~er(in)** *m* -s,- (*f* -, -nen) spectator; (*TV*) viewer

Zuschlag *m* surcharge; (*D-Zug-*) supplement. **z~pflichtig** *a* <*Zug*> for which a supplement is payable

zuschließen† *v sep* ● *vt* lock ● *vi* (*haben*) lock up

zuschneiden† *vt sep* cut out; cut to size <*Holz*>

zuschreiben† *vt sep* attribute (*dat* to); jdm die Schuld z~ blame s.o.

Zuschrift *f* letter; (*auf Annonce*) reply

zuschulden *adv* sich (*dat*) etwas z~ kommen lassen do wrong

Zuschuss *m* contribution; (*staatlich*) subsidy

zusehends *adv* visibly

zusein* *vi sep* (*sein*) zu sein, *s.* zu

zusenden† *vt sep* send (*dat* to)

zusetzen *v sep* ● *vt* add; (*einbüßen*) lose

zusicher|n *vt sep* promise. **Z~ung** *f* promise.

zuspielen *vt sep* (*Sport*) pass

zuspitzen (sich) *vr sep* (*fig*) become critical

Zustand *m* condition, state

zustande *adv* z~ bringen/kommen bring/come about

zuständig *a* competent; (*verantwortlich*) responsible

zustehen† *vi sep* (*haben*) jdm z~ be s.o.'s right; <*Urlaub:*> be due to s.o.

zusteigen† *vi sep* (*sein*) get on; noch jemand zugestiegen? tickets please; (*im Bus*) any more fares please?

zustell|en *vt sep* block; (*bringen*) deliver. **Z~ung** *f* delivery

zusteuern *v sep* ● *vi* (*sein*) head (auf + *acc* for) ● *vt* contribute

zustimm|en *vi sep* (*haben*) agree; (*billigen*) approve (*dat* of). **Z~ung** *f* consent; approval

zustoßen† *vi sep* (*sein*) happen (*dat* to)

Zustrom *m* influx

Zutat *f* (*Culin*) ingredient

zuteil|en *vt sep* allocate; assign <*Aufgabe*>. **Z~ung** *f* allocation

zutiefst *adv* deeply

zutragen† *vt sep* carry/(*fig*) report (*dat* to); **sich z~** happen

zutrau|en *vt sep* **jdm etw z~** believe s.o. capable of sth. **Z~en** *nt* **-s** confidence

zutreffen† *vi sep* (*haben*) be correct; **z~ auf** (+ *acc*) apply to

Zutritt *m* admittance

zuunterst *adv* right at the bottom

zuverlässig *a* reliable. **Z~keit** *f* - reliability

Zuversicht *f* - confidence. **z~lich** *a* confident

zuviel* *pron & adv* **zu viel**, *s.* **viel**

zuvor *adv* before; (*erst*) first

zuvorkommen† *vi sep* (*sein*) (+ *dat*) anticipate. **z~d** *a* obliging

Zuwachs *m* **-es** increase

zuwege *adv* **z~ bringen** achieve

zuweilen *adv* now and then

zuweisen† *vt sep* assign

Zuwendung *f* donation; (*Fürsorge*) care

zuwenig* *pron & adv* **zu wenig**, *s.* **wenig**

zuwerfen† *vt sep* slam <*Tür*>; **jdm etw z~** throw s.o. sth

zuwider *adv* **jdm z~ sein** be repugnant to s.o. ● *prep* (+ *dat*) contrary to

zuzahlen *vt sep* pay extra

zuziehen† *v sep* ● *vt* pull tight; draw <*Vorhänge*>; (*hinzu-*) call in; **sich** (*dat*) **etw z~** contract <*Krankheit*>; sustain <*Verletzung*>; incur <*Zorn*> ● *vi* (*sein*) move into the area

zuzüglich *prep* (+ *gen*) plus

Zwang *m* **-[e]s,ˆe** compulsion; (*Gewalt*) force; (*Verpflichtung*) obligation

zwängen *vt* squeeze

zwanglos *a* informal. **Z~igkeit** *f* - informality

Zwangsjacke *f* straitjacket

zwanzig *inv a* twenty. **z~ste(r,s)** *a* twentieth

zwar *adv* admittedly

Zweck *m* **-[e]s, -e** purpose; (*Sinn*) point. **z~los** *a* pointless. **z~mäßig** *a* suitable; (*praktisch*) functional

zwei *inv a*, **Z~** *f* **-, -en** two; (*Sch*) ≈ B. **Z~bettzimmer** *nt* twin-bedded room

zweideutig *a* ambiguous

zwei|erlei *inv a* two kinds of ● *pron* two things. **z~fach** *a* double

Zweifel *m* **-s,-** doubt. **z~haft** *a* doubtful; (*fragwürdig*) dubious. **z~los** *adv* undoubtedly. **z~n** *vi* (*haben*) doubt (**an etw** *dat* sth)

Zweig *m* **-[e]s, -e** branch. **Z~stelle** *f* branch [office]

Zwei|kampf *m* duel. **z~mal** *adv* twice. **z~reihig** *a* <*Anzug*> double-breasted. **z~sprachig** *a* bilingual

zweit *adv* **zu z~** in twos; **wir waren zu z~** there were two of us. **z~beste(r,s)** *a* second-best. **z~e(r,s)** *a* second

zweitens *adv* secondly

Zwerchfell *nt* diaphragm

Zwerg *m* **-[e]s, -e** dwarf

Zwickel *m* **-s,-** gusset

zwicken *vt/i* (*haben*) pinch

Zwieback *m* **-[e]s,ˆe** rusk

Zwiebel *f* **-, -n** onion; (*Blumen-*)bulb

Zwielicht *nt* half-light; (*Dämmerlicht*) twilight. **z~ig** *a* shady

Zwiespalt *m* conflict

Zwilling *m* **-s, -e** twin; **Z~e** (*Astr*) Gemini

zwingen† *vt* force; **sich z~** force oneself. **z~d** *a* compelling

Zwinger *m* **-s,-** run; (*Zucht-*) kennels *pl*

zwinkern *vi* (*haben*) blink; (*als Zeichen*) wink

Zwirn *m* **-[e]s** button thread

zwischen *prep* (+ *dat/acc*) between; (*unter*) among[st]. **Z~bemerkung** *f* interjection. **z~durch** *adv* in between; (*in der Z~zeit*) in the meantime. **Z~fall** *m* incident. **Z~landung** *f* stopover. **Z~raum** *m* gap, space. **Z~wand** *f* partition. **Z~zeit** *f* **in der Z~zeit** in the meantime

z

Zwist *m* -[e]s, -e discord; (*Streit*) feud

zwitschern *vi* (*haben*) chirp

zwo *inv a* two

zwölf *inv a* twelve. **z~te(r,s)** *a* twelfth

Zylind|er *m* -s,- cylinder; (*Hut*) top hat. **z~risch** *a* cylindrical

Zyn|iker *m* -s,- cynic. **z~isch** *a* cynical. **Z~ismus** *m* - cynicism

Zypern *nt* -s Cyprus

Zypresse *f* -, -n cypress

Zyste /ˈtsʏstə/ *f* -, -n cyst

English–German Dictionary

Aa

a

vor einem Vokal **an**

● *indefinite article*

⋯▸ ein (*m*), eine (*f*), ein (*nt*). **a problem** ein Problem. **an apple** ein Apfel. **a cat** eine Katze. **have you got a pencil?** hast du einen Bleistift? **I gave it to a beggar** ich gab es einem Bettler

❗ There are some cases where **a** is not translated, such as when talking about people's professions or nationalities: **she is a lawyer** sie ist Rechsanwältin. **he's an Italian** er ist Italiener

⋯▸ (*with 'not'*) kein (*m*), keine (*f*), kein (*nt*), keine (*pl*). **that's not a problem/not a good idea** das ist kein Problem/keine gute Idee. **there was not a chance that …** es bestand keine Möglichkeit, dass …. **she did not say a word** sie sagte kein Wort. **I didn't tell a soul** ich habe es keinem Menschen gesagt

⋯▸ (*per; each*) pro. **£300 a week** 300 Pfund pro Woche. **30 miles an hour** 30 Meilen pro Stunde. (*in prices*) **it costs 90p a pound** es kostet 90 Pence das Pfund.

aback *adv* **be taken ~** verblüfft sein

abandon *vt* verlassen; (*give up*) aufgeben

abate *vi* nachlassen

abattoir *n* Schlachthof *m*

abb|ey *n* Abtei *f*. **~ot** *n* Abt *m*

abbreviat|e *vt* abkürzen. **~ion** *n* Abkürzung *f*

abdicat|e *vi* abdanken. **~ion** *n* Abdankung *f*

abdom|en *n* Unterleib *m*. **~inal** *a* Unterleibs-

abduct *vt* entführen. **~ion** *n* Entführung *f*

aberration *n* Abweichung *f*; (*mental*) Verwirrung *f*

abeyance *n* **in ~** [zeitweilig] außer Kraft

abhor *vt* (*pt/pp* abhorred) verabscheuen. **~rent** *a* abscheulich

abid|e *vt* (*pt/pp* abided) (*tolerate*) aushalten; ausstehen <*person*>

ability *n* Fähigkeit *f*; (*talent*) Begabung *f*

abject *a* erbärmlich; (*humble*) demütig

ablaze *a* in Flammen

able *a* (**-r, -st**) fähig; **be ~ to do sth** etw tun können. **~-bodied** *a* körperlich gesund

ably *adv* gekonnt

abnormal *a* anormal; (*Med*) abnorm. **~ity** *n* Abnormität *f*. **~ly** *adv* ungewöhnlich

aboard *adv & prep* an Bord (+ *gen*)

abol|ish *vt* abschaffen. **~ition** *n* Abschaffung *f*

abominable *a*, **-bly** *adv* abscheulich

aborigines *npl* Ureinwohner *pl*

abort *vt* abtreiben. **~ion** *n* Abtreibung *f*. **~ive** *a* <*attempt*> vergeblich

about *adv* umher, herum; (*approximately*) ungefähr; **be ~** (*in circulation*) umgehen; (*in existence*) vorhanden sein; **be ~ to do sth** im Begriff sein, etw zu tun; **there was no one ~** es war kein Mensch da; **run/play ~** herumlaufen/-spielen ● *prep* um (+ *acc*) [… herum]; (*concerning*) über (+ *acc*); **what is it ~?** worum geht es? <*book:*> wovon handelt es? **I know nothing ~ it** ich weiß nichts davon; **talk/know ~** reden/wissen von

about: ~-face *n*, **~-turn** *n* Kehrtwendung *f*

above *adv* oben ● *prep* über (+ *dat/acc*); **~ all** vor allem

above: ~-board *a* legal. **~-mentioned** *a* oben erwähnt

a

abrasive *a* Scheuer-; <*remark*> verletzend ● *n* Scheuermittel *nt*; (*Techn*) Schleifmittel *nt*

abreast *adv* nebeneinander; **keep ~** **of** Schritt halten mit

abridge *vt* kürzen

abroad *adv* im Ausland; **go ~** ins Ausland fahren

abrupt *a*, **-ly** *adv* abrupt; (*sudden*) plötzlich; (*curt*) schroff

abscess *n* Abszess *m*

absence *n* Abwesenheit *f*

absent *a* abwesend; **be ~** fehlen

absentee *n* Abwesende(r) *m/f*

absent-minded *a*, **-ly** *adv* geistesabwesend; (*forgetful*) zerstreut

absolute *a*, **-ly** *adv* absolut

absorb *vt* absorbieren, aufsaugen; **~ed in** vertieft in (+ *acc*). **~ent** *a* saugfähig

absorption *n* Absorption *f*

abstain *vi* sich enthalten (**from** *gen*)

abstemious *a* enthaltsam

abstention *n* (*Pol*) [Stimm]enthaltung *f*

abstract *a* abstrakt ● *n* (*summary*) Abriss *m*

absurd *a*, **-ly** *adv* absurd. **~ity** *n* Absurdität *f*

abundan|ce *n* Fülle *f* (**of** an + *dat*). **~t** *a* reichlich

abuse[1] *vt* missbrauchen; (*insult*) beschimpfen

abus|e[2] *n* Missbrauch *m*; (*insults*) Beschimpfungen *pl*. **~ive** ausfallend

abysmal *a* ⚠ katastrophal

abyss *n* Abgrund *m*

academic *a*, **-ally** *adv* akademisch

academy *n* Akademie *f*

accelerat|e *vt/i* beschleunigen. **~ion** *n* Beschleunigung *f*. **~or** *n* (*Auto*) Gaspedal *nt*

accent *n* Akzent *m*

accept *vt* annehmen; (*fig*) akzeptieren ● *vi* zusagen. **~able** *a* annehmbar. **~ance** *n* Annahme *f*; (*of invitation*) Zusage *f*

access *n* Zugang *m*. **~ible** *a* zugänglich

accessor|y *n* (*Jur*) Mitschuldige(r) *m/f*; **~ies** *pl* (*fashion*) Accessoires *pl*; (*Techn*) Zubehör *nt*

accident *n* Unfall *m*; (*chance*) Zufall *m*; **by ~** zufällig; (*unintentionally*) versehentlich. **~al**, **-ly** *adv* zufällig; (*unintentional*) versehentlich

acclaim *vt* feiern (**as** als)

acclimatize *vt* **become ~d** sich akklimatisieren

accommodat|e *vt* unterbringen. **~ing** *a* entgegenkommend. **~ion** *n* (*rooms*) Unterkunft *f*

accompan|iment *n* Begleitung *f*. **~ist** *n* (*Mus*) Begleiter(in) *m(f)*

accompany *vt* (*pt/pp* **-ied**) begleiten

accomplice *n* Komplize/-zin *m/f*

accomplish *vt* erfüllen <*task*>; (*achieve*) erreichen. **~ed** *a* fähig. **~ment** *n* Fertigkeit *f*; (*achievement*) Leistung *f*

accord *n* **of one's own ~** aus eigenem Antrieb. **~ance** *n* **in ~ance with** entsprechend (+ *dat*)

according *adv* **~ to** nach (+ *dat*). **~ly** *adv* entsprechend

accordion *n* Akkordeon *nt*

account *n* Konto *nt*; (*bill*) Rechnung *f*; (*description*) Darstellung *f*; (*report*) Bericht *m*; **~s** *pl* (*Comm*) Bücher *pl*; **on ~ of** wegen (+ *gen*); **on no ~** auf keinen Fall; **take into ~** in Betracht ziehen, berücksichtigen ● *vi* **~ for** Rechenschaft ablegen für; (*explain*) erklären

accountant *n* Buchhalter(in) *m(f)*; (*chartered*) Wirtschaftsprüfer *m*

accumulat|e *vt* ansammeln, anhäufen ● *vi* sich ansammeln, sich anhäufen. **~ion** *n* Ansammlung *f*, Anhäufung *f*

accura|cy *n* Genauigkeit *f*. **~te** *a*, **-ly** *adv* genau

accusation *n* Anklage *f*

accusative *a* & *n* **~ [case]** (*Gram*) Akkusativ *m*

accuse *vt* (*Jur*) anklagen (**of** *gen*); **~ s.o. of doing sth** jdn beschuldigen, etw getan zu haben

accustom vt gewöhnen (**to** an + dat); **grow** or **get ~ed to** sich gewöhnen an (+ acc). **~ed** a gewohnt

ace n (Cards, Sport) Ass nt

ache n Schmerzen pl ● vi weh tun, schmerzen

achieve vt leisten; (gain) erzielen; (reach) erreichen. **~ment** n (feat) Leistung f

acid a sauer; (fig) beißend ● n Säure f. **~ity** n Säure f. **~ rain** n saurer Regen m

acknowledge vt anerkennen; (admit) zugeben; erwidern <greeting>; **~ receipt of** den Empfang bestätigen (+ gen). **~ment** n Anerkennung f; (of letter) Empfangsbestätigung f

acne n Akne f

acorn n Eichel f

acoustic a, **-ally** adv akustisch. **~s** npl Akustik f

acquaint vt **be ~ed with** kennen; vertraut sein mit <fact>. **~ance** n (person) Bekannte(r) m/f; **make s.o.'s ~ance** jdn kennen lernen

acquire vt erwerben

acquisit|ion n Erwerb m; (thing) Erwerbung f. **~ive** a habgierig

acquit vt (pt/pp acquitted) freisprechen

acre n ≈ Morgen m

acrimonious a bitter

acrobat n Akrobat(in) m(f). **~ic** a akrobatisch

across adv hinüber/herüber; (wide) breit; (not lengthwise) quer; (in crossword) waagerecht; **come ~** sth auf etw (acc) stoßen; **go ~** hinübergehen; **bring ~** herüberbringen ● prep über (+ acc); (on the other side of) auf der anderen Seite (+ gen)

act n Tat f; (action) Handlung f; (law) Gesetz nt; (Theat) Akt m; (item) Nummer f ● vi handeln; (behave) sich verhalten; (Theat) spielen; (pretend) sich verstellen; **~ as** fungieren als ● vt spielen <role>.

~ing a (deputy) stellvertretend ● n (Theat) Schauspielerei f

action n Handlung f; (deed) Tat f; (Mil) Einsatz m; (Jur) Klage f; (effect) Wirkung f; (Techn) Mechanismus m; **out of ~** <machine:> außer Betrieb; **take ~** handeln; **killed in ~** gefallen

activate vt betätigen

activ|e a, **-ly** adv aktiv; **on ~e service** im Einsatz. **~ity** n Aktivität f

act|or n Schauspieler m. **~ress** n Schauspielerin f

actual a, **-ly** adv eigentlich; (real) tatsächlich

acupuncture n Akupunktur f

acute a scharf; <angle> spitz; <illness> akut. **~ly** adv sehr

ad n 🛈 = advertisement

AD abbr (Anno Domini) n.Chr.

adamant a **be ~ that** darauf bestehen, dass

adapt vt anpassen; bearbeiten <play> ● vi sich anpassen. **~able** a anpassungsfähig

adaptation n (Theat) Bearbeitung f

add vt hinzufügen; (Math) addieren ● vi zusammenzählen, addieren; **~ to** hinzufügen zu; (fig: increase) steigern; (compound) verschlimmern. **~ up** vt zusammenzählen <figures> ● vi zusammenzählen, addieren

adder n Kreuzotter f

addict n Süchtige(r) m/f

addict|ed a süchtig; **~ed to drugs** drogensüchtig. **~ion** n Sucht f

addition n Hinzufügung f; (Math) Addition f; (thing added) Ergänzung f; **in ~** zusätzlich. **~al** a, **-ly** adv zusätzlich

additive n Zusatz m

address n Adresse f, Anschrift f; (speech) Ansprache f ● vt adressieren (**to** an + acc); (speak to) anreden <person>; sprechen vor (+ dat) <meeting>. **~ee** n Empfänger m

adequate a, **-ly** adv ausreichend

adhere vi kleben/(fig) festhalten (**to** an + dat)

adhesive a klebend ● n Klebstoff m

adjacent *a* angrenzend

adjective *n* Adjektiv *nt*

adjoin *vt* angrenzen an (+ *acc*). ~**ing** *a* angrenzend

adjourn *vt* vertagen (**until** auf + *acc*) ● *vi* sich vertagen. ~**ment** *n* Vertagung *f*

adjudicate *vi* (*in competition*) Preisrichter sein

adjust *vt* einstellen; (*alter*) verstellen ● *vi* sich anpassen (**to** *dat*). ~**able** *a* verstellbar. ~**ment** *n* Einstellung *f*; Anpassung *f*

ad lib *adv* aus dem Stegreif ● *vi* (*pt/pp* ad libbed) 🔢 improvisieren

administer *vt* verwalten; verabreichen <*medicine*>

administration *n* Verwaltung *f*; (*Pol*) Regierung *f*

admirable *a* bewundernswert

admiral *n* Admiral *m*

admiration *n* Bewunderung *f*

admire *vt* bewundern. ~**r** *n* Verehrer(in) *m(f)*

admission *n* Eingeständnis *nt*; (*entry*) Eintritt *m*

admit *vt* (*pt/pp* admitted) (*let in*) hereinlassen; (*acknowledge*) zugeben; ~ **to sth** etw zugeben. ~**tance** *n* Eintritt *m*. ~**tedly** *adv* zugegebenermaßen

admonish *vt* ermahnen

adolescen|ce *n* Jugend *f*, Pubertät *f*. ~**t** *a* Jugend-; <*boy, girl*> halbwüchsig ● *n* Jugendliche(r) *m/f*

adopt *vt* adoptieren; ergreifen <*measure*>; (*Pol*) annehmen <*candidate*>. ~**ion** *n* Adoption *f*

ador|able *a* bezaubernd. ~**ation** *n* Anbetung *f*

adore *vt* (*worship*) anbeten; (🔢 *like*) lieben

adorn *vt* schmücken. ~**ment** *n* Schmuck *m*

Adriatic *a & n* ~ [**Sea**] Adria *f*

adrift *a* **be** ~ treiben

adroit *a*, **-ly** *adv* gewandt, geschickt

adulation *n* Schwärmerei *f*

adult *n* Erwachsene(r) *m/f*

adulterate *vt* verfälschen; panschen <*wine*>

adultery *n* Ehebruch *m*

advance *n* Fortschritt *m*; (*Mil*) Vorrücken *nt*; (*payment*) Vorschuss *m*; **in** ~ im Voraus ● *vi* vorankommen; (*Mil*) vorrücken; (*make progress*) Fortschritte machen ● *vt* fördern <*cause*>; vorbringen <*idea*>; vorschießen <*money*>. ~**d** *a* fortgeschritten; (*progressive*) fortschrittlich. ~**ment** *n* Förderung *f*; (*promotion*) Beförderung *f*

advantage *n* Vorteil *m*; **take** ~ **of** ausnutzen. ~**ous** *a* vorteilhaft

adventur|e *n* Abenteuer *nt*. ~**er** *n* Abenteurer *m*. ~**ous** *a* abenteuerlich; <*person*> abenteuerlustig

adverb *n* Adverb *nt*

adverse *a* ungünstig

advert *n* 🔢 = **advertisement**

advertise *vt* Reklame machen für; (*by small ad*) inserieren ● *vi* Reklame machen; inserieren

advertisement *n* Anzeige *f*; (*publicity*) Reklame *f*; (*small ad*) Inserat *nt*

advertis|er *n* Inserent *m*. ~**ing** *n* Werbung *f*

advice *n* Rat *m*

advisable *a* ratsam

advis|e *vt* raten (**s.o.** jdm); (*counsel*) beraten; (*inform*) benachrichtigen; ~**e s.o. against sth** jdm von etw abraten ● *vi* raten. ~**er** *n* Berater(in) *m(f)*. ~**ory** *a* beratend

advocate¹ *n* (*supporter*) Befürworter *m*

advocate² *vt* befürworten

aerial *a* Luft- ● *n* Antenne *f*

aerobics *n* Aerobic *nt*

aero|drome *n* Flugplatz *m*. ~**plane** *n* Flugzeug *nt*

aerosol *n* Spraydose *f*

aesthetic *a* ästhetisch

affair *n* Angelegenheit *f*, Sache *f*; (*scandal*) Affäre *f*; [**love-**]~ [Liebes]verhältnis *nt*

affect *vt* sich auswirken auf (+ *acc*); (*concern*) betreffen; (*move*) rühren;

(*pretend*) vortäuschen. **~ation** *n* Affektiertheit *f*. **~ed** *a* affektiert

affection *n* Liebe *f*. **~ate** *a*, **-ly** *adv* liebevoll

affirm *vt* behaupten

affirmative *a* bejahend ● *n* Bejahung *f*

afflict *vt* be **~ed** with behaftet sein mit. **~ion** *n* Leiden *nt*

affluen|ce *n* Reichtum *m*. **~t** *a* wohlhabend. **~t society** *n* Wohlstandsgesellschaft *f*

afford *vt* be able to **~** sth sich (*dat*) etw leisten können. **~able** *a* erschwinglich

affront *n* Beleidigung *f* ● *vt* beleidigen

afloat *a* be **~** <*ship:*> flott sein; keep **~** <*person:*> sich über Wasser halten

afraid *a* be **~** Angst haben (of vor + *dat*); I'm **~** not leider nicht; I'm **~** so [ja] leider

Africa *n* Afrika *nt*. **~n** *a* afrikanisch ● *n* Afrikaner(in) *m(f)*

after *adv* danach ● *prep* nach (+ *dat*); **~** that danach; **~** all schließlich; the day **~** tomorrow übermorgen; be **~** aus sein auf (+ *acc*) ● *conj* nachdem

after: ~-effect *n* Nachwirkung *f*. **~math** *n* Auswirkungen *pl*. **~noon** *n* Nachmittag *m*; good **~noon!** guten Tag! **~-sales service** *n* Kundendienst *m*. **~shave** *n* Rasierwasser *nt*. **~thought** *n* nachträglicher Einfall *m*. **~wards** *adv* nachher

again *adv* wieder; (*once more*) noch einmal; **~** and **~** immer wieder

against *prep* gegen (+ *acc*)

age *n* Alter *nt*; (*era*) Zeitalter *nt*; **~s** 🄸 ewig; under **~** minderjährig; of **~** volljährig; two years of **~** zwei Jahre alt ● *v* (*pres p* ageing) ● *vt* älter machen ● *vi* altern; (*mature*) reifen

aged[1] *a* **~** two zwei Jahre alt

aged[2] *a* betagt ● *n* the **~** *pl* die Alten

ageless *a* ewig jung

agency *n* Agentur *f*; (*office*) Büro *nt*

agenda *n* Tagesordnung *f*

agent *n* Agent(in) *m(f)*; (*Comm*) Vertreter(in) *m(f)*; (*substance*) Mittel *nt*

aggravat|e *vt* verschlimmern; (🄸 *annoy*) ärgern. **~ion** *n* 🄸 Ärger *m*

aggregate *a* gesamt ● *n* Gesamtzahl *f*; (*sum*) Gesamtsumme *f*

aggress|ion *n* Aggression *f*. **~ive** *a*, **-ly** *adv* aggressiv. **~or** *n* Angreifer(in) *m(f)*

aggro *n* 🄸 Ärger *m*

aghast *a* entsetzt

agil|e *a* flink, behände; <*mind*> wendig. **~ity** *n* Flinkheit *f*, Behändigkeit *f*

agitat|e *vt* bewegen; (*shake*) schütteln ● *vi* (*fig*) **~** for agitieren für. **~ed** *a*, **-ly** *adv* erregt. **~ion** *n* Erregung *f*; (*Pol*) Agitation *f*

ago *adv* vor (+ *dat*); a long time **~** vor langer Zeit; how long **~** is it? wie lange ist es her?

agony *n* Qual *f*; be in **~** furchtbare Schmerzen haben

agree *vt* vereinbaren; (*admit*) zugeben; **~** to do sth sich bereit erklären, etw zu tun ● *vi* <*people, figures:*> übereinstimmen; (*reach agreement*) sich einigen; (*get on*) gut miteinander auskommen; (*consent*) einwilligen (to in + *acc*); **~** with s.o. jdm zustimmen; <*food:*> jdm bekommen; **~** with sth (*approve of*) mit etw einverstanden sein

agreeable *a* angenehm

agreed *a* vereinbart

agreement *n* Übereinstimmung *f*; (*consent*) Einwilligung *f*; (*contract*) Abkommen *nt*; reach **~** sich einigen

agricultur|al *a* landwirtschaftlich. **~e** *n* Landwirtschaft *f*

aground *a* gestrandet; run **~** <*ship:*> stranden

ahead *adv* straight **~** geradeaus; be **~** of s.o./sth vor jdm/etw sein; (*fig*) voraus sein; go on **~** vorgehen; get **~** vorankommen; go **~!** 🄸 bitte! look/plan **~** vorausblicken/-planen

aid n Hilfe f; (financial) Unterstützung f; **in ~ of** zugunsten (+ gen) ● vt helfen (+ dat)

Aids n Aids nt

aim n Ziel nt; **take ~** zielen ● vt richten (**at** auf + acc); ● vi zielen (**at** auf + acc); **~ to do sth** beabsichtigen, etw zu tun. **~less** a, **-ly** adv ziellos

air n Luft f; (expression) Miene f; (appearance) Anschein m; **be on the ~** <programme:> gesendet werden; <person:> auf Sendung sein; **by ~** auf dem Luftweg; (airmail) mit Luftpost ● vt lüften; vorbringen <views>

air: **~-conditioned** a klimatisiert. **~-conditioning** n Klimaanlage f. **~craft** n Flugzeug nt. **~field** n Flugplatz m. **~ force** n Luftwaffe f. **~ freshener** n Raumspray nt. **~gun** n Luftgewehr nt. **~ hostess** n Stewardess f. **~ letter** n Aerogramm nt. **~line** n Fluggesellschaft f. **~mail** n Luftpost f. **~man** n Flieger m. **~plane** n (Amer) Flugzeug nt. **~port** n Flughafen m. **~-raid** n Luftangriff m. **~-raid shelter** n Luftschutzbunker m. **~ship** n Luftschiff nt. **~ ticket** n Flugschein m. **~tight** a luftdicht. **~-traffic controller** n Fluglotse m

airy a (-ier, -iest) luftig; <manner> nonchalant

aisle n Gang m

ajar a angelehnt

alarm n Alarm m; (device) Alarmanlage f; (clock) Wecker m; (fear) Unruhe f ● vt erschrecken

alas int ach!

album n Album nt

alcohol n Alkohol m. **~ic** a alkoholisch ● n Alkoholiker(in) m(f). **~ism** n Alkoholismus m

alert a aufmerksam ● n Alarm m

algebra n Algebra f

Algeria n Algerien nt

alias n Deckname m ● adv alias

alibi n Alibi nt

alien a fremd ● n Ausländer(in) m(f)

alienate vt entfremden

alight[1] vi aussteigen (**from** aus)

alight[2] a **be ~** brennen; **set ~** anzünden

align vt ausrichten. **~ment** n Ausrichtung f

alike a & adv ähnlich; (same) gleich; **look ~** sich (dat) ähnlich sehen

alive a lebendig; **be ~** leben; **be ~ with** wimmeln von

all
● adjective
····▸ (plural) alle. **all [the] children** alle Kinder. **all our children** alle unsere Kinder. **all the books** alle Bücher. **all the others** alle anderen
····▸ (singular = whole) ganz. **all the wine** der ganze Wein. **all the town** die ganze Stadt. **all my money** mein ganzes Geld; all mein Geld. **all day** den ganzen Tag. **all Germany** ganz Deutschland
● pronoun
····▸ (plural = all persons/things) alle. **all are welcome** alle sind willkommen. **they all came** sie sind alle gekommen. **are we all here?** sind wir alle da? **the best pupils of all** die besten Schüler (von allen). **the most beautiful of all** der/die/das schönste von allen
····▸ (singular = everything) alles. **that is all** das ist alles. **all that I possess** alles, was ich besitze
····▸ **all of** ganz; (with plural) alle. **all of the money** das ganze Geld. **all of the paintings** alle Gemälde. **all of you/ them** Sie/sie alle
····▸ (in phrases) **all in all** in allem. **in all** insgesamt. **most of all** am meisten. **once and for all** ein für alle Mal. **not at all** gar nicht
● adverb
····▸ (completely) ganz. **she was all alone** sie war ganz allein. **I was all dirty** ich war ganz schmutzig
····▸ (in scores) **four all** vier zu vier
····▸ **all right** (things) in Ordnung. **is everything all right?** ist alles in Ordnung? **is that all right for you?** passt das Ihnen? **I'm all right** mir geht es gut. **did you get home all**

right? sind Sie gut nach Hause gekommen? is it all right to go in? kann ich reingehen? yes, all right ja, gut. work out all right gut gehen; klappen ⚀
····▸ (in phrases) all but (almost) fast. all at once auf einmal. all the better umso besser. all the same (nevertheless) trotzdem

allege vt behaupten

allegiance n Treue f

allerg|ic a allergisch (to gegen). ~y n Allergie f

alleviate vt lindern

alley n Gasse f; (for bowling) Bahn f

alliance n Verbindung f; (Pol) Bündnis nt

allied a alliiert

alligator n Alligator m

allocat|e vt zuteilen; (share out) verteilen. ~ion n Zuteilung f

allot vt (pt/pp allotted) zuteilen (s.o. jdm)

allow vt erlauben; (give) geben; (grant) gewähren; (reckon) rechnen; (agree, admit) zugeben; ~ for berücksichtigen; ~ s.o. to do sth jdm erlauben, etw zu tun; be ~ed to do sth etw tun dürfen

allowance n [finanzielle] Unterstützung f; make ~s for berücksichtigen

alloy n Legierung f

allude vi anspielen (to auf + acc)

allusion n Anspielung f

ally[1] n Verbündete(r) m/f; the Allies pl die Alliierten

ally[2] vt (pt/pp -ied) verbinden; ~ oneself with sich verbünden mit

almighty a allmächtig; (⚀ big) Riesen- ● n the A~ der Allmächtige

almond n (Bot) Mandel f

almost adv fast, beinahe

alone a & adv allein; leave me ~ lass mich in Ruhe; leave that ~! lass die Finger davon! let ~ ganz zu schweigen von

along prep entlang (+ acc); ~ the river den Fluss entlang ● adv ~ with zusammen mit; all ~ die ganze Zeit;

come ~ komm doch; I'll bring it ~ ich bringe es mit

alongside adv daneben ● prep neben (+ dat)

aloud adv laut

alphabet n Alphabet nt. ~ical a, -ly adv alphabetisch

alpine a alpin; A ~ Alpen-

Alps npl Alpen pl

already adv schon

Alsace n Elsass nt

Alsatian n (dog) [deutscher] Schäferhund m

also adv auch

altar n Altar m

alter vt ändern ● vi sich verändern. ~ation n Änderung f

alternate[1] vi [sich] abwechseln ● vt abwechseln

alternate[2] a, -ly adv abwechselnd; on ~ days jeden zweiten Tag

alternative a andere(r,s); ~ medicine Alternativmedizin f ● n Alternative f. ~ly adv oder aber

although conj obgleich, obwohl

altitude n Höhe f

altogether adv insgesamt; (on the whole) alles in allem

aluminium n, (Amer) **aluminum** n Aluminium nt

always adv immer

am see be

a.m. abbr (ante meridiem) vormittags

amass vt anhäufen

amateur n Amateur m ● attrib Amateur-; (Theat) Laien-. ~ish a laienhaft

amaze vt erstaunen. ~d a erstaunt. ~ment n Erstaunen nt

amazing a, -ly adv erstaunlich

ambassador n Botschafter m

amber n Bernstein m ● a (colour) gelb

ambigu|ity n Zweideutigkeit f. ~ous a -ly adv zweideutig

ambiti|on n Ehrgeiz m; (aim) Ambition f. ~ous a ehrgeizig

amble vi schlendern

ambulance n Krankenwagen m. ~ man n Sanitäter m

ambush n Hinterhalt m ● vt aus dem Hinterhalt überfallen

amen int amen

amend vt ändern. ~ment n Änderung f

amenities npl Einrichtungen pl

America n Amerika nt. ~n a amerikanisch ● n Amerikaner(in) m(f). ~nism n Amerikanismus m

amiable a nett

amicable a, -bly adv freundschaftlich; <agreement> gütlich

amid[st] prep inmitten (+ gen)

ammonia n Ammoniak nt

ammunition n Munition f

amnesty n Amnestie f

among[st] prep unter (+ dat/acc); ~ yourselves untereinander

amoral a amoralisch

amorous a zärtlich

amount n Menge f; (sum of money) Betrag m; (total) Gesamtsumme f ● vi ~ to sich belaufen auf (+ acc); (fig) hinauslaufen auf (+ acc)

amphibi|an n Amphibie f. ~ous a amphibisch

amphitheatre n Amphitheater nt

ample a (-r, -st), -ly adv reichlich; (large) füllig

amplif|ier n Verstärker m. ~y vt (pt/pp -ied) weiter ausführen; verstärken <sound>

amputat|e vt amputieren. ~ion n Amputation f

amuse vt amüsieren, belustigen; (entertain) unterhalten. ~ment n Belustigung f; Unterhaltung f

amusing a amüsant

an see a

anaem|ia n Blutarmut f, Anämie f. ~ic a blutarm

anaesthetic n Narkosemittel nt, Betäubungsmittel nt; under [an] ~ in Narkose

anaesthetist n Narkosearzt m

analogy n Analogie f

analyse vt analysieren

analysis n Analyse f

analyst n Chemiker(in) m(f); (Psych) Analytiker m

analytical a analytisch

anarch|ist n Anarchist m. ~y n Anarchie f

anatom|ical a, -ly adv anatomisch. ~y n Anatomie f

ancest|or n Vorfahr m. ~ry n Abstammung f

anchor n Anker m ● vi ankern ● vt verankern

ancient a alt

and conj und; ~ so on und so weiter; six hundred ~ two sechshundertzwei; more ~ more immer mehr; nice ~ warm schön warm

anecdote n Anekdote f

angel n Engel m. ~ic a engelhaft

anger n Zorn m ● vt zornig machen

angle n Winkel m; (fig) Standpunkt m; at an ~ schräg

angler n Angler m

Anglican a anglikanisch ● n Anglikaner(in) m(f)

Anglo-Saxon a angelsächsich ● n Angelsächsisch nt

angry a (-ier, -iest), -ily adv zornig; be ~ with böse sein auf (+ acc)

anguish n Qual f

angular a eckig; <features> kantig

animal n Tier nt ● a tierisch

animat|e vt beleben. ~ed a lebhaft

animosity n Feindseligkeit f

ankle n [Fuß]knöchel m

annex[e] n Nebengebäude nt; (extension) Anbau m

annihilate vt vernichten

anniversary n Jahrestag m

annotate vt kommentieren

announce vt bekannt geben; (over loudspeaker) durchsagen; (at reception) ankündigen; (Radio, TV) ansagen; (in newspaper) anzeigen. ~ment n Bekanntgabe f, Bekanntmachung f; Durchsage f; Ansage f; Anzeige f. ~r n Ansager(in) m(f)

annoy vt ärgern; (*pester*) belästigen; get ~ed sich ärgern. **~ance** n Ärger m. **~ing** a ärgerlich

annual a, **-ly** adv jährlich ● n (*book*) Jahresalbum nt

anonymous a, **-ly** adv anonym

anorak n Anorak m

anorexi|a n Magersucht f. **~c** a be ~c an Magersucht leiden

another a & pron ein anderer/eine andere/ein anderes; (*additional*) noch ein(e); ~ [one] noch einer/ eine/eins; ~ time ein andermal; one ~ einander

answer n Antwort f; (*solution*) Lösung f ● vt antworten (**s.o.** jdm); beantworten <*question, letter*>; ~ the door/telephone an die Tür/ans Telefon gehen ● vi antworten; (*Teleph*) sich melden; ~ **back** eine freche Antwort geben. **~ing machine** n (*Teleph*) Anrufbeantworter m

ant n Ameise f

antagonis|m n Antagonismus m. **~tic** a feindselig

Antarctic n Antarktis f

antelope n Antilope f

antenatal a ~ care Schwangerschaftsfürsorge f

antenna n Fühler m; (*Amer: aerial*) Antenne f

anthem n Hymne f

anthology n Anthologie f

anthropology n Anthropologie f

antibiotic n Antibiotikum nt

anticipat|e vt vorhersehen; (*forestall*) zuvorkommen (+ *dat*); (*expect*) erwarten. **~ion** n Erwartung f

anticlimax n Enttäuschung f

anticlockwise a & adv gegen den Uhrzeigersinn

antics npl Mätzchen pl

antidote n Gegengift nt

antifreeze n Frostschutzmittel nt

antipathy n Abneigung f, Antipathie f

antiquated a veraltet

antique a antik ● n Antiquität f. ~ **dealer** n Antiquitätenhändler m

antiquity n Altertum nt

antiseptic a antiseptisch ● n Antiseptikum nt

antisocial a asozial; [T] ungesellig

antlers npl Geweih nt

anus n After m

anvil n Amboss m

anxiety n Sorge f

anxious a, **-ly** adv ängstlich; (*worried*) besorgt; be ~ to do sth etw gerne machen wollen

any a irgendein(e); pl irgendwelche; (*every*) jede(r,s); pl alle; (*after negative*) kein(e); pl keine; ~ colour/number you like eine beliebige Farbe/Zahl; have you ~ wine/apples? haben Sie Wein/Äpfel? ● pron [irgend]einer/eine/eins; pl [irgend]welche; (*some*) welche(r,s); pl welche; (*all*) alle pl; (*negative*) keiner/keine/keins; pl keine; I don't want ~ of it ich will nichts davon; there aren't ~ es gibt keine ● adv noch; ~ quicker/slower noch schneller/langsamer; is it ~ better? geht es etwas besser? would you like ~ more? möchten Sie noch [etwas]? I can't eat ~ more ich kann nichts mehr essen

anybody pron [irgend]jemand; (*after negative*) niemand; ~ can do that das kann jeder

anyhow adv jedenfalls; (*nevertheless*) trotzdem; (*badly*) irgendwie

anyone pron = anybody

anything pron [irgend]etwas; (*after negative*) nichts; (*everything*) alles

anyway adv jedenfalls; (*in any case*) sowieso

anywhere adv irgendwo; (*after negative*) nirgendwo; <*be, live*> überall; <*go*> überallhin

apart adv auseinander; live ~ getrennt leben; ~ **from** abgesehen von

apartment n Zimmer nt; (*flat*) Wohnung f

ape n [Menschen]affe m ● vt
nachäffen

aperitif n Aperitif m

apologetic a, **-ally** adv
entschuldigend; **be** ~ sich
entschuldigen

apologize vi sich entschuldigen (**to**
bei)

apology n Entschuldigung f

apostle n Apostel m

apostrophe n Apostroph m

appal vt (pt/pp appalled) entsetzen.
~**ling** a entsetzlich

apparatus n Apparatur f; (Sport)
Geräte pl; (single piece) Gerät nt

apparent a offenbar; (seeming)
scheinbar. ~**ly** adv offenbar,
anscheinend

appeal n Appell m, Aufruf m;
(request) Bitte f; (attraction) Reiz m;
(Jur) Berufung f ● vi appellieren (**to**
an + acc); (ask) bitten (**for** um); (be
attractive) zusagen (**to** dat); (Jur)
Berufung einlegen. ~**ing** a
ansprechend

appear vi erscheinen; (seem)
scheinen; (Theat) auftreten. ~**ance**
n Erscheinen nt; (look) Aussehen nt;
to all ~**ances** allem Anschein nach

appendicitis n
Blinddarmentzündung f

appendix n (pl **-ices**) (of book)
Anhang m ● (pl **-es**) (Anat)
Blinddarm m

appetite n Appetit m

appetizing a appetitlich

applau|d vt/i Beifall klatschen (+
dat). ~**se** n Beifall m

apple n Apfel m

appliance n Gerät nt

applicable a anwendbar (**to** auf +
acc); (on form) **not** ~ nicht
zutreffend

applicant n Bewerber(in) m(f)

application n Anwendung f;
(request) Antrag m; (for job)
Bewerbung f; (diligence) Fleiß m

applied a angewandt

apply vt (pt/pp **-ied**) auftragen
<paint>; anwenden <force, rule> ● vi

zutreffen (**to** auf + acc); ~ **for**
beantragen; sich bewerben um <job>

appoint vt ernennen; (fix) festlegen.
~**ment** n Ernennung f; (meeting)
Verabredung f; (at doctor's,
hairdresser's) Termin m; (job) Posten
m; **make an** ~**ment** sich anmelden

appreciable a merklich;
(considerable) beträchtlich

appreciat|e vt zu schätzen wissen;
(be grateful for) dankbar sein für;
(enjoy) schätzen; (understand)
verstehen ● vi (increase in value) im
Wert steigen. ~**ion** n (gratitude)
Dankbarkeit f. ~**ive** a dankbar

apprehens|ion n Festnahme f;
(fear) Angst f. ~**ive** a ängstlich

apprentice n Lehrling m. ~**ship** n
Lehre f

approach n Näherkommen nt; (of
time) Nahen nt; (access) Zugang m;
(road) Zufahrt f ● vi sich nähern;
<time:> nahen ● vt sich nähern (+
dat); (with request) herantreten an (+
acc); (set about) sich heranmachen
an (+ acc). ~**able** a zugänglich

appropriate a angebracht,
angemessen

approval n Billigung f; **on** ~ zur
Ansicht

approv|e vt billigen ● vi ~**e of** sth/
s.o. mit etw/jdm einverstanden sein.
~**ing** a, **-ly** adv anerkennend

approximate a, **-ly** adv ungefähr

approximation n Schätzung f

apricot n Aprikose f

April n April m; **make an** ~ **fool of** in
den April schicken

apron n Schürze f

apt a, **-ly** adv passend; **be** ~ **to do
sth** dazu neigen, etw zu tun

aqualung n Tauchgerät nt

aquarium n Aquarium nt

aquatic a Wasser-

Arab a arabisch ● n Araber(in) m(f).
~**ian** a arabisch

Arabic a arabisch

arbitrary a, **-ily** adv willkürlich

arbitrat|e vi schlichten. ~**ion** n
Schlichtung f

arc n Bogen m

arcade n Laubengang m; (shops) Einkaufspassage f

arch n Bogen m; (of foot) Gewölbe nt ● vt ~ its back <cat:> einen Buckel machen

archaeological a archäologisch

archaeolog|ist n Archäologe m/ -login f. ~y n Archäologie f

archaic a veraltet

archbishop n Erzbischof m

archer n Bogenschütze m. ~y n Bogenschießen nt

architect n Architekt(in) m(f). ~ural a, -ly adv architektonisch

architecture n Architektur f

archives npl Archiv nt

archway n Torbogen m

Arctic a arktisch ● n the ~ die Arktis

ardent a, -ly adv leidenschaftlich

ardour n Leidenschaft f

arduous a mühsam

are see be

area n (surface) Fläche f; (Geom) Flächeninhalt m; (region) Gegend f; (fig) Gebiet nt

arena n Arena f

Argentina n Argentinien nt

Argentin|e, ~ian a argentinisch

argue vi streiten (about über + acc); <two people:> sich streiten; (debate) diskutieren; **don't ~!** keine Widerrede! ● vt (debate) diskutieren; (reason) ~ **that** argumentieren, dass

argument n Streit m, Auseinandersetzung f; (reasoning) Argument nt; **have an ~** sich streiten. ~**ative** a streitlustig

aria n Arie f

arise vi (pt arose, pp arisen) sich ergeben (from aus)

aristocracy n Aristokratie f

aristocrat n Aristokrat(in) m(f). ~**ic** a aristokratisch

arithmetic n Rechnen nt

arm n Arm m; (of chair) Armlehne f; ~**s** pl (weapons) Waffen pl; (Heraldry) Wappen nt ● vt bewaffnen

armament n Bewaffnung f; ~**s** pl Waffen pl

armchair n Sessel m

armed a bewaffnet; ~ **forces** Streitkräfte pl

armour n Rüstung f. ~**ed** a Panzer-

armpit n Achselhöhle f

army n Heer nt; (specific) Armee f; **join the ~** zum Militär gehen

aroma n Aroma nt, Duft m. ~**tic** a aromatisch

arose see arise

around adv [all] ~ rings herum; **he's not ~** er ist nicht da; **travel ~** herumreisen ● prep um (+ acc) … herum; (approximately) gegen

arouse vt aufwecken; (excite) erregen

arrange vt arrangieren; anordnen <furniture, books>; (settle) abmachen. ~**ment** n Anordnung f; (agreement) Vereinbarung f; (of flowers) Gesteck nt; **make ~ments** Vorkehrungen treffen

arrest n Verhaftung f; **under ~** verhaftet ● vt verhaften

arrival n Ankunft f; **new ~s** pl Neuankömmlinge pl

arrive vi ankommen; ~ **at** (fig) gelangen zu

arrogan|ce n Arroganz f. ~**t** a, -ly adv arrogant

arrow n Pfeil m

arse n (vulg) Arsch m

arson n Brandstiftung f. ~**ist** n Brandstifter m

art n Kunst f; **work of ~** Kunstwerk nt; ~**s and crafts** pl Kunstgewerbe nt; **A~s** pl (Univ) Geisteswissenschaften pl

artery n Schlagader f, Arterie f

art gallery n Kunstgalerie f

arthritis n Arthritis f

artichoke n Artischocke f

article n Artikel m; (object) Gegenstand m; ~ **of clothing** Kleidungsstück nt

artificial a, -ly adv künstlich

artillery n Artillerie f

artist n Künstler(in) m(f)

artiste n (Theat) Artist(in) m(f)

artistic a, -ally adv künstlerisch

a

as *conj* (*because*) da; (*when*) als; (*while*) während ● *prep* als; **as a child/foreigner** als Kind/Ausländer ● *adv* as well auch; **as soon as** sobald; **as much as** so viel wie; **as quick as you** so schnell wie du; **as you know** wie Sie wissen; **as far as I'm concerned** was mich betrifft

asbestos *n* Asbest *m*

ascend *vi* [auf]steigen ● *vt* besteigen <*throne*>

ascent *n* Aufstieg *m*

ascertain *vt* ermitteln

ash[1] *n* (*tree*) Esche *f*

ash[2] *n* Asche *f*

ashamed *a* beschämt; **be ~** sich schämen (**of** über + *acc*)

ashore *adv* an Land

ashtray *n* Aschenbecher *m*

Asia *n* Asien *nt*. **~n** *a* asiatisch ● *n* Asiat(in) *m(f)*. **~tic** *a* asiatisch

aside *adv* beiseite

ask *vt/i* fragen; stellen <*question*>; (*invite*) einladen; **~ for** bitten um; verlangen <*s.o.*>; **~ after** sich erkundigen nach; **~ s.o. in** jdn hereinbitten; **~ s.o. to do sth** jdn bitten, etw zu tun

asleep *a* **be ~** schlafen; **fall ~** einschlafen

asparagus *n* Spargel *m*

aspect *n* Aspekt *m*

asphalt *n* Asphalt *m*

aspire *vi* **~ to** streben nach

ass *n* Esel *m*

assail *vt* bestürmen. **~ant** *n* Angreifer(in) *m(f)*

assassin *n* Mörder(in) *m(f)*. **~ate** *vt* ermorden. **~ation** *n* [politischer] Mord *m*

assault *n* (*Mil*) Angriff *m*; (*Jur*) Körperverletzung *f* ● *vt* [tätlich] angreifen

assemble *vi* sich versammeln ● *vt* versammeln; (*Techn*) montieren

assembly *n* Versammlung *f*; (*Sch*) Andacht *f*; (*Techn*) Montage *f*. **~ line** *n* Fließband *nt*

assent *n* Zustimmung *f*

assert *vt* behaupten; **~ oneself** sich durchsetzen. **~ion** *n* Behauptung *f*

assess *vt* bewerten; (*fig & for tax purposes*) einschätzen: schätzen <*value*>. **~ment** *n* Einschätzung *f*; (*of tax*) Steuerbescheid *m*

asset *n* Vorteil *m*; **~s** *pl* (*money*) Vermögen *nt*; (*Comm*) Aktiva *pl*

assign *vt* zuweisen (**to** *dat*). **~ment** *n* (*task*) Aufgabe *f*

assist *vt/i* helfen (+ *dat*). **~ance** *n* Hilfe *f*. **~ant** *a* Hilfs- ● *n* Assistent(in) *m(f)*; (*in shop*) Verkäufer(in) *m(f)*

associat|e[1] *vt* verbinden; (*Psych*) assoziieren ● *vi* **~ with** verkehren mit. **~ion** *n* Verband *m*

associate[2] *a* assoziiert ● *n* Kollege *m*/-gin *f*

assort|ed *a* gemischt. **~ment** *n* Mischung *f*

assum|e *vt* annehmen; übernehmen <*office*>; **~ing that** angenommen, dass

assumption *n* Annahme *f*; **on the ~** in der Annahme (**that** dass)

assurance *n* Versicherung *f*; (*confidence*) Selbstsicherheit *f*

assure *vt* versichern (**s.o.** jdm); **I ~ you** [of that] das versichere ich Ihnen. **~d** *a* sicher

asterisk *n* Sternchen *nt*

asthma *n* Asthma *nt*

astonish *vt* erstaunen. **~ing** *a* erstaunlich. **~ment** *n* Erstaunen *nt*

astray *adv* **go ~** verloren gehen; <*person:*> sich verlaufen

astride *adv* rittlings ● *prep* rittlings auf (+ *dat/acc*)

astrolog|er *n* Astrologe *m*/-gin *f*. **~y** *n* Astrologie *f*

astronaut *n* Astronaut(in) *m(f)*

astronom|er *n* Astronom *m*. **~ical** *a* astronomisch. **~y** *n* Astronomie *f*

astute *a* scharfsinnig

asylum *n* Asyl *nt*; **[lunatic] ~** Irrenanstalt *f*

at
● *preposition*

····▶ (*expressing place*) an (+ *dat*). at the station am Bahnhof. **at the end** am Ende. **at the corner** an der Ecke. **at the same place** an der gleichen Stelle

····▶ (*at s.o.'s house or shop*) bei (+ *dat*). **at Lisa's** bei Lisa. **at my uncle's** bei meinem Onkel. **at the baker's/ butcher's** beim Bäcker/Fleischer

····▶ (*inside a building*) in (+ *dat*). **at the theatre/supermarket** im Theater/ Supermarkt. **we spent the night at a hotel** wir übernachteten in einem Hotel. **he is still at the office** er ist noch im Büro

····▶ (*expressing time*) (*with clock time*) um; (*with main festivals*) zu. **at six o'clock** um sechs Uhr. **at midnight** um Mitternacht. **at midday** um zwölf Uhr mittags. **at Christmas/Easter** zu Weihnachten/Ostern

····▶ (*expressing age*) mit. **at [the age of] forty** mit vierzig; im Alter von vierzig

····▶ (*expressing price*) zu. **at £2.50 [each]** zu *od* für [je] 2,50 Pfund

····▶ (*expressing speed*) mit. **at 30 m.p.h.** mit dreißig Meilen pro Stunde

····▶ (*in phrases*) **good/bad at languages** gut/schlecht in Sprachen. **two at a time** zwei auf einmal. **at that** (*at that point*) dabei; (*at that provocation*) daraufhin; (*moreover*) noch dazu

ate *see* eat
atheist n Atheist(in) *m(f)*
athlet|e n Athlet(in) *m(f)*. ∼**ic** *a* sportlich. ∼**ics** n Leichtathletik *f*
Atlantic *a & n* the ∼ [Ocean] der Atlantik
atlas n Atlas *m*
atmosphere n Atmosphäre *f*
atom n Atom *nt*. ∼ **bomb** n Atombombe *f*
atomic *a* Atom-
atrocious *a* abscheulich
atrocity n Gräueltat *f*
attach *vt* befestigen (to an + *dat*); beimessen <*importance*> (to *dat*); be ∼ed to (*fig*) hängen an (+ *dat*)
attack n Angriff *m*; (*Med*) Anfall *m* ● *vt/i* angreifen. ∼**er** n Angreifer *m*

attain *vt* erreichen. ∼**able** *a* erreichbar
attempt n Versuch *m* ● *vt* versuchen
attend *vt* anwesend sein bei; (*go regularly to*) besuchen; (*take part in*) teilnehmen an (+ *dat*); (*accompany*) begleiten; <*doctor:*> behandeln ● *vi* anwesend sein; (*pay attention*) aufpassen; ∼ **to** sich kümmern um; (*in shop*) bedienen. ∼**ance** n Anwesenheit *f*; (*number*) Besucherzahl *f*. ∼**ant** n Wärter(in) *m(f)*; (*in car park*) Wächter *m*
attention n Aufmerksamkeit *f*; ∼! (*Mil*) stillgestanden! **pay** ∼ aufpassen; **pay** ∼ **to** beachten, achten auf (+ *acc*)
attentive *a*, **-ly** *adv* aufmerksam
attic n Dachboden *m*
attitude n Haltung *f*
attorney n (*Amer: lawyer*) Rechtsanwalt *m*; **power of** ∼ Vollmacht *f*
attract *vt* anziehen; erregen <*attention*>; ∼ **s.o.'s attention** jds Aufmerksamkeit auf sich (*acc*) lenken. ∼**ion** n Anziehungskraft *f*; (*charm*) Reiz *m*; (*thing*) Attraktion *f*. ∼**ive** *a*, **-ly** *adv* attraktiv
attribute *vt* zuschreiben (to *dat*)
aubergine n Aubergine *f*
auburn *a* kastanienbraun
auction n Auktion *f* Versteigerung *f* ● *vt* versteigern. ∼**eer** n Auktionator *m*
audaci|ous *a*, **-ly** *adv* verwegen. ∼**ty** n Verwegenheit *f*; (*impudence*) Dreistigkeit *f*
audible *a*, **-bly** *adv* hörbar
audience n Publikum *nt*; (*Theat, TV*) Zuschauer *pl*; (*Radio*) Zuhörer *pl*; (*meeting*) Audienz *f*
audit n Bücherrevision *f* ● *vt* (*Comm*) prüfen
audition n (*Theat*) Vorsprechen *nt*; (*Mus*) Vorspielen *nt*; (*for singer*) Vorsingen *nt* ● *vi* vorsprechen; vorspielen; vorsingen
auditor n Buchprüfer *m*
auditorium n Zuschauerraum *m*

August n August m

aunt n Tante f

au pair n ~ [girl] Au-pair-Mädchen nt

aura n Fluidum nt

auspicious a günstig; <occasion> freudig

auster|e a streng; (simple) nüchtern. **~ity** n Strenge f; (hardship) Entbehrung f

Australia n Australien nt. **~n** a australisch ● n Australier(in) m(f)

Austria n Österreich nt ● **~n** a österreichisch ● n Österreicher(in) m(f)

authentic a echt, authentisch. **~ate** vt beglaubigen. **~ity** n Echtheit f

author n Schriftsteller m, Autor m; (of document) Verfasser m

authoritarian a autoritär

authoritative a maßgebend

authority n Autorität f; (public) Behörde f; in ~ verantwortlich

authorization n Ermächtigung f

authorize vt ermächtigen <s.o.>; genehmigen <sth>

autobiography n Autobiographie f

autograph n Autogramm nt

automatic a, **-ally** adv automatisch

automation n Automation f

automobile n Auto nt

autonom|ous a autonom. **~y** n Autonomie f

autumn n Herbst m. **~al** a herbstlich

auxiliary a Hilfs- ● n Helfer(in) m(f), Hilfskraft f

avail n to no ~ vergeblich

available a verfügbar; (obtainable) erhältlich

avalanche n Lawine f

avenge vt rächen

avenue n Allee f

average a Durchschnitts-, durchschnittlich ● n Durchschnitt m; on ~ im Durchschnitt,

durchschnittlich ● vt durchschnittlich schaffen

averse a not be ~e to sth etw (dat) nicht abgeneigt sein

avert vt abwenden

aviary n Vogelhaus nt

aviation n Luftfahrt f

avocado n Avocado f

avoid vt vermeiden; ~ s.o. jdm aus dem Weg gehen. **~able** a vermeidbar. **~ance** n Vermeidung f

await vt warten auf (+ acc)

awake a wach; wide ~ hellwach ● vi (pt awoke, pp awoken) erwachen

awaken vt wecken ● vi erwachen. **~ing** n Erwachen nt

award n Auszeichnung f; (prize) Preis m ● vt zuerkennen (to s.o. dat); verleihen <prize>

aware a become ~ gewahr werden (of gen); be ~ that wissen, dass. **~ness** n Bewusstsein nt

away adv weg, fort; (absent) abwesend; **four kilometres** ~ vier Kilometer entfernt; **play** ~ (Sport) auswärts spielen. **~ game** n Auswärtsspiel nt

awful a, **-ly** adv furchtbar

awkward a schwierig; (clumsy) ungeschickt; (embarrassing) peinlich; (inconvenient) ungünstig. **~ly** adv ungeschickt; (embarrassedly) verlegen

awning n Markise f

awoke(n) see awake

axe n Axt f ● vt (pres p axing) streichen

axle n (Techn) Achse f

Bb

B n (Mus) H nt

baboon n Pavian m

baby n Baby nt; (Amer 🔢) Schätzchen nt

baby: ~**ish** a kindisch. ~**-sit** vi babysitten. ~**-sitter** n Babysitter m

bachelor n Junggeselle m

back n Rücken m; (reverse) Rückseite f; (of chair) Rückenlehne f; (Sport) Verteidiger m; at/(Auto) in the ~ hinten; on the ~ auf der Rückseite; ~ to front verkehrt ● a Hinter- ● adv zurück; ~ here/there hier/da hinten; ~ at home zu Hause; go/pay ~ zurückgehen/-zahlen ● vt (support) unterstützen; (with money) finanzieren; (Auto) zurücksetzen; (Betting) [Geld] setzen auf (+ acc); (cover the back of) mit einer Verstärkung versehen ● vi (Auto) zurücksetzen. ~ **down** vi klein beigeben. ~ **in** vi rückwärts hineinfahren. ~ **out** vi rückwärts hinaus-/herausfahren; (fig) aussteigen (of aus). ~ **up** vt unterstützen; (confirm) bestätigen ● vi (Auto) zurücksetzen

back: ~**ache** n Rückenschmerzen pl. ~**biting** n gehässiges Gerede nt. ~**bone** n Rückgrat nt. ~**date** vt rückdatieren; ~**dated to** rückwirkend von. ~ **door** n Hintertür f

backer n Geldgeber m

back: ~**fire** vi (Auto) fehlzünden; (fig) fehlschlagen. ~**ground** n Hintergrund m; family ~**ground** Familienverhältnisse pl. ~**hand** n (Sport) Rückhand f. ~**handed** a <compliment> zweifelhaft

backing n (support) Unterstützung f; (material) Verstärkung f

back: ~**lash** n (fig) Gegenschlag m. ~**log** n Rückstand m (of an + dat). ~**pack** n Rucksack m. ~ **seat** n Rücksitz m. ~**side** n 🔢 Hintern m. ~**stroke** n Rückenschwimmen nt. ~**-up** n Unterstützung f; (Amer: traffic jam) Stau m

backward a zurückgeblieben; <country> rückständig ● adv rückwärts. ~**s** rückwärts; ~**s and forwards** hin und her

back yard n Hinterhof m; **not in my** ~ **yard** 🔢 nicht vor meiner Haustür

bacon n [Schinken]speck m

bacteria npl Bakterien pl

bad a (worse, worst) schlecht; (serious) schwer, schlimm; (naughty) unartig; ~ **language** gemeine Ausdrucksweise f; **feel** ~ sich schlecht fühlen; (feel guilty) ein schlechtes Gewissen haben

badge n Abzeichen nt

badger n Dachs m ● vt plagen

badly adv schlecht; (seriously) schwer; ~ **off** schlecht gestellt; ~ **behaved** unerzogen; **want** ~ sich (dat) sehnsüchtig wünschen; **need** ~ dringend brauchen

bad-mannered a mit schlechten Manieren

badminton n Federball m

bad-tempered a schlecht gelaunt

baffle vt verblüffen

bag n Tasche f; (of paper) Tüte f; (pouch) Beutel m; ~**s of** 🔢 jede Menge ● vt (🔢 reserve) in Beschlag nehmen

baggage n [Reise]gepäck nt

baggy a <clothes> ausgebeult

bagpipes npl Dudelsack m

bail n Kaution f; **on** ~ gegen Kaution ● vt ~ **s.o. out** jdn gegen Kaution freibekommen; (fig) jdm aus der Patsche helfen

bait n Köder m ● vt mit einem Köder versehen; (fig: torment) reizen

bake vt/i backen

baker n Bäcker m; ~**'s [shop]** Bäckerei f. ~**y** n Bäckerei f

baking n Backen nt. ~**-powder** n Backpulver nt

balance n (equilibrium) Gleichgewicht nt, Balance f; (scales) Waage f; (Comm) Saldo m; (outstanding sum) Restbetrag m; [bank] ~ Kontostand m; **in the** ~ (fig) in der Schwebe ● vt balancieren; (equalize) ausgleichen; (Comm) abschließen <books> ● vi balancieren; (fig & Comm) sich ausgleichen. ~**d** a ausgewogen

balcony n Balkon m

bald a (-er, -est) kahl; <*person*> kahlköpfig

bald|ly adv unverblümt. ~**ness** n Kahlköpfigkeit f

ball¹ n Ball m; (*Billiards, Croquet*) Kugel f; (*of yarn*) Knäuel m & nt; on the ~ 🔢 auf Draht

ball² n (*dance*) Ball m

ball-bearing n Kugellager nt

ballerina n Ballerina f

ballet m Ballett nt. ~ **dancer** n Balletttänzer(in) m(f)

balloon n Luftballon m; (*Aviat*) Ballon m

ballot n [geheime] Wahl f; (*on issue*) [geheime] Abstimmung f. ~**-box** n Wahlurne f. ~**-paper** n Stimmzettel m

ball: ~**point [pen]** n Kugelschreiber m. ~**room** n Ballsaal m

balm n Balsam m

balmy a (-ier, -iest) a sanft

Baltic a & n the ~ **[Sea]** die Ostsee

bamboo n Bambus m

ban n Verbot nt ● vt (*pt/pp* banned) verbieten

banal a banal. ~**ity** n Banalität f

banana n Banane f

band n Band nt; (*stripe*) Streifen m; (*group*) Schar f; (*Mus*) Kapelle f

bandage n Verband m; (*for support*) Bandage f ● vt verbinden; bandagieren <*limb*>

b. & b. abbr of bed and breakfast

bandit n Bandit m

band: ~**stand** n Musikpavillon m. ~**wagon** n jump on the ~**wagon** (*fig*) sich einer erfolgreichen Sache anschließen

bang n (*noise*) Knall m; (*blow*) Schlag m ● adv go ~ knallen ● int bums! peng! ● vt knallen; (*shut noisily*) zuknallen; (*strike*) schlagen auf (+ acc); ~ one's head sich (*dat*) den Kopf stoßen (on an + acc) ● vi schlagen; <*door:*> zuknallen

banger n (*firework*) Knallfrosch m; (🔢 *sausage*) Wurst f; old ~ (🔢 *car*) Klapperkiste f

bangle n Armreifen m

banish vt verbannen

banisters npl [Treppen]geländer nt

banjo n Banjo nt

bank¹ n (*of river*) Ufer nt; (*slope*) Hang m ● vi (*Aviat*) in die Kurve gehen

bank² n Bank f ● ~ **on** vt sich verlassen auf (+ acc)

bank account n Bankkonto nt

banker n Bankier m

bank: ~ **holiday** n gesetzlicher Feiertag m. ~**ing** n Bankwesen nt. ~**note** n Banknote f

bankrupt a bankrott; go ~ Bankrott machen ● n Bankrotteur m ● vt Bankrott machen. ~**cy** n Bankrott m

banner n Banner nt; (*carried by demonstrators*) Transparent nt, Spruchband nt

banquet n Bankett nt

baptism n Taufe f

baptize vt taufen

bar n Stange f; (*of cage*) [Gitter]stab m; (*of gold*) Barren m; (*of chocolate*) Tafel f; (*of soap*) Stück nt; (*long*) Riegel m; (*café*) Bar f; (*counter*) Theke f; (*Mus*) Takt m; (*fig: obstacle*) Hindernis nt; **parallel** ~**s** (*Sport*) Barren m; **behind** ~**s** 🔢 hinter Gittern ● vt (*pt/pp* barred) versperren <*way, door*>; ausschließen <*person*>

barbar|ic a barbarisch. ~**ity** n Barbarei f. ~**ous** a barbarisch

barbecue n Grill m; (*party*) Grillfest nt ● vt [im Freien] grillen

barbed a ~ **wire** Stacheldraht m

barber n [Herren]friseur m

bar code n Strichkode m

bare a (-r, -st) nackt, bloß; <*tree*> kahl; (*empty*) leer; (*mere*) bloß

bare: ~**back** adv ohne Sattel. ~**faced** a schamlos. ~**foot** adv barfuß. ~**headed** a mit unbedecktem Kopf

barely adv kaum

bargain n (*agreement*) Geschäft nt; (*good buy*) Gelegenheitskauf m; **into the** ~ noch dazu; **make a** ~ sich einigen ● *vi* handeln; (*haggle*) feilschen; **~ for** (*expect*) rechnen mit

barge *n* Lastkahn *m*; (*towed*) Schleppkahn *m* ● *vi* **~ in** 🅸 hereinplatzen

baritone *n* Bariton *m*

bark¹ *n* (*of tree*) Rinde *f*

bark² *n* Bellen *nt* ● *vi* bellen

barley *n* Gerste *f*

bar: **~maid** *n* Schankmädchen *nt*. **~man** Barmann *m*

barmy *a* 🅸 verrückt

barn *n* Scheune *f*

barometer *n* Barometer *nt*

baron *n* Baron *m*. **~ess** *n* Baronin *f*

barracks *npl* Kaserne *f*

barrage *n* (*in river*) Wehr *nt*; (*Mil*) Sperrfeuer *nt*; (*fig*) Hagel *m*

barrel *n* Fass *nt*; (*of gun*) Lauf *m*; (*of cannon*) Rohr *nt*. **~organ** *n* Drehorgel *f*

barren *a* unfruchtbar; <*landscape*> öde

barricade *n* Barrikade *f* ● *vt* verbarrikadieren

barrier *n* Barriere *f*; (*across road*) Schranke *f*; (*Rail*) Sperre *f*; (*fig*) Hindernis *nt*

barrow *n* Karre *f*, Karren *m*

base *n* Fuß *m*; (*fig*) Basis *f*; (*Mil*) Stützpunkt *m* ● *vt* stützen (**on** auf + *acc*); **be ~d on** basieren auf (+ *dat*)

base: **~ball** *n* Baseball *m*. **~less** *a* unbegründet. **~ment** *n* Kellergeschoss *nt*

bash *n* Schlag *m*; **have a ~!** 🅸 probier es mal! ● *vt* hauen

basic *a* Grund-; (*fundamental*) grundlegend; (*essential*) wesentlich; (*unadorned*) einfach; **the ~s** das Wesentliche. **~ally** *adv* grundsätzlich

basin *n* Becken *nt*; (*for washing*) Waschbecken *nt*; (*for food*) Schüssel *f*

basis *n* (*pl* **-ses**) Basis *f*

bask *vi* sich sonnen

basket *n* Korb *m*. **~ball** *n* Basketball *m*

Basle *n* Basel *nt*

bass *a* Bass-; **~ voice** Bassstimme *f* ● *n* Bass *m*; (*person*) Bassist *m*

bassoon *n* Fagott *nt*

bastard *n* 🆇 Schuft *m*

bat¹ *n* Schläger *m*; **off one's own ~** 🅸 auf eigene Faust ● *vt* (*pt/pp* **batted**) schlagen; **not ~ an eyelid** (*fig*) nicht mit der Wimper zucken

bat² *n* (*Zool*) Fledermaus *f*

batch *n* (*of people*) Gruppe *f*; (*of papers*) Stoß *m*; (*of goods*) Sendung *f*; (*of bread*) Schub *m*

bath *n* (*pl* **-s**) Bad *nt*; (*tub*) Badewanne *f*; **~s** *pl* Badeanstalt *f*; **have a ~** baden

bathe *n* Bad *nt* ● *vt/i* baden. **~r** *n* Badende(r) *m/f*

bathing *n* Baden *nt*. **~cap** *n* Bademütze *f*. **~costume** *n* Badeanzug *m*

bath: **~mat** *n* Badematte *f*. **~room** *n* Badezimmer *nt*. **~towel** *n* Badetuch *nt*

battalion *n* Bataillon *nt*

batter *n* (*Culin*) flüssiger Teig *m* ● *vt* schlagen. **~ed** *a* <*car*> verbeult; <*wife*> misshandelt

battery *n* Batterie *f*

battle *n* Schlacht *f*; (*fig*) Kampf *m* ● *vi* (*fig*) kämpfen (**for** um)

battle: **~field** *n* Schlachtfeld *nt*. **~ship** *n* Schlachtschiff *nt*

batty *a* 🅸 verrückt

Bavaria *n* Bayern *nt*. **~n** *a* bayrisch ● *n* Bayer(in) *m(f)*

bawl *vt/i* brüllen

bay¹ *n* (*Geog*) Bucht *f*; (*Archit*) Erker *m*

bay² *n* (*Bot*) [echter] Lorbeer *m*. **~leaf** *n* Lorbeerblatt *nt*

bayonet *n* Bajonett *nt*

bay window *n* Erkerfenster *nt*

bazaar *n* Basar *m*

BC *abbr* (**before Christ**) v. Chr.

be

(*pres* **am, are, is,** *pl* **are;** *pt* **was,** *pl* **were;** *pp* **been**)

● *intransitive verb*

····▶ (*expressing identity, nature, state, age etc.*) sein. **he is a teacher** er ist Lehrer. **she is French** sie ist Französin. **he is very nice** er ist sehr nett. **I am tall** ich bin groß. **you are thirty** du bist dreißig. **it was very cold** es war sehr kalt

····▶ (*expressing general position*) sein; (*lie*) liegen; (*stand*) stehen. **where is the bank?** wo ist die Bank? **the book is on the table** das Buch liegt auf dem Tisch. **the vase is on the shelf** die Vase steht auf dem Brett

····▶ (*feel*) **I am cold/hot** mir ist kalt/heiß. **I am ill** ich bin krank. **I am well** mir geht es gut. **how are you?** wie geht es Ihnen?

····▶ (*date*) **it is the 5th today** heute haben wir den Fünften

····▶ (*go, come, stay*) sein. **I have been to Vienna** ich bin in Wien gewesen. **have you ever been to London?** bist du schon einmal in London gewesen? **has the postman been?** war der Briefträger schon da? **I've been here for an hour** ich bin seit einer Stunde hier

····▶ (*origin*) **where are you from?** woher stammen *od* kommen Sie? **she is from Australia** sie stammt *od* ist aus Australien

····▶ (*cost*) kosten. **how much are the eggs?** was kosten die Eier?

····▶ (*in calculations*) **two threes are six** zweimal drei ist *od* sind sechs

····▶ (*exist*) **there is/are** es gibt (+ *acc*). **there's no fish left** es gibt keinen Fisch mehr

●*auxiliary verb*

····▶ (*forming continuous tenses: not translated*) **I'm working** ich arbeite. **I'm leaving tomorrow** ich reise morgen [ab]. **they were singing** sie sangen. **they will be coming on Tuesday** sie kommen am Dienstag

····▶ (*forming passive*) werden. **the child was found** das Kind wurde gefunden. **German is spoken here** hier wird Deutsch gesprochen; hier spricht man Deutsch

····▶ (*expressing arrangement, obligation, destiny*) sollen. **I am to go/inform you** ich soll gehen/Sie unterrichten. **they were to fly today**

sie sollten heute fliegen. **you are to do that immediately** das sollst du sofort machen. **you are not to ...** (*prohibition*) du darfst nicht .... **they were never to meet again** (*destiny*) sie sollten sich nie wieder treffen

····▶ (*in short answers*) **Are you disappointed? — Yes I am** Bist du enttäuscht? — Ja. (*negating previous statement*) **Aren't you coming? — Yes I am!** Kommst du nicht? — Doch!

····▶ (*in tag questions*) **isn't it? she? aren't they?** *etc.* nicht wahr. **it's a beautiful house, isn't it?** das Haus ist sehr schön, nicht wahr?

beach *n* Strand *m*

bead *n* Perle *f*

beak *n* Schnabel *m*

beam *n* Balken *m*; (*of light*) Strahl *m* ● *vi* strahlen. **~ing** *a* [freude]strahlend

bean *n* Bohne *f*

bear¹ *n* Bär *m*

bear² *vt/i* (*pt* bore, *pp* borne) tragen; (*endure*) ertragen; gebären <*child*>; **~ right** sich rechts halten. **~able** *a* erträglich

beard *n* Bart *m*. **~ed** *a* bärtig

bearer *n* Träger *m*; (*of news, cheque*) Überbringer *m*; (*of passport*) Inhaber(in) *m(f)*

bearing *n* Haltung *f*; (*Techn*) Lager *nt*; **get one's ~s** sich orientieren

beast *n* Tier *nt*; (🔢 *person*) Biest *nt*

beastly *a* (-ier, -iest) 🔢 scheußlich; <*person*> gemein

beat *n* Schlag *m*; (*of policeman*) Runde *f*; (*rhythm*) Takt *m* ● *vt/i* (*pt* beat, *pp* beaten) schlagen; (*thrash*) verprügeln; klopfen <*carpet*>; (*hammer*) hämmern (**on** an + *acc*); **~ it!** 🔢 hau ab! **it ~s me** 🔢 das begreife ich nicht. **~ up** *vt* zusammenschlagen

beat|en *a* **off the ~en track** abseits. **~ing** *n* Prügel *pl*

beauti|ful *a*, **-ly** *adv* schön. **~fy** *vt* (*pt/pp* -ied) verschönern

beauty *n* Schönheit *f*. **~ parlour** *n* Kosmetiksalon *m*. **~ spot** *n* Schönheitsfleck *m*; (*place*) landschaftlich besonders reizvolles Fleckchen nt.

beaver n Biber m

became see become

because conj weil ● adv ~ of wegen (+ gen)

becom|e vt/i (pt **became**, pp **become**) werden. ~**ing** a <clothes> kleidsam

bed n Bett nt; (layer) Schicht f; (of flowers) Beet nt; in ~ im Bett; go to ~ ins od zu Bett gehen; ~ and breakfast Zimmer mit Frühstück. ~**clothes** npl, ~**ding** n Bettzeug nt. ~**room** n Schlafzimmer nt

bedside n at his ~ an seinem Bett. ~ **lamp** n Nachttischlampe f. ~ **table** n Nachttisch m

bed: ~**sitter** n, ~**sitting-room** n Wohnschlafzimmer nt. ~**spread** n Tagesdecke f. ~**time** n at ~time vor dem Schlafengehen

bee n Biene f

beech n Buche f

beef n Rindfleisch nt. ~**burger** n Hamburger m

bee: ~**hive** n Bienenstock m. ~**line** n make a ~-line for 🄸 zusteuern auf (+ acc)

been see be

beer n Bier nt

beet n (Amer: beetroot) Rote Bete f; [sugar] ~ Zuckerrübe f

beetle n Käfer m

beetroot n Rote Bete f

before prep vor (+ dat/acc); the day ~ yesterday vorgestern; ~ long bald ● adv vorher; (already) schon; never ~ noch nie; ~ that davor ● conj (time) ehe, bevor. ~**hand** adv vorher, im Voraus

beg v (pt/pp begged) ● vi betteln ● vt (entreat) anflehen; (ask) bitten (for um)

began see begin

beggar n Bettler(in) m(f); 🄸 Kerl m

begin vt/i (pt began, pp begun, pres p beginning) anfangen, beginnen; to ~ with anfangs. ~**ner** n Anfänger(in) m(f). ~**ning** n Anfang m, Beginn m

begun see begin

behalf n on ~ of im Namen von; on my ~ meinetwegen

behave vi sich verhalten; ~ oneself sich benehmen

behaviour n Verhalten nt; good/bad ~ gutes/schlechtes Benehmen nt

behind prep hinter (+ dat/acc); be ~ sth hinter etw (dat) stecken ● adv hinten; (late) im Rückstand; a long way ~ weit zurück ● n 🄸 Hintern m. ~**hand** adv im Rückstand

beige a beige

being n Dasein nt; living ~ Lebewesen nt; come into ~ entstehen

belated a, **-ly** adv verspätet

belfry n Glockenstube f; (tower) Glockenturm m

Belgian a belgisch ● n Belgier(in) m(f)

Belgium n Belgien nt

belief n Glaube m

believable a glaubhaft

believe vt/i glauben (s.o. jdm; in an + acc). ~**r** n (Relig) Gläubige(r) m/f

belittle vt herabsetzen

bell n Glocke f; (on door) Klingel f

bellow vt/i brüllen

belly n Bauch m

belong vi gehören (to dat); (be member) angehören (to dat). ~**ings** npl Sachen pl

beloved a geliebt ● n Geliebte(r) m/f

below prep unter (+ dat/acc) ● adv unten; (Naut) unter Deck

belt n Gürtel m; (area) Zone f; (Techn) [Treib]riemen m ● vi (🄸 rush) rasen ● vt (🄸 hit) hauen

bench n Bank f; (work-) Werkbank f

bend n Biegung f; (in road) Kurve f; round the ~ 🄸 verrückt ● v (pt/pp bent) ● vt biegen; beugen <arm, leg> ● vi sich bücken; <thing:> sich biegen; <road:> eine Biegung machen. ~ **down** vi sich bücken. ~ **over** vi sich vornüberbeugen

beneath prep unter (+ dat/acc); ~ him (fig) unter seiner Würde ● adv darunter

b

benefactor n Wohltäter(in) m(f)

beneficial a nützlich

benefit n Vorteil m; (allowance) Unterstützung f; (insurance) Leistung f; sickness ~ Krankengeld nt ● v (pt/pp -fited, pres p -fiting) ● vt nützen (+ dat) ● vi profitieren (from von)

benevolen|ce n Wohlwollen nt. ~t a, -ly adv wohlwollend

bent see bend ● a <person> gebeugt; (distorted) verbogen; (🗓 dishonest) korrupt; be ~ on doing sth darauf erpicht sein, etw zu tun ● n Hang m, Neigung f (for zu); artistic ~ künstlerische Ader f

bequeath vt vermachen (to dat)

bereave|d n the ~d pl die Hinterbliebenen

beret n Baskenmütze f

Berne n Bern nt

berry n Beere f

berth n (on ship) [Schlaf]koje f; (ship's anchorage) Liegeplatz m; give a wide ~ to 🗓 einen großen Bogen machen um

beside prep neben (+ dat/acc); ~ oneself außer sich (dat)

besides prep außer (+ dat) ● adv außerdem

besiege vt belagern

best a & n beste(r,s); the ~ der/die/das Beste; at ~ bestenfalls; all the ~! alles Gute! do one's ~ sein Bestes tun; the ~ part of a year fast ein Jahr; to the ~ of my knowledge so viel ich weiß; make the ~ of it das Beste daraus machen ● adv am besten; as ~ I could so gut ich konnte. ~ man ≈ Trauzeuge m. ~seller n Bestseller m

bet n Wette f ● v (pt/pp bet or betted) ● vt ~ s.o. £5 mit jdm um £5 wetten ● vi wetten; ~ on [Geld] setzen auf (+ acc)

betray vt verraten. ~al n Verrat m

better a besser; get ~ sich bessern; (after illness) sich erholen ● adv besser; ~ off besser dran; ~ not lieber nicht; all the ~ umso besser; the sooner the ~ je eher, desto

besser; think ~ of it sich eines Besseren besinnen; you'd ~ stay du bleibst am besten hier ● vt verbessern; (do better than) übertreffen; ~ oneself sich verbessern

between prep zwischen (+ dat/acc); ~ you and me unter uns; ~ us (together) zusammen ● adv [in] ~ dazwischen

beware vi sich in Acht nehmen (of vor + dat); ~ of the dog! Vorsicht, bissiger Hund!

bewilder vt verwirren. ~ment n Verwirrung f

bewitch vt verzaubern; (fig) bezaubern

beyond prep über (+ acc) ... hinaus; (further) weiter als; ~ reach außer Reichweite; ~ doubt ohne jeden Zweifel; it's ~ me 🗓 das geht über meinen Horizont ● adv darüber hinaus

bias n Voreingenommenheit f; (preference) Vorliebe f; (Jur) Befangenheit f ● vt (pt/pp biased) (influence) beeinflussen. ~ed a voreingenommen; (Jur) befangen

bib n Lätzchen nt

Bible n Bibel f

biblical a biblisch

bibliography n Bibliographie f

bicycle n Fahrrad nt ● vi mit dem Rad fahren

bid n Gebot nt; (attempt) Versuch m ● vt/i (pt/pp bid, pres p bidding) bieten (for auf + acc); (Cards) reizen

bidder n Bieter(in) m(f)

bide vt ~ one's time den richtigen Moment abwarten

big a (bigger, biggest) groß ● adv talk ~ 🗓 angeben

bigam|ist n Bigamist m. ~y n Bigamie f

big-headed a 🗓 eingebildet

bigot n Eiferer m. ~ed a engstirnig

bigwig n 🗓 hohes Tier nt

bike n 🗓 [Fahr]rad nt

bikini n Bikini m

bile n Galle f

bilingual a zweisprachig

b

bilious a (Med) ~ **attack** verdorbener Magen m

bill¹ n Rechnung f; (poster) Plakat nt; (Pol) Gesetzentwurf m; (Amer: note) Banknote f; ~ **of exchange** Wechsel m ● vt eine Rechnung schicken (+ dat)

bill² n (beak) Schnabel m

billfold n (Amer) Brieftasche f

billiards n Billard nt

billion n (thousand million) Milliarde f; (million million) Billion f

bin n Mülleimer m; (for bread) Kasten m

bind vt (pt/pp **bound**) binden (to an + acc); (bandage) verbinden; (Jur) verpflichten; (cover the edge of) einfassen. ~**ing** a verbindlich ● n Einband m; (braid) Borte f; (on ski) Bindung f

binge n Ⅰ **go on the** ~ eine Sauftour machen

binoculars npl [pair of] ~ Fernglas nt

bio|chemistry n Biochemie f. ~**degradable** a biologisch abbaubar

biograph|er n Biograph(in) m(f). ~**y** n Biographie f

biological a biologisch

biolog|ist n Biologe m. ~**y** n Biologie f

birch n Birke f; (whip) Rute f

bird n Vogel m; (Ⅰ girl) Mädchen nt; **kill two** ~**s with one stone** zwei Fliegen mit einer Klappe schlagen

Biro (P) n Kugelschreiber m

birth n Geburt f

birth: ~ **certificate** n Geburtsurkunde f. ~**control** n Geburtenregelung f. ~**day** n Geburtstag m. ~**rate** n Geburtenziffer f

biscuit n Keks m

bishop n Bischof m

bit¹ n Stückchen nt; (for horse) Gebiss nt; (Techn) Bohreinsatz m; **a** ~ ein bisschen; ~ **by** ~ nach und nach; **a** ~ **of bread** ein bisschen Brot; **do one's** ~ sein Teil tun

bit² see **bite**

bitch n Hündin f; Ⅹ Luder nt. ~**y** a gehässig

bit|e n Biss m; [insect] ~ Stich m; (mouthful) Bissen m ● vt/i (pt **bit**, pp **bitten**) beißen; <insect:> stechen; kauen <one's nails>. ~**ing** a beißend

bitten see **bite**

bitter a, **-ly** adv bitter; ~**ly cold** bitterkalt ● n bitteres Bier nt. ~**ness** n Bitterkeit f

bitty a zusammengestoppelt

bizarre a bizarr

black a (-er, -est) schwarz; **be** ~**and blue** grün und blau sein ● n Schwarz nt; (person) Schwarze(r) m/f ● vt schwärzen; boykottieren <goods>

black: ~**berry** n Brombeere f. ~**bird** n Amsel f. ~**board** n (Sch) [Wand]tafel f. ~**currant** n schwarze Johannisbeere f

blacken vt/i schwärzen

black: ~ **eye** n blaues Auge nt. **B**~ **Forest** n Schwarzwald m. ~ **ice** n Glatteis nt. ~**list** vt auf die schwarze Liste setzen. ~**mail** n Erpressung f ● vt erpressen. ~**mailer** n Erpresser(in) m(f). ~ **market** n schwarzer Markt m. ~**out** n **have a** ~**out** (Med) das Bewusstsein verlieren. ~ **pudding** n Blutwurst f

bladder n (Anat) Blase f

blade n Klinge f; (of grass) Halm m

blame n Schuld f ● vt die Schuld geben (+ dat); **no one is to** ~ keiner ist schuld daran. ~**less** a schuldlos

bland a (-er, -est) mild

blank a leer; <look> ausdruckslos ● n Lücke f; (cartridge) Platzpatrone f. ~ **cheque** n Blankoscheck m

blanket n Decke f; **wet** ~ Ⅰ Spielverderber(in) m(f)

blare vt/i schmettern

blasé a blasiert

blast n (gust) Luftstoß m; (sound) Schmettern nt; (of horn) Tuten nt ● vt sprengen ● int Ⅹ verdammt. ~**ed** a Ⅹ verdammt

blast-off n (of missile) Start m

blatant a offensichtlich

blaze n Feuer nt • vi brennen

blazer n Blazer m

bleach n Bleichmittel nt • vt/i bleichen

bleak a (-er, -est) öde; (fig) trostlos

bleary-eyed a mit trüben/(on waking up) verschlafenen Augen

bleat vi blöken

bleed v (pt/pp bled) • vi bluten • vt entlüften <radiator>

bleep n Piepton m • vi piepsen • vt mit dem Piepser rufen. ~er n Piepser m

blemish n Makel m

blend n Mischung f • vt mischen • vi sich vermischen

bless vt segnen. ~ed a heilig; 🅇 verflixt. ~ing n Segen m

blew see blow²

blight n (Bot) Brand m

blind a blind; <corner> unübersichtlich; ~ man/woman Blinde(r) m/f • n [roller] ~ Rouleau nt • vt blenden

blind: ~ alley n Sackgasse f. ~fold a & adv mit verbundenen Augen • n Augenbinde f • vt die Augen verbinden (+ dat). ~ly adv blindlings. ~ness n Blindheit f

blink vi blinzeln; <light:> blinken

bliss n Glückseligkeit f. ~ful a glücklich

blister n (Med) Blase f

blitz n 🅛 Großaktion f

blizzard n Schneesturm m

bloated a aufgedunsen

blob n Klecks m

block n Block m; (of wood) Klotz m; (of flats) [Wohn]block m • vt blockieren. ~ up vt zustopfen

blockade n Blockade f • vt blockieren

blockage n Verstopfung f

block: ~head n 🅛 Dummkopf m. ~ letters npl Blockschrift f

bloke n 🅛 Kerl m

blonde a blond • n Blondine f

blood n Blut nt

blood: ~-curdling a markerschütternd. ~ donor n Blutspender m. ~ group n Blutgruppe f. ~hound n Bluthund m. ~-poisoning n Blutvergiftung f. ~ pressure n Blutdruck m. ~shed n Blutvergießen nt. ~shot a blutunterlaufen. ~ sports npl Jagdsport m. ~-stained a blutbefleckt. ~ test n Blutprobe f. ~thirsty a blutdürstig. ~-vessel n Blutgefäß nt

bloody a (-ier, -iest) blutig; 🅇 verdammt. ~-minded a 🅇 stur

bloom n Blüte f • vi blühen

blossom n Blüte f • vi blühen

blot n [Tinten]klecks m; (fig) Fleck m • ~ out vt (fig) auslöschen

blotch n Fleck m. ~y a fleckig

blotting-paper n Löschpapier nt

blouse n Bluse f

blow¹ n Schlag m

blow² v (pt blew, pp blown) • vt blasen; (fam; squander) verpulvern; ~ one's nose sich (dat) die Nase putzen • vi blasen; <fuse:> durchbrennen. ~ away vt wegblasen • vi wegfliegen. ~ down vt umwehen • vi umfallen. ~ out vt (extinguish) ausblasen. ~ over vi umfallen; (fig: die down) vorübergehen. ~ up vt (inflate) aufblasen; (enlarge) vergrößern; (shatter by explosion) sprengen • vi explodieren

blowlamp n Lötlampe f

blown see blow²

blowtorch n (Amer) Lötlampe f

blowy a windig

blue a (-r, -st) blau; feel ~ deprimiert sein • n Blau nt; have the ~s deprimiert sein; out of the ~ aus heiterem Himmel

blue: ~bell n Sternhyazinthe f. ~berry n Heidelbeere f. ~bottle n Schmeißfliege f. ~ film n Pornofilm m. ~print n (fig) Entwurf m

bluff n Bluff m • vi bluffen

blunder n Schnitzer m • vi einen Schnitzer machen

blunt a stumpf; <person> geradeheraus. ~ly adv unverblümt, geradeheraus

blur n it's all a ~ alles ist verschwommen ● vt (pt/pp **blurred**) verschwommen machen; ~**red** verschwommen

blush n Erröten nt ● vi erröten

bluster n Großtuerei f. ~**y** a windig

boar n Eber m

board n Brett nt; (for notices) schwarzes Brett nt; (committee) Ausschuss m; (of directors) Vorstand m; on ~ an Bord; full ~ Vollpension f; ~ and lodging Unterkunft und Verpflegung pl ● vt einsteigen in (+ acc); (Naut, Aviat) besteigen ● vi an Bord gehen. ~ **up** vt mit Brettern verschlagen

boarder n Pensionsgast m; (Sch) Internatsschüler(in) m(f)

board: ~**game** n Brettspiel nt. ~**ing-house** n Pension f. ~**ing-school** n Internat nt

boast vt sich rühmen (+ gen) ● vi prahlen (**about** mit). ~**ful** a, -**ly** adv prahlerisch

boat n Boot nt; (ship) Schiff nt

bob vi (pt/pp **bobbed**) ~ up and down sich auf und ab bewegen

bob-sleigh n Bob m

bodily a körperlich ● adv (forcibly) mit Gewalt

body n Körper m; (corpse) Leiche f; (corporation) Körperschaft f. ~**guard** n Leibwächter m. ~**work** n (Auto) Karosserie f

bog n Sumpf m

bogus a falsch

boil¹ n Furunkel m

boil² n bring/come to the ~ zum Kochen bringen/kommen ● vt/i kochen; ~ed potatoes Salzkartoffeln pl. ~ **down** vi (fig) hinauslaufen (**to** auf + acc). ~ **over** vi überkochen

boiler n Heizkessel m

boiling point n Siedepunkt m

boisterous a übermütig

bold a (-er, -est), -**ly** adv kühn; (Typ) fett. ~**ness** n Kühnheit f

bolster n Nackenrolle f ● vt ~ up Mut machen (+ dat)

bolt n Riegel m; (Techn) Bolzen m ● vt schrauben (**to** an + acc); verriegeln <door>; hinunterschlingen <food> ● vi abhauen; <horse:> durchgehen

bomb n Bombe f ● vt bombardieren

bombard vt beschießen; (fig) bombardieren

bombastic a bombastisch

bomber n (Aviat) Bomber m; (person) Bombenleger(in) m(f)

bond n (fig) Band nt; (Comm) Obligation f

bone n Knochen m; (of fish) Gräte f ● vt von den Knochen lösen <meat>; entgräten <fish>. ~-**dry** a knochentrocken

bonfire n Gartenfeuer nt; (celebratory) Freudenfeuer nt

bonus n Prämie f; (gratuity) Gratifikation f; (fig) Plus nt

bony a (-ier, -iest) knochig; <fish> grätig

boo int buh! ● vt ausbuhen ● vi buhen

boob n (🄸 mistake) Schnitzer m

book n Buch nt; (of tickets) Heft nt; keep the ~s (Comm) die Bücher führen ● vt/i buchen; (reserve) [vor]bestellen; (for offence) aufschreiben

book: ~**case** n Bücherregal nt. ~-**ends** npl Buchstützen pl. ~**ing-office** n Fahrkartenschalter m. ~**keeping** n Buchführung f. ~**let** n Broschüre f. ~**maker** n Buchmacher m. ~**mark** n Lesezeichen nt. ~**seller** n Buchhändler(in) m(f). ~**shop** n Buchhandlung f. ~**stall** n Bücherstand m

boom n (Comm) Hochkonjunktur f; (upturn) Aufschwung m ● vi dröhnen; (fig) blühen

boon n Segen m

boost n Auftrieb m ● vt Auftrieb geben (+ dat)

boot n Stiefel m; (Auto) Kofferraum m

booth n Bude f; (cubicle) Kabine f

booty n Beute f

booze n 🄸 Alkohol m ● vi 🄸 saufen

border n Rand m; (*frontier*) Grenze f, (*in garden*) Rabatte f ● vi ~ on grenzen an (+ acc). **~line case** n Grenzfall m

bore¹ see **bear²**

bor|e² n (*of gun*) Kaliber nt; (*person*) langweiliger Mensch m; (*thing*) langweilige Sache f ● vt langweilen; be ~ed sich langweilen. **~edom** n Langeweile f. **~ing** a langweilig

born pp be ~ geboren werden ● a geboren

borne see **bear²**

borrow vt [sich (*dat*)] borgen od leihen (**from** von)

bosom n Busen m

boss n 🔊 Chef m ● vt herumkommandieren. **~y** a herrschsüchtig

botanical a botanisch

botan|ist n Botaniker(in) m(f). **~y** n Botanik f

both a & pron beide; ~[of] the children beide Kinder; ~ of them beide [von ihnen] ● adv ~ men and women sowohl Männer als auch Frauen

bother n Mühe f; (*minor trouble*) Ärger m ● int 🔊 verflixt! ● vt belästigen; (*disturb*) stören ● vi sich kümmern (**about** um)

bottle n Flasche f ● vt auf Flaschen abfüllen; (*preserve*) einmachen

bottle: **~-neck** n (*fig*) Engpass m. **~-opener** n Flaschenöffner m

bottom a unterste(r,s) ● n (*of container*) Boden m; (*of river*) Grund m; (*of page, hill*) Fuß m; (*buttocks*) Hintern m; at the ~ unten; get to the ~ of sth (*fig*) hinter etw (*acc*) kommen

bought see **buy**

bounce vi [auf]springen; <*cheque:*> 🔊 nicht gedeckt sein ● vt aufspringen lassen <*ball*>

bouncer n 🔊 Rausschmeißer m

bound¹ n Sprung m ● vi springen

bound² see **bind** ● a ~ for <*ship*> mit Kurs auf (+ acc); be ~ to do sth etw bestimmt machen; (*obliged*) verpflichtet sein, etw zu machen

boundary n Grenze f

bounds npl (*fig*) Grenzen pl; out of ~ verboten

bouquet n [Blumen]strauß m; (*of wine*) Bukett nt

bourgeois a (*pej*) spießbürgerlich

bout n (*Med*) Anfall m; (*Sport*) Kampf m

bow¹ n (*weapon & Mus*) Bogen m; (*knot*) Schleife f

bow² n Verbeugung f ● vi sich verbeugen ● vt neigen <*head*>

bow³ n (*Naut*) Bug m

bowel n Darm m. **~s** pl Eingeweide pl

bowl¹ n Schüssel f; (*shallow*) Schale f

bowl² n (*ball*) Kugel f ● vt/i werfen. ~ over vt umwerfen

bowler n (*Sport*) Werfer m

bowling n Kegeln nt. **~-alley** n Kegelbahn f

bowls n Bowlsspiel nt

bow-tie n Fliege f

box¹ n Schachtel f; (*wooden*) Kiste f; (*cardboard*) Karton m; (*Theat*) Loge f

box² vt/i (*Sport*) boxen

box|er n Boxer m. **~ing** n Boxen nt. **B~ing Day** n zweiter Weihnachtstag m

box: **~-office** n (*Theat*) Kasse f. **~-room** n Abstellraum m

boy n Junge m

boycott n Boykott m ● vt boykottieren

boy: **~friend** n Freund m. **~ish** a jungenhaft

bra n BH m

brace n Strebe f, Stütze f; (*dental*) Zahnspange f; **~s** npl Hosenträger mpl

bracelet n Armband nt

bracing a stärkend

bracket n Konsole f; (*group*) Gruppe f; (*Typ*) round/square **~s** runde/eckige Klammern ● vt einklammern

brag vi (*pt/pp* bragged) prahlen (**about** mit)

braille n Blindenschrift f

brain n Gehirn nt; ~s (fig) Intelligenz f

brain: ~**less** a dumm. ~**wash** vt einer Gehirnwäsche unterziehen. ~**wave** n Geistesblitz m

brainy a (-ier, -iest) klug

brake n Bremse f ● vt/i bremsen. ~**light** n Bremslicht nt

bramble n Brombeerstrauch m

branch n Ast m; (fig) Zweig m; (Comm) Zweigstelle f, (shop) Filiale f ● vi sich gabeln

brand n Marke f ● vt (fig) brandmarken als

brandish vt schwingen

brand-new a nagelneu

brandy n Weinbrand m

brash a nassforsch

brass n Messing nt; (Mus) Blech nt; top ~ 🛈 hohe Tiere pl. ~ **band** n Blaskapelle f

brassy a (-ier, -iest) 🛈 ordinär

brat n (pej) Balg nt

bravado n Forschheit f

brave a (-r, -st), **-ly** adv tapfer ● vt die Stirn bieten (+ dat). ~**ry** n Tapferkeit f

bravo int bravo!

brawl n Schlägerei f

brawn n (Culin) Sülze f

brawny a muskulös

bray vi iahen

brazen a unverschämt

Brazil n Brasilien nt. ~**ian** a brasilianisch. ~ **nut** n Paranuss f

breach n Bruch m; (Mil & fig) Bresche f; ~ **of contract** Vertragsbruch m

bread n Brot nt; **slice of** ~ **and butter** Butterbrot nt. ~**crumbs** npl Brotkrümel pl; (Culin) Paniermehl nt

breadth n Breite f

break n Bruch m; (interval) Pause f; (interruption) Unterbrechung f; (🛈 chance) Chance f ● v (pt **broke**, pp **broken**) ● vt brechen; (smash) zerbrechen; (damage) kaputtmachen 🛈; (interrupt) unterbrechen; ~ **one's arm** sich (dat) den Arm brechen ● vi

brechen; <day:> anbrechen; <storm:> losbrechen; <thing:> kaputtgehen 🛈; <rope, thread:> reißen; <news:> bekannt werden; **his voice is** ~**ing** er ist im Stimmbruch. ~ **away** vi sich losreißen/(fig) sich absetzen (**from** von). ~ **down** vi zusammenbrechen; (Techn) eine Panne haben; <negotiations:> scheitern ● vt aufbrechen <door>; aufgliedern <figures>. ~ **in** vi einbrechen. ~ **off** vt/i abbrechen; lösen <engagement>. ~ **out** vi ausbrechen. ~ **up** vt zerbrechen ● vi <crowd:> sich zerstreuen; <marriage, couple:> auseinander gehen; (Sch) Ferien bekommen

break|able a zerbrechlich. ~**age** n Bruch m. ~**down** n (Techn) Panne f; (Med) Zusammenbruch m; (of figures) Aufgliederung f. ~**er** n (wave) Brecher m

breakfast n Frühstück nt

break: ~**through** n Durchbruch m. ~**water** n Buhne f

breast n Brust f. ~**bone** n Brustbein nt. ~**feed** vt stillen. ~**stroke** n Brustschwimmen nt

breath n Atem m; **out of** ~ außer Atem; **under one's** ~ vor sich (acc) hin

breathe vt/i atmen. ~ **in** vt/i einatmen. ~ **out** vt/i ausatmen

breathing n Atmen nt

breath: ~**less** a atemlos. ~**taking** a atemberaubend

bred see **breed**

breed n Rasse f ● v (pt/pp **bred**) ● vt züchten; (give rise to) erzeugen ● vi sich vermehren. ~**er** n Züchter m. ~**ing** n Zucht f; (fig) [gute] Lebensart f

breez|e n Lüftchen nt; (Naut) Brise f. ~**y** a windig

brevity n Kürze f

brew n Gebräu nt ● vt brauen; kochen <tea>. ~**er** n Brauer m. ~**ery** n Brauerei f

bribe n (money) Bestechungsgeld nt ● vt bestechen. ~**ry** n Bestechung f

brick n Ziegelstein m, Backstein m

bricklayer n Maurer m

bridal *a* Braut-

bride *n* Braut *f*. **~groom** *n* Bräutigam *m*. **~smaid** *n* Brautjungfer *f*

bridge¹ *n* Brücke *f*; (*of nose*) Nasenrücken *m*; (*of spectacles*) Steg *m*

bridge² *n* (*Cards*) Bridge *nt*

bridle *n* Zaum *m*

brief¹ *a* (-er, -est) kurz; be ~ <*person:*> sich kurz fassen

brief² *n* Instruktionen *pl*; (*Jur: case*) Mandat *nt*. **~case** *n* Aktentasche *f*

brief|ing *n* Informationsgespräch *nt*. **~ly** *adv* kurz. **~ness** *n* Kürze *f*

briefs *npl* Slip *m*

brigade *n* Brigade *f*

bright *a* (-er, -est), **-ly** *adv* hell; <*day*> heiter; ~ **red** hellrot

bright|en *v* ~**en** [**up**] ● *vt* aufheitern ● *vi* sich aufheitern. **~ness** *n* Helligkeit *f*

brilliance *n* Glanz *m*; (*of person*) Genialität *f*

brilliant *a*, **-ly** *adv* glänzend; <*person*> genial

brim *n* Rand *m*; (*of hat*) Krempe *f*

bring *vt* (*pt/pp* **brought**) bringen; ~ **them with you** bring sie mit; **I can't ~ myself to do it** ich bringe es nicht fertig. ~ **about** *vt* verursachen. ~ **along** *vt* mitbringen. ~ **back** *vt* zurückbringen. ~ **down** *vt* herunterbringen; senken <*price*>. ~ **off** *vt* vollbringen. ~ **on** *vt* (*cause*) verursachen. ~ **out** *vt* herausbringen. ~ **round** *vt* vorbeibringen; (*persuade*) überreden; wieder zum Bewusstsein bringen <*unconscious person*>. ~ **up** *vt* heraufbringen; (*vomit*) erbrechen; aufziehen <*children*>; erwähnen <*question*>

brink *n* Rand *m*

brisk *a* (-er, -est,) **-ly** *adv* lebhaft; (*quick*) schnell

bristle *n* Borste *f*

Brit|ain *n* Großbritannien *nt*. **~ish** *a* britisch; the **~ish** die Briten *pl*. **~on** *n* Brite *m*/Britin *f*

Brittany *n* die Bretagne

brittle *a* brüchig, spröde

broad *a* (-er, -est) breit; <*hint*> deutlich; **in ~ daylight** am helllichten Tag. ~ **beans** *npl* dicke Bohnen *pl*

broadcast *n* Sendung *f* ● *vt/i* (*pt/pp* -cast) senden. **~er** *n* Rundfunk- und Fernsehpersönlichkeit *f*. **~ing** *n* Funk und Fernsehen *pl*

broaden *vt* verbreitern; (*fig*) erweitern ● *vi* sich verbreitern

broadly *adv* breit; ~ **speaking** allgemein gesagt

broadminded *a* tolerant

broccoli *n inv* Brokkoli *pl*

brochure *n* Broschüre *f*

broke *see* **break** ● *a* 🇬🇧 pleite

broken *see* **break** ● *a* zerbrochen, 🇬🇧 kaputt. **~-hearted** *a* untröstlich

broker *n* Makler *m*

brolly *n* 🇬🇧 Schirm *m*

bronchitis *n* Bronchitis *f*

bronze *n* Bronze *f*

brooch *n* Brosche *f*

brood *vi* (*fig*) grübeln

broom *n* Besen *m*; (*Bot*) Ginster *m*

broth *n* Brühe *f*

brothel *n* Bordell *nt*

brother *n* Bruder *m*

brother: ~-in-law *n* (*pl* -s-in-law) Schwager *m*. **~ly** *a* brüderlich

brought *see* **bring**

brow *n* Augenbraue *f*; (*forehead*) Stirn *f*; (*of hill*) [Berg]kuppe *f*

brown *a* (-er, -est) braun; ~ **paper** Packpapier *nt* ● *n* Braun *nt* ● *vt* bräunen ● *vi* braun werden

browse *vi* (*read*) schmökern; (*in shop*) sich umsehen

bruise *n* blauer Fleck *m* ● *vt* beschädigen <*fruit*>; ~ **one's arm** sich (*dat*) den Arm quetschen

brunette *n* Brünette *f*

brush *n* Bürste *f*; (*with handle*) Handfeger *m*; (*for paint, pastry*) Pinsel *m*; (*bushes*) Unterholz *nt*; (*fig: conflict*) Zusammenstoß *m* ● *vt* bürsten; putzen <*teeth*>; ~ **against** streifen [gegen]; ~ **aside** (*fig*) abtun.

~ off *vt* abbürsten. **~ up** *vt/i* (*fig*) **~ up** [on] auffrischen

brusque *a*, **-ly** *adv* brüsk

Brussels *n* Brüssel *nt*. **~ sprouts** *npl* Rosenkohl *m*

brutal *a*, **-ly** *adv* brutal. **~ity** *n* Brutalität *f*

brute *n* Unmensch *m*. **~ force** *n* rohe Gewalt *f*

bubble *n* [Luft]blase *f* ● *vi* sprudeln

buck[1] *n* (*deer & Gym*) Bock *m*; (*rabbit*) Rammler *m* ● *vi* <*horse:*> bocken

buck[2] *n* (*Amer* 🎧) Dollar *m*

buck[3] *n* pass the **~** die Verantwortung abschieben

bucket *n* Eimer *m*

buckle *n* Schnalle *f* ● *vt* zuschnallen ● *vi* sich verbiegen

bud *n* Knospe *f*

buddy *n* 🎧 Freund *m*

budge *vt* bewegen ● *vi* sich [von der Stelle] rühren

budget *n* Budget *nt*; (*Pol*) Haushaltsplan *m*; (*money available*) Etat *m* ● *vi* (*pt/pp* budgeted) **~ for** sth etw einkalkulieren

buff *a* (*colour*) sandfarben ● *n* Sandfarbe *f*; 🎧 Fan *m* ● *vt* polieren

buffalo *n* (*inv or pl* **-es**) Büffel *m*

buffer *n* (*Rail*) Puffer *m*

buffet[1] *n* Büfett *nt*; (*on station*) Imbissstube *f*

buffet[2] *vt* (*pt/pp* buffeted) hin und her werfen

bug *n* Wanze *f*; (🎧 *virus*) Bazillus *m*; (🎧 *device*) Abhörgerät *nt*, 🎧 Wanze *f* ● *vt* (*pt/pp* bugged) 🎧 verwanzen <*room*>; abhören <*telephone*>; (*Amer: annoy*) ärgern

bugle *n* Signalhorn

build *n* (*of person*) Körperbau *m* ● *vt/i* (*pt/pp* built) bauen. **~ on** *vt* anbauen (**to an** + *acc*). **~ up** *vt* aufbauen ● *vi* zunehmen

builder *n* Bauunternehmer *m*

building *n* Gebäude *nt*. **~ site** *n* Baustelle *f*. **~ society** *n* Bausparkasse *f*

built *see* **build**. **~-in** *a* eingebaut. **~-in cupboard** *n* Einbauschrank *m*. **~-up area** *n* bebautes Gebiet *nt*; (*Auto*) geschlossene Ortschaft *f*

bulb *n* [Blumen]zwiebel *f*; (*Electr*) [Glüh]birne *f*

bulbous *a* bauchig

Bulgaria *n* Bulgarien *nt*

bulg|e *n* Ausbauchung *f* ● *vi* sich ausbauchen. **~ing** *a* prall; <*eyes*> hervorquellend

bulk *n* Masse *f*; (*greater part*) Hauptteil *m*. **~y** *a* sperrig; (*large*) massig

bull *n* Bulle *m*, Stier *m*

bulldog *n* Bulldogge *f*

bulldozer *n* Planierraupe *f*

bullet *n* Kugel *f*

bulletin *n* Bulletin *nt*

bullet-proof *a* kugelsicher

bullfight *n* Stierkampf *m*. **~er** *n* Stierkämpfer *m*

bullfinch *n* Dompfaff *m*

bullock *n* Ochse *m*

bull: ~ring *n* Stierkampfarena *f*. **~'s-eye** *n* score a **~**'s-eye ins Schwarze treffen

bully *n* Tyrann *m* ● *vt* tyrannisieren

bum *n* 🎧 Hintern *m*

bumble-bee *n* Hummel *f*

bump *n* Bums *m*; (*swelling*) Beule *f*; (*in road*) holperige Stelle *f* ● *vt* stoßen; **~ into** stoßen gegen; (*meet*) zufällig treffen. **~ off** *vt* 🎧 um die Ecke bringen

bumper *a* Rekord- ● *n* (*Auto*) Stoßstange *f*

bumpy *a* holperig

bun *n* Milchbrötchen *nt*; (*hair*) [Haar]knoten *m*

bunch *n* (*of flowers*) Strauß *m*; (*of radishes, keys*) Bund *m*; (*of people*) Gruppe *f*; **~ of grapes** [ganze] Weintraube *f*

bundle *n* Bündel *nt* ● *vt* **~** [up] bündeln

bungalow *n* Bungalow *m*

bungle *vt* verpfuschen

bunk *n* [Schlaf]koje *f*. **~-beds** *npl* Etagenbett *nt*

bunker n Bunker m

bunny n 🔲 Kaninchen nt

buoy n Boje f

buoyan|cy n Auftrieb m. ~**t** a be ~**t** schwimmen

burden n Last f

bureau n (pl -**x** or -**s**) (desk) Sekretär m; (office) Büro nt

bureaucracy n Bürokratie f

bureaucratic a bürokratisch

burger n Hamburger m

burglar n Einbrecher m. ~ **alarm** n Alarmanlage f

burglary n Einbruch m

burgle vt einbrechen in (+ acc); they have been ~d bei ihnen ist eingebrochen worden

burial n Begräbnis nt

burly a (-ier, -iest) stämmig

Burm|a n Birma nt. ~**ese** a birmanisch

burn n Verbrennung f; (on skin) Brandwunde f; (on material) Brandstelle f ● v (pt/pp burnt or burned) ● vt verbrennen ● vi brennen; <food:> anbrennen. ~ **down** vt/i niederbrennen

burnt see burn

burp vi 🔲 aufstoßen

burrow n Bau m ● vi wühlen

burst n Bruch m; (surge) Ausbruch m ● v (pt/pp burst) ● vt platzen machen ● vi platzen; <bud:> aufgehen; ~ **into tears** in Tränen ausbrechen

bury vt (pt/pp -ied) begraben; (hide) vergraben

bus n [Auto]bus m

bush n Strauch m; (land) Busch m. ~**y** a (-ier, -iest) buschig

busily adv eifrig

business n Angelegenheit f; (Comm) Geschäft nt; on ~ geschäftlich; he has no ~ er hat kein Recht (to zu); mind one's own ~ sich um seine eigenen Angelegenheiten kümmern; that's none of your ~ das geht Sie nichts an. ~-**like** a geschäftsmäßig. ~**man** n Geschäftsmann m

bus-stop n Bushaltestelle f

bust[1] n Büste f

bust[2] a 🔲 kaputt; go ~ Pleite gehen ● v (pt/pp busted or bust) 🔲 ● vt kaputtmachen ● vi kaputtgehen

busy a (-ier, -iest) beschäftigt; <day> voll; <street> belebt; (with traffic) stark befahren; (Amer Teleph) besetzt; be ~ zu tun haben ● vt ~ oneself sich beschäftigen (with mit)

but conj aber; (after negative) sondern ● prep außer (+ dat); ~ **for** (without) ohne (+ acc); the last ~ one der/die/ das vorletzte; the next ~ one der/ die/das übernächste ● adv nur

butcher n Fleischer m, Metzger m; ~**'s [shop]** Fleischerei f, Metzgerei f ● vt [ab]schlachten

butler n Butler m

butt n (of gun) [Gewehr]kolben m; (fig: target) Zielscheibe f; (of cigarette) Stummel m; (for water) Regentonne f ● vi ~ **in** unterbrechen

butter n Butter f ● vt mit Butter bestreichen. ~ **up** vt 🔲 schmeicheln (+ dat)

butter: ~**cup** a Butterblume f, Hahnenfuß m. ~**fly** n Schmetterling m

buttocks npl Gesäß nt

button n Knopf m ● vt ~ [up] zuknöpfen. ~**hole** n Knopfloch nt

buy n Kauf m ● vt (pt/pp bought) kaufen. ~**er** n Käufer(in) m(f)

buzz n Summen nt ● vi summen

buzzer n Summer m

by prep (close to) bei (+ dat); (next to) neben (+ dat/acc); (past) an (+ dat) ... vorbei; (to the extent of) um (+ acc); (at the latest) bis; (by means of) durch; **by Mozart/Dickens** von Mozart/Dickens; ~ **oneself** allein; ~ **the sea** am Meer; ~ **car/bus** mit dem Auto/Bus; ~ **sea** mit dem Schiff; ~ **day/night** bei Tag/Nacht; ~ **the hour** pro Stunde; ~ **the metre** meterweise; **six metres** ~ **four** sechs mal vier Meter; **win** ~ **a length** mit einer Länge Vorsprung gewinnen; **miss the train** ~ **a minute** den Zug um eine Minute verpassen ● adv ~ **and large** im Großen und Ganzen; **put** ~

beiseite legen; **go/pass ~**
vorbeigehen

bye int 🔲 tschüs

by: ~-election n Nachwahl f.
~pass n Umgehungsstraße f; (Med)
Bypass m ● vt umfahren. **~-
product** n Nebenprodukt m.
~stander n Zuschauer(in) m(f)

Cc

cab n Taxi nt; (of lorry, train)
Führerhaus nt

cabaret n Kabarett nt

cabbage n Kohl m

cabin n Kabine f; (hut) Hütte f

cabinet n Schrank m; [display] ~
Vitrine f; C~ (Pol) Kabinett nt

cable n Kabel nt; (rope) Tau nt. ~
railway n Seilbahn f. ~
television n Kabelfernsehen nt

cackle vi gackern

cactus n (pl **-ti** or **-tuses**) Kaktus m

cadet n Kadett m

cadge vt/i 🔲 schnorren

Caesarean a & n ~ **[section]**
Kaiserschnitt m

café n Café nt

cafeteria n
Selbstbedienungsrestaurant nt

cage n Käfig m

cagey a 🔲 **be ~** mit der Sprache
nicht herauswollen

cake n Kuchen m; (of soap) Stück nt.
~d a verkrustet (**with** mit)

calamity n Katastrophe f

calculat|e vt berechnen; (estimate)
kalkulieren. **~ing** a (fig)
berechnend. **~ion** n Rechnung f,
Kalkulation f. **~or** n Rechner m

calendar n Kalender m

calf¹ n (pl **calves**) Kalb nt

calf² n (pl **calves**) (Anat) Wade f

calibre n Kaliber nt

call n Ruf m; (Teleph) Anruf m; (visit)
Besuch m ● vt rufen; (Teleph)
anrufen; (wake) wecken; ausrufen
<strike>; (name) nennen; **be ~ed**
heißen ● vi rufen; **~ [in** or **round]**
vorbeikommen. **~ back** vt
zurückrufen ● vi noch einmal
vorbeikommen. **~ for** vt rufen nach;
(demand) verlangen; (fetch) abholen.
~ off vt zurückrufen <dog>; (cancel)
absagen. **~ on** vt bitten (**for** um);
(appeal to) appellieren an (+ acc);
(visit) besuchen. **~ out** vt rufen;
aufrufen <names> ● vi rufen. **~ up**
vt (Mil) einberufen; (Teleph) anrufen

call: ~-box n Telefonzelle f. **~er** n
Besucher m; (Teleph) Anrufer m.
~ing n Berufung f. **~-up** n (Mil)
Einberufung f

calm a (**-er, -est**), **-ly** adv ruhig ● n
Ruhe f ● vt ~ **[down]** beruhigen ● vi
~ down sich beruhigen. **~ness** n
Ruhe f; (of sea) Stille f

calorie n Kalorie f

calves npl see **calf¹** & ²

came see **come**

camel n Kamel nt

camera n Kamera f

camouflage n Tarnung f ● vt
tarnen

camp n Lager nt ● vi campen; (Mil)
kampieren

campaign n Feldzug m; (Comm,
Pol) Kampagne f ● vi (Pol) im
Wahlkampf arbeiten

camp: ~-bed n Feldbett nt. **~er** n
Camper m; (Auto) Wohnmobil nt.
~ing n Camping nt. **~site** n
Campingplatz m

can¹ n (for petrol) Kanister m; (tin)
Dose f, Büchse f; **a ~ of beer** eine
Dose Bier

can²

pres **can**, pt **could**

● auxiliary verb

····▸ (be able to) können. **I can't** or
cannot go ich kann nicht gehen. **she
couldn't** or **could not go** (was unable
to) sie konnte nicht gehen; (would
not be able to) sie könnte nicht

gehen. **he could go if he had time** er
könnte gehen, wenn er Zeit hätte. **if I
could go** wenn ich gehen könnte.
that cannot be true das kann nicht
stimmen

···▸ (*know how to*) können. **can you
swim?** können Sie schwimmen? **she
can drive** sie kann Auto fahren

···▸ (*be allowed to*) dürfen. **you can't
smoke here** hier dürfen Sie nicht
rauchen. **can I go?** kann *od* darf ich
gehen?

···▸ (*in requests*) können. **can I have a
glass of water, please?** kann ich ein
Glas Wasser haben, bitte? **could you
ring me tomorrow?** könnten Sie mich
morgen anrufen?

···▸ **could** (*expressing possibility*)
könnte. **that could be so** das könnte
od kann sein. **I could have killed him**
ich hätte ihn umbringen können

Canad|a *n* Kanada *nt*. **~ian** *a*
kanadisch ● *n* Kanadier(in) *m(f)*

canal *n* Kanal *m*

canary *n* Kanarienvogel *m*

cancel *vt/i* (*pt/pp* **cancelled**)
absagen; abbestellen <*newspaper*>;
be ~led ausfallen. **~lation** *n*
Absage *f*

cancer *n*, & (*Astr*) **C~** Krebs *m*.
~ous *a* krebsig

candid *a*, **-ly** *adv* offen

candidate *n* Kandidat(in) *m(f)*

candle *n* Kerze *f*. **~stick** *n*
Kerzenständer *m*, Leuchter *m*

candy *n* (*Amer*) Süßigkeiten *pl*;
[piece of] ~ Bonbon *m*

cane *n* Rohr *nt*; (*stick*) Stock *m* ● *vt*
mit dem Stock züchtigen

canine *a* Hunde-. **~ tooth** *n*
Eckzahn *m*

cannabis *n* Haschisch *nt*

canned *a* Dosen-, Büchsen-

cannibal *n* Kannibale *m*. **~ism** *n*
Kannibalismus *m*

cannon *n inv* Kanone *f*

cannot *see* **can²**

canoe *n* Paddelboot *nt*; (*Sport*) Kanu
nt

can-opener *n* Dosenöffner *m*

can't = **cannot**. *See* **can²**

canteen *n* Kantine *f*; **~ of cutlery**
Besteckkasten *m*

canter *n* Kanter *m* ● *vi* kantern

canvas *n* Segeltuch *nt*; (*Art*)
Leinwand *f*; (*painting*) Gemälde *nt*

canvass *vi* um Stimmen werben

canyon *n* Cañon *m*

cap *n* Kappe *f*, Mütze *f*; (*nurse's*)
Haube *f*; (*top, lid*) Verschluss *m*

capability *n* Fähigkeit *f*

capable *a*, **-bly** *adv* fähig; **be ~ of
doing sth** fähig sein, etw zu tun

capacity *n* Fassungsvermögen *nt*;
(*ability*) Fähigkeit *f*; **in my ~ as** in
meiner Eigenschaft als

cape¹ *n* (*cloak*) Cape *nt*

cape² *n* (*Geog*) Kap *nt*

capital *a* <*letter*> groß ● *n* (*town*)
Hauptstadt *f*; (*money*) Kapital *nt*;
(*letter*) Großbuchstabe *m*

capital|ism *n* Kapitalismus *m*.
~ist *a* kapitalistisch ● *n* Kapitalist
m. **~ letter** *n* Großbuchstabe *m*. **~
punishment** *n* Todesstrafe *f*

capsize *vi* kentern ● *vt* zum
Kentern bringen

captain *n* Kapitän *m*; (*Mil*)
Hauptmann *m* ● *vt* anführen <*team*>

caption *n* Überschrift *f*; (*of
illustration*) Bildtext *m*

captivate *vt* bezaubern

captiv|e *a* <*hold/take*> **~e** gefangen
halten/nehmen ● *n* Gefangene(r) *m/
f*. **~ity** *n* Gefangenschaft *f*

capture *n* Gefangennahme *f* ● *vt*
gefangen nehmen; [ein]fangen
<*animal*>; (*Mil*) einnehmen <*town*>

car *n* Auto *nt*, Wagen *m*; **by ~** mit
dem Auto *od* Wagen

caramel *n* Karamell *m*

carat *n* Karat *nt*

caravan *n* Wohnwagen *m*;
(*procession*) Karawane *f*

carbon *n* Kohlenstoff *m*; (*paper*)
Kohlepapier *nt*; (*copy*) Durchschlag
m

carbon: ~ copy *n* Durchschlag *m*.
~ paper *n* Kohlepapier *nt*

carburettor *n* Vergaser *m*

carcass *n* Kadaver *m*

card n Karte f

cardboard n Pappe f, Karton m. ~ **box** n Pappschachtel f; (large) [Papp]karton m

card-game n Kartenspiel nt

cardigan n Strickjacke f

cardinal a Kardinal- ● n (Relig) Kardinal m

card index n Kartei f

care n Sorgfalt f; (caution) Vorsicht f; (protection) Obhut f; (looking after) Pflege f; (worry) Sorge f; ~ of (on letter abbr **c/o**) bei; **take** ~ vorsichtig sein; **take into** ~ in Pflege nehmen; **take** ~ **of** sich kümmern um ● vi ~ **for** (like) mögen; (look after) betreuen; **I don't** ~ das ist mir gleich

career n Laufbahn f; (profession) Beruf m ● vi rasen

care: ~**free** a sorglos. ~**ful** a, -**ly** adv sorgfältig; (cautious) vorsichtig. ~**less** a, -**ly** adv nachlässig. ~**lessness** n Nachlässigkeit f

caretaker n Hausmeister m

car ferry n Autofähre f

cargo n (pl -es) Ladung f

Caribbean n the ~ die Karibik

caricature n Karikatur f ● vt karikieren

caring a <parent> liebevoll; <profession, attitude> sozial

carnation n Nelke f

carnival n Karneval m

carol n [Christmas] ~ Weihnachtslied nt

carp¹ n inv Karpfen m

carp² vi nörgeln

car park n Parkplatz m; (multi-storey) Parkhaus nt; (underground) Tiefgarage f

carpent|er n Zimmermann m; (joiner) Tischler m. ~**ry** n Tischlerei f

carpet n Teppich m

carriage n Kutsche f; (Rail) Wagen m; (of goods) Beförderung f; (cost) Frachtkosten pl; (bearing) Haltung f

carrier n Träger(in) m(f); (Comm) Spediteur m; ~ **[-bag]** Tragetasche f

carrot n Möhre f, Karotte f

carry vt/i (pt/pp -ied) tragen; **be carried away** Ⓘ hingerissen sein. ~ **off** vt wegtragen; gewinnen <prize>. ~ **on** vi weitermachen; ~ **on with** Ⓘ eine Affäre haben mit ● vt führen; (continue) fortführen. ~ **out** vt hinaus-/heraustragen; (perform) ausführen

cart n Karren m; **put the** ~ **before the horse** das Pferd beim Schwanz aufzäumen ● vt karren; (Ⓘ carry) schleppen

carton n [Papp]karton m; (for drink) Tüte f; (of cream, yoghurt) Becher m

cartoon n Karikatur f; (joke) Witzzeichnung f; (strip) Comic Strips pl; (film) Zeichentrickfilm m. ~**ist** n Karikaturist m

cartridge n Patrone f; (for film) Kassette f

carve vt schnitzen; (in stone) hauen; (Culin) aufschneiden

carving n Schnitzerei f. ~-**knife** n Tranchiermesser nt

car wash n Autowäsche f; (place) Autowaschanlage f

case¹ n Fall m; **in any** ~ auf jeden Fall; **just in** ~ für alle Fälle; **in** ~ **he comes** falls er kommt

case² n Kasten m; (crate) Kiste f; (for spectacles) Etui nt; (suitcase) Koffer m; (for display) Vitrine f

cash n Bargeld nt; **pay [in]** ~ [in] bar bezahlen; ~ **on delivery** per Nachnahme ● vt einlösen <cheque>. ~ **desk** n Kasse f

cashier n Kassierer(in) m(f)

cash register n Registrierkasse f

cassette n Kassette f. ~ **recorder** n Kassettenrecorder m

cast n (mould) Form f; (model) Abguss m; (Theat) Besetzung f; [plaster] (Med) Gipsverband m ● vt (pt/pp cast) (throw) werfen; (shed) abwerfen; abgeben <vote>; gießen <metal>; (Theat) besetzen <role>. ~ **off** vi (Naut) ablegen

castle n Schloss nt; (fortified) Burg f; (Chess) Turm m

cast-offs npl abgelegte Kleidung f

castor n (*wheel*) [Lauf]rolle f
castor sugar n Streuzucker m
casual a, **-ly** adv (*chance*) zufällig; (*offhand*) lässig; (*informal*) zwanglos; (*not permanent*) Gelegenheits-; ～ **wear** Freizeitbekleidung f
casualty n [Todes]opfer nt; (*injured person*) Verletzte(r) m/f; ～ [**department**] Unfallstation f
cat n Katze f
catalogue n Katalog m ● vt katalogisieren
catapult n Katapult nt ● vt katapultieren
cataract n (*Med*) grauer Star m
catarrh n Katarrh m
catastroph|e n Katastrophe f. ～**ic** a katastrophal
catch n (*of fish*) Fang m; (*fastener*) Verschluss m; (*on door*) Klinke f; (🛈 *snag*) Haken m 🛈 ● v (pt/pp caught) ● vt fangen; (*be in time for*) erreichen; (*travel by*) fahren mit; bekommen <*illness*>; ～ **a cold** sich erkälten; ～ **sight of** erblicken; ～ **s.o. stealing** jdn beim Stehlen erwischen; ～ **one's finger in the door** sich (*dat*) den Finger in der Tür [ein]klemmen ● vi (*burn*) anbrennen; (*get stuck*) klemmen. ～ **on** vi 🛈 (*understand*) kapieren; (*become popular*) sich durchsetzen. ～ **up** vt einholen ● vi aufholen; ～ **up with** einholen <*s.o.*>; nachholen <*work*>
catching a ansteckend
catch: ～**phrase** n, ～**word** n Schlagwort nt
catchy a (-ier, -iest) einprägsam
categor|ical a, **-ly** adv kategorisch. ～**y** n Kategorie f
cater vi ～ **for** beköstigen; <*firm:*> das Essen liefern für <*party*>; (*fig*) eingestellt sein auf (+ *acc*). ～**ing** n (*trade*) Gaststättengewerbe nt
caterpillar n Raupe f
cathedral n Dom m, Kathedrale f
Catholic a katholisch ● n Katholik(in) m(f). **C** ～**ism** n Katholizismus m
cattle npl Vieh nt
catty a (-ier, -iest) boshaft

caught *see* **catch**
cauliflower n Blumenkohl m
cause n Ursache f; (*reason*) Grund m; **good** ～ gute Sache f ● vt verursachen; ～ **s.o. to do sth** jdn veranlassen, etw zu tun
caution n Vorsicht f; (*warning*) Verwarnung f ● vt (*Jur*) verwarnen
cautious a, **-ly** adv vorsichtig
cavalry n Kavallerie f
cave n Höhle f ● vi ～ **in** einstürzen
cavern n Höhle f
caviare n Kaviar m
cavity n Hohlraum m; (*in tooth*) Loch nt
CD abbr (**compact disc**) CD f; ～**-ROM** CD-ROM f
cease vt/i aufhören. ～**fire** n Waffenruhe f. ～**less** a, **-ly** adv unaufhörlich
cedar n Zeder f
ceiling n [Zimmer]decke f; (*fig*) oberste Grenze f
celebrat|e vt/i feiern. ～**ed** a berühmt (**for** wegen). ～**ion** n Feier f
celebrity n Berühmtheit f
celery n [Stangen]sellerie m & f
cell n Zelle f
cellar n Keller m
cellist n Cellist(in) m(f)
cello n Cello nt
Celsius a Celsius
Celt n Kelte m/ Keltin f. ～**ic** a keltisch
cement n Zement m; (*adhesive*) Kitt m
cemetery n Friedhof m
censor n Zensor m ● vt zensieren. ～**ship** n Zensur f
census n Volkszählung f
cent n (*coin*) Cent m
centenary n, (*Amer*) **centennial** n Hundertjahrfeier f
center n (*Amer*) = **centre**
centi|grade a Celsius. ～**metre** n Zentimeter m & nt
central a, **-ly** adv zentral. ～ **heating** n Zentralheizung f. ～**ize** vt zentralisieren

centre n Zentrum nt; (middle) Mitte f ● v (pt/pp centred) ● vt zentrieren. **~-forward** n Mittelstürmer m

century n Jahrhundert nt

ceramic a Keramik-

cereal n Getreide nt; (breakfast food) Frühstücksflocken pl

ceremon|ial a, **-ly** adv zeremoniell, feierlich ● n Zeremoniell nt. **~ious** a, **-ly** adv formell

ceremony n Zeremonie f, Feier f

certain a sicher; (not named) gewiss; **for ~** mit Bestimmtheit; **make ~** (check) sich vergewissern (that dass); (ensure) dafür sorgen (that dass); **he is ~ to win** er wird ganz bestimmt siegen. **~ly** adv bestimmt, sicher; **~ly not!** auf keinen Fall! **~ty** n Sicherheit f, Gewissheit f; **it's a ~ty** es ist sicher

certificate n Bescheinigung f; (Jur) Urkunde f; (Sch) Zeugnis nt

certify vt (pt/pp **-ied**) bescheinigen; (declare insane) für geisteskrank erklären

cf. abbr (compare) vgl.

chafe vt wund reiben

chaffinch n Buchfink m

chain n Kette f ● vt ketten (**to an** + acc). **~ up** vt anketten

chain: ~ reaction n Kettenreaktion f. **~-smoker** n Kettenraucher m. **~ store** n Kettenladen m

chair n Stuhl m; (Univ) Lehrstuhl m; (Adm) Vorsitzende(r) m/f. **~-lift** n Sessellift m. **~man** n Vorsitzende(r) m/f

chalet n Chalet nt

chalk n Kreide f

challeng|e n Herausforderung f; (Mil) Anruf m ● vt herausfordern; (Mil) anrufen; (fig) anfechten <statement>. **~er** n Herausforderer m. **~ing** a herausfordernd; (demanding) anspruchsvoll

chamber n Kammer f; **C~ of Commerce** Handelskammer f. **~ music** n Kammermusik f

chamber music n Kammermusik f

chamois n **~[-leather]** Ledertuch nt

champagne n Champagner m

champion n (Sport) Meister(in) m(f); (of cause) Verfechter m ● vt sich einsetzen für. **~ship** n (Sport) Meisterschaft f

chance n Zufall m; (prospect) Chancen pl; (likelihood) Aussicht f; (opportunity) Gelegenheit f; **by ~** zufällig; **take a ~** ein Risiko eingehen; **give s.o. a ~** jdm eine Chance geben ● attrib zufällig ● vt **~ it** es riskieren

chancellor n Kanzler m; (Univ) Rektor m

chancy a riskant

change n Veränderung f; (alteration) Änderung f; (money) Wechselgeld nt; **for a ~** zur Abwechslung ● vt wechseln; (alter) ändern; (exchange) umtauschen (**for** gegen); (transform) verwandeln; trocken legen <baby>; **~ one's clothes** sich umziehen; **~ trains** umsteigen ● vi sich verändern; (**~ clothes**) sich umziehen; (**~ trains**) umsteigen; **all ~!** alles aussteigen!

changeable a wechselhaft

changing-room n Umkleideraum m

channel n Rinne f; (Radio, TV) Kanal m; (fig) Weg m; **the [English] C~** der Ärmelkanal; **the C~ Islands** die Kanalinseln

chant vt singen; <demonstrators:> skandieren

chao|s n Chaos nt. **~tic** a chaotisch

chap n 🄸 Kerl m

chapel n Kapelle f

chaplain n Geistliche(r) m

chapped a <skin> aufgesprungen

chapter n Kapitel nt

character n Charakter m; (in novel, play) Gestalt f; (Typ) Schriftzeichen nt; **out of ~** uncharakteristisch; **quite a ~** 🄸 ein Original

characteristic a, **-ally** adv charakteristisch (**of** für) ● n Merkmal nt

characterize vt charakterisieren

charge n (price) Gebühr f; (Electr) Ladung f; (attack) Angriff m; (Jur) Anklage f; free of ~ kostenlos; be in ~ verantwortlich sein (of für); take ~ die Aufsicht übernehmen (of über + acc) ● vt berechnen <fee>; (Electr) laden; (attack) angreifen; (Jur) anklagen (with gen); ~ s.o. for sth jdm etw berechnen

charitable a wohltätig; (kind) wohlwollend

charity n Nächstenliebe f; (organization) wohltätige Einrichtung f; for ~ für Wohltätigkeitszwecke

charm n Reiz m; (of person) Charme f; (object) Amulett nt ● vt bezaubern. ~ing a, -ly adv reizend; <person, smile> charmant

chart n Karte f; (table) Tabelle f

charter n ~ [flight] Charterflug m ● vt chartern; ~ed accountant Wirtschaftsprüfer(in) m(f)

chase n Verfolgungsjagd f ● vt jagen, verfolgen. ~ away or off vt wegjagen

chassis n (pl chassis) Chassis nt

chaste a keusch

chat n Plauderei f; have a ~ with plaudern mit ● vi (pt/pp chatted) plaudern. ~ show n Talkshow f

chatter n Geschwätz nt ● vi schwatzen; <child:> plappern; <teeth:> klappern. ~box n 🔲 Plappermaul nt

chatty a (-ier, -iest) geschwätzig

chauffeur n Chauffeur m

cheap a & adv (-er, -est), -ly adv billig. ~en vt entwürdigen

cheat n Betrüger(in) m(f); (at games) Mogler m ● vt betrügen ● vi (at games) mogeln 🔲

check¹ a (squared) kariert ● n Karo nt

check² n Überprüfung f; (inspection) Kontrolle f; (Chess) Schach nt; (Amer: bill) Rechnung f; (Amer: cheque) Scheck m; (Amer: tick) Haken m; keep a ~ on kontrollieren ● vt [über]prüfen; (inspect)

kontrollieren; (restrain) hemmen; (stop) aufhalten ● vi [go and] ~ nachsehen. ~ in vi sich anmelden; (Aviat) einchecken ● vt abfertigen; einchecken. ~ out vi sich abmelden. ~ up vi prüfen, kontrollieren; ~ up on überprüfen

checked a kariert

check: ~-out n Kasse f. ~room n (Amer) Garderobe f. ~-up n (Med) [Kontroll]untersuchung f

cheek n Backe f; (impudence) Frechheit f. ~y a, -ily adv frech

cheer n Beifallsruf m; three ~s ein dreifaches Hoch (for auf + acc); ~s! prost! (goodbye) tschüs! ● vt zujubeln (+ dat) ● vi jubeln. ~ up vt aufmuntern; aufheitern ● vi munterer werden. ~ful a, -ly adv fröhlich. ~fulness n Fröhlichkeit f

cheerio int 🔲 tschüs!

cheese n Käse m. ~cake n Käsekuchen m

chef n Koch m

chemical a, -ly adv chemisch ● n Chemikalie f

chemist n (pharmacist) Apotheker(in) m(f); (scientist) Chemiker(in) m(f); ~'s [shop] Drogerie f; (dispensing) Apotheke f. ~ry n Chemie f

cheque n Scheck m. ~-book n Scheckbuch nt. ~ card n Scheckkarte f

cherish vt lieben; (fig) hegen

cherry n Kirsche f ● attrib Kirsch-

chess n Schach nt

chess: ~board n Schachbrett nt. ~-man n Schachfigur f

chest n Brust f; (box) Truhe f

chestnut n Esskastanie f, Marone f; (horse-) [Ross]kastanie f

chest of drawers n Kommode f

chew vt kauen. ~ing-gum n Kaugummi m

chick n Küken nt

chicken n Huhn nt ● attrib Hühner- ● a 🔲 feige

chief a Haupt- ● n Chef m; (of tribe) Häuptling m. ~ly adv hauptsächlich

child n (pl ~ren) Kind nt

child: ∼**birth** n Geburt f. ∼**hood** n Kindheit f. ∼**ish** a kindisch. ∼**less** a kinderlos. ∼**like** a kindlich. ∼**minder** n Tagesmutter f

children npl see **child**

Chile n Chile nt

chill n Kälte f; (illness) Erkältung f ● vt kühlen

chilly a kühl; **I felt** ∼ mich fröstelte [es]

chime vi läuten; <clock:> schlagen

chimney n Schornstein m. ∼**pot** n Schornsteinaufsatz m. ∼**sweep** n Schornsteinfeger m

chin n Kinn nt

china n Porzellan nt

Chin|a n China nt. ∼**ese** a chinesisch ● n (Lang) Chinesisch nt; **the** ∼**ese** pl die Chinesen

chink¹ n (slit) Ritze f

chink² n Geklirr nt ● vi klirren; <coins:> klimpern

chip n (fragment) Span m; (in china, paintwork) angeschlagene Stelle f; (Computing, Gambling) Chip m; ∼**s** pl (Culin) Pommes frites pl; (Amer: crisps) Chips pl ● vt (pt/pp **chipped**) (damage) anschlagen. ∼**ped** a angeschlagen

chirp vi zwitschern; <cricket:> zirpen. ∼**y** a 🔢 munter

chit n Zettel m

chocolate n Schokolade f; (sweet) Praline f

choice n Wahl f; (variety) Auswahl f ● a auserlesen

choir n Chor m. ∼**boy** n Chorknabe m

choke n (Auto) Choke m ● vt würgen; (to death) erwürgen ● vi sich verschlucken; ∼ **on** [fast] ersticken an (+ dat)

choose vt/i (pt **chose**, pp **chosen**) wählen; (select) sich (dat) aussuchen; ∼ **to do/go** [freiwillig] tun/gehen; **as you** ∼ wie Sie wollen

choos[e]y a 🔢 wählerisch

chop n (blow) Hieb m; (Culin) Kotelett nt ● vt (pt/pp **chopped**) hacken. ∼ **down** vt abhacken; fällen <tree>. ∼ **off** vt abhacken

chop|per n Beil nt; 🔢 (helicopter) Hubschrauber m. ∼**py** a kabbelig

chopsticks npl Essstäbchen pl

choral a Chor-

chord n (Mus) Akkord m

chore n lästige Pflicht f; [household] ∼**s** Hausarbeit f

chorus n Chor m; (of song) Refrain m

chose, chosen see **choose**

Christ n Christus m

christen vt taufen

Christian a christlich ● n Christ(in) m(f). ∼**ity** n Christentum nt. ∼ **name** n Vorname m

Christmas n Weihnachten nt. ∼ **card** n Weihnachtskarte f. ∼ **Day** n erster Weihnachtstag m. ∼ **Eve** n Heiligabend m. ∼ **tree** n Weihnachtsbaum m

chrome n, **chromium** n Chrom nt

chronic a chronisch

chronicle n Chronik f

chrysanthemum n Chrysantheme f

chubby a (-ier, -iest) mollig

chuck vt 🔢 schmeißen. ∼ **out** vt 🔢 rausschmeißen

chuckle vi in sich (acc) hineinlachen

chum n Freund(in) m(f)

chunk n Stück nt

church n Kirche f. ∼**yard** n Friedhof m

churn vt ∼ **out** am laufenden Band produzieren

cider n ≈ Apfelwein m

cigar n Zigarre f

cigarette n Zigarette f

cine-camera n Filmkamera f

cinema n Kino nt

cinnamon n Zimt m

circle n Kreis m; (Theat) Rang m ● vt umkreisen ● vi kreisen

circuit n Runde f; (racetrack) Rennbahn f; (Electr) Stromkreis m. ∼**ous** a ∼ route Umweg m

circular a kreisförmig ● n Rundschreiben nt. ∼ **saw** n Kreissäge f. ∼ **tour** n Rundfahrt f

C

circulat|e *vt* in Umlauf setzen ● *vi* zirkulieren. **~ion** *n* Kreislauf *m*; (*of newspaper*) Auflage *f*

circumference *n* Umfang *m*

circumstance *n* Umstand *m*; **~s** *pl* Umstände *pl*; (*financial*) Verhältnisse *pl*

circus *n* Zirkus *m*

cistern *n* (*tank*) Wasserbehälter *m*; (*of WC*) Spülkasten *m*

cite *vt* zitieren

citizen *n* Bürger(in) *m(f)*. **~ship** *n* Staatsangehörigkeit *f*

citrus *n* **~** [**fruit**] Zitrusfrucht *f*

city *n* [Groß]stadt *f*

civic *a* Bürger-

civil *a* bürgerlich; <*aviation, defence*> zivil; (*polite*) höflich. **~ engineering** *n* Hoch- und Tiefbau *m*

civilian *a* Zivil-; **in ~ clothes** in Zivil ● *n* Zivilist *m*

civiliz|ation *n* Zivilisation *f*. **~e** *vt* zivilisieren

civil: **~servant** *n* Beamte(r) *m*/ Beamtin *f*. **C~ Service** *n* Staatsdienst *m*

claim *n* Anspruch *m*; (*application*) Antrag *m*; (*demand*) Forderung *f*; (*assertion*) Behauptung *f* ● *vt* beanspruchen; (*apply for*) beantragen; (*demand*) fordern; (*assert*) behaupten; (*collect*) abholen

clam *n* Klaffmuschel *f*

clamber *vi* klettern

clammy *a* (-ier, -iest) feucht

clamour *n* Geschrei *nt* ● *vi* **~ for** schreien nach

clamp *n* Klammer *f* ● *vt* [ein]spannen ● *vi* 🛈 **~ down on** vorgehen gegen

clan *n* Clan *m*

clang *n* Schmettern *nt*. **~er** *n* 🛈 Schnitzer *m*

clank *vi* klirren

clap *n* **give s.o. a ~** jdm Beifall klatschen; **~ of thunder** Donnerschlag *m* ● *vt/i* (*pt/pp* **clapped**) Beifall klatschen (+ *dat*); **~ one's hands** [in die Hände] klatschen

clari|fication *n* Klärung *f*. **~fy** *vt/i* (*pt/pp* **-ied**) klären

clarinet *n* Klarinette *f*

clarity *n* Klarheit *f*

clash *n* Geklirr *nt*; (*fig*) Konflikt *m* ● *vi* klirren; <*colours:*> sich beißen; <*events:*> ungünstig zusammenfallen

clasp *n* Verschluss *m* ● *vt* ergreifen; (*hold*) halten

class *n* Klasse *f*; **travel first/second ~** erster/zweiter Klasse reisen ● *vt* einordnen

classic *a* klassisch ● *n* Klassiker *m*. **~al** *a* klassisch

classi|fication *n* Klassifikation *f*. **~fy** *vt* (*pt/pp* **-ied**) klassifizieren

classroom *n* Klassenzimmer *nt*

classy *a* (-ier, -iest) 🛈 schick

clatter *n* Geklapper *nt* ● *vi* klappern

clause *n* Klausel *f*; (*Gram*) Satzteil *m*

claw *n* Kralle *f*; (*of bird of prey &* *Techn*) Klaue *f*; (*of crab, lobster*) Schere *f* ● *vt* kratzen

clay *n* Lehm *m*; (*pottery*) Ton *m*

clean *a* (-er, -est) sauber ● *adv* glatt ● *vt* sauber machen; putzen <*shoes, windows*>; **~ one's teeth** sich (*dat*) die Zähne putzen; **have sth ~ed** etw reinigen lassen. **~ up** *vt* sauber machen

cleaner *n* Putzfrau *f*; (*substance*) Reinigungsmittel *nt*; [**dry**] **~'s** chemische Reinigung *f*

cleanliness *n* Sauberkeit *f*

cleanse *vt* reinigen

clear *a* (-er, -est), **-ly** *adv* klar; (*obvious*) eindeutig; (*distinct*) deutlich; <*conscience:*> rein; (*without obstacles*) frei; **make sth ~** etw klarmachen (**to** *dat*) ● *adv* **stand ~** zurücktreten; **keep ~ of** aus dem Wege gehen (+ *dat*) ● *vt* räumen; abräumen <*table*>; (*acquit*) freisprechen; (*authorize*) genehmigen; (*jump over*) überspringen; **~ one's throat** sich räuspern ● *vi* <*fog:*> sich auflösen. **~ away** *vt* wegräumen. **~ off** *vi* 🛈 abhauen. **~ out** *vt* ausräumen ● *vi* 🛈 abhauen. **~ up** *vt* (*tidy*)

aufräumen; (*solve*) aufklären ● *vi*
<*weather*>: sich aufklären

clearance *n* Räumung *f*;
(*authorization*) Genehmigung *f*;
(*customs*) [Zoll]abfertigung *f*; (*Techn*)
Spielraum *m*. ~ **sale** *n*
Räumungsverkauf *m*

clench *vt* ~ one's fist die Faust
ballen; ~ one's teeth die Zähne
zusammenbeißen

clergy *npl* Geistlichkeit *f*. ~**man** *n*
Geistliche(r) *m*

clerk *n* Büroangestellte(r) *m/f*;
(*Amer: shop assistant*) Verkäufer(in)
m(f)

clever *a* (-er, -est), -ly *adv* klug;
(*skilful*) geschickt

cliché *n* Klischee *nt*

click *vi* klicken

client *n* Kunde *m*/ Kundin *f*; (*Jur*)
Klient(in) *m(f)*

cliff *n* Kliff *nt*

climate *n* Klima *nt*

climax *n* Höhepunkt *m*

climb *n* Aufstieg *m* ● *vt* besteigen
<*mountain*>; steigen auf (+ *acc*)
<*ladder, tree*> ● *vi* klettern; (*rise*)
steigen; <*road*:> ansteigen. ~ **down**
vi hinunter-/herunterklettern; (*from
ladder, tree*) heruntersteigen; 🔳
nachgeben

climber *n* Bergsteiger *m*; (*plant*)
Kletterpflanze *f*

cling *vi* (*pt/pp* clung) sich klammern
(to an + *acc*); (*stick*) haften (to an +
dat). ~ **film** *n* Sichtfolie *f* mit
Hafteffekt

clinic *n* Klinik *f*. ~**al** *a*, -ly *adv*
klinisch

clink *vi* klirren

clip¹ *n* Klammer *f*; (*jewellery*) Klipp
m ● *vt* (*pt/pp* clipped) anklammern
(to an + *acc*)

clip² *n* (*extract*) Ausschnitt *m* ● *vt*
schneiden; knipsen <*ticket*>. ~**ping**
n (*extract*) Ausschnitt *m*

cloak *n* Umhang *m*. ~**room** *n*
Garderobe *f*; (*toilet*) Toilette *f*

clobber *n* 🔳 Zeug *nt* ● *vt* (🔳 *hit,
defeat*) schlagen

clock *n* Uhr *f*; (🔳 *speedometer*)
Tacho *m* ● *vi* ~ in/out stechen

clock: ~**wise** *a* & *adv* im
Uhrzeigersinn. ~**work** *n* Uhrwerk
nt; (*of toy*) Aufziehmechanismus *m*;
like ~work 🔳 wie am Schnürchen

clod *n* Klumpen *m*

clog *vt/i* (*pt/pp* clogged) ~ [up]
verstopfen

cloister *n* Kreuzgang *m*

close¹ *a* (-r, -st) nah[e] (to *dat*);
<*friend*> eng; <*weather*> schwül;
have a ~ shave 🔳 mit knapper Not
davonkommen ● *adv* nahe ● *n*
(*street*) Sackgasse *f*

close² *n* Ende *nt*; draw to a ~ sich
dem Ende nähern ● *vt* zumachen,
schließen; (*bring to an end*) beenden;
sperren <*road*> ● *vi* sich schließen;
<*shop*:> schließen, zumachen; (*end*)
enden. ~ **down** *vt* schließen;
stilllegen <*factory*> ● *vi* schließen;
<*factory*:> stillgelegt werden

closely *adv* eng, nah[e]; (*with
attention*) genau

closet *n* (*Amer*) Schrank *m*

close-up *n* Nahaufnahme *f*

closure *n* Schließung *f*; (*of factory*)
Stilllegung *f*; (*of road*) Sperrung *f*

clot *n* [Blut]gerinnsel *nt*; (🔳 *idiot*)
Trottel *m*

cloth *n* Tuch *nt*

clothe *vt* kleiden

clothes *npl* Kleider *pl*. ~**-line** *n*
Wäscheleine *f*

clothing *n* Kleidung *f*

cloud *n* Wolke *f* ● *vi* ~ over sich
bewölken

cloudy *a* (-ier, -iest) wolkig, bewölkt;
<*liquid*> trübe

clout *n* 🔳 Schlag *m*; (*influence*)
Einfluss *m*

clove *n* [Gewürz]nelke *f*; ~ of garlic
Knoblauchzehe *f*

clover *n* Klee *m*. ~ **leaf** *n* Kleeblatt
nt

clown *n* Clown *m* ● *vi* ~ [about]
herumalbern

club *n* Klub *m*; (*weapon*) Keule *f*;
(*Sport*) Schläger *m*; ~**s** *pl* (*Cards*)
Kreuz *nt*, Treff *nt*

clue *n* Anhaltspunkt *m*; (*in crossword*) Frage *f*; **I haven't a ~** ich habe keine Ahnung

clump *n* Gruppe *f*

clumsiness *n* Ungeschicklichkeit *f*

clumsy *a* (-ier, -iest), **-ily** *adv* ungeschickt; (*unwieldy*) unförmig

clung *see* cling

clutch *n* Griff *m*; (*Auto*) Kupplung *f*; be in s.o.'s **~es** 🔢 in jds Klauen sein ● *vt* festhalten; (*grab*) ergreifen ● *vi* **~ at** greifen nach

clutter *n* Kram *m* ● *vt* **~** [up] vollstopfen

c/o *abbr* (**care of**) bei

coach *n* [Reise]bus *m*; (*Rail*) Wagen *m*; (*horse-drawn*) Kutsche *f*; (*Sport*) Trainer *m* ● *vt* Nachhilfestunden geben (+ *dat*); (*Sport*) trainieren

coal *n* Kohle *f*

coalition *n* Koalition *f*

coal-mine *n* Kohlenbergwerk *nt*

coarse *a* (-r, -st), **-ly** *adv* grob

coast *n* Küste *f* ● *vi* (*freewheel*) im Freilauf fahren; (*Auto*) im Leerlauf fahren. **~er** *n* (*mat*) Untersatz *m*

coast: ~guard *n* Küstenwache *f*. **~line** *n* Küste *f*

coat *n* Mantel *m*; (*of animal*) Fell *nt*; (*of paint*) Anstrich *m*; **~ of arms** Wappen *nt* ● *vt* überziehen; (*with paint*) streichen. **~hanger** *n* Kleiderbügel *m*. **~hook** *n* Kleiderhaken *m*

coating *n* Überzug *m*, Schicht *f*; (*of paint*) Anstrich *m*

coax *vt* gut zureden (+ *dat*)

cobble[1] *n* Kopfstein *m*; **~s** *pl* Kopfsteinpflaster *nt*

cobble[2] *vt* flicken. **~r** *n* Schuster *m*

cobweb *n* Spinnengewebe *nt*

cock *n* Hahn *m*; (*any male bird*) Männchen *nt* ● *vt* <*animal:*> **~ its ears** die Ohren spitzen; **~ the gun** den Hahn spannen

cockerel *n* [junger] Hahn *m*

cockney *n* (*dialect*) Cockney *nt*; (*person*) Cockney *m*

cock: ~pit *n* (*Aviat*) Cockpit *nt*. **~roach** *n* Küchenschabe *f*. **~tail** *n*
Cocktail *m*. **~-up** *n* 🗙 **make a ~-up** Mist bauen (**of** bei)

cocky *a* (-ier, -iest) 🔢 eingebildet

cocoa *n* Kakao *m*

coconut *n* Kokosnuß *f*

cod *n inv* Kabeljau *m*

COD *abbr* (**cash on delivery**) per Nachnahme

coddle *vt* verhätscheln

code *n* Kode *m*; (*Computing*) Code *m*; (*set of rules*) Kodex *m*. **~d** *a* verschlüsselt

coerc|e *vt* zwingen. **~ion** *n* Zwang *m*

coffee *n* Kaffee *m*

coffee: ~-grinder *n* Kaffeemühle *f*. **~-pot** *n* Kaffeekanne *f*. **~-table** *n* Couchtisch *m*

coffin *n* Sarg *m*

cogent *a* überzeugend

coherent *a* zusammenhängend; (*comprehensible*) verständlich

coil *n* Rolle *f*; (*Electr*) Spule *f*; (*one ring*) Windung *f* ● *vt* **~** [up] zusammenrollen

coin *n* Münze *f* ● *vt* prägen

coincide *vi* zusammenfallen; (*agree*) übereinstimmen

coinciden|ce *n* Zufall *m*. **~tal** *a*, **-ly** *adv* zufällig

coke *n* Koks *m*

Coke (P) *n* (*drink*) Cola *f*

cold *a* (-er, -est) kalt; **I am** *or* **feel ~** mir ist kalt ● *n* Kälte *f*; (*Med*) Erkältung *f*

cold: ~-blooded *a* kaltblütig. **~-hearted** *a* kaltherzig. **~ly** *adv* (*fig*) kalt, kühl. **~ness** *n* Kälte *f*

collaborat|e *vi* zusammenarbeiten (**with** mit); **~e on sth** mitarbeiten bei etw. **~ion** *n* Zusammenarbeit *f*, Mitarbeit *f*; (*with enemy*) Kollaboration *f*. **~or** *n* Mitarbeiter(in) *m(f)*; Kollaborateur *m*

collaps|e *n* Zusammenbruch *m*; Einsturz *m* ● *vi* zusammenbrechen; <*roof, building*> einstürzen. **~ible** *a* zusammenklappbar

collar n Kragen m; (for animal)
Halsband nt. ~**bone** n
Schlüsselbein nt

colleague n Kollege m/Kollegin f

collect vt sammeln; (fetch) abholen;
einsammeln <tickets>; einziehen
<taxes> ● vi sich [an]sammeln ● adv
call ~ (Amer) ein R-Gespräch führen

collection n Sammlung f; (in
church) Kollekte f; (of post) Leerung
f; (designer's) Kollektion f

collector n Sammler(in) m(f)

college n College nt

collide vi zusammenstoßen

colliery n Kohlengrube f

collision n Zusammenstoß m

colloquial a, -**ly** adv
umgangssprachlich

Cologne n Köln nt

colon n Doppelpunkt

colonel n Oberst m

colonial a Kolonial-

colony n Kolonie f

colossal a riesig

colour n Farbe f, (complexion)
Gesichtsfarbe f; (race) Hautfarbe f;
off ~ 🆒 nicht ganz auf der Höhe
● vt färben; ~ [in] ausmalen

colour: ~**blind** a farbenblind.
~**ed** a farbig ● n (person) Farbige(r)
m/f. ~**fast** a farbecht. ~ **film** n
Farbfilm m. ~**ful** a farbenfroh.
~**less** a farblos. ~ **photo[graph]**
n Farbaufnahme f. ~ **television** n
Farbfernsehen nt

column n Säule f; (of soldiers,
figures) Kolonne f; (Typ) Spalte f;
(Journ) Kolumne f

comb n Kamm m ● vt kämmen;
(search) absuchen; ~ **one's hair** sich
(dat) [die Haare] kämmen

combat n Kampf m

combination n Kombination f

combine[1] vt verbinden ● vi sich
verbinden; <people:> sich
zusammenschließen

combine[2] n (Comm) Konzern m

combustion n Verbrennung f

come vi (pt came, pp come)
kommen; (reach) reichen (to an +

acc); **that ~ s to £10** das macht £10;
~ **into money** zu Geld kommen; ~
true wahr werden; ~ **in two sizes** in
zwei Größen erhältlich sein; **the
years to ~** die kommenden Jahre;
how ~? 🆒 wie das? ~ **about** vi
geschehen. ~ **across** vi
herüberkommen; 🆒 klar werden
● vt stoßen auf (+ acc). ~ **apart** vi
sich auseinander nehmen lassen;
(accidentally) auseinander gehen. ~
away vi weggehen; <thing:>
abgehen. ~ **back** vi
zurückkommen. ~ **by** vi
vorbeikommen ● vt (obtain)
bekommen. ~ **in** vi hereinkommen.
~ **off** vi abgehen; (take place)
stattfinden; (succeed) klappen 🆒. ~
out vi herauskommen; <book:>
erscheinen; <stain:> herausgehen. ~
round vi vorbeikommen; (after
fainting) [wieder] zu sich kommen;
(change one's mind) sich umstimmen
lassen. ~ **to** vi [wieder] zu sich
kommen. ~ **up** vi heraufkommen;
<plant:> aufgehen; (reach) reichen
(to bis); ~ **up with** sich (dat)
einfallen lassen

come-back n Comeback nt

comedian n Komiker m

come-down n Rückschritt m

comedy n Komödie f

comet n Komet m

comfort n Bequemlichkeit f;
(consolation) Trost m ● vt trösten

comfortable a, -**bly** adv bequem

comfort station n (Amer)
öffentliche Toilette f

comfy a 🆒 bequem

comic a komisch ● n Komiker m;
(periodical) Comic-Heft nt

coming a kommend ● n Kommen nt

comma n Komma nt

command n Befehl m; (Mil)
Kommando nt; (mastery)
Beherrschung f ● vt befehlen (+ dat);
kommandieren <army>

command|er n Befehlshaber m.
~**ing officer** n Befehlshaber m

commemorat|e vt gedenken (+
gen). ~**ion** n Gedenken nt

commence vt/i anfangen, beginnen

commend vt loben; (recommend) empfehlen (to dat)

comment n Bemerkung f; no ~! kein Kommentar! ● vi sich äußern (on zu); ~ on (Journ) kommentieren

commentary n Kommentar m; [running] ~ (Radio, TV) Reportage f

commentator n Kommentator m; (Sport) Reporter m

commerce n Handel m

commercial a, -ly adv kommerziell ● n (Radio, TV) Werbespot m

commission n (order for work) Auftrag m; (body of people) Kommission f; (payment) Provision f; (Mil) [Offiziers]patent nt; out of ~ außer Betrieb ● vt beauftragen <s.o.>; in Auftrag geben <thing>; (Mil) zum Offizier ernennen

commit vt (pt/pp committed) begehen; (entrust) anvertrauen (to dat); (consign) einweisen (to in + acc); ~ oneself sich festlegen; (involve oneself) sich engagieren. ~ment n Verpflichtung f; (involvement) Engagement nt. ~ted a engagiert

committee n Ausschuss m, Komitee nt

common a (-er, -est) gemeinsam; (frequent) häufig; (ordinary) gewöhnlich; (vulgar) ordinär ● n Gemeindeland nt; have in ~ gemeinsam haben; House of C~s Unterhaus nt

common: ~ly adv allgemein. C~ Market n Gemeinsamer Markt m. ~place a häufig. ~-room n Aufenthaltsraum m. ~ sense n gesunder Menschenverstand m

commotion n Tumult m

communal a gemeinschaftlich

communicate vt mitteilen (to dat); übertragen <disease> ● vi sich verständigen

communication n Verständigung f; (contact) Verbindung f; (message) Mitteilung f; ~s pl (technology) Nachrichtenwesen nt

communicative a mitteilsam

Communion n [Holy] ~ das [heilige] Abendmahl; (Roman Catholic) die [heilige] Kommunion

communis|m n Kommunismus m. ~t a kommunistisch ● n Kommunist(in) m(f)

community n Gemeinschaft f; local ~ Gemeinde f

commute vi pendeln. ~r n Pendler(in) m(f)

compact a kompakt

companion n Begleiter(in) m(f). ~ship n Gesellschaft f

company n Gesellschaft f; (firm) Firma f; (Mil) Kompanie f; (⊞ guests) Besuch m. ~ car n Firmenwagen m

comparable a vergleichbar

comparative a vergleichend; (relative) relativ ● n (Gram) Komparativ m. ~ly adv verhältnismäßig

compare vt vergleichen (with/to mit) ● vi sich vergleichen lassen

comparison n Vergleich m

compartment n Fach nt; (Rail) Abteil nt

compass n Kompass m

compassion n Mitleid nt. ~ate a mitfühlend

compatible a vereinbar; <drugs> verträglich; (Techn) kompatibel; be ~ <people:> [gut] zueinander passen

compatriot n Landsmann m /-männin f

compel vt (pt/pp compelled) zwingen

compensat|e vt entschädigen. ~ion n Entschädigung f; (fig) Ausgleich m

compete vi konkurrieren; (take part) teilnehmen (in an + dat)

competen|ce n Fähigkeit f. ~t a fähig

competition n Konkurrenz f; (contest) Wettbewerb m; (in newspaper) Preisausschreiben nt

competitive a (Comm) konkurrenzfähig

competitor n Teilnehmer m; (Comm) Konkurrent m

compile vt zusammenstellen

complacen|cy n Selbstzufriedenheit f. ~**t** a, -**ly** adv selbstzufrieden

complain vi klagen (**about/of** über + acc); (formally) sich beschweren. ~**t** n Klage f; (formal) Beschwerde f; (Med) Leiden nt

complement[1] n Ergänzung f; **full ~** volle Anzahl f

complement[2] vt ergänzen

complete a vollständig; (finished) fertig; (utter) völlig ● vt vervollständigen; (finish) abschließen; (fill in) ausfüllen. ~**ly** adv völlig

completion n Vervollständigung f; (end) Abschluss m

complex a komplex ● n Komplex m

complexion n Teint m; (colour) Gesichtsfarbe f

complexity n Komplexität f

complicat|e vt komplizieren. ~**ed** a kompliziert. ~**ion** n Komplikation f

compliment n Kompliment nt; ~**s** pl Grüße pl ● vt ein Kompliment machen (+ dat). ~**ary** a schmeichelhaft; (given free) Frei-

comply vi (pt/pp -ied) ~ **with** nachkommen (+ dat)

compose vt verfassen; (Mus) komponieren; **be** ~**d of** sich zusammensetzen aus. ~**r** n Komponist m

composition n Komposition f; (essay) Aufsatz m

compost n Kompost m

composure n Fassung f

compound a zusammengesetzt; <fracture> kompliziert ● n (Chem) Verbindung f; (Gram) Kompositum nt

comprehen|d vt begreifen, verstehen. ~**sible** a, -**bly** adv verständlich. ~**sion** n Verständnis nt

comprehensive a & n umfassend; ~ [**school**] Gesamtschule f. ~

insurance n (Auto) Vollkaskoversicherung f

compress vt zusammenpressen; ~**ed air** Druckluft f

comprise vt umfassen, bestehen aus

compromise n Kompromiss m ● vt kompromittieren <person> ● vi einen Kompromiss schließen

compuls|ion n Zwang m. ~**ive** a zwanghaft. ~**ory** a obligatorisch

comput|er n Computer m. ~**er game** n Computerspiel. ~**erize** vt computerisieren <data>; auf Computer umstellen <firm>. ~**literate** a mit Computern vertraut. ~**ing** n Computertechnik f

comrade n Kamerad m; (Pol) Genosse m/Genossin f

con[1] see **pro**

con[2] 🄘 Schwindel m ● vt (pt/pp conned) 🄘 beschwindeln

concave a konkav

conceal vt verstecken; (keep secret) verheimlichen

concede vt zugeben; (give up) aufgeben

conceit n Einbildung f. ~**ed** a eingebildet

conceivable a denkbar

conceive vt (Biol) empfangen; (fig) sich (dat) ausdenken ● vi schwanger werden

concentrat|e vt konzentrieren ● vi sich konzentrieren. ~**ion** n Konzentration f

concern n Angelegenheit f; (worry) Sorge f; (Comm) Unternehmen nt ● vt (be about, affect) betreffen; (worry) kümmern; **be** ~**ed about** besorgt sein um; ~ **oneself with** sich beschäftigen mit; **as far as I am** ~**ed** was mich angeht od betrifft. ~**ing** prep bezüglich (+ gen)

concert n Konzert nt

concerto n Konzert nt

concession n Zugeständnis nt; (Comm) Konzession f; (reduction) Ermäßigung f

concise a, -**ly** adv kurz

conclude vt/i schließen

conclusion n Schluss m; in ~ abschließend, zum Schluss

conclusive a schlüssig

concoct vt zusammenstellen; (fig) fabrizieren. ~ion n Zusammenstellung f; (drink) Gebräu nt

concrete a konkret ● n Beton m ● vt betonieren

concurrently adv gleichzeitig

concussion n Gehirnerschütterung f

condemn vt verurteilen; (declare unfit) für untauglich erklären. ~ation n Verurteilung f

condensation n Kondensation f

condense vt zusammenfassen

condescend vi sich herablassen (to zu). ~ing a, -ly adv herablassend

condition n Bedingung f; (state) Zustand m; ~s pl Verhältnisse pl; on ~ that unter der Bedingung, dass ● vt (Psych) konditionieren. ~al a bedingt ● n (Gram) Konditional m. ~er n Pflegespülung f; (for fabrics) Weichspüler m

condolences npl Beileid nt

condom n Kondom nt

condominium n (Amer) ≈ Eigentumswohnung f

conduct[1] n Verhalten nt; (Sch) Betragen nt

conduct[2] vt führen; (Phys) leiten; (Mus) dirigieren. ~or n Dirigent m; (of bus) Schaffner m; (Phys) Leiter m

cone n Kegel m; (Bot) Zapfen m; (for ice-cream) [Eis]tüte f; (Auto) Leitkegel m

confectioner n Konditor m. ~y n Süßwaren pl

conference n Konferenz f

confess vt/i gestehen; (Relig) beichten. ~ion n Geständnis nt; (Relig) Beichte f

confetti n Konfetti nt

confide vt anvertrauen ● vi ~ in s.o. sich jdm anvertrauen

confidence n (trust) Vertrauen nt; (self-assurance) Selbstvertrauen nt; (secret) Geheimnis nt; in ~ im Vertrauen. ~ **trick** n Schwindel m

confident a, -ly adv zuversichtlich; (self-assured) selbstsicher

confidential a, -ly adv vertraulich

confine vt beschränken (to auf + acc). ~d a (narrow) eng

confirm vt bestätigen; (Relig) konfirmieren; (Roman Catholic) firmen. ~ation n Bestätigung f; Konfirmation f; Firmung f

confiscat|e vt beschlagnahmen. ~ion n Beschlagnahme f

conflict[1] n Konflikt m

conflict[2] vi im Widerspruch stehen (with zu). ~ing a widersprüchlich

conform vi <person:> sich anpassen; <thing:> entsprechen (to dat). ~ist n Konformist m

confounded a 🆇 verflixt

confront vt konfrontieren. ~ation n Konfrontation f

confus|e vt verwirren; (mistake for) verwechseln (with mit). ~ing a verwirrend. ~ion n Verwirrung f; (muddle) Durcheinander nt

congenial a angenehm

congest|ed a verstopft; (with people) überfüllt. ~ion n Verstopfung f; Überfüllung f

congratulat|e vt gratulieren (+ dat) (on zu). ~ions npl Glückwünsche pl; ~ions! [ich] gratuliere!

congregation n (Relig) Gemeinde f

congress n Kongress m. ~man n Kongressabgeordnete(r) m

conical a kegelförmig

conifer n Nadelbaum m

conjecture n Mutmaßung f

conjunction n Konjunktion f; in ~ with zusammen mit

conjur|e vi zaubern ● vt ~e up heraufbeschwören. ~or n Zauberkünstler m

conk vi ~ out 🆇 <machine:> kaputtgehen

conker n 🆇 Kastanie f

con-man n 🆇 Schwindler m

connect vt verbinden (to mit); (Electr) anschließen (to an + acc); be ~ed with zu tun haben mit; (be related to) verwandt sein mit● vi verbunden sein; <train:> Anschluss haben (with an + acc)

connection n Verbindung f; (Rail, Electr) Anschluss m; in ~ with in Zusammenhang mit. ~s npl Beziehungen pl

connoisseur n Kenner m

conquer vt erobern; (fig) besiegen. ~or n Eroberer m

conquest n Eroberung f

conscience n Gewissen nt

conscientious a, -ly adv gewissenhaft

conscious a, -ly adv bewusst; [fully] ~ bei [vollem] Bewusstsein; be/become ~ of sth sich (dat) etw (gen) bewusst sein/werden. ~ness n Bewusstsein nt

conscript n Einberufene(r) m

consecrat|e vt weihen; einweihen <church>. ~ion n Weihe f; Einweihung f

consecutive a aufeinanderfolgend. -ly adv fortlaufend

consent n Einwilligung f, Zustimmung f ● vi einwilligen (to in + acc), zustimmen (to dat)

consequen|ce n Folge f. ~t a daraus folgend. ~tly adv folglich

conservation n Erhaltung f, Bewahrung f. ~ist n Umweltschützer m

conservative a konservativ; <estimate> vorsichtig. C~ (Pol) a konservativ ● n Konservative(r) m/f

conservatory n Wintergarten m

conserve vt erhalten, bewahren; sparen <energy>

consider vt erwägen; (think over) sich (dat) überlegen; (take into account) berücksichtigen; (regard as) betrachten als; ~ doing sth erwägen, etw zu tun. ~able a, -bly adv erheblich

consider|ate a, -ly adv rücksichtsvoll. ~ation n Erwägung

f; (thoughtfulness) Rücksicht f; (payment) Entgelt nt; take into ~ation berücksichtigen. ~ing prep wenn man bedenkt (that dass)

consist vi ~ of bestehen aus

consisten|cy n Konsequenz f; (density) Konsistenz f. ~t a konsequent; (unchanging) gleichbleibend. ~tly adv konsequent; (constantly) ständig

consolation n Trost m. ~ prize n Trostpreis m

console vt trösten

consonant n Konsonant m

conspicuous a auffällig

conspiracy n Verschwörung f

constable n Polizist m

constant a, -ly adv beständig; (continuous) ständig

constipat|ed a verstopft. ~ion n Verstopfung f

constituency n Wahlkreis m

constitut|e vt bilden. ~ion n (Pol) Verfassung f; (of person) Konstitution f

constraint n Zwang m; (restriction) Beschränkung f; (strained manner) Gezwungenheit f

construct vt bauen. ~ion n Bau m; (Gram) Konstruktion f; (interpretation) Deutung f; under ~ion im Bau

consul n Konsul m. ~ate n Konsulat nt

consult vt [um Rat] fragen; konsultieren <doctor>; nachschlagen in (+ dat) <book>. ~ant n Berater m; (Med) Chefarzt m. ~ation n Beratung f; (Med) Konsultation f

consume vt verzehren; (use) verbrauchen. ~r n Verbraucher m

consumption n Konsum m; (use) Verbrauch m

contact n Kontakt m; (person) Kontaktperson f ● vt sich in Verbindung setzen mit. ~ lenses npl Kontaktlinsen pl

contagious a direkt übertragbar

contain vt enthalten; (control) beherrschen. ~er n Behälter m; (Comm) Container m

contaminat|e vt verseuchen. **~ion** n Verseuchung f

contemplat|e vt betrachten; (*meditate*) nachdenken über (+ acc). **~ion** n Betrachtung f; Nachdenken nt

contemporary a zeitgenössisch ● n Zeitgenosse m/ -genossin f

contempt n Verachtung f; **beneath ~** verabscheuungswürdig. **~ible** a verachtenswert. **~uous** a, **-ly** adv verächtlich

content[1] n & **contents** pl Inhalt m

content[2] a zufrieden ● n **to one's heart's ~** nach Herzenslust ● vt **~ oneself** sich begnügen (with mit). **~ed** a, **-ly** adv zufrieden

contentment n Zufriedenheit f

contest n Kampf m; (*competition*) Wettbewerb m. **~ant** n Teilnehmer m

context n Zusammenhang m

continent n Kontinent m

continental a Kontinental-. **~ breakfast** n kleines Frühstück nt. **~ quilt** n Daunendecke f

continual a, **-ly** adv dauernd

continuation n Fortsetzung f

continue vt fortsetzen; **~ doing** or **to do sth** fortfahren, etw zu tun; **to be ~d** Fortsetzung folgt ● vi weitergehen; (*doing sth*) weitermachen; (*speaking*) fortfahren; <*weather:*> anhalten

continuity n Kontinuität f

continuous a, **-ly** adv anhaltend, ununterbrochen

contort vt verzerren. **~ion** n Verzerrung f

contour n Kontur f; (*line*) Höhenlinie f

contracep|tion n Empfängnisverhütung f. **~tive** a Empfängnisverhütungsmittel nt

contract[1] n Vertrag m

contract[2] vi sich zusammenziehen. **~or** n Unternehmer m

contradict vt widersprechen (+ dat). **~ion** n Widerspruch m. **~ory** a widersprüchlich

contralto n Alt m; (*singer*) Altistin f

contraption n 🎧 Apparat m

contrary a & adv entgegengesetzt; **~ to** entgegen (+ dat) ● n Gegenteil nt; **on the ~** im Gegenteil

contrast[1] n Kontrast m

contrast[2] vt gegenüberstellen (with dat) ● vi einen Kontrast bilden (with zu). **~ing** a gegensätzlich; <*colour*> Kontrast-

contribut|e vt/i beitragen; beisteuern <*money*>; (*donate*) spenden. **~ion** n Beitrag m; (*donation*) Spende f. **~or** n Beitragende(r) m/f

contrivance n Vorrichtung f

control n Kontrolle f; (*mastery*) Beherrschung f; (*Techn*) Regler m; **~s** pl (*of car, plane*) Steuerung f; **get out of ~** außer Kontrolle geraten ● vt (pt/pp **controlled**) kontrollieren; (*restrain*) unter Kontrolle halten; **~ oneself** sich beherrschen

controvers|ial a umstritten. **~y** n Kontroverse f

convalesce vi sich erholen. **~nce** n Erholung f

convalescent home n Erholungsheim nt

convenience n Bequemlichkeit f; **[public] ~** öffentliche Toilette f; **with all modern ~s** mit allem Komfort

convenient a, **-ly** adv günstig; **be ~ for s.o.** jdm gelegen sein, jdm passen; **if it is ~ [for you]** wenn es Ihnen passt

convent n [Nonnen]kloster nt

convention n (*custom*) Brauch m, Sitte f. **~al** a, **-ly** adv konventionell

converge vi zusammenlaufen

conversation n Gespräch nt; (*Sch*) Konversation f

conversion n Umbau m; (*Relig*) Bekehrung f; (*calculation*) Umrechnung f

convert[1] n Bekehrte(r) m/f, Konvertit m

convert[2] vt bekehren <*person*>; (*change*) umwandeln (into in + acc); umbauen <*building*>; (*calculate*) umrechnen; (*Techn*) umstellen. ∼**ible** a verwandelbar ● n (*Auto*) Kabrio[lett] nt

convex a konvex

convey vt befördern; vermitteln <*idea, message*>. ∼**or belt** n Förderband nt

convict¹ n Sträfling m

convict² vt verurteilen (of wegen). ∼**ion** n Verurteilung f; (*belief*) Überzeugung f; **previous** ∼**ion** Vorstrafe f

convinc|e vt überzeugen. ∼**ing** a, -**ly** adv überzeugend

convoy n Konvoi m

convulse vt be ∼ed sich krümmen (with vor + dat)

coo vi gurren

cook n Koch m/ Köchin f ● vt/i kochen; **is it** ∼**ed?** ist es gar? ∼ **the books** 🔟 die Bilanz frisieren. ∼**book** n (*Amer*) Kochbuch nt

cooker n [Koch]herd m; (*apple*) Kochapfel m. ∼**y** n Kochen nt. ∼**y book** n Kochbuch nt

cookie n (*Amer*) Keks m

cool a (-er, -est), -**ly** adv kühl ● n Kühle f ● vt kühlen ● vi abkühlen. ∼**-box** n Kühlbox f. ∼**ness** n Kühle f

coop vt ∼ up einsperren

co-operat|e vi zusammenarbeiten. ∼**ion** n Kooperation f

co-operative a hilfsbereit ● n Genossenschaft f

cop n 🔟 Polizist m

cope vi 🔟 zurechtkommen; ∼ with fertig werden mit

copious a reichlich

copper¹ n Kupfer nt ● a kupfern

copper² n 🔟 Polizist m

copper beech n Blutbuche f

coppice, copse ns Gehölz nt

copy n Kopie f; (*book*) Exemplar nt ● vt (*pt/pp* -**ied**) kopieren; (*imitate*) nachahmen; (*Sch*) abschreiben

copy: ∼**right** n Copyright nt. ∼**-writer** n Texter m

coral n Koralle f

cord n Schnur f; (*fabric*) Cordsamt m; ∼**s** pl Cordhose f

cordial a, -**ly** adv herzlich ● n Fruchtsirup m

cordon n Kordon m ● vt ∼ off absperren

corduroy n Cordsamt m

core n Kern m; (*of apple, pear*) Kerngehäuse nt

cork n Kork m; (*for bottle*) Korken m. ∼**screw** n Korkenzieher m

corn¹ n Korn nt; (*Amer: maize*) Mais m

corn² n (*Med*) Hühnerauge nt

corned beef n Cornedbeef nt

corner n Ecke f; (*bend*) Kurve f; (*football*) Eckball m ● vt (*fig*) in die Enge treiben; (*Comm*) monopolisieren <*market*>. ∼**-stone** n Eckstein m

cornet n (*Mus*) Kornett nt; (*for ice-cream*) [Eis]tüte f

corn: ∼**flour** n, (*Amer*) ∼**starch** n Stärkemehl nt

corny a 🔟 abgedroschen

coronation n Krönung f

coroner n Beamte(r) m, der verdächtige Todesfälle untersucht

corporal n (*Mil*) Stabsunteroffizier m

corps n (*pl* corps) Korps nt

corpse n Leiche f

correct a, -**ly** adv richtig; (*proper*) korrekt ● vt verbessern; (*Sch, Typ*) korrigieren. ∼**ion** n Verbesserung f; (*Typ*) Korrektur f

correspond vi entsprechen (to dat); <*two things:*> sich entsprechen; (*write*) korrespondieren. ∼**ence** n Briefwechsel m; (*Comm*) Korrespondenz f. ∼**ent** n Korrespondent(in) m(f). ∼**ing** a, -**ly** adv entsprechend

corridor n Gang m; (*Pol, Aviat*) Korridor m

corro|de vt zerfressen ● vi rosten. ∼**sion** n Korrosion f

corrugated a gewellt. ∼ **iron** n Wellblech nt

corrupt a korrupt ● vt korrumpieren; (spoil) verderben. **~ion** n Korruption f

corset n & **-s** pl Korsett nt

Corsica n Korsika nt

cosh n Totschläger m

cosmetic a kosmetisch ● n **~s** pl Kosmetika pl

cosset vt verhätscheln

cost n Kosten pl; **~s** pl (Jur) Kosten; **at all ~s** um jeden Preis ● vt (pt/pp cost) kosten; **it ~ me £20** es hat mich £20 gekostet ● vt (pt/pp costed) **~ [out]** die Kosten kalkulieren für

costly a (-ier, -iest) teuer

cost: ~ of living n Lebenshaltungskosten pl. **~ price** n Selbstkostenpreis m

costume n Kostüm nt; (national) Tracht f. **~ jewellery** n Modeschmuck m

cosy a (-ier, -iest) gemütlich ● n (tea-, egg-) Wärmer m

cot n Kinderbett nt; (Amer: camp bed) Feldbett nt

cottage n Häuschen nt. **~ cheese** n Hüttenkäse m

cotton n Baumwolle f; (thread) Nähgarn nt ● a baumwollen ● vi **~ on** 🔤 kapieren

cotton wool n Watte f

couch n Liege f

couchette n (Rail) Liegeplatz m

cough n Husten m ● vi husten. **~ up** vt/i husten; (🔤 pay) blechen

cough mixture n Hustensaft m

could see can²

council n Rat m; (Admin) Stadtverwaltung f; (rural) Gemeindeverwaltung f. **~ house** n ≈ Sozialwohnung f

councillor n Ratsmitglied nt

council tax n Gemeindesteuer f

count¹ n Graf m

count² n Zählung f; **keep ~** zählen ● vt/i zählen. **~ on** vt rechnen auf (+ acc)

counter¹ n (in shop) Ladentisch m; (in bank) Schalter m; (in café) Theke f; (Games) Spielmarke f

counter² a Gegen- ● vt/i kontern

counteract vt entgegenwirken (+ dat)

counterfeit a gefälscht

counterfoil n Kontrollabschnitt m

counterpart n Gegenstück nt

counter-productive a **be ~** das Gegenteil bewirken

countersign vt gegenzeichnen

countess n Gräfin f

countless a unzählig

country n Land nt; (native land) Heimat f; (countryside) Landschaft f; **in the ~** auf dem Lande. **~man** n [fellow] **~man** Landsmann m. **~side** n Landschaft f

county n Grafschaft f

coup n (Pol) Staatsstreich m

couple n Paar nt; **a ~ of** (two) zwei ● vt verbinden

coupon n Kupon m; (voucher) Gutschein m; (entry form) Schein m

courage n Mut m. **~ous** a, **-ly** adv mutig

courgettes npl Zucchini pl

courier n Bote m; (diplomatic) Kurier m; (for tourists) Reiseleiter(in) m(f)

course n (Naut, Sch) Kurs m; (Culin) Gang m; (for golf) Platz m; **~ of treatment** (Med) Kur f; **of ~** natürlich, selbstverständlich; **in the ~ of** im Lauf[e] (+ gen)

court n Hof m; (Sport) Platz m; (Jur) Gericht nt

courteous a, **-ly** adv höflich

courtesy n Höflichkeit f

court: ~ martial n (pl **~s martial**) Militärgericht nt. **~yard** n Hof m

cousin n Vetter m, Cousin m; (female) Kusine f

cove n kleine Bucht f

cover n Decke f; (of cushion) Bezug m; (of umbrella) Hülle f; (of typewriter) Haube f; (of book, lid) Deckel m; (of magazine) Umschlag m; (protection) Deckung f, Schutz m;

take ~ Deckung nehmen; **under separate ~** mit getrennter Post ● *vt* bedecken; beziehen *<cushion>*; decken *<costs, needs>*; zurücklegen *<distance>*; (*Journ*) berichten über (+ *acc*); (*insure*) versichern. **~ up** *vt* zudecken; (*fig*) vertuschen

coverage *n* (*Journ*) Berichterstattung *f* (of über + *acc*)

cover: ~ing *n* Decke *f*; (*for floor*) Belag *m*. **~-up** *n* Vertuschung *f*

cow *n* Kuh *f*

coward *n* Feigling *m*. **~ice** *n* Feigheit *f*. **~ly** *a* feige

cowboy *n* Cowboy *m*; 🔲 unsolider Handwerker *m*

cower *vi* sich [ängstlich] ducken

cowshed *n* Kuhstall *m*

cox *n*, **coxswain** *n* Steuermann *m*

coy *a* (-er, -est) gespielt schüchtern

crab *n* Krabbe *f*

crack *n* Riss *m*; (*in china, glass*) Sprung *m*; (*noise*) Knall *m*; (🔲 *joke*) Witz *m*; (🔲 *attempt*) Versuch *m* ● *a* 🔲 erstklassig ● *vt* knacken *<nut, code>*; einen Sprung machen in (+ *acc*) *<china, glass>*; 🔲 reißen *<joke>*; 🔲 lösen *<problem>* ● *vi* *<china, glass:>* springen; *<whip:>* knallen. **~ down** *vi* 🔲 durchgreifen

cracked *a* gesprungen; *<rib>* angebrochen; (🔲 *crazy*) verrückt

cracker *n* (*biscuit*) Kräcker *m*; (*firework*) Knallkörper *m*; [Christmas] ~ Knallbonbon *m*. **~s** *a* be **~s** 🔲 einen Knacks haben

crackle *vi* knistern

cradle *n* Wiege *f*

craft *n* Handwerk *nt*; (*technique*) Fertigkeit *f*. **~sman** *n* Handwerker *m*

crafty *a* (-ier, -iest), **-ily** *adv* gerissen

crag *n* Felszacken *m*

cram *v* (*pt/pp* crammed) ● *vt* hineinstopfen (**into** in + *acc*); vollstopfen (**with** mit) ● *vi* (*for exams*) pauken

cramp *n* Krampf *m*. **~ed** *a* eng

cranberry *n* (*Culin*) Preiselbeere *f*

crane *n* Kran *m*; (*bird*) Kranich *m*

crank *n* 🔲 Exzentriker *m*

crankshaft *n* Kurbelwelle *f*

crash *n* (*noise*) Krach *m*; (*Auto*) Zusammenstoß *m*; (*Aviat*) Absturz *m* ● *vi* krachen (**into** gegen); *<cars:>* zusammenstoßen; *<plane:>* abstürzen ● *vt* einen Unfall haben mit *<car>*

crash: ~helmet *n* Sturzhelm *m*. **~-landing** *n* Bruchlandung *f*

crate *n* Kiste *f*

crater *n* Krater *m*

crawl *n* (*Swimming*) Kraul *nt*; **do the ~** kraulen; **at a ~** im Kriechtempo ● *vi* kriechen; *<baby:>* krabbeln; **~ with** wimmeln von

crayon *n* Wachsstift *m*; (*pencil*) Buntstift *m*

craze *n* Mode *f*

crazy *a* (-ier, -iest) verrückt; **be ~ about** verrückt sein nach

creak *vi* knarren

cream *n* Sahne *f*; (*Cosmetic, Med, Culin*) Creme *f* ● *a* (*colour*) cremefarben ● *vt* (*Culin*) cremig rühren. **~y** *a* sahnig; (*smooth*) cremig

crease *n* Falte *f*; (*unwanted*) Knitterfalte *f* ● *vt* falten; (*accidentally*) zerknittern ● *vi* knittern

creat|e *vt* schaffen. **~ion** *n* Schöpfung *f*. **~ive** *a* schöpferisch. **~or** *n* Schöpfer *m*

creature *n* Geschöpf *nt*

crèche *n* Kinderkrippe *f*

credibility *n* Glaubwürdigkeit *f*

credible *a* glaubwürdig

credit *n* Kredit *m*; (*honour*) Ehre *f* ● *vt* glauben; **~ s.o. with sth** (*Comm*) jdm etw gutschreiben; (*fig*) jdm etw zuschreiben. **~able** *a* lobenswert

credit: ~ card *n* Kreditkarte *f*. **~or** *n* Gläubiger *m*

creep *vi* (*pt/pp* crept) schleichen ● *n* 🔲 fieser Kerl *m*; **it gives me the ~s** es ist mir unheimlich. **~er** *n* Kletterpflanze *f*. **~y** *a* gruselig

cremat|e *vt* einäschern. **~ion** *n* Einäscherung *f*

crêpe *n* Krepp *m*. **~ paper** *n* Krepppapier *nt*

crept see creep

crescent n Halbmond m

cress n Kresse f

crest n Kamm m; (*coat of arms*) Wappen nt

crew n Besatzung f; (*gang*) Bande f. ~ **cut** n Bürstenschnitt m

crib[1] n Krippe f

crib[2] vt/i (*pt/pp* cribbed) 🔟 abschreiben

cricket n Kricket nt. ~**er** n Kricketspieler m

crime n Verbrechen nt; (*rate*) Kriminalität f

criminal a kriminell, verbrecherisch; <*law, court*> Straf- ● n Verbrecher m

crimson a purpurrot

crinkle vt/i knittern

cripple n Krüppel m ● vt zum Krüppel machen; (*fig*) lahmlegen. ~**d** a verkrüppelt

crisis n (*pl* -ses) Krise f

crisp a (-er, -est) knusprig. ~**bread** n Knäckebrot nt. ~**s** npl Chips pl

criss-cross a schräg gekreuzt

criterion n (*pl* -ria) Kriterium nt

critic n Kritiker m. ~**al** a kritisch. ~**ally** adv kritisch; ~**ally** ill schwer krank

criticism n Kritik f

criticize vt kritisieren

croak vi krächzen; <*frog:*> quaken

crockery n Geschirr nt

crocodile n Krokodil nt

crocus n (*pl* -es) Krokus m

crony n Kumpel m

crook n (*stick*) Stab m; (🔟 *criminal*) Schwindler m, Gauner m

crooked a schief; (*bent*) krumm; (🔟 *dishonest*) unehrlich

crop n Feldfrucht f; (*harvest*) Ernte f ● v (*pt/pp* cropped) ● vt stutzen ● vi ~ **up** 🔟 zur Sprache kommen; (*occur*) dazwischenkommen

croquet n Krocket nt

cross a, -ly adv (*annoyed*) böse (with auf + *acc*); talk at ~ purposes aneinander vorbeireden ● n Kreuz nt; (*Bot, Zool*) Kreuzung f ● vt kreuzen <*cheque, animals*>; überqueren <*road*>; ~ oneself sich bekreuzigen; ~ one's arms die Arme verschränken; ~ one's legs die Beine übereinander schlagen; keep one's fingers ~ed for s.o. jdm die Daumen drücken; it ~ed my mind es fiel mir ein ● vi (*go across*) hinübergehen/-fahren; <*lines:*> sich kreuzen. ~ out vt durchstreichen

cross: ~-**country** n (*Sport*) Crosslauf m. ~-**eyed** a schielend; be ~-eyed schielen. ~**fire** n Kreuzfeuer nt. ~**ing** n Übergang m; (*sea journey*) Überfahrt f. ~**roads** n [Straßen]kreuzung f. ~-**section** n Querschnitt m. ~**wise** adv quer. ~**word** n ~**word** [puzzle] Kreuzworträtsel nt

crotchety a griesgrämig

crouch vi kauern

crow n Krähe f; as the ~ flies Luftlinie

crowd n [Menschen]menge f ● vi sich drängen. ~**ed** a [gedrängt] voll

crown n Krone f ● vt krönen; überkronen <*tooth*>

crucial a höchst wichtig; (*decisive*) entscheidend (to für)

crude a (-r, -st) primitiv; (*raw*) roh

cruel a (crueller, cruellest), -ly adv grausam (to gegen). ~**ty** n Grausamkeit f

cruis|e n Kreuzfahrt f ● vi kreuzen; <*car:*> fahren. ~**er** n (*Mil*) Kreuzer m; (*motor boat*) Kajütboot nt

crumb n Krümel m

crumble vt/i krümeln; (*collapse*) einstürzen

crumple vt zerknittern ● vi knittern

crunch n 🔟 when it comes to the ~ wenn es [wirklich] drauf ankommt ● vt mampfen ● vi knirschen

crusade n Kreuzzug m; (*fig*) Kampagne f. ~**r** n Kreuzfahrer m; (*fig*) Kämpfer m

crush n (*crowd*) Gedränge nt ● vt zerquetschen; zerknittern <*clothes*>; (*fig: subdue*) niederschlagen

crust n Kruste f

crutch *n* Krücke *f*

cry *n* Ruf *m*; (*shout*) Schrei *m*; **a far ~ from** (*fig*) weit entfernt von ● *vi* (*pt/pp* **cried**) (*weep*) weinen; <*baby:*> schreien; (*call*) rufen

crypt *n* Krypta *f*. **~ic** *a* rätselhaft

crystal *n* Kristall *m*; (*glass*) Kristall *nt*

cub *n* (*Zool*) Junge(s) *nt*

Cuba *n* Kuba *nt*

cubby-hole *n* Fach *nt*

cub|e *n* Würfel *m*. **~ic** *a* Kubik-

cubicle *n* Kabine *f*

cuckoo *n* Kuckuck *m*. **~ clock** *n* Kuckucksuhr *f*

cucumber *n* Gurke *f*

cuddl|e *vt* herzen ● *vi* **~e up to** sich kuscheln an (+ *acc*). **~y** *a* kuschelig

cue¹ *n* Stichwort *nt*

cue² *n* (*Billiards*) Queue *nt*

cuff *n* Manschette *f*; (*Amer: turn-up*) [Hosen]aufschlag *m*; (*blow*) Klaps *m*; **off the ~** 𝕀 aus dem Stegreif. **~-link** *n* Manschettenknopf *m*

cul-de-sac *n* Sackgasse *f*

culinary *a* kulinarisch

culprit *n* Täter *m*

cult *n* Kult *m*

cultivate *vt* anbauen <*crop*>; bebauen <*land*>

cultural *a* kulturell

culture *n* Kultur *f*. **~d** *a* kultiviert

cumbersome *a* hinderlich; (*unwieldy*) unhandlich

cunning *a* listig ● *n* List *f*

cup *n* Tasse *f*; (*prize*) Pokal *m*

cupboard *n* Schrank *m*

Cup Final *n* Pokalendspiel *nt*

curable *a* heilbar

curate *n* Vikar *m*; (*Roman Catholic*) Kaplan *m*

curb *vt* zügeln

curdle *vi* gerinnen

cure *n* [Heil]mittel *nt* ● *vt* heilen; (*salt*) pökeln; (*smoke*) räuchern; gerben <*skin*>

curiosity *n* Neugier *f*; (*object*) Kuriosität *f*

curious *a*, **-ly** *adv* neugierig; (*strange*) merkwürdig, seltsam

curl *n* Locke *f* ● *vt* locken ● *vi* sich locken

curly *a* (**-ier, -iest**) lockig

currant *n* (*dried*) Korinthe *f*

currency *n* Geläufigkeit *f*; (*money*) Währung *f*; **foreign ~** Devisen *pl*

current *a* augenblicklich, gegenwärtig; (*in general use*) geläufig, gebräuchlich ● *n* Strömung *f*; (*Electr*) Strom *m*. **~ affairs** *or* **events** *npl* Aktuelle(s) *nt*. **~ly** *adv* zurzeit

curriculum *n* Lehrplan *m*. **~ vitae** *n* Lebenslauf *m*

curry *n* Curry *nt* & *m*; (*meal*) Currygericht *nt*

curse *n* Fluch *m* ● *vt* verfluchen ● *vi* fluchen

cursory *a* flüchtig

curt *a*, **-ly** *adv* barsch

curtain *n* Vorhang *m*

curtsy *n* Knicks *m* ● *vi* (*pt/pp* **-ied**) knicksen

curve *n* Kurve *f* ● *vi* einen Bogen machen; **~ to the right/left** nach rechts/links biegen. **~d** *a* gebogen

cushion *n* Kissen *nt* ● *vt* dämpfen; (*protect*) beschützen

cushy *a* (**-ier, -iest**) 𝕀 bequem

custard *n* Vanillesoße *f*

custom *n* Brauch *m*; (*habit*) Gewohnheit *f*; (*Comm*) Kundschaft *f*. **~ary** *a* üblich; (*habitual*) gewohnt. **~er** *n* Kunde *m*/Kundin *f*

customs *npl* Zoll *m*. **~ officer** *n* Zollbeamte(r) *m*

cut *n* Schnitt *m*; (*Med*) Schnittwunde *f*; (*reduction*) Kürzung *f*; (*in price*) Senkung *f*; **~ [of meat]** [Fleisch]stück *nt* ● *vt/i* (*pt/pp* **cut**, *pres p* **cutting**) schneiden; (*mow*) mähen; abheben <*cards*>; (*reduce*) kürzen; senken <*price*>; **~ one's finger** sich in den Finger schneiden; **~ s.o.'s hair** jdm die Haare schneiden; **~ short** abkürzen. **~ back** *vt* zurückschneiden; (*fig*) einschränken, kürzen. **~ down** *vt* fällen; (*fig*) einschränken. **~ off** *vt* abschneiden; (*disconnect*) abstellen; be ~ off (*Teleph*) unterbrochen werden. ~ out *vt* ausschneiden; (*delete*) streichen; be ~ out for 🔲 geeignet sein zu. ~ up *vt* zerschneiden; (*slice*) aufschneiden

cut-back *n* Kürzung *f*

cute *a* (-r, -st) 🔲 niedlich

cut glass *n* Kristall *nt*

cutlery *n* Besteck *nt*

cutlet *n* Kotelett *nt*

cut-price *a* verbilligt

cutting *a* <*remark*> bissig ● *n* (*from newspaper*) Ausschnitt *m*; (*of plant*) Ableger *m*

CV *abbr* of curriculum vitae

cycl|e *n* Zyklus *m*; (*bicycle*) [Fahr]rad *nt* ● *vi* mit dem Rad fahren. ~ing *n* Radfahren *nt*. ~ist *n* Radfahrer(in) *m(f)*

cylind|er *n* Zylinder *m*. ~rical *a* zylindrisch

cynic *n* Zyniker *m*. ~al *a*, -ly *adv* zynisch. ~ism *n* Zynismus *m*

Cyprus *n* Zypern *nt*

Czech *a* tschechisch; ~ Republic Tschechische Republik *f* ● *n* Tscheche *m*/ Tschechin *f*

Dd

dab *n* Tupfer *m*; (*of butter*) Klecks *m*

dabble *vi* ~ in sth (*fig*) sich nebenbei mit etw befassen

dachshund *n* Dackel *m*

dad[dy] *n* 🔲 Vati *m*

daddy-long-legs *n* [Kohl]schnake *f*; (*Amer: spider*) Weberknecht *m*

daffodil *n* Osterglocke *f*, gelbe Narzisse *f*

daft *a* (-er, -est) dumm

dagger *n* Dolch *m*

dahlia *n* Dahlie *f*

daily *a* & *adv* täglich

dainty *a* (-ier, -iest) zierlich

dairy *n* Molkerei *f*; (*shop*) Milchgeschäft *nt*. ~ products *pl* Milchprodukte *pl*

daisy *n* Gänseblümchen *nt*

dam *n* [Stau]damm *m* ● *vt* (*pt/pp* dammed) eindämmen

damage *n* Schaden *m* (to an + *dat*); ~s *pl* (*Jur*) Schadenersatz *m* ● *vt* beschädigen; (*fig*) beeinträchtigen

damn *a*, *int* & *adv* 🔲 verdammt ● *n* I don't care or give a ~ 🔲 ich schere mich einen Dreck darum ● *vt* verdammen. ~ation *n* Verdammnis *f*

damp *a* (-er, -est) feucht ● *n* Feuchtigkeit *f*

damp|en *vt* anfeuchten; (*fig*) dämpfen. ~ness *n* Feuchtigkeit *f*

dance *n* Tanz *m*; (*function*) Tanzveranstaltung *f* ● *vt/i* tanzen. ~ music *n* Tanzmusik *f*

dancer *n* Tänzer(in) *m(f)*

dandelion *n* Löwenzahn *m*

dandruff *n* Schuppen *pl*

Dane *n* Däne *m*/Dänin *f*

danger *n* Gefahr *f*; in/out of ~ in/ außer Gefahr. ~ous *a*, -ly *adv* gefährlich; ~ously ill schwer erkrankt

dangle *vi* baumeln ● *vt* baumeln lassen

Danish *a* dänisch. ~ pastry *n* Hefeteilchen *nt*

Danube *n* Donau *f*

dare *vt/i* (*challenge*) herausfordern (to zu); ~ [to] do sth [es] wagen, etw zu tun. ~devil *n* Draufgänger *m*

daring *a* verwegen ● *n* Verwegenheit *f*

dark *a* (-er, -est) dunkel; ~ blue/ brown dunkelblau/ -braun; ~ horse (*fig*) stilles Wasser *nt* ● *n* Dunkelheit *f*; after ~ nach Einbruch der Dunkelheit; in the ~ im Dunkeln

dark|en *vt* verdunkeln ● *vi* dunkler werden. ~ness *n* Dunkelheit *f*

dark-room *n* Dunkelkammer *f*

darling *a* allerliebst ● *n* Liebling *m*

darn *vt* stopfen

dart n Pfeil m; ~s sg (game) [Wurf]pfeil m ● vi flitzen

dash n (Typ) Gedankenstrich m; a ~ of milk ein Schuss Milch ● vi rennen ● vt schleudern. ~ **off** vi losstürzen ● vt (write quickly) hinwerfen

dashboard n Armaturenbrett nt

data npl & sg Daten pl. ~ **processing** n Datenverarbeitung f

date¹ n (fruit) Dattel f

date² n Datum nt; Ⓣ Verabredung f; to ~ bis heute; out of ~ überholt; (expired) ungültig; be up to ~ auf dem Laufenden sein ● vt/i datieren; (Amer Ⓣ: go out with) ausgehen mit

dated a altmodisch

dative a & n (Gram) ~ [case] Dativ m

daub vt beschmieren (with mit); schmieren <paint>

daughter n Tochter f. ~-**in-law** n (pl ~s-in-law) Schwiegertochter f

dawdle vi trödeln

dawn n Morgendämmerung f; at ~ bei Tagesanbruch ● vi anbrechen; it ~ed on me (fig) es ging mir auf

day n Tag m; ~ **by** ~ Tag für Tag; after ~ Tag um Tag; these ~s heutzutage; in those ~s zu der Zeit

day: ~-**dream** n Tagtraum m ● vi [mit offenen Augen] träumen. ~**light** n Tageslicht nt. ~**time** n in the ~time am Tage

daze n in a ~ wie benommen. ~**d** a benommen

dazzle vt blenden

dead a tot; <flower> verwelkt; (numb) taub; ~ **body** Leiche f; ~ **centre** genau in der Mitte ● adv ~ **tired** todmüde; ~ **slow** sehr langsam ● n the ~ pl die Toten; in the ~ of night mitten in der Nacht

deaden vt dämpfen <sound>; betäuben <pain>

dead: ~ **end** n Sackgasse f. ~ **heat** n totes Rennen nt. ~**line** n [letzter] Termin m

deadly a (-ier, -iest) tödlich; (Ⓣ dreary) sterbenslangweilig

deaf a (-er, -est) taub; ~ **and dumb** taubstumm

deaf|en vt betäuben; (permanently) taub machen. ~**ening** a ohrenbetäubend. ~**ness** n Taubheit f

deal n (transaction) Geschäft nt; whose ~? (Cards) wer gibt? a good or great ~ eine Menge; get a raw ~ Ⓣ schlecht wegkommen ● v (pt/pp **dealt**) ● vt (Cards) geben; ~ **out** austeilen ● vi ~ **in** handeln mit; ~ **with** zu tun haben mit; (handle) sich befassen mit; (cope with) fertig werden mit; (be about) handeln von; **that's been dealt with** das ist schon erledigt

dealer n Händler m

dean n Dekan m

dear a (-er, -est) lieb; (expensive) teuer; (in letter) liebe(r,s)/ (formal) sehr geehrte(r,s) ● n Liebe(r) m/f ● int oh ~! oje! ~**ly** adv <love> sehr; <pay> teuer

death n Tod m; **three** ~s **drei** Todesfälle. ~ **certificate** n Sterbeurkunde f

deathly a ~ **silence** Totenstille f ● adv ~ **pale** totenblass

death: ~ **penalty** n Todesstrafe f. ~-**trap** n Todesfalle f

debatable a strittig

debate n Debatte f ● vt/i debattieren

debauchery n Ausschweifung f

debit n ~ [**side**] Soll nt ● vt (pt/pp debited) belasten; abbuchen <sum>

debris n Trümmer pl

debt n Schuld f; in ~ verschuldet. ~ **or** n Schuldner m

debut n Debüt nt

decade n Jahrzehnt nt

decaden|ce n Dekadenz f. ~**t** a dekadent

decaffeinated a koffeinfrei

decay n Verfall m; (rot) Verwesung f; (of tooth) Zahnfäule f ● vi verfallen; (rot) verwesen; <tooth:> schlecht werden

deceased a verstorben ● n the ~**d** der/die Verstorbene

deceit n Täuschung f. ~**ful** a, -**ly** adv unaufrichtig

deceive vt täuschen; (be unfaithful to) betrügen

December n Dezember m

decency n Anstand m

decent a, **-ly** adv anständig

decept|ion n Täuschung f; (fraud) Betrug m. **~ive** a, **-ly** adv täuschend

decide vt entscheiden ● vi sich entscheiden (on für)

decided a, **-ly** adv entschieden

decimal a Dezimal- ● n Dezimalzahl f. **~ point** n Komma nt

decipher vt entziffern

decision n Entscheidung f; (firmness) Entschlossenheit f

decisive a ausschlaggebend; (firm) entschlossen

deck[1] vt schmücken

deck[2] n (Naut) Deck nt; on ~ an Deck; ~ of cards (Amer) [Karten]spiel nt. **~-chair** n Liegestuhl m

declaration n Erklärung f

declare vt erklären; angeben <goods>; **anything to ~?** etwas zu verzollen?

decline n Rückgang m; (in health) Verfall m ● vt ablehnen; (Gram) deklinieren ● vi ablehnen; (fall) sinken; (decrease) nachlassen

décor n Ausstattung f

decorat|e vt (adorn) schmücken; verzieren <cake>; (paint) streichen; (wallpaper) tapezieren; (award medal to) einen Orden verleihen (+ dat). **~ion** n Verzierung f; (medal) Orden m; **~ions** pl Schmuck m. **~ive** a dekorativ. **~or** n painter and **~or** n Maler und Tapezierer m

decoy n Lockvogel m

decrease[1] n Verringerung f; (in number) Rückgang m

decrease[2] vt verringern; herabsetzen <price> ● vi sich verringern <price>; sinken

decrepit a altersschwach

dedicat|e vt widmen; (Relig) weihen. **~ed** a hingebungsvoll; <person> aufopfernd. **~ion** n Hingabe f; (in book) Widmung f

deduce vt folgern (from aus)

deduct vt abziehen

deduction n Abzug m; (conclusion) Folgerung f

deed n Tat f; (Jur) Urkunde f

deep a (-er, -est), **-ly** adv tief; go off the ~ end 🅵 auf die Palme gehen ● adv tief

deepen vt vertiefen

deep-freeze n Gefriertruhe f; (upright) Gefrierschrank m

deer n inv Hirsch m; (roe) Reh nt

deface vt beschädigen

default n win by ~ (Sport) kampflos gewinnen

defeat n Niederlage f; (defeating) Besiegung f; (rejection) Ablehnung f ● vt besiegen; ablehnen <motion>; (frustrate) vereiteln

defect n Fehler m; (Techn) Defekt m. **~ive** a fehlerhaft; (Techn) defekt

defence n Verteidigung f. **~less** a wehrlos

defend vt verteidigen; (justify) rechtfertigen. **~ant** n (Jur) Beklagte(r) m/f; (in criminal court) Angeklagte(r) m/f

defensive a defensiv

defer vt (pt/pp deferred) (postpone) aufschieben

deferen|ce n Ehrerbietung f. **~tial** a, **-ly** adv ehrerbietig

defian|ce n Trotz m; in ~ce of zum Trotz (+ dat). **~t** a, **-ly** adv aufsässig

deficien|cy n Mangel m. **~t** a mangelhaft

deficit n Defizit nt

define vt bestimmen; definieren <word>

definite a, **-ly** adv bestimmt; (certain) sicher

definition n Definition f; (Phot, TV) Schärfe f

definitive a endgültig; (authoritative) maßgeblich

deflat|e vt die Luft auslassen aus. **~ion** n (Comm) Deflation f

deflect vt ablenken

deform|ed a missgebildet. **~ity** n Missbildung f

defraud *vt* betrügen (of um)

defray *vt* bestreiten

defrost *vt* entfrosten; abtauen
<*fridge*>; auftauen <*food*>

deft *a* (-er, -est), **-ly** *adv* geschickt.
~ness *n* Geschicklichkeit *f*

defuse *vt* entschärfen

defy *vt* (*pt/pp* -ied) trotzen (+ *dat*);
widerstehen (+ *dat*) <*attempt*>

degrading *a* entwürdigend

degree *n* Grad *m*; (*Univ*)
akademischer Grad *m*; **20 ~s** 20
Grad

de-ice *vt* enteisen

deity *n* Gottheit *f*

dejected *a*, **-ly** *adv*
niedergeschlagen

delay *n* Verzögerung *f*; (*of train,
aircraft*) Verspätung *f*; **without ~**
unverzüglich ● *vt* aufhalten;
(*postpone*) aufschieben ● *vi* zögern

delegate¹ *n* Delegierte(r) *m/f*

delegat|e² *vt* delegieren. **~ion** *n*
Delegation *f*

delet|e *vt* streichen. **~ion** *n*
Streichung *f*

deliberate *a*, **-ly** *adv* absichtlich;
(*slow*) bedächtig

delicacy *n* Feinheit *f*; Zartheit *f*;
(*food*) Delikatesse *f*

delicate *a* fein; <*fabric, health*>
zart; <*situation*> heikel;
<*mechanism*> empfindlich

delicatessen *n*
Delikatessengeschäft *nt*

delicious *a* köstlich

delight *n* Freude *f* ● *vt* entzücken
● *vi* **~ in** sich erfreuen an (+ *dat*).
~ed *a* hocherfreut; **be ~ed** sich
sehr freuen. **~ful** *a* reizend

delinquent *a* straffällig ● *n*
Straffällige(r) *m/f*

deli|rious *a* **be ~rious** im Delirium
sein. **~rium** *n* Delirium *nt*

deliver *vt* liefern; zustellen <*post,
newspaper*>; halten <*speech*>;
überbringen <*message*>; versetzen
<*blow*>; (*set free*) befreien; **~ a baby**
ein Kind zur Welt bringen. **~y** *n*
Lieferung *f*; (*of post*) Zustellung *f*;

(*Med*) Entbindung *f*; **cash on ~y** per
Nachnahme

delta *n* Delta *nt*

deluge *n* Flut *f*; (*heavy rain*)
schwerer Guss *m*

delusion *n* Täuschung *f*

de luxe *a* Luxus-

demand *n* Forderung *f*; (*Comm*)
Nachfrage *f*; **in ~** gefragt; **on ~** auf
Verlangen ● *vt* verlangen, fordern
(of/from von). **~ing** *a* anspruchsvoll

demented *a* verrückt

demister *n* (*Auto*) Defroster *m*

demo *n* (*pl* **~s**) 🄸 Demonstration *f*

democracy *n* Demokratie *f*

democrat *n* Demokrat *m*. **~ic** *a*,
-ally *adv* demokratisch

demo|lish *vt* abbrechen; (*destroy*)
zerstören. **~lition** *n* Abbruch *m*

demon *n* Dämon *m*

demonstrat|e *vt* beweisen;
vorführen <*appliance*> ● *vi* (*Pol*)
demonstrieren. **~ion** *n* Vorführung
f; (*Pol*) Demonstration *f*

demonstrator *n* Vorführer *m*;
(*Pol*) Demonstrant *m*

demoralize *vt* demoralisieren

demote *vt* degradieren

demure *a*, **-ly** *adv* sittsam

den *n* Höhle *f*; (*room*) Bude *f*

denial *n* Leugnen *nt*; **official ~**
Dementi *nt*

denim *n* Jeansstoff *m*; **~s** *pl* Jeans
pl

Denmark *n* Dänemark *nt*

denounce *vt* denunzieren;
(*condemn*) verurteilen

dens|e *a* (-r, -st), **-ly** *adv* dicht; (🄸
stupid) blöd[e]. **~ity** *n* Dichte *f*

dent *n* Delle *f*, Beule *f* ● *vt*
einbeulen; **~ed** *a* verbeult

dental *a* Zahn-; <*treatment*>
zahnärztlich. **~ floss** *n* Zahnseide *f*.
~ surgeon *n* Zahnarzt *m*

dentist *n* Zahnarzt *m*/-ärztin *f*. **~ry**
n Zahnmedizin *f*

denture *n* Zahnprothese *f*; **~s** *pl*
künstliches Gebiss *nt*

deny *vt* (*pt/pp* **-ied**) leugnen; (*officially*) dementieren; ∼ s.o. sth jdm etw verweigern

deodorant *n* Deodorant *nt*

depart *vi* abfahren; (*Aviat*) abfliegen; (*go away*) weggehen/ -fahren; (*deviate*) abweichen (**from** von)

department *n* Abteilung *f*; (*Pol*) Ministerium *nt*. ∼ **store** *n* Kaufhaus *nt*

departure *n* Abfahrt *f*; (*Aviat*) Abflug *m*; (*from rule*) Abweichung *f*

depend *vi* abhängen (**on** von); (*rely*) sich verlassen (**on** auf + *acc*); it all ∼s das kommt darauf an. ∼**able** *a* zuverlässig. ∼**ant** *n* Abhängige(r) *m/f*. ∼**ence** *n* Abhängigkeit *f*. ∼**ent** *a* abhängig (**on** von)

depict *vt* darstellen

deplor|able *a* bedauerlich. ∼**e** *vt* bedauern

deploy *vt* (*Mil*) einsetzen

depopulate *vt* entvölkern

deport *vt* deportieren, ausweisen. ∼**ation** *n* Ausweisung *f*

depose *vt* absetzen

deposit *n* Anzahlung *f*; (*against damage*) Kaution *f*; (*on bottle*) Pfand *nt*; (*sediment*) Bodensatz *m*; (*Geol*) Ablagerung *f* ● *vt* (*pt/pp* **deposited**) legen; (*for safety*) deponieren; (*Geol*) ablagern. ∼ **account** *n* Sparkonto *nt*

depot *n* Depot *nt*; (*Amer: railway station*) Bahnhof *m*

deprave *vt* verderben. ∼**d** *a* verkommen

depreciat|e *vi* an Wert verlieren. ∼**ion** *n* Wertminderung *f*; (*Comm*) Abschreibung *f*

depress *vt* deprimieren; (*press down*) herunterdrücken. ∼**ed** *a* deprimiert. ∼**ing** *a* deprimierend. ∼**ion** *n* Vertiefung *f*; (*Med*) Depression *f*; (*Meteorol*) Tief *nt*

deprivation *n* Entbehrung *f*

deprive *vt* ∼ s.o. of sth jdm etw entziehen. ∼**d** *a* benachteiligt

depth *n* Tiefe *f*; in ∼ gründlich; in the ∼s of winter im tiefsten Winter

deputize *vi* ∼ for vertreten

deputy *n* Stellvertreter *m* ● *attrib* stellvertretend

derail *vt* be ∼ed entgleisen. ∼**ment** *n* Entgleisung *f*

derelict *a* verfallen; (*abandoned*) verlassen

derisory *a* höhnisch; <*offer*> lächerlich

derivation *n* Ableitung *f*

derivative *a* abgeleitet ● *n* Ableitung *f*

derive *vt/i* (*obtain*) gewinnen (**from** aus); be ∼d from <*word:*> hergeleitet sein aus

derogatory *a* abfällig

derv *n* Diesel[kraftstoff] *m*

descend *vt/i* hinunter-/ heruntergehen; <*vehicle, lift:*> hinunter-/herunterfahren; be ∼ed from abstammen von. ∼**ant** *n* Nachkomme *m*

descent *n* Abstieg *m*; (*lineage*) Abstammung *f*

describe *vt* beschreiben

descrip|tion *n* Beschreibung *f*; (*sort*) Art *f*. ∼**tive** *a* beschreibend; (*vivid*) anschaulich

desecrate *vt* entweihen

desert¹ *n* Wüste *f*. ∼ **island** verlassene Insel *f*

desert² *vt* verlassen ● *vt* desertieren. ∼**ed** *a* verlassen. ∼**er** *n* (*Mil*) Deserteur *m*. ∼**ion** *n* Fahnenflucht *f*

deserv|e *vt* verdienen. ∼**edly** *adv* verdientermaßen. ∼**ing** *a* verdienstvoll

design *n* Entwurf *m*; (*pattern*) Muster *nt*; (*construction*) Konstruktion *f*; (*aim*) Absicht *f* ● *vt* entwerfen; (*construct*) konstruieren; be ∼ed for bestimmt sein für

designer *n* Designer *m*; (*Techn*) Konstrukteur *m*; (*Theat*) Bühnenbildner *m*

desirable *a* wünschenswert; (*sexually*) begehrenswert

desire *n* Wunsch *m*; (*longing*) Verlangen *nt* (**for** nach); (*sexual*)

Begierde *f* ● *vt* [sich (*dat*)] wünschen; (*sexually*) begehren

desk *n* Schreibtisch *m*; (*Sch*) Pult *nt*

desolat|e *a* trostlos. **~ion** *n* Trostlosigkeit *f*

despair *n* Verzweiflung *f*; in **~** verzweifelt ● *vi* verzweifeln

desperat|e *a*, **-ly** *adv* verzweifelt; (*urgent*) dringend; be **~e** for dringend brauchen. **~ion** *n* Verzweiflung *f*

despicable *a* verachtenswert

despise *vt* verachten

despite *prep* trotz (+ *gen*)

despondent *a* niedergeschlagen

dessert *n* Dessert *nt*, Nachtisch *m*. **~ spoon** *n* Dessertlöffel *m*

destination *n* [Reise]ziel *nt*; (*of goods*) Bestimmungsort *m*

destiny *n* Schicksal *nt*

destitute *a* völlig mittellos

destroy *vt* zerstören; (*totally*) vernichten. **~er** *n* (*Naut*) Zerstörer *m*

destruc|tion *n* Zerstörung *f*; Vernichtung *f*. **-tive** *a* zerstörerisch; (*fig*) destruktiv

detach *vt* abnehmen; (*tear off*) abtrennen. **~able** *a* abnehmbar. **~ed** *a* **~ed house** Einzelhaus *nt*

detail *n* Einzelheit *f*, Detail *nt*; in **~** ausführlich ● *vt* einzeln aufführen. **~ed** *a* ausführlich

detain *vt* aufhalten; <*police:*> in Haft behalten; (*take into custody*) in Haft nehmen

detect *vt* entdecken; (*perceive*) wahrnehmen. **~ion** *n* Entdeckung *f*

detective *n* Detektiv *m*. **~ story** *n* Detektivroman *m*

detention *n* Haft *f*; (*Sch*) Nachsitzen *nt*

deter *vt* (*pt/pp* **deterred**) abschrecken; (*prevent*) abhalten

detergent *n* Waschmittel *nt*

deteriorat|e *vi* sich verschlechtern. **~ion** *n* Verschlechterung *f*

determination *n* Entschlossenheit *f*

determine *vt* bestimmen. **~d** *a* entschlossen

deterrent *n* Abschreckungsmittel *nt*

detest *vt* verabscheuen. **~able** *a* abscheulich

detonate *vt* zünden

detour *n* Umweg *m*

detract *vi* **~ from** beeinträchtigen

detriment *n* to the **~** (of) zum Schaden (+ *gen*). **~al** *a* schädlich (to *dat*)

deuce *n* (*Tennis*) Einstand *m*

devaluation *n* Abwertung *f*

devalue *vt* abwerten <*currency*>

devastat|e *vt* verwüsten. **~ing** *a* verheerend. **~ion** *n* Verwüstung *f*

develop *vt* entwickeln; bekommen <*illness*>; erschließen <*area*> ● *vi* sich entwickeln (into zu). **~er** *n* [property] **~er** Bodenspekulant *m*

development *n* Entwicklung *f*

deviat|e *vi* abweichen. **~ion** *n* Abweichung *f*

device *n* Gerät *nt*; (*fig*) Mittel *nt*

devil *n* Teufel *m*. **~ish** *a* teuflisch

devious *a* verschlagen

devise *vt* sich (*dat*) ausdenken

devot|e *vt* widmen (to *dat*). **~ed** *a*, **-ly** *adv* ergeben; <*care*> liebevoll; be **~ed to s.o.** sehr an jdm hängen

devotion *n* Hingabe *f*

devour *vt* verschlingen

devout *a* fromm

dew *n* Tau *m*

dexterity *n* Geschicklichkeit *f*

diabet|es *n* Zuckerkrankheit *f*. **~ic** *n* Diabetiker(in) *m(f)*

diabolical *a* teuflisch

diagnose *vt* diagnostizieren

diagnosis *n* (*pl* **-oses**) Diagnose *f*

diagonal, **-ly** *adv* diagonal ● *n* Diagonale *f*

diagram *n* Diagramm *nt*

dial *n* (*of clock*) Zifferblatt *nt*; (*Techn*) Skala *f*; (*Teleph*) Wählscheibe *f* ● *vt/i* (*pt/pp* **dialled**) (*Teleph*) wählen; **~ direct** durchwählen

dialect *n* Dialekt *m*

dialling: ~ **code** n
Vorwahlnummer f. ~ **tone** n
Amtszeichen nt

dialogue n Dialog m

diameter n Durchmesser m

diamond n Diamant m; (cut)
Brillant m; (shape) Raute f; ~s pl
(Cards) Karo nt

diaper n (Amer) Windel f

diarrhoea n Durchfall m

diary n Tagebuch nt; (for
appointments) [Termin]kalender m

dice n inv Würfel m

dictat|e vt/i diktieren. ~ion n
Diktat nt

dictator n Diktator m. ~ial a
diktatorisch. ~ship n Diktatur f

dictionary n Wörterbuch nt

did see do

didn't = did not

die¹ n (Techn) Prägestempel m;
(metal mould) Gussform f

die² vi (pres p dying) sterben (of an +
dat); <plant, animal:> eingehen;
<flower:> verwelken; **be dying to do
sth** 🔢 darauf brennen, etw zu tun;
be dying for sth 🔢 sich nach etw
sehnen. ~ **down** vi nachlassen;
<fire:> herunterbrennen. ~ **out** vi
aussterben

diesel n Diesel m. ~ **engine** n
Dieselmotor m

diet n Kost f; (restricted) Diät f; (for
slimming) Schlankheitskur f; **be on a**
~ Diät leben; eine Schlankheitskur
machen ● vi diät leben; eine
Schlankheitskur machen

differ vi sich unterscheiden;
(disagree) verschiedener Meinung
sein

differen|ce n Unterschied m;
(disagreement)
Meinungsverschiedenheit f. ~t a
andere(r,s); (various) verschiedene;
be ~t anders sein (**from** als)

differential a Differenzial- ● n
Unterschied m; (Techn) Differenzial
nt

differentiate vt/i unterscheiden
(**between** zwischen + dat)

differently adv anders

difficult a schwierig, schwer. ~y n
Schwierigkeit f

diffiden|ce n Zaghaftigkeit f. ~t a
zaghaft

dig n (poke) Stoß m; (remark) spitze
Bemerkung f; (Archaeol) Ausgrabung
f ● vt/i (pt/pp dug, pres p digging)
graben; umgraben <garden>. ~ **out**
vt ausgraben. ~ **up** vt ausgraben;
umgraben <garden>; aufreißen
<street>

digest vt verdauen. ~**ible** a
verdaulich. ~**ion** n Verdauung f

digit n Ziffer f; (finger) Finger m;
(toe) Zehe f

digital a Digital-

dignified a würdevoll

dignity n Würde f

dilapidated a baufällig

dilatory a langsam

dilemma n Dilemma nt

dilettante n Dilettant(in) m(f)

diligen|ce n Fleiß m. ~**t** a, -**ly** adv
fleißig

dilute vt verdünnen

dim a (dimmer, dimmest). -**ly** adv
(weak) schwach; (dark) trüb[e];
(indistinct) undeutlich; (🔢 stupid)
dumm, 🔢 doof ● v (pt/pp dimmed)
● vt dämpfen

dime n (Amer) Zehncentstück nt

dimension n Dimension f; ~s pl
Maße pl

diminutive a winzig ● n
Verkleinerungsform f

dimple n Grübchen nt

din n Krach m, Getöse nt

dine vi speisen. ~**r** n Speisende(r)
m/f; (Amer: restaurant) Esslokal nt

dinghy n Dinghi nt; (inflatable)
Schlauchboot nt

dingy a (-ier, -iest) trübe

dining: ~-**car** n Speisewagen m.
~-**room** n Esszimmer nt. ~-**table**
n Esstisch m

dinner n Abendessen nt; (at midday)
Mittagessen nt; (formal) Essen nt.
~-**jacket** n Smoking m

dinosaur n Dinosaurier m

diocese n Diözese f

dip n (in ground) Senke f; (Culin) Dip m ● v (pt/pp dipped) vt [ein]tauchen; ∼ one's headlights (Auto) [die Scheinwerfer] abblenden ● vi sich senken

diploma n Diplom nt

diplomacy n Diplomatie f

diplomat n Diplomat m. ∼ic a, -ally adv diplomatisch

dip-stick n (Auto) Ölmessstab m

dire a (-r, -st) bitter; <consequences> furchtbar

direct a & adv direkt ● vt (aim) richten (at auf / (fig) an + acc); (control) leiten; (order) anweisen; ∼ a film/play bei einem Film/ Theaterstück Regie führen

direction n Richtung f; (control) Leitung f; (of play, film) Regie f; ∼s pl Anweisungen pl; ∼s for use Gebrauchsanweisung f

directly adv direkt; (at once) sofort

director n (Comm) Direktor m; (of play, film) Regisseur m

directory n Verzeichnis nt; (Teleph) Telefonbuch nt

dirt n Schmutz m; (soil) Erde f; ∼ cheap 🔲 spottbillig

dirty a (-ier, -iest) schmutzig

dis|ability n Behinderung f. ∼abled a [körper]behindert

disadvantage n Nachteil m; at a ∼ im Nachteil. ∼d a benachteiligt

disagree vi nicht übereinstimmen (with mit); I ∼ ich bin anderer Meinung; oysters ∼ with me Austern bekommen mir nicht

disagreeable a unangenehm

disagreement n Meinungsverschiedenheit f

disappear vi verschwinden. ∼ance n Verschwinden nt

disappoint vt enttäuschen. ∼ment n Enttäuschung f

disapproval n Missbilligung f

disapprove vi dagegen sein; ∼ of missbilligen

disarm vt entwaffnen ● vi (Mil) abrüsten. ∼ament n Abrüstung f. ∼ing a entwaffnend

disast|er n Katastrophe f; (accident) Unglück nt. ∼rous a katastrophal

disbelief n Ungläubigkeit f; in ∼ ungläubig

disc n Scheibe f; (record) [Schall]platte f; (CD) CD f

discard vt ablegen; (throw away) wegwerfen

discerning a anspruchsvoll

discharge[1] n Ausstoßen nt; (Naut, Electr) Entladung f; (dismissal) Entlassung f; (Jur) Freispruch m; (Med) Ausfluss m

discharge[2] vt ausstoßen; (Naut, Electr) entladen; (dismiss) entlassen; (Jur) freisprechen <accused>

disciplinary a disziplinarisch

discipline n Disziplin f ● vt Disziplin beibringen (+ dat); (punish) bestrafen

disc jockey n Diskjockey m

disclaim vt abstreiten. ∼er n Verzichterklärung f

disclos|e vt enthüllen. ∼ure n Enthüllung f

disco n 🔲 Disko f

discolour vt verfärben ● vi sich verfärben

discomfort n Beschwerden pl; (fig) Unbehagen nt

disconnect vt trennen; (Electr) ausschalten; (cut supply) abstellen

discontent n Unzufriedenheit f. ∼ed a unzufrieden

discontinue vt einstellen; (Comm) nicht mehr herstellen

discord n Zwietracht f; (Mus & fig) Missklang m

discothèque n Diskothek f

discount n Rabatt m

discourage vt entmutigen; (dissuade) abraten (+ dat)

discourteous a, -ly adv unhöflich

discover vt entdecken. ∼y n Entdeckung f

discreet a, -ly adv diskret

discretion n Diskretion f; (judgement) Ermessen nt

discriminat|e vi unterscheiden (between zwischen + dat); ∼e

against diskriminieren. **~ing** a anspruchsvoll. **~ion** n Diskriminierung f

discus n Diskus m

discuss vt besprechen; (*examine critically*) diskutieren. **~ion** n Besprechung f; Diskussion f

disdain n Verachtung f

disease n Krankheit f

disembark vi an Land gehen

disenchant vt ernüchtern

disengage vt losmachen

disentangle vt entwirren

disfigure vt entstellen

disgrace n Schande f; in ~ in Ungnade ● vt Schande machen (+ dat). **~ful** a schändlich

disgruntled a verstimmt

disguise n Verkleidung f; in ~ verkleidet ● vt verkleiden; verstellen <voice>

disgust n Ekel m; in ~ empört ● vt anekeln; (*appal*) empören. **~ing** a eklig; (*appalling*) abscheulich

dish n Schüssel f; (*shallow*) Schale f; (*small*) Schälchen nt; (*food*) Gericht nt. ~ **out** vt austeilen. ~ **up** vt auftragen

dishcloth n Spültuch nt

dishearten vt entmutigen

dishonest a **-ly** adv unehrlich. **~y** n Unehrlichkeit f

dishonour n Schande f. **~able** a, **-bly** adv unehrenhaft

dishwasher n Geschirrspülmaschine f

disillusion vt ernüchtern. **~ment** n Ernüchterung f

disinfect vt desinfizieren. **~ant** n Desinfektionsmittel nt

disinherit vt enterben

disintegrate vi zerfallen

disjointed a unzusammenhängend

disk n = disc

dislike n Abneigung f ● vt nicht mögen

dislocate vt ausrenken

dislodge vt entfernen

disloyal a, **-ly** adv illoyal. **~ty** n Illoyalität f

dismal a trüb[e]; <person> trübselig

dismantle vt auseinander nehmen; (*take down*) abbauen

dismay n Bestürzung f. **~ed** a bestürzt

dismiss vt entlassen; (*reject*) zurückweisen. **~al** n Entlassung f; Zurückweisung f

disobedien|ce n Ungehorsam m. **~t** a ungehorsam

disobey vt/i nicht gehorchen (+ dat); nicht befolgen <rule>

disorder n Unordnung f; (*Med*) Störung f. **~ly** a unordentlich

disorganized a unorganisiert

disown vt verleugnen

disparaging a, **-ly** adv abschätzig

dispassionate a, **-ly** adv gelassen; (*impartial*) unparteiisch

dispatch n (*Comm*) Versand m; (*Mil*) Nachricht f; (*report*) Bericht m ● vt [ab]senden; (*kill*) töten

dispel vt (pt/pp dispelled) vertreiben

dispensary n Apotheke f

dispense vt austeilen; ~ **with** verzichten auf (+ acc). **~r** n (*device*) Automat m

disperse vt zerstreuen ● vi sich zerstreuen

dispirited a entmutigt

display n Ausstellung f; (*Comm*) Auslage f; (*performance*) Vorführung f ● vt zeigen; ausstellen <goods>

displease vt missfallen (+ dat)

displeasure n Missfallen nt

disposable a Wegwerf-; <income> verfügbar

disposal n Beseitigung f; be at s.o.'s ~ jdm zur Verfügung stehen

dispose vi ~ **of** beseitigen; (*deal with*) erledigen

disposition n Veranlagung f; (*nature*) Wesensart f

disproportionate a, **-ly** adv unverhältnismäßig

disprove vt widerlegen

dispute n Disput m; (*quarrel*) Streit m ● vt bestreiten

disqualification n Disqualifikation f

disqualify vt disqualifizieren; ~ s.o. from driving jdm den Führerschein entziehen

disregard vt nicht beachten

disrepair n fall into ~ verfallen

disreputable a verrufen

disrepute n Verruf m

disrespect n Respektlosigkeit f. ~**ful** a, -**ly** adv respektlos

disrupt vt stören. ~**ion** n Störung f

dissatisfaction n Unzufriedenheit f

dissatisfied a unzufrieden

dissect vt zergliedern; (Med) sezieren. ~**ion** n Zergliederung f; (Med) Sektion f

dissent n Nichtübereinstimmung f ● vi nicht übereinstimmen

dissident n Dissident m

dissimilar a unähnlich (**to** dat)

dissociate vt ~ oneself sich distanzieren (**from** von)

dissolute a zügellos; <life> ausschweifend

dissolve vt auflösen ● vi sich auflösen

dissuade vt abbringen (**from** von)

distance n Entfernung f; long/short ~ lange/kurze Strecke f; in the/from a ~ in/aus der Ferne

distant a fern; (aloof) kühl; <relative> entfernt

distasteful a unangenehm

distil vt (pt/pp distilled) brennen; (Chem) destillieren. ~**lery** n Brennerei f

distinct a deutlich; (different) verschieden. ~**ion** n Unterschied m; (Sch) Auszeichnung f. ~**ive** a kennzeichnend; (unmistakable) unverwechselbar. ~**ly** adv deutlich

distinguish vt/i unterscheiden; (make out) erkennen; ~ oneself auszeichnen. ~**ed** a angesehen; <appearance> distinguiert

distort vt verzerren; (fig) verdrehen. ~**ion** n Verzerrung f; (fig) Verdrehung f

distract vt ablenken. ~**ion** n Ablenkung f; (despair) Verzweiflung f

distraught a [völlig] aufgelöst

distress n Kummer m; (pain) Schmerz m; (poverty, danger) Not f ● vt Kummer/Schmerz bereiten (+ dat); (sadden) bekümmern; (shock) erschüttern. ~**ing** a schmerzlich; (shocking) erschütternd

distribut|e vt verteilen; (Comm) vertreiben. ~**ion** n Verteilung f; Vertrieb m. ~**or** n Verteiler m

district n Gegend f; (Admin) Bezirk m

distrust n Misstrauen nt ● vt misstrauen (+ dat). ~**ful** a misstrauisch

disturb vt stören; (perturb) beunruhigen; (touch) anrühren. ~**ance** n Unruhe f; (interruption) Störung f. ~**ed** a beunruhigt; [mentally] ~**ed** geistig gestört. ~**ing** a beunruhigend

disused a stillgelegt; (empty) leer

ditch n Graben m ● vt (🄕 abandon) fallen lassen <plan>

dither vi zaudern

ditto n dito; (🄕) ebenfalls

dive n [Kopf]sprung m; (Aviat) Sturzflug m; (🄕 place) Spelunke f ● vi einen Kopfsprung machen; (when in water) tauchen; (Aviat) einen Sturzflug machen; (🄕 rush) stürzen

diver n Taucher m; (Sport) [Kunst]springer m

diverse a verschieden

diversify vt/i (pt/pp -ied) variieren; (Comm) diversifizieren

diversion n Umleitung f; (distraction) Ablenkung f

diversity n Vielfalt f

divert vt umleiten; ablenken <attention>; (entertain) unterhalten

divide vt teilen; (separate) trennen; (Math) dividieren (**by** durch) ● vi sich teilen

dividend n Dividende f

divine a göttlich

diving n (Sport) Kunstspringen nt. ~-**board** n Sprungbrett nt

divinity n Göttlichkeit f; (subject) Theologie f

d

division n Teilung f; (separation)
Trennung f; (Math, Mil) Division f;
(Parl) Hammelsprung m; (line)
Trennlinie f; (group) Abteilung f

divorce n Scheidung f ● vt sich
scheiden lassen von. ~**d** a
geschieden; get ~**d** sich scheiden
lassen

DIY abbr of do-it-yourself

dizziness n Schwindel m

dizzy a (-ier, -iest) schwindlig; I feel
~ mir ist schwindlig

. . . .

do

   3 sg pres tense **does**; pt **did**; pp
   done

● transitive verb

····▸ (perform) machen <homework,
housework, exam, handstand etc>;
tun <duty, favour, something,
nothing>; vorführen <trick, dance>;
durchführen <test>. **what are you
doing?** was tust od machst du? **what
can I do for you?** was kann ich für
Sie tun? **do something!** tu doch
etwas! **have you nothing better to
do?** hast du nichts Besseres zu tun?
do the washing-up /cleaning
abwaschen/sauber machen

····▸ (as job) **what does your father do?**
was macht dein Vater?; was ist dein
Vater von Beruf?

····▸ (clean) putzen; (arrange)
[zurecht]machen <hair>

····▸ (cook) kochen; (roast, fry) braten.
well done (meat) durch[gebraten]. **the
potatoes aren't done yet** die
Kartoffeln sind noch nicht richtig
durch

····▸ (solve) lösen <problem, riddle>;
machen <puzzle>

····▸ (🄵 swindle) reinlegen. **do s.o. out
of sth** jdn um etw bringen

● intransitive verb

····▸ (with as or adverb) es tun; es
machen. **do as they do** mach es wie
sie. **he can do as he likes** er kann
tun od machen, was er will. **you did
well** du hast es gut gemacht

····▸ (get on) vorankommen; (in exams)
abschneiden. **do well/badly at school**
gut/schlecht in der Schule sein. **how**

are you doing? wie geht's dir? **how
do you do?** (formal) guten Tag!

····▸ **will do** (serve purpose) es tun;
(suffice) [aus]reichen; (be suitable)
gehen. **that won't do** das geht nicht.
that will do! jetzt aber genug!

● auxiliary verb

····▸ (in questions) **do you know him?**
kennst du ihn? **what does he want?**
was will er?

····▸ (in negation) **I don't** or **do not wish
to take part** ich will nicht
teilnehmen. **don't be so noisy!** seid
[doch] nicht so laut!

····▸ (as verb substitute) **you mustn't
act as he does** du darfst nicht so wie
er handeln. **come in, do!** komm doch
herein!

····▸ (in tag questions) **don't you,
doesn't he** etc. nicht wahr. **you went
to Paris, didn't you?** du warst in
Paris, nicht wahr?

····▸ (in short questions) **Does he live in
London?** — **Yes, he does** Wohnt er
in London? — Ja [, stimmt]

····▸ (for special emphasis) **I do love
Greece** Griechenland gefällt mir
wirklich gut

····▸ (for inversion) **little did he know
that** ... er hatte keine Ahnung, dass
...

● noun

   pl **do's** or **dos**

····▸ (🄵 celebration) Feier f

● phrasal verbs● **do away with** vt
abschaffen. ● **do for** vt 🄵: **do for
s.o.** jdn fertig machen 🄵; **be done
for** erledigt sein. ● **do in** vt (🄴 kill)
kaltmachen 🄴. ● **do up** vt (fasten)
zumachen; binden <shoe-lace, bow-
tie>; (wrap) einpacken; (renovate)
renovieren. ● **do with** vt: **I could do
with** ... ich brauche .... ● **do
without** vt: **do without sth** auf etw
(acc) verzichten; vi darauf verzichten

docile a fügsam

dock[1] n (Jur) Anklagebank f

dock[2] n Dock nt ● vi anlegen. ~**er** n
Hafenarbeiter m. ~**yard** n Werft f

doctor n Arzt m/ Ärztin f; (Univ)
Doktor m ● vt kastrieren; (spay)
sterilisieren

doctrine n Lehre f

document n Dokument nt. **~ary** a Dokumentar- ● n Dokumentarbericht m; (film) Dokumentarfilm m

dodge n 🔲 Trick m, Kniff m ● vt/i ausweichen (+ dat)

dodgy a (-ier, -iest) 🔲 (awkward) knifflig; (dubious) zweifelhaft

doe n Ricke f; (rabbit) [Kaninchen]weibchen nt

does see do

doesn't = does not

dog n Hund m

dog: **~-biscuit** n Hundekuchen m. **~-collar** n Hundehalsband nt; (Relig 🔲) Kragen m eines Geistlichen. **~-eared** a be **~-eared** Eselsohren haben

dogged a, -ly adv beharrlich

dogma n Dogma nt. **~tic** a dogmatisch

do-it-yourself n Heimwerken nt. **~ shop** n Heimwerkerladen m

doldrums npl be in the **~** niedergeschlagen sein; <business:> daniederliegen

dole n 🔲 Stempelgeld nt; be on the **~** arbeitslos sein ● vt **~ out** austeilen

doll n Puppe f ● vt 🔲 **~ oneself up** sich herausputzen

dollar n Dollar m

dolphin n Delphin m

domain n Gebiet nt

dome n Kuppel m

domestic a häuslich; (Pol) Innen-; (Comm) Binnen-. **~ animal** n Haustier nt. **~ flight** n Inlandflug m

dominant a vorherrschend

dominat|e vt beherrschen ● vi dominieren. **~ion** n Vorherrschaft f

domineering a herrschsüchtig

domino n (pl -es) Dominostein m; **~es** sg (game) Domino nt

donat|e vt spenden. **~ion** n Spende f

done see do

donkey n Esel m; **~'s years** 🔲 eine Ewigkeit. **~-work** n Routinearbeit f

donor n Spender(in) m(f)

don't = do not

doom n Schicksal nt; (ruin) Verhängnis nt

door n Tür f; out of **~s** im Freien

door: **~man** n Portier m. **~mat** n [Fuß]abtreter m. **~step** n Türschwelle f; on the **~step** vor der Tür. **~way** n Türöffnung f

dope n 🔲 Drogen pl; (🔲 information) Informationen pl; (🔲 idiot) Trottel m ● vt betäuben; (Sport) dopen

dormant a ruhend

dormitory n Schlafsaal m

dormouse n Haselmaus f

dosage n Dosierung f

dose n Dosis f

dot n Punkt m; on the **~** pünktlich. **~-com** n Dot-com-Firma f

dote vi **~ on** vernarrt sein in (+ acc)

dotted a **~ line** punktierte Linie f; be **~ with** bestreut sein mit

dotty a (-ier, -iest) 🔲 verdreht

double a & adv doppelt; <bed, chin> Doppel-; <flower> gefüllt ● n das Doppelte; (person) Doppelgänger m; **~s** pl (Tennis) Doppel nt; ● vt verdoppeln; (fold) falten ● vi sich verdoppeln. **~ up** vi sich krümmen (with vor + dat)

double: **~-bass** n Kontrabass m. **~-breasted** a zweireihig. **~-cross** vt ein Doppelspiel treiben mit. **~-decker** n Doppeldecker m. **~ glazing** n Doppelverglasung f. **~ room** n Doppelzimmer nt

doubly adv doppelt

doubt n Zweifel m ● vt bezweifeln. **~ful** a, -ly adv zweifelhaft; (disbelieving) skeptisch. **~less** adv zweifellos

dough n [fester] Teig m; (🔲 money) Pinke f. **~nut** n Berliner [Pfannkuchen] m

dove n Taube f

dowdy a (-ier, -iest) unschick

down[1] n (feathers) Daunen pl

down[2] adv unten; (with movement) nach unten; go **~** hinuntergehen; come **~** herunterkommen; **~ there**

da unten; **£50** ~ £50 Anzahlung; ~! (*to dog*) Platz! ~ **with** ...! nieder mit ...! ● *prep* ~ **the road/stairs** die Straße/Treppe hinunter; ~ **the river** den Fluss abwärts ● *vt* 🔲 (*drink*) runterkippen; ~ **tools** die Arbeit niederlegen

down: ~**cast** *a* niedergeschlagen. ~**fall** *n* Sturz *m*; (*ruin*) Ruin *m*. ~**hearted** *a* entmutigt. ~**hill** *adv* bergab. ~ ~ **payment** *n* Anzahlung *f*. ~**pour** *n* Platzregen *m*. ~**right** *a* & *adv* ausgesprochen. ~**stairs** *adv* unten; <*go*> nach unten ● *a* im Erdgeschoss. ~**stream** *adv* stromabwärts. ~**-to-earth** *a* sachlich. ~**town** *adv* (*Amer*) im Stadtzentrum. ~**ward** *a* nach unten; <*slope*> abfallend ● *adv* ~**[s]** abwärts, nach unten

doze *n* Nickerchen *nt* ● *vi* dösen. ~ **off** *vi* einnicken

dozen *n* Dutzend *nt*

Dr *abbr of* **doctor**

draft[1] *n* Entwurf *m*; (*Comm*) Tratte *f*; (*Amer Mil*) Einberufung *f* ● *vt* entwerfen; (*Amer Mil*) einberufen

draft[2] *n* (*Amer*) = **draught**

drag *n* **in** ~ 🔲 <*man*> als Frau gekleidet ● *vt* (*pt/pp* **dragged**) schleppen; absuchen <*river*>. ~ **on** *vi* sich in die Länge ziehen

dragon *n* Drache *m*. ~**-fly** *n* Libelle *f*

drain *n* Abfluss *m*; (*underground*) Kanal *m*; **the** ~**s** die Kanalisation ● *vt* entwässern <*land*>; ablassen <*liquid*>; das Wasser ablassen aus <*tank*>; abgießen <*vegetables*>; austrinken <*glass*> ● *vi* ~ **[away]** ablaufen

drain|age *n* Kanalisation *f*; (*of land*) Dränage *f*. ~**ing board** *n* Abtropfbrett *nt*. ~**-pipe** *n* Abflussrohr *nt*

drake *n* Enterich *m*

drama *n* Drama *nt*

dramatic *a*, **-ally** *adv* dramatisch

dramat|ist *n* Dramatiker *m*. ~**ize** *vt* für die Bühne bearbeiten; (*fig*) dramatisieren

drank *see* **drink**

drape *n* (*Amer*) Vorhang *m* ● *vt* drapieren

drastic *a*, **-ally** *adv* drastisch

draught *n* [Luft]zug *m*; ~**s** *sg* (*game*) Damespiel *nt*; **there is a** ~ es zieht

draught beer *n* Bier *nt* vom Fass

draughty *a* zugig

draw *n* Attraktion *f*; (*Sport*) Unentschieden *nt*; (*in lottery*) Ziehung *f* ● *v* (*pt* **drew**, *pp* **drawn**) ● *vt* ziehen; (*attract*) anziehen; zeichnen <*picture*>; abheben <*money*>; ~ **the curtains** die Vorhänge zuziehen/ (*back*) aufziehen ● *vi* (*Sport*) unentschieden spielen. ~ **back** *vt* zurückziehen ● *vi* (*recoil*) zurückweichen. ~ **in** *vt* einziehen ● *vi* einfahren. ~ **out** *vt* herausziehen; abheben <*money*> ● *vi* ausfahren. ~ **up** *vt* aufsetzen <*document*>; herrücken <*chair*> ● *vi* [an]halten

draw: ~**back** *n* Nachteil *m*. ~**bridge** *n* Zugbrücke *f*

drawer *n* Schublade *f*

drawing *n* Zeichnung *f*

drawing: ~**-board** *n* Reißbrett *nt*. ~**-pin** *n* Reißzwecke *f*. ~**-room** *n* Wohnzimmer *nt*

drawl *n* schleppende Aussprache *f*

drawn *see* **draw**

dread *n* Furcht *f* (**of** vor + *dat*) ● *vt* fürchten. ~**ful** *a*, **-fully** *adv* fürchterlich

dream *n* Traum *m* ● *vt/i* (*pt/pp* **dreamt** *or* **dreamed**) träumen (**about/ of** von)

dreary *a* (**-ier**, **-iest**) trüb[e]; (*boring*) langweilig

dregs *npl* Bodensatz *m*

drench *vt* durchnässen

dress *n* Kleid *nt*; (*clothing*) Kleidung *f* ● *vt* anziehen; (*Med*) verbinden; ~ **oneself**, **get** ~**ed** sich anziehen ● *vi* sich anziehen. ~ **up** *vi* sich schön anziehen; (*in disguise*) sich verkleiden (**as** als)

dress: ~ **circle** *n* (*Theat*) erster Rang *m*. ~**er** *n* (*furniture*) Anrichte *f*; (*Amer: dressing-table*) Frisiertisch *m*

dressing *n* (*Culin*) Soße *f*; (*Med*) Verband *m*

dressing: **~-gown** *n* Morgenmantel *m*. **~-room** *n* Ankleidezimmer *nt*; (*Theat*) [Künstler]garderobe *f*. **~-table** *n* Frisiertisch *m*

dress: **~maker** *n* Schneiderin *f*. **~ rehearsal** *n* Generalprobe *f*

drew *see* draw

dried *a* getrocknet; **~ fruit** Dörrobst *nt*

drier *n* Trockner *m*

drift *n* Abtrift *f*; (*of snow*) Schneewehe *f*; (*meaning*) Sinn *m* ● *vi* treiben; (*off course*) abtreiben; <*snow:*> Wehen bilden; (*fig*) <*person:*> sich treiben lassen

drill *n* Bohrer *m*; (*Mil*) Drill *m* ● *vt/i* bohren (**for** nach); (*Mil*) drillen

drily *adv* trocken

drink *n* Getränk *nt*; (*alcoholic*) Drink *m*; (*alcohol*) Alkohol *m* ● *vt/i* (*pt* **drank**, *pp* **drunk**) trinken. **~ up** *vt/i* austrinken

drink|able *a* trinkbar. **~er** *n* Trinker *m*

drinking-water *n* Trinkwasser *nt*

drip *n* Tropfen *nt*; (*drop*) Tropfen *m*; (*Med*) Tropf *m*; (🔢 *person*) Niete *f* ● *vi* (*pt/pp* **dripped**) tropfen

drive *n* [Auto]fahrt *f*; (*entrance*) Einfahrt *f*; (*energy*) Elan *m*; (*Psych*) Trieb *m*; (*Pol*) Aktion *f*; (*Sport*) Treibschlag *m*; (*Techn*) Antrieb *m* ● *v* (*pt* **drove**, *pp* **driven**) ● *vt* treiben; fahren <*car*>; (*Sport: hit*) schlagen; (*Techn*) antreiben; **~ s.o. mad** 🔢 jdn verrückt machen; **what are you driving at?** 🔢 worauf willst du hinaus? ● *vi* fahren. **~ away** *vt* vertreiben ● *vi* abfahren. **~ off** *vt* vertreiben ● *vi* abfahren. **~ on** *vi* weiterfahren. **~ up** *vi* vorfahren

drivel *n* 🔢 Quatsch *m*

driven *see* drive

driver *n* Fahrer(in) *m(f)*; (*of train*) Lokführer *m*

driving: **~ lesson** *n* Fahrstunde *f*. **~ licence** *n* Führerschein *m*. **~ school** *n* Fahrschule *f*. **~ test** *n* Fahrprüfung *f*

drizzle *n* Nieselregen *m* ● *vi* nieseln

drone *n* (*sound*) Brummen *nt*

droop *vi* herabhängen

drop *n* Tropfen *m*; (*fall*) Fall *m*; (*in price, temperature*) Rückgang *m* ● *v* (*pt/pp* **dropped**) ● *vt* fallen lassen; abwerfen <*bomb*>; (*omit*) auslassen; (*give up*) aufgeben ● *vi* fallen; (*fall lower*) sinken; <*wind:*> nachlassen. **~ in** *vi* vorbeikommen. **~ off** *vt* absetzen <*person*> ● *vi* abfallen; (*fall asleep*) einschlafen. **~ out** *vi* herausfallen; (*give up*) aufgeben

drought *n* Dürre *f*

drove *see* drive

drown *vi* ertrinken ● *vt* ertränken; übertönen <*noise*>; **be ~ed** ertrinken

drowsy *a* schläfrig

drudgery *n* Plackerei *f*

drug *n* Droge *f* ● *vt* (*pt/pp* **drugged**) betäuben

drug: **~ addict** *n* Drogenabhängige(r) *m/f*. **~store** *n* (*Amer*) Drogerie *f*; (*dispensing*) Apotheke *f*

drum *n* Trommel *f*; (*for oil*) Tonne *f* ● *v* (*pt/pp* **drummed**) ● *vi* trommeln ● *vt* **~sth into s.o.** 🔢 jdm etw einbläuen. **~mer** *n* Trommler *m*; (*in pop-group*) Schlagzeuger *m*. **~stick** *n* Trommelschlegel *m*; (*Culin*) Keule *f*

drunk *see* drink ● *a* betrunken; **get ~** sich betrinken ● *n* Betrunkene(r) *m*

drunk|ard *n* Trinker *m*. **~en** *a* betrunken

dry *a* (**drier, driest**) trocken ● *vt/i* trocknen. **~ up** *vt/i* austrocknen

dry: **~-clean** *vt* chemisch reinigen. **~-cleaner's** *n* (*shop*) chemische Reinigung *f*. **~ness** *n* Trockenheit *f*

dual *a* doppelt

dual carriageway *n* ≈ Schnellstraße *f*

dubious *a* zweifelhaft

duchess *n* Herzogin *f*

duck n Ente f ● vt (in water) untertauchen ● vi sich ducken

duct n Rohr nt; (Anat) Gang m

dud a 🄸 nutzlos; <coin> falsch; <cheque> ungedeckt; (forged) gefälscht

due a angemessen; be ~ fällig sein; <baby:> erwartet werden; <train:> planmäßig ankommen; ~ to (owing to) wegen (+ gen); be ~ to zurückzuführen sein auf (+ acc) ● adv ~ west genau westlich

duel n Duell nt

duet n Duo nt; (vocal) Duett nt

dug see dig

duke n Herzog m

dull a (-er, -est) (overcast, not bright) trüb[e]; (not shiny) matt; <sound> dumpf; (boring) langweilig; (stupid) schwerfällig

duly adv ordnungsgemäß

dumb a (-er, -est) stumm

dummy n (tailor's) [Schneider]puppe f; (for baby) Schnuller m; (Comm) Attrappe f

dump n Abfallhaufen m; (for refuse) Müllhalde f, Deponie f, (🄸 town) Kaff nt; be down in the ~s 🄸 deprimiert sein ● vt abladen

dumpling n Kloß m

dunce n Dummkopf m

dune n Düne f

dung n Mist m

dungarees npl Latzhose f

dungeon n Verlies nt

dunk vt eintunken

duo n Paar nt; (Mus) Duo nt

dupe n Betrogene(r) m/f ● vt betrügen

duplicate[1] n Doppel nt; in ~ in doppelter Ausfertigung f

duplicate[2] vt kopieren; (do twice) zweimal machen

durable a haltbar

duration n Dauer f

during prep während (+ gen)

dusk n [Abend]dämmerung f

dust n Staub m ● vt abstauben; (sprinkle) bestäuben (with mit) ● vi Staub wischen

dust: ~bin n Mülltonne f. ~cart n Müllwagen m. ~er n Staubtuch nt. ~jacket n Schutzumschlag m. ~man n Müllmann m. ~pan n Kehrschaufel f

dusty a (-ier, -iest) staubig

Dutch a holländisch ● n (Lang) Holländisch nt; the ~ pl die Holländer. ~man n Holländer m

dutiful a, -ly adv pflichtbewusst

duty n Pflicht f; (task) Aufgabe f; (tax) Zoll m; be on ~ Dienst haben. ~-free a zollfrei

duvet n Steppdecke f

dwarf n (pl -s or dwarves) Zwerg m

dwell vi (pt/pp dwelt); ~ on (fig) verweilen bei. ~ing n Wohnung f

dwindle vi abnehmen, schwinden

dye n Farbstoff m ● vt (pres p dyeing) färben

dying see die[2]

dynamic a dynamisch

dynamite n Dynamit nt

dyslex|ia n Legasthenie f. ~ic a legasthenisch; be ~ic Legastheniker sein

Ee

each a & pron jede(r,s); (per) je; ~ other einander; £1 ~ £1 pro Person; (for thing) pro Stück

eager a, -ly adv eifrig; be ~ to do sth etw gerne machen wollen. ~ness n Eifer m

eagle n Adler m

ear n Ohr nt. ~ache n Ohrenschmerzen pl. ~drum n Trommelfell nt

earl n Graf m

early a & adv (-ier, -iest) früh; <reply> baldig; be ~ früh dran sein

earn vt verdienen

earnest *a*, **-ly** *adv* ernsthaft ● *n* in ~ im Ernst

earnings *npl* Verdienst *m*

ear: **~phones** *npl* Kopfhörer *pl*. **~ring** *n* Ohrring *m*; (clip-on) Ohrklips *m*. **~shot** *n* **within/out of ~shot** in/außer Hörweite

earth *n* Erde *f*; (of fox) Bau *m* ● *vt* (Electr) erden

earthenware *n* Tonwaren *pl*

earthly *a* irdisch; **be no ~ use** 🛇 völlig nutzlos sein

earthquake *n* Erdbeben *nt*

earthy *a* erdig; (coarse) derb

ease *n* Leichtigkeit *f* ● *vt* erleichtern; lindern <*pain*> ● *vi* <*pain:*> nachlassen; <*situation:*> sich entspannen

easily *adv* leicht, mit Leichtigkeit

east *n* Osten *m*; **to the ~ of** östlich von ● *a* Ost-, ost- ● *adv* nach Osten

Easter *n* Ostern *nt* ● *attrib* Oster-. **~ egg** *n* Osterei *nt*

east|erly *a* östlich. **~ern** *a* östlich. **~ward[s]** *adv* nach Osten

easy *a* (-ier, -iest) leicht; **take it ~** 🛇 sich schonen; **go ~ with** 🛇 sparsam umgehen mit

easy: **~ chair** *n* Sessel *m*. **~going** *a* gelassen

eat *vt/i* (*pt* ate, *pp* eaten) essen; <*animal:*> fressen. **~ up** *vt* aufessen

eatable *a* genießbar

eau-de-Cologne *n* Kölnisch Wasser *nt*

eaves *npl* Dachüberhang *m*. **~drop** *vi* (*pt/pp* ~ dropped) [heimlich] lauschen

ebb *n* (tide) Ebbe *f* ● *vi* zurückgehen; (fig) verebben

ebony *n* Ebenholz *nt*

EC *abbr* (European Community) EG *f*

eccentric *a* exzentrisch ● *n* Exzentriker *m*

ecclesiastical *a* kirchlich

echo *n* (*pl* -es) Echo *nt*, Widerhall *m* ● *v* (*pt/pp* echoed, *pres p* echoing) ● *vi* widerhallen (**with** von)

eclipse *n* (Astr) Finsternis *f*

ecolog|ical *a* ökologisch. **~y** *n* Ökologie *f*

economic *a* wirtschaftlich. **~al** *a* sparsam. **~ally** *adv* wirtschaftlich; (thriftily) sparsam. **~s** *n* Volkswirtschaft *f*

economist *n* Volkswirt *m*; (Univ) Wirtschaftswissenschaftler *m*

economize *vi* sparen (**on** an + *dat*)

economy *n* Wirtschaft *f*; (thrift) Sparsamkeit *f*

ecstasy *n* Ekstase *f*

ecstatic *a*, **-ally** *adv* ekstatisch

eczema *n* Ekzem *nt*

eddy *n* Wirbel *m*

edge *n* Rand *m*; (of table, lawn) Kante *f*; (of knife) Schneide *f*; **on ~** 🛇 nervös ● *vt* einfassen. **~ forward** *vi* sich nach vorn schieben

edgy *a* 🛇 nervös

edible *a* essbar

edifice *n* [großes] Gebäude *nt*

edit *vt* (*pt/pp* edited) redigieren; herausgeben <*anthology, dictionary*>; schneiden <*film, tape*>

edition *n* Ausgabe *f*; (impression) Auflage *f*

editor *n* Redakteur *m*; (of anthology, dictionary) Herausgeber *m*; (of newspaper) Chefredakteur *m*; (of film) Cutter(in) *m(f)*

editorial *a* redaktionell, Redaktions- ● *n* (Journ) Leitartikel *m*

educate *vt* erziehen. **~d** *a* gebildet

education *n* Erziehung *f*; (culture) Bildung *f*. **~al** *a* pädagogisch; <*visit*> kulturell

eel *n* Aal *m*

eerie *a* (-ier, -iest) unheimlich

effect *n* Wirkung *f*, Effekt *m*; **take ~** in Kraft treten

effective *a*, **-ly** *adv* wirksam, effektiv; (striking) wirkungsvoll, effektvoll; (actual) tatsächlich. **~ness** *n* Wirksamkeit *f*

effeminate *a* unmännlich

effervescent *a* sprudelnd

efficiency *n* Tüchtigkeit *f*; (of machine, organization) Leistungsfähigkeit *f*

efficient *a* tüchtig; <*machine, organization*> leistungsfähig; <*method*> rationell. **∼ly** *adv* gut; <*function*> rationell

effort *n* Anstrengung *f*; make an ∼ sich (*dat*) Mühe geben. **∼less** *a*, **-ly** *adv* mühelos

e.g. *abbr* z.B.

egalitarian *a* egalitär

egg *n* Ei *nt*. **∼-cup** *n* Eierbecher *m*. **∼shell** *n* Eierschale *f*

ego *n* Ich *nt*. **∼ism** *n* Egoismus *m*. **∼ist** *n* Egoist *m*. **∼tism** *n* Ichbezogenheit *f*. **∼tist** *n* ichbezogener Mensch *m*

Egypt *n* Ägypten *nt*. **∼ian** *a* ägyptisch ● *n* Ägypter(in) *m(f)*

eiderdown *n* (*quilt*) Daunendecke *f*

eigh|t *a* acht ● *n* Acht *f*; (*boat*) Achter *m*. **∼teen** *a* achtzehn. **∼teenth** *a* achtzehnte(r,s)

eighth *a* achte(r,s) ● *n* Achtel *nt*

eightieth *a* achtzigste(r,s)

eighty *a* achtzig

either *a & pron* ∼ [of them] einer von [den] beiden; (*both*) beide; on ∼ side auf beiden Seiten ● *adv* I don't ∼ ich auch nicht ● *conj* ∼ ... or entweder ... oder

eject *vt* hinauswerfen

elaborate *a*, **-ly** *adv* kunstvoll; (*fig*) kompliziert

elapse *vi* vergehen

elastic *a* elastisch. **∼ band** *n* Gummiband *nt*

elasticity *n* Elastizität *f*

elated *a* überglücklich

elbow *n* Ellbogen *m*

elder[1] *n* Holunder *m*

eld|er[2] *a* ältere(r,s) ● the **∼er** der/die Ältere. **∼erly** *a* alt. **∼est** *a* älteste(r,s) ● *n* the **∼est** der/die Älteste

elect *vt* wählen. **∼ion** *n* Wahl *f*

elector *n* Wähler(in) *m(f)*. **∼ate** *n* Wählerschaft *f*

electric *a*, **-ally** *adv* elektrisch

electrical *a* elektrisch; **∼ engineering** Elektrotechnik *f*

electric: **∼ blanket** *n* Heizdecke *f*. **∼ fire** *n* elektrischer Heizofen *m*

electrician *n* Elektriker *m*

electricity *n* Elektrizität *f*; (*supply*) Strom *m*

electrify *vt* (*pt/pp* **-ied**) elektrifizieren. **∼ing** *a* (*fig*) elektrisierend

electrocute *vt* durch einen elektrischen Schlag töten

electrode *n* Elektrode *f*

electronic *a* elektronisch. **∼s** *n* Elektronik *f*

elegance *n* Eleganz *f*

elegant *a*, **-ly** *adv* elegant

elegy *n* Elegie *f*

element *n* Element *nt*. **∼ary** *a* elementar

elephant *n* Elefant *m*

elevat|e *vt* heben; (*fig*) erheben. **∼ion** *n* Erhebung *f*

elevator *n* (*Amer*) Aufzug *m*, Fahrstuhl *m*

eleven *a* elf ● *n* Elf *f*. **∼th** *a* elfte(r,s); at the **∼th hour** 🗊 in letzter Minute

eligible *a* berechtigt

eliminate *vt* ausschalten

élite *n* Elite *f*

elm *n* Ulme *f*

elocution *n* Sprecherziehung *f*

elope *vi* durchbrennen 🗊

eloquen|ce *n* Beredsamkeit *f*. **∼t** *a*, **∼ly** *adv* beredt

else *adv* sonst; **nothing ∼** sonst nichts; **or ∼** oder; (*otherwise*) sonst; **someone/somewhere ∼** jemand/ irgendwo anders; **anyone ∼** jeder andere; (*as question*) sonst noch jemand? **anything ∼** alles andere; (*as question*) sonst noch etwas? **∼where** *adv* woanders

elucidate *vt* erläutern

elusive *a* be ∼ schwer zu fassen sein

emaciated *a* abgezehrt

e-mail *n* E-Mail *f*. **∼ address** *n* E-Mail-Adresse *f*. **∼ message** *n* E-Mail *f* ● *vt* per E-Mail übermitteln

<Ergebnisse, Datei usw.>; ~ **s.o.** jdm eine E-Mail schicken

emancipat|ed *a* emanzipiert. **~ion** *n* Emanzipation *f*; *(of slaves)* Freilassung *f*

embankment *n* Böschung *f*; *(of railway)* Bahndamm *m*

embark *vi* sich einschiffen. **~ation** *n* Einschiffung *f*

embarrass *vt* in Verlegenheit bringen. **~ed** *a* verlegen. **~ing** *a* peinlich. **~ment** *n* Verlegenheit *f*

embassy *n* Botschaft *f*

embellish *vt* verzieren; *(fig)* ausschmücken

embezzle *vt* unterschlagen. **~ment** *n* Unterschlagung *f*

emblem *n* Emblem *nt*

embodiment *n* Verkörperung *f*

embody *vt* *(pt/pp* -ied*)* verkörpern; *(include)* enthalten

embrace *n* Umarmung *f* ● *vt* umarmen; *(fig)* umfassen ● *vi* sich umarmen

embroider *vt* besticken; sticken *<design>* ● *vi* sticken. **~y** *n* Stickerei *f*

embryo *n* Embryo *m*

emerald *n* Smaragd *m*

emer|ge *vi* auftauchen (from aus); *(become known)* sich herausstellen; *(come into being)* entstehen. **~gence** *n* Auftauchen *nt*; Entstehung *f*

emergency *n* Notfall *m*. **~ exit** *n* Notausgang *m*

emigrant *n* Auswanderer *m*

emigrat|e *vi* auswandern. **~ion** *n* Auswanderung *f*

eminent *a*, **-ly** *adv* eminent

emission *n* Ausstrahlung *f*; *(of pollutant)* Emission *f*

emit *vt* *(pt/pp* emitted*)* ausstrahlen *<light, heat>*; ausstoßen *<smoke, fumes, cry>*

emotion *n* Gefühl *nt*. **~al** *a* emotional; **become ~al** sich erregen

empathy *n* Einfühlungsvermögen *nt*

emperor *n* Kaiser *m*

emphasis *n* Betonung *f*

emphasize *vt* betonen

emphatic *a*, **-ally** *adv* nachdrücklich

empire *n* Reich *nt*

employ *vt* beschäftigen; *(appoint)* einstellen; *(fig)* anwenden. **~ee** *n* Beschäftigte(r) *m/f*; *(in contrast to employer)* Arbeitnehmer *m*. **~er** *n* Arbeitgeber *m*. **~ment** *n* Beschäftigung *f*; *(work)* Arbeit *f*. **~ment agency** *n* Stellenvermittlung *f*

empress *n* Kaiserin *f*

emptiness *n* Leere *f*

empty *a* leer ● *vt* leeren; ausleeren *<container>* ● *vi* sich leeren

emulsion *n* Emulsion *f*

enable *vt* ~ **s.o. to** es jdm möglich machen, zu

enact *vt* *(Theat)* aufführen

enamel *n* Email *nt*; *(on teeth)* Zahnschmelz *m*; *(paint)* Lack *m*

enchant *vt* bezaubern. **~ing** *a* bezaubernd. **~ment** *n* Zauber *m*

encircle *vt* einkreisen

enclos|e *vt* einschließen; *(in letter)* beilegen (with *dat*). **~ure** *n* *(at zoo)* Gehege *nt*; *(in letter)* Anlage *f*

encore *n* Zugabe *f* ● *int* bravo!

encounter *n* Begegnung *f* ● *vt* begegnen (+ *dat*); *(fig)* stoßen auf (+ *acc*)

encourag|e *vt* ermutigen; *(promote)* fördern. **~ement** *n* Ermutigung *f*. **~ing** *a* ermutigend

encroach *vi* ~ **on** eindringen in (+ *acc*) *<land>*

encyclopaed|ia *n* Enzyklopädie *f*, Lexikon *nt*. **~ic** *a* enzyklopädisch

end *n* Ende *nt*; *(purpose)* Zweck *m*; **in the ~** schließlich; **at the ~ of May** Ende Mai; **on ~** hochkant; **for days on ~** tagelang; **make ~s meet** 🅵 [gerade] auskommen; **no ~ of** 🅵 unheimlich viel(e) ● *vt* beenden ● *vi* enden; **~ up in** (🅵 *arrive at*) landen in (+ *dat*)

endanger *vt* gefährden

endeavour *n* Bemühung *f* ● *vi* sich bemühen (**to** zu)

ending *n* Schluss *m*, Ende *nt*;
(*Gram*) Endung *f*

endless *a*, **-ly** *adv* endlos

endorse *vt* (*Comm*) indossieren;
(*confirm*) bestätigen. **~ment** *n*
(*Comm*) Indossament *nt*; (*fig*)
Bestätigung *f*; (*on driving licence*)
Strafvermerk *m*

endow *vt* stiften; **be ~ed with** (*fig*)
haben

endurance *n* Durchhaltevermögen
nt; **beyond ~** unerträglich

endure *vt* ertragen

enemy *n* Feind *m* ● *attrib* feindlich

energetic *a* tatkräftig; **be ~** voller
Energie sein

energy *n* Energie *f*

enforce *vt* durchsetzen. **~d** *a*
unfreiwillig

engage *vt* einstellen *<staff>*; (*Theat*)
engagieren; (*Auto*) einlegen *<gear>*
● *vi* sich beteiligen (**in** an + *dat*);
(*Techn*) ineinandergreifen. **~d** *a*
besetzt; *<person>* beschäftigt; (*to be
married*) verlobt; **get ~d** sich
verloben (**to** mit). **~ment** *n*
Verlobung *f*; (*appointment*)
Verabredung *f*; (*Mil*) Gefecht *nt*

engaging *a* einnehmend

engine *n* Motor *m*; (*Naut*) Maschine
f; (*Rail*) Lokomotive *f*; (*of jet plane*)
Triebwerk *nt*. **~-driver** *n*
Lokomotivführer *m*

engineer *n* Ingenieur *m*; (*service,
installation*) Techniker *m*; (*Naut*)
Maschinist *m*; (*Amer*)
Lokomotivführer *m*. **~ing** *n*
[mechanical] **~ing** Maschinenbau *m*

England *n* England *nt*

English *a* englisch; **the ~ Channel**
der Ärmelkanal ● *n* (*Lang*) Englisch
nt; **in ~** auf Englisch; **into ~** ins
Englische; **the ~** *pl* die Engländer.
~man *n* Engländer *m*. **~woman** *n*
Engländerin *f*

engrav|e *vt* eingravieren. **~ing** *n*
Stich *m*

enhance *vt* verschönern; (*fig*)
steigern

enigma *n* Rätsel *nt*. **~tic** *a*
rätselhaft

enjoy *vt* genießen; **~ oneself** sich
amüsieren; **~ cooking** gern kochen; **I
~ed it** es hat mir gut gefallen/
<food:> geschmeckt. **~able** *a*
angenehm, nett. **~ment** *n*
Vergnügen *nt*

enlarge *vt* vergrößern. **~ment** *n*
Vergrößerung *f*

enlist *vt* (*Mil*) einziehen; **~ s.o.'s
help** jdn zur Hilfe heranziehen ● *vi*
(*Mil*) sich melden

enliven *vt* beleben

enmity *n* Feindschaft *f*

enormity *n* Ungeheuerlichkeit *f*

enormous *a*, **-ly** *adv* riesig

enough *a*, *adv* & *n* genug; **be ~**
reichen; **funnily ~** komischerweise

enquir|e *vi* sich erkundigen (**about**
nach). **~y** *n* Erkundigung *f*;
(*investigation*) Untersuchung *f*

enrage *vt* wütend machen

enrich *vt* bereichern

enrol *v* (*pt/pp* **-rolled**) ● *vt*
einschreiben ● *vi* sich einschreiben

ensemble *n* (*clothing & Mus*)
Ensemble *nt*

enslave *vt* versklaven

ensue *vi* folgen; (*result*) sich ergeben
(**from** aus)

ensure *vt* sicherstellen; **~ that** dafür
sorgen, dass

entail *vt* erforderlich machen; **what
does it ~?** was ist damit verbunden?

entangle *vt* **get ~d** sich verfangen
(**in** in + *dat*)

enter *vt* eintreten/ *<vehicle:>*
einfahren in (+ *acc*); einreisen in (+
acc) *<country>*; (*register*) eintragen;
sich anmelden zu *<competition>* ● *vi*
eintreten; *<vehicle:>* einfahren;
(*Theat*) auftreten; (*register as
competitor*) sich anmelden; (*take
part*) sich beteiligen (**in** an + *dat*)

enterpris|e *n* Unternehmen *nt*;
(*quality*) Unternehmungsgeist *m*.
~ing *a* unternehmend

entertain *vt* unterhalten; (*invite*)
einladen; (*to meal*) bewirten *<guest>*
● *vi* unterhalten; (*have guests*) Gäste
haben. **~er** *n* Unterhalter *m*.
~ment *n* Unterhaltung *f*

enthral vt (pt/pp **enthralled**) be ~**led** gefesselt sein (**by** von)

enthuse vi ~ **over** schwärmen von

enthusias|m n Begeisterung f. ~**t** n Enthusiast m. ~**tic** a, -**ally** adv begeistert

entice vt locken. ~**ment** n Anreiz m

entire a ganz. ~**ly** adv ganz, völlig. ~**ty** n **in its** ~**ty** in seiner Gesamtheit

entitle vt berechtigen; ~**d** ... mit dem Titel ...; **be** ~**d to sth** das Recht auf etw (acc) haben. ~**ment** n Berechtigung f; (claim) Anspruch m (**to** auf + acc)

entrance n Eintritt m; (Theat) Auftritt m; (way in) Eingang m; (for vehicle) Einfahrt f. ~ **fee** n Eintrittsgebühr f

entrant n Teilnehmer(in) m(f)

entreat vt anflehen (**for** um)

entrust vt ~ **s.o. with sth**, ~ **sth to s.o.** jdm etw anvertrauen

entry n Eintritt m; (into country) Einreise f; (on list) Eintrag m; **no** ~ Zutritt/ (Auto) Einfahrt verboten

envelop vt (pt/pp **enveloped**) einhüllen

envelope n [Brief]umschlag m

enviable a beneidenswert

envious a, -**ly** adv neidisch (**of** auf + acc)

environment n Umwelt f

environmental a Umwelt-. ~**ist** n Umweltschützer m. ~**ly** adv ~**ly friendly** umweltfreundlich

envisage vt sich (dat) vorstellen

envoy n Gesandte(r) m

envy n Neid m ● vt (pt/pp -**ied**) ~ **s.o. sth** jdn um etw beneiden

epic a episch ● n Epos nt

epidemic n Epidemie f

epilep|sy n Epilepsie f. ~**tic** a epileptisch ● n Epileptiker(in) m(f)

epilogue n Epilog m

episode n Episode f; (instalment) Folge f

epitome n Inbegriff m

epoch n Epoche f. ~**-making** a epochemachend

equal a gleich (**to** dat); **be** ~ **to a task** einer Aufgabe gewachsen sein ● n Gleichgestellte(r) m/f ● vt (pt/pp **equalled**) gleichen (+ dat); (fig) gleichkommen (+ dat). ~**ity** n Gleichheit f

equalize vt/i ausgleichen

equally adv gleich; <divide> gleichmäßig; (just as) genauso

equat|e vt gleichsetzen (**with** mit). ~**ion** n (Math) Gleichung f

equator n Äquator m

equestrian a Reit-

equilibrium n Gleichgewicht nt

equinox n Tagundnachtgleiche f

equip vt (pt/pp **equipped**) ausrüsten; (furnish) ausstatten. ~**ment** n Ausrüstung f; Ausstattung f

equity n Gerechtigkeit f

equivalent a gleichwertig; (corresponding) entsprechend ● n Äquivalent nt; (value) Gegenwert m; (counterpart) Gegenstück nt

era n Ära f, Zeitalter nt

eradicate vt ausrotten

erase vt ausradieren; (from tape) löschen

erect a aufrecht ● vt errichten. ~**ion** n Errichtung f; (building) Bau m; (Biol) Erektion f

ero|de vt <water:> auswaschen; <acid:> angreifen. ~**sion** n Erosion f

erotic a erotisch

errand n Botengang m

erratic a unregelmäßig; <person> unberechenbar

erroneous a falsch; <belief, assumption> irrig

error n Irrtum m; (mistake) Fehler m; **in** ~ irrtümlicherweise

erupt vi ausbrechen. ~**ion** n Ausbruch m

escalat|e vt/i eskalieren. ~**or** n Rolltreppe f

escape n Flucht f; (from prison) Ausbruch m; **have a narrow** ~ gerade noch davonkommen ● vi flüchten; <prisoner:> ausbrechen;

entkommen (**from** aus; **from s.o.** jdm); <*gas:*> entweichen ● *vt* **the name ~s me** der Name entfällt mir

escapism *n* Eskapismus *m*

escort[1] *n* (*of person*) Begleiter *m*; (*Mil*) Eskorte *f*

escort[2] *vt* begleiten; (*Mil*) eskortieren

Eskimo *n* Eskimo *m*

esoteric *a* esoterisch

especially *adv* besonders

espionage *n* Spionage *f*

essay *n* Aufsatz *m*

essence *n* Wesen *nt*; (*Chem, Culin*) Essenz *f*

essential *a* wesentlich; (*indispensable*) unentbehrlich ● *n* **the ~s** das Wesentliche; (*items*) das Nötigste. **~ly** *adv* im Wesentlichen

establish *vt* gründen; (*form*) bilden; (*prove*) beweisen

estate *n* Gut *nt*; (*possessions*) Besitz *m*; (*after death*) Nachlass *m*; (*housing*) [Wohn]siedlung *f*. **~ agent** *n* Immobilienmakler *m*. **~ car** *n* Kombi[wagen] *m*

esteem *n* Achtung *f* ● *vt* hochschätzen

estimate[1] *n* Schätzung *f*; (*Comm*) [Kosten]voranschlag *m*; **at a rough ~** grob geschätzt

estimat|e[2] *vt* schätzen. **~ion** *n* Einschätzung *f*

estuary *n* Mündung *f*

etc. *abbr* (**et cetera**) und so weiter, usw.

eternal *a*, **-ly** *adv* ewig

eternity *n* Ewigkeit *f*

ethic|al *a* ethisch; (*morally correct*) moralisch einwandfrei. **~s** *n* Ethik *f*

Ethiopia *n* Äthiopien *nt*

ethnic *a* ethnisch. **~ cleansing** *n* ethnische Säuberung

etiquette *n* Etikette *f*

EU *abbr* (**European Union**) EU *f*

eulogy *n* Lobrede *f*

euphemis|m *n* Euphemismus. **~tic** *a*, **-ally** *adv* verhüllend

Euro *n* Euro *m*. **~cheque** *n* Euroscheck *m*

Europe *n* Europa *nt*

European *a* europäisch; **~ Union** Europäische Union *f* ● *n* Europäer(in) *m(f)*

evacuat|e *vt* evakuieren; räumen <*building, area*>. **~ion** *n* Evakuierung *f*; Räumung *f*

evade *vt* sich entziehen (+ *dat*); hinterziehen <*taxes*>

evaluate *vt* einschätzen

evange|lical *a* evangelisch. **~list** *n* Evangelist *m*

evaporat|e *vi* verdunsten. **~ion** *n* Verdampfung *f*

evasion *n* Ausweichen *nt*; **tax ~** Steuerhinterziehung *f*

evasive *a*, **-ly** *adv* ausweichend; **be ~** ausweichen

even *a* (*level*) eben; (*same, equal*) gleich; (*regular*) gleichmäßig; <*number*> gerade; **get ~ with** 🛈 es jdm heimzahlen ● *adv* sogar, selbst; **~ so** trotzdem; **not ~** nicht einmal ● *vt* **~ the score** ausgleichen

evening *n* Abend *m*; **this ~** heute Abend; **in the ~** abends, am Abend. **~ class** *n* Abendkurs *m*

evenly *adv* gleichmäßig

event *n* Ereignis *nt*; (*function*) Veranstaltung *f*; (*Sport*) Wettbewerb *m*. **~ful** *a* ereignisreich

eventual *a* **his ~ success** der Erfolg, der ihm schließlich zuteil wurde. **~ly** *adv* schließlich

ever *adv* je[mals]; **not ~** nie; **for ~** für immer; **hardly ~** fast nie; **~ since** seitdem

evergreen *n* immergrüner Strauch *m*/ (*tree*) Baum *m*

everlasting *a* ewig

every *a* jede(r,s); **~ one** jede(r,s) Einzelne; **~ other day** jeden zweiten Tag

every: ~body *pron* jeder[mann]; alle *pl*. **~day** *a* alltäglich. **~ one** *pron* jeder[mann]; alle *pl*. **~thing** *pron* alles. **~where** *adv* überall

evict *vt* [aus der Wohnung] hinausweisen. **~ion** *n* Ausweisung *f*

eviden|ce *n* Beweise *pl*; (*Jur*) Beweismaterial *nt*; (*testimony*)

Aussage *f;* **give ~ce** aussagen. **~t** *a,*
-ly *adv* offensichtlich

evil *a* böse ● *n* Böse *nt*

evoke *vt* heraufbeschwören

evolution *n* Evolution *f*

evolve *vt* entwickeln ● *vi* sich
entwickeln

ewe *n* Schaf *nt*

exact *a,* **-ly** *adv* genau; **not ~ly**
nicht gerade. **~ness** *n* Genauigkeit
f

exaggerat|e *vt/i* übertreiben.
~ion *n* Übertreibung *f*

exam *n* 🔝 Prüfung *f*

examination *n* Untersuchung *f;*
(*Sch*) Prüfung *f*

examine *vt* untersuchen; (*Sch*)
prüfen

example *n* Beispiel *nt* (**of** für); **for
~** zum Beispiel; **make an ~ of** ein
Exempel statuieren an (+ *dat*)

exasperat|e *vt* zur Verzweiflung
treiben. **~ion** *n* Verzweiflung *f*

excavat|e *vt* ausschachten;
(*Archaeol*) ausgraben. **~ion** *n*
Ausgrabung *f*

exceed *vt* übersteigen. **~ingly** *adv*
äußerst

excel *v* (*pt/pp* **excelled**) *vi* sich
auszeichnen ● *vt* **~ oneself** sich
selbst übertreffen

excellen|ce *n* Vorzüglichkeit *f.* **~t**
a, **-ly** *adv* ausgezeichnet, vorzüglich

except *prep* außer (+ *dat*); **~ for**
abgesehen von ● *vt* ausnehmen

exception *n* Ausnahme *f.* **~al** *a,*
-ly *adv* außergewöhnlich

excerpt *n* Auszug *m*

excess *n* Übermaß *nt* (**of** an + *dat*);
(*surplus*) Überschuss *m;* **~es** *pl*
Exzesse *pl*

excessive *a,* **-ly** *adv* übermäßig

exchange *n* Austausch *m;* (*Teleph*)
Fernsprechamt *nt;* (*Comm*)
[Geld]wechsel *m;* **in ~** dafür ● *vt*
austauschen (**for** gegen); tauschen
<*places*>. **~ rate** *n* Wechselkurs *m*

excitable *a* [leicht] erregbar

excit|e *vt* aufregen; (*cause*) erregen.
~ed *a,* **-ly** *adv* aufgeregt; **get ~ed**
sich aufregen. **~ement** *n*

Aufregung *f;* Erregung *f.* **~ing** *a*
aufregend; <*story*> spannend

exclaim *vt/i* ausrufen

exclamation *n* Ausruf *m.* **~
mark** *n,* (*Amer*) **~ point** *n*
Ausrufezeichen *nt*

exclu|de *vt* ausschließen. **~ding**
prep ausschließlich (+ *gen*). **~sion**
n Ausschluss *m*

exclusive *a,* **-ly** *adv* ausschließlich;
(*select*) exklusiv

excrement *n* Kot *m*

excrete *vt* ausscheiden

excruciating *a* grässlich

excursion *n* Ausflug *m*

excusable *a* entschuldbar

excuse[1] *n* Entschuldigung *f;*
(*pretext*) Ausrede *f*

excuse[2] *vt* entschuldigen; **~ me!**
Entschuldigung!

ex-directory *a* **be ~** nicht im
Telefonbuch stehen

execute *vt* ausführen; (*put to death*)
hinrichten

execution *n* Ausführung *f;*
Hinrichtung *f*

executive *a* leitend ● *n* leitende(r)
Angestellte(r) *m/f;* (*Pol*) Exekutive *f*

exemplary *a* beispielhaft

exemplify *vt* (*pt/pp* **-ied**)
veranschaulichen

exempt *a* befreit ● *vt* befreien (**from**
von). **~ion** *n* Befreiung *f*

exercise *n* Übung *f;* **physical ~**
körperliche Bewegung *f* ● *vt* (*use*)
ausüben; bewegen <*horse*> ● *vi* sich
bewegen. **~ book** *n* [Schul]heft *nt*

exert *vt* ausüben; **~ oneself** sich
anstrengen. **~ion** *n* Anstrengung *f*

exhale *vt/i* ausatmen

exhaust *n* (*Auto*) Auspuff *m;*
(*fumes*) Abgase *pl* ● *vt* erschöpfen.
~ed *a* erschöpft. **~ing** *a*
anstrengend. **~ion** *n* Erschöpfung *f.*
~ive *a* (*fig*) erschöpfend

exhibit *n* Ausstellungsstück *nt;*
(*Jur*) Beweisstück *nt* ● *vt* ausstellen

exhibition *n* Ausstellung *f;* (*Univ*)
Stipendium *nt.* **~ist** *n*
Exhibitionist(in) *m(f)*

exhibitor *n* Aussteller *m*

exhilarat|ing *a* berauschend.
~**ion** *n* Hochgefühl *nt*

exhume *vt* exhumieren

exile *n* Exil *nt*; (*person*) im Exil
Lebende(r) *m/f* ● *vt* ins Exil
schicken

exist *vi* bestehen, existieren.
~**ence** *n* Existenz *f*; be in ~**ence**
existieren

exit *n* Ausgang *m*; (*Auto*) Ausfahrt *f*;
(*Theat*) Abgang *m*

exorbitant *a* übermäßig hoch

exotic *a* exotisch

expand *vt* ausdehnen; (*explain
better*) weiter ausführen ● *vi* sich
ausdehnen; (*Comm*) expandieren

expans|e *n* Weite *f*. ~**ion** *n*
Ausdehnung *f*; (*Techn, Pol, Comm*)
Expansion *f*

expect *vt* erwarten; (*suppose*)
annehmen; I ~ so wahrscheinlich

expectan|cy *n* Erwartung *f*. ~**t** *a*,
-ly *adv* erwartungsvoll; ~**t mother**
werdende Mutter *f*

expectation *n* Erwartung *f*

expedient *a* zweckdienlich

expedite *vt* beschleunigen

expedition *n* Expedition *f*

expel *vt* (*pt/pp* expelled) ausweisen
(**from** aus); (*from school*) von der
Schule verweisen

expenditure *n* Ausgaben *pl*

expense *n* Kosten *pl*; **business
~s** *pl* Spesen *pl*; **at my ~** auf meine
Kosten

expensive *a*, **-ly** *adv* teuer

experience *n* Erfahrung *f*; (*event*)
Erlebnis *nt* ● *vt* erleben. ~**d** *a*
erfahren

experiment *n* Versuch *m*,
Experiment *nt* ● *vi*
experimentieren. ~**al** *a*
experimentell

expert *a*, **-ly** *adv* fachmännisch ● *n*
Fachmann *m*, Experte *m*

expertise *n* Sachkenntnis *f*

expire *vi* ablaufen

expiry *n* Ablauf *m*

explain *vt* erklären

explana|tion *n* Erklärung *f*.
~**tory** *a* erklärend

explicit *a*, **-ly** *adv* deutlich

explode *vi* explodieren ● *vt* zur
Explosion bringen

exploit¹ *n* [Helden]tat *f*

exploit² *vt* ausbeuten. ~**ation** *n*
Ausbeutung *f*

exploration *n* Erforschung *f*

explore *vt* erforschen. ~**r** *n*
Forschungsreisende(r) *m*

explos|ion *n* Explosion *f*. ~**ive** *a*
explosiv ● *n* Sprengstoff *m*

export¹ *n* Export *m*, Ausfuhr *f*

export² *vt* exportieren, ausführen.
~**er** *n* Exporteur *m*

expos|e *vt* freilegen; (*to danger*)
aussetzen (**to** *dat*); (*reveal*)
aufdecken; (*Phot*) belichten. ~**ure** *n*
Aussetzung *f*; (*Med*) Unterkühlung *f*;
(*Phot*) Belichtung *f*; 24 ~**ures** 24
Aufnahmen

express *adv* <*send*> per Eilpost ● *n*
(*train*) Schnellzug *m* ● *vt*
ausdrücken; ~ **oneself** sich
ausdrücken. ~**ion** *n* Ausdruck *m*.
~**ive** *a* ausdrucksvoll. ~**ly** *adv*
ausdrücklich

expulsion *n* Ausweisung *f*; (*Sch*)
Verweisung *f* von der Schule

exquisite *a* erlesen

extend *vt* verlängern; (*stretch out*)
ausstrecken; (*enlarge*) vergrößern
● *vi* sich ausdehnen; <*table:*> sich
ausziehen lassen

extension *n* Verlängerung *f*; (*to
house*) Anbau *m*; (*Teleph*)
Nebenanschluss *m*

extensive *a* weit; (*fig*) umfassend.
~**ly** *adv* viel

extent *n* Ausdehnung *f*; (*scope*)
Ausmaß *nt*, Umfang *m*; **to a certain
~** in gewissem Maße

exterior *a* äußere(r,s) ● *n* **the ~** das
Äußere

exterminat|e *vt* ausrotten. ~**ion**
n Ausrottung *f*

external *a* äußere(r,s); **for ~ use
only** (*Med*) nur äußerlich. ~**ly** *adv*
äußerlich

extinct *a* ausgestorben; *<volcano>* erloschen. **~ion** *n* Aussterben *nt*

extinguish *vt* löschen. **~er** *n* Feuerlöscher *m*

extort *vt* erpressen. **~ion** *n* Erpressung *f*

extortionate *a* übermäßig hoch

extra *a* zusätzlich ● *adv* extra; *(especially)* besonders ● *n* (*Theat*) Statist(in) *m(f)*; **~s** *pl* Nebenkosten *pl*; (*Auto*) Extras *pl*

extract¹ *n* Auszug *m*

extract² *vt* herausziehen; ziehen *<tooth>*

extraordinary *a*, **-ily** *adv* außerordentlich; *(strange)* seltsam

extravagan|ce *n* Verschwendung *f*; **an ~ce** ein Luxus *m*. **~t** *a* verschwenderisch

extrem|e *a* äußerste(r,s); *(fig)* extrem ● *n* Extrem *nt*; **in the ~e** im höchsten Grade. **~ely** *adv* äußerst. **~ist** *n* Extremist *m*

extricate *vt* befreien

extrovert *n* extravertierter Mensch *m*

exuberant *a* überglücklich

exude *vt* absondern; *(fig)* ausstrahlen

exult *vi* frohlocken

eye *n* Auge *nt*; *(of needle)* Öhr *nt*; *(for hook)* Öse *f*; **keep an ~ on** aufpassen auf (+ *acc*) ● *vt* (*pt/pp* **eyed**, *pres p* **ey[e]ing**) ansehen

eye: **~brow** *n* Augenbraue *f*. **~lash** *n* Wimper *f*. **~lid** *n* Augenlid *nt*. **~-shadow** *n* Lidschatten *m*. **~sight** *n* Sehkraft *f*. **~sore** *n* 🗉 Schandfleck *m*. **~witness** *n* Augenzeuge *m*

fabric *n* Stoff *m*

fabrication *n* Erfindung *f*

fabulous *a* 🗉 phantastisch

façade *n* Fassade *f*

face *n* Gesicht *nt*; *(surface)* Fläche *f*; *(of clock)* Zifferblatt *nt*; **pull ~s** Gesichter schneiden; **in the ~ of** angesichts (+ *gen*); **on the ~ of it** allem Anschein nach ● *vt/i* gegenüberstehen (+ *dat*); **~ north** *<house>:* nach Norden liegen; **~ the fact that** sich damit abfinden, dass

face: **~-flannel** *n* Waschlappen *m*. **~less** *a* anonym. **~-lift** *n* Gesichtsstraffung *f*

facet *n* Facette *f*; *(fig)* Aspekt *m*

facetious *a*, **-ly** *adv* spöttisch

facial *a* Gesichts-

facile *a* oberflächlich

facilitate *vt* erleichtern

facility *n* Leichtigkeit *f*; *(skill)* Gewandtheit *f*; **~ies** *pl* Einrichtungen *pl*

facsimile *n* Faksimile *nt*

fact *n* Tatsache *f*; **in ~** tatsächlich; *(actually)* eigentlich

faction *n* Gruppe *f*

factor *n* Faktor *m*

factory *n* Fabrik *f*

factual *a*, **-ly** *adv* sachlich

faculty *n* Fähigkeit *f*; *(Univ)* Fakultät *f*

fad *n* Fimmel *m*

fade *vi* verblassen; *<material>:* verbleichen; *<sound>:* abklingen; *<flower>:* verwelken.

fag *n* *(chore)* Plage *f*; (🗉 *cigarette*) Zigarette *f*

fail *n* **without ~** unbedingt ● *vi* *<attempt>:* scheitern; *(grow weak)* nachlassen; *(break down)* versagen; *(in exam)* durchfallen; **~ to do sth** etw nicht tun ● *vt* nicht bestehen *<exam>*; durchfallen lassen *<candidate>*; *(disappoint)* enttäuschen

failing *n* Fehler *m*

failure *n* Misserfolg *m*; *(breakdown)* Versagen *nt*; *(person)* Versager *m*

Ff

fable *n* Fabel *f*

faint a (-er, -est), **-ly** adv schwach; I feel ~ mir ist schwach ● n Ohnmacht f ● vi ohnmächtig werden. ~**ness** n Schwäche f

fair[1] n Jahrmarkt m; (Comm) Messe f

fair[2] a (-er, -est) <hair> blond; <skin> hell; <weather> heiter; (just) gerecht, fair; (quite good) ziemlich gut; (Sch) genügend; **a** ~ **amount** ziemlich viel ● adv **play** ~ fair sein. ~**ly** adv gerecht; (rather) ziemlich. ~**ness** n Blondheit f; Helle f; Gerechtigkeit f; (Sport) Fairness f

fairy n Elfe f; **good/wicked** ~ gute/böse Fee f. ~ **story,** ~**-tale** n Märchen nt

faith n Glaube m; (trust) Vertrauen nt (in zu)

faithful a, **-ly** adv treu; (exact) genau; **Yours** ~**ly** Hochachtungsvoll. ~**ness** n Treue f; Genauigkeit f

fake a falsch ● n Fälschung f; (person) Schwindler m ● vt fälschen; (pretend) vortäuschen

falcon n Falke m

fall n Fall m; (heavy) Sturz m; (in prices) Fallen nt; (Amer: autumn) Herbst m; **have a** ~ fallen ● vi (pt fell, pp fallen) fallen; (heavily) stürzen; <night:> anbrechen; ~ **in love** sich verlieben; ~ **back on** zurückgreifen auf (+ acc); ~ **for s.o.** [] sich in jdn verlieben; ~ **for sth** [] auf etw (acc) hereinfallen. ~ **about** vi (with laughter) sich [vor Lachen] kringeln. ~ **down** vi umfallen; <thing:> herunterfallen; <building:> einstürzen. ~ **in** vi hineinfallen; (collapse) einfallen; (Mil) antreten; ~ **in with** sich anschließen (+ dat). ~ **off** vi herunterfallen; (diminish) abnehmen. ~ **out** vi herausfallen; <hair:> ausfallen; (quarrel) sich überwerfen. ~ **over** vi hinfallen. ~ **through** vi durchfallen; <plan:> ins Wasser fallen

fallacy n Irrtum m

fallible a fehlbar

fall-out n [radioaktiver] Niederschlag m

false a falsch; (artificial) künstlich. ~**hood** n Unwahrheit f. ~**ly** adv falsch

false teeth npl [künstliches] Gebiss nt

falsify vt (pt/pp -ied) fälschen

falter vi zögern

fame n Ruhm m.

familiar a vertraut; (known) bekannt; **too** ~ familiär. ~**ity** n Vertrautheit f. ~**ize** vt vertraut machen (**with** mit)

family n Familie f

family: ~ **doctor** n Hausarzt m. ~ **life** n Familienleben nt. ~ **planning** n Familienplanung f. ~ **tree** n Stammbaum m

famine n Hungersnot f

famished a sehr hungrig

famous a berühmt

fan[1] n Fächer m; (Techn) Ventilator m

fan[2] n (admirer) Fan m

fanatic n Fanatiker m. ~**al** a, **-ly** adv fanatisch. ~**ism** n Fanatismus m

fanciful a phantastisch; (imaginative) phantasiereich

fancy n Phantasie f; **I have taken a real** ~ **to him** er hat es mir angetan ● a ausgefallen ● vt (believe) meinen; (imagine) sich (dat) einbilden; ([] want) Lust haben auf (+ acc); ~ **that!** stell dir vor! (really) tatsächlich! ~ **dress** n Kostüm nt

fanfare n Fanfare f

fang n Fangzahn m

fan heater n Heizlüfter m

fantas|ize vi fantasieren. ~**tic** a fantastisch. ~**y** n Fantasie f

far adv weit; (much) viel; **by** ~ bei weitem; ~ **away** weit weg; **as** ~ **as I know** soviel ich weiß; **as** ~ **as the church** bis zur Kirche ● a **at the** ~ **end** am anderen Ende; **the F**~ **East** der Ferne Osten

farc|e n Farce f. ~**ical** a lächerlich

fare n Fahrpreis m; (money) Fahrgeld nt; (food) Kost f; **air** ~ Flugpreis m

farewell int (liter) lebe wohl! ● n Lebewohl nt

far-fetched *a* weit hergeholt

farm *n* Bauernhof *m* ● *vi* Landwirtschaft betreiben ● *vt* bewirtschaften <*land*>. **~er** *n* Landwirt *m*

farm: ~house *n* Bauernhaus *nt*. **~ing** *n* Landwirtschaft *f*. **~yard** *n* Hof *m*

far: ~-reaching *a* weit reichend. **~-sighted** *a* (*fig*) umsichtig; (*Amer: long-sighted*) weitsichtig

farther *adv* weiter; **~ off** weiter entfernt

fascinat|e *vt* faszinieren. **~ing** *a* faszinierend. **~ion** *n* Faszination *f*

fascis|m *n* Faschismus *m*. **~t** *n* Faschist *m* ● *a* faschistisch

fashion *n* Mode *f*; (*manner*) Art *f*. **~able** *a*, **-bly** *adv* modisch

fast *a* & *adv* (*-er, -est*) schnell; (*firm*) fest; <*colour*> waschecht; **be ~** <*clock*:> vorgehen; **be ~ asleep** fest schlafen

fasten *vt* zumachen; (*fix*) befestigen (**to** an + *dat*). **~er** *n*, **~ing** *n* Verschluss *m*

fastidious *a* wählerisch; (*particular*) penibel

fat *a* (**fatter, fattest**) dick; <*meat*> fett ● *n* Fett *nt*

fatal *a* tödlich; <*error*> verhängnisvoll. **~ity** *n* Todesopfer *nt*. **~ly** *adv* tödlich

fate *n* Schicksal *nt*. **~ful** *a* verhängnisvoll

fat-head *n* 🔲 Dummkopf *m*

father *n* Vater *m*; **F ~ Christmas** der Weihnachtsmann ● *vt* zeugen

father: ~hood *n* Vaterschaft *f*. **~-in-law** *n* (*pl* **~s-in-law**) Schwiegervater *m*. **~ly** *a* väterlich

fathom *n* (*Naut*) Faden *m* ● *vt* verstehen

fatigue *n* Ermüdung *f*

fatten *vt* mästen <*animal*>

fatty *a* fett; <*foods*> fetthaltig

fatuous *a*, **-ly** *adv* albern

fault *n* Fehler *m*; (*Techn*) Defekt *m*; (*Geol*) Verwerfung *f*; **at ~** im Unrecht; **find ~ with** etwas auszusetzen haben an (+ *dat*); **it's**

your ~ du bist schuld. **~less** *a*, **-ly** *adv* fehlerfrei

faulty *a* fehlerhaft

favour *n* Gunst *f*; **I am in ~** ich bin dafür; **do s.o. a ~** jdm einen Gefallen tun ● *vt* begünstigen; (*prefer*) bevorzugen. **~able** *a*, **-bly** *adv* günstig; <*reply*> positiv

favourit|e *a* Lieblings- ● *n* Liebling *m*; (*Sport*) Favorit(in) *m(f)*. **~ism** *n* Bevorzugung *f*

fawn *a* rehbraun ● *n* Hirschkalb *nt*

fax *n* Fax *nt* ● *vt* faxen (**s.o.** jdm). **~ machine** *n* Faxgerät *nt*

fear *n* Furcht *f*, Angst *f* (**of** vor + *dat*) ● *vt/i* fürchten

fear|ful *a* besorgt; (*awful*) furchtbar. **~less** *a*, **-ly** *adv* furchtlos

feas|ibility *n* Durchführbarkeit *f*. **~ible** *a* durchführbar; (*possible*) möglich

feast *n* Festmahl *nt*; (*Relig*) Fest *nt* ● *vi* **~ [on]** schmausen

feat *n* Leistung *f*

feather *n* Feder *f*

feature *n* Gesichtszug *m*; (*quality*) Merkmal *nt*; (*Journ*) Feature *nt* ● *vt* darstellen

February *n* Februar *m*

fed ● *a* **be ~ up** 🔲 die Nase voll haben (**with** von)

federal *a* Bundes-

federation *n* Föderation *f*

fee *n* Gebühr *f*; (*professional*) Honorar *nt*

feeble *a* (**-r, -st**), **-bly** *adv* schwach

feed *n* Futter *nt*; (*for baby*) Essen *nt* ● *v* (*pt/pp* **fed**) ● *vt* füttern; (*support*) ernähren; (*into machine*) eingeben; speisen <*computer*> ● *vi* sich ernähren (**on** von)

feedback *n* Feedback *nt*

feel *v* (*pt/pp* **felt**) ● *vt* fühlen; (*experience*) empfinden; (*think*) meinen ● *vi* sich fühlen; **~ soft/hard** sich weich/hart anfühlen; **I ~ hot/ill** mir ist heiß/schlecht; **~ing** *n* Gefühl *nt*; **no hard ~ings** nichts für ungut

feet *see* **foot**

feline *a* Katzen-; (*catlike*) katzenartig

fell¹ *vt* fällen

fell² *see* fall

fellow *n* (🔲 *man*) Kerl *m*

fellow: ~**-countryman** *n* Landsmann *m*. ~ **men** *pl* Mitmenschen *pl*

felt¹ *see* feel

felt² *n* Filz *m*. ~**[-tipped] pen** *n* Filzstift *m*

female *a* weiblich ● *nt* Weibchen *nt*; (*pej: woman*) Weib *nt*

femin|ine *a* weiblich ● *n* (*Gram*) Femininum *nt*. ~**inity** *n* Weiblichkeit *f*. ~**ist** *a* feministisch ● *n* Feminist(in) *m(f)*

fenc|e *n* Zaun *m*; (🔲 *person*) Hehler *m* ● *vi* (*Sport*) fechten ● *vt* ~**e in** einzäunen. ~**er** *n* Fechter *m*. ~**ing** *n* Zaun *m*; (*Sport*) Fechten *nt*

fender *n* Kaminvorsetzer *m*; (*Naut*) Fender *m*; (*Amer: wing*) Kotflügel *m*

ferment *vi* gären ● *vt* gären lassen

fern *n* Farn *m*

feroc|ious *a* wild. ~**ity** *n* Wildheit *f*

ferry *n* Fähre *f*

fertil|e *a* fruchtbar. ~**ity** *n* Fruchtbarkeit *f*

fertilize *vt* befruchten; düngen <*land*>. ~**r** *n* Dünger *m*

fervent *a* leidenschaftlich

fervour *n* Leidenschaft *f*

festival *n* Fest *nt*; (*Mus, Theat*) Festspiele *pl*

festiv|e *a* festlich. ~**ities** *npl* Feierlichkeiten *pl*

festoon *vt* behängen (with mit)

fetch *vt* holen; (*collect*) abholen; (*be sold for*) einbringen

fetching *a* anziehend

fête *n* Fest *nt* ● *vt* feiern

feud *n* Fehde *f*

feudal *a* Feudal-

fever *n* Fieber *nt*. ~**ish** *a* fiebrig; (*fig*) fieberhaft

few *a* (-er, -est) wenige; every ~ days alle paar Tage ● *n* a ~ ein paar; quite a ~ ziemlich viele

fiancé *n* Verlobte(r) *m*. **fiancée** *n* Verlobte *f*

fiasco *n* Fiasko *nt*

fib *n* kleine Lüge

fibre *n* Faser *f*

fiction *n* Erfindung *f*; [works of] ~ Erzählungsliteratur *f*. ~**al** *a* erfunden

fictitious *a* [frei] erfunden

fiddle *n* 🔲 Geige *f*; (*cheating*) Schwindel *m* ● *vi* herumspielen (with mit) ● *vt* 🔲 frisieren <*accounts*>

fiddly *a* knifflig

fidelity *n* Treue *f*

fidget *vi* zappeln. ~**y** *a* zappelig

field *n* Feld *nt*; (*meadow*) Wiese *f*; (*subject*) Gebiet *nt*

field: ~ **events** *npl* Sprung- und Wurfdisziplinen *pl*. **F~ Marshal** *n* Feldmarschall *m*

fiendish *a* teuflisch

fierce *a* (-r, -st), **-ly** *adv* wild; (*fig*) heftig. ~**ness** *n* Wildheit *f*; (*fig*) Heftigkeit *f*

fiery *a* (-ier, -iest) feurig

fifteen *a* fünfzehn ● *n* Fünfzehn *f*. ~**th** *a* fünfzehnte(r,s)

fifth *a* fünfte(r,s)

fiftieth *a* fünfzigste(r,s)

fifty *a* fünfzig

fig *n* Feige *f*

fight *n* Kampf *m*; (*brawl*) Schlägerei *f*; (*between children, dogs*) Rauferei *f* ● *v* (*pt/pp* fought) ● *vt* kämpfen gegen; (*fig*) bekämpfen ● *vi* kämpfen; (*brawl*) sich schlagen; <*children, dogs:*> sich raufen. ~**er** *n* Kämpfer *m*; (*Aviat*) Jagdflugzeug *nt*. ~**ing** *n* Kampf *m*

figurative *a*, **-ly** *adv* bildlich, übertragen

figure *n* (*digit*) Ziffer *f*; (*number*) Zahl *f*; (*sum*) Summe *f*; (*carving, sculpture, woman's*) Figur *f*; (*form*) Gestalt *f*; (*illustration*) Abbildung *f*; good at ~s gut im Rechnen ● *vi* (*appear*) erscheinen ● *vt* (*Amer: think*) glauben

filch *vt* 🔲 klauen

file¹ *n* Akte *f*; (*for documents*) [Akten]ordner *m* ● *vt* ablegen <*documents*>; (*Jur*) einreichen

file² n (line) Reihe f; **in single ~** im Gänsemarsch

file³ n (Techn) Feile f ● vt feilen

fill n eat one's **~** sich satt essen ● vt füllen; plombieren <tooth> ● vi sich füllen. **~ in** vt auffüllen; ausfüllen <form>. **~ out** vt ausfüllen <form>. **~ up** vi sich füllen ● vt vollfüllen; (Auto) volltanken; ausfüllen <form>

fillet n Filet nt ● vt (pt/pp filleted) entgräten

filling n Füllung f; (of tooth) Plombe f. **~ station** n Tankstelle f

filly n junge Stute f

film n Film m ● vt/i filmen; verfilmen <book>. **~ star** n Filmstar m

filter n Filter m ● vt filtern

filth n Dreck m. **~y** a (-ier, -iest) dreckig

fin n Flosse f

final a letzte(r,s); (conclusive) endgültig ● n (Sport) Endspiel nt; **~s** pl (Univ) Abschlussprüfung f

finale n Finale nt

final|ist n Finalist(in) m(f)

final|ize vt endgültig festlegen. **~ly** adv schließlich

finance n Finanz f ● vt finanzieren

financial a, **-ly** adv finanziell

find n Fund m ● vt (pt/pp found) finden; (establish) feststellen; **go and ~** holen; **try to ~** suchen. **~ out** vt herausfinden; (learn) erfahren ● vi (enquire) sich erkundigen

fine¹ n Geldstrafe f ● vt zu einer Geldstrafe verurteilen

fine² a (-r, -st,) **-ly** adv fein; <weather> schön; **he's ~** es geht ihm gut ● adv gut; **cut it ~** Ⅰ sich (dat) wenig Zeit lassen

finesse n Gewandtheit f

finger n Finger m ● vt anfassen

finger: ~-nail n Fingernagel m. **~print** n Fingerabdruck m. **~tip** n Fingerspitze f

finicky a knifflig; (choosy) wählerisch

finish n Schluss m; (Sport) Finish nt; (line) Ziel nt; (of product) Ausführung f ● vt beenden; (use up) aufbrauchen; **~ one's drink**

austrinken; **~ reading** zu Ende lesen ● vi fertig werden; <performance:> zu Ende sein; <runner:> durchs Ziel gehen

Finland n Finnland nt

Finn n Finne m/ Finnin f. **~ish** a finnisch

fir n Tanne f

fire n Feuer nt; (forest, house) Brand m; **be on ~** brennen; **catch ~** Feuer fangen; **set ~ to** anzünden; <arsonist:> in Brand stecken; **under ~** unter Beschuss ● vt brennen <pottery>; abfeuern <shot>; schießen mit <gun>; (Ⅰ dismiss) feuern ● vi schießen (at auf + acc); <engine:> anspringen

fire: ~ alarm n Feuermelder m. **~ brigade** n Feuerwehr f. **~-engine** n Löschfahrzeug nt. **~ extinguisher** n Feuerlöscher m. **~man** n Feuerwehrmann m. **~place** n Kamin m. **~side** n by or at the **~side** am Kamin. **~ station** n Feuerwache f. **~wood** n Brennholz nt. **~work** n Feuerwerkskörper m; **~works** pl (display) Feuerwerk nt

firm¹ n Firma f

firm² a (-er, -est), **-ly** adv fest; (resolute) entschlossen; (strict) streng

first a & n erste(r,s); **at ~** zuerst; **at ~ sight** auf den ersten Blick; **from the ~** von Anfang an ● adv zuerst; (firstly) erstens

first: ~ aid n erste Hilfe. **~-aid kit** n Verbandkasten m. **~-class** a erstklassig; (Rail) erster Klasse ● adv <travel> erster Klasse. **~ floor** n erster Stock; (Amer: ground floor) Erdgeschoss nt. **~ly** adv erstens. **~name** n Vorname m. **~-rate** a erstklassig

fish n Fisch m ● vt/i fischen; (with rod) angeln

fish: ~bone n Gräte f. **~erman** n Fischer m. **~ finger** n Fischstäbchen nt

fishing n Fischerei f. **~ boat** n Fischerboot nt. **~-rod** n Angel[rute] f

fish: **~monger** n Fischhändler m.
~y a Fisch-; (🅸 *suspicious*)
verdächtig

fission n (*Phys*) Spaltung f

fist n Faust f

fit¹ n (*attack*) Anfall m

fit² a (fitter, fittest) (*suitable*) geeignet;
(*healthy*) gesund; (*Sport*) fit; **~ to eat**
essbar

fit³ n (*of clothes*) Sitz m; be a good **~**
gut passen ● v (*pt/pp* fitted) ● vi (*be
the right size*) passen ● vt anbringen
(**to** an + *dat*); (*install*) einbauen; **~
with** versehen mit. **~ in** vi
hineinpassen; (*adapt*) sich einfügen
(**with** in + *acc*) ● vt (*accommodate*)
unterbringen

fit|ness n Eignung f; [*physical*]
~ness Gesundheit f; (*Sport*) Fitness
f. **~ted** a eingebaut; <*garment*>
tailliert

fitted: **~ carpet** n Teppichboden
m. **~ kitchen** n Einbauküche f. **~
sheet** n Spannlaken nt

fitting a passend ● n (*of clothes*)
Anprobe f; (*of shoes*) Weite f; (*Techn*)
Zubehörteil nt; **~s** pl Zubehör nt

five a fünf ● n Fünf f. **~r** n
Fünfpfundschein m

fix n (🆇 *drugs*) Fix m; be in a **~** 🅸 in
der Klemme sitzen ● vt befestigen
(**to** an + *dat*); (*arrange*) festlegen;
(*repair*) reparieren; (*Phot*) fixieren;
~ a meal Essen machen

fixed a fest

fixture n (*Sport*) Veranstaltung f; **~s
and fittings** zu einer Wohnung
gehörende Einrichtungen pl

fizz vi sprudeln

fizzle vi **~ out** verpuffen

fizzy a sprudelnd. **~ drink** n
Brause[limonade] f

flabbergasted a be **~** platt sein
🅸

flabby a schlaff

flag n Fahne f; (*Naut*) Flagge f

flag-pole n Fahnenstange f

flagrant a flagrant

flagstone n [Pflaster]platte f

flair n Begabung f

flake n Flocke f ● vi **~ [off]**
abblättern

flamboyant a extravagant

flame n Flamme f

flan n [fruit] **~** Obsttorte f

flank n Flanke f

flannel n Flanell m; (*for washing*)
Waschlappen m

flap n Klappe f; in a **~** 🅸 aufgeregt
● v (*pt/pp* flapped) vi flattern; 🅸
sich aufregen ● vt **~ its wings** mit
den Flügeln schlagen

flare n Leuchtsignal nt. ● vi **~ up**
auflodern; (🅸 *get angry*) aufbrausen

flash n Blitz m; in a **~** 🅸 im Nu ● vi
blitzen; (*repeatedly*) blinken; **~ past**
vorbeirasen

flash: **~back** n Rückblende f. **~er**
n (*Auto*) Blinker m. **~light** n (*Phot*)
Blitzlicht nt; (*Amer: torch*)
Taschenlampe f. **~y** a auffällig

flask n Flasche f

flat a (flatter, flattest) flach; <*surface*>
eben; <*refusal*> glatt; <*beer*> schal;
<*battery*> verbraucht; (*Auto*) leer;
<*tyre*> platt; (*Mus*) **A ~** As nt; **B ~** B
nt ● n Wohnung f; (🅸 *puncture*)
Reifenpanne f

flat: **~ly** adv <*refuse*> glatt. **~ rate**
n Einheitspreis m

flatten vt platt drücken

flatter vt schmeicheln (+ *dat*). **~y** n
Schmeichelei f

flat tyre n Reifenpanne f

flaunt vt prunken mit

flautist n Flötist(in) m(f)

flavour n Geschmack m ● vt
abschmecken. **~ing** n Aroma nt

flaw n Fehler m. **~less** a tadellos;
<*complexion*> makellos

flea n Floh m

fleck n Tupfen m

fled see flee

flee v (*pt/pp* fled) ● vi fliehen (**from**
vor + *dat*) ● vt flüchten aus

fleece n Vlies nt ● vt 🅸 schröpfen

fleet n Flotte f; (*of cars*) Wagenpark
m

fleeting a flüchtig

Flemish a flämisch

flesh n Fleisch nt

flew see fly²

flex¹ vt anspannen <muscle>

flex² n (Electr) Schnur f

flexib|ility n Biegsamkeit f; (fig) Flexibilität f. ~**le** a biegsam; (fig) flexibel

flick vt schnippen

flicker vi flackern

flier n = flyer

flight¹ n (fleeing) Flucht f

flight² n (flying) Flug m; ~ **of stairs** Treppe f

flight recorder n Flugschreiber m

flimsy a (-ier, -iest) dünn; <excuse> fadenscheinig

flinch vi zurückzucken

fling vt (pt/pp flung) schleudern

flint n Feuerstein m

flip vt/i schnippen; ~ **through** durchblättern

flippant a, **-ly** adv leichtfertig

flirt n kokette Frau f ● vi flirten

flirtat|ion n Flirt m. ~**ious** a kokett

flit vi (pt/pp flitted) flattern

float n Schwimmer m; (in procession) Festwagen m; (money) Wechselgeld nt ● vi <thing:> schwimmen; <person:> sich treiben lassen; (in air) schweben

flock n Herde f; (of birds) Schwarm m ● vi strömen

flog vt (pt/pp flogged) auspeitschen; (🔢 sell) verkloppen

flood n Überschwemmung f; (fig) Flut f ● vt überschwemmen

floodlight n Flutlicht nt ● vt (pt/pp floodlit) anstrahlen

floor n Fußboden m; (storey) Stock m

floor: ~ **board** n Dielenbrett nt. ~**polish** n Bohnerwachs nt. ~ **show** n Kabarettvorstellung f

flop n 🔢 (failure) Reinfall m; (Theat) Durchfall m ● vi (pt/pp flopped) 🔢 (fail) durchfallen

floppy a schlapp. ~ **disc** n Diskette f

floral a Blumen-

florid a <complexion> gerötet; <style> blumig

florist n Blumenhändler(in) m(f)

flounder vi zappeln

flour n Mehl nt

flourish n große Geste f; (scroll) Schnörkel m ● vi gedeihen; (fig) blühen ● vt schwenken

flout vt missachten

flow n Fluss m; (of traffic, blood) Strom m ● vi fließen

flower n Blume f ● vi blühen

flower: ~**bed** n Blumenbeet nt. ~**pot** n Blumentopf m. ~**y** a blumig

flown see fly²

flu n 🔢 Grippe f

fluctuat|e vi schwanken. ~**ion** n Schwankung f

fluent a, **-ly** adv fließend

fluff n Fusseln pl; (down) Flaum m. ~**y** a (-ier, -iest) flauschig

fluid a flüssig, (fig) veränderlich ● n Flüssigkeit f

fluke n [glücklicher] Zufall m

flung see fling

fluorescent a fluoreszierend

fluoride n Fluor nt

flush n (blush) Erröten nt ● vi rot werden ● vt spülen ● a in einer Ebene (with mit); (🔢 affluent) gut bei Kasse

flustered a nervös

flute n Flöte f

flutter n Flattern nt ● vi flattern

fly¹ n (pl flies) Fliege f

fly² v (pt flew, pp flown) ● vi fliegen; <flag:> wehen; (rush) sausen ● vt fliegen; führen <flag>

fly³ n & **flies** pl (on trousers) Hosenschlitz m

flyer n Flieger(in) m(f); (leaflet) Flugblatt nt

foal n Fohlen nt

foam n Schaum m; (synthetic) Schaumstoff m ● vi schäumen

fob vt (pt/pp fobbed) ~ **sth off** etw andrehen (on s.o. jdm); ~ **s.o. off** jdn abspeisen (with mit)

focal n Brenn-

focus n Brennpunkt m; **in ~** scharf eingestellt ● v (pt/pp **focused** or **focussed**) ● vt einstellen (**on** auf + acc) ● vi (fig) sich konzentrieren (**on** auf + acc)

fog n Nebel m

foggy a (**foggier, foggiest**) neblig

fog-horn n Nebelhorn nt

foible n Eigenart f

foil¹ n Folie f; (Culin) Alufolie f

foil² vt (thwart) vereiteln

foil³ n (Fencing) Florett nt

fold n Falte f; (in paper) Kniff m ● vt falten; **~ one's arms** die Arme verschränken ● vi sich falten lassen; (fail) eingehen. **~ up** vt zusammenfalten; zusammenklappen <chair> ● vi sich zusammenfalten/-klappen lassen; [T] <business:> eingehen

fold|er n Mappe f. **~ing** a Klapp-

foliage n Blätter pl; (of tree) Laub nt

folk npl Leute pl

folk: ~-dance n Volkstanz m. **~-song** n Volkslied nt

follow vt/i folgen (+ dat); (pursue) verfolgen; (in vehicle) nachfahren (+ dat). **~ up** vt nachgehen (+ dat)

follow|er n Anhänger(in) m(f). **~ing** a folgend ● n Folgende(s) nt; (supporters) Anhängerschaft f ● prep im Anschluss an (+ acc)

folly n Torheit f

fond a (-er, -est), **-ly** adv liebevoll; **be ~ of** gern haben; gern essen <food>

fondle vt liebkosen

fondness n Liebe f (**for** zu)

food n Essen nt; (for animals) Futter nt; (groceries) Lebensmittel pl. **~ poisoning** n Lebensmittelvergiftung f

food poisoning n Lebensmittelvergiftung f

fool¹ n (Culin) Fruchtcreme f

fool² n Narr m; **make a ~ of oneself** sich lächerlich machen ● vt hereinlegen ● vi **~ around** herumalbern

fool|hardy a tollkühn. **~ish** a, **-ly** adv dumm. **~ishness** n Dummheit f. **~proof** a narrensicher

foot n (pl **feet**) Fuß m; (measure) Fuß m (30,48 cm); (of bed) Fußende nt; **on ~** zu Fuß; **on one's feet** auf den Beinen; **put one's ~ in it** [T] ins Fettnäpfchen treten; **7 ~ or feet** 7 fuß

foot: ~ball n Fußball m. **~baller** n Fußballspieler m. **~ball pools** npl Fußballtoto nt. **~bridge** n Fußgängerbrücke f. **~hills** npl Vorgebirge nt. **~hold** n Halt m. **~ing** n Halt m. **~lights** npl Rampenlicht nt. **~note** n Fußnote f. **~path** n Fußweg m. **~print** n Fußabdruck m. **~step** n Schritt m; **follow in s.o.'s ~steps** (fig) in jds Fußstapfen treten. **~wear** n Schuhwerk nt

for

● preposition

····▸ (on behalf of; in place of; in favour of) für (+ acc). **I did it for you** ich habe es für dich gemacht. **I work for him/for a bank** ich arbeite für ihn/für eine Bank. **be for doing sth** dafür sein, etw zu tun. **cheque/bill for £5** Scheck/Rechnung über 5 Pfund. **for nothing** umsonst. **what have you got for a cold?** was haben Sie gegen Erkältungen?

····▸ (expressing reason) wegen (+ gen); (with emotion) aus. **famous for these wines** berühmt wegen dieser Weine od für diese Weine. **he was sentenced to death for murder** er wurde wegen Mordes zum Tode verurteilt. **were it not for you/your help** ohne dich/deine Hilfe. **for fear/love of** aus Angst vor (+ dat)/aus Liebe zu (+ dat)

····▸ (expressing purpose) (with action, meal) zu (+ dat); (with object) für (+ acc). **it's for washing the car** es ist zum Autowaschen. **we met for a discussion** wir trafen uns zu einer Besprechung. **for pleasure** zum Vergnügen. **meat for lunch** Fleisch zum Mittagessen. **what is that for?** wofür od wozu ist das? **a dish for nuts** eine Schale für Nüsse

····▸ (expressing direction) nach (+ dat); (less precise) in Richtung. **the train for Oxford** der Zug nach Oxford. **they**

were heading *or* making for London
sie fuhren in Richtung London
····▸ (*expressing time*) (*completed process*) … lang; (*continuing process*) seit (+ *dat*). I lived here for two years ich habe zwei Jahre [lang] hier gewohnt. I have been living here for two years ich wohne hier seit zwei Jahren. we are staying for a week wir werden eine Woche bleiben
····▸ (*expressing difficulty, impossibility, embarrassment etc.*) + *dat*. it's impossible/inconvenient for her es ist ihr unmöglich/ungelegen. it was embarrassing for our teacher unserem Lehrer war es peinlich
● *conjunction*
····▸ denn. he's not coming for he has no money er kommt nicht mit, denn er hat kein Geld

forbade *see* forbid
forbid *vt* (*pt* forbade, *pp* forbidden) verbieten (**s.o.** jdm). ~**ding** *a* bedrohlich; (*stern*) streng
force *n* Kraft *f*; (*of blow*) Wucht *f*; (*violence*) Gewalt *f*; in ~ gültig; (*in large numbers*) in großer Zahl; **come into** ~ in Kraft treten; **the** ~**s** *pl* die Streitkräfte *pl* ● *vt* zwingen; (*break open*) aufbrechen
forced *a* gezwungen; ~ **landing** Notlandung *f*
force: ~**feed** *vt* (*pt/pp* -fed) zwangsernähren. ~**ful** *a*, -**ly** *adv* energisch
forceps *n inv* Zange *f*
forcible *a* gewaltsam
ford *n* Furt *f* ● *vt* durchwaten; (*in vehicle*) durchfahren
fore *a* vordere(r,s)
fore: ~**arm** *n* Unterarm *m*. ~**cast** *n* Voraussage *f* ● *vt* (*pt/pp* -cast) voraussagen, vorhersagen. ~**finger** *n* Zeigefinger *m*. ~**gone** *a* be a ~**gone conclusion** von vornherein feststehen. ~**ground** *n* Vordergrund *m*. ~**head** *n* Stirn *f*. ~**hand** *n* Vorhand *f*
foreign *a* ausländisch; <*country*> fremd; **he is** ~ er ist Ausländer. ~ **currency** *n* Devisen *pl*. ~**er** *n*

Ausländer(in) *m(f)*. ~ **language** *n* Fremdsprache *f*
Foreign: ~ **Office** *n* ≈ Außenministerium *nt*. ~ **Secretary** *n* ≈ Außenminister *m*
fore: ~**leg** *n* Vorderbein *nt*. ~**man** *n* Vorarbeiter *m*. ~**most** *a* führend ● *adv* **first and** ~**most** zuallererst. ~**name** *n* Vorname *m*. ~**runner** *n* Vorläufer *m*
foresee *vt* (*pt* -saw, *pp* -seen) voraussehen, vorhersehen. ~**able** *a* **in the** ~**able future** in absehbarer Zeit
foresight *n* Weitblick *m*
forest *n* Wald *m*. ~**er** *n* Förster *m*
forestry *n* Forstwirtschaft *f*
foretaste *n* Vorgeschmack *m*
forever *adv* für immer
forewarn *vt* vorher warnen
foreword *n* Vorwort *nt*
forfeit *n* (*in game*) Pfand *nt* ● *vt* verwirken
forgave *see* forgive
forge *n* Schmiede *f* ● *vt* schmieden; (*counterfeit*) fälschen. ~**r** *n* Fälscher *m*. ~**ry** *n* Fälschung *f*
forget *vt/i* (*pt* -got, *pp* -gotten) vergessen; verlernen <*language, skill*>. ~**ful** *a* vergesslich. ~**fulness** *n* Vergesslichkeit *f*. ~**me-not** *n* Vergissmeinnicht *nt*
forgive *vt* (*pt* -gave, *pp* -given) ~ **s.o. for sth** jdm etw vergeben *od* verzeihen
forgot(ten) *see* forget
fork *n* Gabel *f*; (*in road*) Gabelung *f* ● *vi* <*road:*> sich gabeln; ~ **right** rechts abzweigen
fork-lift truck *n* Gabelstapler *m*
forlorn *a* verlassen; <*hope*> schwach
form *n* Form *f*; (*document*) Formular *nt*; (*bench*) Bank *f*; (*Sch*) Klasse *f* ● *vt* formen (**into** zu); (*create*) bilden ● *vi* sich bilden; <*idea:*> Gestalt annehmen
formal *a*, -**ly** *adv* formell, förmlich. ~**ity** *n* Förmlichkeit *f*; (*requirement*) Formalität *f*
format *n* Format *nt* ● *vt* formatieren

formation n Formation f

former a ehemalig; **the ~** der/die/das Erstere. **~ly** adv früher

formidable a gewaltig

formula n (pl **-ae** or **-s**) Formel f

formulate vt formulieren

forsake vt (pt **-sook**, pp **-saken**) verlassen

fort n (Mil) Fort nt

forth adv **back and ~** hin und her; **and so ~** und so weiter

forth: **~coming** a bevorstehend; (🅸 communicative) mitteilsam. **~right** a direkt

fortieth a vierzigste(r,s)

fortification n Befestigung f

fortify vt (pt/pp **-ied**) befestigen; (fig) stärken

fortnight n vierzehn Tage pl. **~ly** a vierzehntäglich ● adv alle vierzehn Tage

fortress n Festung f

fortunate a glücklich; **be ~** Glück haben. **~ly** adv glüklicherweise

fortune n Glück nt; (money) Vermögen nt. **~-teller** n Wahrsagerin f

forty a vierzig

forward adv vorwärts; (to the front) nach vorn ● a Vorwärts-; (presumptuous) anmaßend ● n (Sport) Stürmer m ● vt nachsenden <letter>. **~s** adv vorwärts

fossil n Fossil nt

foster vt fördern; in Pflege nehmen <child>. **~-child** n Pflegekind nt. **~-mother** n Pflegemutter f

fought see fight

foul a (-er, -est) widerlich; <language> unflätig; **~ play** (Jur) Mord m ● n (Sport) Foul nt ● vt verschmutzen; (obstruct) blockieren; (Sport) foulen

found[1] see find

found[2] vt gründen

foundation n (basis) Gundlage f; (charitable) Stiftung f; **~s** pl Fundament nt

founder n Gründer(in) m(f)

foundry n Gießerei f

fountain n Brunnen m

four a vier ● n Vier f

four: **~teen** a vierzehn ● n Vierzehn f. **~teenth** a vierzehnte(r,s)

fourth a vierte(r,s)

fowl n Geflügel nt

fox n Fuchs m ● vt (puzzle) verblüffen

foyer n Foyer nt; (in hotel) Empfangshalle f

fraction n Bruchteil m; (Math) Bruch m

fracture n Bruch m ● vt/i brechen

fragile a zerbrechlich

fragment n Bruchstück nt, Fragment nt

fragran|ce n Duft m. **~t** a duftend

frail a (-er, -est) gebrechlich

frame n Rahmen m; (of spectacles) Gestell nt; (Anat) Körperbau m ● vt einrahmen; (fig) formulieren; 🗶 ein Verbrechen anhängen (+ dat). **~work** n Gerüst nt; (fig) Gerippe nt

franc n (French, Belgian) Franc m; (Swiss) Franken m

France n Frankreich nt

franchise n (Pol) Wahlrecht nt; (Comm) Franchise nt

frank a, **-ly** adv offen

frankfurter n Frankfurter f

frantic a, **-ally** adv verzweifelt; außer sich (dat) (**with** vor)

fraternal a brüderlich

fraud n Betrug m; (person) Betrüger(in) m(f)

fray vi ausfransen

freak n Missbildung f; (person) Missgeburt f ● a anormal

freckle n Sommersprosse f

free a (freer, freest) frei; <ticket, copy, time> Frei-; (lavish) freigebig; **~ [of charge]** kostenlos; **set ~** freilassen; (rescue) befreien ● vt (pt/pp **freed**) freilassen; (rescue) befreien; (disentangle) freibekommen

free: **~dom** n Freiheit f. **~hold** n [freier] Grundbesitz m. **~lance** a & adv freiberuflich. **~ly** adv frei; (voluntarily) freiwillig; (generously) großzügig. **F~mason** n Freimaurer m. **~range** a ~-range eggs Landeier pl. **~ sample** n Gratisprobe f. **~style** n Freistil m. **~way** n (Amer) Autobahn f

freez|e vt (pt froze, pp frozen) einfrieren; stoppen <wages> ● vi it's ~ing es friert. **~er** n Gefriertruhe f; (upright) Gefrierschrank m. **~ing** a eiskalt ● n below ~ing unter Null

freight n Fracht f. **~er** n Frachter m. **~ train** n Güterzug m

French a französisch ● n (Lang) Französisch nt; **the ~** pl die Franzosen

French: ~ beans npl grüne Bohnen pl. **~ bread** n Stangenbrot nt. **~ fries** npl Pommes frites pl. **~man** n Franzose m. **~ window** n Terrassentür f. **~woman** n Französin f

frenzy n Raserei f

frequency n Häufigkeit f; (Phys) Frequenz f

frequent[1] a, **-ly** adv häufig

frequent[2] vt regelmäßig besuchen

fresh a (-er, -est), **-ly** adv frisch; (new) neu; (cheeky) frech

freshness n Frische f

freshwater a Süßwasser-

fret vi (pt/pp fretted) sich grämen. **~ful** a weinerlich

fretsaw n Laubsäge f

friction n Reibung f; (fig) Reibereien pl

Friday n Freitag m

fridge n Kühlschrank m

fried see fry[2] ● a gebraten; **~ egg** Spiegelei nt

friend n Freund(in) m(f). **~liness** n Freundlichkeit f. **~ly** a (-ier, -iest) freundlich; ~ly with befreundet mit. **~ship** n Freundschaft f

fright n Schreck m

frighten vt Angst machen (+ dat); (startle) erschrecken; be ~ed Angst haben (of vor + dat). **~ing** a Angst erregend

frightful a, **-ly** adv schrecklich

frigid a frostig; (Psych) frigide. **~ity** n Frostigkeit f; Frigidität f

frill n Rüsche f; (paper) Manschette f. **~y** a rüschenbesetzt

fringe n Fransen pl; (of hair) Pony m; (fig: edge) Rand m

frisk vi herumspringen ● vt (search) durchsuchen

frisky a (-ier, -iest) lebhaft

fritter vt ~ [away] verplempern ⊞

frivol|ity n Frivolität f. **~ous** a, **-ly** adv frivol, leichtfertig

fro see to

frock n Kleid nt

frog n Frosch m. **~man** n Froschmann m

frolic vi (pt/pp frolicked) herumtollen

from prep von (+ dat); (out of) aus (+ dat); (according to) nach (+ dat); ~ Monday ab Montag; ~ that day seit dem Tag

front n Vorderseite f; (fig) Fassade f; (of garment) Vorderteil nt; (sea~) Strandpromenade f; (Mil, Pol, Meteorol) Front f; in ~ of vor; in or at the ~ vorne; to the ~ nach vorne ● a vordere(r,s); <page, row> erste(r,s); <tooth, wheel> Vorder-

front: ~ door n Haustür f. **~ garden** n Vorgarten m

frontier n Grenze f

frost n Frost m; (hoar-~) Raureif m; ten degrees of ~ zehn Grad Kälte. **~bite** n Erfrierung f. **~bitten** a erfroren

frost|ed a ~ed glass Mattglas nt. **~ing** n (Amer Culin) Zuckerguss m. **~y** a, **-ily** adv frostig

froth n Schaum m ● vi schäumen. **~y** a schaumig

frown n Stirnrunzeln nt ● vi die Stirn runzeln

froze see freeze

frozen see freeze ● a gefroren; (Culin) tiefgekühlt; I'm ~ ⊞ mir ist eiskalt. **~ food** n Tiefkühlkost f

frugal a, **-ly** adv sparsam; <meal> frugal

fruit n Frucht f; (collectively) Obst nt. **~ cake** n englischer [Tee]kuchen m

fruitful a fruchtbar

fruit: ~ **juice** n Obstsaft m. ~**less** a, **-ly** adv fruchtlos. ~ **salad** n Obstsalat m

fruity a fruchtig

frustrat|e vt vereiteln; (Psych) frustrieren. ~**ion** n Frustration f

fry vt/i (pt/pp fried) [in der Pfanne] braten. ~**ing-pan** n Bratpfanne f

fuel n Brennstoff m; (for car) Kraftstoff m; (for aircraft) Treibstoff m

fugitive n Flüchtling m

fulfil vt (pt/pp -filled) erfüllen. ~**ment** n Erfüllung f

full a & adv (-er, -est) voll; (detailed) ausführlich; <skirt> weit; ~ **of** voll von (+ dat), voller (+ gen); **at** ~ **speed** in voller Fahrt ● n **in** ~ vollständig

full: ~ **moon** n Vollmond m. ~-**scale** a <model> in Originalgröße; <rescue, alert> großangelegt. ~ **stop** n Punkt m. ~-**time** a ganztägig ● adv ganztags

fully adv völlig; (in detail) ausführlich

fumble vi herumfummeln (with an + dat)

fume vi vor Wut schäumen

fumes npl Dämpfe pl; (from car) Abgase pl

fun n Spaß m; **for** ~ aus od zum Spaß; **make** ~ **of** sich lustig machen über (+ acc); **have** ~! viel Spaß!

function n Funktion f; (event) Veranstaltung f ● vi funktionieren; (serve) dienen (as als). ~**al** a zweckmäßig

fund n Fonds m; (fig) Vorrat m; ~**s** pl Geldmittel pl ● vt finanzieren

fundamental a grundlegend; (essential) wesentlich

funeral n Beerdigung f; (cremation) Feuerbestattung f

funeral: ~ **march** n Trauermarsch m. ~ **service** n Trauergottesdienst m

funfair n Jahrmarkt m

fungus n (pl -gi) Pilz m

funnel n Trichter m; (on ship, train) Schornstein m

funnily adv komisch; ~ **enough** komischerweise

funny a (-ier, -iest) komisch

fur n Fell nt; (for clothing) Pelz m; (in kettle) Kesselstein m. ~ **coat** n Pelzmantel m

furious a, **-ly** adv wütend (with auf + acc)

furnace n (Techn) Ofen m

furnish vt einrichten; (supply) liefern. ~**ed** a ~**ed room** möbliertes Zimmer nt. ~**ings** npl Einrichtungsgegenstände pl

furniture n Möbel pl

further a weitere(r,s); **at the** ~ **end** am anderen Ende; **until** ~ **notice** bis auf weiteres ● adv weiter; ~ **off** weiter entfernt ● vt fördern

furthest a am weitesten entfernt ● adv am weitesten

fury n Wut f

fuse¹ n (of bomb) Zünder m; (cord) Zündschnur f

fuse² n (Electr) Sicherung f ● vt/i verschmelzen; **the lights have** ~**d** die Sicherung [für das Licht] ist durchgebrannt. ~-**box** n Sicherungskasten m

fuselage n (Aviat) Rumpf m

fuss n Getue nt; **make a** ~ **of** verwöhnen; (caress) liebkosen ● vi Umstände machen

fussy a (-ier, -iest) wählerisch; (particular) penibel

futil|e a zwecklos. ~**ity** n Zwecklosigkeit f

future a zukünftig ● n Zukunft f; (Gram) [erstes] Futur nt

futuristic a futuristisch

fuzzy a (-ier, -iest) <hair> kraus; (blurred) verschwommen

Gg

gabble *vi* schnell reden

gable *n* Giebel *m*

gadget *n* [kleines] Gerät *nt*

Gaelic *n* Gälisch *nt*

gag *n* Knebel *m*; (*joke*) Witz *m*; (*Theat*) Gag *m* ● *vt* (*pt/pp* **gagged**) knebeln

gaiety *n* Fröhlichkeit *f*

gaily *adv* fröhlich

gain *n* Gewinn *m*; (*increase*) Zunahme *f* ● *vt* gewinnen; (*obtain*) erlangen; ~ **weight** zunehmen ● *vi* <*clock:*> vorgehen

gait *n* Gang *m*

gala *n* Fest *nt* ● *attrib* Gala-

galaxy *n* Galaxie *f*; **the G**~ die Milchstraße

gale *n* Sturm *m*

gallant *a*, **-ly** *adv* tapfer; (*chivalrous*) galant. ~**ry** *n* Tapferkeit *f*

gall-bladder *n* Gallenblase *f*

gallery *n* Galerie *f*

galley *n* (*ship's kitchen*) Kombüse *f*; ~ [**proof**] [Druck]fahne *f*

gallon *n* Gallone *f* (= *4,5 l*; *Amer* = *3,785 l*)

gallop *n* Galopp *m* ● *vi* galoppieren

gallows *n* Galgen *m*

galore *adv* in Hülle und Fülle

gamble *n* (*risk*) Risiko *nt* ● *vi* [um Geld] spielen; ~ **on** (*rely*) sich verlassen auf (+ *acc*). ~**r** *n* Spieler(in) *m(f)*

game *n* Spiel *nt*; (*animals, birds*) Wild *nt*; ~**s** (*Sch*) Sport *m* ● *a* (*brave*) tapfer; (*willing*) bereit (**for** zu). ~**keeper** *n* Wildhüter *m*

gammon *n* [geräucherter] Schinken *m*

gang *n* Bande *f*; (*of workmen*) Kolonne *f*

gangling *a* schlaksig

gangrene *n* Wundbrand *m*

gangster *n* Gangster *m*

gangway *n* Gang *m*; (*Naut, Aviat*) Gangway *f*

gaol *n* Gefängnis *nt* ● *vt* ins Gefängnis sperren. ~**er** *n* Gefängniswärter *m*

gap *n* Lücke *f*; (*interval*) Pause *f*; (*difference*) Unterschied *m*

gap|e *vi* gaffen; ~**e at** anstarren. ~**ing** *a* klaffend

garage *n* Garage *f*; (*for repairs*) Werkstatt *f*; (*for petrol*) Tankstelle *f*

garbage *n* Müll *m*. ~ **can** *n* (*Amer*) Mülleimer *m*

garbled *a* verworren

garden *n* Garten *m*; [**public**] ~**s** *pl* [öffentliche] Anlagen *pl* ● *vi* im Garten arbeiten. ~**er** *n* Gärtner(in) *m(f)*. ~**ing** *n* Gartenarbeit *f*

gargle *n* (*liquid*) Gurgelwasser *nt* ● *vi* gurgeln

garish *a* grell

garland *n* Girlande *f*

garlic *n* Knoblauch *m*

garment *n* Kleidungsstück *nt*

garnet *n* Granat *m*

garnish *n* Garnierung *f* ● *vt* garnieren

garrison *n* Garnison *f*

garrulous *a* geschwätzig

garter *n* Strumpfband *nt*; (*Amer*: *suspender*) Strumpfhalter *m*

gas *n* Gas *nt*; (*Amer* 🄸: *petrol*) Benzin *m* ● *v* (*pt/pp* **gassed**) ● *vt* vergasen ● *vi* 🄸 schwatzen. ~ **cooker** *n* Gasherd *m*. ~ **fire** *n* Gasofen *m*

gash *n* Schnitt *m*; (*wound*) klaffende Wunde *f*

gasket *n* (*Techn*) Dichtung *f*

gas: ~ **mask** *n* Gasmaske *f*. ~- **meter** *n* Gaszähler *m*

gasoline *n* (*Amer*) Benzin *nt*

gasp *vi* keuchen; (*in surprise*) hörbar die Luft einziehen

gas station *n* (*Amer*) Tankstelle *f*

gastric *a* Magen-

gastronomy *n* Gastronomie *f*

gate n Tor nt; (to field) Gatter nt; (barrier) Schranke f, (at airport) Flugsteig m

gate: ~**crasher** n ungeladener Gast m. ~**way** n Tor nt

gather vt sammeln; (pick) pflücken; (conclude) folgern (from aus) ● vi sich versammeln; <storm:> sich zusammenziehen. ~**ing** n family ~ing Familientreffen nt

gaudy a (-ier, -iest) knallig

gauge n Stärke f, (Rail) Spurweite f, (device) Messinstrument nt

gaunt a hager

gauze n Gaze f

gave see give

gawky a (-ier, -iest) schlaksig

gay a (-er, -est) fröhlich; 🔲 homosexuell, 🔲 schwul

gaze n [langer] Blick m ● vi sehen; ~ **at** ansehen

GB abbr of Great Britain

gear n Ausrüstung f, (Techn) Getriebe nt; (Auto) Gang m; **change** ~ schalten

gear: ~**box** n (Auto) Getriebe nt. ~**lever** n, (Amer) ~**shift** n Schalthebel m

geese see goose

gel n Gel nt

gelatine n Gelatine f

gem n Juwel nt

gender n (Gram) Geschlecht nt

gene n Gen nt

genealogy n Genealogie f

general a allgemein ● n General m; **in** ~ im Allgemeinen. ~ **election** n allgemeine Wahlen pl

generaliz|ation n Verallgemeinerung f. ~**e** vi verallgemeinern

generally adv im Allgemeinen

general practitioner n praktischer Arzt m

generate vt erzeugen

generation n Generation f

generator n Generator m

generosity n Großzügigkeit f

generous a, -**ly** adv großzügig

Geneva n Genf nt

genial a, -**ly** adv freundlich

genitals pl [äußere] Geschlechtsteile pl

genitive a & n ~ **[case]** Genitiv m

genius n (pl -uses) Genie nt; (quality) Genialität f

genre n Gattung f, Genre nt

gent n 🔲 Herr m; **the** ~**s** sg die Herrentoilette f

genteel a vornehm

gentle a (-r, -st) sanft

gentleman n Herr m; (well-mannered) Gentleman m

gent|leness n Sanftheit f. ~**ly** adv sanft

genuine a echt; (sincere) aufrichtig. ~**ly** adv (honestly) ehrlich

geograph|ical a, -**ly** adv geographisch. ~**y** n Geographie f, Erdkunde f

geological a, -**ly** adv geologisch

geolog|ist n Geologe m/-gin f. ~**y** n Geologie f

geometr|ic(al) a geometrisch. ~**y** n Geometrie f

geranium n Geranie f

geriatric a geriatrisch ● n geriatrischer Patient m

germ n Keim m; ~**s** pl 🔲 Bazillen pl

German a deutsch ● n (person) Deutsche(r) m/f, (Lang) Deutsch nt; **in** ~ auf Deutsch; **into** ~ ins Deutsche

Germanic a germanisch

Germany n Deutschland nt

germinate vi keimen

gesticulate vi gestikulieren

gesture n Geste f

get v

pt **got**, pp **got** (Amer also **gotten**), pres p **getting**

● transitive verb

····▸ (obtain, receive) bekommen, 🔲 kriegen; (procure) besorgen; (buy) kaufen; (fetch) holen. **get a job/taxi for s.o.** jdm einen Job verschaffen/ein Taxi besorgen. **I must get some bread** ich muss Brot holen. **get permission** die Erlaubnis erhalten. I couldn't get her on the phone ich konnte sie nicht telefonisch erreichen

····▸ (*prepare*) machen <*meal*>. he got the breakfast er machte das Frühstück

····▸ (*cause*) get s.o. to do sth jdn dazu bringen, etw zu tun. get one's hair cut sich (*dat*) die Haare schneiden lassen. get one's hands dirty sich (*dat*) die Hände schmutzig machen

····▸ get the bus/train (*travel by*) den Bus/Zug nehmen; (*be in time for, catch*) den Bus/Zug erreichen

····▸ have got (Ⅱ *have*) haben. I've got a cold ich habe eine Erkältung

····▸ have got to do sth etw tun müssen. I've got to hurry ich muss mich beeilen

····▸ (Ⅱ *understand*) kapieren Ⅱ. I don't get it ich kapiere nicht

● *intransitive verb*

····▸ (*become*) werden. get older älter werden. the weather got worse das Wetter wurde schlechter. get to kommen zu/nach <*town*>; (*reach*) erreichen. get dressed sich anziehen. get married heiraten.

● *phrasal verbs* ● **get about** *vi* (*move*) sich bewegen; (*travel*) herumkommen; (*spread*) sich verbreiten. ● **get at** *vt* (*have access*) herankommen an (+ *acc*); (Ⅱ *criticize*) anmachen Ⅱ. (*mean*) what are you getting at? worauf willst du hinaus? ● **get away** *vi* (*leave*) wegkommen; (*escape*) entkommen. ● **get back** *vi* zurückkommen; *vt* (*recover*) zurückbekommen; get one's own back sich revanchieren. ● **get by** *vi* vorbeikommen; (*manage*) sein Auskommen haben. ● **get down** *vi* heruntersteigen; get down to sich [heran]machen an (+ *acc*); *vt* (*depress*) deprimieren. ● **get in** *vi* (*into bus*) einsteigen; *vt* (*fetch*) hereinholen. ● **get off** *vi* (*dismount*) absteigen; (*from bus*) aussteigen; (*leave*) wegkommen; (*Jur*) freigesprochen werden; *vt* (*remove*) abbekommen. ● **get on** *vi* (*mount*) aufsteigen; (*to bus*) einsteigen; (*be on good terms*) gut auskommen (with mit + *dat*); (*make progress*)

Fortschritte machen; how are you getting on? wie geht's? ● **get out** *vi* herauskommen; (*of car*) aussteigen; get out of (*avoid doing*) sich drücken um; *vt* (*take out*) herausholen; herausbekommen <*cork, stain*>. ● **get over** *vi* hinübersteigen; *vt* (*fig*) hinwegkommen über (+ *acc*). ● **get round** *vi* herumkommen; I never get round to it ich komme nie dazu; *vt* herumkriegen; (*avoid*). umgehen. ● **get through** *vi* durchkommen. ● **get up** *vi* aufstehen

get: ~**away** *n* Flucht *f*. ~**-up** *n* Aufmachung *f*

ghastly *a* (-ier, -iest) grässlich; (*pale*) blass

gherkin *n* Essiggurke *f*

ghost *n* Geist *m*, Gespenst *nt*. ~**ly** *a* geisterhaft

ghoulish *a* makaber

giant *n* Riese *m* ● *a* riesig

gibberish *n* Kauderwelsch *nt*

giblets *npl* Geflügelklein *nt*

giddiness *n* Schwindel *m*

giddy *a* (-ier, -iest) schwindlig

gift *n* Geschenk *nt*; (*to charity*) Gabe *f*, (*talent*) Begabung *f*. ~**ed** *a* begabt

gigantic *a* riesig, riesengroß

giggle *n* Kichern *nt* ● *vi* kichern

gild *vt* vergolden

gilt *a* vergoldet ● *n* Vergoldung *f*. ~**-edged** *a* (*Comm*) mündelsicher

gimmick *n* Trick *m*

gin *n* Gin *m*

ginger *a* rotblond; <*cat*> rot ● *n* Ingwer *m*. ~**bread** *n* Pfefferkuchen *m*

gingerly *adv* vorsichtig

gipsy *n* = gypsy

giraffe *n* Giraffe *f*

girder *n* (*Techn*) Träger *m*

girl *n* Mädchen *nt*; (*young woman*) junge Frau *f*. ~**friend** *n* Freundin *f*. ~**ish** *a*, -**ly** *adv* mädchenhaft

gist *n* the ~ das Wesentliche

give *n* Elastizität *f* ● *v* (*pt* gave, *pp* given) ● *vt* geben/(*as present*) schenken (to *dat*); (*donate*) spenden;

<lecture> halten; <one's name> angeben ● vi geben; (yield) nachgeben. **~ away** vt verschenken; (betray) verraten; (distribute) verteilen. **~ back** vt zurückgeben. **~ in** vt einreichen ● vi (yield) nachgeben. **~ off** vt abgeben ● vi aufgeben; **~ oneself up** sich stellen. **~ way** vi nachgeben; (Auto) die Vorfahrt beachten

glacier n Gletscher m

glad a froh (of über + acc)

gladly adv gern[e]

glamorous a glanzvoll; <film star> glamourös

glamour n [betörender] Glanz m

glance n [flüchtiger] Blick m ● vi ~ at einen Blick werfen auf (+ acc). **~ up** vi aufblicken

gland n Drüse f

glare n grelles Licht nt; (look) ärgerlicher Blick m ● vi ~ at böse ansehen

glaring a grell; <mistake> krass

glass n Glas nt; (mirror) Spiegel m; **~es** n pl (spectacles) Brille f. **~y** a glasig

glaze n Glasur f

gleam n Schein m ● vi glänzen

glib a, **-ly** adv (pej) gewandt

glid|e vi gleiten; (through the air) schweben. **~er** n Segelflugzeug nt. **~ing** n Segelfliegen nt

glimmer n Glimmen nt ● vi glimmen

glimpse vt flüchtig sehen

glint n Blitzen nt ● vi blitzen

glisten vi glitzern

glitter vi glitzern

global a, **-ly** adv global

globaliz|e vt globalisieren. **~ation** n Globalisierung f

globe n Kugel f; (map) Globus m

gloom n Düsterkeit f; (fig) Pessimismus m

gloomy a (-ier, -iest), **-ily** adv düster; (fig) pessimistisch

glorify vt (pt/pp -ied) verherrlichen

glorious a herrlich; <deed, hero> glorreich

glory n Ruhm m; (splendour) Pracht f ● vi ~ in genießen

gloss n Glanz m ● a Glanz- ● vi ~ over beschönigen

glossary n Glossar nt

glossy a (-ier, -iest) glänzend

glove n Handschuh m

glow n Glut f; (of candle) Schein m ● vi glühen; <candle:> scheinen. **~ing** a glühend; <account> begeistert

glucose n Traubenzucker m, Glukose f

glue n Klebstoff m ● vt (pres p gluing) kleben (to an + acc)

glum a (glummer, glummest), **-ly** adv niedergeschlagen

glut n Überfluss m (of an + dat)

glutton n Vielfraß m

GM abbr (genetically modified); **~ crops/food** gentechnisch veränderte Feldfrüchte/Nahrungsmittel

gnash vt ~ one's teeth mit den Zähnen knirschen

gnat n Mücke f

gnaw vt/i nagen (at an + dat)

go

3 sg pres tense **goes**; pt **went**; pp **gone**

● intransitive verb

····▸ gehen; (in vehicle) fahren. **go by air** fliegen. **where are you going?** wo gehst du hin? **I'm going to France** ich fahre nach Frankreich. **go to the doctor's/dentist's** zum Arzt/Zahnarzt gehen. **go to the theatre/cinema** ins Theater/Kino gehen. **I must go to Paris/to the doctor's** ich muss nach Paris/zum Arzt. **go shopping** einkaufen gehen. **go swimming** schwimmen gehen. **go to see s.o.** jdn besuchen [gehen]

····▸ (leave) weggehen; (on journey) abfahren. **I must go now** ich muss jetzt gehen. **we're going on Friday** wir fahren am Freitag

····▸ (work, function) <engine, clock> gehen

····➤ (*become*) werden. **go deaf** taub werden. **go mad** verrückt werden. **he went red** er wurde rot

····➤ (*pass*) <*time*> vergehen

····➤ (*disappear*) weggehen; <*coat, hat, stain*> verschwinden. **my headache/ my coat/the stain has gone** mein Kopfweh/mein Mantel/der Fleck ist weg

····➤ (*turn out, progress*) gehen; verlaufen. **everything's going very well** alles geht *od* verläuft sehr gut. **how did the party go?** wie war die Party? **go smoothly/according to plan** reibungslos/planmäßig verlaufen

····➤ (*match*) zusammenpassen. **the two colours don't go [together]** die beiden Farben passen nicht zusammen

····➤ (*cease to function*) kaputtgehen; <*fuse*> durchbrennen. **his memory is going** sein Gedächtnis lässt nach

● *auxiliary verb*

····➤ **be going to** werden + *inf*. **it's going to rain** es wird regnen. **I'm not going to** ich werde es nicht tun

● *noun*

     pl **goes**

····➤ (*turn*) **it's your go** du bist jetzt an der Reihe *od* dran

····➤ (*attempt*) Versuch. **have a go at doing sth** versuchen, etw zu tun. **have another go!** versuch's noch mal!

····➤ (*energy, drive*) Energie

····➤ (*in phrases*) **on the go** auf Trab. **make a go of sth** das Beste aus etw machen

● *phrasal verbs*

● **go across** *vi* hinübergehen/-fahren; *vt* überqueren. ● **go after** *vt* (*pursue*) jagen. ● **go away** *vi* weggehen/-fahren; (*on holiday or business*) verreisen. ● **go back** *vi* zurückgehen/-fahren. ● **go back on** *vt* nicht [ein]halten <*promise*>. ● **go by** *vi* vorbeigehen/-fahren; <*time*> vergehen. ● **go down** *vi* hinuntergehen/-fahren; <*sun, ship*> untergehen; <*prices*> fallen; <*temperature, swelling*> zurückgehen. ● **go for** *vt* holen; ([T]

attack) losgehen auf (+ *acc*). ● **go in** *vi* hineingehen/-fahren; ● **go in for** *vt* teilnehmen an (+ *dat*) <*competition*>; (*take up*) sich verlegen auf (+ *acc*). ● **go off** *vi* weggehen/-fahren; <*alarm clock*> klingeln; <*alarm, gun, bomb*> losgehen; <*light*> ausgehen; (*go bad*) schlecht werden; **go off well** gut verlaufen; *vt*: **go off sth** von etw abkommen. ● **go on** *vi* weitergehen/-fahren; <*light*> angehen; (*continue*) weitermachen; (*talking*) fortfahren; (*happen*) vorgehen. ● **go on at** *vt* [T] herumnörgeln an (+ *dat*). ● **go out** *vi* (*from home*) ausgehen; (*leave*) hinausgehen/-fahren; <*fire, light*> ausgehen; **go out to work/for a meal** arbeiten/essen gehen; **go out with s.o.** ([T] *date s.o.*) mit jdm gehen [T]. ● **go over** *vi* hinübergehen/-fahren; *vt* (*rehearse*) durchgehen. ● **go round** *vi* herumgehen/-fahren; (*visit*) vorbeigehen; (*turn*) sich drehen; (*be enough*) reichen. ● **go through** *vi* durchgehen/-fahren; *vt* (*suffer*) durchmachen; (*rehearse*) durchgehen; <*bags*> durchsuchen. ● **go through with** *vt* zu Ende machen. ● **go under** *vi* untergehen/-fahren; (*fail*) scheitern. ● **go up** *vi* hinaufgehen/-fahren; <*lift*> hochfahren; <*prices*> steigen. ● **go without** *vt*: **go without sth** auf etw (*acc*) verzichten; *vi* darauf verzichten

go-ahead *a* fortschrittlich; (*enterprising*) unternehmend ● *n* (*fig*) grünes Licht *nt*

goal *n* Ziel *nt*; (*sport*) Tor *nt*. ~**keeper** *n* Torwart *m*. ~**-post** *n* Torpfosten *m*

goat *n* Ziege *f*

gobble *vt* hinunterschlingen

God, god *n* Gott *m*

god: ~**child** *n* Patenkind *nt*. ~**daughter** *n* Patentochter *f*. ~**dess** *n* Göttin *f*. ~**father** *n* Pate *m*. ~**mother** *n* Patin *f*. ~**parents** *npl* Paten *pl*. ~**send** *n* Segen *m*. ~**son** *n* Patensohn *m*

goggles *npl* Schutzbrille *f*

going *a* <*price, rate*> gängig; <*concern*> gut gehend ● *n* **it is hard ~** es ist schwierig

gold *n* Gold *nt* ● *a* golden

golden *a* golden. **~ wedding** *n* goldene Hochzeit *f*

gold: ~fish *n inv* Goldfisch *m*. **~-mine** *n* Goldgrube *f*. **~-plated** *a* vergoldet. **~smith** *n* Goldschmied *m*

golf *n* Golf *nt*

golf: ~-club *n* Golfklub *m*; (*implement*) Golfschläger *m*. **~-course** *n* Golfplatz *m*. **~er** *m* Golfspieler(in) *m(f)*

gone *see* go

good *a* (**better, best**) gut; (*well-behaved*) brav, artig; **~ at** gut in (+ *dat*); **a ~ deal** ziemlich viel; **~ morning/evening** guten Morgen/Abend ● *n* **for ~** für immer; **do ~** Gutes tun; **do s.o. ~** jdm gut tun; **it's no ~** es ist nutzlos; (*hopeless*) da ist nichts zu machen

goodbye *int* auf Wiedersehen; (*Teleph, Radio*) auf Wiederhören

good: G~ Friday *n* Karfreitag *m*. **~-looking** *a* gut aussehend. **~-natured** *a* gutmütig

goodness *n* Güte *f*; **thank ~!** Gott sei Dank!

goods *npl* Waren *pl*. **~ train** *n* Güterzug *m*

goodwill *n* Wohlwollen *nt*; (*Comm*) Goodwill *m*

gooey *a* 🗈 klebrig

goose *n* (*pl* **geese**) Gans *f*

gooseberry *n* Stachelbeere *f*

goose: ~-flesh *n*, **~-pimples** *npl* Gänsehaut *f*

gorge *n* (*Geog*) Schlucht *f* ● *vt* **~ oneself** sich vollessen

gorgeous *a* prachtvoll; 🗈 herrlich

gorilla *n* Gorilla *m*

gormless *a* 🗈 doof

gorse *n inv* Stechginster *m*

gory *a* (**-ier, -iest**) blutig; <*story*> blutrünstig

gosh *int* 🗈 Mensch!

gospel *n* Evangelium *nt*

gossip *n* Klatsch *m*; (*person*) Klatschbase *f* ● *vi* klatschen

got *see* get; **have ~** haben; **have ~ to** müssen; **have ~ to do sth** etw tun müssen

Gothic *a* gotisch

gotten *see* get

goulash *n* Gulasch *nt*

gourmet *n* Feinschmecker *m*

govern *vt/i* regieren; (*determine*) bestimmen

government *n* Regierung *f*

governor *n* Gouverneur *m*; (*on board*) Vorstandsmitglied *nt*; (*of prison*) Direktor *m*; (🗈 *boss*) Chef *m*

gown *n* [elegantes] Kleid *nt*; (*Univ, Jur*) Talar *m*

GP *abbr of* general practitioner

grab *vt* (*pt/pp* **grabbed**) ergreifen; **~ [hold of]** packen

grace *n* Anmut *f*; (*before meal*) Tischgebet *nt*; **three days' ~** drei Tage Frist. **~ful** *a*, **-ly** *adv* anmutig

gracious *a* gnädig; (*elegant*) vornehm

grade *n* Stufe *f*, (*Comm*) Güteklasse *f*; (*Sch*) Note *f*; (*Amer, Sch: class*) Klasse *f*; (*Amer*) = **gradient** ● *vt* einstufen; (*Comm*) sortieren. **~ crossing** *n* (*Amer*) Bahnübergang *m*

gradient *n* Steigung *f*; (*downward*) Gefälle *nt*

gradual *a*, **-ly** *adv* allmählich

graduate *n* Akademiker(in) *m(f)*

graffiti *npl* Graffiti *pl*

graft *n* (*Bot*) Pfropfreis *nt*; (*Med*) Transplantat *nt*; (🗈 *hard work*) Plackerei *f*

grain *n* (*sand, salt, rice*) Korn *nt*; (*cereals*) Getreide *nt*; (*in wood*) Maserung *f*

gram *n* Gramm *nt*

grammar *n* Grammatik *f*. **~ school** *n* ≈ Gymnasium *nt*

grammatical *a*, **-ly** *adv* grammatisch

grand *a* (**-er, -est**) großartig

grandad *n* 🗈 Opa *m*

grandchild n Enkelkind nt
granddaughter n Enkelin f
grandeur n Pracht f
grandfather n Großvater m. ~ **clock** n Standuhr f
grandiose a grandios
grand: ~**mother** n Großmutter f. ~**parents** npl Großeltern pl. ~ **piano** n Flügel m. ~**son** n Enkel m. ~**stand** n Tribüne f
granite n Granit m
granny n 🇮 Oma f
grant n Subvention f; (Univ) Studienbeihilfe f ● vt gewähren; (admit) zugeben; take sth for ~ed etw als selbstverständlich hinnehmen
grape n [Wein]traube f; bunch of ~s [ganze] Weintraube f
grapefruit n invar Grapefruit f
graph n grafische Darstellung f
graphic a, -**ally** adv grafisch; (vivid) anschaulich
graph paper n Millimeterpapier nt
grapple vi ringen
grasp n Griff m ● vt ergreifen; (understand) begreifen. ~**ing** a habgierig
grass n Gras nt; (lawn) Rasen m. ~**hopper** n Heuschrecke f
grassy a grasig
grate¹ n Feuerrost m; (hearth) Kamin m
grate² vt (Culin) reiben
grateful a, -**ly** adv dankbar (to dat)
grater n (Culin) Reibe f
gratify vt (pt/pp -ied) befriedigen. ~**ing** a erfreulich
gratis adv gratis
gratitude n Dankbarkeit f
gratuitous a (uncalled for) überflüssig
grave¹ a (-r, -st), -**ly** adv ernst; ~**ly** ill schwer krank
grave² n Grab nt. ~-**digger** n Totengräber m
gravel n Kies m
grave: ~**stone** n Grabstein m. ~**yard** n Friedhof m

gravity n Ernst m; (force) Schwerkraft f
gravy n [Braten]soße f
gray a (Amer) = grey
graze¹ vi <animal:> weiden
graze² n Schürfwunde f ● vt <car> streifen; <knee> aufschürfen
grease n Fett nt; (lubricant) Schmierfett nt ● vt einfetten; (lubricate) schmieren
greasy a (-ier, -iest) fettig
great a (-er, -est) groß; (🇮 marvellous) großartig
great: ~-**aunt** n Großtante f. **G**~ **Britain** n Großbritannien nt. ~-**grandchildren** npl Urenkel pl. ~-**grandfather** n Urgroßvater m. ~-**grandmother** n Urgroßmutter f
great|ly adv sehr. ~**ness** n Größe f
great-uncle n Großonkel m
Greece n Griechenland nt
greed n [Hab]gier f
greedy a (-ier, -iest), -**ily** adv gierig
Greek a griechisch ● n Grieche m/ Griechin f; (Lang) Griechisch nt
green a (-er, -est) grün; (fig) unerfahren ● n Grün nt; (grass) Wiese f; ~s pl Kohl m; the **G**~s pl (Pol) die Grünen pl
greenery n Grün nt
green: ~**fly** n Blattlaus f. ~**grocer** n Obst- und Gemüsehändler m. ~**house** n Gewächshaus nt
Greenland n Grönland nt
greet vt grüßen; (welcome) begrüßen. ~**ing** n Gruß m; (welcome) Begrüßung f
grew see grow
grey a (-er, -est) grau ● n Grau nt ● vi grau werden. ~**hound** n Windhund m
grid n Gitter nt
grief n Trauer f
grievance n Beschwerde f
grieve vi trauern (for um)
grill n Gitter nt; (Culin) Grill m; mixed ~ Gemischtes nt vom Grill ● vt/i grillen; (interrogate) [streng] verhören
grille n Gitter nt

grim a (grimmer, grimmest), **-ly** adv ernst; <*determination*> verbissen

grimace n Grimasse f ● vi Grimassen schneiden

grime n Schmutz m

grimy a (-ier, -iest) schmutzig

grin n Grinsen nt ● vi (pt/pp grinned) grinsen

grind n (🇬🇧 hard work) Plackerei f ● vt (pt/pp ground) mahlen; (smooth, sharpen) schleifen; (Amer: mince) durchdrehen

grip n Griff m; (bag) Reisetasche f ● vt (pt/pp gripped) ergreifen; (hold) festhalten

gripping a fesselnd

grisly a (-ier, -iest) grausig

gristle n Knorpel m

grit n [grober] Sand m; (for roads) Streugut nt; (courage) Mut m ● vt (pt/pp gritted) streuen <road>

groan n Stöhnen nt ● vi stöhnen

grocer n Lebensmittelhändler m; ~'s [shop] Lebensmittelgeschäft nt. ~ies npl Lebensmittel pl

groin n (Anat) Leiste f

groom n Bräutigam m; (for horse) Pferdepfleger(in) m(f) ● vt striegeln <horse>

groove n Rille f

grope vi tasten (for nach)

gross a (-er, -est) fett; (coarse) derb; (glaring) grob; (Comm) brutto; <salary, weight> Brutto-. ~ly adv (very) sehr

grotesque a, **-ly** adv grotesk

ground¹ see grind

ground² n Boden m; (terrain) Gelände nt; (reason) Grund m; (Amer, Electr) Erde f; ~s pl (park) Anlagen pl; (of coffee) Satz m

ground: ~ **floor** n Erdgeschoss nt. ~ing n Grundlage f. ~less a grundlos. ~sheet n Bodenplane f. ~work n Vorarbeiten pl

group n Gruppe f ● vt gruppieren ● vi sich gruppieren

grouse vi 🇬🇧 meckern

grovel vi (pt/pp grovelled) kriechen

grow v (pt grew, pp grown) ● vi wachsen; (become) werden; (increase) zunehmen ● vt anbauen. ~ **up** vi aufwachsen; <town:> entstehen

growl n Knurren nt ● vi knurren

grown see grow. ~-**up** a erwachsen ● n Erwachsene(r) m/f

growth n Wachstum nt; (increase) Zunahme f; (Med) Gewächs nt

grub n (larva) Made f; (fam: food) Essen nt

grubby a (-ier, -iest) schmuddelig

grudg|e n Groll m ● vt ~e s.o. sth jdm etw missgönnen. ~ing a, **-ly** adv widerwillig

gruelling a strapaziös

gruesome a grausig

gruff a, **-ly** adv barsch

grumble vi schimpfen (at mit)

grumpy a (-ier, -iest) griesgrämig

grunt n Grunzen nt ● vi grunzen

guarantee n Garantie f; (document) Garantieschein m ● vt garantieren; garantieren für <quality, success>

guard n Wache f; (security) Wächter m; (on train) ≈ Zugführer m; (Techn) Schutz m; be on ~ Wache stehen; on one's ~ auf der Hut ● vt bewachen; (protect) schützen ● vi ~ against sich hüten vor (+ dat). ~-**dog** n Wachhund m

guarded a vorsichtig

guardian n Vormund m

guess n Vermutung f ● vt erraten ● vi raten; (Amer: believe) glauben. ~**work** n Vermutung f

guest n Gast m. ~-**house** n Pension f

guidance n Führung f, Leitung f; (advice) Beratung f

guide n Führer(in) m(f); (book) Führer m; [Girl] G~ Pfadfinderin f ● vt führen, leiten. ~**book** n Führer m

guided a ~ tour Führung f

guide: ~-**dog** n Blindenhund m. ~**lines** npl Richtlinien pl

guilt n Schuld f. ~**ily** adv schuldbewusst

guilty a (-ier, -iest) a schuldig (of gen); ⟨look⟩ schuldbewusst; ⟨conscience⟩ schlecht

guinea-pig n Meerschweinchen nt; (person) Versuchskaninchen nt

guitar n Gitarre f. ∼**ist** n Gitarrist(in) m(f)

gulf n (Geog) Golf m; (fig) Kluft f

gull n Möwe f

gullible a leichtgläubig

gully n Schlucht f; (drain) Rinne f

gulp n Schluck m ● vi schlucken ● vt ∼ **down** hinunterschlucken

gum¹ n & -s pl (Anat) Zahnfleisch nt

gum² n Gummi[harz] nt; (glue) Klebstoff m; (chewing gum) Kaugummi m

gummed see gum² ● a ⟨label⟩ gummiert

gun n Schusswaffe f; (pistol) Pistole f; (rifle) Gewehr nt; (cannon) Geschütz nt

gun: ∼**fire** n Geschützfeuer nt. ∼**man** bewaffneter Bandit m

gunner n Artillerist m

gunpowder n Schießpulver nt

gurgle vi gluckern; (of baby) glucksen

gush vi strömen; (enthuse) schwärmen (over von)

gust n (of wind) Windstoß m; (Naut) Bö f

gusto n with ∼ mit Schwung

gusty a böig

gut n Darm m; ∼**s** pl Eingeweide pl; (🄵 courage) Schneid m ● vt (pt/pp gutted) (Culin) ausnehmen; ∼**ted by fire** ausgebrannt

gutter n Rinnstein m; (fig) Gosse f; (on roof) Dachrinne f

guy n 🄵 Kerl m

guzzle vt/i schlingen; (drink) schlürfen

gym n 🄵 Turnhalle f; (gymnastics) Turnen nt

gymnasium n Turnhalle f

gymnast n Turner(in) m(f). ∼**ics** n Turnen nt

gym shoes pl Turnschuhe pl

gynaecolog|ist n Frauenarzt m /-ärztin f. ∼**y** n Gynäkologie f

gypsy n Zigeuner(in) m(f)

Hh

habit n Gewohnheit f; (Relig: costume) Ordenstracht f; **be in the** ∼ die Angewohnheit haben (of zu)

habitat n Habitat nt

habitation n unfit for human ∼ für Wohnzwecke ungeeignet

habitual a gewohnt; (inveterate) gewohnheitsmäßig. ∼**ly** adv gewohnheitsmäßig; (constantly) ständig

hack¹ n (writer) Schreiberling m; (hired horse) Mietpferd nt

hack² vt hacken; ∼ **to pieces** zerhacken

hackneyed a abgedroschen

hacksaw n Metallsäge f

had see have

haddock n inv Schellfisch m

haggard a abgehärmt

haggle vi feilschen (over um)

hail¹ vt begrüßen; herbeirufen ⟨taxi⟩ ● vi ∼ **from** kommen aus

hail² n Hagel m ● vi hageln. ∼**stone** n Hagelkorn nt

hair n Haar nt; **wash one's** ∼ sich (dat) die Haare waschen

hair: ∼**brush** n Haarbürste f. ∼**cut** n Haarschnitt m; **have a** ∼**cut** sich (dat) die Haare schneiden lassen. ∼**-do** n 🄵 Frisur f. ∼**dresser** n Friseur m/Friseuse f. ∼**drier** n Haartrockner m; (hand-held) Föhn m. ∼**pin** n Haarnadel f. ∼**pin bend** n Haarnadelkurve f. ∼**-raising** a haarsträubend. ∼**-style** n Frisur f

hairy a (-ier, -iest) behaart; (excessively) haarig; (fam; frightening) brenzlig

hake n inv Seehecht m

half n (pl **halves**) Hälfte f; cut in ~ halbieren; one and a ~ eineinhalb, anderthalb; ~ a **dozen** ein halbes Dutzend; ~ **an hour** eine halbe Stunde ● a & adv halb; ~ **past two** halb drei; [at] ~ **price** zum halben Preis

half: ~**-hearted** a lustlos. ~**-term** n schulfreie Tage nach dem halben Trimester. ~**-timbered** a Fachwerk-. ~**-time** n (Sport) Halbzeit f. ~**way** a the ~way mark/stage die Hälfte ● adv auf halbem Weg

halibut n inv Heilbutt m

hall n Halle f; (room) Saal m; (Sch) Aula f; (entrance) Flur m; (mansion) Gutshaus nt; ~ **of residence** (Univ) Studentenheim nt

hallmark n [Feingehalts]stempel m; (fig) Kennzeichen nt (of für)

hallo int [guten] Tag! 🇬🇧 hallo!

hallucination n Halluzination f

halo n (pl **-es**) Heiligenschein m; (Astr) Hof m

halt n Halt m; come to a ~ stehen bleiben; <traffic:> zum Stillstand kommen ● vi Halt machen; ~! halt! ~**ing** a, adv **-ly** zögernd

halve vt halbieren; (reduce) um die Hälfte reduzieren

ham n Schinken m

hamburger n Hamburger m

hammer n Hammer m ● vt/i hämmern (**at an** + acc)

hammock n Hängematte f

hamper vt behindern

hamster n Hamster m

hand n Hand f; (of clock) Zeiger m; (writing) Handschrift f; (worker) Arbeiter(in) m(f); (Cards) Blatt nt; **on the one/other** ~ einer-/andererseits; **out of** ~ außer Kontrolle; (summarily) kurzerhand; **in** ~ unter Kontrolle; (available) verfügbar; **give s.o. a** ~ jdm behilflich sein ● vt reichen (**to** dat). ~ **in** vt abgeben. ~ **out** vt austeilen. ~ **over** vt überreichen

hand: ~**bag** n Handtasche f. ~**book** n Handbuch nt. ~**brake** n Handbremse f. ~**cuffs** npl Handschellen pl. ~**ful** n Handvoll f; **be [quite] a** ~**ful** 🇬🇧 nicht leicht zu haben sein

handicap n Behinderung f; (Sport & fig) Handikap nt. ~**ped** a mentally/physically ~**ped** geistig/körperlich behindert

handkerchief n (pl ~**s** & **-chieves**) Taschentuch nt

handle n Griff m; (of door) Klinke f; (of cup) Henkel m; (of broom) Stiel m ● vt handhaben; (treat) umgehen mit; (touch) anfassen. ~**bars** npl Lenkstange f

hand: ~**made** a handgemacht. ~**shake** n Händedruck m

handsome a gut aussehend; (generous) großzügig; (large) beträchtlich

hand: ~**writing** n Handschrift f. ~**written** a handgeschrieben

handy a (**-ier, -iest**) handlich; <person> geschickt; **have/keep** ~ griffbereit haben/halten

hang vt/i (pt/pp hung) hängen; ~ **wallpaper** tapezieren ● vt (pt/pp hanged) hängen <criminal> ● n **get the** ~ **of it** 🇬🇧 den Dreh herauskriegen. ~ **about** vi sich herumdrücken. ~ **on** vi sich festhalten (**to** an + dat); (🇬🇧 wait) warten. ~ **out** vi heraushängen; (🇬🇧 live) wohnen ● vt draußen aufhängen <washing>. ~ **up** vt/i aufhängen

hangar n Flugzeughalle f

hanger n [Kleider]bügel m

hang: ~**-glider** n Drachenflieger m. ~**-gliding** n Drachenfliegen nt. ~**man** n Henker m. ~**over** n 🇬🇧 Kater m 🇬🇧. ~**-up** n 🇬🇧 Komplex m

hanker vi ~ **after sth** sich (dat) etw wünschen

hanky n 🇬🇧 Taschentuch nt

haphazard a, **-ly** adv planlos

happen vi geschehen, passieren; I ~**ed to be there** ich war zufällig da; **what has** ~**ed to him?** was ist mit ihm los? (*become of*) was ist aus ihm geworden? **∼ing** n Ereignis nt

happi|ly adv glücklich; (*fortunately*) glücklicherweise. **∼ness** n Glück nt

happy a (-ier, -iest) glücklich. **∼-go-lucky** a sorglos

harass vt schikanieren. **∼ed** a abgehetzt. **∼ment** n Schikane f; (*sexual*) Belästigung f

harbour n Hafen m

hard a (-er, -est) hart; (*difficult*) schwer; **∼ of hearing** schwerhörig ● adv hart; <*work*> schwer; <*pull*> kräftig; <*rain, snow*> stark; **be ∼ up** 🔲 knapp bei Kasse sein; **be ∼ done by** 🔲 ungerecht behandelt werden

hard: **∼back** n gebundene Ausgabe f. **∼board** n Hartfaserplatte f. **∼-boiled** a hart gekocht

harden vi hart werden

hard-hearted a hartherzig

hard|ly adv kaum; **∼ly ever** kaum [jemals]. **∼ness** n Härte f. **∼ship** n Not f

hard: **∼ shoulder** n (*Auto*) Randstreifen m. **∼ware** n Haushaltswaren pl; (*Computing*) Hardware f. **∼-wearing** a strapazierfähig. **∼-working** a fleißig

hardy a (-ier, -iest) abgehärtet; <*plant*> winterhart

hare n Hase m

harm n Schaden m; **it won't do any ∼** es kann nichts schaden ● vt **∼ s.o.** jdm etwas antun. **∼ful** a schädlich. **∼less** a harmlos

harmonious a, **-ly** adv harmonisch

harmon|ize vi (*fig*) harmonieren. **∼y** n Harmonie f

harness n Geschirr nt; (*of parachute*) Gurtwerk nt ● vt anschirren <*horse*>; (*use*) nutzbar machen

harp n Harfe f. **∼ist** n Harfenist(in) m(f)

harpsichord n Cembalo nt

harrowing a grauenhaft

harsh a (-er, -est), **-ly** adv hart; <*voice*> rau; <*light*> grell. **∼ness** n Härte f; Rauheit f

harvest n Ernte f ● vt ernten

has see **have**

hassle n 🔲 Ärger m ● vt schikanieren

haste n Eile f

hasten vi sich beeilen (**to** zu); (*go quickly*) eilen ● vt beschleunigen

hasty a (-ier, -iest), **-ily** adv hastig; <*decision*> voreilig

hat n Hut m; (*knitted*) Mütze f

hatch[1] n (*for food*) Durchreiche f; (*Naut*) Luke f

hatch[2] vi **∼[out]** ausschlüpfen ● vt ausbrüten

hatchback n (*Auto*) Modell nt mit Hecktür

hate n Hass m ● vt hassen. **∼ful** a abscheulich

hatred n Hass m

haughty a (-ier, -iest), **-ily** adv hochmütig

haul n (*loot*) Beute f ● vt/i ziehen (**on** an + dat)

haunt n Lieblingsaufenthalt m ● vt umgehen in (+ dat); **this house is ∼ed** in diesem Haus spukt es

have

3 sg pres tense **has**; *pt and pp* **had**

● *transitive verb*

····▸ (*possess*) haben. **he has [got] a car** er hat ein Auto. **she has [got] a brother** sie hat einen Bruder. **we have [got] five minutes** wir haben fünf Minuten

····▸ (*eat*) essen; (*drink*) trinken; (*smoke*) rauchen. **have a cup of tea** eine Tasse Tee trinken. **have a pizza** eine Pizza essen. **have a cigarette** eine Zigarette rauchen. **have breakfast/dinner/lunch** frühstücken/zu Abend essen/zu Mittag essen

····▸ (*take esp. in shop, restaurant*) nehmen. **I'll have the soup/the red dress** ich nehme die Suppe/das rote Kleid. **have a cigarette!** nehmen Sie eine Zigarette!

····▸ (*get, receive*) bekommen. **I had a letter from her** ich bekam einen Brief

h

von ihr. **have a baby** ein Baby bekommen

····▸ (*suffer*) haben <*illness, pain, disappointment*>; erleiden <*shock*>

····▸ (*organize*) **have a party** eine Party veranstalten. **they had a meeting** sie hielten eine Versammlung ab

····▸ (*take part in*) **have a game of football** Fußball spielen. **have a swim** schwimmen

····▸ (*as guest*) **have s.o. to stay** jdn zu Besuch haben

····▸ **have had it** 🄸 <*thing*> ausgedient haben; <*person*> geliefert sein. **you've had it now** jetzt ist es aus

····▸ **have sth done** etw machen lassen. **we had the house painted** wir haben das Haus malen lassen. **have a dress made** sich (*dat*) ein Kleid machen lassen. **have a tooth out** sich (*dat*) einen Zahn ziehen lassen. **have one's hair cut** sich (*dat*) die Haare schneiden lassen

····▸ **have to do sth** etw tun müssen. **I have to go now** ich muss jetzt gehen

● *auxiliary verb*

····▸ (*forming perfect and past perfect tenses*) haben; (*with verbs of motion and some others*) sein. **I have seen him** ich habe ihn gesehen. **he has never been there** er ist nie da gewesen. **I had gone** ich war gegangen. **if I had known ...** wenn ich gewusst hätte ...

····▸ (*in tag questions*) nicht wahr. **you've met her, haven't you?** du kennst sie, nicht wahr?

····▸ (*in short answers*) **Have you seen the film? — Yes, I have** Hast du den Film gesehen? — Ja [, stimmt]

●● **have on** *vt* (*be wearing*) anhaben; (*dupe*) anführen

havoc *n* Verwüstung *f*

hawk *n* Falke *m*

hawthorn *n* Hagedorn *m*

hay *n* Heu *nt*. ~ **fever** *n* Heuschnupfen *m*. ~**stack** *n* Heuschober *m*

hazard *n* Gefahr *f*; (*risk*) Risiko *nt* ● *vt* riskieren. ~**ous** *a* gefährlich; (*risky*) riskant

haze *n* Dunst *m*

hazel *n* Haselbusch *m*. ~-**nut** *n* Haselnuss *f*

hazy *a* (-ier, -iest) dunstig; (*fig*) unklar

he *pron* er

head *n* Kopf *m*; (*chief*) Oberhaupt *nt*; (*of firm*) Chef(in) *m(f)*; (*of school*) Schulleiter(in) *m(f)*; (*on beer*) Schaumkrone *f*; (*of bed*) Kopfende *nt*; ~ **first** kopfüber ● *vt* anführen; (*Sport*) köpfen <*ball*> ● *vi* ~ **for** zusteuern auf (+ *acc*). ~**ache** *n* Kopfschmerzen *pl*

head|**er** *n* Kopfball *m*; (*dive*) Kopfsprung *m*. ~**ing** *n* Überschrift *f*

head: ~**lamp**, ~**light** *n* (*Auto*) Scheinwerfer *m*. ~**line** *n* Schlagzeile *f*. ~**long** *adv* kopfüber. ~**master** *n* Schulleiter *m*. ~**mistress** *n* Schulleiterin *f*. ~-**on** *a & adv* frontal. ~**phones** *npl* Kopfhörer *pl*. ~**quarters** *npl* Hauptquartier *nt*; (*Pol*) Zentrale *f*. ~-**rest** *n* Kopfstütze *f*. ~**room** *n* lichte Höhe *f*. ~**scarf** *n* Kopftuch *nt*. ~**strong** *a* eigenwillig. ~**way** *n* make ~**way** Fortschritte machen. ~**word** *n* Stichwort *nt*

heady *a* berauschend

heal *vt/i* heilen

health *n* Gesundheit *f*

health: ~ **farm** *n* Schönheitsfarm *f*. ~ **foods** *npl* Reformkost *f*. ~-**food shop** *n* Reformhaus *nt*. ~ **insurance** *n* Krankenversicherung *f*

healthy *a* (-ier, -iest), -**ily** *adv* gesund

heap *n* Haufen *m*; ~**s** 🄸 jede Menge ● *vt* ~ [**up**] häufen

hear *vt/i* (*pt/pp* **heard**) hören; ~, ~! hört, hört! **he would not** ~ **of it** er ließ es nicht zu

hearing *n* Gehör *nt*; (*Jur*) Verhandlung *f*. ~-**aid** *n* Hörgerät *nt*

hearse *n* Leichenwagen *m*

heart *n* Herz *nt*; (*courage*) Mut *m*; ~**s** *pl* (*Cards*) Herz *nt*; **by** ~ auswendig

heart: ~**ache** *n* Kummer *m*. ~**attack** *n* Herzanfall *m*. ~**beat** *n* Herzschlag *m*. ~-**breaking** *a* herzzerreißend. **~broken** a untröstlich. **~burn** n Sodbrennen nt. **~en** vt ermutigen. **~felt** a herzlich[st]

hearth n Herd m; (*fireplace*) Kamin m

heart|ily adv herzlich; <*eat*> viel. **~less** a, **-ly** adv herzlos. **~y** a herzlich; <*meal*> groß; <*person*> burschikos

heat n Hitze f; (*Sport*) Vorlauf m ● vt heiß machen; heizen <*room*>. **~ed** a geheizt; <*swimming pool*> beheizt; <*discussion*> hitzig. **~er** n Heizgerät nt; (*Auto*) Heizanlage f

heath n Heide f

heathen a heidnisch ● n Heide m/ Heidin f

heather n Heidekraut nt

heating n Heizung f

heat wave n Hitzewelle f

heave vt/i ziehen; (*lift*) heben; (🆃 *throw*) schmeißen

heaven n Himmel m. **~ly** a himmlisch

heavy a (-ier, -iest), **-ily** adv schwer; <*traffic, rain*> stark. **~weight** n Schwergewicht nt

heckle vt [durch Zwischenrufe] unterbrechen. **~r** n Zwischenrufer m

hectic a hektisch

hedge n Hecke f. **~hog** n Igel m

heed vt beachten

heel[1] n Ferse f; (*of shoe*) Absatz m; down at **~** heruntergekommen

heel[2] vi **~ over** (*Naut*) sich auf die Seite legen

hefty a (-ier, -iest) kräftig; (*heavy*) schwer

height n Höhe f; (*of person*) Größe f. **~en** vt (*fig*) steigern

heir n Erbe m. **~ess** n Erbin f. **~loom** n Erbstück nt

held see hold[2]

helicopter n Hubschrauber m

hell n Hölle f; go to **~**! 🆇 geh zum Teufel! ● int verdammt!

hello int [guten] Tag! 🆃 hallo!

helm n [Steuer]ruder nt

helmet n Helm m

help n Hilfe f; (*employees*) Hilfskräfte pl; that's no **~** das nützt nichts ● vt/ i helfen (s.o. jdm); **~** oneself to sth sich (*dat*) etw nehmen; **~** yourself (*at table*) greif zu; I could not **~** laughing ich musste lachen; it cannot be **~ed** es lässt sich nicht ändern; I can't **~** it ich kann nichts dafür

help|er n Helfer(in) m(f). **~ful** a, **-ly** adv hilfsbereit; <*advice*> nützlich. **~ing** n Portion f. **~less** a, **-ly** adv hilflos

hem n Saum m ● vt (pt/pp hemmed) säumen; **~** in umzingeln

hemisphere n Hemisphäre f

hem-line n Rocklänge f

hen n Henne f; (*any female bird*) Weibchen nt

hence adv daher; five years **~** in fünf Jahren. **~forth** adv von nun an

henpecked a **~** husband Pantoffelheld m

her a ihr ● pron (acc) sie; (dat) ihr

herald vt verkünden. **~ry** n Wappenkunde f

herb n Kraut nt

herbaceous a **~** border Staudenrabatte f

herd n Herde f. **~** together vt zusammentreiben

here adv hier; (*to this place*) hierher; in **~** hier drinnen; come/bring **~** herkommen/herbringen

hereditary a erblich

here|sy n Ketzerei f. **~tic** n Ketzer(in) m(f)

herewith adv (Comm) beiliegend

heritage n Erbe nt

hero n (pl -es) Held m

heroic a, **-ally** adv heldenhaft

heroin n Heroin nt

hero|ine n Heldin f. **~ism** n Heldentum nt

heron n Reiher m

herring n Hering m

hers poss pron ihre(r), ihrs; a friend of **~** ein Freund von ihr; that is **~** das gehört ihr

herself pron selbst; (refl) sich; by ~ allein

hesitant a, **-ly** adv zögernd

hesitat|e vi zögern. **~ion** n Zögern nt; without **~ion** ohne zu zögern

hexagonal a sechseckig

heyday n Glanzzeit f

hi int he! (hallo) Tag!

hiatus n (pl **-tuses**) Lücke f

hibernat|e vi Winterschlaf halten. **~ion** n Winterschlaf m

hiccup n Hick m; ([I] hitch) Panne f; have the ~s den Schluckauf haben ● vi hick machen

hid, hidden see hide[2]

hide v (pt hid, pp hidden) ● vt verstecken; (keep secret) verheimlichen ● vi sich verstecken

hideous a, **-ly** adv hässlich; (horrible) grässlich

hide-out n Versteck nt

hiding[1] n [I] give s.o. a ~ jdn verdreschen

hiding[2] n go into ~ untertauchen

hierarchy n Hierarchie f

high a (**-er, -est**) hoch; attrib hohe(r,s); <meat> angegangen; <wind> stark; (on drugs) high; it's ~ time es ist höchste Zeit ● adv hoch; ~ and low überall ● n Hoch nt; (temperature) Höchsttemperatur f

high: ~brow a intellektuell. **~chair** n Kinderhochstuhl m. **~-handed** a selbstherrlich. **~-heeled** a hochhackig. **~ jump** n Hochsprung m

highlight n (fig) Höhepunkt m; **~s** pl (in hair) helle Strähnen pl ● vt (emphasize) hervorheben

highly adv hoch; speak ~ of loben; think ~ of sehr schätzen. **~-strung** a nervös

Highness n Hoheit f

high: ~ season n Hochsaison f. **~ street** n Hauptstraße f. **~ tide** n Hochwasser nt. **~way** n public **~way** öffentliche Straße f

hijack vt entführen. **~er** n Entführer m

hike n Wanderung f ● vi wandern. **~r** n Wanderer m

hilarious a sehr komisch

hill n Berg m; (mound) Hügel m; (slope) Hang m

hill: ~side n Hang m. **~y** a hügelig

him pron (acc) ihn; (dat) ihm. **~self** pron selbst; (refl) sich; by **~self** allein

hind a Hinter-

hind|er vt hindern. **~rance** n Hindernis nt

hindsight n with ~ rückblickend

Hindu n Hindu m ● a Hindu-. **~ism** n Hinduismus m

hinge n Scharnier nt; (on door) Angel f

hint n Wink m, Andeutung f; (advice) Hinweis m; (trace) Spur f ● vi ~ at anspielen auf (+ acc)

hip n Hüfte f

hip pocket n Gesäßtasche f

hippopotamus n (pl **-muses** or **-mi**) Nilpferd nt

hire vt mieten <car>; leihen <suit>; einstellen <person>; **~[out]** vermieten; verleihen

his a sein ● poss pron seine(r), seins; a friend of ~ ein Freund von ihm; that is ~ das gehört ihm

hiss n Zischen nt ● vt/i zischen

historian n Historiker(in) m(f)

historic a historisch. **~al** a, **-ly** adv geschichtlich, historisch

history n Geschichte f

hit n (blow) Schlag m; ([I] success) Erfolg m; direct ~ Volltreffer m ● vt/i (pt/pp hit, pres p hitting) schlagen; (knock against, collide with, affect) treffen; ~ the target das Ziel treffen; ~ on (fig) kommen auf (+ acc); ~ it off gut auskommen (with mit); ~ one's head on sth sich (dat) den Kopf an etw (dat) stoßen

hitch n Problem nt; technical ~ Panne f ● vt festmachen (to an + dat); ~ up hochziehen. **~-hike** vi [I] trampen. **~-hiker** n Anhalter(in) m(f)

hive n Bienenstock m

hoard n Hort m ● vt horten, hamstern

hoarding n Bauzaun m; (with advertisements) Reklamewand f

hoar-frost n Raureif m

hoarse a (-r, -st), **-ly** adv heiser. **~ness** n Heiserkeit f

hoax n übler Scherz m; (false alarm) blinder Alarm m

hobble vi humpeln

hobby n Hobby nt. **~-horse** n (fig) Lieblingsthema nt

hockey n Hockey nt

hoe n Hacke f ● vt (pres p hoeing) hacken

hog vt (pt/pp hogged) ▣ mit Beschlag belegen

hoist n Lastenaufzug m ● vt hochziehen; hissen <flag>

hold¹ n (Naut) Laderaum m

hold² n Halt m; (Sport) Griff m; (fig: influence) Einfluss m; **get ~ of** fassen; (▣ contact) erreichen ● v (pt/pp held) ● vt halten; <container:> fassen; (believe) meinen; (possess) haben; anhalten <breath> ● vi <rope:> halten; <weather:> sich halten. **~ back** vt zurückhalten ● vi zögern. **~ on** vi (wait) warten; (on telephone) am Apparat bleiben; **~ on to** (keep) behalten; (cling to) sich festhalten an (+ dat). **~ out** vt hinhalten ● vi (resist) aushalten. **~ up** vt hochhalten; (delay) aufhalten; (rob) überfallen

hold|all n Reisetasche f. **~er** n Inhaber(in) m(f); (container) Halter m. **~-up** n Verzögerung f; (attack) Überfall m

hole n Loch nt

holiday n Urlaub m; (Sch) Ferien pl; (public) Feiertag m; (day off) freier Tag m; **go on ~** in Urlaub fahren

holiness n Heiligkeit f

Holland n Holland nt

hollow a hohl; <promise> leer ● n Vertiefung f; (in ground) Mulde f. **~ out** vt aushöhlen

holly n Stechpalme f

holster n Pistolentasche f

holy a (-ier, -est) heilig. **H~ Ghost** or **Spirit** n Heiliger Geist m

homage n Huldigung f; **pay ~ to** huldigen (+ dat)

home n Zuhause nt (house) Haus nt; (institution) Heim nt; (native land) Heimat f ● adv **at ~** zu Hause; **come/go ~** nach Hause kommen/gehen

home: **~ address** n Heimatanschrift f. **~ game** n Heimspiel nt. **~ help** n Haushaltshilfe f. **~land** n Heimatland nt. **~less** a obdachlos

homely a (-ier, -iest) a gemütlich; (Amer: ugly) unscheinbar

home: **~-made** a selbst gemacht. **H~ Office** n Innenministerium nt. **H~ Secretary** Innenminister m. **~sick** a **be ~sick** Heimweh haben (for nach). **~sickness** n Heimweh nt. **~ town** n Heimatstadt f. **~work** n (Sch) Hausaufgaben pl

homosexual a homosexuell ● n Homosexuelle(r) m/f

honest a, **-ly** adv ehrlich. **~y** n Ehrlichkeit f

honey n Honig m; (▣ darling) Schatz m

honey: **~comb** n Honigwabe f. **~moon** n Flitterwochen pl; (journey) Hochzeitsreise f

honorary a ehrenamtlich; <member, doctorate> Ehren-

honour n Ehre f ● vt ehren; honorieren <cheque>. **~able** a, **-bly** adv ehrenhaft

hood n Kapuze f; (of car, pram) [Klapp]verdeck nt; (over cooker) Abzugshaube f; (Auto, Amer) Kühlerhaube f

hoof n (pl ~s or hooves) Huf m

hook n Haken m ● vt festhaken (to an + acc)

hook|ed a **~ed nose** Hakennase f; **~ed on** ▣ abhängig von; (keen on) besessen von. **~er** n (Amer ▣) Nutte f

hookey n play ~ (Amer ▣) schwänzen

hooligan n Rowdy m. **~ism** n Rowdytum nt

hooray int & n = hurrah

h

hoot n Ruf m; ~s of laughter schallendes Gelächter nt ● vi <owl:> rufen; <car:> hupen; (jeer) johlen. ~er n (of factory) Sirene f; (Auto) Hupe f

hoover n H~ (P) Staubsauger m ● vt/i [staub]saugen

hop¹ n, & ~s pl Hopfen m

hop² vi (pt/pp hopped) hüpfen; ~ it! 🔲 hau ab!

hope n Hoffnung f; (prospect) Aussicht f (of auf + acc) ● vt/i hoffen (for auf + acc); I ~ so hoffentlich

hope|ful a hoffnungsvoll; be ~ful that hoffen, dass. ~fully adv hoffnungsvoll; (it is hoped) hoffentlich. ~less a, -ly adv hoffnungslos; (useless) nutzlos; (incompetent) untauglich

horde n Horde f

horizon n Horizont m

horizontal a, -ly adv horizontal. ~ bar n Reck nt

horn n Horn nt; (Auto) Hupe f

hornet n Hornisse f

horoscope n Horoskop nt

horrible a, -bly adv schrecklich

horrid a grässlich

horrific a entsetzlich

horrify vt (pt/pp -ied) entsetzen

horror n Entsetzen nt

hors-d'œuvre n Vorspeise f

horse n Pferd nt

horse: ~back n on ~back zu Pferde. ~man n Reiter m. ~power n Pferdestärke f. ~racing n Pferderennen nt. ~radish n Meerrettich m. ~shoe n Hufeisen nt

horticulture n Gartenbau m

hose n (pipe) Schlauch m ● vt ~ down abspritzen

hosiery n Strumpfwaren pl

hospitable a, -bly adv gastfreundlich

hospital n Krankenhaus nt

hospitality n Gastfreundschaft f

host¹ n Gastgeber m

hostage n Geisel f

hostel n [Wohn]heim nt

hostess n Gastgeberin f

hostile a feindlich; (unfriendly) feindselig

hostilit|y n Feindschaft f; ~ies pl Feindseligkeiten pl

hot a (hotter, hottest) heiß; <meal> warm; (spicy) scharf; I am or feel ~ mir ist heiß

hotel n Hotel nt

hot: ~head n Hitzkopf m. ~house n Treibhaus nt. ~ly adv (fig) heiß, heftig. ~plate n Tellerwärmer m; (of cooker) Kochplatte f. ~ tap n Warmwasserhahn m. ~-tempered a jähzornig. ~-water bottle n Wärmflasche f

hound n Jagdhund m ● vt (fig) verfolgen

hour n Stunde f. ~ly a & adv stündlich

house¹ n Haus nt; at my ~ bei mir

house² vt unterbringen

house: ~breaking n Einbruch m. ~hold n Haushalt m. ~holder n Hausinhaber(in) m(f). ~keeper n Haushälterin f. ~keeping n Hauswirtschaft f; (money) Haushaltsgeld nt. ~-plant n Zimmerpflanze f. ~-trained a stubenrein. ~-warming n have a ~-warming party Einstand feiern. ~wife n Hausfrau f. ~work n Hausarbeit f

housing n Wohnungen pl; (Techn) Gehäuse nt

hovel n elende Hütte f

hover vi schweben. ~craft n Luftkissenfahrzeug nt

how adv wie; ~ do you do? guten Tag!; and ~! und ob!

however adv (in question) wie; (nevertheless) jedoch, aber; ~ small wie klein es auch sein mag

howl n Heulen nt ● vi heulen; <baby:> brüllen

hub n Nabe f

huddle vi ~ together sich zusammendrängen

huff n in a ~ beleidigt

hug n Umarmung f ● vt (pt/pp hugged) umarmen

huge *a*, **-ly** *adv* riesig

hull *n* (*Naut*) Rumpf *m*

hullo *int* = hallo

hum *n* Summen *nt*; Brummen *nt*
● *vt/i* (*pt/pp* hummed) summen;
<*motor:*> brummen

human *a* menschlich ● *n* Mensch *m*.
∼ **being** *n* Mensch *m*

humane *a*, **-ly** *adv* human

humanitarian *a* humanitär

humanity *n* Menschheit *f*

humble *a* (-r, -st), **-bly** *adv* demütig
● *vt* demütigen

humdrum *a* eintönig

humid *a* feucht. ∼**ity** *n* Feuchtigkeit
f

humiliat|e *vt* demütigen. ∼**ion** *n*
Demütigung *f*

humility *n* Demut *f*

humorous *a*, **-ly** *adv* humorvoll;
<*story*> humoristisch

humour *n* Humor *m*; (*mood*) Laune
f; have a sense of ∼ Humor haben

hump *n* Buckel *m*; (*of camel*) Höcker
m ● *vt* schleppen

hunch *n* (*idea*) Ahnung *f*

hunchback *n* Bucklige(r) *m/f*

hundred *a* one/a ∼ [ein]hundert
● *n* Hundert *nt*; (*written figure*)
Hundert *f*. ∼**th** *a* hundertste(r,s) ● *n*
Hundertstel *nt*. ∼**weight** *n* ≈
Zentner *m*

hung *see* hang

Hungarian *a* ungarisch ● *n*
Ungar(in) *m(f)*

Hungary *n* Ungarn *nt*

hunger *n* Hunger *m*. ∼**-strike** *n*
Hungerstreik *m*

hungry *a* (-ier, -iest), **-ily** *adv*
hungrig; be ∼ Hunger haben

hunt *n* Jagd *f*; (*for criminal*)
Fahndung *f* ● *vt/i* jagen; fahnden
nach <*criminal*>; ∼ **for** suchen. ∼**er**
n Jäger *m*; (*horse*) Jagdpferd *nt*.
∼**ing** *n* Jagd *f*

hurdle *n* (*Sport & fig*) Hürde *f*

hurl *vt* schleudern

hurrah, hurray *int* hurra! ● *n* Hurra
nt

hurricane *n* Orkan *m*

hurried *a*, **-ly** *adv* eilig; (*superficial*)
flüchtig

hurry *n* Eile *f*; be in a ∼ es eilig
haben ● *vi* (*pt/pp* -ied) sich beeilen;
(*go quickly*) eilen. ∼ **up** *vi* sich
beeilen ● *vt* antreiben

hurt *n* Schmerz *m* ● *vt/i* (*pt/pp* hurt)
weh tun (+ *dat*); (*injure*) verletzen;
(*offend*) kränken

hurtle *vi* ∼ along rasen

husband *n* [Ehe]mann *m*

hush *n* Stille *f* ● *vt* ∼ **up** vertuschen.
∼**ed** *a* gedämpft

husky *a* (-ier, -iest) heiser; (*burly*)
stämmig

hustle *vt* drängen ● *n* Gedränge *nt*

hut *n* Hütte *f*

hutch *n* [Kaninchen]stall *m*

hybrid *a* hybrid ● *n* Hybride *f*

hydraulic *a*, **-ally** *adv* hydraulisch

hydroelectric *a* hydroelektrisch

hydrogen *n* Wasserstoff *m*

hygien|e *n* Hygiene *f*. ∼**ic** *a*, **-ally**
adv hygienisch

hymn *n* Kirchenlied *nt*. ∼**-book** *n*
Gesangbuch *nt*

hyphen *n* Bindestrich *m*. ∼**ate** *vt*
mit Bindestrich schreiben

hypno|sis *n* Hypnose *f*. ∼**tic** *a*
hypnotisch

hypno|tism *n* Hypnotik *f*. ∼**tist** *n*
Hypnotiseur *m*. ∼**tize** *vt*
hypnotisieren

hypochondriac *n* Hypochonder *m*

hypocrisy *n* Heuchelei *f*

hypocrite *n* Heuchler(in) *m(f)*

hypodermic *a & n* ∼ [syringe]
Injektionsspritze *f*

hypothe|sis *n* Hypothese *f*. ∼**tical**
a, **-ly** *adv* hypothetisch

hyster|ia *n* Hysterie *f*. ∼**ical** *a*, **-ly**
adv hysterisch. ∼**ics** *npl*
hysterischer Anfall *m*

h

I *pron* ich

ice *n* Eis *nt* ● *vt* mit Zuckerguss überziehen <*cake*>

ice: ~**berg** *n* Eisberg *m*. ~**box** *n* (*Amer*) Kühlschrank *m*. ~-**cream** *n* [Speise]eis *nt*. ~-**cube** *n* Eiswürfel *m*

Iceland *n* Island *nt*

ice: ~ **lolly** *n* Eis *nt* am Stiel. ~ **rink** *n* Eisbahn *f*

icicle *n* Eiszapfen *m*

icing *n* Zuckerguss *m*. ~ **sugar** *n* Puderzucker *m*

icon *n* Ikone *f*

icy *a* (-ier, -iest), -**ily** *adv* eisig; <*road*> vereist

idea *n* Idee *f*; (*conception*) Vorstellung *f*; **I have no** ~! ich habe keine Ahnung!

ideal *a* ideal ● *n* Ideal *nt*. ~**ism** *n* Idealismus *m*. ~**ist** *n* Idealist(in) *m(f)*. ~**istic** *a* idealistisch. ~**ize** *vt* idealisieren. ~**ly** *adv* ideal; (*in ideal circumstances*) idealerweise

identical *a* identisch; <*twins*> eineiig

identi|fication *n* Identifizierung *f*; (*proof of identity*) Ausweispapiere *pl*. ~**fy** *vt* (*pt/pp* -**ied**) identifizieren

identity *n* Identität *f*. ~ **card** *n* [Personal]ausweis *m*

idiom *n* [feste] Redewendung *f*. ~**atic** *a*, -**ally** *adv* idiomatisch

idiosyncrasy *n* Eigenart *f*

idiot *n* Idiot *m*. ~**ic** *a* idiotisch

idle *a* (-r, -st), -**ly** *adv* untätig; (*lazy*) faul; (*empty*) leer; <*machine*> nicht in Betrieb ● *vi* faulenzen; <*engine:*> leer laufen. ~**ness** *n* Untätigkeit *f*; Faulheit *f*

idol *n* Idol *nt*. ~**ize** *vt* vergöttern

idyllic *a* idyllisch

i.e. *abbr* (**id est**) d.h.

if *conj* wenn; (*whether*) ob; **as if** als ob

ignition *n* (*Auto*) Zündung *f*. ~ **key** *n* Zündschlüssel *m*

ignoramus *n* Ignorant *m*

ignoran|ce *n* Unwissenheit *f*. ~**t** *a* unwissend

ignore *vt* ignorieren

ill *a* krank; (*bad*) schlecht; **feel** ~ **at ease** sich unbehaglich fühlen ● *adv* schlecht

illegal *a*, -**ly** *adv* illegal

illegible *a*, -**bly** *adv* unleserlich

illegitimate *a* unehelich; <*claim*> unberechtigt

illicit *a*, -**ly** *adv* illegal

illiterate *a* **be** ~**te** nicht lesen und schreiben können

illness *n* Krankheit *f*

illogical *a*, -**ly** *adv* unlogisch

ill-treat *vt* misshandeln. ~**ment** *n* Misshandlung *f*

illuminat|e *vt* beleuchten. ~**ion** *n* Beleuchtung *f*

illusion *n* Illusion *f*; **be under the** ~ **that** sich (*dat*) einbilden, dass

illustrat|e *vt* illustrieren. ~**ion** *n* Illustration *f*

illustrious *a* berühmt

image *n* Bild *nt*; (*statue*) Standbild *nt*; (*exact likeness*) Ebenbild *nt*; [public] ~ Image *nt*

imagin|able *a* vorstellbar. ~**ary** *a* eingebildet

imagination *n* Fantasie *f*; (*fancy*) Einbildung *f*. ~**ive** *a*, -**ly** *adv* fantasievoll; (*full of ideas*) einfallsreich

imagine *vt* sich (*dat*) vorstellen; (*wrongly*) sich (*dat*) einbilden

imbalance *n* Unausgeglichenheit *f*

imbecile *n* Schwachsinnige(r) *m/f*; (*pej*) Idiot *m*

imitat|e *vt* nachahmen, imitieren. ~**ion** *n* Nachahmung *f*, Imitation *f*

immaculate *a*, -**ly** *adv* tadellos; (*Relig*) unbefleckt

immature *a* unreif

immediate *a* sofortig; (*nearest*) nächste(r,s). ~**ly** *adv* sofort; ~**ly**

next to unmittelbar neben ● *conj* sobald

immemorial *a* **from time** ~ seit Urzeiten

immense *a*, **-ly** *adv* riesig; Ⓘ enorm

immerse *vt* untertauchen

immigrant *n* Einwanderer *m*

immigration *n* Einwanderung *f*

imminent *a* **be** ~ unmittelbar bevorstehen

immobile *a* unbeweglich

immodest *a* unbescheiden

immoral *a*, **-ly** *adv* unmoralisch. ~**ity** *n* Unmoral *f*

immortal *a* unsterblich. ~**ity** *n* Unsterblichkeit *f*. ~**ize** *vt* verewigen

immune *a* immun (**to/from** gegen)

immunity *n* Immunität *f*

imp *n* Kobold *m*

impact *n* Aufprall *m*; (*collision*) Zusammenprall *m*; (*of bomb*) Einschlag *m*; (*fig*) Auswirkung *f*

impair *vt* beeinträchtigen

impart *vt* übermitteln (**to** *dat*); vermitteln <*knowledge*>

impartial *a* unparteiisch. ~**ity** *n* Unparteilichkeit *f*

impassable *a* unpassierbar

impassioned *a* leidenschaftlich

impassive *a*, **-ly** *adv* unbeweglich

impatien|ce *n* Ungeduld *f*. ~**t** *a*, **-ly** *adv* ungeduldig

impeccable *a*, **-bly** *adv* tadellos

impede *vt* behindern

impediment *n* Hindernis *nt*; (*in speech*) Sprachfehler *m*

impel *vt* (*pt/pp* impelled) treiben

impending *a* bevorstehend

impenetrable *a* undurchdringlich

imperative *a* **be** ~ dringend notwendig sein ● *n* (*Gram*) Imperativ *m*

imperceptible *a* nicht wahrnehmbar

imperfect *a* unvollkommen; (*faulty*) fehlerhaft ● *n* (*Gram*) Imperfekt *nt*. ~**ion** *n*

Unvollkommenheit *f*; (*fault*) Fehler *m*

imperial *a* kaiserlich. ~**ism** *n* Imperialismus *m*

impersonal *a* unpersönlich

impersonat|e *vt* sich ausgeben als; (*Theat*) nachahmen, imitieren. ~**or** *n* Imitator *m*

impertinen|ce *n* Frechheit *f*. ~**t** *a* frech

imperturbable *a* unerschütterlich

impetuous *a*, **-ly** *adv* ungestüm

impetus *n* Schwung *m*

implacable *a* unerbittlich

implant *vt* einpflanzen

implement[1] *n* Gerät *nt*

implement[2] *vt* ausführen

implication *n* Verwicklung *f*; ~**s** *pl* Auswirkungen *pl*; **by** ~ implizit

implicit *a*, **-ly** *adv* unausgesprochen; (*absolute*) unbedingt

implore *vt* anflehen

imply *vt* (*pt/pp* **-ied**) andeuten; **what are you** ~**ing?** was wollen Sie damit sagen?

impolite *a*, **-ly** *adv* unhöflich

import[1] *n* Import *m*, Einfuhr *f*

import[2] *vt* importieren, einführen

importan|ce *n* Wichtigkeit *f*. ~**t** *a* wichtig

importer *n* Importeur *m*

impos|e *vt* auferlegen (**on** *dat*) ● *vi* sich aufdrängen (**on** *dat*). ~**ing** *a* eindrucksvoll

impossibility *n* Unmöglichkeit *f*

impossible *a*, **-bly** *adv* unmöglich

impostor *n* Betrüger(in) *m(f)*

impoten|ce *n* Machtlosigkeit *f*; (*Med*) Impotenz *f*. ~**t** *a* machtlos; (*Med*) impotent

impoverished *a* verarmt

impracticable *a* undurchführbar

impractical *a* unpraktisch

imprecise *a* ungenau

impress *vt* beeindrucken; ~ **sth [up]on s.o.** jdm etw einprägen

impression *n* Eindruck *m*; (*imitation*) Nachahmung *f*; (*edition*)

Auflage f. **~ism** n Impressionismus m

impressive a eindrucksvoll

imprison vt gefangen halten; (*put in prison*) ins Gefängnis sperren

improbable a unwahrscheinlich

impromptu a improvisiert ● adv aus dem Stegreif

improper a, **-ly** adv inkorrekt; (*indecent*) unanständig

impropriety n Unkorrektheit f

improve vt verbessern; verschönern <*appearance*> ● vi sich bessern; ~ [up]on übertreffen. **~ment** n Verbesserung f; (*in health*) Besserung f

improvise vt/i improvisieren

imprudent a unklug

impuden|ce n Frechheit f. **~t** a, **-ly** adv frech

impuls|e n Impuls m; on [an] ~e impulsiv. **~ive** a, **-ly** adv impulsiv

impur|e a unrein. **~ity** n Unreinheit f

in prep in (+ dat/(into) + acc); **sit in the garden** im Garten sitzen; **go in the garden** in den Garten gehen; **in May** im Mai; **in 1992** [im Jahre] 1992; **in this heat** bei dieser Hitze; **in the evening** am Abend; **in the sky** am Himmel; **in the world** auf der Welt; **in the street** auf der Straße; **deaf in one ear** auf einem Ohr taub; **in the army** beim Militär; **in English/German** auf Englisch/Deutsch; **in ink/pencil** mit Tinte/Bleistift; **in a soft/loud voice** mit leiser/lauter Stimme; **in doing this, he ...** indem er das tut/tat, ... er ● adv (*at home*) zu Hause; (*indoors*) drinnen; **he's not in yet** er ist noch nicht da; **all in** alles inbegriffen; (⊞ *exhausted*) kaputt; **day in, day out** tagaus, tagein; **have it in for s.o.** ⊞ es auf jdn abgesehen haben; **send/go in** hineinschicken/-gehen; **come/ bring in** hereinkommen/-bringen ● a (⊞ *in fashion*) in ● n **the ins and outs** alle Einzelheiten pl

inability n Unfähigkeit f

inaccessible a unzugänglich

inaccura|cy n Ungenauigkeit f. **~te** a, **-ly** adv ungenau

inac|tive a untätig. **~tivity** n Untätigkeit f

inadequate a, **-ly** adv unzulänglich

inadmissible a unzulässig

inadvertently adv versehentlich

inadvisable a nicht ratsam

inane a, **-ly** adv albern

inanimate a unbelebt

inapplicable a nicht zutreffend

inappropriate a unangebracht

inarticulate a undeutlich; **be ~** sich nicht gut ausdrücken können

inattentive a unaufmerksam

inaudible a, **-bly** adv unhörbar

inaugural a Antritts-

inauspicious a ungünstig

inborn a angeboren

inbred a angeboren

incalculable a nicht berechenbar; (*fig*) unabsehbar

incapable a unfähig; **be ~ of doing sth** nicht fähig sein, etw zu tun

incapacitate vt unfähig machen

incarnation n Inkarnation f

incendiary a & n ~ [bomb] Brandbombe f

incense¹ n Weihrauch m

incense² vt wütend machen

incentive n Anreiz m

incessant a, **-ly** adv unaufhörlich

incest n Inzest m, Blutschande f

inch n Zoll m ● vi ~ **forward** sich ganz langsam vorwärts schieben

incident n Zwischenfall m

incidental a nebensächlich; <*remark*> beiläufig; <*expenses*> Neben-. **~ly** adv übrigens

incinerate vt verbrennen

incision n Einschnitt m

incisive a scharfsinnig

incite vt aufhetzen. **~ment** n Aufhetzung f

inclement a rau

inclination n Neigung f

incline vt neigen; **be ~d to do sth** dazu neigen, etw zu tun ● vi sich neigen

inclu|de *vt* einschließen; (*contain*) enthalten; (*incorporate*) aufnehmen (in in + *acc*). **~ding** *prep* einschließlich (+ *gen*). **~sion** *n* Aufnahme *f*

inclusive *a* Inklusiv-; **~ of** einschließlich (+ *gen*)

incognito *adv* inkognito

incoherent *a*, **-ly** *adv* zusammenhanglos; (*incomprehensible*) unverständlich

income *n* Einkommen *nt*. **~ tax** *n* Einkommensteuer *f*

incoming *a* ankommend; <*mail, call*> eingehend

incomparable *a* unvergleichlich

incompatible *a* unvereinbar; be **~** <*people:*> nicht zueinander passen

incompeten|ce *n* Unfähigkeit *f*. **~t** *a* unfähig

incomplete *a* unvollständig

incomprehensible *a* unverständlich

inconceivable *a* undenkbar

inconclusive *a* nicht schlüssig

incongruous *a* unpassend

inconsiderate *a* rücksichtslos

inconsistent *a*, **-ly** *adv* widersprüchlich; (*illogical*) inkonsequent; be **~** <*things:*> nicht übereinstimmen

inconsolable *a* untröstlich

inconspicuous *a* unauffällig

incontinen|ce *n* Inkontinenz *f*. **~t** *a* inkontinent

inconvenien|ce *n* Unannehmlichkeit *f*; (*drawback*) Nachteil *m*. **~t** *a*, **-ly** *adv* ungünstig; be **~t** for s.o. jdm nicht passen

incorporate *vt* aufnehmen; (*contain*) enthalten

incorrect *a*, **-ly** *adv* inkorrekt

incorrigible *a* unverbesserlich

incorruptible *a* unbestechlich

increase¹ *n* Zunahme *f*; (*rise*) Erhöhung *f*; be on the **~** zunehmen

increase² *vt* vergrößern; (*raise*) erhöhen ● *vi* zunehmen; (*rise*) sich erhöhen. **~ing** *a*, **-ly** *adv* zunehmend

incredible *a*, **-bly** *adv* unglaublich

incredulous *a* ungläubig

incriminate *vt* (*Jur*) belasten

incur *vt* (*pt/pp* **incurred**) sich (*dat*) zuziehen; machen <*debts*>

incurable *a*, **-bly** *adv* unheilbar

indebted *a* verpflichtet (to *dat*)

indecent *a*, **-ly** *adv* unanständig

indecision *n* Unentschlossenheit *f*

indecisive *a* ergebnislos; <*person*> unentschlossen

indeed *adv* in der Tat, tatsächlich; very much **~** sehr

indefatigable *a* unermüdlich

indefinite *a* unbestimmt. **~ly** *adv* unbegrenzt; <*postpone*> auf unbestimmte Zeit

indent *vt* (*Typ*) einrücken. **~ation** *n* Einrückung *f*; (*notch*) Kerbe *f*

independen|ce *n* Unabhängigkeit *f*, (*self-reliance*) Selbstständigkeit *f*. **~t** *a*, **-ly** *adv* unabhängig; selbstständig

indescribable *a*, **-bly** *adv* unbeschreiblich

indestructible *a* unzerstörbar

indeterminate *a* unbestimmt

index *n* Register *nt*

index: ~ card *n* Karteikarte *f*. **~ finger** *n* Zeigefinger *m*. **~-linked** *a* <*pension*> dynamisch

India *n* Indien *nt*. **~n** *a* indisch; (*American*) indianisch ● *n* Inder(in) *m(f)*; (*American*) Indianer(in) *m(f)*

Indian summer *n* Nachsommer *m*

indicat|e *vt* zeigen; (*point at*) zeigen auf (+ *acc*); (*hint*) andeuten; (*register*) anzeigen ● *vi* <*car:*> blinken. **~ion** *n* Anzeichen *nt*

indicative *n* (*Gram*) Indikativ *m*

indicator *n* (*Auto*) Blinker *m*

indifferen|ce *n* Gleichgültigkeit *f*. **~t** *a*, **-ly** *adv* gleichgültig; (*not good*) mittelmäßig

indigest|ible *a* unverdaulich; (*difficult to digest*) schwer verdaulich. **~ion** *n* Magenverstimmung *f*

indigna|nt *a*, **-ly** *adv* entrüstet, empört. **∼tion** *n* Entrüstung *f*, Empörung *f*

indignity *n* Demütigung *f*

indirect *a*, **-ly** *adv* indirekt

indiscreet *a* indiskret

indiscretion *n* Indiskretion *f*

indispensable *a* unentbehrlich

indisposed *a* indisponiert

indisputable *a*, **-bly** *adv* unbestreitbar

indistinct *a*, **-ly** *adv* undeutlich

indistinguishable *a* be ∼ nicht zu unterscheiden sein

individual *a*, **-ly** *adv* individuell; (*single*) einzeln ● *n* Individuum *nt*. **∼ity** *n* Individualität *f*

indivisible *a* unteilbar

indoctrinate *vt* indoktrinieren

indolen|ce *n* Faulheit *f*. **∼t** *a* faul

indomitable *a* unbeugsam

indoor *a* Innen-; <*clothes*> Haus-; <*plant*> Zimmer-; (*Sport*) Hallen-. **∼s** *adv* im Haus, drinnen; **go ∼s** ins Haus gehen

indulge *vt* frönen (+ *dat*); verwöhnen <*child*> ● *vi* ∼ in frönen (+ *dat*). **∼nce** *n* Nachgiebigkeit *f*; (*leniency*) Nachsicht *f*. **∼nt** *a* [zu] nachgiebig; nachsichtig

industrial *a* Industrie-. **∼ist** *n* Industrielle(r) *m*

industr|ious *a*, **-ly** *adv* fleißig. **∼y** *n* Industrie *f*; (*zeal*) Fleiß *m*

inebriated *a* betrunken

inedible *a* nicht essbar

ineffective *a*, **-ly** *adv* unwirksam; <*person*> untauglich

inefficient *a* unfähig; <*organization*> nicht leistungsfähig; <*method*> nicht rationell

ineligible *a* nicht berechtigt

inept *a* ungeschickt

inequality *n* Ungleichheit *f*

inertia *n* Trägheit *f*

inescapable *a* unvermeidlich

inestimable *a* unschätzbar

inevitab|le *a* unvermeidlich. **∼ly** *adv* zwangsläufig

inexact *a* ungenau

inexcusable *a* unverzeihlich

inexhaustible *a* unerschöpflich

inexpensive *a*, **-ly** *adv* preiswert

inexperience *n* Unerfahrenheit *f*. **∼d** *a* unerfahren

inexplicable *a* unerklärlich

infallible *a* unfehlbar

infamous *a* niederträchtig; (*notorious*) berüchtigt

infan|cy *n* frühe Kindheit *f*; (*fig*) Anfangsstadium *nt*. **∼t** *n* Kleinkind *nt*. **∼tile** *a* kindisch

infantry *n* Infanterie *f*

infatuated *a* vernarrt (with in + *acc*)

infect *vt* anstecken, infizieren; **become ∼ed** <*wound:*> sich infizieren. **∼ion** *n* Infektion *f*. **∼ious** *a* ansteckend

inferior *a* minderwertig; (*in rank*) untergeordnet ● *n* Untergebene(r) *m|f*

inferiority *n* Minderwertigkeit *f*. **∼ complex** *n* Minderwertigkeitskomplex *m*

infern|al *a* höllisch. **∼o** *n* flammendes Inferno *nt*

infertile *a* unfruchtbar

infest *vt* **be ∼ed with** befallen sein von; <*place*> verseucht sein mit

infidelity *n* Untreue *f*

infighting *n* (*fig*) interne Machtkämpfe *pl*

infinite *a*, **-ly** *adv* unendlich

infinitive *n* (*Gram*) Infinitiv *m*

infinity *n* Unendlichkeit *f*

inflame *vt* entzünden. **∼d** *a* entzündet

inflammable *a* feuergefährlich

inflammation *n* Entzündung *f*

inflammatory *a* aufrührerisch

inflat|e *vt* aufblasen; (*with pump*) aufpumpen. **∼ion** *n* Inflation *f*. **∼ionary** *a* inflationär

inflexible *a* starr; <*person*> unbeugsam

inflict *vt* zufügen (on *dat*); versetzen <*blow*> (on *dat*)

influen|ce *n* Einfluss *m* ● *vt* beeinflussen. **∼tial** *a* einflussreich

influenza n Grippe f

inform vt benachrichtigen; (officially) informieren; ~ s.o. of sth jdm etw mitteilen; keep s.o. ~ed jdn auf dem Laufenden halten ● vi ~ against denunzieren

informal a, -ly adv zwanglos; (unofficial) inoffiziell. ~ity n Zwanglosigkeit f

informant n Gewährsmann m

informat|ion n Auskunft f; a piece of ~ion eine Auskunft. ~ive a aufschlussreich; (instructive) lehrreich

informer n Spitzel m; (Pol) Denunziant m

infra-red a infrarot

infrequent a, -ly adv selten

infringe vt/i [on] verstoßen gegen. ~ment n Verstoß m

infuriat|e vt wütend machen. ~ing a ärgerlich

ingenious a erfinderisch; <thing> raffiniert

ingenuity n Geschicklichkeit f

ingrained a eingefleischt; be ~ <dirt> tief sitzen

ingratiate vt ~ oneself sich einschmeicheln (with bei)

ingratitude n Undankbarkeit f

ingredient n (Culin) Zutat f

ingrowing a <nail> eingewachsen

inhabit vt bewohnen. ~ant n Einwohner(in) m(f)

inhale vt/i einatmen; (Med & when smoking) inhalieren

inherent a natürlich

inherit vt erben. ~ance n Erbschaft f, Erbe nt

inhibit|ed a gehemmt. ~ion n Hemmung f

inhospitable a ungastlich

inhuman a unmenschlich

inimitable a unnachahmlich

initial a anfänglich, Anfangs- ● n Anfangsbuchstabe m; my ~s meine Initialen. ~ly adv anfangs, am Anfang

initiat|e vt einführen. ~ion n Einführung f

initiative n Initiative f

inject vt einspritzen, injizieren. ~ion n Spritze f, Injektion f

injur|e vt verletzen. ~y n Verletzung f

injustice n Ungerechtigkeit f; do s.o. an ~ jdm unrecht tun

ink n Tinte f

inlaid a eingelegt

inland a Binnen- ● adv landeinwärts

in-laws npl 🅸 Schwiegereltern pl

inlay n Einlegearbeit f

inlet n schmale Bucht f; (Techn) Zuleitung f

inmate n Insasse m

inn n Gasthaus nt

innate a angeboren

inner a innere(r,s). ~most a innerste(r,s)

innocen|ce n Unschuld f. ~t a unschuldig. ~tly adv in aller Unschuld

innocuous a harmlos

innovat|ion n Neuerung f. ~ive a innovativ. ~or n Neuerer m

innumerable a unzählig

inoculat|e vt impfen. ~ion n Impfung f

inoffensive a harmlos

inoperable a nicht operierbar

inopportune a unpassend

inorganic a anorganisch

in-patient n [stationär behandelter] Krankenhauspatient m

input n Input m & nt

inquest n gerichtliche Untersuchung f der Todesursache

inquir|e vi sich erkundigen (about nach); ~e into untersuchen ● vt sich erkundigen nach. ~y n Erkundigung f; (investigation) Untersuchung f

inquisitive a, -ly adv neugierig

insane a geisteskrank; (fig) wahnsinnig

insanitary a unhygienisch

insanity n Geisteskrankheit f

insatiable a unersättlich

inscription n Inschrift f

inscrutable a unergründlich; <*expression*> undurchdringlich

insect n Insekt nt. ~**icide** n Insektenvertilgungsmittel nt

insecur|e a nicht sicher; (*fig*) unsicher. ~**ity** n Unsicherheit f

insensitive a gefühllos; ~ **to** unempfindlich gegen

inseparable a untrennbar; (*people*) unzertrennlich

insert[1] n Einsatz m

insert[2] vt einfügen, einsetzen; einstecken <*key*>; einwerfen <*coin*>. ~**ion** n (*insert*) Einsatz m; (*in text*) Einfügung f

inside n Innenseite f; (*of house*) Innere(s) nt ● attrib Innen- ● adv innen; (*indoors*) drinnen; **go** ~ hineingehen; **come** ~ hereinkommen; ~ **out** links [herum]; **know sth** ~ **out** etw in- und auswendig kennen ● prep ~ [**of**] in (+ *dat/* (*into*) + *acc*)

insight n Einblick m (**into** in + *acc*); (*understanding*) Einsicht f

insignificant a unbedeutend

insincere a unaufrichtig

insinuat|e vt andeuten. ~**ion** n Andeutung f

insipid a fade

insist vi darauf bestehen; ~ **on** bestehen auf (+ *dat*) ● vt ~ **that** darauf bestehen, dass. ~**ence** n Bestehen nt. ~**ent** a, **-ly** adv beharrlich; **be** ~**ent** darauf bestehen

insole n Einlegesohle f

insolen|ce n Unverschämtheit f. ~**t** a, **-ly** adv unverschämt

insoluble a unlöslich; (*fig*) unlösbar

insolvent a zahlungsunfähig

insomnia n Schlaflosigkeit f

inspect vt inspizieren; (*test*) prüfen; kontrollieren <*ticket*>. ~**ion** n Inspektion f. ~**or** n Inspektor m; (*of tickets*) Kontrolleur m

inspiration n Inspiration f

inspire vt inspirieren

instability n Unbeständigkeit f; (*of person*) Labilität f

install vt installieren. ~**ation** n Installation f

instalment n (*Comm*) Rate f; (*of serial*) Fortsetzung f; (*Radio, TV*) Folge f

instance n Fall m; (*example*) Beispiel nt; **in the first** ~ zunächst; **for** ~ zum Beispiel

instant a sofortig; (*Culin*) Instant- ● n Augenblick m, Moment m. ~**aneous** a unverzüglich, unmittelbar

instant coffee n Pulverkaffee m

instantly adv sofort

instead adv statt dessen; ~ **of** statt (+ *gen*), anstelle von; ~ **of me** an meiner Stelle; ~ **of going** anstatt zu gehen

instep n Spann m, Rist m

instigat|e vt anstiften; einleiten <*proceedings*>. ~**ion** n Anstiftung f; **at his** ~**ion** auf seine Veranlassung

instil vt (*pt/pp* instilled) einprägen (**into s.o.** jdm)

instinct n Instinkt m. ~**ive** a, **-ly** adv instinktiv

institut|e n Institut nt. ~**ion** n Institution f; (*home*) Anstalt f

instruct vt unterrichten; (*order*) anweisen. ~**ion** n Unterricht m; Anweisung f; ~**ions** pl **for use** Gebrauchsanweisung f. ~**ive** a lehrreich. ~**or** n Lehrer(in) m(f); (*Mil*) Ausbilder m

instrument n Instrument nt. ~**al** a Instrumental-

insubordi|nate a ungehorsam. ~**nation** n Ungehorsam m; (*Mil*) Insubordination f

insufficient a, **-ly** adv nicht genügend

insulat|e vt isolieren. ~**ing tape** n Isolierband nt. ~**ion** n Isolierung f

insult[1] n Beleidigung f

insult[2] vt beleidigen

insur|ance n Versicherung f. ~**e** vt versichern

intact a unbeschädigt; (*complete*) vollständig

intake n Aufnahme f

intangible a nicht greifbar

integral a wesentlich

integrat|e *vt* integrieren ● *vi* sich integrieren. **∼ion** *n* Integration *f*

integrity *n* Integrität *f*

intellect *n* Intellekt *m*. **∼ual** *a* intellektuell

intelligen|ce *n* Intelligenz *f*; (*Mil*) Nachrichtendienst *m*; (*information*) Meldungen *pl*. **∼t** *a*, **-ly** *adv* intelligent

intelligible *a* verständlich

intend *vt* beabsichtigen; be **∼ed for** bestimmt sein für

intense *a* intensiv; <*pain*> stark. **∼ly** *adv* äußerst; <*study*> intensiv

intensify *v* (*pt/pp* **-ied**) ● *vt* intensivieren ● *vi* zunehmen

intensity *n* Intensität *f*

intensive *a*, **-ly** *adv* intensiv; be in **∼ care** auf der Intensivstation sein

intent *a*, **-ly** *adv* aufmerksam; **∼ on** (*absorbed in*) vertieft in (+ *acc*) ● *n* Absicht *f*

intention *n* Absicht *f*. **∼al** *a*, **-ly** *adv* absichtlich

interacti|on *n* Wechselwirkung *f*. **∼ve** *a* interaktiv

intercede *vi* Fürsprache einlegen (**on behalf of** für)

intercept *vt* abfangen

interchange *n* Austausch *m*; (*Auto*) Autobahnkreuz *nt*

intercom *n* [Gegen]sprechanlage *f*

intercourse *n* (*sexual*) Geschlechtsverkehr *m*

interest *n* Interesse *nt*; (*Comm*) Zinsen *pl* ● *vt* interessieren; be **∼ed** sich interessieren (**in** für). **∼ing** *a* interessant. **∼ rate** *n* Zinssatz *m*

interfere *vi* sich einmischen. **∼nce** *n* Einmischung *f*; (*Radio, TV*) Störung *f*

interim *a* Zwischen-; (*temporary*) vorläufig

interior *a* innere(r,s), Innen- ● *n* Innere(s) *nt*

interject *vt* einwerfen. **∼ion** *n* Interjektion *f*; (*remark*) Einwurf *m*

interlude *n* Pause *f*; (*performance*) Zwischenspiel *nt*

intermarry *vi* untereinander heiraten; <*different groups:*> Mischehen schließen

intermediary *n* Vermittler(in) *m(f)*

intermediate *a* Zwischen-

interminable *a* endlos [lang]

intermittent *a* in Abständen auftretend

internal *a* innere(r,s); <*matter, dispute*> intern; **∼ly** *adv* innerlich; <*deal with*> intern

international *a*, **-ly** *adv* international ● *n* Länderspiel *nt*; (*player*) Nationalspieler(in) *m(f)*

Internet *n* Internet *nt*; **on the ∼** im Internet

internment *n* Internierung *f*

interplay *n* Wechselspiel *nt*

interpolate *vt* einwerfen

interpret *vt* interpretieren; auslegen <*text*>; deuten <*dream*>; (*translate*) dolmetschen ● *vi* dolmetschen. **∼ation** *n* Interpretation *f*. **∼er** *n* Dolmetscher(in) *m(f)*

interrogat|e *vt* verhören. **∼ion** *n* Verhör *nt*

interrogative *a & n* **∼ [pronoun]** Interrogativpronomen *nt*

interrupt *vt/i* unterbrechen; don't **∼!** red nicht dazwischen! **∼ion** *n* Unterbrechung *f*

intersect *vi* sich kreuzen; (*Geom*) sich schneiden. **∼ion** *n* Kreuzung *f*

interspersed *a* **∼ with** durchsetzt mit

intertwine *vi* sich ineinanderschlingen

interval *n* Abstand *m*; (*Theat*) Pause *f*; (*Mus*) Intervall *nt*; **at hourly ∼s** alle Stunde; **bright ∼s** *pl* Aufheiterungen *pl*

interven|e *vi* eingreifen; (*occur*) dazwischenkommen. **∼tion** *n* Eingreifen *nt*; (*Mil, Pol*) Intervention *f*

interview *n* (*Journ*) Interview *nt*; (*for job*) Vorstellungsgespräch *nt* ● *vt* interviewen; ein Vorstellungsgespräch führen mit. **∼er** *n* Interviewer(in) *m(f)*

intimacy n Vertrautheit f; (sexual) Intimität f

intimate a, -ly adv vertraut; <friend> eng; (sexually) intim

intimidat|e vt einschüchtern. ~**ion** n Einschüchterung f

into prep in (+ acc); be ~ 🗊 sich auskennen mit; 7 ~ 21 21 [geteilt] durch 7

intolerable a unerträglich

intoleran|ce n Intoleranz f. ~**t** a intolerant

intonation n Tonfall m

intoxicat|ed a betrunken; (fig) berauscht. ~**ion** n Rausch m

intransigent a unnachgiebig

intransitive a, -ly adv intransitiv

intrepid a kühn, unerschrocken

intricate a kompliziert

intrigu|e n Intrige f ● vt faszinieren. ~**ing** a faszinierend

intrinsic a ~ value Eigenwert m

introduce vt vorstellen; (bring in, insert) einführen

introduct|ion n Einführung f; (to person) Vorstellung f; (to book) Einleitung f. ~**ory** a einleitend

introvert n introvertierter Mensch m

intru|de vi stören. ~**der** n Eindringling m. ~**sion** n Störung f

intuit|ion n Intuition f. ~**ive** a, -ly adv intuitiv

inundate vt überschwemmen

invade vt einfallen in (+ acc). ~**r** n Angreifer m

invalid[1] n Kranke(r) m/f

invalid[2] a ungültig

invaluable a unschätzbar; <person> unersetzlich

invariab|le a unveränderlich. ~**ly** adv immer

invasion n Invasion f

invent vt erfinden. ~**ion** n Erfindung f. ~**ive** a erfinderisch. ~**or** n Erfinder m

inventory n Bestandsliste f

invert vt umkehren. ~**ed commas** npl Anführungszeichen pl

invest vt investieren, anlegen; ~ in (🗊 buy) sich (dat) zulegen

investigat|e vt untersuchen. ~**ion** n Untersuchung f

invest|ment n Anlage f; be a good ~**ment** (fig) sich bezahlt machen. ~**or** n Kapitalanleger m

invidious a unerfreulich; (unfair) ungerecht

invincible a unbesiegbar

inviolable a unantastbar

invisible a unsichtbar

invitation n Einladung f

invit|e vt einladen. ~**ing** a einladend

invoice n Rechnung f ● vt ~ s.o. jdm eine Rechnung schicken

involuntary a, -ily adv unwillkürlich

involve vt beteiligen; (affect) betreffen; (implicate) verwickeln; (entail) mit sich bringen; (mean) bedeuten; be ~d in beteiligt sein an (+ dat); (implicated) verwickelt sein in (+ acc); get ~d with s.o. sich mit jdm einlassen. ~**d** a kompliziert

invulnerable a unverwundbar; <position> unangreifbar

inward a innere(r,s). ~**s** adv nach innen

iodine n Jod nt

IOU abbr Schuldschein m

Iran n der Iran

Iraq n der Irak

irascible a aufbrausend

irate a wütend

Ireland n Irland nt

iris n (Anat) Regenbogenhaut f, Iris f; (Bot) Schwertlilie f

Irish a irisch ● n the ~ pl die Iren. ~**man** n Ire m. ~**woman** n Irin f

iron a Eisen-; (fig) eisern ● n Eisen nt; (appliance) Bügeleisen nt ● vt/i bügeln

ironic[al] a ironisch

ironing n Bügeln nt; (articles) Bügelwäsche f. ~**board** n Bügelbrett nt

ironmonger n ~**'s** [shop] Haushaltswarengeschäft nt

irony *n* Ironie *f*

irrational *a* irrational

irreconcilable *a* unversöhnlich

irrefutable *a* unwiderlegbar

irregular *a*, **-ly** *adv* unregelmäßig; (*against rules*) regelwidrig. **~ity** *n* Unregelmäßigkeit *f*; Regelwidrigkeit *f*

irrelevant *a* irrelevant

irreparable *a* nicht wieder gutzumachen

irreplaceable *a* unersetzlich

irrepressible *a* unverwüstlich; be ~ <*person.*> nicht unterzukriegen sein

irresistible *a* unwiderstehlich

irresolute *a* unentschlossen

irrespective *a* ~ **of** ungeachtet (+ *gen*)

irresponsible *a*, **-bly** *adv* unverantwortlich; <*person*> verantwortungslos

irreverent *a*, **-ly** *adv* respektlos

irrevocable *a*, **-bly** *adv* unwiderruflich

irrigat|e *vt* bewässern. **~ion** *n* Bewässerung *f*

irritable *a* reizbar

irritant *n* Reizstoff *m*

irritat|e *vt* irritieren; (*Med*) reizen. **~ion** *n* Ärger *m*; (*Med*) Reizung *f*

is *see* be

Islam *n* der Islam. **~ic** *a* islamisch

island *n* Insel *f*. **~er** *n* Inselbewohner(in) *m(f)*

isolat|e *vt* isolieren. **~ed** *a* (*remote*) abgelegen; (*single*) einzeln. **~ion** *n* Isoliertheit *f*; (*Med*) Isolierung *f*

Israel *n* Israel *nt*. **~i** *a* israelisch ● *n* Israeli *m/f*

issue *n* Frage *f*; (*outcome*) Ergebnis *nt*; (*of magazine, stamps*) Ausgabe *f*; (*offspring*) Nachkommen *pl* ● *vt* ausgeben; ausstellen <*passport*>; erteilen <*order*>; herausgeben <*book*>; be ~d with sth etw erhalten

it
● *pronoun*
····▸ (*as subject*) er (*m*), sie (*f*), es (*nt*); (*in impersonal sentence*) es. where is the spoon? It's on the table wo ist der Löffel? Er liegt auf dem Tisch. it was very kind of you es war sehr nett von Ihnen. it's five o'clock es ist fünf Uhr
····▸ (*as direct object*) ihn (*m*), sie (*f*), es (*nt*). that's my pencil — give it to me das ist mein Bleistift — gib ihn mir.
····▸ (*as dative object*) ihm (*m*), ihr (*f*), ihm (*nt*). he found a track and followed it er fand eine Spur und folgte ihr.
····▸ (*after prepositions*)

> **!** Combinations such as *with it*, *from it*, *to it* are translated by the prepositions with the prefix da- (damit, davon, dazu). Prepositions beginning with a vowel insert an 'r' (daran, darauf, darüber). I can't do anything with it ich kann nichts damit anfangen. don't lean on it! lehn dich nicht daran!

····▸ (*the person in question*) es. it's me ich bin's. is it you, Dad? bist du es, Vater? who is it? wer ist da?

Italian *a* italienisch ● *n* Italiener(in) *m(f)*; (*Lang*) Italienisch *nt*

italics *npl* Kursivschrift *f*; in ~s kursiv

Italy *n* Italien *nt*

itch *n* Juckreiz *m*; I have an ~ es juckt mich ● *vi* jucken; I'm ~ing [☐] es juckt mich (to zu). **~y** *a* be ~y jucken

item *n* Gegenstand *m*; (*Comm*) Artikel *m*; (*on agenda*) Punkt *m*; (*on invoice*) Posten *m*; (*act*) Nummer *f*

itinerary *n* [Reise]route *f*

its *poss pron* sein; (*f*) ihr

it's = it is, it has

itself *pron* selbst; (*refl*) sich; by ~ von selbst; (*alone*) allein

ivory *n* Elfenbein *nt* ● *attrib* Elfenbein-

ivy *n* Efeu *m*

Jj

jab n Stoß m; (🔟 injection) Spritze f ● vt (pt/pp **jabbed**) stoßen

jabber vi plappern

jack n (Auto) Wagenheber m; (Cards) Bube m ● vt ~ **up** (Auto) aufbocken

jacket n Jacke f; (of book) Schutzumschlag m

jackpot n hit the ~ das große Los ziehen

jade n Jade m

jagged a zackig

jail = gaol

jam¹ n Marmelade f

jam² n Gedränge nt; (Auto) Stau m; (fam. difficulty) Klemme f ● v (pt/pp jammed) ● vt klemmen (in in + acc); stören <broadcast> ● vi klemmen

Jamaica n Jamaika nt

jangle vi klimpern ● vt klimpern mit

January n Januar m

Japan n Japan nt. ~**ese** a japanisch ● n Japaner(in) m(f); (Lang) Japanisch nt

jar n Glas nt; (earthenware) Topf m

jargon n Jargon m

jaunt n Ausflug m

jaunty a (-ier, -iest) -ily adv keck

javelin n Speer m

jaw n Kiefer m

jazz n Jazz m. ~**y** a knallig

jealous a, -ly adv eifersüchtig (of auf + acc). ~**y** n Eifersucht f

jeans npl Jeans pl

jeer vi johlen; ~ **at** verhöhnen

jelly n Gelee nt; (dessert) Götterspeise f. ~**fish** n Qualle f

jeopar|dize vt gefährden. ~**dy** n in ~**dy** gefährdet

jerk n Ruck m ● vt stoßen; (pull) reißen ● vi rucken; <limb, muscle:> zucken. ~**ily** adv ruckweise. ~**y** a ruckartig

jersey n Pullover m; (Sport) Trikot nt; (fabric) Jersey m

jest n in ~ im Spaß

jet n (of water) [Wasser]strahl m; (nozzle) Düse f; (plane) Düsenflugzeug nt

jet: ~**-black** a pechschwarz. ~**-propelled** a mit Düsenantrieb

jetty n Landesteg m; (breakwater) Buhne f

Jew n Jude m /Jüdin f

jewel n Edelstein m; (fig) Juwel nt. ~**ler** n Juwelier m; ~**ler's** [shop] Juweliergeschäft nt. ~**lery** n Schmuck m

Jew|ess n Jüdin f. ~**ish** a jüdisch

jib vi (pt/pp jibbed) (fig) sich sträuben (at gegen)

jigsaw n ~ [puzzle] Puzzlespiel nt

jilt vt sitzen lassen

jingle n (rhyme) Verschen nt ● vi klimpern

jinx n 🔟 it's got a ~ on it es ist verhext

jittery a 🔟 nervös

job n Aufgabe f; (post) Stelle f, 🔟 Job m; be a ~ 🔟 nicht leicht sein; it's a good ~ that es ist [nur] gut, dass. ~**less** a arbeitslos

jockey n Jockei m

jocular a, -ly adv spaßhaft

jog n Stoß m ● v (pt/pp jogged) ● vt anstoßen; ~ **s.o.'s memory** jds Gedächtnis nachhelfen ● vi (Sport) joggen. ~**ging** n Jogging nt

john n (Amer 🔟) Klo nt

join n Nahtstelle f ● vt verbinden (to mit); sich anschließen (+ dat) <person>; (become member of) beitreten (+ dat); eintreten in (+ acc) <firm> ● vi <roads:> sich treffen. ~ **in** vi mitmachen. ~ **up** vi (Mil) Soldat werden ● vt zusammenfügen

joint a, -ly adv gemeinsam ● n Gelenk nt; (in wood, brickwork) Fuge f; (Culin) Braten m; (🔟 bar) Lokal nt

jok|e n Scherz m; (funny story) Witz m; (trick) Streich m ● vi scherzen. ~**er** n Witzbold m; (Cards) Joker m.

∼ing n ∼ing apart Spaß beiseite.
∼ingly adv im Spaß

jolly a (-ier, -iest) lustig ● adv Ⓘ sehr

jolt n Ruck m ● vt einen Ruck
versetzen (+ dat) ● vi holpern

Jordan n Jordanien nt

jostle vt anrempeln

jot vt (pt/pp jotted) ∼ [down] sich
(dat) notieren

journal n Zeitschrift f; (diary)
Tagebuch nt. **∼ese** n
Zeitungsjargon m. **∼ism** n
Journalismus m. **∼ist** n
Journalist(in) m(f)

journey n Reise f

jovial a lustig

joy n Freude f. **∼ful** a, **-ly** adv
freudig, froh. **∼ride** n Ⓘ Spritztour
f [im gestohlenen Auto]

jubil|ant a überglücklich. **∼ation** n
Jubel m

jubilee n Jubiläum nt

judder vi rucken

judge n Richter m; (of competition)
Preisrichter m ● vt beurteilen;
(estimate) [ein]schätzen ● vi urteilen
(by nach). **∼ment** n Beurteilung f;
(Jur) Urteil nt; (fig) Urteilsvermögen
nt

judic|ial a gerichtlich. **∼ious** a
klug

jug n Kanne f; (small) Kännchen nt;
(for water, wine) Krug m

juggle vi jonglieren. **∼r** n Jongleur
m

juice n Saft m

juicy a (-ier, -iest) saftig; Ⓘ <story>
pikant

juke-box n Musikbox f

July n Juli m

jumble n Durcheinander nt ● vt ∼
[up] durcheinander bringen. **∼ sale**
n [Wohltätigkeits]basar m

jump n Sprung m; (in prices) Anstieg
m; (in horse racing) Hindernis nt
● vi springen; (start)
zusammenzucken; **make s.o. ∼** jdn
erschrecken; **∼ at** (fig) sofort
zugreifen bei <offer>; **∼ to
conclusions** voreilige Schlüsse

ziehen ● vt überspringen. **∼ up** vi
aufspringen

jumper n Pullover m, Pulli m

jumpy a nervös

junction n Kreuzung f; (Rail)
Knotenpunkt m

June n Juni m

jungle n Dschungel m

junior a jünger; (in rank)
untergeordnet; (Sport) Junioren- ● n
Junior m

junk n Gerümpel nt, Trödel m

junkie n ⊠ Fixer m

junk-shop n Trödelladen m

jurisdiction n Gerichtsbarkeit f

jury n the **∼** die Geschworenen pl;
(for competition) die Jury

just a gerecht ● adv gerade; (only)
nur; (simply) einfach; (exactly)
genau; **∼ as tall** ebenso groß; **I'm ∼
going** ich gehe schon

justice n Gerechtigkeit f; **do ∼ to**
gerecht werden (+ dat)

justifiab|le a berechtigt. **∼ly** adv
berechtigterweise

justi|fication n Rechtfertigung f.
∼fy vt (pt/pp -ied) rechtfertigen

justly adv zu Recht

jut vi (pt/pp jutted) **∼ out** vorstehen

juvenile a jugendlich; (childish)
kindisch ● n Jugendliche(r) m/f. **∼
delinquency** n Jugendkriminalität
f

Kk

kangaroo n Känguru nt

kebab n Spießchen nt

keel n Kiel m ● vi **∼ over** umkippen;
(Naut) kentern

keen a (-er, -est) (sharp) scharf;
(intense) groß; (eager) eifrig,
begeistert; **∼ on** Ⓘ erpicht auf (+
acc); **∼ on s.o.** von jdm sehr

k

angetan; **be ∼ to do sth** etw gerne machen wollen. **∼ly** adv tief. **∼ness** n Eifer m, Begeisterung f

keep n (maintenance) Unterhalt m; (of castle) Bergfried m; **for ∼s** für immer ● v (pt/pp kept) ● vt behalten; (store) aufbewahren; (not throw away) aufheben; (support) unterhalten; (detain) aufhalten; freihalten <seat>; halten <promise, animals>; führen, haben <shop>; einhalten <law, rules>; ∼ **s.o. waiting** jdn warten lassen; ∼ **sth to oneself** etw nicht weitersagen ● vi (remain) bleiben; <food:> sich halten; ∼ **left/right** sich links/rechts halten; ∼ **on doing sth** etw weitermachen; (repeatedly) etw dauernd machen; ∼ **in with** sich gut stellen mit. ∼ **up** vi Schritt halten ● vt (continue) weitermachen

keep|er n Wärter(in) m(f). **∼ing** n **be in ∼ing with** passen zu

kennel n Hundehütte f; **∼s** pl (boarding) Hundepension f; (breeding) Zwinger m

Kenya n Kenia nt

kept see keep

kerb n Bordstein m

kernel n Kern m

ketchup n Ketschup m

kettle n [Wasser]kessel m; **put the ∼ on** Wasser aufsetzen

key n Schlüssel m; (Mus) Tonart f; (of piano, typewriter) Taste f ● vt ∼ **in** eintasten

key: ∼board n Tastatur f; (Mus) Klaviatur f. **∼hole** n Schlüsselloch nt. **∼-ring** n Schlüsselring m

khaki a khakifarben ● n Khaki nt

kick n [Fuß]tritt m; **for ∼s** 🛈 zum Spaß ● vt treten; ∼ **the bucket** 🛈 abkratzen ● vi <animal> ausschlagen

kid n (🛈 child) Kind nt ● vt (pt/pp kidded) 🛈 ∼ **s.o.** jdm etwas vormachen

kidnap vt (pt/pp -napped) entführen. **∼per** n Entführer m. **∼ping** n Entführung f

kidney n Niere f

kill vt töten; 🛈 totschlagen <time>: ∼ **two birds with one stone** zwei Fliegen mit einer Klappe schlagen. **∼er** n Mörder(in) m(f). **∼ing** n Tötung f; (murder) Mord m

killjoy n Spielverderber m

kilo n Kilo nt

kilo:: ∼gram n Kilogramm nt. **∼metre** n Kilometer m. **∼watt** n Kilowatt nt

kilt n Schottenrock m

kind¹ n Art f, (brand, type) Sorte f; **what ∼ of car?** was für ein Auto? ∼ **of** 🛈 irgendwie

kind² a (-er, -est) nett; ∼ **to animals** gut zu Tieren

kind|ly a (-ier, -iest) nett ● adv netterweise; (if you please) gefälligst. **∼ness** n Güte f; (favour) Gefallen m

king n König m; (Draughts) Dame f. **∼dom** n Königreich nt; (fig & Relig) Reich nt

king: ∼fisher n Eisvogel m. **∼-sized** a extragroß

kink n Knick m. **∼y** a 🛈 pervers

kiosk n Kiosk m

kip n **have a ∼** 🛈 pennen ● vi (pt/pp kipped) 🛈 pennen

kipper n Räucherhering m

kiss n Kuss m ● vt/i küssen

kit n Ausrüstung f; (tools) Werkzeug nt; (construction ∼) Bausatz m ● vt (pt/pp kitted) **∼out** ausrüsten

kitchen n Küche f ● attrib Küchen-. **∼ette** n Kochnische f

kitchen: ∼garden n Gemüsegarten m. **∼sink** n Spülbecken nt

kite n Drachen m

kitten n Kätzchen nt

kitty n (money) [gemeinsame] Kasse f

knack n Trick m, Dreh m

knead vt kneten

knee n Knie nt. **∼cap** n Kniescheibe f

kneel vi (pt/pp knelt) knien; ∼ **[down]** sich [nieder]knien

knelt see kneel

knew see know

knickers npl Schlüpfer m

knife n (pl **knives**) Messer nt ● vt einen Messerstich versetzen (+ dat)

knight n Ritter m; (Chess) Springer m ● vt adeln

knit vt/i (pt/pp **knitted**) stricken; ~ one's brow die Stirn runzeln. **~ting** n Stricken nt; (work) Strickzeug nt. **~ting-needle** n Stricknadel f. **~wear** n Strickwaren pl

knives npl see **knife**

knob n Knopf m; (on door) Knauf m; (small lump) Beule f. **~bly** a knorrig; (bony) knochig

knock n Klopfen nt; (blow) Schlag m; there was a ~ es klopfte ● vt anstoßen; (🔢 criticize) heruntermachen; ~ a hole in sth ein Loch in etw (acc) schlagen; ~ one's head sich (dat) den Kopf stoßen (on an + dat) ● vi klopfen. ~ about vt schlagen ● vi 🔢 herumkommen. ~ down vt herunterwerfen; (with fist) niederschlagen; (in car) anfahren; (demolish) abreißen; (🔢 reduce) herabsetzen. ~ off vt herunterwerfen; (🔢 steal) klauen; (🔢 complete quickly) hinhauen ● vi (🔢 cease work) Feierabend machen. ~ out vt ausschlagen; (make unconscious) bewusstlos schlagen; (Boxing) k.o. schlagen. ~ over vt umwerfen; (in car) anfahren

knock: **~-down** a ~-down prices Schleuderpreise pl. **~er** n Türklopfer m. **~-out** n (Boxing) K.o. m

knot n Knoten m ● vt (pt/pp **knotted**) knoten

know vt/i (pt **knew**, pp **known**) wissen; kennen <person>; können <language>; get to ~ kennen lernen ● n in the ~ 🔢 im Bild

know: **~-all** n 🔢 Alleswisser m. **~-how** n 🔢 [Sach]kenntnis f. **~ing** a wissend. **~ingly** adv wissend; (intentionally) wissentlich

knowledge n Kenntnis f (of von/ gen); (general) Wissen nt; (specialized) Kenntnisse pl. **~able** a be ~able viel wissen

knuckle n [Finger]knöchel m; (Culin) Hachse f

kosher a koscher

kudos n 🔢 Prestige nt

Ll

lab n 🔢 Labor nt

label n Etikett nt ● vt (pt/pp **labelled**) etikettieren

laboratory n Labor nt

laborious a, **-ly** adv mühsam

labour n Arbeit f; (workers) Arbeitskräfte pl; (Med) Wehen pl; **L~** (Pol) die Labourpartei ● attrib Labour- ● vi arbeiten ● vt (fig) sich lange auslassen über (+ acc). **~er** n Arbeiter m

labour-saving a arbeitssparend

lace n Spitze f; (of shoe) Schnürsenkel m ● vt schnüren

lack n Mangel m (of an + dat) ● vt I ~ the time mir fehlt die Zeit ● vi be **~ing** fehlen

laconic a, **-ally** adv lakonisch

lacquer n Lack m; (for hair) [Haar]spray m

lad n Junge m

ladder n Leiter f; (in fabric) Laufmasche f

ladle n [Schöpf]kelle f ● vt schöpfen

lady n Dame f; (title) Lady f

lady: **~bird** n, (Amer) **~bug** n Marienkäfer m. **~like** a damenhaft

lag[1] vi (pt/pp **lagged**) ~ behind zurückbleiben; (fig) nachhinken

lag[2] vt (pt/pp **lagged**) umwickeln <pipes>

lager n Lagerbier nt

laid see **lay**[3]

lain see **lie**[2]

lake n See m

lamb n Lamm nt

lame a (-r, -st) lahm

lament n Klage f; (song) Klagelied nt ● vt beklagen ● vi klagen

k
l

laminated a laminiert

lamp n Lampe f; (in street) Laterne f. **~post** n Laternenpfahl m. **~shade** n Lampenschirm m

lance vt (Med) aufschneiden

land n Land nt; plot of **~** Grundstück nt ● vt/i landen; **~ s.o. with sth** ⓣ jdm etw aufhalsen

landing n Landung f; (top of stairs) Treppenflur m. **~-stage** n Landesteg m

land: **~lady** n Wirtin f. **~lord** n Wirt m; (of land) Grundbesitzer m; (of building) Hausbesitzer m. **~mark** n Erkennungszeichen nt; (fig) Meilenstein m. **~owner** n Grundbesitzer m. **~scape** n Landschaft f. **~slide** n Erdrutsch m

lane n kleine Landstraße f; (Auto) Spur f; (Sport) Bahn f; 'get in **~**' (Auto) 'bitte einordnen'

language n Sprache f; (speech, style) Ausdrucksweise f

languid a, **-ly** adv träge

languish vi schmachten

lanky a (-ier, -iest) schlaksig

lantern n Laterne f

lap¹ n Schoß m

lap² n (Sport) Runde f; (of journey) Etappe f ● vi (pt/pp lapped) plätschern (against gegen)

lap³ vt (pt/pp lapped) **~ up** aufschlecken

lapel n Revers nt

lapse n Fehler m; (moral) Fehltritt m; (of time) Zeitspanne f ● vi (expire) erlöschen; **~ into** verfallen in (+ acc)

lard n [Schweine]schmalz nt

larder n Speisekammer f

large a (-r, -st) & adv groß; **by and ~** im Großen und Ganzen; **at ~** auf freiem Fuß. **~ly** adv großenteils

lark¹ n (bird) Lerche f

lark² n (joke) Jux m ● vi **~ about** herumalbern

laryngitis n Kehlkopfentzündung f

larynx n Kehlkopf m

laser n Laser m

lash n Peitschenhieb m; (eyelash) Wimper f ● vt peitschen; (tie)

festbinden (**to** an + acc). **~ out** vi um sich schlagen; (spend) viel Geld ausgeben (**on** für)

lass n Mädchen nt

lasso n Lasso nt

last a & n letzte(r,s); **~ night** heute od gestern Nacht; (evening) gestern Abend; **at ~** endlich; **for the ~ time** zum letzten Mal; **the ~ but one** der/ die/das vorletzte ● adv zuletzt; (last time) das letzte Mal; **he/she went ~** er/sie ging als Letzter/Letzte ● vi dauern; <weather:> sich halten; <relationship:> halten. **~ing** a dauerhaft. **~ly** adv schließlich, zum Schluss

latch n [einfache] Klinke f

late a & adv (-r, -st) spät; (delayed) verspätet; (deceased) verstorben; **the ~st news** die neuesten Nachrichten; **stay up ~** bis spät aufbleiben; **arrive ~** zu spät ankommen; **I am ~** ich komme zu spät od habe mich verspätet; **the train is ~** der Zug hat Verspätung. **~comer** n Zuspätkommende(r) m/f. **~ly** adv in letzter Zeit. **~ness** n Zuspätkommen nt; (delay) Verspätung f

later a & adv später; **~ on** nachher

lateral a seitlich

lather n [Seifen]schaum m

Latin a lateinisch ● n Latein nt. **~ America** n Lateinamerika nt

latitude n (Geog) Breite f; (fig) Freiheit f

latter a & n **the ~** der/die/das Letztere

Latvia n Lettland nt

laudable a lobenswert

laugh n Lachen nt; **with a ~** lachend ● vi lachen (**at/about** über + acc); **~ at s.o.** (mock) jdn auslachen. **~able** a lachhaft, lächerlich

laughter n Gelächter nt

launch¹ n (boat) Barkasse f

launch² n Stapellauf m; (of rocket) Abschuss m; (of product) Lancierung f ● vt vom Stapel lassen <ship>; zu Wasser lassen <lifeboat>; abschießen

<*rocket*>; starten <*attack*>; (*Comm*) lancieren <*product*>

laund(e)rette n Münzwäscherei f

laundry n Wäscherei f; (*clothes*) Wäsche f

laurel n Lorbeer m

lava n Lava f

lavatory n Toilette f

lavender n Lavendel m

lavish a, **-ly** adv großzügig; (*wasteful*) verschwenderisch ● vt ~ sth on s.o. jdn mit etw überschütten

law n Gesetz nt; (*system*) Recht nt; study ~ Jura studieren; ~ and order Recht und Ordnung

law: ~**-abiding** a gesetzestreu. ~ **court** n Gerichtshof m. ~**ful** a rechtmäßig. ~**less** a gesetzlos

lawn n Rasen m. ~**-mower** n Rasenmäher m

lawyer n Rechtsanwalt m /-anwältin f

lax a lax, locker

laxative n Abführmittel nt

laxity n Laxheit f

lay¹ see **lie²**

lay² vt (pt/pp laid) legen; decken <*table*>; ~ a trap eine Falle stellen. ~ **down** vt hinlegen; festlegen <*rules, conditions*>. ~ **off** vt entlassen <*workers*> ● vi (🄵 stop) aufhören. ~ **out** vt hinlegen; aufbahren <*corpse*>; anlegen <*garden*>; (*Typ*) gestalten

lay-by n Parkbucht f

layer n Schicht f

lay: ~**man** n Laie m. ~**out** n Anordnung f; (*design*) Gestaltung f; (*Typ*) Layout nt

laze vi ~[about] faulenzen

laziness n Faulheit f

lazy a (-ier, -iest) faul. ~**-bones** n Faulenzer m

lead¹ n Blei nt; (*of pencil*) [Bleistift]mine f

lead² n Führung f; (*leash*) Leine f; (*flex*) Schnur f; (*clue*) Hinweis m, Spur f; (*Theat*) Hauptrolle f; (*distance ahead*) Vorsprung m; be in the ~ in Führung liegen ● vt/i (pt/pp led) führen; leiten <*team*>; (*induce*)

bringen; (*at cards*) ausspielen; ~ the way vorangehen; ~ up to sth (*fig*) etw (*dat*) vorangehen

leader n Führer m; (*of expedition, group*) Leiter(in) m(f); (*of orchestra*) Konzertmeister m; (*in newspaper*) Leitartikel m. ~**ship** n Führung f; Leitung f

leading a führend; ~ lady Hauptdarstellerin f

leaf n (pl leaves) Blatt nt ● vi ~ through sth etw durchblättern. ~**let** n Merkblatt nt; (*advertising*) Reklameblatt nt; (*political*) Flugblatt nt

league n Liga f

leak n (*hole*) undichte Stelle f; (*Naut*) Leck nt; (*of gas*) Gasausfluss m ● vi undicht sein; <*ship:*> leck sein, lecken; <*liquid:*> auslaufen; <*gas:*> ausströmen ● vt auslaufen lassen; ~ sth to s.o. (*fig*) jdm etw zuspielen. ~**y** a undicht; (*Naut*) leck

lean¹ a (-er, -est) mager

lean² v (pt/pp leaned or leant) ● vt lehnen (against/on an + acc) ● vi <*person*> sich lehnen (against/on an + acc); (*not be straight*) sich neigen; be ~ing against lehnen an (+ dat). ~ **back** vi sich zurücklehnen. ~ **forward** vi sich vorbeugen. ~ **out** vi sich hinauslehnen. ~ **over** vi sich vorbeugen

leaning a schief ● n Neigung f

leap n Sprung m ● vi (pt/pp leapt or leaped) springen; he leapt at it 🄵 er griff sofort zu. ~ **year** n Schaltjahr nt

learn vt/i (pt/pp learnt or learned) lernen; (*hear*) erfahren; ~ to swim schwimmen lernen

learn|ed a gelehrt. ~**er** n Anfänger m; ~**er [driver]** Fahrschüler(in) m(f). ~**ing** n Gelehrsamkeit f

lease n Pacht f; (*contract*) Mietvertrag m ● vt pachten

leash n Leine f

least a geringste(r,s) ● n the ~ das wenigste; at ~ wenigstens, mindestens; not in the ~ nicht im Geringsten ● adv am wenigsten

leather n Leder nt

leave n Erlaubnis f; (holiday) Urlaub m; on ~ auf Urlaub; take one's ~ sich verabschieden ● v (pt/pp left) ● vt lassen; (go out of, abandon) verlassen; (forget) liegen lassen; (bequeath) vermachen (to dat); ~ it to me! überlassen Sie es mir! there is nothing left es ist nichts mehr übrig ● vi [weg]gehen/-fahren; <train, bus:> abfahren. ~ **behind** vt zurücklassen; (forget) liegen lassen. ~ **out** vt liegen lassen; (leave outside) draußen lassen; (omit) auslassen

leaves see leaf

Lebanon n Libanon m

lecherous a lüstern

lecture n Vortrag m; (Univ) Vorlesung f; (reproof) Strafpredigt f ● vi einen Vortrag/eine Vorlesung halten (on über + acc) ● vt ~ **s.o.** jdm eine Strafpredigt halten. ~**r** n Vortragende(r) m/f; (Univ) Dozent(in) m(f)

led see lead²

ledge n Leiste f; (shelf, of window) Sims m; (in rock) Vorsprung m

ledger n Hauptbuch nt

leech n Blutegel m

leek n Stange f Porree; ~**s** pl Porree m

left¹ see leave

left² a linke(r,s) ● adv links; <go> nach links ● n linke Seite f; on the ~ links; from/to the ~ von/nach links; the ~ (Pol) die Linke

left: ~**-handed** a linkshändig. ~**-luggage [office]** n Gepäckaufbewahrung f. ~**overs** npl Reste pl. ~**wing** a (Pol) linke(r,s)

leg n Bein nt; (Culin) Keule f; (of journey) Etappe f

legacy n Vermächtnis nt, Erbschaft f

legal a, **-ly** adv gesetzlich; <matters> rechtlich; <department, position> Rechts-; be ~ [gesetzlich] erlaubt sein

legality n Legalität f

legend n Legende f. ~**ary** a legendär

legible a, **-bly** adv leserlich

legion n Legion f

legislat|e vi Gesetze erlassen. ~**ion** n Gesetzgebung f; (laws) Gesetze pl

legislative a gesetzgebend

legitimate a rechtmäßig; (justifiable) berechtigt

leisure n Freizeit f; at your ~ wenn Sie Zeit haben. ~**ly** a gemächlich

lemon n Zitrone f. ~**ade** n Zitronenlimonade f

lend vt (pt/pp lent) leihen (s.o. sth jdm etw)

length n Länge f; (piece) Stück nt; (of wallpaper) Bahn f; (of time) Dauer f

length|en vt länger machen ● vi länger werden. ~**ways** adv der Länge nach

lengthy a (-ier, -iest) langwierig

lenien|t a, **-ly** adv nachsichtig

lens n Linse f; (Phot) Objektiv nt; (of spectacles) Glas nt

lent see lend

Lent n Fastenzeit f

lentil n (Bot) Linse f

leopard n Leopard m

leotard n Trikot nt

lesbian a lesbisch ● n Lesbierin f

less a, adv, n & prep weniger; ~ and ~ immer weniger

lessen vt verringern ● vi nachlassen; <value:> abnehmen

lesser a geringere(r,s)

lesson n Stunde f; (in textbook) Lektion f; (Relig) Lesung f; teach s.o. a ~ (fig) jdm eine Lehre erteilen

lest conj (liter) damit ... nicht

let vt (pt/pp let, pres p letting) lassen; (rent) vermieten; ~ alone (not to mention) geschweige denn; ~ us go gehen wir; ~ me know sagen Sie mir Bescheid; ~ oneself in for sth ⚀ sich (dat) etw einbrocken. ~ **down** vt hinunter-/herunterlassen; (lengthen) länger machen; ~ **s.o.** down ⚀ jdn im Stich lassen; (disappoint) jdn enttäuschen. ~ **in** vt hereinlassen. ~ **off** vt abfeuern <gun>; hochgehen lassen <firework, bomb>; (emit) ausstoßen; (excuse from) befreien von; (*not punish*) frei ausgehen lassen. **∼ out** vt hinaus-/herauslassen; (*make larger*) auslassen. **∼ through** vt durchlassen. **∼ up** vi 🔲 nachlassen

let-down n Enttäuschung f, 🔲 Reinfall m

lethal a tödlich

letharg|ic a lethargisch. **∼y** n Lethargie f

letter n Brief m; (*of alphabet*) Buchstabe m. **∼-box** n Briefkasten m. **∼-head** n Briefkopf m. **∼ing** n Beschriftung f

lettuce n [Kopf]salat m

let-up n 🔲 Nachlassen nt

level a eben; (*horizontal*) waagerecht; (*in height*) auf gleicher Höhe; <*spoonful*> gestrichen; one's **∼ best** sein Möglichstes ● n Höhe f; (*fig*) Ebene f, Niveau nt; (*stage*) Stufe f; on the **∼** 🔲 ehrlich ● vt (*pt/pp* levelled) einebnen

level crossing n Bahnübergang m

lever n Hebel m ● vt **∼ up** mit einem Hebel anheben. **∼age** n Hebelkraft f

lewd a (-er, -est) anstößig

liabilit|y n Haftung f; **∼ies** pl Verbindlichkeiten pl

liable a haftbar; be **∼ to do sth** etw leicht tun können

liaise vi 🔲 Verbindungsperson sein

liaison n Verbindung f; (*affair*) Verhältnis nt

liar n Lügner(in) m(f)

libel n Verleumdung f ● vt (*pt/pp* libelled) verleumden. **∼lous** a verleumderisch

liberal a, -ly adv tolerant; (*generous*) großzügig. **L∼** a (*Pol*) liberal ● n Liberale(r) m/f

liberat|e vt befreien. **∼ed** a <*woman*> emanzipiert. **∼ion** n Befreiung f. **∼or** n Befreier m

liberty n Freiheit f; take liberties sich (*dat*) Freiheiten erlauben

librarian n Bibliothekar(in) m(f)

library n Bibliothek f

Libya n Libyen nt

lice *see* louse

licence n Genehmigung f; (*Comm*) Lizenz f; (*for TV*) ≈ Fernsehgebühr f; (*for driving*) Führerschein m; (*for alcohol*) Schankkonzession f

license vt eine Genehmigung/(*Comm*) Lizenz erteilen (+ *dat*); be **∼d** <*car:*> zugelassen sein; <*restaurant:*> Schankkonzession haben. **∼-plate** n (*Amer*) Nummernschild nt

lick n Lecken nt; a **∼ of paint** ein bisschen Farbe ● vt lecken; (🔲 defeat) schlagen

lid n Deckel m; (*of eye*) Lid nt

lie¹ n Lüge f; tell a **∼** lügen ● vi (*pt/pp* lied, *pres p* lying) lügen; **∼ to** belügen

lie² vi (*pt* lay, *pp* lain, *pres p* lying) liegen; here **∼s** ... hier ruht ... **∼ down** vi sich hinlegen

lie-in n have a **∼** [sich] ausschlafen

lieu n in **∼ of** statt (+ *gen*)

lieutenant n Oberleutnant m

life n (*pl* lives) Leben nt; lose one's **∼** ums Leben kommen

life: **∼-boat** n Rettungsboot nt. **∼-guard** n Lebensretter m. **∼-jacket** n Schwimmweste f. **∼less** a leblos. **∼like** a naturgetreu. **∼long** a lebenslang. **∼ preserver** n (*Amer*) Rettungsring m. **∼-size(d)** a ... in Lebensgröße. **∼time** n Leben nt; in s.o.'s **∼time** zu jds Lebzeiten; the chance of a **∼time** eine einmalige Gelegenheit

lift n Aufzug m, Lift m; give s.o. a **∼** jdn mitnehmen; get a **∼** mitgenommen werden ● vt heben; aufheben <*restrictions*> ● vi <*fog:*> sich lichten. **∼ up** vt hochheben

light¹ a (-er, -est) (*not dark*) hell; **∼ blue** hellblau ● n Licht nt; (*lamp*) Lampe f; have you [got] a **∼**? haben Sie Feuer? ● vt (*pt/pp* lit *or* lighted) anzünden <*fire, cigarette*>; (*illuminate*) beleuchten. **∼ up** vi <*face:*> sich erhellen

light² a (-er, -est) (*not heavy*) leicht; **∼ sentence** milde Strafe f ● adv travel **∼** mit wenig Gepäck reisen

light-bulb n Glühbirne f

lighten¹ vt heller machen

lighten² vt leichter machen <load>

lighter n Feuerzeug nt

light: ~-hearted a unbekümmert. ~house n Leuchtturm m. ~ing n Beleuchtung f. ~ly adv leicht; **get off** ~ly glimpflich davonkommen

lightning n Blitz m

lightweight a leicht ● n (Boxing) Leichtgewicht nt

like¹ a ähnlich; (same) gleich ● prep wie; (similar to) ähnlich (+ dat); ~ **this** so; **what's he** ~? wie ist er denn? ● conj (🗓 as) wie; (Amer: as if) als ob

like² vt mögen; **I should/would** ~ ich möchte; **I** ~ **the car** das Auto gefällt mir; ~ **dancing/singing** gern tanzen/singen ● n ~**s and dislikes** pl Vorlieben und Abneigungen pl

like|able a sympathisch. ~**lihood** n Wahrscheinlichkeit f. ~**ly** a (-ier, -iest) & adv wahrscheinlich; **not** ~**ly!** 🗓 auf gar keinen Fall!

like-minded a gleich gesinnt

liken vt vergleichen (**to** mit)

like|ness n Ähnlichkeit f. ~**wise** adv ebenso

liking n Vorliebe f; **is it to your** ~? gefällt es Ihnen?

lilac n Flieder m

lily n Lilie f

limb n Glied nt

lime n (fruit) Limone f; (tree) Linde f. ~**light** n **be in the** ~**light** im Rampenlicht stehen

limit n Grenze f; (limitation) Beschränkung f; **that's the** ~! 🗓 das ist doch die Höhe! ● vt beschränken (**to** auf + acc). ~**ation** n Beschränkung f; ~**ed** a beschränkt. ~**ed company** Gesellschaft f mit beschränkter Haftung

limousine n Limousine f

limp¹ n Hinken nt ● vi hinken

limp² a (-er -est), -**ly** adv schlaff

limpid a klar

line¹ n Linie f; (length of rope, cord) Leine f; (Teleph) Leitung f; (of writing) Zeile f; (row) Reihe f; (wrinkle) Falte f; (of business)

Branche f; (Amer: queue) Schlange f; **in** ~ **with** gemäß (+ dat) ● vt säumen <street>

line² vt füttern <garment>; (Techn) auskleiden

lined¹ a (wrinkled) faltig; <paper> liniert

lined² a <garment> gefüttert

linen n Leinen nt; (articles) Wäsche f

liner n Passagierschiff nt

linesman n (Sport) Linienrichter m

linger vi [zurück]bleiben

lingerie n Damenunterwäsche f

linguist n Sprachkundige(r) m/f

linguistic a, -**ally** adv sprachlich

lining n (of garment) Futter nt; (Techn) Auskleidung f

link n (of chain) Glied nt (fig) Verbindung f ● vt verbinden; ~ **arms** sich unterhaken

links n or npl Golfplatz m

lint n Verbandstoff m

lion n Löwe m; ~'**s share** (fig) Löwenanteil m. ~**ess** n Löwin f

lip n Lippe f; (edge) Rand m; (of jug) Schnabel m

lip: ~-**reading** n Lippenlesen nt. ~-**service** n **pay** ~-**service** ein Lippenbekenntnis ablegen (**to** zu). ~**stick** n Lippenstift m

liqueur n Likör m

liquid n Flüssigkeit f ● a flüssig

liquidation n Liquidation f

liquidize vt [im Mixer] pürieren. ~**r** n Mixer m

liquor n Alkohol m. ~ **store** n (Amer) Spirituosengeschäft nt

lisp n Lispeln nt ● vt/i lispeln

list¹ n Liste f ● vt aufführen

list² vi <ship:> Schlagseite haben

listen vi zuhören (**to** dat); ~ **to the radio** Radio hören. ~**er** n Zuhörer(in) m(f); (Radio) Hörer(in) m(f)

listless a, -**ly** adv lustlos

lit see **light¹**

literacy n Lese- und Schreibfertigkeit f

literal a wörtlich. ~**ly** adv buchstäblich

literary *a* literarisch

literate *a* be ~ lesen und schreiben können

literature *n* Literatur *f*; Ⓘ Informationsmaterial *nt*

lithe *a* geschmeidig

Lithuania *n* Litauen *nt*

litre *n* Liter *m & nt*

litter *n* Abfall *m*; (*Zool*) Wurf *m*. ~-**bin** *n* Abfalleimer *m*

little *a* klein; (*not much*) wenig ● *adv & n* wenig; **a** ~ ein bisschen/wenig; ~ **by** ~ nach und nach

live¹ *a* lebendig; <*ammunition*> scharf; ~ **broadcast** Live-Sendung *f*; **be** ~ (*Electr*) unter Strom stehen

live² *vi* leben; (*reside*) wohnen. ~ **on** *vt* leben von; (*eat*) sich ernähren von ● *vi* weiterleben

liveli|hood *n* Lebensunterhalt *m*. ~**ness** *n* Lebendigkeit *f*

lively *a* (-ier, -iest) lebhaft, lebendig

liver *n* Leber *f*

lives *see* life

livid *a* Ⓘ wütend

living *a* lebend ● *n* **earn one's** ~ seinen Lebensunterhalt verdienen. ~-**room** *n* Wohnzimmer *nt*

lizard *n* Eidechse *f*

load *n* Last *f*; (*quantity*) Ladung *f*; (*Electr*) Belastung *f*; ~**s of** Ⓘ jede Menge ● *vt* laden <*goods, gun*>; beladen <*vehicle*>; ~ **a camera** einen Film in eine Kamera einlegen. ~**ed** *a* beladen; (Ⓘ *rich*) steinreich

loaf *n* (*pl* loaves) Brot *nt*

loan *n* Leihgabe *f*; (*money*) Darlehen *nt*; **on** ~ geliehen ● *vt* leihen (*to dat*)

loath *a* be ~ **to do sth** etw ungern tun

loath|e *vt* verabscheuen. ~**ing** *n* Abscheu *m*

loaves *see* loaf¹

lobby *n* Foyer *nt*; (*anteroom*) Vorraum *m*; (*Pol*) Lobby *f*

lobster *n* Hummer *m*

local *a* hiesig; <*time, traffic*> Orts-; ~ **anaesthetic** örtliche Betäubung; **I'm not** ~ ich bin nicht von hier ● *n* Hiesige(r) *m/f*; (Ⓘ *public house*)

Stammkneipe *f*. ~ **call** *n* (*Teleph*) Ortsgespräch *nt*

locality *n* Gegend *f*

locally *adv* am Ort

locat|e *vt* ausfindig machen; **be** ~**ed** sich befinden. ~**ion** *n* Lage *f*; **filmed on** ~**ion** als Außenaufnahme gedreht

lock¹ *n* (*hair*) Strähne *f*

lock² *n* (*on door*) Schloss *nt*; (*on canal*) Schleuse *f* ● *vt* abschließen ● *vi* sich abschließen lassen. ~ **in** *vt* einschließen. ~ **out** *vt* ausschließen. ~ **up** *vt* abschließen; einsperren <*person*>

locker *n* Schließfach *nt*; (*Mil*) Spind *m*

lock: ~-**out** *n* Aussperrung *f*. ~**smith** *n* Schlosser *m*

locomotive *n* Lokomotive *f*

locum *n* Vertreter(in) *m(f)*

locust *n* Heuschrecke *f*

lodge *n* (*porter's*) Pförtnerhaus *nt* ● *vt* (*submit*) einreichen; (*deposit*) deponieren ● *vi* zur Untermiete wohnen (**with** bei); (*become fixed*) stecken bleiben. ~**r** *n* Untermieter(in) *m(f)*

lodging *n* Unterkunft *f*; ~**s** *npl* möbliertes Zimmer *nt*

loft *n* Dachboden *m*

lofty *a* (-ier, -iest) hoch

log *n* Baumstamm *m*; (*for fire*) [Holz]scheit *nt*; **sleep like a** ~ Ⓘ wie ein Murmeltier schlafen ● *vi* ~ **off** sich abmelden; ~ **on** sich anmelden

loggerheads *npl* **be at** ~ Ⓘ sich in den Haaren liegen

logic *n* Logik *f*. ~**al** *a*, -**ly** *adv* logisch

logo *n* Symbol *nt*, Logo *nt*

loiter *vi* herumlungern

loll *vi* sich lümmeln

loll|ipop *n* Lutscher *m*. ~**y** *n* Lutscher *m*; (Ⓘ *money*) Moneten *pl*

London *n* London *nt* ● *attrib* Londoner. ~**er** *n* Londoner(in) *m(f)*

lone *a* einzeln. ~**liness** *n* Einsamkeit *f*

lonely *a* (-ier, -iest) einsam

lone|r n Einzelgänger m. ∼**some** a einsam

long[1] a (**-er, -est**) lang; <*journey*> weit; a ∼ **time** lange; a ∼ **way** weit; **in the** ∼ **run** auf lange Sicht; (*in the end*) letzten Endes ● adv lange; **all day** ∼ den ganzen Tag; **not** ∼ **ago** vor kurzem; **before** ∼ bald; **no** ∼**er** nicht mehr; **as** or **so** ∼**as** solange; **so** ∼! 🛈 tschüs!

long[2] vi ∼ **for** sich sehnen nach

long-distance a Fern-; (*Sport*) Langstrecken-

longing a, **-ly** adv sehnsüchtig ● n Sehnsucht f

longitude n (*Geog*) Länge f

long: ∼ **jump** n Weitsprung m. ∼**lived** a langlebig. ∼**range** a (*Mil, Aviat*) Langstrecken-; <*forecast*> langfristig. ∼**sighted** a weitsichtig. ∼**sleeved** a langärmelig. ∼**suffering** a langmütig. ∼**term** a langfristig. ∼**wave** n Langwelle. ∼**winded** a langatmig

loo n 🛈 Klo nt

look n Blick m; (*appearance*) Aussehen nt; **[good]** ∼**s** pl [gutes] Aussehen nt; **have a** ∼ **at** sich (*dat*) ansehen; **go and have a** ∼ sieh mal nach ● vi sehen; (*search*) nachsehen; (*seem*) aussehen; **don't** ∼ sieh nicht hin; ∼ **here!** hören Sie mal! ∼ **at** ansehen; ∼ **for** suchen; ∼ **forward to** sich freuen auf (+ *acc*); ∼ **in on** vorbeischauen bei; ∼ **into** (*examine*) nachgehen (+ *dat*); ∼ **like** aussehen wie; ∼ **on to** <*room:*> gehen auf (+ *acc*). ∼ **after** vt betreuen. ∼ **down** vi hinuntersehen; ∼ **down on s.o.** (*fig*) auf jdn herabsehen. ∼ **out** vi hinaus-/heraussehen; (*take care*) aufpassen; ∼ **out for** Ausschau halten nach; ∼ **out!** Vorsicht! ∼ **round** vi sich umsehen. ∼ **up** vi aufblicken; ∼ **up to s.o.** (*fig*) zu jdm aufsehen ● vt nachschlagen <*word*>

look-out n Wache f; (*prospect*) Aussicht f; **be on the** ∼ **for** Ausschau halten nach

loom[1] n Webstuhl m

loom[2] vi auftauchen

loony a 🛈 verrückt

loop n Schlinge f; (*in road*) Schleife f. ∼**hole** n Hintertürchen nt; (*in the law*) Lücke f

loose a (**-r, -st**), **-ly** adv lose; (*not tight enough*) locker; (*inexact*) frei; **be at a** ∼ **end** nichts zu tun haben. ∼ **change** n Kleingeld nt

loosen vt lockern

loot n Beute f ● vt/i plündern. ∼**er** n Plünderer m

lop vt (*pt/pp* **lopped**) stutzen

lopsided a schief

lord n Herr m; (*title*) Lord m; **House of L**∼**s** ≈ Oberhaus nt; **the L**∼**'s Prayer** das Vaterunser

lorry n Last[kraft]wagen m

lose v (*pt/pp* **lost**) ● vt verlieren; (*miss*) verpassen ● vi verlieren; <*clock:*> nachgehen; **get lost** verloren gehen; <*person*> sich verlaufen. ∼**r** n Verlierer m

loss n Verlust m; **be at a** ∼ nicht mehr weiter wissen

lost see **lose.** ∼ **property office** n Fundbüro nt

lot[1] n Los nt; (*at auction*) Posten m; **draw** ∼**s** losen (**for** um)

lot[2] n **the** ∼ alle; (*everything*) alles; **a** ∼ **[of]** viel; (*many*) viele; ∼**s of** 🛈 eine Menge; **it has changed a** ∼ es hat sich sehr verändert

lotion n Lotion f

lottery n Lotterie f. ∼ **ticket** n Los nt

loud a (**-er, -est**), **-ly** adv laut; <*colours*> grell ● adv **[out]** ∼ laut. ∼**speaker** n Lautsprecher m

lounge n Wohnzimmer nt; (*in hotel*) Aufenthaltsraum m. ● vi sich lümmeln

louse n (*pl* **lice**) Laus f

lousy a (**-ier, -iest**) 🛈 lausig

lout n Flegel m, Lümmel m

lovable a liebenswert

love n Liebe f; (*Tennis*) null; **in** ∼ verliebt ● vt lieben; ∼ **doing sth** etw sehr gerne machen. ∼**affair** n Liebesverhältnis nt. ∼ **letter** n Liebesbrief m

lovely a (**-ier, -iest**) schön

lover *n* Liebhaber *m*

love: ~ **song** *n* Liebeslied *nt*. ~ **story** *n* Liebesgeschichte *f*

loving *a*, **-ly** *adv* liebevoll

low *a* (**-er**, **-est**) tief; *<cloud, note>* tief; *<voice>* leise; *(depressed)* niedergeschlagen ● *adv* niedrig; *<fly, sing>* tief; *<speak>* leise ● *n.* *(Meteorol)* Tief *nt*; *(fig)* Tiefstand *m*.

low: ~**brow** *a* geistig anspruchslos. ~**-cut** *a* *<dress>* tief ausgeschnitten

lower *a & adv see* **low** ● *vt* niedriger machen; *(let down)* herunterlassen; *(reduce)* senken

low: ~**-fat** *a* fettarm. ~**lands** *npl* Tiefland *nt*. ~ **tide** *n* Ebbe *f*

loyal *a*, **-ly** *adv* treu. ~**ty** *n* Treue *f*

lozenge *n* Pastille *f*

Ltd *abbr* (Limited) GmbH

lubricant *n* Schmiermittel *nt*

lubricat|e *vt* schmieren. ~**ion** *n* Schmierung *f*

lucid *a* klar. ~**ity** *n* Klarheit *f*

luck *n* Glück *nt*; bad ~ Pech *nt*; good ~! viel Glück! ~**ily** *adv* glücklicherweise, zum Glück

lucky *a* (**-ier**, **-iest**) glücklich; *<day, number>* Glücks-; be ~ Glück haben; *<thing:>* Glück bringen

lucrative *a* einträglich

ludicrous *a* lächerlich

lug *vt* (*pt/pp* **lugged**) 🔲 schleppen

luggage *n* Gepäck *nt*

luggage: ~**-rack** *in* Gepäckablage *f*. ~**-van** *n* Gepäckwagen *m*

lukewarm *a* lauwarm

lull *n* Pause *f* ● *vt* ~ to sleep einschläfern

lullaby *n* Wiegenlied *nt*

lumber *n* Gerümpel *nt*; *(Amer: timber)* Bauholz *nt* ● *vt* ~ s.o. with sth jdm etw aufhalsen. ~**jack** *n* *(Amer)* Holzfäller *m*

luminous *a* leuchtend

lump *n* Klumpen *m*; *(of sugar)* Stück *nt*; *(swelling)* Beule *f*; *(in breast)* Knoten *m*; *(tumour)* Geschwulst *f*; a ~ in one's throat 🔲 ein Kloß im Hals

lump: ~ **sugar** *n* Würfelzucker *m*. ~ **sum** *n* Pauschalsumme *f*

lumpy *a* (**-ier**, **-iest**) klumpig

lunacy *n* Wahnsinn *m*

lunar *a* Mond-

lunatic *n* Wahnsinnige(r) *m/f*

lunch *n* Mittagessen *nt* ● *vi* zu Mittag essen

luncheon *n* Mittagessen *nt*. ~ **voucher** *n* Essensbon *m*

lunch: ~**-hour** *n* Mittagspause *f*. ~**-time** *n* Mittagszeit *f*

lung *n* Lungenflügel *m*; ~**s** *pl* Lunge *f*

lunge *vi* sich stürzen (**at** auf + *acc*)

lurch[1] *n* leave in the ~ 🔲 im Stich lassen

lurch[2] *vi* *<person:>* torkeln

lure *vt* locken

lurid *a* grell; *(sensational)* reißerisch

lurk *vi* lauern

luscious *a* lecker, köstlich

lush *a* üppig

lust *n* Begierde *f*. ~**ful** *a* lüstern

lustre *n* Glanz *m*

lusty *a* (**-ier**, **-iest**) kräftig

luxuriant *a* üppig

luxurious *a*, **-ly** *adv* luxuriös

luxury *n* Luxus *m* ● *attrib* Luxus-

lying *see* **lie**[1], **lie**[2]

lynch *vt* lynchen

lyric *a* lyrisch. ~**al** *a* lyrisch; *(enthusiastic)* schwärmerisch. ~ **poetry** *n* Lyrik *f*. ~**s** *npl* [Lied]text *m*

Mm

mac *n* 🔲 Regenmantel *m*

macabre *a* makaber

macaroni *n* Makkaroni *pl*

machinations *pl* Machenschaften *pl*

machine n Maschine f ● vt (sew) mit der Maschine nähen; (Techn) maschinell bearbeiten. **~-gun** n Maschinengewehr nt

machinery n Maschinerie f

mackerel n inv Makrele f

mackintosh n Regenmantel m

mad a (madder, maddest) verrückt; (dog) tollwütig; (fam: angry) böse (at auf + acc)

madam n gnädige Frau f

madden vt (make angry) wütend machen

made see make; **~ to measure** maßgeschneidert

mad|ly adv 🖩 wahnsinnig. **~man** n Irre(r) m. **~ness** n Wahnsinn m

madonna n Madonna f

magazine n Zeitschrift f; (Mil, Phot) Magazin nt

maggot n Made f

magic n Zauber m; (tricks) Zauberkunst f ● a magisch; <word, wand> Zauber-. **~al** a zauberhaft

magician n Zauberer m; (entertainer) Zauberkünstler m

magistrate n ≈ Friedensrichter m

magnet n Magnet m. **~ic** a magnetisch. **~ism** n Magnetismus m

magnification n Vergrößerung f

magnificen|ce n Großartigkeit f. **~t** a, **-ly** adv großartig

magnify vt (pt/pp -ied) vergrößern; (exaggerate) übertreiben. **~ing glass** n Vergrößerungsglas nt

magnitude n Größe f; (importance) Bedeutung f

magpie n Elster f

mahogany n Mahagoni nt

maid n Dienstmädchen nt; old **~** (pej) alte Jungfer f

maiden a <speech, voyage> Jungfern-. **~ name** n Mädchenname m

mail n Post f ● vt mit der Post schicken

mail: ~-bag n Postsack m. **~box** n (Amer) Briefkasten m. **~ing list** n Postversandliste f. **~man** n (Amer)

Briefträger m. **~-order firm** n Versandhaus nt

maim vt verstümmeln

main a Haupt- ● n (water, gas, electricity) Hauptleitung f

main: ~land n Festland nt. **~ly** adv hauptsächlich. **~stay** n (fig) Stütze f. **~ street** n Hauptstraße f

maintain vt aufrechterhalten; (keep in repair) instand halten; (support) unterhalten; (claim) behaupten

maintenance n Aufrechterhaltung f; (care) Instandhaltung f; (allowance) Unterhalt m

maize n Mais m

majestic a, **-ally** adv majestätisch

majesty n Majestät f

major a größer ● n (Mil) Major m; (Mus) Dur nt ● vi **~** in als Hauptfach studieren

majority n Mehrheit f; **in the ~** in der Mehrzahl

major road n Hauptverkehrsstraße f

make n (brand) Marke f ● v (pt/pp made) ● vt machen; (force) zwingen; (earn) verdienen; halten <speech>; treffen <decision>; erreichen <destination> ● vi **~ do** vi zurechtkommen (with mit). **~ for** vi zusteuern auf (+ acc). **~ off** vi sich davonmachen (with mit). **~ out** vt (distinguish) ausmachen; (write out) ausstellen; (assert) behaupten. **~ up** vt (constitute) bilden; (invent) erfinden; (apply cosmetics to) schminken; **~ up one's mind** sich entschließen ● vi sich versöhnen; **~ up for sth** etw wieder gutmachen; **~ up for lost time** verlorene Zeit aufholen

make-believe n Phantasie f

maker n Hersteller m

make: ~ shift a behelfsmäßig ● n Notbehelf m. **~-up** n Make-up nt

maladjusted a verhaltensgestört

male a männlich ● n Mann m; (animal) Männchen nt. **~ nurse** n Krankenpfleger m. **~ voice choir** n Männerchor m

malice n Bosheit f

malicious *a*, **-ly** *adv* böswillig

malign *vt* verleumden

malignant *a* bösartig

mallet *n* Holzhammer *m*

malnutrition *n* Unterernährung *f*

malpractice *n* Berufsvergehen *nt*

malt *n* Malz *m*

maltreat *vt* misshandeln. **~ment** *n* Misshandlung *f*

mammal *n* Säugetier *nt*

mammoth *a* riesig

man *n* (*pl* **men**) Mann *m*; (*mankind*) der Mensch; (*chess*) Figur *f*; (*draughts*) Stein *m* ● *vt* (*pt/pp* **manned**) bemannen <*ship*>; bedienen <*pump*>; besetzen <*counter*>

manage *vt* leiten; verwalten <*estate*>; (*cope with*) fertig werden mit; **~ to do sth** es schaffen, etw zu tun ● *vi* zurechtkommen; **~ on** auskommen mit. **~able** *a* <*tool*> handlich; <*person*> fügsam. **~ment** *n* Leitung *f*; **the ~ment** die Geschäftsleitung *f*

manager *n* Geschäftsführer *m*; (*of bank*) Direktor *m*; (*of estate*) Verwalter *m*; (*Sport*) [Chef]trainer *m*. **~ess** *n* Geschäftsführerin *f*. **~ial** *a* **~ial staff** Führungskräfte *pl*

managing *a* **~ director** Generaldirektor *m*

mandat|e *n* Mandat *nt*. **~ory** *a* obligatorisch

mane *n* Mähne *f*

manful *a*, **-ly** *adv* mannhaft

man: **~handle** *vt* grob behandeln <*person*>. **~hole** *n* Kanalschacht *m*. **~hood** *n* Mannesalter *nt*; (*quality*) Männlichkeit *f*. **~-hour** *n* Arbeitsstunde *f*. **~-hunt** *n* Fahndung *f*

mania *n* Manie *f*. **~c** *n* Wahnsinnige(r) *m/f*

manicure *n* Maniküre *f* ● *vt* maniküren

manifest *a*, **-ly** *adv* offensichtlich

manifesto *n* Manifest *nt*

manifold *a* mannigfaltig

manipulat|e *vt* handhaben; (*pej*) manipulieren. **~ion** *n* Manipulation *f*

mankind *n* die Menschheit

manly *a* männlich

man-made *a* künstlich. **~ fibre** *n* Kunstfaser *f*

manner *n* Weise *f*; (*kind, behaviour*) Art *f*; **[good/bad] ~s** [gute/schlechte] Manieren *pl*. **~ism** *n* Angewohnheit *f*

manœuvrable *a* manövrierfähig

manœuvre *n* Manöver *nt* ● *vt/i* manövrieren

manor *n* Gutshof *m*; (*house*) Gutshaus *nt*

manpower *n* Arbeitskräfte *pl*

mansion *n* Villa *f*

manslaughter *n* Totschlag *m*

mantelpiece *n* Kaminsims *m* & *nt*

manual *a* Hand- ● *n* Handbuch *nt*

manufacture *vt* herstellen ● *n* Herstellung *f*. **~r** *n* Hersteller *m*

manure *n* Mist *m*

manuscript *n* Manuskript *nt*

many *a* viele ● *n* **a good/great ~** sehr viele

map *n* Landkarte *f*; (*of town*) Stadtplan *m*

maple *n* Ahorn *m*

mar *vt* (*pt/pp* **marred**) verderben

marathon *n* Marathon *m*

marble *n* Marmor *m*; (*for game*) Murmel *f*

March *n* März *m*

march *n* Marsch *m* ● *vi* marschieren ● *vt* marschieren lassen; **~ s.o. off** jdn abführen

mare *n* Stute *f*

margarine *n* Margarine *f*

margin *n* Rand *m*; (*leeway*) Spielraum *m*; (*Comm*) Spanne *f*. **~al** *a*, **-ly** *adv* geringfügig

marigold *n* Ringelblume *f*

marina *n* Jachthafen *m*

marine *a* Meeres- ● *n* Marine *f*; (*sailor*) Marineinfanterist *m*

marital *a* ehelich. **~ status** *n* Familienstand *m*

maritime *a* See-

mark¹ n (currency) Mark f

mark² n Fleck m; (sign) Zeichen nt; (trace) Spur f; (target) Ziel nt; (Sch) Note f ● vt markieren; (spoil) beschädigen; (characterize) kennzeichnen; (Sch) korrigieren; (Sport) decken; ~ **time** (Mil) auf der Stelle treten; (fig) abwarten. ~ **out** vt markieren

marked a, ~**ly** adv deutlich; (pronounced) ausgeprägt

market n Markt m ● vt vertreiben; (launch) auf den Markt bringen. ~**ing** n Marketing nt. ~ **research** n Marktforschung f

marking n Markierung f; (on animal) Zeichnung f

marksman n Scharfschütze m

marmalade n Orangenmarmelade f

maroon a dunkelrot

marooned a (fig) von der Außenwelt abgeschnitten

marquee n Festzelt nt

marquetry n Einlegearbeit f

marriage n Ehe f; (wedding) Hochzeit f. ~**able** a heiratsfähig

married see marry ● a verheiratet. ~ **life** n Eheleben nt

marrow n (Anat) Mark nt; (vegetable) Kürbis m

marr|y vt/i (pt/pp married) heiraten; (unite) trauen; **get** ~**ied** heiraten

marsh n Sumpf m

marshal n Marschall m; (steward) Ordner m

marshy a sumpfig

martial a kriegerisch. ~ **law** n Kriegsrecht nt

martyr n Märtyrer(in) m(f). ~**dom** n Martyrium nt

marvel n Wunder nt ● vi (pt/pp marvelled) staunen (at über + acc). ~**lous** a, -ly adv wunderbar

Marxis|m n Marxismus m. ~**t** a marxistisch ● n Marxist(in) m(f)

marzipan n Marzipan nt

mascot n Maskottchen nt

masculin|e a männlich ● n (Gram) Maskulinum nt. ~**ity** n Männlichkeit f

mash n Ⓘ, ~**ed potatoes** npl Kartoffelpüree nt

mask n Maske f ● vt maskieren

masochis|m n Masochismus m. ~**t** n Masochist m

mason n Steinmetz m. ~**ry** n Mauerwerk nt

mass¹ n (Relig) Messe f

mass² n Masse f ● vi sich sammeln; (Mil) sich massieren

massacre n Massaker nt ● vt niedermetzeln

massage n Massage f ● vt massieren

masseu|r n Masseur m. ~**se** n Masseuse f

massive a massiv; (huge) riesig

mass: ~ **media** npl Massenmedien pl. ~-**produce** vt in Massenproduktion herstellen. ~ **production** n Massenproduktion f

mast n Mast m

master n Herr m; (teacher) Lehrer m; (craftsman, artist) Meister m; (of ship) Kapitän m ● vt meistern; beherrschen <language>

master: ~**ly** a meisterhaft. ~-**mind** n führender Kopf m ● vt der führende Kopf sein von. ~**piece** n Meisterwerk nt. ~**y** n (of subject) Beherrschung f

mat n Matte f; (on table) Untersatz m

match¹ n Wettkampf m; (in ball games) Spiel nt; (Tennis) Match nt; (marriage) Heirat f; **be a good** ~ <colours:> gut zusammenpassen; **be no** ~ **for s.o.** jdm nicht gewachsen sein ● vt (equal) gleichkommen (+ dat); (be like) passen zu; (find sth similar) etwas Passendes finden zu ● vi zusammenpassen

match² n Streichholz nt. ~**box** n Streichholzschachtel f

mate¹ n Kumpel m; (assistant) Gehilfe m; (Naut) Maat m; (Zool) Männchen nt; (female) Weibchen nt ● vi sich paaren

mate² n (Chess) Matt nt

material n Material nt; (fabric) Stoff m; **raw** ~**s** Rohstoffe pl ● a materiell

material|ism n Materialismus m.
~**istic** a materialistisch. ~**ize** vi
sich verwirklichen

maternal a mütterlich

maternity n Mutterschaft f. ~
clothes npl Umstandskleidung f. ~
ward n Entbindungsstation f

mathematic|al a, **-ly** adv
mathematisch. ~**ian** n
Mathematiker(in) m(f)

mathematics n Mathematik f

maths n 🔲 Mathe f

matinée n (Theat)
Nachmittagsvorstellung f

matrimony n Ehe f

matron n (of hospital) Oberin f; (of
school) Hausmutter f

matt a matt

matted a verfilzt

matter n (affair) Sache f; (Phys:
substance) Materie f; money ~s
Geldangelegenheiten pl; what is the
~? was ist los? ● vi wichtig sein; ~
to s.o. jdm etwas ausmachen; it
doesn't ~ es macht nichts. ~-**of-
fact** a sachlich

mattress n Matratze f

matur|e a reif; (Comm) fällig ● vi
reifen; <person:> reifer werden;
(Comm) fällig werden ● vt reifen
lassen. ~**ity** n Reife f; (Comm)
Fälligkeit f

mauve a lila

maximum a maximal ● n (pl **-ima**)
Maximum nt. ~ **speed** n
Höchstgeschwindigkeit f

may

pres **may**, pt **might**

● auxiliary verb

····▸ (expressing possibility) können.
she may come es kann sein, dass sie
kommt; es ist möglich, dass sie
kommt. **she might come** (more
distant possibility) sie könnte
kommen. **it may/might rain** es könnte
regnen. **I may be wrong** vielleicht
irre ich mich. **he may have missed
his train** vielleicht hat er seinen Zug
verpasst

····▸ (expressing permission) dürfen.
may I come in? darf ich
reinkommen? **you may smoke** Sie
dürfen rauchen

····▸ (expressing wish) **may the best
man win!** auf dass der Beste gewinnt!

····▸ (expressing concession) **he may be
slow but he's accurate** mag od kann
sein, dass er langsam ist, aber dafür
ist er auch genau

····▸ **may/might as well** ebenso gut
können. **we may/might as well go**
wir könnten eigentlich ebensogut
[auch] gehen. **we might as well give
up** da können wir gleich aufgeben

May n Mai m

maybe adv vielleicht

May Day n der Erste Mai

mayonnaise n Mayonnaise f

mayor n Bürgermeister m. ~**ess** n
Bürgermeisterin f; (wife of mayor)
Frau Bürgermeister f

maze n Irrgarten m; (fig) Labyrinth
nt

me pron (acc) mich; (dat) mir; **it's ~**
🔲 ich bin es

meadow n Wiese f

meagre a dürftig

meal n Mahlzeit f; (food) Essen nt;
(grain) Schrot m

mean¹ a (**-er, -est**) (miserly) geizig;
(unkind) gemein; (poor) schäbig

mean² a mittlere(r,s) ● n (average)
Durchschnitt m

mean³ vt (pt/pp **meant**) heißen;
(signify) bedeuten; (intend)
beabsichtigen; **I ~ it** das ist mein
Ernst; ~ **well** es gut meinen; **be
meant for** <present:> bestimmt sein
für; <remark:> gerichtet sein an (+
acc)

meaning n Bedeutung f. ~**ful** a
bedeutungsvoll. ~**less** a
bedeutungslos

means n Möglichkeit f, Mittel nt; ~
of transport Verkehrsmittel nt; **by ~
of** durch; **by all ~!** aber natürlich! **by
no ~** keineswegs ● npl (resources)
[Geld]mittel pl

meant see **mean³**

m

meantime n in the ~ in der Zwischenzeit ● adv inzwischen

meanwhile adv inzwischen

measles n Masern pl

measure n Maß nt; (action) Maßnahme f ● vt/i messen; ~ up to (fig) herankommen an (+ acc). ~d a gemessen. ~ment n Maß nt

meat n Fleisch nt

mechan|ic n Mechaniker m. ~ical a, -ly adv mechanisch. ~ical engineering Maschinenbau m

mechan|ism n Mechanismus m. ~ize vt mechanisieren

medal n Orden m; (Sport) Medaille f

medallist n Medaillengewinner(in) m(f)

meddle vi sich einmischen (in in + acc); (tinker) herumhantieren (with an + acc)

media see medium ● n pl the ~ die Medien pl

mediat|e vi vermitteln. ~or n Vermittler(in) m(f)

medical a medizinisch; (treatment) ärztlich ● n ärztliche Untersuchung f. ~ insurance n Krankenversicherung f. ~ student n Medizinstudent m

medicat|ed a medizinisch. ~ion n (drugs) Medikamente pl

medicinal a medizinisch; (plant) heilkräftig

medicine n Medizin f; (preparation) Medikament nt

medieval a mittelalterlich

mediocr|e a mittelmäßig. ~ity n Mittelmäßigkeit f

meditat|e vi nachdenken (on über + acc). ~ion n Meditation f

Mediterranean n Mittelmeer nt ● a Mittelmeer-

medium a mittlere(r,s); (steak) medium; of ~ size von mittlerer Größe ● n (pl media) Medium nt; (means) Mittel nt

medium: ~-sized a mittelgroß. ~ wave n Mittelwelle f

medley n Gemisch nt; (Mus) Potpourri nt

meek a (-er, -est), -ly adv sanftmütig; (unprotesting) widerspruchslos

meet v (pt/pp met) ● vt treffen; (by chance) begegnen (+ dat); (at station) abholen; (make the acquaintance of) kennen lernen; stoßen auf (+ acc) <problem>; bezahlen <bill>; erfüllen <requirements> ● vi sich treffen; (for the first time) sich kennen lernen

meeting n Treffen nt; (by chance) Begegnung f; (discussion) Besprechung f; (of committee) Sitzung f; (large) Versammlung f

megalomania n Größenwahnsinn m

megaphone n Megaphon nt

melancholy a melancholisch ● n Melancholie f

mellow a (-er, -est) <fruit> ausgereift; <sound, person> sanft ● vi reifer werden

melodious a melodiös

melodramatic a, -ally adv melodramatisch

melody n Melodie f

melon n Melone f

melt vt/i schmelzen

member n Mitglied nt; (of family) Angehörige(r) m/f; M~ of Parliament Abgeordnete(r) m/f. ~ship n Mitgliedschaft f; (members) Mitgliederzahl f

memento n Andenken nt

memo n Mitteilung f

memoirs n pl Memoiren pl

memorable a denkwürdig

memorial n Denkmal nt. ~ service n Gedenkfeier f

memorize vt sich (dat) einprägen

memory n Gedächtnis nt; (thing remembered) Erinnerung f; (of computer) Speicher m; from ~ auswendig; in ~ of zur Erinnerung an (+ acc)

men see man

menac|e n Drohung f; (nuisance) Plage f ● vt bedrohen. ~ing a, ~ly adv drohend

mend vt reparieren; (patch) flicken; ausbessern <clothes>

menfolk n pl Männer pl

menial a niedrig

menopause n Wechseljahre pl

mental a, **-ly** adv geistig; (□ mad) verrückt. ~ **arithmetic** n Kopfrechnen nt. ~ **illness** n Geisteskrankheit f

mentality n Mentalität f

mention n Erwähnung f ● vt erwähnen; don't ~ it keine Ursache; bitte

menu n Speisekarte f

merchandise n Ware f

merchant n Kaufmann m; (dealer) Händler m. ~ **navy** n Handelsmarine f

merci|ful a barmherzig. ~**fully** adv □ glücklicherweise. ~**less** a, **-ly** adv erbarmungslos

mercury n Quecksilber nt

mercy n Barmherzigkeit f, Gnade f; be at s.o.'s ~ jdm ausgeliefert sein

mere a, **-ly** adv bloß

merest a kleinste(r,s)

merge vi zusammenlaufen; (Comm) fusionieren

merger n Fusion f

meringue n Baiser nt

merit n Verdienst nt; (advantage) Vorzug m; (worth) Wert m ● vt verdienen

merry a (-ier, -iest) fröhlich

merry-go-round n Karussell nt

mesh n Masche f

mesmerized a (fig) [wie] gebannt

mess n Durcheinander nt; (trouble) Schwierigkeiten pl; (something spilt) Bescherung f □; (Mil) Messe f; **make a** ~ **of** (botch) verpfuschen ● vt ~ **up** in Unordnung bringen; (botch) verpfuschen ● vi ~ **about** herumalbern; (tinker) herumspielen (with mit)

message n Nachricht f; give s.o. a ~ jdm etwas ausrichten

messenger n Bote m

Messrs n pl see Mr; (on letter) ~ Smith Firma Smith

messy a (-ier, -iest) schmutzig; (untidy) unordentlich

met see meet

metal n Metall nt ● a Metall-. ~**lic** a metallisch

metaphor n Metapher f. ~**ical** a, **-ly** adv metaphorisch

meteor n Meteor m. ~**ic** a kometenhaft

meteorological a Wetter-

meteorolog|ist n Meteorologe m/ -gin f. ~**y** n Meteorologie f

meter[1] n Zähler m

meter[2] n (Amer) = metre

method n Methode f; (Culin) Zubereitung f

methodical a, **-ly** adv systematisch, methodisch

methylated a ~ **spirit[s]** Brennspiritus m

meticulous a, **-ly** adv sehr genau

metre n Meter m & n; (rhythm) Versmaß nt

metric a metrisch

metropolis n Metropole f

metropolitan a haupstädtisch; (international) weltstädtisch

mew n Miau nt ● vi miauen

Mexican a mexikanisch ● n Mexikaner(in) m(f). **Mexico** n Mexiko nt

miaow n Miau nt ● vi miauen

mice see mouse

micro: ~**film** n Mikrofilm m. ~**phone** n Mikrofon nt. ~**scope** n Mikroskop nt. ~**scopic** a mikroskopisch. ~**wave [oven]** n Mikrowellenherd m

mid a ~ May Mitte Mai; in ~ air in der Luft

midday n Mittag m

middle a mittlere(r,s); the M~ Ages das Mittelalter; the ~ class[es] der Mittelstand; the M~ East der Nahe Osten ● n Mitte f; in the ~ of the night mitten in der Nacht

middle: ~**-aged** a mittleren Alters. ~**-class** a bürgerlich

midge n [kleine] Mücke f

midget n Liliputaner(in) m(f)

Midlands npl the ~ Mittelengland n

midnight n Mitternacht f

midriff n Ⓣ Taille f

midst n in the ~ of mitten in (+ dat); in our ~ unter uns

mid: ~**summer** n Hochsommer m. ~**way** adv auf halbem Wege. ~**wife** n Hebamme f. ~**winter** n Mitte f des Winters

might¹ v aux I ~ vielleicht; it ~ be true es könnte wahr sein; he asked if he ~ go er fragte, ob er gehen dürfte; you ~ have drowned du hättest ertrinken können

might² n Macht f

mighty a (-ier, -iest) mächtig

migraine n Migräne f

migrat|e vi abwandern; <birds:> ziehen. ~**ion** n Wanderung f; (of birds) Zug m

mike n Ⓣ Mikrofon nt

mild a (-er, -est) mild

mild|ly adv leicht; to put it ~ly gelinde gesagt. ~**ness** n Milde f

mile n Meile f (= 1,6 km); ~s too big Ⓣ viel zu groß

mile|age n Meilenzahl f; (of car) Meilenstand m

militant a militant

military a militärisch. ~ **service** n Wehrdienst m

milk n Milch f ● vt melken

milk: ~**man** n Milchmann m. ~**shake** n Milchmixgetränk nt. ~**tooth** n Milchzahn m

milky a (-ier, -iest) milchig. **M~Way** n (Astr) Milchstraße f

mill n Mühle f; (factory) Fabrik f

millennium n Jahrtausend nt

milli|gram n Milligramm nt. ~**metre** n Millimeter m & nt

million n Million f; a ~ pounds eine Million Pfund. ~**aire** n Millionär(in) m(f)

mime n Pantomime f ● vt pantomimisch darstellen

mimic n Imitator m ● vt (pt/pp mimicked) nachahmen

mince n Hackfleisch nt ● vt (Culin) durchdrehen; **not ~ words** kein Blatt vor den Mund nehmen

mince: ~**meat** n Masse f aus Korinthen, Zitronat usw; **make ~meat of** (fig) vernichtend schlagen. ~ **pie** n mit 'mincemeat' gefülltes Pastetchen nt

mincer n Fleischwolf m

mind n Geist m; (sanity) Verstand m; **give s.o. a piece of one's ~** jdm gehörig die Meinung sagen; **make up one's ~** sich entschließen; **be out of one's ~** nicht bei Verstand sein; **have sth in ~** etw im Sinn haben; **bear sth in ~** an etw (acc) denken; **have a good ~ to** große Lust haben, zu; **I have changed my ~** ich habe es mir anders überlegt ● vt aufpassen auf (+ acc); **I don't ~ the noise** der Lärm stört mich nicht; ~ **the step!** Achtung Stufe! ● vi (care) sich kümmern (about um); **I don't ~** mir macht es nichts aus; **never ~!** macht nichts! **do you ~ if?** haben Sie etwas dagegen, wenn? ~ **out** vi aufpassen

mindless a geistlos

mine¹ poss pron meine(r), meins; a friend of ~ ein Freund von mir; **that is ~** das gehört mir

mine² n Bergwerk nt; (explosive) Mine f ● vt abbauen; (Mil) verminen

miner n Bergarbeiter m

mineral n Mineral nt. ~ **water** n Mineralwasser nt

minesweeper n Minenräumboot nt

mingle vi ~ with sich mischen unter (+ acc)

miniature a Klein- ● n Miniatur f

mini|bus n Kleinbus m. ~**cab** n Kleintaxi nt

minim|al a minimal. ~**um** n (pl -ima) Minimum nt ● a Mindest-

mining n Bergbau m

miniskirt n Minirock m

minister n Minister m; (Relig) Pastor m. ~**ial** a ministeriell

ministry n (Pol) Ministerium nt

mink n Nerz m

minor a kleiner; (less important) unbedeutend ● n Minderjährige(r) m/f; (Mus) Moll nt

minority n Minderheit f

minor road *n* Nebenstraße *f*

mint¹ *n* Münzstätte *f* ● *a* <*stamp*>
postfrisch; **in ~ condition** wie neu
● *vt* prägen

mint² *n* (*herb*) Minze *f*; (*sweet*)
Pfefferminzbonbon *m & nt*

minus *prep* minus, weniger; (⏣
without) ohne

minute¹ *n* Minute *f*; **in a ~** (*shortly*)
gleich; **~s** *pl* (*of meeting*) Protokoll
nt

minute² *a* winzig

mirac|le *n* Wunder *nt*. **~ulous** *a*
wunderbar

mirror *n* Spiegel *m* ● *vt*
widerspiegeln

mirth *n* Heiterkeit *f*

misadventure *n* Missgeschick *nt*

misapprehension *n*
Missverständnis *nt*; **be under a ~**
sich irren

misbehav|e *vi* sich schlecht
benehmen. **~iour** *n* schlechtes
Benehmen *nt*

miscalcu|late *vt* falsch berechnen
● *vi* sich verrechnen. **~lation** *n*
Fehlkalkulation *f*

miscarriage *n* Fehlgeburt *f*

miscellaneous *a* vermischt

mischief *n* Unfug *m*

mischievous *a*, **-ly** *adv*
schelmisch; (*malicious*) boshaft

misconception *n* falsche
Vorstellung *f*

misconduct *n* unkorrektes
Verhalten *nt*; (*adultery*) Ehebruch *m*

miser *n* Geizhals *m*

miserable *a*, **-bly** *adv* unglücklich;
(*wretched*) elend

miserly *adv* geizig

misery *n* Elend *nt*; (⏣ *person*)
Miesepeter *m*

misfire *vi* fehlzünden; (*go wrong*)
fehlschlagen

misfit *n* Außenseiter(in) *m(f)*

misfortune *n* Unglück *nt*

misgivings *npl* Bedenken *pl*

misguided *a* töricht

mishap *n* Missgeschick *nt*

misinform *vt* falsch unterrichten

misinterpret *vt* missdeuten

misjudge *vt* falsch beurteilen

mislay *vt* (*pt/pp* **-laid**) verlegen

mislead *vt* (*pt/pp* **-led**) irreführen.
~ing *a* irreführend

mismanage *vt* schlecht verwalten.
~ment *n* Misswirtschaft *f*

misnomer *n* Fehlbezeichnung *f*

misprint *n* Druckfehler *m*

misquote *vt* falsch zitieren

misrepresent *vt* falsch darstellen

miss *n* Fehltreffer *m* ● *vt* verpassen;
(*fail to hit or find*) verfehlen; (*fail to
attend*) versäumen; (*fail to notice*)
übersehen; (*feel the loss of*)
vermissen ● *vi* (*fail to hit*) nicht
treffen. **~ out** *vt* auslassen

Miss *n* (*pl* **-es**) Fräulein *nt*

missile *n* [Wurf]geschoss *nt*; (*Mil*)
Rakete *f*

missing *a* fehlend; (*lost*)
verschwunden; (*Mil*) vermisst; **be ~**
fehlen

mission *n* Auftrag *m*; (*Mil*) Einsatz
m; (*Relig*) Mission *f*

missionary *n* Missionar(in) *m(f)*

misspell *vt* (*pt/pp* **-spelt** or **-spelled**)
falsch schreiben

mist *n* Dunst *m*; (*fog*) Nebel *m*; (*on
window*) Beschlag *m* ● *vi* **~ up**
beschlagen

mistake *n* Fehler *m*; **by ~** aus
Versehen ● *vt* (*pt* **mistook**, *pp*
mistaken); **~ for** verwechseln mit

mistaken *a* falsch; **be ~** sich irren.
~ly *adv* irrtümlicherweise

mistletoe *n* Mistel *f*

mistress *n* Herrin *f*; (*teacher*)
Lehrerin *f*; (*lover*) Geliebte *f*

mistrust *n* Misstrauen *nt* ● *vt*
misstrauen (+ *dat*)

misty *a* (**-ier**, **-iest**) dunstig; (*foggy*)
neblig; (*fig*) unklar

misunderstand *vt* (*pt/pp* **-stood**)
missverstehen. **~ing** *n*
Missverständnis *nt*

misuse¹ *vt* missbrauchen

misuse² *n* Missbrauch *m*

mitigating *a* mildernd

mix n Mischung f ● vt mischen ● vi sich mischen; ~ **with** (*associate with*) verkehren mit. ~ **up** vt mischen; (*muddle*) durcheinander bringen; (*mistake for*) verwechseln (with mit)

mixed a gemischt; be ~ up durcheinander sein

mixer n Mischmaschine f; (*Culin*) Küchenmaschine f

mixture n Mischung f; (*medicine*) Mixtur f; (*Culin*) Teig m

mix-up n Durcheinander nt; (*confusion*) Verwirrung f, (*mistake*) Verwechslung f

moan n Stöhnen nt ● vi stöhnen; (*complain*) jammern

mob n Horde f; (*rabble*) Pöbel m; (🔲 *gang*) Bande f ● vt (*pt/pp* mobbed) herfallen über (+ *acc*); belagern <*celebrity*>

mobile a beweglich ● n Mobile nt; (*telephone*) Handy nt. ~ **home** n Wohnwagen m. ~ **phone** n Handy nt

mobility n Beweglichkeit f

mock a Schein- ● vt verspotten. ~**ery** n Spott m

mock-up n Modell nt

mode n [Art und] Weise f; (*fashion*) Mode f

model n Modell nt; (*example*) Vorbild nt; [**fashion**] ~ Mannequin nt ● a Modell-; (*exemplary*) Muster- ● v (*pt/pp* modelled) ● vt formen, modellieren; vorführen <*clothes*> ● vi Mannequin sein; (*for artist*) Modell stehen

moderate¹ vt mäßigen

moderate² a mäßig; <*opinion*> gemäßigt. ~**ly** adv mäßig; (*fairly*) einigermaßen

moderation n Mäßigung f; in ~ mit Maß[en]

modern a modern. ~**ize** vt modernisieren. ~ **languages** npl neuere Sprachen pl

modest a bescheiden; (*decorous*) schamhaft. ~**y** n Bescheidenheit f

modif|ication n Abänderung f. ~**y** vt (*pt/pp* -fied) abändern

moist a (-er, -est) feucht

moisten vt befeuchten

moistur|e n Feuchtigkeit f. ~**izer** n Feuchtigkeitscreme f

molar n Backenzahn m

mole¹ n Leberfleck m

mole² n (*Zool*) Maulwurf m

molecule n Molekül nt

molest vt belästigen

mollify vt (*pt/pp* -ied) besänftigen

mollycoddle vt verzärteln

molten a geschmolzen

mom n (*Amer fam*) Mutti f

moment n Moment m, Augenblick m; at the ~ im Augenblick, augenblicklich. ~**ary** a vorübergehend

momentous a bedeutsam

momentum n Schwung m

monarch n Monarch(in) m(f). ~**y** n Monarchie f

monastery n Kloster nt

Monday n Montag m

money n Geld nt

money: ~-**box** n Sparbüchse f. ~-**lender** n Geldverleiher m. ~ **order** n Zahlungsanweisung f

mongrel n Promenadenmischung f

monitor n (*Techn*) Monitor m ● vt überwachen <*progress*>; abhören <*broadcast*>

monk n Mönch m

monkey n Affe m

mono n Mono nt

monogram n Monogramm nt

monologue n Monolog m

monopol|ize vt monopolisieren. ~**y** n Monopol nt

monosyllable n einsilbiges Wort nt

monotone n in a ~ mit monotoner Stimme

monoton|ous a, -**ly** adv eintönig, monoton; (*tedious*) langweilig. ~**y** n Eintönigkeit f, Monotonie f

monster n Ungeheuer nt; (*cruel person*) Unmensch m

monstrosity n Monstrosität f

monstrous a ungeheuer; (*outrageous*) ungeheuerlich

month n Monat m. **~ly** a & adv monatlich ● n (periodical) Monatszeitschrift f

monument n Denkmal nt. **~al** a (fig) monumental

moo n Muh nt ● vi (pt/pp mooed) muhen

mood n Laune f; be in a good/bad ~ gute/schlechte Laune haben

moody a (-ier, -iest) launisch

moon n Mond m; over the ~ 🗓 überglücklich

moon: **~light** n Mondschein m. **~lighting** n 🗓 ≈ Schwarzarbeit f. **~lit** a mondhell

moor¹ n Moor nt

moor² vt (Naut) festmachen ● vi anlegen

mop n Mopp m; ~ of hair Wuschelkopf m ● vt (pt/pp mopped) wischen. ~ **up** vt aufwischen

moped n Moped nt

moral a, **-ly** adv moralisch, sittlich; (virtuous) tugendhaft ● n Moral f; **~s** pl Moral f

morale n Moral f

morality n Sittlichkeit f

morbid a krankhaft; (gloomy) trübe

more a, adv & n mehr; (in addition) noch; a few ~ noch ein paar; any ~ noch etwas; once ~ noch einmal; ~ or less mehr oder weniger; some ~ tea? noch etwas Tee? ~ interesting interessanter; ~ [and ~] quickly [immer] schneller

moreover adv außerdem

morgue n Leichenschauhaus nt

morning n Morgen m; in the ~ morgens, am Morgen; (tomorrow) morgen früh

Morocco n Marokko nt

moron n 🗓 Idiot m

morose a, **-ly** adv mürrisch

morsel n Happen m

mortal a sterblich; (fatal) tödlich ● n Sterbliche(r) m/f. **~ity** n Sterblichkeit f. **~ly** adv tödlich

mortar n Mörtel m

mortgage n Hypothek f ● vt hypothekarisch belasten

mortuary n Leichenhalle f, (public) Leichenschauhaus nt; (Amer: undertaker's) Bestattungsinstitut nt

mosaic n Mosaik nt

Moscow n Moskau nt

mosque n Moschee f

mosquito n (pl -es) [Stech]mücke f, Schnake f; (tropical) Moskito m

moss n Moos nt. **~y** a moosig

most a der/die/das meiste; (majority) die meisten; for the ~ part zum größten Teil ● adv am meisten; (very) höchst; the ~ interesting day der interessanteste Tag; ~ unlikely höchst unwahrscheinlich ● n das meiste; ~ of them die meisten [von ihnen]; at [the] ~ höchstens; ~ of the time die meiste Zeit. **~ly** adv meist

MOT n ≈ TÜV m

motel n Motel nt

moth n Nachtfalter m; [clothes-] ~ Motte f

mothball n Mottenkugel f

mother n Mutter f

mother: **~hood** n Mutterschaft f. **~-in-law** (pl ~s-in-law) Schwiegermutter f. **~land** n Mutterland nt. **~ly** a mütterlich. **~-of-pearl** n Perlmutter f. **~-to-be** n werdende Mutter f

mothproof a mottenfest

motif n Motiv nt

motion n Bewegung f; (proposal) Antrag m. **~less** a, **-ly** adv bewegungslos

motivat|e vt motivieren. **~ion** n Motivation f

motive n Motiv nt

motor n Motor m; (car) Auto nt ● a Motor-; (Anat) motorisch ● vi [mit dem Auto] fahren

motor: **~bike** n 🗓 Motorrad nt. **~ boat** n Motorboot nt. ~ **car** n Auto nt, Wagen m. **~cycle** n Motorrad nt. **~cyclist** n Motorradfahrer m. **~ing** n Autofahren nt. **~ist** n Autofahrer(in) m(f). ~ **vehicle** n Kraftfahrzeug nt. **~way** n Autobahn f

mottled a gesprenkelt

m

motto n (pl -es) Motto nt

mould[1] n (fungus) Schimmel m

mould[2] n Form f ● vt formen (into zu). **~ing** n (Archit) Fries m

mouldy a schimmelig; (🔢 worthless) schäbig

mound n Hügel m; (of stones) Haufen m

mount n (animal) Reittier nt; (of jewel) Fassung f; (of photo, picture) Passepartout nt ● vt (get on) steigen auf (+ acc); (on pedestal) montieren auf (+ acc); besteigen <horse>; fassen <jewel>; aufziehen <photo, picture> ● vi aufsteigen; <tension:> steigen. **~ up** vi sich häufen; (add up) sich anhäufen

mountain n Berg m

mountaineer n Bergsteiger(in) m(f). **~ing** n Bergsteigen nt

mountainous a bergig, gebirgig

mourn vt betrauern ● vi trauern (for um). **~er** n Trauernde(r) m/f. **~ful** a, **-ly** adv trauervoll. **~ing** n Trauer f

mouse n (pl mice) Maus f. **~trap** n Mausefalle f

moustache n Schnurrbart m

mouth[1] vt **~** sth etw lautlos mit den Lippen sagen

mouth[2] n Mund m; (of animal) Maul nt; (of river) Mündung f

mouth: **~ful** n Mundvoll m; (bite) Bissen m. **~organ** n Mundharmonika f. **~wash** n Mundwasser nt

movable a beweglich

move n Bewegung f; (fig) Schritt m; (moving house) Umzug m; (in board game) Zug m; **on the ~** unterwegs; **get a ~ on** 🔢 sich beeilen ● vt bewegen; (emotionally) rühren; (move along) rücken; (in board game) ziehen; (take away) wegnehmen; wegfahren <car>; (rearrange) umstellen; (transfer) versetzen <person>; verlegen <office>; (propose) beantragen; **~ house** umziehen ● vi sich bewegen; (move house) umziehen; **don't ~!** stillhalten! (stop) stillstehen! **~ along** vt/i weiterrücken. **~ away**

vt/i wegrücken; (move house) wegziehen. **~ in** vi einziehen. **~ off** vi <vehicle:> losfahren. **~ out** vi ausziehen. **~ over** vt/i [zur Seite] rücken. **~ up** vi aufrücken

movement n Bewegung f; (Mus) Satz m; (of clock) Uhrwerk nt

movie n (Amer) Film m; **go to the ~s** ins Kino gehen

moving a beweglich; (touching) rührend

mow vt (pt mowed, pp mown or mowed) mähen

mower n Rasenmäher m

MP abbr see **Member of Parliament**

Mr n (pl **Messrs**) Herr m

Mrs n Frau f

Ms n Frau f

much a, adv & n viel; **as ~ as** so viel wie; **~ loved** sehr geliebt

muck n Mist m; (🔢 filth) Dreck m. **~ about** vi herumalbern; (tinker) herumspielen (with mit). **~ out** vt ausmisten. **~ up** vt 🔢 vermasseln; (make dirty) schmutzig machen

mucky a (-ier, -iest) dreckig

mud n Schlamm m

muddle n Durcheinander nt; (confusion) Verwirrung f ● vt **~ [up]** durcheinander bringen

muddy a (-ier, -iest) schlammig; <shoes> schmutzig

mudguard n Kotflügel m; (on bicycle) Schutzblech nt

muffle vt dämpfen

muffler n Schal m; (Amer, Auto) Auspufftopf m

mug[1] n Becher m; (for beer) Bierkrug m; (🔢 face) Visage f; (🔢 simpleton) Trottel m

mug[2] vt (pt/pp mugged) überfallen. **~ger** n Straßenräuber m. **~ging** n Straßenraub m

muggy a (-ier, -iest) schwül

mule n Maultier nt

mulled a **~ wine** Glühwein m

multi: **~coloured** a vielfarbig, bunt. **~lingual** a mehrsprachig. **~national** a multinational

multiple a vielfach; (with pl) mehrere ● n Vielfache(s) nt

multiplication n Multiplikation f

multiply v (pt/pp -ied) ● vt multiplizieren (by mit) ● vi sich vermehren

multistorey a ~ car park Parkhaus nt

mum n 🔲 Mutti f

mumble vt/i murmeln

mummy¹ n 🔲 Mutti f

mummy² n (Archaeol) Mumie f

mumps n Mumps m

munch vt/i mampfen

municipal a städtisch

munitions npl Kriegsmaterial nt

mural n Wandgemälde nt

murder n Mord m ● vt ermorden. ~er n Mörder m. ~ess n Mörderin f. ~ous a mörderisch

murky a (-ier, -iest) düster

murmur n Murmeln nt ● vt/i murmeln

muscle n Muskel m

muscular a Muskel-; (strong) muskulös

museum n Museum nt

mushroom n [essbarer] Pilz m, esp Champignon m ● vi (fig) wie Pilze aus dem Boden schießen

mushy a breiig

music n Musik f; (written) Noten pl; set to ~ vertonen

musical a musikalisch ● n Musical nt. ~ **box** n Spieldose f. ~ **instrument** n Musikinstrument nt

musician n Musiker(in) m(f)

music-stand n Notenständer m

Muslim a mohammedanisch ● n Mohammedaner(in) m(f)

must v aux (nur Präsens) müssen; (with negative) dürfen ● n a ~ 🔲 ein Muss nt

mustard n Senf m

musty a (-ier, -iest) muffig

mute a stumm

mutilat|e vt verstümmeln. ~ion n Verstümmelung f

mutin|ous a meuterisch. ~y n Meuterei f ● vi (pt/pp -ied) meutern

mutter n Murmeln nt ● vt/i murmeln

mutton n Hammelfleisch nt

mutual a gegenseitig; (🔲 common) gemeinsam. ~ly adv gegenseitig

muzzle n (of animal) Schnauze f; (of firearm) Mündung f; (for dog) Maulkorb m

my a mein

myself pron selbst; (refl) mich; by ~ allein; I thought to ~ ich habe mir gedacht

mysterious a, -ly adv geheimnisvoll; (puzzling) mysteriös, rätselhaft

mystery n Geheimnis nt; (puzzle) Rätsel nt; ~ [story] Krimi m

mysti|c[al] a mystisch. ~cism n Mystik f

mystified a be ~ vor einem Rätsel stehen

mystique n geheimnisvoller Zauber m

myth n Mythos m; (🔲 untruth) Märchen nt. ~ical a mythisch; (fig) erfunden

mythology n Mythologie f

Nn

nab vt (pt/pp nabbed) 🔲 erwischen

nag¹ n (horse) Gaul m

nag² vt/i (pp/pp nagged) herumnörgeln (s.o. an jdm)

nail n (Anat, Techn) Nagel m; on the ~ 🔲 sofort ● vt nageln (to an + acc)

nail: ~-**brush** n Nagelbürste f. ~-**file** n Nagelfeile f. ~ **scissors** npl Nagelschere f. ~ **varnish** n Nagellack m

naïve a, -ly adv naiv. ~ty n Naivität f

naked *a* nackt; *<flame>* offen; with the ∼ eye mit bloßem Auge. **∼ness** *n* Nacktheit *f*

name *n* Name *m*; *(reputation)* Ruf *m*; by ∼ dem Namen nach; by the ∼ of namens; call s.o. ∼s 🔢 jdn beschimpfen ● *vt* nennen; *(give a name to)* einen Namen geben (+ *dat*); *(announce publicly)* den Namen bekannt geben von. **∼less** *a* namenlos. **∼ly** *adv* nämlich

name: **∼-plate** *n* Namensschild *nt*. **∼sake** *n* Namensvetter *m*/ Namensschwester *f*

nanny *n* Kindermädchen *nt*

nap *n* Nickerchen *nt*

napkin *n* Serviette *f*

nappy *n* Windel *f*

narcotic *n* *(drug)* Rauschgift *nt*

narrat|e *vt* erzählen. **∼ion** *n* Erzählung *f*

narrative *n* Erzählung *f*

narrator *n* Erzähler(in) *m(f)*

narrow *a* (-er, -est) schmal; *(restricted)* eng; *<margin, majority>* knapp; **have a ∼ escape** mit knapper Not davonkommen ● *vi* sich verengen. **∼-minded** *a* engstirnig

nasal *a* nasal; *(Med & Anat)* Nasen-

nasty *a* (-ier, -iest) übel; *(unpleasant)* unangenehm; *(unkind)* boshaft; *(serious)* schlimm

nation *n* Nation *f*; *(people)* Volk *nt*

national *a* national; *<newspaper>* überregional; *<campaign>* landesweit ● *n* Staatsbürger(in) *m(f)*

national: **∼ anthem** *n* Nationalhymne *f*. **N∼ Health Service** *n* staatlicher Gesundheitsdienst *m*. **N∼ Insurance** *n* Sozialversicherung *f*

nationalism *n* Nationalismus *m*

nationality *n* Staatsangehörigkeit *f*

national|ization *n* Verstaatlichung *f*. **∼ize** *vt* verstaatlichen

native *a* einheimisch; *(innate)* angeboren ● *n* Eingeborene(r) *m/f*; *(local inhabitant)* Einheimische(r) *m/f*; **a ∼ of Vienna** ein gebürtiger Wiener

native: **∼ land** *n* Heimatland *nt*. **∼ language** *n* Muttersprache *f*

natter *vi* 🔢 schwatzen

natural *a*, **-ly** *adv* natürlich; **∼[-coloured]** naturfarben

natural: **∼ gas** *n* Erdgas *nt*. **∼ history** *n* Naturkunde *f*

naturalist *n* Naturforscher *m*

natural|ization *n* Einbürgerung *f*. **∼ize** *vt* einbürgern

nature *n* Natur *f*; *(kind)* Art *f*; by ∼ von Natur aus. **∼ reserve** *n* Naturschutzgebiet *nt*

naughty *a* (-ier, -iest), **-ily** *adv* unartig; *(slightly indecent)* gewagt

nausea *n* Übelkeit *f*

nautical *a* nautisch. **∼ mile** *n* Seemeile *f*

naval *a* Marine-

nave *n* Kirchenschiff *nt*

navel *n* Nabel *m*

navigable *a* schiffbar

navigat|e *vi* navigieren ● *vt* befahren *<river>*. **∼ion** *n* Navigation *f*

navy *n* [Kriegs]marine *f* ● *a* ∼ [blue] marineblau

near *a* (-er, -est) nah[e]; the ∼est bank die nächste Bank ● *adv* nahe; **draw ∼** sich nähern ● *prep* nahe an (+ *dat/acc*); in der Nähe von

near: **∼by** *a* nahe gelegen, nahe liegend. **∼ly** *adv* fast, beinahe; **not ∼ly** bei weitem nicht. **∼ness** *n* Nähe *f*. **∼ side** *n* Beifahrerseite *f*. **∼-sighted** *a* (Amer) kurzsichtig

neat *a* (-er, -est), **-ly** *adv* adrett; *(tidy)* ordentlich; *(clever)* geschickt; *(undiluted)* pur. **∼ness** *n* Ordentlichkeit *f*

necessarily *adv* notwendigerweise; **not ∼** nicht unbedingt

necessary *a* nötig, notwendig

necessit|ate *vt* notwendig machen. **∼y** *n* Notwendigkeit *f*; **work from ∼y** arbeiten, weil man es nötig hat

neck *n* Hals *m*; ∼ **and** ∼ Kopf an Kopf

necklace *n* Halskette *f*

neckline n Halsausschnitt m

née a ~ X geborene X

need n Bedürfnis nt; (misfortune) Not f; be in ~ of brauchen; in case of ~ notfalls; if ~ be wenn nötig; there is a ~ for es besteht ein Bedarf an (+ dat); there is no ~ for that das ist nicht nötig ● vt brauchen; you ~ not go du brauchst nicht zu gehen; ~ I come? muss ich kommen? I ~ to know ich muss es wissen

needle n Nadel f

needless a, -ly adv unnötig; ~ to say selbstverständlich, natürlich

needlework n Nadelarbeit f

needy a (-ier, -iest) bedürftig

negation n Verneinung f

negative a negativ ● n Verneinung f; (photo) Negativ nt

neglect n Vernachlässigung f ● vt vernachlässigen; (omit) versäumen (to zu). ~ed a verwahrlost. ~ful a nachlässig

negligen|ce n Nachlässigkeit f. ~t a, -ly adv nachlässig

negligible a unbedeutend

negotiat|e vt aushandeln; (Auto) nehmen <bend> ● vi verhandeln. ~ion n Verhandlung f. ~or n Unterhändler(in) m(f)

Negro a Neger- ● n (pl -es) Neger m

neigh vi wiehern

neighbour n Nachbar(in) m(f). ~hood n Nachbarschaft f. ~ing a Nachbar-. ~ly a [gut]nachbarlich

neither a & pron keine(r, s) [von beiden] ● adv ~... nor weder ... noch ● conj auch nicht

neon n Neon nt

nephew n Neffe m

nepotism n Vetternwirtschaft f

nerve n Nerv m; (☐ courage) Mut m; (☐ impudence) Frechheit f. ~-racking a nervenaufreibend

nervous a, -ly adv (afraid) ängstlich; (highly strung) nervös; (Anat, Med) Nerven-. ~ break-down n Nervenzusammenbruch m. ~ness Ängstlichkeit f

nervy a (-ier, -iest) nervös; (Amer: impudent) frech

nest n Nest nt ● vi nisten

nestle vi sich schmiegen (against an + acc)

net¹ n Netz nt; (curtain) Store m

net² a netto; <salary, weight> Netto-

netball n ≈ Korbball m

Netherlands npl the ~ die Niederlande pl

nettle n Nessel f

network n Netz nt

neurolog|ist n Neurologe m/ -gin f. ~y n Neurologie f

neur|osis n (pl -oses) Neurose f. ~otic a neurotisch

neuter a (Gram) sächlich ● n (Gram) Neutrum nt ● vt kastrieren; (spay) sterilisieren

neutral a neutral ● n in ~ (Auto) im Leerlauf. ~ity n Neutralität f

never adv nie, niemals; (☐ not) nicht; ~ mind macht nichts; well I ~! ja so was! ~-ending a endlos

nevertheless adv dennoch, trotzdem

new a (-er, -est) neu

new: ~comer n Neuankömmling m. ~fangled a (pej) neumodisch. ~-laid a frisch gelegt

newly adv frisch. ~-weds npl Jungverheiratete pl

new: ~ moon n Neumond m. ~ness n Neuheit f

news n Nachricht f; (Radio, TV) Nachrichten pl; piece of ~ Neuigkeit f

news: ~agent n Zeitungshändler m. ~ bulletin n Nachrichten-sendung f. ~letter n Mitteilungs-blatt nt. ~paper n Zeitung f; (material) Zeitungspapier nt. ~reader n Nachrichtensprecher(in) m(f)

New: ~ Year's Day n Neujahr nt. ~ Year's Eve n Silvester nt. ~ Zealand n Neuseeland nt

next a & n nächste(r, s); who's ~? wer kommt als Nächster dran? the ~ best das nächstbeste; ~ door nebenan; my ~ of kin mein nächster

Verwandter; ~ **to nothing** fast gar nichts; **the week after** ~ übernächste Woche ● *adv* als Nächstes; ~ **to** neben

nib *n* Feder *f*

nibble *vt/i* knabbern (**at** an + *dat*)

nice *a* (**-r, -st**) nett; *<day, weather>* schön; *<food>* gut; *<distinction>* fein. ~**ly** *adv* nett; (*well*) gut

niche *n* Nische *f*; (*fig*) Platz *m*

nick *n* Kerbe *f*; (① *prison*) Knast *m*; (① *police station*) Revier *nt*; **in good** ~ ① in gutem Zustand ● *vt* einkerben; (*steal*) klauen; (① *arrest*) schnappen

nickel *n* Nickel *nt*; (*Amer*) Fünfcentstück *nt*

nickname *n* Spitzname *m*

nicotine *n* Nikotin *nt*

niece *n* Nichte *f*

Nigeria *n* Nigeria *nt*. ~**n** *a* nigerianisch ● *n* Nigerianer(in) *m(f)*

night *n* Nacht *f*; (*evening*) Abend *m*; **at** ~ nachts

night: ~**club** *n* Nachtklub *m*. ~**dress** *n* Nachthemd *nt*. ~**fall** *n* at ~**fall** bei Einbruch der Dunkelheit. ~**gown** *n*, ① ~**ie** *n* Nachthemd *nt*

nightingale *n* Nachtigall *f*

night: ~**life** *n* Nachtleben *nt*. ~**ly** *a* nächtlich ● *adv* jede Nacht. ~**mare** *n* Albtraum *m*. ~**-time** *n* at ~**-time** bei Nacht

nil *n* null

nimble *a* (**-r, -st**), **-bly** *adv* flink

nine *a* neun ● *n* Neun *f*. ~**teen** *a* neunzehn. ~**teenth** *a* neunzehnte(r, s)

ninetieth *a* neunzigste(r, s)

ninety *a* neunzig

ninth *a* neunte(r, s)

nip *vt* kneifen; (*bite*) beißen; ~ **in the bud** (*fig*) im Keim ersticken ● *vi* (① *run*) laufen

nipple *n* Brustwarze *f*; (*Amer: on bottle*) Sauger *m*

nitwit *n* ① Dummkopf *m*

no *adv* nein ● *n* (*pl* **noes**) Nein *nt* ● *a* kein(e); (*pl*) keine; **in no time** [sehr] schnell; **no parking/smoking**

Parken/Rauchen verboten; **no one** = **nobody**

nobility *n* Adel *m*

noble *a* (**-r, -st**) edel; (*aristocratic*) adlig. ~**man** *n* Adlige(r) *m*

nobody *pron* niemand, keiner ● *n* **a** ~ ein Niemand *m*

nocturnal *a* nächtlich; *<animal, bird>* Nacht-

nod *n* Nicken *nt* ● *v* (*pt/pp* **nodded**) ● *vi* nicken ● *vt* ~ **one's head** mit dem Kopf nicken

noise *n* Geräusch *nt*; (*loud*) Lärm *m*. ~**less** *a*, **-ly** *adv* geräuschlos

noisy *a* (**-ier, -iest**), **-ily** *adv* laut; *<eater>* geräuschvoll

nomad *n* Nomade *m*. ~**ic** *a* nomadisch; *<life, tribe>* Nomaden-

nominal *a*, **-ly** *adv* nominell

nominat|e *vt* nominieren, aufstellen; (*appoint*) ernennen. ~**ion** *n* Nominierung *f*; Ernennung *f*

nominative *a & n* (*Gram*) ~**[case]** Nominativ *m*

nonchalant *a*, **-ly** *adv* nonchalant; *<gesture>* lässig

nondescript *a* unbestimmbar; *<person>* unscheinbar

none *pron* keine(r)/keins; ~ **of it/this** nichts davon ● *adv* ~ **too** nicht gerade; ~ **too soon** [um] keine Minute zu früh; ~ **the less** dennoch

nonentity *n* Null *f*

non-existent *a* nicht vorhanden

non-fiction *n* Sachliteratur *f*

nonplussed *a* verblüfft

nonsens|e *n* Unsinn *m*. ~**ical** *a* unsinnig

non-smoker *n* Nichtraucher *m*

non-stop *adv* ununterbrochen; *<fly>* nonstop

non-swimmer *n* Nichtschwimmer *m*

non-violent *a* gewaltlos

noodles *npl* Bandnudeln *pl*

noon *n* Mittag *m*; **at** ~ um 12 Uhr mittags

noose *n* Schlinge *f*

nor *adv* noch ● *conj* auch nicht

Nordic *a* nordisch

norm n Norm f

normal a normal. **~ity** n Normalität f. **~ly** adv normal; (usually) normalerweise

north n Norden m; **to the ~ of** nördlich von ● a Nord-, nord- ● adv nach Norden

north: N~ America n Nordamerika nt. **~-east** a Nordost- ● n Nordosten m

norther|ly a nördlich. **~n** a nördlich. **N~n Ireland** n Nordirland nt

north: N~ Pole n Nordpol m. **N~ Sea** n Nordsee f. **~ward[s]** adv nach Norden. **~-west** a Nordwest- ● n Nordwesten m

Nor|way n Norwegen nt. **~wegian** a norwegisch ● n Norweger(in) m(f)

nose n Nase

nosebleed n Nasenbluten nt

nostalg|ia n Nostalgie f. **~ic** a nostalgisch

nostril n Nasenloch nt

nosy a (-ier, -iest) 🗓 neugierig

not
● adverb
····▸ nicht. **I don't know** ich weiß nicht. **isn't she pretty?** ist sie nicht hübsch?
····▸ not a kein. **he is not a doctor** er ist kein Arzt. **she didn't wear a hat** sie trug keinen Hut. **there was not a person to be seen** es gab keinen Menschen zu sehen. **not a thing** gar nichts. **not a bit** kein bisschen
····▸ (in elliptical phrases) **I hope not** ich hoffe nicht. **of course not** natürlich nicht. **not at all** überhaupt nicht; (in polite reply to thanks) keine Ursache; gern geschehen. **certainly not!** auf keinen Fall! **not I** ich nicht
····▸ not ... but ... nicht ... sondern .... **it was not a small town but a big one** es war keine kleine Stadt, sondern eine große

notab|le a bedeutend; (remarkable) bemerkenswert. **~ly** adv insbesondere

notation n Notation f; (Mus) Notenschrift f

notch n Kerbe f

note n (written comment) Notiz f, Anmerkung f; (short letter) Briefchen nt, Zettel m; (bank ~) Banknote f, Schein m; (Mus) Note f; (sound) Ton m; (on piano) Taste f; **half/whole** ~ (Amer) halbe/ganze Note f; **of** ~ von Bedeutung; **make a** ~ **of** notieren ● vt beachten; (notice) bemerken (that dass)

notebook n Notizbuch nt

noted a bekannt (for für)

note: ~paper n Briefpapier nt. **~worthy** a beachtenswert

nothing n, pron & adv nichts; **for** ~ umsonst; ~ **but** nichts als; ~ **much** nicht viel; ~ **interesting** nichts Interessantes

notice n (on board) Anschlag m, Bekanntmachung f; (announcement) Anzeige f; (review) Kritik f; (termination of lease, employment) Kündigung f; **give [in one's]** ~ kündigen; **give s.o.** ~ jdm kündigen; **take no** ~! ignoriere es! ● vt bemerken. **~able**, a, **-bly** adv merklich. **~-board** n Anschlagbrett nt

noti|fication n Benachrichtigung f. **~fy** vt (pt/pp -ied) benachrichtigen

notion n Idee f

notorious a berüchtigt

notwithstanding prep trotz (+ gen) ● adv trotzdem, dennoch

nought n Null f

noun n Substantiv nt

nourish vt nähren. **~ing** a nahrhaft. **~ment** n Nahrung f

novel a neu[artig] ● n Roman m. **~ist** n Romanschriftsteller(in) m(f). **~ty** n Neuheit f

November n November m

novice n Neuling m; (Relig) Novize m/Novizin f

now adv & conj jetzt; ~ **[that]** jetzt, wo; **just** ~ gerade, eben; **right** ~ sofort; ~ **and again** hin und wieder; **now, now!** na, na!

nowadays adv heutzutage

n

nowhere *adv* nirgendwo, nirgends

nozzle *n* Düse *f*

nuance *n* Nuance *f*

nuclear *a* Kern-. **~ deterrent** *n* nukleares Abschreckungsmittel *nt*

nucleus *n* (*pl* -lei) Kern *m*

nude *a* nackt ● *n* (*Art*) Akt *m*; **in the ~** nackt

nudge *vt* stupsen

nud|ist *n* Nudist *m*. **~ity** *n* Nacktheit *f*

nuisance *n* Ärgernis *nt*; (*pest*) Plage *f*; **be a ~** ärgerlich sein

null *a* **~ and void** null und nichtig

numb *a* gefühllos, taub ● *vt* betäuben

number *n* Nummer *f*; (*amount*) Anzahl *f*; (*Math*) Zahl *f* ● *vt* nummerieren; (*include*) zählen (**among** zu). **~-plate** *n* Nummernschild *nt*

numeral *n* Ziffer *f*

numerical *a*, **-ly** *adv* numerisch; **in ~ order** zahlenmäßig geordnet

numerous *a* zahlreich

nun *n* Nonne *f*

nurse *n* [Kranken]schwester *f*; (*male*) Krankenpfleger *m*; **children's ~** Kindermädchen *nt* ● *vt* pflegen

nursery *n* Kinderzimmer *nt*; (*Hort*) Gärtnerei *f*; **[day] ~** Kindertagesstätte *f*. **~ rhyme** *n* Kinderreim *m*. **~ school** *n* Kindergarten *m*

nursing *n* Krankenpflege *f*. **~ home** *n* Pflegeheim *nt*

nut *n* Nuss *f*; (*Techn*) [Schrauben]mutter *f*; (🄸 *head*) Birne *f* 🄸; **be ~s** 🄸 spinnen 🄸. **~crackers** *npl* Nussknacker *m*. **~meg** *n* Muskat *m*

nutrient *n* Nährstoff *m*

nutrit|ion *n* Ernährung *f*. **~ious** *a* nahrhaft

nutshell *n* Nussschale *f*; **in a ~** (*fig*) kurz gesagt

nylon *n* Nylon *nt*

O *n* (*Teleph*) null

oak *n* Eiche *f*

OAP *abbr* (**old-age pensioner**) Rentner(in) *m(f)*

oar *n* Ruder *nt*. **~sman** *n* Ruderer *m*

oasis *n* (*pl* **oases**) Oase *f*

oath *n* Eid *m*; (*swear-word*) Fluch *m*

oatmeal *n* Hafermehl *nt*

oats *npl* Hafer *m*; (*Culin*) **[rolled] ~** Haferflocken *pl*

obedien|ce *n* Gehorsam *m*. **~t** *a*, **-ly** *adv* gehorsam

obey *vt/i* gehorchen (+ *dat*); befolgen <*instructions, rules*>

obituary *n* Nachruf *m*; (*notice*) Todesanzeige *f*

object[1] *n* Gegenstand *m*; (*aim*) Zweck *m*; (*intention*) Absicht *f*; (*Gram*) Objekt *nt*; **money is no ~** Geld spielt keine Rolle

object[2] *vi* Einspruch erheben (**to** gegen); (*be against*) etwas dagegen haben

objection *n* Einwand *m*; **have no ~** nichts dagegen haben. **~able** *a* anstößig; <*person*> unangenehm

objectiv|e *a*, **-ly** *adv* objektiv ● *n* Ziel *nt*. **~ity** *n* Objektivität *f*

objector *n* Gegner *m*

obligation *n* Pflicht *f*; **without ~** unverbindlich

obligatory *a* obligatorisch; **be ~** Vorschrift sein

oblig|e *vt* verpflichten; (*compel*) zwingen; (*do a small service*) einen Gefallen tun (+ *dat*). **~ing** *a* entgegenkommend

oblique *a* schräg; <*angle*> schief; (*fig*) indirekt

obliterate *vt* auslöschen

oblivion *n* Vergessenheit *f*

oblivious *a* **be ~** sich (*dat*) nicht bewusst sein (**of** *gen*)

oblong a rechteckig ● n Rechteck nt
obnoxious a widerlich
oboe n Oboe f
obscen|e a obszön. ~**ity** n Obszönität f
obscur|e a dunkel; (*unknown*) unbekannt ● vt verdecken; (*confuse*) verwischen. ~**ity** n Dunkelheit f; Unbekanntheit f
observa|nce n (*of custom*) Einhaltung f. ~**nt** a aufmerksam. ~**tion** n Beobachtung f; (*remark*) Bemerkung f
observatory n Sternwarte f
observe vt beobachten; (*say, notice*) bemerken; (*keep, celebrate*) feiern; (*obey*) einhalten. ~**r** n Beobachter m
obsess vt be ~ed by besessen sein von. ~**ion** n Besessenheit f; (*persistent idea*) fixe Idee f. ~**ive** a, **-ly** adv zwanghaft
obsolete a veraltet
obstacle n Hindernis nt
obstina|cy n Starrsinn m. ~**te** a, **-ly** adv starrsinnig; (*refusal*) hartnäckig
obstruct vt blockieren; (*hinder*) behindern. ~**ion** n Blockierung f; Behinderung f; (*obstacle*) Hindernis nt. ~**ive** a be ~ive Schwierigkeiten bereiten
obtain vt erhalten. ~**able** a erhältlich
obtrusive a aufdringlich; <*thing*> auffällig
obtuse a begriffsstutzig
obvious a, **-ly** adv offensichtlich, offenbar
occasion n Gelegenheit f; (*time*) Mal nt; (*event*) Ereignis nt; (*cause*) Anlass m, Grund m; on the ~ of anlässlich (+ gen)
occasional a gelegentlich. ~**ly** adv gelegentlich, hin und wieder
occult a okkult
occupant n Bewohner(in) m(f); (*of vehicle*) Insasse m
occupation n Beschäftigung f; (*job*) Beruf m; (*Mil*) Besetzung f; (*period*) Besatzung f. ~**al** a Berufs-.

~**al therapy** n Beschäftigungstherapie f
occupier n Bewohner(in) m(f)
occupy vt (*pt/pp occupied*) besetzen <*seat, (Mil) country*>; einnehmen <*space*>; in Anspruch nehmen <*time*>; (*live in*) bewohnen; (*fig*) bekleiden <*office*>; (*keep busy*) beschäftigen
occur vi (*pt/pp occurred*) geschehen; (*exist*) vorkommen, auftreten; it ~red to me that es fiel mir ein, dass. ~**rence** n Auftreten nt; (*event*) Ereignis nt
ocean n Ozean m
o'clock adv [at] 7 ~ [um] 7 Uhr
octagonal a achteckig
October n Oktober m
octopus n (*pl* **-puses**) Tintenfisch m
odd a (**-er, -est**) seltsam, merkwürdig; <*number*> ungerade; (*not of set*) einzeln; **forty** ~ über vierzig; ~ **jobs** Gelegenheitsarbeiten pl; **the** ~ **one out** die Ausnahme; **at** ~ **moments** zwischendurch
odd|ity n Kuriosität f. ~**ly** adv merkwürdig; ~**ly enough** merkwürdigerweise ~**ment** n (*of fabric*) Rest m
odds npl (*chances*) Chancen pl; **at** ~ uneinig; ~ **and ends** Kleinkram m
ode n Ode f
odious a widerlich
odour n Geruch m. ~**less** a geruchlos

··

of
● *preposition*
····▸ (*indicating belonging, origin*) von (+ *dat*); genitive. **the mother of twins** die Mutter von Zwillingen. **the mother of the twins** die Mutter der Zwillinge *or* von den Zwillingen. **the Queen of England** die Königin von England. **a friend of mine** ein Freund von mir. **a friend of the teacher's** ein Freund des Lehrers. **the brother of her father** der Bruder ihres Vaters. **the works of Shakespeare** Shakespeares Werke. **it was nice of him** es war nett von ihm

····▸ *(made of)* aus (+ *dat*). **a dress of cotton** ein Kleid aus Baumwolle
····▸ *(following number)* **five of us** fünf von uns. **the two of us** wir zwei. **there were four of us waiting** wir waren vier, die warteten
····▸ *(followed by number, description)* von (+ *dat*). **a girl of ten** ein Mädchen von zehn Jahren. **a distance of 50 miles** eine Entfernung von 50 Meilen. **a man of character** ein Mann von Charakter. **a woman of exceptional beauty** eine Frau von außerordentlicher Schönheit. **a person of strong views** ein Mensch mit festen Ansichten

!
of is not translated after measures and in some other cases: **a pound of apples** ein Pfund Äpfel; **a cup of tea** eine Tasse Tee; **a glass of wine** ein Glas Wein; **the city of Chicago** die Stadt Chicago; **the fourth of January** der vierte Januar

off *prep* von (+ *dat*); ~ **the coast** vor der Küste; **get ~ the ladder/bus** von der Leiter/aus dem Bus steigen ● *adv* weg; *<button, lid, handle>* ab; *<light>* aus; *<brake>* los; *<machine>* abgeschaltet; *<tap>* zu; *(on appliance)* 'off' 'aus'; **2 kilometres ~** 2 Kilometer entfernt; **a long way ~** weit weg; *(time)* noch lange hin; ~ **and on** hin und wieder; **with his hat/coat ~** ohne Hut/Mantel; **20% ~** 20% Nachlass; **be ~** *(leave)* [weg]gehen; *(Sport)* starten; *<food:>* schlecht sein; **be well ~** gut dran sein; *(financially)* wohlhabend sein; **have a day ~** einen freien Tag haben

offal *n (Culin)* Innereien *pl*

offence *n (illegal act)* Vergehen *nt*; **give/take ~** Anstoß erregen/nehmen (**at** an + *dat*)

offend *vt* beleidigen. **~er** *n (Jur)* Straftäter *m*

offensive *a* anstößig; *(Mil, Sport)* offensiv ● *n* Offensive *f*

offer *n* Angebot *nt*; **on (special) ~** im Sonderangebot ● *vt* anbieten (**to** *dat*);

leisten *<resistance>*; ~ **to do sth** sich anbieten, etw zu tun. **~ing** *n* Gabe *f*

offhand *a* brüsk; *(casual)* lässig

office *n* Büro *nt*; *(post)* Amt *nt*

officer *n* Offizier *m*; *(official)* Beamte(r) *m*/ Beamtin *f*; *(police)* Polizeibeamte(r) *m*/-beamtin *f*

official *a* offiziell, amtlich ● *n* Beamte(r) *m*/ Beamtin *f*; *(Sport)* Funktionär *m*. **~ly** *adv* offiziell

officious *a*, **-ly** *adv* übereifrig

off-licence *n* Wein und Spirituosenhandlung *f*

off-load *vt* ausladen

off-putting *a* 🗊 abstoßend

offset *vt (pt/pp* **-set**, *pres p* **-setting)** ausgleichen

offshoot *n* Schössling *m*; *(fig)* Zweig *m*

offshore *a* Offshore-

offside *a (Sport)* abseits

offspring *n* Nachwuchs *m*

offstage *adv* hinter den Kulissen

off-white *a* fast weiß

often *adv* oft; **every so ~** von Zeit zu Zeit

oh *int* oh! ach! **oh dear!** o weh!

oil *n* Öl *nt*; *(petroleum)* Erdöl *nt* ● *vt* ölen

oil: ~field *n* Ölfeld *nt*. **~-painting** *n* Ölgemälde *nt*. ~ **refinery** *n* [Erd]ölraffinerie *f*. **~-tanker** *n* Öltanker *m*. ~ **well** *n* Ölquelle *f*

oily *a* (**-ier**, **-iest**) ölig

ointment *n* Salbe *f*

OK *a & int* 🗊 in Ordnung; okay ● *adv (well)* gut ● *vt (auch* **okay)** *(pt/pp* **okayed)** genehmigen

old *a* (**-er**, **-est**) alt; *(former)* ehemalig

old: ~ **age** *n* Alter *nt*. **~-age pensioner** *n* Rentner(in) *m(f)*. ~ **boy** *n* ehemaliger Schüler. **~-fashioned** *a* altmodisch. ~ **girl** *n* ehemalige Schülerin *f*

olive *n* Olive *f*; *(colour)* Oliv *nt* ● *a* olivgrün. ~ **oil** *n* Olivenöl *nt*

Olympic *a* olympisch ● *n* **the ~s** die Olympischen Spiele *pl*

omelette *n* Omelett *nt*

ominous *a* bedrohlich

omission n Auslassung f; (failure to do) Unterlassung f

omit vt (pt/pp omitted) auslassen; ~ **to do sth** es unterlassen, etw zu tun

omnipotent a allmächtig

on prep auf (+ dat/(on to) + acc); (on vertical surface) an (+ dat/(on to) + acc); (about) über (+ acc); **on Monday** [am] Montag; **on Mondays** montags; **on the first of May** am ersten Mai; **on arriving** als ich ankam; **on one's finger** am Finger; **on the right/left** rechts/links; **on the Rhine** am Rhein; **on the radio/television** im Radio/ Fernsehen; **on the bus/train** im Bus/ Zug; **go on the bus/train** mit dem Bus/Zug fahren; **on me** (with me) bei mir; **it's on me** 🛈 das spendiere ich ● adv (further on) weiter; (switched on) an; <brake> angezogen; <machine> angeschaltet; (on appliance) 'on' 'ein'; **with/without his hat/coat** on mit/ohne Hut/Mantel; **be on** <film:> laufen; <event:> stattfinden; **be on at** 🛈 bedrängen (zu to); **it's not on** 🛈 das geht nicht; **on and on** immer weiter; **on and off** hin und wieder; **and so on** und so weiter

once adv einmal; (formerly) früher; **at** ~ sofort; (at the same time) gleichzeitig; ~ **and for all** ein für alle Mal ● conj wenn; (with past tense) als

oncoming a ~ **traffic** Gegenverkehr m

one a ein(e); (only) einzig; **not** ~ kein(e); ~ **day/evening** eines Tages/ Abends ● n Eins f ● pron eine(r)/ eins; (impersonal) man; **which** ~ welche(r,s); ~ **another** einander; ~ **by** ~ einzeln; ~ **never knows** man kann nie wissen

one: ~**-parent family** n Einelternfamilie f. ~**self** pron selbst; (refl) sich; **by** ~**self** allein. ~**-sided** a einseitig. ~**-way** a <street> Einbahn-; <ticket> einfach

onion n Zwiebel f

onlooker n Zuschauer(in) m(f)

only a einzige(r,s); **an** ~ **child** ein Einzelkind nt ● adv & conj nur; ~ **just** gerade erst; (barely) gerade noch

onset n Beginn m; (of winter) Einsetzen nt

onward[s] adv vorwärts; **from then** ~ von der Zeit an

ooze vi sickern

opaque a undurchsichtig

open a, -ly adv offen; **be** ~ <shop:> geöffnet sein; **in the** ~ **air** im Freien ● n **in the** ~ im Freien ● vt öffnen, aufmachen; (start, set up) eröffnen ● vi sich öffnen; <flower:> aufgehen; <shop:> öffnen, aufmachen; (be started) eröffnet werden. ~ **up** vt öffnen, aufmachen

open day n Tag m der offenen Tür

opener n Öffner m

opening n Öffnung f; (beginning) Eröffnung f; (job) Einstiegs- möglichkeit f. ~ **hours** npl Öffnungszeiten pl

open: ~**-minded** a aufgeschlossen. ~ **sandwich** n belegtes Brot nt

opera n Oper f. ~**-house** n Opernhaus nt. ~**-singer** n Opernsänger(in) m(f)

operate vt bedienen <machine, lift>; betätigen <lever, brake>; (fig: run) betreiben ● vi (Techn) funktionieren; (be in action) in Betrieb sein; (Mil & fig) operieren; ~ **[on]** (Med) operieren

operatic a Opern-

operation n (see operate) Bedienung f; Betätigung f; Operation f; **in** ~ (Techn) in Betrieb; **come into** ~ (fig) in Kraft treten; **have an** ~ (Med) operiert werden. ~**al** a **be** ~**al** in Betrieb sein; <law:> in Kraft sein

operative a wirksam

operator n (user) Bedienungsperson f; (Teleph) Vermittlung f

operetta n Operette f

opinion n Meinung f; **in my** ~ meiner Meinung nach. ~**ated** a rechthaberisch

opponent n Gegner(in) m(f)

opportun|e *a* günstig. **~ist** *n* Opportunist *m*

opportunity *n* Gelegenheit *f*

oppos|e *vt* Widerstand leisten (+ *dat*); (*argue against*) sprechen gegen; **be ~ed to sth** gegen etw sein; **as ~ed to** im Gegensatz zu. **~ing** *a* gegnerisch

opposite *a* entgegengesetzt; <*house, side*> gegenüberliegend; **~ number** (*fig*) Gegenstück *nt*; **the ~ sex** das andere Geschlecht ● *n* Gegenteil *nt* ● *adv* gegenüber ● *prep* gegenüber (+ *dat*)

opposition *n* Widerstand *m*; (*Pol*) Opposition *f*

oppress *vt* unterdrücken. **~ion** *n* Unterdrückung *f*. **~ive** *a* tyrannisch; <*heat*> drückend

opt *vi* **~ for** sich entscheiden für

optical *a* optisch

optician *n* Optiker *m*

optimis|m *n* Optimismus *m*. **~t** *n* Optimist *m*. **~tic** *a*, **-ally** *adv* optimistisch

optimum *a* optimal

option *n* Wahl *f*; (*Comm*) Option *f*. **~al** *a* auf Wunsch erhältlich; <*subject*> wahlfrei

opu|lence *n* Prunk *m*. **~lent** *a* prunkvoll

or *conj* oder; (*after negative*) noch; **or [else]** sonst; **in a year or two** in ein bis zwei Jahren

oral *a*, **-ly** *adv* mündlich; (*Med*) oral ● *n* Mündliche(s) *nt*

orange *n* Apfelsine *f*, Orange *f*; (*colour*) Orange *nt* ● *a* orangefarben

oratorio *n* Oratorium *nt*

oratory *n* Redekunst *f*

orbit *n* Umlaufbahn *f* ● *vt* umkreisen

orchard *n* Obstgarten *m*

orches|tra *n* Orchester *nt*. **~tral** *a* Orchester-. **~trate** *vt* orchestrieren

ordeal *n* (*fig*) Qual *f*

order *n* Ordnung *f*; (*sequence*) Reihenfolge *f*; (*condition*) Zustand *m*; (*command*) Befehl *m*; (*in restaurant*) Bestellung *f*; (*Comm*) Auftrag *m*; (*Relig, medal*) Orden *m*; **out of ~** <*machine*> außer Betrieb; **in ~ that** damit; **in ~ to help** um zu helfen ● *vt* (*put in ~*) ordnen; (*command*) befehlen (+ *dat*); (*Comm, in restaurant*) bestellen; (*prescribe*) verordnen

orderly *a* ordentlich; (*not unruly*) friedlich ● *n* (*Mil, Med*) Sanitäter *m*

ordinary *a* gewöhnlich, normal

ore *n* Erz *nt*

organ *n* (*Biol & fig*) Organ *nt*; (*Mus*) Orgel *f*

organic *a*, **-ally** *adv* organisch; (*without chemicals*) biodynamisch; <*crop*> biologisch angebaut; <*food*> Bio-. **~ farming** *n* biologischer Anbau *m*

organism *n* Organismus *m*

organist *n* Organist *m*

organization *n* Organisation *f*

organize *vt* organisieren; veranstalten <*event*>. **~r** *n* Organisator *m*; Veranstalter *m*

orgy *n* Orgie *f*

Orient *n* Orient *m*. **o~al** *a* orientalisch ● *n* Orientale *m*/ Orientalin *f*

orientation *n* Orientierung *f*

origin *n* Ursprung *m*; (*of person, goods*) Herkunft *f*

original *a* ursprünglich; (*not copied*) original; (*new*) originell ● *n* Original *nt*. **~ity** *n* Originalität *f*. **~ly** *adv* ursprünglich

originate *vi* entstehen

ornament *n* Ziergegenstand *m*; (*decoration*) Verzierung *f*. **~al** *a* dekorativ

ornate *a* reich verziert

ornithology *n* Vogelkunde *f*

orphan *n* Waisenkind *nt*, Waise *f*. **~age** *n* Waisenhaus *nt*

orthodox *a* orthodox

ostensible *a*, **-bly** *adv* angeblich

ostentat|ion *n* Protzerei *f* ⚠. **~ious** *a* protzig ⚠

osteopath *n* Osteopath *m*

ostrich *n* Strauß *m*

other *a*, *pron* & *n* andere(r,s); **the ~ [one]** der/die/das andere; **the ~ two** die zwei anderen; **no ~s** sonst keine;

any ~ questions? sonst noch Fragen? **every ~ day** jeden zweiten Tag; **the ~ day** neulich; **the ~ evening** neulich abends; **someone/ something or ~** irgendjemand/-etwas ● *adv* anders; **~ than him** außer ihm; **somehow/somewhere or ~** irgendwie/irgendwo

otherwise *adv* sonst; (*differently*) anders

ought *v aux* I/we **~ to stay** ich sollte/wir sollten eigentlich bleiben; **he ~ not to have done it** er hätte es nicht machen sollen

ounce *n* Unze *f* (*28, 35 g*)

our *a* unser

ours *poss pron* unsere(r,s); **a friend of ~** ein Freund von uns; **that is ~** das gehört uns

ourselves *pron* selbst; (*refl*) uns; **by ~** allein

out *adv* (*not at home*) weg; (*outside*) draußen; (*not alight*) aus; (*unconscious*) bewusstlos; **be ~** *<sun:>* scheinen; *<flower>* blühen; *<workers>* streiken; *<calculation:>* nicht stimmen; (*Sport*) aus sein; (*fig: not feasible*) nicht infrage kommen; **~ and about** unterwegs; **have it ~ with s.o.** 🄸 jdn zur Rede stellen; **get ~!** 🄸 raus! **~ with it!** 🄸 heraus damit! ● *prep* **~ of** aus (+ *dat*); **go ~ (of) the door** zur Tür hinausgehen; **be ~ of bed/ the room** nicht im Bett/im Zimmer sein; **~ of breath/ danger** außer Atem/Gefahr; **~ of work** arbeitslos; **nine ~ of ten** neun von zehn; **be ~ of sugar** keinen Zucker mehr haben

outboard *a* **~ motor** Außenbordmotor *m*

outbreak *n* Ausbruch *m*

outbuilding *n* Nebengebäude *nt*

outburst *n* Ausbruch *m*

outcast *n* Ausgestoßene(r) *m/f*

outcome *n* Ergebnis *nt*

outcry *n* Aufschrei *m* [der Entrüstung]

outdated *a* überholt

outdo *vt* (*pt* -did, *pp* -done) übertreffen, übertrumpfen

outdoor *a* *<life, sports>* im Freien; **~ swimming pool** Freibad *nt*

outdoors *adv* draußen; **go ~** nach draußen gehen

outer *a* äußere(r,s)

outfit *n* Ausstattung *f*; (*clothes*) Ensemble *nt*; (🄸 *organization*) Laden *m*

outgoing *a* ausscheidend; *<mail>* ausgehend; (*sociable*) kontaktfreudig, **~s** *npl* Ausgaben *pl*

outgrow *vi* (*pt* -grew, *pp* -grown) herauswachsen aus

outing *n* Ausflug *m*

outlaw *n* Geächtete(r) *m/f* ● *vt* ächten

outlay *n* Auslagen *pl*

outlet *n* Abzug *m*; (*for water*) Abfluss *m*; (*fig*) Ventil *nt*; (*Comm*) Absatzmöglichkeit *f*

outline *n* Umriss *m*; (*summary*) kurze Darstellung *f* ● *vt* umreißen

outlive *vt* überleben

outlook *n* Aussicht *f*; (*future prospect*) Aussichten *pl*; (*attitude*) Einstellung *f*

outmoded *a* überholt

outnumber *vt* zahlenmäßig überlegen sein (+ *dat*)

out-patient *n* ambulanter Patient *m*

outpost *n* Vorposten *m*

output *n* Leistung *f*; Produktion *f*

outrage *n* Gräueltat *f*; (*fig*) Skandal *m*; (*indignation*) Empörung *f*. **~ous** *a* empörend

outright[1] *a* völlig, total; *<refusal>* glatt

outright[2] *adv* ganz; (*at once*) sofort; (*frankly*) offen

outset *n* Anfang *m*

outside[1] *a* äußere(r,s); **~ wall** Außenwand *f* ● *n* Außenseite *f*; **from the ~** von außen; **at the ~** höchstens

outside[2] *adv* außen; (*out of doors*) draußen; **go ~** nach draußen gehen ● *prep* außerhalb (+ *gen*); (*in front of*) vor (+ *dat/acc*)

outsider *n* Außenseiter *m*

outsize *a* übergroß

outskirts *npl* Rand *m*

outspoken *a* offen; **be ~** kein Blatt vor den Mund nehmen

outstanding *a* hervorragend; (*conspicuous*) bemerkenswert; (*Comm*) ausstehend

outstretched *a* ausgestreckt

outvote *vt* überstimmen

outward *a* äußerlich; **~ journey** Hinreise *f* ● *adv* nach außen. **~ly** *adv* nach außen hin, äußerlich. **~s** *adv* nach außen

outwit *vt* (*pt/pp* -**witted**) überlisten

oval *a* oval ● *n* Oval *nt*

ovation *n* Ovation *f*

oven *n* Backofen *m*

over *prep* über (+ *acc/dat*); **~ dinner** beim Essen; **~ the phone** am Telefon; **~ the page** auf der nächsten Seite ● *adv* (*remaining*) übrig; (*ended*) zu Ende; **~ again** noch einmal; **~ and ~** immer wieder; **~ here/there** hier/da drüben; **all ~** (*everywhere*) überall; **it's all ~** es ist vorbei; **I ache all ~** mir tut alles weh

overall[1] *n* Kittel *m*; **~s** *pl* Overall *m*

overall[2] *a* gesamt; (*general*) allgemein ● *adv* insgesamt

overbalance *vi* das Gleichgewicht verlieren

overbearing *a* herrisch

overboard *adv* (*Naut*) über Bord

overcast *a* bedeckt

overcharge *vt* **~ s.o.** jdm zu viel berechnen ● *vi* zu viel verlangen

overcoat *n* Mantel *m*

overcome *vt* (*pt* -**came**, *pp* -**come**) überwinden; **be ~ by** überwältigt werden von

overcrowded *a* überfüllt

overdo *vt* (*pt* -**did**, *pp* -**done**) übertreiben; (*cook too long*) zu lange kochen; **~ it** (F do too much) sich übernehmen

overdose *n* Überdosis *f*

overdraft *n* [Konto]überziehung *f*; **have an ~** sein Konto überzogen haben

overdue *a* überfällig

overestimate *vt* überschätzen

overflow[1] *n* Überschuss *m*; (*outlet*) Überlauf *m*

overflow[2] *vi* überlaufen

overgrown *a* <*garden*> überwachsen

overhang[1] *n* Überhang *m*

overhang[2] *vt/i* (*pt/pp* -**hung**) überhängen (über + *acc*)

overhaul[1] *n* Überholung *f*

overhaul[2] *vt* (*Techn*) überholen

overhead[1] *adv* oben

overhead[2] *a* Ober-; (*ceiling*) Decken-. **~s** *npl* allgemeine Unkosten *pl*

overhear *vt* (*pt/pp* -**heard**) mit anhören <*conversation*>

overheat *vi* zu heiß werden

overjoyed *a* überglücklich

overland *a & adv* auf dem Landweg; **~ route** Landroute *f*

overlap *vi* (*pt/pp* -**lapped**) sich überschneiden

overleaf *adv* umseitig

overload *vt* überladen

overlook *vt* überblicken; (*fail to see, ignore*) übersehen

overnight[1] *adv* über Nacht; **stay ~** übernachten

overnight[2] *a* Nacht-; **~ stay** Übernachtung *f*

overpass *n* Überführung *f*

overpay *vt* (*pt/pp* -**paid**) überbezahlen

overpopulated *a* übervölkert

overpower *vt* überwältigen. **~ing** *a* überwältigend

overpriced *a* zu teuer

overrated *a* überbewertet

overreact *vi* überreagieren. **~ion** *n* Überreaktion *f*

overriding *a* Haupt-

overrule *vt* ablehnen; **we were ~d** wir wurden überstimmt

overrun *vt* (*pt* -**ran**, *pp* -**run**, *pres p* -**running**) überrennen; überschreiten <*time*>; **be ~ with** überlaufen sein von

overseas[1] *adv* in Übersee; **go ~** nach Übersee gehen

overseas[2] *a* Übersee-

oversee vt (pt -saw, pp -seen) beaufsichtigen

overshadow vt überschatten

overshoot vt (pt/pp -shot) hinausschießen über (+ acc)

oversight n Versehen nt

oversleep vi (pt/pp -slept) [sich] verschlafen

overstep vt (pt/pp -stepped) überschreiten

overt a offen

overtake vt/i (pt -took, pp -taken) überholen

overthrow vt (pt -threw, pp -thrown) (Pol) stürzen

overtime n Überstunden pl ● adv work ~ Überstunden machen

overtired a übermüdet

overture n (Mus) Ouvertüre f; ~s pl (fig) Annäherungsversuche pl

overturn vt umstoßen ● vi umkippen

overweight a übergewichtig; be ~ Übergewicht haben

overwhelm vt überwältigen. ~ing a überwältigend

overwork n Überarbeitung f ● vt überfordern ● vi sich überarbeiten

overwrought a überreizt

ow|e vt schulden/ (fig) verdanken ([to] s.o. jdm); ~e s.o. sth jdm etw schuldig sein. ~ing to prep wegen (+ gen)

owl n Eule f

own¹ a & pron eigen; it's my ~ es gehört mir; a car of my ~ mein eigenes Auto; on one's ~ allein; get one's ~ back Ⓘ sich revanchieren

own² vt besitzen; I don't ~ it es gehört mir nicht. ~ up vi es zugeben

owner n Eigentümer(in) m(f), Besitzer(in) m(f); (of shop)Inhaber(in) m(f). ~ship n Besitz m

oxygen n Sauerstoff m

oyster n Auster f

Pp

pace n Schritt m; (speed) Tempo nt; keep ~ with Schritt halten mit ● vi ~ up and down auf und ab gehen. ~-maker n (Sport & Med) Schrittmacher m

Pacific a & n the ~ [Ocean] der Pazifik

pacifist n Pazifist m

pacify vt (pt/pp -ied) beruhigen

pack n Packung f; (Mil) Tornister m; (of cards) [Karten]spiel nt; (gang) Bande f; (of hounds) Meute f; (of wolves) Rudel nt; a ~ of lies ein Haufen Lügen ● vt/i packen; einpacken <article>; be ~ed (crowded) [gedrängt] voll sein. ~ up vt einpacken ● vi Ⓘ <machine:> kaputtgehen

package n Paket nt. ~ holiday n Pauschalreise f

packet n Päckchen nt

packing n Verpackung f

pact n Pakt m

pad n Polster nt; (for writing) [Schreib]block m ● vt (pt/pp padded) polstern

padding n Polsterung f; (in written work) Füllwerk nt

paddle¹ n Paddel nt ● vt (row) paddeln

paddle² vi waten

paddock n Koppel f

padlock n Vorhängeschloss nt ● vt mit einem Vorhängeschloss verschließen

paediatrician n Kinderarzt m /-ärztin f

pagan a heidnisch ● n Heide m/ Heidin f

page¹ n Seite f

page² n (boy) Page m ● vt ausrufen <person>

paid *see* pay ● *a* bezahlt; **put ~ to** 🔲 zunichte machen

pail *n* Eimer *m*

pain *n* Schmerz *m*; **be in ~** Schmerzen haben; **take ~s** sich (*dat*) Mühe geben; **~ in the neck** 🔲 Nervensäge *f*

pain: ~ful *a* schmerzhaft; (*fig*) schmerzlich. **~-killer** *n* schmerzstillendes Mittel *nt*. **~less** *a*, **-ly** *adv* schmerzlos

painstaking *a* sorgfältig

paint *n* Farbe *f* ● *vt/i* streichen; <*artist:*> malen. **~brush** *n* Pinsel *m*. **~er** *n* Maler *m*; (*decorator*) Anstreicher *m*. **~ing** *n* Malerei *f*; (*picture*) Gemälde *nt*

pair *n* Paar *nt*; **~ of trousers** Hose *f* ● *vi* **~ off** Paare bilden

pajamas *n pl* (*Amer*) Schlafanzug *m*

Pakistan *n* Pakistan *nt*. **~i** *a* pakistanisch ● *n* Pakistaner(in) *m(f)*

pal *n* Freund(in) *m(f)*

palace *n* Palast *m*

palatable *a* schmackhaft

palate *n* Gaumen *m*

palatial *a* palastartig

pale *a* (-r, -st) blass ● *vi* blass werden. **~ness** *n* Blässe *f*

Palestin|e *n* Palästina *nt*. **~ian** *a* palästinensisch ● *n* Palästinenser(in) *m(f)*

palette *n* Palette *f*

palm *n* Handfläche *f*; (*tree, symbol*) Palme *f* ● *vt* **~ sth off on s.o.** jdm etw andrehen. **P~ Sunday** *n* Palmsonntag *m*

palpable *a* tastbar; (*perceptible*) spürbar

palpitations *npl* Herzklopfen *nt*

paltry *a* (-ier, -iest) armselig

pamper *vt* verwöhnen

pamphlet *n* Broschüre *f*

pan *n* Pfanne *f*; (*saucepan*) Topf *m*; (*of scales*) Schale *f*

panacea *n* Allheilmittel *nt*

pancake *n* Pfannkuchen *m*

panda *n* Panda *m*

pandemonium *n* Höllenlärm *m*

pane *n* [Glas]scheibe *f*

panel *n* Tafel *f*, Platte *f*; **~ of experts** Expertenrunde *f*; **~ of judges** Jury *f*. **~ling** *n* Täfelung *f*

pang *n* **~s of hunger** Hungergefühl *nt*; **~s of conscience** Gewissensbisse *pl*

panic *n* Panik *f* ● *vi* (*pt/pp* panicked) in Panik geraten. **~-stricken** *a* von Panik ergriffen

panoram|a *n* Panorama *nt*. **~ic** *a* Panorama-

pansy *n* Stiefmütterchen *nt*

pant *vi* keuchen; <*dog:*> hecheln

panther *n* Panther *m*

panties *npl* [Damen]slip *m*

pantomime *n* [zu Weihnachten aufgeführte] Märchenvorstellung *f*

pantry *n* Speisekammer *f*

pants *npl* Unterhose *f*; (*woman's*) Schlüpfer *m*; (*trousers*) Hose *f*

pantyhose *n* (*Amer*) Strumpfhose *f*

paper *n* Papier *nt*; (*newspaper*) Zeitung *f*; (*exam ~*) Testbogen *m*; (*exam*) Klausur *f*; (*treatise*) Referat *nt*; **~s** *pl* (*documents*) Unterlagen *pl*; (*for identification*) [Ausweis]papiere *pl* ● *vt* tapezieren

paper: ~back *n* Taschenbuch *nt*. **~-clip** *n* Büroklammer *f*. **~weight** *n* Briefbeschwerer *m*. **~work** *n* Schreibarbeit *f*

par *n* (*Golf*) Par *nt*; **on a ~** gleichwertig (**with** *dat*)

parable *n* Gleichnis *nt*

parachut|e *n* Fallschirm *m* ● *vi* [mit dem Fallschirm] abspringen. **~ist** *n* Fallschirmspringer *m*

parade *n* Parade *f*; (*procession*) Festzug *m* ● *vt* (*show off*) zur Schau stellen

paradise *n* Paradies *nt*

paradox *n* Paradox *nt*. **~ical** *a* paradox

paraffin *n* Paraffin *nt*

paragraph *n* Absatz *m*

parallel *a & adv* parallel ● *n* (*Geog*) Breitenkreis *m*; (*fig*) Parallele *f*

paralyse *vt* lähmen; (*fig*) lahmlegen

paralysis *n* (*pl* -ses) Lähmung *f*

paranoid a [krankhaft] misstrauisch

parapet n Brüstung f

paraphernalia n Kram m

parasite n Parasit m, Schmarotzer m

paratrooper n Fallschirmjäger m

parcel n Paket nt

parch vt austrocknen; be ~ed <person:> einen furchtbaren Durst haben

parchment n Pergament nt

pardon n Verzeihung f; (Jur) Begnadigung f; ~? Ⓣ bitte? I beg your ~ wie bitte? (sorry) Verzeihung! ● vt verzeihen; (Jur) begnadigen

parent n Elternteil m; ~s pl Eltern pl. ~al a elterlich

parenthesis n (pl -ses) Klammer f

parish n Gemeinde f. ~ioner n Gemeindemitglied nt

park n Park m ● vt/i parken

parking n Parken nt; 'no ~' 'Parken verboten'. ~-lot n (Amer) Parkplatz m. ~-meter n Parkuhr f. ~ space n Parkplatz m

parliament n Parlament nt. ~ary a parlamentarisch

parochial a Gemeinde-; (fig) beschränkt

parody n Parodie f ● vt (pt/pp -ied) parodieren

parole n on ~ auf Bewährung

parquet n ~ floor Parkett nt

parrot n Papagei m

parsley n Petersilie f

parsnip n Pastinake f

parson n Pfarrer m

part n Teil m; (Techn) Teil nt; (area) Gegend f; (Theat) Rolle f; (Mus) Part m; spare ~ Ersatzteil nt; for my ~ meinerseits; on the ~ of vonseiten (+ gen); take s.o.'s ~ für jdn Partei ergreifen; take ~ in teilnehmen an (+ dat) ● adv teils ● vt trennen; scheiteln <hair> ● vi <people:> sich trennen; ~ with sich trennen von

partial a Teil-; be ~ to mögen. -ly adv teilweise

particip|ant n Teilnehmer(in) m(f). ~ate vi teilnehmen (in an + dat). ~ation n Teilnahme f

particle n Körnchen nt; (Phys) Partikel nt; (Gram) Partikel f

particular a besondere(r,s); (precise) genau; (fastidious) penibel; in ~ besonders. ~ly adv besonders. ~s npl nähere Angaben pl

parting n Abschied m; (in hair) Scheitel m

partition n Trennwand f; (Pol) Teilung f ● vt teilen

partly adv teilweise

partner n Partner(in) m(f); (Comm) Teilhaber m. ~ship n Partnerschaft f; (Comm) Teilhaberschaft f

partridge n Rebhuhn n

part-time a & adv Teilzeit-; be or work ~ Teilzeitarbeit machen

party n Party f, Fest nt; (group) Gruppe f; (Pol, Jur) Partei f

pass n Ausweis m; (Geog, Sport) Pass m; (Sch) ≈ ausreichend; get a ~ bestehen ● vt vorbeigehen/-fahren an (+ dat); (overtake) überholen; (hand) reichen; (Sport) abgeben, abspielen; (approve) annehmen; (exceed) übersteigen; bestehen <exam>; machen <remark>; fällen <judgement>; (Jur) verhängen <sentence>; ~ the time sich (dat) die Zeit vertreiben; ~ one's hand over sth mit der Hand über etw (acc) fahren ● vi vorbeigehen/-fahren; (get by) vorbeikommen; (overtake) überholen; <time:> vergehen; (in exam) bestehen; ~ away vi sterben. ~ down vt herunterreichen; (fig) weitergeben. ~ out vi ohnmächtig werden. ~ round vt herumreichen. ~ up vt heraufreichen; (Ⓣ miss) vorübergehen lassen

passable a <road> befahrbar; (satisfactory) passabel

passage n Durchgang m; (corridor) Gang m; (voyage) Überfahrt f; (in book) Passage f

passenger n Fahrgast m; (Naut, Aviat) Passagier m; (in car) Mitfahrer m. ~ seat n Beifahrersitz m

p

passer-by n (pl **-s-by**) Passant(in) m(f)

passion n Leidenschaft f. ~**ate** a, **-ly** adv leidenschaftlich

passive a passiv ● n Passiv nt

pass: ~**port** n [Reise]pass m. ~**word** n Kennwort nt; (Mil) Losung f

past a vergangene(r,s); (former) ehemalig; **that's all** ~ das ist jetzt vorbei ● n Vergangenheit f ● prep an (+ dat) ... vorbei; (after) nach; **at ten** ~ **two** um zehn nach zwei ● adv vorbei; **go** ~ vorbeigehen

pasta n Nudeln pl

paste n Brei m; (adhesive) Kleister m; (jewellery) Strass m ● vt kleistern

pastel n Pastellfarbe f, (drawing) Pastell ● attrib Pastell-

pastime n Zeitvertreib m

pastry n Teig m; **cakes and** ~**ies** Kuchen und Gebäck

pasture n Weide f

pasty n Pastete f

pat n Klaps m; (of butter) Stückchen nt ● vt (pt/pp **patted**) tätscheln; ~ **s.o. on the back** jdm auf die Schulter klopfen

patch n Flicken m; (spot) Fleck m; **not a** ~ **on** 🇮 gar nicht zu vergleichen mit ● vt flicken. ~ **up** vt [zusammen]flicken; beilegen <quarrel>

patchy a ungleichmäßig

patent n Patent nt ● vt patentieren. ~ **leather** n Lackleder nt

paternal a väterlich

path n (pl **-s**) [Fuß]weg m, Pfad m; (orbit, track) Bahn f; (fig) Weg m

pathetic a mitleiderregend; <attempt> erbärmlich

patience n Geduld f; (game) Patience f

patient a, **-ly** adv geduldig ● n Patient(in) m(f)

patio n Terrasse f

patriot n Patriot(in) m(f). ~**ic** a patriotisch. ~**ism** n Patriotismus m

patrol n Patrouille f ● vt/i patrouillieren [in (+ dat)]; <police:> auf Streife gehen/fahren [in (+ dat)]. ~ **car** n Streifenwagen m

patron n Gönner m; (of charity) Schirmherr m; (of the arts) Mäzen m; (customer) Kunde m/Kundin f; (Theat) Besucher m. ~**age** n Schirmherrschaft f

patroniz|e vt (fig) herablassend behandeln. ~**ing** a, **-ly** adv gönnerhaft

patter n (speech) Gerede nt

pattern n Muster nt

paunch n [Schmer]bauch m

pause n Pause f ● vi innehalten

pave vt pflastern; ~ **the way** den Weg bereiten (**for** dat). ~**ment** n Bürgersteig m

paw n Pfote f, (of large animal) Pranke f, Tatze f

pawn¹ n (Chess) Bauer m; (fig) Schachfigur f

pawn² vt verpfänden. ~ **broker** n Pfandleiher m

pay n Lohn m; (salary) Gehalt nt; **be in the** ~ **of** bezahlt werden von ● v (pt/pp **paid**) ● vt bezahlen; zahlen <money>; ~ **s.o. a visit** jdm einen Besuch abstatten; ~ **s.o. a compliment** jdm ein Kompliment machen ● vi zahlen; (be profitable) sich bezahlt machen; (fig) sich lohnen; ~ **for sth** etw bezahlen. ~ **back** vt zurückzahlen. ~ **in** vt einzahlen. ~ **off** vt abzahlen <debt> ● vi (fig) sich auszahlen

payable a zahlbar; **make** ~ **to** ausstellen auf (+ acc)

payment n Bezahlung f, (amount) Zahlung f

pea n Erbse f

peace n Frieden m; **for my** ~ **of mind** zu meiner eigenen Beruhigung

peace|ful a, **-ly** adv friedlich. ~**maker** n Friedensstifter m

peach n Pfirsich m

peacock n Pfau m

peak n Gipfel m; (fig) Höhepunkt m. ~**ed cap** n Schirmmütze f. ~ **hours** npl Hauptbelastungszeit f, (for traffic) Hauptverkehrszeit f

peal n (of bells) Glockengeläut nt; ~s of laughter schallendes Gelächter nt

peanut n Erdnuss f

pear n Birne f

pearl n Perle f

peasant n Bauer m

peat n Torf m

pebble n Kieselstein m

peck n Schnabelhieb m; (kiss) flüchtiger Kuss m ● vt/i picken/(nip) hacken (at nach)

peculiar a eigenartig, seltsam; ~ to eigentümlich (+ dat). ~ity n Eigenart f

pedal n Pedal nt ● vt fahren <bicycle> ● vi treten

pedantic a, -ally adv pedantisch

pedestal n Sockel m

pedestrian n Fußgänger(in) m(f) ● a (fig) prosaisch. ~ crossing n Fußgängerüberweg m. ~ precinct n Fußgängerzone f

pedigree n Stammbaum m ● attrib <animal> Rasse-

pedlar n Hausierer m

peek vi 🛈 gucken

peel n Schale f ● vt schälen; ● vi <skin:> sich schälen; <paint:> abblättern. ~ings npl Schalen pl

peep n kurzer Blick m ● vi gucken. ~-hole n Guckloch nt

peer¹ vi ~ at forschend ansehen

peer² n Peer m; his ~s pl seinesgleichen

peg n (hook) Haken m; (for tent) Pflock m, Hering m; (for clothes) [Wäsche]klammer f; off the ~ 🛈 von der Stange

pejorative a, -ly adv abwertend

pelican n Pelikan m

pellet n Kügelchen nt

pelt¹ n (skin) Pelz m, Fell nt

pelt² vt bewerfen ● vi ~ [down] <rain:> [hernieder]prasseln

pelvis n (Anat) Becken nt

pen¹ n (for animals) Hürde f

pen² n Federhalter m; (ballpoint) Kugelschreiber m

penal a Straf-. ~ize vt bestrafen; (fig) benachteiligen

penalty n Strafe f; (fine) Geldstrafe f; (Sport) Strafstoß m; (Football) Elfmeter m

penance n Buße f

pence see penny

pencil n Bleistift m ● vt (pt/pp pencilled) mit Bleistift schreiben. ~-sharpener n Bleistiftspitzer m

pendulum n Pendel nt

penetrat|e vt durchdringen; ~e into eindringen in (+ acc). ~ing a durchdringend. ~ion n Durchdringen nt

penfriend n Brieffreund(in) m(f)

penguin n Pinguin m

penicillin n Penizillin nt

peninsula n Halbinsel f

penis n Penis m

penitentiary n (Amer) Gefängnis nt

pen: ~knife n Taschenmesser nt. ~-name n Pseudonym nt

penniless a mittellos

penny n (pl pence; single coins pennies) Penny m; (Amer) Centstück nt; the ~'s dropped 🛈 der Groschen ist gefallen

pension n Rente f, (of civil servant) Pension f. ~er n Rentner(in) m(f); Pensionär(in) m(f)

pensive a nachdenklich

pent-up a angestaut

penultimate a vorletzte(r,s)

people npl Leute pl, Menschen pl; (citizens) Bevölkerung f; the ~ das Volk; English ~ die Engländer; ~ say man sagt; for four ~ für vier Personen ● vt bevölkern

pepper n Pfeffer m; (vegetable) Paprika m

pepper: ~mint n Pfefferminz nt; (Bot) Pfefferminze f. ~pot n Pfefferstreuer m

per prep pro; ~ cent Prozent nt

percentage n Prozentsatz m; (part) Teil m

perceptible a wahrnehmbar

percept|ion n Wahrnehmung f. ~ive a feinsinnig

perch¹ *n* Stange *f* ● *vi* <*bird*:> sich niederlassen

perch² *n inv* (*fish*) Barsch *m*

percussion *n* Schlagzeug *nt*. ∼ **instrument** *n* Schlaginstrument *nt*

perennial *a* <*problem*> immer wiederkehrend ● *n* (*Bot*) mehrjährige Pflanze *f*

perfect¹ *a* perfekt, vollkommen; (Ⅰ *utter*) völlig ● *n* (*Gram*) Perfekt *nt*

perfect² *vt* vervollkommnen. ∼**ion** *n* Vollkommenheit *f*; **to** ∼**ion** perfekt

perfectly *adv* perfekt; (*completely*) vollkommen, völlig

perforated *a* perforiert

perform *vt* ausführen; erfüllen <*duty*>; (*Theat*) aufführen <*play*>; spielen <*role*> ● *vi* (*Theat*) auftreten; (*Techn*) laufen. ∼**ance** *n* Aufführung *f*; (*at theatre, cinema*) Vorstellung *f*; (*Techn, Sport*) Leistung *f*. ∼**er** *n* Künstler(in) *m(f)*

perfume *n* Parfüm *nt*; (*smell*) Duft *m*

perhaps *adv* vielleicht

perilous *a* gefährlich

perimeter *n* [äußere] Grenze *f*; (*Geom*) Umfang *m*

period *n* Periode *f*; (*Sch*) Stunde *f*; (*full stop*) Punkt *m* ● *attrib* <*costume*> zeitgenössisch; <*furniture*> antik. ∼**ic** *a*, **-ally** *adv* periodisch. ∼**ical** *n* Zeitschrift *f*

peripher|al *a* nebensächlich. ∼**y** *n* Peripherie *f*

perish *vi* <*rubber*:> verrotten; <*food*:> verderben; (*liter: die*) ums Leben kommen. ∼**able** *a* leicht verderblich. ∼**ing** *a* (Ⅰ *cold*) eiskalt

perjur|e *vt* ∼**e oneself** einen Meineid leisten. ∼**y** *n* Meineid *m*

perk¹ *n* Ⅰ [Sonder]vergünstigung *f*

perk² *vi* ∼ **up** munter werden

perm *n* Dauerwelle *f* ● *vt* ∼ **s.o.'s hair** jdm eine Dauerwelle machen

permanent *a* ständig; <*job, address*> fest. ∼**ly** *adv* ständig; <*work, live*> dauernd, permanent; <*employed*> fest

permissible *a* erlaubt

permission *n* Erlaubnis *f*

permit¹ *vt* (*pt/pp* **-mitted**) erlauben (**s.o.** jdm)

permit² *n* Genehmigung *f*

perpendicular *a* senkrecht ● *n* Senkrechte *f*

perpetual *a*, **-ly** *adv* ständig, dauernd

perpetuate *vt* bewahren; verewigen <*error*>

perplex *vt* verblüffen. ∼**ed** *a* verblüfft

persecut|e *vt* verfolgen. ∼**ion** *n* Verfolgung *f*

perseverance *n* Ausdauer *f*

persevere *vi* beharrlich weitermachen

Persia *n* Persien *nt*

Persian *a* persisch; <*cat, carpet*> Perser-

persist *vi* beharrlich weitermachen; (*continue*) anhalten; <*view*:> weiter bestehen; ∼ **in doing sth** dabei bleiben, etw zu tun. ∼**ence** *n* Beharrlichkeit *f*. ∼**ent** *a*, **-ly** *adv* beharrlich; (*continuous*) anhaltend

person *n* Person *f*; **in** ∼ persönlich

personal *a*, **-ly** *adv* persönlich. ∼ **hygiene** *n* Körperpflege *f*

personality *n* Persönlichkeit *f*

personify *vt* (*pt/pp* **-ied**) personifizieren, verkörpern

personnel *n* Personal *nt*

perspective *n* Perspektive *f*

persp|iration *n* Schweiß *m*. ∼**ire** *vi* schwitzen

persua|de *vt* überreden; (*convince*) überzeugen. ∼**sion** *n* Überredung *f*; (*powers of* ∼**sion**) Überredungskunst *f*

persuasive *a*, **-ly** *adv* beredsam; (*convincing*) überzeugend

pertinent *a* relevant (**to** für)

perturb *vt* beunruhigen

peruse *vt* lesen

pervers|e *a* eigensinnig. ∼**ion** *n* Perversion *f*

pervert¹ *vt* verdrehen; verführen <*person*>

pervert² *n* Perverse(r) *m*

p

pessimis|m n Pessimismus m. ~t
n Pessimist m. ~tic a, -ally adv
pessimistisch

pest n Schädling m; (🔲 person)
Nervensäge f

pester vt belästigen

pesticide n
Schädlingsbekämpfungsmittel nt

pet n Haustier nt; (favourite) Liebling
m ● vt (pt/pp petted) liebkosen

petal n Blütenblatt nt

peter vi ~ out allmählich aufhören

petition n Bittschrift f

pet name n Kosename m

petrified a vor Angst wie
versteinert

petrol n Benzin nt

petroleum n Petroleum nt

petrol: ~-pump n Zapfsäule f. ~
station n Tankstelle f. ~ tank n
Benzintank m

petticoat n Unterrock m

petty a (-ier, -iest) kleinlich. ~
cash n Portokasse f

petulant a gekränkt

pew n [Kirchen]bank f

pharmaceutical a
pharmazeutisch

pharmac|ist n Apotheker(in) m(f).
~y n Pharmazie f; (shop) Apotheke f

phase n Phase f ● vt ~ in/out
allmählich einführen/abbauen

Ph.D. (abbr of Doctor of Philosophy)
Dr. phil.

pheasant n Fasan m

phenomen|al a phänomenal. ~on
n (pl -na) Phänomen nt

philharmonic n (orchestra)
Philharmoniker pl

Philippines npl Philippinen pl

philistine n Banause m

philosoph|er n Philosoph m.
~ical a, -ly adv philosophisch. ~y
n Philosophie f

phlegmatic a phlegmatisch

phobia n Phobie f

phone n Telefon nt; be on the ~
Telefon haben; (be phoning)
telefonieren ● vt anrufen ● vi
telefonieren. ~ back vt/i

zurückrufen. ~ book n
Telefonbuch nt. ~ box n
Telefonzelle f. ~ card n
Telefonkarte f. ~-in n (Radio)
Hörersendung f. ~ number n
Telefonnummer f

phonetic a phonetisch. ~s n
Phonetik f

phoney a (-ier, -iest) falsch; (forged)
gefälscht

photo n Foto nt, Aufnahme f.
~copier n Fotokopiergerät nt.
~copy n Fotokopie f ● vt
fotokopieren

photogenic a fotogen

photograph n Fotografie f,
Aufnahme f ● vt fotografieren

photograph|er n Fotograf(in) m(f).
~ic a, -ally adv fotografisch. ~y n
Fotografie f

phrase n Redensart f ● vt
formulieren. ~-book n
Sprachführer m

physical a, -ly adv körperlich

physician n Arzt m/ Ärztin f

physic|ist n Physiker(in) m(f). ~s
n Physik f

physiotherap|ist n
Physiotherapeut(in) m(f). ~y n
Physiotherapie f

physique n Körperbau m

pianist n Klavierspieler(in) m(f);
(professional) Pianist(in) m(f)

piano n Klavier nt

pick¹ n Spitzhacke f

pick² n Auslese f; take one's ~ sich
(dat) aussuchen ● vt/i (pluck)
pflücken; (select) wählen, sich (dat)
aussuchen; ~ and choose
wählerisch sein; ~ a quarrel einen
Streit anfangen; ~ holes in 🔲
kritisieren; ~ at one's food im
Essen herumstochern. ~ on vt
wählen; (🔲 find fault with)
herumhacken auf (+ dat). ~ up vt
in die Hand nehmen; (off the ground)
aufheben; hochnehmen <baby>;
(learn) lernen; (acquire) erwerben;
(buy) kaufen; (Teleph) abnehmen
<receiver>; auffangen <signal>;
(collect) abholen; aufnehmen
<passengers>; <police:> aufgreifen

p

<criminal>; sich holen <illness>; ⊞
aufgabeln <girl>; ～ oneself up
aufstehen ● vi (improve) sich
bessern

pickaxe n Spitzhacke f

picket n Streikposten m

pickle n (Amer: gherkin) Essiggurke
f; ～s pl [Mixed] Pickles pl ● vt
einlegen

pick: ～pocket n Taschendieb m.
～-up n (truck) Lieferwagen m

picnic n Picknick nt ● vi (pt/pp
-nicked) picknicken

picture n Bild nt; (film) Film m; as
pretty as a ～ bildhübsch; put s.o. in
the ～ (fig) jdn ins Bild setzen ● vt
(imagine) sich (dat) vorstellen

picturesque a malerisch

pie n Pastete f; (fruit) Kuchen m

piece n Stück nt; (of set) Teil nt; (in
game) Stein m; (Journ) Artikel m; a
～ of bread/paper ein Stück Brot/
Papier; a ～ of news/advice eine
Nachricht/ein Rat; take to ～s
auseinander nehmen ● vt ～ together
zusammensetzen; (fig)
zusammenstückeln. ～meal adv
stückweise

pier n Pier m; (pillar) Pfeiler m

pierc|e vt durchstechen. ～ing a
durchdringend

pig n Schwein nt

pigeon n Taube f. ～hole n Fach nt

piggy|back n give s.o. a ～back jdn
huckepack tragen. ～ bank n
Sparschwein nt

pigheaded a ⊞ starrköpfig

pigment n Pigment nt

pig: ～skin n Schweinsleder nt.
～sty n Schweinestall m. ～tail n ⊞
Zopf m

pilchard n Sardine f

pile¹ n (of fabric) Flor m

pile² n Haufen m ● vt ～ sth on to sth
etw auf etw (acc) häufen. ～ up vt
häufen ● vi sich häufen

piles npl Hämorrhoiden pl

pile-up n Massenkarambolage f

pilgrim n Pilger(in) m(f). ～age n
Pilgerfahrt f, Wallfahrt f

pill n Pille f

pillar n Säule f. ～-box n
Briefkasten m

pillow n Kopfkissen nt. ～case n
Kopfkissenbezug m

pilot n Pilot m; (Naut) Lotse m ● vt
fliegen <plane>; lotsen <ship>. ～-
light n Zündflamme f

pimple n Pickel m

pin n Stecknadel f; (Techn) Bolzen m,
Stift m; (Med) Nagel m; I have ～s
and needles in my leg ⊞ mein Bein
ist eingeschlafen ● vt (pt/pp pinned)
anstecken (to/on an + acc); (sewing)
stecken; (hold down) festhalten

pinafore n Schürze f. ～ dress n
Kleiderrock m

pincers npl Kneifzange f; (Zool)
Scheren pl

pinch n Kniff m; (of salt) Prise f; at a
～ ⊞ zur Not ● vt kneifen, zwicken;
(fam; steal) klauen; ～ one's finger
sich (dat) den Finger klemmen ● vi
<shoe:> drücken

pine¹ n (tree) Kiefer f

pine² vi ～ for sich sehnen nach

pineapple n Ananas f

ping-pong n Tischtennis nt

pink a rosa

pinnacle n Gipfel m; (on roof)
Turmspitze f

pin: ～point vt genau festlegen.
～stripe n Nadelstreifen m

pint n Pint nt (0,57 l, Amer: 0,47 l)

pioneer n Pionier m ● vt
bahnbrechende Arbeit leisten für

pious a, -ly adv fromm

pip¹ n (seed) Kern m

pip² n (sound) Tonsignal nt

pipe n Pfeife f; (for water, gas) Rohr
nt ● vt in Rohren leiten; (Culin)
spritzen

pipe: ～dream n Luftschloss nt.
～line n Pipeline f; in the ～line ⊞
in Vorbereitung

piping a ～ hot kochend heiß

pirate n Pirat m

piss vi ⊠ pissen

pistol n Pistole f

piston n (Techn) Kolben m

pit n Grube f; (for orchestra) Orchestergraben m

pitch¹ n (steepness) Schräge f; (of voice) Stimmlage f; (of sound) [Ton]höhe f; (Sport) Feld nt; (of street trader) Standplatz m; (fig: degree) Grad m ● vt werfen; aufschlagen <tent> ● vi fallen

pitch² n (tar) Pech nt. **~-black** a pechschwarz. **~-dark** a stockdunkel

piteous a erbärmlich

pitfall n (fig) Falle f

pith n (Bot) Mark nt; (of orange) weiße Haut f

pithy a (-ier, -iest) (fig) prägnant

piti|ful a bedauernswert. **~less** a mitleidslos

pittance n Hungerlohn m

pity n Mitleid nt, Erbarmen nt; [what a] ~! [wie] schade! take ~ on sich erbarmen über (+ acc) ● vt bemitleiden

pivot n Drehzapfen m ● vi sich drehen (on um)

pizza n Pizza f

placard n Plakat nt

placate vt beschwichtigen

place n Platz m; (spot) Stelle f; (town, village) Ort m; (🔲 house) Haus nt; out of ~ fehl am Platze; take ~ stattfinden ● vt setzen; (upright) stellen; (flat) legen; (remember) unterbringen 🔲; ~ an order eine Bestellung aufgeben; be ~d (in race) sich platzieren. **~-mat** n Set nt

placid a gelassen

plague n Pest f ● vt plagen

plaice n inv Scholle f

plain a (-er, -est) klar; (simple) einfach; (not pretty) nicht hübsch; (not patterned) einfarbig; <chocolate> zartbitter; in ~ clothes in Zivil ● adv (simply) einfach ● n Ebene f. **~ly** adv klar, deutlich; (simply) einfach; (obviously) offensichtlich

plait n Zopf m ● vt flechten

plan n Plan m ● vt (pt/pp planned) planen; (intend) vorhaben

plane¹ n (tree) Platane f

plane² n Flugzeug nt; (Geom & fig) Ebene f

plane³ n (Techn) Hobel m ● vt hobeln

planet n Planet m

plank n Brett nt; (thick) Planke f

planning n Planung f

plant n Pflanze f; (Techn) Anlage f; (factory) Werk nt ● vt pflanzen; (place in position) setzen; ~ oneself sich hinstellen. **~ation** n Plantage f

plaque n [Gedenk]tafel f; (on teeth) Zahnbelag m

plaster n Verputz m; (sticking ~) Pflaster nt; ~ [of Paris] Gips m ● vt verputzen <wall>; (cover) bedecken mit

plastic n Kunststoff m, Plastik nt ● a Kunststoff-, Plastik-; (malleable) formbar, plastisch

plastic surgery n plastische Chirurgie f

plate n Teller m; (flat sheet) Platte f; (with name, number) Schild nt; (gold and silverware) vergoldete/ versilberte Ware f; (in book) Tafel f ● vt (with gold) vergolden; (with silver) versilbern

platform n Plattform f; (stage) Podium nt; (Rail) Bahnsteig m; ~ 5 Gleis 5

platinum n Platin nt

platitude n Plattitüde f

plausible a plausibel

play n Spiel nt; [Theater]stück nt; (Radio) Hörspiel nt; (TV) Fernsehspiel nt; ~ on words Wortspiel nt ● vt/i spielen; ausspielen <card>; ~ safe sichergehen. **~ down** vt herunterspielen. ~ **up** vi 🔲 Mätzchen machen

play: ~**er** n Spieler(in) m(f). **~ful** a, **-ly** adv verspielt. ~**ground** n Spielplatz m; (Sch) Schulhof m. ~**group** n Kindergarten m

playing: ~**-card** n Spielkarte f. ~**field** n Sportplatz m

play: ~**mate** n Spielkamerad m. ~**thing** n Spielzeug nt. ~**wright** n Dramatiker m

p

plc *abbr* (public limited company) ≈ GmbH

plea *n* Bitte *f*; **make a ~ for** bitten um

plead *vi* flehen (**for** um); **~ guilty** sich schuldig bekennen; **~ with s.o.** jdn anflehen

pleasant *a* angenehm; <*person*> nett. **~ly** *adv* angenehm; <*say, smile*> freundlich

pleas|e *adv* bitte ● *vt* gefallen (+ *dat*); **~e s.o.** jdm eine Freude machen; **~e oneself** tun, was man will. **~ed** *a* erfreut; **be ~ed with/ about sth** sich über etw (*acc*) freuen. **~ing** *a* erfreulich

pleasure *n* Vergnügen *nt*; (*joy*) Freude *f*; **with ~** gern[e]

pleat *n* Falte *f* ● *vt* fälteln

pledge *n* Versprechen *nt* ● *vt* verpfänden; versprechen

plentiful *a* reichlich

plenty *n* eine Menge; (*enough*) reichlich; **~ of money/people** viel Geld/viele Leute

pliable *a* biegsam

pliers *npl* [Flach]zange *f*

plight *n* [Not]lage *f*

plinth *n* Sockel *m*

plod *vi* (*pt/pp* plodded) trotten; (*work*) sich abmühen

plonk *n* 🔲 billiger Wein *m*

plot *n* Komplott *nt*; (*of novel*) Handlung *f*; **~ of land** Stück *nt* Land ● *vt* einzeichnen ● *vi* ein Komplott schmieden

plough *n* Pflug *m* ● *vt/i* pflügen

ploy *n* 🔲 Trick *m*

pluck *n* Mut *m* ● *vt* zupfen; rupfen <*bird*>; pflücken <*flower*>; **~ up courage** Mut fassen

plucky *a* (-ier, -iest) tapfer, mutig

plug *n* Stöpsel *m*; (*wood*) Zapfen *m*; (*cotton wool*) Bausch *m*; (*Electr*) Stecker *m*; (*Auto*) Zündkerze *f*; (🔲 *advertisement*) Schleichwerbung *f* ● *vt* zustopfen; (🔲 *advertise*) Schleichwerbung machen für. **~ in** *vt* (*Electr*) einstecken

plum *n* Pflaume *f*

plumage *n* Gefieder *nt*

plumb|er *n* Klempner *m*. **~ing** *n* Wasserleitungen *pl*

plume *n* Feder *f*

plump *a* (-er, -est) mollig, rundlich ● *vt* **~ for** wählen

plunge *n* Sprung *m*; **take the ~** 🔲 den Schritt wagen ● *vt/i* tauchen

plural *a* pluralisch ● *n* Mehrzahl *f*, Plural *m*

plus *prep* plus (+ *dat*) ● *a* Plus- ● *n* Pluszeichen *nt*; (*advantage*) Plus *nt*

plush[y] *a* luxuriös

ply *vt* (*pt/pp* plied) ausüben <*trade*>; **~ s.o. with drink** jdm ein Glas nach dem anderen eingießen. **~wood** *n* Sperrholz *nt*

p.m. *adv* (*abbr of* post meridiem) nachmittags

pneumatic *a* pneumatisch. **~ drill** *n* Presslufthammer *m*

pneumonia *n* Lungenentzündung *f*

poach *vt* (*Culin*) pochieren; (*steal*) wildern. **~er** *n* Wilddieb *m*

pocket *n* Tasche *f*; **be out of ~** [an einem Geschäft] verlieren ● *vt* einstecken. **~-book** *n* Notizbuch *nt*; (*wallet*) Brieftasche *f*. **~-money** *n* Taschengeld *nt*

pod *n* Hülse *f*

poem *n* Gedicht *nt*

poet *n* Dichter(in) *m(f)*. **~ic** *a* dichterisch

poetry *n* Dichtung *f*

poignant *a* ergreifend

point *n* Punkt *m*; (*sharp end*) Spitze *f*; (*meaning*) Sinn *m*; (*purpose*) Zweck *m*; (*Electr*) Steckdose *f*; **~s** *pl* (*Rail*) Weiche *f*; **~ of view** Standpunkt *m*; **good/bad ~s** gute/schlechte Seiten; **what is the ~?** wozu? **the ~ is** es geht darum; **up to a ~** bis zu einem gewissen Grade; **be on the ~ of doing sth** im Begriff sein, etw zu tun ● *vt* richten (**at** auf + *acc*); ausfugen <*brickwork*> ● *vi* deuten (**at/to** auf + *acc*); (*with finger*) mit dem Finger zeigen. **~ out** *vt* zeigen auf (+ *acc*); **~ sth out to s.o.** jdn auf etw (*acc*) hinweisen

point-blank *a* aus nächster Entfernung; (*fig*) rundweg

point|ed a spitz; <*question*> gezielt. ~**less** a zwecklos, sinnlos

poise n Haltung f

poison n Gift nt ● vt vergiften. ~**ous** a giftig

poke n Stoß m ● vt stoßen; schüren <*fire*>; (*put*) stecken

poker[1] n Schüreisen nt

poker[2] n (*Cards*) Poker nt

poky a (-ier, -iest) eng

Poland n Polen nt

polar a Polar-. ~**bear** n Eisbär m

Pole n Pole m/Polin f

pole[1] n Stange f

pole[2] n (*Geog, Electr*) Pol m

pole-vault n Stabhochsprung m

police npl Polizei f

police: ~**man** n Polizist m. ~**station** n Polizeiwache f. ~**woman** n Polizistin f

policy[1] n Politik f

policy[2] n (*insurance*) Police f

Polish a polnisch

polish n (*shine*) Glanz m; (*for shoes*) [Schuh]creme f; (*for floor*) Bohnerwachs m; (*for furniture*) Politur f; (*for silver*) Putzmittel nt; (*for nails*) Lack m; (*fig*) Schliff m ● vt polieren; bohnern <*floor*>. ~**off** vt 🇮 verputzen <*food*>; erledigen <*task*>

polite a, -**ly** adv höflich. ~**ness** n Höflichkeit f

politic|al a, -**ly** adv politisch. ~**ian** n Politiker(in) m(f)

politics n Politik f

poll n Abstimmung f, (*election*) Wahl f; [opinion] ~ [Meinungs]umfrage f

pollen n Blütenstaub m, Pollen m

polling: ~-**booth** n Wahlkabine f. ~-**station** n Wahllokal nt

pollut|e vt verschmutzen. ~**ion** n Verschmutzung f

polo n Polo nt. ~-**neck** n Rollkragen m

polystyrene n Polystyrol nt; (*for packing*) Styropor (P) nt

polythene n Polyäthylen nt. ~**bag** n Plastiktüte f

pomp n Pomp m

pompous a, -**ly** adv großspurig

pond n Teich m

ponder vi nachdenken

ponderous a schwerfällig

pony n Pony nt. ~**tail** n Pferdeschwanz m

poodle n Pudel m

pool n [Schwimm]becken nt; (*pond*) Teich m; (*of blood*) Lache f; (*common fund*) [gemeinsame] Kasse f; ~**s** pl [Fußball]toto nt ● vt zusammenlegen

poor a (-er, -est) arm; (*not good*) schlecht; in ~ health nicht gesund. ~**ly** a be ~**ly** krank sein ● adv ärmlich; (*badly*) schlecht

pop[1] n Knall m ● v (*pt/pp* popped) ● vt (🇮 *put*) stecken (in in + acc) ● vi knallen; (*burst*) platzen. ~ in vi 🇮 reinschauen. ~ out vi 🇮 kurz rausgehen

pop[2] n 🇮 Popmusik f, Pop m ● attrib Pop-

popcorn n Puffmais m

pope n Papst m

poplar n Pappel f

poppy n Mohn m

popular a beliebt, populär; <*belief*> volkstümlich. ~**ity** n Beliebtheit f, Popularität f

populat|e vt bevölkern. ~**ion** n Bevölkerung f

porcelain n Porzellan nt

porch n Vorbau m; (*Amer*) Veranda f

porcupine n Stachelschwein nt

pore n Pore f

pork n Schweinefleisch nt

porn n 🇮 Porno m

pornograph|ic a pornographisch. ~**y** n Pornographie f

porridge n Haferbrei m

port[1] n Hafen m; (*town*) Hafenstadt f

port[2] n (*Naut*) Backbord nt

port[3] n (*wine*) Portwein m

portable a tragbar

porter n Portier m; (*for luggage*) Gepäckträger m

porthole n Bullauge nt

portion n Portion f; (*part, share*) Teil nt

portrait n Porträt nt

p

portray vt darstellen. ~**al** n Darstellung f

Portug|al n Portugal nt. ~**uese** a portugiesisch ● n Portugiese m/-giesin f

pose n Pose f ● vt aufwerfen <problem>; stellen <question> ● vi posieren; (for painter) Modell stehen

posh a 🔢 feudal

position n Platz m; (posture) Haltung f; (job) Stelle f; (situation) Lage f, Situation f; (status) Stellung f ● vt platzieren; ~ oneself sich stellen

positive a, **-ly** adv positiv; (definite) eindeutig; (real) ausgesprochen ● n Positiv nt

possess vt besitzen. ~**ion** n Besitz m; ~**ions** pl Sachen pl

possess|ive a Possessiv-; be ~ive about s.o. zu sehr an jdm hängen

possibility n Möglichkeit f

possib|le a möglich. ~**ly** adv möglicherweise; not ~**ly** unmöglich

post¹ n (pole) Pfosten m

post² n (place of duty) Posten m; (job) Stelle f

post³ n (mail) Post f; by ~ mit der Post ● vt aufgeben <letter>; (send by ~) mit der Post schicken; keep s.o. ~ed jdn auf dem Laufenden halten

postage n Porto nt

postal a Post-. ~ **order** n ≈ Geldanweisung f

post: ~**box** n Briefkasten m. ~**card** n Postkarte f; (picture) Ansichtskarte f. ~**code** n Postleitzahl f. ~**date** vt vordatieren

poster n Plakat nt

posterity n Nachwelt f

posthumous a, **-ly** adv postum

post: ~**man** n Briefträger m. ~**mark** n Poststempel m

post-mortem n Obduktion f

post office n Post f

postpone vt aufschieben; ~ until verschieben auf (+ acc). ~**ment** n Verschiebung f

postscript n Nachschrift f

posture n Haltung f

pot n Topf m; (for tea, coffee) Kanne f; ~**s of money** 🔢 eine Menge Geld

potato n (pl -es) Kartoffel f

potent a stark

potential a, **-ly** adv potenziell ● n Potenzial nt

pot: ~**hole** n Höhle f; (in road) Schlagloch nt. ~**shot** n take a ~-shot at schießen auf (+ acc)

potter n Töpfer(in) m(f). ~**y** n Töpferei f; (articles) Töpferwaren pl

potty a (-ier, -iest) 🔢 verrückt ● n Töpfchen nt

pouch n Beutel m

poultry n Geflügel nt

pounce vi zuschlagen; ~ **on** sich stürzen auf (+ acc)

pound¹ n (money & 0,454 kg) Pfund nt

pound² vi <heart:> hämmern; (run heavily) stampfen

pour vt gießen; einschenken <drink> ● vi strömen; (with rain) gießen. ~ **out** vi ausströmen ● vt ausschütten; einschenken <drink>

pout vi einen Schmollmund machen

poverty n Armut f

powder n Pulver nt; (cosmetic) Puder m ● vt pudern

power n Macht f; (strength) Kraft f; (Electr) Strom m; (nuclear) Energie f; (Math) Potenz f. ~ **cut** n Stromsperre f. ~**ed** a betrieben (by mit); ~**ed by electricity** mit Elektroantrieb. ~**ful** a mächtig; (strong) stark. ~**less** a machtlos. ~**station** n Kraftwerk nt

practicable a durchführbar, praktikabel

practical a, **-ly** adv praktisch. ~ **joke** n Streich m

practice n Praxis f; (custom) Brauch m; (habit) Gewohnheit f; (exercise) Übung f; (Sport) Training nt; in ~ (in reality) in der Praxis; out of ~ außer Übung; put into ~ ausführen

practise vt üben; (carry out) praktizieren; ausüben <profession> ● vi üben; <doctor:> praktizieren. ~**d** a geübt

praise n Lob nt ● vt loben.
~**worthy** a lobenswert
pram n Kinderwagen m
prank n Streich m
prawn n Garnele f, Krabbe f
pray vi beten. ~**er** n Gebet nt
preach vt/i predigen. ~**er** n
Prediger m
pre-arrange vt im Voraus
arrangieren
precarious a, -**ly** adv unsicher
precaution n Vorsichtsmaßnahme
f
precede vt vorangehen (+ dat)
preceden|ce n Vorrang m. ~**t** n
Präzedenzfall m
preceding a vorhergehend
precinct n Bereich m; (traffic-free)
Fußgängerzone f; (Amer: district)
Bezirk m
precious a kostbar; <style> preziös
● adv 🛈 ~ **little** recht wenig
precipice n Steilabfall m
precipitation n (Meteorol)
Niederschlag m
precis|e a, -**ly** adv genau. ~**ion** n
Genauigkeit f
precocious a frühreif
pre|conceived a vorgefasst.
~**conception** n vorgefasste
Meinung f
predator n Raubtier nt
predecessor n Vorgänger(in) m(f)
predicat|e n (Gram) Prädikat nt.
~**ive** a, -**ly** adv prädikativ
predict vt voraussagen. ~**able** a
voraussehbar; <person>
berechenbar. ~**ion** n Voraussage f
predomin|ant a vorherrschend.
~**antly** adv hauptsächlich,
überwiegend. ~**ate** vi vorherrschen
preen vt putzen
prefab n 🛈 [einfaches] Fertighaus
nt. ~**ricated** a vorgefertigt
preface n Vorwort nt
prefect n Präfekt m
prefer vt (pt/pp preferred) vorziehen;
I ~ **to walk** ich gehe lieber zu Fuß; I
~ **wine** ich trinke lieber Wein

prefera|ble a be ~**ble** vorzuziehen
sein (to dat). ~**bly** adv vorzugsweise
preferen|ce n Vorzug m. ~**tial** a
bevorzugt
pregnan|cy n Schwangerschaft f.
~**t** a schwanger; <animal> trächtig
prehistoric a prähistorisch
prejudice n Vorurteil nt; (bias)
Voreingenommenheit f ● vt
einnehmen (against gegen). ~**d** a
voreingenommen
preliminary a Vor-
prelude n Vorspiel nt
premature a vorzeitig; <birth>
Früh-. ~**ly** adv zu früh
premeditated a vorsätzlich
premier a führend ● n (Pol)
Premier[minister] m
premiere n Premiere f
premises npl Räumlichkeiten pl;
on the ~ im Haus
premium n Prämie f; be at a ~
hoch im Kurs stehen
premonition n Vorahnung f
preoccupied a [in Gedanken]
beschäftigt
preparation n Vorbereitung f;
(substance) Präparat nt
preparatory a Vor-
prepare vt vorbereiten; anrichten
<meal> ● vi sich vorbereiten (for auf
+ acc); ~**d** to bereit zu
preposition n Präposition f
preposterous a absurd
prerequisite n Voraussetzung f
Presbyterian a presbyterianisch
● n Presbyterianer(in) m(f)
prescribe vt vorschreiben; (Med)
verschreiben
prescription n (Med) Rezept nt
presence n Anwesenheit f,
Gegenwart f; ~ of mind
Geistesgegenwart f
present[1] a gegenwärtig; be ~
anwesend sein; (occur) vorkommen
● n Gegenwart f; (Gram) Präsens nt;
at ~ zurzeit; for the ~ vorläufig
present[2] n (gift) Geschenk nt
present[3] vt überreichen; (show)
zeigen; vorlegen <cheque>;

(introduce) vorstellen; ~ s.o. with sth jdm etw überreichen. **~able** *a* be ~able sich zeigen lassen können

presentation *n* Überreichung *f*

presently *adv* nachher; *(Amer: now)* zurzeit

preservation *n* Erhaltung *f*

preservative *n* Konservierungsmittel *nt*

preserve *vt* erhalten; *(Culin)* konservieren; *(bottle)* einmachen ● *n* *(Hunting & fig)* Revier *nt*; *(jam)* Konfitüre *f*

preside *vi* den Vorsitz haben **(over bei)**

presidency *n* Präsidentschaft *f*

president *n* Präsident *m*; *(Amer: chairman)* Vorsitzende(r) *m/f*. **~ial** *a* Präsidenten-; *<election>* Präsidentschafts-

press *n* Presse *f* ● *vt/i* drücken; drücken auf (+ *acc*) *<button>*; pressen *<flower>*; *(iron)* bügeln; *(urge)* bedrängen; ~ for drängen auf (+ *acc*); be ~ed for time in Zeitdruck sein. ~ on *vi* weitergehen/-fahren; *(fig)* weitermachen

press: ~ cutting *n* Zeitungsausschnitt *m*. **~ing** *a* dringend

pressure *n* Druck *m*. **~-cooker** *n* Schnellkochtopf *m*

pressurize *vt* Druck ausüben auf (+ *acc*). **~d** *a* Druck-

prestig|e *n* Prestige *nt*. **~ious** *a* Prestige-

presumably *adv* vermutlich

presume *vt* vermuten

presumpt|ion *n* Vermutung *f*; *(boldness)* Anmaßung *f*. **~uous** *a*, **-ly** *adv* anmaßend

pretence *n* Verstellung *f*; *(pretext)* Vorwand *m*

pretend *vt* *(claim)* vorgeben; ~ that so tun, als ob; ~ to be sich ausgeben als

pretentious *a* protzig

pretext *n* Vorwand *m*

pretty *a* (-ier, -iest), **-ily** *adv* hübsch ● *adv* (ⓘ *fairly*) ziemlich

prevail *vi* siegen; *<custom:>* vorherrschen; ~ on s.o. to do sth jdn dazu bringen, etw zu tun

prevalen|ce *n* Häufigkeit *f*. **~t** *a* vorherrschend

prevent *vt* verhindern, verhüten; ~ s.o. [from] doing sth jdn daran hindern, etw zu tun. **~ion** *n* Verhinderung *f*, Verhütung *f*. **~ive** *a* vorbeugend

preview *n* Voraufführung *f*

previous *a* vorhergehend; ~ to vor (+ *dat*). **~ly** *adv* vorher, früher

prey *n* Beute *f*; bird of ~ Raubvogel *m*

price *n* Preis *m* ● *vt* *(Comm)* auszeichnen. **~less** *a* unschätzbar; *(fig)* unbezahlbar

prick *n* Stich *m* ● *vt/i* stechen

prickl|e *n* Stachel *m*; *(thorn)* Dorn *m*. **~y** *a* stachelig; *<sensation>* stechend

pride *n* Stolz *m*; *(arrogance)* Hochmut *m* ● *vt* ~ oneself on stolz sein auf (+ *acc*)

priest *n* Priester *m*

prim *a* (primmer, primmest) prüde

primarily *adv* hauptsächlich, in erster Linie

primary *a* Haupt-. ~ school *n* Grundschule *f*

prime[1] *a* Haupt-; *(first-rate)* erstklassig

prime[2] *vt* scharf machen *<bomb>*; grundieren *<surface>*

Prime Minister *n* Premierminister(in) *m(f)*

primitive *a* primitiv

primrose *n* gelbe Schlüsselblume *f*

prince *n* Prinz *m*

princess *n* Prinzessin *f*

principal *a* Haupt- ● *n* *(Sch)* Rektor(in) *m(f)*

principally *adv* hauptsächlich

principle *n* Prinzip *nt*, Grundsatz *m*; in/on ~ im/aus Prinzip

print *n* Druck *m*; *(Phot)* Abzug *m*; in ~ gedruckt; *(available)* erhältlich; out of ~ vergriffen ● *vt* drucken; *(write in capitals)* in Druckschrift schreiben; *(Computing)* ausdrucken;

(*Phot*) abziehen. **~ed matter** *n* Drucksache *f*

print|er *n* Drucker *m*. **~ing** *n* Druck *m*

printout *n* (*Computing*) Ausdruck *m*

prior *a* frühere(r,s); **~ to** vor (+ *dat*)

priority *n* Priorität *f*, Vorrang *m*

prise *vt* **~ open/up** aufstemmen/ hochstemmen

prison *n* Gefängnis *nt*. **~er** *n* Gefangene(r) *m/f*

privacy *n* Privatsphäre *f*; **have no ~** nie für sich sein

private *a*, **-ly** *adv* privat; (*confidential*) vertraulich; <*car, secretary, school*> Privat- ● *n* (*Mil*) [einfacher] Soldat *m*; **in ~** privat; (*confidentially*) vertraulich

privation *n* Entbehrung *f*

privilege *n* Privileg *nt*. **~d** *a* privilegiert

prize *n* Preis *m* ● *vt* schätzen

pro *n* 🗓 Profi *m*; **the ~s and cons** das Für und Wider

probability *n* Wahrscheinlichkeit *f*

probable *a*, **-bly** *adv* wahrscheinlich

probation *n* (*Jur*) Bewährung *f*

probe *n* Sonde *f*; (*fig: investigation*) Untersuchung *f*

problem *n* Problem *nt*; (*Math*) Textaufgabe *f*. **~atic** *a* problematisch

procedure *n* Verfahren *nt*

proceed *vi* gehen; (*in vehicle*) fahren; (*continue*) weitergehen/ -fahren; (*speaking*) fortfahren; (*act*) verfahren

proceedings *npl* Verfahren *nt*; (*Jur*) Prozess *m*

proceeds *npl* Erlös *m*

process *n* Prozess *m*; (*procedure*) Verfahren *nt*; **in the ~** dabei ● *vt* verarbeiten; (*Admin*) bearbeiten; (*Phot*) entwickeln

procession *n* Umzug *m*, Prozession *f*

proclaim *vt* ausrufen

proclamation *n* Proklamation *f*

procure *vt* beschaffen

prod *n* Stoß *m* ● *vt* stoßen

prodigy *n* [**infant**] **~** Wunderkind *nt*

produce[1] *n* landwirtschaftliche Erzeugnisse *pl*

produce[2] *vt* erzeugen, produzieren; (*manufacture*) herstellen; (*bring out*) hervorholen; (*cause*) hervorrufen; inszenieren <*play*>; (*Radio, TV*) redigieren. **~r** *n* Erzeuger *m*, Produzent *m*; Hersteller *m*; (*Theat*) Regisseur *m*; (*Radio, TV*) Redakteur(in) *m(f)*

product *n* Erzeugnis *nt*, Produkt *nt*. **~ion** *n* Produktion *f*; (*Theat*) Inszenierung *f*

productiv|e *a* produktiv; <*land, talks*> fruchtbar. **~ity** *n* Produktivität *f*

profession *n* Beruf *m*. **~al** *a*, **-ly** *adv* beruflich; (*not amateur*) Berufs-; (*expert*) fachmännisch; (*Sport*) professionell ● *n* Fachmann *m*; (*Sport*) Profi *m*

professor *n* Professor *m*

proficien|cy *n* Können *nt*. **~t** *a* **be ~t in** beherrschen

profile *n* Profil *nt*; (*character study*) Porträt *nt*

profit *n* Gewinn *m*, Profit *m* ● *vi* **~ from** profitieren von. **~able** *a*, **-bly** *adv* gewinnbringend; (*fig*) nutzbringend

profound *a*, **-ly** *adv* tief

program (*Amer & Computing*) *n* Programm *nt* ● *vt* (*pt/pp* **programmed**) programmieren

programme *n* Programm *nt*; (*Radio, TV*) Sendung *f*. **~r** *n* (*Computing*) Programmierer(in) *m(f)*

progress[1] *n* Vorankommen *nt*; (*fig*) Fortschritt *m*; **in ~** im Gange; **make ~** (*fig*) Fortschritte machen

progress[2] *vi* vorankommen; (*fig*) fortschreiten. **~ion** *n* Folge *f*; (*development*) Entwicklung *f*

progressive *a* fortschrittlich. **~ly** *adv* zunehmend

prohibit *vt* verbieten (**s.o.** jdm). **~ive** *a* unerschwinglich

project[1] *n* Projekt *nt*; (*Sch*) Arbeit *f*

p

project² vt projizieren <film>; (plan) planen ● vi (jut out) vorstehen

projector n Projektor m

prolific a fruchtbar; (fig) produktiv

prologue n Prolog m

prolong vt verlängern

promenade n Promenade f ● vi spazieren gehen

prominent a vorstehend; (important) prominent; (conspicuous) auffällig

promiscuous a be ~ous häufig den Partner wechseln

promis|e n Versprechen nt ● vt/i versprechen (s.o. jdm). ~ing a viel versprechend

promot|e vt befördern; (advance) fördern; (publicize) Reklame machen für; be ~ed (Sport) aufsteigen. ~ion n Beförderung f; (Sport) Aufstieg m; (Comm) Reklame f

prompt a prompt, unverzüglich; (punctual) pünktlich ● adv pünktlich ● vt/i veranlassen (to zu); (Theat) soufflieren (+ dat). ~er n Souffleur m/Souffleuse f. ~ly adv prompt

prone a be or lie ~ auf dem Bauch liegen; be ~ to neigen zu

pronoun n Fürwort nt, Pronomen nt

pronounce vt aussprechen; (declare) erklären. ~d a ausgeprägt; (noticeable) deutlich. ~ment n Erklärung f

pronunciation n Aussprache f

proof n Beweis m; (Typ) Korrekturbogen m. ~-reader n Korrektor m

prop¹ n Stütze f ● vt (pt/pp propped) ~ against lehnen an (+ acc). ~ up vt stützen

prop² n (Theat 🔲) Requisit nt

propaganda n Propaganda f

propel vt (pt/pp propelled) [an]treiben. ~ler n Propeller m

proper a, -ly adv richtig; (decent) anständig

property n Eigentum nt; (quality) Eigenschaft f; (Theat) Requisit nt; (land) [Grund]besitz m; (house) Haus nt

prophecy n Prophezeiung f

prophesy vt (pt/pp -ied) prophezeien

prophet n Prophet m. ~ic a prophetisch

proportion n Verhältnis nt; (share) Teil m; ~s pl Proportionen; (dimensions) Maße. ~al a, -ly adv proportional

proposal n Vorschlag m; (of marriage) [Heirats]antrag m

propose vt vorschlagen; (intend) vorhaben; einbringen <motion> ● vi einen Heiratsantrag machen

proposition n Vorschlag m

proprietor n Inhaber(in) m(f)

propriety n Korrektheit f; (decorum) Anstand m

prose n Prosa f

prosecut|e vt strafrechtlich verfolgen. ~ion n strafrechtliche Verfolgung f; the ~ion die Anklage. ~or n [Public] P~or Staatsanwalt m

prospect n Aussicht f

prospect|ive a (future) zukünftig. ~or n Prospektor m

prospectus n Prospekt m

prosper vi gedeihen, florieren; <person> Erfolg haben. ~ity n Wohlstand m

prosperous a wohlhabend

prostitut|e n Prostituierte f. ~ion n Prostitution f

prostrate a ausgestreckt

protagonist n Kämpfer m; (fig) Protagonist m

protect vt schützen (from vor + dat); beschützen <person>. ~ion n Schutz m. ~ive a Schutz-; (fig) beschützend. ~or n Beschützer m

protein n Eiweiß nt

protest¹ n Protest m

protest² vi protestieren

Protestant a protestantisch ● n Protestant(in) m(f)

protester n Protestierende(r) m/f

prototype n Prototyp m

protrude vi [her]vorstehen

proud a, -ly adv stolz (of auf + acc)

prove vt beweisen ● vi ~ to be sich erweisen als

proverb n Sprichwort nt

provide vt zur Verfügung stellen; spenden <*shade*>; ~ s.o. with sth jdn mit etw versorgen od versehen ● vi ~ for sorgen für

provided conj ~ [that] vorausgesetzt [dass]

providen|ce n Vorsehung f. ~tial a be ~tial ein Glück sein

provinc|e n Provinz f; (fig) Bereich m. ~ial a provinziell

provision n Versorgung f (of mit); ~s pl Lebensmittel pl. ~al a, -ly adv vorläufig

provocat|ion n Provokation f. ~ive a, -ly adv provozierend; (sexually) aufreizend

provoke vt provozieren; (cause) hervorrufen

prow n Bug m

prowl vi herumschleichen

proximity n Nähe f

pruden|ce n Umsicht f. ~t a, -ly adv umsichtig; (wise) klug

prudish a prüde

prune[1] n Backpflaume f

prune[2] vt beschneiden

pry vi (pt/pp pried) neugierig sein

psalm n Psalm m

psychiatric a psychiatrisch

psychiatr|ist n Psychiater(in) m(f). ~y n Psychiatrie f

psychic a übersinnlich

psycho|analysis n Psychoanalyse f. ~analyst n Psychoanalytiker(in) m(f)

psychological a, -ly adv psychologisch; <*illness*> psychisch

psycholog|ist n Psychologe m/ -login f. ~y n Psychologie f

P.T.O. abbr (please turn over) b.w.

pub n 🄸 Kneipe f

puberty n Pubertät f

public a, -ly adv öffentlich; make ~ publik machen ● n the ~ die Öffentlichkeit

publican n [Gast]wirt m

publication n Veröffentlichung f

public: ~ holiday n gesetzlicher Feiertag m. ~ house n [Gast]wirtschaft f

publicity n Publicity f; (advertising) Reklame f

publicize vt Reklame machen für

public: ~ school n Privatschule f; (Amer) staatliche Schule f. ~-spirited a be ~-spirited Gemeinsinn haben

publish vt veröffentlichen. ~er n Verleger(in) m(f); (firm) Verlag m. ~ing n Verlagswesen nt

pudding n Pudding m; (course) Nachtisch m

puddle n Pfütze f

puff n (of wind) Hauch m; (of smoke) Wölkchen nt ● vt blasen, pusten; ~ out ausstoßen. ~ vi keuchen; ~ at paffen an (+ dat) <*pipe*>. ~ed a (out of breath) aus der Puste. ~ pastry n Blätterteig m

pull n Zug m; (jerk) Ruck m; (🄸 influence) Einfluss m ● vt ziehen; ziehen an (+ dat) <*rope*>; ~ a muscle sich (dat) einen Muskel zerren; ~ oneself together sich zusammennehmen; ~ one's weight tüchtig mitarbeiten; ~ s.o.'s leg 🄸 jdn auf den Arm nehmen. ~ down vt herunterziehen; (demolish) abreißen. ~ in vt hereinziehen ● vi (Auto) einscheren. ~ off vt abziehen; 🄸 schaffen. ~ out vt herausziehen ● vi (Auto) ausscheren. ~ through vt durchziehen ● vi (recover) durchkommen. ~ up vt heraufziehen; ausziehen <*plant*> ● vi (Auto) anhalten

pullover n Pullover m

pulp n Brei m; (of fruit) [Frucht]fleisch nt

pulpit n Kanzel f

pulse n Puls m

pulses npl Hülsenfrüchte pl

pummel vt (pt/pp pummelled) mit den Fäusten bearbeiten

pump n Pumpe f ● vt pumpen; 🄸 aushorchen. ~ up vt (inflate) aufpumpen

pumpkin n Kürbis m

pun n Wortspiel nt

punch¹ n Faustschlag m; (device) Locher m ● vt boxen; lochen <ticket>; stanzen <hole>

punch² n (drink) Bowle f

punctual a, **-ly** adv pünktlich. **~ity** n Pünktlichkeit f

punctuat|e vt mit Satzzeichen versehen. **~ion** n Interpunktion f

puncture n Loch nt; (tyre) Reifenpanne f ● vt durchstechen

punish vt bestrafen. **~able** a strafbar. **~ment** n Strafe f

punt n (boat) Stechkahn m

puny a (-ier, -iest) mickerig

pup n = puppy

pupil n Schüler(in) m(f); (of eye) Pupille f

puppet n Puppe f; (fig) Marionette f

puppy n junger Hund m

purchase n Kauf m; (leverage) Hebelkraft f ● vt kaufen. **~r** n Käufer m

pure a (-r, -st,) **-ly** adv rein

purge n (Pol) Säuberungsaktion f ● vt reinigen

puri|fication n Reinigung f. **~fy** vt (pt/pp -ied) reinigen

puritanical a puritanisch

purity n Reinheit f

purple a [dunkel]lila

purpose n Zweck m; (intention) Absicht f; (determination) Entschlossenheit f; on ~ absichtlich. **~ful** a, **-ly** adv entschlossen. **~ly** adv absichtlich

purr vi schnurren

purse n Portemonnaie nt; (Amer: handbag) Handtasche f

pursue vt verfolgen; (fig) nachgehen (+ dat). **~r** n Verfolger m

pursuit n Verfolgung f; Jagd f; (pastime) Beschäftigung f

pus n Eiter m

push n Stoß m; get the ~ 🄸 hinausfliegen ● vt/i schieben; (press) drücken; (roughly) stoßen. ~ **off** vt hinunterstoßen ● vi (🄸 leave) abhauen. ~ **on** vi (continue) weitergehen/-fahren; (with activity) weitermachen. ~ **up** vt hochschieben; hochtreiben <price>

push: **~-button** n Druckknopf m. **~-chair** n [Kinder]sportwagen m

pushy a 🄸 aufdringlich

puss n, **pussy** n Mieze f

put vt (pt/pp put, pres p putting) tun; (place) setzen; (upright) stellen; (flat) legen; (express) ausdrücken; (say) sagen; (estimate) schätzen (at auf + acc); ~ **aside** or by beiseite legen ● vi ~ to sea auslaufen ● a stay ~ dableiben. ~ **away** vt wegräumen. ~ **back** vt wieder hinsetzen/ -stellen/-legen; zurückstellen <clock>. ~ **down** vt hinsetzen/ -stellen/-legen; (suppress) niederschlagen; (kill) töten; (write) niederschreiben; (attribute) zuschreiben (to dat). ~ **forward** vt vorbringen; vorstellen <clock>. ~ **in** vt hineinsetzen/-stellen/-legen; (insert) einstecken; (submit) einreichen ● vi ~ **in for** beantragen. ~ **off** vt ausmachen <light>; (postpone) verschieben; ~ **s.o. off** jdn abbestellen; (disconcert) jdn aus der Fassung bringen. ~ **on** vt anziehen <clothes, brake>; sich (dat) aufsetzen <hat>; (Culin) aufsetzen; anmachen <light>; aufführen <play>; annehmen <accent>; ~ **on weight** zunehmen. ~ **out** vt hinaussetzen/ -stellen/-legen; ausmachen <fire, light>; ausstrecken <hand>; (disconcert) aus der Fassung bringen; ~ **s.o./oneself out** jdm/sich Umstände machen. ~ **through** vt durchstecken; (Teleph) verbinden (to mit). ~ **up** vt errichten <building>; aufschlagen <tent>; aufspannen <umbrella>; anschlagen <notice>; erhöhen <price>; unterbringen <guest> ● vi (at hotel) absteigen in (+ dat); ~ **up with sth** sich (dat) etw bieten lassen

putrid a faulig

putty n Kitt m

puzzl|e n Rätsel nt; (jigsaw) Puzzlespiel nt ● vt it ~es me es ist mir rätselhaft. **~ing** a rätselhaft

pyjamas npl Schlafanzug m

pylon n Mast m
pyramid n Pyramide f
python n Pythonschlange f

Qq

quack n Quaken nt; (*doctor*)
Quacksalber m ● vi quaken
quadrangle n Viereck nt; (*court*)
Hof m
quadruped n Vierfüßer m
quadruple a vierfach ● vt
vervierfachen ● vi sich
vervierfachen
quaint a (-er, -est) malerisch; (*odd*)
putzig
quake n ⊞ Erdbeben nt ● vi beben;
(*with fear*) zittern
qualif|ication n Qualifikation f;
(*reservation*) Einschränkung f. ~**ied**
a qualifiziert; (*trained*) ausgebildet;
(*limited*) bedingt
qualify v (*pt/pp* -ied) ● vt
qualifizieren; (*entitle*) berechtigen;
(*limit*) einschränken ● vi sich
qualifizieren
quality n Qualität f; (*characteristic*)
Eigenschaft f
qualm n Bedenken pl
quantity n Quantität f, Menge f; in
~ in großen Mengen
quarantine n Quarantäne f
quarrel n Streit m ● vi (*pt/pp*
quarrelled) sich streiten. ~**some** a
streitsüchtig
quarry¹ n (*prey*) Beute f
quarry² n Steinbruch m
quart n Quart nt
quarter n Viertel nt; (*of year*)
Vierteljahr nt; (*Amer*) 25-Cent-Stück
nt; ~**s** pl Quartier nt; at [a] ~ to six
um Viertel vor sechs ● vt vierteln;
(*Mil*) einquartieren (on bei). ~-**final**
n Viertelfinale nt

quarterly a & adv vierteljährlich
quartet n Quartett nt
quartz n Quarz m
quay n Kai m
queasy a I feel ~ mir ist übel
queen n Königin f; (*Cards, Chess*)
Dame f
queer a (-er, -est) eigenartig;
(*dubious*) zweifelhaft; (*ill*) unwohl
quell vt unterdrücken
quench vt löschen
query n Frage f; (*question mark*)
Fragezeichen nt ● vt (*pt/pp* -ied)
infrage stellen; reklamieren <*bill*>
quest n Suche f (for nach)
question n Frage f; (*for discussion*)
Thema nt; out of the ~
ausgeschlossen; the person in ~ die
fragliche Person ● vt infrage stellen;
~ s.o. jdn ausfragen; <*police:*> jdn
verhören. ~**able** a zweifelhaft. ~
mark n Fragezeichen nt
questionnaire n Fragebogen m
queue n Schlange f ● vi ~ [up]
Schlange stehen, sich anstellen (for
nach)
quibble vi Haarspalterei treiben
quick a (-er, -est), -**ly** adv schnell; be
~! mach schnell! ● adv schnell.
~**en** vt beschleunigen ● vi sich
beschleunigen
quick: ~**sand** n Treibsand m. ~-
tempered a aufbrausend
quid n inv ⊞ Pfund nt
quiet a (-er, -est), -**ly** adv still; (*calm*)
ruhig; (*soft*) leise; keep ~ about ⊞
nichts sagen von ● n Stille f; Ruhe f
quiet|en vt beruhigen ● vi ~**en**
down ruhig werden. ~**ness** n Stille
f; Ruhe f
quilt n Steppdecke f. ~**ed** a Stepp-
quintet n Quintett nt
quirk n Eigenart f
quit v (*pt/pp* quitted or quit) ● vt
verlassen; (*give up*) aufgeben; ~
doing sth aufhören, etw zu tun ● vi
gehen
quite adv ganz; (*really*) wirklich; ~
[so]! genau! ~ a few ziemlich viele
quits a quitt

p
q

quiver *vi* zittern

quiz *n* Quiz *nt* ● *vt* (*pt/pp* quizzed) ausfragen. **~zical** *a*, **-ly** *adv* fragend

quota *n* Anteil *m*; (*Comm*) Kontingent *nt*

quotation *n* Zitat *nt*; (*price*) Kostenvoranschlag *m*; (*of shares*) Notierung *f*. **~ marks** *npl* Anführungszeichen *pl*

quote *n* 🔲 = quotation; in **~s** in Anführungszeichen ● *vt/i* zitieren

Rr

rabbi *n* Rabbiner *m*; (*title*) Rabbi *m*

rabbit *n* Kaninchen *nt*

rabid *a* fanatisch; <*animal*> tollwütig

rabies *n* Tollwut *f*

race[1] *n* Rasse *f*

race[2] *n* Rennen *nt*; (*fig*) Wettlauf *m* ● *vi* [am Rennen] teilnehmen; <*athlete, horse*:> laufen; (🔲 *rush*) rasen ● *vt* um die Wette laufen mit; an einem Rennen teilnehmen lassen <*horse*>

race: **~course** *n* Rennbahn *f*. **~horse** *n* Rennpferd *nt*. **~-track** *n* Rennbahn *f*

racial *a*, **-ly** *adv* rassisch; <*discrimination*> Rassen-

racing *n* Rennsport *m*; (*horse-*) Pferderennen *nt*. **~ car** *n* Rennwagen *m*. **~ driver** *n* Rennfahrer *m*

racis|m *n* Rassismus *m*. **~t** *a* rassistisch ● *n* Rassist *m*

rack[1] *n* Ständer *m*; (*for plates*) Gestell *nt* ● *vt* **~** one's brains sich (*dat*) den Kopf zerbrechen

rack[2] *n* go to **~** and ruin verfallen; (*fig*) herunterkommen

racket *n* (*Sport*) Schläger *m*; (*din*) Krach *m*; (*swindle*) Schwindelgeschäft *nt*

racy *a* (**-ier**, **-iest**) schwungvoll; (*risqué*) gewagt

radar *n* Radar *m*

radian|ce *n* Strahlen *nt*. **~t** *a*, **-ly** *adv* strahlend

radiat|e *vt* ausstrahlen ● *vi* <*heat*:> ausgestrahlt werden; <*roads*:> strahlenförmig ausgehen. **~ion** *n* Strahlung *f*

radiator *n* Heizkörper *m*; (*Auto*) Kühler *m*

radical *a*, **-ly** *adv* radikal ● *n* Radikale(r) *m/f*

radio *n* Radio *nt*; by **~** über Funk ● *vt* funken <*message*>

radio|active *a* radioaktiv. **~activity** *n* Radioaktivität *f*

radish *n* Radieschen *nt*

radius *n* (*pl* **-dii**) Radius *m*, Halbmesser *m*

raffle *n* Tombola *f*

raft *n* Floß *nt*

rafter *n* Dachsparren *m*

rag *n* Lumpen *m*; (*pej: newspaper*) Käseblatt *nt*

rage *n* Wut *f*; all the **~** 🔲 der letzte Schrei ● *vi* rasen

ragged *a* zerlumpt; <*edge*> ausgefranst

raid *n* Überfall *m*; (*Mil*) Angriff *m*; (*police*) Razzia *f* ● *vt* überfallen; (*Mil*) angreifen; <*police*> eine Razzia durchführen in (+ *dat*); (*break in*) eindringen in (+ *acc*). **~er** *n* Eindringling *m*; (*of bank*) Bankräuber *m*

rail *n* Schiene *f*; (*pole*) Stange *f*; (*hand~*) Handlauf *m*; (*Naut*) Reling *f*; by **~** mit der Bahn

railings *npl* Geländer *nt*

railroad *n* (*Amer*) = railway

railway *n* [Eisen]bahn *f*. **~ station** *n* Bahnhof *m*

rain *n* Regen *m* ● *vi* regnen

rain: **~bow** *n* Regenbogen *m*. **~coat** *n* Regenmantel *m*. **~fall** *n* Niederschlag *m*

rainy *a* (**-ier**, **-iest**) regnerisch

raise n (Amer) Lohnerhöhung f ● vt
erheben; (upright) aufrichten; (make
higher) erhöhen; (lift) [hoch]heben;
aufziehen <child, animal>;
aufwerfen <question>; aufbringen
<money>

raisin n Rosine f

rake n Harke f, Rechen m ● vt
harken, rechen

rally n Versammlung f, (Auto) Rallye
f, (Tennis) Ballwechsel m ● vt
sammeln

ram n Schafbock m ● vt (pt/pp
rammed) rammen

rambl|e n Wanderung f ● vi
wandern; (in speech) irrereden. **~er**
n Wanderer m; (rose) Kletterrose f.
~ing a weitschweifig; <club>
Wander-

ramp n Rampe f, (Aviat) Gangway f

rampage[1] n be/go on the **~**
randalieren

rampage[2] vi randalieren

ramshackle a baufällig

ran see run

ranch n Ranch f

random a willkürlich; a **~ sample**
eine Stichprobe ● n at **~** aufs
Geratewohl; <choose> willkürlich

rang see ring[2]

range n Serie f, Reihe f, (Comm)
Auswahl f, Angebot nt (of an + dat);
(of mountains) Kette f, (Mus) Umfang
m; (distance) Reichweite f, (for
shooting) Schießplatz m; (stove)
Kohlenherd m ● vi reichen; **~ from**
… **to** gehen von … bis. **~r** n
Aufseher m

rank n (row) Reihe f, (Mil) Rang m;
(social position) Stand m; **the ~ and
file** die breite Masse ● vt/i einstufen;
~ among zählen zu

ransack vt durchwühlen; (pillage)
plündern

ransom n Lösegeld nt; **hold s.o. to
~** Lösegeld für jdn fordern

rape n Vergewaltigung f ● vt
vergewaltigen

rapid a, **-ly** adv schnell. **~ity** n
Schnelligkeit f

rapist n Vergewaltiger m

raptur|e n Entzücken nt. **~ous** a,
-ly adv begeistert

rare[1] a (-r, -st), **-ly** adv selten

rare[2] a (Culin) englisch gebraten

rarefied a dünn

rarity n Seltenheit f

rascal n Schlingel m

rash[1] n (Med) Ausschlag m

rash[2] a (-er, -est), **-ly** adv voreilig

rasher n Speckscheibe f

raspberry n Himbeere f

rat n Ratte f, (🄙 person) Schuft m;
smell a ~ 🄙 Lunte riechen

rate n Rate f, (speed) Tempo nt; (of
payment) Satz m; (of exchange) Kurs
m; **~s** pl (taxes) ≈ Grundsteuer f, **at
any ~** auf jeden Fall; **at this ~** auf
diese Weise ● vt einschätzen; **~
among** zählen zu ● vi **~ as** gelten
als

rather adv lieber; (fairly) ziemlich;
~! und ob!

rating n Einschätzung f, (class)
Klasse f, (sailor) [einfacher] Matrose
m; **~s** pl (Radio, TV) ≈
Einschaltquote f

ratio n Verhältnis nt

ration n Ration f ● vt rationieren

rational a, **-ly** adv rational. **~ize**
vt/i rationalisieren

rattle n Rasseln nt; (of windows)
Klappern nt; (toy) Klapper f ● vi
rasseln; klappern ● vt rasseln mit

raucous a rau

rave vi toben; **~ about** schwärmen
von

raven n Rabe m

ravenous a heißhungrig

ravine n Schlucht f

raving a **~ mad** 🄙 total verrückt

ravishing a hinreißend

raw a (-er, -est) roh; (not processed)
Roh-; <skin> wund; <weather>
nasskalt; (inexperienced) unerfahren;
get a ~ deal 🄙 schlecht
wegkommen. **~ materials** npl
Rohstoffe pl

ray n Strahl m

razor n Rasierapparat m. **~ blade** n
Rasierklinge f

r

re prep betreffs (+ gen)

reach n Reichweite f; (of river) Strecke f; **within/out of** ~ in/außer Reichweite ● vt erreichen; (arrive at) ankommen in (+ dat); (~ as far as) reichen bis zu; kommen zu <decision, conclusion>; (pass) reichen ● vi reichen (to bis zu); ~ **for** greifen nach

react vi reagieren (to auf + acc)

reaction n Reaktion f. ~**ary** a reaktionär

reactor n Reaktor m

read vt/i (pt/pp read) lesen; (aloud) vorlesen (to dat); (Univ) studieren; ablesen <meter>. ~ **out** vt vorlesen

readable a lesbar

reader n Leser(in) m(f); (book) Lesebuch nt

readily adv bereitwillig; (easily) leicht

reading n Lesen nt; (Pol, Relig) Lesung f

readjust vt neu einstellen ● vi sich umstellen (to auf + acc)

ready a (-ier, -iest) fertig; (willing) bereit; (quick) schnell; **get** ~ sich fertig machen; (prepare to) sich bereitmachen

ready: ~-**made** a fertig. ~-**to-wear** a Konfektions-

real a wirklich; (genuine) echt; (actual) eigentlich ● adv (Amer 🔢) echt. ~ **estate** n Immobilien pl

realis|m n Realismus m. ~**t** n Realist m. ~**tic** a, -**ally** adv realistisch

reality n Wirklichkeit f

realization n Erkenntnis f

realize vt einsehen; (become aware) gewahr werden; verwirklichen <hopes, plans>; einbringen <price>

really adv wirklich; (actually) eigentlich

realm n Reich nt

realtor n (Amer) Immobilienmakler m

reap vt ernten

reappear vi wiederkommen

rear[1] a Hinter-; (Auto) Heck- ● n the ~ der hintere Teil; **from the** ~ von hinten

rear[2] vt aufziehen ● vi ~ [up] <horse:> sich aufbäumen

rearrange vt umstellen

reason n Grund m; (good sense) Vernunft f; (ability to think) Verstand m; **within** ~ in vernünftigen Grenzen ● vi argumentieren; ~ **with** vernünftig reden mit. ~**able** a vernünftig; (not expensive) preiswert. ~**ably** adv (fairly) ziemlich

reassur|ance n Beruhigung f; Versicherung f. ~**e** vt beruhigen; ~**e s.o. of sth** jdm etw (gen) versichern

rebel[1] n Rebell m

rebel[2] vi (pt/pp rebelled) rebellieren. ~**lion** n Rebellion f. ~**lious** a rebellisch

rebound[1] vi abprallen

rebound[2] n Rückprall m

rebuild vt (pt/pp -built) wieder aufbauen

rebuke n Tadel m ● vt tadeln

recall n Erinnerung f ● vt zurückrufen; abberufen <diplomat>; (remember) sich erinnern an (+ acc)

recant vi widerrufen

recap vt/i 🔢 = recapitulate

recapitulate vt/i zusammenfassen; rekapitulieren

recapture vt wieder gefangen nehmen <person>; wieder einfangen <animal>

reced|e vi zurückgehen. ~**ing** a <forehead, chin> fliehend

receipt n Quittung f; (receiving) Empfang m; ~**s** pl (Comm) Einnahmen pl

receive vt erhalten, bekommen; empfangen <guests>. ~**r** n (Teleph) Hörer m; (of stolen goods) Hehler m

recent a kürzlich erfolgte(r,s). ~**ly** adv vor kurzem

receptacle n Behälter m

reception n Empfang m; ~ [**desk**] (in hotel) Rezeption f. ~**ist** n Empfangsdame f

receptive *a* aufnahmefähig; ~ **to** empfänglich für

recess *n* Nische *f*; (*holiday*) Ferien *pl*

recession *n* Rezession *f*

recharge *vt* [wieder] aufladen

recipe *n* Rezept *nt*

recipient *n* Empfänger *m*

recital *n* (*of poetry, songs*) Vortrag *m*; (*of instrumental music*) Konzert *nt*

recite *vt* aufsagen; (*before audience*) vortragen

reckless *a*, **-ly** *adv* leichtsinnig; (*careless*) rücksichtslos. ~**ness** *n* Leichtsinn *m*; (*carelessness*) Rücksichtslosigkeit *f*

reckon *vt* rechnen; (*consider*) glauben ● *vi* ~ **on/with** rechnen mit

reclaim *vt* zurückfordern; zurückgewinnen <*land*>

reclin|e *vi* liegen. ~**ing seat** *n* Liegesitz *m*

recluse *n* Einsiedler(in) *m(f)*

recognition *n* Erkennen *nt*; (*acknowledgement*) Anerkennung *f*; **in** ~ als Anerkennung (**of** *gen*)

recognize *vt* erkennen; (*know again*) wieder erkennen; (*acknowledge*) anerkennen

recoil *vi* zurückschnellen; (*in fear*) zurückschrecken

recollect *vt* sich erinnern an (+ *acc*). ~**ion** *n* Erinnerung *f*

recommend *vt* empfehlen. ~**ation** *n* Empfehlung *f*

recon|cile *vt* versöhnen; ~**cile oneself to** sich abfinden mit. ~**ciliation** *n* Versöhnung *f*

reconnaissance *n* (*Mil*) Aufklärung *f*

reconnoitre *vi* (*pres p* -**tring**) auf Erkundung ausgehen

reconsider *vt* sich (*dat*) noch einmal überlegen

reconstruct *vt* wieder aufbauen; rekonstruieren <*crime*>

record[1] *vt* aufzeichnen; (*register*) registrieren; (*on tape*) aufnehmen

record[2] *n* Aufzeichnung *f*; (*Jur*) Protokoll *nt*; (*Mus*) [Schall]platte *f*; (*Sport*) Rekord *m*; ~**s** *pl* Unterlagen *pl*; **off the** ~ inoffiziell; **have a [criminal]** ~ vorbestraft sein

recorder *n* (*Mus*) Blockflöte *f*

recording *n* Aufnahme *f*

re-count[1] *vt* nachzählen

re-count[2] *n* (*Pol*) Nachzählung *f*

recover *vt* zurückbekommen ● *vi* sich erholen. ~**y** *n* Wiedererlangung *f*; (*of health*) Erholung *f*

recreation *n* Erholung *f*; (*hobby*) Hobby *nt*. ~**al** *a* Freizeit-; **be** ~**al** erholsam sein

recruit *n* (*Mil*) Rekrut *m*; **new** ~ (*member*) neues Mitglied *nt*; (*worker*) neuer Mitarbeiter *m* ● *vt* rekrutieren; anwerben <*staff*>. ~**ment** *n* Rekrutierung *f*; Anwerbung *f*

rectang|le *n* Rechteck *nt*. ~**ular** *a* rechteckig

rectify *vt* (*pt/pp* -**ied**) berichtigen

rector *n* Pfarrer *m*; (*Univ*) Rektor *m*. ~**y** *n* Pfarrhaus *nt*

recur *vi* (*pt/pp* **recurred**) sich wiederholen; <*illness:*> wiederkehren

recurren|ce *n* Wiederkehr *f*. ~**t** *a* wiederkehrend

recycle *vt* wieder verwerten

red *a* (**redder, reddest**) rot ● *n* Rot *nt*

redd|en *vt* röten ● *vi* rot werden. ~**ish** *a* rötlich

redecorate *vt* renovieren; (*paint*) neu streichen; (*wallpaper*) neu tapezieren

redeem *vt* einlösen; (*Relig*) erlösen

redemption *n* Erlösung *f*

red: ~**-haired** *a* rothaarig. ~**handed** *a* **catch s.o.** ~**-handed** jdn auf frischer Tat ertappen. ~**herring** *n* falsche Spur *f*. ~**-hot** *a* glühend heiß. ~ **light** *n* (*Auto*) rote Ampel *f*. ~**ness** *n* Röte *f*

redo *vt* (*pt* -**did**, *pp* -**done**) noch einmal machen

redouble *vt* verdoppeln

red tape *n* 🄵 Bürokratie *f*

reduc|e *vt* verringern, vermindern; (*in size*) verkleinern; ermäßigen <*costs*>; herabsetzen <*price, goods*>; (*Culin*) einkochen lassen. ~**tion** *n*

Verringerung f; (in price) Ermäßigung f; (in size) Verkleinerung f

redundan|cy n Beschäftigungslosigkeit f. **~t** a überflüssig; **make ~t** entlassen; **be made ~t** beschäftigungslos werden

reed n [Schilf]rohr nt; **~s** pl Schilf nt

reef n Riff nt

reek vi riechen (**of** nach)

reel n Rolle f, Spule f ● vi (stagger) taumeln ● vt **~ off** (fig) herunterrasseln

refectory n Refektorium nt; (Univ) Mensa f

refer v (pt/pp referred) ● vt verweisen (**to** an + acc); übergeben, weiterleiten <matter> (**to** an + acc) ● vi **~ to** sich beziehen auf (+ acc); (mention) erwähnen; (concern) betreffen; (consult) sich wenden an (+ acc); nachschlagen in (+ dat) <book>; **are you ~ring to me?** meinen Sie mich?

referee n Schiedsrichter m; (Boxing) Ringrichter m; (for job) Referenz f ● vt/i (pt/pp refereed) Schiedsrichter/Ringrichter sein (bei)

reference n Erwähnung f; (in book) Verweis m; (for job) Referenz f; **with ~ to** in Bezug auf (+ acc); **make [a] ~ to** erwähnen. **~ book** n Nachschlagewerk nt

referendum n Volksabstimmung f

refill¹ vt nachfüllen

refill² n (for pen) Ersatzmine f

refine vt raffinieren. **~d** a fein, vornehm. **~ment** n Vornehmheit f; (Techn) Verfeinerung f. **~ry** n Raffinerie f

reflect vt reflektieren; <mirror:> [wider]spiegeln; **be ~ed in** sich spiegeln in (+ dat) ● vi nachdenken (**on** über + acc). **~ion** n Reflexion f; (image) Spiegelbild nt; **on ~ion** nach nochmaliger Überlegung. **~or** n Rückstrahler m

reflex n Reflex m

reflexive a reflexiv

reform n Reform f ● vt reformieren ● vi sich bessern

refrain¹ n Refrain m

refrain² vi **~ from doing sth** etw nicht tun

refresh vt erfrischen. **~ing** a erfrischend. **~ments** npl Erfrischungen pl

refrigerat|e vt kühlen. **~or** n Kühlschrank m

refuel vt/i (pt/pp -fuelled) auftanken

refuge n Zuflucht f; **take ~** Zuflucht nehmen

refugee n Flüchtling m

refund¹ n **get a ~** sein Geld zurückbekommen

refund² vt zurückerstatten

refusal n (see refuse¹) Ablehnung f; Weigerung f

refuse¹ vt ablehnen; (not grant) verweigern; **~ to do sth** sich weigern, etw zu tun ● vi ablehnen; sich weigern

refuse² n Müll m

refute vt widerlegen

regain vt wiedergewinnen

regal a, **-ly** adv königlich

regard n (heed) Rücksicht f; (respect) Achtung f; **~s** pl Grüße pl; **with ~ to** in Bezug auf (+ acc) ● vt ansehen, betrachten (**as** als). **~ing** prep bezüglich (+ gen). **~less** adv ohne Rücksicht (**of** auf + acc)

regatta n Regatta f

regime n Regime nt

regiment n Regiment nt. **~al** a Regiments-

region n Region f; **in the ~ of** (fig) ungefähr. **~al** a, **-ly** adv regional

register n Register nt; (Sch) Anwesenheitsliste f ● vt registrieren; (report) anmelden; einschreiben <letter>; aufgeben <luggage> ● vi (report) sich anmelden

registrar n Standesbeamte(r) m

registration n Registrierung f; Anmeldung f. **~ number** n Autonummer f

registry office n Standesamt nt

regret n Bedauern nt ● vt (pt/pp **regretted**) bedauern. **~fully** adv mit Bedauern

regrettab|le a bedauerlich. **~ly** adv bedauerlicherweise

regular a, **-ly** adv regelmäßig; (usual) üblich ● n (in pub) Stammgast m; (in shop) Stammkunde m. **~ity** n Regelmäßigkeit f

regulat|e vt regulieren. **~ion** n (rule) Vorschrift f

rehears|al n (Theat) Probe f. **~e** vt proben

reign n Herrschaft f ● vi herrschen, regieren

rein n Zügel m

reindeer n inv Rentier nt

reinforce vt verstärken. **~ment** n Verstärkung f; **send ~ments** Verstärkung schicken

reiterate vt wiederholen

reject vt ablehnen. **~ion** n Ablehnung f

rejects npl (Comm) Ausschussware f

rejoic|e vi (liter) sich freuen. **~ing** n Freude f

rejoin vt sich wieder anschließen (+ dat); wieder beitreten (+ dat) <club, party>

rejuvenate vt verjüngen

relapse n Rückfall m ● vi einen Rückfall erleiden

relate vt (tell) erzählen; (connect) verbinden

relation n Beziehung f; (person) Verwandte(r) m/f. **~ship** n Beziehung f; (link) Verbindung f; (blood tie) Verwandtschaft f; (affair) Verhältnis nt

relative n Verwandte(r) m/f ● a relativ; (Gram) Relativ-. **~ly** adv relativ, verhältnismäßig

relax vt lockern, entspannen ● vi sich lockern, sich entspannen. **~ation** n Entspannung f. **~ing** a entspannend

relay[1] vt (pt/pp **-layed**) weitergeben; (Radio, TV) übertragen

relay[2] n. **~ [race]** n Staffel f

release n Freilassung f, Entlassung f; (Techn) Auslöser m ● vt freilassen; (let go of) loslassen; (Techn) auslösen; veröffentlichen <information>

relent vi nachgeben. **~less** a, **-ly** adv erbarmungslos; (unceasing) unaufhörlich

relevan|ce n Relevanz f. **~t** a relevant (to für)

reliab|ility n Zuverlässigkeit f. **~le** a, **-ly** adv zuverlässig

relian|ce n Abhängigkeit f (on von). **~t** a angewiesen (on auf + acc)

relic n Überbleibsel nt; (Relig) Reliquie f

relief n Erleichterung f; (assistance) Hilfe f; (replacement) Ablösung f; (Art) Relief nt

relieve vt erleichtern; (take over from) ablösen; **~ of** entlasten von

religion n Religion f

religious a religiös

relinquish vt loslassen; (give up) aufgeben

relish n Genuss m; (Culin) Würze f ● vt genießen

reluctan|ce n Widerstreben nt. **~t** a widerstrebend; **be ~t** zögern (to zu). **~tly** adv ungern; widerstrebend

rely vi (pt/pp **-ied**) **~ on** sich verlassen auf (+ acc); (be dependent on) angewiesen sein auf (+ acc)

remain vi bleiben; (be left) übrig bleiben. **~der** n Rest m. **~ing** a restlich. **~s** npl Reste pl; [mortal] **~s** [sterbliche] Überreste pl

remand n **on ~** in Untersuchungshaft ● vt **~ in custody** in Untersuchungshaft schicken

remark n Bemerkung f ● vt bemerken. **~able** a, **-bly** adv bemerkenswert

remarry vi wieder heiraten

remedy n [Heil]mittel nt (for gegen); (fig) Abhilfe f ● vt (pt/pp **-ied**) abhelfen (+ dat); beheben <fault>

remember vt sich erinnern an (+ acc); **~ to do sth** daran denken, etw zu tun ● vi sich erinnern

r

remind *vt* erinnern (**of** an + *acc*). **~er** *n* Andenken *nt*; (*letter, warning*) Mahnung *f*

reminisce *vi* sich seinen Erinnerungen hingeben. **~nces** *npl* Erinnerungen *pl*. **~nt** *a* be **~nt of** erinnern an (+ *acc*)

remnant *n* Rest *m*

remorse *n* Reue *f*. **~ful** *a*, **-ly** *adv* reumütig. **~less** *a*, **-ly** *adv* unerbittlich

remote *a* fern; (*isolated*) abgelegen; (*slight*) gering. **~ control** *n* Fernsteuerung *f*; (*for TV*) Fernbedienung *f*

remotely *adv* entfernt; **not ~** nicht im Entferntesten

removable *a* abnehmbar

removal *n* Entfernung *f*; (*from house*) Umzug *m*. **~ van** *n* Möbelwagen *m*

remove *vt* entfernen; (*take off*) abnehmen; (*take out*) herausnehmen

render *vt* machen; erweisen <*service*>; (*translate*) wiedergeben; (*Mus*) vortragen

renegade *n* Abtrünnige(r) *m/f*

renew *vt* erneuern; verlängern <*contract*>. **~al** *n* Erneuerung *f*; Verlängerung *f*

renounce *vt* verzichten auf (+ *acc*)

renovat|e *vt* renovieren. **~ion** *n* Renovierung *f*

renown *n* Ruf *m*. **~ed** *a* berühmt

rent *n* Miete *f* ● *vt* mieten; (*hire*) leihen; **~ [out]** vermieten; verleihen. **~al** *n* Mietgebühr *f*; Leihgebühr *f*

renunciation *n* Verzicht *m*

reopen *vt/i* wieder aufmachen

reorganize *vt* reorganisieren

rep *n* 🔟 Vertreter *m*

repair *n* Reparatur *f*; **in good/bad ~** in gutem/schlechtem Zustand ● *vt* reparieren

repatriate *vt* repatriieren

repay *vt* (*pt/pp* **-paid**) zurückzahlen; **~ s.o. for sth** jdm etw zurückzahlen. **~ment** *n* Rückzahlung *f*

repeal *n* Aufhebung *f* ● *vt* aufheben

repeat *n* Wiederholung *f* ● *vt/i* wiederholen; **~ after me** sprechen Sie mir nach. **~ed** *a*, **-ly** *adv* wiederholt

repel *vt* (*pt/pp* **repelled**) abwehren; (*fig*) abstoßen. **~lent** *a* abstoßend

repent *vi* Reue zeigen. **~ance** *n* Reue *f*. **~ant** *a* reuig

repercussions *npl* Auswirkungen *pl*

repertoire, repertory *n* Repertoire *nt*

repetit|ion *n* Wiederholung *f*. **~ive** *a* eintönig

replace *vt* zurücktun; (*take the place of*) ersetzen; (*exchange*) austauschen. **~ment** *n* Ersatz *m*

replay *n* (*Sport*) Wiederholungsspiel *nt*; [**action**] **~** Wiederholung *f*

replenish *vt* auffüllen <*stocks*>; (*refill*) nachfüllen

replica *n* Nachbildung *f*

reply *n* Antwort *f* (**to** auf + *acc*) ● *vt/i* (*pt/pp* **replied**) antworten

report *n* Bericht *m*; (*Sch*) Zeugnis *nt*; (*rumour*) Gerücht *nt*; (*of gun*) Knall *m* ● *vt* berichten; (*notify*) melden; **~ s.o. to the police** jdn anzeigen ● *vi* berichten (**on** über + *acc*); (*present oneself*) sich melden (**to** bei). **~er** *n* Reporter(in) *m(f)*

reprehensible *a* tadelnswert

represent *vt* darstellen; (*act for*) vertreten, repräsentieren. **~ation** *n* Darstellung *f*

representative *a* repräsentativ (**of** für) ● *n* Bevollmächtigte(r) *m/(f)*; (*Comm*) Vertreter(in) *m(f)*; (*Amer, Pol*) Abgeordnete(r) *m/f*

repress *vt* unterdrücken. **~ion** *n* Unterdrückung *f*. **~ive** *a* repressiv

reprieve *n* Begnadigung *f*; (*fig*) Gnadenfrist *f* ● *vt* begnadigen

reprimand *n* Tadel *m* ● *vt* tadeln

reprint[1] *n* Nachdruck *m*

reprint[2] *vt* neu auflegen

reprisal *n* Vergeltungsmaßnahme *f*

reproach *n* Vorwurf *m* ● *vt* Vorwürfe *pl* machen (+ *dat*). **~ful** *a*, **-ly** *adv* vorwurfsvoll

reproduc|e *vt* wiedergeben, reproduzieren ● *vi* sich fortpflanzen.

~tion n Reproduktion f; (Biol) Fortpflanzung f

reptile n Reptil nt

republic n Republik f. **~an** a republikanisch ● n Republikaner(in) m(f)

repugnan|ce n Widerwille m. **~t** a widerlich

repuls|ion n Widerwille m. **~ive** a abstoßend, widerlich

reputable a <firm> von gutem Ruf; (respectable) anständig

reputation n Ruf m

request n Bitte f ● vt bitten

require vt (need) brauchen; (demand) erfordern; be **~d** to do sth etw tun müssen. **~ment** n Bedürfnis nt; (condition) Erfordernis nt

resale n Weiterverkauf m

rescue n Rettung f ● vt retten. **~r** n Retter m

research n Forschung f ● vt erforschen; (Journ) recherchieren. **~er** n Forscher m; (Journ) Rechercheur m

resem|blance n Ähnlichkeit f. **~ble** vt ähneln (+ dat)

resent vt übel nehmen; einen Groll hegen gegen <person>. **~ful** a, **-ly** adv verbittert. **~ment** n Groll m

reservation n Reservierung f; (doubt) Vorbehalt m; (enclosure) Reservat nt

reserve n Reserve f; (for animals) Reservat nt; (Sport) Reservespieler(in) m(f) ● vt reservieren; <client:> reservieren lassen; (keep) aufheben; sich (dat) vorbehalten <right>. **~d** a reserviert

reservoir n Reservoir nt

reshuffle n (Pol) Umbildung f ● vt (Pol) umbilden

residence n Wohnsitz m; (official) Residenz f; (stay) Aufenthalt m

resident a ansässig (in in + dat); <housekeeper, nurse> im Haus wohnend ● n Bewohner(in) m(f); (of street) Anwohner m. **~ial** a Wohn-

residue n Rest m; (Chem) Rückstand m

resign vt **~** oneself to sich abfinden mit ● vi kündigen; (from public office) zurücktreten. **~ation** n Resignation f; (from job) Kündigung f; Rücktritt m. **~ed** a, **-ly** adv resigniert

resilient a federnd; (fig) widerstandsfähig

resin n Harz nt

resist vt/i sich widersetzen (+ dat), (fig) widerstehen (+ dat). **~ance** n Widerstand m. **~ant** a widerstandsfähig

resolut|e a, **-ly** adv entschlossen. **~ion** n Entschlossenheit f; (intention) Vorsatz m; (Pol) Resolution f

resolve n Entschlossenheit f; (decision) Beschluss m ● vt beschließen; (solve) lösen

resort n (place) Urlaubsort m; as a last **~** wenn alles andere fehlschlägt ● vi **~** to (fig) greifen zu

resound vi widerhallen

resource n **~s** pl Ressourcen pl. **~ful** a findig

respect n Respekt m, Achtung f (for vor + dat); (aspect) Hinsicht f; with **~** to in Bezug auf (+ acc) ● vt respektieren, achten

respect|able a, **-bly** adv ehrbar; (decent) anständig; (considerable) ansehnlich. **~ful** a, **-ly** adv respektvoll

respective a jeweilig. **~ly** adv beziehungsweise

respiration n Atmung f

respite n [Ruhe]pause f; (delay) Aufschub m

respond vi antworten; (react) reagieren (to auf + acc)

response n Antwort f; Reaktion f

responsibility n Verantwortung f; (duty) Verpflichtung f

responsib|le a verantwortlich; (trustworthy) verantwortungsvoll. **~ly** adv verantwortungsbewusst

rest¹ n Ruhe f; (holiday) Erholung f; (interval & Mus) Pause f; have a **~**

r

eine Pause machen; (*rest*) sich ausruhen ● *vt* ausruhen; (*lean*) lehnen (on an/auf + *acc*) ● *vi* ruhen; (*have a rest*) sich ausruhen

rest² *n* the ∼ der Rest; (*people*) die Übrigen *pl* ● *vi* it ∼s with you es ist an Ihnen (to zu)

restaurant *n* Restaurant *nt*, Gaststätte *f*

restful *a* erholsam

restive *a* unruhig

restless *a*, **-ly** *adv* unruhig

restoration *n* (*of building*) Restaurierung *f*

restore *vt* wiederherstellen; restaurieren <*building*>

restrain *vt* zurückhalten; ∼ oneself sich beherrschen. ∼ed *a* zurückhaltend. ∼t *n* Zurückhaltung *f*

restrict *vt* einschränken; ∼ to beschränken auf (+ *acc*). ∼ion *n* Einschränkung *f*; Beschränkung *f*. ∼ive *a* einschränkend

rest room *n* (*Amer*) Toilette *f*

result *n* Ergebnis *nt*, Resultat *nt*; (*consequence*) Folge *f*; as a ∼ als Folge (of *gen*) ● *vi* sich ergeben (from aus); ∼ in enden in (+ *dat*); (*lead to*) führen zu

resume *vt* wieder aufnehmen ● *vi* wieder beginnen

résumé *n* Zusammenfassung *f*

resumption *n* Wiederaufnahme *f*

resurrect *vt* (*fig*) wieder beleben. ∼ion the R ∼ion (*Relig*) die Auferstehung

resuscitat|e *vt* wieder beleben. ∼ion *n* Wiederbelebung *f*

retail *n* Einzelhandel *m* ● *a* Einzelhandels- ● *adv* im Einzelhandel ● *vt* im Einzelhandel verkaufen ● *vi* ∼ at im Einzelhandel kosten. ∼er *n* Einzelhändler *m*

retain *vt* behalten

retaliat|e *vi* zurückschlagen. ∼ion *n* Vergeltung *f*; in ∼ion als Vergeltung

retarded *a* zurückgeblieben

reticen|ce *n* Zurückhaltung *f*. ∼t *a* zurückhaltend

retina *n* Netzhaut *f*

retinue *n* Gefolge *nt*

retire *vi* in den Ruhestand treten; (*withdraw*) sich zurückziehen. ∼d *a* im Ruhestand. ∼ment *n* Ruhestand *m*

retiring *a* zurückhaltend

retort *n* scharfe Erwiderung *f*; (*Chem*) Retorte *f* ● *vt* scharf erwidern

retrace *vt* ∼ one's steps denselben Weg zurückgehen

retrain *vt* umschulen ● *vi* umgeschult werden

retreat *n* Rückzug *m*; (*place*) Zufluchtsort *m* ● *vi* sich zurückziehen

retrial *n* Wiederaufnahmeverfahren *nt*

retrieve *vt* zurückholen; (*from wreckage*) bergen; (*Computing*) wieder auffinden

retrograde *a* rückschrittlich

retrospect *n* in ∼ rückblickend. ∼ive *a*, **-ly** *adv* rückwirkend; (*looking back*) rückblickend

return *n* Rückkehr *f*; (*giving back*) Rückgabe *f*; (*Comm*) Ertrag *m*; (*ticket*) Rückfahrkarte *f*; (*Aviat*) Rückflugschein *m*; by ∼ [of post] postwendend; in ∼ dafür; in ∼ for für; many happy ∼s! herzlichen Glückwunsch zum Geburtstag! ● *vt* zurückgehen/-fahren; (*come back*) zurückkommen ● *vt* zurückgeben; (*put back*) zurückstellen/-legen; (*send back*) zurückschicken

return ticket *n* Rückfahrkarte *f*; (*Aviat*) Rückflugschein *m*

reunion *n* Wiedervereinigung *f*; (*social gathering*) Treffen *nt*

reunite *vt* wieder vereinigen

reuse *vt* wieder verwenden

rev *n* (*Auto* 🔢) Umdrehung *f* ● *vt/i* ∼ [up] den Motor auf Touren bringen

reveal *vt* zum Vorschein bringen; (*fig*) enthüllen. ∼ing *a* (*fig*) aufschlussreich

revel *vi* (*pt/pp* revelled) ∼ in sth etw genießen

revelation n Offenbarung f, Enthüllung f

revenge n Rache f; (fig & Sport) Revanche f ● vt rächen

revenue n [Staats]einnahmen pl

revere vt verehren. **~nce** n Ehrfurcht f

Reverend a the ~ X Pfarrer X; (Catholic) Hochwürden X

reverent a, **-ly** adv ehrfürchtig

reversal n Umkehrung f

reverse a umgekehrt ● n Gegenteil nt; (back) Rückseite f; (Auto) Rückwärtsgang m ● vt umkehren; (Auto) zurücksetzen ● vi zurücksetzen

revert vi ~ **to** zurückfallen an (+ acc)

review n Rückblick m (of auf + acc); (re-examination) Überprüfung f; (Mil) Truppenschau f; (of book, play) Kritik f, Rezension f ● vt zurückblicken auf (+ acc); überprüfen <situation>; rezensieren <book, play>. **~er** n Kritiker m, Rezensent m

revis|e vt revidieren; (for exam) wiederholen. **~ion** n Revision f; (for exam) Wiederholung f

revival n Wiederbelebung f

revive vt wieder beleben; (fig) wieder aufleben lassen ● vi wieder aufleben

revolt n Aufstand m ● vi rebellieren ● vt anwidern. **~ing** a widerlich, eklig

revolution n Revolution f; (Auto) Umdrehung f. **~ary** a revolutionär. **~ize** vt revolutionieren

revolve vi sich drehen; ~ **around** kreisen um

revolv|er n Revolver m. **~ing** a Dreh-

revue n Revue f; (satirical) Kabarett nt

revulsion n Abscheu m

reward n Belohnung f ● vt belohnen. **~ing** a lohnend

rewrite vt (pt rewrote, pp rewritten) noch einmal [neu] schreiben; (alter) umschreiben

rhetoric n Rhetorik f. **~al** a rhetorisch

rheumatism n Rheumatismus m, Rheuma nt

Rhine n Rhein m

rhinoceros n Nashorn nt, Rhinozeros nt

rhubarb n Rhabarber m

rhyme n Reim m ● vt reimen ● vi sich reimen

rhythm n Rhythmus m. **~ic[al]** a, **-ally** adv rhythmisch

rib n Rippe f

ribbon n Band nt; (for typewriter) Farbband nt

rice n Reis m

rich a (-er, -est), **-ly** adv reich; <food> gehaltvoll; (heavy) schwer ● n the ~ pl die Reichen; **~es** pl Reichtum m

ricochet vi abprallen

rid vt (pt/pp rid, pres p ridding) befreien (of von); get ~ of loswerden

riddance n good ~! auf Nimmerwiedersehen!

ridden see ride

riddle n Rätsel nt

riddled a ~ with durchlöchert mit

ride n Ritt m; (in vehicle) Fahrt f; take s.o. for a ~ 🔢 jdn reinlegen ● v (pt rode, pp ridden) ● vt reiten <horse>; fahren mit <bicycle> ● vi reiten; (in vehicle) fahren. **~r** n Reiter(in) m(f); (on bicycle) Fahrer(in) m(f)

ridge n Erhebung f; (on roof) First m; (of mountain) Grat m, Kamm m

ridicule n Spott m ● vt verspotten, spotten über (+ acc)

ridiculous a, **-ly** adv lächerlich

riding n Reiten nt ● attrib Reit-

riff-raff n Gesindel nt

rifle n Gewehr nt ● vt plündern; ~ **through** durchwühlen

rift n Spalt m; (fig) Riss m

rig n Ölbohrturm m; (at sea) Bohrinsel f ● vt (pt/pp rigged) ~ **out** ausrüsten; ~ **up** aufbauen

right a richtig; (not left) rechte(r,s); be ~ <person:> Recht haben;

r

<clock:> richtig gehen; **put ~** wieder in Ordnung bringen; (*fig*) richtig stellen; **that's ~!** das stimmt! ● *adv* richtig; (*directly*) direkt; (*completely*) ganz; (*not left*) rechts; <*go*> nach rechts; **~ away** sofort ● *n* Recht *nt*; (*not left*) rechte Seite *f*; **on the ~** rechts; **from/to the ~** von/nach rechts; **be in the ~** Recht haben; **by ~s** eigentlich; **the R~** (*Pol*) die Rechte. **~ angle** *n* rechter Winkel *m*

rightful *a*, **-ly** *adv* rechtmäßig
right-handed *a* rechtshändig
rightly *adv* mit Recht
right-wing *a* (*Pol*) rechte(r,s)
rigid *a* starr; (*strict*) streng. **~ity** *n* Starrheit *f*; Strenge *f*
rigorous *a*, **-ly** *adv* streng
rigour *n* Strenge *f*
rim *n* Rand *m*; (*of wheel*) Felge *f*
rind *n* (*on fruit*) Schale *f*; (*on cheese*) Rinde *f*; (*on bacon*) Schwarte *f*
ring¹ *n* Ring *m*; (*for circus*) Manege *f*; **stand in a ~** im Kreis stehen ● *vt* umringen
ring² *n* Klingeln *nt*; **give s.o. a ~** (*Teleph*) jdn anrufen ● *v* (*pt* **rang**, *pp* **rung**) ● *vt* läuten; **~ [up]** (*Teleph*) anrufen ● *vi* <*bells:*> läuten; <*telephone:*> klingeln. **~ back** *vt/i* (*Teleph*) zurückrufen
ring: ~leader *n* Rädelsführer *m*. **~ road** *n* Umgehungsstraße *f*
rink *n* Eisbahn *f*
rinse *n* Spülung *f*; (*hair colour*) Tönung *f* ● *vt* spülen
riot *n* Aufruhr *m*; **~s** *pl* Unruhen *pl*; **run ~** randalieren ● *vi* randalieren. **~er** *n* Randalierer *m*. **~ous** *a* aufrührerisch; (*boisterous*) wild
rip *n* Riss *m* ● *vt/i* (*pt/pp* **ripped**) zerreißen; **~ open** aufreißen. **~ off** *vt* 🔲 neppen
ripe *a* (**-r**, **-st**) reif
ripen *vi* reifen ● *vt* reifen lassen
ripeness *n* Reife *f*
rip-off *n* 🔲 Nepp *m*
ripple *n* kleine Welle *f*
rise *n* Anstieg *m*; (*fig*) Aufstieg *m*; (*increase*) Zunahme *f*; (*in wages*)

Lohnerhöhung *f*; (*in salary*) Gehaltserhöhung *f*; **give ~ to** Anlass geben zu ● *vi* (*pt* **rose**, *pp* **risen**) steigen; <*ground:*> ansteigen; <*sun, dough:*> aufgehen; <*river:*> entspringen; (*get up*) aufstehen; (*fig*) aufsteigen (**to** zu). **~r** *n* **early ~r** Frühaufsteher *m*
rising *a* steigend; <*sun*> aufgehend ● *n* (*revolt*) Aufstand *m*
risk *n* Risiko *nt*; **at one's own ~** auf eigene Gefahr ● *vt* riskieren
risky *a* (**-ier**, **-iest**) riskant
rite *n* Ritus *m*
ritual *a* rituell ● *n* Ritual *nt*
rival *a* rivalisierend ● *n* Rivale *m*/ Rivalin *f*. **~ry** *n* Rivalität *f*; (*Comm*) Konkurrenzkampf *m*
river *n* Fluss *m*
rivet *n* Niete *f* ● *vt* [ver]nieten; **~ed by** (*fig*) gefesselt von
road *n* Straße *f*; (*fig*) Weg *m*
road: ~map *n* Straßenkarte *f*. **~ safety** *n* Verkehrssicherheit *f*. **~side** *n* Straßenrand *m*. **~way** *n* Fahrbahn *f*. **~-works** *npl* Straßenarbeiten *pl*. **~worthy** *a* verkehrssicher
roam *vi* wandern
roar *n* Gebrüll *nt*; **~s of laughter** schallendes Gelächter *nt* ● *vi* brüllen; (*with laughter*) schallend lachen. **~ing** *a* <*fire*> prasselnd; **do a ~ing trade** 🔲 ein Bombengeschäft machen
roast *a* gebraten, Brat-; **~ beef/pork** Rinder-/Schweinebraten *m* ● *n* Braten *m* ● *vt/i* braten; rösten <*coffee, chestnuts*>
rob *vt* (*pt/pp* **robbed**) berauben (**of** *gen*); ausrauben <*bank*>. **~ber** *n* Räuber *m*. **~bery** *n* Raub *m*
robe *n* Robe *f*; (*Amer: bathrobe*) Bademantel *m*
robin *n* Rotkehlchen *nt*
robot *n* Roboter *m*
robust *a* robust
rock¹ *n* Fels *m*; **on the ~s** <*ship*> aufgelaufen; <*marriage*> kaputt; <*drink*> mit Eis
rock² *vt/i* schaukeln

rock³ n (Mus) Rock m

rockery n Steingarten m

rocket n Rakete f

rocking: ~-chair n Schaukelstuhl m. **~-horse** n Schaukelpferd nt

rocky a (-ier, -iest) felsig; (unsteady) wackelig

rod n Stab m; (stick) Rute f; (for fishing) Angel[rute] f

rode see ride

rodent n Nagetier nt

rogue n Gauner m

role n Rolle f

roll n Rolle f; (bread) Brötchen nt; (list) Liste f; (of drum) Wirbel m ● vi rollen; **be ~ing in money** 🔳 Geld wie Heu haben ● vt rollen; walzen <lawn>; ausrollen <pastry>. **~ over** vi sich auf die andere Seite rollen. **~ up** vt aufrollen; hochkrempeln <sleeves> ● vi 🔳 auftauchen

roller n Rolle f; (lawn, road) Walze f; (hair) Lockenwickler m. **~ blind** n Rollo nt. **~-coaster** n Berg-und-Talbahn f. **~-skate** n Rollschuh m

rolling-pin n Teigrolle f

Roman a römisch ● n Römer(in) m(f)

romance n Romantik f; (love-affair) Romanze f; (book) Liebesgeschichte f

Romania n Rumänien nt. **~n** a rumänisch ● n Rumäne m/-nin f

romantic a, **-ally** adv romantisch. **~ism** n Romantik f

Rome n Rom nt

romp vi [herum]tollen

roof n Dach nt; (of mouth) Gaumen m ● vt **~ [over]** überdachen. **~-top** n Dach nt

rook n Saatkrähe f; (Chess) Turm m

room n Zimmer nt; (for functions) Saal m; (space) Platz m. **~y** a geräumig

roost n Hühnerstange f

root¹ n Wurzel f; **take ~** anwachsen ● vi Wurzeln schlagen. **~ out** vt (fig) ausrotten

root² vi **~ about** wühlen; **~ for s.o.** 🔳 für jdn sein

rope n Seil nt; **know the ~s** 🔳 sich auskennen. **~ in** vt 🔳 einspannen

rose¹ n Rose f; (of watering-can) Brause f

rose² see rise

rostrum n Podium nt

rosy a (-ier, -iest) rosig

rot n Fäulnis f; (🔳 nonsense) Quatsch m ● vi (pt/pp rotted) [ver]faulen

rota n Dienstplan m

rotary a Dreh-; (Techn) Rotations-

rotat|e vt drehen ● vi sich drehen; (Techn) rotieren. **~ion** n Drehung f; **in ~ion** im Wechsel

rote n **by ~** auswendig

rotten a faul; 🔳 mies; <person> fies

rough a (-er, -est) rau; (uneven) uneben; (coarse, not gentle) grob; (brutal) roh; (turbulent) stürmisch; (approximate) ungefähr ● adv **sleep ~** im Freien übernachten ● vt **~ it** primitiv leben. **~ out** vt im Groben entwerfen

roughage n Ballaststoffe pl

rough draft n grober Entwurf m

rough|ly adv (see rough) rau; grob; roh; ungefähr. **~ness** n Rauheit f

rough paper n Konzeptpapier nt

round a (-er, -est) rund ● n Runde f; (slice) Scheibe f; **do one's ~s** seine Runde machen ● prep um (+ acc); **~ the clock** rund um die Uhr ● adv **all ~** ringsherum; **ask s.o. ~** jdn einladen ● vt biegen um <corner>. **~ off** vt abrunden. **~ up** vt aufrunden; zusammentreiben <animals>; festnehmen <criminals>

roundabout a **~ route** Umweg m ● n Karussell nt; (for traffic) Kreisverkehr m

round trip n Rundreise f

rous|e vt wecken; (fig) erregen. **~ing** a mitreißend

route n Route f; (of bus) Linie f

routine a, **-ly** adv routinemäßig ● n Routine f; (Theat) Nummer f

row¹ n (line) Reihe f

row² vt/i rudern

row³ n 🔳 Krach m ● vi 🔳 sich streiten

r

rowdy *a* (**-ier, -iest**) laut

rowing boat *n* Ruderboot *nt*

royal *a*, **-ly** *adv* königlich

royalt|y *n* Königtum *nt*; (*persons*) Mitglieder *pl* der königlichen Familie; **-ies** *pl* (*payments*) Tantiemen *pl*

rub *vt* (*pt/pp* **rubbed**) reiben; (*polish*) polieren; **don't ~ it in** 🔢 reib es mir nicht unter die Nase. **~ off** *vt* abreiben ● *vi* abgehen. **~ out** *vt* ausradieren

rubber *n* Gummi *m*; (*eraser*) Radiergummi *m*. **~ band** *n* Gummiband *nt*

rubbish *n* Abfall *m*, Müll *m*; (🔢 *nonsense*) Quatsch *m*; (🔢 *junk*) Plunder *m*. **~ bin** *n* Abfalleimer *m*. **~ dump** *n* Abfallhaufen *m*; (*official*) Müllhalde *f*

rubble *n* Trümmer *pl*

ruby *n* Rubin *m*

rudder *n* [Steuer]ruder *nt*

rude *a* (**-r, -st**), **-ly** *adv* unhöflich; (*improper*) unanständig. **~ness** *n* Unhöflichkeit *f*

rudimentary *a* elementar; (*Biol*) rudimentär

ruffian *n* Rüpel *m*

ruffle *vt* zerzausen

rug *n* Vorleger *m*, [kleiner] Teppich *m*; (*blanket*) Decke *f*

rugged *a* <*coastline*> zerklüftet

ruin *n* Ruine *f*; (*fig*) Ruin *m* ● *vt* ruinieren

rule *n* Regel *f*; (*control*) Herrschaft *f*; (*government*) Regierung *f*; (*for measuring*) Lineal *nt*; **as a ~** in der Regel ● *vt* regieren, herrschen über (+ *acc*); (*fig*) beherrschen; (*decide*) entscheiden; ziehen <*line*> ● *vi* regieren, herrschen. **~ out** *vt* ausschließen

ruled *a* <*paper*> liniert

ruler *n* Herrscher(in) *m(f)*; (*measure*) Lineal *nt*

ruling *a* herrschend; <*factor*> entscheidend; (*Pol*) regierend ● *n* Entscheidung *f*

rum *n* Rum *m*

rumble *n* Grollen *nt* ● *vi* grollen; <*stomach:*> knurren

rummage *vi* wühlen; **~ through** durchwühlen

rumour *n* Gerücht *nt* ● *vt* **it is ~ed that** es geht das Gerücht, dass

rump *n* Hinterteil *nt*. **~ steak** *n* Rumpsteak *nt*

run *n* Lauf *m*; (*journey*) Fahrt *f*; (*series*) Serie *f*, Reihe *f*; (*Theat*) Laufzeit *f*; (*Skiing*) Abfahrt *f*; (*enclosure*) Auslauf *m*; (*Amer: ladder*) Laufmasche *f*; **~ of bad luck** Pechsträhne *f*; **be on the ~** flüchtig sein; **in the long ~** auf lange Sicht ● *v* (*pt* **ran**, *pp* **run**, *pres p* **running**) ● *vi* laufen; (*flow*) fließen; <*eyes:*> tränen; <*bus:*> verkehren; <*butter, ink:*> zerfließen; <*colours:*> [ab]färben; (*in election*) kandidieren ● *vt* laufen lassen; einlaufen lassen <*bath*>; (*manage*) führen, leiten; (*drive*) fahren; eingehen <*risk*>; (*Journ*) bringen <*article*>; **~ one's hand over sth** mit der Hand über etw (*acc*) fahren. **~ away** *vi* weglaufen. **~ down** *vi* hinunter-/ herunterlaufen; <*clockwork:*> ablaufen; <*stocks:*> sich verringern ● *vt* (*run over*) überfahren; (*reduce*) verringern; (🔢 *criticize*) heruntermachen. **~ in** *vi* hinein-/ hereinlaufen. **~ off** *vi* weglaufen ● *vt* abziehen <*copies*>. **~ out** *vi* hinaus-/herauslaufen; <*supplies, money:*> ausgehen; **I've ~ out of sugar** ich habe keinen Zucker mehr. **~ over** *vt* überfahren. **~ up** *vi* hinauf-/herauflaufen; (*towards*) hinlaufen ● *vt* machen <*debts*>; auflaufen lassen <*bill*>; (*sew*) schnell nähen

runaway *n* Ausreißer *m*

run-down *a* <*area*> verkommen

rung[1] *n* (*of ladder*) Sprosse *f*

rung[2] *see* **ring**[1]

runner *n* Läufer *m*; (*Bot*) Ausläufer *m*; (*on sledge*) Kufe *f*. **~ bean** *n* Stangenbohne *f*. **~-up** *n* Zweite(r) *m/f*

running *a* laufend; <*water*> fließend; **four times ~** viermal nacheinander

● *n* Laufen *nt*; (*management*) Führung *f*, Leitung *f*; **be/not be in the ~** eine/keine Chance haben

runny *a* flüssig

run: ~-up *n* (*Sport*) Anlauf *m*; (*to election*) Zeit *f* vor der Wahl. **~way** *n* Start- und Landebahn *f*

rupture *n* Bruch *m* ● *vt/i* brechen

rural *a* ländlich

ruse *n* List *f*

rush¹ *n* (*Bot*) Binse *f*

rush² *n* Hetze *f*; **in a ~** in Eile ● *vi* sich hetzen; (*run*) rasen; <*water:*> rauschen ● *vt* hetzen, drängen. **~-hour** *n* Hauptverkehrszeit *f*, Stoßzeit *f*

Russia *n* Russland *nt*. **~n** *a* russisch ● *n* Russe *m*/Russin *f*; (*Lang*) Russisch *nt*

rust *n* Rost *m* ● *vi* rosten

rustle *vi* rascheln ● *vt* rascheln mit; (*Amer*) stehlen <*cattle*>. **~ up** *vt* 🄸 improvisieren

rustproof *a* rostfrei

rusty *a* (-ier, -iest) rostig

rut *n* Furche *f*

ruthless *a*, **-ly** *adv* rücksichtslos. **~ness** *n* Rücksichtslosigkeit *f*

rye *n* Roggen *m*

Ss

sabbath *n* Sabbat *m*

sabotage *n* Sabotage *f* ● *vt* sabotieren

sachet *n* Beutel *m*; (*scented*) Kissen *nt*

sack *n* Sack *m*; **get the ~** 🄸 rausgeschmissen werden ● *vt* 🄸 rausschmeißen

sacred *a* heilig

sacrifice *n* Opfer *nt* ● *vt* opfern

sacrilege *n* Sakrileg *nt*

sad *a* (**sadder, saddest**) traurig: <*loss, death*> schmerzlich. **~den** *vt* traurig machen

saddle *n* Sattel *m* ● *vt* satteln; **~ s.o. with sth** 🄸 jdm etw aufhalsen

sadist *n* Sadist *m*. **~ic** *a*, **-ally** *adv* sadistisch

sad|ly *adv* traurig; (*unfortunately*) leider. **~ness** *n* Traurigkeit *f*

safe *a* (-r, -st) sicher; <*journey*> gut; (*not dangerous*) ungefährlich; **~ and sound** gesund und wohlbehalten ● *n* Safe *m*. **~guard** *n* Schutz *m* ● *vt* schützen. **~ly** *adv* sicher; <*arrive*> gut

safety *n* Sicherheit *f*. **~-belt** *n* Sicherheitsgurt *m*. **~-pin** *n* Sicherheitsnadel *f*. **~-valve** *n* [Sicherheits]ventil *nt*

sag *vi* (*pt/pp* **sagged**) durchhängen

saga *n* Saga *f*; (*fig*) Geschichte *f*

said *see* say

sail *n* Segel *nt*; (*trip*) Segelfahrt *f* ● *vi* segeln; (*on liner*) fahren; (*leave*) abfahren (**for** nach) ● *vt* segeln mit

sailing *n* Segelsport *m*. **~-boat** *n* Segelboot *nt*. **~-ship** *n* Segelschiff *nt*

sailor *n* Seemann *m*; (*in navy*) Matrose *m*

saint *n* Heilige(r) *m/f*. **~ly** *a* heilig

sake *n* **for the ~ of** ... um ... (*gen*) willen; **for my/your ~** um meinet-/deinetwillen

salad *n* Salat *m*. **~-dressing** *n* Salatsoße *f*

salary *n* Gehalt *nt*

sale *n* Verkauf *m*; (*event*) Basar *m*; (*at reduced prices*) Schlussverkauf *m*; **for ~** zu verkaufen

sales|man *n* Verkäufer *m*. **~woman** *n* Verkäuferin *f*

saliva *n* Speichel *m*

salmon *n* Lachs *m*

saloon *n* Salon *m*; (*Auto*) Limousine *f*; (*Amer: bar*) Wirtschaft *f*

salt *n* Salz *nt* ● *a* salzig; <*water, meat*> Salz- ● *vt* salzen; (*cure*) pökeln; streuen <*road*>. **~-cellar** *n* Salzfass *nt*. **~ water** *n* Salzwasser *nt*. **~y** *a* salzig

r

s

salute n (*Mil*) Gruß m ● vt/i (*Mil*) grüßen

salvage n (*Naut*) Bergung f ● vt bergen

salvation n Rettung f; (*Relig*) Heil nt

same a & pron **the ~** der/die/das gleiche; (*pl*) die gleichen; (*identical*) der-/die-/dasselbe; (*pl*) dieselben ● adv **the ~** gleich; **all the ~** trotzdem

sample n Probe f; (*Comm*) Muster nt ● vt probieren; kosten <*food*>

sanatorium n Sanatorium nt

sanction n Sanktion f ● vt sanktionieren

sanctuary n (*Relig*) Heiligtum nt; (*refuge*) Zuflucht f; (*for wildlife*) Tierschutzgebiet nt

sand n Sand m ● vt ~ **[down]** [ab]schmirgeln

sandal n Sandale f

sand: ~**bank** n Sandbank f. ~**paper** n Sandpapier nt. ~**-pit** n Sandkasten m

sandwich n; Sandwich m ● vt ~**ed between** eingeklemmt zwischen

sandy a (-ier, -iest) sandig; <*beach, soil*> Sand-; <*hair*> rotblond

sane a (-r, -st) geistig normal; (*sensible*) vernünftig

sang see **sing**

sanitary a hygienisch; <*system*> sanitär. ~ **napkin** n (*Amer*), ~ **towel** n [Damen]binde f

sanitation n Kanalisation und Abfallbeseitigung pl

sanity n [gesunder] Verstand m

sank see **sink**

sap n (*Bot*) Saft m ● vt (pt/pp sapped) schwächen

sarcas|m n Sarkasmus m. ~**tic** a, -**ally** adv sarkastisch

sardine n Sardine f

sash n Schärpe f

sat see **sit**

satchel n Ranzen m

satellite n Satellit m. ~ **television** n Satellitenfernsehen nt

satin n Satin m

satire n Satire f

satirical a, -**ly** adv satirisch

satir|ist n Satiriker(in) m(f)

satisfaction n Befriedigung f; **to my ~** zu meiner Zufriedenheit

satisfactory a, -**ily** adv zufrieden stellend

satisfy vt (pp/pp -ied) befriedigen; zufrieden stellen <*customer*>; (*convince*) überzeugen; **be ~ied** zufrieden sein. ~**ing** a befriedigend; <*meal*> sättigend

saturate vt durchtränken; (*Chem & fig*) sättigen

Saturday n Samstag m

sauce n Soße f; (*cheek*) Frechheit f. ~**pan** n Kochtopf m

saucer n Untertasse f

saucy a (-ier, -iest) frech

Saudi Arabia n Saudi-Arabien n

sauna n Sauna f

saunter vi schlendern

sausage n Wurst f

savage a wild; (*fierce*) scharf; (*brutal*) brutal ● n Wilde(r) m/f. ~**ry** n Brutalität f

save n (*Sport*) Abwehr f ● vt retten (**from** vor + dat); (*keep*) aufheben; (*not waste*) sparen; (*collect*) sammeln; (*avoid*) ersparen; (*Sport*) verhindern <*goal*> ● vi ~ **[up]** sparen

saver n Sparer m

saving n (*see* save) Rettung f; Sparen nt; Ersparnis f; ~**s** pl (*money*) Ersparnisse pl

savour n Geschmack m ● vt auskosten. ~**y** a würzig

saw¹ see **see¹**

saw² n Säge f ● vt/i (pt sawed, pp sawn or sawed) sägen

saxophone n Saxophon nt

say n Mitspracherecht nt; **have one's ~** seine Meinung sagen ● vt/i (pt/pp said) sagen; sprechen <*prayer*>; **that is to ~** das heißt; **that goes without ~ing** das versteht sich von selbst. ~**ing** n Redensart f

scab n Schorf m; (*pej*) Streikbrecher m

scaffolding n Gerüst nt

scald *vt* verbrühen

scale¹ *n* (*of fish*) Schuppe *f*

scale² *n* Skala *f*; (*Mus*) Tonleiter *f*; (*ratio*) Maßstab *m* ● *vt* (*climb*) erklettern. **~ down** *vt* verkleinern

scales *npl* (*for weighing*) Waage *f*

scalp *n* Kopfhaut *f*

scamper *vi* huschen

scan *n* (*Med*) Szintigramm *nt* ● *v* (*pt/pp* **scanned**) ● *vt* absuchen; (*quickly*) flüchtig ansehen; (*Med*) szintigraphisch untersuchen

scandal *n* Skandal *m*; (*gossip*) Skandalgeschichten *pl*. **~ize** *vt* schockieren. **~ous** *a* skandalös

Scandinavia *n* Skandinavien *nt*. **~n** *a* skandinavisch ● *n* Skandinavier(in) *m(f)*

scanner *n* Scanner *m*

scanty *a* (**-ier**, **-iest**), **-ily** *adv* spärlich; <*clothing*> knapp

scapegoat *n* Sündenbock *m*

scar *n* Narbe *f*

scarc|e *a* (**-r**, **-st**) knapp; **make oneself ~e** 🛈 sich aus dem Staub machen. **~ely** *adv* kaum. **~ity** *n* Knappheit *f*

scare *n* Schreck *m*; (*panic*) [allgemeine] Panik *f* ● *vt* Angst machen (+ *dat*); **be ~d** Angst haben (of vor + *dat*)

scarf *n* (*pl* **scarves**) Schal *m*; (*square*) Tuch *nt*

scarlet *a* scharlachrot

scary *a* unheimlich

scathing *a* bissig

scatter *vt* verstreuen; (*disperse*) zerstreuen ● *vi* sich zerstreuen. **~ed** *a* verstreut; <*showers*> vereinzelt

scatty *a* (**-ier**, **-iest**) 🛈 verrückt

scene *n* Szene *f*; (*sight*) Anblick *m*; (*place of event*) Schauplatz *m*; **behind the ~s** hinter den Kulissen

scenery *n* Landschaft *f*; (*Theat*) Szenerie *f*

scenic *a* landschaftlich schön

scent *n* Duft *m*; (*trail*) Fährte *f*; (*perfume*) Parfüm *nt*. **~ed** *a* parfümiert

sceptic|al *a*, **-ly** *adv* skeptisch. **~ism** *n* Skepsis *f*

schedule *n* Programm *nt*; (*of work*) Zeitplan *m*; (*timetable*) Fahrplan *m*; **behind ~** im Rückstand; **according to ~** planmäßig ● *vt* planen

scheme *n* Programm *nt*; (*plan*) Plan *m*; (*plot*) Komplott *nt* ● *vi* Ränke schmieden

schizophrenic *a* schizophren

scholar *n* Gelehrte(r) *m/f*. **~ly** *a* gelehrt. **~ship** *n* Gelehrtheit *f*; (*grant*) Stipendium *nt*

school *n* Schule *f*; (*Univ*) Fakultät *f* ● *vt* schulen

school: ~boy *n* Schüler *m*. **~girl** *n* Schülerin *f*. **~ing** *n* Schulbildung *f*. **~master** *n* Lehrer *m*. **~mistress** *n* Lehrerin *f*. **~teacher** *n* Lehrer(in) *m(f)*

scien|ce *n* Wissenschaft *f*. **~tific** *a* wissenschaftlich. **~tist** *n* Wissenschaftler *m*

scissors *npl* Schere *f*; **a pair of ~** eine Schere

scoff¹ *vi* **~ at** spotten über (+ *acc*)

scoff² *vt* 🛈 verschlingen

scold *vt* ausschimpfen

scoop *n* Schaufel *f*; (*Culin*) Portionierer *m*; (*Journ*) Exklusivmeldung *f* ● *vt* **~ out** aushöhlen; (*remove*) auslöffeln

scooter *n* Roller *m*

scope *n* Bereich *m*; (*opportunity*) Möglichkeiten *pl*

scorch *vt* versengen. **~ing** *a* glühend heiß

score *n* [Spiel]stand *m*; (*individual*) Punktzahl *f*; (*Mus*) Partitur *f*; (*Cinema*) Filmmusik *f*; **on that ~** was das betrifft ● *vt* erzielen; schießen <*goal*>; (*cut*) einritzen ● *vi* Punkte erzielen; (*Sport*) ein Tor schießen; (*keep score*) Punkte zählen. **~r** *n* Punktezähler *m*; (*of goals*) Torschütze *m*

scorn *n* Verachtung *f* ● *vt* verachten. **~ful** *a*, **-ly** *adv* verächtlich

Scot *n* Schotte *m*/Schottin *f*

Scotch a schottisch ● n (whisky) Scotch m

Scot|land n Schottland nt. ~s, ~tish a schottisch

scoundrel n Schurke m

scour vt (search) absuchen; (clean) scheuern

scout n (Mil) Kundschafter m; [Boy] S~ Pfadfinder m

scowl n böser Gesichtsausdruck m ● vi ein böses Gesicht machen

scram vi 🗵 abhauen

scramble n Gerangel nt ● vi klettern; ~ for sich drängen nach. ~d egg[s] n[pl] Rührei nt

scrap¹ n (🗵 fight) Rauferei f ● vi sich raufen

scrap² n Stückchen nt; (metal) Schrott m; ~s pl Reste; not a ~ kein bisschen ● vt (pt/pp scrapped) aufgeben

scrapbook n Sammelalbum nt

scrape vt schaben; (clean) abkratzen; (damage) [ver]schrammen. ~ through vi gerade noch durchkommen. ~ together vt zusammenkriegen

scrappy a lückenhaft

scrapyard n Schrottplatz m

scratch n Kratzer m; start from ~ von vorne anfangen; not be up to ~ zu wünschen übrig lassen ● vt/i kratzen; (damage) zerkratzen

scrawl n Gekrakel nt ● vt/i krakeln

scream n Schrei m ● vt/i schreien

screech n Kreischen nt ● vt/i kreischen

screen n Schirm m; (Cinema) Leinwand f; (TV) Bildschirm m ● vt schützen; (conceal) verdecken; vorführen <film>; (examine) überprüfen; (Med) untersuchen

screw n Schraube f ● vt schrauben. ~ up vt festschrauben; (crumple) zusammenknüllen; zusammenkneifen <eyes>; (🗵 bungle) vermasseln

screwdriver n Schraubenzieher m

scribble n Gekritzel nt ● vt/i kritzeln

script n Schrift f; (of speech, play) Text m; (Radio, TV) Skript nt; (of film) Drehbuch nt

scrounge vt/i schnorren. ~r n Schnorrer m

scrub¹ n (land) Buschland nt, Gestrüpp nt

scrub² vt/i (pt/pp scrubbed) schrubben

scruff n by the ~ of the neck beim Genick

scruffy a (-ier, -iest) vergammelt

scrum n Gedränge nt

scruple n Skrupel m

scrupulous a, -ly adv gewissenhaft

scuffle n Handgemenge nt

sculpt|or n Bildhauer(in) m(f). ~ure n Bildhauerei f; (piece of work) Skulptur f, Plastik f

scum n Schmutzschicht f; (people) Abschaum m

scurry vi (pt/pp -ied) huschen

scuttle¹ vt versenken <ship>

scuttle² vi schnell krabbeln

sea n Meer nt, See f; at ~ auf See; by ~ mit dem Schiff. ~food n Meeresfrüchte pl. ~gull n Möwe f

seal¹ n (Zool) Seehund m

seal² n Siegel nt ● vt versiegeln; (fig) besiegeln. ~ off vt abriegeln

sea-level n Meeresspiegel m

seam n Naht f; (of coal) Flöz nt

seaman n Seemann m; (sailor) Matrose m

seance n spiritistische Sitzung f

search n Suche f; (official) Durchsuchung f ● vt durchsuchen; absuchen <area> ● vi suchen (for nach). ~ing a prüfend, forschend

search: ~light n [Such]scheinwerfer m. ~-party n Suchmannschaft f

sea: ~sick a seekrank. ~side n at/to the ~side am/ans Meer

season n Jahreszeit f; (social, tourist, sporting) Saison f ● vt (flavour) würzen. ~al a Saison-. ~ing n Gewürze pl

season ticket n Dauerkarte f

seat n Sitz m; (*place*) Sitzplatz m; (*bottom*) Hintern m; **take a ~** Platz nehmen ● vt setzen; (*have seats for*) Sitzplätze bieten (+ dat); **remain ~ed** sitzen bleiben. **~-belt** n Sicherheitsgurt m; **fasten one's ~-belt** sich anschnallen

sea: **~weed** n [See]tang m. **~worthy** a seetüchtig

seclu|ded a abgelegen. **~sion** n Zurückgezogenheit f

second a zweite(r,s); **on ~ thoughts** nach weiterer Überlegung ● n Sekunde f; (*Sport*) Sekundant m; **~s** pl (*goods*) Waren zweiter Wahl ● adv (*in race*) an zweiter Stelle ● vt unterstützen <*proposal*>

secondary a zweitrangig; (*Phys*) Sekundär-. **~ school** n höhere Schule f

second: **~-best** a zweitbeste(r,s). **~ class** adv <*travel, send*> zweiter Klasse. **~-class** a zweitklassig

second hand n (*on clock*) Sekundenzeiger m

second-hand a gebraucht ● adv aus zweiter Hand

secondly adv zweitens

second-rate a zweitklassig

secrecy n Heimlichkeit f

secret a geheim; <*agent, police*> Geheim-; <*drinker, lover*> heimlich ● n Geheimnis nt

secretarial a Sekretärinnen-; <*work, staff*> Sekretariats-

secretary n Sekretär(in) m(f)

secretive a geheimtuerisch

secretly adv heimlich

sect n Sekte f

section n Teil m; (*of text*) Abschnitt m; (*of firm*) Abteilung f; (*of organization*) Sektion f

sector n Sektor m

secular a weltlich

secure a, **-ly** adv sicher; (*firm*) fest; (*emotionally*) geborgen ● vt sichern; (*fasten*) festmachen; (*obtain*) sich (dat) sichern

securit|y n Sicherheit f; (*emotional*) Geborgenheit f; **~ies** pl Wertpapiere pl

sedan n (*Amer*) Limousine f

sedate a, **-ly** adv gesetzt

sedative a beruhigend ● n Beruhigungsmittel nt

sediment n [Boden]satz m

seduce vt verführen

seduct|ion n Verführung f. **~ive** a, **-ly** adv verführerisch

see v (pt **saw**, pp **seen**) ● vt sehen; (*understand*) einsehen; (*imagine*) sich (dat) vorstellen; (*escort*) begleiten; **go and ~** nachsehen; (*visit*) besuchen; **~ you later!** bis nachher! **~ing that** da ● vi sehen; (*check*) nachsehen; **~ about** sich kümmern um. **~ off** vt verabschieden; (*chase away*) vertreiben. **~ through** vt (*fig*) durchschauen <*person*>

seed n Samen m; (*of grape*) Kern m; (*fig*) Saat f; (*Tennis*) gesetzter Spieler m; **go to ~** Samen bilden; (*fig*) herunterkommen. **~ed** a (*Tennis*) gesetzt

seedy a (**-ier**, **-iest**) schäbig; <*area*> heruntergekommen

seek vt (pt/pp **sought**) suchen

seem vi scheinen

seen see **see**[1]

seep vi sickern

seethe vi **~ with anger** vor Wut schäumen

see-through a durchsichtig

segment n Teil m; (*of worm*) Segment nt; (*of orange*) Spalte f

segregat|e vt trennen. **~ion** n Trennung f

seize vt ergreifen; (*Jur*) beschlagnahmen; **~ s.o. by the arm** jdn am Arm packen. **~ up** vi (*Techn*) sich festfressen

seldom adv selten

select a ausgewählt; (*exclusive*) exklusiv ● vt auswählen; aufstellen <*team*>. **~ion** n Auswahl f

self n (pl **selves**) Ich nt

self: **~-assurance** n Selbstsicherheit f. **~-assured** a selbstsicher. **~-catering** n Selbstversorgung f. **~-centred** a egozentrisch. **~-confidence** n

S

Selbstbewusstsein *nt*, Selbstvertrauen *nt*. **~-confident** *a* selbstbewusst. **~-conscious** *a* befangen. **~-contained** *a* <*flat*> abgeschlossen. **~-control** *n* Selbstbeherrschung *f*. **~-defence** *n* Selbstverteidigung *f*; (*Jur*) Notwehr *f*. **~-employed** selbstständig. **~-esteem** *n* Selbstachtung *f*. **~-evident** *a* offensichtlich. **~-indulgent** *a* maßlos. **~-interest** *n* Eigennutz *m*

self|ish *a*, **-ly** *adv* egoistisch, selbstsüchtig. **~less** *a*, **-ly** *adv* selbstlos

self: **~-pity** *n* Selbstmitleid *nt*. **~-portrait** *n* Selbstporträt *nt*. **~-respect** *n* Selbstachtung *f*. **~-righteous** *a* selbstgerecht. **~-sacrifice** *n* Selbstaufopferung *f*. **~-satisfied** *a* selbstgefällig. **~-service** *n* Selbstbedienung *f* ● *attrib* Selbstbedienungs-. **~-sufficient** *a* selbstständig

sell *v* (*pt/pp* sold) ● *vt* verkaufen; be sold out ausverkauft sein ● *vi* sich verkaufen. **~ off** *vt* verkaufen

seller *n* Verkäufer *m*

Sellotape (P), *n* ≈ Tesafilm (P) *m*

sell-out *n* be a ~ ausverkauft sein; (॒ *betrayal*) Verrat sein

selves *see* self

semester *n* (*Amer*) Semester *nt*

semi|breve *n* (*Mus*) ganze Note *f*. **~circle** *n* Halbkreis *m*. **~circular** *a* halbkreisförmig. **~colon** *n* Semikolon *nt*. **~-detached** *a & n* **~-detached [house]** Doppelhaushälfte *f*. **~-final** *n* Halbfinale *nt*

seminar *n* Seminar *nt*

senat|e *n* Senat *m*. **~or** *n* Senator *m*

send *vt/i* (*pt/pp* sent) schicken; ~ for kommen lassen <*person*>; sich (*dat*) schicken lassen <*thing*>. **~er** *n* Absender *m*. **~-off** *n* Verabschiedung *f*

senile *a* senil

senior *a* älter; (*in rank*) höher ● *n* Ältere(r) *m/f*; (*in rank*)

Vorgesetzte(r) *m/f*. ~ **citizen** *n* Senior(in) *m(f)*

seniority *n* höheres Alter *nt*; (*in rank*) höherer Rang *m*

sensation *n* Sensation *f*; (*feeling*) Gefühl *nt*. **~al** *a*, **-ly** *adv* sensationell

sense *n* Sinn *m*; (*feeling*) Gefühl *nt*; (*common* ~) Verstand *m*; make ~ Sinn ergeben ● *vt* spüren. **~less** *a*, **-ly** *adv* sinnlos; (*unconscious*) bewusstlos

sensible *a*, **-bly** *adv* vernünftig; <*suitable*> zweckmäßig

sensitiv|e *a*, **-ly** *adv* empfindlich; (*understanding*) einfühlsam. **~ity** *n* Empfindlichkeit *f*

sensual *a* sinnlich. **-ity** *n* Sinnlichkeit *f*

sensuous *a* sinnlich

sent *see* send

sentence *n* Satz *m*; (*Jur*) Urteil *nt*; (*punishment*) Strafe *f* ● *vt* verurteilen

sentiment *n* Gefühl *nt*; (*opinion*) Meinung *f*; (*sentimentality*) Sentimentalität *f* **~al** *a* sentimental. **~ality** *n* Sentimentalität *f*

sentry *n* Wache *f*

separable *a* trennbar

separate¹ *a*, **-ly** *adv* getrennt, separat

separat|e² *vt* trennen ● *vi* sich trennen. **~ion** *n* Trennung *f*

September *n* September *m*

septic *a* vereitert

sequel *n* Folge *f*; (*fig*) Nachspiel *nt*

sequence *n* Reihenfolge *f*

serenade *n* Ständchen *nt* ● *vt* ~ s.o. jdm ein Ständchen bringen

seren|e *a*, **-ly** *adv* gelassen. **~ity** *n* Gelassenheit *f*

sergeant *n* (*Mil*) Feldwebel *m*; (*in police*) Polizeimeister *m*

serial *n* Fortsetzungsgeschichte *f*; (*Radio, TV*) Serie *f*. **~ize** *vt* in Fortsetzungen veröffentlichen/ (*Radio, TV*) senden

series *n inv* Serie *f*

serious *a*, **-ly** *adv* ernst; <*illness, error*> schwer. **~ness** *n* Ernst *m*

sermon n Predigt f

servant n Diener(in) m(f)

serve n (*Tennis*) Aufschlag m ● vt dienen (+ dat); bedienen <*customer, guest*>; servieren <*food*>; verbüßen <*sentence*>; it ∼s you right! das geschieht dir recht! ● vi dienen; (*Tennis*) aufschlagen

service n Dienst m; (*Relig*) Gottesdienst m; (*in shop, restaurant*) Bedienung f; (*transport*) Verbindung f; (*maintenance*) Wartung f; (*set of crockery*) Service nt; (*Tennis*) Aufschlag m; ∼s pl Dienstleistungen pl; (*on motorway*) Tankstelle und Raststätte f; in the ∼s beim Militär; out of/in ∼ <*machine:*> außer/in Betrieb ● vt (*Techn*) warten

service: ∼ **area** n Tankstelle und Raststätte f. ∼ **charge** n Bedienungszuschlag m. ∼**man** n Soldat m. ∼ **station** n Tankstelle f

serviette n Serviette f

servile a unterwürfig

session n Sitzung f

set n Satz m; (*of crockery*) Service nt; (*of cutlery*) Garnitur f; (*TV, Radio*) Apparat m; (*Math*) Menge f; (*Theat*) Bühnenbild nt; (*Cinema*) Szenenaufbau m; (*of people*) Kreis m ● a (*ready*) fertig, bereit; (*rigid*) fest; <*book*> vorgeschrieben; be ∼ on doing sth entschlossen sein, etw zu tun ● v (*pt/pp* set, *pres p* setting) ● vt setzen; (*adjust*) einstellen; stellen <*task, alarm clock*>; festsetzen, festlegen <*date, limit*>; aufgeben <*homework*>; zusammenstellen <*questions*>; [ein]fassen <*gem*>; einrichten <*bone*>; legen <*hair*>; decken <*table*> ● vi <*sun:*> untergehen; (*become hard*) fest werden. ∼ **back** vt zurücksetzen; (*hold up*) aufhalten; (⚠ *cost*) kosten. ∼ **off** vi losgehen; (*in vehicle*) losfahren ● vt auslösen <*alarm*>; explodieren lassen <*bomb*>. ∼ **out** vi losgehen; (*in vehicle*) losfahren ● vt auslegen; (*state*) darlegen. ∼ **up** vt aufbauen; (*fig*) gründen

settee n Sofa nt, Couch f

setting n Rahmen m; (*surroundings*) Umgebung f

settle vt (*decide*) entscheiden; (*agree*) regeln; (*fix*) festsetzen; (*calm*) beruhigen; (*pay*) bezahlen ● vi sich niederlassen; <*snow, dust:*> liegen bleiben; (*subside*) sich senken; <*sediment:*> sich absetzen. ∼ **down** vi sich beruhigen; (*permanently*) sesshaft werden. ∼ **up** vi abrechnen

settlement n (*see* settle) Entscheidung f; Regelung f; Bezahlung f; (*Jur*) Vergleich m; (*colony*) Siedlung f

settler n Siedler m

set-up n System nt

seven a sieben. ∼**teen** a siebzehn. ∼**teenth** a siebzehnte(r,s)

seventh a siebte(r,s)

seventieth a siebzigste(r,s)

seventy a siebzig

several a & pron mehrere, einige

sever|e a (-r, -st,) **-ly** adv streng; <*pain*> stark; <*illness*> schwer. ∼**ity** n Strenge f; Schwere f

sew vt/i (*pt* sewed, *pp* sewn *or* sewed) nähen

sewage n Abwasser nt

sewer n Abwasserkanal m

sewing n Nähen nt; (*work*) Näharbeit f. ∼ **machine** n Nähmaschine f

sewn *see* sew

sex n Geschlecht nt; (*sexuality, intercourse*) Sex m. ∼**ist** a sexistisch

sexual a, **-ly** adv sexuell. ∼ **intercourse** n Geschlechtsverkehr m

sexuality n Sexualität f

sexy a (-ier, -iest) sexy

shabby a (-ier, -iest), **-ily** adv schäbig

shack n Hütte f

shade n Schatten m; (*of colour*) [Farb]ton m; (*for lamp*) [Lampen]schirm m; (*Amer: window-blind*) Jalousie f ● vt beschatten

shadow n Schatten m ● vt (*follow*) beschatten

S

shady a (-ier, -iest) schattig; (🔲 disreputable) zwielichtig

shaft n Schaft m; (Techn) Welle f; (of light) Strahl m; (of lift) Schacht m

shaggy a (-ier, -iest) zottig

shake n Schütteln nt ● v (pt shook, pp shaken) ● vt schütteln; (shock) erschüttern; ~ hands with s.o. jdm die Hand geben ● vi wackeln; (tremble) zittern. ~ off vt abschütteln

shaky a (-ier, -iest) wackelig; <hand, voice> zittrig

shall v aux we ~ see wir werden sehen; what ~ I do? was soll ich machen?

shallow a (-er, -est) seicht; <dish> flach; (fig) oberflächlich

sham a unecht ● n Heuchelei f ● vt (pt/pp shammed) vortäuschen

shambles n Durcheinander nt

shame n Scham f; (disgrace) Schande f; be a ~ schade sein; what a ~! wie schade!

shame|ful a, -ly adv schändlich. ~less a, -ly adv schamlos

shampoo n Shampoo nt ● vt schamponieren

shan't = shall not

shape n Form f; (figure) Gestalt f ● vt formen (into zu). ~less a formlos; <clothing> unförmig

share n [An]teil m; (Comm) Aktie f ● vt/i teilen. ~holder n Aktionär(in) m(f)

shark n Hai[fisch] m

sharp a (-er, -est), -ly adv scharf; (pointed) spitz; (severe) heftig; (sudden) steil; (alert) clever; (unscrupulous) gerissen ● adv scharf; (Mus) zu hoch; at six o'clock ~ Punkt sechs Uhr ● n (Mus) Kreuz nt. ~en vt schärfen; [an]spitzen <pencil>

shatter vt zertrümmern; (fig) zerstören; ~ed <person:> erschüttert; (🔲 exhausted) kaputt ● vi zersplittern

shave n Rasur f; have a ~ sich rasieren ● vt rasieren ● vi sich rasieren. ~r n Rasierapparat m

shawl n Schultertuch nt

she pron sie

shears npl [große] Schere f

shed¹ n Schuppen m

shed² vt (pt/pp shed, pres p shedding) verlieren; vergießen <blood, tears>; ~ light on Licht bringen in (+ acc)

sheep n inv Schaf nt. ~-dog n Hütehund m

sheepish a, -ly adv verlegen

sheer a rein; (steep) steil; (transparent) hauchdünn

sheet n Laken nt, Betttuch nt; (of paper) Blatt nt; (of glass, metal) Platte f

shelf n (pl shelves) Brett nt, Bord nt; (set of shelves) Regal nt

shell n Schale f; (of snail) Haus nt; (of tortoise) Panzer m; (on beach) Muschel f; (Mil) Granate f ● vt pellen; enthülsen <peas>; (Mil) [mit Granaten] beschießen. ~ out vi 🔲 blechen

shellfish n inv Schalentiere pl; (Culin) Meeresfrüchte pl

shelter n Schutz m; (air-raid ~) Luftschutzraum m ● vt schützen (from vor + dat) ● vi sich unterstellen. ~ed a geschützt; <life> behütet

shelve vt auf Eis legen; (abandon) aufgeben

shelving n (shelves) Regale pl

shepherd n Schäfer m ● vt führen

sherry n Sherry m

shield n Schild m; (for eyes) Schirm m; (Techn & fig) Schutz m ● vt schützen (from vor + dat)

shift n Verschiebung f; (at work) Schicht f ● vt rücken; (take away) wegnehmen; (rearrange) umstellen; schieben <blame> (on to auf + acc) ● vi sich verschieben; (🔲 rush) rasen

shifty a (-ier, -iest) (pej) verschlagen

shimmer n Schimmer m ● vi schimmern

shin n Schienbein nt

shine n Glanz m ● v (pt/pp shone) ● vi leuchten; (reflect light) glänzen;

<sun.> scheinen ● *vt* ~ **a light on** beleuchten

shingle *n* (*pebbles*) Kiesel *pl*

shiny *a* (-ier, -iest) glänzend

ship *n* Schiff *nt* ● *vt* (*pt/pp* shipped) verschiffen

ship: ~**building** *n* Schiffbau *m*. ~**ment** *n* Sendung *f*. ~**per** *n* Spediteur *m*. ~**ping** *n* Versand *m*; (*traffic*) Schifffahrt *f*. ~**shape** *a* & *adv* in Ordnung. ~**wreck** *n* Schiffbruch *m*. ~**wrecked** *a* schiffbrüchig. ~**yard** *n* Werft *f*

shirt *n* [Ober]hemd *nt*; (*for woman*) Hemdbluse *f*

shit *n* (*vulg*) Scheiße *f* ● *vi* (*pt/pp* shit) (*vulg*) scheißen

shiver *n* Schauder *m* ● *vi* zittern

shoal *n* (*fish*) Schwarm *m*

shock *n* Schock *m*; (*Electr*) Schlag *m*; (*impact*) Erschütterung *f* ● *vt* einen Schock versetzen (+ *dat*); (*scandalize*) schockieren. ~**ing** *a* schockierend; (🗓 *bad*) fürchterlich

shoddy *a* (-ier, -iest) minderwertig

shoe *n* Schuh *m*; (*of horse*) Hufeisen *nt* ● *vt* (*pt/pp* shod, *pres p* shoeing) beschlagen *<horse>*

shoe: ~**horn** *n* Schuhanzieher *m*. ~**lace** *n* Schnürsenkel *m*. ~**string** *n* on a ~string 🗓 mit ganz wenig Geld

shone *see* shine

shoo *vt* scheuchen ● *int* sch!

shook *see* shake

shoot *n* (*Bot*) Trieb *m*; (*hunt*) Jagd *f* ● *v* (*pt/pp* shot) ● *vt* schießen; (*kill*) erschießen; drehen *<film>* ● *vi* schießen. ~ **down** *vt* abschießen. ~ **out** *vi* (*rush*) herausschießen. ~ **up** *vi* (*grow*) in die Höhe schießen/ *<prices:>* schnellen

shop *n* Laden *m*, Geschäft *nt*; (*workshop*) Werkstatt *f*; talk ~ 🗓 fachsimpeln ● *vi* (*pt/pp* shopped, *pres p* shopping) einkaufen; go ~ping einkaufen gehen

shop: ~ **assistant** *n* Verkäufer(in) *m*(*f*). ~**keeper** *n* Ladenbesitzer(in) *m*(*f*). ~**lifter** *n* Ladendieb *m*. ~**lifting** *n* Ladendiebstahl *m*

shopping *n* Einkaufen *nt*; (*articles*) Einkäufe *pl*; do the ~ einkaufen. ~ **bag** *n* Einkaufstasche *f*. ~ **centre** *n* Einkaufszentrum *nt*. ~ **trolley** *n* Einkaufswagen *m*

shop-window *n* Schaufenster *nt*

shore *n* Strand *m*; (*of lake*) Ufer *nt*

short *a* (-er, -est) kurz; *<person>* klein; (*curt*) schroff; a ~ time ago vor kurzem; be ~ of ... zu wenig ... haben; be in ~ supply knapp sein ● *adv* kurz; (*abruptly*) plötzlich; (*curtly*) kurz angebunden; in ~ kurzum; ~ of (*except*) außer; go ~ Mangel leiden

shortage *n* Mangel *m* (of an + *dat*); (*scarcity*) Knappheit *f*

short: ~**bread** *n* ≈ Mürbekekse *pl*. ~ **circuit** *n* Kurzschluss *m*. ~**coming** *n* Fehler *m*. ~ **cut** *n* Abkürzung *f*

shorten *vt* [ab]kürzen; kürzer machen *<garment>*

short: ~**hand** *n* Kurzschrift *f*, Stenographie *f*. ~**list** *n* engere Auswahl *f*

short|ly *adv* in Kürze; ~ly before/ after kurz vorher/danach. ~**ness** *n* Kürze *f*; (*of person*) Kleinheit *f*

shorts *npl* Shorts *pl*

short: ~**sighted** *a* kurzsichtig. ~**sleeved** *a* kurzärmelig. ~ **story** *n* Kurzgeschichte *f*. ~**tempered** *a* aufbrausend. ~**term** *a* kurzfristig. ~ **wave** *n* Kurzwelle *f*

shot *see* shoot ● *n* Schuss *m*; (*pellets*) Schrot *m*; (*person*) Schütze *m*; (*Phot*) Aufnahme *f*; (*injection*) Spritze *f*; (🗓 *attempt*) Versuch *m*; like a ~ 🗓 sofort. ~**gun** *n* Schrotflinte *f*. ~**put** *n* (*Sport*) Kugelstoßen *nt*

should *v aux* you ~ go du solltest gehen; I ~ have seen him ich hätte ihn sehen sollen; I ~ like ich möchte; this ~ be enough das müsste eigentlich reichen; if he ~ be there falls er da sein sollte

shoulder *n* Schulter *f* ● *vt* schultern; (*fig*) auf sich (*acc*) nehmen. ~**blade** *n* Schulterblatt *nt*

shout *n* Schrei *m* ● *vt/i* schreien. ~ **down** *vt* niederschreien

S

shouting n Geschrei nt

shove n Stoß m ● vt stoßen; (🔲 put) tun ● vi drängeln. ~ **off** vi 🔲 abhauen

shovel n Schaufel f ● vt (pt/pp **shovelled**) schaufeln

show n (display) Pracht f; (exhibition) Ausstellung f, Schau f; (performance) Vorstellung f; (Theat, TV) Show f; **on** ~ ausgestellt ● v (pt **showed**, pp **shown**) ● vt zeigen; (put on display) ausstellen; vorführen <film> ● vi sichtbar sein; <film:> gezeigt werden. ~ **in** vt hereinführen. ~ **off** vi 🔲 angeben ● vt vorführen; (flaunt) angeben mit. ~ **up** vi [deutlich] zu sehen sein; (🔲 arrive) auftauchen ● vt deutlich zeigen; (🔲 embarrass) blamieren

shower n Dusche f; (of rain) Schauer m; **have a** ~ duschen ● vt ~ **with** überschütten mit ● vi duschen

show-jumping n Springreiten nt

shown see show

show: ~**-off** n Angeber(in) m(f). ~**room** n Ausstellungsraum m

showy a protzig

shrank see shrink

shred n Fetzen m; (fig) Spur f ● vt (pt/pp **shredded**) zerkleinern; (Culin) schnitzeln. ~**der** n Reißwolf m; (Culin) Schnitzelwerk nt

shrewd a (-er, -est), **-ly** adv klug. ~**ness** n Klugheit f

shriek n Schrei m ● vt/i schreien

shrill a, **-y** adv schrill

shrimp n Garnele f, Krabbe f

shrink vi (pt **shrank**, pp **shrunk**) schrumpfen; <garment:> einlaufen; (draw back) zurückschrecken (**from** vor + dat)

shrivel vi (pt/pp **shrivelled**) verschrumpeln

Shrove n ~ **Tuesday** Fastnachtsdienstag m

shrub n Strauch m

shrug n Achselzucken nt ● vt/i (pt/pp **shrugged**) ~ [**one's shoulders**] die Achseln zucken

shrunk see shrink

shudder n Schauder m ● vi schaudern; (tremble) zittern

shuffle vi schlurfen ● vt mischen <cards>

shun vt (pt/pp **shunned**) meiden

shunt vt rangieren

shut v (pt/pp **shut**, pres p **shutting**) ● vt zumachen, schließen ● vi sich schließen; <shop:> schließen, zumachen; stilllegen <factory> ● vi schließen. ~ **up** vt abschließen; (lock in) einsperren ● vi 🔲 den Mund halten

shutter n [Fenster]laden m; (Phot) Verschluss m

shuttle n (Tex) Schiffchen nt

shuttle service n Pendelverkehr m

shy a (-er, -est), **-ly** adv schüchtern; (timid) scheu. ~**ness** n Schüchternheit f

siblings npl Geschwister pl

Sicily n Sizilien nt

sick a krank; <humour> makaber; **be** ~ (vomit) sich übergeben; **be** ~ **of sth** 🔲 etw satt haben; **I feel** ~ mir ist schlecht

sick|ly a (-ier, -iest) kränklich. ~**ness** n Krankheit f; (vomiting) Erbrechen nt

side n Seite f; **on the** ~ (as sideline) nebenbei; ~ **by** ~ nebeneinander; (fig) Seite an Seite; **take** ~s Partei ergreifen (**with** für) ● attrib Seiten- ● vi ~ **with** Partei ergreifen für

side: ~**board** n Anrichte f. ~**-effect** n Nebenwirkung f. ~**lights** npl Standlicht nt. ~**line** n Nebenbeschäftigung f. ~**-show** n Nebenattraktion f. ~**-step** vt ausweichen (+ dat). ~**walk** n (Amer) Bürgersteig m. ~**ways** adv seitwärts

siding n Abstellgleis nt

siege n Belagerung f; (by police) Umstellung f

sieve n Sieb nt ● vt sieben

sift vt sieben; (fig) durchsehen

sigh n Seufzer m ● vi seufzen

sight n Sicht f; (faculty) Sehvermögen nt; (spectacle) Anblick *m*; (*on gun*) Visier *nt*; **~s** *pl* Sehenswürdigkeiten *pl*; **at first ~** auf den ersten Blick; **lose ~ of** aus dem Auge verlieren; **know by ~** vom Sehen kennen ● *vt* sichten

sightseeing *n* **go ~** die Sehenswürdigkeiten besichtigen

sign *n* Zeichen *nt*; (*notice*) Schild *nt* ● *vt/i* unterschreiben; <*author, artist:*> signieren. **~ on** *vi* (*as unemployed*) sich arbeitslos melden; (*Mil*) sich verpflichten

signal *n* Signal *nt* ● *vt/i* (*pt/pp* **signalled**) signalisieren; **~ to s.o.** jdm ein Signal geben

signature *n* Unterschrift *f*; (*of artist*) Signatur *f*

significan|ce *n* Bedeutung *f*. **~t** *a*, **-ly** *adv* (*important*) bedeutend

signify *vt* (*pt/pp* **-ied**) bedeuten

signpost *n* Wegweiser *m*

silence *n* Stille *f*; (*of person*) Schweigen *nt* ● *vt* zum Schweigen bringen. **~r** *n* (*on gun*) Schalldämpfer *m*; (*Auto*) Auspufftopf *m*

silent *a*, **-ly** *adv* still; (*without speaking*) schweigend; **remain ~** schweigen

silhouette *n* Silhouette *f*; (*picture*) Schattenriss *m* ● *vt* **be ~d** sich als Silhouette abheben

silicon *n* Silizium *nt*

silk *n* Seide *f* ● *attrib* Seiden-

silky *a* (**-ier**, **-iest**) seidig

sill *n* Sims *m* & *nt*

silly *a* (**-ier**, **-iest**) dumm, albern

silver *a* silbern; <*coin, paper*> Silber- ● *n* Silber *nt*

silver: ~-plated *a* versilbert. **~ware** *n* Silber *nt*

similar *a*, **-ly** *adv* ähnlich. **~ity** *n* Ähnlichkeit *f*

simmer *vi* leise kochen, ziehen ● *vt* ziehen lassen

simple *a* (**-r**, **-st**) einfach; <*person*> einfältig. **~-minded** *a* einfältig

simplicity *n* Einfachheit *f*

simpli|fication *n* Vereinfachung *f*. **~fy** *vt* (*pt/pp* **-ied**) vereinfachen

simply *adv* einfach

simulate *vt* vortäuschen; (*Techn*) simulieren

simultaneous *a*, **-ly** *adv* gleichzeitig

sin *n* Sünde *f* ● *vi* (*pt/pp* **sinned**) sündigen

---

since
● *preposition*
····▸ seit (+ *dat*). **he's been living here since 1991** er wohnt* seit 1991 hier. **I had been waiting since 8 o'clock** ich wartete* [schon] seit 8 Uhr. **since seeing you** seit ich dich gesehen habe. **how long is it since your interview?** wie lange ist es seit deinem Vorstellungsgespräch?
● *adverb*
····▸ seitdem. **I haven't spoken to her since** seitdem habe ich mit ihr nicht gesprochen. **the house has been empty ever since** das Haus steht seitdem leer. **he has since remarried** er hat danach wieder geheiratet. **long since** vor langer Zeit
● *conjunction*
····▸ seit. **since she has been living in Germany** seit sie in Deutschland wohnt*. **since they had been in London** seit sie in London waren*. **how long is it since he left?** wie lange ist es her, dass er weggezogen ist? **it's a year since he left** es ist ein Jahr her, dass er weggezogen ist
····▸ (*because*) da. **since she was ill, I had to do it** da sie krank war, musste ich es tun

⚠ *Note the different tenses in German

---

sincere *a* aufrichtig; (*heartfelt*) herzlich. **~ly** *adv* aufrichtig; **Yours ~ly** Mit freundlichen Grüßen

sincerity *n* Aufrichtigkeit *f*

sinful *a* sündhaft

sing *vt/i* (*pt* **sang**, *pp* **sung**) singen

singe *vt* (*pres p* **singeing**) versengen

singer *n* Sänger(in) *m(f)*

single *a* einzeln; (*one only*) einzig; (*unmarried*) ledig; <*ticket*> einfach; <*room, bed*> Einzel- ● *n* (*ticket*) einfache Fahrkarte *f*; (*record*) Single

S

f; ∼**s** *pl* (*Tennis*) Einzel *nt* ● *vt* ∼
out auswählen

single: ∼**-handed** *a & adv* allein.
∼ **parent** *n* Alleinerziehende(r) *m/f*

singly *adv* einzeln

singular *a* eigenartig; (*Gram*) im
Singular ● *n* Singular *m*

sinister *a* finster

sink *n* Spülbecken *nt* ● *v* (*pt* sank, *pp*
sunk) ● *vt* versenken
<*ship*>; senken <*shaft*>. ∼ **in** *vi*
einsinken; (🄸 *be understood*) kapiert
werden

sinner *n* Sünder(in) *m(f)*

sip *n* Schlückchen *nt* ● *vt* (*pt/pp*
sipped) in kleinen Schlucken
trinken

siphon *n* (*bottle*) Siphon *m*. ∼ **off** *vt*
mit einem Saugheber ablassen

sir *n* mein Herr; S∼ (*title*) Sir; **Dear
S∼s** Sehr geehrte Herren

siren *n* Sirene *f*

sister *n* Schwester *f*; (*nurse*)
Oberschwester *f*. ∼**-in-law** *n*
Schwägerin *f*

sit *v* (*pt/pp* sat, *pres p* sitting) ● *vi*
sitzen; (*sit down*) sich setzen;
<*committee*:> tagen ● *vt* setzen;
machen <*exam*>. ∼ **back** *vi* sich
zurücklehnen. ∼ **down** *vi* sich
setzen. ∼ **up** *vi* [aufrecht] sitzen;
(*rise*) sich aufsetzen; (*not slouch*)
gerade sitzen

site *n* Gelände *nt*; (*for camping*) Platz
m; (*Archaeol*) Stätte *f*

sitting *n* Sitzung *f*; (*for meals*) Schub
m

situat|e *vt* legen; be ∼ed liegen.
∼**ion** *n* Lage *f*; (*circumstances*)
Situation *f*; (*job*) Stelle *f*

six *a* sechs. ∼**teen** *a* sechzehn.
∼**teenth** *a* sechzehnte(r,s)

sixth *a* sechste(r,s)

sixtieth *a* sechzigste(r,s)

sixty *a* sechzig

size *n* Größe *f*

sizzle *vi* brutzeln

skate *n* Schlittschuh *m* ● *vi*
Schlittschuh laufen. ∼**r** *n*
Eisläufer(in) *m(f)*

skating *n* Eislaufen *nt*. ∼**-rink** *n*
Eisbahn *f*

skeleton *n* Skelett *nt*. ∼ **key** *n*
Dietrich *m*

sketch *n* Skizze *f*; (*Theat*) Sketch *m*
● *vt* skizzieren

sketchy *a* (-ier, -iest), -ily *adv*
skizzenhaft

ski *n* Ski *m* ● *vi* (*pt/pp* skied, *pres p*
skiing) Ski fahren *or* laufen

skid *n* Schleudern *nt* ● *vi* (*pt/pp*
skidded) schleudern

skier *n* Skiläufer(in) *m(f)*

skiing *n* Skilaufen *nt*

skilful *a*, -ly *adv* geschickt

skill *n* Geschick *nt*. ∼**ed** *a* geschickt;
(*trained*) ausgebildet

skim *vt* (*pt/pp* skimmed) entrahmen
<*milk*>

skimp *vt* sparen an (+ *dat*)

skimpy *a* (-ier, -iest) knapp

skin *n* Haut *f*; (*on fruit*) Schale *f* ● *vt*
(*pt/pp* skinned) häuten; schälen
<*fruit*>

skin: ∼**-deep** *a* oberflächlich. ∼**-
diving** *n* Sporttauchen *nt*

skinny *a* (-ier, -iest) dünn

skip¹ *n* Container *m*

skip² *n* Hüpfer *m* ● *v* (*pt/pp* skipped)
vi hüpfen; (*with rope*) seilspringen
● *vt* überspringen

skipper *n* Kapitän *m*

skipping-rope *n* Sprungseil *nt*

skirmish *n* Gefecht *nt*

skirt *n* Rock *m* ● *vt* herumgehen um

skittle *n* Kegel *m*

skive *vi* 🄸 blaumachen

skull *n* Schädel *m*

sky *n* Himmel *m*. ∼**light** *n* Dachluke
f. ∼**scraper** *n* Wolkenkratzer *m*

slab *n* Platte *f*; (*slice*) Scheibe *f*; (*of
chocolate*) Tafel *f*

slack *a* (-er, -est) schlaff, locker;
<*person*> nachlässig; (*Comm*) flau
● *vi* bummeln

slacken *vi* sich lockern; (*diminish*)
nachlassen ● *vt* lockern; (*diminish*)
verringern

slain *see* slay

slam v (pt/pp **slammed**) ● vt
zuschlagen; (put) knallen 🔲; (🔲
criticize) verreißen ● vi zuschlagen

slander n Verleumdung f ● vt
verleumden

slang n Slang m. **~y** a salopp

slant n Schräge f; **on the ~** schräg
● vt abschrägen; (fig) färben
<report> ● vi sich neigen

slap n Schlag m ● vt (pt/pp **slapped**)
schlagen; (put) knallen 🔲 ● adv
direkt

slapdash a 🔲 schludrig

slash n Schlitz m ● vt aufschlitzen;
[drastisch] reduzieren <prices>

slat n Latte f

slate n Schiefer m ● vt 🔲
heruntermachen; verreißen
<performance>

slaughter n Schlachten nt;
(massacre) Gemetzel nt ● vt
schlachten; abschlachten <men>

Slav a slawisch ● n Slawe m/ Slawin
f

slave n Sklave m/ Sklavin f ● vi **~**
[away] schuften

slavery n Sklaverei f

slay vt (pt **slew**, pp **slain**) ermorden

sledge n Schlitten m

sleek a (-er, -est) seidig; (well-fed)
wohlgenährt

sleep n Schlaf m; **go to ~**
einschlafen; **put to ~** einschläfern
● v (pt/pp **slept**) ● vi schlafen ● vt
(accommodate) Unterkunft bieten
für. **~er** n Schläfer(in) m(f); (Rail)
Schlafwagen m; (on track) Schwelle f

sleeping: ~-bag n Schlafsack m.
~-pill n Schlaftablette f

sleep: ~less a schlaflos. **~-
walking** n Schlafwandeln nt

sleepy a (-ier, -iest), **-ily** adv
schläfrig

sleet n Schneeregen m

sleeve n Ärmel m; (for record) Hülle
f. **~less** a ärmellos

sleigh n [Pferde]schlitten m

slender a schlank; (fig) gering

slept see **sleep**

slew see **slay**

slice n Scheibe f ● vt in Scheiben
schneiden

slick a clever

slid|e n Rutschbahn f; (for hair)
Spange f; (Phot) Dia nt ● v (pt/pp
slid) ● vi rutschen ● vt schieben.
~ing a gleitend; <door, seat>
Schiebe-

slight a (-er, -est), **-ly** adv leicht;
<importance> gering;
<acquaintance> flüchtig; (slender)
schlank; **not in the ~est** nicht im
Geringsten; **~ly better** ein bisschen
besser ● vt kränken, beleidigen ● n
Beleidigung f

slim a (slimmer, slimmest) schlank;
<volume> schmal; (fig) gering ● vi
eine Schlankheitskur machen

slim|e n Schleim m. **~y** a schleimig

sling n (Med) Schlinge f ● vt (pt/pp
slung) 🔲 schmeißen

slip n (mistake) Fehler m, 🔲 Patzer
m; (petticoat) Unterrock m; (paper)
Zettel m; **give s.o. the ~** 🔲 jdm
entwischen; **~ of the tongue**
Versprecher m ● v (pt/pp **slipped**)
● vi rutschen; (fall) ausrutschen; (go
quickly) schlüpfen ● vt schieben; **~
s.o.'s mind** jdm entfallen. **~ away**
vi sich fortschleichen. **~ up** vi 🔲
einen Schnitzer machen

slipper n Hausschuh m

slippery a glitschig; <surface> glatt

slipshod a schludrig

slip-up n 🔲 Schnitzer m

slit n Schlitz m ● vt (pt/pp **slit**)
aufschlitzen

slither vi rutschen

slog n [hard] **~** Schinderei f ● vi (pt/
pp **slogged**) schuften

slogan n Schlagwort nt;
(advertising) Werbespruch m

slop|e n Hang m; (inclination)
Neigung f ● vi sich neigen. **~ing** a
schräg

sloppy a (-ier, -iest) schludrig;
(sentimental) sentimental

slosh vi 🔲 schwappen

slot n Schlitz m; (TV) Sendezeit f ● v
(pt/pp **slotted**) ● vt einfügen ● vi
sich einfügen (**in** in + acc)

S

slot-machine n Münzautomat m; (for gambling) Spielautomat m

slouch vi sich schlecht halten

slovenly a schlampig

slow a (-er, -est), **-ly** adv langsam; be ~ <clock:> nachgehen; in ~ motion in Zeitlupe ● adv langsam ● vt verlangsamen ● vi ~ down, ~ up langsamer werden. **~ness** n Langsamkeit f

sludge n Schlamm m

slug n Nacktschnecke f

sluggish a, **-ly** adv träge

sluice n Schleuse f

slum n Elendsviertel nt

slumber n Schlummer m ● vi schlummern

slump n Sturz m ● vi fallen; (crumple) zusammensacken; <prices:> stürzen; <sales:> zurückgehen

slung see sling

slur vt (pt/pp slurred) undeutlich sprechen

slurp vt/i schlürfen

slush n [Schnee]matsch m; (fig) Kitsch m

slut n Schlampe f 🛈

sly a (-er, -est), **-ly** adv verschlagen ● n on the ~ heimlich

smack n Schlag m, Klaps m ● vt schlagen ● adv 🛈 direkt

small a (-er, -est) klein ● adv chop up ~ klein hacken ● n ~ of the back Kreuz nt

small: ~ **ads** npl Kleinanzeigen pl. ~ **change** n Kleingeld nt. ~**pox** n Pocken pl. ~ **talk** n leichte Konversation f

smart a (-er, -est), **-ly** adv schick; (clever) schlau, clever; (brisk) flott; (Amer 🛈: cheeky) frech ● vi brennen

smarten vt ~ oneself up mehr auf sein Äußeres achten

smash n Krach m; (collision) Zusammenstoß m; (Tennis) Schmetterball m ● vt zerschlagen; (strike) schlagen; (Tennis) schmettern ● vi zerschmettern; (crash) krachen (into gegen). ~**ing** a 🛈 toll

smear n verschmierter Fleck m; (Med) Abstrich m; (fig) Verleumdung f ● vt schmieren; (coat) beschmieren (with mit); (fig) verleumden ● vi schmieren

smell n Geruch m; (sense) Geruchssinn m ● v (pt/pp smelt or smelled) ● vt riechen; (sniff) riechen an (+ dat) ● vi riechen (of nach)

smelly a (-ier, -iest) übel riechend

smelt see smell

smile n Lächeln nt ● vi lächeln; ~ at anlächeln

smirk vi feixen

smith n Schmied m

smock n Kittel m

smog n Smog m

smoke n Rauch m ● vt/i rauchen; (Culin) räuchern. ~**less** a rauchfrei; <fuel> rauchlos

smoker n Raucher m; (Rail) Raucherabteil nt

smoking n Rauchen nt; 'no ~' 'Rauchen verboten'

smoky a (-ier, -iest) verraucht; <taste> rauchig

smooth a (-er, -est), **-ly** adv glatt ● vt glätten. ~ **out** vt glatt streichen

smother vt ersticken; (cover) bedecken; (suppress) unterdrücken

smoulder vi schwelen

smudge n Fleck m ● vt verwischen ● vi schmieren

smug a (smugger, smuggest), **-ly** adv selbstgefällig

smuggl|e vt schmuggeln. ~**er** n Schmuggler m. ~**ing** n Schmuggel m

snack n Imbiss m. ~**-bar** n Imbissstube f

snag n Schwierigkeit f, 🛈 Haken m

snail n Schnecke f; at a ~'s pace im Schneckentempo

snake n Schlange f

snap n Knacken nt; (photo) Schnappschuss m ● attrib <decision> plötzlich ● v (pt/pp snapped) ● vi [entzwei]brechen; ~ at (bite) schnappen nach; (speak sharply) [scharf] anfahren ● vt zerbrechen;

(*say*) fauchen; (*Phot*) knipsen. **~ up**
vt wegschnappen

snappy *a* (-ier, -iest) (*smart*) flott;
make it ~! ein bisschen schnell!

snapshot *n* Schnappschuss *m*

snare *n* Schlinge *f*

snarl *vi* [mit gefletschten Zähnen]
knurren

snatch *n* (*fragment*) Fetzen *pl* ● *vt*
schnappen; (*steal*) klauen; entführen
<*child*>; **~ sth from s.o.** jdm etw
entreißen

sneak *n* 〔T〕 Petze *f* ● *vi* schleichen;
(〔T〕 *tell tales*) petzen ● *vt* (*take*)
mitgehen lassen ● *vi* **~ in/out** sich
hinein-/hinausschleichen

sneakers *npl* (*Amer*) Turnschuhe
pl

sneer *vi* höhnisch lächeln; (*mock*)
spotten

sneeze *n* Niesen *nt* ● *vi* niesen

snide *a* 〔T〕 abfällig

sniff *vi* schnüffeln ● *vt* schnüffeln an
(+ *dat*)

snigger *vi* [boshaft] kichern

snip *n* Schnitt *m* ● *vt/i* **~ [at]**
schnippeln an (+ *dat*)

snippet *n* Schnipsel *m*; (*of
information*) Bruchstück *nt*

snivel *vi* (*pt/pp* snivelled) flennen

snob *n* Snob *m*. **~bery** *n* Snobismus
m. **~bish** *a* snobistisch

snoop *vi* 〔T〕 schnüffeln

snooty *a* 〔T〕 hochnäsig

snooze *n* Nickerchen *nt* ● *vi* dösen

snore *vi* schnarchen

snorkel *n* Schnorchel *m*

snort *vi* schnauben

snout *n* Schnauze *f*

snow *n* Schnee *m* ● *vi* schneien;
~ed under with (*fig*) überhäuft mit

snow: ~ball *n* Schneeball *m*. **~-
drift** *n* Schneewehe *f*. **~drop** *n*
Schneeglöckchen *nt*. **~fall** *n*
Schneefall *m*. **~flake** *n*
Schneeflocke *f*. **~man** *n*
Schneemann *m*. **~plough** *n*
Schneepflug *m*

snub *n* Abfuhr *f* ● *vt* (*pt/pp* snubbed)
brüskieren

snub-nosed *a* stupsnasig

snuffle *vi* schnüffeln

snug *a* (snugger, snuggest)
behaglich, gemütlich

snuggle *vi* sich kuscheln (**up to** an
+ *acc*)

so *adv* so; **so am I** ich auch; **so I see**
das sehe ich; **that is so** das stimmt;
so much the better umso besser; **if so**
wenn ja; **so as to** um zu; **so long!** 〔T〕
tschüs! ● *pron* **I hope so** hoffentlich;
I think so ich glaube schon; **I'm afraid
so** leider ja; **so saying/doing, he/she
... indem er/sie das sagte/tat, ...**
● *conj* (*therefore*) also; **so that** damit;
so what! na und! **so you see** wie du
siehst

soak *vt* nass machen; (*steep*)
einweichen; (〔T〕 *fleece*) schröpfen ● *vi*
weichen; <*liquid*:> sickern. **~ up** *vt*
aufsaugen

soaking *a* & *adv* **~ [wet]** patschnass
〔T〕

soap *n* Seife *f*. **~ opera** *n*
Seifenoper *f*. **~ powder** *n*
Seifenpulver *nt*

soapy *a* (-ier, -iest) seifig

soar *vi* aufsteigen; <*prices*:> in die
Höhe schnellen

sob *n* Schluchzer *m* ● *vi* (*pt/pp*
sobbed) schluchzen

sober *a*, **-ly** *adv* nüchtern; (*serious*)
ernst; <*colour*:> gedeckt. **~ up** *vi*
nüchtern werden

so-called *a* sogenannt

soccer *n* 〔T〕 Fußball *m*

sociable *a* gesellig

social *a* gesellschaftlich; (*Admin,
Pol, Zool*) sozial

socialis|m *n* Sozialismus *m*. **~t** *a*
sozialistisch ● *n* Sozialist *m*

socialize *vi* [gesellschaftlich]
verkehren

socially *adv* gesellschaftlich; **know
~** privat kennen

social: ~ security *n* Sozialhilfe *f*.
~ worker *n* Sozialarbeiter(in) *m(f)*

society *n* Gesellschaft *f*; (*club*)
Verein *m*

sociolog|ist *n* Soziologe *m*. **~y** *n*
Soziologie *f*

S

sock n Socke f; (kneelength) Kniestrumpf m

socket n (of eye) Augenhöhle f; (of joint) Gelenkpfanne f; (wall plug) Steckdose f

soda n Soda nt; (Amer) Limonade f. ~ **water** n Sodawasser nt

sodden a durchnässt

sofa n Sofa nt. ~ **bed** n Schlafcouch f

soft a (-er, -est), **-ly** adv weich; (quiet) leise; (gentle) sanft; (I silly) dumm. ~ **drink** n alkoholfreies Getränk nt

soften vt weich machen; (fig) mildern ● vi weich werden

soft: ~ **toy** n Stofftier nt. ~**ware** n Software f

soggy a (-ier, -iest) aufgeweicht

soil¹ n Erde f, Boden m

soil² vt verschmutzen

solar a Sonnen-

sold see sell

soldier n Soldat m ● vi ~ on [unbeirrbar] weitermachen

sole¹ n Sohle f

sole² n (fish) Seezunge f

sole³ a einzig. ~**ly** adv einzig und allein

solemn a, **-ly** adv feierlich; (serious) ernst

solicitor n Rechtsanwalt m/ -anwältin f

solid a fest; (sturdy) stabil; (not hollow, of same substance) massiv; (unanimous) einstimmig; (complete) ganz

solidarity n Solidarität f

solidify vi (pt/pp -ied) fest werden

solitary a einsam; (sole) einzig

solitude n Einsamkeit f

solo n Solo nt ● a Solo-; <flight> Allein- ● adv solo. ~**ist** n Solist(in) m(f)

solstice n Sonnenwende f

soluble a löslich

solution n Lösung f

solvable a lösbar

solve vt lösen

solvent n Lösungsmittel nt

sombre a dunkel; <mood> düster

some a & pron etwas; (a little) ein bisschen; (with pl noun) einige; (a few) ein paar; (certain) manche(r,s); (one or the other) [irgend]ein; ~ **day** eines Tages; **I want** ~ ich möchte etwas/ (pl) welche; **will you have** ~ **wine?** möchten Sie Wein? **do** ~ **shopping** einkaufen

some: ~**body** pron & n jemand; (emphatic) irgendjemand. ~**how** adv irgendwie. ~**one** pron & n = somebody

somersault n Purzelbaum m I; (Sport) Salto m; **turn a** ~ einen Purzelbaum schlagen/einen Salto springen

something pron & adv etwas; (emphatic) irgendetwas; ~ **different** etwas anderes; ~ **like this** so etwas [wie das]

some: ~**time** adv irgendwann ● a ehemalig. ~**times** adv manchmal. ~**what** adv ziemlich. ~**where** adv irgendwo; <go> irgendwohin

son n Sohn m

song n Lied nt. ~**bird** n Singvogel m

son-in-law n (pl ~s-in-law) Schwiegersohn m

soon adv (-er, -est) bald; (quickly) schnell; **too** ~ zu früh; **as** ~ **as possible** so bald wie möglich; ~**er or later** früher oder später; **no** ~**er had I arrived than** ... kaum war ich angekommen, da ...; **I would** ~**er stay** ich würde lieber bleiben

soot n Ruß m

sooth|e vt beruhigen; lindern <pain>. ~**ing** a, **-ly** adv beruhigend; lindernd

sophisticated a weltgewandt; (complex) hoch entwickelt

sopping a & adv ~ **[wet]** durchnässt

soppy a (-ier, -iest) I rührselig

soprano n Sopran m; (woman) Sopranistin f

sordid a schmutzig

sore a (-r, -st) wund; (painful) schmerzhaft; **have a** ~ **throat**

Halsschmerzen haben ● n wunde Stelle f. ~ly adv sehr

sorrow n Kummer m

sorry a (-ier, -iest) (sad) traurig; (wretched) erbärmlich; I am ~ es tut mir Leid; she is or feels ~ for him er tut ihr Leid; I am ~ to say leider; ~! Entschuldigung!

sort n Art f; (brand) Sorte f; he's a good ~ 🅸 er ist in Ordnung ● vt sortieren. ~ out vt sortieren; (fig) klären

sought see seek

soul n Seele f

sound¹ a (-er, -est) gesund; (sensible) vernünftig; (secure) solide; (thorough) gehörig ● adv be ~ asleep fest schlafen

sound² n (strait) Meerenge f

sound³ n Laut m; (noise) Geräusch nt; (Phys) Schall m; (Radio, TV) Ton m; (of bells, music) Klang m; I don't like the ~ of it 🅸 das hört sich nicht gut an ● vi [er]tönen; (seem) sich anhören ● vt (pronounce) aussprechen; schlagen <alarm>; (Med) abhorchen <chest>

soundly adv solide; <sleep> fest; <defeat> vernichtend

soundproof a schalldicht

soup n Suppe f

sour a (-er, -est) sauer; (bad-tempered) griesgrämig, verdrießlich

source n Quelle f

south n Süden m; to the ~ of südlich von ● a Süd-, süd- ● adv nach Süden

south: S~ **Africa** n Südafrika nt. S~ **America** n Südamerika nt. ~-**east** n Südosten m

southerly a südlich

southern a südlich

southward[s] adv nach Süden

souvenir n Andenken nt, Souvenir nt

Soviet a <History> sowjetisch; ~ **Union** Sowjetunion f

sow¹ n Sau f

sow² vt (pt sowed, pp sown or sowed) säen

soya n ~ **bean** Sojabohne f

spa n Heilbad nt

space n Raum m; (gap) Platz m; (Astr) Weltraum m ● vt ~ [out] [in Abständen] verteilen

space: ~**craft** n Raumfahrzeug nt. ~**ship** n Raumschiff nt

spacious a geräumig

spade n Spaten m; (for child) Schaufel f; ~s pl (Cards) Pik nt

Spain n Spanien nt

span¹ n Spanne f; (of arch) Spannweite f ● vt (pt/pp spanned) überspannen; umspannen <time>

span² see spick

Span|iard n Spanier(in) m(f). ~**ish** a spanisch ● n (Lang) Spanisch nt; **the** ~**ish** pl die Spanier

spank vt verhauen

spanner n Schraubenschlüssel m

spare a (surplus) übrig; (additional) zusätzlich; <seat, time> frei; <room> Gäste-; <bed, cup> Extra- ● n (part) Ersatzteil nt ● vt ersparen; (not hurt) verschonen; (do without) entbehren; (afford to give) erübrigen. ~ **wheel** n Reserverad nt

sparing a, -ly adv sparsam

spark n Funke nt. ~[**ing**]-**plug** n (Auto) Zündkerze f

sparkl|e n Funkeln nt ● vi funkeln. ~**ing** a funkelnd; <wine> Schaum-

sparrow n Spatz m

sparse a spärlich. ~**ly** adv spärlich; <populated> dünn

spasm n Anfall m; (cramp) Krampf m. ~**odic** a, -**ally** adv sporadisch

spastic a spastisch [gelähmt] ● n Spastiker(in) m(f)

spat see spit²

spatter vt spritzen; ~ **with** bespritzen mit

spawn n Laich m ● vt (fig) hervorbringen

speak v (pt spoke, pp spoken) ● vi sprechen (to mit) ~**ing!** (Teleph) am Apparat! ● vt sprechen; sagen <truth>. ~ **up** vi lauter sprechen; ~ up for oneself seine Meinung äußern

speaker n Sprecher(in) m(f); (in public) Redner(in) m(f); (loudspeaker) Lautsprecher m

S

spear n Speer m ● vt aufspießen

spec n on ~ 🔲 auf gut Glück

special a besondere(r,s), speziell. ~**ist** n Spezialist m; (Med) Facharzt m/-ärztin f. ~**ity** n Spezialität f

special|ize vi sich spezialisieren (in auf + acc). ~**ly** adv speziell; (particularly) besonders

species n Art f

specific a bestimmt; (precise) genau; (Phys) spezifisch. ~**ally** adv ausdrücklich

specification n & ~**s** pl genaue Angaben pl

specify vt (pt/pp -ied) [genau] angeben

specimen n Exemplar nt; (sample) Probe f; (of urine) Urinprobe f

speck n Fleck m

speckled a gesprenkelt

spectacle n (show) Schauspiel nt; (sight) Anblick m. ~**s** npl Brille f

spectacular a spektakulär

spectator n Zuschauer(in) m(f)

speculat|e vi spekulieren. ~**ion** n Spekulation f. ~**or** n Spekulant m

sped see speed

speech n Sprache f; (address) Rede f. ~**less** a sprachlos

speed n Geschwindigkeit f; (rapidity) Schnelligkeit f ● vi (pt/pp sped) schnell fahren ● (pt/pp speeded) (go too fast) zu schnell fahren. ~ up (pt/pp speeded up) ● vt/i beschleunigen

speed: ~boat n Rennboot nt. ~**ing** n Geschwindigkeitsüberschreitung f. ~ **limit** n Geschwindigkeitsbeschränkung f

speedometer n Tachometer m

speedy a (-ier, -iest), **-ily** adv schnell

spell¹ n Weile f; (of weather) Periode f

spell² v (pt/pp spelled or spelt) ● vt schreiben; (aloud) buchstabieren; (fig: mean) bedeuten ● vi richtig schreiben; (aloud) buchstabieren. ~ **out** vt buchstabieren; (fig) genau erklären

spell³ n Zauber m; (words) Zauberspruch m. ~**bound** a wie verzaubert

spelling n (of a word) Schreibweise f; (orthography) Rechtschreibung f

spelt see spell²

spend vt/i (pt/pp spent) ausgeben; verbringen <time>

spent see spend

sperm n Samen m

sphere n Kugel f; (fig) Sphäre f

spice n Gewürz nt; (fig) Würze f

spicy a würzig, pikant

spider n Spinne f

spik|e n Spitze f; (Bot, Zool) Stachel m; (on shoe) Spike m. ~**y** a stachelig

spill v (pt/pp spilt or spilled) ● vt verschütten ● vi überlaufen

spin v (pt/pp spun, pres p spinning) ● vt drehen; spinnen <wool>; schleudern <washing> ● vi sich drehen

spinach n Spinat m

spindl|e n Spindel f. ~**y** a spindeldürr

spin-drier n Wäscheschleuder f

spine n Rückgrat nt; (of book) [Buch]rücken m; (Bot, Zool) Stachel m. ~**less** a (fig) rückgratlos

spin-off n Nebenprodukt nt

spinster n ledige Frau f

spiral a spiralig ● n Spirale f ● vi (pt/pp spiralled) sich hochwinden. ~ **staircase** n Wendeltreppe f

spire n Turmspitze f

spirit n Geist m; (courage) Mut m; ~**s** pl (alcohol) Spirituosen pl; in low ~**s** niedergedrückt. ~ **away** vt verschwinden lassen

spirited a lebhaft; (courageous) beherzt

spiritual a geistig; (Relig) geistlich

spit¹ n (for roasting) [Brat]spieß m

spit² n Spucke f ● vt/i (pt/pp spat, pres p spitting) spucken; <cat:> fauchen; <fat:> spritzen; it's ~**ting** with rain es tröpfelt

spite n Boshaftigkeit f; in ~ of trotz (+ gen) ● vt ärgern. ~**ful** a, **-ly** adv gehässig

splash n Platschen nt; (🚫 drop) Schuss m; ~ **of colour** Farbfleck m ● vt spritzen; ~ **s.o. with sth** jdn mit etw bespritzen ● vi spritzen. ~ **about** vi planschen

splendid a herrlich, großartig

splendour n Pracht f

splint n (Med) Schiene f

splinter n Splitter m ● vi zersplittern

split n Spaltung f; (Pol) Bruch m; (tear) Riss m ● v (pt/pp **split**, pres p **splitting**) ● vt spalten; (share) teilen; (tear) zerreißen ● vi sich spalten; (tear) zerreißen; ~ **on s.o.** 🚫 verpfeifen. ~ **up** vt aufteilen ● vi <couple:> sich trennen

splutter vi prusten

spoil n ~**s** pl Beute f ● v (pt/pp **spoilt** or **spoiled**) ● vt verderben; verwöhnen <person> ● vi verderben. ~**sport** n Spielverderber m

spoke¹ n Speiche f

spoke², **spoken** see **speak**

spokesman n Sprecher m

sponge n Schwamm m ● vt abwaschen ● vi ~ **on** schmarotzen bei. ~**bag** n Waschbeutel m. ~**cake** n Biskuitkuchen m

sponsor n Sponsor m; (godparent) Pate m/Patin f ● vt sponsern

spontaneous a, **-ly** adv spontan

spoof n 🚫 Parodie f

spooky a (-ier, -iest) 🚫 gespenstisch

spool n Spule f

spoon n Löffel m ● vt löffeln. ~**ful** n Löffel m

sporadic a, **-ally** adv sporadisch

sport n Sport m ● vt [stolz] tragen. ~**ing** a sportlich

sports: ~ **car** n Sportwagen m. ~ **coat** n, ~ **jacket** n Sakko m. ~**man** n Sportler m. ~**woman** n Sportlerin f

sporty a (-ier, -iest) sportlich

spot n Fleck m; (place) Stelle f (dot) Punkt m; (drop) Tropfen m; (pimple) Pickel m; ~**s** pl (rash) Ausschlag m; **on the** ~ auf der Stelle ● vt (pt/pp **spotted**) entdecken

spot: ~ **check** n Stichprobe f. ~**less** a makellos; (🚫 very clean) blitzsauber. ~**light** n Scheinwerfer m; (fig) Rampenlicht nt

spotted a gepunktet

spouse n Gatte m/Gattin f

spout n Schnabel m, Tülle f ● vi schießen (from aus)

sprain n Verstauchung f ● vt verstauchen

sprang see **spring²**

sprawl vi sich ausstrecken

spray¹ n (of flowers) Strauß m

spray² n Sprühnebel m; (from sea) Gischt m; (device) Spritze f; (container) Sprühdose f; (preparation) Spray nt ● vt spritzen; (with aerosol) sprühen

spread n Verbreitung f; (paste) Aufstrich m; (🚫 feast) Festessen nt ● v (pt/pp **spread**) ● vt ausbreiten; streichen <butter, jam>; bestreichen <bread, surface>; streuen <sand, manure>; verbreiten <news, disease>; verteilen <payments> ● vi sich ausbreiten. ~ **out** vt ausbreiten; (space out) verteilen ● vi sich verteilen

spree n 🚫 **go on a shopping** ~ groß einkaufen gehen

sprightly a (-ier, -iest) rüstig

spring¹ n Frühling m ● attrib Frühlings-

spring² n (jump) Sprung m; (water) Quelle f; (device) Feder f; (elasticity) Elastizität f ● v (pt **sprang**, pp **sprung**) ● vi springen; (arise) entspringen (from dat) ● vt ~ **sth on s.o.** jdn mit etw überfallen

spring: ~**cleaning** n Frühjahrsputz m. ~**time** n Frühling m

sprinkl|e vt sprengen; (scatter) streuen; bestreuen <surface>. ~**ing** n dünne Schicht f

sprint n Sprint m ● vi rennen; (Sport) sprinten. ~**er** n Kurzstreckenläufer(in) m(f)

sprout n Trieb m; [**Brussels**] ~**s** pl Rosenkohl m ● vi sprießen

sprung see **spring²**

spud n ⚀ Kartoffel f

spun see spin

spur n Sporn m; (stimulus) Ansporn m; **on the ~ of the moment** ganz spontan ● vt (pt/pp **spurred**) ~ **[on]** (fig) anspornen

spurn vt verschmähen

spurt n (Sport) Spurt m; **put on a ~** spurten ● vi spritzen

spy n Spion(in) m(f) ● vi spionieren; **~ on s.o.** jdm nachspionieren. ● vt (⚀ see) sehen

spying n Spionage f

squabble n Zank m ● vi sich zanken

squad n Gruppe f; (Sport) Mannschaft f

squadron n (Mil) Geschwader nt

squalid a, -ly adv schmutzig

squall n Bö f ● vi brüllen

squalor n Schmutz m

squander vt vergeuden

square a quadratisch; <metre, mile> Quadrat-; <meal> anständig; **all ~** ⚀ quitt ● n Quadrat nt; (area) Platz m; (on chessboard) Feld nt ● vt (settle) klären; (Math) quadrieren

squash n Gedränge nt; (drink) Fruchtsaftgetränk nt; (Sport) Squash nt ● vt zerquetschen; (suppress) niederschlagen. **~y** a weich

squat a gedrungen ● vi (pt/pp **squatted**) hocken; **~ in a house** ein Haus besetzen. **~ter** n Hausbesetzer m

squawk vi krächzen

squeak n Quieken nt; (of hinge, brakes) Quietschen nt ● vi quieken; quietschen

squeal n Kreischen nt ● vi kreischen

squeamish a empfindlich

squeeze n Druck m; (crush) Gedränge nt ● vt drücken; (to get juice) ausdrücken; (force) zwängen

squiggle n Schnörkel m

squint n Schielen nt ● vi schielen

squirm vi sich winden

squirrel n Eichhörnchen nt

squirt n Spritzer m ● vt/i spritzen

St abbr (Saint) St.; (Street) Str.

stab n Stich m; (⚀ attempt) Versuch m ● vt (pt/pp **stabbed**) stechen; (to death) erstechen

stability n Stabilität f

stable¹ a (-r, -st) stabil

stable² n Stall m; (establishment) Reitstall m

stack n Stapel m; (of chimney) Schornstein m ● vt stapeln

stadium n Stadion nt

staff n (stick & Mil) Stab m ● (& pl) (employees) Personal nt; (Sch) Lehrkräfte pl ● vt mit Personal besetzen. **~-room** n (Sch) Lehrerzimmer nt

stag n Hirsch m

stage n Bühne f; (in journey) Etappe f; (in process) Stadium nt; **by** or **in ~s** in Etappen ● vt aufführen; (arrange) veranstalten

stagger vi taumeln ● vt staffeln <holidays>; versetzt anordnen <seats>; **I was ~ed** es hat mir die Sprache verschlagen. **~ing** a unglaublich

stagnant a stehend; (fig) stagnierend

stagnate vi (fig) stagnieren

stain n Fleck m; (for wood) Beize f ● vt färben; beizen <wood>; **~ed glass** farbiges Glas nt. **~less** a <steel> rostfrei

stair n Stufe f; **~s** pl Treppe f. **~case** n Treppe f

stake n Pfahl m; (wager) Einsatz m; (Comm) Anteil m; **be at ~** auf dem Spiel stehen ● vt **~ a claim to sth** Anspruch auf etw (acc) erheben

stale a (-r, -st) alt; <air> verbraucht. **~mate** n Patt nt

stalk n Stiel m, Stängel m

stall n Stand m; **~s** pl (Theat) Parkett nt ● vi <engine:> stehen bleiben; (fig) ausweichen ● vt abwürgen <engine>

stalwart a treu ● n treuer Anhänger m

stamina n Ausdauer f

stammer n Stottern nt ● vt/i stottern

stamp n Stempel m; (postage ~) [Brief]marke f ● vt stempeln; (impress) prägen; (put postage on) frankieren ● vi stampfen. ~ **out** vt [aus]stanzen; (fig) ausmerzen

stampede n wilde Flucht f ● vi in Panik fliehen

stance n Haltung f

stand n Stand m; (rack) Ständer m; (pedestal) Sockel m; (Sport) Tribüne f; (fig) Einstellung f ● v (pt/pp stood) ● vi stehen; (rise) aufstehen; (be candidate) kandidieren; (stay valid) gültig bleiben; ~ **still** stillstehen; ~ **firm** (fig) festbleiben; ~ **to reason** logisch sein; ~ **in for** vertreten; ~ **for** (mean) bedeuten ● vt stellen; (withstand) standhalten (+ dat); (endure) ertragen; vertragen <climate>; (put up with) aushalten; haben <chance>; ~ **s.o. a beer** jdm ein Bier spendieren; **I can't ~ her** ☒ ich kann sie nicht ausstehen. ~ **by** vi daneben stehen; (be ready) sich bereithalten ● vt ~ **by s.o.** (fig) zu jdm stehen. ~ **down** vi (retire) zurücktreten. ~ **out** vi hervorstehen; (fig) herausragen. ~ **up** vi aufstehen; ~ **up for** eintreten für; ~ **up to** sich wehren gegen

standard a Normal- ● n Maßstab m; (Techn) Norm f; (level) Niveau nt; (flag) Standarte f; ~**s** pl (morals) Prinzipien pl. ~**ize** vt standardisieren; (Techn) normen

stand-in n Ersatz m

standing a (erect) stehend; (permanent) ständig ● n Rang m; (duration) Dauer f. ~**-room** n Stehplätze pl

stand: ~**-offish** a distanziert. ~**point** n Standpunkt m. ~**still** n Stillstand m; **come to a** ~**still** zum Stillstand kommen

stank see stink

staple[1] a Grund-

staple[2] n Heftklammer f ● vt heften. ~**r** n Heftmaschine f

star n Stern m; (asterisk) Sternchen nt; (Theat, Sport) Star m ● vi (pt/pp starred) die Hauptrolle spielen

starboard n Steuerbord nt

starch n Stärke f ● vt stärken. ~**y** a stärkehaltig; (fig) steif

stare n Starren nt ● vt starren; ~ **at** anstarren

stark a (-er, -est) scharf; <contrast> krass

starling n Star m

start n Anfang m, Beginn m; (departure) Aufbruch m; (Sport) Start m; **from the** ~ von Anfang an; **for a** ~ erstens ● vi anfangen, beginnen; (set out) aufbrechen; <engine:> anspringen; (Auto, Sport) starten; (jump) aufschrecken; **to** ~ **with** zuerst ● vt anfangen, beginnen; (cause) verursachen; (found) gründen; starten <car, race>; in Umlauf setzen <rumour>. ~**er** n (Culin) Vorspeise f; (Auto, Sport) Starter m. ~**ing-point** n Ausgangspunkt m

startle vt erschrecken

starvation n Verhungern nt

starve vi hungern; (to death) verhungern ● vt verhungern lassen

state n Zustand m; (Pol) Staat m; ~ **of play** Spielstand m; **be in a** ~ <person:> aufgeregt sein ● attrib Staats-, staatlich ● vt erklären; (specify) angeben

stately a (-ier, -iest) stattlich. ~ **home** n Schloss nt

statement n Erklärung f; (Jur) Aussage f; (Banking) Auszug m

statesman n Staatsmann m

static a statisch; **remain** ~ unverändert bleiben

station n Bahnhof m; (police) Wache f; (radio) Sender m; (space, weather) Station f; (Mil) Posten m; (status) Rang m ● vt stationieren; (post) postieren. ~**ary** a stehend; **be** ~**ary** stehen

stationery n Briefpapier nt; (writing materials) Schreibwaren pl

station-wagon n (Amer) Kombi[wagen] n

statistic n statistische Tatsache f. ~**al** a, **-ly** adv statistisch. ~**s** n & pl Statistik f

statue n Statue f

S

stature n Statur f; (fig) Format nt

status n Status m, Rang m

statut|e n Statut nt. ~**ory** a gesetzlich

staunch a (-er, -est), **-ly** adv treu

stave vt ~ **off** abwenden

stay n Aufenthalt m ● vi bleiben; (reside) wohnen; ~ **the night** übernachten. ~ **behind** vi zurückbleiben. ~ **in** vi zu Hause bleiben; (Sch) nachsitzen. ~ **up** vi <person:> aufbleiben

steadily adv fest; (continually) stetig

steady a (-ier, -iest) fest; (not wobbly) stabil; <hand> ruhig; (regular) regelmäßig; (dependable) zuverlässig

steak n Steak nt

steal vt/i (pt stole, pp stolen) stehlen (from dat). ~ **in/out** vi sich hinein-/hinausstehlen

stealthy a heimlich

steam n Dampf m ● vt (Culin) dämpfen, dünsten ● vi dampfen. ~ **up** vi beschlagen

steam engine n Dampfmaschine f; (Rail) Dampflokomotive f

steamer n Dampfer m

steamy a dampfig

steel n Stahl m

steep a, **-ly** adv steil; (🄵 exorbitant) gesalzen

steeple n Kirchturm m

steer vt/i (Auto) lenken; (Naut) steuern; ~ **clear of s.o./sth** jdm/ etw aus dem Weg gehen. ~**ing** n (Auto) Lenkung f. ~**ing-wheel** n Lenkrad nt

stem[1] n Stiel m; (of word) Stamm m

stem[2] vt (pt/pp stemmed) eindämmen; stillen <bleeding>

stench n Gestank m

stencil n Schablone f

step n Schritt m; (stair) Stufe f; ~**s** pl (ladder) Trittleiter f; **in** ~ im Schritt; ~ **by** ~ Schritt für Schritt; **take** ~**s** (fig) Schritte unternehmen ● vi (pt/pp stepped) treten; ~ **in** (fig) eingreifen. ~ **up** vt (increase) erhöhen, steigen; verstärken <efforts>

step: ~**brother** n Stiefbruder m. ~**child** n Stiefkind nt. ~**daughter** n Stieftochter f. ~**father** n Stiefvater m. ~**ladder** n Trittleiter f. ~**mother** n Stiefmutter f. ~**sister** n Stiefschwester f. ~**son** n Stiefsohn m

stereo n Stereo nt; (equipment) Stereoanlage f. ~**phonic** a stereophon

stereotype n stereotype Figur f

steril|e a steril. ~**ize** vt sterilisieren

sterling a Sterling-; (fig) gediegen ● n Sterling m

stern[1] a (-er, -est), **-ly** adv streng

stern[2] n (of boat) Heck nt

stew n Eintopf m; **in a** ~ 🄵 aufgeregt ● vt/i schmoren; ~**ed fruit** Kompott nt

steward n Ordner m; (on ship, aircraft) Steward m. ~**ess** n Stewardess f

stick[1] n Stock m; (of chalk) Stück nt; (of rhubarb) Stange f; (Sport) Schläger m

stick[2] v (pt/pp stuck) ● vt stecken; (stab) stechen; (glue) kleben; (🄵 put) tun; (🄵 endure) aushalten ● vi stecken; (adhere) kleben, haften (**to an** + dat); (jam) klemmen; ~ **at it** 🄵 dranbleiben; ~ **up for** 🄵 eintreten für; **be stuck** nicht weiterkönnen; <vehicle:> festsitzen, festgefahren sein; <drawer:> klemmen; **be stuck with sth** 🄵 etw am Hals haben. ~ **out** vi abstehen; (project) vorstehen ● vt hinausstrecken; herausstrecken <tongue>

sticker n Aufkleber m

sticking plaster n Heftpflaster nt

sticky a (-ier, -iest) klebrig; (adhesive) Klebe-

stiff a (-er, -est), **-ly** adv steif; <brush; <dough> fest; (difficult) schwierig; <penalty> schwer; **be bored** ~ 🄵 sich zu Tode langweilen. ~**en** vt steif machen ● vi steif werden. ~**ness** n Steifheit f

stifl|e *vt* ersticken; *(fig)* unterdrücken. **~ing** *a* be **~ing** zum Ersticken sein

still *a* still; *<drink>* ohne Kohlensäure; **keep ~** stillhalten; **stand ~** stillstehen ● *adv* noch; *(emphatic)* immer noch; *(nevertheless)* trotzdem; **~ not** immer noch nicht

stillborn *a* tot geboren

still life *n* Stillleben *nt*

stilted *a* gestelzt, geschraubt

stimulant *n* Anregungsmittel *nt*

stimulat|e *vt* anregen. **~ion** *n* Anregung *f*

stimulus *n* (*pl* **-li**) Reiz *m*

sting *n* Stich *m*; *(from nettle, jellyfish)* Brennen *nt*; *(organ)* Stachel *m* ● *v* (*pt/pp* **stung**) ● *vt* stechen ● *vi* brennen; *<insect:>* stechen

stingy *a* (**-ier, -iest**) geizig, Ⓘ knauserig

stink *n* Gestank *m* ● *vi* (*pt* **stank**, *pp* **stunk**) stinken (**of** nach)

stipulat|e *vt* vorschreiben. **~ion** *n* Bedingung *f*

stir *n* (*commotion*) Aufregung *f* ● *v* (*pt/pp* **stirred**) *vt* rühren ● *vi* sich rühren

stirrup *n* Steigbügel *m*

stitch *n* Stich *m*; *(Knitting)* Masche *f*; *(pain)* Seitenstechen *nt*; **be in ~es** Ⓘ sich kaputtlachen ● *vt* nähen

stock *n* Vorrat *m* (**of** an + *dat*); *(in shop)* [Waren]bestand *m*; *(livestock)* Vieh *nt*; *(lineage)* Abstammung *f*; *(Finance)* Wertpapiere *pl*; *(Culin)* Brühe *f*; *(plant)* Levkoje *f*; **in/out of ~** vorrätig/nicht vorrätig; **take ~** *(fig)* Bilanz ziehen ● *a* Standard- ● *vt* *<shop:>* führen; auffüllen *<shelves>*. **~ up** *vi* sich eindecken (**with** mit)

stock: ~broker *n* Börsenmakler *m*. **S~ Exchange** *n* Börse *f*

stocking *n* Strumpf *m*

stock: ~market *n* Börse *f*. **~taking** *n* (*Comm*) Inventur *f*

stocky *a* (**-ier, -iest**) untersetzt

stodgy *a* pappig [und schwer verdaulich]

stoke *vt* heizen

stole, stolen *see* **steal**

stomach *n* Magen *m*. **~ache** *n* Magenschmerzen *pl*

stone *n* Stein *m*; *(weight)* 6,35kg ● *a* steinern; *<wall, Age>* Stein- ● *vt* mit Steinen bewerfen; entsteinen *<fruit>*. **~-cold** *a* eiskalt. **~-deaf** *n* Ⓘ stocktaub

stony *a* steinig

stood *see* **stand**

stool *n* Hocker *m*

stoop *n* **walk with a ~** gebeugt gehen ● *vi* sich bücken

stop *n* Halt *m*; *(break)* Pause *f*; *(for bus)* Haltestelle *f*; *(for train)* Station *f*; *(Gram)* Punkt *m*; *(on organ)* Register *nt*; **come to a ~** stehen bleiben; **put a ~ to sth** etw unterbinden ● *v* (*pt/pp* **stopped**) ● *vt* anhalten, stoppen; *(switch off)* abstellen; *(plug, block)* zustopfen; *(prevent)* verhindern; **~ s.o. doing sth** jdn daran hindern, etw zu tun; **~ doing sth** aufhören, etw zu tun; **~ that!** hör auf damit! ● *vi* anhalten; *(cease)* aufhören; *<clock:>* stehen bleiben ● *int* halt!

stop: ~gap *n* Notlösung *f*. **~over** *n* *(Aviat)* Zwischenlandung *f*

stoppage *n* Unterbrechung *f*; *(strike)* Streik *m*

stopper *n* Stöpsel *m*

stop-watch *n* Stoppuhr *f*

storage *n* Aufbewahrung *f*; *(in warehouse)* Lagerung *f*; *(Computing)* Speicherung *f*

store *n* (*stock*) Vorrat *m*; *(shop)* Laden *m*; *(department ~)* Kaufhaus *nt*; *(depot)* Lager *nt*; **in ~** auf Lager; **be in ~ for s.o.** *(fig)* jdm bevorstehen ● *vt* aufbewahren; *(in warehouse)* lagern; *(Computing)* speichern. **~room** *n* Lagerraum *m*

storey *n* Stockwerk *nt*

stork *n* Storch *m*

storm *n* Sturm *m*; *(with thunder)* Gewitter *nt* ● *vt/i* stürmen. **~y** *a* stürmisch

story *n* Geschichte *f*; *(in newspaper)* Artikel *m*; (Ⓘ *lie*) Märchen *nt*

S

stout *a* (-er, -est) beleibt; (*strong*) fest

stove *n* Ofen *m*; (*for cooking*) Herd *m*

stow *vt* verstauen. **~away** *n* blinder Passagier *m*

straggl|e *vi* hinterherhinken. **~er** *n* Nachzügler *m*. **~y** *a* strähnig

straight *a* (-er, -est) gerade; (*direct*) direkt; (*clear*) klar; <*hair*> glatt; <*drink*>; pur; **be ~** (*tidy*) in Ordnung sein ● *adv* gerade; (*directly*) direkt, geradewegs; (*clearly*) klar; **~ away** sofort; **~ on** *or* **ahead** geradeaus; **~ out** (*fig*) geradeheraus; **sit/stand up ~** gerade sitzen/stehen

straighten *vt* gerade machen; (*put straight*) gerade richten ● *vi* gerade werden; **~ [up]** <*person*:> sich aufrichten. **~ out** *vt* gerade biegen

straightforward *a* offen; (*simple*) einfach

strain *n* Belastung *f*; **~s** *pl* (*of music*) Klänge *pl* ● *vt* belasten; (*overexert*) überanstrengen; (*injure*) zerren <*muscle*>; (*Culin*) durchseihen; abgießen <*vegetables*>. **~ed** *a* <*relations*> gespannt. **~er** *n* Sieb *nt*

strait *n* Meerenge *f*; **in dire ~s** in großen Nöten

strand[1] *n* (*of thread*) Faden *m*; (*of hair*) Strähne *f*

strand[2] *vt* **be ~ed** festsitzen

strange *a* (-r, -st) fremd; (*odd*) seltsam, merkwürdig. **~ly** *adv* seltsam, merkwürdig; **~ enough** seltsamerweise. **~r** *n* Fremde(r) *m/f*

strangle *vt* erwürgen; (*fig*) unterdrücken

strap *n* Riemen *m*; (*for safety*) Gurt *m*; (*to grasp in vehicle*) Halteriemen *m*; (*of watch*) Armband *nt*; (*shoulder* ~) Träger *m* ● *vt* (*pt/pp* **strapped**) schnallen

strapping *a* stramm

strategic *a*, **-ally** *adv* strategisch

strategy *n* Strategie *f*

straw *n* Stroh *nt*; (*single piece, drinking*) Strohhalm *m*; **that's the last ~** jetzt reicht's aber

strawberry *n* Erdbeere *f*

stray *a* streunend ● *n* streunendes Tier *nt* ● *vi* sich verirren; (*deviate*) abweichen

streak *n* Streifen *m*; (*in hair*) Strähne *f*; (*fig: trait*) Zug *m*

stream *n* Bach *m*; (*flow*) Strom *m*; (*current*) Strömung *f*; (*Sch*) Parallelzug *m* ● *vi* strömen

streamline *vt* (*fig*) rationalisieren. **~d** *a* stromlinienförmig

street *n* Straße *f*. **~car** *n* (*Amer*) Straßenbahn *f*. **~lamp** *n* Straßenlaterne *f*

strength *n* Stärke *f*; (*power*) Kraft *f*; **on the ~ of** auf Grund (+ *gen*). **~en** *vt* stärken; (*reinforce*) verstärken

strenuous *a* anstrengend

stress *n* (*emphasis*) Betonung *f*; (*strain*) Belastung *f*; (*mental*) Stress *m* ● *vt* betonen; (*put a strain on*) belasten. **~ful** *a* stressig ⚠

stretch *n* (*of road*) Strecke *f*; (*elasticity*) Elastizität *f*; **at a ~** ohne Unterbrechung; **have a ~** sich strecken ● *vt* strecken; (*widen*) dehnen; (*spread*) ausbreiten; fordern <*person*>; **~ one's legs** sich (*dat*) die Beine vertreten ● *vt* sich erstrecken; (*become wider*) sich dehnen; <*person*:> sich strecken. **~er** *n* Tragbahre *f*

strict *a* (-er, -est), **-ly** *adv* streng; **~ly speaking** streng genommen

stride *n* [großer] Schritt *m*; **take sth in one's ~** mit etw gut fertig werden ● *vi* (*pt* **strode**, *pp* **stridden**) [mit großen Schritten] gehen

strident *a*, **-ly** *adv* schrill; <*colour*> grell

strife *n* Streit *m*

strike *n* Streik *m*; (*Mil*) Angriff *m*; **be on ~** streiken ● *v* (*pt/pp* **struck**) ● *vt* schlagen; (*knock against, collide with*) treffen; anzünden <*match*>; stoßen auf (+ *acc*) <*oil, gold*>; abbrechen <*camp*>; (*impress*) beeindrucken; (*occur to*) einfallen (+ *dat*); **~ s.o. a blow** jdm einen Schlag versetzen ● *vi* treffen; *<lightning:>* einschlagen; *<clock:>* schlagen; (*attack*) zuschlagen; *<workers:>* streiken

striker *n* Streikende(r) *m/f*

striking *a* auffallend

string *n* Schnur *f*; (*thin*) Bindfaden *m*; (*of musical instrument, racket*) Saite *f*; (*of bow*) Sehne *f*; (*of pearls*) Kette *f*; **the ~s** (*Mus*) die Streicher *pl*; **pull ~s** 🔲 seine Beziehungen spielen lassen ● *vt* (*pt/pp* **strung**) (*thread*) aufziehen *<beads>*

stringent *a* streng

strip *n* Streifen *m* ● *v* (*pt/pp* **stripped**) ● *vt* ablösen; ausziehen *<person, clothes>*; abziehen *<bed>*; abbeizen *<wood, furniture>*; auseinander nehmen *<machine>*; (*deprive*) berauben (*of gen*); **~ sth off** **sth** etw von etw entfernen ● *vi* (*undress*) sich ausziehen

stripe *n* Streifen *m*. **~d** *a* gestreift

stripper *n* Stripperin *f*; (*male*) Stripper *m*

strive *vi* (*pt* **strove**, *pp* **striven**) sich bemühen (**to** zu); **~ for** streben nach

strode *see* **stride**

stroke¹ *n* Schlag *m*; (*of pen*) Strich *m*; (*Swimming*) Zug *m*; (*style*) Stil *m*; (*Med*) Schlaganfall *m*; **~ of luck** Glücksfall *m*

stroke² ● *vt* streicheln

stroll *n* Bummel *m* 🔲 ● *vi* bummeln 🔲. **~er** *n* (*Amer: pushchair*) [Kinder]sportwagen *m*

strong *a* (-er, -est), **-ly** *adv* stark; (*powerful, healthy*) kräftig; (*severe*) streng; (*sturdy*) stabil; (*convincing*) gut

strong: ~hold *n* Festung *f*; (*fig*) Hochburg *f*. **~-room** *n* Tresorraum *m*

strove *see* **strive**

struck *see* **strike**

structural *a*, **-ly** *adv* baulich

structure *n* Struktur *f*; (*building*) Bau *m*

struggle *n* Kampf *m*; **with a ~** mit Mühe ● *vt* kämpfen; **~ to do sth** sich abmühen, etw zutun

strum *v* (*pt/pp* **strummed**) ● *vt* klimpern auf (+ *dat*) ● *vi* klimpern

strung *see* **string**

strut¹ *n* Strebe *f*

strut² *vi* (*pt/pp* **strutted**) stolzieren

stub *n* Stummel *m*; (*counterfoil*) Abschnitt *m*. **~ out** *vt* (*pt/pp* **stubbed**) ausdrücken *<cigarette>*

stubble *n* Stoppeln *pl*

stubborn *a*, **-ly** *adv* starrsinnig; *<refusal>* hartnäckig

stubby *a*, (-ier, -iest) kurz und dick

stuck *see* **stick²**. **~-up** *a* 🔲 hochnäsig

stud *n* Nagel *m*; (*on clothes*) Niete *f*; (*for collar*) Kragenknopf *m*; (*for ear*) Ohrstecker *m*

student *n* Student(in) *m(f)*; (*Sch*) Schüler(in) *m(f)*

studio *n* Studio *nt*; (*for artist*) Atelier *nt*

studious *a* lerneifrig; (*earnest*) ernsthaft

stud|y *n* Studie *f*; (*room*) Arbeitszimmer *nt*; (*investigation*) Untersuchung *f*; **~ies** *pl* Studium *nt* ● *v* (*pt/pp* **studied**) ● *vt* studieren; (*examine*) untersuchen ● *vi* lernen; (*at university*) studieren

stuff *n* Stoff *m*; (🔲 *things*) Zeug *nt* ● *vt* vollstopfen; (*with padding, Culin*) füllen; ausstopfen *<animal>*; (*cram*) [hinein]stopfen. **~ing** *n* Füllung *f*

stuffy *a* (-ier, -iest) stickig; (*old-fashioned*) spießig

stumbl|e *vi* stolpern; **~e across** zufällig stoßen auf (+ *acc*). **~ing-block** *n* Hindernis *nt*

stump *n* Stumpf *m* ● **~ up** *vt/i* 🔲 blechen. **~ed** *a* 🔲 überfragt

stun *vt* (*pt/pp* **stunned**) betäuben

stung *see* **sting**

stunk *see* **stink**

stunning *a* 🔲 toll

stunt *n* 🔲 Kunststück *nt*

stupendous *a*, **-ly** *adv* enorm

stupid *a* dumm. **~ity** *n* Dummheit *f*. **~ly** *adv* dumm; **~ly [enough]** dummerweise

S

sturdy a (-ier, -iest) stämmig; <*furniture*> stabil; <*shoes*> fest

stutter n Stottern nt ● vt/i stottern

sty n (pl sties) Schweinestall m

style n Stil m; (*fashion*) Mode f; (*sort*) Art f; (*hair~*) Frisur f; **in ~** in großem Stil

stylish a, -ly adv stilvoll

stylist n Friseur m/ Friseuse f. **~ic** a, -ally adv stilistisch

suave a (*pej*) gewandt

subconscious a, -ly adv unterbewusst ● n Unterbewusstsein nt

subdivi|de vt unterteilen. **~sion** n Unterteilung f

subdue vt unterwerfen. **~d** a gedämpft; <*person*> still

subject[1] a **be ~ to sth** etw (*dat*) unterworfen sein ● n Staatsbürger(in) m(f); (*of ruler*) Untertan m; (*theme*) Thema nt; (*of investigation*) Gegenstand m; (*Sch*) Fach nt; (*Gram*) Subjekt nt

subject[2] vt unterwerfen (to *dat*); (*expose*) aussetzen (to *dat*)

subjective a, -ly adv subjektiv

subjunctive n Konjunktiv m

sublime a, -ly adv erhaben

submarine n Unterseeboot nt

submerge vt untertauchen; **be ~d** unter Wasser stehen ● vi tauchen

submission n Unterwerfung f

submit v (pt/pp -mitted, pres p -mitting) ● vt vorlegen (to *dat*); (*hand in*) einreichen ● vi sich unterwerfen (to *dat*)

subordinate[1] a untergeordnet ● n Untergebene(r) m/f

subordinate[2] vt unterordnen (to *dat*)

subscribe vi spenden; **~ to** (*fig*); abonnieren <*newspaper*>. **~r** n Spender m; Abonnent m

subscription n (to *club*) [Mitglieds]beitrag m; (to *newspaper*) Abonnement nt; **by ~** mit Spenden; <*buy*> im Abonnement

subsequent a, -ly adv folgend; (*later*) später

subside vi sinken; <*ground:*> sich senken; <*storm:*> nachlassen

subsidiary a untergeordnet ● n Tochtergesellschaft f

subsid|ize vt subventionieren. **~y** n Subvention f

substance n Substanz f

substandard a unzulänglich; <*goods*> minderwertig

substantial a solide; <*meal*> reichhaltig; (*considerable*) beträchtlich. **~ly** adv solide; (*essentially*) im Wesentlichen

substitut|e n Ersatz m; (*Sport*) Ersatzspieler(in) m(f) ● vt **~e A for B** B durch A ersetzen ● vi **~e for s.o.** jdn vertreten. **~ion** n Ersetzung f

subterranean a unterirdisch

subtitle n Untertitel m

subtle a (-r, -st), -tly adv fein; (*fig*) subtil

subtract vt abziehen, subtrahieren. **~ion** n Subtraktion f

suburb n Vorort m. **~an** a Vorort-. **~ia** n die Vororte pl

subway n Unterführung f; (*Amer: railway*) U-Bahn f

succeed vi Erfolg haben; <*plan:*> gelingen; (*follow*) nachfolgen (+ *dat*); **I ~ed** es ist mir gelungen; **he ~ed in escaping** es gelang ihm zu entkommen ● vt folgen (+ *dat*)

success n Erfolg m. **~ful** a,-ly adv erfolgreich

succession n Folge f; (*series*) Serie f; (to *title, office*) Nachfolge f; (to *throne*) Thronfolge f; **in ~** hintereinander

successive a aufeinander folgend

successor n Nachfolger(in) m(f)

succumb vi erliegen (to *dat*)

such
● *adjective*
⋯▸ (*of that kind*) solch. **such a book** ein solches Buch; so ein Buch Ⓣ. **such a person** ein solcher Mensch; so ein Mensch Ⓣ. **such people** solche Leute. **such a thing** so etwas. **no such example** kein solches

Beispiel. **there is no such thing** so etwas gibt es nicht; das gibt es gar nicht. **there is no such person** eine solche Person gibt es nicht. **such writers as Goethe and Schiller** Schriftsteller wie Goethe und Schiller

····▸ (*so great*) solch; derartig. **I've got such a headache!** ich habe solche Kopfschmerzen! **it was such fun!** das machte solchen Spaß! **I got such a fright that** ... ich bekam einen derartigen *od* 🛈 so einen Schrecken, dass ...

····▸ (*with adjective*) so. **such a big house** ein so großes Haus. **he has such lovely blue eyes** er hat so schöne blaue Augen. **such a long time** so lange

● *pronoun*

····▸ **as such** als solcher/solche/ solches. **the thing as such** die Sache als solche. (*strictly speaking*) **this is not a promotion as such** dies ist im Grunde genommen keine Beförderung

····▸ **such is: such is life** so ist das Leben. **such is not the case** das ist nicht der Fall

····▸ **such as** wie [zum Beispiel]

suchlike *pron* 🛈 dergleichen
suck *vt/i* saugen; lutschen <*sweet*>. ~ **up** *vt* aufsaugen ● *vi* ~ **up to s.o.** 🛈 sich bei jdm einschmeicheln
suction *n* Saugwirkung *f*
sudden *a*, **-ly** *adv* plötzlich; (*abrupt*) jäh ● *n* **all of a** ~ auf einmal
sue *vt* (*pres p* **suing**) verklagen (**for** auf + *acc*) ● *vi* klagen
suede *n* Wildleder *nt*
suet *n* [Nieren]talg *m*
suffer *vi* leiden (**from** an + *dat*) ● *vt* erleiden; (*tolerate*) dulden
suffice *vi* genügen
sufficient *a*, **-ly** *adv* genug, genügend; **be** ~ genügen
suffocat|e *vt/i* ersticken. ~**ion** *n* Ersticken *nt*
sugar *n* Zucker *m* ● *vt* zuckern; (*fig*) versüßen. ~ **basin,** ~**-bowl** *n* Zuckerschale *f.* ~**y** *a* süß; (*fig*) süßlich

suggest *vt* vorschlagen; (*indicate, insinuate*) andeuten. ~**ion** *n* Vorschlag *m*; Andeutung *f*; (*trace*) Spur *f.* ~**ive** *a*, **-ly** *adv* anzüglich
suicidal *a* selbstmörderisch
suicide *n* Selbstmord *m*
suit *n* Anzug *m*; (*woman's*) Kostüm *nt*; (*Cards*) Farbe *f*; (*Jur*) Prozess *m* ● *vt* (*adapt*) anpassen (**to** *dat*); (*be convenient for*) passen (+ *dat*); (*go with*) passen zu; <*clothing:*> stehen (**s.o.** *jdm*); **be** ~**ed for** geeignet sein für; ~ **yourself!** wie du willst!
suit|able *a* geeignet; (*convenient*) passend; (*appropriate*) angemessen; (*for weather, activity*) zweckmäßig. ~**ably** *adv* angemessen; zweckmäßig
suitcase *n* Koffer *m*
suite *n* Suite *f*; (*of furniture*) Garnitur *f*
sulk *vi* schmollen. ~**y** *a* schmollend
sullen *a*, **-ly** *adv* mürrisch
sultry *a* (**-ier, -iest**) <*weather*> schwül
sum *n* Summe *f*; (*Sch*) Rechenaufgabe *f* ● *vt/i* (*pt/pp* **summed**) ~ **up** zusammenfassen; (*assess*) einschätzen
summar|ize *vt* zusammenfassen. ~**y** *n* Zusammenfassung *f* ● *a*, **-ily** *adv* summarisch; <*dismissal*> fristlos
summer *n* Sommer *m*. ~**time** *n* Sommer *m*
summery *a* sommerlich
summit *n* Gipfel *m*. ~ **conference** *n* Gipfelkonferenz *f*
summon *vt* rufen; holen <*help*>; (*Jur*) vorladen
summons *n* (*Jur*) Vorladung *f* ● *vt* vorladen
sumptuous *a*, **-ly** *adv* prunkvoll; <*meal*> üppig
sun *n* Sonne *f* ● *vt* (*pt/pp* **sunned**) ~ **oneself** sich sonnen
sun: ~**bathe** *vi* sich sonnen. ~**-bed** *n* Sonnenbank *f.* ~**burn** *n* Sonnenbrand *m*
Sunday *n* Sonntag *m*
sunflower *n* Sonnenblume *f*

sung see **sing**

sunglasses npl Sonnenbrille f

sunk see **sink**

sunny a (-ier, -iest) sonnig

sun: ~**rise** n Sonnenaufgang m. ~**roof** n (Auto) Schiebedach nt. ~**set** n Sonnenuntergang m. ~**shade** n Sonnenschirm m. ~**shine** n Sonnenschein m. ~**stroke** n Sonnenstich m. ~**tan** n [Sonnen]bräune f. ~**tanned** a braun [gebrannt]. ~**tan oil** n Sonnenöl nt

super a 🔢 prima, toll

superb a erstklassig

superficial a, -ly adv oberflächlich

superfluous a überflüssig

superintendent n (of police) Kommissar m

superior a überlegen; (in rank) höher ● n Vorgesetzte(r) m/f. ~**ity** n Überlegenheit f

superlative a unübertrefflich ● n Superlativ m

supermarket n Supermarkt m

supernatural a übernatürlich

supersede vt ersetzen

superstiti|on n Aberglaube m. ~**ous** a, -ly adv abergläubisch

supervis|e vt beaufsichtigen; überwachen <work>. ~**ion** n Aufsicht f; Überwachung f. ~**or** n Aufseher(in) m(f)

supper n Abendessen nt

supple a geschmeidig

supplement n Ergänzung f; (addition) Zusatz m; (to fare) Zuschlag m; (book) Ergänzungsband m; (to newspaper) Beilage f ● vt ergänzen. ~**ary** a zusätzlich

supplier n Lieferant m

supply n Vorrat m; **supplies** pl (Mil) Nachschub m ● vt (pt/pp -ied) liefern; ~ s.o. with sth jdn mit etw versorgen

support n Stütze f; (fig) Unterstützung f ● vt stützen; (bear weight of) tragen; (keep) ernähren; (give money to) unterstützen; (speak in favour of) befürworten; (Sport)

Fan sein von. ~**er** n Anhänger(in) m(f); (Sport) Fan m

suppose vt annehmen; (presume) vermuten; (imagine) sich (dat) vorstellen; be ~d to do sth etw tun sollen; not be ~d to 🔢 nicht dürfen; I ~ so vermutlich. ~**dly** adv angeblich

supposition n Vermutung f

suppress vt unterdrücken. ~**ion** n Unterdrückung f

supremacy n Vorherrschaft f

supreme a höchste(r,s); <court> oberste(r,s)

sure a (-r, -st) sicher; make ~ sich vergewissern (of gen); (check) nachprüfen ● adv (Amer 🔢) klar; ~ enough tatsächlich. ~**ly** adv sicher; (for emphasis) doch; (Amer: gladly) gern

surf n Brandung f

surface n Oberfläche f ● vi (emerge) auftauchen

surfboard n Surfbrett nt

surfing n Surfen nt

surge n (of sea) Branden nt; (fig) Welle f ● vi branden; ~ **forward** nach vorn drängen

surgeon n Chirurg(in) m(f)

surgery n Chirurgie f; (place) Praxis f; (room) Sprechzimmer nt; (hours) Sprechstunde f; have ~ operiert werden

surgical a, -ly adv chirurgisch

surly a (-ier, -iest) mürrisch

surname n Nachname m

surpass vt übertreffen

surplus a überschüssig ● n Überschuss m (of an + dat)

surpris|e n Überraschung f ● vt überraschen; be ~**ed** sich wundern (at über + acc). ~**ing** a, -ly adv überraschend

surrender n Kapitulation f ● vi sich ergeben; (Mil) kapitulieren ● vt aufgeben

surround vt umgeben; (encircle) umzingeln; ~**ed by** umgeben von. ~**ing** a umliegend. ~**ings** npl Umgebung f

surveillance *n* Überwachung *f;* **be under ~** überwacht werden

survey¹ *n* Überblick *m; (poll)* Umfrage *f; (investigation)* Untersuchung *f; (of land)* Vermessung *f; (of house)* Gutachten *nt*

survey² *vt* betrachten; vermessen *<land>;* begutachten *<building>.* **~or** *n* Landvermesser *m;* Gutachter *m*

survival *n* Überleben *nt; (of tradition)* Fortbestand *m*

surviv|e *vt* überleben ● *vi* überleben; *<tradition.>* erhalten bleiben. **~or** *n* Überlebende(r) *m/f;* **be a ~or** nicht unterzukriegen sein

susceptible *a* empfänglich/ *(Med)* anfällig **(for für)**

suspect¹ *vt* verdächtigen; *(assume)* vermuten; **he ~s nothing** er ahnt nichts

suspect² *a* verdächtig ● *n* Verdächtige(r) *m/f*

suspend *vt* aufhängen; *(stop)* [vorläufig] einstellen; *(from duty)* vorläufig beurlauben. **~ders** *npl (Amer: braces)* Hosenträger *pl*

suspense *n* Spannung *f*

suspension *n (Auto)* Federung *f.* **~ bridge** *n* Hängebrücke *f*

suspici|on *n* Verdacht *m; (mistrust)* Misstrauen *nt; (trace)* Spur *f.* **~ous** *a*, **-ly** *adv* misstrauisch; *(arousing suspicion)* verdächtig

sustain *vt* tragen; *(fig)* aufrechterhalten; erhalten *<life>;* erleiden *<injury>*

sustenance *n* Nahrung *f*

swagger *vi* stolzieren

swallow¹ *vt/i* schlucken. **~ up** *vt* verschlucken; verschlingen *<resources>*

swallow² *n (bird)* Schwalbe *f*

swam *see* **swim**

swamp *n* Sumpf *m* ● *vt* überschwemmen

swan *n* Schwan *m*

swank *vi* 🄸 angeben

swap *n* 🄸 Tausch *m* ● *vt/i (pt/pp swapped)* 🄸 tauschen **(for gegen)**

swarm *n* Schwarm *m* ● *vi* schwärmen; **be ~ing with** wimmeln von

swat *vt (pt/pp swatted)* totschlagen

sway *vi* schwanken; *(gently)* sich wiegen ● *vt (influence)* beeinflussen

swear *v (pt swore, pp sworn)* ● *vt* schwören ● *vi* schwören **(by auf +** *acc); (curse)* fluchen. **~-word** *n* Kraftausdruck *m*

sweat *n* Schweiß *m* ● *vi* schwitzen

sweater *n* Pullover *m*

Swed|e *n* Schwede *m/*Schwedin *f.* **~en** *n* Schweden *nt.* **~ish** *a* schwedisch

sweep *n* Schornsteinfeger *m; (curve)* Bogen *m; (movement)* ausholende Bewegung *f* ● *v (pt/pp swept)* ● *vt* fegen, kehren ● *vi (go swiftly)* rauschen; *<wind:>* fegen

sweeping *a* ausholend; *<statement>* pauschal; *<changes>* weit reichend

sweet *a (-er, -est)* süß; **have a ~ tooth** gern Süßes mögen ● *n* Bonbon *m & nt; (dessert)* Nachtisch *m*

sweeten *vt* süßen

sweet: ~heart *n* Schatz *m.* **~ness** *n* Süße *f.* **~ pea** *n* Wicke *f.* **~-shop** *n* Süßwarenladen *m*

swell *n* Dünung *f* ● *v (pt swelled, pp swollen or swelled)* ● *vi* [an]schwellen; *<wood:>* aufquellen ● *vt* anschwellen lassen; *(increase)* vergrößern. **~ing** *n* Schwellung *f*

swelter *vi* schwitzen

swept *see* **sweep**

swerve *vi* einen Bogen machen

swift *a (-er, -est)*, **-ly** *adv* schnell

swig *n* 🄸 Schluck *m*

swim *n* **have a ~** schwimmen ● *vi (pt swam, pp swum)* schwimmen; **my head is ~ming** mir dreht sich der Kopf. **~mer** *n* Schwimmer(in) *m(f)*

swimming *n* Schwimmen *nt.* **~-baths** *npl* Schwimmbad *nt.* **~-pool** *n* Schwimmbecken *nt; (private)* Swimmingpool *m*

swimsuit *n* Badeanzug *m*

swindle *n* Schwindel *m*, Betrug *m* ● *vt* betrügen. **~r** *n* Schwindler *m*

S

swine n (pej) Schwein nt

swing n Schwung m; (shift) Schwenk m; (seat) Schaukel f; **in full ~** in vollem Gange ● (pt/pp swung) ● vi schwingen; (on swing) schaukeln; (dangle) baumeln; (turn) schwenken ● vt schwingen; (influence) beeinflussen

swipe n 🅘 Schlag m ● vt 🅘 knallen; (steal) klauen

swirl n Wirbel m ● vt/i wirbeln

Swiss a Schweizer, schweizerisch ● n Schweizer(in) m(f); **the ~** pl die Schweizer. **~ roll** n Biskuitrolle f

switch n Schalter m; (change) Wechsel m; (Amer, Rail) Weiche f ● vt wechseln; (exchange) tauschen ● vi wechseln; **~ to** umstellen auf (+ acc). **~ off** vt ausschalten; abschalten <engine>. **~ on** vt einschalten

switchboard n [Telefon]zentrale f

Switzerland n die Schweiz

swivel v (pt/pp swivelled) ● vt drehen ● vi sich drehen

swollen see swell

swoop n (by police) Razzia f ● vi **~ down** herabstoßen

sword n Schwert nt

swore see swear

sworn see swear

swot n 🅘 Streber m ● vt (pt/pp swotted) 🅘 büffeln

swum see swim

swung see swing

syllable n Silbe f

syllabus n Lehrplan m; (for exam) Studienplan m

symbol n Symbol nt (of für). **~ic** a, -ally adv symbolisch **~ism** n Symbolik f. **~ize** vt symbolisieren

symmetr|ical a, -ly adv symmetrisch. **~y** n Symmetrie f

sympathetic a, -ally adv mitfühlend; (likeable) sympathisch

sympathize vi mitfühlen

sympathy n Mitgefühl nt; (condolences) Beileid nt

symphony n Sinfonie f

symptom n Symptom nt

synagogue n Synagoge f

synchronize vt synchronisieren

synonym n Synonym nt. **~ous** a, -ly adv synonym

synthesis n (pl -ses) Synthese f

synthetic a synthetisch

Syria n Syrien nt

syringe n Spritze f

syrup n Sirup m

system n System nt. **~atic** a, -ally adv systematisch

Tt

tab n (projecting) Zunge f; (with name) Namensschild nt; (loop) Aufhänger m; **pick up the ~** 🅘 bezahlen

table n Tisch m; (list) Tabelle f; **at [the] ~** bei Tisch. **~-cloth** n Tischdecke f. **~spoon** n Servierlöffel m

tablet n Tablette f; (of soap) Stück nt

table tennis n Tischtennis nt

tabloid n kleinformatige Zeitung f; (pej) Boulevardzeitung f

taciturn a wortkarg

tack n (nail) Stift m; (stitch) Heftstich m; (Naut & fig) Kurs m ● vt festnageln; (sew) heften ● vi (Naut) kreuzen

tackle n Ausrüstung f ● vt angehen <problem>; (Sport) angreifen

tact n Takt m, Taktgefühl nt. **~ful** a, -ly adv taktvoll

tactic|al a, -ly adv taktisch. **~s** npl Taktik f

tactless a, -ly adv taktlos. **~ness** n Taktlosigkeit f

tag n (label) Schild nt ● vi (pt/pp tagged) **~ along** mitkommen

tail n Schwanz m; **~s** pl (tailcoat) Frack m; **heads or ~s?** Kopf oder

Zahl? ● *vt* (🔢 *follow*) beschatten ● *vi*
~ **off** zurückgehen

tail: ~**back** *n* Rückstau *m.* ~ **light**
n Rücklicht *nt*

tailor *n* Schneider *m.* ~**-made** *a*
maßgeschneidert

taint *vt* verderben

take *v* (*pt* **took**, *pp* **taken**) ● *vt*
nehmen: (*with one*) mitnehmen; (*take
to a place*) bringen; (*steal*) stehlen;
(*win*) gewinnen; (*capture*)
einnehmen; (*require*) brauchen; (*last*)
dauern; (*teach*) geben; machen
<*exam, subject, holiday,
photograph*>; messen <*pulse,
temperature*>; ~ **sth to the cleaner's**
etw in die Reinigung bringen; **be ~n
ill** krank werden; ~ **sth calmly** etw
gelassen aufnehmen ● *vi* <*plant:*>
angehen; ~ **after s.o.** jdm
nachschlagen; (*in looks*) jdm ähnlich
sehen; ~ **to** (*like*) mögen; (*as a habit*)
sich (*dat*) angewöhnen. ~ **away** *vt*
wegbringen; (*remove*) wegnehmen;
(*subtract*) abziehen; **'to ~ away'** 'zum
Mitnehmen'. ~ **back** *vt*
zurücknehmen; (*return*)
zurückbringen. ~ **down** *vt*
herunternehmen; (*remove*)
abnehmen; (*write down*)
aufschreiben. ~ **in** *vt*
hineinbringen; (*bring indoors*)
hereinholen; (*to one's home*)
aufnehmen; (*understand*) begreifen;
(*deceive*) hereinlegen; (*make smaller*)
enger machen. ~ **off** *vt* abnehmen;
ablegen <*coat*>; sich (*dat*) ausziehen
<*clothes*>; (*deduct*) abziehen; (*mimic*)
nachmachen ● *vi* (*Aviat*) starten. ~
on *vt* annehmen; (*undertake*)
übernehmen; (*engage*) einstellen; (*as
opponent*) antreten gegen. ~ **out** *vt*
hinausbringen; (*for pleasure*)
ausgehen mit; ausführen <*dog*>;
(*remove*) herausnehmen; (*withdraw*)
abheben <*money*>; (*from library*)
ausleihen; ~ **it out on s.o.** 🔢 seinen
Ärger an jdm auslassen. ~ **over** *vt*
hinüberbringen; übernehmen <*firm,
control*> ● *vi* ~ **over from s.o.** jdn
ablösen. ~ **up** *vt* hinaufbringen;
annehmen <*offer*>; ergreifen
<*profession*>; sich (*dat*) zulegen

<*hobby*>; in Anspruch nehmen
<*time*>; einnehmen <*space*>;
aufreißen <*floorboards*>; ~ **sth up
with s.o.** mit jdm über etw (*acc*)
sprechen

take: ~**-away** *n* Essen *nt* zum
Mitnehmen; (*restaurant*) Restaurant
nt mit Straßenverkauf. ~**-off** *n*
(*Aviat*) Start *m*, Abflug *m.* ~**-over** *n*
Übernahme *f*

takings *npl* Einnahmen *pl*

talcum *n* ~ **[powder]** Körperpuder
m

tale *n* Geschichte *f*

talent *n* Talent *nt*

talk *n* Gespräch *nt*; (*lecture*) Vortrag
m ● *vi* reden, sprechen (**to/with** mit)
● *vt* reden; ~ **s.o. into sth** jdn zu etw
überreden. ~ **over** *vt* besprechen

talkative *a* gesprächig

tall *a* (**-er, -est**) groß; <*building, tree*>
hoch. ~ **story** *n* übertriebene
Geschichte *f*

tally *vi* übereinstimmen

tame *a* (**-r, -st**), **-ly** *adv* zahm; (*dull*)
lahm 🔢 ● *vt* zähmen. ~**r** *n*
Dompteur *m*

tamper *vi* ~ **with** sich (*dat*) zu
schaffen machen an (+ *dat*)

tampon *n* Tampon *m*

tan *a* gelbbraun ● *n* Gelbbraun *nt*;
(*from sun*) Bräune *f* ● *v* (*pt/pp
tanned*) ● *vt* gerben <*hide*> ● *vi*
braun werden

tang *n* herber Geschmack *m*; (*smell*)
herber Geruch *m*

tangible *a* greifbar

tangle *n* Gewirr *nt*; (*in hair*)
Verfilzung *f* ● *vt* ~ **[up]** verheddern
● *vi* sich verheddern

tank *n* Tank *m*; (*Mil*) Panzer *m*

tanker *n* Tanker *m*; (*lorry*)
Tank[last]wagen *m*

tantrum *n* Wutanfall *m*

tap *n* Hahn *m*; (*knock*) Klopfen *nt*; **on
~** zur Verfügung ● *v* (*pt/pp* **tapped**)
● *vt* klopfen an (+ *acc*); anzapfen
<*barrel, tree*>; erschließen
<*resources*>; abhören <*telephone*>
● *vi* klopfen. ~**-dance** *n*

t

Stepp[tanz] *m* ● *vi* Stepp tanzen,
steppen

tape *n* Band *nt*; (*adhesive*)
Klebstreifen *m*; (*for recording*)
Tonband *nt* ● *vt* mit Klebstreifen
zukleben; (*record*) auf Band
aufnehmen

tape-measure *n* Bandmaß *nt*

taper *vi* sich verjüngen

tape recorder *n* Tonbandgerät *nt*

tar *n* Teer *m* ● *vt* (*pt/pp* tarred) teeren

target *n* Ziel *nt*; (*board*)
[Ziel]scheibe *f*

tarnish *vi* anlaufen

tarpaulin *n* Plane *f*

tart¹ *a* (-er, -est) sauer

tart² *n* ≈ Obstkuchen *m*; (*individual*)
Törtchen *nt*; (🗷 *prostitute*) Nutte *f*
● *vt* ~ oneself up 🖪 sich auftakeln

tartan *n* Schottenmuster *nt*; (*cloth*)
Schottenstoff *m*

task *n* Aufgabe *f*; take s.o. to ~ jdm
Vorhaltungen machen. ~ **force** *n*
Sonderkommando *nt*

tassel *n* Quaste *f*

taste *n* Geschmack *m*; (*sample*)
Kostprobe *f* ● *vt* kosten, probieren;
schmecken <*flavour*> ● *vi*
schmecken (of nach). ~**ful** *a*, -**ly**
adv (*fig*) geschmackvoll. ~**less** *a*,
-**ly** *adv* geschmacklos

tasty *a* (-ier, -iest) lecker

tat *see* tit²

tatters *npl* in ~s in Fetzen

tattoo *n* Tätowierung *f* ● *vt*
tätowieren

tatty *a* (-ier, -iest) schäbig; <*book*>
zerfleddert

taught *see* teach

taunt *n* höhnische Bemerkung *f* ● *vt*
verhöhnen

taut *a* straff

tawdry *a* (-ier, -iest) billig und
geschmacklos

tax *n* Steuer *f* ● *vt* besteuern; (*fig*)
strapazieren. ~**able** *a*
steuerpflichtig. ~**ation** *n*
Besteuerung *f*

taxi *n* Taxi *nt* ● *vi* (*pt/pp* taxied, *pres
p* taxiing) <*aircraft:*> rollen. ~

driver *n* Taxifahrer *m*. ~ **rank** *n*
Taxistand *m*

taxpayer *n* Steuerzahler *m*

tea *n* Tee *m*. ~**-bag** *n* Teebeutel *m*.
~**-break** *n* Teepause *f*

teach *vt/i* (*pt/pp* taught)
unterrichten; ~ s.o. sth jdm etw
beibringen. ~**er** *n* Lehrer(in) *m(f)*.
~**ing** *n* Unterrichten *nt*

tea: ~**-cloth** *n* (*for drying*)
Geschirrtuch *nt*. ~**cup** *n* Teetasse *f*

teak *n* Teakholz *nt*

team *n* Mannschaft *f*; (*fig*) Team *nt*;
(*of animals*) Gespann *nt*

teapot *n* Teekanne *f*

tear¹ *n* Riss *m* ● *v* (*pt* tore, *pp* torn)
● *vt* reißen; (*damage*) zerreißen; ~
oneself away sich losreißen ● *vi*
[zer]reißen; (*run*) rasen. ~ **up** *vt*
zerreißen

tear² *n* Träne *f*. ~**ful** *a* weinend.
~**fully** *adv* unter Tränen. ~**gas** *n*
Tränengas *nt*

tease *vt* necken

tea: ~**-set** *n* Teeservice *nt*. ~ **shop**
n Café *nt*. ~**spoon** *n* Teelöffel *m*

teat *n* Zitze *f*; (*on bottle*) Sauger *m*

tea-towel *n* Geschirrtuch *nt*

technical *a* technisch; (*specialized*)
fachlich. ~**ity** *n* technisches Detail
nt; (*Jur*) Formfehler *m*. ~**ly** *adv*
technisch; (*strictly*) streng
genommen. ~ **term** *n*
Fachausdruck *m*

technician *n* Techniker *m*

technique *n* Technik *f*

technological *a*, -**ly** *adv*
technologisch

technology *n* Technik *f*

teddy *n* ~ [bear] Teddybär *m*

tedious *a* langweilig

tedium *n* Langeweile *f*

teenage *a* Teenager-; ~ boy/girl
Junge *m*/Mädchen *nt* im
Teenageralter. ~**r** *n* Teenager *m*

teens *npl* the ~ die Teenagerjahre
pl

teeter *vi* schwanken

teeth *see* tooth

teeth|e vi zahnen. **~ing troubles** npl (fig) Anfangsschwierigkeiten pl

teetotal a abstinent. **~ler** n Abstinenzler m

telecommunications npl Fernmeldewesen nt

telegram n Telegramm nt

telegraph pole n Telegrafenmast m

telephone n Telefon nt; **be on the ~** Telefon haben; (be telephoning) telefonieren ● vt anrufen ● vi telefonieren

telephone: **~ booth** n, **~ box** n Telefonzelle f. **~ directory** n Telefonbuch nt. **~ number** n Telefonnummer f

telephoto a **~ lens** Teleobjektiv nt

telescop|e n Teleskop nt, Fernrohr nt. **~ic** a (collapsible) ausziehbar

televise vt im Fernsehen übertragen

television n Fernsehen nt; **watch ~** fernsehen; **~ [set]** Fernseher m Ⓣ

tell vt/i (pt/pp told) sagen (s.o. jdm); (relate) erzählen; (know) wissen; (distinguish) erkennen; **~ the time** die Uhr lesen; **time will ~** das wird man erst sehen; **his age is beginning to ~** sein Alter macht sich bemerkbar. **~ off** vt ausschimpfen

telly n Ⓣ = television

temp n Ⓣ Aushilfssekretärin f

temper n (disposition) Naturell; (mood) Laune f; (anger) Wut f; **lose one's ~** wütend werden ● vt (fig) mäßigen

temperament n Temperament nt. **~al** a temperamentvoll; (moody) launisch

temperate a gemäßigt

temperature n Temperatur f; **have or run a ~** Fieber haben

temple[1] n Tempel m

temple[2] n (Anat) Schläfe f

tempo n Tempo nt

temporary a, **-ily** adv vorübergehend; <measure, building> provisorisch

tempt vt verleiten; (Relig) versuchen; herausfordern <fate>; (entice) [ver]locken; **be ~ed** versucht sein (to zu). **~ation** n Versuchung f. **~ing** a verlockend

ten a zehn

tenaci|ous a, **-ly** adv hartnäckig. **~ty** n Hartnäckigkeit f

tenant n Mieter(in) m(f); (Comm) Pächter(in) m(f)

tend vi **~ to do sth** dazu neigen, etw zu tun

tendency n Tendenz f; (inclination) Neigung f

tender a zart; (loving) zärtlich; (painful) empfindlich. **~ly** adv zärtlich. **~ness** n Zartheit f; Zärtlichkeit f

tendon n Sehne f

tenner n Ⓣ Zehnpfundschein m

tennis n Tennis nt. **~-court** n Tennisplatz m

tenor n Tenor m

tense a (-r, -st) gespannt ● vt anspannen <muscle>

tension n Spannung f

tent n Zelt nt

tentative a, **-ly** adv vorläufig; (hesitant) zaghaft

tenterhooks npl **be on ~** wie auf glühenden Kohlen sitzen

tenth a zehnte(r,s) ● n Zehntel nt

tenuous a schwach

tepid a lauwarm

term n Zeitraum m; (Sch) ≈ Halbjahr nt; (Univ) ≈ Semester nt; (expression) Ausdruck m; **~s** pl (conditions) Bedingungen pl; **in the short/long ~** kurz-/langfristig; **be on good/bad ~s** gut/nicht gut miteinander auskommen

terminal a End-; (Med) unheilbar ● n (Aviat) Terminal m; (of bus) Endstation f; (on battery) Pol m; (Computing) Terminal nt

terminat|e vt beenden; lösen <contract>; unterbrechen <pregnancy> ● vi enden

terminology n Terminologie f

terminus n (pl -ni) Endstation f

terrace n Terrasse f; (houses) Häuserreihe f. **~d house** n Reihenhaus nt

t

terrain n Gelände nt

terrible a, **-bly** adv schrecklich

terrific a ⊡ (*excellent*) sagenhaft; (*huge*) riesig

terri|fy vt (*pt/pp* **-ied**) Angst machen (+ *dat*); **be ∼fied** Angst haben. **∼fying** a Furcht erregend

territorial a Territorial-

territory n Gebiet nt

terror n [panische] Angst f; (*Pol*) Terror m. **∼ism** n Terrorismus m. **∼ist** n Terrorist m. **∼ize** vt terrorisieren

terse a, **-ly** adv kurz, knapp

test n Test m; (*Sch*) Klassenarbeit f; **put to the ∼** auf die Probe stellen ● vt prüfen; (*examine*) untersuchen (for auf + *acc*)

testament n Testament nt

testify v (*pt/pp* **-ied**) ● vt beweisen; **∼ that** bezeugen, dass ● vi aussagen

testimonial n Zeugnis nt

testimony n Aussage f

test-tube n Reagenzglas nt

tether n be at the end of one's ∼ am Ende seiner Kraft sein ● vt anbinden

text n Text m. **∼book** n Lehrbuch nt

textile a Textil- ● n **∼s** pl Textilien pl

texture n Beschaffenheit f; (*Tex*) Struktur f

Thai a thailändisch. **∼land** n Thailand nt

Thames n Themse f

than conj als

thank vt danken (+ *dat*); **∼ you [very much]** danke [schön]. **∼ful** a, **-ly** adv dankbar. **∼less** a undankbar

thanks npl Dank m; **∼!** ⊡ danke! **∼ to** dank (+ *dat or gen*)

---

that

pl **those**

● *adjective*

····▸ der (m), die (f), das (nt), die (pl); (*just seen or experienced*) dieser (m), diese (f), dieses (nt), diese (pl). **I'll never forget that day** den Tag werde ich nie vergessen. **I liked that house** dieses Haus hat mir gut gefallen

● *pronoun*

····▸ der (m), die (f), das (nt), die (pl). **that is not true** das ist nicht wahr. **who is that in the garden?** wer ist das [da] im Garten? **I'll take that** ich nehme den/die/das. **I don't like those** die mag ich nicht. **is that you?** bist du es? **that is why** deshalb

····▸ **like that** so. **don't be like that!** sei doch nicht so! **a man like that** ein solcher Mann; so ein Mann ⊡

····▸ (*after prepositions*) da .... ⊡ **after that** danach. **with that** damit. **apart from that** außerdem

····▸ (*relative pronoun*) der (m), die (f), das (nt), die (pl). **the book that I'm reading** das Buch, das ich lese. **the people that you got it from** die Leute, von denen du es bekommen hast. **everyone that I know** jeder, den ich kenne. **that is all that I have** das ist alles, was ich habe

● *adverb*

····▸ so. **he's not that stupid** so blöd ist er [auch wieder] nicht. **it wasn't that bad** so schlecht war es auch nicht. **a nail about that long** ein etwa so langer Nagel

····▸ (*relative adverb*) der (m), die (f), das (nt), die (pl). **the day that I first met her** der Tag, an dem ich sie zum ersten Mal sah. **at the speed that he was going** bei der Geschwindigkeit, die er hatte

● *conjunction*

····▸ dass. **I don't think that he'll come** ich denke nicht, dass er kommt. **we know that you're right** wir wissen, dass du Recht hast. **I'm so tired that I can hardly walk** ich bin so müde, dass ich kaum gehen kann

····▸ **so that** (*purpose*) damit; (*result*) sodass. **he came earlier so that they would have more time** er kam früher, damit sie mehr Zeit hatten. **it was late, so that I had to catch the bus** es war spät, sodass ich den Bus nehmen musste

---

thatch n Strohdach nt. **∼ed** a strohgedeckt

thaw n Tauwetter nt ● vt/i auftauen; it's ~ing es taut

the def art der/die/das; (pl) die; **play ~ piano/violin** Klavier/Geige spielen ● adv ~ **more** ~ **better** je mehr, desto besser; **all** ~ **better** umso besser

theatre n Theater nt; (Med) Operationssaal m

theatrical a Theater-; (showy) theatralisch

theft n Diebstahl m

their a ihr

theirs poss pron ihre(r), ihrs; **a friend of** ~ ein Freund von ihnen; **those are** ~ die gehören ihnen

them pron (acc) sie; (dat) ihnen

theme n Thema nt

themselves pron selbst; (refl) sich; **by** ~ allein

then adv dann; (at that time in past) damals; **by** ~ bis dahin; **since** ~ seitdem; **before** ~ vorher; **from** ~ **on** von da an; **now and** ~ dann und wann; **there and** ~ auf der Stelle ● a damalig

theology n Theologie f

theoretical a, **-ly** adv theoretisch

theory n Theorie f; **in** ~ theoretisch

therap|ist n Therapeut(in) m(f). ~**y** n Therapie f

there adv da; (with movement) dahin, dorthin; **down/up** ~ da unten/oben; ~ **is/are** da ist/sind; (in existence) es gibt ~, ~! nun, nun!

there: ~**abouts** adv da [in der Nähe]; **or** ~**abouts** (roughly) ungefähr. ~**fore** adv deshalb, also

thermometer n Thermometer nt

Thermos (P) n ~ [flask] Thermosflasche (P) f

thermostat n Thermostat m

these see this

thesis n (pl **-ses**) Dissertation f; (proposition) These f

they pron sie; ~ **say** (generalizing) man sagt

thick a (**-er**, **-est**), **-ly** adv dick; (dense) dicht; <liquid> dickflüssig; (𝕀 stupid) dumm ● adv dick ● n **in the** ~ **of** mitten in (+ dat). ~**en** vt dicker machen; eindicken <sauce> ● vi dicker werden; <fog:> dichter werden; <plot:> komplizierter werden. ~**ness** n Dicke f; (density) Dichte f; (of liquid) Dickflüssigkeit f

thief n (pl **thieves**) Dieb(in) m(f)

thigh n Oberschenkel m

thimble n Fingerhut m

thin a (**thinner**, **thinnest**), **-ly** adv dünn ● adv dünn ● v (pt/pp **thinned**) ● vt verdünnen <liquid> ● vi sich lichten

thing n Ding nt; (subject, affair) Sache f; ~**s** pl (belongings) Sachen pl; **for one** ~ erstens; **just the** ~! genau das Richtige! **how are** ~**s**? wie geht's? **the latest** ~ 𝕀 der letzte Schrei

think vt/i (pt/pp **thought**) denken (**about/of** an + acc); (believe) meinen; (consider) nachdenken; (regard as) halten für; **I** ~ **so** ich glaube schon; **what do you** ~ **of it?** was halten Sie davon? ~ **over** vt sich (dat) überlegen. ~ **up** vt sich (dat) ausdenken

third a dritte(r,s) ● n Drittel nt. ~**ly** adv drittens. ~**-rate** a drittrangig

thirst n Durst m. ~**y** a, **-ily** adv durstig; **be** ~**y** Durst haben

thirteen a dreizehn. ~**th** a dreizehnte(r,s)

thirtieth a dreißigste(r,s)

thirty a dreißig

this a (pl **these**) diese(r,s); (pl) diese; ~ **one** diese(r,s) da; **I'll take** ~ ich nehme diesen/diese/ dieses; ~ **evening/morning** heute Abend/ Morgen; **these days** heutzutage ● pron (pl **these**) das, dies[es]; (pl) die, diese; ~ **and that** dies und das; ~ **or that** dieses oder das da; **like** ~ so; ~ **is Peter** das ist Peter; (Teleph) hier [spricht] Peter; **who is** ~? wer ist das? (Teleph, Amer) wer ist am Apparat?

thistle n Distel f

thorn n Dorn m

thorough a gründlich

thoroughbred n reinrassiges Tier nt; (horse) Rassepferd nt

thorough|ly *adv* gründlich; (*completely*) völlig; (*extremely*) äußerst. **~ness** *n* Gründlichkeit *f*

those *see* that

though *conj* obgleich, obwohl; **as ~** als ob ● *adv* 🛈 doch

thought *see* think ● *n* Gedanke *m*; (*thinking*) Denken *nt*. **~ful** *a*, **-ly** *adv* nachdenklich; (*considerate*) rücksichtsvoll. **~less** *a*, **-ly** *adv* gedankenlos

thousand *a* one/a **~** [ein]tausend ● *n* Tausend *nt*. **~th** *a* tausendste(r,s) ● *n* Tausendstel *nt*

thrash *vt* verprügeln; (*defeat*) [vernichtend] schlagen

thread *n* Faden *m*; (*of screw*) Gewinde *nt* ● *vt* einfädeln; auffädeln <*beads*>. **~bare** *a* fadenscheinig

threat *n* Drohung *f*; (*danger*) Bedrohung *f*

threaten *vt* drohen (+ *dat*); (*with weapon*) bedrohen; **~ s.o. with sth** jdm etw androhen ● *vi* drohen. **~ing**, **-ly** *adv* drohend; (*ominous*) bedrohlich

three *a* drei. **~fold** *a* & *adv* dreifach

thresh *vt* dreschen

threshold *n* Schwelle *f*

threw *see* throw

thrift *n* Sparsamkeit *f*. **~y** *a* sparsam

thrill *n* Erregung *f*; 🛈 Nervenkitzel *m* ● *vt* (*excite*) erregen; **be ~ed with** sich sehr freuen über (+ *acc*). **~er** *n* Thriller *m*. **~ing** *a* erregend

thrive *vi* (*pt* thrived *or* throve, *pp* thrived *or* thriven) gedeihen (on bei); <*business:*> florieren

throat *n* Hals *m*; cut s.o.'s **~** jdm die Kehle durchschneiden

throb *n* Pochen *nt* ● *vi* (*pt/pp* throbbed) pochen; (*vibrate*) vibrieren

throes *npl* in the **~** of (*fig*) mitten in (+ *dat*)

throne *n* Thron *m*

throttle *vt* erdrosseln

through *prep* durch (+ *acc*); (*during*) während (+ *gen*); (*Amer: up to &*
including) bis einschließlich ● *adv* durch; wet **~** durch und durch nass;

read sth **~** etw durchlesen ● *a* <*train*> durchgehend; be **~** (*finished*) fertig sein; (*Teleph*) durch sein

throughout *prep* **~ the country** im ganzen Land; **~ the night** die Nacht durch ● *adv* ganz; (*time*) die ganze Zeit

throve *see* thrive

throw *n* Wurf *m* ● *vt* (*pt* threw, *pp* thrown) werfen; schütten <*liquid*>; betätigen <*switch*>; abwerfen <*rider*>; (🛈 *disconcert*) aus der Fassung bringen; 🛈 geben <*party*>; **~ sth to s.o.** jdm etw zuwerfen. **~ away** *vt* wegwerfen. **~ out** *vt* hinauswerfen; (**~** *away*) wegwerfen; verwerfen <*plan*>. **~ up** *vt* hochwerfen ● *vi* sich übergeben

throw-away *a* Wegwerf-

thrush *n* Drossel *f*

thrust *n* Stoß *m*; (*Phys*) Schub *m* ● *vt* (*pt/pp* thrust) stoßen; (*insert*) stecken

thud *n* dumpfer Schlag *m*

thug *n* Schläger *m*

thumb *n* Daumen *m* ● *vt* **~ a lift** 🛈 per Anhalter fahren. **~tack** *n* (*Amer*) Reißzwecke *f*

thump *n* Schlag *m*; (*noise*) dumpfer Schlag *m* ● *vt* schlagen ● *vi* hämmern; <*heart:*> pochen

thunder *n* Donner *m* ● *vi* donnern. **~clap** *n* Donnerschlag *m*. **~storm** *n* Gewitter *nt*. **~y** *a* gewittrig

Thursday *n* Donnerstag *m*

thus *adv* so

thwart *vt* vereiteln; **~ s.o.** jdm einen Strich durch die Rechnung machen

tick¹ *n* on**~** 🛈 auf Pump

tick² *n* (*sound*) Ticken *nt*; (*mark*) Häkchen *nt*; (🛈 *instant*) Sekunde *f* ● *vi* ticken ● *vt* abhaken. **~ off** *vt* abhaken; 🛈 rüffeln

ticket *n* Karte *f*; (*for bus, train*) Fahrschein *m*; (*Aviat*) Flugschein *m*; (*for lottery*) Los *nt*; (*for article deposited*) Schein *m*; (*label*) Schild *nt*; (*for library*) Lesekarte *f*; (*fine*) Strafzettel *m*. **~ collector** *n*

Fahrkartenkontrolleur m. ~ **office** n Fahrkartenschalter m; (for entry) Kasse f

tick|le n Kitzeln nt ● vt/i kitzeln. **~lish** a kitzlig

tidal a ~ **wave** Flutwelle f

tide n Gezeiten pl; (of events) Strom m; the ~ is in/out es ist Flut/Ebbe ● vt ~ **s.o. over** jdm über die Runden helfen

tidiness n Ordentlichkeit f

tidy a (-ier, -iest), **-ily** adv ordentlich ● vt ~ **[up]** aufräumen

tie n Krawatte f; Schlips m; (cord) Schnur f; (fig: bond) Band nt; (restriction) Bindung f; (Sport) Unentschieden nt; (in competition) Punktgleichheit f ● v (pres p **tying**) ● vt binden; machen <knot>; ● vi (Sport) unentschieden spielen; (have equal scores, votes) punktgleich sein. ~ **up** vt festbinden; verschnüren <parcel>; fesseln <person>; be ~d up (busy) beschäftigt sein

tier n Stufe f; (of cake) Etage f; (in stadium) Rang m

tiger n Tiger m

tight a (-er, -est), **-ly** adv fest; (taut) straff; <clothes> eng; <control> streng; (⊞ drunk) blau ● adv fest

tighten vt fester ziehen; straffen <rope>; anziehen <screw>; verschärfen <control> ● vi sich spannen

tightrope n Hochseil nt

tights npl Strumpfhose f

tile n Fliese f; (on wall) Kachel f; (on roof) [Dach]ziegel m ● vt mit Fliesen auslegen; kacheln <wall>; decken <roof>

till¹ prep & conj = until

till² n Kasse f

tilt n Neigung f ● vt kippen; [zur Seite] neigen <head> ● vi sich neigen

timber n [Nutz]holz nt

time n Zeit f; (occasion) Mal nt; (rhythm) Takt m; ~s (Math) mal; at ~s manchmal; ~ **and again** immer wieder; **two at a** ~ zwei auf einmal; **on** ~ pünktlich; **in** ~ rechtzeitig; (eventually) mit der Zeit; **in no** ~ im Handumdrehen; **in a year's** ~ in einem Jahr; **behind** ~ verspätet; **behind the** ~s rückständig; **for the** ~ **being** vorläufig; **what is the** ~? wie spät ist es? wie viel Uhr ist es? **did you have a nice** ~? hat es dir gut gefallen? ● vt stoppen <race>; **be well** ~d gut abgepaßt sein

time: ~ **bomb** n Zeitbombe f. ~**less** a zeitlos. ~**ly** a rechtzeitig. ~-**switch** n Zeitschalter m. ~-**table** n Fahrplan m; (Sch) Stundenplan m

timid a, **-ly** adv scheu; (hesitant) zaghaft

timing n (Sport, Techn) Timing nt

tin n Zinn nt; (container) Dose f ● vt (pt/pp **tinned**) in Dosen konservieren. ~ **foil** n Stanniol nt; (Culin) Alufolie f

tinge n Hauch m

tingle vi kribbeln

tinker vi herumbasteln (with an + dat)

tinkle n Klingeln nt ● vi klingeln

tinned a Dosen-

tin opener n Dosenöffner m

tinsel n Lametta nt

tint n Farbton m ● vt tönen

tiny a (-ier, -iest) winzig

tip¹ n Spitze f

tip² n (money) Trinkgeld nt; (advice) Rat m, ⊞ Tipp m; (for rubbish) Müllhalde f ● v (pt/pp **tipped**) ● vt (tilt) kippen; (reward) Trinkgeld geben (**s.o.** jdm) ● vi kippen. ~ **out** vt auskippen. ~ **over** vt/i umkippen

tipped a Filter-

tipsy a ⊞ beschwipst

tiptoe n **on** ~ auf Zehenspitzen

tiptop a ⊞ erstklassig

tire vt/i ermüden. ~**d** a müde; **be** ~**d of sth** etw satt haben; ~**d out** [völlig] erschöpft. ~**less** a, **-ly** adv unermüdlich. ~**some** a lästig

tiring a ermüdend

tissue n Gewebe nt; (handkerchief) Papiertaschentuch nt

tit n (bird) Meise f

titbit n Leckerbissen m

t

title *n* Titel *m*

to
● *preposition*
····➤ *(destinations: most cases)* zu (+ *dat*). **go to work/the station** zur Arbeit/zum Bahnhof gehen. **from house to house** von Haus zu Haus. **go/come to s.o.** zu jdm gehen/kommen
····➤ *(with name of place or points of compass)* nach. **to Paris/Germany** nach Paris/Deutschland. **to Switzerland** in die Schweiz. **from East to West** von Osten nach Westen. **I've never been to Berlin** ich war noch nie in Berlin
····➤ *(to cinema, theatre, bed)* in (+ *acc*). **to bed with you!** ins Bett mit dir!
····➤ *(to wedding, party, university, the toilet)* auf (+ *acc*).
····➤ *(up to)* bis zu (+ *dat*). **to the end** bis zum Schluss. **to this day** bis heute. **5 to 6 pounds** 5 bis 6 Pfund
····➤ <*give, say, write*> + *dat*. **give/say sth to s.o.** jdm etw geben/sagen. **she wrote to him/the firm** sie hat ihm/an die Firma geschrieben
····➤ <*address, send, fasten*> an (+ *acc*). **she sent it to her brother** sie schickte es an ihren Bruder
····➤ *(in telling the time)* vor. **five to eight** fünf vor acht. **a quarter to ten** Viertel vor zehn
● *before infinitive*
····➤ *(after modal verb)* *(not translated)*. **I want to go** ich will gehen. **he is learning to swim** er lernt schwimmen. **you have to** du musst [es tun]
····➤ *(after adjective)* zu. **it is easy to forget** es ist leicht zu vergessen
····➤ *(expressing purpose, result)* um ... zu. **he did it to annoy me** er tat es, um mich zu ärgern. **she was too tired to go** sie war zu müde um zu gehen
● *adverb*
····➤ **be to** <*door, window*> angelehnt sein. **pull a door to** eine Tür anlehnen
····➤ **to and fro** hin und her

toad *n* Kröte *f*

toast *n* Toast *m* ● *vt* toasten <*bread*>; *(drink a ~ to)* trinken auf (+ *acc*). **~er** *n* Toaster *m*

tobacco *n* Tabak *m*. **~nist's [shop]** *n* Tabakladen *m*

toboggan *n* Schlitten *m* ● *vi* Schlitten fahren

today *n* & *adv* heute; **~ week** heute in einer Woche

toddler *n* Kleinkind *nt*

toe *n* Zeh *m*; *(of footwear)* Spitze *f* ● *vt* **~ the line** spuren. **~nail** *n* Zehennagel *m*

toffee *n* Karamell *m* & *nt*

together *adv* zusammen; *(at the same time)* gleichzeitig

toilet *n* Toilette *f*. **~ bag** *n* Kulturbeutel *m*. **~ paper** *n* Toilettenpapier *nt*

toiletries *npl* Toilettenartikel *pl*

token *n* Zeichen *nt*; *(counter)* Marke *f*; *(voucher)* Gutschein *m* ● *attrib* symbolisch

told *see* tell ● *a* **all ~** insgesamt

tolerable *a*, **-bly** *adv* erträglich; *(not bad)* leidlich

toleran|ce *n* Toleranz *f*. **~t** *a*, **-ly** *adv* tolerant

tolerate *vt* dulden, tolerieren; *(bear)* ertragen

toll *n* Gebühr *f*; *(for road)* Maut *f* *(Aust)*; **death ~** Zahl *f* der Todesopfer

tomato *n* (*pl* **-es**) Tomate *f*

tomb *n* Grabmal *nt*

tombstone *n* Grabstein *m*

tom-cat *n* Kater *m*

tomorrow *n* & *adv* morgen; **~ morning** morgen früh; **the day after ~** übermorgen; **see you ~!** bis morgen!

ton *n* Tonne *f*; **~s of** 🔢 jede Menge

tone *n* Ton *m*; *(colour)* Farbton *m* ● *vt* **~ down** dämpfen; *(fig)* mäßigen. **~ up** *vt* kräftigen; straffen <*muscles*>

tongs *npl* Zange *f*

tongue *n* Zunge *f*; **~ in cheek** 🔢 nicht ernst

tonic n Tonikum nt; (for hair) Haarwasser nt; (fig) Wohltat f; ~ [water] Tonic nt

tonight n & adv heute Nacht; (evening) heute Abend

tonne n Tonne f

tonsil n (Anat) Mandel f. ~**itis** n Mandelentzündung f

too adv zu; (also) auch; ~ **much/little** zu viel/zu wenig

took see take

tool n Werkzeug nt; (for gardening) Gerät nt

tooth n (pl teeth) Zahn m

tooth: ~**ache** n Zahnschmerzen pl. ~**brush** n Zahnbürste f. ~**less** a zahnlos. ~**paste** n Zahnpasta f. ~**pick** n Zahnstocher m

top¹ n (toy) Kreisel m

top² n oberer Teil m; (apex) Spitze f; (summit) Gipfel m; (Sch) Erste(r) m/f; (top part or half) Oberteil nt; (head) Kopfende nt; (of road) oberes Ende nt; (upper surface) Oberfläche f; (lid) Deckel m; (of bottle) Verschluss m; (garment) Top nt; at the/on ~ oben; on ~ of oben auf (+ dat/acc); on ~ of that (besides) obendrein; from ~ to bottom von oben bis unten ● a oberste(r,s); (highest) höchste(r,s); (best) beste(r,s) ● vt (pt/pp topped) an erster Stelle stehen auf (+ dat) <list>; (exceed) übersteigen; (remove the ~ of) die Spitze abschneiden von. ~ **up** vt nachfüllen, auffüllen

top: ~ **hat** n Zylinder[hut] m. ~-**heavy** a kopflastig

topic n Thema nt. ~**al** a aktuell

topple vt/i umstürzen

torch n Taschenlampe f; (flaming) Fackel f

tore see tear¹

torment¹ n Qual f

torment² vt quälen

torn see tear¹ ● a zerrissen

torpedo n (pl -es) Torpedo m ● vt torpedieren

torrent n reißender Strom m. ~**ial** a <rain> wolkenbruchartig

tortoise n Schildkröte f. ~**shell** n Schildpatt nt

tortuous a verschlungen; (fig) umständlich

torture n Folter f; (fig) Qual f ● vt foltern; (fig) quälen

toss vt werfen; (into the air) hochwerfen; (shake) schütteln; (unseat) abwerfen; mischen <salad>; wenden <pancake>; ~ **a coin** mit einer Münze losen ● vi ~ **and turn** (in bed) sich [schlaflos] im Bett wälzen

tot¹ n kleines Kind nt; (🅸 of liquor) Gläschen nt

tot² vt (pt/pp totted) ~ **up** 🅸 zusammenzählen

total a gesamt; (complete) völlig, total ● n Gesamtzahl f; (sum) Gesamtsumme f ● vt (pt/pp totalled); (amount to) sich belaufen auf (+ acc)

totalitarian a totalitär

totally adv völlig, total

totter vi taumeln

touch n Berührung f; (sense) Tastsinn m; (Mus) Anschlag m; (contact) Kontakt m; (trace) Spur f; (fig) Anflug m; **get/be in** ~ sich in Verbindung setzen/in Verbindung stehen (with mit) ● vt berühren; (get hold of) anfassen; (lightly) tippen auf/an (+ acc); (brush against) streifen [gegen]; (fig: move) rühren; anrühren <food, subject>; **don't** ~ **that!** fass das nicht an! ● vi sich berühren; ~ **on** (fig) berühren. ~ **down** vi (Aviat) landen. ~ **up** vt ausbessern

touch|ing a rührend. ~**y** a empfindlich

tough a (-er, -est) zäh; (severe, harsh) hart; (difficult) schwierig; (durable) strapazierfähig

toughen vt härten; ~ **up** abhärten

tour n Reise f, Tour f; (of building, town) Besichtigung f; (Theat, Sport) Tournee f; (of duty) Dienstzeit f ● vt fahren durch ● vi herumreisen

touris|m n Tourismus m, Fremdenverkehr m. ~**t** n Tourist(in) m(f) ● attrib Touristen-. ~**t office** n Fremdenverkehrsbüro nt

tournament n Turnier nt

tour operator n Reiseveranstalter m

tousle vt zerzausen

tow n give s.o./a car a ~ jdn/ein Auto abschleppen ● vt schleppen; ziehen <trailer>

toward[s] prep zu (+ dat); (with time) gegen (+ acc); (with respect to) gegenüber (+ dat)

towel n Handtuch nt. ~ling n (Tex) Frottee nt

tower n Turm m ● vi ~ above überragen. ~ **block** n Hochhaus nt. ~ing a hoch aufragend

town n Stadt f. ~ **hall** n Rathaus nt

tow-rope n Abschleppseil nt

toxic a giftig

toy n Spielzeug nt ● vi ~ with spielen mit; stochern in (+ dat) <food>. ~shop n Spielwarengeschäft nt

trace n Spur f ● vt folgen (+ dat); (find) finden; (draw) zeichnen; (with tracing-paper) durchpausen

track n Spur f; (path) [unbefestigter] Weg m; (Sport) Bahn f; (Rail) Gleis nt; keep ~ of im Auge behalten ● vt verfolgen. ~ **down** vt aufspüren; (find) finden

tracksuit n Trainingsanzug m

tractor n Traktor m

trade n Handel m; (line of business) Gewerbe nt; (business) Geschäft nt; (craft) Handwerk nt; by ~ von Beruf ● vt tauschen; ~ **in** (give in part exchange) in Zahlung geben ● vi handeln (in mit)

trade mark n Warenzeichen nt

trader n Händler m

trade: ~ **union** n Gewerkschaft f. ~ **unionist** n Gewerkschaftler(in) m(f)

trading n Handel m

tradition n Tradition f. ~al a, -ly adv traditionell

traffic n Verkehr m; (trading) Handel m

traffic: ~ **circle** n (Amer) Kreisverkehr m. ~ **jam** n [Verkehrs]stau m. ~ **lights** npl [Verkehrs]ampel f. ~ **warden** n ≈ Hilfspolizist m; (woman) Politesse f

tragedy n Tragödie f

tragic a, -ally adv tragisch

trail n Spur f; (path) Weg m, Pfad m ● vi schleifen; <plant:> sich ranken ● vt verfolgen, folgen (+ dat); (drag) schleifen

trailer n (Auto) Anhänger m; (Amer: caravan) Wohnwagen m; (film) Vorschau f

train n Zug m; (of dress) Schleppe f ● vt ausbilden; (Sport) trainieren; (aim) richten auf (+ acc); erziehen <child>; abrichten/(to do tricks) dressieren <animal>/(to); ziehen <plant> ● vi eine Ausbildung machen; (Sport) trainieren. ~ed a ausgebildet

trainee n Auszubildende(r) m/f; (Techn) Praktikant(in) m(f)

train|er n (Sport) Trainer m; (in circus) Dompteur m; ~ers pl Trainingsschuhe pl. ~ing n Ausbildung f; (Sport) Training nt; (of animals) Dressur f

trait n Eigenschaft f

traitor n Verräter m

tram n Straßenbahn f

tramp n Landstreicher m ● vi stapfen; (walk) marschieren

trample vt/i trampeln

trance n Trance f

tranquil a ruhig. ~lity n Ruhe f

tranquillizer n Beruhigungsmittel nt

transaction n Transaktion f

transcend vt übersteigen

transfer¹ n (see transfer²) Übertragung f; Verlegung f; Versetzung f; Überweisung f; (Sport) Transfer m; (design) Abziehbild nt

transfer² v (pt/pp transferred) ● vt übertragen; verlegen <firm, prisoners>; versetzen <employee>; überweisen <money>; (Sport) transferieren ● vi [über]wechseln; (when travelling) umsteigen

transform vt verwandeln. ~ation n Verwandlung f. ~er n Transformator m

transfusion n Transfusion f

transistor n Transistor m

transit n Transit m; (of goods) Transport m; **in** ~ <goods> auf dem Transport

transition n Übergang m. ~**al** a Übergangs-

translat|e vt übersetzen. ~**ion** n Übersetzung f. ~**or** n Übersetzer(in) m(f)

transmission n Übertragung f

transmit vt (pt/pp **transmitted**) übertragen. ~**ter** n Sender m

transparen|cy n (Phot) Dia nt. ~**t** a durchsichtig

transplant¹ n Verpflanzung f, Transplantation f

transplant² vt umpflanzen; (Med) verpflanzen

transport¹ n Transport m

transport² vt transportieren. ~**ation** n Transport m

transpose vt umstellen

trap n Falle f; (🅸 mouth) Klappe f; **pony and** ~ Einspänner m ● vt (pt/pp **trapped**) [mit einer Falle] fangen; (jam) einklemmen; **be** ~**ped** festsitzen; (shut in) eingeschlossen sein. ~**door** n Falltür f

trash n Schund m; (rubbish) Abfall m; (nonsense) Quatsch m. ~**can** n (Amer) Mülleimer m. ~**y** a Schund-

trauma n Trauma nt. ~**tic** a traumatisch

travel n Reisen nt ● v (pt/pp **travelled**) ● vi reisen; (go in vehicle) fahren; <light, sound:> sich fortpflanzen; (Techn) sich bewegen ● vt bereisen; fahren <distance>. ~ **agency** n Reisebüro nt. ~ **agent** n Reisebürokaufmann m

traveller n Reisende(r) m/f; (Comm) Vertreter m; ~**s** pl (gypsies) Zigeuner pl. ~'**s cheque** n Reisescheck m

trawler n Fischdampfer m

tray n Tablett nt; (for baking) [Back]blech nt; (for documents) Ablagekorb m

treacher|ous a treulos; (dangerous, deceptive) tückisch. ~**y** n Verrat m

tread n Schritt m; (step) Stufe f; (of tyre) Profil nt ● v (pt **trod**, pp **trodden**) ● vi (walk) gehen; ~ **on/in** treten auf/ in (+ acc) ● vt treten

treason n Verrat m

treasure n Schatz m ● vt in Ehren halten. ~**r** n Kassenwart m

treasury n Schatzkammer f; **the T~** das Finanzministerium

treat n [besonderes] Vergnügen nt ● vt behandeln; ~ **s.o. to sth** jdm etw spendieren

treatment n Behandlung f

treaty n Vertrag m

treble a dreifach; ~ **the amount** dreimal so viel ● n (Mus) Diskant m; (voice) Sopran m ● vt verdreifachen ● vi sich verdreifachen

tree n Baum m

trek n Marsch m ● vi (pt/pp **trekked**) latschen

trellis n Gitter nt

tremble vi zittern

tremendous a, **-ly** adv gewaltig; (🅸 excellent) großartig

tremor n Zittern nt; [earth] ~ Beben nt

trench n Graben m; (Mil) Schützengraben m

trend n Tendenz f; (fashion) Trend m. ~**y** a (-ier, -iest) 🅸 modisch

trepidation n Beklommenheit f

trespass vi ~ **on** unerlaubt betreten

trial n (Jur) [Gerichts]verfahren nt, Prozess m; (test) Probe f; (ordeal) Prüfung f; **be on** ~ auf Probe sein; (Jur) angeklagt sein (**for** wegen); **by** ~ **and error** durch Probieren

triang|le n Dreieck nt; (Mus) Triangel m. ~**ular** a dreieckig

tribe n Stamm m

tribunal n Schiedsgericht nt

tributary n Nebenfluss m

tribute n Tribut m; **pay** ~ Tribut zollen (**to** dat)

trick n Trick m; (joke) Streich m; (Cards) Stich m; (feat of skill) Kunststück nt ● vt täuschen, 🅸 hereinlegen

trickle vi rinnen

trick|ster n Schwindler m. ~**y** a (**-ier, -iest**) a schwierig

tricycle n Dreirad nt

tried see try

trifl|e n Kleinigkeit f; (Culin) Trifle nt. ~**ing** a unbedeutend

trigger n Abzug m; (fig) Auslöser m ● vt ~ [**off**] auslösen

trim a (**trimmer, trimmest**) gepflegt ● n (cut) Nachschneiden nt; (decoration) Verzierung f, (condition) Zustand m ● vt schneiden; (decorate) besetzen. ~**ming** n Besatz m; ~**mings** pl (accessories) Zubehör nt; (decorations) Verzierungen pl

trio n Trio nt

trip n Reise f; (excursion) Ausflug m ● v (pt/pp **tripped**) ● vt ~ **s.o. up** jdm ein Bein stellen ● vi stolpern (**on/over** über + acc)

tripe n Kaldaunen pl; (nonsense) Quatsch m

triple a dreifach ● vt verdreifachen ● vi sich verdreifachen

triplets npl Drillinge pl

triplicate n **in** ~ in dreifacher Ausfertigung

tripod n Stativ nt

tripper n Ausflügler m

trite a banal

triumph n Triumph m ● vi triumphieren (**over** über + acc). ~**ant** a, **-ly** adv triumphierend

trivial a belanglos. ~**ity** n Belanglosigkeit f

trod, trodden see tread

trolley n (for food) Servierwagen m; (for shopping) Einkaufswagen m; (for luggage) Kofferkuli m; (Amer: tram) Straßenbahn f

trombone n Posaune f

troop n Schar f; ~**s** pl Truppen pl

trophy n Trophäe f; (in competition) ≈ Pokal m

tropic|s npl Tropen pl. ~**al** a tropisch; <fruit> Süd-

trot n Trab m ● vi (pt/pp **trotted**) traben

trouble n Ärger m; (difficulties) Schwierigkeiten pl; (inconvenience) Mühe f, (conflict) Unruhe f; (Med) Beschwerden pl; (Techn) Probleme pl; **get into** ~ Ärger bekommen; **take** ~ sich (dat) Mühe geben ● vt (disturb) stören; (worry) beunruhigen ● vi sich bemühen. ~**maker** n Unruhestifter m. ~**some** a schwierig; <flies, cough> lästig

trough n Trog m

troupe n Truppe f

trousers npl Hose f

trousseau n Aussteuer f

trout n inv Forelle f

trowel n Kelle f

truant n **play** ~ die Schule schwänzen

truce n Waffenstillstand m

truck n Last[kraft]wagen m; (Rail) Güterwagen m

trudge vi latschen

true a (**-r, -st**) wahr; (loyal) treu; (genuine) echt; **come** ~ in Erfüllung gehen; **is that** ~? stimmt das?

truly adv wirklich; (faithfully) treu; **Yours** ~ mit freundlichen Grüßen

trump n (Cards) Trumpf m ● vt übertrumpfen

trumpet n Trompete f. ~**er** n Trompeter m

truncheon n Schlagstock m

trunk n [Baum]stamm m; (body) Rumpf m; (of elephant) Rüssel m; (for travelling) [Übersee]koffer m; (Amer: of car) Kofferraum m; ~**s** pl Badehose f

trust n Vertrauen nt; (group of companies) Trust m; (organization) Treuhandgesellschaft f; (charitable) Stiftung f ● vt trauen (+ dat); vertrauen (+ dat); (hope) hoffen ● vi vertrauen (**in/to** auf + acc)

trustee n Treuhänder m

trust|ful a, **-ly** adv, ~**ing** a vertrauensvoll. ~**worthy** a vertrauenswürdig

truth n (pl **-s**) Wahrheit f. ~**ful** a, **-ly** adv ehrlich

try n Versuch m ● v (pt/pp **tried**) ● vt versuchen; (sample, taste) probieren;

(*be a strain on*) anstrengen; (*Jur*) vor Gericht stellen; verhandeln <*case*> ● *vi* versuchen; (*make an effort*) sich bemühen. **∼ on** *vt* anprobieren; aufprobieren <*hat*>. **∼ out** *vt* ausprobieren

trying *a* schwierig

T-shirt *n* T-Shirt *nt*

tub *n* Kübel *m*; (*carton*) Becher *m*; (*bath*) Wanne *f*

tuba *n* (*Mus*) Tuba *f*

tubby *a* (-ier, -iest) rundlich

tube *n* Röhre *f*; (*pipe*) Rohr *nt*; (*flexible*) Schlauch *m*; (*of toothpaste*) Tube *f*; (*Rail* Ⓔ) U-Bahn *f*

tuberculosis *n* Tuberkulose *f*

tubular *a* röhrenförmig

tuck *n* Saum *m*; (*decorative*) Biese *f* ● *vt* (*put*) stecken. **∼ in** *vt* hineinstecken; **∼ s.o. in** *or* **up** jdn zudecken ● *vi* (Ⓔ *eat*) zulangen

Tuesday *n* Dienstag *m*

tuft *n* Büschel *nt*

tug *n* Ruck *m*; (*Naut*) Schleppdampfer *m* ● *v* (*pt/pp* tugged) ● *vt* ziehen ● *vi* zerren (**at** an + *dat*)

tuition *n* Unterricht *m*

tulip *n* Tulpe *f*

tumble *n* Sturz *m* ● *vi* fallen. **∼down** *a* verfallen. **∼-drier** *n* Wäschetrockner *m*

tumbler *n* Glas *nt*

tummy *n* Ⓔ Bauch *m*

tumour *n* Tumor *m*

tumult *n* Tumult *m*

tuna *n* Thunfisch *m*

tune *n* Melodie *f*; **out of ∼** <*instrument*> verstimmt ● *vt* stimmen; (*Techn*) einstellen. **∼ in** *vt* einstellen: ● *vi* **∼ in to a station** einen Sender einstellen. **∼ up** *vi* (*Mus*) stimmen

tuneful *a* melodisch

Tunisia *n* Tunesien *nt*

tunnel *n* Tunnel *m* ● *vi* (*pt/pp* tunnelled) einen Tunnel graben

turban *n* Turban *m*

turbine *n* Turbine *f*

turbulen|ce *n* Turbulenz *f*. **∼t** *a* stürmisch

turf *n* Rasen *m*; (*segment*) Rasenstück *nt*

Turk *n* Türke *m*/Türkin *f*

turkey *n* Truthahn *m*

Turk|ey *n* die Türkei. **∼ish** *a* türkisch; **the ∼ish** die Türken

turmoil *n* Aufruhr *m*; (*confusion*) Durcheinander *nt*

turn *n* (*rotation*) Drehung *f*; (*bend*) Kurve *f*; (*change of direction*) Wende *f*; (*Theat*) Nummer *f*; (Ⓔ *attack*) Anfall *m*; **do s.o. a good ∼** jdm einen guten Dienst erweisen; **take ∼s** sich abwechseln; **in ∼** der Reihe nach; **out of ∼** außer der Reihe; **it's your ∼** du bist an der Reihe ● *vt* drehen; (**∼ over**) wenden; (*reverse*) umdrehen; (*Techn*) drechseln <*wood*>; **∼ the page** umblättern; **∼ the corner** um die Ecke biegen ● *vi* sich drehen; (**∼ round**) sich umdrehen; <*car:*> wenden; <*leaves:*> sich färben; <*weather:*> umschlagen; (*become*) werden; **∼ right/left** nach rechts/links abbiegen; **∼ to s.o.** sich an jdn wenden. **∼ away** *vt* abweisen ● *vi* sich abwenden. **∼ down** *vt* herunterschlagen <*collar*>; herunterdrehen <*heat, gas*>; leiser stellen <*sound*>; (*reject*) ablehnen; abweisen <*person*>. **∼ in** *vt* einschlagen <*edges*> ● *vi* <*car:*> einbiegen; (Ⓔ *go to bed*) ins Bett gehen. **∼ off** *vt* zudrehen <*tap*>; ausschalten <*light, radio*>; abstellen <*water, gas, engine, machine*> ● *vi* abbiegen. **∼ on** *vt* aufdrehen <*tap*>; einschalten <*light, radio*>; anstellen <*water, gas, engine, machine*>. **∼ out** *vt* (*expel*) vertreiben, Ⓔ hinauswerfen; ausschalten <*light*>; abdrehen <*gas*>; (*produce*) produzieren; (*empty*) ausleeren; [gründlich] aufräumen <*room, cupboard*> ● *vi* (*go out*) hinausgehen; (*transpire*) sich herausstellen. **∼ over** *vt* umdrehen. **∼ up** *vt* hochschlagen <*collar*>; aufdrehen <*heat, gas*>; lauter stellen <*sound, radio*> ● *vi* auftauchen

turning *n* Abzweigung *f*. **∼-point** *n* Wendepunkt *m*

turnip *n* weiße Rübe *f*

turn: **~-out** n (of people) Beteiligung f. **~over** n (Comm) Umsatz m; (of staff) Personalwechsel m. **~pike** n (Amer) gebührenpflichtige Autobahn f. **~table** n Drehscheibe f; (on record player) Plattenteller m. **~-up** n [Hosen]aufschlag m

turquoise a türkis[farben] ● n (gem) Türkis m

turret n Türmchen nt

turtle n Seeschildkröte f

tusk n Stoßzahn m

tutor n [Privat]lehrer m

tuxedo n (Amer) Smoking m

TV abbr of television

tweed n Tweed m

tweezers npl Pinzette f

twelfth a zwölfter(r,s)

twelve a zwölf

twentieth a zwanzigste(r,s)

twenty a zwanzig

twice adv zweimal

twig n Zweig m

twilight n Dämmerlicht nt

twin n Zwilling m ● attrib Zwillings-

twine n Bindfaden m

twinge n Stechen nt; **~ of conscience** Gewissensbisse pl

twinkle n Funkeln nt ● vi funkeln

twin town n Partnerstadt f

twirl vt/i herumwirbeln

twist n Drehung f; (curve) Kurve f; (unexpected occurrence) überraschende Wendung f ● vt drehen; (distort) verdrehen; (🅃 swindle) beschummeln; **~ one's ankle** sich (dat) den Knöchel verrenken ● vi sich drehen; <road:> sich winden. **~er** n 🅃 Schwindler m

twit n 🅃 Trottel m

twitch n Zucken nt ● vi zucken

twitter n Zwitschern nt ● vi zwitschern

two a zwei

two: **~-faced** a falsch. **~-piece** a zweiteilig. **~-way** a **~-way traffic** Gegenverkehr m

tycoon n Magnat m

tying see tie

type n Art f, Sorte f; (person) Typ m; (printing) Type f ● vt mit der Maschine schreiben, 🅃 tippen ● vi Maschine schreiben, 🅃 tippen. **~writer** n Schreibmaschine f. **~written** a maschinegeschrieben

typical a, **-ly** adv typisch (of für)

typify vt (pt/pp -ied) typisch sein für

typing n Maschineschreiben nt

typist n Schreibkraft f

tyrannical a tyrannisch

tyranny n Tyrannei f

tyrant n Tyrann m

tyre n Reifen m

Uu

ugl|iness n Hässlichkeit f. **~y** a (-ier, -iest) hässlich; (nasty) übel

UK abbr see United Kingdom

ulcer n Geschwür nt

ultimate a letzte(r,s); (final) endgültig; (fundamental) grundlegend, eigentlich. **~ly** adv schließlich

ultimatum n Ultimatum nt

ultraviolet a ultraviolett

umbrella n [Regen]schirm m

umpire n Schiedsrichter m ● vt/i Schiedsrichter sein (bei)

umpteen a 🅃 zig. **~th** a 🅃 zigste(r,s)

unable a **be ~ to do sth** etw nicht tun können

unabridged a ungekürzt

unaccompanied a ohne Begleitung; <luggage> unbegleitet

unaccountable a unerklärlich

unaccustomed a ungewohnt; **be ~ to sth** etw (acc) nicht gewohnt sein

unaided a ohne fremde Hilfe

unanimous a, **-ly** adv einmütig; <vote, decision> einstimmig

unarmed *a* unbewaffnet

unassuming *a* bescheiden

unattended *a* unbeaufsichtigt

unauthorized *a* unbefugt

unavoidable *a* unvermeidlich

unaware *a* be ~ of sth sich (*dat*) etw (*gen*) nicht bewusst sein. **~s** *adv* catch s.o. ~s jdn überraschen

unbearable *a*, **-bly** *adv* unerträglich

unbeat|able *a* unschlagbar. **~en** *a* ungeschlagen; <*record*> ungebrochen

unbelievable *a* unglaublich

unbiased *a* unvoreingenommen

unblock *vt* frei machen

unbolt *vt* aufriegeln

unbreakable *a* unzerbrechlich

unbutton *vt* aufknöpfen

uncalled-for *a* unangebracht

uncanny *a* unheimlich

unceasing *a* unaufhörlich

uncertain *a* (*doubtful*) ungewiss; <*origins*> unbestimmt; be ~ nicht sicher sein. **~ty** *n* Ungewissheit *f*

unchanged *a* unverändert

uncharitable *a* lieblos

uncle *n* Onkel *m*

uncomfortable *a*, **-bly** *adv* unbequem; feel ~ (*fig*) sich nicht wohl fühlen

uncommon *a* ungewöhnlich

uncompromising *a* kompromisslos

unconditional *a*, **~ly** *adv* bedingungslos

unconscious *a* bewusstlos; (*unintended*) unbewusst; be ~ of sth sich (*dat*) etw (*gen*) nicht bewusst sein. **~ly** *adv* unbewusst

unconventional *a* unkonventionell

uncooperative *a* nicht hilfsbereit

uncork *vt* entkorken

uncouth *a* ungehobelt

uncover *vt* aufdecken

undecided *a* unentschlossen; (*not settled*) nicht entschieden

undeniable *a*, **-bly** *adv* unbestreitbar

under *prep* unter (+ *dat/acc*); ~ it darunter; ~ there da drunter; ~ repair in Reparatur; ~ construction im Bau; ~ age minderjährig ● *adv* darunter

undercarriage *n* (*Aviat*) Fahrwerk *nt*, Fahrgestell *nt*

underclothes *npl* Unterwäsche *f*

undercover *a* geheim

undercurrent *n* Unterströmung *f*; (*fig*) Unterton *m*

underdog *n* Unterlegene(r) *m*

underdone *a* nicht gar; (*rare*) nicht durchgebraten

underestimate *vt* unterschätzen

underfed *a* unterernährt

underfoot *adv* am Boden

undergo *vt* (*pt* -went, *pp* -gone) durchmachen; sich unterziehen (+ *dat*) <*operation, treatment*>

undergraduate *n* Student(in) *m(f)*

underground¹ *adv* unter der Erde; <*mining*> unter Tage

underground² *a* unterirdisch; (*secret*) Untergrund- ● *n* (*railway*) U-Bahn *f*. ~ **car park** *n* Tiefgarage *f*

undergrowth *n* Unterholz *nt*

underhand *a* hinterhältig

underlie *vt* (*pt* -lay, *pp* -lain, *pres p* -lying) zugrunde liegen (+ *dat*)

underline *vt* unterstreichen

underlying *a* eigentlich

undermine *vt* (*fig*) unterminieren, untergraben

underneath *prep* unter (+ *dat/acc*) ● *adv* darunter

underpants *npl* Unterhose *f*

underpass *n* Unterführung *f*

underprivileged *a* unterprivilegiert

underrate *vt* unterschätzen

undershirt *n* (*Amer*) Unterhemd *nt*

understand *vt/i* (*pt/pp* -stood) verstehen; I ~ that ... (*have heard*) ich habe gehört, dass ... **~able** *a* verständlich. **~ably** *adv* verständlicherweise

understanding *a* verständnisvoll ● *n* Verständnis *nt*; (*agreement*)

u

Vereinbarung *f*; **reach an** ∼ sich verständigen

understatement *n* Untertreibung *f*

undertake *vt* (*pt* **-took**, *pp* **-taken**) unternehmen; ∼ **to do sth** sich verpflichten, etw zu tun

undertaker *n* Leichenbestatter *m*; [firm of] ∼**s** Bestattungsinstitut *n*

undertaking *n* Unternehmen *nt*; (*promise*) Versprechen *nt*

undertone *n* (*fig*) Unterton *m*; **in an** ∼ mit gedämpfter Stimme

undervalue *vt* unterbewerten

underwater[1] *a* Unterwasser-

underwater[2] *adv* unter Wasser

underwear *n* Unterwäsche *f*

underweight *a* untergewichtig; **be** ∼ Untergewicht haben

underworld *n* Unterwelt *f*

undesirable *a* unerwünscht

undignified *a* würdelos

undo *vt* (*pt* **-did**, *pp* **-done**) aufmachen; (*fig*) ungeschehen machen

undone *a* offen; (*not accomplished*) unerledigt

undoubted *a* unzweifelhaft. ∼**ly** *adv* zweifellos

undress *vt* ausziehen; **get** ∼**ed** sich ausziehen ● *vi* sich ausziehen

undue *a* übermäßig

unduly *adv* übermäßig

unearth *vt* ausgraben; (*fig*) zutage bringen. ∼**ly** *a* unheimlich; **at an** ∼**ly hour** 🗓 in aller Herrgottsfrühe

uneasy *a* unbehaglich

uneconomic *a*, **-ally** *adv* unwirtschaftlich

unemployed *a* arbeitslos ● *npl* **the** ∼ die Arbeitslosen

unemployment *n* Arbeitslosigkeit *f*

unending *a* endlos

unequal *a* unterschiedlich; <*struggle*> ungleich. ∼**ly** *adv* ungleichmäßig

unequivocal *a*, **-ly** *adv* eindeutig

unethical *a* unmoralisch; **be** ∼ gegen das Berufsethos verstoßen

uneven *a* uneben; (*unequal*) ungleich; (*not regular*) ungleichmäßig; <*number*> ungerade

unexpected *a*, **-ly** *adv* unerwartet

unfair *a*, **-ly** *adv* ungerecht, unfair. ∼**ness** *n* Ungerechtigkeit *f*

unfaithful *a* untreu

unfamiliar *a* ungewohnt; (*unknown*) unbekannt

unfasten *vt* aufmachen; (*detach*) losmachen

unfavourable *a* ungünstig

unfeeling *a* gefühllos

unfit *a* ungeeignet; (*incompetent*) unfähig; (*Sport*) nicht fit; ∼ **for work** arbeitsunfähig

unfold *vt* auseinander falten, entfalten; (*spread out*) ausbreiten ● *vi* sich entfalten

unforeseen *a* unvorhergesehen

unforgettable *a* unvergesslich

unforgivable *a* unverzeihlich

unfortunate *a* unglücklich; (*unfavourable*) ungünstig; (*regrettable*) bedauerlich; **be** ∼ <*person:*> Pech haben. ∼**ly** *adv* leider

unfounded *a* unbegründet

unfurl *vt* entrollen

unfurnished *a* unmöbliert

ungainly *a* unbeholfen

ungrateful *a*, **-ly** *adv* undankbar

unhappiness *n* Kummer *m*

unhappy *a* unglücklich; (*not content*) unzufrieden

unharmed *a* unverletzt

unhealthy *a* ungesund

unhurt *a* unverletzt

unification *n* Einigung *f*

uniform *a*, **-ly** *adv* einheitlich ● *n* Uniform *f*

unify *vt* (*pt/pp* **-ied**) einigen

unilateral *a*, **-ly** *adv* einseitig

unimaginable *a* unvorstellbar

unimportant *a* unwichtig

uninhabited *a* unbewohnt

unintentional *a*, **-ly** *adv* unabsichtlich

union *n* Vereinigung *f*; (*Pol*) Union *f*; (*trade* ∼) Gewerkschaft *f*

unique *a* einzigartig. **~ly** *adv* einmalig

unison *n* in **~** einstimmig

unit *n* Einheit *f*; (*Math*) Einer *m*; (*of furniture*) Teil *nt*, Element *nt*

unite *vt* vereinigen ● *vi* sich vereinigen

united *a* einig. **U~ Kingdom** *n* Vereinigtes Königreich *nt*. **U~ Nations** *n* Vereinte Nationen *pl*. **U~ States [of America]** *n* Vereinigte Staaten *pl* [von Amerika]

unity *n* Einheit *f*; (*harmony*) Einigkeit *f*

universal *a*, **-ly** *adv* allgemein

universe *n* [Welt]all *nt*, Universum *nt*

university *n* Universität *f* ● *attrib* Universitäts-

unjust *a*, **-ly** *adv* ungerecht

unkind *a*, **-ly** *adv* unfreundlich; (*harsh*) hässlich

unknown *a* unbekannt

unlawful *a*, **-ly** *adv* gesetzwidrig

unleaded *a* bleifrei

unleash *vt* (*fig*) entfesseln

unless *conj* wenn ... nicht; **~ I am mistaken** wenn ich mich nicht irre

unlike *prep* im Gegensatz zu (+ *dat*)

unlikely *a* unwahrscheinlich

unlimited *a* unbegrenzt

unload *vt* entladen; ausladen <*luggage*>

unlock *vt* aufschließen

unlucky *a* unglücklich; <*day, number*> Unglücks-; **be ~** Pech haben; <*thing:*> Unglück bringen

unmarried *a* unverheiratet. **~ mother** *n* ledige Mutter *f*

unmask *vt* (*fig*) entlarven

unmistakable *a*, **-bly** *adv* unverkennbar

unnatural *a*, **-ly** *adv* unnatürlich; (*not normal*) nicht normal

unnecessary *a*, **-ily** *adv* unnötig

unnoticed *a* unbemerkt

unobtainable *a* nicht erhältlich

unobtrusive *a*, **-ly** *adv* unaufdringlich; <*thing*> unauffällig

unofficial *a*, **-ly** *adv* inoffiziell

unpack *vt/i* auspacken

unpaid *a* unbezahlt

unpleasant *a*, **-ly** *adv* unangenehm

unplug *vt* (*pt/pp* **-plugged**) den Stecker herausziehen von

unpopular *a* unbeliebt

unprecedented *a* beispiellos

unpredictable *a* unberechenbar

unprepared *a* nicht vorbereitet

unpretentious *a* bescheiden

unprofitable *a* unrentabel

unqualified *a* unqualifiziert; (*fig: absolute*) uneingeschränkt

unquestionable *a* unbezweifelbar; <*right*> unbestreitbar

unravel *vt* (*pt/pp* **-ravelled**) entwirren; (*Knitting*) aufziehen

unreal *a* unwirklich

unreasonable *a* unvernünftig

unrelated *a* unzusammenhängend; **be ~** nicht verwandt sein; <*events:*> nicht miteinander zusammenhängen

unreliable *a* unzuverlässig

unrest *n* Unruhen *pl*

unrivalled *a* unübertroffen

unroll *vt* aufrollen ● *vi* sich aufrollen

unruly *a* ungebärdig

unsafe *a* nicht sicher

unsatisfactory *a* unbefriedigend

unsavoury *a* unangenehm; (*fig*) unerfreulich

unscathed *a* unversehrt

unscrew *vt* abschrauben

unscrupulous *a* skrupellos

unseemly *a* unschicklich

unselfish *a* selbstlos

unsettled *a* ungeklärt; <*weather*> unbeständig; <*bill*> unbezahlt

unshakeable *a* unerschütterlich

unshaven *a* unrasiert

unsightly *a* unansehnlich

unskilled *a* ungelernt; <*work*> unqualifiziert

unsociable *a* ungesellig

unsophisticated *a* einfach

unsound *a* krank, nicht gesund; <*building*> nicht sicher; <*advice*>

u

unzuverlässig; *<reasoning>* nicht stichhaltig

unstable *a* nicht stabil; *(mentally)* labil

unsteady *a*, **-ily** *adv* unsicher; *(wobbly)* wackelig

unstuck *a* come ~ sich lösen; (🔢 *fail)* scheitern

unsuccessful *a*, **-ly** *adv* erfolglos; be ~ keinen Erfolg haben

unsuitable *a* ungeeignet; *(inappropriate)* unpassend; *(for weather, activity)* unzweckmäßig

unthinkable *a* unvorstellbar

untidiness *n* Unordentlichkeit *f*

untidy *a*, **-ily** *adv* unordentlich

untie *vt* aufbinden; losbinden *<person, boat, horse>*

until *prep* bis (+ *acc*); not ~ erst; ~ the evening bis zum Abend ● *conj* bis; not ~ erst wenn; *(in past)* erst als

untold *a* unermesslich

untrue *a* unwahr; that's ~ das ist nicht wahr

unused¹ *a* unbenutzt; *(not utilized)* ungenutzt

unused² *a* be ~ to sth etw nicht gewohnt sein

unusual *a*, **-ly** *adv* ungewöhnlich

unveil *vt* enthüllen

unwanted *a* unerwünscht

unwelcome *a* unwillkommen

unwell *a* be *or* feel ~ sich nicht wohl fühlen

unwieldy *a* sperrig

unwilling *a*, **-ly** *adv* widerwillig; be ~ to do sth etw nicht tun wollen

unwind *v* (*pt/pp* unwound) ● *vt* abwickeln ● *vi* sich abwickeln; (🔢 *relax)* sich entspannen

unwise *a*, **-ly** *adv* unklug

unworthy *a* unwürdig

unwrap *vt* (*pt/pp* **-wrapped**) auswickeln; auspacken *<present>*

unwritten *a* ungeschrieben

up *adv* oben; *(with movement)* nach oben; *(not in bed)* auf; *<road>* aufgerissen; *<price>* gestiegen; be up for sale zu verkaufen sein; up there

da oben; up to *(as far as)* bis; time's up die Zeit ist um; what's up? 🔢 was ist los? what's he up to? 🔢 was hat er vor? I don't feel up to it ich fühle mich dem nicht gewachsen; go up hinaufgehen; come up heraufkommen ● *prep* be up on sth [oben] auf etw (*dat*) sein; up the mountain oben am Berg; *(movement)* den Berg hinauf; be up the tree oben im Baum sein; up the road die Straße entlang; up the river stromaufwärts; go up the stairs die Treppe hinaufgehen

upbringing *n* Erziehung *f*

update *vt* auf den neuesten Stand bringen

upgrade *vt* aufstufen

upheaval *n* Unruhe *f*; *(Pol)* Umbruch *m*

uphill *a* *(fig)* mühsam ● *adv* bergauf

uphold *vt* (*pt/pp* upheld) unterstützen; bestätigen *<verdict>*

upholster *vt* polstern. ~**y** *n* Polsterung *f*

upkeep *n* Unterhalt *m*

upmarket *a* anspruchsvoll

upon *prep* auf (+ *dat/acc*)

upper *a* obere(r,s); *<deck, jaw, lip>* Ober-; have the ~ hand die Oberhand haben ● *n* *(of shoe)* Obermaterial *nt*

upper class *n* Oberschicht *f*

upright *a* aufrecht

uprising *n* Aufstand *m*

uproar *n* Aufruhr *m*

upset¹ *vt* (*pt/pp* upset, *pres p* upsetting) umstoßen; *(spill)* verschütten; durcheinander bringen *<plan>*; *(distress)* erschüttern; *<food:>* nicht bekommen (+ *dat*); get ~ about sth sich über etw (*acc*) aufregen

upset² *n* Aufregung *f*; have a stomach ~ einen verdorbenen Magen haben

upshot *n* Ergebnis *nt*

upside down *adv* verkehrt herum; turn ~ umdrehen

upstairs¹ *adv* oben; *<go>* nach oben

upstairs² *a* im Obergeschoss

upstart n Emporkömmling m

upstream adv stromaufwärts

uptake n slow on the ~ schwer von Begriff; be quick on the ~ schnell begreifen

upturn n Aufschwung m

upward a nach oben; <movement> Aufwärts-; ~ slope Steigung f ● adv ~[s] aufwärts, nach oben

uranium n Uran nt

urban a städtisch

urge n Trieb m, Drang m ● vt drängen; ~ on antreiben

urgen|cy n Dringlichkeit f. ~t a, -ly adv dringend

urine n Urin m, Harn m

us pron uns; it's us wir sind es

US[A] abbr USA pl

usable a brauchbar

usage n Brauch m; (of word) [Sprach]gebrauch m

use¹ n (see use²) Benutzung f; Verwendung f; Gebrauch m; be (of) no ~ nichts nützen; it is no ~ es hat keinen Zweck; what's the ~? wozu?

use² vt benutzen <implement, room, lift>; verwenden <ingredient, method, book, money>; gebrauchen <words, force, brains>; ~ [up] aufbrauchen

used¹ a gebraucht; <towel> benutzt; <car> Gebraucht-

used² pt be ~ to sth an etw (acc) gewöhnt sein; get ~ to sich gewöhnen an (+ acc); he ~ to say er hat immer gesagt; he ~ to live here er war früher hier gewohnt

useful a nützlich. ~ness n Nützlichkeit f

useless a nutzlos; (not usable) unbrauchbar; (pointless) zwecklos

user n Benutzer(in) m(f)

usher n Platzanweiser m; (in court) Gerichtsdiener m

usherette n Platzanweiserin f

USSR abbr (History) UdSSR f

usual a üblich. ~ly adv gewöhnlich

utensil n Gerät nt

utility a Gebrauchs-

utilize vt nutzen

utmost a äußerste(r,s), größte(r,s) ● n do one's ~ sein Möglichstes tun

utter¹ a, -ly adv völlig

utter² vt von sich geben <sigh, sound>; sagen <word>

U-turn n (fig) Kehrtwendung f; 'no ~s' (Auto) 'Wenden verboten'

Vv

vacan|cy n (job) freie Stelle f; (room) freies Zimmer nt; 'no ~cies' 'belegt'. ~t a frei; <look> [gedanken]leer

vacate vt räumen

vacation n (Univ & Amer) Ferien pl

vaccinat|e vt impfen. ~ion n Impfung f

vaccine n Impfstoff m

vacuum n Vakuum nt, luftleerer Raum m ● vt saugen. ~ cleaner n Staubsauger m

vagina n (Anat) Scheide f

vague a (-r, -st), -ly adv vage; <outline> verschwommen

vain a (-er, -est) eitel; <hope, attempt> vergeblich; in ~ vergeblich. ~ly adv vergeblich

valiant a, -ly adv tapfer

valid a gültig; <claim> berechtigt; <argument> stichhaltig; <reason> triftig. ~ity n Gültigkeit f

valley n Tal nt

valour n Tapferkeit f

valuable a wertvoll. ~s npl Wertsachen pl

valuation n Schätzung f

value n Wert m; (usefulness) Nutzen m ● vt schätzen. ~ added tax n Mehrwertsteuer f

valve n Ventil nt; (Anat) Klappe f; (Electr) Röhre f

van n Lieferwagen m

vandal n Rowdy m. **~ism** n
mutwillige Zerstörung f. **~ize** vt
demolieren

vanilla n Vanille f

vanish vi verschwinden

vanity n Eitelkeit f

vapour n Dampf m

variable a unbeständig; (Math)
variabel; (adjustable) regulierbar

variant n Variante f

variation n Variation f; (difference)
Unterschied m

varied a vielseitig; <diet:>
abwechslungsreich

variety n Abwechslung f; (quantity)
Vielfalt f; (Comm) Auswahl f; (type)
Art f; (Bot) Abart f; (Theat) Varieté
nt

various a verschieden. **~ly** adv
unterschiedlich

varnish n Lack m ● vt lackieren

vary v (pt/pp -ied) ● vi sich ändern;
(be different) verschieden sein ● vt
[ver]ändern; (add variety to)
abwechslungsreicher gestalten

vase n Vase f

vast a riesig; <expanse> weit. **~ly**
adv gewaltig

vat n Bottich m

VAT abbr (value added tax)
Mehrwertsteuer f, MwSt.

vault¹ n (roof) Gewölbe nt; (in bank)
Tresor m; (tomb) Gruft f

vault² n Sprung m ● vt/i ~ **[over]**
springen über (+ acc)

VDU abbr (visual display unit)
Bildschirmgerät nt

veal n Kalbfleisch nt ● attrib Kalbs-

veer vi sich drehen; (Auto)
ausscheren

vegetable n Gemüse nt; **~s** pl
Gemüse nt ● attrib Gemüse-; <oil,
fat> Pflanzen-

vegetarian a vegetarisch ● n
Vegetarier(in) m(f)

vegetation n Vegetation f

vehement a, **-ly** adv heftig

vehicle n Fahrzeug nt

veil n Schleier m ● vt verschleiern

vein n Ader f; (mood) Stimmung f;
(manner) Art f

velocity n Geschwindigkeit f

velvet n Samt m

vending-machine n
[Verkaufs]automat m

vendor n Verkäufer(in) m(f)

veneer n Furnier nt; (fig) Tünche f.
~ed a furniert

venerable a ehrwürdig

Venetian a venezianisch. **v~
blind** n Jalousie f

vengeance n Rache f; with a ~
gewaltig

Venice n Venedig nt

venison n (Culin) Reh(fleisch) nt

venom n Gift nt; (fig) Hass m.
~ous a giftig

vent n Öffnung f

ventilat|e vt belüften. **~ion** n
Belüftung f; (installation) Lüftung f.
~or n Lüftungsvorrichtung f; (Med)
Beatmungsgerät nt

ventriloquist n Bauchredner m

venture n Unternehmung f ● vt
wagen ● vi sich wagen

venue n (for event)
Veranstaltungsort m

veranda n Veranda f

verb n Verb nt. **~al** a, **-ly** adv
mündlich; (Gram) verbal

verbose a weitschweifig

verdict n Urteil nt

verge n Rand m ● vi ~ **on** (fig)
grenzen an (+ acc)

verify vt (pt/pp -ied) überprüfen;
(confirm) bestätigen

vermin n Ungeziefer nt

vermouth n Wermut m

versatil|e a vielseitig. **~ity** n
Vielseitigkeit f

verse n Strophe f; (of Bible) Vers m;
(poetry) Lyrik f

version n Version f; (translation)
Übersetzung f; (model) Modell nt

versus prep gegen (+ acc)

vertical a, **-ly** adv senkrecht ● n
Senkrechte f

vertigo n (Med) Schwindel m

verve n Schwung m

very adv sehr; ~ **much** sehr; (quantity) sehr viel; ~ **probably** höchstwahrscheinlich; at the ~ **most** allerhöchstens ● a (mere) bloß; the ~ **first** der/die/das allererste; the ~ **thing** genau das Richtige; at the ~ **end/beginning** ganz am Ende/ Anfang; only a ~ **little** nur ein ganz kleines bisschen

vessel n Schiff nt; (receptacle & Anat) Gefäß nt

vest n [Unter]hemd nt; (Amer: waistcoat) Weste f

vestige n Spur f

vestry n Sakristei f

vet n Tierarzt m /-ärztin f ● vt (pt/pp **vetted**) überprüfen

veteran n Veteran m

veterinary a tierärztlich. ~ **surgeon** n Tierarzt m /-ärztin f

veto n (pl -es) Veto nt

VHF abbr (very high frequency) UKW

via prep über (+ acc)

viable a lebensfähig; (fig) realisierbar; <firm> rentabel

viaduct n Viadukt nt

vibrat|e vi vibrieren. ~**ion** n Vibrieren nt

vicar n Pfarrer m. ~**age** n Pfarrhaus nt

vice¹ n Laster nt

vice² n (Techn) Schraubstock m

vice³ a Vize-; ~ **chairman** stellvertretender Vorsitzender m

vice versa adv umgekehrt

vicinity n Umgebung f; in the ~ of in der Nähe von

vicious a, -ly adv boshaft; <animal> bösartig

victim n Opfer nt. ~**ize** vt schikanieren

victor n Sieger m

victor|ious a siegreich. ~**y** n Sieg m

video n Video nt; (recorder) Videorecorder m ● attrib Video-

video: ~ **cassette** n Videokassette f. ~ **game** n Videospiel nt. ~ **recorder** n Videorecorder m

Vienn|a n Wien nt. ~**ese** a Wiener

view n Sicht f; (scene) Aussicht f, Blick m; (picture, opinion) Ansicht f; in my ~ meiner Ansicht nach; in ~ of angesichts (+ gen); be on ~ besichtigt werden können ● vt sich (dat) ansehen; besichtigen <house>; (consider) betrachten ● vi (TV) fernsehen. ~**er** n (TV) Zuschauer(in) m(f)

view: ~**finder** n (Phot) Sucher m. ~**point** n Standpunkt m

vigilan|ce n Wachsamkeit f. ~**t** a, -ly adv wachsam

vigorous a, -ly adv kräftig; (fig) heftig

vigour n Kraft f; (fig) Heftigkeit f

vile a abscheulich

villa n (for holidays) Ferienhaus nt

village n Dorf nt. ~**r** n Dorfbewohner(in) m(f)

villain n Schurke m; (in story) Bösewicht m

vindicat|e vt rechtfertigen. ~**ion** n Rechtfertigung f

vindictive a nachtragend

vine n Weinrebe f

vinegar n Essig m

vineyard n Weinberg m

vintage a erlesen ● n (year) Jahrgang m. ~ **car** n Oldtimer m

viola n (Mus) Bratsche f

violat|e vt verletzen; (break) brechen; (disturb) stören; (defile) schänden. ~**ion** n Verletzung f; Schändung f

violen|ce n Gewalt f; (fig) Heftigkeit f. ~**t** a gewalttätig; (fig) heftig. ~**tly** adv brutal; (fig) heftig

violet a violett ● n (flower) Veilchen nt

violin n Geige f, Violine f. ~**ist** n Geiger(in) m(f)

VIP abbr (very important person) Prominente(r) m/f

viper n Kreuzotter f

virgin a unberührt ● n Jungfrau f. ~**ity** n Unschuld f

viril|e a männlich. ~**ity** n Männlichkeit f

virtual a a ~ ... praktisch ein ... ~**ly** adv praktisch

V

virtu|e n Tugend f; (advantage) Vorteil m; **by** or **in ∼e of** auf Grund (+ gen)

virtuoso n (pl -si) Virtuose m

virtuous a tugendhaft

virus n Virus nt

visa n Visum nt

visibility n Sichtbarkeit f; (Meteorol) Sichtweite f

visible a, -bly adv sichtbar

vision n Vision f; (sight) Sehkraft f; (foresight) Weitblick m

visit n Besuch m ● vt besuchen; besichtigen <town, building>. **∼or** n Besucher(in) m(f); (in hotel) Gast m; **have ∼ors** Besuch haben

visor n Schirm m; (Auto) [Sonnen]blende f

vista n Aussicht f

visual a, -ly adv visuell. **∼ display unit** n Bildschirmgerät nt

visualize vt sich (dat) vorstellen

vital a unbedingt notwendig; (essential to life) lebenswichtig. **∼ity** n Vitalität f. **∼ly** adv äußerst

vitamin n Vitamin nt

vivaci|ous a, -ly adv lebhaft. **∼ty** n Lebhaftigkeit f

vivid a, -ly adv lebhaft; <description> lebendig

vocabulary n Wortschatz m; (list) Vokabelverzeichnis nt; **learn ∼** Vokabeln lernen

vocal a, -ly adv stimmlich; (vociferous) lautstark

vocalist n Sänger(in) m(f)

vocation n Berufung f. **∼al** a Berufs-

vociferous a lautstark

vodka n Wodka m

vogue n Mode f

voice n Stimme f ● vt zum Ausdruck bringen

void a leer; (not valid) ungültig; **∼ of** ohne ● n Leere f

volatile a flüchtig; <person> sprunghaft

volcanic a vulkanisch

volcano n Vulkan m

volley n (of gunfire) Salve f; (Tennis) Volley m

volt n Volt nt. **∼age** n (Electr) Spannung f

voluble a, -bly adv redselig; <protest> wortreich

volume n (book) Band m; (Geom) Rauminhalt m; (amount) Ausmaß nt; (Radio, TV) Lautstärke f

voluntary a, -ily adv freiwillig

volunteer n Freiwillige(r) m/f ● vt anbieten; geben <information> ● vi sich freiwillig melden

vomit n Erbrochene(s) nt ● vt erbrechen ● vi sich übergeben

voracious a gefräßig; <appetite> unbändig

vot|e n Stimme f; (ballot) Abstimmung f; (right) Wahlrecht nt ● vi abstimmen; (in election) wählen. **∼er** n Wähler(in) m(f)

vouch vi **∼ for** sich verbürgen für. **∼er** n Gutschein m

vowel n Vokal m

voyage n Seereise f; (in space) Reise f, Flug m

vulgar a vulgär, ordinär. **∼ity** n Vulgarität f

vulnerable a verwundbar

vulture n Geier m

Ww

wad n Bausch m; (bundle) Bündel nt. **∼ding** n Wattierung f

waddle vi watscheln

wade vi waten

wafer n Waffel f

waffle¹ vi 🆃 schwafeln

waffle² n (Culin) Waffel f

waft vt/i wehen

wag v (pt/pp wagged) ● vt wedeln mit ● vi wedeln

wage n, & **∼s** pl Lohn m

wager n Wette f

wagon n Wagen m; (Rail) Waggon m

wail n [klagender] Schrei m ● vi heulen; (lament) klagen

waist n Taille f. ~**coat** n Weste f. ~**line** n Taille f

wait n Wartezeit f; lie in ~ for auflauern (+ dat) ● vi warten (for auf + acc); (at table) servieren; ~ on bedienen ● vt ~ one's turn warten, bis man an der Reihe ist

waiter n Kellner m; ~! Herr Ober!

waiting: ~**-list** n Warteliste f. ~**room** n Warteraum m; (doctor's) Wartezimmer nt

waitress n Kellnerin f

waive vt verzichten auf (+ acc)

wake[1] n Totenwache f ● v (pt woke, pp woken) ~ [up] ● vt [auf]wecken ● vi aufwachen

wake[2] n (Naut) Kielwasser nt; in the ~ of im Gefolge (+ gen)

Wales n Wales nt

walk n Spaziergang m; (gait) Gang m; (path) Weg m; go for a ~ spazieren gehen ● vi gehen; (not ride) laufen, zu Fuß gehen; (ramble) wandern; learn to ~ laufen lernen ● vt ausführen <dog>. ~ **out** vi hinausgehen; <workers:> in den Streik treten; ~ **out on s.o.** jdn verlassen

walker n Spaziergänger(in) m(f); (rambler) Wanderer m/Wanderin f

walking n Gehen nt; (rambling) Wandern nt. ~**-stick** n Spazierstock m

wall n Wand f; (external) Mauer f; drive s.o. up the ~ 🔲 jdn auf die Palme bringen ● vt ~ up zumauern

wallet n Brieftasche f

wallflower n Goldlack m

wallop vt (pt/pp walloped) 🔲 schlagen

wallow vi sich wälzen; (fig) schwelgen

wallpaper n Tapete f ● vt tapezieren

walnut n Walnuss f

waltz n Walzer m ● vi Walzer tanzen

wander vi umherwandern, 🔲 bummeln; (fig: digress) abschweifen. ~ **about** vi umherwandern

wangle vt 🔲 organisieren

want n Mangel m (of an + dat); (hardship) Not f; (desire) Bedürfnis nt ● vt wollen; (need) brauchen; ~ [to have] sth etw haben wollen; ~ to do sth etw tun wollen; I ~ you to go ich will, dass du gehst; it ~s painting es müsste gestrichen werden ● vi he doesn't ~ for anything ihm fehlt es an nichts. ~**ed** a <criminal> gesucht

war n Krieg m; be at ~ sich im Krieg befinden

ward n [Kranken]saal m; (unit) Station f; (of town) Wahlbezirk m; (child) Mündel nt ● vt ~ **off** abwehren

warden n (of hostel) Heimleiter(in) m(f); (of youth hostel) Herbergsvater m; (supervisor) Aufseher(in) m(f)

warder n Wärter(in) m(f)

wardrobe n Kleiderschrank m; (clothes) Garderobe f

warehouse n Lager nt; (building) Lagerhaus nt

wares npl Waren pl

war: ~**fare** n Krieg m. ~**like** a kriegerisch

warm a (-er, -est), -ly adv warm; <welcome> herzlich; I am ~ mir ist warm ● vt wärmen. ~ **up** vt aufwärmen ● vi warm werden; (Sport) sich aufwärmen. ~**-hearted** a warmherzig

warmth n Wärme f

warn vt warnen (of vor + dat). ~**ing** n Warnung f; (advance notice) Vorwarnung f; (caution) Verwarnung f

warp vt verbiegen ● vi sich verziehen

warrant n (for arrest) Haftbefehl m; (for search) Durchsuchungsbefehl m ● vt (justify) rechtfertigen; (guarantee) garantieren

warranty n Garantie f

warrior n Krieger m

warship n Kriegsschiff nt

wart n Warze f

wartime n Kriegszeit f

wary a (-ier, -iest), **-ily** adv vorsichtig; (suspicious) misstrauisch

was see be

wash n Wäsche f; (Naut) Wellen pl; have a ~ sich waschen ● vt waschen; spülen <dishes>; aufwischen <floor>; ~ one's hands sich (dat) die Hände waschen ● vi sich waschen. ~ **out** vt auswaschen; ausspülen <mouth>. ~ **up** vt/i abwaschen, spülen ● vi (Amer) sich waschen

washable a waschbar

wash-basin n Waschbecken nt

washer n (Techn) Dichtungsring m; (machine) Waschmaschine f

washing n Wäsche f. ~**-machine** n Waschmaschine f. ~**-powder** n Waschpulver nt. ~**up** n Abwasch m; do the ~**up** abwaschen, spülen. ~**-up liquid** n Spülmittel nt

wasp n Wespe f

waste n Verschwendung f; (rubbish) Abfall m; ~**s** pl Öde f ● a <product> Abfall- ● vt verschwenden ● vi ~ **away** immer mehr abmagern

waste: ~**ful** a verschwenderisch. ~ **land** n Ödland nt. ~ **paper** n Altpapier nt. ~**-paper basket** n Papierkorb m

watch n Wache f; (timepiece) [Armband]uhr f ● vt beobachten; sich (dat) ansehen <film, match>; (keep an eye on) achten auf (+ acc); ~ **television** fernsehen ● vi zusehen. ~ **out** vi Ausschau halten (**for** nach); (be careful) aufpassen

watch: ~**dog** n Wachhund m. ~**ful** a, **-ly** adv wachsam. ~**man** n Wachmann m

water n Wasser nt; ~**s** pl Gewässer nt ● vt gießen <garden, plant>; (dilute) verdünnen ● vi <eyes:> tränen; **my mouth was** ~**ing** mir lief das Wasser im Munde zusammen. ~ **down** vt verwässern

water: ~**colour** n Wasserfarbe f; (painting) Aquarell nt. ~**cress** n Brunnenkresse f. ~**fall** n Wasserfall m

watering-can n Gießkanne f

water: ~**lily** n Seerose f. ~**logged** a **be** ~**logged** <ground:> unter Wasser stehen. ~ **polo** n Wasserball m. ~**proof** a wasserdicht. ~**skiing** n Wasserskilaufen nt. ~**tight** a wasserdicht. ~**way** n Wasserstraße f

watery a wässrig

watt n Watt nt

wave n Welle f; (gesture) Handbewegung f; (as greeting) Winken nt ● vt winken mit; (brandish) schwingen; wellen <hair>; ~ one's hand winken ● vi winken (**to** dat); <flag:> wehen. ~**length** n Wellenlänge f

waver vi schwanken

wavy a wellig

wax n Wachs nt; (in ear) Schmalz nt ● vt wachsen. ~**works** n Wachsfigurenkabinett nt

way n Weg m; (direction) Richtung f; (respect) Hinsicht f; (manner) Art f; (method) Art und Weise f, ~**s** pl Gewohnheiten pl; **on the** ~ auf dem Weg (**to** nach/zu); (under way) unterwegs; **a little/long** ~ ein kleines/ganzes Stück; **a long** ~ **off** weit weg; **this** ~ hierher; (like this) so; **which** ~ in welche Richtung; (how) wie; **by the** ~ übrigens; **in some** ~**s** in gewisser Hinsicht; **either** ~ so oder so; **in this** ~ auf diese Weise; **in a** ~ in gewisser Weise; **lead the** ~ vorausgehen; **make** ~ Platz machen (**for** dat); '**give** ~' (Auto) 'Vorfahrt beachten'; **go out of one's** ~ (fig) sich (dat) besondere Mühe geben (**to** zu); **get one's [own]** ~ seinen Willen durchsetzen ● adv weit; ~ **behind** weit zurück. ~ **in** n Eingang m

way out n Ausgang m; (fig) Ausweg m

WC abbr WC nt

we pron wir

weak a (-er, -est), **-ly** adv schwach; <liquid> dünn. ~**en** vt schwächen ● vi schwächer werden. ~**ling** n

Schwächling *m*. **~ness** *n* Schwäche *f*

wealth *n* Reichtum *m*; (*fig*) Fülle *f* (of an + *dat*). **~y** *a* (-ier, -iest) reich

weapon *n* Waffe *f*

wear *n* (*clothing*) Kleidung *f*; **~ and tear** Abnutzung *f*, Verschleiß *m* ● *v* (*pt* wore, *pp* worn) ● *vt* tragen; (*damage*) abnutzen; **what shall I ~?** was soll ich anziehen? ● *vi* sich abnutzen; (*last*) halten. **~ off** *vi* abgehen; <*effect:*> nachlassen. **~ out** *vt* abnutzen; (*exhaust*) erschöpfen ● *vi* sich abnutzen

weary *a* (-ier, -iest), **-ily** *adv* müde

weather *n* Wetter *nt*; **in this ~** bei diesem Wetter; **under the ~** 🈁 nicht ganz auf dem Posten ● *vt* abwettern <*storm*>; (*fig*) überstehen

weather: ~-beaten *a* verwittert; wettergegerbt <*face*>. **~ forecast** *n* Wettervorhersage *f*

weave¹ *vi* (*pt/pp* weaved) sich schlängeln (**through** durch)

weave² *n* (*Tex*) Bindung *f* ● *vt* (*pt* wove, *pp* woven) weben. **~r** *n* Weber *m*

web *n* Netz *nt*. **~site** *n* Website *f*

wed *vt/i* (*pt/pp* wedded) heiraten. **~ding** *n* Hochzeit *f*

wedding: ~ day *n* Hochzeitstag *m*. **~ dress** *n* Hochzeitskleid *nt*. **~ ring** *n* Ehering *m*, Trauring *m*

wedge *n* Keil *m* ● *vt* festklemmen

Wednesday *n* Mittwoch *m*

wee *a* 🈁 klein ● *vi* Pipi machen

weed *n & ~s* *pl* Unkraut *nt* ● *vt/i* jäten. **~ out** *vt* (*fig*) aussieben

weedkiller *n* Unkrautvertilgungsmittel *nt*

weedy *a* 🈁 spillerig

week *n* Woche *f*. **~day** *n* Wochentag *m*. **~end** *n* Wochenende *nt*

weekly *a & adv* wöchentlich ● *n* Wochenzeitschrift *f*

weep *vi* (*pt/pp* wept) weinen

weigh *vt/i* wiegen. **~ down** *vt* (*fig*) niederdrücken. **~ up** *vt* (*fig*) abwägen

weight *n* Gewicht *nt*; **put on/lose ~** zunehmen/abnehmen

weight-lifting *n* Gewichtheben *nt*

weighty *a* (-ier, -iest) schwer; (*important*) gewichtig

weir *n* Wehr *nt*.

weird *a* (-er, -est) unheimlich; (*bizarre*) bizarr

welcome *a* willkommen; **you're ~!** nichts zu danken! **you're ~ to (have) it** das können Sie gerne haben ● *n* Willkommen *nt* ● *vt* begrüßen

weld *vt* schweißen. **~er** *n* Schweißer *m*

welfare *n* Wohl *nt*; (*Admin*) Fürsorge *f*. **W ~ State** *n* Wohlfahrtsstaat *m*

well¹ *n* Brunnen *m*; (*oil ~*) Quelle *f*

well² *adv* (better, best) gut; **as ~** auch; **as ~ as** (*in addition*) sowohl ... als auch; **~ done!** gut gemacht! ● *a* gesund; **he is not ~** es geht ihm nicht gut; **get ~ soon!** gute Besserung! ● *int* nun, na

well: ~-behaved *a* artig. **~-being** *n* Wohl *nt*

wellingtons *npl* Gummistiefel *pl*

well: ~-known *a* bekannt. **~-off** *a* wohlhabend; **be ~-off** gut dransein. **~-to-do** *a* wohlhabend

Welsh *a* walisisch ● *n* (*Lang*) Walisisch *nt*; **the ~** *pl* die Waliser. **~man** *n* Waliser *m*

went *see* go

wept *see* weep

were *see* be

west *n* Westen *m*; **to the ~ of** westlich von ● *a* West-, west- ● *adv* nach Westen. **~erly** *a* westlich. **~ern** *a* westlich ● *n* Western *m*

West: ~ Germany *n* Westdeutschland *nt*. **~ Indian** *a* westindisch ● *n* Westinder(in) *m(f)*. **~ Indies** *npl* Westindische Inseln *pl*

westward[s] *adv* nach Westen

wet *a* (wetter, wettest) nass; <🈁 *person*> weichlich, lasch; **'~ paint'** 'frisch gestrichen' ● *vt* (*pt/pp* wet or wetted) nass machen

whack *vt* 🔲 schlagen. **~ed** *a* 🔲 kaputt

whale *n* Wal *m*

wharf *n* Kai *m*

what

● *pronoun*

····▸ (*in questions*) was. **what is it?** was ist das? **what do you want?** was wollen Sie? **what is your name?** wie heißen Sie? **what?** (🔲 *say that again*) wie?; was? **what is the time?** wie spät ist es? (*indirect*) **I didn't know what to do** ich wusste nicht, was ich machen sollte

❗ The equivalent of a preposition with **what** in English is a special word in German beginning with *wo-* (*wor-* before a vowel): **for what? what for?** = wofür? wozu? **from what?** wovon? **on what?** worauf? **under what?** worunter? **with what?** womit? etc. **what do you want the money for?** wozu willst du das Geld? **what is he talking about?** wovon redet er?

····▸ (*relative pronoun*) was. **do what I tell you** tu, was ich dir sage. **give me what you can** gib mir, so viel du kannst. **what little I know** das bisschen, das ich weiß. **I don't agree with what you are saying** ich stimme dem nicht zu, was Sie sagen

····▸ (*in phrases*) **what about me?** was ist mit mir? **what about a cup of coffee?** wie wäre es mit einer Tasse Kaffee? **what if she doesn't come?** was ist, wenn sie nicht kommt? **what of it?** was ist dabei?

● *adjective*

····▸ (*asking for selection*) welcher (*m*), welche (*f*), welches (*nt*), welche (*pl*). **what book do you want?** welches Buch willst du haben? **what colour are the walls?** welche Farbe haben die Wände? **I asked him what train to take** ich habe ihn gefragt, welchen Zug ich nehmen soll

····▸ (*asking how much/many*) **what money does he have?** wie viel Geld hat er? **what time is it?** wie spät ist

es? **what time does it start?** um wie viel Uhr fängt es an?

····▸ **what kind of ...?** was für [ein(e)]? **what kind of man is he?** was für ein Mensch ist er?

····▸ (*in exclamations*) was für (+ *nom*). **what a fool you are!** was für ein Dummkopf du doch bist! **what cheek/luck!** was für eine Frechheit/ ein Glück! **what a huge house!** was für ein riesiges Haus! **what a lot of people!** was für viele Leute!

whatever *a* [egal] welche(r,s) ● *pron* was ... auch; **~ is it?** was ist das bloß? **~ he does** was er auch tut; **nothing ~** überhaupt nichts

whatsoever *pron & a* ≈ **whatever**

wheat *n* Weizen *m*

wheel *n* Rad *nt*; (*pottery*) Töpferscheibe *f*; (*steering* **~**) Lenkrad *nt*; **at the ~** am Steuer ● *vt* (*push*) schieben ● *vi* kehrtmachen; (*circle*) kreisen

wheel: ~barrow *n* Schubkarre *f*. **~chair** *n* Rollstuhl *m*. **~-clamp** *n* Parkkralle *f*

when *adv* wann; **the day ~** der Tag, an dem ● *conj* wenn; (*in the past*) als; (*although*) wo ... doch; **~ swimming/reading** beim Schwimmen/Lesen

whenever *conj & adv* [immer] wenn; (*at whatever time*) wann immer; **~ did it happen?** wann ist das bloß passiert?

where *adv & conj* wo; **~ [to]** wohin; **~ [from]** woher

whereabouts[1] *adv* wo

whereabouts[2] *n* Verbleib *m*; (*of person*) Aufenthaltsort *m*

whereas *conj* während; (*in contrast*) wohingegen

whereupon *adv* worauf[hin]

wherever *conj & adv* wo immer; (*to whatever place*) wohin immer; (*from whatever place*) woher immer; (*everywhere*) überall wo; **~ possible** wenn irgend möglich

whether *conj* ob

which
● *adjective*
····➤ (*in questions*) welcher (*m*), welche (*f*), welches (*nt*), welche (*pl*). **which book do you need?** welches Buch brauchst du? **which one?** welcher/welche/welches? **which ones?** welche? **which one of you did it?** wer von euch hat es getan? **which way?** (*which direction*) welche Richtung?; (*where*) wohin?; (*how*) wie?
····➤ (*relative*) **he always comes at one, at which time I'm having lunch/by which time I've finished** er kommt immer um ein Uhr; dann esse ich gerade zu Mittag/bis dahin bin ich schon fertig
● *pronoun*
····➤ (*in questions*) welcher (*m*), welche (*f*), welches (*nt*), welche (*pl*). **which is which?** welcher/welche/welches ist welcher/welche/welches? **which of you?** wer von euch?
····➤ (*relative*) der (*m*), die (*f*), das (*nt*), die (*pl*); (*genitive*) dessen (*m, nt*), deren (*f, pl*); (*dative*) dem (*m, nt*), der (*f*), denen (*pl*); (*referring to a clause*) was. **the book which I gave you** das Buch, das ich dir gab. **the trial, the result of which we are expecting** der Prozess, dessen Ergebnis wir erwarten. **the house of which I was speaking** das Haus, von dem *od* wovon ich redete. **after which** wonach; nach dem. **on which** worauf; auf dem. **the shop opposite which we parked** der Laden, gegenüber dem wir parkten. **everything which I tell you** alles, was ich dir sage

whichever *a & pron* [egal] welche(r,s); ~ **it is** was es auch ist

while *n* Weile *f*; **a long** ~ lange; **be worth** ~ sich lohnen; **it's worth my** ~ es lohnt sich für mich ● *conj* während; (*as long as*) solange; (*although*) obgleich ● *vt* ~ **away** sich (*dat*) vertreiben

whilst *conj* während

whim *n* Laune *f*

whimper *vi* wimmern; <*dog:*> winseln

whine *vi* winseln

whip *n* Peitsche *f*; (*Pol*) Einpeitscher *m* ● *vt* (*pt/pp* **whipped**) peitschen; (*Culin*) schlagen. ~**ped cream** *n* Schlagsahne *f*

whirl *vt/i* wirbeln. ~**pool** *n* Strudel *m*. ~**wind** *n* Wirbelwind *m*

whirr *vi* surren

whisk *n* (*Culin*) Schneebesen *m* ● *vt* (*Culin*) schlagen

whisker *n* Schnurrhaar *nt*

whisky *n* Whisky *m*

whisper *n* Flüstern *nt* ● *vt/i* flüstern

whistle *n* Pfiff *m*; (*instrument*) Pfeife *f* ● *vt/i* pfeifen

white *a* (-r, -st) weiß ● *n* Weiß *nt*; (*of egg*) Eiweiß *nt*; (*person*) Weiße(r) *m/f*

white: ~ **coffee** *n* Kaffee *m* mit Milch. ~**collar worker** *n* Angestellte(r) *m*. ~ **lie** *n* Notlüge *f*

whiten *vt* weiß machen ● *vi* weiß werden

whiteness *n* Weiß *nt*

Whitsun *n* Pfingsten *nt*

whiz[z] *vi* (*pt/pp* **whizzed**) zischen. ~**kid** *n* ⊞ Senkrechtstarter *m*

who *pron* wer; (*acc*) wen; (*dat*) wem ● *rel pron* der/die/das, (*pl*) die

whoever *pron* wer [immer]; ~ **he is** wer er auch ist; ~ **is it?** wer ist das bloß?

whole *a* ganz; <*truth*> voll ● *n* Ganze(s) *nt*; **as a** ~ als Ganzes; **on the** ~ im Großen und Ganzen; **the** ~ **of Germany** ganz Deutschland

whole: ~**food** *n* Vollwertkost *f*. ~**hearted** *a* rückhaltlos. ~**meal** *a* Vollkorn-

wholesale *a* Großhandels- ● *adv* en gros; (*fig*) in Bausch und Bogen. ~**r** *n* Großhändler *m*

wholly *adv* völlig

whom *pron* wen; **to** ~ wem ● *rel pron* den/die/das, (*pl*) die; (*dat*) dem/dem, (*pl*) denen

whopping *a* ⊞ Riesen-

whore *n* Hure *f*

whose *pron* wessen; ~ **is that?** wem gehört das? ● *rel pron* dessen/deren/dessen, (*pl*) deren

W

why *adv* warum; (*for what purpose*) wozu; **that's ~** darum

wick *n* Docht *m*

wicked *a* böse; (*mischievous*) frech, boshaft

wicker *n* Korbgeflecht *nt* ● *attrib* Korb-

wide *a* (-r, -st) weit; (*broad*) breit; (*fig*) groß ● *adv* weit; (*off target*) daneben; **~ awake** hellwach; **far and ~** weit und breit. **~ly** *adv* weit; *<known, accepted>* weithin; *<differ>* stark

widen *vt* verbreitern; (*fig*) erweitern ● *vi* sich verbreitern

widespread *a* weit verbreitet

widow *n* Witwe *f*. **~ed** *a* verwitwet. **~er** *n* Witwer *m*

width *n* Weite *f*; (*breadth*) Breite *f*

wield *vt* schwingen; ausüben *<power>*

wife *n* (*pl* **wives**) [Ehe]frau *f*

wig *n* Perücke *f*

wiggle *vi* wackeln ● *vt* wackeln mit

wild *a* (-er, -est), **-ly** *adv* wild; *<animal>* wild lebend; *<flower>* wild wachsend; (*furious*) wütend ● *adv* wild; **run ~** frei herumlaufen ● *n* **in the ~** wild; **the ~s** *pl* die Wildnis *f*

wilderness *n* Wildnis *f*; (*desert*) Wüste *f*

wildlife *n* Tierwelt *f*

will¹

● *auxiliary verb*

past **would**

····▸ (*expressing the future*) werden. **she will arrive tomorrow** sie wird morgen ankommen. **he will be there by now** er wird jetzt schon da sein

····▸ (*expressing intention*) (*present tense*) **will you go?** gehst du? **I promise I won't do it again** ich verspreche, ich machs nicht noch mal

····▸ (*in requests*) **will/would you please tidy up?** würdest du bitte aufräumen? **will you be quiet!** willst du ruhig sein!

····▸ (*in invitations*) **will you have/ would you like some wine?** wollen Sie/möchten Sie Wein?

····▸ (*negative: refuse to*) nicht wollen. **they won't help me** sie wollen mir nicht helfen. **the car won't start** das Auto will nicht anspringen

····▸ (*in tag questions*) nicht wahr. **you'll be back soon, won't you?** du kommst bald wieder, nicht wahr? **you will help her, won't you?** du hilfst ihr doch, nicht wahr?

····▸ (*in short answers*) **Will you be there? — Yes I will** Wirst du da sein? — Ja

will² *n* Wille *m*; (*document*) Testament *nt*

willing *a* willig; (*eager*) bereitwillig; **be ~** bereit sein. **~ly** *adv* bereitwillig; (*gladly*) gern. **~ness** *n* Bereitwilligkeit *f*

willow *n* Weide *f*

will-power *n* Willenskraft *f*

wilt *vi* welk werden, welken

wily *a* (-ier, -iest) listig

win *n* Sieg *m* ● *v* (*pt/pp* **won**; *pres p* **winning**) ● *vt* gewinnen; bekommen *<scholarship>* ● *vi* gewinnen; (*in battle*) siegen. **~ over** *vt* auf seine Seite bringen

wince *vi* zusammenzucken

winch *n* Winde *f* ● *vt* **~ up** hochwinden

wind¹ *n* Wind *m*; (🗓 *flatulence*) Blähungen *pl* ● *vt* **~ s.o.** jdm den Atem nehmen

wind² *v* (*pt/pp* **wound**) ● *vt* (*wrap*) wickeln; (*move by turning*) kurbeln; aufziehen *<clock>* *vi* *<road:>* sich winden. **~ up** *vt* aufziehen *<clock>*; schließen *<proceedings>*

wind: ~ instrument *n* Blasinstrument *nt*. **~mill** *n* Windmühle *f*

window *n* Fenster *nt*; (*of shop*) Schaufenster *nt*

window: ~-box *n* Blumenkasten *m*. **~-cleaner** *n* Fensterputzer *m*. **~-pane** *n* Fensterscheibe *f*. **~-shopping** *n* Schaufensterbummel *m*. **~-sill** *n* Fensterbrett *nt*

w

windpipe n Luftröhre f

windscreen n, (Amer) **windshield** n Windschutzscheibe f. **~-wiper** n Scheibenwischer m

wind surfing n Windsurfen nt

windy a (-ier, -iest) windig

wine n Wein m

wine: **~-bar** n Weinstube f. **~ glass** n Weinglas nt. **~-list** n Weinkarte f

winery n (Amer) Weingut nt

wine-tasting n Weinprobe f

wing n Flügel m; (Auto) Kotflügel m; **~s** pl (Theat) Kulissen pl

wink n Zwinkern nt; **not sleep a ~** kein Auge zutun ● vi zwinkern; <light:> blinken

winner n Gewinner(in) m(f); (Sport) Sieger(in) m(f)

winning a siegreich; <smile> gewinnend. **~-post** n Zielpfosten m. **~s** npl Gewinn m

wint|er n Winter m. **~ry** a winterlich

wipe n give sth a ~ etw abwischen ● vt abwischen; aufwischen <floor>; (dry) abtrocknen. **~ out** vt (cancel) löschen; (destroy) ausrotten. **~ up** vt aufwischen

wire n Draht m

wiring n [elektrische] Leitungen pl

wisdom n Weisheit f; (prudence) Klugheit f. **~ tooth** n Weisheitszahn m

wise a (-r, -st), **-ly** adv weise; (prudent) klug

wish n Wunsch m ● vt wünschen; **~ s.o. well** jdm alles Gute wünschen; **I ~ you could stay** ich wünschte, du könntest hier bleiben ● vi sich (dat) etwas wünschen. **~ful** a **~ful thinking** Wunschdenken nt

wistful a, **-ly** adv wehmütig

wit n Geist m, Witz m; (intelligence) Verstand m; (person) geistreicher Mensch m; **be at one's ~s' end** sich (dat) keinen Rat mehr wissen

witch n Hexe f. **~craft** n Hexerei f

with prep mit (+ dat); **~ fear/cold** vor Angst/Kälte; **~ it** damit; **I'm going ~ you** ich gehe mit; **take it ~**

you nimm es mit; **I haven't got it ~ me** ich habe es nicht bei mir

withdraw v (pt -drew, pp -drawn) ● vt zurückziehen; abheben <money> ● vi sich zurückziehen. **~al** n Zurückziehen nt; (of money) Abhebung f; (from drugs) Entzug m

wither vi [ver]welken

withhold vt (pt/pp -held) vorenthalten (**from** s.o. jdm)

within prep innerhalb (+ gen) ● adv innen

without prep ohne (+ acc); **~ my noticing it** ohne dass ich es merkte

withstand vt (pt/pp -stood) standhalten (+ dat)

witness n Zeuge m/Zeugin f ● vt Zeuge/Zeugin sein (+ gen); bestätigen <signature>

witticism n geistreicher Ausspruch m

witty a (-ier, -iest) witzig, geistreich

wives see **wife**

wizard n Zauberer m

wizened a verhutzelt

wobb|le vi wackeln. **~ly** a wackelig

woke, woken see **wake**[1]

wolf n (pl wolves) Wolf m

woman n (pl women) Frau f. **~izer** n Schürzenjäger m

womb n Gebärmutter f

women npl see **woman**

won see **win**

wonder n Wunder nt; (surprise) Staunen nt ● vt/i sich fragen; (be surprised) sich wundern; **I ~ da** frage ich mich; **I ~ whether she is ill** ob sie wohl krank ist? **~ful** a, **-ly** adv wunderbar

won't = will not

wood n Holz nt; (forest) Wald m; **touch ~!** unberufen!

wood: **~ed** a bewaldet. **~en** a Holz-; (fig) hölzern. **~pecker** n Specht m. **~wind** n Holzbläser pl. **~work** n (wooden parts) Holzteile pl; (craft) Tischlerei f. **~worm** n Holzwurm m

wool n Wolle f ● attrib Woll-. **~len** a wollen

w

woolly a (-ier, -iest) wollig; (fig) unklar

word n Wort nt; (news) Nachricht f; by ~ of mouth mündlich; have a ~ with sprechen mit; have ~s einen Wortwechsel haben. ~ing n Wortlaut m. ~ **processor** n Textverarbeitungssystem nt

wore see wear

work n Arbeit f; (Art, Literature) Werk nt; ~s pl (factory, mechanism) Werk nt; at ~ bei der Arbeit; out of ~ arbeitslos ● vi arbeiten; <machine, system:> funktionieren; (have effect) wirken; (study) lernen; it won't ~ (fig) es klappt nicht ● vt arbeiten lassen; bedienen <machine>; betätigen <lever>. ~ **off** vt abarbeiten. ~ **out** vt ausrechnen; (solve) lösen ● vi gut gehen, 🇮 klappen. ~ **up** vt aufbauen; sich (dat) holen <appetite>; get ~ed up sich aufregen

workable a (feasible) durchführbar

worker n Arbeiter(in) m(f)

working a berufstätig; <day, clothes> Arbeits-; be in ~ **order** funktionieren. ~ **class** n Arbeiterklasse f

work: ~**man** n Arbeiter m; (craftsman) Handwerker m. ~**manship** n Arbeit f. ~**shop** n Werkstatt f

world n Welt f; in the ~ auf der Welt; think the ~ of s.o. große Stücke auf jdn halten. ~**ly** a weltlich; <person> weltlich gesinnt. ~**-wide** a & adv weltweit

worm n Wurm m

worn see wear ● a abgetragen. ~**out** a abgetragen; <carpet> abgenutzt; <person> erschöpft

worried a besorgt

worry n Sorge f ● v (pt/pp worried) ● vt beunruhigen; (bother) stören ● vi sich beunruhigen, sich (dat) Sorgen machen. ~**ing** a beunruhigend

worse a & adv schlechter; (more serious) schlimmer ● n Schlechtere(s) nt; Schlimmere(s) nt

worsen vt verschlechtern ● vi sich verschlechtern

worship n Anbetung f; (service) Gottesdienst m ● vt (pt/pp -shipped) anbeten

worst a schlechteste(r,s); (most serious) schlimmste(r,s) ● adv am schlechtesten; am schlimmsten ● n the ~ das Schlimmste

worth n Wert m; £10's ~ of petrol Benzin für £10 ● a be ~ £5 £5 wert sein; be ~ it (fig) sich lohnen. ~**less** a wertlos. ~**while** a lohnend

worthy a würdig

would v aux I ~ do it ich würde es tun, ich täte es; ~ you go? würdest du gehen? he said he ~n't er sagte, er würde es nicht tun; what ~ you like? was möchten Sie?

wound[1] n Wunde f ● vt verwunden

wound[2] see wind[2]

wove, woven see weave[2]

wrangle n Streit m

wrap n Umhang m ● vt (pt/pp wrapped) ~ [up] wickeln; einpacken <present> ● vi ~ up warmly sich warm einpacken. ~**per** n Hülle f. ~**ping** n Verpackung f

wrath n Zorn m

wreath n (pl -s) Kranz m

wreck n Wrack nt ● vt zerstören; zunichte machen <plans>; zerrütten <marriage>. ~**age** n Wrackteile pl; (fig) Trümmer pl

wren n Zaunkönig m

wrench n Ruck m; (tool) Schraubenschlüssel m; be a ~ (fig) weh tun ● vt reißen; ~ sth from s.o. jdm etw entreißen

wrestl|e vi ringen. ~**er** n Ringer m. ~**ing** n Ringen nt

wretch n Kreatur f. ~**ed** a elend; (very bad) erbärmlich

wriggle n Zappeln nt ● vi zappeln; (move forward) sich schlängeln; ~ out of sth 🇮 sich vor etw (dat) drücken

wring vt (pt/pp wrung) wringen; (~ out) auswringen; umdrehen <neck>; ringen <hands>

wrinkle *n* Falte *f*; (*on skin*) Runzel *f*
● *vt* kräuseln ● *vi* sich kräuseln,
sich falten. **~d** *a* runzlig

wrist *n* Handgelenk *nt*. **~-watch** *n*
Armbanduhr *f*

write *vt/i* (*pt* **wrote**, *pp* **written**, *pres p*
writing) schreiben. **~ down** *vt*
aufschreiben. **~ off** *vt* abschreiben;
zu Schrott fahren <*car*>

write-off *n* ≈ Totalschaden *m*

writer *n* Schreiber(in) *m(f)*; (*author*)
Schriftsteller(in) *m(f)*

writhe *vi* sich winden

writing *n* Schreiben *nt*;
(*handwriting*) Schrift *f*; **in ~**
schriftlich. **~-paper** *n*
Schreibpapier *nt*

written *see* write

wrong *a*, **-ly** *adv* falsch; (*morally*)
unrecht; (*not just*) ungerecht; **be ~**
nicht stimmen; <*person:*> Unrecht
haben; **what's ~?** was ist los? ● *adv*
falsch; **go ~** <*person:*> etwas falsch
machen; <*machine:*> kaputtgehen;
<*plan:*> schief gehen ● *n* Unrecht *nt*
● *vt* Unrecht tun (+ *dat*). **~ful** *a*
ungerechtfertigt. **~fully** *adv*
<*accuse*> zu Unrecht

wrote *see* write

wrung *see* wring

wry *a* (**-er**, **-est**) ironisch; <*humour*>
trocken

Xmas *n* 🇬🇧 Weihnachten *nt*

X-ray *n* (*picture*) Röntgenaufnahme *f*;
~s *pl* Röntgenstrahlen *pl* ● *vt*
röntgen; durchleuchten <*luggage*>

Yy

yacht *n* Jacht *f*; (*for racing*)
Segeljacht *f*. **~ing** *n* Segeln *nt*

yank *vt* 🇬🇧 reißen

Yank *n* 🇬🇧 Ami *m* 🇬🇧

yap *vi* (*pt/pp* **yapped**) <*dog:*>
kläffen

yard[1] *n* Hof *m*; (*for storage*) Lager *nt*

yard[2] *n* Yard *nt* (= 0,91 m)

yarn *n* Garn *nt*; (🇬🇧 *tale*) Geschichte
f

yawn *n* Gähnen *nt* ● *vi* gähnen

year *n* Jahr *nt*; (*of wine*) Jahrgang *m*;
for ~s jahrelang. **~ly** *a* & *adv*
jährlich

yearn *vi* sich sehnen (**for** nach).
~ing *n* Sehnsucht *f*

yeast *n* Hefe *f*

yell *n* Schrei *m* ● *vi* schreien

yellow *a* gelb ● *n* Gelb *nt*

yelp *vi* jaulen

yes *adv* ja; (*contradicting*) doch ● *n*
Ja *nt*

yesterday *n* & *adv* gestern; **~'s
paper** die gestrige Zeitung; **the day
before ~** vorgestern

yet *adv* noch; (*in question*) schon;
(*nevertheless*) doch; **as ~** bisher; **not
~** noch nicht; **the best ~** das bisher
beste ● *conj* doch

Yiddish *n* Jiddisch *nt*

yield *n* Ertrag *m* ● *vt* bringen;
abwerfen <*profit*> ● *vi* nachgeben;
(*Amer, Auto*) die Vorfahrt
beachten

yoga *n* Yoga *m*

yoghurt *n* Joghurt *m*

yoke *n* Joch *nt*; (*of garment*) Passe
f

yolk *n* Dotter *m*, Eigelb *nt*

you *pron* du; (*acc*) dich; (*dat*) dir; (*pl*)
ihr; (*acc, dat*) euch; (*formal*) (*nom &
acc, sg & pl*) Sie; (*dat, sg & pl*) Ihnen;
(*one*) man; (*acc*) einen; (*dat*) einem;

w
x
y

all of ~ ihr/Sie alle; **I know ~** ich
kenne dich/euch/Sie; **I'll give ~**
the money ich gebe dir/euch/Ihnen
das Geld; **it does ~ good** es tut
einem gut; **it's bad for ~** es ist
ungesund

young *a* (-er, -est) jung ● *npl*
(*animals*) Junge *pl*; **the ~** die Jugend
f. **~ster** *n* Jugendliche(r) *m/f*;
(*child*) Kleine(r) *m/f*

your *a* dein; (*pl*) euer; (*formal*)
Ihr

yours *poss pron* deine(r), deins; (*pl*)
eure(r), euers; (*formal, sg & pl*)
Ihre(r), Ihr[e]s; **a friend of ~** ein
Freund von dir/Ihnen/euch; **that is**
~ das gehört dir/Ihnen/euch

yourself *pron* (*pl* **-selves**) selbst;
(*refl*) dich; (*dat*) dir; (*pl*) euch;
(*formal*) sich; **by ~** allein

youth *n* (*pl* **-s**) Jugend *f*; (*boy*)
Jugendliche(r) *m*. **~ful** *a* jugendlich.
~ hostel *n* Jugendherberge *f*

Yugoslavia *n* Jugoslawien *nt*

zero *n* Null *f*

zest *n* Begeisterung *f*

zigzag *n* Zickzack *m* ● *vi* (*pt/pp*
-zagged) im Zickzack laufen/ (*in*
vehicle) fahren

zinc *n* Zink *nt*

zip *n* **~** [**fastener**] Reißverschluss *m*
● *vt* **~** [**up**] den Reißverschluss
zuziehen an (+ *dat*)

zip code *n* (*Amer*) Postleitzahl *f*

zipper *n* Reißverschluss *m*

zodiac *n* Tierkreis *m*

zone *n* Zone *f*

zoo *n* Zoo *m*

zoological *a* zoologisch

zoolog|ist *n* Zoologe *m*/gin *f*. **~y** *n*
Zoologie *f*

zoom *vi* sausen. **~ lens** *n*
Zoomobjektiv *nt*

Zz

zeal *n* Eifer *m*

zealous *a*, **-ly** *adv* eifrig

zebra *n* Zebra *nt*. **~ crossing** *n*
Zebrastreifen *m*

German irregular verbs

1st, 2nd, and 3rd person present are given after the infinitive, and past subjunctive after the past indicative, where there is a change of vowel or any other irregularity.

Compound verbs are only given if they do not take the same forms as the corresponding simple verb, e.g. *befehlen*, or if there is no corresponding simple verb, e.g. *bewegen*.

An asterisk (*) indicates a verb which is also conjugated regularly.

Infinitive	Past tense	Past participle
abwägen	wog (wöge) ab	abgewogen
ausbedingen	bedang (bedänge) aus	ausbedungen
backen (du bäckst, er bäckt)	buk (büke)	gebacke
befehlen (du befiehlst, er befiehlt)	befahl (beföhle, befähle)	befohlen
beginnen	begann (begänne)	begonnen
beißen (du/er beißt)	biss (bisse)	gebissen
bergen (du birgst, er birgt)	barg (bärge)	geborgen
bewegen[2]	bewog (bewöge)	bewogen
biegen[2]	bog (böge)	gebogen
bieten	bot (böte)	geboten
binden	band (bände)	gebunden
bitten	bat (bäte)	gebeten
blasen (du/er bläst)	blies	geblasen
bleiben	blieb	geblieben
bleichen*	blich	geblichen
braten (du brätst, er brät)	briet	gebraten
brechen (du brichst, er bricht)	brach (bräche)	gebrochen
brennen	brannte (brennte)	gebrannt
bringen	brachte (brächte)	gebracht
denken	dachte (dächte)	gedacht
dreschen (du drischst, er drischt)	drosch (drösche)	gedroschen
dringen	drang (dränge)	gedrungen
dürfen (ich/er darf, du darfst)	durfte (dürfte)	gedurft
empfehlen (du empfiehlst, er empfiehlt)	empfahl (empföhle)	empfohlen
erlöschen (du erlischst, er erlischt)	erlosch (erlösche)	erloschen
erschrecken (du erschrickst, er erschrickt)	erschrak (erschäke)	erschrocken
erwägen	erwog (erwöge)	erwogen
essen (du/er isst)	aß (äße)	gegessen
fahren (du fährst, er fährt)	fuhr (führe)	gefahren
fallen (du fällst, er fällt)	fiel	gefallen
fangen (du fängst, er fängt)	fing	gefangen
fechten (du fichtst, er ficht)	focht (föchte)	gefochten

Infinitive	Past tense	Past participle
finden	fand (fände)	gefunden
flechten (du flichtst, er flicht)	flocht (flöchte)	geflochten
fliegen	flog (flöge)	geflogen
fliehen	floh (flöhe)	geflohen
fließen (du/er fließt)	floss (flösse)	geflossen
fressen (du/er frisst)	fraß (fräße)	gefressen
frieren	fror (fröre)	gefroren
gären*	gor (göre)	gegoren
gebären (du gebierst, sie gebiert)	gebar (gebäre)	geboren
geben (du gibst, er gibt)	gab (gäbe)	gegeben
gedeihen	gedieh	gediehen
gehen	ging	gegangen
gelingen	gelang (gelänge)	gelungen
gelten (du giltst, er gilt)	galt (gölte, gälte)	gegolten
genesen (du/er genest)	genas (genäse)	genesen
genießen (du/er genießt)	genoss (genösse)	genossen
geschehen (es geschieht)	geschah (geschähe)	geschehen
gewinnen	gewann (gewönne, gewänne)	gewonnen
gießen (du/er gießt)	goss (gösse)	gegossen
gleichen	glich	geglichen
gleiten	glitt	geglitten
glimmen	glomm (glömme)	geglommen
graben (du gräbst, er gräbt)	grub (grübe)	gegraben
greifen	griff	gegriffen
haben (du hast, er hat)	hatte (hätte)	gehabt
halten (du hältst, er hält)	hielt	gehalten
hängen²	hing	gehangen
hauen	haute	gehauen
heben	hob (höbe)	gehoben
heißen (du/er heißt)	hieß	geheißen
helfen (du hilfst, er hilft)	half (hülfe)	geholfen
kennen	kannte (kennte)	gekannt
klingen	klang (klänge)	geklungen
kneifen	kniff	gekniffen
kommen	kam (käme)	gekommen
können (ich/er kann, du kannst)	konnte (könnte)	gekonnt
kriechen	kroch (kröche)	gekrochen
laden (du lädst, er lädt)	lud (lüde)	geladen
lassen (du/er lässt)	ließ	gelassen
lassen (du/er lässt)	ließ	gelassen
laufen (du läufst, er läuft)	lief	gelaufen
leiden	litt	gelitten
leihen	lieh	geliehen
lesen (du/er liest)	las (läse)	gelesen
liegen	lag (läge)	gelegen
lügen	log (löge)	gelogen
mahlen	mahlte	gemahlen
meiden	mied	gemieden
melken	molk (mölke)	gemolken
messen (du/er misst)	maß (mäße)	gemessen
misslingen	misslang (misslänge)	misslungen

Infinitive	Past tense	Past participle
mögen (ich/er mag, du magst)	mochte (möchte)	gemocht
müssen (ich/er muss, du musst)	musste (müsste)	gemusst
nehmen (du nimmst, er nimmt)	nahm (nähme)	genommen
nennen	nannte (nennte)	genannt
pfeifen	pfiff	gepfiffen
preisen (du/er preist)	pries	gepriesen
raten (du rätst, er rät)	riet	geraten
reiben	rieb	gerieben
reißen (du/er reißt)	riss	gerissen
reiten	ritt	geritten
rennen	rannte (rennte)	gerannt
riechen	roch (röche)	gerochen
ringen	rang (ränge)	gerungen
rinnen	rann (ränne)	geronnen
rufen	rief	gerufen
salzen* (du/er salzt)	salzte	gesalzen
saufen (du säufst, er säuft)	soff (söffe)	gesoffen
saugen*	sog (söge)	gesogen
schaffen[1]	schuf (schüfe)	geschaffen
scheiden	schied	geschieden
scheinen	schien	geschienen
scheißen (du/er scheißt)	schiss	geschissen
schelten (du schiltst, er schilt)	schalt (schölte)	gescholten
scheren[1]	schor (schöre)	geschoren
schieben	schob (schöbe)	geschoben
schießen (du/er schießt)	schoss (schösse)	geschossen
schlafen (du schläfst, er schläft)	schlief	geschlafen
schlagen (du schlägst, er schlägt)	schlug (schlüge)	geschlagen
schleichen	schlich	geschlichen
schleifen[2]	schliff	geschliffen
schließen (du/er schießt)	schloss (schlösse)	geschlossen
schlingen	schlang (schlänge)	geschlungen
schmeißen (du/er schmeißt)	schmiss (schmisse)	geschmissen
schmelzen (du/er schmilzt)	schmolz (schmölze)	geschmolzen
schneiden	schnitt	geschnitten
schrecken* (du schrickst, er schrickt)	schrak (schräke)	geschreckt
schreiben	schrieb	geschrieben
schreien	schrie	geschrie[e]n
schreiten	schritt	geschritten
schweigen	schwieg	geschwiegen
schwellen (du schwillst, er schwillt)	schwoll (schwölle)	geschwollen
schwimmen	schwamm (schwömme)	geschwommen
schwinden	schwand (schwände)	geschwunden
schwingen	schwang (schwänge)	geschwungen
schwören	schwor (schwüre)	geschworen
sehen (du siehst, er sieht)	sah (sähe)	gesehen
sein (ich bin, du bist, er ist, wir sind, ihr seid, sie sind)	war (wäre)	gewesen
l**senden**[1]	sandte (sendete)	gesandt
sieden	sott (sötte)	gesotten
singen	sang (sänge)	gesungen
sinken	sank (sänke)	gesunken

Infinitive	Past tense	Past participle
sitzen (du/er sitzt)	saß (säße)	gesessen
sollen (ich/er soll, du sollst)	sollte	gesollt
spalten*	spaltete	gespalten
spinnen	spann (spönne, spänne)	gesponnen
sprechen (du sprichst, er spricht)	sprach (spräche)	gesprochen
sprießen (du/er sprießt)	spross (sprösse)	gesprossen
springen	sprang (spränge)	gesprungen
stechen (du stichst, er sticht)	stach (stäche)	gestochen
stehen	stand (stünde, stände)	gestanden
stehlen (du stiehlst, er stiehlt)	stahl (stähle)	gestohlen
steigen	stieg	gestiegen
sterben (du stirbst, er stirbt)	starb (stürbe)	gestorben
stinken	stank (stänke)	gestunken
stoßen (du/er stößt)	stieß	gestoßen
streichen	strich	gestrichen
streiten	stritt	gestritten
tragen (du trägst, er trägt)	trug (trüge)	getragen
treffen (du triffst, er trifft)	traf (träfe)	getroffen
treiben	trieb	getrieben
treten (du trittst, er tritt)	trat (träte)	getreten
triefen*	troff (tröffe)	getroffen
trinken	trank (tränke)	getrunken
trügen	trog (tröge)	getrogen
tun (du tust, er tut)	tat (täte)	getan
verderben (du verdirbst, er verdirbt)	verdarb (verdürbe)	verdorben
vergessen (du/er vergisst)	vergaß (vergäße)	vergessen
verlieren	verlor (verlöre)	verloren
verzeihen	verzieh	verziehen
wachsen[1] (du/er wächst)	wuchs (wüchse)	gewachsen
waschen (du wäschst, er wäscht)	wusch (wüsche)	gewaschen
wenden[2]*	wandte (wendete)	gewandt
werben (du wirbst, er wirbt)	warb (würbe)	geworben
werden (du wirst, er wird)	wurde (würde)	geworden
werfen (du wirfst, er wirft)	warf (würfe)	geworfen
wiegen[1]	wog (wöge)	gewogen
winden	wand (wände)	gewunden
wissen (ich/er weiß, du weißt)	wusste (wüsste)	gewusst
wollen (ich/er will, du willst)	wollte	gewollt
wringen	wrang (wränge)	gewrungen
ziehen	zog (zöge)	gezogen
zwingen	zwang (zwänge)	gezwungen